lonely planet

Chile
& Easter Island

Wayne Bernhardson

LONELY PLANET PUBLICATIONS
Melbourne · Oakland · London · Paris

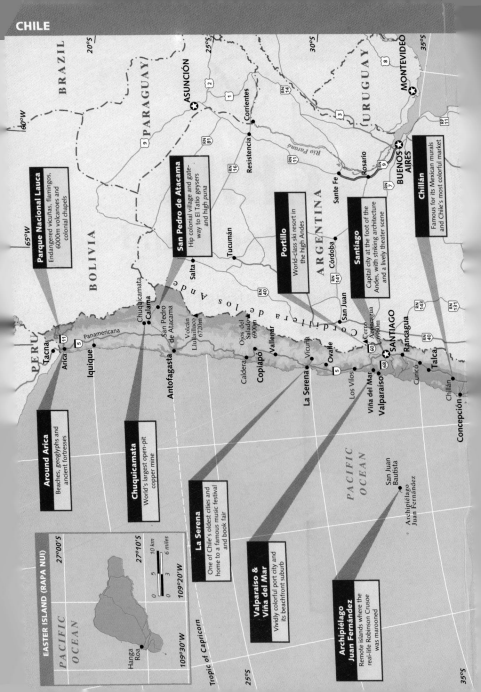

BRAZIL

20°S

25°S

30°S

35°S

65°W

60°W

PARAGUAY

ASUNCIÓN

URUGUAY

MONTEVIDEO

BUENOS AIRES

2

1

14 RN

3

9 RN

7 RN

Corrientes

Resistencia

Santa Fe

Córdoba

Tucumán

Salta

San Juan

RN 141

RN 40

RN 143

RN 131

RN 40

RN 16

RN 81

BOLIVIA

PERU

ARGENTINA

Cordillera de los Andes

Rosario

Rio Paraná

Parque Nacional Lauca
Endangered vicuñas, flamingos, 6000m volcanoes and colonial chapels

San Pedro de Atacama
Hip colonial village and gateway to El Tatio geysers and high puna

Portillo
World-class ski resort in the high Andes

Santiago
Capital city at the foot of the Andes, with striking architecture and a lively theater scene

Chillán
Famous for its Mexican murals and Chile's most colorful market

Around Arica
Beaches, geoglyphs and ancient fortresses

Chuquicamata
World's largest open-pit copper mine

La Serena
One of Chile's oldest cities and home to a famous music festival and book fair

Valparaíso & Viña del Mar
Vividly colorful port city and its beachfront suburb

Archipiélago Juan Fernández
Remote islands where the real-life Robinson Crusoe was marooned

Tacna

Arica

Iquique

Antofagasta

Calama

Chuquicamata

San Pedro de Atacama

Caldera

Copiapó

Vallenar

La Serena

Vicuña

Ovalle

Los Vilos

Viña del Mar

Valparaíso

Rancagua

Curicó

Talca

Chillán

Concepción

SANTIAGO

Panamericana

11

5

5

60

68

Volcán Llullaillaco 6720m

Ojos del Salado 6900m

Cerro Aconcagua 6960m

PACIFIC OCEAN

San Juan Bautista

Archipiélago Juan Fernández

EASTER ISLAND (RAPA NUI)

PACIFIC OCEAN

27°00'S

27°10'S

109°30'W

109°20'W

Hanga Roa

0 5 10 km
0 3 6 miles

Tropic of Capricorn

25°S

35°S

CHILE

Elevation
- 4000m
- 3000m
- 2000m
- 1000m
- 500m
- Sea Level

ATLANTIC OCEAN

FALKLAND ISLANDS
(ISLAS MALVINAS; UK)

★ STANLEY

Cordillera de los Andes

Cabo de Hornos (Cape Horn)

Strait of Magellan

Río Biobío
World-class white-water rafting

Pucón
Adventure travel mecca in the shadow of Volcán Villarrica

The Camino Austral
Pinochet's infamous public works project

Temuco
Metropolis of indigenous Chile, gateway to the lakes and volcanoes of the south

Puerto Montt
Starting point for lake cruises to Argentina and the ferry journey through southern fjords

Chiloé
Heartland of Chilean folklore

Parque Nacional Torres del Paine
One of South America's most spectacular parks, with a popular trekking circuit

Punta Arenas
Onetime Gold Rush port and Patagonia's liveliest city

Neuquén
Bahía Blanca
Los Angeles
Temuco
Villarrica
Pucón
Licán Ray
Valdivia
Osorno
Puerto Varas
Puerto Montt
Bariloche
Ancud
Castro
Archipiélago de Chiloé
Quellón
Chaitén
Coihaique
El Calafate
Puerto Natales
Punta Arenas
Porvenir
Río Grande
Ushuaia

Río Biobío

0 200 400 km
0 125 250 miles

Chile
5th edition – June 2000
First published – July 1987

Published by
Lonely Planet Publications Pty Ltd A.C.N. 005 607 983
192 Burwood Rd, Hawthorn, Victoria 3122, Australia

Lonely Planet Offices
Australia PO Box 617, Hawthorn, Victoria 3122
USA 150 Linden St, Oakland, CA 94607
UK 10a Spring Place, London NW5 3BH
France 1 rue du Dahomey, 75011 Paris

Photographs
Judi L Baker/GeoIMAGERY, Wayne Bernhardson, Victor Engelbert,
David Frazier, Robert Frerck/Odyssey/Chicago, Robert Fried,
Robert Holmes, James Lyon, Aaron McCoy, Andrew Peters, Daniel
Rivadamar/Odyssey/Chicago, Galen Rowell/Odyssey/Chicago,
Kevin Schafer, David Tipling, Woods Wheatcroft, Eric Wheater,
Tony Wheeler

Many of the images in this guide are available for licensing from
Lonely Planet Images.
email: lpi@lonelyplanet.com.au

Illustrators
Hugh D'Andrade, Shelley Firth, Hayden Foell, Justin Marler, Hannah
Reineck, Jim Swanson, Wendy Yanagihara

Front cover photograph
Chris Anderson, Aurora/PNI

ISBN 1 86450 088 3

Contents

INTRODUCTION   15

FACTS ABOUT CHILE   17

History 17
Geography & Climate . . . 28
Ecology & Environment . . 33
Flora & Fauna 33
Government & Politics . . 39
Economy 43
Population & People 45
Education 46
Arts 46
Society & Conduct 50
Religion 50
Language 51

FACTS FOR THE VISITOR   52

Suggested Itineraries 52
Planning 52
Tourist Offices 53
Visas & Documents 54
Customs 55
Money 55
Post & Communications . 59
Books 62
Film 67
Newspapers & Magazines . 67
Radio & TV 68
Photography & Video . . . 68
Time 69
Electricity 69
Weights & Measures 69
Laundry 69
Toilets 69
Health 69
Women Travelers 73
Gay & Lesbian Travelers . 73
Disabled Travelers 73
Senior Travelers 74
Travel with Children 74
Useful Organizations 74
Dangers & Annoyances . . 75
Legal Matters 76
Business Hours 76
Public Holidays
& Special Events 76
Activities 77
Courses 78
Work 79
Accommodations 79
Food 81
Drinks 84
Entertainment 85
Spectator Sports 86
Shopping 87

GETTING THERE & AWAY   88

Air 88
Land 99
Organized Tours 103

GETTING AROUND   106

Air 106
Bus 107
Train 110
Car & Motorcycle 111
Bicycle 114
Hitchhiking 114
Ferry 115
Local Transport 115
Organized Tours 116

SANTIAGO   118

History 118
Orientation 120
Information 122
Language Courses 140
Organized Tours 140
Special Events 141
Places to Stay 141
Places to Eat 144
Entertainment 148
Spectator Sports 150
Shopping 151
Getting There & Away . 152
Getting Around 152
Around Santiago 154
Templo Votivo de Maipú . 154
Pomaire 155
Wineries 155
Cajón del Maipo 156
Ski Resorts 159

MIDDLE CHILE   161

**Valparaíso & the Central
Coast 161**
Valparaíso 161
Around Valparaíso 173
Viña Del Mar 174
Around Viña Del Mar . . 182
La Ligua 183
PN La Campana 183
Los Andes 186
Southern Heartland 187
Rancagua 187
Around Rancagua 189
RN Río de Los Cipreses . 190
Hacienda Los Lingues . . 191
Lago Rapel 191
Pichilemu 191
Curicó 192
Around Curicó 194

RN Radal Siete Tazas . . . 194
Talca 196
Around Talca 199
RN Altos del Lircay 200
Chillán 201

Around Chillán 205
Concepción 206
Around Concepción . . . 214
Los Angeles 216
Around Los Angeles . . . 218

PN Laguna del Laja 219
Angol 222
PN Nahuelbuta 223

NORTE GRANDE 226

Arica 228
Around Arica 237
Putre 239
PN Lauca 241
RN Las Vicuñas 245
Monumento Natural Salar
de Surire 246
Pisagua 246
Iquique 248
Around Iquique 257
Pozo Almonte 259

Mamiña 259
RN Pampa del Tamarugal . 260
Pica 261
Antofagasta Region . . . 262
Antofagasta 263
Around Antofagasta . . . 269
Mejillones 270
Cobija & Gatico 270
Baquedano 271
María Elena 271
Around María Elena . . . 272

Tocopilla 272
Calama 273
Around Calama 277
San Pedro de Atacama . 280
Around San Pedro
de Atacama 285
RN Los Flamencos 286
El Tatio Geysers 287
Toconao 287
Taltal 288
Around Taltal 289

NORTE CHICO 290

History 290
Copiapó 292
Around Copiapó 297
PN Nevado Tres Cruces . 298
Caldera & Bahía Inglesa . 299
Around Caldera 301
Chañaral 301
PN Pan de Azúcar 302
El Salvador 303

Vallenar 304
Around Vallenar 306
RN Pingüino
de Humboldt 307
La Serena 308
Around La Serena 315
Coquimbo 316
Guanaqueros 317
Tongoy 317

Vicuña 317
Around Vicuña 320
Pisco Elqui 322
Ovalle 322
Around Ovalle 324
PN Fray Jorge 325
Los Vilos 326
Laguna Conchalí 328
Pichidangui 328

LA ARAUCANÍA & LOS LAGOS 329

History 329
Temuco 332
Chol Chol 340
PN Tolhuaca 340
PN Conguillío 341
Curacautín 344
Termas de Tolhuaca . . . 344
Lonquimay
& Upper Biobío 344
Melipeuco 345
Villarrica 345
Pucón 349
Around Pucón 354
PN Huerquehue 356
PN Villarrica 357

Lican Ray 358
Coñaripe 359
Centro Turístico Termal
Coñaripe 360
Liquiñe 360
Panguipulli 360
Choshuenco 362
Valdivia 362
Corral, Niebla & Isla
Mancera 368
Futrono 369
Llifén 369
Lago Ranco 369
Río Bueno 370
Osorno 370

Around Osorno 375
PN Puyehue 376
Puerto Octay 379
Las Cascadas 380
Frutillar 380
Puerto Varas 383
Ensenada 387
PN Vicente Pérez Rosales . 388
Cochamó 391
Puerto Montt 392
Around Puerto Montt . . 402
PN Alerce Andino 403
Hornopirén 404

ARCHIPIÉLAGO DE CHILOÉ 406

Ancud 408
Dalcahue 412
Castro 413

Achao 418
Around Achao 419
Chonchi 419

PN Chiloé 420
Quellón 422

AISÉN & THE CAMINO AUSTRAL 425

Coihaique 430	Puerto Puyuhuapi 440	RN Cerro Castillo 450
RN Coihaique 434	Termas De Puyuhuapi . . 440	Villa Cerro Castillo 450
Monumento Natural	La Junta 441	Puerto Río Tranquilo . . . 450
Dos Lagunas 435	Lago Yelcho 441	Puerto Guadal 450
RN Río Simpson 435	Futaleufú 442	Chile Chico 451
Puerto Chacabuco 436	Palena 443	Puerto Bertrand 454
PN Laguna San Rafael . . 436	Caleta Gonzalo	Cochrane 455
Northern Aisén 438	(PN Pumalín) 443	Caleta Tortel 455
Villa Mañihuales 438	Chaitén 446	Puerto Yungay 456
Villa Amengual 438	Termas El Amarillo 449	Villa O'Higgins 456
Puerto Cisnes 439	**Southern Aisén 449**	
PN Queulat 439	Puerto Ingeniero Ibáñez . 449	

MAGALLANES & TIERRA DEL FUEGO 457

Magallanes 457	Estancia El Galpón 488	Puerto Williams 500
Punta Arenas 457	PN Los Glaciares (Arg) . . 488	Ushuaia (Arg) 501
Around Punta Arenas . . 469	Fitzroy Range (Arg) 492	Around Ushuaia 508
Puerto Natales 471	Tierra del Fuego 495	PN Tierra del Fuego (Arg) . 509
Around Puerto Natales . 476	Porvenir 497	Río Grande (Arg) 511
Villa Cerro Castillo 477	Cerro Sombrero 499	Around Río Grande 513
PN Torres del Paine 478	Lago Blanco 499	
El Calafate (Arg) 484	Estancia Yendegaia 500	

ARCHIPIÉLAGO JUAN FERNÁNDEZ 514

History 514	Books 519	PN Juan Fernández 523
Geography & Climate . . 516	Getting There & Away . . 519	Isla Alejandro Selkirk . . . 525
Flora 518	Getting Around 520	
Fauna 519	San Juan Bautista 520	

EASTER ISLAND (RAPA NUI) 526

History 526	Rapa Nui Antiquities . . . 536	Getting Around 542
Geography & Geology . . 535	Books & Film 539	Hanga Roa 544
Climate 535	Maps 540	PN Rapa Nui 550
Flora & Fauna 535	Getting There & Away . . 540	

FALKLAND ISLANDS (ISLAS MALVINAS) 557

Facts About the Islands . 557	Getting Around 563	Camp 566
Facts for the Visitor 560	Stanley 563	
Getting There & Away . 563	Around Stanley 566	

LANGUAGE 571

GLOSSARY 576

CLIMATE CHARTS 582

ACKNOWLEDGMENTS 583

INDEX 590

MAP INDEX

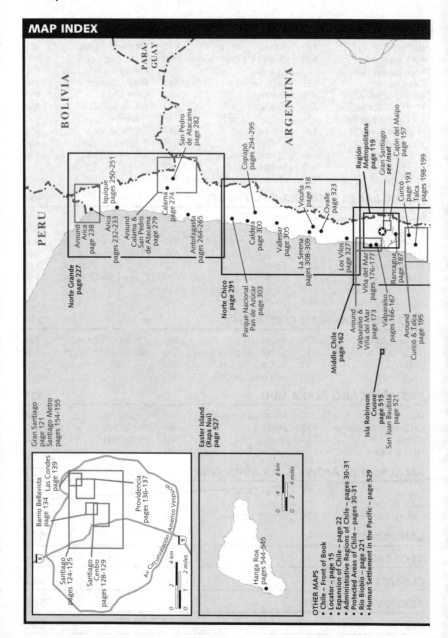

PARAGUAY

BOLIVIA

ARGENTINA

PERU

San Pedro de Atacama page 282

Around Arica page 238

Iquique pages 250-251

Arica pages 232-233

Around Calama & San Pedro de Atacama page 279

Calama page 274

Antofagasta pages 264-265

Norte Grande page 227

Copiapó pages 294-295

Vicuña page 318

Ovalle page 323

Región Metropolitana page 119 Gran Santiago see inset

Cajón del Maipo page 157

Curicó page 193

Talca pages 198-199

Caldera page 300

Vallenar page 305

La Serena pages 308-309

Los Vilos page 327

Viña del Mar pages 176-177

Rancagua page 187

Parque Nacional Pan de Azúcar page 303

Norte Chico page 291

Middle Chile page 162

Around Valparaíso & Viña del Mar page 173

Valparaíso pages 166-167

Curicó & Talca page 195

Gran Santiago page 121 Santiago Metro pages 154-155

Barrio Bellavista page 134   Las Condes page 139

Providencia pages 136-137

Santiago pages 124-125

Santiago Centro pages 128-129

Av Circunvalación Américo Vespucio

5

5

0   2   4 km
0   1   2 miles

Easter Island (Rapa Nui) page 527

Isla Robinson Crusoe page 515 San Juan Bautista page 521

0   4   8 km
0   2   4 miles

Hanga Roa pages 544-545

OTHER MAPS
• Chile – Front of Book
• Locator – page 15
• Expansion of Chile – page 22
• Administrative Regions of Chile – pages 30-31
• Protected Areas of Chile – pages 30-31
• Río Biobío – page 221
• Human Settlement in the Pacific – page 529

MAP INDEX

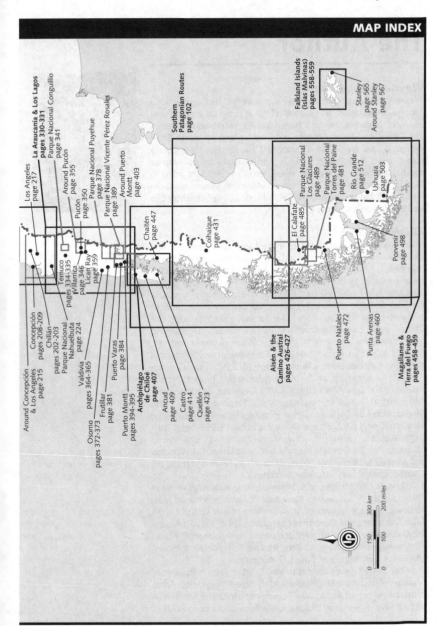

La Araucania & Los Lagos
pages 330-331

Parque Nacional Conguillio
page 341

Around Pucón
page 355

Pucón
page 350

Parque Nacional Puyehue
page 378

Parque Nacional Vicente Pérez Rosales
page 389

Around Puerto Montt
page 403

Los Angeles
page 217

Temuco
pages 334-335

Villarrica
page 346

Lican Ray
page 359

Chaitén
page 447

Southern
Patagonian Routes
page 102

Falkland Islands
(Islas Malvinas)
pages 558-559

Stanley
page 565
Around Stanley
page 567

Parque Nacional
Los Glaciares
page 489

Parque Nacional
Torres del Paine
page 481

Río Grande
page 512

Ushuaia
page 503

El Calafate
page 485

Coihaique
page 431

Porvenir
page 498

Around Concepción
& Los Angeles
page 215

Concepción
pages 208-209

Chillán
pages 202-203

Parque Nacional
Nahuelbuta
page 224

Valdivia
pages 364-365

Osorno
pages 372-373

Frutillar
page 381

Puerto Varas
page 384

Puerto Montt
pages 394-395

Archipiélago
de Chiloé
page 407

Ancud
page 409

Castro
page 414

Quellón
page 423

Aisén & the
Camino Austral
pages 426-427

Puerto Natales
page 472

Punta Arenas
page 460

Magallanes &
Tierra del Fuego
pages 458-459

0   150   300 km
0   100   200 miles

The Author

Wayne Bernhardson

Wayne Bernhardson was born in Fargo, North Dakota, grew up in Tacoma, Washington, and earned a PhD in geography at the University of California, Berkeley. He has traveled extensively in Mexico and Central and South America and lived for long periods in Chile, Argentina and the Falkland (Malvinas) Islands. His other Lonely Planet credits include *Buenos Aires*, *South America on a Shoestring* and *Baja California*. 'The gringo who knows Chile best,' according to Santiago's principal daily newspaper, *El Mercurio*, Wayne resides in Oakland, California, with María Laura Massolo, their daughter Clio and his Alaskan malamute Gardel.

FROM WAYNE

Many friends and acquaintances in Santiago and elsewhere were exceptionally helpful and hospitable in the process of pulling this all together. The list could go on forever, but special mention to Yerko Ivelic of Cascada Expediciones, for harboring my truck in San Alfonso while I returned to California to write up my Argentine material and for reviewing material on Chilean rivers; and to customs agent Juan Alarcón Rojas for navigating through the Chilean bureaucracy. Thanks also to Pablo Fernández of Hostelling International, for arranging long-term accommodation in Santiago; Eduardo Núñez of Conaf, Santiago, for easing access to national parks and other reserves; Claudia Aguirre N of Patagonia Connection; Steve Anderson of the Chile Information Project; Harold Beckett of the Guía Aérea Oficial; Carlos Casanova, Marco Vergara and Cristina Carrillo of Navimag; María Fernanda Daza of the Municipalidad de Santiago; Simon Hosking of the British Embassy, Santiago; Douglas Koneff and Diana Page of the US Embassy, Santiago; Alejandra Belart of Lassa; Víctor Maldonado and Marisa Blásquez; Hernán, Carmen, Marcela and Paula Torres; Pato Ovando and Marializ Maldonado; Claudio Parra of Los Jaivas and his agent Claudia Schlegel; and Mauricio Carmona.

In Middle Chile, thanks go to Veronique Arancet Rodríguez of the Municipalidad de Valparaíso; Paola Lara of Sernatur, Viña del Mar; Verónica Morgado Saldivia of Sernatur, Talca; Alexis Villa of Conaf, Talca; Doris Sandoval Gutiérrez of Sernatur, Chillán; Claudia Alejandra García Niño of Los Angeles; John and Louise Jackson of Fundo Curanilahue; Nelson Oyarzo Barrientos of Sernatur, Concepción; and Rolando Rodríguez of Conaf, Concepción.

In the Norte Grande, thanks to José Gustavo Cuevas Ramírez of Sernatur, Arica; Michel Cinquin and Charlie Dekeyser of Arica; Barbara Knapton of Putre; Juan Torres Santibáñez and Mario Marroquín Silva of Sernatur, Iquique; César Eduardo Cardozo Rojas of

Reserva Nacional Pampa del Tamarugal; Gerda Alcaide López of Sernatur, Antofagasta; Alejandro Santoro of Conaf, Antofagasta; Carlos Reygadas of Calama; and Martín Beeris of Cosmo Andino, San Pedro de Atacama.

In the Norte Chico, thanks to Fernando Bascuñán of Conaf, Copiapó; Washington Hernández and Leila Manterola of Sernatur, Copiapó; Cecilia Prats Cuthbert and Alicia Díaz Fraile of Sernatur, La Serena; Rodrigo Sugg Pierry of La Serena; and David González of La Serena and Cerro Tololo International Observatory.

In La Araucanía and Los Lagos, thanks to Javier Ibar Muñoz of the Municipalidad de Angol; Alex Hernández Montanares of Parque Nacional Conguillío; Carolina Morgado of Puerto Varas for information on Pumalín; Luis Canales Leyton of Puerto Varas's municipal tourist office Rony Pollak and William Hatcher of Pucón; Béat and Claudia Zbiden of Villarrica; Patricio Yáñez Strange of Sernatur, Valdivia; Clark Stede of Puerto Varas; Adrian Turner and Marcela Benavides of Puerto Montt; and Andrés Añazco P of Puerto Octay. On Chiloé, thanks to Andrea González of Hotelga, Castro, Carl Grady of Chonchi and Rosa Díaz Santana of Quellón.

In the Aisén region and along the Camino Austral, thanks to Nicholas La Penna of Chaitén; Gabriela Neira Morales of Sernatur, Coihaique; Carlos Lezama Nagel of Conaf, Coihaique; and Jonathan Leidich of Puerto Bertrand.

In Magallanes, thanks to Julio Arenas Coloma and Andrea Lagunas Flores of Sernatur, Punta Arenas; British Consul John Rees Jones of Punta Arenas; Ivette Martínez of Turismo Cordillera Darwin, Punta Arenas; Miguel Angel Muñoz of Sernatur, Puerto Natales; Edmundo Martínez G of Andescape, Puerto Natales; Werner and Cecilia Ruf-Chaura, of Casa Cecilia, Puerto Natales, and Hernán Jofré of Concepto Indigo, Puerto Natales; Carlos Barria Díaz of Parque Nacional Torres del Paine; and Wolf Kloss of Puerto Williams.

On Juan Fernández, special mention to Hernán González of Conaf and to Juanita Díaz. In Hanga Roa, Rapa Nui, thanks to Francisco Edmunds of Sernatur, Ramón Edmunds, Martín Hereveri and particularly Conny Martin.

In Argentina, thanks to Julio César Lovece and Natalie Prosser de Goodall of Ushuaia, Tierra del Fuego; Mariano Besio of El Calafate, and the staff at the Casa de Santa Cruz in Buenos Aires; Rubén Vásquez of El Chaltén, Santa Cruz; and Lilián Díaz and Mario Feldman of El Calafate. Jeff Rubin, author of Lonely Planet's *Antarctica*, passed along useful notes on Ushuaia.

In the Falkland Islands, thanks to Stanley residents John Fowler and Deborah Gilding of the Falkland Islands Tourist Board, former governor Richard Ralph, Ian and Maria Strange, Kay McCallum, Sue Binnie, Jane Cameron, Tony Smith, Montana Short, John and Margaret Leonard, Shirley Peck, Dave Eynon, and Ray and Nancy Poole. In camp, thanks to Dave and Pat Grey of Sea Lion Island, Richard and Toni Stevens of Port Sussex, Tony McMullen of Goose Green,

William and Lynda Anderson of San Carlos, James McGhie of Pebble Island, John Ferguson of Weddell Island, all the Pole-Evanses on Saunders Island, Robin Lee and Ron Reeves of Port Howard, Richard and Griz Cockwell of Fox Bay East for lunch and transport back to Port Howard, and Jerome and Sally Poncet of Beaver Island.

Stateside, thanks to Scott Stine of California State University, Hayward, for sharing the results of his research on the Moreno Glacier. Georgia Lee of Los Osos, California, made a huge contribution to the Easter Island chapter, overturning misconceptions that I shared with many other people. Chilean consul Alberto Joacham of San Francisco aided immensely with customs paperwork. James T Smith of Oakland and Elaine Pilz of Grand Junction, Colorado, were great companions on Juan Fernández and Easter Island.

In Los Angeles, Iván Zika of LanChile was most helpful in arranging flight details along with Alberto Cortés of LanChile in Miami. Cecilia Aguayo of Miami and Silber Editores also deserves a mention. Chris Spelius of Expediciones Chile and Bryson, North Carolina, kept me up-to-date on Chilean rivers. Thanks also to Paul and Philip Garber of the Chilean consulate in Boston. Amy Eisenberg of Tucson shared the results of her recent research in Parque Nacional Lauca.

Thanks again to Tony and Maureen Wheeler, for keeping me employed for nearly a decade, and to Eric Kettunen and other Oakland office editors, cartographers and staff.

My apologies to anyone I've overlooked.

This Book

The first two editions of *Chile & Easter Island* were written by Alan Samalgalski. The 3rd edition was researched again from scratch, rewritten and considerably expanded by Wayne Bernhardson, who also updated and expanded the 4th edition.

Wayne also researched and wrote this 5th edition of *Chile & Easter Island*.

From the Publisher

This 5th edition of *Chile & Easter Island* was produced in Lonely Planet's Oakland office. Under the supervision of peerless (and fearless) senior editors Jacqueline Volin and Michele Posner, text and maps were edited by Tullan Spitz, with immeasurable help from Kevin Anglin. Karen O'Donnell-Stein, Wade Fox, China Williams and Carolyn Hubbard also deserve hearty thanks. Tullan, Kevin, Karen and Rachel Bernstein proofed the text and maps. Ken DellaPenta indexed the book. With unflagging patience, lead cartographer Heather Haskell and cartographers Andy Rebold, Chris Gillis, John Spelman and Patrick Phelan created the maps, guided by senior cartographers Amy Dennis, Tracey Croom and Kimra McAfee. Alex Guilbert supervised the cartography crew. Shelley Firth artfully designed the color pages and managed layout with help from Ruth Askevold and guidance from Susan Rimerman. Hayden Foell, Shelley, Wendy Yanagihara, Justin Marler, Hannah Reineck, Hugh D'Andrade and Jim Swanson drew the illustrations. Simon Bracken designed the cover.

Many thanks to Scott Summers for his expertise and kindness; to Kate Hoffman for editorial advice; and to Wendy Taylor-Hall, Paige Penland, Christine Lee, Maria Donohoe, Rachel Bernstein and David Zingarelli for moral support.

Warning & Request

Things change – prices go up, schedules change, good places go bad and bad places go bankrupt – nothing stays the same. So if you find things better or worse, recently opened or long since closed, please write and tell us and help make the next edition better!

Your letters will be used to help update future editions and, where possible, important changes will also be included as a Stop Press section in reprints.

All information is greatly appreciated and the best letters will receive a free copy of the next edition, or any other Lonely Planet book of your choice.

Foreword

ABOUT LONELY PLANET GUIDEBOOKS

The story begins with a classic travel adventure: Tony and Maureen Wheeler's 1972 journey across Europe and Asia to Australia. Useful information about the overland trail did not exist at that time, so Tony and Maureen published the first Lonely Planet guidebook to meet a growing need.

From a kitchen table, then from a tiny office in Melbourne (Australia), Lonely Planet has become the largest independent travel publisher in the world, an international company with offices in Melbourne, Oakland (USA), London (UK) and Paris (France).

Today Lonely Planet guidebooks cover the globe. There is an ever-growing list of books, and there's information in a variety of forms and media. Some things haven't changed. The main aim is still to help make it possible for adventurous travelers to get out there – to explore and better understand the world.

At Lonely Planet we believe travelers can make a positive contribution to the countries they visit – if they respect their host communities and spend their money wisely. Since 1986 a percentage of the income from each book has been donated to aid projects and human-rights campaigns.

Updates Lonely Planet thoroughly updates each guidebook as often as possible. This usually means there are around two years between editions, although for more unusual or more stable destinations the gap can be longer. Check the imprint page (following the color map at the beginning of the book) for publication dates.

Between editions, up-to-date information is available in two free newsletters – the paper *Planet Talk* and email *Comet* (to subscribe, contact any Lonely Planet office) – and on our website at www.lonelyplanet.com. The *Upgrades* section of the website covers a number of important and volatile destinations and is regularly updated by Lonely Planet authors. *Scoop* covers news and current affairs relevant to travelers. And, lastly, the *Thorn Tree* bulletin board and *Postcards* section of the site carry unverified, but fascinating, reports from travelers.

Correspondence The process of creating new editions begins with the letters, postcards and emails received from travelers. This correspondence often includes suggestions, criticisms and comments about the current editions. Interesting excerpts are immediately passed on via newsletters and the website, and everything goes to our authors to be verified when they're researching on the road. We're keen to get more feedback from organizations or individuals who represent communities visited by travelers.

Lonely Planet gathers information for everyone who's curious about the planet – and especially for those who explore it first-hand. Through guidebooks, phrasebooks, activity guides, maps, literature, newsletters, image library, TV series and website, we act as an information exchange for a worldwide community of travelers.

Research Authors aim to gather sufficient practical information to enable travelers to make informed choices and to make the mechanics of a journey run smoothly. They also research historical and cultural background to help enrich the travel experience and allow travelers to understand and respond appropriately to cultural and environmental issues.

Authors don't stay in every hotel because that would mean spending a couple of months in each medium-size city and, no, they don't eat at every restaurant because that would mean stretching belts beyond capacity. They do visit hotels and restaurants to check standards and prices, but feedback based on readers' direct experiences can be very helpful.

Many of our authors work undercover; others aren't so secretive. None of them accept freebies in exchange for positive write-ups. And none of our guidebooks contain any advertising.

Production Authors submit their raw manuscripts and maps to offices in Australia, the USA, the UK or France. Editors and cartographers – all experienced travelers themselves – then begin the process of assembling the pieces. When the book finally hits the shops, some things are already out of date, we start getting feedback from readers and the process begins again....

WARNING & REQUEST

Things change – prices go up, schedules change, good places go bad and bad places go bankrupt – nothing stays the same. So, if you find things better or worse, recently opened or long since closed, please tell us and help make the next edition even more accurate and useful. We genuinely value all the feedback we receive. Julie Young coordinates a well-traveled team that reads and acknowledges every letter, postcard and email and ensures that every morsel of information finds its way to the appropriate authors, editors and cartographers for verification.

Everyone who writes to us will find their name in the next edition of the appropriate guidebook. They will also receive the latest issue of *Planet Talk*, our quarterly printed newsletter, or *Comet*, our monthly email newsletter. Subscriptions to both newsletters are free. The very best contributions will be rewarded with a free guidebook.

Excerpts from your correspondence may appear in new editions of Lonely Planet guidebooks, the Lonely Planet website, *Planet Talk* or *Comet*, so please let us know if you *don't* want your letter published or your name acknowledged.

Send all correspondence to the Lonely Planet office closest to you:

Australia: PO Box 617, Hawthorn, Victoria 3122
USA: 150 Linden St, Oakland, CA 94607
UK: 10A Spring Place, London NW5 3BH
France: 1 rue du Dahomey, 75011 Paris

Or email us at: talk2us@lonelyplanet.com.au

For news, views and updates, see our website: www.lonelyplanet.com

HOW TO USE A LONELY PLANET GUIDEBOOK

The best way to use a Lonely Planet guidebook is any way you choose. At Lonely Planet, we believe the most memorable travel experiences are often those that are unexpected, and the finest discoveries are those you make yourself. Guidebooks are not intended to be used as if they provided a detailed set of infallible instructions!

Contents All Lonely Planet guidebooks follow the same format. The Facts about the Country chapters or sections give background information ranging from history to weather. Facts for the Visitor gives practical information on issues like visas and health. Getting There & Away gives a brief starting point for researching travel to and from the destination. Getting Around gives an overview of the transport options available when you arrive.

The peculiar demands of each destination determine how subsequent chapters are broken up, but some things remain constant. We always start with background, then proceed to sights, places to stay, places to eat, entertainment, getting there and away, and getting around information – in that order.

Heading Hierarchy Lonely Planet headings are used in a strict hierarchical structure that can be visualized as a set of Russian dolls. Each heading (and its following text) is encompassed by any preceding heading that is higher on the hierarchical ladder.

Entry Points We do not assume guidebooks will be read from beginning to end, but that people will dip into them. The traditional entry points are the list of contents and the index. In addition, however, some books have a complete list of maps and an index map illustrating map coverage.

There may also be a color map that shows highlights. These highlights are dealt with in greater detail later in the book, along with planning questions. Each chapter covering a geographical region usually begins with a locator map and another list of highlights. Once you find something of interest in a list of highlights, turn to the index.

Maps Maps play a crucial role in Lonely Planet guidebooks and include a huge amount of information. A legend is printed on the back page. We seek to have complete consistency between maps and text, and to have every important place in the text captured on a map. Map key numbers usually start in the top left corner.

Although inclusion in a guidebook usually implies a recommendation, we cannot list every good place. Exclusion does not necessarily imply criticism. In fact, there are a number of reasons why we might exclude a place – sometimes it is simply inappropriate to encourage an influx of travelers.

Introduction

On South America's Pacific coast, stretching from the tropics nearly to the Antarctic, Chile is a string bean country rarely wider than 180 km. For nearly all its length, the imposing Andes Mountains isolate it from Bolivia and Argentina, but it also shares a short border with Peru in the Atacama desert. Chile, whose coastline stretches 4300km, features a great variety of environments: the nearly waterless Atacama, the Mediterranean-like central valley, a mountainous but temperate lakes district and Patagonia's spectacular alpine glaciers and fjords, where national parks such as Torres del Paine and Queulat offer some of the world's finest trekking and fishing. Even from popular Pacific beaches, the massive Andean crest is almost always within sight; surfing and skiing on the same day is not beyond possibility.

For nearly two decades, Chile was an international pariah because of the bloody 1973 coup that took the life of socialist Salvador Allende, the constitutional president, and resulted in his replacement by military dictator General Augusto Pinochet. Since Pinochet's rejection by Chilean voters in a referendum and the return to constitutional government in 1989, the country has become an increasingly popular destination. General Pinochet's regime was a remarkably durable anomaly in the history of Chile, where military intervention has been the exception rather than the rule since the country's independence from Spain in the early 19th century.

Chile is a mestizo country, of mixed European and indigenous extraction, and the indigenous tradition is still visible and viable in several parts of the country. In the desert

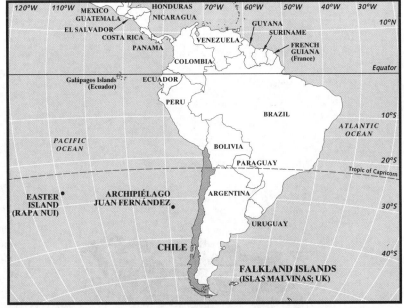

north, once part of the Inka empire, are important archaeological sites. Aymara Indians still farm the valleys and terraces of the Andean foothills and tend flocks of llamas and alpacas on the altiplano.

South of the Chilean heartland in the central valley, hundreds of thousands of Mapuche Indians live in communities whose symbolic status in Chilean life exceeds their political and economic significance. The Mapuche maintained an effective and heroic resistance to the southward advance of Chilean rule nearly into the 20th century, earning a grudging respect from the expansionist Chilean state. Cities such as Temuco and Osorno are proud of their indigenous heritage.

For visitors with a taste for the exotic or the romantic, Chile has two unique insular possessions. Distant Easter Island (Rapa Nui), with its giant stylized statues, has long attracted explorers, adventurers, anthropologists and archaeologists. Tourist access is better than ever, and the island's Polynesian hospitality is an unexpected bonus. Nearer the mainland, the Juan Fernández Archipelago was the refuge of marooned Scotsman Alexander Selkirk, whose solitary experiences inspired Daniel Defoe's classic novel *Robinson Crusoe*. The archipelago is a national park, and its many endemic plant species have made it a World Biosphere Reserve.

Chile's people are remarkably friendly and hospitable to foreigners. No longer a place to avoid because of its turbulent history, the country is drawing increasing numbers of travelers whose itineraries once included only Peru, Bolivia and Argentina. Its tremendous geographic diversity and surprising cultural variety have made it an important destination in its own right.

Facts about Chile

HISTORY
Indigenous Cultures

When Europeans first arrived in present-day Chile in the 16th century, they encountered a number of native peoples whose customs and economies differed greatly. While politically subject to the Inkas, most cultures in the region predated the lords of Cuzco by centuries or even millennia. In the canyons of the desert north, sedentary Aymara farmers cultivated maize in transverse valleys irrigated by the rivers descending from the Andes. At higher elevations, they grew potatoes and tended flocks of llamas and alpacas. To the south, beyond the Río Loa, Atacameño peoples practiced a similar livelihood, while Chango fisherfolk occupied coastal areas from Arica almost to the Río Choapa, south of present-day La Serena. Diaguita Indians inhabited the interior of this latter region, which comprises the drainages of the Copiapó, Huasco and Elqui Rivers.

Inka rule barely touched the central valley and the forests of the south, where Araucanian Indians (Picunche and Mapuche) Indians fiercely resisted incursions from the north. The Picunche lived in permanent agricultural settlements, while the Mapuche, who practiced shifting cultivation, were more mobile and much more difficult for the Inkas, and later the Spaniards, to subdue. Several groups closely related to the Mapuche – the Pehuenche, Huilliche and Puelche – lived in the southern lakes region, while the Cunco fished and farmed on the island of Chiloé and along the shores of the gulfs of Reloncaví and Ancud. Not until the late 19th century did the descendants of Europeans establish a permanent presence beyond the Río Biobío.

South of the Chilean mainland, numerous small populations of Indians subsisted through hunting and fishing – the Chonos, Qawashqar (Alacalufes), Yamaná (Yahgan), Tehuelche and Ona (Selknam). These isolated archipelagic peoples long avoided contact with Europeans, but they are now extinct or nearly so.

Spanish Invasion

In 1494, the papal Treaty of Tordesillas ratified the Spanish-Portuguese division of the Americas, granting all territory west of Brazil to Spain, which rapidly consolidated its formal authority and, by the mid-16th century, dominated most of an area extending from Florida and Mexico to central Chile. In the same period, most of South America's important cities were founded, including Lima, Peru; Santiago, Chile; Asunción, Paraguay; and La Paz, Bolivia.

Spain's successful invasion of the Americas was accomplished by groups of adventurers, lowlifes and soldiers-of-fortune against whom the penal colonists of Australia's Botany Bay look like saints. Diego de Almagro, one of the early explorers of Chile and northern Argentina, arrived in Panama after fleeing a Spanish murder charge. Few in number (Francisco Pizarro took Peru with only 180 men), the conquerors were determined and ruthless, exploiting factionalism among indigenous groups and frightening native peoples with their horses, vicious dogs and firearms, but their greatest ally was infectious disease to which the natives lacked immunity.

Before Pizarro's assassination in 1541, he assigned the task of conquering Chile to Pedro de Valdivia. After some difficulty in recruitment (Almagro's earlier expedition had suffered terribly, especially during its winter crossing, from Argentina, of the bitterly cold and nearly waterless Puna de Atacama), Valdivia's expedition left Peru in 1540, crossed the desert and reached Chile's fertile Mapocho Valley in 1541, subduing local Indians and founding the city of Santiago on February 12. Only six months later, the Indians counterattacked, destroyed the city and nearly wiped out the settlers' supplies. But the Spaniards held out, and six years later their numbers had grown to

Pedro de Valdivia

nearly 500 with assistance and reinforcements from Peru. Meanwhile, they founded settlements at La Serena and Valparaíso. Valdivia also worked southward, founding Concepción, Valdivia and Villarrica. Despite his death at the battle of Tucapel in 1553, at the hands of Mapuche forces led by the famous *caciques* (chiefs) Caupolicán and Lautaro, Valdivia had laid the groundwork for a new society.

Colonial Society

Ironically, throughout the Americas, the structure of indigenous societies influenced the economic and political structure of early colonial life to a greater extent than the directives of European authorities. The Spaniards' primary goal was the acquisition of gold and silver, and they ruthlessly appropriated precious metals through outright robbery when possible, and by other, no less brutal, means when necessary. El Dorado, the legendary city of gold, proved elusive, but the Spaniards soon realized that the true wealth of the New World consisted of the large Indian populations of Mexico, Peru and other lands.

Disdaining physical labor themselves, the Spaniards exploited the indigenous populations of the New World through mechanisms such as the *encomienda*, best translated as 'entrustment,' by which the Crown granted an individual Spaniard *(encomendero)* rights to Indian labor and tribute in a particular village or area. Institutions such as the Catholic Church also held encomiendas. In theory, Spanish legislation required the encomendero to reciprocate with instruction in the Spanish language and the Catholic religion, but in practice imperial administration was inadequate to ensure compliance and avoid the worst abuses. Spanish overseers worked Indians mercilessly in the mines and extracted the maximum in agricultural produce.

In the most densely populated parts of the Americas, some encomenderos became extraordinarily wealthy, but the encomienda system failed when Indian populations declined rapidly, not so much from overwork and physical punishment as from epidemic disease. Isolated for at least 10,000 years from Old World diseases, the Indians could not withstand the onslaught of smallpox, influenza, typhus and other such killers: in some parts of the New World, these diseases reduced the native population by more than 95%.

In Chile, the encomienda was most important in the irrigated valleys of the desert north (then part of Peru), where the population was large and sedentary – the most highly organized Indian peoples were the easiest to subdue and control, since they were accustomed to similar forms of exploitation. In hierarchical states such as the Inka empire, the Spaniards easily replaced established local authority.

The Spaniards also established dominance in central Chile, but the semi-sedentary and nomadic peoples of the south mounted vigorous resistance, and even into the late 19th century the area remained unsafe for white settlers. Crossing the Andes, the Mapuche had tamed the feral horses that had multiplied rapidly on the fine pastures of the Argentine pampas; they soon became expert riders, which increased their mobility and enhanced their ability to strike.

Even in places where Spanish supremacy went unchallenged, Indians outnumbered Spaniards. Since few women accompanied the early settlers, Spanish men, especially of the lower classes, had both formal and informal relationships with Indian women; the resulting *mestizo* children, of mixed Spanish and Indian parentage, soon outnumbered the Indian population as many of the natives died through epidemics, forced labor abuses and warfare. As the Indian population declined, encomiendas became nearly worthless, and Spaniards sought new economic alternatives.

Rise of the Latifundio

In Chile, unlike many other parts of Spanish America, the encomienda became highly correlated with land ownership; Chile was too remote for adequate imperial oversight and, despite the Crown's disapproval, Valdivia rewarded his followers with enormous land grants, some stretching from the Andes to the Pacific. More than anywhere else in the Americas, the system of control resembled the great feudal estates of Valdivia's homeland of Extremadura in Spain. Such estates *(latifundios)*, many intact as late as the 1960s, became an enduring feature of Chilean agriculture and the dominant force in Chilean society.

As the encomienda system declined, Chile's neoaristocracy had to look elsewhere for labor. The country's growing mestizo population, systematically excluded from land ownership, provided the solution. Landless and vagrant, these ostensible Spaniards soon attached themselves as *inquilinos* (tenant farmers) to the large rural estates, which evolved from livestock *estancias* into agricultural haciendas or, as they became more commonly known in Chile, *fundos*.

In becoming inquilinos, laborers and their families also became personally dependent on the *hacendado* (master) for certain rights. Paying little or no rent, they could occupy a shack on the estate, graze livestock on its more remote sections, and cultivate a patch of land for household use.

In return, they provided labor during annual rodeos and watched out for their master's interests. American geographer George McCutcheon McBride found this relationship of 'man and master' endured well into the 20th century and permeated all aspects of Chilean society:

There was a landholding aristocracy, well educated, far-traveled, highly cultured, in full control of the national life; and, quite apart from them, a lower class, often spoken of with mixed disdain and affection as the *rotos* (ragged ones), constituting the fixed tenantry of the rural estates. This distinction, clearly an agrarian one in its origin, was carried into the social structure of the entire people. It gave its cast to the nation.

Other groups gave their cast to the nation as well. Even though the large estates remained intact, they did not always remain in the same hands. Later immigrants, especially Basques, became a major influence from the late 17th century to the end of the colonial era. Surnames such as Eyzaguirre, Urrutia and Larraín became prominent in Chilean commerce, and these families purchased many landed estates, including ones that had been confiscated when the Spaniards expelled the Jesuits and offered at public auction. Basque families adopted the pseudoaristocratic values of the early landed gentry and have remained important in Chilean politics, society and business.

In colonial times, mining and business brought greater wealth than did land. Only after political independence, having broken the mercantile links with imperial Spain, did Chile's agricultural economy begin to flourish.

Independence Movements

Within a few decades of Columbus' Caribbean landing, Spain possessed an empire twice the size of Europe, stretching from California to Cape Horn. Yet the empire disintegrated in less than two decades; by the late 1820s, only Puerto Rico and Cuba remained in Spanish hands.

Many factors contributed to the rise of Latin American independence movements. One was the emergence of the *criollo* (creole) class – American-born Spaniards who soon distinguished themselves from the Iberians. In every Latin American country, the development of a definable American identity increased people's desire for self-government. Of equal importance, influential criollo merchants resented Spain's rigid mercantile trade system. To facilitate tax collection, Madrid decreed that all trade to the mother country must pass overland through Panama to the Caribbean and Havana, rather than directly by ship from the port of Valparaíso. This cumbersome system hampered the commerce of Chile and other Spanish colonies and eventually cost Spain its empire.

Spain's own stagnant economy could not provide the manufactured goods that the American colonies demanded. Spain also had to contend with interloping European countries, as Britain, Holland and France all acquired minor bases in the Caribbean and elsewhere in the New World. By the late 18th century the British had obtained trade concessions from Spain and were surreptitiously encouraging criollo political aspirations.

Several other factors contributed, directly and indirectly, to the independence drive that began between 1808 and 1810: the successful North American rebellion against England, the overthrow of the French monarchy, Napoleon's invasion of Spain (which disrupted communications between Spain and America and allowed the colonies a period of temporary autonomy) and European intellectual trends. The fact that colonial armies consisted mainly of criollos and mestizos, rather than troops from Spain, made it easier for them to challenge Spanish authority.

Revolutionary Wars
During colonial times, the formal jurisdiction of the Audiencia de Chile stretched roughly from present-day Chañaral in the north to Puerto Aisén in the south; it also encompassed the trans-Andean Cuyo region of modern Argentina, comprising the provinces of Mendoza, San Juan and San Luis.

The Audiencia was an administrative subdivision of the much larger Viceroyalty of Peru, whose capital, Lima, was South America's most important city. But Chile was distant from Lima and developed in near isolation from Peru, with an identity distinct from its northern neighbor.

Independence movements throughout South America united to expel Spain from the continent by the 1820s. From Venezuela, a criollo army under Simón Bolívar fought its way across the Andes to the Pacific and then south toward Peru. José de San Martín's Ejército de los Andes (Army of the Andes) – nearly a third of them liberated slaves – marched over the *cordillera* (mountain range) from Argentina into Chile, occupied Santiago and sailed north to Lima.

San Martín's army also included numerous Chileans who had fled the reimposition of Spanish colonial rule after the Napoleonic Wars. The Argentine liberator appointed Bernardo O'Higgins second-in-command of his forces. O'Higgins, the illegitimate son of an Irishman who had served the Spaniards as Viceroy of Peru, became supreme director of the new Chilean republic. San Martín helped drive Spain from Peru, transporting his army in ships either seized from the Spaniards or purchased from Britons or North Americans. British and North American merchants also financed the purchase of arms and ammunition, knowing that expulsion of the Spaniards would create new commercial opportunities. Scotsman Thomas Cochrane, a colorful former Royal Navy officer, founded and commanded Chile's navy.

Early Republic
Spanish administrative divisions provided the framework for the political geography of the new South American republics. At independence, Chile was but a fraction of its present size, consisting of the *intendencias* (administrative units of the Spanish Empire) of Santiago and Concepción and sharing ambiguous boundaries with Bolivia in the north, Argentina to the east, and the hostile Mapuche nation south of the Río Biobío.

Chile lost the trans-Andean region of Cuyo to the Provincias Unidas del Río de la Plata (United Provinces of the River Plate), forerunner of modern Argentina.

Although other Latin American countries emerged from the wars with severe economic difficulties, Chile quickly achieved a degree of political stability, permitting rapid development of agriculture, mining, industry and commerce. Regional quarrels were less serious and violent than they were, for example, in Argentina. Despite social and economic cleavages, the population was relatively homogeneous and less afflicted by racial problems than most other Latin American states. The country was well situated to take advantage of international economic trends; the port of Valparaíso, for instance, became an important outlet for Chilean wheat, which satisfied the unprecedented demand of the California gold rush.

O'Higgins dominated Chilean politics for five years after formal independence in 1818, enacting political, social, religious and educational reforms, but the landowning elite that first supported him soon objected to increased taxes, abolition of titles and limitations on the inheritance of landed estates. Pressured by military forces allied with the aristocracy, he resigned in 1823 and went into exile in Peru. He died there in 1842, never having returned to his homeland.

Apart from deposing the Spaniards, political independence did not alter the structure of Chilean society, which was dominated by major landowners. The embodiment of landowning interests was Diego Portales, a businessman who, as interior minister, was de facto dictator until his execution after an uprising in 1837. His custom-drawn constitution centralized power in Santiago and established Roman Catholicism as the state religion. It also limited suffrage to literate and propertied adult males and established indirect elections for the presidency and the Senate; only the lower Chamber of Deputies was chosen directly by voters. Portales' constitution lasted, with some changes, until 1925.

Territorial Expansion & Political Reform

At independence, Chile was a compact country whose northern limit was the southern border of the present-day region of Antofagasta, and whose southern limit was the Río Biobío. From the mid-19th century, railroad construction began to revolutionize internal transport. Military triumphs over Peru and Bolivia in the War of the Pacific (1879–83) and treaties with the Mapuche (1881) incorporated the nitrate-rich Atacama and temperate southern territories under Chilean authority. At the same time, however, Chile had to abandon its claims to most of enormous, sparsely populated Patagonia to Argentina.

Santiago's intervention in the Atacama, ostensibly to protect the interests of Chilean nationals laboring in the nitrate fields, proved a bonanza. Just as guano financed Peruvian independence, so nitrates brought prosperity to Chile, or at least to certain sectors of Chilean society. British, North American and German investors supplied most of the capital.

Ever since the California gold rush, Valparaíso had been a critical port. Soon the nitrate ports of Antofagasta and Iquique also became important in international commerce, until the opening of the Panama Canal in 1914 nearly eliminated traffic around the Horn, and the later development of petroleum-based fertilizers made mineral nitrates obsolete.

Chile also sought a broader Pacific presence, and Chilean naval vessels sailed to Australia, Asia and Polynesia. Extremists even advocated annexation of the Philippines, still under Spanish control at the time. Chile's only imperial possession, however, was tiny, remote Easter Island (Isla de Pascua or Rapa Nui), annexed in 1888.

Chile emerged from the War of the Pacific enriched not only by the Atacama's nitrates but also, later, by copper. Mining expansion created a new working class, as well as a class of nouveaux riches, both of which challenged the political power of the landowning oligarchy.

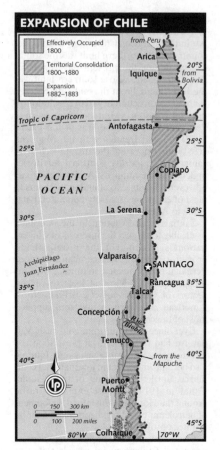

EXPANSION OF CHILE

Effectively Occupied 1800

Territorial Consolidation 1800–1880

Expansion 1882–1883

from Peru
Arica
Iquique   20°S   from Bolivia
Tropic of Capricorn
Antofagasta
25°S   25°S
PACIFIC OCEAN
Copiapó
La Serena   30°S
30°S
Archipiélago Juan Fernández
Valparaíso
35°S   SANTIAGO
Rancagua 35°S
Talca
Concepción   Río Biobío
Temuco
40°S   from the Mapuche   40°S
Puerto Montt
0   150   300 km
0   100   200 miles
80°W   Coihaique   70°W   45°S

The first political figure to tackle the dilemma of Chile's badly distributed wealth and power was President José Manuel Balmaceda, elected in 1886. Balmaceda's administration undertook major public works projects, expanding the rail network and building new roads, bridges and docks, extending telegraph lines and postal services, and improving hospitals and schools.

Balmaceda's policies met resistance from a conservative Congress, which in 1890 rejected his budget, voted to depose him, and appointed Naval Commander Jorge Montt to head a provisional government. More than 10,000 Chileans died in the ensuing civil war, in which Montt's navy controlled the country's ports and eventually defeated the government despite army support for Balmaceda. After several months' asylum in the Argentine embassy, Balmaceda shot himself.

Although they weakened the presidential system, Balmaceda's immediate successors continued many of his public works projects and also opened Congress to popular rather than indirect elections. Major reform, though, wouldn't come until after WWII.

20th Century

Despite economic hardship due to a declining nitrate industry, the election of President Arturo Alessandri Palma was a hopeful sign for Chile's working class. To reduce landowners' power, he proposed greater political autonomy for the provinces and land and income taxes to finance social benefits to improve working conditions, public health, education and welfare. Congressional conservatives obstructed these reforms, though, and army opposition forced Alessandri's resignation in 1924.

For several years, the dictatorial General Carlos Ibáñez del Campo occupied the presidency and other positions of power, but his misguided or miscarried economic policies (exacerbated by global depression) led to widespread opposition, forcing him into Argentine exile in 1931.

After Ibáñez's ouster, Chilean political parties realigned. Several leftist groups briefly imposed a socialist republic and merged to form the Socialist Party. Splits between Stalinists and Trotskyites divided the Communist Party, while splinter groups from existing radical and reformist parties created a bewildering mix of new political organizations. For most of the 1930s and '40s the democratic left dominated Chilean politics, and government intervention in the economy through Corfo, the state development corporation, became increasingly important.

Meanwhile, the US role in the Chilean economy also grew steadily, since German investment had declined after WWI and development of synthetic nitrates undercut British economic influence. In the first two decades of the 20th century, North American companies had gained control of the copper mines, the cornerstone – then and now – of the Chilean economy. WWII augmented the demand for Chilean copper, promoting economic growth even as Chile remained neutral in the conflict.

Politics of Land Reform
In the 1920s as much as 75% of Chile's rural population still depended on haciendas that controlled 80% of prime agricultural land. Inquilinos remained at the mercy of landowners for access to housing, soil and subsistence. Their votes belonged to landowners, who used them to influence Congress and maintain the existing land tenure system.

To some degree, the Alessandri government avoided antagonizing the landed elite, partly because urban leftists pressed for lower food prices and restrictions on exports of agricultural produce. Controls kept food prices artificially low, pleasing urban consumers but also satisfying landowners, who could maintain control over their land and workers, and thus their influence.

As protected industry expanded and the government promoted public works, employment increased and the lot of urban workers improved. That of rural workers, however, deteriorated rapidly; real wages fell, forcing day laborers to the cities in search of work. Inquilinos suffered reduced land allotments, seed and fertilizer supplies, as well as rights to graze animals, and yet had to supply more labor. Given abundant labor, haciendas had little incentive to modernize and production stagnated, a situation that changed little until the 1960s.

In 1952, the former dictator Ibáñez del Campo won the presidency as an authoritarian but 'apolitical' candidate, largely because of widespread disenchantment with predecessor Gabriel González Videla and political parties in general. Surprisingly, Ibáñez tried to curtail landowners' political power by reducing their control over the votes of their tenants and laborers; he also revoked an earlier law banning the Communist Party, but his government faltered in the face of high inflation and partisan politicking.

In 1958, socialist Salvador Allende headed a new leftist coalition known as FRAP (Frente de Acción Popular, or Popular Action Front), while Jorge Alessandri, son of Arturo Alessandri, represented a coalition between the conservative and liberal parties. Eduardo Frei Montalva represented the recently formed Democracia Cristiana (Christian Democrats), a reformist party whose goals resembled those of FRAP but whose philosophical basis was Catholic humanism.

Alessandri won the election with less than 32% of the vote, while Allende managed 29% and Frei 21%, the best showing ever by a Christian Democrat. An opposition congress forced Alessandri to accept modest land reform legislation, beginning a decade's battle with the haciendas. Alessandri's term saw little concrete progress in this matter, but the new laws provided a legal basis for expropriation of large estates.

Christian Democratic Period
The 1964 presidential election was a choice between Allende and Frei, who also drew support from conservative groups who detested the leftist physician. During the campaign, both FRAP and the Christian Democrats promised agrarian reform, supported rural unionization and promised an end to the hacienda system. Frei won with 56% as Allende, undermined by leftist factionalism, polled only 39%.

Genuinely committed to social transformation, the Christian Democrats attempted to control inflation, improve the balance of payments between imports and exports, implement agrarian reform and improve public health, education and social services. Their policies, however, threatened both the traditional elite's privileges and the radical left's working-class support. Fearful of losing their influence, the FRAP coalition urged faster and more radical action. According to Chilean analyst César Caviedes, the 1964 election marked a shift in Chilean politics: ideology superseded personal charisma.

The Chile-California Connection

Flying into Santiago, first-time visitors to Chile are often struck by the country's resemblance to California. Toward the Pacific, covered with Mediterranean scrub, the coastal range rises out of the sea, just as it does in California from the Mexican border north to the San Francisco Bay Area. To the east, the towering Andean crest is a reminder of California's lower but still impressive Sierra Nevada. Middle Chile's climate, with its extended summer drought, nearly constant coastal fogs and brief but intense winter rains, completes the picture of what, to lay observers at least, are two barely distinguishable physical environments.

Yet the two places also have a common history no less significant than their physical similarities. Both, of course, were backwaters of the Spanish empire, though California was an even more remote appendage of colonial Mexico than Chile was of Peru. After the colonial wars of the early 19th century, the two territories' political status diverged as Chile's larger population allowed it to be independent of Peru, while California remained a dependency of the new Mexican state.

By the mid-19th century, Chile's achievements seemed far greater than California's potential. On a continent notorious for political chaos, Chile had managed a prosperous stability that made it seem a model for the region. Since the end of Spanish rule, northern European immigrants had found Chile a congenial place to live and work, so much so that the port city of Valparaíso even boasted two English-language daily newspapers. California, by contrast, was a restive place where friction reigned between Mexican authorities and the growing number of foreigners, mostly from the United States, who found their way west. By the mid-1840s, foreign residents briefly declared California a republic in the so-called Bear Flag Revolt before it became part of the United States after the Mexican-American war.

What really spurred the convergence of Chile and California was the gold rush of 1849. For ships rounding the Horn, Valparaíso's strategic location made it the first stop westbound and the last stop eastbound; rumors of gold arrived here from San Francisco even before they did at the Peruvian settlement of Callao, the port of Lima. These rumors were slow to take hold, partly because of a healthy skepticism toward hearsay, but confirmation eventually resulted in the northward migration of many prominent figures from Valparaíso. Among them were Faxon Atherton (a merchant whose name survives in a wealthy suburb south of San Francisco); James Lick (a piano builder and hotelier memorialized today by an observatory on

The Christian Democrats had other difficulties. In the last years of Jorge Alessandri's presidency, the country's economy had declined, and limited opportunities in the countryside drove the dispossessed to the cities, where spontaneous squatter settlements or *callampas* (mushrooms), sprang up almost overnight. As the Christian Democrats inherited these problems, one common response was to attack the visible export sector, dominated by US interests; President Frei advocated 'Chileanization' of the copper industry (getting rid of foreign investors in favor of Chileans), while Allende and his backers supported the industry's

'nationalization' (placing the industry under state control).

The Christian Democrats also faced challenges from violent groups such as the MIR (Movimiento de Izquierda Revolucionario, or Leftist Revolutionary Movement), which had begun among upper-middle-class students in Concepción, a southern university town and important industrial center. MIR's activism appealed to coal miners, textile workers and other urban laborers who formed the allied Frente de Trabajadores Revolucionarios (Revolutionary Workers Front). Activism also caught on with peasants who longed for land reform.

The Chile-California Connection

Hamilton near the California city of San Jose); and Irish engineer Jasper O'Farrell, who laid out much of San Francisco's present-day grid (O'Farrell actually had become a California surveyor under Mexican rule, but remained under US rule).

Not only those of Anglo origins made their way north, though. While largely unremembered as individuals, Chilean miners staked many claims in the Sierra Nevada foothills – only to be dispossessed by Anglo-Americans who attacked and ousted them. Chilean technology remained, however; the so-called Chili wheel, in which heavy rotating stone wheels crushed gold-bearing ores, was a refinement of the earlier but cruder *arrastre*. Place-names such as Chili Bar, near the town of Placerville, are another reminder of the miners' presence.

One Chilean whose reputation survives is Vicente Pérez Rosales, an explorer and writer whose *Recuerdos del Pasado* appeared in English as *California Adventure*; Pérez Rosales, whose name graces Chile's oldest national park, detailed the discrimination that Hispanic Chilean immigrants suffered in the mines and in barrios such as San Francisco's Little Chile, at the foot of Telegraph Hill.

Another intriguing but more ambiguous figure of the era is Joaquín Murieta, a Robin Hood character romanticized in numerous sources, including a poem by Oakland eccentric Joaquín Miller (real name: Cincinnatus Hiner Miller) and a play by Nobel Prize-winning poet Pablo Neruda. There is no unequivocal evidence that Murieta even existed, and if he did he was probably Mexican, but many Chileans remain convinced he was one of theirs, born in the town of Quillota near Viña del Mar.

Contemporary connections between Chile and California are less fanciful but more meaningful. The University of California and the Universidad de Chile have long provided reciprocal assistance to academics conducting research far from home, and the Chile-California Chamber of Commerce encourages business contacts between Chile and the US state. In the aftermath of the military coup d'état of 1973, many political exiles found refuge in California, among them novelist Isabel Allende of Marin County – where place-names such as Chileno Creek are still common. Allende herself has linked Valparaíso and San Francisco in her 1999 novel, *Daughter of Fortune*.

Readers interested in the commonalities between the west coasts of North and South America in the 19th century should consult Jay Monaghan's 1973 book *Chile, Peru and the California Gold Rush of 1849*.

Other leftist groups supported strikes and land seizures by Mapuche Indians and rural laborers.

Too slow to appease the leftists, Frei's reforms were too rapid for the conservative National Party and even for some Christian Democrats. Despite improved living conditions for many rural workers and impressive gains in education and public health, the country was plagued by increasing inflation, dependence on foreign markets and capital, and inequitable income distribution. The Christian Democrats could not satisfy rising expectations in an increasingly militant and polarized society.

Allende's Rise to Power

As the presidential election approached in 1970, the new leftist coalition UP (Unidad Popular, or Popular Unity) chose Allende as its candidate. The UP's radical program included the nationalization of mines, banks and insurance companies, plus the expropriation and redistribution of large landholdings.

The other major candidates were Christian Democrat Radomiro Tomic (too left-wing for conservatives) and aged Jorge Alessandri, standing for the National Party. In one of Chile's closest elections ever, Allende won a plurality of 36%, while

Salvador Allende

country out of recession. This worked briefly, but apprehensive businessmen and landowners, worried over expropriation and nationalization, sold off stock and disposed of farm machinery and livestock. Industrial production nose-dived, leading to shortages, hyperinflation and black marketeering.

Peasants, frustrated with an agrarian reform that favored collectives of inquilinos (resident laborers who had rights to a small patch of land for household use) over share-croppers (contract farmers who owed half their crop to the hacienda) and *afuerinos* (outside laborers), seized land, and agricultural production fell. The government had to use scarce foreign currency to import food.

Chilean politics grew increasingly polarized and confrontational, as many of Allende's supporters resented his indirect approach to transformation of the state and its economy. MIR intensified its guerrilla activities, and stories circulated in Santiago's factories about the creation of armed communist organizations.

Expropriation of US-controlled copper mines and other enterprises, plus conspicuously friendly relations with Cuba, provoked US hostility. Later hearings in the US Congress indicated that President Richard Nixon and Secretary of State Henry Kissinger had actively undercut Allende by discouraging credit from international finance organizations and providing both financial and moral support to his opponents. Until the late 1980s, except during the Carter administration, the US maintained friendly relations with the Chilean military.

Faced with such difficulties, the government tried to forestall conflict by proposing clearly defined limits on nationalization. Unfortunately, neither extreme leftists, who believed that only force could achieve socialism, nor their rightist counterparts, who believed only force could prevent it, were open to compromise.

Rightist Backlash

In late 1972, independent truckers led a widespread strike by an alliance of shopkeepers, professionals, bank clerks, right-

Alessandri drew 35% and Tomic 28%. Under the constitution, if no candidate obtained an absolute majority, Congress had to confirm the result and could in theory choose the runner-up, although by custom it had never done so. Since no party had a congressional majority, Christian Democrats pressured Allende for constitutional guarantees to preserve the democratic process in return for their support. Agreeing to these guarantees, Allende assumed the presidency in October 1970.

Allende's own multiparty coalition of socialists, communists and radicals disagreed on the new government's objectives. Lacking any real electoral mandate, he faced an opposition Congress and a suspicious US government, and right-wing extremists even advocated his overthrow by violent means.

Allende's economic program, accomplished by evading rather than confronting Congress, included state takeover of many private enterprises and massive income redistribution. By increasing government spending, the new president expected to stimulate demand and encourage private enterprise to increase production and reduce unemployment, thereby bringing the

wing students and even some urban and rural laborers. Demanding that the government abandon plans for a state-owned trucking enterprise and supported by both the Christian Democrats and the National Party, the strikers threatened the government's viability. As the government's authority crumbled, a desperate Allende invited constitutionalist army commander General Carlos Prats to occupy the critical post of interior minister, and he included an admiral and an air force general in his cabinet. Despite the economic crisis, results of the March 1973 congressional elections demonstrated that Allende's support had actually increased since 1970 – but the unified opposition nevertheless strengthened its control of Congress, underscoring the polarization of Chilean politics. In June 1973 there was an unsuccessful military coup.

. The next month, truckers and other rightists once again went on strike, supported by the entire opposition. Having lost military support, General Prats resigned, to be replaced by the relatively obscure General Augusto Pinochet Ugarte, whom both Prats and Allende thought loyal to constitutional government. On September 11, 1973, Pinochet unleashed a brutal *golpe de estado* (coup d'état) which overthrew the UP government and resulted in Allende's death (an apparent suicide) and the death of thousands of his supporters.

Police and the military apprehended thousands of leftists, suspected leftists and sympathizers. Many were herded into Santiago's National Stadium, where they suffered beatings, torture and even execution. Estimates of deaths range from as few as 2500 to as many as 80,000, though the former is probably much closer to the truth. Hundreds of thousands went into exile.

The military argued that force was necessary to remove Allende because his government had fomented political and economic chaos and he was himself planning to overthrow the constitutional order by force. Certainly, inept policies brought about this 'economic chaos,' but reactionary sectors, encouraged and abetted from abroad, exacerbated scarcities, producing a black market that further undercut order. Allende's record of persistently standing for election and his pledge to the opposition implied commitment to the democratic process, but his inability or unwillingness to control factions to his left terrified the middle class as well as the oligarchy. His last words, part of a radio address just before the attacks on the government palace, La Moneda, expressed his ideals but underlined his failure:

My words are not spoken in bitterness, but in disappointment. They will be a moral judgment on those who have betrayed the oath they took as soldiers of Chile...They have the might and they can enslave us, but they cannot halt the world's social processes, not with crimes, nor with guns...May you go forward in the knowledge that, sooner rather than later, the great avenues will open once again, along which free citizens will march in order to build a better society. Long live Chile! Long live the people! Long live the workers! These are my last words, and I am sure that this sacrifice will constitute a moral lesson which will punish cowardice, perfidy and treason.

Military Dictatorship

Many opposition leaders, some of whom had encouraged the coup, expected a quick return to civilian government, but General Pinochet had other ideas. From 1973 to 1989, he headed a durable junta that dissolved Congress, banned leftist parties and suspended all others, prohibited nearly all political activity and ruled by decree. Assuming the presidency in 1974, Pinochet sought to reorder the country's political and economic culture through repression, torture and murder. Detainees came from all sectors of society, from peasant to professional (including doctors, lawyers and university professors).

The CNI (Centro Nacional de Informaciones, or National Information Center) and its predecessor DINA (Directoria de Inteligencia Nacional, or National Intelligence Directorate) were the most notorious practitioners of state terrorism. International assassinations were not unusual – a car bomb killed General Prats in Buenos Aires a year after the coup, and Christian Democrat leader Bernardo Leighton barely survived a shooting in Rome in 1975. Perhaps the most notorious case was the 1976 murder of Allende's foreign minister, Orlando Letelier, by a car bomb in Washington, DC.

By 1977 even air force general Gustavo Leigh, a member of the junta, thought the campaign against 'subversion' so successful that he proposed a return to civilian rule, but Pinochet forced Leigh's resignation, ensuring the army's dominance and perpetuating himself in power. By 1980, Pinochet felt confident enough to submit a new, customized constitution to the electorate and wager his own political future on it. In a plebiscite with narrow options, about two-thirds of the voters approved the constitution and ratified Pinochet's presidency until 1989, though many voters abstained in protest.

Return to Democracy

Political parties began to function openly again in 1987. In late 1988, trying to extend his presidency until 1997, Pinochet held another plebiscite, but this time voters rejected him. In multiparty elections in 1989, Christian Democrat Patricio Aylwin, compromise candidate of a coalition of opposition parties known as the Concertación para la Democracia, defeated Pinochet protégé Hernán Büchi, a conservative economist and candidate of Renovación Nacional (National Renovation).

Consolidating the return to democracy, Aylwin's relatively uneventful four-year term expired in 1994; in late 1993, Chileans elected Eduardo Frei Ruiz-Tagle, son of the late president Eduardo Frei Montalva, to a six-year term. Despite uninterrupted civilian government, the military retains considerable power and the constitution institutionalizes this, at least in the short term. Pinochet's senate appointees, with help from elected conservatives, can still block reform, and he himself assumed a senate seat upon retirement from the army in 1997 – at least in part because it conferred immunity from prosecution in Chile.

The September 1998 arrest of General Pinochet in London at the request of Spanish judge Báltazar Garzón, who was in-

vestigating deaths and disappearances of Spanish citizens in the aftermath of the 1973 coup, caused an international uproar that has not completely subsided within Chile. The Concertación government, feeling obliged to uphold its part of the transition agreement with the general, protested the arrest and has worked for his release (claiming, disingenuously, that the general should face charges in Chilean rather than Spanish courts, but failing to request extradition). Whatever the final outcome, however, the arrest opened up political dialogue on issues that had been wallpapered over for a quarter century. For more details, see Human Rights later in this chapter.

GEOGRAPHY & CLIMATE

Few countries of Chile's size – slightly larger than Texas at about 800,000 sq km (288,000 sq miles) – can boast such varied landscapes; rocky Andean peaks, snow-capped volcanoes, broad river valleys and deep canyons, waterless deserts, icy fjords, deep-blue glaciers, turquoise lakes, sandy beaches and precipitous headlands. It owes this diversity – a 'crazy geography' or 'geographical extravaganza,' in the words of Chilean writer Benjamín Subercaseaux – to extremes of latitude and altitude: not counting Antarctic claims, Chilean territory extends some 4300km (2666 miles) north to south between the Andes and the Pacific Ocean, equivalent to the distance from Havana to Hudson Bay. On average less than 200km (124 miles) wide from east to west, it rises from sea level to more than 6000m (19,680 feet). Describing these geographical contrasts, British diplomat James Bryce observed, 'The difference is as great as that between the verdure of Ireland and the sterility of the Sahara.'

Chile's present boundaries are the result of conquest and expansion, first by Spain and later by the republic itself. Only at the end of the 19th century did Chile reach its present extent, from the city of Arica in the northern Atacama desert to the archipelago of Tierra del Fuego in the south. Chile also possesses the Pacific islands of Easter Island (Isla de Pascua, or Rapa Nui in the local

Polynesian language) and the Juan Fernández Archipelago. It has disputes with Argentina and with Britain over Antarctic claims.

Administrative Regions

For administrative purposes, Chile consists of 13 regions. Except for the Metropolitan Region of Santiago, they are numbered ordinally from north to south but are normally written in Roman numerals. Chileans usually abbreviate the longer formal names, such as O'Higgins and Aisén. See the Administrative Regions of Chile map.

Geographical Regions

Chile's customary, rather than formal, regional divisions reflect ecological zonation and human economy rather than arbitrary political boundaries. Described here, north to south, are the geographical regions covered by this book's chapters. The Andes cut across these divisions and are described in several of the book's chapters. Archipiélago Juan Fernández and Easter Island (Rapa Nui) are discussed in separate chapters.

Norte Grande The regions of Tarapacá and Antofagasta together comprise the Norte Grande (Great North), running from the Peruvian border to the province of Chañaral and dominated by the Atacama desert. Transverse river valleys, subterranean water sources and springs, and diversions of distant streams sustain cities such as Arica, Iquique and Antofagasta, which occupy narrow coastal plains. These sources also irrigate the limited but productive farmland even though, in the entire Norte Grande, only the Río Loa regularly reaches the sea. Since the colonial era, mining of silver, nitrates and copper has been the principal economic activity, although irrigated agriculture and native livestock herding are locally significant.

Despite its aridity and tropical latitude, the Atacama is a remarkably temperate desert, moderated by the Pacific Ocean's cool, north-flowing Peru (Humboldt) Current, which parallels the coast. High humidity produces an extensive cloud cover and thick fogs known as *camanchaca*, which condense on coastal range escarpments. Toward the Bolivian border, the canyons of the *precordillera* (foothills) lead to the *altiplano*, or high steppe, where Aymara herders graze their llamas and alpacas, and to high mountain passes.

Norte Chico South of Chañaral, the regions of Atacama and Coquimbo form the transitional Norte Chico (Little North), whose approximate southern boundary is the Río Aconcagua. The desert relents to support scrub and occasional forest, which becomes denser as rainfall increases to the south. Like the Norte Grande, the Norte Chico is rich in minerals, but there is also irrigated agriculture in the major river valleys, especially the Elqui. In those rare years of substantial rainfall, the landscape erupts with wildflowers.

Middle Chile South of the Aconcagua begins the fertile heartland of Middle Chile. The intermontane Valle Central (central valley) extends through most of this area, which contains the capital, Santiago (with at least a third of the country's population), the ports of Valparaíso and San Antonio, and the bulk of the country's industry and employment, plus important copper mines. The industrial city of Concepción and its port of Talcahuano, at the mouth of the Río Biobío, mark the region's southern boundary. Middle Chile is also the country's chief agricultural zone and, in total, holds perhaps 75% of the country's population.

The heartland enjoys a Mediterranean climate, with maximum temperatures averaging 28°C (82°F) in January and 10°C (50°F) in July; the rainy season lasts from May to August. Evenings and nights can be cool, even during summer. At the highest elevations, snow lasts into early summer, permitting excellent skiing much of the year.

La Araucanía & Los Lagos South of Concepción, the Río Biobío marks Chile's 19th-century frontier, homeland of the Mapuche Indians and now an area of cereal and pastoral production, extensive native forests and plantations of introduced conifers. Although (continued on page 32)

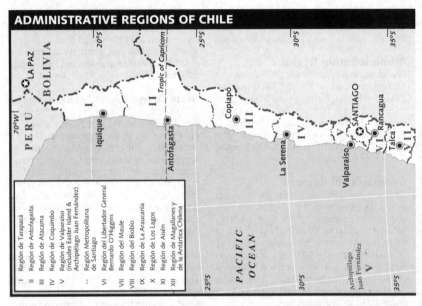

ADMINISTRATIVE REGIONS OF CHILE

I   Región de Tarapacá
II   Región de Antofagasta
III   Región de Atacama
IV   Región de Coquimbo
V   Región de Valparaíso (includes Easter Island & Archipiélago Juan Fernández)
--   Región Metropolitana de Santiago
VI   Región del Libertador General Bernardo O'Higgins
VII   Región del Maule
VIII Región del Biobío
IX   Región de La Araucanía
X   Región de Los Lagos
XI   Región de Aisén
XII   Región de Magallanes y de la Antártica Chilena

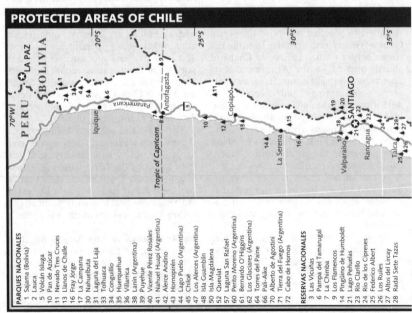

PROTECTED AREAS OF CHILE

PARQUES NACIONALES

1   Sajama (Bolivia)
2   Lauca
5   Volcán Isluga
10 Pan de Azúcar
11 Nevado Tres Cruces
13 Llanos de Challe
16 Fray Jorge
17 La Campana
30 Nahuelbuta
31 Laguna del Laja
33 Tolhuaca
34 Conguillío
35 Huerquehue
36 Villarrica
38 Lanín (Argentina)
39 Puyehue
40 Vicente Pérez Rosales
41 Nahuel Huapi (Argentina)
42 Alerce Andino
43 Hornopirén
44 Lago Puelo (Argentina)
45 Chiloé
47 Los Alerces (Argentina)
48 Isla Guamblín
50 Isla Magdalena
52 Queulat
57 Laguna San Rafael
60 Perito Moreno (Argentina)
61 Bernardo O'Higgins
62 Los Glaciares (Argentina)
64 Torres del Paine
66 Pali-Aike
70 Alberto de Agostini
71 Tierra del Fuego (Argentina)
72 Cabo de Hornos

RESERVAS NACIONALES

3   Las Vicuñas
6   Pampa del Tamarugal
9   La Chimba
14 Los Flamencos
21 Pingüino de Humboldt
22 Lago Peñuelas
23 Río Clarillo
24 Río de los Cipreses
25 Federico Albert
26 Los Ruiles
27 Altos del Lircay
28 Radal Siete Tazas

ADMINISTRATIVE REGIONS OF CHILE

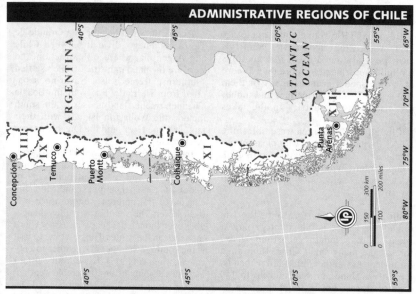

PROTECTED AREAS OF CHILE

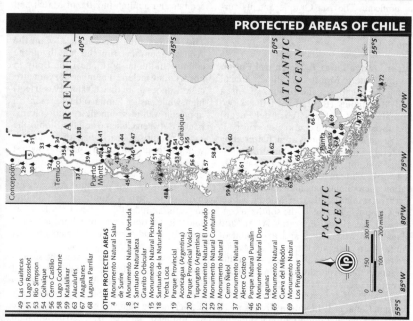

49 Las Guaitecas
51 Lago Rosselot
53 Río Simpson
54 Coihaique
56 Cerro Castillo
58 Lago Cochrane
59 Katalalixar
63 Alacalufes
67 Magallanes
68 Laguna Parrillar

OTHER PROTECTED AREAS

4   Monumento Natural Salar
    de Surire
8   Monumento Natural la Portada
12 Santuario Naturaleza
    Granito Orbicular
15 Monumento Natural Pichasca
18 Santuario de la Naturaleza
    Yerba Loca
19 Parque Provincial
    Aconcagua (Argentina)
20 Parque Provincial Volcán
    Tupungato (Argentina)
22 Monumento Natural El Morado
29 Monumento Natural Contulmo
32 Monumento Natural
    Cerro Ñielol
37 Monumento Natural
    Alerce Costero
46 Parque Natural Pumalín
55 Monumento Natural Dos
    Lagunas
65 Monumento Natural
    Cueva del Milodón
69 Monumento Natural
    Los Pingüinos

rural population is fairly dense, most of the population lives in towns and cities.

Beyond the Río Toltén, south of the city of Temuco, Los Lagos is the country's most popular tourist area, its numerous foothill lakes framed by more than a score of snowcapped volcanoes, many of them still active. Fishing, agriculture and timber are also major industries in the lakes region.

Climatically, the area resembles the USA's Pacific Northwest, with pleasant but changeable summer weather and cool, damp winters. Winter brings snow to the Andes, occasionally blocking the passes to Argentina.

Chiloé South of Puerto Montt, the Isla Grande de Chiloé is the country's largest island, with a lengthy coastline, dense forests and many small farms. Renowned for inclement weather, it has fewer than 60 days of sunshine per year and up to 150 days of storms, but in summer it can be magnificent. The Isla Grande and its surrounding offshore islands are the country's greatest repository of traditional culture and folklore.

Aisén, Magallanes & Tierra del Fuego

South of Puerto Montt and Chiloé, Chilean Patagonia comprises the regions of Aisén and Magallanes (the latter of these two formal regions includes Tierra del Fuego) and about 30% of the country's territory. It is a rugged, mountainous area, battered by westerly winds and storms that drop enormous amounts of snow and rain on the seaward Andean slopes, although the balmy microclimate around Lago General Carrera resembles that of Middle Chile. The Campo de Hielo Sur, the southern continental ice field, separates Aisén and Magallanes. Magallanes and its capital of Punta Arenas, on the Strait of Magellan, are more easily accessible from Argentine Patagonia than from the Chilean mainland (generally speaking, north of the Campo de Hielo Sur). Before the opening of the Panama Canal in 1914, Punta Arenas was a major port of call for international shipping,

but its prosperity now depends on oil, gas, fishing and wool.

Across the strait lies the Isla Grande de Tierra del Fuego, divided between Chile and Argentina, where oil extraction and wool are the main industries. Chile's settled southern extreme is Isla Navarino, separated from Tierra del Fuego by the Beagle Channel; smaller land masses to the south include the Wollaston Islands, with their famous Cape Horn, and the Diego Ramírez Archipelago.

In Magallanes and Tierra del Fuego, temperatures drop to a summer average of just 11°C (52°F), and to a winter average of about 4°C (39°F). Dampness and wind chill can make the ambient temperature feel even lower. The weather is highly changeable, even though the nearly incessant winds moderate in the winter. The best time to visit is the southern summer (December to February), when very long days permit outdoor activities despite the unpredictable weather, but the spring months of November and December and autumn months of March and April can be nearly as good.

The Andes Like the Pacific Ocean, the Andes mountains run the length of the country. In the far north, near the Bolivian border, they include a number of symmetrical volcanoes more than 6000m (19,680 feet) high, while east of Santiago they present an imposing wall of sedimentary and volcanic peaks. Between Copiapó and the Biobío, the range comprises nearly half the country's width, with some of South America's highest peaks. Despite numerous passes, transport and communications are difficult, isolating Chile from the rest of South America for most of its history. South of the Biobío, lower in altitude, the Andes are a less formidable barrier – except where seasonal snowfields and permanent glaciers obstruct passage between east and west.

Despite their scenic grandeur, the seismically unstable Andes are a significant hazard throughout Chile. Many of the country's major cities (including Santiago, Valparaíso, La Serena and Valdivia) have suffered severe earthquake damage or destruction, and volcanic eruptions are a potential menace in other areas.

ECOLOGY & ENVIRONMENT

The Chilean public's growing awareness of environmental issues often seems at odds with the recent government's single-minded commitment to economic growth, which led to dubious development projects such as a series of hydroelectric dams on the Río Biobío and a proposed large-scale effort to harvest native beech forest in one of Tierra del Fuego's most remote areas. In 1995–96, however, French nuclear tests in the Pacific caused so much ill feeling within Chile that the government felt obliged to lodge formal protests with the French government.

For most Chileans, the single most palpable environmental issue is the cloud of smog that so often hangs over the city of Santiago, which, like Los Angeles, sits in a basin between two mountain ranges and has a virtually identical climate; it's mild year-round. Air pollution, which on some days is so severe that schoolchildren may not take physical education and older citizens are advised to stay indoors, stems from the growing number of private automobiles, the presence of diesel buses and the concentration of polluting industries. While some efforts have been made to reduce air pollution, for example, by improving the quality of public transport vehicles, the government seems more willing to promote automobile ownership (through construction of new roads and highways) than restrict vehicular congestion in the crowded central city or shut down industrial polluters.

From Region VIII south, the felling of native forest and its replacement by plantations of fast-growing exotics such as eucalyptus and Monterey pine have attracted international attention. Native forests of araucaria (monkey-puzzle trees) and alerce (a long-lived conifer resembling the redwood) have declined precipitously over the past decades; the alerce, in particular, has been vulnerable to clandestine cutting because of the export value of its wood chips.

Throughout the south, the burgeoning salmon farming industry has drawn criticism for polluting both freshwater and saltwater areas. Another issue is the ever more intensive use of agricultural chemicals and pesticides to promote Chile's flourishing fruit exports, which during the southern summer furnish the Northern Hemisphere with fresh produce. A related matter is agricultural water usage in drought-prone Middle Chile and in the Norte Chico, where water is even more scarce. Water contamination and air pollution by the mining industry are also major concerns throughout the country.

The growing hole in the ozone layer over Antarctica, due to global atmospheric aerosols, has become such an issue that medical authorities recommend wearing protective clothing and heavy sunblock to avoid cancer-causing ultraviolet radiation, especially in Patagonia.

FLORA & FAUNA

Chile's northern deserts and high-altitude steppes, soaring mountains, alpine and sub-Antarctic forests and lengthy coastline all support distinctive flora and fauna that will be unfamiliar to most visitors, or at least to those from the Northern Hemisphere. To protect these environments, Chile's Corporación Nacional Forestal (Conaf) administers an extensive system of national parks and reserves, the more accessible of which are briefly described in the section Protected Areas. More detailed descriptions can be found in individual chapters. A handful of reserves are not part of the Conaf system; these are mentioned in the appropriate chapters.

Jürgen Rottmann's bilingual *Bosques de Chile/Chile's Woodlands* (1988), published in cooperation with the World Wide Fund for Nature, is a well-illustrated, generalist's introduction to the country's forests and their fauna, despite its superficial 'Smokey the Bear' approach to fire ecology.

Flora

Thanks to its latitudinal extent and great altitudinal range, Chile has an extraordinary variety of plants. The northern coastal deserts are virtually devoid of vegetation

Endangered Species

The Convention on International Trade in Endangered Species of Wild Fauna and Flora (CITES) is a diplomatic agreement regulating trade in biotic resources, including plants and animals, which are either in immediate danger of extinction or are threatened or declining so rapidly that they may soon be in danger of extinction. Regulations are complex, but in general, such species are either protected from commercial or noncommercial exploitation or such activity is subject to severe restrictions. In many instances, all commerce involving a given species is prohibited; in most others, the export of plants and animals in a given country is prohibited without express authorization from that country's government.

Under CITES, most species are assigned either to Appendix I (endangered, under immediate threat of extinction without remedial action) or Appendix II (threatened, perhaps regionally

Appendix I

Mammals
Andean cat *(Felis jacobita)*
Beaked whales
  (Berardius or *Mesoplodon* species*)
Blue whale *(Balaenoptera musculus)*
Bottlenosed dolphins *(Hyperodon* species)
Fin whale *(Balaenoptera physalus)*
Giant armadillo *(Priodontes maximus)*
Humpback whale
  (Megaptera novaeangliae)
Jaguarundi *(Felis yagouarundi)*
Long-tailed otter *(Lutra platensis)*
Marine otter *(Lutra felina)*
Minke whale *(Balaenoptera acutorostrata)*
North Andean huemul
  (Hippocamelus antisensis)
Pink fairy armadillo *(Clamyphorus truncatus)*
Pudú *(Pudu pudu)*
Pygmy right whale *(Caperea marginata)*
Sei whale *(Balaenoptera borealis)*

South Andean huemul
  (Hippocamelus bisulcus)
Southern right whale *(Eubalaena australis*
Southern river otter *(Lutra provocax)*
Sperm whale *(Physeter catodon)*
Vicuña *(Vicugna vicugna**)*

Birds
Andean condor *(Vultur gryphus)*
Black-fronted piping-guan *(Pipile jacutinga)*
Darwin's rhea
  (Pterocnemia pennata pennata)
Eskimo curlew *(Numenius borealis)*
Humboldt penguin *(Spheniscus humboldtii)*
Lesser rhea *(Pterocnemia pennata)*
Solitary tinamou *(Tinamus solitarius)*

Flora
Alerce (Chilean false larch)
  (Fitzroya cupressoides)

except in river valleys. The cacti at slightly higher elevations give way to the patchy grasslands of the very high altiplano, where there are also scrub forests of queñoa *(Polylepis tarapacana)*.

From the Norte Chico through most of Middle Chile, the native flora consist mostly of shrubs whose sclerophyllous (glossy) leaves help conserve water during the long summer dry season. At some higher elevations in the coastal ranges there are forests of southern beech *(Nothofagus* species), but

the native Chilean palm is in decline. Farther south, beyond the Biobío, the distinctive araucaria is related to the Northern Hemisphere pines. At the southern end of the lakes region, the alerce *(Fitzroya cupressoides)*, belonging to the cypress family, has become the focus of international conservation efforts.

In the far south of Aisén and Magallanes, verdant upland forests consist of several species of the widespread genus *Nothofagus*. On the eastern plains of Magallanes and

Endangered Species

endangered); some recovering species have been reassigned from Appendix I to Appendix II. Appendix III listings cover species that require close monitoring to determine their degree of vulnerability to extinction.

Travelers should take special care not to hunt, purchase or collect the following species of plants and animals found in Chile, Argentina and the Falkland Islands, nor should they purchase products made from these plants and animals. The following list is partial, and travelers should consult their own country's customs service before attempting to import any such products. Note that US customs no longer permits the importation of birds even with CITES permits from the appropriate country, and that the US Marine Mammal Protection Act prohibits the importation of any marine mammal products whatsoever.

Appendix II

Mammals

Argentine gray fox *(Dusicyon griseus)*
Guanaco *(Lamo guanicoe)*
Juan Fernández fur seal
 (Arctocephalus philippi)
Mountain lion *(Felis concolor)*
Southern elephant seal
 Mirounga leonina)
Southern fur seal *(Arctocephalus australis)*

Birds

Andean flamingo
 (Phoenicoparrus andinus)
Black-necked swan
 (Cygnus melanocoryphus)
Caracaras
 (Falconidae, all species in family except
 those on Appendix I)
Chilean flamingo
 (Phoenicopterus ruber chilensis)

Coscoroba swan
 (Coscoroba coscoroba)
James flamingo *(Phoenicoparrus jamesi)*
Greater rhea
 (Rhea americana albescens)
Patagonian conure
 (Cyanoliseus patagonus byroni)
Peregrine falcon *(Falco peregrinus)*

Flora

Cacti (all species not on Appendix I)

*All cetaceans (whales and porpoises) not on Appendix I are on Appendix II, but not all are listed individually here.

**In some areas, specifically Parque Nacional Lauca, the vicuña is on Appendix II rather than Appendix I, permitting the export of cloth only.

Tierra del Fuego, decreased rainfall supports extensive grasslands.

Chile's major Pacific island possessions, Easter Island (Rapa Nui) and the Juan Fernández Archipelago, are a special case. The latter, in particular, is a major storehouse of biological diversity that has been named a UNESCO World Biosphere Reserve. See their chapters for more information.

Specialists interested in Middle Chile's Mediterranean-like environments and their comparison with similar settings elsewhere

in the world should consult Mary Kalin Arroyo's edited collection *Ecology & Biology of Mediterranean Ecosystems in Chile, California and Australia* in *Ecological Studies* No 108 (1995). Another interesting book, despite its somewhat shallow approach to socioeconomic issues in the Norte Chico, is Conrad Bahre's *Destruction of the Natural Vegetation of North Central Chile* (1978). A more recent publication worth reading is *La Tragedia del Bosque Chileno,* edited by Adriana Hoffman (1998).

Fauna

Chile's fauna is as varied as its flora, even though less conspicuously abundant. Notable mammals include the wide-ranging (though not common) puma; the camel-like guanaco (in both the desert north and Patagonia) and its close relative the vicuña (only in the high steppes of the altiplano); the huemul or Chilean deer (with separate subspecies in the Norte Grande and in Patagonia); the vizcacha (a wild relative of the chinchilla); the rare and diminutive deer known as the pudú; and several species of foxes. Though more often associated with Peru or Bolivia, the domestic llama and alpaca are abundant in the northern highlands.

Chile's long coastline features many marine mammals, including sea lions, otters and fur seals, along with the finfish and shellfish that have made the country's fisheries some of the world's most important. See the Food section of the Facts for the Visitor chapter for detailed information on the role of seafood in the Chilean diet.

Most foreign visitors will find the country's bird life more easily accessible and very different from that of the Northern Hemisphere. The legendary Andean condor is widespread though not numerous, while the ostrichlike rhea (called ñandú in Spanish) inhabits both the far north and the far south. Parque Nacional Lauca, a world biosphere reserve in the northern altiplano, contains a variety of bird life, from Andean gulls and giant coots to three species of flamingos, thanks in large part to the habitat of extensive high-altitude wetlands. The extensive shoreline is home to many species, including penguins, while Patagonian reserves like Parque Nacional Torres del Paine are home to particularly rich concentrations of bird life.

Visitors interested in birds should look for Mark Pearman's *Essential Guide to Birding in Chile* (1995), Nigel Wheatley's *Where to Watch Birds in South America* (1995), Martín R de la Peña and Maurice Rumbold's *Birds of Southern South America and Antarctica* (1998), or Braulio Araya and Sharon Chester's *Birds of Chile: A Field Guide* (1993). Those competent in Spanish should look for the *Guía de Campo de las Aves de Chile* (1986) by Araya and Guillermo Millie. H Wayne Lynch's *Penguins of the World* (1997) is a high-quality coffee-table-style book dealing exclusively with the Southern Hemisphere's flightless birds, several species of which inhabit Chilean territory (though only one is easily seen).

Protected Areas

Since the establishment of Parque Nacional Vicente Pérez Rosales in the mid-1920s, Chile's national parks have become a major international attraction. As part of its 'Sistema Nacional de Areas Silvestres Protegidas del Estado' (Snaspe, or National System of State-Protected Wild Areas), the government has created many other parks and reserves, administered by Conaf, mostly but not exclusively in the Andean range.

Before leaving Santiago, travelers should visit Conaf's central information office (☎ 390-0282), Av Bulnes 291, for inexpensive maps and brochures, which may be in short supply in the parks themselves. Regional Conaf offices, listed in the appropriate city entries, will sometimes assist in transportation to more isolated areas.

Chilean protected areas are of five main types: *parques nacionales* (national parks), *reservas nacionales* (national reserves), *monumentos naturales* (natural monuments), *áreas de protección turística* (tourist protection areas) and *santuarios de la naturaleza* (nature sanctuaries). Chilean law also permits the creation of private nature reserves, of which there are a handful.

National parks are generally extensive areas with a variety of natural ecosystems. National reserves are areas open to economic exploitation on a sustainable basis and may include some relatively pristine areas. Natural monuments are smaller but more strictly protected, usually with a single outstanding natural feature. Tourist protection areas are usually private lands where management practices limit economic exploitation in the interest of scenic resources. Nature sanctuaries are primarily intended for research.

Now difficult to find and outdated in its coverage, the beautifully illustrated but expensive *Chile: Sus Parques Nacionales y Otras Areas Protegidas* (1982) is still a good introduction to Chile's environmental diversity. For English-speakers, William C Leitch's eloquent survey *South America's National Parks* (1990) contains a valuable chapter on the history and natural history of half a dozen of Chile's most popular parks. It could use an update, however.

For locations of many of Chile's protected areas, see the Protected Areas of Chile map on pages 28 and 29. Regional chapters in this book describe relevant parks and preserves not included in the following list.

National Parks In the northern region of Tarapacá, east of the city of Arica, the 138,000-hectare (532-sq-mile) Lauca offers extraordinary natural attractions, including active and dormant volcanoes, clear blue lakes with abundant bird life and extensive steppes that support flourishing populations of the endangered vicuña, a wild relative of the llama and alpaca. Living in tiny villages with picturesque colonial churches, Aymara Indian shepherds graze their animals on the same pastures. Adjacent to the park are two other protected areas, which are less accessible, the Reserva Nacional Las Vicuñas and Monumento Natural Salar de Surire. The latter features huge nesting colonies of flamingos.

Rarely visited and relatively inaccessible, 175,000-hectare (675-sq-mile) Volcán Isluga in the altiplano of Iquique, bears many similarities to Lauca, but its cultural resources may be even more impressive.

Set in the coastal desert of the regions of Antofagasta and Atacama, near the small port of Chañaral, Pan de Azúcar is a 44,000-hectare (170-sq-mile) park featuring a stark but beautiful shoreline and unique vegetation that draws moisture from the coastal fog. The park is home to pelicans, penguins, otters and sea lions.

East of Copiapó, in the high Andes along the Argentine border, the 62,000-hectare (239-sq-mile) Nevado de Tres Cruces is destined to attract more travelers in coming years. The area's outstanding feature is not its 6330m (20,762-foot) namesake peak, but the even more prominent 6900m (22,637-foot) Ojos del Salado, a prime climber's destination once thought to be higher than Argentina's Aconcagua, the highest peak in the Western Hemisphere.

On the coastal plain of the Norte Chico, north of the port of Huasco, the 45,000-hectare (174-sq-mile) Llanos de Challe is the best site to view the spectacular 'flowering of the desert' after one of the region's rare heavy rains.

In Region IV, 75km (46 miles) from the city of Ovalle, 10,000-hectare (39-sq-mile) Bosque Fray Jorge is an ecological island of the type of humid forest usually found several hundred kilometers to the south. Like Pan de Azúcar, its vegetation depends on coastal fog.

Easily accessible both from Santiago and Valparaíso/Viña del Mar, La Campana's 8000 hectares (31 sq miles) are good at any time of year for short hikes through tranquil forests of native oaks and palms.

Consisting of three islands several hundred kilometers west of Valparaíso, Archipiélago de Juan Fernández, a 9100-hectare (35-sq-mile) unit, is one of Chile's hidden ecological treasures, with spectacular scenery and a great variety of endemic plant species. It is best known as the site of exile for Scottish mariner Alexander Selkirk, immortalized as Robinson Crusoe in Daniel Defoe's novel.

Rapa Nui is the proper Polynesian name for 6600-hectare (25-sq-mile) Easter Island, with its huge, enigmatic stone statues, 3700km (2294 miles) west of Valparaíso. Despite its isolation, distance from the continent, and the expense of getting there, it remains a popular tourist destination.

In the Andean foothills of Region VIII, 12,000-hectare (46-sq-mile) Laguna del Laja has a great deal to offer: waterfalls, lakes, volcanoes, bird life and numerous hiking trails.

In the high coastal range of Region IX, Nahuelbuta's 7000 hectares (27 sq miles) preserve the area's largest remaining araucaria forests. In the same region, at the end of a narrow mountain road east of the town of Victoria and north of Curacautín, 6400-hectare (25-sq-mile) Tolhuaca is a remote forested getaway in the headwaters of the Río Malleco. The southern approach from Curacautín is very difficult for non-4WD vehicles beyond Termas de Tolhuaca, but it's short enough for hikers and mountain bikers.

In the Andean portion of the Araucanía, 80km (50 miles) from Temuco, 61,000-hectare (235-sq-mile) Conguillío features mixed forests of araucaria, cypress and southern beech surrounding the active, snowcapped Volcán Llaima. Small but scenic, 12,500-hectare (48-sq-mile) Huerquehue has excellent hiking trails with outstanding views of nearby Villarrica (see below). It is 120km (74 miles) from Temuco and only a short distance from Pucón.

One of the lakes region's gems, Volcán Villarrica's smoking, symmetrical cone overlooks the lake and town of the same name. Its 61,000 hectares (235 sq miles) make a popular destination for trekkers and climbers.

One of the country's most-visited parks, 107,000-hectare (413-sq-mile) Puyehue is only 80km (50 miles) from the city of Osorno but still offers scenery and solitude to dedicated visitors. There are outstanding hiking spots and hidden hot springs near Volcán Puyehue, which erupted in 1960 to form a striking volcanic desert as yet colonized by only a few hardy plants.

Founded in 1926, Vicente Pérez Rosales is Chile's oldest national park, named for a Chilean explorer, politician and writer who helped found the city of Puerto Montt. Its 254,000 hectares (980 sq miles) include the spectacular Lago Todos los Santos, which provides a scenic alternate route to Bariloche, Argentina, via Argentina's Parque Nacional Nahuel Huapi. Just 50km (31 miles) from Puerto Montt, the 40,000-hectare (154-sq-mile) Alerce Andino preserves tracts of the last remaining alerce trees.

Largely undeveloped, 48,000-hectare (185-sq-mile) Hornopirén rewards determined hikers with verdant rain forest. It's near its namesake village, the last mainland ferry port southbound on the Camino Austral.

On the remote western shore of Chile's misty southern island, the 43,000-hectare (165-sq-mile) Chiloé features excellent hiking trails across sweeping dunes and broad sandy beaches, along blue lagoons and through the forbidding forests that fostered the island's colorful and enigmatic folklore.

An increasingly popular destination since the opening of the Camino Austral between Puerto Montt and Cochrane, Queulat consists of 154,000 hectares (594 sq miles) of truly wild evergreen forest, mountains and glaciers, 150km (93 miles) north of Coihaique and 200km (124 miles) south of Chaitén.

Glaciers reach the sea at Laguna San Rafael, one of Chile's most impressive parks, which is part of the Campo de Hielo Norte (northern Patagonian ice field). Two hundred kilometers (124 miles) south of Puerto Chacabuco, it is accessible only by air or sea. Its nearly 1.8 million hectares (6947 sq miles) deserve a visit, but it is either expensive or time-consuming to do so.

Largely inaccessible except at a few points, the massive 3.5 million-hectare (13,508-sq-mile) Bernardo O'Higgins straddles the Patagonian ice fields in Regions XI and XII. Torres del Paine is Chile's showpiece, a world biosphere reserve with all the diverse scenery of Alaska in only 181,000 hectares (698 sq miles), and a wealth of wildlife, including the Patagonian guanaco, a wild relative of the Andean llama. It is 150km (93 miles) from Puerto Natales and 400km (248 miles) from Punta Arenas, in Region XII. Near the Argentine border, on the eastern mainland of Region XII, 5000-hectare (19-sq-mile) Pali Aike is one of southern South America's major sites for the study of early human habitation. It also supports a notable variety of Patagonian wildlife.

National Reserves Just north of Antofagasta, La Chimba is a 2583-hectare area conserving a representative sample of Tocopilla coastal desert and a lesser sample of interior desert. At present, it is closed to the public.

Comprising seven scattered sectors in and around San Pedro de Atacama, the 73,986-hectare (285-sq-mile) Reserva Nacional Los Flamencos protects a variety of salt lakes and high-altitude lagoons that host several species of flamingos, as well as eerie desert landforms and hot springs.

On the border of Regions III and IV, Pingüino de Humboldt is a 859-hectare 3½-sq-mile) reserve consisting of several off-shore islands with breeding populations of Humboldt's penguin and many other sea-birds. Access is improving, and camping is possible.

Only 45km (28 miles) from Santiago and suitable for a day trip, 10,000-hectare (39-sq-mile) Río Clarillo encompasses a variety of Andean ecosystems.

The Andes east of Rancagua are best known for massive El Teniente copper mine, but the 37,000-hectare (143-sq-mile) Río de los Cipreses is the area's outstanding recreational resource.

A virtual staircase of falls and pools along the Río Claro is the major attraction of the 7700-hectare (30-sq-mile) Radal Siete Tazas in the precordillera of Talca. Recently reclassified and renamed, with excellent access from Talca, 17,000-hectare (66-sq-mile) Altos del Lircay (formerly Parque Nacional Vilches) is one of central Chile's natural highlights. In addition to spectacular views of the Andean divide, its many hiking trails include a loop trek to Radal Siete Tazas, for a which a local guide is desirable.

Despite Coihaique's proximity to its city namesake, and less than an hour's walk away, this 2150-hectare (15-sq-mile) reserve is surprisingly wild and attractive, with exceptional views of the surrounding area and good opportunities for camping and hiking.

Downgraded from national park status, the 41,000-hectare (158-sq-mile) Río Simpson, which straddles the highway between Coihaique and Puerto Aisén, is still a pleasant and accessible destination with verdant forests, waterfalls and a spectacular canyon.

Wild, high and remote, the 180,000-hectare (695-sq-mile) Cerro Castillo, south of Coihaique, is increasingly popular with hikers, who take advantage of two convenient access points along the Camino Austral.

Just 7km (4 miles) west of Punta Arenas, Magallanes is a hilly forest reserve consisting of 13,500 hectares (52 sq miles) of southern beech and Magellanic steppe, plus a small ski area.

Other Protected Areas Symbol of Antofagasta, the offshore Monumento Natural La Portada and its immediate surroundings, totaling about 31 hectares, are a popular day-trip destination for residents.

In Region IV, midway between Vicuña and Ovalle, 128-hectare (316-acre) Monumento Natural Pichasca's main attraction is its petrified forest, but scavengers have absconded with many of the best specimens.

In the Andean foothills of the Santiago suburb of Lo Barnechea, 39,000-hectare (150-sq-mile) Santuario de la Naturaleza Yerba Loca is a popular weekend destination for residents of the capital. It's an excellent place to view Middle Chile's diverse Mediterranean vegetation.

The easily accessible 3000-hectare (740-acre) Andean Monumento Nacional El Morado featuring the San Francisco Glacier, source of the Río Morales, is only 93km (58 miles) from Santiago.

Only 16km (10 miles) from Punta Arenas, the area known as Monumento Natural Cueva del Milodón (only 150 hectares, or 370 acres) contains the cave where pioneers found remains of a milodon, a huge Pleistocene ground sloth.

Accessible only by boat from Punta Arenas, the small offshore Monumento Natural Los Pingüinos consists of two islands in the Strait of Magellan, honeycombed with burrowing Magellanic penguins and other seabirds. There is also a historic lighthouse here.

GOVERNMENT & POLITICS

Chile's constitution, ratified by the electorate in a controversial plebiscite in 1980, is a custom document that was largely the work of Pinochet supporter Jaime Guzmán, then a conservative law professor and later a senator, assassinated by leftists in 1990. It provides for a popularly elected president and a bicameral congress, with a 46-member Senado (Senate) and a 120-member Cámara de Diputados (Chamber of Deputies); eight senators are 'institutional,' appointed by the president and not subject to popular vote. Although the president continues to reside in Santiago and work at the Palacio de la Moneda there, the congress now meets in Valparaíso.

Administratively, the country consists of a Metropolitan Region, including the capital of Santiago and its surroundings, plus a dozen other distinct regions, one of which includes the Chilean Antarctic (where territorial claims are on hold by international agreement). The regions, in turn, are subdivided into provinces, which are further subdivided into *comunas*, the units of local government. Traditionally, Chilean politics is highly centralized, with nearly all important decisions made in Santiago.

Political Parties & Trade Unions

Since 1987, conventional political parties have operated legally, and the armed resistance that continued into the early years of the constitutional transition has ceased. Many prominent exiles have returned to Chile, and the trade union movement, generally allied with center-left parties, also operates freely, but the influence of the trade union movement is greatly diminished by discriminatory legislation passed during the Pinochet dictatorship. Only about 22% of Chile's 3.5-million-person work force belongs to unions, whose principal representative is the Central Unitaria de Trabajadores (CUT; Central Union of Workers).

The range and variation of political parties and their incessant transformations make it difficult for any but the most experienced observer to follow Chilean electoral politics. In the 1989 elections, 17 parties with little in common except their opposition to Pinochet formed an unlikely coalition known as the Concertación para la Democracia, choosing Christian Democrat Patricio Aylwin as a compromise candidate for the presidency. Aylwin easily defeated Pinochet's reluctant protégé Hernán Büchi, who stood for Renovación Nacional (RN, a direct descendant of the conservative National Party), and independent businessman Francisco Errázuriz, a right-wing populist. The right-wing Unión Democrática Independiente (UDI), founded by the late senator Guzmán, has at least temporarily consolidated a once-shaky Alianza para Chile (Alliance for Chile) with the more moderate RN.

In the 1993 presidential elections, the Concertación easily got Christian Democrat Eduardo Frei Ruiz-Tagle elected over RN candidate Arturo Alessandri for a six-year term, but the 1999 election brought increasing internal disagreement over presidential politics. In the January, 2000, runoff election, Concertación candidate, socialist Ricardo Lagos (a onetime Allende associate) won the presidency with just over 51% of the vote. The Alianza candidate, former Las Condes mayor Joaquín Lavín, who had attempted to overcome the reactionary UDI stereotype by supporting constitutional reform and reaching out to human rights groups, took a little more than 48½% of the vote.

Former president Frei's efforts at reforming the constitution to eliminate the institutional senators failed, despite official RN cooperation, when the recalcitrant UDI and the most conservative RN senators failed to go along. The proposed reform, incidentally, would have prevented Frei (or any other president) from choosing replacements for Pinochet appointees whose terms have expired.

The Military

Prussian officer Emilio Körner, contracted to reform the Chilean officer-training academy in the late 19th century, is responsible for creating the army's current system of organization. As head of its general staff from 1891 to 1910, he introduced German instructors, uniforms, discipline and modern equipment. Even after more than a decade of civilian rule, Chilean soldiers in parade dress bear a disconcerting resemblance to the jackbooted German troops of the 1930s and '40s.

Although the Pinochet regime is often seen as an aberration and the army as apolitical, Chile has suffered four civil wars, 10 successful coups and many uprisings and mutinies since independence from Spain. Military service is obligatory (though not universal – university students can get out of it) for males, but there is growing sentiment for eliminating conscription.

All the services enjoy wide autonomy – the civilian president lacks authority over their chiefs or even junior officers – and are highly disciplined and cohesive and far more loyal to their commanders than to the civilian head of state. Still, civilians have sometimes exploited interservice rivalries, especially between the older army and navy and the newer air force.

Unlike neighboring Argentina, where ignominious defeat in the Falklands war of 1982 undercut military privilege, the triumphant Chilean military is nearly unrepentant about human rights abuses under its dictatorship. Only General Máximo Venegas of the FACh (Chile's air force, the most reluctant participant in the 1973 coup) has shown any contrition, saying his branch of the armed forces asks forgiveness 'if wrong deeds were committed.'

Pinochet (born 1915) remains a force in Chilean politics, but his age, his declining health and of course his detention in Britain have reduced his influence. The influence of the military remains strong, however, as the civilian president could choose Pinochet's replacement only from a list provided by the army itself. President Frei's choice of general Ricardo Izurieta for the post obliged the other more senior candidates, closely identified with Pinochet, to retire, but the military still constitutes a powerful caste.

In addition, the heads of the armed services comprise a Consejo de Seguridad Nacional (Cosena; National Security Council) that, in case of state emergencies, can suspend the constitution and impose martial law. Nevertheless, the Pinochet situation appears to be slowly eroding military power and influence, and some observers have even speculated that Izurieta actually welcomes Pinochet's detention in England, since it frees him from the elderly, stubborn general's meddling. Publicly, though, Izurieta has supported Pinochet's release from detention, even traveling to London to show his solidarity.

According to the British-based International Institute for Strategic Studies (IISS), Chile has 93,000 professional military personnel, plus another 30,000 conscripts in uniform. In 1997 Chile devoted 3.5% of its GDP to military spending (the highest percentage of any Latin American country), and the forces are insulated from budgetary responsibility in part by a legal provision that guarantees them 10% of the profits from state copper sales, about US$240 million in 1998, for arms purchases. By law, the military budget cannot fall below 1989 levels, nor can it go down in real terms.

Geopolitics

One of the mainstays of military ideology and influence is the idea of geopolitics, a 19th-century European doctrine first elaborated by German geographer Friedrich Ratzel and later exaggerated in National Socialist (Nazi) ideology in the 1930s. According to this world view, the state resembles a biological organism that must expand or die. This means that the state must effectively occupy the territories it claims, in which process it comes into conflict with other states. Historically, this has been the justification for Chilean expansion into Tarapacá and the Pacific islands, as well as Antarctica.

General Pinochet, who has even written a textbook, *Geopolítica*, on this philosophy, isn't the only South American leader to hold such a view. His Argentine and Brazilian counterparts expound on topics such as the 'Fifth Column' of Chilean immigrants in Patagonia (largely humble and illiterate sheep shearers from economically depressed Chiloé) or the justification of territorial claims in the Antarctic in accordance with each country's longitudinal 'frontage' on the icebound continent. Chile has gone so far as to establish a 'permanent' settlement of families in Antarctica, with formal state services such as banking and housing. The tenets of geopolitics are most popular among, but not restricted to, the military. At the same time, the country has finally settled all of its long-standing border disputes with neighboring Argentina.

Among the last geopolitical disputes between Argentina and Chile have been the Laguna del Desierto on the border between the regions of Aisén and Magallanes, settled in Argentina's favor, and the Campo de Hielo Sur, the southern Patagonian ice field. When Chile submitted to arbitration at Laguna del Desierto, it expected to gain something and was shocked when arbitrators awarded the entire disputed area to Argentina. After going through an appeal process to save face, the Chilean government has also had to endure exaggerated criticism from right-wing parties over a proposed – but not yet approved – settlement in the Campo de Hielo Sur. The Chilean air force, for its part, quickly built an airfield and training base directly on the ice.

Human Rights

Despite the military's self-serving amnesty laws, human rights issues have not gone away. On this theme, the biggest news of 1998–99 was the London arrest, detention and requested extradition of former dictator Pinochet, on charges of torture, at the request of Spain. Fearful that Pinochet's possible extradition to Spain could destabilize Chile's ostensibly fragile democracy, and under pressure from the military, the timid Concertación government pressed for the general's release, but most Chileans seemed to take the events in stride – if not with satisfaction.

For the vast majority of Chileans, Pinochet's arrest and the future of his case (it now seems likely that, due to failing health, Pinochet will not be extradited to Spain but may, eventually, face trail in Chile) are not everyday concerns, even though the arrest was a surprise. It has brought the subject into the open, but it is for the most part less polemical than it would have been before the arrest. Those who demonstrate loudly against the arrest are die-hard right-wingers. The more thoughtful conservatives, such as Joaquín Lavín, unsuccesful presidential candidate in the January, 2000, election, realize they must distance themselves from Pinochet and his associates to have any hope of taking power.

Visitors to Chile should be circumspect about raising the topic of the former dictator's arrest unless they know their audience. Britons and Spaniards are unlikely to run into any specific problems; they may even be more likely to be congratulated than hassled for their governments' actions.

Related news included indictments of five army officers linked to the infamous 'Caravan of Death,' under the direction of General Sergio Arellano Stark, at Pinochet's instigation, which resulted in summary executions of numerous political prisoners in the dictatorship's early months. Chilean judge Juan Guzmán sidestepped the Pinochet-era amnesty law by ruling that, because many of the victims' fates remain unknown, the disappearances are continuing offenses.

There was even evidence that the military's code of silence was eroding. Retired Army colonel Olagier Benavente Bustos stated publicly that Pinochet's favorite helicopter pilot had admitted dumping bodies of the disappeared into the remote Andes and the Pacific Ocean during the dictatorship's early years. (Unlike its Argentine counterparts, however,

VICTOR ENGLEBERT

Chileans sound off about Pinochet.

the Chilean military apparently did not toss live victims from helicopters.) In August 1999, the heads of the armed forces agreed to help 'reconstruct' the facts behind the disappearances, while simultaneously denying that they had any information. This was not, however, sufficient for human rights activists and victims' families, who continue to seek justice through the courts.

The release of formerly confidential documents from US government archives may also shed light upon the dictatorship's abuses, and the Clinton administration was reportedly even considering Pinochet's indictment in the Letelier murder case. Former DINA chief Manuel Contreras and his deputy Pedro Espinosa went to prison several years ago for their roles in the Letelier case, though critics consider their incarceration in a custom-built facility near Santiago only a slap on the wrist (some defenders of Contreras and Espinosa consider them scapegoats for the rest of the military). It's worth mentioning that General Contreras' 'cell' sports custom furniture, a large personal library, outside phone lines and an Internet connection, plus his own cook, waiter and full-time nurse.

Another worry for the former military rulers is the Buenos Aires trial of ex-DINA agent Enrique Arancibia Clavel for the assassination of General Prats, since it could reveal details of covert operations outside the shield of military courts and hand-picked judges. In April 1999, US attorney general Janet Reno decided to release to the Argentine courts details of testimony by former DINA agent Michael Townley, a US citizen who turned in state's evidence in the Letelier case in return for a lighter sentence. This could implicate many Chilean military officials of the Pinochet dictatorship.

The Chilean government, for its part, has supported the Prats family in the murder trial of Arancibia Clavel, who has been held for two years in Buenos Aires but has refused to cooperate on charges of 'illicit association,' which could lead to broader action against Pinochet and his associates.

In addition, while the Spanish government has dropped its demand for extradition and prosecution of the killers of Carmelo Soria (a Spanish diplomat working under UN auspices in 1978) because Chile's supreme court invoked the amnesty law, Soria's family continues to pursue the case in Spanish and international courts.

On the other hand, the government of Uruguay has closed an investigation of the mysterious death of Eugenio Berríos, a former Chilean intelligence agent who disappeared in 1992 after seeking police protection in that country against his former DINA colleagues. An Uruguayan judge ruled the case 'unsolved.'

ECONOMY

When Pinochet's junta seized power, it had no strategy beyond an urge to eradicate leftist influence and stabilize the economy. Its pledge to reduce inflation and return confiscated property appealed to conservatives and professionals opposed to Allende, but it soon adopted a more radical economic program.

Pinochet appointed civilian economists, disciples of the economics department at the University of Chicago, to direct government policy. To encourage commerce, the Chicago Boys favored measures that slashed government expenditures and eliminated regulatory functions, abolished price controls, reduced tariffs in the interests of free trade and sold most state-owned industries to private entrepreneurs; new financial codes encouraged foreign investment. Codelco (Corporación del Cobre, the national copper company) remained under state ownership, but the Chilean government compensated foreign mining companies for their losses. State-owned banks froze interest rates for savings, but private banks raised them, causing a flow of personal savings into private institutions.

For some years, inflation remained high despite shrinking domestic demand and declining imports. Industrial production also declined and some inefficient industries disappeared, although growth of 'nontraditional' exports, such as off-season temperate fruits to Europe and North America, helped compensate for falling copper prices. Despite falling wages, unemployment reached nearly 20% by early 1976.

In some callampas, where unemployment reached as high as 80% or more, only church-organized soup kitchens prevented starvation. The government's response was the PEM (Programa de Empleo Mínimo, Minimum Employment Program), which paid a token monthly salary to individuals who swept streets or performed other minor public-works duties.

As private owners acquired former state banks, interest rates escaped government controls and subsequently soared. Firms borrowing money to avoid bankruptcy fell into debt to private banks and finance companies. Not surprisingly, financiers – some of them Chicago Boys using foreign loan money – obtained failed enterprises at little cost, creating their own personal business empires.

When inflation finally fell, real wages and salaries rose slowly, but demand increased for goods and services. Since local industry could not satisfy the demand, duty-free zones in the northern city of Iquique and the southern city of Punta Arenas fueled an import boom. But Chile continued to rely on the export of products such as minerals, timber, fruit and seafood in order to earn foreign exchange. In the early 1980s, global recession reduced the price of copper and other mineral exports, and Chile's international debt (almost all of it created by foreign loans to private banks and firms) skyrocketed. By the end of 1981, loan repayments were consuming 75% of export earnings. Interest rates climbed, bankruptcies increased and unemployment soared.

In 1982 the government sought to promote exports by devaluing the peso and further reducing real wages, but inflation soon wiped out any benefits for exporters. Rising local and global interest rates exacerbated the banks' debt problems. Allowed to float, the peso plummeted by 40% against the US dollar and, with the Chicago Boys' policies in shambles, the junta backtracked and bailed out key private banks and finance houses in early 1983.

Until very recently, the Chilean economy had improved greatly on a macro scale,

enjoying a decade of uninterrupted growth at rates of 6% or higher, but close economic ties across the Pacific made the country especially vulnerable to the Asian meltdown of 1998, when the growth rate slipped to only 3.4%. In the first half of 1999, GDP actually fell to a figure of -2.9%, Chile's first serious recession in recent memory. On the positive side, but perhaps predictably, inflation fell to 3.4% per annum.

The elite have benefited more from economic growth than the poor, and unemployment remains distressingly high, exceeding 10% in mid-1999. Countless city dwellers earn a precarious subsistence as street vendors of ice cream, candy, cigarettes and other cheap goods such as audiocassettes. The minimum wage, for those fortunate enough to have regular employment, is only about US$206 per month, and the gap between rich and poor is widening.

While both the Aylwin and Frei administrations displayed a more sympathetic attitude toward the plight of the poor and dispossessed, they largely continued the junta's macroeconomic policies despite some advances in social spending. The inequalities of wealth now resemble the inequalities of land distribution in earlier times. According to a mid-1990s report by the United Nations' Santiago-based Economic Commission for Latin America and the Caribbean (Cepal), the wealthiest 10% of Chileans receive more than 40% of the national income; the poorest 40% earn just 13%. Although these figures were among the worst in the region, the number of Chileans living in poverty fell by half, from 46% to 23%, between 1987 and 1996.

At the same time, since the return to representative government, there has been an influx of foreign capital from companies that were clearly reluctant to invest in the dictatorship, but the recent economic slump has diminished hopes that vigorous economic growth would further reduce poverty. Since 1987, Chile has enjoyed an increasing trade surplus; its most important trading partners are the USA, Japan, Germany, Brazil and Argentina.

The export economy is now more diverse and less vulnerable to fluctuations in international markets; the mining sector, for instance, no longer relies exclusively on copper but also produces less-traditional commodities such as lithium. Still, Chilean copper represents nearly 40% of the country's exports, 8% of its GDP, 16% of domestic investment, 34% of social expenditure, 34% of world copper production and 37% of world reserves. Nevertheless, export items such as fresh fruit have also increased and diversified.

International travel and tourism are flourishing – in 1997, 1.7 million foreign visitors spent US$1 billion in Chile, constituting about 4% of GDP and 6% of total export income. Forest products are a rapidly growing but increasingly controversial sector, given the country's declining native forests, the apparent unsustainability of the present level of exports, and dubious reforestation programs of fast-growing exotic species such as Monterey pine and eucalyptus.

POPULATION & PEOPLE

Chile's population of about 14.8 million is unevenly distributed. About a third, perhaps 4.5 million, reside in Gran Santiago, which includes the capital and its immediate suburbs; this includes 70% of all Chileans between the ages of 15 and 24. No other city population is greater than about 300,000. Moreover, almost 75% live in the Chilean heartland (including the conurbations of Valparaíso-Viña del Mar and Concepción-Talcahuano), which comprises only 20% of the country's total land area. More than 80% of Chileans live in cities or towns, but south of the Río Biobío, there is still a dense rural population. The last formal census was in 1992.

In the desert north, nearly everyone lives in the large coastal cities of Arica, Iquique, Antofagasta, La Serena and Coquimbo, although the mining centers of Calama-Chuquicamata, El Salvador and Copiapó are relatively large as well. South of Santiago, the most important cities are Rancagua, Concepción-Talcahuano, Valdivia, Osorno and Puerto Montt. Beyond Puerto Montt, where the fractured landscape complicates communications, the only notable towns are Coihaique, in Region XI, and Punta Arenas, in Region XII.

Most Chileans are mestizos, although many can still claim purely European descent. Throughout much of the country, social class is still a greater issue than race – working-class people and others resentfully call the country's wealthier elite *momios* (mummies) because, to paraphrase the words of film director Miguel Littín, they are so resistant to change that they might as well be embalmed. In the southern region of La Araucanía, there is a large, visible and increasingly militant Mapuche Indian population, mostly in and around the city of Temuco. Above the once densely peopled river valleys of the desert north, Aymara and Atacameño peoples farm the terraces of the precordillera and pasture their llamas and alpacas in the altiplano.

Chile did not experience the massive 19th- and 20th-century European immigration that neighboring Argentina did – at the end of the 19th century, only a small percentage of Chileans were foreign-born. After the European upheavals of 1848, many Germans settled near present-day Valdivia, Osorno and Puerto Montt in southern Chile, where use of the German language is still vigorous, if not widespread. Other immigrant groups included the French, Italians, Yugoslavs (particularly in Magallanes and Tierra del Fuego), European Jews and Palestinians.

European immigration did not alter the structure of Chilean society, but added non-Spanish elements to the middle and upper classes. The established aristocracy (the original landed gentry), of mostly Spanish Basque origin, welcomed wealthy immigrants with British, French or German surnames like Edwards, Subercaseaux and Gildemeister. Despite their small numbers, European immigrants became economically powerful, controlling rural estates and commercial, financial and industrial institutions.

EDUCATION

Chile's 95% literacy rate is one of Latin America's highest. From the age of five to 12, education is free and compulsory, although school attendance is low in some rural areas.

Traditionally, universities are free and open, but after the 1973 coup the military government installed its own rectors throughout the country; its sweeping university reform of the 1980s reduced state funding, raised student fees and downgraded or eliminated ostensibly 'subversive' careers such as sociology and psychology. The Universidad de Chile was a particular target because of its reputation for aggressive dissent. It underwent further downsizing during the Frei administration.

Like other Latin American countries, Chile suffers from a glut of lawyers and other professionals and a shortage of trained people in engineering and other more practical fields. The military reform of higher education made it easy to open private 'universities,' but most of these are glorified trade schools with part-time faculty, limited curriculum and dubious standards. Some, however, are rapidly improving.

ARTS

Although derivative of European precedents in many ways, Chilean art, literature and music have been influential beyond the country's borders. Many Chilean intellectuals have been educated in European capitals, particularly Paris. In the 19th and early 20th centuries Santiago self-consciously emulated European – especially French – cultural trends in art, music and architecture. There are many art museums and galleries.

Poetry

Pablo Neruda and Gabriela Mistral, both Nobel Prize-winning poets, are major figures in Chilean, Latin American and world literature. Much of their work is available in English translation, such as Neruda's *Heights of Macchu Picchu, Canto General, Passions and Impressions* (1993) and his rambling, selective, but still readable *Memoirs* (1977). For an interestingly conceived view of Neruda and his work, see Luis Poirot's *Pablo Neruda, Absence and Presence* (1990), a collection of outstanding black-and-white photos with accompanying text from Neruda, friends and admirers (both Chilean and foreign). Especially poignant are the photos of Neruda's houses in Santiago, Valparaíso and Isla Negra after their vandalization by the military.

US poet Langston Hughes translated some of Gabriela Mistral's work in *Selected Poems of Gabriela Mistral* (1957), while a different book with the same title was published by the Library of Congress and Johns Hopkins Press in 1971. For an interpretation of her work, try Margot Arce de Vásquez's *Gabriela Mistral, the Poet and Her Work* (1964).

Important contemporary poets include Nicanor Parra, who has drawn Nobel Prize attention, and Jorge Teillier, whose work has been translated and analyzed by Carolyne Wright in *In Order to Talk with the Dead* (1993).

Fiction

With novels in the 'magical realism' tradition of Latin American fiction, Isabel Allende (niece of the late president Salvador Allende) has become a popular writer overseas as well as in Chile. Among her works are *House of the Spirits* (1986), *Of Love and Shadows* (1988), *Eva Luna* (1989) and *Daughter of Fortune* (1999).

Chile's best contemporary novelist, José Donoso, died in late 1996. His *Curfew* (1988) offers a portrait of life under the dictatorship through the eyes of a returned exile. Antonio Skármeta's *I Dreamt the Snow Was Burning* (1985) is a novel of the early post-coup years, but Skármeta has become famous for his novel *Burning Patience* (1987), adapted into the award-winning Italian film *Il Postino* (The Postman). Luis Sepúlveda's misleadingly titled novella *The Old Man Who Read Love Stories* (1993) is a fictional account of life and society on Ecuador's Amazonian frontier.

Marco Antonio de la Parra's *Secret Holy War of Santiago de Chile* (1994) is a surrealistic novel of contemporary Chile, with numerous geographical and cultural references that anyone who has visited the capital will find fascinating and challenging.

Roberto Ampuero writes mystery novels whose main character, Cayetano Brulé, is a Valparaíso-based Cuban expatriate detective who gets around the country, visiting many places that will be recognizable to foreign visitors. While none of Ampuero's work has yet appeared in English, his straightforward writing style makes stories like *El Alemán de Atacama (The German of Atacama*, 1996) accessible to nonnative speakers.

Music

Probably the best-known manifestation of Chilean popular culture is *La Nueva Canción Chilena (New Chilean Song Movement)*, whose practitioners wedded the country's folkloric heritage to the political passions of the late 1960s and early '70s. Its most legendary figure is Violeta Parra, best known for her enduring theme *Gracias a la Vida (Thanks to Life)*, but her children Isabel and Angel, also performers, established the first of many *peñas* (musical and cultural centers) in Santiago in the mid-1960s. Individual performers such as Victor Jara, brutally executed during the 1973 military coup, and groups like Quilapayún and Inti-Illimani acquired international reputations for both their music and their political commitment.

Many Chilean folk musicians, exiled during the Pinochet dictatorship, performed regularly in Europe, North America and Australia, and their recordings are available both in Chile and overseas.

Chilean rock music is less widely known, but there are several groups worth hearing, most notably the Paris-based Los Jaivas, who frequently perform in Europe and also tour Chile every summer; Los Tres (who, despite their name, are a four-piece band); La Ley (based in Mexico); and Los Dioses (a reincarnated version of Los Prisioneros, probably the country's most popular rock band ever).

Film

Until the 1973 coup, Chilean cinema was among the most experimental in Latin America. Director Alejandro Jodorowsky's surrealistic *El Topo (The Mole)*, an underground success overseas, included a performance by Country Joe and the Fish. Then-exiled director Miguel Littín's *Alsino and the Condor* (1983), nominated for an Academy Award as Best Foreign Film, is readily available on video. Littín has recently gone over budget in the historical epic *Tierra del Fuego*.

Paris-based Raúl Ruiz, another exile, has been prolific in his adopted country but only recently released his first English-language film, the psychological thriller *Shattered Image* (1998). Starring William Baldwin and Anne Parillaud (best known for *La Femme Nikita)*, it drew mostly tepid and critical reviews for its portrayal of a woman unable to distinguish between dream and reality.

Director Gustavo Graef-Marino's *Johnny 100 Pesos*, based on a true story about a group of robbers who become trapped in a Santiago high-rise, made a favorable impression at 1994's Sundance Film Festival and led to a Hollywood contract for a thriller shot in Romania in 1998–99 with Tom Berenger and Daryl Hannah in starring roles. It has just been released in Chile as *El Enemigo de mi Enemigo*.

Several films about Chile, all available on video, deal with politics to a greater or lesser degree. Costa-Gavras' *Missing* (1982), with Jack Lemmon and Sissy Spacek, was based on Thomas Hauser's book *The Execution of Charles Horman: An American Sacrifice*, which chronicled the disappearance of a US activist following the coup. Ben Kingsley and Sigourney Weaver were the protagonists in Roman Polanski's English-language adaptation of Ariel Dorfman's play *Death and the Maiden* (1994), for which Dorfman also wrote the screenplay. Antonio Skármeta's novel *Burning Patience* was the template for British director Michael Radford's award-winning Italian-language film *Il Postino (The Postman*, 1994), a fictional exploration of Pablo Neruda's counsel to a shy but lovestruck mail carrier.

The Paths of Mistral & Neruda

Gabriela Mistral and Pablo Neruda have opened a window on Chile and Latin America through their poetry, but their biographies are no less revealing. In some ways, no two individuals could be more different than these Nobel Prize winners, but the parallels and divergences in their lives disclose both unifying and contrasting aspects of Chilean life and culture.

They were contemporaries, but of different generations; Mistral was born in 1889, Neruda in 1904. Both belonged to the provinces: Mistral to the remote Elqui Valley of the Norte Chico, Neruda to the southern city of Temuco, though his birthplace was Parral, in the heartland province of Maule, and he lived in Santiago, Valparaíso and a small beach community at Isla Negra. Both poets used pseudonyms: Gabriela Mistral's given name was Lucila Godoy Alcayaga; Pablo Neruda's was Neftalí Ricardo Reyes Basoalto. Both adopted their aliases out of timidity: the young rural schoolmistress Lucila Godoy sat in the audience at Santiago's Teatro Municipal while a surrogate received a prize for her series 'Sonnets on Death,' in memory of a young suitor who had committed suicide; Neftalí Reyes feared the ridicule of his working-class family.

Both enjoyed literary success at a young age. The government rewarded both with diplomatic posts that subsidized their creative writing; in consequence, both traveled extensively and became celebrities outside their own country and the South American continent, which hadn't produced a Nobel Prize winner in literature until Mistral's award in 1945. In 1971, Neruda became the third Latin American writer to receive the Swedish Academy's prize (Guatemalan novelist Miguel Angel Asturias was the second, in 1967).

Despite these similarities, the two poets were very different in other respects. After the death of her beloved, Mistral never married, devoted her life to children and their education at schools from La Serena to Punta Arenas. When she taught in Temuco, the young Neruda and his friends worshipped her. She even traveled abroad to reform the Mexican system of public instruction. She lived austerely, but her stern features masked the sensitivity of a woman whose poetry was compassionate and mystical. Though friendly with political figures, most notably President Pedro Aguirre Cerda, her politics were not a matter of public controversy.

Neruda, by contrast, became a flamboyant figure whose private life was public knowledge, who built eccentric houses and filled them with outlandish objects, and whose politics more than once landed him in trouble. Unlike the somber Mistral, his face was usually smiling, often pensive, but never grim. While consul in Java in the 1930s, he married a Dutch woman, left her for Delia del Carril (a decade older than himself) a few years later, and after nearly 20 years left Delia for the much younger Matilde Urrutia. For her, he built and named La Chascona (her nickname, for her unruly mane of hair), his Santiago house at the foot of Cerro San Cristóbal.

Theater

Even in the provinces, live theater is an important medium of expression. While traditional venues such as Santiago's Teatro Municipal operated more or less normally during the Pinochet dictatorship, the end of military government has meant a major burst of growth in central neighborhoods like Barrio Bellavista and even suburban comunas such as Ñuñoa. Look for small experimental companies: one is La Tropa, a three-person outfit that plays public parks such as Plaza Ñuñoa.

One of Chile's best-known playwrights is Ariel Dorfman, whose *Death and the Maiden* explored issues of brutality and reconciliation

The Paths of Mistral & Neruda

Neruda's houses, including his beachfront favorite at Isla Negra and La Sebastiana in Valparaíso, were material expressions of his personality, improvised with eclectic assemblies of objects amassed during his travels and at his diplomatic posts. Entire rooms are filled with shells, bowsprit figureheads, ships in bottles and, of course, books, all of which delighted him and his guests and now draw thousands of visitors. The houses themselves break all the rules of standard architecture and, for that reason, intrigue visitors as much as they pleased the owner. In his autobiography, Neruda wrote, 'I have . . . built my house like a toy house and I play in it from morning till night.'

After Franco's rebels defeated the Spanish republic, the Chilean diplomat devoted his energies to helping refugees escape the dictator's revenge. In Spain he had made a personal commitment to the Communist Party, although he did not enroll officially until his return to Chile, where he was elected senator for Tarapacá and Antofagasta, the mining provinces of the Norte Grande. After managing Gabriel González Videla's successful presidential campaign of 1946, he fell afoul of the president's caprice and went into hiding and then exile in Argentina, escaping by foot and horseback across the southern Andes.

After González Videla left office, Neruda returned to Chile and continued his political activities without reducing his prolific output of poetry. In 1969 he was the Communist candidate for the presidency, but he withdrew in support of Salvador Allende's candidacy and later became Allende's ambassador to France. He received the Nobel Prize during his tenure in France. Neruda died less than a fortnight after the military coup of 1973.

For all his wealth, Neruda never forgot his modest origins nor abandoned his political convictions and did not consider his privileged lifestyle incompatible with his leftist beliefs. Lacking heirs, he left everything to the Chilean people through a foundation.

Mistral's reflective and mystical verse was uncontroversial, but Neruda's poetry could be committed and combative. And although no government could suppress literature that could be found in almost every household that could spare a penny to buy it, General Pinochet's dictatorship did its best to erase his memory. After Neruda's death, his houses were vandalized with police and military complicity, but his widow Matilde and dedicated volunteers persisted to establish the Fundación Neruda in spite of legal and extralegal obstacles. It administers the estate and has successfully restored all three houses, now open to the public. Chileans and foreigners flock to them, and with a very few truly extreme exceptions, even those who disagreed with his politics enjoy and respect his work.

Gabriela Mistral, meanwhile, remains a modest but reassuring presence in Chilean life and literature. Every day, thousands of Santiago's citizens pass the mural of Gabriela and her 'children' on the Alameda, at the base of Cerro Santa Lucía, while many more pay her homage at the museum bearing her name in the village of Vicuña, in her native Elqui Valley. Although she died in New York, she is buried in her natal hamlet of Montegrande.

in the postmilitary years. The versatile Dorfman was once notorious for his deconstruction of Disney in *How to Read Donald Duck* (1971), a clever but indignant critique of cultural imperialism coauthored with Belgian sociologist Armand Mattelart. Dorfman is also a poet and novelist. His memoir is *Heading South, Looking North* (1998).

Of a younger generation, playwright Marco Antonio de la Parra remained in Santiago during the years of the Pinochet dictatorship, despite censorship of such works as *Lo Crudo, lo Cocido y lo Podrido (The Raw, the Cooked and the Rotten)*. Many of his plays have been performed in Europe and North America.

Painting & Sculpture

Chile has many art museums, but with a handful of exceptions, their focus is historical rather than contemporary and the work is unexceptional. Venues such as Santiago's Palacio de Bellas Artes tend to focus on traveling international exhibitions, but others, such as Providencia's Parque de las Esculturas (an open-air sculpture museum along the Río Mapocho) and Castro's Museo de Arte Moderno focus on Chilean artists.

Valparaíso's Museo de Bellas Artes, presently undergoing renovation, stresses 19th-century Chilean landscapes such as English painter Thomas Somerscales' *Crepúsculo sobre Aconcagua (Dusk over Aconcagua)*, which uses Andean light superbly. Public murals, inspired by the Mexican muralists who left a visible legacy in Chillán and Concepción, deserve a look.

Manuel González, the father of Chilean impressionism, painted *El Pago de Chile (The Payment of Chile)*, depicting a mutilated soldier from the War of the Pacific; glory-conscious agents of the Pinochet dictatorship changed its title to *Capitán Dinamita (Captain Dynamite)*.

Chile's best-known living painter is Paris-based Roberto Matta (born 1911), the Latin American artist most closely identified with surrealism. Jesuit-educated in Chile, he went to France in 1934 to study architecture with Le Corbusier, but he has also lived in New York and Mexico City. Influenced by Mexican landscapes, his painting is nevertheless more abstract than that influence would suggest; he has also worked in media such as sculpture and engraving.

Among Chile's notable contemporary artists are Máximo Pincheira, whose grim works deal with the anxieties of life under the dictatorship, and María José Romero (daughter of painter Carmen Aldunate), whose 'frivolous' oils, as she has called them, deal more with personal than political issues. Mario Irarrázaval (born 1940) is responsible for work such as *El Juicio (The Judgment)*, showing a bound prisoner at the mercy of three judges – perhaps symbolizing Chile under military rule.

SOCIETY & CONDUCT

On the surface, English-speaking visitors will find Chile, like Argentina, more accessible than other Latin American countries because it is a more immigrant-based, European-derived society. Foreign travelers are less conspicuous than in Peru or Bolivia, which have large indigenous populations, and can more easily integrate themselves into everyday life. Chileans are hospitable and often invite foreigners to visit their homes and participate in daily activities, but they may also be very reserved at times.

Travelers should be circumspect in their behavior around indigenous peoples, especially in areas like the altiplano of Arica, around San Pedro de Atacama, and in the Mapuche south. Aggressive picture-taking and rowdiness may be particularly offensive.

RELIGION

Traditionally about 90% of Chileans are Roman Catholic, but evangelical Protestantism is rapidly gaining converts. There are also Lutherans, Jews, Presbyterians, Mormons and Pentecostals. The proselytizing Mormons have caused great controversy, and their churches have been the target of numerous bombings by leftist groups.

Catholicism has provided Chile with some of its most compelling cultural monuments – the colonial adobe churches of the Norte Grande, Santiago's Catedral Metropolitana and colonial Iglesia San Francisco, and the modest but dignified shingled chapels of Chiloé. Countless roadside shrines, some of them extraordinary manifestations of folk art, also testify to the pervasiveness of religion in Chilean society.

Like Chilean political parties, the church has serious factions, but its Vicaria de la Solidaridad compiled such an outstanding human rights record during the dictatorship that it became the major object of the general's vitriolic scorn in his four-volume autobiography. At great risk to themselves, Chilean priests frequently worked in the shantytowns of Santiago and other large cities. Such activism has continued in today's more lenient political climate.

On the other hand, the church's attitude toward other social issues is starkly reactionary. Its obstinate attitude has contributed to the fact that Chile is the world's only democracy without a divorce law, though annulments are not unusual for those who can pay for the legal maneuvering (a new but still very restrictive divorce law is now under consideration by the Congress). The government has found it difficult to institute critically important sex education programs over ecclesiastical opposition.

LANGUAGE

Spanish is Chile's official language and is almost universally understood, but there are also a handful of native languages, some spoken by a very few individuals. In the desert north, more than 20,000 people speak Aymara, although most are bilingual; in the south, there are about 400,000 Mapudungun (Mapuche) speakers and a few thousand Huilliches, whose language shares many common elements with Mapudungun, though the languages are not mutually intelligible. Perhaps the most intriguing linguistic minorities are the 2200 speakers of Rapanui, the Polynesian language of most of Easter Island's population, and the roughly 50 remaining Qawashqar speakers of the southern fjords, near Puerto Edén.

See the Language chapter at the back of the book for pronunciation details and useful phrases.

Facts for the Visitor

SUGGESTED ITINERARIES

Depending on the length of your trip, Chile offers many possible itineraries. A week's trip could include a stay in Santiago and excursions in the vicinity, especially during ski season, or a whirlwind trip to the desert north, taking in sights such as Parque Nacional Lauca, or south, to Patagonian attractions such as Torres del Paine. A two-week trip might allow you to take in all of these sights. Alternately, you could visit the southern lakes region and take a four-day cruise through the Chilean fjords to Puerto Natales to get to Torres del Paine, or make a side trip to Easter Island (Rapa Nui).

With more time, say a month, it's possible to do all of the above, though the long distances make flying to certain destinations desirable or even essential. If you're lucky enough to have two months or more, it's possible to make an intimate acquaintance with Chile by traveling overland, stopping at many points of interest. The fact that nearly everything is on or near one or two major highways, with frequent and comfortable bus service, makes organizing a trip easy.

PLANNING

If you're planning your first big trip, or if you're a seasoned traveler but have never been to Chile before, you may want to check out Lonely Planet's *Read This First: Central & South America*. The Read This First series, aimed at first-time travelers, is packed with useful predeparture information on planning, buying tickets, visa applications and health issues. A section, with full-color maps, is devoted to Chile.

When to Go

The country's geographical variety can make a visit rewarding in any season. Santiago and Middle Chile are best in the verdant spring (September through November) or during the fall harvest (late February into April), while popular natural attractions such as Parque Nacional Torres del Paine in

Magallanes and the lakes region are best in summer (December through March). Conversely, Chilean ski resorts draw many visitors during the Northern Hemisphere's summer (June through August).

The Atacama desert is temperate and attractive at any time of year, although nights are always cold at higher altitudes. In the northern altiplano, summer is the rainy season, but this usually means only a brief afternoon thunderstorm. Still, the dry spring months are probably best for explorations off the main highways.

Easter Island is cooler, slightly cheaper and far less crowded outside the summer months. The same is true of the Juan Fernández Archipelago, which can be inaccessible if winter rains gully the dirt airstrip; March is an ideal time for a visit.

Maps

Lonely Planet's *Chile & Easter Island travel atlas* maps the entire country in full color at a scale of 1:1,000,000. For members of the American Automobile Association (AAA) and its affiliates, there is a general South American road map that is adequate for initial planning.

ITMB's widely available *Southern South America*, at a scale of 1:4,000,000, includes most of Chile, as does its *Argentina*, at an identical scale. ITMB also publishes maps of Easter Island at 1:30,000 and Tierra del Fuego at 1:750,000.

Several useful maps of Chile are available from kiosks and street vendors in the main towns and cities. Atlas de Chile's *Plano de Santiago y Mini Atlas Caminero de Chile 1995* combines an indexed plan of the capital (1:25,000) with a respectable highway map (1:2,000,000). Inupal's *Gran Mapa Caminero de Chile* provides comparable highway coverage but lacks city maps.

The Instituto Geográfico Militar's *Guía Caminera* (1992) is a reasonably good highway map in a convenient ring-binder format, with scales ranging from 1:500,000 to

1:1,500,000; it also includes several city maps at varying scales. If you can find it, the IGM's *Plano Guía del Gran Santiago* (1989) is the local equivalent of *London A–Z*, at a scale of 1:20,000, but the binding is flimsy; a new edition would be welcome.

The IGM's 1:50,000 topographic series is valuable for trekkers, although maps of some sensitive border areas (where most national parks are) may not be available. Individual maps cost about US$15 each in Santiago, where the IGM (☎ 02-696-8221) is at Dieciocho 369, just south of the Alameda. It's open 9 am to 5:30 pm Monday, 9 am to 5:50 pm Tuesday through Friday.

The popular Turistel guidebook series (see Guidebooks, later in this chapter) contains detailed highway maps and excellent plans of Chilean cities and towns, but lacks scales. JLM Cartografía (☎ 02-225-1365, jmatassi@interactiva.cl), General del Canto 105, Oficina 1506, Providencia, Santiago, publishes specialized maps for tourist areas such as San Pedro de Atacama, Torres del Paine and surroundings at scales ranging from 1:50,000 to 1:500,000.

Some of these maps may be available at specialist bookstores such as Stanford's in London, or in the map rooms of major university libraries. In most major Chilean cities, the Automóvil Club de Chile (Acchi) has an office that sells maps, although not all of them are equally well stocked. If you belong to an auto club at home, ask for a discount.

What to Bring

Chile is a mostly temperate, midlatitude country, and seasonally appropriate clothing for North America or Europe will be equally suitable here. In the desert north, lightweight cottons are a good idea, but at the higher elevations of the Andes and in Patagonia you should carry warm clothing even in summer. From Temuco south, rain is possible at any time of the year, and a small, light umbrella is useful in the city (but not in the gales of Magallanes, where heavier rain gear is desirable). In winter, budget hotels in the south may not provide sufficient blankets, so a warm sleeping bag is a good idea even if you're not camping.

There is no prejudice against backpackers, and during the summer, many young Chileans themselves visit remote parts of the country on a shoestring budget. The selection and quality of outdoor equipment are improving, but prices are still relatively high compared to North America or Europe, so it's better to bring camping gear from home.

Personal preference largely determines the best way to carry your baggage. A large zip-up bag or duffel with a wide shoulder strap is convenient for buses, trains and planes but is awkward to carry for long distances. A backpack is most convenient if you expect to do a lot of walking. Internal frame packs, with a cover that protects the straps from getting snagged in storage on buses or planes, can be a good compromise.

Don't overlook small essentials like a Swiss Army knife, needle and thread, a small pair of scissors, contraceptives, sunglasses and swimming gear. Basic supplies such as toothbrushes and toothpaste, shaving cream, shampoo and tampons are readily available, except in very small, remote places. Visitors staying in budget hotels and traveling on buses or trains will find a good pair of earplugs useful. It's also a good idea to carry toilet paper at all times, since many Chilean bathrooms lack it.

Travelers interested in wildlife, particularly birds, should remember to bring a pair of binoculars.

See Health later in this chapter for a list of medical items to bring.

TOURIST OFFICES

Every regional capital and some other Chilean cities have a local representative of Sernatur, the national tourist service, while many municipalities have their own tourist office, usually on the main plaza or at the bus terminal. In some areas, these offices may be open during the summer only.

Abroad, Chilean embassies and consulates in major cities usually have a tourist representative in their delegation. You should also try representatives of LanChile, Chile's only intercontinental airline, for tourist information.

VISAS & DOCUMENTS
Passport & Visas

Except for nationals of Argentina, Brazil, Uruguay and Paraguay, who need only their national identity cards, passports are obligatory. Citizens of Canada, the UK, the USA, Australia, New Zealand and most Western European countries need passports only. Countries whose nationals need advance visas include Korea, Poland, India, Thailand, Jamaica and Russia. Do not arrive at the border without one, or you may be sent back to the nearest Chilean consulate. For up-to-date visa information, check Lonely Planet's website, www.lonelyplanet.com.

Note that the Chilean government now collects a US$45 processing fee from arriving US citizens in response to the US government's imposition of a similar fee on Chilean citizens applying for US visas; this payment is valid for the life of the passport. Canadians pay US$55, Australians US$30.

It is advisable to carry your passport: even though the military are keeping a low profile under the present civilian government, Chile's *carabineros* (national police) can still demand identification at any moment. In general, Chileans are document oriented, and a passport is essential for cashing traveler's checks, checking into a hotel and many other routine activities.

If your passport is lost or stolen, notify the carabineros, get a statement and then notify your consulate as soon as possible.

Tourist Cards On arrival, visitors receive a tourist card and entry stamp that allow a stay of up to 90 days but are renewable for an additional 90. To renew an expiring tourist card, make a visit to the Departamento de Extranjería (☎ 02-672-5320), Moneda 1342 in Santiago, between 9 am and 1:30 pm. You may also visit the Departamento de Extranjería in any of Chile's regional capitals. However, since this now costs about US$100, many visitors prefer a quick dash across the Argentine border and back. Even the quickest trip to Mendoza and back won't cost much less than that, and it's probably more interesting than standing in lines for several days.

If you plan on staying longer than six months, it's simplest to make a brief visit to Argentina, Peru or Bolivia, then return and start your six months all over again. There is no formal obstacle to doing so, although border officials sometimes question returnees from Mendoza, Argentina, to determine whether they are working illegally in Chile. Do not lose your tourist card, which border authorities take very seriously; for a replacement, visit the Policía Internacional (☎ 02-737-1292) at General Borgoño 1052 in the Santiago comuna of Independencia, near the old Mapocho station, from 8:30 am to 12:30 pm or 3 to 7 pm. One reader reports that, with the help of the airline staff, a card can be replaced more quickly at the international airport.

Onward Tickets

Theoretically, Chile requires a return or onward ticket for arriving travelers, and some airlines may ask for evidence of an onward ticket if the date of your return ticket is beyond the initial 90-day tourist-card limit. However, some travelers report having crossed numerous Chilean border posts, including international airports, dozens of times over many years without ever being asked for an onward ticket.

Travel Insurance

Insurance bought at relatively small cost can pay great benefits if you get sick. Look for a policy that will pay return travel costs and reimburse you for lost air tickets and other fixed expenses if you become ill. Such policies often cover losses from theft as well (a policy that protects baggage and valuables like cameras and camcorders is a good idea). The international travel policies handled by STA or other budget travel organizations are usually a good value. Keep insurance records separate from your other possessions in case you have to make a claim.

Driver's Licenses & Permits

Foreigners residing in Chile may obtain a Chilean driver's license through the municipality in which they live. Visiting motorists need an International Driving Permit to complement their national or state licenses. Carabineros at highway checkpoints or on the road are generally firm but courteous and fair, with a much higher reputation for personal integrity than most Latin American police. *Never* attempt to bribe them.

Permits for temporarily imported tourist vehicles may now be extended beyond the initial 90-day period, but not all customs officials are aware of this; it may be easier to cross the border into Argentina and return with new paperwork. For information on purchasing and registering a car in Chile, see the Getting Around chapter.

Hostel Card

Chile has a small but growing network of official hostels and affiliates throughout the country. Contact the Asociación Chilena de Albergues Turísticos Juveniles (☎/fax 02-233-3220, achatj@entelchile.net), the local affiliate of Hostelling International, at Hernando de Aguirre 201, Oficina 602, in Providencia in Santiago (Metro: Tobalaba). Hostel cards can also be purchased at the Santiago hostel, Cienfuegos 151.

Student & Youth Cards

The Instituto Nacional de la Juventud (INJ; ☎ 02-688-1071), Agustinas 1564 in Santiago (Metro: Universidad Católica), issues an inexpensive *Tarjeta Joven* (youth card) that entitles the holder to discounts on many travel services, including some airline fares and admission to national parks. There's no clear policy as to whether the card is available only to Chilean nationals and permanent residents, or to young people from all over.

International Health Card

Chile does not require an International Health Certificate, but it may be a good idea if you are visiting other South American countries, especially in the tropics. It's advisable to have a medical checkup before your trip.

Photocopies

It's advisable to keep photocopies of the data pages of your passport and other documents, as well as airline tickets, travel insurance documents with emergency numbers, credit cards (and phone numbers to contact in case of loss), driver's license and vehicle documentation. Keep all of this, and a list of traveler's checks, separate from the originals, and leave a copy with someone reliable at home.

CUSTOMS

There are no restrictions on import and export of local and foreign currency. Duty-free allowances include 400 cigarettes or 50 cigars or 500 grams of tobacco, 2½ liters of alcoholic beverages and perfume for personal use. Though Chilean officials generally defer to foreign visitors, travelers crossing the border frequently and carrying electronic equipment like camcorders or laptop computers should keep a typed list of these items, with serial numbers, stamped by authorities.

Inspections are usually routine, although some travelers have had to put up with more thorough examinations because of drug smuggling from Peru and Bolivia. Travelers from Regions I (Tarapacá) and XII (Magallanes), both of which enjoy *zona franca* (duty-free) status, are subject to internal customs inspections when leaving those regions.

At international borders, officials of the SAG (Servicio Agrícola-Ganadero, Agriculture and Livestock Service) rigorously check luggage for fruit, the importation of which is strictly controlled to prevent the spread of diseases and pests that might threaten Chile's booming fruit exports. Since Chile has officially eliminated the Mediterranean fruit fly, SAG no longer maintains checkpoints along north-south routes in the Atacama desert.

Photographers should note that at major international border crossings such as Los Libertadores (the crossing from Mendoza, Argentina) and Pajaritos (the crossing from Bariloche, Argentina), Chilean customs officials put baggage through x-ray machines; do not leave your film in your luggage.

MONEY

A combination of cash, traveler's checks and credit or ATM cards is the best way to take money to Chile.

Embassies & Consulates

Chilean Embassies & Consulates Abroad

Chile has diplomatic representation in most parts of the world; those listed are the ones most likely to be useful to intending visitors. In some places there is a tourist information section with a separate address.

Argentina
(☎ 4394-6582)
San Martín 439, 9th floor
Buenos Aires

Australia
(☎ 6286-2430)
10 Culgoa Circuit
O'Malley, ACT 2606

Bolivia
(☎ 785-275)
Av H Siles 5843
Barrio Obrajes, La Paz

Brazil
(☎ 552-5349)
Praia do Flamengo 344,
7th floor, Flamengo
Rio de Janeiro
(☎ 284-2044)
Av Paulista 1009, 10th floor
São Paulo

Canada
(☎ 613-235-4402)
50 O'Connor St, Suite 1413
Ottawa, Ontario K1P 6L2

Consulates:
(☎ 416-924-0106)
2 Bloor St West, Suite 1801
Toronto, Ontario M4W 3E2

France
(☎ 470-54661)
64 Blvd de la Tour
Maubourg, Paris

Germany
(☎ 204-4990)
Leipzigerstrasse 63, Berlin

New Zealand
(☎ 471-6270)
7th floor, Willis Corroon
House, 1-3 Welleston St
Wellington

Paraguay
(☎ 600671)
Guido Spano 1687
Asunción

Peru
(☎ 221-2817)
Javier Prado Oeste 790
San Isidro, Lima

UK
(☎ 0171-580-1032)
12 Devonshire St
London W1N 2DS

Uruguay
(☎ 908-2223)
Andes 1365, 1st floor
Montevideo

USA
(☎ 202-785-3159)
1736 Massachusetts Ave NW
Washington, DC 20036

Consulates:
(☎ 212-980-3706)
866 United Nations Plaza,
Suite 302, New York,
NY 10017
(☎ 312-654-8780)
875 N Michigan Ave,
Suite 3352
Chicago, IL 60611
(☎ 415-982-7662)
870 Market St, Suite 1062
San Francisco, CA 94105
(☎ 310-785-0047)
1900 Avenue of the Stars,
Suite 2450
Los Angeles, CA 90067
(☎ 619-232-6361)
550 West C St, Suite 1820,
San Diego, CA 92101
(☎ 808-949-28501)
1860 Ala Moana Blvd,
No 1900, Honolulu,
HI 96815

Foreign Embassies & Consulates in Chile

There are many embassies and consulates of European and South American countries in Santiago. Some countries have representation in other Chilean cities as well.

Argentina
(☎ 02-222-8977)
Vicuña Mackenna 41,
Santiago
(☎ 55-256-279)
Díaz Gana 1274,
Antofagasta

(☎ 65-253-996)
Cauquenes 94,
2nd floor,
Puerto Montt
(☎ 61-261-912)
21 de Mayo 1878,
Punta Arenas

Australia
(☎ 02-228-5065)
Gertrudis Echeñique 420,
Las Condes, Santiago

Embassies & Consulates

Bolivia
(☎ 02-232-8180)
Av Santa María 2796,
Providencia, Santiago

Brazil
(☎ 02-639-8867)
MacIver 225, 15th floor,
Santiago

(☎ 61-241-093)
Arauco 769, Punta Arenas

Canada
(☎ 02-362-9660)
Nueva Tajamar 481,
12th floor, Las Condes,
Santiago

France
(☎ 02-225-1030)
Condell 65, Providencia,
Santiago

Germany
(☎ 02-633-5031)
Agustinas 785, 7th floor,
Santiago

(☎ 32-356-749)
Blanco 1215, 11th floor
Valparaíso

(☎ 64-232-151)
Edificio Paillahue at
Mackenna 967, Oficina 4
Osorno

Netherlands
(☎ 02-223-6825)
Las Violetas 2368,
Providencia, Santiago

New Zealand
(☎ 02-231-4204)
Isidora Goyenechea 3516,
Las Condes, Santiago

Paraguay
(☎ 02-639-4640)
Huérfanos 886,
Oficina 514, Santiago

Peru
(☎ 02-235-4600)
Padre Mariano 10,
Oficina 309, Providencia,
Santiago

(☎ 32-253-403)
Blanco 1215, Oficina 1404
Santiago

(☎ 58-231-020)
San Marcos 786, Arica

(☎ 57-411-466)
Zegers 570, Iquique

UK
(☎ 02-231-3737)
Av El Bosque Norte 0125,
3rd floor, Las Condes,
Santiago

(☎ 32-256-117)
Blanco 725, Oficina 26
Valparaíso

(☎ 61-244-727) Roca 924
Punta Arenas

Uruguay
(☎ 02-223-8398)
Pedro de Valdivia 711,
Providencia, Santiago

USA
(☎ 02-232-2600)
Av Costanera Andrés Bello
2800 Las Condes
Santiago

Your Own Embassy

All major European and South American countries, and many others as well, have embassies in Santiago. The neighboring countries of Argentina, Bolivia and Peru have consulates in a number of other cities.

As a tourist, it's important to realize what your own embassy – the embassy of the country of which you are a citizen – can and can't do. Generally speaking, it won't be much help in emergencies if the trouble you're in is remotely your own fault. Remember that you are bound by the laws of the country you are in. Your embassy will not be sympathetic if you end up in jail after committing a crime locally, even if such actions are legal in your own country.

In genuine emergencies you might get some assistance, but only if other channels have been exhausted. For example, if you need to get home urgently, a free ticket home is exceedingly unlikely – the embassy would expect you to have insurance. If you have all your money and documents stolen, it might assist in getting a new passport, but a loan for onward travel is out of the question.

Embassies used to keep letters for travelers or have a small reading room with home newspapers, but these days the mail-holding service has been stopped and even newspapers tend to be out of date.

Currency

The unit of currency is the peso (Ch$). Bank notes come in denominations of 500, 1000, 5000 and 10,000 pesos, with a new 2000 peso in circulation, but still relatively uncommon. Coin values are 1, 5, 10, 50 and 100 pesos, although one-peso coins are rare. Copper-colored coins have replaced light-weight aluminum coins, which are no longer legal tender. In small villages, it can be difficult to change bills larger than Ch$1000.

There is no restriction on export or import of local currency, but demand for pesos is minimal outside Chile, except in a few border towns and capitals.

Exchange Rates

Exchange rates are usually best in Santiago. Generally, only Santiago will have a ready market for European currencies, although the German mark may find purchasers in the southern lakes region. The following exchange rates, current as of early 2000, provide an idea of relative values:

country	unit	peso
Argentina	Arg$1	Ch$529
Australia	A$1	Ch$349
Bolivia	Bol1	Ch$89
Canada	Can$1	Ch$365
euro	€1	Ch$547
France	FFr1	Ch$83
Germany	DM1	Ch$279
Italy	It£1000	Ch$282
Japan	¥100	Ch$507
New Zealand	NZ$1	Ch$275
Peru	Sol1	Ch$151
Spain	Pta100	Ch$329
Switzerland	SwFr1	Ch$341
UK	UK£1	Ch$869
USA	US$1	Ch$529

For the most current information, see *Estrategia* (Chile's equivalent of the *Wall Street Journal* or *Financial Times)*, the financial pages of *El Mercurio*, or the online *Santiago Times*. Conversion rates are also available at www.xe.net/ucc/full.shtml.

Exchanging Money

Cash US dollars are by far the preferred foreign currency, although Argentine pesos can be readily exchanged in Santiago, at border crossings and in tourist centers such as Viña del Mar and the southern lakes region. The dollar has gradually been gaining strength against the Chilean peso, ranging from about Ch$450 to just upward of Ch$500 during the period of research, with some fluctuations. Cash dollars can be exchanged at banks, *casas de cambio* (exchange houses), hotels, and some travel agencies, and often in shops or on the street. Cash dollars earn a slightly better exchange rate and allow you to avoid commissions sometimes levied on traveler's checks; if you are confident of your ability to carry cash safely, it's a much better alternative.

If arriving from Argentina, it's better to change surplus Argentine currency directly into Chilean pesos: although the rate is a little lower than for dollars, the double exchange is more costly. Commissions are insignificant except on traveler's checks in some areas, most notably Easter Island.

Chile has no black market at present, though some businesses may give an especially favorable exchange rate for purchases in cash US dollars. There is nothing illegal about this.

Traveler's Checks Traveler's checks are unquestionably safer than cash, but in smaller towns and out-of-the-way locations, it can be difficult to find a bank that will change them, so carrying some cash dollars is a good idea. Some travelers have reported that lost Thomas Cook checks will not be replaced unless you notify the Santiago office of the loss within 24 hours; contact the local representative Turismo Tajamar (☎ 02-231-5112), Orrego Luco 023, Providencia, or phone the US office (☎ 609-987-7300) collect.

If you have traveler's checks in US dollars, it may be better advantageous to convert them to cash and then change the cash for pesos. This is more problematic than it once was, but some cambios along Agustinas in Santiago will still do it.

ATMs Automated teller machines affiliated with the Plus and Cirrus systems make it easy to get withdrawals or cash advances in most Chilean cities, but Banco del Estado's ATMs in smaller towns are incompatible with foreign ATM or credit cards.

Credit Cards Credit cards, particularly those that allow cash advances or traveler's check purchases (American Express, Visa and MasterCard), can be very useful. Revaluation of local currency can make your bill higher than anticipated (though devaluations can make it lower), so be aware of fluctuations in the rate. Credit cards are also useful if you must show that you have 'sufficient funds' before entering another South American country, or in an emergency.

International Transfers To receive money from abroad, have your home bank send a draft. Money transferred by cable should arrive in a few days; Chilean banks will give you your money in US dollars on request.

Security

Chile is not a high-crime country, but pick-pocketing is not unknown and travelers should avoid carrying large amounts of money in vulnerable spots such as the back pocket. Money belts and leg pouches are two secure means of carrying cash and other important monetary documents, such as traveler's checks.

Costs

While Chile's inflation has been slightly higher than that of neighboring Argentina, gradual devaluation has meant stabilization, at least in dollar terms. It's still relatively expensive compared with the Andean republics of Peru and Bolivia, but modest lodging, food and transport are still more economical than in Europe, North America or even Argentina.

Shoestring travelers should budget a minimum of US$25 per day for food and lodging, but if you purchase food at markets or eat at modest restaurants you may be able to get by more cheaply. It's possible to

lunch economically at some very fine restaurants that offer fixed menus.

Mid-range travelers can do very well on about US$50 per day, though some of the best family-style accommodations are better values than mid-range hotels. Visitors for whom budget concerns are not primary will find some outstanding values, both in accommodations and food.

Tipping & Bargaining

In restaurants, it's customary to tip about 10% of the bill except in exclusively family-run places, which rarely expect a tip. In general, waiters and waitresses are poorly paid, so if you can afford to eat out you can afford to tip, and even a small *propina* will be appreciated. Taxi drivers do not require tips, although you may round off the fare for convenience.

Usually only purchases from handicrafts markets will be subject to bargaining. Hotel prices are generally fixed and prominently displayed, but in the off-season or a slow summer, haggling may be possible; for long-term stays it is definitely possible. It's worth asking if the first price quoted is their best.

On occasion, long-distance bus or *taxi colectivo* (shared taxi) fares are open to negotiation, especially those between Santiago and Mendoza, Argentina.

Taxes & Refunds

At many mid-range and top-end hotels, payment in US dollars (either cash or credit) legally sidesteps the crippling 18% IVA *(impuesto de valor agregado*, or, value-added tax). If there is any question as to whether IVA is included in the rates, clarify before paying. A few places that get only a handful of foreign visitors can't be bothered with the extra paperwork, but most find it advantageous to be able to offer the discount (for which it's imperative to show your tourist card).

POST & COMMUNICATIONS

Correos de Chile's postal services are reasonably dependable but sometimes rather slow. Over the past decade or so, telephone infrastructure has gone from Paleolithic to postmodern and is probably the best on the continent. Telegraph, telex and fax services are of equally high quality. Every major city and most tourist-oriented areas have Internet and email access.

Postal Rates

Within Chile, an ordinary letter costs about US$0.25. An airmail letter costs about US$0.85 to North America and US$1 to other overseas destinations; aerograms cost US$0.75 to anywhere. Postcards are slightly cheaper.

Addresses

In Chilean cities and towns, names of streets, plazas and other features are often very long and elaborate, such as Calle Cardenal José Maria Caro or Avenida Libertador General Bernardo O'Higgins. Long names are often shortened in writing and speech, and on maps. So the former might appear on a map as JM Caro, or just Caro, while the latter might appear as Avenida Gral O'Higgins, Avenida B O'Higgins, just O'Higgins or even by a colloquial alternative (Alameda). The word *calle* (street) is usually omitted on maps.

Some addresses include the expression *local* (locale) followed by a number, for example Cochrane 56, Local 5. 'Local' means it's one of several offices at the same street address. Some street numbers begin with a zero, eg, Bosque Norte 084. This confusing practice usually happens when an older street is extended in the opposite direction, beyond the original number 1. If, for example, street numbers are increasing from north to south, El Bosque Norte 084 will be north of El Bosque 84, which will be north of El Bosque 184.

The abbreviation 's/n' following a street address stands for *sin número* (without number) and indicates that the address has no specific street number.

Sending Mail

Chilean post offices are open 9 am to 6 pm weekdays and 9 am to noon Saturdays. Send important overseas mail *certificado* (registered) to ensure its arrival. Mail that appears to contain cash is unlikely to arrive at its final destination.

Sending parcels is straightforward, although a customs official may have to inspect your package before a postal clerk will accept it. Vendors in or near the post office will wrap parcels upon request. International courier services are readily available in Santiago, less so outside the capital.

Receiving Mail

You can receive mail via *lista de correos* or poste restante (equivalent to general delivery) at any Chilean post office. Santiago's American Express office offers client mail services, while some consulates will also hold correspondence for their citizens. To collect your mail from a post office (or from American Express or an embassy), you need your passport as proof of identity. Instruct your correspondents to address letters clearly and to indicate a date until which the post office should hold them; otherwise, they may be returned or destroyed. There is usually a small charge, about US$0.25 per item.

Chilean post offices literally maintain separate lists of correspondence for men and women, so check both if your correspondent has not addressed the letter 'Señor,' 'Señora' or 'Señorita.' If expected correspondence does not arrive, ask the clerk to check under every possible combination of your initials, even 'M' (for Mr, Ms, etc). There may be particular confusion if correspondents use your middle name, since Chileans use both paternal and maternal surnames for identification, with the former listed first. Thus a letter to 'Augusto Pinochet Ugarte' will be found under the listing for 'P' rather than 'U,' while a letter to 'Ronald Wilson Reagan' may be found under 'W' even though 'Reagan' is the proper surname.

Telephone

Chile's country code is ☎ 56. All telephone numbers in Santiago and the Metropolitan Region have seven digits; all other telephone numbers have six digits except for certain toll-free and emergency numbers, and cellular telephones throughout the country, which have seven digits prefixed by

09. The toll-free number for the carabineros is ☎ 133. You'll reach directory assistance at ☎ 103.

Despite occasional glitches due to rapid technological change, Chilean telephone services are among the best and cheapest in the world. The former state telephone monopoly Entel, (CTC) Telefónica and several other carriers offer domestic and international long-distance services throughout most of the country. In Regions X and XI, the unrelated Telefónica del Sur provides most long-distance service.

Local calls from public phones cost Ch$100 (about US$0.20) for five minutes, but outside peak hours (8 am to 8 pm weekdays, 8 am to 2 pm Saturdays) they cost only Ch$50. A liquid-crystal readout indicates the remaining credit on your call; when it reaches zero and you hear a beeping sound, insert another coin unless you plan to finish soon. Public phones do not make change, but if there is at least Ch$50 credit remaining you may make another call by pressing a button rather than inserting another coin.

Some CTC phones accept only coins, some take only magnetic phone cards; some take both. *Cobro revertido* (reverse-charge or collect) calls overseas are simple, as are credit card calls. Only a handful of phones have direct fiber-optic connections to operators in North America and Europe.

CTC magnetic phone cards are available in values of Ch$2000 to Ch$5000, valid at most but not all CTC phones. Entel's 'Entel Ticket' has a similar appearance but has an individual number instead of a magnetic strip. Dial ☎ 800-800-123, then 2, then the ticket number; at this point, a computer voice states the remaining peso amount and, after you dial the number, tells you the time that amount will permit you to speak.

Because of the so-called multicarrier system, whereby a number of companies compete for long-distance services, charges for both foreign and domestic calls can be astonishingly cheap, but the system is complicated. Most Entel and CTC offices close by 10 pm. To make a collect call, dial the number of the carrier, then 182 for an operator.

Carrier Codes

Both Entel and CTC (Telefónica) have access codes to overseas operators, though it is often cheaper to pay for the calls in Chile (the opposite is true in neighboring Argentina and most other Latin American countries). The following are local carrier codes, but rates change on a weekly or even daily basis – for the latest, consult the English-language *News Review* or any Santiago daily. If it's a CTC or Entel public phone, you don't need to dial the carrier code.

carrier	code
BellSouth	(181)
Chilesat	(171)
CTC (Telefónica)	(188)
Entel	(123)
Firstcom Chile	(155)
Manquehue	(122)
Telefónica del Sur	(121)
Transam	(113)
VTR	(120)

Following are international codes for Entel; for countries not on this list, phone ☎ 800-123-123.

country	Entel code
Australia	☎ 800-360-150
Belgium	☎ 800-360-121
Canada	☎ 800-360-280
France	☎ 800-360-110
Germany	☎ 123-003-491
Israel	☎ 123-003-9721
Italy	☎ 800-360-099
Netherlands	☎ 123-003-311
Spain	☎ 800-360-055
UK (BT)	☎ 800-360-066
USA (AT&T)	☎ 800-800-311
USA (MCI)	☎ 800-360-180
USA (Sprint)	☎ 800-360-777

Following are international codes for CTC. For other countries, you can contact CTC at ☎ 800-200-300.

country	CTC code
Australia	☎ 800-800-287
Canada	☎ 800-800-226
France	☎ 800-800-372
Germany	☎ 800-800-049
Italy	☎ 800-800-039
Spain	☎ 800-207-334
UK (BT)	☎ 800-800-044
USA (AT&T)	☎ 800-800-288
USA (MCI)	☎ 800-207-300
USA (Sprint)	☎ 800-800-777

A great way to make calls is by using Lonely Planet's eKno Communication Card, which is aimed at independent travelers and provides budget international calls, a range of messaging services, free email and travel information – for local calls, use a local card. You can join at www.eKno.lonelyplanet.com or by phone from Chile by dialing ☎ 800-360-193. To use eKno from Chile once you have joined, dial the same number.

When calling or answering the telephone, the proper salutation is *aló* or *hola* (hello). Exchange pleasantries before getting to the point of your conversation.

Cellular Communications Cell phones have become very common, thanks to companies like BellSouth, which rent them for about US$50 per month, plus additional charges beyond a certain amount of usage. Services often include voice mail, call waiting and three-way calling. In early 1999, all cellular service switched to a 'caller-pays' format, which eats up magnetic phone cards very quickly.

Cell phones throughout the country have seven digits, even in areas where conventional telephones have six; when calling a cell phone, dial the prefix ☎ 09 first.

Fax & Telegraph
Entel, CTC, Telex-Chile and VTR offer telex, telegraph and fax services at their long-distance telephone offices; there are also many small private offices with fax service. Like other telecommunications services in Chile, prices are very reasonable.

Email & Internet Access
It's becoming more routine for Chilean businesses and individuals to have email and Internet access. The increasing number of Internet cafés and other public outlets is the most convenient; otherwise you need your own phone line, usually possible only at top-end hotels that place surcharges on local calls (which are, in any event, on a metered rather than flat-fee basis). Rates at Internet cafés are around US$5 to US$6 per hour; some charge by the minute, others in 15-minute or half-hour increments.

If you do intend to rely on cybercafes, you'll need to carry three pieces of information with you to enable you to access your Internet mail account: your incoming (POP or IMAP) mail server name, your account name and your password. Your ISP or network supervisor will be able to give you these. Armed with this information, you should be able to access your Internet mail account from any net-connected machine in the world, provided it runs some kind of email software (remember that Netscape and Internet Explorer both have mail modules). It pays to become familiar with the process for doing this before you leave home. A final option to collect mail through cybercafes is to open a free Web-based email account such as HotMail (www.hotmail.com) or Yahoo! Mail (mail.yahoo.com). You can then access your mail from anywhere in the world from any net-connected machine running a standard Web browser.

Some Internet service providers, such as AOL and Compuserve, have local dial-in numbers in Chile. Otherwise, for suggestions, contact the following local providers: CTC (☎ 800-200-300), Entel (info@entelchile.net) or Chilesat (nfo@chilepac.net).

For information on traveling with a portable computer, see www.teleadapt.com or www.warrior.com.

BOOKS
See the Arts section of the Facts about Chile chapter for information on Chilean literature and reading recommendations.

Lonely Planet

Additional guidebooks can supplement or complement this one, especially if you are visiting countries other than Chile. As well as this book, Lonely Planet's guidebook series includes the following titles: *Santiago*; *Argentina, Uruguay & Paraguay*; *Buenos Aires*; *Ecuador & the Galápagos Islands*; *Bolivia*; *Peru*; and *Brazil*. Budget travelers covering a large part of the continent should look for *South America on a shoestring*.

If you're interested in trekking, Lonely Planet's *Trekking in the Patagonian Andes* has detailed descriptions and maps of extensive walks in Chile, plus others across the border in Argentina. Lonely Planet's *Latin American Spanish phrasebook* is helpful for beginners.

Guidebooks

Chile and Argentina: Backpacking and Hiking (1998) by Tim Burford and John Dixon, has information about hiking and camping in the Southern Cone countries. For Chile's national parks, do not miss William Leitch's beautifully written but also selective *South America's National Parks* (1990), which is superb on environment and natural history but much weaker on practical aspects of South American travel. Rae Natalie Prosser de Goodall's bilingual guidebook *Tierra del Fuego* (1978), published in Argentina and still available if hard to find, contains valuable thematic material despite the dated practical information.

One of the most useful sources of information is the Turistel guide series, published by the CTC (Telefónica), which is annually updated and reasonably priced. However, the single-volume English translation *Chile: A Remote Corner of the Earth* is badly out of date. The Spanish version has separate volumes on the north, center and south of the country, plus an additional volume on camping and campgrounds that has more detailed maps of some important areas.

Oriented toward motorists, Turistel guides provide excellent highway and city maps (the latter beautifully drawn, despite frequent minor errors and the absence of scales) and

thorough background information, but they rarely cover budget accommodations. Their biggest drawback, though, is the flimsy paper binding that makes them unusable after one season – handle with care.

Travel Literature

Chile has inspired some fine travel writing. Although Bruce Chatwin's classic *In Patagonia* (1977) deals more with Argentina than with Chile, it's one of the most informed syntheses of life and landscape about any part of South America. His collection *What Am I Doing Here?* (1989) contains a beautiful essay on the village of Cucao, on the Isla Grande de Chiloé.

Sara Wheeler's *Travels in a Thin Country* (1996) is humorous and sometimes insightful, but suffers from an irritating 'product placement' approach to a certain international car rental agency. Luis Sepúlveda's *Full Circle: A South American Journey* (1996), part of the Lonely Planet Journeys series, is a hybrid work combining an exile's political insights on his own country with travel observations that border on fiction (the author is a novelist as well as a journalist).

Ariel Dorfman's *Heading South, Looking North* (1998) is the personal and political memoir of a bicultural activist, also one of contemporary Chile's major literary figures, that fits partly into the travel literature category. John Hickman's *News from the End of the Earth: A Portrait of Chile* (1998) uses the author's five years (1982-87) as British ambassador to Santiago as a takeoff point for an interpretation of the country.

Don't overlook works of greater antiquity. Charles Darwin's *Voyage of the Beagle*, available in many editions, is as fresh as yesterday. His accounts of Chiloé and other parts of the Chilean landscape are truly memorable, and a lightweight paperback copy is a perfect companion for any trip to Chile. Besides insights on the early Chilean polity, María Graham's *Journal of a Residence in Chile* (1824) conveys the beauty of the landscape in both words and illustrations.

There is a voluminous amount of literature on Rapa Nui, spanning the 250 years since

Online Services

The World Wide Web is a rich resource. You can hunt down bargain air fares, book hotels, check on weather or chat with others about the best places to visit. The rapid growth of the Web has meant a bewildering variety of sites of varying quality, some short-lived, others rarely updated.

There's no better place to start your Web explorations than the Lonely Planet Web site (www.lonelyplanet.com). Here you'll find succinct travel summaries, postcards from other travelers and the Thorn Tree bulletin board, where you can ask questions before you go or dispense advice when you get back. You can also find travel news and updates to many of our most popular guidebooks, and the subWWWay section links you to the most useful travel resources elsewhere on the Web. Lonely Planet's 'Destination Chile' page at www.lonelyplanet.com/dest/sam/chile.htm includes most recent travelers' tips.

Altué Active Travel – Santiago adventure travel agency emphasizing sea kayaking in and around Dalcahue, Chiloé
www.chile-travel.com/altue.htm
email: altue@netline.cl
www.altueseakayak.co.cl
email: altue@entelchile.net

Andescape – Puerto Natales agency with lodges and campgrounds in Torres del Paine
www.chileaustral.com/andescape
email: andescape@chileaustral.com

Anytime Adventures – Osorno-based agency offering bus tours
www.pearshaped.com/anytime

Austral Adventures – agency offering yacht charters from Puerto Montt southwards
www.austral-adventures.com

Carnegie Observatories Home Page – information on astronomical observatory at Las Campanas
www.ociw.edu/

Cascada Expediciones – adventure travel agency specializes in rafting and horseback trips
www.cascada-expediciones.com
email: cascada@ibm.net

Centro de Ski Portillo – South America's premier ski resort, northeast of Santiago
www.skiportillo.com
email: info@skiportillo.com

Cerro Tololo International Observatory – information on this observatory, east of La Serena
ctios2.ctio.noao.edu/ctio.html

Chip News – English-language site including the *Santiago Times* summary of current events and more
www.chip.cl

Cruceros Australis – site detailing cruises of the Fuegian fjords, as well as Navimag's trip

from Puerto Montt to Puerto Natales
www.australis.com

Easter Island Home Page – information on Chile's distant Pacific possession
www.netaxs.com/~trance/rapanui.html

El Mercurio – Santiago's most prestigious daily newspaper; in Spanish
www.elmercurio.cl

Estrategia – Chile's financial daily; in Spanish
www.estrategia.cl

Explora – site for hotel chain whose Torres del Paine construction is a marvel, but is also responsible for an ill-advised and environmentally disastrous facility in San Pedro de Atacama
www.interknowledge.com/Chile/explora
email: explora@entelchile.net

FutaFriends – US-based non-profit river conservation organization
www.futafriends.org

Hotel Antumalal – upscale lakeside hotel near Pucón
www.antumalal.com

Hostería Las Torres/Fantástico Sur – backcountry hostels, camping, hotel and tours at estancia near Torres del Paine
www.chileaustral.com/lastorres

Intijalsu – professional astronomers offering excursions in the Norte Chico.
www.intijalsu.cv.cl/

La Brújula – index of Chilean websites
www.brujula.cl

LanChile – Chile's national airline
www.lanchile.com/

Observatorio Comunal Cerro Mamalluca – site for small-scale non-research observatory near Vicuña; open to visitors for night-sky viewing in the Norte Chico
www.angelfire.com/wy/obsermamalluca

Online Services

Onas Patagónica – tour operator offering maritime and riverine approach to Parque Nacional Torres del Paine
www.chileaustral.com/onas

Osterinsel – German-language site of Easter Island-based tour operator
www.osterinsel.de
email: mw@entdecke.de, pacific_images@entelchile.net

Patagonia Connection – agency that operates luxury catamaran from Puerto Chacabuco to Parque Nacional Laguna San Rafael
www.patagoniaconnex.cl
email: info@patagoniaconnec.cl

ProChile – official Chilean government promotional site, including travel- and tourism-oriented material; in English
www.chileinfo.com

Publiguías – Chilean yellow pages
www.amarillas.cl

Sernatur – official Chilean government tourist agency; in Spanish
www.segegob.cl/sernatur/inicio.html

Termas de Chillán – major ski resort and spa
www.termaschillan.com

Travel House – comprehensive site on the Puerto Montt-Puerto Varas area
www.travelhouse.cl

Travellers – Puerto Montt-based travel agency
email: gochile@entelchile.net

TravelSur – Puerto Varas-based tour operator
www.travelsur.com

Trancura Expediciones – Pucón-based adventure travel operator
www.trancura.com

Transportes Aéreos Isla Robinson Crusoe – air-taxi service to Juan Fernández Archipelago
www.tairc.cl/
email: tairc@cmet.net

Turismo Cordillera Darwin – Punta Arenas start-up promoting the isolated Cordillera Darwin on Tierra del Fuego
www.patagonian.com/c_darwin
email: c_darwin@patagonian.com

Turismo 21 de Mayo – Puerto Natales-based cruises to Serrano glacier
www.chileaustral.com/21demayo

Valle Nevado – major ski resort just outside Santiago
www.vallenevado.com
email: info@vallenevado.com

North American Tour Companies

Bio Bio Expeditions – California-based rafting company operating on the Biobío and Futaleufú Rivers
www.bbxrafting.com
Email: H2Omarc@aol.com

Earth River Expeditions – New York-based rafting company that also provides complementary activities such as horseback riding and hiking
www.earthriver.com
email: earthriv@ulster.com

Eldertreks – Toronto-based company catering to vigorous over-50s
www.eldertreks.com
email: eldertreks@eldertreks.com

Expediciones Chile – US-Chilean operator specializing in kayaking
www.kayakchile.com
email: office@kayakchile.com

Far Horizons Archaeological & Cultural Trips – US-based tour operator that specializes in Easter Island with trips led by leading scholars; trips to the Norte Grande also.
www.farhorizon.com

Mountain Travel Sobek – well-established adventure travel agency
www.mtsobek.com/

Nantahala Outdoor Center – US-based kayaking specialist
www.nocweb.com/
email: adtrav@nocweb.com

National Outdoor Leadership School – outdoors-skills training institution with Chilean base at Coihaique
www.nols.edu
email: admissions@nols.edu

Nature Expeditions International
email: NaturExp@aol.com

Off the Beaten Path – fly-fishing specialists
www.offbeatenpath.com

Usenet Discussion Groups

Soc.culture.chile – wide-ranging but often polemical discussion group

Rec.travel.latin-america – regional travel discussion group with frequent though not numerous items on Chile

Europeans first landed on the island. See the Easter Island chapter for more details.

History

For an account of early European exploration of Chile and other parts of South America, see JH Parry's *Discovery of South America* (1979). Another good source is Edward J Goodman's *Explorers of South America* (1992).

Although it does not focus specifically on Chile, James Lockhart and Stuart Schwartz's *Early Latin America* (1983) makes an original, persuasive argument that the structures of native societies such as the Mapuche were more important than Spanish domination in the cultural transitions of the colonial period. Uruguayan journalist-historian Eduardo Galeano presents a bitter indictment of European invasion and its consequences in *The Open Veins of Latin America, Five Centuries of the Pillage of a Continent* (1973). Do not miss Alfred Crosby's fascinating account of southern South America's ecological transformations in comparison with other mid-latitude lands that were settled by Europeans in *Ecological Imperialism: The Biological Expansion of Europe, 900-1900* (1986).

On the South American wars of independence, the standard work is John Lynch's *Spanish-American Revolutions 1808-1826* (1973). Richard W Slatta's comparison of Argentine gauchos and Chilean huasos to stockmen of other countries in the beautifully illustrated *Cowboys of the Americas* (1990) is well worth a look.

Several readable texts integrate Latin American history with geography. Ones to try are Arthur Morris' *South America* (1979), the detailed chapter on Chile in Harold Blakemore and Clifford Smith's collection *Latin America* (1983) and *The Cambridge Encyclopedia of Latin America* (1985), which is broader in conception.

Allende & the Unidad Popular

Publishing on the Allende years is a minor industry in its own right and as in the 1970s, it's still hard to find a middle ground. Try *Allende's Chile* (1977) by Edward Boorstein,

a US economist who worked for the UP government. A more recent and wide-ranging attempt to explain the UP's failure is Edy Kaufman's *Crisis in Allende's Chile: New Perspectives* (1988).

For a firsthand account of the countryside during these years, read Kyle Steenland's *Agrarian Reform under Allende: Peasant Revolt in the South* (1977), based on research in Cautín province from 1972 to '73.

For a Marxist analysis of US involvement in the campaign against Allende, try *The United States and Chile: Imperialism and the Overthrow of the Allende Government* (1975) by James Petras and Morris Morley. For a more thorough historical perspective, see Robert J Alexander's *Tragedy of Chile* (1978). Nathaniel Davis, former US ambassador to Chile, relates his side of the story in *The Last Two Years of Salvador Allende* (1985).

For a more conservative view, tempered by its critical assessment of extremism among Chile's right-wing elements, see *A Small Earthquake in Chile* (1972), by Alistair Horne. Sergio Bitar, a onetime member of Allende's cabinet and now a senator, provides systematic analysis of the UP's achievements and failures in *Chile, Experiment in Democracy* (1986).

Joan Jara, the English wife of murdered folk singer Victor Jara, has written a personal account of life during the 1960s and '70s in *Victor: An Unfinished Song* (1983). The death of a politically involved US citizen in the 1973 coup was the subject of Thomas Hauser's book *The Execution of Charles Horman: An American Sacrifice* (1978), which implicated US officials and was the basis of the film *Missing*.

The assassination of Orlando Letelier, a career diplomat and foreign minister under Allende, has been the subject of several books, including John Dinges and Saul Landau's *Assassination on Embassy Row* (1980) and Taylor Branch and Eugene Popper's *Labyrinth* (1983).

The Military Dictatorship

Chile: The Pinochet Decade, by Phil O'Brien and Jackie Roddick (1983), covers the junta's early years, concentrating on the economic measures of the Chicago Boys. Pinochet himself has offered the autobiographical *Camino Recorrido: Memorias de Un Soldado* in four volumes (Instituto Geográfico Militar, Santiago, 1990, 1991; Geniart, Santiago, 1993, 1994). As a counterpoint, consult Genaro Arriagada's *Pinochet: The Politics of Power* (1988), a critical account by a Christian Democrat intellectual who details the evolution of the military regime from a collegial junta to a personalistic but institutionalized dictatorship.

A riveting account of an exile's secret return is Colombian writer Gabriel García Márquez's *Clandestine in Chile* (1987), which tells the story of filmmaker Miguel Littín's secret working visit to Chile in 1985. Argentine writer Jacobo Timerman, famous for criticism of his country's military dictatorship of the late 1970s, has written *Chile: Death in the South* (1987).

Politics, the Military & Geopolitics

An outstanding, nonpolemical explanation of the complexities of 20th-century Chilean politics is *The Politics of Chile: A Sociogeographical Assessment* (1979), by César Caviedes (1979). For an account of the Pinochet years and their aftermath that eschews partisan rhetoric and focuses on the complexities of political events over two decades, see *A Nation of Enemies* (1991), by Pamela Constable and Arturo Valenzuela.

One classic overview of the military in Latin America is John J Johnson's *Military and Society in Latin America* (1964). For analysis of geopolitics in Chile, see *Geopolitics of the Southern Cone and Antarctica* (1985), edited by Philip Kelly and Jack Child. A more general account, dealing with Argentina, Brazil and Paraguay as well, is *The Southern Cone: Realities of the Authoritarian State* (1984), by César Caviedes.

General

One widely available book on Chile from the Spanish conquest to the late 1970s is Brian Loveman's rather glib *Chile: The Legacy of Hispanic Capitalism* (1979), which, despite its polemical and condescending tone, presents a common point of view. A better choice, though more restricted in its coverage, is the collection *Chile since Independence* (1993), edited by Leslie Bethell.

With a narrower focus, based on painstaking archival research, Arnold Bauer's *Chilean Rural Society from the Spanish Conquest to 1930* (1975) traces the evolution of the Chilean countryside. Though dated in many ways, George McCutcheon McBride's *Chile: Land and Society* (1936) is a vivid portrait of life on the *latifundio* (large landholding, such as a hacienda), which changed little until the late 1960s.

Chile's early 20th-century development, based on the nitrate boom, is the subject of many books. Two of the best written in English are Thomas F O'Brien's *Nitrate Industry and Chile's Crucial Transition* (1982) and Michael Monteón's *Chile in the Nitrate Era* (1982). German writer Theodor Plivier's *Revolt on the Pampas* (1937) is a hard-to-find fictional account of uprisings in the nitrate enterprises.

FILM

See the Arts section of the Facts about Chile chapter for information on Chilean film.

NEWSPAPERS & MAGAZINES

Still recovering from the repression of the Pinochet years, the quality of Chilean journalism is rapidly improving, but conditions are far from perfect. State security laws favor the powerful, even when allegations may be true. In 1999, when journalist Alejandra Matús published *El Negro Libro de la Justicia Chilena* (The Black Book of Chilean Justice), exposing corruption in the supreme court, the chief justice ordered it confiscated and briefly jailed the publishers, forcing Matús to flee to Miami.

El Mercurio de Valparaíso, founded in 1827, is Chile's most venerable daily, but Santiago is the country's media center. *El Mercurio*, the capital's oldest and most prestigious daily, follows a conservative editorial policy but has a diverse letters section, excellent cultural coverage and an outstanding Sunday travel magazine; its *Wikén* supplement, which comes out Fridays, is a guide to entertainment in the capital. *Mercurio*'s parent corporation also owns the sleazy tabloids *La Segunda* and *Ultimas Noticias*, which sensationalize crime and radical political dissent (which they seem to consider synonymous).

La Tercera, another tabloid, has improved coverage and broadened its editorial stance but is still relatively conservative. *La Nación* is the official government daily, but the editorial dominance of its conservative competition makes it sound like an opposition paper. *Estrategia* is the daily voice of Chile's financial community and the best source on trends in the exchange rate.

Because of difficulties in attracting advertising, the radical press has not fared well. *El Siglo*, voice of the Communist Party, has become a monthly rather than a weekly because of financial difficulties; the other major leftist paper is the uncompromising fortnightly *Punto Final*.

Since its beginning in late 1991, Santiago's English-language *News Review* has improved substantially, but it's had to cut back from twice weekly to weekly only. It's still hard to find outside the capital, but try upscale hotels in the regions. The *News Review*'s German-language counterpart is *El Cóndor*, now in its 59th year.

The weekday English-language digest of the Chilean press, *Santiago Times* (☎ 02-777-5376, fax 735-2267, www.chipnews.cl), Casilla 53331, Correo Central, Santiago, is available by fax or email subscription.

The following Chilean news sources have World Wide Web addresses:

El Mercurio
  www.elmercurio.cl/

Estrategia
  www.estrategia.cl

La Tercera
  www.tercera.cl

Santiago Times
  www.chipnews.cl

Chilean news magazines include the general-interest weekly *Ercilla* and the monthly *Rocinante*, which specializes in the arts, culture and society.

RADIO & TV

In recent years, the end of government monopoly in the electronic media has opened the airwaves to a greater variety of programming. Broadcasting is less regulated than before and there are many stations on both AM and FM bands. Television stations include the government-owned Televisión Nacional (TVN) and the Universidad Católica's Channel 13, plus several private stations. International cable service is widely available and is common even in many hospedajes and residenciales.

Chile's most famous television personality is Mario Kreuzberger, popularly known as 'Don Francisco,' host of the weekly variety program *Sábado Gigante*, also seen on Spanish-language TV stations in the USA. The portly, multilingual Don Francisco, whose smiling visage endorses products on billboards throughout the country, also hosts the annual *Teletón* to raise money for disabled children. He conspicuously absents himself when military donors appear on the *Teletón*.

PHOTOGRAPHY & VIDEO

The latest in consumer electronics is available in Chile at lower prices than in neighboring countries, especially at the duty-free zones at Iquique (Region I, Norte Grande) and Punta Arenas (Region XII, Magallanes), which are good places to replace a lost or stolen camera. Color slide film can also be purchased cheaply at Iquique but is harder to find in Punta Arenas. Developing color prints is fairly inexpensive; slides are much more costly, especially with frames.

At high altitudes, especially in northern Chile, the bright tropical sun can wash out photographs; a polarizing filter is virtually essential. Photographers should be particularly circumspect about indigenous peoples, who often resent the intrusion. When in doubt, don't do it.

At major international border crossings such as Los Libertadores (from Mendoza, Argentina) and Pajaritos (from Bariloche, Argentina), Chilean customs officials put baggage through X-ray machines; do not leave your film in your luggage.

TIME

For most of the year, Chile is four hours behind GMT, but from mid-December to late March, because of daylight saving time (summer time), the difference is three hours. The exact date of the changeover varies from year to year. Because of Chile's great latitudinal range, this means that summer sunrise in the desert tropics of Arica, where the durations of day and night are roughly equal throughout the year, occurs after 8 am. Easter Island is two hours behind the mainland.

ELECTRICITY

Electric current operates on 220 volts, 50 cycles. In Santiago, numerous electrical supply stores on Calle San Pablo, west of the Puente pedestrian mall, sell transformers for appliances.

WEIGHTS & MEASURES

The metric system is official, but for weight the traditional *quintal* of 46 kilos is still common. For motorists, it's common to find tire pressure measured in pounds per square inch, and the Chilean military often uses feet as a standard measure, for instance for airport elevations.

LAUNDRY

In recent years, self-service *lavanderías* (laundromats) have become more common in Santiago and in other cities, but it's only slightly more expensive to leave your clothes and pick them up later. Most inexpensive hotels will have a place where you can wash your own clothes and hang them to dry. In some places, laundry service in batch will be reasonable, but agree on charges in advance.

TOILETS

Ordinary toilet paper does not readily disintegrate in Chilean sewers, so most bathrooms have a basket where you discard what you have used. Cheaper accommodations and public toilets rarely provide toilet paper, so carry your own wherever you go. For the squeamish, the better restaurants and cafes are good alternatives to public toilets, which are often dirty. There are separate facilities for men and women.

HEALTH

In general, Chile presents few serious health hazards, though there were localized outbreaks of cholera after the major 1991 epidemic in Peru. The Ministry of Health prohibited restaurants from serving raw vegetables that grow in the ground (such as lettuce, cabbage, celery, cauliflower, beets and carrots) and raw seafood in the form of *ceviche*, which is also suspect (ceviche must now be made with seafood that is cooked and then cooled). Santiago's drinking water is adequately treated and you can drink tap water in most other parts of the country without problems, but if you have any doubts, stay with bottled mineral waters.

US residents can call the Centers for Disease Control's International Traveler's Hotline (☎ 404-332-4559), where, by punching in the country's phone code (56 for Chile), you can get recorded information on vaccinations, food and water and current health problems. They also have a fax-back service and a website.

Travelers who wear glasses should bring an extra pair and a copy of their prescription. Losing your glasses can be a real nuisance, although in many places you can get new spectacles made up quickly, cheaply and competently.

If you require a particular medication, take an adequate supply and a copy of the prescription, with the generic rather than the brand name. Many US and European prescription items are available over the counter in Chile.

Travel Health Guides

Lonely Planet's handy, pocket-size *Healthy Travel: Central and South America* is packed with useful information including pretrip planning, emergency first aid, immunization and disease information and advice on what to do if you get sick on the road. Lonely Planet's *Travel with Children* by Lonely Planet cofounder Maureen Wheeler includes useful information on travel health for younger children.

For basic health information when traveling, a good source is Richard Dawood's *Travellers' Health: How to Stay Healthy Abroad* (1994). Another possibility is David Werner's *Where There is No Doctor* (1992).

Predeparture Preparations

Vaccinations Chile doesn't require vaccinations for entry from any country, but visitors to nearby tropical countries should definitely consider prophylaxis against typhoid, malaria and other diseases. Typhoid, polio, tetanus and hepatitis immunization are also recommended. All vaccinations should be recorded on an International Health Certificate, available from your physician or health department.

Typhoid protection lasts three years and is useful if traveling in rural areas. You may suffer side effects such as pain at the point of injection site, fever, headache and general discomfort.

A complete series of oral polio vaccines is essential if you haven't ever had them before. Tetanus and diphtheria boosters are necessary every 10 years and are highly recommended.

Injections of gamma globulin, not a vaccine but a ready-made antibody, provide some protection against infectious hepatitis (hepatitis A).

Malaria does not exist in Chile, but if you are coming from a malarial zone, you should continue to take antimalarial drugs for six weeks.

Medical Kit All standard medications are available in well-stocked pharmacies. Many common prescription drugs can be purchased legally over the counter in Chile. However, it's wise to carry a small medical kit with you. This should include

- Aspirin or Panadol – for pain or fever
- Antihistamine (such as Benadryl) – useful as a decongestant for colds, allergies, to ease the itch from insect bites or stings or to help prevent motion sickness
- Antibiotics – useful if you're traveling well off the beaten track, but they must be prescribed and you should carry the prescription with you

- Kaolin preparation (Pepto-Bismol), Imodium or Lomotil – for stomach upsets
- Rehydration mixture – for treatment of severe diarrhea; this is particularly important if traveling with children
- Antiseptic, mercurochrome and antibiotic powder or similar 'dry' spray – for cuts and grazes
- Calamine lotion – to ease irritation from bites or stings
- Bandages and Band-Aids – for minor injuries
- Scissors, tweezers and a thermometer – mercury thermometers are prohibited by airlines
- Insect repellent, sunblock, lip balm and water-purification tablets

Food & Water

Most North Americans, Europeans and Australians will find that Chilean food is generally easy on the stomach, but the great variety of shellfish may take some adaptation. Since the cholera scare has subsided, salad greens and other fresh, unpeeled vegetables are safe to eat, but eating raw shellfish is not advisable. The water supply of Santiago and most other cities is safe, with little danger of dysentery or similar ailments, but take precautions in rural areas, where latrines may be close to wells and untreated water may be taken from rivers or irrigation ditches. Water in the Atacama desert and its cities has a strong mineral content. Easter Island's water has a similar reputation, but is both safe and tasty.

Geographical & Climatic Considerations

Altitude Sickness From the passes between Chile and the Argentine city of Mendoza northward to the Bolivian border, altitude sickness (*apunamiento* or *soroche*) represents a potential health hazard. Lack of oxygen at high altitudes (over 2500m) affects most people to some extent. The effect may be mild or severe and occurs because less oxygen reaches the muscles and the brain at high altitude, requiring the heart and lungs to compensate by working harder. Symptoms of Acute Mountain Sickness (AMS) usually develop during the first 24 hours at altitude but may be delayed up to three weeks. Mild symptoms include headache, lethargy, dizziness, difficulty sleeping and loss of appetite. AMS may become more severe without warning and can be fatal. Severe symptoms include breathlessness, a dry, irritative cough (which may progress to the production of pink, frothy sputum), severe headache, lack of coordination and balance, confusion, irrational behavior, vomiting, drowsiness and unconsciousness. There is no hard-and-fast rule as to what is too high: AMS has been fatal at 3000m, although 3500m to 4500m is the usual range.

Treat mild symptoms by resting at the same altitude until recovery, usually a day or two. Paracetamol or aspirin can be taken for headaches. If symptoms persist or become worse, however, *immediate descent is necessary*; even 500m can help. Drug treatments should never be used to avoid descent or to enable further ascent.

The drugs acetazolamide (Diamox) and dexamethasone are recommended by some doctors for the prevention of AMS, however their use is controversial. They can reduce the symptoms, but they may also mask warning signs; severe and fatal AMS has occurred in people taking these drugs. In general, we do not recommend them for travelers.

To prevent acute mountain sickness:

- Ascend slowly – take frequent rest days, spending two to three nights at each rise of 1000m. If you reach a high altitude by trekking, acclimatization takes place gradually and you are less likely to be affected than if you fly directly to high altitude.

- It is always wise to sleep at a lower altitude than the greatest height reached during the day, if possible. Also, once above 3000m, care should be taken not to increase the sleeping altitude by more than 300m per day.

- Drink extra fluids. The mountain air is dry and cold and moisture is lost as you breathe. Evaporation of sweat may occur unnoticed and result in dehydration.

- Eat light, high-carbohydrate meals for more energy.

- Avoid alcohol, as it may increase the risk of dehydration.

- Avoid sedatives.

Heat Exhaustion & Sunburn Although Chile is mostly a temperate country, its northern regions lie within the tropic of Capricorn and the sun's nearly direct rays can be devastating, especially at high altitude. In the desert, summer temperatures are usually not oppressive, but dehydration can still be a serious problem. Drink plenty of liquids and keep your body well covered with light cotton clothing. Wear a hat that shades your head and neck. Damage to the ozone layer has increased the level of ultraviolet radiation in southern South America, so protection from the sun is especially important – use an effective sunscreen on exposed parts of your body and good-quality sunglasses. Sweating can also lead to a loss of salt, so adding some salt to your food can be a good idea. Salt tablets should be taken only to treat heat exhaustion caused by salt deficiency.

Hypothermia Hypothermia occurs when the body loses heat faster than it can produce it and the core temperature of your body falls. At high altitudes and in Patagonia, changeable weather can leave you vulnerable to exposure: after dark, temperatures can drop from balmy to below freezing, while a sudden soaking and high winds can lower your body temperature so rapidly that you may not survive. Disorientation, dizziness, slurred speech, stumbling, shivering, numb skin and physical exhaustion are all symptoms of hypothermia and are indications that you should seek warmth, shelter and food. Avoid traveling alone; partners are less likely to fall victim to hypothermia.

Always be prepared for cold, wet or windy conditions, even if you're just out walking or hitchhiking. Wear woolen clothing or synthetics that retain warmth when wet. Carry high-energy, easily digestible snacks such as chocolate or dried fruit, both of which are readily available in Chile. If bad weather is approaching, seek shelter before you are caught outside.

Diarrhea & Dysentery
Stomach problems don't necessarily mean you've caught something: they can arise

from dietary changes. Although Chilean public health standards are reasonably high, introduce yourself gradually to exotic or highly spiced foods (the latter not very common in Chile).

Avoid rushing to the pharmacy and gulping antibiotics at the first signs of trouble. The best thing to do is to rest, avoid eating solids and drink plenty of liquids (tea or herbal solutions, without sugar or milk). Many cafés in Chile serve excellent chamomile tea *(agua de manzanilla)* or other herbal teas; otherwise, try mineral water *(agua mineral)*. As you recover, keep to simple foods like yoghurt, lemon juice and boiled vegetables.

Ordinary 'traveler's diarrhea' rarely lasts more than a few days, so if it lasts more than a week, you must get treatment, move on to antibiotics or see a doctor. Lomotil or Imodium can relieve symptoms but do not actually cure the problem. For children, Imodium is preferable, but do not use such drugs if you have a high fever or are severely dehydrated.

After a severe bout of diarrhea or dysentery, you will probably be dehydrated, with painful cramps. Relieve these symptoms with fruit juices or tea, with a tiny bit of dissolved salt. Antibiotics can help treat severe diarrhea, especially if accompanied by nausea, vomiting, stomach cramps or mild fever.

Sexually Transmitted Diseases

Sexual contact with an infected partner spreads these diseases. While abstinence is the only certain preventative, condoms are also effective. Gonorrhea and syphilis are the most common of these diseases; sores, blisters or rashes around the genitals and discharge or pain when urinating are common symptoms. Symptoms may be less obvious – or even absent – in women. The symptoms of syphilis eventually disappear completely, but the disease can cause severe problems in later years. Both gonorrhea and syphilis can be treated effectively with antibiotics.

There are numerous other sexually transmitted diseases, and effective treatment is available for most. However, there is no cure for either herpes or the far more serious AIDS.

HIV/AIDS

AIDS (Acquired Immune Deficiency Syndrome) is most commonly transmitted by unsafe sexual activity – in Chile, this is the source of about 85% of all cases. Apart from abstinence, avoiding such unsafe activity and using condoms are the most effective preventatives. As of December 1998, Chile had 2736 registered cases of AIDS and another 3601 carriers of HIV (the Human Immunodeficiency Virus). About 90% are males, mostly between the ages of 20 and 49. The port city of Valparaíso has the highest rate of infection.

AIDS can also be spread by dirty needles (vaccinations, acupuncture and tattooing are potentially as dangerous as intravenous drug use if the equipment is not clean) or through infected blood transfusions. If you need an injection or a blood test (obligatory if you are a driver involved in an auto accident), purchase a new syringe from a pharmacy and ask the doctor or nurse to use it.

Fear of HIV infection should never preclude treatment for serious medical conditions. Although there may be a risk of infection, it is very small indeed. A good resource for help and information is the US Centers for Disease Control AIDS hot line (☎ 800-343-2347). In Santiago contact the Corporación Chilena de Prevención del Sida (☎ 02-222-5255), General Jofré 179, Santiago, or Información sobre Sida y Enfermedades de Transmisión Sexual (☎ 02-736-5542), Melipilla 3432, Conchalí, Santiago, which also provides medical and legal advice.

Women's Health

Gynecological Problems Poor diet, lowered resistance due to the use of antibiotics for stomach upsets and even contraceptive pills can lead to vaginal infections when traveling in hot climates. Yeast infections, characterized by rash, itch and discharge, can be treated with a vinegar or even lemon juice douche or with yogurt. Nystatin suppositories are the usual medical prescription. Trichomonas is a more serious infection with a discharge and a burning sensation when urinating. Male sexual partners must also be treated; if a vinegar-water douche is not effective, seek medical attention. Flagyl is the prescribed drug.

Pregnancy The first three months of pregnancy are riskiest time to travel, since most miscarriages occur during this trimester. The last three months should also be spent within reasonable distance of good medical care. Pregnant women should avoid all unnecessary medication, but vaccinations and malarial prophylactics should still be taken where possible. Take additional care to prevent illness and pay particular attention to diet and nutrition.

WOMEN TRAVELERS
Attitudes Toward Women
Chilean men are very *machista* (chauvinist) but rarely violent in public behavior toward women. The main nuisances are unwelcome attention and vulgar language, which usually emphasizes feminine physical attributes, generally in the presence of other males. If you respond aggressively ('Are you talking to me?' or, in Spanish, '¿Estás hablando a mí?'), you will probably put the aggressor to shame.

Single women checking in at low-budget hotels, both in Santiago and elsewhere, may find themselves objects of curiosity or suspicion, since prostitutes often frequent such places. If you otherwise like the place, ignore this and it should disappear. Outside the larger cities, women traveling alone are also objects of curiosity, since Chilean women generally do not travel alone. You should interpret questions as to whether you are running away from parents or husband as expressions of concern.

Some foreign women living in Chile have complained that they find it difficult to make female friends, since some Chilean women view them as competitors for Chilean men. This sometimes contributes to a sense of social isolation.

Women who appear to be Scandinavian may find that some Chilean men associate them with liberal attitudes toward sex and pornography.

Safety Precautions
For women traveling alone, Chile is probably safer than most other Latin American countries, although you should not be complacent. Unwelcome physical contact, particularly on crowded buses or trains, is not unusual, but if you're physically confident, a slap or a well-aimed elbow should discourage any further incident. If not, try a scream – another very effective measure.

Should you hitchhike, exercise caution and especially avoid getting into a vehicle with more than one man. Though hitchhiking is never totally safe, it is much safer in pairs. Lonely Planet does not recommend hitchhiking.

GAY & LESBIAN TRAVELERS
While Chile is a strongly Catholic country and homosexuality or even talk of it is considered taboo by many, there are enclaves of tolerance, most notably in Santiago. Since Chilean males are often more physically demonstrative than their counterparts in Europe or North America, behaviors like a vigorous embrace will seem innocuous even to some who dislike homosexuals. Likewise, lesbians walking hand-in-hand will attract little attention, since Chilean women frequently do so, but this would be very indiscreet behavior for males.

After unwarranted raids on gay bars in Santiago in early 1996, homosexual rights advocates managed to get the Policía de Investigaciones to destroy videotapes of the raids, which had resulted in arrests but no charges, and to pledge not to repeat the incidents. In June 1999, about 250 gay activists marched through downtown Santiago in a gay pride celebration.

Chile's main gay rights organization is Movimiento Unificado de Minorías Sexuales (MUMS, ☎ 02-634-7557), Viollier 87, Santiago, which also has its own website (www.minorias.in.cl) in both Spanish and imperfect but readable English.

DISABLED TRAVELERS
Travelers with disabilities may find Chile somewhat difficult; in particular those in wheelchairs will find the narrow sidewalks,

which are frequently in a state of disrepair, difficult to negotiate. Crossing streets can also be a problem, though most Chilean drivers are courteous toward individuals with obvious handicaps.

According to Chile's last census (1992), 288,000 Chileans claimed some sort of disability, while one recent government study suggests a figure around 616,000. However, the Fondo Nacional del Descapacitado (National Fund for the Handicapped, abbreviated as Fonadis) believes the World Health Organization (WHO) figure of 1.4 million is closer to the truth. Law now requires new public buildings to provide disabled access, but public transport remains poor in this regard – though the Metro's new Línea 5 has been retrofitted.

Santiago's Tixi Service (☎ 800-223-097 toll-free) caters specifically to disabled individuals, with hydraulic elevators to accommodate wheelchairs. Trips within the capital generally cost around US$12.

SENIOR TRAVELERS

Senior travelers should encounter no particular difficulties traveling in Chile, where older citizens typically enjoy a great deal of respect. On crowded buses, for instance, most Chileans will readily offer their seat to an older person.

TRAVEL WITH CHILDREN

Chile is child-friendly in terms of safety, health, people's attitudes and family-oriented activities. For small children, a folding stroller is a good idea, especially where there is a chance of getting lost in crowds. People are also very helpful on public transport; often someone will give up a seat for parent and child, but if that does not happen, an older person may offer to put the child on his or her lap.

In terms of food and health, there are no special concerns in most of the country, but bottled water may be a good idea for delicate stomachs. Most restaurants offer a wide variety of dishes suitable for children (vegetables, pasta, meat, chicken, fish), and Chilean cuisine is generally bland despite the occasional hot sauce. Portions are abundant enough that smaller children probably will not need a separate meals, and there is usually no problem in securing additional cutlery.

In general, public toilets are poorly maintained; always carry toilet paper, which is almost nonexistent. While a woman may take a young boy into the ladies' room, it would be socially unacceptable for a man to take a girl into the men's room.

Unless you are traveling by plane, remember that distances are long and trips seem endless, so bring a comfortable blanket and enough toys and games to amuse your child. Santiago and most other cities have large public parks with playgrounds, so it's easy for children to make international friendships. There are also many activities specifically for children; consult newspapers like *El Mercurio* for listings.

For general information on the subject, look for Lonely Planet's *Travel with Children* (1995), by Lonely Planet cofounder Maureen Wheeler.

USEFUL ORGANIZATIONS

Travelers interested in environmental conservation may wish to contact Codeff (Comité Pro Defensa de la Fauna y Flora (☎ 02-251-0287, fax 02-251-8433, info@codeff.mic.cl), Av Francisco Bilbao 691, Providencia, Santiago; Greenpeace Pacífico Sur (☎ 02-777-9570, fax 735-8990, greenpeacechile@dialb.greenpeace .org), the Chilean branch of the international conservation organization, at Montecarmelo 37, Providencia, Santiago; Defensores del Bosque Chileno (☎ 02-204-1914), Diagonal Oriente 1413, Ñuñoa; and Fundación Lahuen (☎ 02-234-2617), Orrego Luco 054, Providencia. Ancient Forests International (☎/fax 707-923-3015), Box 1850, Redway, CA 95560, USA, has close links to Chilean forest conservation organizations.

German visitors, business people or intending residents may wish to contact the Deutsch-Chilenischer Bund (☎ 02-212-6474), Av Vitacura 5875, Vitacura, Santiago, which publishes the useful guide *Chile: Ein Land zum Leben, Arbeiten und Investieren* (1997).

The Instituto Nacional de la Juventud (INJ; ☎ 02-688-1072), Agustinas 1564, Santiago, issues the *Tarjeta Joven* (Youth Card), which entitles its holders to discounts on many services throughout the country.

DANGERS & ANNOYANCES

Chile is much less hazardous than most other Latin American countries and many other parts of the world, but certain precautions will nevertheless reduce risks and make your trip more enjoyable.

Personal Security & Theft

Although many Chileans find street crime alarming, personal security problems are minor compared with many other South American countries. Truly violent crime is still unusual in Santiago; both men or women can travel in most parts of the city at any time of day or night without excessive apprehension. The crowded Metro and buses can be havens for pickpockets, however.

Valparaíso has an unfortunate reputation for robberies in some of its southern neighborhoods. Summer is the crime season in beach resorts like Viña del Mar, Reñaca and La Serena. Though these are by no means violent places, be alert for pickpockets and avoid leaving valuables on the beach while you go for a swim.

Take precautions against petty theft, such as purse snatching. Be especially wary of calculated distractions, such as someone tapping you on the shoulder or spilling something on you, since these 'accidents' are often part of a team effort to relieve you of your backpack or other valuables. Grip your bag or purse firmly, carry your wallet in a front pocket and avoid conspicuous displays of expensive jewelry. Valuables such as passports and air tickets can be conveniently carried in a light jacket or vest with one or two zip-up or button-up pockets. Money belts and neck pouches are common alternatives, though some travelers find them uncomfortable; an elastic leg pouch is less cumbersome but can get very sweaty in hot weather.

Baggage insurance is a good idea. Since the doors to rooms in many budget hotels have only token locks or none at all, do not leave valuables such as cash or cameras in your hotel room. You may want to bring your own: many of the doors have hasps that can be used with a small combination or key lock. Lower to mid-range accommodations usually have secure left-luggage areas, while upscale hotels often have secure strongboxes in each room.

Unauthorized political demonstrations still take place and can be very disputatious; the police will sometimes use tear gas or truck-mounted water cannons – known as *guanacos*, after the spitting wild New World camels – to break them up. The single most contentious site in Chile may be Providencia's Av 11 de Septiembre, named by the dictatorship for the date of the coup that overthrew the Allende government; on every anniversary of the coup, truculent demonstrators demand that the street be renamed.

Natural & Recreational Hazards

The Pacific coast of South America is part of the 'ring of fire' that stretches from Asia to Alaska to Tierra del Fuego. Volcanic eruptions are not unusual. In 1991, for example, the explosion of Aisén's Volcán Hudson buried Chile Chico and Los Antiguos, Argentina, knee-deep in ash. Earthquakes are common.

Volcanic activity is unlikely to pose any immediate threat to travelers, since volcanoes usually give some notice before a big eruption. A few popular resorts are especially vulnerable, particularly the town of Pucón, at the base of Volcán Villarrica.

Earthquakes are another matter, since they occur without warning. Local construction often does not meet seismic safety standards; adobe buildings tend to be especially vulnerable. Travelers in budget accommodations should make contingency plans for safety, including evacuation, before falling asleep at night.

Many of Chile's finest beach areas have dangerous offshore rip currents, so ask before entering the water and be sure someone on shore knows your whereabouts. The water at some beaches, such as Iquique's Playa Brava, is unsafe under any conditions.

In wilderness areas such as Parque Nacional Torres del Paine, accidents have become common enough that authorities no longer permit solo trekking.

LEGAL MATTERS

Chile's carabineros, less known for corruption than other South American police, behave professionally and politely in ordinary circumstances, but there have been credible reports of mistreatment of foreign travelers, especially in Santiago. In one 1999 case, police apparently attempted to frame a French citizen on weapons charges during a pro-Mapuche demonstration in the southern city of Traiguén, though a judge later dismissed the complaint.

Carabineros can demand identification at any time, so carry your passport. Throughout the country, the toll-free emergency telephone number for carabineros is ☎ 133.

Chileans often refer to carabineros as *pacos*, a disrespectful (though not obscene) term that should *never* be used to a policeman's face. Speed bumps are sometimes known as *pacos acostados* (sleeping police officers).

Members of the military still take themselves seriously, even under civilian government, so avoid photographing military installations. In the event of a national emergency, the military-dominated Consejo de Seguridad Nacional (National Security Council) may impose martial law, suspending all civil rights, so make sure someone knows your whereabouts; contact your embassy or consulate for advice.

If you are involved in any automobile accident, your license (usually your international permit) will be confiscated until the case is resolved, although local officials will usually issue a temporary driving permit within a few days. A blood alcohol test is obligatory; purchase a sterile syringe at the hospital or clinic pharmacy when the carabineros take you there. After this you will be taken to the police station to make a statement and then, under most circumstances, released. Ordinarily you cannot leave Chile until the matter is resolved; consult your consulate, insurance carrier and a lawyer at home.

Carabineros do not harass drivers for minor equipment violations (unlike the police in neighboring Argentina). You should *never* attempt to bribe the carabineros, whose reputation for institutional integrity is high.

BUSINESS HOURS

Traditionally, business hours in Chile commence by 9 am, but shops close at about 1 pm for three or even four hours, when people often return home for lunch and a brief siesta. After the siesta, shops reopen until 8 or 9 pm. In Santiago, government offices and many businesses have adopted a more conventional 9 am to 6 pm schedule. Banks and government offices are often open to the public only in the morning.

PUBLIC HOLIDAYS & SPECIAL EVENTS

Throughout the year but especially in summer, Chileans from Arica to Punta Arenas celebrate a variety of local and national cultural festivals. Other than religious holidays such as Easter and Christmas, the most significant are mid-September's Fiestas Patrias, but many localities have their own favorites. For listings, see individual city entries.

There are numerous national holidays, on which government offices and businesses are closed. There is pressure to reduce these or to eliminate so-called sandwich holidays, which many Chileans take between an actual holiday and the weekend, by moving some of them to the nearest Monday.

Año Nuevo (New Year)
   January 1

Semana Santa (Easter Week)

Día del Trabajo (Labor Day)
   May 1

Glorias Navales (commemorating the naval Battle of Iquique)
   May 21

Corpus Christi
   May 30

Día de San Pedro y San Pablo (St Peter & St Paul's Day)
   June 29

Asunción de la Virgen (Assumption)
   August 15

Día de la Unidad Nacional (Day of National Unity, replacing the controversial *Pronunciamiento Militar de 1973*, the military coup of 1973). The future of this holiday is in doubt as it was not formally celebrated in 1999 due to General Pinochet's detention in London.
First Monday in September

Día de la Independencia Nacional (National Independence Day)
September 18

Día del Ejército (Armed Forces Day)
September 19

Día de la Raza (Columbus Day)
October 12

Todo los Santos (All Saints' Day)
November 1

Inmaculada Concepción (Immaculate Conception)
December 8

Navidad (Christmas Day)
December 25

ACTIVITIES

Chileans are fond of a variety of sports, both as participants and spectators, but the most popular is soccer. In the callampas, children will clear a vacant lot, mark the goal with stones and make a ball of old rags and socks to pursue their pastime. Even in exclusive country clubs the sport is popular.

In the summer, the beach is the most popular vacation spot. Paddleball, a game like tennis, has gained major popularity. Courts have sprung up around the country, and many people play on the beach.

Other popular sports include tennis, basketball, volleyball and cycling. And outdoor activities such as canoeing, climbing, kayaking, trekking, windsurfing and hang gliding are gaining popularity. Rivers, including the Maipo, Claro, Biobío and Futaleufú are increasingly popular for white-water rafting and kayaking, although hydroelectric development seriously threatens the Biobío. Chile has an increasing number of Santiago-based agencies specializing in adventure travel; See Organized Tours in the Getting Around chapter for more information.

Cycling & Mountain Biking

Cycling is increasingly popular, both as a recreational activity and as a way to get around the country. Because even some paved roads suffer from potholes and frequent construction, a mountain bike with wide tires is the best choice; on unpaved highways like the Camino Austral, it is utterly essential. Travel agencies like Santiago's Pared Sur, in Las Condes, organize weekend and longer mountain-bike trips.

Skiing

Skiing in Chile, though increasingly expensive, can be world class. The most internationally renowned resort is Portillo, the site of several downhill speed records, northeast of Santiago near the Argentine border crossing to Mendoza. Other major resorts are within an hour of the capital, at La Parva, El Colorado and Valle Nevado; east of Chillán at Termas de Chillán; in Parque Nacional Villarrica near the resort town of Pucón; and at Antillanca in Parque Nacional Puyehue, east of Osorno. There are a handful of lesser ski resorts in the Aisén region near Coihaique and near Punta Arenas.

Prospective skiers should try to locate Chris Lizza's *South America Ski Guide* (1992), which contains substantial chapters on both Chile and Argentina but has gone out of print. Most of the ski areas mentioned above have elaborate websites (see boxed text 'Online Services' and regional chapters).

Hiking & Trekking

More people enjoy hiking and trekking than any other single activity, thanks to Chile's numerous national parks, most of which have decent – and sometimes very good – trail networks. International showpieces like Torres del Paine get the most attention, but there are excellent alternatives only a short bus ride from major cities; for instance, Parque Nacional El Morado near Santiago and Parque Nacional La Campana near Viña del Mar. See Lonely Planet's *Trekking in the Patagonian Andes* (1997), by Clem Lindenmayer, for information on extended treks in southern Chile and Argentina.

Hikers and trekkers visiting the Southern Hemisphere for the first time should look for a compensated needle compass such as the Recta DP 10; Northern Hemisphere compasses can be deceptive as an indicator of direction in far southern latitudes.

Andescape (☎/fax 061-412-877, fax 412-592, andescape@chileaustral.com), Eberhard 599 in Puerto Natales, operates moderately priced trekking lodges in Parque Nacional Torres del Paine. Fantástico Sur (☎ 061-226-054, fax 222-641, lastorres@chileaustral .com), Magallanes 960 in Punta Arenas, is a private operator with more elaborate lodges on the legendary Paine Circuit but just outside the park boundaries.

Mountaineering

Chile has great mountaineering country, ranging from the Pallachatas volcanoes of the northern altiplano to Ojos del Salado east of Copiapó, the numerous volcanic cones of Araucanía and Los Lagos and the international magnet of Torres del Paine. Climbers should be aware of bureaucratic obstacles, however, most notably Conaf's US$800 fee for climbing in Parque Nacional Torres del Paine. It is also advisable to check in with Conaf or the local carabineros office before starting a climb.

Climbers intending to scale border peaks like the Pallachatas or Ojos del Salado must have permission from Chile's Dirección de Fronteras y Límites (Difrol; ☎ 02-671-4110, fax 697-1909, 672-2536) at Bandera 52, 4th floor, Santiago. For other information on climbing and help with the bureaucracy, contact the Federación de Andinismo (☎ 02-222-0888) at Almirante Simpson 77, Providencia, Santiago.

Surfing

Chile's almost endless coastline offers plenty of surfing possibilities, but only at Arica is the water comfortably warm, so wet suits are imperative. Rough surf and rip currents make some areas inadvisable, and it's best not to surf alone anywhere.

Many of the best surfing areas are in or near Arica, Iquique and Antofagasta in the Norte Grande; the paving of coastal Ruta 1 has opened this area to surfers, but has also brought mountains of trash from careless campers. Pichilemu, in Region V, is another popular area.

For detailed information on surfing in Chile, contact Surfer Publications (☎ 714-496-5922, fax 496-7849), PO Box 1028, Dana Point, CA 92629, USA. Its monthly *Surf Report* includes issues on Region I (vol 10, No 5, May 1989; revised in vol 16, No 6, June 1995); Regions II, III and IV (vol 10, No 6, October 1989); and Regions V and VI (vol 14, No 8, August 1993).

White-Water Rafting & Kayaking

White-water enthusiasts agree that Chile's rivers are world-class for both rafting and kayaking, with plenty of Class V challenges on the Biobío, Futaleufú and other spots in the southern lakes and Aisén. There are respectable white-water runs even in the suburbs of Santiago, for instance, in the Cajón del Maipo, organized by agencies like Cascada Expediciones and Altué Active Travel. Sea kayaking is becoming increasingly popular in and around the sheltered archipelagic waters of Chiloé, where Altué has a center at the market town of Dalcahue.

For more information on rafting and kayaking, with details on North American operators, see the Organized Tours section in the Getting There & Away chapter.

Diving

Chile is not known for diving or snorkeling, since even the tropical segments of its long coastline experience cold currents. The best places for diving are its Pacific island possessions, the Juan Fernández Archipelago and Easter Island, and offshore islands like Isla Damas in Reserva Nacional Pingüino de Humboldt, but even then it's unlikely anyone would come to Chile just for the diving.

Paragliding

Paragliding is still in its early stages in Chile, but there are ideal conditions in and near the city of Iquique, in the Norte Grande, where several operators teach paragliding; see the Iquique section of the Norte Grande chapter for details.

COURSES

Santiago is the main center in Chile for language courses, but there are also possibilities in Iquique and Pucón. See the respective city entries for more details.

Santiago's Escuela de Vino (☎ (02-207-3520, fax 207-0581), Av Vitacura 3446 in Vitacura, offers introductory, middle and advanced wine-appreciation courses, consisting of four to seven two-hour sessions each, with instruction by Chilean vintners, enologists and university faculty. Classes take place Monday through Thursday, monthly between March and December in Spanish only, but the students are international. The cost is about US$100, and there are about 20 students per class.

With Chilean headquarters at Coihaique, the National Outdoor Leadership School (NOLS; ☎ 307-332-6973; fax 307-332-1220, admissions@nols.edu, www.nols.edu), 288 Main St, Lander, WY 82520, USA, offers a 'Semester in Patagonia' program, emphasizing wilderness skills and natural history courses, with university credit available.

WORK

It's increasingly difficult to obtain residence and work permits for Chile. Consequently, many foreigners do not bother to do so, but the most reputable employers will insist on the proper visa. If you need one, go to the Departamento de Extranjería (☎ 02-672-5320), Moneda 1342, Santiago. Business hours are 9 am to 1:30 pm.

A good orientation to working and living in Chile, including suggestions on obtaining residence and starting a business, is *The International Settler*, an informational booklet published by the *News Review*, Santiago's weekly English-language newspaper. If you're unable to find it around town, try to contact the *News Review* (☎ 02-236-1423, newrevi@mcl.cl), Almirante Pastene 222, Providencia, Santiago.

It is not unusual for visiting travelers to work as English-language instructors in Santiago. Wages are fairly good on a per-hour basis, but full-time employment is hard to come by without a commitment to stay for some time.

Options for volunteer work are worth exploring, especially with social and environmental organizations. Two good sources to consult are the comprehensive, biannual *Directorio de Instituciones de Chile* (popularly known as the 'Guía Silber' after its publisher Silber Editores), a directory of political, labor, church, cultural and other institutions both official and nongovernmental; and the annual *Directorio de Organizaciones Miembros* published by Renace (Red Nacional de Acción Ecológica), a loosely affiliated network of environmental organizations throughout the country.

The best options for bar work are in Santiago, especially in the numerous pubs along Avenida Suecia and General Holley (Metro: Los Leones), in Barrio Bellavista and in seasonally popular resorts like Pucón. Wages, however, are much lower than they would be in Europe or North America.

Street musicians and theater performers are a staple of Chilean life, so the competition is stiff. Without some unique skill, foreign visitors are unlikely to attract enough attention to earn a living. In some cases, the police can be a nuisance.

ACCOMMODATIONS

Chile's broad spectrum of accommodations ranges from hostels and campgrounds to five-star luxury hotels. Where you stay will depend on your budget and your standards, where you are, and how hard you look, but you should be able to find something reasonable. You may also find yourself invited into Chilean homes and generally should not hesitate to accept this hospitality.

Reservations

Nearly all hotels, even the cheapest, have telephones and many have fax machines, so it's easy to make reservations. While reservations are usually unnecessary, if you'll be arriving at an awkward hour or during the peak summer season or a holiday weekend, they can be a good idea.

Camping & Refugios

Sernatur's Santiago headquarters has a free pamphlet called *Camping* that lists and describes campgrounds throughout Chile. The sites are usually in wooded areas and have excellent facilities: hot showers, toilets and laundry, fire pits for cooking, restaurants or snack bars and grocery stores. Some even have swimming pools or lake access. CTC (Telefónica) publishes an annually updated Turistel camping guide with detailed information and excellent maps – for some areas, the maps are better than those in the regular Turistel guides.

Chilean campgrounds are not the bargain they once were, since many sites charge a five-person minimum; this means that for singles or couples they can be more expensive than basic *hospedajes* or *residenciales*. This is true both at private campgrounds and in national parks where concessionaires control the franchise. In some remote parts of Chile, there is free camping, but drinkable water and sanitary facilities are often lacking.

For comfort, invest in a good, dome-style tent with a rain fly before coming to South America, where camping equipment is more expensive. With a good tent, a three-season sleeping bag should be adequate for almost any weather conditions. A camp stove that can burn a variety of fuels is a good idea, since white gas *(bencina blanca)* is available only at chemical supply shops or hardware stores. Firewood is a limited and often expensive resource, which, in any event, smudges your pots and pans. Bring or buy mosquito repellent, since many campsites are near rivers or lakes.

There are also *refugios*, which are rustic – sometimes *very* rustic – shelters for hikers and trekkers in the national parks. The more rustic of these are free or very cheap, but some newer ones are comfortable commercial enterprises, complete with bunks, mattresses, showers and even restaurants, that charge plenty for the privilege of staying there.

Travelers with their own vehicles will find that many *servicentros* along Ruta 5, the Panamericana, have spacious lots suitable for parking and sleeping, if the maneuvers of 18-wheelers don't disturb your sleep. In addition to clean toilet facilities (for which there is a token charge), most of these places offer hot showers for less than US$1.

Long-Term Rentals
If you're staying in a place for an extended period, house and apartment rentals can save you money. In Santiago, check listings in Sunday's *El Mercurio* or in the weekly classified paper *El Rastro*. In resorts such as Viña del Mar, La Serena or Villarrica, you can lodge several people for the price of one by renting an apartment and cooking your own meals. In towns such as Valdivia and La Serena, people line the highway approaches in summer to offer houses and apartments. You can also check the tourist office or local papers.

Casas de Familia
In summer, especially from Temuco south, families often rent rooms to visitors. A *casa de familia* can be an excellent bargain, with access to cooking and laundry facilities, hot showers and Chilean hospitality. Tourist offices often maintain lists of such accommodations.

Hostels
Chile has two types of youth hostels. The first is the growing but limited number affiliated with Hostelling International (HI), whose central office is the Asociación Chilena de Albergues Turísticos Juveniles (☎ 02-233-3220, fax 233-2555, achatj@entelchile.net), Hernando de Aguirre 201, Oficina 602, Providencia, Santiago. A hostel card, valid worldwide, costs about US$15.

HI has its own custom-built facility in Santiago's Barrio Brasil, but elsewhere its affiliates are usually budget hotels that have set aside a few beds or rooms for hostelers. In addition to Santiago, there are currently hostel affiliates in La Serena, Viña del Mar, Hanga Roa (Rapa Nui/Easter Island), Salto del Laja (near Los Angeles), Temuco, Pucón, Valdivia, Frutillar, Puerto Montt, Ancud and Punta Arenas. Under consideration for inclusion in the system are facilities in Arica, Iquique and Antofagasta.

The second system is coordinated by the Dirección General de Deportes y Recreación (Digeder; ☎ 02-223-8099), Fidel Oteíza 1956, 5th floor, Providencia, whose *albergues juveniles* cater mainly to schoolchildren and students on holiday and occupy temporary sites at sports stadiums, campgrounds, schools or churches. Usually open in January and February only, they charge a mere few dollars per night for a dormitory bed, making them just about the cheapest accommodations in Chile. Since these hostel sites often change from year to year, it is very useful to have the most current listing, but if you don't, local tourist offices can often refer you to them.

Hospedajes, Pensiones & Residenciales

All these offer very reasonable accommodations, but the differences among them are sometimes ill-defined; all may be called hotels. Rooms and furnishings are modest, usually including beds with clean sheets and blankets, but never hesitate to ask to see a room. A few have private baths, but more commonly you will share toilet and shower facilities with other guests. Since the owners do not wish to waste hot water, you will usually have to ask them to turn on the *calefón* (hot water heater) before taking a shower.

A *hospedaje* is usually a large family home that has a few extra bedrooms for guests. Typically, the bathroom is shared. Some are not permanent businesses but temporary expedients in times of economic distress. Similarly, a *pensión* offers short-term accommodations in a family home but may also house permanent lodgers. Meals are sometimes available.

Residenciales, which are permanent businesses but sometimes only seasonal, more commonly figure in tourist office lists. In general, they occupy buildings designed for short-stay accommodations, although some cater to clients who intend only *very* short stays – say two hours or so. Prostitutes have been known to frequent them, but so do young couples with no other indoor alternative for their passion. Except for occasional noise, the proximity of such activities should not deter you, even if you have children.

Several travelers have complained of fleas at the cheapest budget hotels throughout Chile and recommend carrying some sort of bug bomb or insect repellent. Others have had no such problems.

Hotels & Motels

Hotels vary from one-star austerity to five-star luxury, but correlation between these categories and their standards is less than perfect; many one-star places seem to be a better value than their three- and four-star brethren. In general, hotels provide a room with attached private bath, often a telephone and sometimes *música funcional* (Muzak) or a TV. Normally they will have a restaurant; breakfast is often, but not always, included in the price. Upper mid-range to top-end places have room service and laundry service, international cable TV, swimming pools, bars, shopping galleries and other luxuries; these are most common in major cities and resorts.

In some areas, motels are what North Americans and Europeans expect: rural or suburban roadside accommodations with convenient parking. However, the term 'motel' can also be a euphemism for a place catering almost exclusively to unmarried couples (or individuals married to others) with no other alternative for privacy. The external decor (in one case a building was decorated with a heart-pierced-by-an-arrow symbol) usually makes it obvious what sort of place a given establishment is. Within cities, its counterpart is known as a *hotel parejero*.

FOOD

From the tropics to the pole, Chile's varied cuisine features seafood, beef, fresh fruit and vegetables. Upwelling of the waters from the Pacific Ocean's cool Humboldt Current sustains a cornucopia of fish and shellfish for Chilean kitchens, while the fields, orchards and pastures of Middle Chile fill the table with superb produce.

Chilean restaurants range from hole-in-the-wall snack bars to sumptuous venues. Most cities feature a central market with many small, cheap restaurants, usually known as *cocinerías* or *comedores*, of surprisingly high quality. Nearly every sizable town also has a *casino de bomberos* (fire station restaurant) with excellent and inexpensive meals.

There are several categories of eating establishments. Bars serve snacks and both alcoholic and nonalcoholic drinks, while *fuentes de soda* are similar but do not serve alcohol. Snack bars sell fast food. *Cafeterías* serve modest meals; *hosterías* are more elaborate and usually located outside the main cities. A *salón de té* is not quite literally a teahouse but is a bit more upscale than a cafetería. Full-fledged *restaurantes* are distinguished by quality and service. Distinctions are less than exact, and the term 'restaurante' can be applied to every category of establishment. Almost all serve alcoholic and nonalcoholic drinks.

Except in strictly family-run establishments, it is customary – and expected – to leave a 10% tip. The menu is *la carta*; the bill is *la cuenta*.

Snacks

Cheap and available almost everywhere in Chile, one of the world's finest snacks is the *empanada*, a tasty turnover with vegetables, hard-boiled egg, olive, beef, chicken, ham and cheese or other filling. The most common fillings you'll find, however, are *pino* (ground beef) and *queso* (cheese). Empanadas *al horno* (baked) are lighter than empanadas *fritas* (fried). Travelers arriving from Argentina will find the Chilean empanada larger and more filling than its Argentine counterpart, so don't order a dozen for lunch or your bus trip.

Humitas are corn tamales, frequently wrapped in corn husks and steamed; when served in this manner they are *humitas en chala* – a popular and tasty snack. There are numerous breads, including *chapalele*, made with potatoes and flour and boiled; *milcao*, another type of potato bread; and *sopaipa*, recognizable by its dark brown exterior, which is made from wheat flour and fruit, but not baked. *Pebre* is a tasty condiment made with chopped tomatoes, onion, garlic, chili peppers, cilantro and parsley.

Sandwiches are popular snacks throughout the day. Among sandwich fillings, *churrasco* (steak), *jamón* (ham) and queso are most widely available. Cold ham and cheese make an *aliado*, while a sandwich with ham and melted cheese constitutes a *Barros Jarpa*, after a Chilean painter known for consuming them in large quantities. A steak sandwich with melted cheese is a *Barros Luco*, the favorite of Ramón Barros Luco, who was president from 1910 to '15. Beefsteak with tomato and other vegetables is a *chacarero*.

Chile's cheapest fast food is the *completo*, a hot dog with absolutely everything (including a massive cholesterol infusion).

Breakfast

Breakfast *(desayuno)* usually comprises toast *(pan tostado)* with butter *(mantequilla)* or jam *(mermelada)* and tea *(té)*; eggs or sandwiches are also common. *Huevos fritos* are fried eggs, usually served in a *paila* (small frying pan). *Huevos revueltos* are scrambled, *huevos pasados* are boiled, and *huevos a la copa* are poached. *Bien cocidos* means well-cooked and *duros* means hard-boiled.

Main Dishes

Many places offer a cheap set meal *(comida corrida* or *almuerzo del día)* for lunch *(almuerzo* or *colación)* and, less often, for dinner *(cena)*. Some of the most common dishes are listed below, but there are many other possibilities. Do not hesitate to ask waiters for an explanation of any dish.

Lunch can be the biggest meal of the day. Set menus tend to be almost identical at cheaper restaurants, generally consisting of *cazuela*, a stew of potato or maize with a piece of beef or chicken, a main course of rice with chicken or meat, (usually beef) and a simple dessert. Soup is *caldo* or *sopa*. *Porotos* (beans) are a common budget entrée, but there are more elaborate versions with a variety of vegetables and condiments. One of Chile's most delicious and filling traditional dishes is *pastel de choclo*, a maize casserole filled with vegetables, chicken and beef, but this may be available only during the summer maize harvest.

The biggest standard meal in Chile is *lomo a lo pobre*, an enormous slab of beef topped with two fried eggs and buried in french fries. This is not a low-calorie snack, and you may wish to monitor your cholesterol level before and after eating. *Ajiaco* is a spiced beef stew that, traditionally, uses a variety of leftovers.

Beef, in a variety of cuts and styles of preparation, is the most popular main course at *parrillas* – restaurants that grill everything from steak to sausages over charcoal. The *parrillada* proper is an assortment of steak and other cuts that will appall vegetarians and heart specialists. A traditional parrillada includes offal like *chunchules* (small intestines), *tripa gorda* (large intestine), *ubre* (udder), *riñones* (kidneys) and *morcilla* (blood sausage). A token green salad *(ensalada)* will usually accompany the meal.

Many restaurants of all kinds offer *pollo con papas fritas* (chicken with fries) and *pollo con arroz* (chicken with rice).

Seafood

What really distinguishes Chilean cuisine is its varied seafood, among the world's best. Popular seafood dishes include the delicious *sopa de mariscos*, or *cazuela de mariscos* (shellfish soup), which is more of a shellfish stew. *Paila marina* is a fish and shellfish chowder, while *sopa de pescado* is a fish soup. Try *chupe de cóngrio* (conger eel stew) or, if available, *chupe de locos* (abalone stew), both cooked in a thick sauce of butter, bread crumbs, cheese and spices. Locos may be in *veda* (quarantine) because of overexploitation.

Do not overlook the market restaurants in cities like Iquique, Concepción, Temuco and Puerto Montt. Some dishes, like *erizos* (sea urchins) are acquired tastes, but they will rarely upset your stomach. Do insist on all shellfish being thoroughly cooked, which has been obligatory since the cholera scare of 1991–92; even the traditional *ceviche* (marinated raw fish or shellfish) must now be cooked, although it is still served cold.

In southern Chile and especially on Chiloé, one of the typical specialties is *curanto*, a hearty stew of fish, shellfish, chicken, pork, lamb, beef and potato. Curanto is eaten with chapalele or milcao (potato breads).

A few seafood terms worth knowing are:

clams	*almejas*
crab	*cangrejo* or *jaiva*
fish	*pescado*
giant barnacle	*picoroco*
king crab	*centolla*
mussels	*cholgas*
octopus	*pulpo*
oysters	*ostras*
prawns	*camarones grandes*
razor clams	*machas*
scallops	*ostiones*
sea urchins	*erizos*
shellfish	*mariscos*
shrimp	*camarones*
squid	*calamares*

Many basic restaurants prepare their fish by frying in heavy oil, which besides its dietary shortcomings also destroys the flavor; on request, however, most will prepare fish *al vapor* (steamed) or *a la plancha* (grilled).

Desserts

Dessert *(postre)* is commonly fresh fruit or *helado* (ice cream). The latter has improved greatly over the past several years, at least at those ice creameries featuring *elaboración artesanal* (small-scale rather than industrial production). Also try *arroz con leche* (rice pudding), *flan* (egg custard) and *tortas* (cakes). In the southern lakes region, Chileans of German descent bake exquisite *kuchen* (pastries) filled with local fruit (Chile's raspberries are the world's tastiest).

Ethnic Food

Santiago has a large and increasing selection of 'ethnic' restaurants. French, Italian, Spanish, German and Chinese are the most common, but Brazilian, Mexican, Middle Eastern and other national cuisines are also available. Another good place to look for restaurants is the Santiago entry in the Turistel Centro guidebook.

In northern coastal cities like Arica and Iquique, there are many Chinese restaurants.

These *chifas* are generally cheap, good values and pleasant changes.

Vegetarian Dishes

While most Chileans are carnivores, vegetarianism is no longer the mark of an eccentric. Santiago has some excellent vegetarian fare, but in other than strictly vegetarian restaurants, you may have to make a special request. If presented with meat that you don't want, it may help to claim allergy *(alergia)*.

Every town has a market with a wide variety of fruits and vegetables – produce from the Chilean heartland reaches the limits of the republic and overseas. Remember that agricultural regulations forbid importing fruit from foreign countries, including neighboring Argentina.

Fast Food

Fast-food restaurants are mostly inferior clones of Kentucky Fried Chicken or McDonald's, although these foreign franchises are themselves increasingly common. Except at better Italian restaurants, pizzas are generally small, greasy and not very yummy. The nationwide Dino's and Bavaria chains offer passable standard fare.

DRINKS
Nonalcoholic Drinks

Soft Drinks & Water Chileans guzzle prodigious amounts of soft drinks, from the ubiquitous Coca Cola to 7-Up, Sprite and sugary local brands such as Bilz. Mineral water, both carbonated *(con gas)* and plain *(sin gas)*, is widely available, but tap water is potable almost everywhere. The most popular mineral waters are Cachantún and Chusmiza, but others are equally good.

Fruit Juices & Licuados *Jugos* (juices) are varied and excellent. Besides the common *naranja* (orange), *toronja* (grapefruit), *limón* (lemon), *damasco* (apricot) and *piña* (pineapple), *mora* (blackberry), *maracuyá* (passion fruit) and *sandía* (watermelon) are also available. The distinctively Chilean *mote con huesillo* is a peach nectar with barley kernels, sold by countless street vendors but closely monitored for hygiene.

Licuados are milk-blended fruit drinks; on request they can be made with water. Common flavors are banana, *durazno* (peach) and *pera* (pear). Unless you like yours *very* sweet, ask them to hold the sugar ('sin azúcar, por favor').

Coffee & Tea While the situation is improving, Chilean coffee will dismay serious caffeine addicts. Except in upscale restaurants and specialized coffee bars such as Santiago's Café Haití and Café Caribe, which serve espresso, semisoluble Nescafé is the norm. *Café con leche* is literally milk with coffee – a teaspoonful of coffee dissolved in hot milk. *Café solo* or *café negro* is coffee with hot water alone.

Likewise, *té con leche* is a tea bag submerged in warm milk. Tea is normally served black, with at least three packets of sugar. If you prefer just a touch of milk, a habit most Chileans find bizarre, it is easier to ask for *un poquito de leche* later rather than try to explain your eccentric habits in advance.

Yerba mate, or 'Paraguayan tea,' is consumed much more widely in the River Plate countries (Argentina, Uruguay and Paraguay) than in Chile, but some Chilean supermarkets do carry it. Chileans consume herbal teas *(aguas)* such as *manzanilla* (chamomile), *rosa mosqueta* and *boldo* in considerable quantities.

Alcoholic Drinks

Wines & Wine Regions Chilean wines are South America's best and rate among the finest in the world; reds *(tintos)* and whites *(blancos)* are both excellent. The country's commercial wine-growing district stretches from the Copiapó valley of the Norte Chico's Region III (Atacama) to the drainage of the Río Biobío in Region VIII.

From north to south, rainfall increases and irrigation decreases. In the Copiapó area, known as the *zona pisquera*, irrigated vineyards produce grapes with a high sugar content, which are made into *pisco* (grape brandy). From the drainage of the Río Aconcagua to the Río Maule is a middle zone with a Mediterranean climate in which irrigation is also crucial. A reduced need for irrigation characterizes the more humid area south of the Maule. The Biobío drainage receives sufficient rainfall to make irrigation unnecessary, but that same weather makes the harvest unsuitable for finer wines.

Chile's variety of growing conditions, made even more complex by its abrupt topography, produces a considerable variety of wines. Atacama wineries specialize in the brandylike pisco and the tasty dessert wine known as *pajarete* and also produce small quantities of whites and sparkling wines. Middle Chile's *zona de regadío* produces the country's best-known wines, mostly Cabernet Sauvignon and other types of reds planted under French tutelage in the 19th century. Acreages planted to whites such as Chardonnay and Riesling are increasing. Many major wineries in this zone lack sufficient acreage to produce the quantity they require and buy quality grapes on contract. Major labels include Concha y Toro (and its subsidiary Santa Emiliana), Undurraga, Cousiño Macul, Errázuriz Panquehue, Ochagavía, Santa Rita, Santa Carolina, Manquehue, San Pedro Canepa, Tarapacá and Carmen. Several of these wineries are open to the public.

To the south, in the transitional zone of the Maule, reds give way to whites such as Sauvignon Blanc and Sémillon. Curicó and Talca are the centers of production for brands like Miguel Torres and Viña San Pedro, whose wineries also welcome visitors. Like the zone around Copiapó, the Biobío drainage is a peripheral, pioneer zone for wine grapes, with relatively small yields of common reds and whites that are mostly blended and used for jug wines. Farther south, in the Araucanía, there are some scattered vineyards, but commercial production is precarious.

Wine aficionados who plan a trip to South America should look at Harm de Blij's *Wine Regions of the Southern Hemisphere* (1985), which contains excellent chapters on the Chilean, Argentine and Brazilian wine industries. A locally published wine guide is Fred Purdy's *Gringo's Guide to Chilean Wine*.

Other Alcoholic Drinks Chile's table wines should satisfy most visitors' alcoholic thirst, but don't refrain from trying the tasty but powerful pisco, often served in the form of a pisco sour, with lemon juice, egg white and powdered sugar. It may also be served with ginger ale *(chilcano)* or vermouth *(capitán)*.

Escudo is the best bottled beer and Cristal the most popular, but Becker has recently gained popularity. Bars and restaurants commonly sell draft beer (known as *chopp* and pronounced 'shop'), which is cheaper than bottled beer *(cerveza)* and often better.

Gol is a translucent alcoholic mixture of butter, sugar and milk, left to ferment for a fortnight. It's drunk in the south, mostly in private homes, but not readily available in restaurants. *Guinda* is a cherrylike fruit that is the basis of *guindado*, a fermented alcoholic drink with brandy, cinnamon, and cloves. A popular holiday drink is the powerful but deceptively sweet *cola de mono* ('tail of the monkey'), which consists of *aguardiente* (cane alcohol), coffee, cloves and vanilla.

ENTERTAINMENT
Cinemas

Traditionally, Chileans flock to the cinema, although outside Santiago the video revolution has meant the closure of many theaters that were once the only show in town. Still, in the capital and large cities such as Valparaíso and Viña del Mar, major theaters offer the

latest films from Europe, the USA and Latin America. Prices have risen in recent years, but many cinemas offer substantial midweek discounts. Repertory houses, cultural centers and universities provide a chance to see classics or less commercial films you may have missed. Films are usually shown in the original language, with Spanish subtitles, but animated features and children's films are invariably dubbed.

Bars & Clubs

Pubs and bars are often proving grounds for young bands on the way up, but are also prone to derivative entertainment such as Beatles tribute bands and Neil Diamond impersonators. Every once in a while, though, you will stumble onto something really worthwhile.

Santiago has an array of dance clubs and discotheques. Many but not all of those in the Bellavista neighborhood north of the Mapocho are sterile, expensive techno-pop venues, but this is also the mecca of the capital's gay life. Pubs in the area around Avenida Suecia and General Holley in the Providencia neighborhood more commonly feature live bands. Beach resorts like Viña del Mar, Reñaca, Concón and La Serena also have numerous dance clubs.

In cities such as Santiago and Viña del Mar, Chilean nightclubs tend to be tacky affairs, where traditional music and dances are sanitized and presented in glitzy but costly settings for foreign visitors. In ports like Valparaíso and Iquique, they can be disreputable *boites*, frequented by prostitutes and sailors.

Theater

Both in Santiago and the provinces, live theater is well attended and of high quality, from the classics and serious drama to burlesque. In the southern lakes region, many towns offer summer theater presentations in their annual cultural festivals.

Music

Santiago's most prestigious music venues, like the Teatro Municipal and the Teatro de la Universidad de Chile, are the main sites for classical concerts. See the Santiago chapter for details.

Chile's best-known rock groups, including La Ley and Los Tres, play at stadium venues, though only visiting acts like the Rolling Stones can fill the massive Estadio Nacional in the Santiago suburb of Ñuñoa. There's a flourishing, credible rock and blues scene in the less flashy venues of Bellavista and a few other areas.

Live jazz is not widespread in Chile, but the quality is often good. Santiago's Club de Jazz (☎ 02-274-1937), José Pedro Alessandri 85 in Ñuñoa, is the most reliable venue.

Peñas are nightclubs whose performers offer unapologetically political material based on folk themes. The famous *Nueva Canción Chilena* (New Chilean Song Movement) had its origins in the peñas of the 1960s, and many Chilean performers exiled after the military coup of 1973 kept the flame alive in similar venues in their adopted countries.

In the archipelago of Chiloé, folk groups often present music and dance resembling those of the Appalachian region of the eastern USA. These expansive family-oriented groups usually include a bevy of female singers, dancers of both sexes, at least three guitarists, accordion players and a variety of percussionists. Summer folk festivals are the best places to see them.

SPECTATOR SPORTS

By far the most popular spectator sport is soccer, whose British origins are apparent in the names of teams like Santiago Morning and Everton. The professional season begins in March and ends in November, though the playoffs run almost until Christmas.

The most popular teams are Colo Colo (named for the legendary Mapuche cacique), Universidad de Chile and the more elitist Universidad Católica. Followers of Colo Colo are popularly known as *garras blancas* (the white claws), while those of the Universidad de Chile are called *los de abajo* (the underdogs).

Other popular spectator sports include tennis, boxing, horse racing and basketball. Internationally, the best-known Chilean athletes are soccer forwards Iván Zamorano (a star with Spain's Real Madrid and Italy's Inter Milan) and Marcelo Salas, and tennis player Marcelo (Chino) Ríos, who recently was ranked No 1 in the world for a brief period of time.

SHOPPING

In artisans' *ferias*, found throughout the country, it is often difficult to choose among a variety of quality handicrafts. There are especially good choices in Santiago's Barrio Bellavista and the suburban comuna of Las Condes; Viña del Mar; Valdivia; the Puerto Montt suburb of Angelmó; and the village of Dalcahue, near Castro on the island of Chiloé. Copper and leather goods are excellent choices. Woolens from the Andean north are often made of llama and alpaca wool woven in geometric designs, resembling those from Peru or Bolivia.

In the Araucanía, Mapuche artisans produce a wide variety of quality ceramics, basketry, silverwork and weavings (some travelers will find parallels with the Navajo of North America) and carvings. These are widely available in popular tourist destinations like Temuco, Villarrica and Pucón.

Many cities have good antiques markets, most notably Santiago's Mercado Franklin and Valparaíso's Plaza O'Higgins. Flea markets are commonly known as *Ferias Persas* (Persian Fairs).

Getting There & Away

Chile has direct overseas air connections from North America, the UK, Europe and Australia/New Zealand. The transpacific route from Australia via Tahiti, though expensive, permits a stopover on Easter Island (Rapa Nui).

Another alternative is to fly to a neighboring country like Argentina, Bolivia or Peru, and continue to Chile by air or land. International flights within South America, however, tend to be costly unless purchased as part of intercontinental travel, but there are real bargain roundtrip fares between Buenos Aires and Santiago.

Warning

The information in this chapter is particularly vulnerable to change: Prices for international travel are volatile, routes are introduced and canceled, schedules change, special deals come and go, and rules and visa requirements are amended. Airlines and governments seem to take a perverse pleasure in making price structures and regulations as complicated as possible. You should check directly with the airline or a travel agent to make sure you understand how a fare (and any ticket you may buy) works. In addition, the travel industry is highly competitive and there are many hidden costs and benefits.

The upshot of this is that you should get opinions, quotes and advice from as many airlines and travel agents as possible before you part with your hard-earned cash. The details given in this chapter should be regarded as pointers and are not a substitute for your own careful, up-to-date research. Use fares quoted in this book as a guide only. They are approximate and based on rates advertised by travel agents and airlines at press time. Quoted airfares do not necessarily constitute a recommendation for the carrier.

AIR

Always reconfirm onward flights or return bookings by the specified time – at least 72 hours before departure on intercontinental flights. Otherwise you risk missing your flight because of rescheduling or else being classified as a 'no-show.'

Airports & Airlines

Most long-distance flights to Chile arrive at Santiago, landing at Aeropuerto Internacional Arturo Merino Benítez in the suburb of Pudahuel. There are also flights from neighboring countries to regional airports such as Arica, Iquique, Temuco, Puerto Montt and Punta Arenas.

LanChile is the national carrier, with the most extensive system of connecting internal routes, but many other reputable airlines also serve Santiago. Many major international airlines have offices or representatives in Santiago. The following list includes the most important ones:

Aeroflot
    (☎ 02-331-0244) Guardia Vieja 255,
    Oficina 1010, Providencia, Santiago

Aerolíneas Argentinas
    (☎ 02-639-3922) Moneda 756, Santiago

Aeroméxico
    (☎ 02-234-0001) Ebro 2738, Las Condes,
    Santiago

Air France
    (☎ 02-290-9330) Alcántara 44, 6th floor,
    Las Condes, Santiago

Air New Zealand
    (☎ 02-231-8626) Andrés de Fuenzalida 17,
    Oficina 62, Providencia, Santiago

Alitalia
    (☎ 02-698-3336) Alameda 949, Oficina 1003,
    Santiago

American Airlines
    (☎ 02-679-0000) Huérfanos 1199, Santiago
    (☎ 02-231-0299) Las Urbinas 043,
    Providencia, Santiago
    (☎ 02-334-4746) Av El Bosque Norte 0107,
    Local 11, Las Condes,
    Santiago

Avianca
(☎ 02-231-6646) Santa Magdalena 116, Local 106, Providencia, Santiago

British Airways
(☎ 02-330-8600) Isidora Goyenechea 2934, Oficina 302, Las Condes, Santiago

Canadian Airlines International
(☎ 02-679-0100) Huérfanos 1199, Santiago

Continental
(☎ 02-204-4000) Av Nueva Tajamar 481, Oficina 905, Santiago

Copa
(☎ 02-209-4838) Fidel Oteíza 1921, Oficina 703, Providencia, Santiago

Cubana de Aviación
(☎ 02-274-1819) Fidel Oteíza 1971, Oficina 201, Providencia, Santiago

Ecuatoriana
(☎ 02-671-2334) Moneda 1170, Santiago

Iberia
(☎ 02-698-1716) Bandera 206, 8th floor, Santiago

KLM
(☎ 02-233-0991) San Sebastián 2839, Oficina 202, Las Condes, Santiago

LanChile
(☎ 02-632-3442) Agustinas 640, Santiago
(☎ 02-232-3448) Pedro de Valdivia Norte 0139, Providencia, Santiago

Líneas Aéreas de Costa Rica (Lacsa)
(☎ 02-235-5500) Manuel Barros Borgoño 105, 2nd floor, Providencia, Santiago

Lloyd Aéreo Boliviano (LAB)
(☎ 02-672-6163) Moneda 1170, Santiago

Lufthansa
(☎ 02-630-1655) Moneda 970, 16th floor, Santiago

Northwest
(☎ 02-233-4343) Av 11 de Septiembre 2155, Torre B, Oficina 1204, Providencia, Santiago

Pluna
(☎ 02-707-8008) Av El Bosque Norte 0177, 9th floor, Santiago

Qantas
(☎ 02-232-9562) Isidora Goyenechea 2934, Oficina 301, Las Condes, Santiago

SAS
(☎ 02-233-5283) Fernández 128, Oficina 502, Providencia, Santiago

Saeta
(☎ 02-334-4427) Santa Magdalena 75, Oficina 410, Providencia, Santiago

Swissair
(☎ 02-244-2888) Alfredo Barros Errázuriz 1954, Oficina 810, Providencia, Santiago

Transportes Aéreos Mercosur (TAM)
(☎ 02-381-1333) Santa Magdalena 94, Providencia, Santiago

TAME (Ecuador)
(☎ 02-334-1758) Ebro 2747, Las Condes, Santiago

United Airlines
(☎ 02-632-0279) Tenderini 171, Santiago
(☎ 02-337-0000) El Bosque Norte 0177, 19th floor, Las Condes, Santiago

Varig
(☎ 02-707-8000) Av El Bosque Norte 0177, Oficina 903, Las Condes, Santiago

Buying Tickets

From almost everywhere, South America is a relatively expensive destination, but discount fares can reduce the bite considerably. One alternative to a straightforward round-trip is a Round-the-World ticket. If possible, take advantage of seasonal discounts and try to avoid peak times such as Christmas, New Year's or Easter. Advance purchase for a given period of time, usually two to six months, will normally provide the best, but not necessarily most flexible, deal.

The plane ticket will probably be the single most expensive item in your budget, and buying it can be intimidating. It is always worth putting aside a few hours to research the current state of the market. Start shopping for a ticket early – some of the cheapest tickets must be purchased months in advance, and some popular flights sell out early. Talk to recent travelers – they just might be able to stop you from making some of the same old mistakes. Look at the ads in newspapers and magazines, consult reference books, and watch for special offers.

Airlines can supply information on routes and timetables, but they do not supply the cheapest tickets except during fare wars and the competitive low season. Travel agents are usually a better source of bargains. Whether you go directly through an airline or use an agent, always ask the representative to clarify the fare, the route, the duration of the journey and any restrictions on the ticket.

Air Travel Glossary

Baggage Allowance This will be written on your ticket and usually includes one 20kg item to go in the hold, plus one item of hand luggage.

Bucket Shops These are unbonded travel agencies specializing in discounted airline tickets.

Bumped Just because you have a confirmed seat doesn't mean you're going to get on the plane (see Overbooking).

Cancellation Penalties If you have to cancel or change a discounted ticket, there are often heavy penalties involved; insurance can sometimes be taken out against these penalties. Some airlines impose penalties on regular tickets as well, particularly against 'no-show' passengers.

Check-In Airlines ask you to check in a certain amount of time ahead of the flight departure (usually one to two hours on international flights). If you fail to check in on time and the flight is overbooked, the airline can cancel your booking and give your seat to somebody else.

Confirmation Having a ticket written out with the flight and date you want doesn't mean you actually have a seat until the agent has checked with the airline that your status is 'OK' or confirmed. Meanwhile you could just be 'on request.'

ITX An ITX, or 'independent inclusive tour excursion,' is often available on tickets to popular holiday destinations. Officially it's a package deal combined with hotel accommodation, but many agents will sell you one of these for the flight only and give you phony hotel vouchers in the unlikely event that you're challenged at the airport.

Lost Tickets If you lose your airline ticket, an airline will usually treat it like a traveler's check and, after inquiries, issue you another one. Legally, however, an airline is entitled to treat it like cash; and if you lose it, then it's gone forever. Take good care of your tickets.

No-Shows No-shows are passengers who fail to show up for their flight. Full-fare passengers who fail to turn up are sometimes entitled to travel on a later flight. The rest are penalized (see Cancellation Penalties).

Most major airlines have ticket 'consolidators' who offer substantial discounts on fares to Latin America, but things change so rapidly that even newspaper listings can be quickly out of date. Among the best sources of information are the Sunday travel pages of major dailies like the *New York Times*, the *Los Angeles Times* or the *San Francisco Examiner*. If you're in a university town, look for bargains in the campus newspapers, such as Berkeley's *Daily Californian*. There will usually be a listing for a local affiliate of the Council on International Education Exchange (CIEE, or Council Travel), or the Student Travel Network (STA); you needn't be a student to take advantage of their services. See regional sections in this chapter for discount travel agencies and bucket shops.

Similar listings are available in the travel sections of the magazines like *Time Out* and *TNT* in the UK, or the Saturday editions of newspapers like the *Sydney Morning Herald* and the *Age* in Australia. Ads in these publications offer cheap fares, but don't be surprised if they happen to be sold out when you contact the agents: they're usually low-

Air Travel Glossary

On Request This is an unconfirmed booking for a flight.

Onward Tickets An entry requirement for many countries is that you have a ticket out of the country. If you're unsure of your next move, the easiest solution is to buy the cheapest onward ticket to a neighboring country or a ticket from a reliable airline that can later be refunded if you do not use it.

Open Jaw Tickets These are return tickets on which you fly out to one place but return from another. If available, these can save you backtracking to your arrival point.

Overbooking Airlines hate to fly with empty seats and since every flight has some passengers who fail to show up, airlines often book more passengers than they have seats. Usually excess passengers make up for the no-shows, but occasionally somebody gets bumped. Can you guess who it is most likely to be? The passengers who check in late.

Reconfirmation At least 72 hours prior to departure time of an onward or return flight, you must contact the airline and 'reconfirm' that you intend to be on the flight. If you don't do this, the airline can delete your name from the passenger list and you could lose your seat.

Restrictions Discounted tickets often have various restrictions on them – such as advance payment, minimum and maximum periods you must be away (eg, a minimum of two weeks or a maximum of one year), and penalties for changing the tickets.

Stand-by This is a discounted ticket on which you only fly if there is a seat free at the last moment. Stand-by fares are usually available only on domestic routes.

Travel Periods Ticket prices vary with the time of year. There is a low (off-peak) season and a high (peak) season, and often a low-shoulder season and a high-shoulder season as well. Usually the fare depends on your outward flight – if you depart in the high season and return in the low season, you pay the high-season fare.

season fares on obscure airlines with conditions attached.

Cheap fares fall into two distinct categories: official and consolidator. Official ones have a variety of names including advance-purchase fares, budget fares, Apex, and super-Apex. Consolidator tickets are simply discounted tickets that the airlines release through selected travel agents (not through airline offices). The cheapest fares are often non-refundable and require an extra fee for changing your flight. Many insurance policies will cover this loss if you

have to change your flight for emergency reasons. Roundtrip (return) tickets usually work out cheaper than two one-way fares – often *much* cheaper.

See the boxed text 'Ticket Options' on the types of tickets you can purchase. Discounts on such fares are often available from travel agents, but usually not in Latin America, where discount ticketing is unusual. Standby can be a cheap way of getting from Europe to the US, but there are no such flights to Chile or other parts of South America. Foreigners in Chile may pay for international air

Ticket Options

There are several types of discount tickets to South America. The main ones are:

Apex Advance purchase excursion (Apex) tickets must be bought well before departure, but they can be a good deal if you know exactly where you will be going and how long you will be staying. Usually only available on a roundtrip basis, with a 14- or 21-day advance purchase requirement, these have minimum- and maximum-stay requirements (usually 14 and 180 days respectively), allow no stopovers and stipulate cancellation charges.

Courier Flights This relatively new system, which businesses use to ensure the arrival of urgent freight without excessive customs hassles, can mean phenomenal bargains for travelers who can tolerate fairly strict requirements, such as short turnaround time – some tickets are valid for only a week or so, others for a month, but rarely any longer. In effect, the courier company ships business freight as your baggage, so that you can usually take only carry-on luggage, but you may pay as little as US$500 from New York to Buenos Aires and back.

Discounted Tickets There are two types of discounted fares – officially discounted (see Promotional Fares) and unofficially discounted. The lowest prices often impose limitations such as flying with unpopular airlines, inconvenient schedules or unpleasant routes and connections. A discounted ticket can save you things other than money – you may be able to pay Apex prices without the associated Apex advance booking and other requirements. Discounted tickets only exist where there is fierce competition.

Economy Class Valid for 12 months, economy-class (Y) tickets have the greatest flexibility within their time period. However, if you try to extend beyond a year, you'll have to pay the difference of any interim price increase.

Excursion Fares Priced midway between Apex and full economy fare, these have no advance booking requirements but may require a minimum stay. Their advantage over advance purchase is that you can change bookings and stopovers without surcharges.

Full Fares Airlines traditionally offer first-class (coded F), business-class (coded J) and economy-class (coded Y) tickets. These days there are so many promotional and discounted fares available from the regular economy class that few passengers pay full economy fare.

MCO 'Miscellaneous charges orders' (MCOs) are open vouchers for a fixed US dollar amount, which can be exchanged for a ticket on any IATA (International Air Transport Association) airline. In countries that require an onward ticket as a condition for entry, such as Panama or Colombia, this will usually satisfy immigration authorities. In a pinch, you can turn it into cash at the local offices of the airline from which you purchased it.

Point-to-Point These are discount tickets that can be bought on some routes in return for passengers waiving their rights to a stopover.

Promotional Fares These are officially discounted fares like Apex fares that are available from travel agents or direct from the airline.

RTW Some excellent bargains are possible on 'Round-the-World' tickets. See the Round-the-World Tickets section in this chapter.

Standby A discounted ticket with which you can fly only if there is a seat free at the last moment. Standby fares are usually only available on domestic routes.

tickets in local currency, but the disappearance of differential exchange rates has eliminated any incentive to do so.

One of the cheapest means of getting to South America is via courier flights, in which travelers trade all or part of their baggage allowance for a highly discounted fare and agree to accompany business equipment or documents. The major drawbacks to this, in addition to baggage being limited to carry-on items, are the relatively short travel period and the limited number of gateway airports in Europe and North America.

You may decide to pay more than the rock-bottom fare by opting for the safety of a better-known travel agent. Established firms such as worldwide STA Travel, the USA's Council Travel and Canada's Travel CUTS are viable alternatives, offering good prices to most destinations.

Once you have your ticket, write down its number, together with the flight numbers and other details, and keep the information in a separate location. If the ticket is lost or stolen, this will help you get a replacement. Remember to buy travel insurance as early as possible.

Round-the-World Tickets Having become popular in the last few years, Round-the-World (RTW) tickets are often real bargains and can work out to be no more expensive or even cheaper than an ordinary roundtrip ticket. Partnerships among various airlines are changing rapidly and prices vary dramatically depending on departure dates and length of ticket, so this is one more issue that requires thorough research before you commit.

The official airline RTW tickets are usually put together by a combination of two airlines, and they permit you to fly anywhere on their routes so long as you do not backtrack. Other restrictions are that you must usually book the first segment in advance, and cancellation penalties apply. There may be restrictions on the number of stops permitted, and tickets are usually valid from 90 days to one year. An alternative type of RTW ticket is one put together by a travel agent using a combination of discounted tickets.

Although most airlines restrict the number of segments that can be flown within the USA and Canada to four, and some airlines black out heavily traveled routes like Honolulu to Tokyo, stopovers are otherwise generally unlimited. In most cases a 14-day advance purchase is required. After the ticket is purchased, dates can be changed without penalty and tickets can be rewritten to add or delete stops for US$50 each.

Examples of RTW tickets from Australia include the British Airways/Qantas Global Explorer (the only fare that takes in Easter Island, as a LanChile codeshare with Qantas and BA), for A$2375 low season, A$2775 high season; and the BA/Qantas European Explorer, which can take in Bangkok, London, and Santiago for A$2019 low season, A$2550 high season.

Circle Pacific Tickets Similar in conception to RTW tickets, 'Circle Pacific' fares can include a US gateway, Lima, Santiago, Easter Island, Tahiti, Sydney and Singapore, starting at around US$2680.

Baggage & Other Restrictions

On most domestic and international flights you are limited to two checked bags. There could be a charge if you bring more or if the size of the bags exceeds the airline's limits. It's best to check with the individual airline if you are worried about this. On some international flights the luggage allowance is based on weight, not numbers; again, check with the airline.

If your luggage is delayed upon arrival (which is rare), some airlines will give a cash advance to purchase necessities. If sporting equipment is misplaced, the airline may pay for rentals. Should the luggage be lost, it's important to submit a claim. The airline doesn't have to pay the full amount of the claim; rather, they can estimate the value of your lost items. It may take them anywhere from six weeks to three months to process the claim and pay.

Smoking Smoking is not allowed on flights to and from Chile; within Chile, all flights are also tobacco-free except those to Easter

Island, which have both smoking and non-smoking sections.

Illegal Items Items that are illegal to take on a plane, either in checked or carry-on baggage, include aerosols of polishes, waxes and so on; tear gas and pepper spray; camp stoves with fuel; and diver's tanks that are full. Matches should not be checked.

Travelers with Special Needs

If you have special needs of any sort – vegetarianism or other dietary restrictions, a broken leg, dependence on a wheelchair, responsibility for a baby, fear of flying – let the airline know as soon as possible so that they can make arrangements accordingly. You should remind them when you reconfirm your booking (at least 72 hours before departure) and again when you check in at the airport. It may also be worth telephoning the airlines before making your booking to find out how they can handle your particular needs.

Airports and airlines can be helpful, but need advance warning. Most international airports provide escorts from check-in desk to plane where needed, and there should be ramps, lifts, accessible toilets and accessible phones. Aircraft toilets, on the other hand, are likely to present a problem; discuss this with the airline at an early stage and, if necessary, with their doctor.

Guide dogs for the blind will often have to travel in a specially pressurized baggage compartment with other animals, away from their owner; though smaller guide dogs may be admitted to the cabin. All guide dogs are subject to the same quarantine laws (six months in isolation, etc) as any other animal when entering or returning to rabies-free countries such as the UK or Australia (UK regulations are due to change soon, however).

Deaf travelers can ask for airport and in-flight announcements to be written down for them.

Children under two years old travel for 10% of the standard fare (free on some airlines) as long as they don't occupy a seat, al-though they get no baggage allowance. 'Skycots' should be provided by the airline if requested in advance; these will take a child weighing up to about 10 kg (22 pounds). Children between two and 12 years old can usually occupy a seat for half fare and do get a baggage allowance. Strollers can often be taken as hand luggage.

Departure Tax

Chilean departure tax for international flights is US$18 or its equivalent in local currency. For domestic flights, there is a departure tax of about US$8.

Note that *arriving* US air passengers pay a one-time fee of US$45, valid for the life of the passport. Chilean authorities imposed this fee after US officials increased a onetime US$20 visa application fee for Chilean nationals and have since applied it to Australians, who pay US$30 and Canadians, who pay US$55.

The USA

From the USA, the principal gateways to South America are Miami, New York and Los Angeles. Airlines that serve Santiago from the USA include LanChile, Aerolíneas Argentinas (via Buenos Aires), American, Avianca (via Bogotá and Buenos Aires), Continental, Copa (via Panama), Ecuatoriana, Líneas Aéreas de Costa Rica (Lacsa), Lloyd Aéreo Boliviano (LAB), Saeta, Trans-Brasil, United and Varig (via Brazil).

One alternative to landing in Santiago is to fly to Lima (Peru) and on to the Peruvian border city of Tacna, or to Arica (in northern Chile). Lloyd Aéreo Boliviano flies from Miami to Arica, but the routing is rather convoluted, via Manaus (Brazil), Santa Cruz de la Sierra and La Paz. For visitors to the Atacama Desert, though, this would save a long trip north from Santiago. Depending on the season, the fare ranges from US$717 to US$906, departing Monday and Wednesday only.

CIEE or Council Travel (☎ 800-226-8624 in the USA; cts@ciee.org) has agencies in the following cities and in many other college towns:

Austin, TX
(☎ 512-472-4931) 2000 Guadalupe St

Berkeley, CA
(☎ 510-848-8604) 2486 Channing Way

Boston, MA
(☎ 617-266-1926) 273 Newbury St

Denver, CO
(☎ 303-571-0630) 900 Auraria Parkway,
Tivoli Bldg

La Jolla, CA
(☎ 619-452-0630) UCSD Price Center B-023

Los Angeles, CA
(☎ 213-208-3551) 10904 Lindbrook Drive

Miami, FL
(☎ 305-670-9261) 9100 S Dadeland Blvd,
Suite 220

New York, NY
(☎ 212-822-2700) 205 E 42nd St, ground floor

Pacific Beach, CA
(☎ 619-270-6401) 953 Garnett Ave

San Francisco, CA
(☎ 415-421-3473) 530 Bush St

Seattle, WA
(☎ 206-632-2448) 1314 NE 43rd St, Suite 210

Washington, DC
(☎ 202-337-6464) 3300 M Street, NW,
2nd floor

Like Council Travel, the Student Travel Network (STA, ☎ 800-777-0112) has offices in the following cities plus many other college towns:

Berkeley, CA
(☎ 510-642-3000) ASUC Travel Center,
Univ of California

Boston, MA
(☎ 617-266-6014) 297 Newbury St

Chicago, IL
(☎ 312-786-9050) 429 S Dearborn St

Los Angeles, CA
(☎ 213-934-8722) 7202 Melrose Ave
(☎ 310-824-1574) 920 Westwood Blvd

Coral Gables, FL
(☎ 305-284-1044) Univ of Miami,
1306 Stanford Dr

New York, NY
(☎ 212-627-3111) 10 Downing St

Philadelphia, PA
(☎ 215-382-2928) 3730 Walnut St

San Francisco, CA
(☎ 415-391-8407) 51 Grant Ave

Seattle, WA
(☎ 206-633-5000) 4341 University Way NE

Washington, DC
(☎ 202-887-0912) 2401 Pennsylvania Ave,
Suite G

Courier Flights In the USA, New York and Miami are the only choices for courier flights to South America. For the widest selection of destinations, try Now Voyager (☎ 212-431-1616, fax 334-5253), 74 Varick St, Suite 307, New York, NY 10013; or Air Facility (☎ 718-712-1769), 153 Rockaway Blvd, Jamaica, NY 11434.

For up-to-date information on courier and other budget fares, send US$5 for the latest newsletter or US$25 for a year's subscription to Travel Unlimited, PO Box 1058, Allston, MA 02134. Another source of information is the International Association of Air Travel Couriers (☎ 407-582-8320, fax 582-1581, iaatc@courier.org), PO Box 1349, Lake Worth, FL 33460; its US$45 annual membership fee includes the monthly newsletter *Shoestring Traveler* (not related to Lonely Planet). It also maintains a website (www.courier.org).

Canada

LanChile no longer has direct service to Canada, but Canadian Airlines offers good connections to Toronto via Miami and to Vancouver via Los Angeles.

Travel CUTS (☎ 888-838-2887 toll-free or 416-977-2185, fax 977-4796), the Canadian counterpart of Council Travel and STA, is at 243 College St, 5th floor, Toronto, Ontario M5T 2Y1.

Mexico & Central America

Aeroméxico and LanChile combine for eight flights weekly to Mexico City. LanChile also flies twice weekly to Cancún. Copa flies daily to Panama via Lima, while Lacsa flies daily to Costa Rica and Guatemala City via Lima.

The UK & Europe

It is no longer necessarily cheaper to fly through New York or Miami than it is to go directly from Europe. There are no non-stops, but many airlines have direct flights to Santiago via Buenos Aires, Rio de Janeiro and São Paulo from major European cities like Paris, Rome, Zurich, London, Moscow, Frankfurt and Amsterdam.

London's so-called 'bucket shops' can provide the best deals; check out newspapers or magazines such as the *Evening Standard* or *Time Out* for suggestions. Advertised fares from London to Santiago have fallen recently and now start as low as £380 roundtrip.

Since bucket shops come and go, it's worth inquiring about their affiliation with the Association of British Travel Agents (ABTA), which will guarantee a refund or alternative if the agent goes out of business. The following are reputable London bucket shops:

Bridge the World
  (☎ 0171-922-0900, www.b-t-w.co.uk)
  47 Chalk Farm Rd,
  London NW1 8AN

Campus Travel
  (☎ 0171-730-3402) 52 Grovsenor Gardens,
  London SW1W 0AG

Journey Latin America
  (☎ 0181-747-3108) 16 Devonshire Rd
  Chiswick,
  London W4 2HD

Passage to South America
  (☎ 0181-767-8989) Fovant Mews,
  12 Noyna Rd, London SW17 7PH

South American Experience
  (☎ 0171-976-5511) 47 Causton St,
  London SW1

STA Travel
  (☎ 0171-361-9962) 86 Old Brompton Rd,
  London SW7 3LQ
  (☎ 0171-361-9962) 117 Euston Rd
  London NW1 2SX

Trailfinders
  (☎ 0171-938-3939) 194 Kensington High St,
  London W8
  (☎ 0171-938-3366) 42-50 Earls Court Rd,
  London W8

In Berlin, check out the magazine *Zitty* for bargain-fare ads. In Berlin and other European capitals, the following agencies are good possibilities for bargain fares:

France
  Council Travel
    (☎ 01-44-41-89-80), 1 Place de l'Odeon,
    75006 Paris

Germany
  STA Travel
    (☎ 030-283-3903) Marienstraße 25, Berlin
    (☎ 069-430191) Bergerstrasse 118, Frankfurt
  Travel Overland, Barerstrasse 73, München
    (☎ 089-27-276-300)

Ireland
  USIT Travel Office
    (☎ 01-602-1600) 19 Aston Quay, Dublin

Italy
  CTS
    (☎ 06-462-0431) Via Genova 16, Rome

Netherlands
  NBBS
    (☎ 020-642-0989) Rokin 38, Amsterdam
  Malibu Travel
    (☎ 020-623-6814) Damrak 30 Amsterdam

Spain
  TIVE
    (☎ 91-347-7778) José Ortega y Gasset 71,
    Madrid

Switzerland
  SSR
    (☎ 01-297-1111) Leonhardstrasse 10,
    Zürich

The only apparent Europe-South America courier flights are with British Airways (☎ 0870-606-1133), which offers roundtrip tickets to Buenos Aires in Argentina for £400, taxes included; given falling bucket-shop prices, the incentive to be a courier is also falling. More information is available by sending a stamped, self-addressed envelope to British Airways Travel Shop, Room E328, E Block, BA Crane Bank S551, Off Jubilee Way, PO Box 10, Heathrow Airport, Hounslow TW6 2JA.

Australia & New Zealand

Fares from Australia and New Zealand to South American have fallen, so that it is no longer cheaper to get a roundtrip flight to Los Angeles or Miami and buy a roundtrip ticket to South America from there, though that's still an option for those who plan to visit the USA anyway. Qantas flies direct to Buenos Aires and, in partnership with Lan-Chile, to Tahiti (stopovers permitted) and

Santiago. It's also possible to make the Tahiti connection with Air New Zealand.

From Australia, return fares to Santiago, which also permit a stopover on Easter Island, start at A$1659 low season, A$1925 high season and also allow a side trip to another South American city, such as Lima or Buenos Aires. Qantas' direct flights to Buenos Aires also permit a side trip to another South American city, say Santiago, with Aerolíneas Argentinas; fares start at A$1689 low season, A$1909 high season. The Aerolíneas transpolar flight from Sydney to Buenos Aires also stops in Río Gallegos for easy connections to Chilean Patagonia and Tierra del Fuego.

STA Travel (☎ 1-800-637-444), with the following Australian locations, is a good place to inquire for bargain airfares; again, student status is not necessary to use their services.

Adelaide
   (☎ 08-223-6620/6244) Level 4, Union House, Adelaide Univ
Brisbane
   (☎ 07-3221-3722) Shop 25 & 26, 111-117 Adelaide St
Canberra
   (☎ 06-247-0800) Arts Centre, ANU
Hobart
   (☎ 02-243-496) Ground Floor, Union Bldg, Univ of Tasmania
Melbourne
   (☎ 03-9349-2411) 220 Faraday St, Carlton
Perth
   (☎ 09-380-2302) 1st floor, New Guild Bldg, Univ of W Australia, Crawley
Sydney
   (☎ 02-360-1822) 9 Oxford St, Paddington

STA also has offices at the following New Zealand locations:

Auckland
   (☎ 09-307-0555) 2nd Floor, Union Bldg, Auckland Univ
Christchurch
   (☎ 03-379-909) 90 Cashel St
Wellington
   (☎ 04-385-0561) 233 Cuba St

Asia & Africa

Carriers serving Santiago from Asia, usually via North America, include All Nippon Airways (with LanChile) via Los Angeles and Varig (via Brazil). Varig also flies to Johannesburg via São Paulo.

Malaysia Airlines (with LanChile) connects Santiago with Kuala Lumpur via Buenos Aires, Johannesburg and Capetown, while South African Airways (with British Airways) flies from Santiago to Johannesburg via Buenos Aires, São Paulo and Rio de Janeiro.

Neighboring Countries

Peru LanChile has three daily flights from Lima to Santiago for US$357 one-way, but there are many discount roundtrip fares. Lacsa, Copa and Saeta all fly daily; Aeroflot flies twice weekly.

Peruvian domestic airline Aerocontinente flies from Lima to the southern city of Tacna, only 50km from the Chilean border city of Arica, for US$90 one-way. Crossing overland from Tacna and flying from Arica to Santiago is substantially cheaper than flying nonstop from Lima to Santiago.

Bolivia LanChile flies daily from Santiago to La Paz via Iquique and Arica. LAB flies weekdays to Iquique and La Paz, Tuesday to Arica and Santa Cruz, Wednesday and Sunday to Iquique and Santa Cruz, and Thursday and Saturday to Arica and La Paz.

Argentina Many airlines fly between Santiago and Buenos Aires from about US$190 one-way, but European airlines that pick up and discharge most of their passengers in Buenos Aires try to fill empty seats by selling roundtrips between the Argentine and Chilean capitals for around US$160 – not much more than the bus fare. Even throwing away the return portion, one-way passengers still come out ahead.

There are also LanChile (twice daily) and Avant (twice weekly) flights from Santiago to Mendoza (around US$98 one-way, with discount roundtrips for as little as US$90), and LanChile flights to Córdoba (twice daily, US$175 one-way, but with discount

Visiting Argentina

Even travelers who don't plan to spend a lot of time in Argentina may want to pay some brief visits, making one of the crossings through the lakes region or in order to reach far-southern Chile, which has no road connections except through Argentine Patagonia. For full details, see Lonely Planet's *Argentina, Uruguay & Paraguay*.

Visas Nationals of the USA, Canada and most Western European countries do not require visas. Australians no longer need visas, but New Zealanders, who do need them, must submit their passports with a payment of US$24 and may need to show a return or onward ticket; ordinarily, the visa will be ready the following day. Argentina's consulate in Santiago is particularly efficient. Verify whether the visa is valid for 90 days from date of issue, or 90 days from first entry.

Customs On entering Argentina, customs officers will probably check your bags for fresh fruit, but nothing else. Officials usually don't hassle foreign visitors, but if you cross the border frequently and carry electronic equipment such as a camera or a laptop computer, it's helpful to have a typed list of these belongings, with serial numbers, stamped by authorities.

Money In recent years, Argentina has controlled inflation with strict fiscal measures, including a fixed exchange rate placing the peso at par with the US dollar. Outside large cities, changing traveler's checks may be difficult or impossible without paying a very high commission, so carry a supply of cash dollars. Since the 'dollarization' of the Argentine economy, many merchants readily accept US dollars in lieu of Argentine pesos, thus avoiding currency dilemmas – but expect to receive your change in pesos. Many Argentina ATMs conveniently dispense both pesos and cash dollars.

Health Argentina requires no vaccinations for visitors entering from any country and, in general, the country presents few serious health hazards, especially in Patagonia.

Getting Around In Argentine Patagonia distances are immense, roads can be appalling and the desert can seem monotonous to some travelers: the occasional flight is a welcome relief. Argentina's two major airlines, Austral and Aerolíneas Argentinas, have extensive networks in southern Patagonia and Tierra del Fuego, but their fares are much higher than competitors such as LAPA, LADE and Kaikén Líneas Aéreas. In increasingly rare instances, fares may be less than the bus fare for the same route, but demand is high, especially in summer; try the airport if LADE staff insist that flights are completely booked.

Argentine buses, resembling those in Chile, are modern, comfortable and fast. Most large towns have a central bus terminal, though some companies operate from their own private offices. In certain more-remote and less-populated areas, buses are few or even nonexistent, so be patient. Southern Patagonia has no passenger railways.

Hitchhiking is relatively easy in Argentina, but traffic in Patagonia and Tierra del Fuego is sparse and there may be long waits between lifts. Since it is never entirely safe, Lonely Planet does not recommend hitchhiking.

roundtrips for as little as US$139). TAN, the regional carrier of Argentina's Neuquén province, connects Temuco with the Argentine city of Neuquén and Puerto Montt with Bariloche and Neuquén.

In southern Patagonia, LanChile's weekly flights to the Falkland Islands stop in Río Gallegos, Argentina, on the third Saturday of each month; return flights from the Falklands stop in Río Gallegos on the fourth Saturday. Regional carriers also link Punta to Río Gallegos and Río Grande (Tierra del Fuego), but there are no direct flights to Ushuaia.

Other Countries LanChile flies from Santiago to Guayaquil (Ecuador), Bogotá

(Colombia), Caracas (Venezuela) and Asunción (Paraguay) in conjunction with TAM, and to São Paulo and Rio de Janeiro (Brazil), and from Iquique to Asunción three times weekly in conjunction with TAM.

Avianca links Santiago with Bogotá daily, either nonstop or via Buenos Aires. Ecuatoriana flies five times weekly to and from Quito and Guayaquil, while Saeta flies to Guayaquil and Quito daily except Sunday. TAME flies three times weekly to Guayaquil and Quito.

Pluna flies five times weekly to Montevideo, the only nonstop service to the Uruguayan capital. TransBrasil and Varig fly to Brazilian destinations.

LAND

Chile has a handful of border crossings with Peru and Bolivia, and many with Argentina, only a few of which are served by public transportation. Chile's Ministerio de Obras Públicas (MOP, Public Works Ministry) continues to improve border crossings to these countries, but especially those to Argentina, to facilitate contact with the Mercosur free-trade zone. Photographers should note that at major land borders, such as Los Libertadores complex between Santiago and Mendoza, and the Pajaritos crossing between Osorno and Bariloche, Chilean customs officials x-ray the baggage of arriving bus passengers.

Most international buses depart from (and arrive at) Terminal de Buses Santiago. There are direct buses to every country on the continent except the Guianas and Bolivia, but only masochists are likely to attempt the 4½ - to 10-day marathons to destinations like Quito, Ecuador (US$110); Bogotá, Colombia (US$160); and Caracas, Venezuela (US$200). Tepsa ($\pi$ 02-779-5263) and Ormeño (π 02-779-3443) cover these northern routes, with stops in Lima, Peru (US$70, 48 hours), about the single longest stretch any traveler is likely to undertake.

Argentina is the most frequent destination; the city of Mendoza has a much wider selection of buses and destinations within Argentina than is available from Santiago. Lines crossing the Andes to Mendoza (seven

hours, US$25) and Buenos Aires (18 hours, US$65) include Ahumada ($\pi$ 02-778-2703; also at Terminal Los Héroes, (π 02-696-9798), Covalle Bus (π 02-778-7576), Fénix (π 02-776-3253), Nueva O'Higgins San Martín (π 02-779-5727), TAC (π 02-779-6920), Tur-Bus (π 02-776-3690) and Cata (π 02-779-3660).

Chile Bus (π 02-776-5557) goes to Mendoza; São Paulo, Brazil (72 hours, US$112), Rio de Janeiro (US$107) and intermediates, and to Bolivia via the Norte Grande. Pluma (π 02-779-6054) goes to Mendoza; Montevideo, Uruguay (US$80, 25 hours); and Brazilian destinations. Tas Choapa (π 02-779-4925) serves Mendoza, Córdoba (15 hours, US$57), Buenos Aires (US$64), Montevideo (US$70) and Bariloche (21 hours, US$36). EGAS ($\pi$ 02-779-3536) also goes to Montevideo and Brazilian destinations, while El Rápido Internacional (π 02-779-0316) goes to Argentina and Uruguay. Pullman Bus (π 02-779-5243) goes to Asunción, Paraguay (US$70, 30 hours) Tuesday and Friday at 1 pm.

Igi Llaima (π 02-779-1751) and Buses Jac (π 02-776-1582) go to Junín de los Andes, San Martín de Los Andes and Neuquén via Temuco, as does Cruz del Sur (π 02-779-0607).

From Terminal Santiago, Coitram (π 02-776-1891) and Nevada (π 02-776-4116) run taxi colectivos to Mendoza, which are only slightly more expensive (about US$28) and far quicker than buses – and drivers may stop on request for photo opportunities on the spectacular Andean crossing. Prices may be open to haggling outside the peak summer season.

Peru

Tacna to Arica is the only overland crossing between Peru and Chile. There is a choice of bus, taxi or train. For details, see the Arica entry in the Norte Grande chapter.

Bolivia

Road connections between Bolivia and Chile have improved dramatically, with the highway from Arica to La Paz completely paved and the route from Iquique to

Colchane and beyond to Oruro and La Paz well under way. There is bus service on both routes, but more on the former.

The only train is a weekly service from Calama to the border village of Ollagüe, with connections to Oruro and La Paz; there is a parallel but mostly unpaved highway here.

It's possible to travel from Uyuni, Bolivia to San Pedro de Atacama via the Portezuelo del Cajón, near the juncture of the Chilean, Bolivian and Argentine borders, but no regularly scheduled public transport exists in this area. See the San Pedro de Atacama entry for details.

Argentina

Except in Patagonia, every land crossing to Argentina involves crossing the Andes. There is public transportation on only a few of these crossings, and some passes are closed in winter.

Calama to Jujuy & Salta Currently being paved, Ruta 27 over the Paso de Jama is now the main route over the Andes via San Pedro de Atacama and has regular bus service (advance booking is advisable, as seats are limited). Slightly farther south, motorists will find the 4079m Paso de Lago Sico a reasonable summer alternative that goes to Salta without passing through Jujuy, but the higher Paso de Huaytiquina is more difficult. Chilean customs are at San Pedro.

There is an occasional Argentine passenger train from Salta to the border at Socompa, but only freight service beyond, although the uncomfortable Chilean freight will sometimes carry passengers to the abandoned station of Augusta Victoria (where it's possible to hitch to Antofagasta), or to Baquedano on Ruta 5 (the Panamericana), where it's easy to catch a bus. See the entries on Antofagasta and Baquedano for details.

Copiapó to Catamarca & La Rioja There is no public transportation over the 4726m Paso de San Francisco, but an increasing amount of vehicle traffic is using this improving route.

La Serena to San Juan Dynamited by the Argentine military during the Beagle Channel dispute of 1978-79, the 4779m Paso del Agua Negra is open for automobile traffic, but the road is rough. Bus services continue to use Los Libertadores crossing west of Mendoza. It is a good bicycle route, however, and tours from La Serena may soon carry passengers to hot springs on the Argentine side.

Santiago or Valparaíso to Mendoza & Buenos Aires Many bus companies service this most popular of crossing points between the two countries, along Ruta 60 through the Los Libertadores tunnel. Taxi colectivos are faster, more comfortable and only slightly more expensive. Winter snow sometimes closes the route, but rarely for long.

Talca to Malargüe & San Rafael Occasional minibuses now use Ruta 115 to cross the 2553m Paso Pehuenche, southeast of Talca. A new crossing is under consideration from Curicó over the 2938m Paso del Planchón, also to San Rafael.

Southern Mainland Routes There are a number of scenic crossings from Temuco south to Puerto Montt, some involving bus-boat shuttles. These are popular in summer, so make advance bookings whenever possible.

Temuco to Zapala & Neuquén

This route crosses the Andes over the 1884m Paso de Pino Hachado, directly east of Temuco via Curacautín and Lonquimay, along the upper Río Biobío. A slightly more southerly route is the 1298m Paso de Icalma. Both have occasional bus traffic in summer.

Temuco to San Martín de los Andes

The most popular route from Temuco passes Lago Villarrica, Pucón and Curarrehue en route to the Paso de Mamuil Malal (known to Argentines as Paso Tromen). On the Argentine side, the road skirts the northern slopes of Volcán Lanín. There is regular summer bus service, but the pass is closed in winter.

Valdivia to San Martín de los Andes

This route starts with a bus from Valdivia to Panguipulli, Choshuenco and Puerto Fuy, followed by a ferry across Lago Pirehueico to the village of Pirehueico. From Pirehueico a local bus goes to Argentine customs at 659m Paso Huahum, where travelers can catch a bus to San Martín.

Osorno to Bariloche via Paso Cardenal Samoré

This crossing, commonly known as Pajaritos, is the quickest land route in the southern lakes region, passing through Parque Nacional Puyehue on the Chilean side and Parque Nacional Nahuel Huapi on the Argentine side. It has frequent bus service all year.

Puerto Montt/Puerto Varas to Bariloche

Very popular in summer but open all year, this bus-ferry combination via Parque Nacional Vicente Pérez Rosales starts in Puerto Montt or Puerto Varas. A ferry goes from Petrohué, at the west end of Lago Todos Los Santos, to Peulla, and a bus crosses 1022m Paso de Pérez Rosales to Argentine immigration at Puerto Frías. After crossing Lago Frías by launch, there's a short bus hop to Puerto Blest on Lago Nahuel Huapi and another ferry to Puerto Pañuelo (Llao Llao). From Llao Llao, there is frequent bus service to Bariloche.

Southern Patagonian Routes

Since the opening of the Camino Austral (Southern Highway) south of Puerto Montt, it's become more common to cross between Chile and Argentina in this area. There are also several crossing points in extreme southern Patagonia and Tierra del Fuego. See also boxed text 'Traveling through Argentine Patagonia' in the Aisén & the Camino Austral chapter.

Puerto Ramírez to Esquel

There are two options here. From the village of Villa Santa Lucía, on the Camino Austral, there is a good lateral that forks at Puerto Ramírez, at the southeastern end of Lago Yelcho. The north fork goes to Futaleufú, where a bridge crosses the river to the Argentine side where you can catch colectivos to Esquel. The south fork goes to Palena and Argentine customs at Carrenleufú, which has bus service to Corcovado, Trevelin and Esquel. Customs and immigration are much more efficient at Futaleufú.

Puerto Cisnes to José de San Martín

At Villa Amengual, a lateral off the Camino Austral climbs the valley of the Río Cisnes to Paso de Río Frías and the Argentine province of Chubut. This crossing may close because so little traffic uses it.

Coihaique to Comodoro Rivadavia

There are several buses per week, often heavily booked, from Coihaique to Comodoro Rivadavia via Río Mayo. For private vehicles, there is an alternative route via Balmaceda to Perito Moreno via the 502m Paso Huemules.

Puerto Ingeniero Ibáñez to Perito Moreno

This route follows the north shore of Lago General Carrera (Lago Buenos Aires on the Argentine side). There is no public transport, but since all vehicles must pass through the *carabineros* (national police) post on the lakefront in Puerto Ibáñez, patient waiting may yield a lift.

Chile Chico to Los Antiguos

From Puerto Ibáñez, take the ferry to Chile Chico on the southern shore of Lago Carrera and a bus to Los Antiguos, which has connections to the Patagonian coastal town of Caleta Olivia or south to El Chaltén or El Calafate. There is also a narrow mountain road with regular bus services to Chile Chico from Cruce El Maitén at the southwestern end of Lago General Carrera.

Cochrane to Bajo Caracoles

Perhaps the most desolate crossing in the Aisén region, 647m Paso Roballos links the hamlet of Cochrane with a flyspeck outpost in Argentina's Santa Cruz province.

Puerto Natales to Río Turbio & El Calafate

Frequent buses connect Puerto Natales to the Argentine coal town of Río Turbio, where many Chileans work; from Río Turbio there are further connections to Río Gallegos and El Calafate. All year, but far more frequently in summer, there are buses from Puerto Natales to El Calafate, the gateway to Argentina's Parque Nacional Los Glaciares, via Paso Río don Guillermo. Improvements on Argentine RN 40 have cut the time on this route nearly in half, from about 10 to six hours.

Punta Arenas to Río Gallegos

Daily, many buses travel on the improved highway between Punta Arenas and Río Gallegos. It's a six-hour trip because of slow customs checks and a rough segment of Argentine RN 3. There are also occasional flights.

Punta Arenas to Tierra del Fuego

From Punta Arenas, a 2½-hour ferry trip or a 10-minute flight takes you to Porvenir, on Chilean Tierra del Fuego, where there are two buses weekly to the Argentine city of Río Grande, which has connections to Ushuaia. Direct buses travel from Punta Arenas to

SOUTHERN PATAGONIAN ROUTES

Ushuaia via the more northerly, more frequent and shorter ferry crossing at Primera Angostura. Regular air service connects Punta Arenas with Río Grande but not directly with Ushuaia.

Puerto Williams to Ushuaia

Because of local commercial-political intrigues, mostly on the Argentine side, passenger boat service from Puerto Williams, on Isla Navarino (reached by plane or boat from Punta Arenas) opposite the Argentine city of Ushuaia is sporadic, undependable and frequently interrupted. Small boats sometimes use the small Argentine landing spot of Puerto Almanza.

ORGANIZED TOURS

Increasingly, both Chilean and foreign companies have become involved in nature-oriented tourism (popularly, but not always accurately, known as *turismo ecológico* or *turismo aventura*). More conventional tours are also available. For visitors with limited time, especially in areas such as Patagonia where logistics can be awkward, a tour may be ideal. Almost all of these companies have websites with more details on their offerings.

From the USA

Festival Tours (☎ 407-850-0680, 800-225-0117, fax 407-240-1480), 737 W Oak Ridge Rd, Orlando, FL 32809, arranges a variety of trips to Chile, including ski weeks at Portillo and Valle Nevado, four-day excursions to Easter Island, and visits to Laguna San Rafael, Chilean and Argentine Patagonia, Isla Grande de Tierra del Fuego and Antarctica.

For travelers of at least 55 years of age, Elderhostel (☎ 617-426-8056), 76 Federal St, Boston, MA 02110, operates several two-week tours including Patagonia and the lakes region, starting in Buenos Aires and ending in Santiago; the Chilean heartland, taking in Valparaíso, Viña del Mar, Santiago and Los Andes; the Atacama desert, including San Pedro de Atacama and Iquique; and the Mapuche territory, including Temuco, Valdivia and Puerto Varas. Eldertreks (☎ 416-588-5000, 800-741-7956, fax 416-588-9839, eldertreks@eldertreks.com), 597 Markham St, Toronto, Ontario M6G 2L7, specializes in trips for vigorous over-50s to destinations such as Easter Island.

Well-established North American adventure companies operating Patagonian trips, which sometimes begin in Argentina but take in substantial parts of Chilean Patagonia, include Wilderness Travel (☎ 510-548-0420, 800-247-6700), 801 Allston Way, Berkeley, CA 94710, and Mountain Travel Sobek (☎ 510-527-8100, 800-227-2384, see the boxed text 'Online Services' in the Facts for the Visitor chapter), 6420 Fairmount Ave, El Cerrito, CA 94530. Both have lavishly illustrated catalogs of their numerous excursions to Patagonia and the Andean lakes. Itineraries range from easy day hikes, with stays at hotels and campgrounds, to strenuous treks and climbs, bivouacking in the backcountry. These companies also offer white-water rafting and kayaking on the Biobío and Futaleufú Rivers, and sea kayaking in the Chilean fjords.

The company Wildland Adventures (☎ 206-365-0686, 800-345-4453, fax 206-363-6615, info@wildland.com), 3516 NE 155th St, Seattle, WA 98155, arranges 10-day itineraries through local guides and outfitters in Patagonia for two or more people from around US$1800 per person (land cost – does not include your airfare to Chile). Another organization to try is Lost World Adventures (☎ 404-373-5820, 800-999-0558, fax 404-377-1902, info@lostworldadventures.com), 220 Second Ave, Decatur, GA 30030.

Natural Habitat Adventures (☎ 303-449-3711, 800-543-8917, fax 449-3712), at 2945 Center Green Court, Boulder, CO 80301, runs 21-day tours to the Falkland Islands, South Georgia and Antarctica via Santiago or Ushuaia (Argentina), starting around US$8900.

Nature Expeditions International (☎ 800-869-0639, (see the boxed text 'Online Services' in the Facts for the Visitor chapter), 6400 E El Dorado Circle, Suite 210, Tucson, AZ 85715, offers a variety of Chilean tours, including a 15-day trip to Easter Island (US$2490), a combination lakes region-Rapa Nui tour in a 17-day excursion (US$2890) or the lakes region and Chilean Patagonia on a 16-day trip (US$3690). Some of the company's 10- to 20-day Pacific cruises (US$2325 to US$10,950) visit Rapa Nui, while their 15- to 21-day Antarctica cruises (US$4865 to US$13,335) visit the Chilean fjords, the Falkland Islands and South Georgia as well. Grand Circle Travel (☎ 800-221-2610), 347 Congress St, Boston, MA 02210, offers discount fares for Norwegian Cruise Line's 21-day sail through the Chilean fjords and on to the Falkland Islands and Buenos Aires.

Kayaker Chris Spelius, a former US Olympian who's now a Chilean resident, runs white-water trips on the Biobío, Fuy and Futaleufú Rivers through Expediciones Chile (☎ 847-400-0790, 888-488-9082, office@kayakchile.com, www.raftingchile.com), PO Box 1640, Bryson, NC 28713. Class IV and V white-water descents run from December through February, last one to three weeks, and are mostly in the US$2400 to US$2600 range. Trip videos, including material on the environmental crisis facing Chilean rivers, are available through the above address. Rafting, fishing, horseback riding and other activities are also possible.

Several other reputable professional rafting and kayaking companies frequent the Futaleufú and other Chilean rivers, with similar conservation commitments, including the Nantahala Outdoor Center (☎ 888-662-1662, ext 333, adtrav@noc.com), 13077 Hwy 19 West, Bryson, NC 28713; Earth River Expeditions (☎ 914-626-2665, 800-643-2784, fax 914-626-4423, earthriv@ulster.net), 180 Towpath Rd, Accord, NY 12404; and Bío Bío Expeditions (☎ 800-246-7238, fax 530-582-6565, H2Omarc@aol.com), PO Box 2028, Truckee, CA 96160.

Backroads (☎ 510-527-1555, 800-462-2848, fax 510-527-1444, www.backroads.com), 801 Cedar St, Berkeley, CA 94710, conducts 11-day mountain-biking trips (US$3298) and hiking expeditions (US$3398) in the Chilean-Argentine lake district, with accommodations in comfortable lodges. The company also offers a cycling trip that takes in parts of Patagonia along with the Chilean wine region.

Rocky Mountain Adventures (☎ 970-493-4005, 800-858-6808), PO Box 1989, Fort Collins, CO 80522, arranges 10-day tours of Chile's Futaleufú area that stress hiking,

horseback riding, rafting, kayaking and fly-fishing for around US$1500 (not including airfare). Another company, Off the Beaten Path (☎ 406-586-1311, 800-445-2995, fax 406-587-4147, caesars@offbeatenpath.com), 27 East Main, Bozeman, MT 59715, specializes in fly-fishing trips in the Aisén region.

Far Horizons Archaeological & Cultural Trips (☎ 505-343-9400, 800-552-4585, fax 505-343-8076, journey@farhorizon.com), PO Box 91900, Albuquerque, NM 87199-1900, specializes in trips to Rapa Nui, including one during the Tapati festival. The company's excursions also take in important archaeological sites in the Norte Grande. Trip leaders are well-known scholars of the archaeology and culture of Easter Island.

Smithsonian Study Tours (☎ 202-357-4700), 1100 Jefferson Drive SW, Suite 3077, Washington DC 20560, does a 14-day tour taking in Santiago, Puerto Varas and vicinity, Punta Arenas, Puerto Natales and Torres del Paine. With roundtrip airfare from Miami, the cost is US$5835 per person.

From the UK & Europe

Journey Latin America (☎ 0181-747-3108), 16 Devonshire Rd, Chiswick, London W4 2HD, takes smallish groups to Latin America, specializing in tours for one or two people. Explore Worldwide (info@explore.co.uk), 1 Frederick St, Aldershot, Hants GU11 1LQ, is also a Latin America specialist.

OTT Expeditions (☎ 0114-258-8508, fax 255-1603, www.ottexpeditions.co.uk), Southwest Centre, Suite 5b, Troutbeck Road, Sheffield S7 2QA, is primarily a mountaineering company but also does three-week trekking excursions in Patagonia, including Torres del Paine, for £1995 including airfare.

From Australia

In Australia, try World Expeditions at three locations: 441 Kent St, Sydney, NSW 2000 (☎ 02-9264-3366, fax 9261-1974, enquiries@worldexpeditions.com.au); 1/393 Little Bourke St, Melbourne, Victoria 3000 (☎ 03-9670-8400, fax 9670-7474, travel@worldexpeditions.com.au); and Shop 2, 36 Agnes Street,

Fortitude Valley (Brisbane) 4006 (☎ 07-3216-0823, fax 07-3216 0827, adventure@worldexpeditions.com.au).

Peregrine Bird Tours (☎ 03-9727-3343), 2 Drysdale Place, Mooroolbark, Victoria 3138, often schedules trips to Argentina. Peregrine Adventures (not affiliated with Peregrine Bird Tours), 258 Lonsdale St, Melbourne, Victoria 3000 (☎ 03-9662-2800, fax 9662-2422), also sometimes runs tours.

Condor Ski Tours (☎ 02-9299-7363, fax 9262-1713, condorsouthamerica@msn.com.au), 350 Kent St, 1st floor, Sydney NSW 2000, arranges weeklong skiing tours to all of the major resorts around Santiago, as well as Termas de Chillán and some resorts across the Andes in Argentina. You can contact them at their mailing address which is PO Box R 96, Royal Exchange, Sydney NSW 2000.

Getting Around

Transportation within Chile is generally straightforward. The fast, punctual, modern and comfortable buses on the main highways are preferable to trains running on railways that have been neglected since the early 1970s. Flights tend to be reasonably priced, with occasional bargain discounts, and there are several interesting and scenic passenger ferries.

AIR

Because of Chile's latitudinal extension, you may want to avoid tiresome and time-consuming backtracking by taking an occasional flight. For instance, you can travel overland through Chilean and Argentine Patagonia to Tierra del Fuego and then fly from Punta Arenas to Puerto Montt or Santiago. The return flight should be no more expensive than a combination of bus fares and accommodations.

Domestic Air Services

Most cities have domestic airports with commercial air service, except for some larger cities near Santiago and towns near other major cities. Santiago's Aeropuerto Internacional Arturo Merino Benítez has a separate domestic terminal; Santiago also has smaller airfields for air taxi services to the Juan Fernández archipelago. Major domestic airports are in Arica, Iquique, Calama, Copiapó, La Serena, Temuco, Valdivia, Puerto Montt, Balmaceda (Coihaique) and Punta Arenas.

Two major airlines, LanChile and Ladeco, offer domestic services, but onetime upstart Avant Airlines is now a well established carrier. There are rumors of further competition, but nothing concrete as yet. LanChile has several daily northbound flights to Antofagasta, Calama, Iquique and Arica, as well as southbound flights to Puerto Montt and Punta Arenas. Some of these flights also make some intermediate stops. They also fly two or three times weekly to Easter Island.

Owned by LanChile, Ladeco has daily flights to La Serena, Antofagasta, Calama, Iquique, Arica, Puerto Montt and Punta Arenas. They also have less-frequent flights to Temuco, Valdivia, Osorno and Balmaceda-Coihaique. The independent Avant Airlines, which is part of the Tur-Bus conglomerate, serves the same destinations less frequently than the other carriers but is growing rapidly.

All three major airlines have computerized booking services, so you can make reservations for domestic and international flights from their offices anywhere in the country or overseas. Both also publish detailed flight timetables to which they adhere closely. Telephone reservations are also a breeze to make. A list of central airline offices in Santiago and regional cities appears in the Getting There & Away chapter.

LanChile is a frequent-flyer partner of American Airlines. Do not be surprised, however, if credits for Chilean international and domestic flights fail to show up on your quarterly mileage statements – be sure to save your tickets and boarding passes so you'll be able to corroborate your flights when you return home.

Minor regional airlines include DAP, which connects Punta Arenas with Tierra del Fuego, Puerto Williams and Antarctica; Lassa, Líneas Aéreas Robinson Crusoe and Servicios Aéreos Ejecutivos, which all operate air taxis to the Juan Fernández Archipelago (for more information, see the Juan Fernández chapter); and several air taxi companies that connect isolated settlements in the Aisén region, south of Puerto Montt.

Smoking is prohibited on all domestic flights, except LanChile's Easter Island (Rapa Nui) service, which offers its passengers a choice of either smoking or non-smoking.

The following is a list of domestic airline locations in Santiago:

Avant
(☎ 02-290-5000) Alameda 107
(☎ 02-639-8969) Huérfanos 885
(☎ 02-252-0300) Av Pedro de Valdivia 041

Ladeco
(☎ 02-639-5053, fax 633-8343) Huérfanos 1157
(☎ 02-334-7629) Av Providencia 2286

Lassa
(☎ 02-273-4354/5209, fax 273-4309)
Av Larraín 7941

Servicios Aéreos Ejecutivos (SAE)
(☎/fax 02-229-3419) Av Apoquindo 7850,
Torres 3, Local 4

Transportes Aéreos Robinson Crusoe
(☎ 02-534-4650, fax 531-3772) Av Pajaritos
3030, Oficina 604

Fares

Ranges of one-way, domestic coach airfares
from Santiago appear in the table, but remember that cheap return fares, which
change frequently, may be available. Lan-
Chile and Ladeco have nearly identical rates;
Avant fares are slightly cheaper. On most
flights, a certain number of discount seats are
available and, if your travel schedule is flexible, you may be able to take advantage of
these. Usually discount ticket purchases must
be made at least three days in advance.

For fare information from other cities in
Chile, see Air in individual cities' Getting
There & Away sections.

destination	one-way fare from Santiago
Antofagasta	US$108 to US$183
Arica	US$126 to US$208
Calama	US$117 to US$179
Coihaique (Balmaceda)	US$115 to US$193
Concepción	US$68 to US$88
Copiapó	US$82 to US$142
Iquique	US$123 to US$206
La Serena	US$67 to US$97
Puerto Montt	US$81 to US$159
Punta Arenas	US$133 to US$283
Temuco	US$73 to US$120

Air Passes

For US$250, LanChile and Ladeco offer a
'Visit Chile Pass,' valid for 30 days, that includes three separate flight coupons so that it

would be possible, for example, to fly from
Santiago to Punta Arenas and back, with a
stop in Puerto Montt. Additional coupons
cost US$60 up to a maximum of six. Destina-
tions include Arica, Iquique, Calama, Antofagasta, Copiapó, Concepción, Puerto Montt,
Balmaceda/Coihaique and Punta Arenas.

Passes, which must be purchased outside
Chile, are available only to foreigners and
nonresidents of Chile. Note that if your international travel is not with LanChile, the
pass costs US$350, and US$80 for each additional coupon. It is no longer possible to
use the pass to travel to Easter Island.

BUS

Major highways and some others are paved,
except for large parts of the Camino Austral
south of Puerto Montt, but many secondary
roads are gravel or dirt. Buses on main roads
are comfortable, some are luxurious, and
nearly all are well maintained, fast and punctual. They generally have toilet facilities and
often serve coffee, tea and even meals on
board; if not, they make regular stops. By
European or North American standards,
fares are a bargain.

Most Chilean cities have a central bus terminal, but in some the companies have separate offices. Offices of bus companies tend
to be within a few blocks of each other. The
bus stations are well organized, with destinations, schedules and fares prominently
displayed.

Santiago has four main bus terminals.
Since closure of the dilapidated Terminal de
Buses Norte, most northbound long-distance
services now use the rejuvenated Terminal
San Borja (☎ 02-776-0645; Metro: Estación
Central), Alameda 3250, whose inconspicuous access is via the market alongside the
main railway station. All services are likely
to be in flux as companies relocate to better
facilities.

Tur-Bus and Pullman Bus, however, use
the Terminal de Buses Alameda (☎ 02-776-
2424) at the corner of Alameda and Jotabeche (Metro: Universidad de Santiago),
while buses for Valparaíso and Viña del Mar
and many southbound destinations leave
from the adjacent Terminal de Buses Santiago

(also known as Terminal de Buses Sur, ☎ 02-779-1385), Alameda 3850 between Ruiz Tagle and Nicasio Retamales.

Some northbound buses also leave from Terminal Los Héroes, on Tucapel Jiménez near the Alameda, where some long-distance buses from Terminal Santiago make an additional stop for passengers.

Several companies also have ticket offices at the Torres de Tajamar, Av Providencia 1100, including Tur-Bus (☎ 02-236-2595), Tas Choapa (☎ 02-235-2405), Pullman Bus (☎ 02-235-8142), Los Corsarios (☎ 02-235-4810), Tramaca (☎ 02-235-1695), Fénix Pullman Norte (☎ 02-235-9707), Buses Jac (☎ 02-235-2484) and Libac (☎ 02-235-2520).

Classes

Long-distance buses now employ a bewildering variety of terms to describe their seating arrangements – about the only one common to all is *Pullman*, which means 44 ordinary reclining seats, two on each side of the aisle. *Executivo* and *semi-cama* usually mean 32 seats, providing extra legroom and calfrests, while *salón cama* sleepers seat only 24 passengers, with only three seats per row and additional legroom. If you have any doubt about the type of service offered, ask for a seat diagram; obviously, seat No 44 is not going to provide the same amenities that No 24 would on a bus with fewer seats.

Normally departing at night, these premium bus services cost upwards of 50% more than ordinary buses, but on long hauls like Arica to Santiago, they merit consideration. Regular buses are also comfortable enough for most purposes, however. Smoking is now prohibited on buses throughout the country.

On back roads, which include about 70,000km of gravel or dirt roads, transport is slower and buses are less frequent, older and more basic. These *micros*, which often lack reclining seats, may be packed with peasants and their produce, but journeys are usually short.

Reservations & Fares

Except during the holiday season (Christmas, January and February, Easter and mid-September's patriotic holidays), it is rarely necessary to book more than a few hours in advance. On very long trips, like Arica to Santiago, or rural routes with limited services (along the Camino Austral, for instance), advance booking is a good idea.

Fares can vary dramatically among companies, so explore several possibilities. Promotions *(ofertas)* can reduce normal fares by half; student reductions, by 25%. Discounts are common outside the peak summer season, and bargaining may even be possible. Try it if the bus is soon to leave and appears to have empty seats. Fares between important destinations are listed throughout this book. For long journeys, especially to the desert north, consider a *salón cama* bus, which has reclining sleeperette seats with footrests, calfrests and extra legroom. Chile's best bus line, Tur-Bus, is more expensive than most but also has a frequent user program that allows members to reserve by phone at a 10% discount.

For a general idea of how much bus travel costs – and how long trips take – see the table 'Sample Bus Fares from Santiago' later in this chapter.

The following is a list of companies serving coastal and northern destinations from Terminal San Borja in Santiago:

Buses Al Sur – to Rancagua
  (☎ 02-778-6637)

Carmelita – to Iquique, Arica and intermediates
  (☎ 02-778-7579)

Combarbalá – to various parts of the Norte Chico
  (02-696-0313)

Cóndor Bus – Valparaíso/Viña del Mar, Norte Chico beaches, Puerto Montt and intermediates
  (☎ 02-778-7089)

Covalle Bus – to La Serena
  (☎ 02-778-7576)

Elqui Bus – to the Norte Chico
  (☎ 02-778-7045)

Expreso Norte – to Norte Chico
  (☎ 02-778-7570)

Evans – to Arica and intermediate points along the Panamericana
  (☎ 02-778-7361)

Fénix Pullman Norte – to Arica and intermediate points
  (☎ 02-778-7074)

Flota Barrios – to Valparaíso/Viña del Mar;
   north to Arica and intermediates
   (☎ 02-778-7076)

Géminis – to Arica and intermediates
   (☎ 02-697-2132)

Golondrina – to Calera, Olmué, Limache
   (Parque Nacional Las Campanas)
   (☎ 02-778-7336)

Lasval – to the Norte Chico
   (☎ 02-672-1817)

Libac – to the Norte Chico
   (☎ 02-778-7071)

Ligua – to La Ligua
   (☎ 02-698-7339)

Lit – to Los Vilos, Coquimbo and La Serena
   (☎ 02-778-6857)

Los Corsarios – to Norte Chico and Antofagasta
   (☎ 02-778-7087)

Los Diamantes de Elqui – to Los Vilos,
   La Serena and Copiapó
   (☎ 02-672-4415)

Pullman Fichtur – to Arica and intermediates
   (☎ 02-778-7086)

Ramos Cholele – to Iquique and Arica
   (☎ 02-671-7388)

Ruta 57 – to Los Andes and San Felipe
   (☎ 02-779-4224)

Tas Choapa – to Los Vilos, Copiapó and
   intermediates
   (☎ 02-778-6827)

Tramaca – to Antofagasta, Calama, Arica and
   intermediate points
   (02-764-5863)

Tur-Bus – to Panamericana destinations from
   Arica to Puerto Montt
   (☎ 02-778-7336)¶

Vía Choapa – to the Norte Chico
   (☎ 02-778-7570)

Companies serving northern and southern
destinations from Santiago's Terminal Los
Héroes include:

Ahumada – to the central coast, and to Puerto
   Montt and intermediates
   (☎ 02-696-9798)

Cruz del Sur – to Los Lagos and Chiloé
   (☎ 02-696-9324)

Fénix Pullman Norte – to Arica and intermediate
   points
   (☎ 02-696-9321)

Flota Barrios – to Valparaíso/Viña del Mar; north
   to Arica and intermediates
   (☎ 02-696-9311)

Lasval – to the Norte Chico
   (☎ 02-672-4904)

Libac – to the Norte Chico
   (☎ 02-698-5974)

Pullman del Sur – to Talco
   (☎ unlisted)

Tas Choapa – to Los Vilos, Copiapó and
   intermediates
   (☎ 02-696-9326)

Tramaca – to Antofagasta, Calama, Arica and
   intermediates
   (☎ 02-695-8009)

Buses serving various destinations from the
smaller Terminal de Buses Alameda,
Alameda 3750, at the southern exit from the
Universidad de Santiago Metro station,
include:

Pullman Bus – to Arica and intermediate points
   northbound; Valparaíso/Viña del Mar
   (☎ 02-776-2569)

Tur-Bus – to Panamericana destinations, from
   Arica to Puerto Montt; Valparaíso/Viña del Mar
   (☎ 02-778-0808)

Companies serving southern and some
northern destinations from the Terminal de
Buses Santiago (☎ 02-779-1385) include:

Ahumada – to the central coast, and to Puerto
   Montt and intermediates
   (☎ 02-778-2703)

Andimar – to the south central coast
   (☎ 02-779-3810)

Bus Norte – to southern Los Lagos and Punta
   Arenas
   (☎ 02-779-5433)

Buses Al Sur – to Rancagua and Talca
   (☎ 02-779-2305)

Buses Jac – to Temuco, Villarrica and Pucón
   (☎ 02-776-1582)

Cóndor Bus – to Valparaíso/Viña,
   central coast, Puerto Montt and
   intermediates
   (☎ 02-779-3721)

Cruz del Sur – to Los Lagos and Chiloé
   (☎ 02-779-0607)

Sample Bus Fares from Santiago

Travelers should remember that bus fares are subject to substantial variations among companies and can also rise dramatically on and near holidays.

destination	hours	pullman	salón cama
Antofagasta	18	US$31	US$42
Arica	28	US$38	US$56
Castro	19	US$27	US$45
Chillán	6	US$9	n/a
Concepción	8	US$14	n/a
Copiapó	11	US$20	US$30
Iquique	26	US$37	US$46
La Serena	7	US$15	US$22
Osorno	14	US$19	US$32
Puerto Montt	16	US$20	US$35
Punta Arenas	60	US$100	
Temuco	11	US$14	US$29
Valdivia	13	US$17	US$32
Valparaíso	2	US$4	n/a
Villarrica	13	US$15	US$29
Viña del Mar	2	US$4	n/a

Fénix – to Los Angeles, Angol, Valdivia and intermediate points
(☎ 02-779-4648)

Flota Barrios – to Valparaíso/Viña del Mar; north to Arica and intermediates
(☎ 02-776-0665)

Igi Llaima – to Los Lagos and Panamericana destinations
(☎ 02-779-1751)

Inter Sur – to many destinations in the Los Lagos region
(☎ 02-779-6312)

Lit – to Los Vilos, Coquimbo and La Serena
(☎ 02-779-5710)

Panguisur – to Panguipulli and Los Lagos
(☎ 02-778-1278)

Pullman Fichtur – to Arica and intermediates
(☎ 02-779-9285)

Tas Choapa – to Chillán, Concepción, Temuco, Puerto Montt and intermediate stops on the Panamericana
(☎ 02-779-4694

Tur-Bus – to Panamericana destinations between Arica and Puerto Montt
(☎ 02-776-3690)

Turibús – to southern Los Lagos and Punta Arenas
(☎ 02-779-0607)

Varmontt – to southern Los Lagos
(☎ 02-231-3505)

Vía Tur – to Chillán, Concepción and mainland points south to Puerto Montt
(☎ 02-779-3839)

TRAIN

Chilean trains are rarely worth the effort except for dedicated rail fans; buses are more frequent and convenient. Southbound trains from Santiago pass through Talca and Chillán to Temuco; a spur that leaves the main longitudinal line at Chillán provides direct service from Santiago to Concepción.

With the exception of the Calama-Oruro line between Chile and Bolivia, there are no long-distance passenger services north of Santiago. It's difficult but not impossible to travel by freight from Baquedano (on the Panamericana northeast of Antofagasta) to the border town of Socompa, and on to Salta in Argentina.

Classes & Fares

Trains have three classes: *economía*, *salón* and *cama*. Cama refers to 'sleeper' class, which has upper and lower bunks; the latter are more expensive. On long overnight journeys, the charming between-the-wars sleepers may be worth consideration, but travelers have observed that decades of heavy use have left the bunks much less comfortable than they once were.

Typical one-way fares (in US dollars) for the three classes, as well as approximate travel times. are listed in the boxed text Sample Train Fares from Santiago, below; a roundtrip fare is slightly cheaper than two singles.

Reservations

All trains from Santiago depart from the Estación Central (☎ 02-689-5199), Alameda 3322 (Metro: Estación Central), which is open 7 am to 11 pm daily. Santiago's Empresa de Ferrocarriles del Estado (EFE) runs southbound passenger service to Chillán, Concepción, Temuco and intermediates from the station. Trains to Chillán leave at 8:30 am, and 2:15 and 6:30 pm. Temuco-bound service leaves at 8 pm only, while the overnighter to Concepción leaves at 10:30 pm. Station hours are 7 am to 11 pm daily. EFE also runs frequent commuter service between Santiago and Rancagua, capital of Region VI, for about US$2 (one hour).

If the Estación Central is inconvenient, book passage at Santiago's Venta de Pasajes (☎ 02-639-8247) in the Galería Libertador, Alameda 853, Local 21. It's open 8:30 am to 1 pm weekdays, 9 am to 1 pm Saturday. There is another office (☎ 02-228-2983) at the Galería Comercial Sur, Local 25, at the Escuela Militar Metro station, open 9 am to 1 pm weekdays.

Tickets are also available at the Venta de Pasajes (ticket office) in the Galería Libertador (☎ 02-632-2801), Alameda 853, Local 21.

CAR & MOTORCYCLE

Even though Chile's public transport system is extensive, many interesting areas are easily accessible only by motor vehicle. Off the main highways, where buses may be few or nonexistent, it's not easy to stop where you want and then continue by public transport.

Advantages of driving include freedom from timetables, the ability to stay wherever you like (particularly if you have camping equipment), the opportunity to get off the beaten track and the flexibility to stop whenever you see something interesting. In some areas – such as the Atacama desert, the Camino Austral or Easter Island – a car is definitely the best way to get around. Security problems are minor, but always lock your vehicle and leave valuables out of sight. Note that because of smog problems there are frequent restrictions on private vehicle use in Santiago and the surrounding region; usually these are organized according to the terminal digit of the license plate of the car.

Motorists with their own vehicles should be aware that a customs regulation that once stipulated that the 90-day import permit for foreign vehicles could not be extended (unlike tourist cards) is no longer in effect, and some border officials routinely issue 180-day permits. Not all customs officials are aware of this change, however, and it may be easier to leave the country and return.

You'll notice distance markers every five kilometers along Chile's two major roads, the Panamericana and the Camino Austral,

Sample Train Fares from Santiago				
destination	time/hours	economía	salón	cama, upper/lower
Talca	5	US$5	US$9	n/a
Chillán	7	US$8	US$14	n/a
Concepción	9	US$11	US$19	US$21/27
Temuco	13	US$14	US$24	US$27/35

and you may be given directions that refer to these kilometer markers.

Road Rules

While Chileans sometimes drive carelessly or a bit too fast (especially in the cities), if you have come from Argentina you will think them saints. Most Chilean drivers are courteous to pedestrians, and rarely willfully do anything dangerous. Driving after dark is not advisable, especially in rural areas in southern Chile, where pedestrians, domestic animals and wooden carts are difficult to see on or near the highways. If you are involved in an automobile accident, consult the entry on Legal Matters in the Facts for the Visitor chapter.

Unless otherwise posted, speed limits are 50kmh in town and 100kmh in rural areas. In contrast to neighboring Argentina, Chile's carabineros enforce speed limits with US$75 fines; bribing them is not an option.

Road Atlases

Lonely Planet's *Chile & Easter Island Travel Atlas* (1997), is an obvious choice. The annual Turistel guides, detailed in the guidebooks entry in the Facts for the Visitor chapter, are a good source on recent changes, particularly with regard to newly paved roads. Published under the auspices of the Argentine oil company YPF but the product of the Turistel group, the *Atlas Vial*, available across the border, also includes Chile from Antofagasta south, and is good at delineating border crossings.

Road Assistance

The Automóvil Club de Chile (Acchi) has offices in most major Chilean cities, provides useful information, sells maps and rents cars. It also offers member services and grants discounts to members of its foreign counterparts, such as the American Automobile Association (AAA) in the USA or the Automobile Association (AA) in the UK. Acchi's central office (☎ 02-212-5702) is at Av Vitacura 8620, Vitacura, Santiago. Its tourism and member services office (☎ 02-225-3790) is at Fidel Oteíza 1960, Providencia, Santiago. Membership includes free towing and other roadside services within 25km of an Automóvil Club office.

Costs

Operating a car in Chile is cheaper than in Europe but dearer than in the USA. The Santiago price of *bencina* (gasoline) ranges from about US$0.50 to US$0.55 per liter, depending on the grade, while *gas-oil* (diesel fuel) is somewhat cheaper. Fuel prices in the regions are generally higher than in Santiago. The 93-octane *común* is available both unleaded *(sin plomo)* and leaded *(con plomo)*, while 95- and 97-octane grades are invariably unleaded.

Rental

Major international rental agencies like Hertz, Avis and Budget have offices in Santiago, and in major cities and other tourist areas. The Automóvil Club also rents cars at some of its offices. To rent a car, you must have a valid driver's license, be at least 25 years of age (some younger readers have managed to rent cars, however) and present either a credit card such as MasterCard or Visa, or a large cash deposit.

Even at smaller agencies, basic rental charges are now very high, the cheapest and smallest vehicles going for about US$50 to US$65 per day with 150 to 200km included, or sometimes with unlimited mileage. Adding the cost of insurance, petrol and IVA *(impuesto de valor agregado,* the value added tax, or VAT), it becomes very pricey indeed to operate a rental vehicle without several others to share expenses. Weekend or weekly rates, with unlimited mileage, are a better bargain. Small vehicles with unlimited mileage cost about US$340 to US$450 per week, while 4WD vehicles cost in excess of US$100 per day. Some companies will give discounts for extended rentals, say a month or more.

One-way rentals can be awkward or impossible to arrange. Some companies, most notably Hertz, will arrange such rentals but with a substantial drop-off charge. With smaller, local agencies, this is next to impossible. Some of these smaller agencies will, however, usually arrange paperwork for taking cars into Argentina, so long as the car is returned to the original office. There may be a substantial charge, around US$90, for taking a car into Argentina; Chilean insurance is not valid in Argentina.

When traveling in remote areas, where fuel may not be readily available, carry extra fuel. Rental agencies often provide a spare *bidón* (fuel container) for this purpose.

Purchase

If you are planning on spending several months in Chile, purchasing a car merits consideration. However, it has both advantages and disadvantages. On the one hand, driving is more flexible than taking public transport and likely to be cheaper than multiple rentals; reselling it at the end of your stay can make it even more economical. On the other hand, any used car can be a risk, especially on the many rugged back roads. Fortunately, even the smallest hamlet seems to have a competent and resourceful mechanic.

Chile's domestic automobile industry is insignificant – nearly 90% of vehicles are imported – but good imported vehicles are available at prices higher than in Europe or the USA, though more reasonable than in Argentina. Japanese and Korean vehicles such as Toyota and Hyundai are especially popular, but Argentine Peugeots are also common. Parts are readily available, except for some older models. Do not expect to find a reliable used car for less than about US$3000, much more for recent models.

If you purchase a car you must change the title within 30 days; failure to do so can result in a fine of several hundred dollars. In order to buy a vehicle, you must have a RUT (Rol Unico Tributario) tax identification number, available through Impuestos Internos, the Chilean tax office; issuance of the RUT takes about 10 days. The actual title transfer is done at any notary through a *compraventa* for about US$10.

All vehicles must carry so-called *seguro obligatorio* (minimum insurance), which covers personal injuries up to a maximum of about US$3000 at a cost of about US$20 per year. All companies issue these policies, which run from April 1 to March 31 of the following year. Additional liability insurance is highly desirable.

Since Chilean policies are not valid in Argentina, but Argentine policies are valid in Chile and other neighboring countries, it is worth buying a reasonably priced Argentine policy across the border if you plan to visit several countries.

Note that, while many inexpensive vehicles are for sale in the duty-free zones of Regions I and XII (Tarapacá and Magallanes), only legal permanent residents of those regions may take a vehicle outside of those regions, for a maximum of 90 days per calendar year.

Shipping a Vehicle

Given its openness toward foreign trade and tourism, Chile is probably the best country on the continent to ship an overseas vehicle to. After I shipped my pickup truck from California to the port of San Antonio, southwest of Santiago, it took less than two hours of routine paperwork to get the vehicle out of customs. If the car is more than a few days in customs, however, storage charges can add up.

To find a reliable shipper, check the yellow pages of your local phone directory under Automobile Transporters. Most transporters are more accustomed to arranging shipments between North America and Europe than from North America or Europe to South America, so it may take some of them time to work out details. One reliable US shipper is McClary, Swift & Co (☎ 650-872-2121), 360 Swift Ave, South San Francisco, CA 94080.

When shipping a vehicle into Chile, do not leave anything whatsoever of value in the vehicle if at all possible. Theft, of tools in particular, is very common.

For shipping a car from Chile back to your home country, try the consolidator Ultramar (☎ 02-630-1817, fax 02-698-6552, italia@ultramar.cl), Moneda 970, 18th floor, Santiago. For completing the paperwork, it also helps to have assistance from a reliable, conscientious customs agent, such as Juan Alarcón Rojas (☎ 02-225-2780, fax 02-204-5302, alrcon@entelchile.net), Fidel Oteíza 1921, 12th floor, Providencia, Santiago.

BICYCLE

Bicycling is an interesting and inexpensive alternative for traveling around Chile, although camping is not a bargain for the solo cyclist, and it will probably be cheaper to stay at residenciales. Because even the best paved roads often lack adequate shoulders, a *todo terreno* (mountain bike), or a touring bike with beefy tires, is a better choice than a racing bike. In areas such as the increasingly popular and almost completely unpaved Camino Austral, a racing bike is almost useless.

Cycling is an increasingly popular recreational activity and there are many good routes, but the weather can be a drawback. From Temuco south, it is changeable and you must be prepared for rain; from Santiago north, especially in the Atacama, water sources are infrequent. In some areas, the wind can slow your progress to a crawl; north to south is generally easier than south to north, but some readers report strong headwinds southbound in summer. Chilean motorists are usually courteous, but on narrow, two-lane highways without shoulders, passing cars can be a real hazard.

LP reader Paul Arundale, who has cycled extensively through the Southern Cone, offers the following suggestions on travel in Chile:

Chile offers ideal cycling conditions on rough unsurfaced roads in the north and south of the country, but in the middle it is difficult to avoid using the Panamericana; while this is not dangerous, having a wide hard shoulder for much of the central part, it is certainly no fun with the mountains far away and the diesel fumes all too close. January and February are months best avoided as all of Santiago seems to be on the road in pickup trucks and vans heading north or south and the unsurfaced roads are usually little more than one-vehicle wide, making continual traffic in either direction a frazzling experience. For those on a longer tour, Chile has the best-stocked bike shops in South America and even the smallest town has at least one bike shop offering all the latest Japanese parts. If flying between New Zealand and Chile, LanChile carries bikes wrapped in cardboard free between Chile, Easter Island and Tahiti.

Another reader claims that spare parts are hard to come by, though easier for mountain bikes than for racing bikes; 27-inch tires are particularly hard to find. There's a cluster of shops along Calle San Diego in Santiago.

Arundale adds:

Cyclists en route from Argentina will find several unsurfaced routes crossing the Andes into Chile such, as the Bajo Caracoles to Cochrane road in the south, and the Bardas Blancas to Talca and Jáchal to Vicuña routes either side of Santiago. These offer ideal traffic-free cycling for well-prepared riders. There are few fences alongside these roads and a tent can be pitched anywhere.

Readers interested in detailed information on cycling in South America can find more material in Walter Sienko's *Cycling in Latin America* (1993).

HITCHHIKING

Along with Argentina, Chile is probably the best country for hitchhiking in all of South America. The major drawback, however, is that Chilean vehicles are often packed with families, but truck drivers will often help backpackers. At *servicentros* on the outskirts of Chilean cities on the Panamericana, where truckers gas up their vehicles, it is often worth soliciting a ride.

Women can and do hitchhike alone but should exercise caution and especially avoid getting into a car with more than one man. In Patagonia, where distances are great and vehicles few, hitchhikers should expect long waits and carry warm, windproof clothing. It's also a good idea to carry some snack food and a water bottle, especially in the desert north.

Along the Panamericana, from Arica to Puerto Montt, hitchhiking is fairly reliable, but competition may be great in the summer months, when Chilean students hit the highway with their backpacks. In the Atacama you may wait for some time, but almost every ride will be a long one. Along the Camino Austral, in Region XI (Aisén), vehicles of any kind are few except between Coihaique and Puerto Aisén, and hitchhiking requires great patience. Readers report that increasing traffic between Chaitén and Coihaique has made that stretch of highway easier to hitchhike.

Hitchhiking is never entirely safe in any country in the world, and Lonely Planet does not recommend it. Travelers who decide to hitchhike should understand that they are taking a small but potentially serious risk. People who do choose to hitchhike will be safer if they travel in pairs and let someone know where they are planning to go.

FERRY

Most bus services between Puerto Montt and Coihaique, in Region XI, pass through Argentina; to explore the less easily accessible parts of the Camino Austral Longitudinal (Southern Longitudinal Highway), it is necessary to take Naviera Magallanes (Navimag) or Transportes Marítimos Chiloé Aysén (Transmarchilay) ferries from Puerto Montt, Hornopirén or Chiloé to Chaitén or Puerto Chacabuco. Navimag's enormously popular ferry service from Puerto Montt to Puerto Natales is one of the continent's great travel experiences.

The Santiago addresses of these companies appear below; for representatives in the regions, see the appropriate city entries.

Navimag
  (☎ 02-203-5030, fax 203-5025) Av El Bosque Norte 0440, 11th floor
Transmarchilay
  (☎/fax 02-633-5959) Agustinas 715, Oficina 403

Puerto Montt to Puerto Chacabuco

Navimag and Transmarchilay operate services from Puerto Montt to Puerto Chacabuco, with bus service continuing on to Coihaique, and on to Parque Nacional Laguna San Rafael. For details of schedules and fares, see the Puerto Montt entry in the La Araucanía & Los Lagos chapter. There's also a tourist ship, the *Skorpios*, from Puerto Chacabuco to Laguna San Rafael, while Patagonia Connection runs a luxury catamaran on the same route.

Puerto Montt to Puerto Natales

The Navimag ferry *Puerto Edén* departs Puerto Montt weekly, usually Monday, taking about three days to reach Puerto Natales, but erratic Patagonian weather can play havoc with schedules. For details of schedules and fares, see the Puerto Montt entry and the boxed text 'Sailing the Fjords' in the La Araucanía & Los Lagos chapter.

La Arena to Puelche

Transmarchilay's shuttle ferry, about 45km southeast of Puerto Montt, runs back and forth constantly, connecting two northerly segments of the Camino Austral all year.

Hornopirén to Caleta Gonzalo

The last mainland stop southbound on the Camino Austral, Hornopirén is a scenic village where, in summer, Transmarchilay ferries sail to Caleta Gonzalo, about 60km north of Chaitén.

Chiloé to the Mainland

There are four connections between Chiloé and the mainland. The most frequent is either with Transmarchilay or with Cruz del Sur ferries between Chacao, at the northern tip of the Isla Grande, and Pargua, on the mainland. For details of fares and schedules, see the Chiloé chapter.

The other main connections are by Transmarchilay ferries between the port of Quellón on Chiloé, and Chaitén or Puerto Chacabuco on the mainland, but there is also a new private service from Chonchi to Chaitén. For details of fares and schedules, see the La Araucanía & Los Lagos, Chiloé and Aisén & the Camino Austral chapters.

Patagonia & Tierra del Fuego

Naviera Sotramin operates a daily automobile/passenger ferry between Puerto Ibáñez, on Lago General Carrera south of Coihaique, to the border town of Chile Chico.

There's a daily ferry link between Punta Arenas and Porvenir, the only town in Chilean Tierra del Fuego. For details of fares and schedules, see the Punta Arenas entry in the Magallanes chapter.

LOCAL TRANSPORT
To/From the Airport

In Santiago, inexpensive (US$1.60 to US$2) airport buses are frequent, but travelers who carry heavy luggage might take advantage of door-to-door airport services for around US$6 to US$7.50. See the Santiago chapter for more details.

In the regions, airlines often arrange bus service between downtown and the airport – either their own bus or one run by a local company. Sometimes the cost is included in your air ticket, sometimes it's extra. Top-end hotels may provide transportation for their clients, but in a few places you must use public transport or a taxi.

Bus

Even small towns have extensive bus systems that can seem chaotic to the novice rider. Buses, however, are clearly numbered and usually carry a placard indicating their final destination. Since many identically numbered buses serve slightly different routes, pay attention to these placards. On boarding, tell the driver your final destination and he will tell you the fare and give you a ticket. Do not lose this ticket, which may be checked en route.

Bus fares in Santiago, the most expensive in the country, are around Ch$210 (approximately US$0.40). Automatic machines are currently being installed, but the process has been slower than authorities would prefer.

Train

Both Santiago and Valparaíso have commuter rail networks. The former runs from Rancagua, capital of Region VI, to Estación Central on the Alameda in Santiago, while the latter runs from Quillota to Viña del Mar and Valparaíso. For details, see the respective city entries.

Metro

Santiago is the only Chilean city with a subway, the Metro, which is efficient, clean and cheap. For details, see the Santiago chapter.

Taxi

Most Chilean cabs are metered, but fares vary. In Santiago, it costs Ch$300 (about US$0.60) to *bajar la bandera* ('lower the flag'), plus Ch$100 (US$0.20) per 200m. Each cab carries a placard indicating its authorized fare.

In some towns, such as Viña del Mar, cabs may cost twice as much. In others, such as Coquimbo, meters are less common, so it is wise to agree upon a fare in advance if possible. Drivers are generally polite and honest, but there are exceptions. Tipping is not necessary, but you may tell the driver to keep small change.

Nearly all Chilean cities also have *taxi colectivos*, which cover fixed routes and are faster than buses and less expensive than regular taxis.

ORGANIZED TOURS

Chile has an increasing number of Santiago-based agencies specializing in adventure travel; many of these also maintain summer offices in the lakes region or elsewhere in the country. Several are described in detail here.

Cascada Expediciones (☎ 02-232-7214, fax 233-9768, cascada@ibm.net), Orrego Luco 040 in Providencia, Santiago, runs a variety of adventure trips throughout the country, including custom day and weekend excursions in the mountains near Santiago, horseback expeditions across the Andes into Argentina, tours of the Juan Fernández Archipelago, treks in Araucaria forests near Pucón and in Torres del Paine, explorations of the Atacama Desert and the northern altiplano, sea-kayaking stints in the fjords of Chiloé, dives at Easter Island and whitewater rafting and kayaking trips on the Biobío and Futaleufú.

Altué Active Travel (☎ (02-232-1103, fax 233-6679, altue@netline.cl, altue@entelchile .net), Encomenderos 83, 2nd floor, Las Condes, Santiago, also arranges white-water rafting on the Maipo as well as the Biobío and Futaleufú, operates a sea-kayaking center near Dalcahue on the Isla Grande de Chiloé, and organizes many other adventure activities.

US-run Austral Adventures (☎/fax 02-735-6224, tours@australadventures.com), Casilla 34, Correo No 4, Recoleta, Santiago, arranges yacht charters from Puerto Montt southwards.

Patagonia Connection (☎ 02-225-6489, fax 274-8111, patagonia@chilnet.cl), Fidel

Oteíza 1921, Oficina 1006, Providencia, Santiago, offers packages to Hotel Termas de Puyuhuapi, in the Aisén region, and also operates the luxury catamaran *Patagonia Express* from Puerto Chacabuco to Parque Nacional Laguna San Rafael. Four-day, three-night packages from Puerto Montt include two nights at the Termas and a full-day catamaran excursion to Laguna San Rafael with a night in Puerto Chacabuco; rates with full board range from US$750 to US$1900 per person, depending on the room and the season. Six-day, five-night packages are also available.

Explora (☎ 02-206-6060, fax 228-4655, explora@entelchile.net), Américo Vespucio Sur 80, 5th floor, Las Condes, Santiago, offers all-inclusive packages, including luxury accommodations and excursions, in Parque Nacional Torres del Paine and in and around San Pedro de Atacama. They also have contact numbers in the USA (☎ 800-858-0855), Canada (☎ 800-275-1129) and Germany (☎ 01-30-822-353).

Cruceros Australis (☎ 02-203-5030, fax 203-5205, terra@australis.com), Av El Bosque Norte 0440, 11th floor, Las Condes, Santiago, arranges weeklong luxury cruises on the 100-passenger *Terra Australis* from Punta Arenas through the Cordillera de Darwin, the Beagle Channel, and Puerto Williams, Ushuaia (Argentina) and back. While these cruises are expensive, starting at US$1047 per person, double occupancy, in low season (September to October and April) and reaching US$3132 for a high-season single (mid-December through February), all meals are included and they do offer a chance to visit

parts of the region that are otherwise very difficult and even more expensive to reach independently. It's possible to do the leg between Punta Arenas and Ushuaia (four nights) or vice-versa (three nights) separately and, obviously, less expensively.

Yanko Motor Tour (yanko@entelchile.net, www.patagonia-moto-tour.co.cl/), Casilla 749, Chillán, specializes in motorcycle tours. Among the options are a nine-day trip across the Libertadores pass to Mendoza and back across the Pehuenche pass to Talca and Santiago (US$2800 including bike, or US$2100 with own bike), or a 17-day Patagonian tour (US$4500 or US$3500).

French-run Les Vagabonds (☎/fax 063-213-760, vagabonds@libertad7.com), Casilla 462, Valdivia, conducts a variety of day tours in and around Valdivia, as well as longer excursions around the lakes region and to Chiloé. English and German are spoken as well as French.

In addition to Altué Active Travel, and Cascadia Expediciones, described above, the following companies have English-speaking staff:

Adventure Expedition
  (☎ 02-211-7571, fax 219-2301) Las Tranqueras 62, Las Condes, Santiago

Grado Diez
  (☎ 02-234-4130) Las Urbinas 56, Providencia, Santiago

Mountain Service
  (☎ 02-242-9723) Ebro 2805, Las Condes, Santiago

Pared Sur
  (☎ 02-207-3525) Juan Estéban Montero 5497, Las Condes, Santiago

Santiago

☎ 02

Santiago is a city of contrasts, a modern metropolis whose shining international air terminal greets foreigners rushing to invest money in what, before recent setbacks, was South America's most dynamic economy. Prosperous professionals still pack fine restaurants, and cell phones and car alarms have become status symbols to a burgeoning middle class – but at the same time, struggling street vendors board city buses to hawk everything from pins and needles to pens and ice cream, and housemaids commute for hours to scrub floors in exclusive suburbs where gardeners lug rakes and push-mowers on the backs of bicycles. The glitzy exterior of Santiago's skyline reflects more than a decade of vigorous economic growth – though improvements have come at a price.

Unfortunately, most streets are too narrow for the heavy rush-hour traffic, and a blanket of smog frequently lurks overhead as the phalanx of the Andes, rarely visible except immediately after a rain, blocks the dispersal of pollutants. Many beautifully landscaped parks provide refuge from air pollution, but it's sometimes hard to overlook the visual pollution, from billboards and neon signs, that an increasingly consumerist society has inflicted on the cityscape.

Chile's sprawling capital is really many cities in one: Santiago proper, the former colonial core, is surrounded by another 31 *comunas* of greater or lesser antiquity that have coalesced to form the present megacity. Each comuna has its own separate municipal administration, including mayor and council, but the national government legislates and administers many urban services, such as public transportation, throughout the Región Metropolitana.

Besides growing out, the city has grown up, as more and more skyscrapers dominate the landscape, both downtown and rising toward the Andes in comunas such as Providencia and Las Condes, which have been usurping downtown's historical role as the city's commercial and financial center. Most areas of interest to visitors are between downtown Santiago and the Andes, along with the surrounding central comunas of Ñuñoa, Estación Central, Quinta Normal, Recoleta and Independencia.

HISTORY

Gazing west from the rocky overlook of Cerro Santa Lucía to the skyscrapers and apartment blocks of metropolitan Santiago, it's hard to imagine that just six months after Pedro de Valdivia founded the city in 1541, Mapuche warriors nearly obliterated it. Spanish troops regrouped on the fortified summit of Santa Lucía and Valdivia made immediate plans to rebuild the precarious settlement.

Valdivia had laid out a regular grid from the present-day Plaza de Armas, but for two years 'Santiago del Nuevo Extremo' was little more than a besieged hillside camp. Its tile-roofed adobe houses survived fire, but colonists nearly starved under Indian pressure. Two years passed before assistance arrived from Peru; after returning to Peru himself for new troops and supplies, Valdivia pushed southwards, founding Concepción in 1550 and Valdivia in 1552.

All these early settlements were merely fortified villages. In Santiago, most houses were built around central patios and enhanced with gardens and grapevine arbors. Open sewers ran down the middle of the streets. As the settlements became more secure, soldiers formed households with Indian women. Tradesmen such as shoemakers, blacksmiths, armorers and tanners provided services for the colonists. In the beginning, the towns were administrative centers for the new colony and bases for sorties into Mapuche territory, but most of the population lived in the countryside.

By the late 16th century, Santiago was a settlement of just 200 houses, inhabited by not more than 700 Spaniards and mestizos,

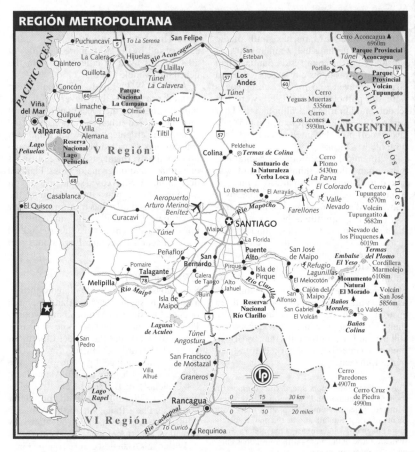

REGIÓN METROPOLITANA

plus several thousand Indian laborers and servants. Occasionally flooded by the Río Mapocho, it nevertheless lacked a safe water supply. Also, communications between town and countryside were difficult. Despite their precarious position, wealthy encomenderos and other elite elements emulated European nobility, acquiring platoons of servants and importing products from Europe and China. Although wealthy households still enjoyed luxuries such as velvet and silk, shortages of resources such as weapons, ammunition and horses contributed to the Spaniards' expul-

sion by the Mapuche from the area south of the Biobío.

Subject to the Viceroyalty of Peru, Chile remained a backwater of imperial Spain for nearly three centuries, yielding little exportable wealth. Nevertheless, by the late 18th century, Santiago began to acquire the infrastructure of a proper city, as new *tajamares* (dikes) restrained the Mapocho, improved roads handled increased commerce between the capital and its port of Valparaíso, and authorities targeted various beautification projects to please the landowning aristocracy.

As colonial rule ended in the early 19th century, Chile's population – including 100,000 sovereign Mapuches south of the Biobío – was perhaps half a million, 90% of which lived in the countryside. Santiago had barely 30,000 residents, city streets remained largely unpaved and most country roads were still potholed tracks. There were few schools and libraries and, although the Universidad de San Felipe (founded in 1758 as a law school) provided intellectual spark, cultural life was bleak.

By the mid-19th century, the capital had more than 100,000 inhabitants and was linked to the port of Valparaíso, a bustling commercial center of 60,000 people, by a railway and telegraph line. The landed aristocracy built sumptuous houses, adorned them with imported luxuries, founded prestigious social clubs and visited their fundos during the holidays. Social life revolved around clubs, the track, the opera and outings to exclusive Parque Cousiño. Those of the governing class fashioned themselves as ladies and gentlemen who valued civilized customs, tradition and breeding, sending their children to be educated in Europe. It's still true, at least for the elite, that, as British diplomat James Bryce remarked at the end of the 19th century:

The leading landowners spend the summers in their country houses and the winter and spring in Santiago, which has thus a pleasant society, with plenty of talent and talk among the men, a society more enlightened and abreast of the modern world than are those of the more northern republics, and with a more stimulating atmosphere.

From its inauspicious beginnings, Santiago has become one of South America's largest cities – the Región Metropolitana contains well over four million inhabitants. The Museo de Santiago, in the colonial Casa Colorada off the Plaza de Armas, documents the city's phenomenal growth, in large part a function of oppression in the countryside. Poverty, lack of opportunity and paternalistic fundos drove farm laborers and tenants north to the nitrate mines, and also into the cities; between 1865 and 1875, Santiago's population increased from 115,000 to more than 150,000, mainly due to domestic migration. This trend continued in the 20th century and, by the 1970s, more than 70% of all Chileans lived in cities, mostly in the heartland (Middle Chile).

After WWII, rapid industrialization created urban jobs, but never enough to satisfy demand. In the 1960s continued rural turmoil fostered urban migration, resulting in squatter settlements known as *callampas* (mushrooms, so called because they sprang up virtually overnight) around the outskirts of Santiago and other major cities. Planned decentralization has eased some pressure on Santiago and regularization, including the granting of land titles, has transformed many callampas. They still stand in contrast, however, to affluent eastern suburbs like El Golf, Vitacura, La Reina, Las Condes and Lo Curro.

ORIENTATION

Santiago is immense, but Santiago Centro is a relatively small, roughly triangular area bounded by the Río Mapocho and woodsy Parque Forestal to the north, the Vía Norte Sur to the west, and the Av del Libertador General Bernardo O'Higgins (more commonly and manageably known as the Alameda, short for the earlier 'Alameda de las Delicias') to the south. The triangle's apex of is Plaza Baquedano, popularly known as Plaza Italia, where the Alameda intersects two other main thoroughfares, Av Providencia and Av Vicuña Mackenna.

Within this triangle, centered on the Plaza de Armas, downtown Santiago's street plan largely conforms to the standard grid that the Spaniards imposed on all their American possessions. Surrounding the plaza are many of the most notable public buildings, including the Municipalidad (city hall), the Catedral Metropolitana and the Correo Central (main post office). Paseo Ahumada, a pedestrian mall, leads south to the Alameda, while a block south of the Plaza de Armas it intersects with Paseo Huérfanos, another pedestrian mall. Other public buildings, including the presidential palace, dominate the Barrio Cívico around Plaza de

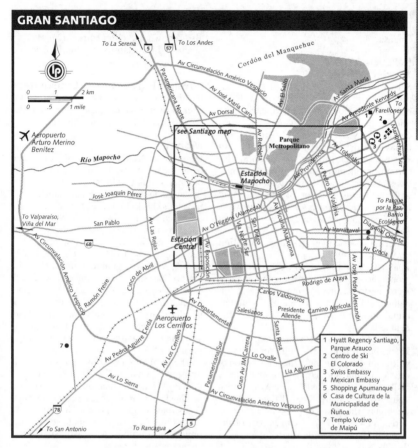

GRAN SANTIAGO

1 Hyatt Regency Santiago,
  Parque Arauco
2 Centro de Ski
  El Colorado
3 Swiss Embassy
4 Mexican Embassy
5 Shopping Apumanque
6 Casa de Cultura de la
  Municipalidad de
  Ñuñoa
7 Templo Votivo
  de Maipú

la Constitución, west of Paseo Ahumada and just north of the Alameda.

One of Santiago's most attractive parks, Cerro Santa Lucía, overlooks the Alameda between the Plaza de Armas and Plaza Baquedano. Across the Mapocho from Plaza Baquedano, on either side of Av Pío Nono, Barrio Bellavista is Santiago's lively 'Paris quarter.' Overlooking Bellavista is the enormous Cerro San Cristóbal, which rises dramatically from the plain to the north of Av Providencia, the thoroughfare that leads eastward toward the comunas of Providencia, Las Condes, Vitacura and Lo Barnechea.

Av Vicuña Mackenna leads southeast toward increasingly fashionable Ñuñoa.

West of the Via Norte Sur, Barrio Brasil is an intriguing enclave of early-20th-century architecture that is presently experiencing an urban renaissance. Farther west and south are the agreeable open spaces of Parque Quinta Normal and Parque O'Higgins, both popular weekend refuges for Santiaguinos and their families.

Travelers planning an extended stay in Santiago might acquire Carlos Ossandón Guzmán's *Guía de Santiago* (Editorial Universitaria). Especially strong on architectural history, it also contains useful maps and illustrations, and a valuable summary in English.

INFORMATION
Tourist Offices

Sernatur (☎ 236-1420, 236-1416), Chile's national tourist service, occupies most of the old market building at Av Providencia 1550, midway between Manuel Montt and Pedro de Valdivia Metro stations. The friendly and capable staff, which always includes an English speaker, offers maps and other information, including lists of accommodations, restaurants and bars, museums and art galleries, transport out of Santiago and leaflets on other parts of the country. It's open 9 am to 5 pm weekdays, 9 am to 1 pm Saturday.

Sernatur also operates an information booth (☎ 601-9320), open 9 am to 9 pm weekdays, 9 am to 5:30 pm weekends, on the ground floor of the international terminal at Aeropuerto Arturo Merino Benítez at Pudahuel, and another at the San Borja bus terminal, alongside the train station on the Alameda.

The Municipalidad maintains a tourist kiosk, helpful but less well stocked with written information, near the intersection of the Ahumada and Huérfanos pedestrian malls, a block from the Plaza de Armas, open 9 am to 9 pm daily. Open 10 am to 6 pm weekdays, the main municipal Oficina de Turismo (☎ 632-7785) occupies part of the colonial Casa Colorada, Merced 860, near the Plaza de Armas; there's also a branch (☎ 664-4206, tur-ims@entelchile.net) on Cerro Santa Lucía, open 9 am to 6 pm Monday through Thursday, 9 am to 5 pm Friday.

All these offices distribute free maps detailing downtown, Providencia and other inner comunas of the capital, with the main Metro stations included. More detailed maps are available from the Municipalidad for about US$2, but the best city map is *Santiago* by Mapas de Matassi (☎ 236-4808), General del Canto 105, Oficina 1506, Providencia, also available at various bookstores and travel agencies around town.

Most hotels distribute *What's On*, a thorough bilingual guide to events around town, also known as *Que Hacer, Que Ver* in Spanish. It has maps of key tourist-oriented areas.

Foreign Embassies & Consulates

For the addresses of diplomatic representatives of overseas and neighboring countries, see the Facts for the Visitor chapter.

Money

Ubiquitous ATMs have made exchange houses less important than they used to be, but numerous cambios on Agustinas, between Bandera and Ahumada, still change traveler's checks and foreign cash. There are also exchange facilities and ATMs in Providencia (where, since rates are slightly lower than downtown, you get a few pesos less) and at the airport (where rates are notably lower), so change minimal amounts at the airport unless you're arriving on a weekend.

Cambios pay slightly less for traveler's checks than for US cash, but they do not usually charge any additional commission. It's still possible to locate street changers by strolling down Paseo Ahumada, but for the most part this is no longer necessary.

The local Thomas Cook representative is Turismo Tajamar (☎ 232-9595), Orrego Luco 023, Providencia, which deals only with replacing lost or stolen checks; Cambio Andes, Agustinas 1036, changes Thomas Cook checks for US cash. Readers have also recommended Cambios Afex, Moneda 1140, to change checks for cash.

Financial Emergencies The following local representatives of major international banking institutions can deal with replacement credit cards and/or traveler's checks:

American Express	(☎ 528-4800)
Diner's Club	(☎ 252-6100)
Visa/MasterCard	(☎ 638-6162)

Post & Communications

The Correo Central (main post office), on the north side of the Plaza de Armas, handles poste restante and also has a philatelic desk.

It's open 8 am to 10 pm weekdays, 8 am to 6 pm Saturdays. Kiosks at the entrance sell envelopes and postcards and will also wrap parcels for a small fee. Correos de Chile has another large downtown post office at Moneda 1155, and a convenient Providencia branch at Av Providencia 1466.

For private international courier service, try Federal Express (☎ 231-5250), Av Providencia 1951 (Metro: Pedro de Valdivia); or DHL Express (☎ 639-2171), Av Santa Rosa 135 (☎ 639-2171), Paseo Huérfanos 1109 or General Holley 70, Providencia (Metro: Los Leones).

For overseas calls, Entel, Paseo Huérfanos 1133, is open 8:30 am to 10 pm daily; there's a branch at Av 11 de Septiembre 1919, Providencia. Chilesat is almost next door at Av 11 de Septiembre 1949. CTC (Telefónica) has many long-distance offices downtown and at Metro stations.

For telegrams and telexes, try VTR Telecomunicaciones, Bandera 168. For cell phones, contact BellSouth Celular downtown at Agustinas 1019 (☎ 339-5506), at Av El Bosque Norte 0134 (☎ 339-5000) in Las Condes (Metro: Tobalaba), or at the international airport (☎ 601-9845).

For Internet access, try the Café Virtual (☎ 638-6846), Alameda 145; Dity Office (☎ 269-2610), Fidel Oteíza 1930, Providencia (Metro: Pedro de Valdivia); or CyberCenter (☎ 231-4207), General Holley 170, Providencia (Metro: Los Leones), open 11 am to 10 pm daily except Sunday. The South Central American Information Club (☎ 673-3166), in the Hotel Indiana at Rosas 1339, also has Internet access.

Travel Agencies

Santiago seems to have travel agencies on nearly every corner, on downtown streets such as Agustinas, Teatinos and Huérfanos, and in affluent Providencia. For good prices on air tickets, contact the Student Flight Center (☎ 335-0395, fax 335-0394, stflictr@ ctc-mundo.net), Hernando de Aguirre 201, Oficina 401, Providencia (Metro: Tobalaba).

The American Express representative is Turismo Cocha (☎ 230-1000, fax 203-5110), Av El Bosque Norte 0430, Las Condes (Metro: Tobalaba). The Thomas Cook representative is Turismo Tajamar (☎ 232-9595), Orrego Luco 023, Providencia (Metro: Pedro de Valdivia).

Several agencies in Providencia and Las Condes specialize in adventure or ecotourism excursions, arranging climbing and horseback riding trips in the Cajón del Maipo east of Santiago, other nearby destinations like Parque Nacional La Campana, and throughout the country. For more information, see the Cajón del Maipo entry at the end of this chapter, and the Activities entry in the Facts for the Visitor chapter.

Bookstores & Newsstands

Santiago's largest and best-stocked bookstore is the Feria Chilena del Libro, Paseo Huérfanos 623, a fine place to browse an excellent selection of books in both Spanish and English; there are several other branches scattered around town. Other good, serious stores include Librería Manantial (☎ 696-7463) at Plaza de Armas 444 (the entrance is a corridor on the south side of the cathedral) and Librería El Cid (☎ 632-1540) at Merced 343, with a good selection of used books. Fondo de Cultura Económica (☎ 695-4843), Paseo Bulnes 152, is a Latin American institution with branches throughout the region, specializing in literature, social sciences, history and economics.

Calle San Diego, south of the Alameda, contains Santiago's largest concentration of used bookstores, although quality varies. One of the best, Librería Rivano at San Diego 119, Local 7, has a fine collection on Chilean history, not all of which is displayed to the public. In the Plaza Mulato Gil de Castro complex at Lastarria 307, Local 100, Ricardo Bravo Murúa (☎ 639-7141) is another good antiquarian bookseller who also stocks maps and postcards.

Behind the grape arbor at the Phone Box Pub, Av Providencia 1652, Librería Chile Ilustrado (☎ 235-8145) has a superb selection of books on Chilean history, archaeology, anthropology and folklore. Specializing in rare materials, but with much general-interest stock, it's open 9:30 am to 1:30 pm and 4 to 7:30 pm weekdays, *(continued on p 126)*

SANTIAGO

SANTIAGO

PLACES TO STAY
21 Residencial del Norte
31 Hotel Ducado
43 Hotel Conde Ansurez
44 Residencial Mery
45 Residencial Alemana

PLACES TO EAT
3 Enoteca
9 Da Dino
12 El Rinconcito
14 Fausto
19 El Chachachá
27 Puro Chile
28 Ocean Pacific's
29 Tú y Yo
30 Pizzería Gigino
32 Las Vacas Gordas
35 Plaza Garibaldi
36 Tongoy
37 Tongoy
38 Ostras Azócar
39 Ostras Squella
41 Puente de los Suspiros
48 Solar de Sancho
   Panza
49 Walhalla
53 La Terraza
56 Café de la Isla
57 República de Ñuñoa
58 El Amor Nunca
   Muere

OTHER
1 Casa de la Cultura
2 Piscina Tupahue
4 Jardín Botánico
   Mapulemu
5 Universidad Católica
   soccer offices
6 Bolivian Embassy
7 Air France
8 Dollar

10 Policía Internacional
   (Lost Tourist Cards)
11 Clínica Dávila
13 Greenpeace
15 Netherlands Embassy
16 French Embassy
17 First Rent a Car
18 Italian Embassy
20 N'aitún
22 Corporación Chilena de
   Prevención del SIDA
23 Defensores del Bosque
   Chileno
24 Museo de Ciencia
   y Tecnología
25 Museo Infantil
26 Museo Nacional de
   Historia Natural
33 Parque Museo
   Ferroviario
34 Museo Artequín
40 Lavandería Lolos
42 Museo de la Solidaridad
   Salvador Allende
46 Instituto Geográfico
   Militar (IGM)
47 Palacio Cousiño
50 Universidad de Chile
   soccer offices
51 Club de Jazz
52 Bar Sin Nombre
54 La Batuta
55 Teatro de la Universidad
   Católica
59 Terminal de
   Buses Santiago
   (Terminal de Buses Sur)
60 Terminal de
   Buses Alameda
61 Terminal San Borja
62 Fantasilandia
63 El Pueblito,
   Museo del Huaso

Av Einstein

Hipódromo
Chile

México

0   300   600 m
0   300   600 yards

Cementerio
General

Cementerio
Católico

Av La Paz

Av Perú

INDEPENDENCIA

Los Olivos

Dorhinica

Av Fermín Vivaceta

Av Independencia

Dávila Baeza

RECOLETA

11

Av Recoleta

12

Panamericana
Norte

5

Río Mapocho

Artesanos

10 ★

Av Balmaceda

Av Santa María

**Estación
Mapocho**

Puente Cal
y Canto

**Bellas
Artes**

Via Norte Sur

Plaza de
Armas

Ricardo Cumming

Av Brasil

19

21

SANTIAGO

Cerro
Santa Lucía ▲
630m

Santa Ana

20

Plaza
Brasil

32

29

Santa
Lucía

Catedral

24   25

26

Lagoon

Compañía   27

28   30

31

**Universidad
de Chile**

Parque
Quinta
Normal

33

Paseo Huérfanos

Agustinas

35

La Moneda

Av Portales

36

40

Moneda

37   39

41

34

Erasmo Escala

38

Malucana

República

Los Héroes

Universidad
de Santiago

Romero

Apóstol Santiago

Estación
Central

Av O'Higgins (Alameda)

44

42   43

see Santiago Centro map

Parque
Diego de
Almagro

46

47

**Estación
Central**

Unión
Latinoamericana

45

Toesca

Plaza
Las
Heras

Av Diez de Julio

Universidad
de Santiago

Saze

Av República

60

61

San Borja

Av Exposición

Aconcagua

5

59

Pila del
Ganso

Cinco de Abril

Bernardo del Mercado

Almirante Blanco Encalada

San Diego

San Francisco

Lord Cochrane

Natanil Cox

**ESTACIÓN
CENTRAL**

Av Velásquez

Club
Hípico

62

Parque
O'Higgins

63

Parque
O'Higgins

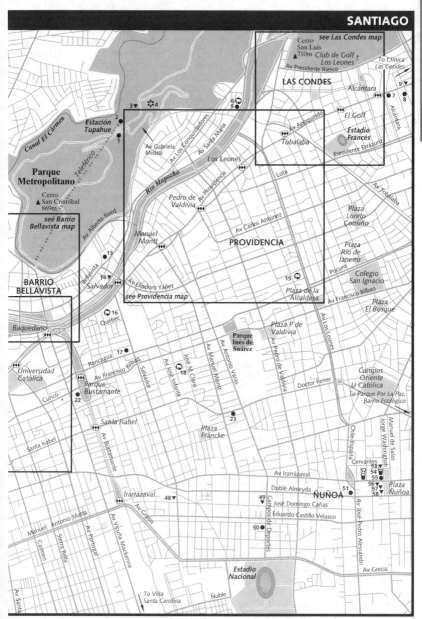

Cerro San Luis
▲710m *Club de Golf*
Los Leones
Av Presidente Riesco
To Clínica Las Condes

LAS CONDES

Alcántara

El Golf

Av Apoquindo

Estadio
Francés

Tobalaba

Presidente Errázuriz

Cerro
San Luis

Estación
Tupahue

Canal El Cármen

Teleférico

Av Gabriela
Mistral

Av Los Conquistadores

Av Santa María

Río Mapocho

Los Leones

Av Providencia

Pedro de
Valdivia

Parque
Metropolitano

Cerro
▲ San Cristóbal
869m

see Barrio
Bellavista map

Av Alberto Reed

Manuel
Montt

Av Carlos Antúnez

PROVIDENCIA

Plaza
Loreto
Cousiño

Av Tobalaba

Plaza
Río de
Janeiro

Colegio
San Ignacio

Plaza de la
Alcaldesa

Av Francisco Bilbao

Plaza
El Bosque

BARRIO
BELLAVISTA

Bellavista

Salvador

Av Eliodoro Yáñez

see Providencia map

Baquedano

Quebec

Plaza P de
Valdivia

Parque
Inés de
Suárez

Av Los Leones

Av Pedro de Valdivia

Universidad
Católica

Rancagua

Av Francisco Bilbao

Salvador

José M Claro

José Infante

Av Antonio Varas

Av Manuel Montt

Campus
Oriente
U Católica
To Parque Por La Paz,
Barrio Ecológico

Curicó

Parque
Bustamante

Doctor Ferrer

Santa Isabel

Av Bustamante

Plaza
Francke

Chile-España

Jorge Washington

Manuel de Salas

Santa Isabel

Cervantes

Plaza
Ñuñoa

Av Irarrázaval

Manuel Antonio Matta

Sierra Bella

Carmen

Av Portugal

Irarrázaval

Av Vicuña Mackenna

Av Grecia

Dublé Almeyda

José Domingo Cañas

Eduardo Castillo Velasco

NUÑOA

Campos de Deportes

Av José Pedro Alessandri

Estadio
Nacional

To Viña
Santa Carolina

Ñuble

Av Grecia

Av Santa

10 am to 1:30 pm Saturday. Two other booksellers occupy the same complex: Books (☎ 235-1205), with a good selection of used but fairly expensive English-language paperbacks, and the feminist bookshop Lila.

For new books in English, try Librería Inglesa at Paseo Huérfanos 669, Local 11, or at Av Pedro de Valdivia 47 in Providencia. For magazines and newspapers, Libro's has locations downtown (☎ 699-0319) at Huérfanos 1178 and in Providencia (☎ 2328-839) at Av Pedro de Valdivia 039. French-speakers will find reading material at the Librería Francesa (☎ 639-2407) at Paseo Estado 337, Local 22.

For a nearly complete selection of Lonely Planet titles, and many other books in both English and German, make a visit to Librería Eduardo Albers (☎ 218-5371), Av Vitacura 5648, Vitacura. Take any bus out Av Vitacura from Av Santa María.

Newspapers and magazines in English and many other European languages, as well as from other Latin American countries, are available at two kiosks at the junction of the Ahumada and Huérfanos pedestrian malls. If a newspaper appears to have been around more than a few days, you can often haggle over the price. Before buying anything, check to see that no pages are missing, as vendors often salvage papers off incoming international flights.

N'aitún (☎ 671-8410), Av Ricardo Cumming 453 in Santiago's Barrio Brasil, is a leftist bookstore-community center that doubles as a venue for live music and theater; drinks and snacks are available as well.

Cultural Centers

Where passenger trains to Viña del Mar and Valparaíso once arrived and departed, the Corporación Cultural de la Estación Mapocho (☎ 361-1761) has become Santiago's premier cultural center, offering live theater, concerts, art exhibits and a café. The center also hosts special events such as the annual book fair. It's on the south bank of the Río Mapocho at the north end of Bandera (Metro: Puente Cal y Canto). The Centro de Extensión de la Universidad Católica (☎ 222-0275), at Alameda 390 (Metro:

Universidad Católica), also regularly presents artistic and photographic exhibits. The Centro de Arte Violeta Parra (☎ 635-2387), Carmen 340, shows films, presents live folkloric music performances and has occasional art exhibits.

The Instituto Chileno-Norteamericano de Cultura (☎ 696-3215), Moneda 1467, offers frequent photographic and artistic exhibits on various topics in various media. It also has a decent English-language library, which carries North American newspapers and magazines, and free films. Other comparable cultural centers include the Instituto Chileno-Británico (☎ 638-2156), Santa Lucía 124, with current British newspapers and periodicals; the Instituto Goethe (☎ 638-3815), Esmeralda 650; and the Instituto Chileno-Francés (☎ 633-5465), Merced 298.

Several suburban comunas have their own cultural centers, all of which change programs frequently. The Instituto Cultural de Providencia (☎ 209-4341), Av 11 de Septiembre 1995, offers free lectures, film cycles and art exhibits. Others possibilities include the Casa de la Cultura de la Municipalidad de Ñuñoa (☎ 225-3919) at Av Irarrázaval 4055 (open 10 am to 8 pm daily) and the Instituto Cultural de Las Condes (☎ 212-8503) at Av Apoquindo 6570 (open 10:30 am to 1:30 pm and 3:30 to 7 pm daily except Monday). The Centro Cultural de España (☎ 235-0657), Av Providencia 927 (Metro: Salvador), is one of Santiago's most active foreign cultural representatives.

National Parks

For trekking and mountaineering information, as well as inexpensive maps and other national parks publications, visit the new information center of the Corporación Nacional Forestal (☎ 390-0282, 390-0125), known by its acronym Conaf, at Paseo Bulnes 291. Hours are 9 am to 1 pm and 2 to 4:30 pm weekdays only.

Laundry

Dry cleaners are abundant, but self-service laundries are relatively few. At most of these, 'self-service' means dropping off your clothes and picking them up later. Most of the inexpensive hotels will wash clothes for a reasonable price.

Lavandería Autoservicio (☎ 632-1772) is at Monjitas 507, south of the Parque Forestal in central Santiago. Lavandería Lolos (☎ 699-5376) is at Moneda 2296 in Barrio Brasil (Metro: República). There's also Laverap at Av Providencia 1645 (Metro: Pedro de Valdivia).

Camera Repair

For prompt and efficient – but not cheap – camera repair service, contact Harry Müller Thierfelder (☎ 698-3596), Ahumada 312, Oficina 312. Other possibilities are Tec-Fo (☎ 695-2969), Nueva York 52, Oficina 204, and, in Providencia, Photo von Stowasser (☎ 232-1138), Santa Magdalena 16 (Metro: Los Leones).

Medical Services

For medical emergencies, try the Posta Central (☎ 634-1650) at Av Portugal 125 (Metro: Universidad Católica), which has English-speaking personnel. Private clinics include the Clínica Universidad Católica (☎ 633-4122) at Lira 40; the Clínica Dávila (☎ 735-4030) at Av Recoleta 464 in Recoleta; or the Clínica Las Condes (☎ 211-1002) at Lo Fontecilla 411, Las Condes, which is more distant than the others.

Dangers & Annoyances

Santiago has a growing reputation for petty street crime, especially downtown and in areas such as Cerro Santa Lucía (though security has improved here recently). The US consulate recommends that visitors take cabs everywhere after dark and avoid city buses, which are said to crawl with pickpockets, but adds that a visit to Chile is usually without incident. Be alert, but not obsessed with personal security. Do take special care with your personal belongings when seated at sidewalk cafés in heavily traveled areas.

Every year, around the September 11 anniversary of the 1973 coup, Providencia's Av 11 de Septiembre becomes the site of very contentious demonstrations, and many visitors prefer to avoid the area at that time.

SANTIAGO CENTRO
Walking Tour

An appropriate starting point for an orientation walk through downtown Santiago is the **Estación Mapocho**, at the corner of Bandera and Balmaceda on the south bank of the Río Mapocho, where rail passengers from Valparaíso and Viña del Mar used to arrive, from 1912 until the mid-1980s. It is now the city's foremost cultural center. Across Balmaceda, between 21 de Mayo and Puente, the wrought-iron **Mercado Central**, designed by architect Fermín Vivaceta in 1872, is one of Santiago's most colorful attractions; any of its numerous seafood locales is a fine choice for lunch or an early dinner.

Two blocks southeast, at Esmeralda 749, the **Posada del Corregidor** (1765) is a whitewashed, two-story adobe structure with an attractive wooden balcony; its art gallery (☎ 633-5573) is open to the public 10 am to 5 pm weekdays, 10 am to noon Saturdays. Continue down MacIver to the corner of Santo Domingo, where the **Casa Manso de Velasco** (1730) resembles the Posada del Corregidor, then head west to the **Templo de Santo Domingo** (1808), a massive stone church at Santo Domingo 961.

One block south is the **Plaza de Armas**, the city's historical center, flanked by the **Correo Central** (main post office, 1882), the Museo Histórico Nacional in the **Palacio de la Real Audiencia** (1804), the **Municipalidad de Santiago** (1785) and the **Catedral Metropolitana** (1745). Half a block east of the plaza, the colonial **Casa Colorada** (1769) houses the city museum and tourist office.

Two blocks west of the plaza, at Morandé 441, the former **Congreso Nacional** (1876) has become the Ministerio de Relaciones Exteriores (Foreign Ministry) since the Congreso moved to Valparaíso. The Ministry's Academia Diplomática (Diplomatic Academy) occupies the nearby **Palacio Edwards**, Catedral 1183, once the mansion of an elite Anglo-Chilean family. Immediately south of the ex-Congreso, fronting on Compañía, are the **Tribunales de Justicia** (Law Courts).

Across the street, at Bandera and Compañía, the late-colonial **Real Casa de Aduana**

SANTIAGO CENTRO

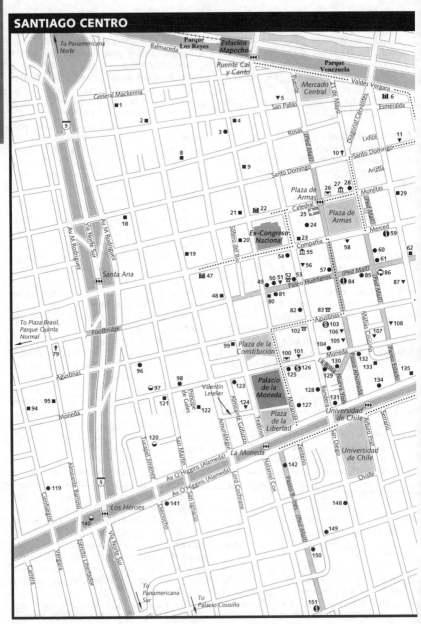

To Panamericana Norte

Parque Los Reyes

Balmaceda

Estación Mapocho

Puente Cal y Canto

Parque Venezuela

Valdés Vergara

General Mackenna

■ 1

2 ■

■ 4

3 ●

8 ■

■ 9

Mercado Central

Diagonal Cervantes

Esmeralda

▼ 5

San Pablo

21 de Mayo

Rosas

(red Mall)

Lidice

11

10 †

Santo Domingo

Ariztía

Santo Domingo

Plaza de Armas

26 ● 27 ● 28 ●

Monjitas

■ 29

21 ■

■ 22

Catedral

25 ●

Plaza de Armas

● 24

Merced

❶ 59

■ 18

Ex-Congreso Nacional

● 20

■ 23

Compañía

58 ▼

● 60

● 61

62

Sotero del Río

■ 19

54 ●

■ 55

● 56

57 ●

(Ped Mall)

❶ 84

● 85

86

87 ▼

Santa Ana

Av M Rodríguez

Av Norte Sur

■ 47

49 ● 50 51 52 53 ●

80 ●

81 ●

82 ●

83 ☎

Paseo Huérfanos

48 ■

To Plaza Brasil, Parque Quinta Normal

Footbridge

Agustinas

❽ 103

106 ▼

102 ☎

104 ●

105 ▼

▼ 108

107 ●

† 79

99 ■

Plaza de la Constitución

100 ● 101 ●

Moneda

130 ●

132 ●

133 ●

135 ●

96 ●

97 ●

98 ●

123 ●

125 ● 126 ●

129 ●

134 ●

121 ●

122 ■

Valentín Leteller

124 ▼

Palacio de la Moneda

128 ●

131 ❶

95 ■

94 ■

Moneda

120 ●

127 ●

Plaza de la Libertad

Universidad de Chile

Universidad de Chile

La Moneda

● 119

Los Héroes

● 141

142 ●

148 ●

140 ●

149 ●

150 ●

To Panamericana Sur

To Palacio Cousiño

151 ❶

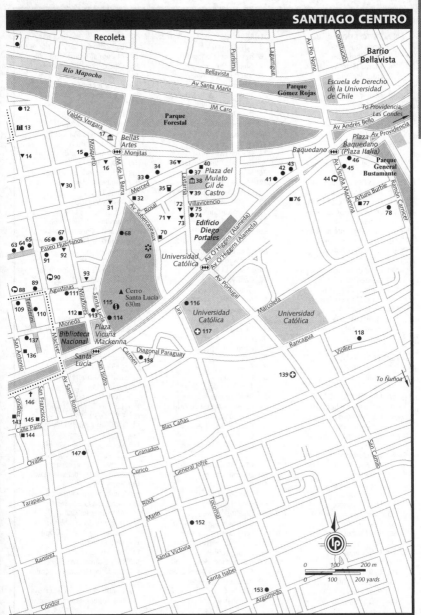

SANTIAGO CENTRO

PLACES TO STAY
1 Hotel Caribe
2 Hotel Pudahuel
4 Nuevo Hotel Valparaíso
8 Hotel Indiana
9 Hotel Cervantes
18 Majestic Hotel
19 Hotel Europa
20 Hotel Metrópoli
21 Hotel España
23 City Hotel
29 Hotel Tupahue
32 Hotel Foresta
40 Hostal del Parque
48 Hotel Panamericano
62 Hotel Santa Lucía
70 Hotel Montecarlo
76 Holiday Inn Crowne Plaza
77 Hotel Principado
80 Hotel Gran Palace
94 Hostelling International
95 Hotel Turismo Japón
99 Hotel Carrera
112 Hotel Riviera
121 Hotel di Maurier
122 Residencial Tabita
133 Hotel El Conquistador
135 Hotel El Libertador
136 Hotel Galerías
143 Hotel Las Vegas
144 Residencial Londres
145 Hotel París

PLACES TO EAT
5 Bar Central
11 Kam-Thu
14 Da Carla
16 Kintaro
30 El Puente de Bórquez
31 Izakaya Yoko
36 Les Assassins
38 Pérgola de la Plaza
39 Cocoa
51 Bar Nacional 2
56 Bar Nacional 1
58 Chez Henry
71 Rincón Español
72 Gatopardo
73 Don Victorino
75 Café del Biógrafo
87 Le Due Torri
92 San Marcos
93 Au Bon Pain
101 El Novillero
105 Café Caribe
106 Café Haiti
107 Café Cousiño
108 Pizza Napoli
124 100% Natural

OTHER
3 Sala Agustín Sire
6 Posada del Corregidor
7 Chip Day Tours
8 South Central American
   Information Club
10 Templo de Santo Domingo
12 Instituto Goethe
13 Casa Manso de Velasco
15 Lavandería Autoservicio
17 Palacio de Bellas Artes
22 Palacio Edwards
24 Librería Manantial
25 Catedral Metropolitana
26 Main Post Office
27 Museo Histórico Nacional
   (Palacio de la Real Audiencia)
28 Municipalidad de Santiago
33 Teatro La Comedia
34 Librería El Cid
35 Bar Berri
37 Instituto Chileno-Francés
38 Museo Arqueológico de
   Santiago
41 Cine Alameda
42 Café Virtual
43 Avant
44 Argentine Consulate
45 Natalis Language Center
46 Teatro Universidad de Chile
47 Palacio La Alhambra
49 American Airlines, Canadian
   Airlines International
50 Ladeco
52 Entel
53 DHL Express
54 Tribunales de Justicia
55 Real Casa de Aduana
   (Museo Chileno de Arte
   Precolombino)
57 Harry Müller Thierfelder
   (Camera Repair)
59 Casa Colorada (Museo de
   Santiago),
   Main Municipal Tourist Office
60 Librería Francesa
61 Avant
63 Cine Huelen
64 Cine Hoyts
65 Cine Rex
66 Librería Inglesa
67 Feria Chilena del Libro
68 Ascensor (Elevator)
69 Jardín Japonés
74 Cine El Biógrafo
78 Federación de Andinismo
79 Basílica del Salvador
80 Libro's, Cine Gran Palace 4
81 Huimpalay

82 Iberia
83 BellSouth Celular
84 Municipal Tourist Kiosk
85 Cine Central, Cine Huérfanos
86 Paraguayan Embassy
88 German Embassy
89 Transmarchilay
90 Brazilian Consulate
91 Cine Lido
96 INJ
97 Tour Express (Airport Buses)
98 Instituto Chileno-
   Norteamericano de Cultura
100 Post Office
102 VTR Telecomunicaciones
103 Cambio Andes
104 Chile Típico
109 Teatro Municipal
110 United Airlines
111 LanChile
113 Instituto Chileno-Británico
114 Centro de Exposición de Arte
   Indígena
115 Tourist Office
116 Centro de Extensión de la
   Universidad Católica
117 Clínica Universidad Católica
118 MUMS
119 Colo Colo
120 Terminal Los Héroes
123 Departamento de Extranjería
   (Tourist Card Extensions)
125 Lloyd Aéreo Boliviano (LAB),
   Ecuatoriana
126 Cambios Afex
127 Teatro Nacional Chileno
128 Difrol
129 Stock Exchange
130 Tec-Fo (Camera Repair)
131 Club de La Unión
132 Lufthansa, Sportstour
134 Alitalia
135 Venta de Pasajes, Galería
   Libertador (train tickets)
137 Aerolíneas Argentinas
138 Centro Artesanal Santa Lucía
139 Posta Central
140 Centropuerto (Airport Buses)
141 Confitería Las Torres
142 Altar de la Patria
146 Iglesia de San Francisco
   (Museo de Arte Colonial)
147 DHL Express
148 Librería Rivano
149 Cine Normandie
150 Fondo de Cultura Económica
151 Conaf
152 Centro de Arte Violeta Parra
153 Los Adobes de Argomedo

(royal customhouse) contains the outstanding Museo Chileno de Arte Precolombino. Two blocks west, at Compañía 1340, Chañarcillo silver magnate Francisco Ignacio Ossa Mercado lived in the Moorish-style **Palacio La Alhambra** (1862); it's now an art gallery and cultural center (☎ 689-0875), open 11 am to 1 pm and 5 to 7:30 pm weekdays.

Running south from the Plaza de Armas, **Paseo Ahumada** is Santiago's main pedestrian thoroughfare. Municipal pressure has reduced the number of street vendors, but buskers of diverse style and varied quality still congregate in the evening (even though shrill Protestant evangelicals often drown out all others). The perpendicular **Paseo Huérfanos** crosses Paseo Ahumada a block south of the plaza. One block east, between the Plaza and the Alameda, **Paseo Estado** is a pedestrian mall.

Southwest of the plaza, between Teatinos and Morandé, **Plaza de la Constitución** offers unobstructed views of the late-colonial **Palacio de La Moneda**, which occupies an entire block. Formerly the presidential residence, La Moneda was badly damaged by air force attacks during the 1973 military coup d'état but restored before the return to democracy. On the opposite side of La Moneda, facing the Alameda, the smaller **Plaza de la Libertad** faces in turn, across the Alameda, the **Altar de la Patria**, which crowns the crypt of Chilean liberator General Bernardo O'Higgins.

Other nearby buildings of note are the **Bolsa de Comercio** (stock exchange, 1917) at La Bolsa 64, and the **Club de La Unión** (1925) at Alameda 1091, where Santiago's stockbrokers hold their power lunches. A short walk across the Alameda (the Metro underpass is safer if not quicker) is the imposing **Universidad de Chile** (1874), Alameda 1058. A few blocks east, at Alameda 834, the striking **Iglesia de San Francisco** (1618, with subsequent modifications) is one of Santiago's oldest buildings, housing the **Museo de Arte Colonial**, an important collection of colonial art. Across the Alameda, at the corner of MacIver, sits the monolithic **Biblioteca Nacional**; two blocks north at Agustinas 794, another impressive building,

the **Teatro Municipal** (1857) is Santiago's prime performing arts venue.

Palacio de la Moneda

Under the direction of Italian-born architect Joaquín Toesca, construction of a royal mint started in 1788 near the current Mercado Central on the Río Mapocho. When the flood-prone site proved inadequate, the project was soon moved to its present location, a former Jesuit farm, where it was finally completed in 1805. Toesca also contributed his architectural talents to Santiago's Catedral Metropolitana, on the Plaza de Armas.

In the mid-19th century, La Moneda became the residence of Chilean presidents, but the last to actually live there was Carlos Ibáñez del Campo, during his second term (1952–58). After his military coup d'état of 1973 left the building unusable, General Pinochet governed from the Edificio Diego Portales, on the Alameda near Cerro Santa Lucía, but since La Moneda's 1981 restoration, Pinochet and elected presidents Patricio Aylwin and Eduardo Frei have kept their offices here. On alternate days at 10 am, the carabineros hold a changing-of-the-guard ceremony here.

The building itself occupies the entire block bounded by Morandé and Teatinos, between Plaza Libertad and Plaza de la Constitución; the main entrance on Moneda faces the latter. With 20 days' advance notice, it's possible to take a guided tour of the interior by contacting the Dirección Administrativa del Palacio de La Moneda (☎ 671-4103). This can often be done more quickly, however, by making an in-person appearance at the subterranean office on Plaza de la Constitución, entered from Morandé.

Mercado Central

Occupying an entire block bounded by San Pablo, Puente, 21 de Mayo and Av Balmaceda, next to the Río Mapocho, Santiago's central market is a distinctive wrought-iron edifice dating from 1872; in its superstructure, note the Chilean star that repeats all the way around the building. Besides an appealing selection of fresh fruit, vegetables and fish, there are a number of eating places ranging from modest to the finest.

Downtown Museums

For a complete listing of museums in downtown Santiago, ask for Sernatur's leaflet *Galerías de Arte y Museos*, which also gives opening hours and transport details. Most museums are free Sundays and closed Mondays.

Museo de Santiago Part of the colonial Casa Colorada, this museum documents the capital's growth from its modest nucleus to the current sprawl. Permanent exhibits include maps, paintings, dioramas and colonial dress. Particularly intriguing are the dioramas of the 1647 earthquake (when 10% of the population died) and the departure of troops for the north in the War of the Pacific. Also of note are a model of the Iglesia de La Compañía after the fire of 1863 and a life-size re-creation of a *sarao*, a parlor gathering of Santiago's late-colonial elite.

At Merced 860, the museum (☎ 633-0723) is open 10 am to 6 pm Tuesday to Friday, 10 am to 5 pm Saturday and 11 am to 2 pm Sundays and holidays. Admission is US$1. There is also a combination bookstore and gift shop.

Museo Chileno de Arte Precolombino In the late-colonial (1805) Real Casa de Aduana (royal customs house), this beautifully arranged museum chronicles 4500 years of pre-Columbian civilization. There are separate halls for Mesoamerica (Mexico and Central America), the central Andes (Peru and Bolivia), the northern Andes (Colombia and Ecuador) and the southern Andes (modern Chile and Argentina plus, anomalously, parts of Brazil). Most of the well-preserved items come from the personal collections of the Larraín family, but special exhibits run from time to time.

At Bandera 361, the Museum (☎ 695-3851) is open 10 am to 6 pm Tuesday to Saturday, 10 am to 2 pm Sundays and holidays, though it's closed during Semana Santa, May 1, September 18, Christmas and New

Year's Eve. Admission is about US$3. It also has a good bookstore and an excellent, attractive café.

Convento y Museo de San Francisco Exhibits at Santiago's landmark church, Iglesia de San Francisco (Museo de Arte Colonial), include a wall-size painting, attributed to an 18th-century artist, detailing the genealogy of the Franciscan order and its patrons. The several rooms depicting the life of St Francis of Assisi will test the endurance of all but the most earnestly devout. At Londres 4, just off the Alameda, the museum (☎ 639-8737) is open 10 am to 1:30 pm and 3 to 6 pm Tuesday to Saturday, 10 am to 2 pm Sundays and holidays. Admission costs US$1 for adults, US$0.50 for children.

Palacio de Bellas Artes Santiago's early-20th-century fine arts museum, modeled on the Petit Palais in Paris, fronts an entire block in the Parque Forestal, on José M de La Barra near Av José María Caro. It has permanent collections of French, Italian, Dutch and Chilean paintings, plus occasional special exhibitions, some of which have been spectacular.

Hours at the museum (☎ 633-0655) are 11 am to 7 pm Tuesday to Saturday, 11 am to 2 pm Sundays and holidays. Admission is US$1; children pay half.

Palacio Cousiño Originally of Portuguese descent, this prominent Chilean wine family enjoyed additional successes in coal and silver mining, which enabled them to build what was probably Santiago's foremost mansion, dating from 1871, embellished with French-style artwork and featuring one of the country's first elevators. Some years back, fire destroyed the 3rd-floor interior, but the remaining floors are well-preserved reminders of elite life in the late 19th century.

Probably the most elaborate of Santiago's 19th-century mansions open to the public, the Palacio (☎ 698-5063) is south of the Alameda at Dieciocho 438, near Parque Almagro (Metro: Los Héroes or, more conveniently, Toesca). It's open 9:30 am to

1:30 pm daily except Monday and 2:30 to 5 pm weekdays. Admission is US$2 for adults, US$1 for children, including excellent guided tours in Spanish or sometimes in English. Interior photography of the palacio is prohibited, but the building's exterior and the surrounding gardens, designed by Spanish landscaper Miguel Arana Bórica, may be photographed.

Museo de la Solidaridad Salvador Allende Having begun in 1971 with donations from artists around the world in sympathy with Chile's socialist experiment, this museum went underground after the military coup of 1973 – the entire collection spent 17 years in the warehouses of the Museo de Arte Contemporáneo, awaiting the return of civilian rule.

Supplemented by works from Chilean artists in exile, a part of the collection is now on display in this small museum (☎ 697-1033) in a cul-de-sac at Virginia Opazo 38 (Metro: República). While the paintings and sculptures themselves are less overtly political than one might expect, the museum also includes a video salon for viewing the history of Allende and the Unidad Popular. Hours are 11 am to 1 pm and 2 to 7 pm weekdays; admission is free (Santiago map).

Cerro Santa Lucía

Honeycombed with gardens, footpaths and fountains, Cerro Santa Lucía (known to the Mapuche as Welen) has been a handy hilltop sanctuary from the bustle of downtown Santiago since 1875. At its base, on the Alameda, sits a large stone engraved with the text of a letter in which Pedro de Valdivia extolled the beauty of the newly conquered territories to Spain's King Carlos V. A short distance north is a striking tiled mural of Nobel Prize-winning poet Gabriela Mistral.

Also fronting the Alameda, at the southwest corner of Cerro Santa Lucía, is the refurbished, attractive **Plaza Neptuno**, around whose fountains staircases ascend to the summit, where a parapet reveals a perfect view of the city, Cerro San Cristóbal and the Andes – smog permitting. The north side of the park, along Av Subercaseaux, features a

pleasant **Jardín Japonés** (Japanese Garden). Santa Lucía's landscaping is a modern development – Bryce noted in 1914 that 'The buildings which had defaced it having been nearly all removed, it is now laid out as a pleasure ground, and planted with trees.' These improvements were the legacy of Santiago mayor Benjamín Vicuña Mackenna, whose tomb lies in a chapel near the summit.

Cerro Santa Lucía is an easy walk from downtown to the east end of Huérfanos, where a glass *ascensor* (elevator) carries passengers up the steep hillside, or a short ride on the Metro to Estación Santa Lucía. It has acquired an unfortunate reputation for nighttime muggings but is generally safe during the day, although visitors should not be complacent.

The municipal tourist office branch on Cerro Santa Lucía offers informative 1½-hour guided tours, in Spanish and English, Thursdays at 11 am. These include a visit to Vicuña Mackenna's tomb and the traditional midday cannon shot; ear protection is provided, but the recoil is powerful and the explosion loud enough to set off car alarms in the street below.

Museo Arqueológico de Santiago Featuring outstanding exhibits on Chile's indigenous peoples from colonial times to the present, this misleadingly named museum is ethnohistorical rather than archaeological. Its major defect is some outdated rhetoric that presents its subjects as Chilean possessions instead of as people in their own right.

At the Plaza del Mulato Gil de Castro, Lastarria 321 on the east side of Cerro Santa Lucía, the Museum (☎ 638-3502) is part of an interesting neighborhood that includes many art galleries, excellent bookstores and varied restaurants. It's open 10 am to 2 pm and 3:30 to 6:30 pm weekdays, 10 am to 2 pm Saturdays. Admission is free.

BARRIO BELLAVISTA

Across the Río Mapocho beneath Cerro San Cristóbal, on both sides of shady Av Pío Nono and many side streets, Bellavista is one of Santiago's liveliest neighborhoods on weekends, but it is usually quiet the rest of

SANTIAGO

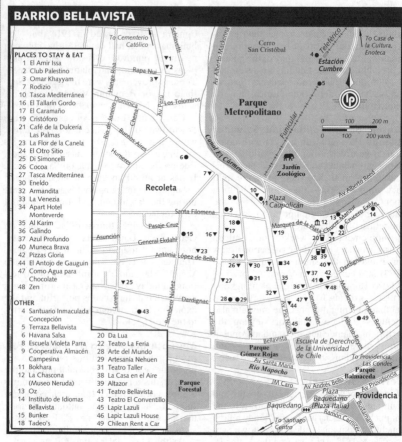

BARRIO BELLAVISTA

PLACES TO STAY & EAT
1   El Amir Issa
2   Club Palestino
3   Omar Khayyam
7   Rodizio
10 Tasca Mediterránea
16 El Tallarín Gordo
17 El Caramaño
19 Cristóforo
21 Café de la Dulcería
    Las Palmas
23 La Flor de la Canela
24 El Otro Sitio
25 Di Simoncelli
26 Cocoa
27 Tasca Mediterránea
30 Eneldo
32 Armandita
33 La Venezia
34 Apart Hotel
    Monteverde
35 Al Karim
36 Galindo
37 Azul Profundo
40 Muneca Brava
42 Pizzas Gloria
44 El Antojo de Gauguin
47 Como Agua para
    Chocolate
48 Zen

OTHER
4   Santuario Inmaculada
    Concepción
5   Terraza Bellavista
6   Havana Salsa
8   Escuela Violeta Parra
9   Cooperativa Almacén
    Campesina
11 Bokhara
12 La Chascona
    (Museo Neruda)
13 Oz
14 Instituto de Idiomas
    Bellavista
15 Bunker
18 Tadeo's
20 Da Lua
22 Teatro La Feria
28 Arte del Mundo
29 Artesanía Nehuen
31 Teatro Taller
38 La Casa en el Aire
39 Altazor
41 Teatro Bellavista
43 Teatro El Conventillo
45 Lapiz Lazuli
46 Lapiz Lazuli House
49 Chilean Rent a Car

---

the time. Its houses painted in lively pastels like those of Valparaíso's hill areas, Bellavista has countless ethnic restaurants and a very active Friday and Saturday evening crafts fair, starting at Parque Gómez Rojas across from the Escuela de Derecho de la Universidad de Chile (law school) and continuing up Av Pío Nono.

Parque Metropolitano (Cerro San Cristóbal)
Crowned by a 36m white statue of the Virgin Mary, 869m-tall Cerro San Cristóbal towers above downtown Santiago from the north

side of the Mapocho. Reached by funicular railway, *teleférico* (aerial tramway), bus or foot, it dominates Parque Metropolitano, central Santiago's largest open space and a major recreational resource for residents of the capital. There are several restaurants, snack bars and coffee shops.

The most direct route to San Cristóbal's summit is via the funicular, which climbs 485m from Plaza Caupolicán, at the north end of Pío Nono. Built in 1925, the funicular makes an intermediate stop at the **Jardín Zoológico** (zoo), which has a modest collection of scandalously neglected exotic animals (a tiger actually escaped and roamed the area for several hours one day in 1996); improvements are supposedly underway. The climb continues to the **Terraza Bellavista** where, on a rare clear day, there are extraordinary views of the city and its surroundings. At the summit proper, Pope John Paul II said mass at the **Santuario Inmaculada Concepción** during his Santiago visit in 1984.

A short walk from the Terraza is the Estación Cumbre, the start of the 2000m-long **teleférico**, which goes from Cerro San Cristóbal, via Tupahue, to a station near the north end of Av Pedro de Valdivia Norte (about 1200m from the Pedro de Valdivia Metro station).

At the Tupahue teleférico station is the **Piscina Tupahue**, a large swimming pool. A short walk east from Tupahue are the **Casa de la Cultura** (an art museum, open 9 am to 5 pm daily), Santiago's famous **Enoteca** (a restaurant and wine museum) and the **Jardín Botánico Mapulemu** (the botanical garden). Further east, there's another large pool at **Piscina Antilén**, reachable only by bus or on foot.

The funicular operates 10 am to 7 pm weekdays, 10 am to 8 pm weekends and holidays. The teleférico keeps slightly different hours, 10:30 am to 6:30 pm weekdays, extended to 7:30 pm weekends and holidays. From either direction, the funicular-teleférico combination (about US$3.50 for adults, US$1.75 for children), plus the Metro, is a good way to orient yourself to Santiago's complex geography. The funicular alone costs US$1.25 to Estación Cumbre, US$2 roundtrip. From Plaza Caupolicán, Buses Tortuga Tour also reaches Av Pedro de Valdivia Norte via Tupahue, on a winding, roundabout road.

La Chascona (Museo Neruda)

Nicknamed for the poet's widow Matilde Urrutia's unruly hair, Pablo Neruda's eclectic Bellavista house sits on a shady cul-de-sac at the foot of Cerro San Cristóbal, a short distance off Pío Nono.

The Fundación Neruda (☎ 737-8712), Márquez de La Plata 0192, conducts tours of La Chascona on a first-come, first-served basis 10 am to 1 pm and 3 to 6 pm daily except Monday. Admission costs US$2.50 for adults, half that for children; tours last an hour and are very thorough. The Fundación also arranges one-day bus tours, with lunch, which take in the poet's three houses: here, at Isla Negra and in Valparaíso (see the Middle Chile chapter for descriptions of the latter two).

Cementerio General

Both Chile's distant and recent history are on display here, where the tombs of figures such as José Manuel Balmaceda, Salvador Allende and diplomat Orlando Letelier are reminders of political turmoil from the 19th century to the present. A recent addition, erected in 1994, is a memorial to the 'disappeared' victims of the Pinochet dictatorship.

At the north end of Av La Paz, north of the Río Mapocho via the Cal y Canto bridge, the Cementerio General is open every day during daylight hours (Santiago map).

PROVIDENCIA

West of Barrio Bellavista is the comuna of Providencia. Its pleasant **Parque de las Esculturas** is an open-air sculpture garden on the banks of the Mapocho. There is also an indoor exhibition hall (☎ 340-7303) at Av Santa María 2201, a short walk across the river from the Pedro de Valdivia Metro station. It's open 9 am to 6 pm weekdays, 10 am to 6 pm weekends.

BARRIO BRASIL

Undergoing a renaissance in recent years, the area immediately southwest of the Via Norte Sur, reached via the new Paseo Huérfanos pedestrian suspension bridge and several surface streets, features good but affordable accommodations and restaurants, plus universities and cultural centers, in what remains one of Santiago's best-preserved traditional neighborhoods (Santiago map).

The barrio's centerpiece is re-landscaped **Plaza Brasil**, which includes a small memorial to samba musician Antonio Carlos Jobim, dedicated by Brazilian President Fernando Enrique Cardoso. Other landmarks

SANTIAGO

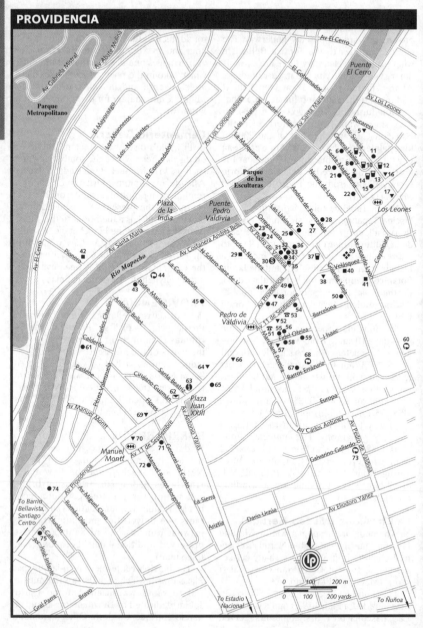

PROVIDENCIA

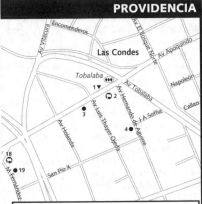

PROVIDENCIA

Encomenderos
Las Condes
Tobalaba
Napoleón
Callao
San Pío X

PLACES TO STAY
29 Hotel Aloha
35 Hotel Orly
40 Hotel Diego de Velásquez
41 Santiago Park Plaza
42 Sheraton San Cristóbal

PLACES TO EAT
1   La Vera Pizza
5   Casa de la Cultura
    de México
16 Freddo
17 Sbarro
27 Sebastián
32 El Huerto, La Huerta
38 Der Münchner Hof
46 Au Bon Pain
48 La Pizza Nostra
52 Pizza Napoli
57 Peters
64 Phone Box Pub,
    Café del Patio
66 La Escarcha
69 Bravíssimo
70 Liguria

OTHER
2   Belgian Consulate
3   Cine Tobalaba
4   Student Flight Center,
    Hostelling International
6   CyberCenter
7   Mister Ed
8   DHL Express
9   Saeta
10 Wall Street
11 Kasbba
12 Brannigans
13 The Old Boston Pub
14 Boomerang
15 Ladeco
18 Swedish Consulate,
    Spanish Consulate
19 SAS
20 Avianca
21 Transportes Aéreos
    Mercosur (TAM)
22 Photo von Stowasser
    (Camera Repair)

23 LanChile
24 Teatro Oriente
25 Grado Diez
26 American Airlines
28 Air New Zealand
30 Cambio Guiñazú
31 Avant
32 Fundación Lahuen
33 Expediciones Las
    Cascadas
34 Libro's
36 Turismo Tajamar
    (Thomas Cook)
37 Electric Cowboy
39 Mall Panorámico,
    Alamo Rent a Car,
    Northwest Airlines
43 United Rent a Car
44 Peruvian Embassy
45 Centro de Ski la Parva
47 Federal Express
49 Librería Inglesa
50 Aeroflot
51 Entel
53 Chilesat
54 Instituto Cultural de
    Providencia
55 Dity Office
56 Automóvil Club de
    Chile (Acchi)
58 Copa
59 Cubana de Aviación
60 Japanese Embassy
61 Hertz Rent a Car
62 Post Office
63 Sernatur
64 Librería Chile Ilustrado,
    Books, Lila
65 Laverap
67 Swissair
68 Austrian Embassy
71 Mapas de Matassi
72 Líneas Aéreas de
    Costa Rica (Lacsa)
73 Uruguayan Embassy
74 Torres de Tajamar,
    Atal Rent a Car
75 Centro Cultural
    de España

include the quake-damaged, neo-Gothic **Basílica del Salvador** (1892), and the gargoyle-festooned **Club Colo Colo** (1926) at Cienfuegos 41. Headquarters of the famous soccer club but originally built by architects Guillermo Edwards Matte and Federico Bieregel for the Ismael Edwards family, the latter building is one of the most outlandish in the city.

PARQUE QUINTA NORMAL

Once an area of prestigious mansions, the comuna of Quinta Normal is now much less exclusive but of great historical interest. West of downtown, the cool, woodsy 40-hectare Parque Quinta Normal attracts strolling Santiaguinos, family picnickers, impromptu soccer games and (on Sundays) increasing numbers of parading evangelicals.

The most notable of several museums in the park is the **Museo Nacional de Historia Natural** (☎ 681-4095), whose exhibits include a credible replica of the mummified body of a 12-year-old child, sacrificed at least 500 years ago. It was discovered in 1954 by a team from the Universidad de Chile on the icy summit of El Plomo, a 5000m-high peak near Santiago. Bone fragments of the giant Pleistocene ground sloth known as the 'milodon,' from the famous cave near Puerto Natales in southern Chile (see the Magallanes chapter), are also on display. Open 10 am to 5:30 pm Tuesday through Saturday, all year, it has varying Sunday hours: 11 am to 6:30 pm September to March, noon to 5:30 pm the rest of the year. Admission is US$1 for adults, US$0.50 for children.

In the middle of the park, there's an artificial lagoon where you can rent rowboats and, for children, the floating equivalent of bumper cars. Beyond the lagoon, visit the **Museo de Ciencia y Tecnología** (☎ 681-6022), open 10 am to 5:30 pm Tuesday to Friday, all year; weekend hours are 11 am to 7 pm October to mid-March, 11 am to 6 pm the rest of the year. Admission is US$1.50 for adults, US$1 for children.

Specifically for children, about 50m north, is the **Museo Infantil** (☎ 681-6022). It's open 9:30 am to 5 pm weekdays; admission is just US$1.

Near the southern entrance, the lovingly maintained steam locomotives at the open-air **Parque Museo Ferroviario** (☎ 681-4627) are a tribute to pioneers of the Chilean railroads. It's open 10 am to 6 pm Tuesday to Friday, 11 am to 7 pm weekends, from mid-October to mid-March; the rest of the year it's open 10 am to 5:30 pm Tuesday to Friday, 11 am to 5:45 pm weekends. Admission is US$1 for adults, US$0.60 for children.

Across from the southern entrance, at Av Portales 3530, housed in an offbeat structure designed for the Paris Exhibition of 1889 and dismantled and installed opposite the Quinta Normal in the early 1900s, the **Museo Artequín** (☎ 681-8687) is an interactive museum of replica art, mostly the work of European masters. December to February, it's open 10:30 am to 6:30 pm Tuesday to Friday, 11 am to 7:30 pm weekends; the rest of the year, hours are 9 am to 5 pm Tuesday to Friday, 11 am to 6 pm weekends. Admission is by voluntary contribution.

To get to the park, take the Metro to Estación Central and then walk or catch a northbound bus up Matucana. There are park entrances on Av Portales, Matucana, Santo Domingo and Apostól Santiago. Public hours are 8 am to 8:30 pm daily except Monday (Santiago map).

PARQUE O'HIGGINS

In a previous incarnation as Parque Cousiño, 80-hectare Parque O'Higgins was the preserve of Santiago's elite, but it's now a more egalitarian place. Parts of the park are dilapidated, making it less appealing than Parque Quinta Normal, but it provides an entertaining glimpse of what many working-class Chileans do on weekends.

The sector known as **El Pueblito** features full-size replicas of rural buildings and a gaggle of inexpensive restaurants with raucous salsa bands on Sunday afternoon. Its **Museo del Huaso** (☎ 555-0054), honoring Chile's counterpart to the Argentine gaucho, often features good folkloric music. It's open 10 am to 5 pm weekdays, 10 am to 2 pm weekends.

El Pueblito also has a small **Museo Acuario** (Municipal Aquarium, ☎ 556-5680),

a **Museo de Insectas y Caracoles** (Museum of Insects and Snails) and a **Museo de Fauna Menor**, a mini-zoo. All the latter are open 10 am to 7 pm daily.

Fantasilandia (☎ 689-3035) is a children's amusement park. In the summer, it's open 2 to 8 pm weekdays except Mondays, 11 am to 8 pm weekends. The rest of the year, hours are 11 am to 8 pm weekends only. Admission, which includes unlimited rides, is free for children who are shorter than 90cm; those between 91cm and 140cm pay US$7.50; all others pay US$8.50.

To get to Parque O'Higgins, take Línea 2 of the Metro to Parque O'Higgins station and walk west upon leaving the station (Santiago map).

PLAZA ÑUÑOA

As upscale high-rise development dissolves the community feeling of once-suburban areas like Providencia and Las Condes, Santiaguinos have gained a new appreciation of areas like middle-class Ñuñoa, where attractive single-family houses and tree-lined streets recall what other parts of the capital have lost. It's close enough to the Andean front range that the mountains are usually visible despite the city's frequent smog.

Middle-class doesn't necessarily mean dull, however – Ñuñoa has an active cultural life centered around Plaza Ñuñoa, where the Universidad Católica has one of Santiago's most important theater venues, and a progressive municipal administration has promoted live concerts and a crafts and flea market. Restaurants and dance clubs pull visitors from downtown, especially on weekends, the Estadio Nacional hosts soccer matches and rock concerts, and foreign students from the Universidad de Chile's nearby Macul campus add a cosmopolitan element.

To get to Plaza Ñuñoa from elsewhere in the city, take bus Nos 212, 338 or 382 from Plaza Italia (the area around Plaza Baquedano), 433 from Alameda and Vicuña Mackenna, 606 from the Terminal de Buses Santiago, 600 from Estación Central or 243 from Compañía. Metrobús directly connects Estación Salvador with Plaza Ñuñoa.

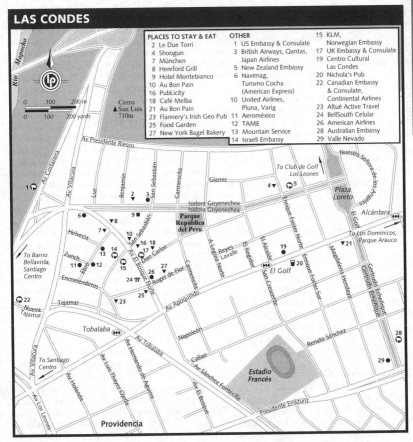

LAS CONDES

PLACES TO STAY & EAT	OTHER	15 KLM,
2 Le Due Torri	1 US Embassy & Consulate	Norwegian Embassy
4 Shoogun	3 British Airways, Qantas,	17 UK Embassy & Consulate
7 München	Japan Airlines	19 Centro Cultural
8 Hereford Grill	5 New Zealand Embassy	Las Condes
9 Hotel Montebianco	6 Navimag,	20 Nichola's Pub
10 Au Bon Pain	Turismo Cocha	22 Canadian Embassy
16 PubLicity	(American Express)	& Consulate,
18 Café Melba	10 United Airlines,	Continental Airlines
21 Au Bon Pain	Pluna, Varig	23 Altué Active Travel
23 Flannery's Irish Geo Pub	11 Aeroméxico	24 BellSouth Celular
25 Food Garden	12 TAME	26 American Airlines
27 New York Bagel Bakery	13 Mountain Service	28 Australian Embassy
	14 Israeli Embassy	29 Valle Nevado

PARQUE POR LA PAZ

In the mostly working-class comuna of Peñalolén, in Santiago's eastern foothills, the onetime estate of Villa Grimaldi was the main detention and torture center for now-imprisoned General Manuel Contreras' notorious DINA. The compound was razed by the military to cover up evidence in the last days of the Pinochet dictatorship, and it has been converted into a memorial park. It's a powerful testament; you need only read the descriptions and see the names of the dead and disappeared to imagine what happened here.

Little remains of the original buildings, except for the former DINA photo lab (containing a model of Villa Grimaldi, ask attendant for key) and the swimming pool, used to frighten people by feigning executions. There are 224 names on a list of those who died here, but only a handful of these appear in military records as executed.

Parque por la Paz, in the 8300 block of José Arrieta near La Capilla, is open 11 am to 8:30 pm daily except Monday. Take bus No 242 from Av Providencia, No 433 from Plaza Italia, or No 337 from Estación Central, on the Alameda.

BARRIO ECOLÓGICO

Also in Peñalolén, where the foothills steepen toward the front range, the so-called Barrio Ecológico began as an agrarian-reform subdivision of a fundo in the late 1960s under President Eduardo Frei Montalva. As wheat crops failed because of poor soils in what was then a remote location, hippies began to move in, acquiring land from campesinos. At the time, this area lacked electricity and running water (now it has both), but the new residents created an innovative community, including some interesting buildings.

Some peasants remain, providing a social mix, and there is an agreement with the Municipalidad of Peñalolén that this should remain a low-density area as a barrier against Santiago's sprawl. None of the streets is paved – a preference of the residents – but some houses have become very elaborate.

At the entrance to the barrio, which is precisely at the end of the No 318 bus line from Mapocho, Santa Lucía or Diagonal Paraguay, there's a small but worthwhile crafts market and a picada serving good, moderately priced lunches. Weekends are the best time to visit.

LANGUAGE COURSES

For intensive (but not inexpensive) language courses, try the Instituto de Idiomas Bellavista (☎ 735-7651), Crucero Exeter 0325, Bellavista. At Ernesto Pinto Lagarrigue 362-A, the Escuela Violeta Parra (☎ 735-8240, fax 229-8246) has drawn praise for emphasizing the social context of language instruction, by arranging field trips to community and environmental organizations, vineyards and the like, as well as tours to nearby national parks.

The Instituto Goethe (☎ 638-3185), in central Santiago at Esmeralda 650, offers intensive Spanish language courses, consisting of four weeks of 25 class-hours per week for US$390; classes are available for beginning, intermediate and advanced students. The Instituto also offers twice-weekly conversation classes for US$120 for four weeks. Classes are no larger than 10 to 12 students.

Another centrally located alternative is the Natalis Language Center (☎/fax 222-6470, natalis@intermedia.cl), Vicuña Mackenna 6, Departamento 3, where month-long courses (20 to 25 hours per week) cost US$340, with a maximum of five students per class. One-on-one conversation classes are also possible.

ORGANIZED TOURS

If your time is limited, consider a tour of Santiago and its surroundings. The municipal tourist kiosk on Paseo Ahumada offers thematic walking tours of the downtown area Tuesday mornings at 10:30 am and Wednesday afternoons at 3 pm; verify these times. Tours include admission to selected museums, and they sometimes accommodate English speakers. You can also arrange tours at the tourist office on Cerro Santa Lucía, taking in Cerro Santa Lucía, the Barrio Cívico Fundacional (the area in and around Plaza de la Constitución), Parque Forestal, museums and the Ruta Herencia Señorial, including Palacio Cousiño and other exclusive buildings.

Several agencies organize day and night tours of the capital (around US$20 each), excursions to Viña del Mar and Valparaíso (around US$40), visits to the Cousiño Macul and Concha y Toro wineries, and ski trips to Farellones, Valle del Nevado and Portillo (see Ski Resorts in the Around Santiago section). Among them are Turismo Cocha (☎ 230-1000) at Av El Bosque Norte 0430 in Las Condes (Metro: Tobalaba) and Sportstour Chile (☎ 549-5200), Moneda 970, 14th floor.

Turismo Frontera (☎ 687-4390 for reservations) leads a city tour of Santiago including La Chascona, the Palacio Cousiño and Parque Metropolitano for US$22, not including admission charges, and a full-day excursion to Isla Negra (US$35), not including lunch. There are also tours to vineyards, Pomaire and the Cajón del Maipo.

Chip Day Tours (☎ 777-5376), Av Santa María 227, Oficina 12, on the north side of the Río Mapocho, offers an unusual, human-rights-oriented 'Historical Memory' tour that includes visits to Parque por la Paz (see that section, earlier in the chapter) and, for a different point of view, the Fundación Pinochet. A half-day tour costs US$35, while a full-day tour, including lunch, costs US$50 to US$75 depending on the number of passengers. Chip also offers tours in the vicinity of Santiago, including Neruda's Isla Negra and regional vineyards.

For other tours and activities outside the city, see the Around Santiago section.

SPECIAL EVENTS

Santiago hosts a variety of special events throughout the year. January's Festival del Barrio Brasil highlights an area currently undergoing a major renewal. Late in the month, the suburban comuna of San Bernardo hosts the Festival Nacional del Folclore.

In March, Aeropuerto Los Cerrillos is the site of the Feria Internacional del Aire y del Espacio, a major international air show attended by an odd combination of arms merchants and the general public. The last Saturday of April, the Gran Premio Hipódromo Chile (at the Hipódromo Chile) determines Chile's best three-year-old race horses. Over the course of the winter, several other racing events take place here and at the Club Hípico.

Santiago's annual Feria Internacional del Libro (International Book Fair) takes place the last two weeks of November in the former Estación Mapocho. Though not so large as Buenos Aires' festival, it attracts authors from throughout the country and the continent, including big names such as Peru's Mario Vargas Llosa and Argentina's Federico Andahazi. Each day focuses on a single country, usually Latin American or European, but there's the occasional oddity such as Iran.

At around the same time, Chile's indigenous peoples – Mapuche, Diaguita, Atacameña, Aymara and Rapa Nui – celebrate their heritage at the Feria Indígena Cerro Huelén, held near the fountain on the south side of Cerro Santa Lucía. Musicians, dancers and others give performances daily, while crafts workers display their weavings, wood carvings, basketry and jewelry. Typical Chilean food is also available.

PLACES TO STAY
Budget

Santiago has abundant budget accommodations, but travelers should be selective – lodgings in this category differ much more in quality than in price.

Hostels Santiago's custom-built *Hostelling International* facility (☎ 671-8532, 688-6434, fax 672-8880, histgoch@entelchile.net, Cienfuegos 151) has a convenient Barrio Brasil location (Metro: Los Héroes). Rates for the 120 beds, in four- and six-bed rooms with locking closets, are US$10 per night for members, US$12.50 for nonmembers, guests automatically become members after six nights. Common areas are ample, including a much-improved cafeteria, TV lounge and patio, and quick, inexpensive laundry service. If the hostel is not crowded, it's possible to have a single or double room for an additional small charge.

About 10 minutes south of the Estación Central by *micro* (a small bus that often travels along the back roads), US-run *SCS Habitat* (☎ 683-3732, San Vicente 1798) is a cramped but still cheap and popular lodging in a quiet but relatively inconvenient neighborhood. Rates are US$7 to US$10 per person with breakfast.

Hotels, Hospedajes & Residenciales

Santiago's main budget hotel zone is a seedy but not really dangerous neighborhood near the former Terminal de Buses Norte, around General Mackenna, Amunátegui, San Pablo and San Martín (Metro: Puente Cal y Canto), where accommodations range from squalid to basic and acceptable. Single women may feel uncomfortable here late at night, especially on General Mackenna, where many prostitutes hang out.

Hotel Indiana (☎ 671-4251, Rosas 1343), a dilapidated mansion with dependable hot water, is Santiago's Israeli hangout; beds cost around US$6. Described by one reader as an 'old, beautiful, European-style building' with large and bright rooms, the odd but friendly *Hotel Pudahuel* (☎ 698-4169, San Pablo 1419) nevertheless has a distinct odor of cat and it can be noisy – not least from its short-term clients. Rates with shared bath are US$6.50 per person; doubles with private bath go for US$15.

The area's best is labyrinthine *Hotel Caribe* (☎ 696-6681, *San Martín 851*), whose spartan rooms, some of them spacious, are a good value at US$7 per person with shared bath and hot showers. It's popular with travelers but there's usually space, although singles may be at a premium. Ask for a room at the back or upstairs, since foot traffic on the squeaky-clean floors makes the lobby and passageway a bit noisy. The doors have flimsy hasps and padlocks, but you can leave valuables in the safe; the manager will happily and securely store your personal belongings at no charge if you go trekking or take some other excursion. Meals, snacks and drinks are available at reasonable prices.

Rivaling the Caribe among budget travelers is the more central, slightly cheaper *Nuevo Hotel Valparaíso* (☎ 671-5698, *San Pablo 1182/Morandé 791*), but the rooms are insecure – store your valuables safely. Even more central, on a cul-de-sac near the corner of Moneda and Amunátegui, *Residencial Tabita* (☎ 671-5700, *fax 696-9492, Príncipe de Gales 81*) charges US$13 per person with shared bath, US$15 with private bath. Rates start around US$11/16 with shared bath, US$16/20 singles/doubles, with private bath at slowly declining *Hotel España* (☎ 698-5245, *Morandé 510*) for clean but stark rooms, some of them dark and with balky plumbing. There may be an additional charge to pay by credit card.

In stylish Barrio París Londres, south of the Alameda near Iglesia San Francisco (Metro: Universidad de Chile), popular *Residencial Londres* (☎/fax 638-2215, *Londres 54*) is an outstanding value at US$11 per person with hot water, clean secure rooms with shared bath, as well as pleasant and helpful staff; rates with private bath are only slightly higher. Make reservations or arrive early, since it fills up quickly – singles are almost impossible to get. If nothing's available, try around the corner at *Hotel París* (☎ 639-4037, *París 813*), where small but clean and comfy singles/doubles with private bath start at US$16/24; some of these lack

windows, but better, more spacious rooms with cable TV and other luxuries go for US$24/32 and up.

Barrio Brasil's highly recommended *Residencial del Norte* (☎ 695-1876, *fax 696-9251, Catedral 2207*) charges US$10 per person, with shared bath and breakfast, in a family atmosphere (Metro: Santa Ana or República); rooms are clean and spacious, with ample furniture and balconies, and some beds are soft and the numerous micros passing nearby make noise – as do occasional evangelical gatherings across the street, although these end mercifully early.

Closer to the main Metro line, aging but still recommended *Residencial Alemana* (☎ 671-2388, *Av República 220*) charges US$14 per person with shared bath, US$19/31 singles/doubles with private bath (Metro: República). Even closer to the Metro, but slightly more expensive, is *Residencial Mery* (☎ 696-8883, *Pasaje República 36*) for US$15/27.

Mid-Range

Santiago's mid-range accommodations sometimes offer a better value than its budget selections. Many of these hotels have agreeable, little rooms with private bath; for a few bucks more there is often telephone, TV and refrigerator.

Friendly *Hotel di Maurier* (☎ 695-7750, *fax 696-6193, Moneda 1510*, is convenient to the airport bus; rates are US$25/33 with private bath but without breakfast. *Hotel Europa* (☎ 695-2448, *fax 697-1378, Amunátegui 449*) has small, simple but tidy rooms in excellent condition for US$30/35 with breakfast; discounts are possible for extended stays.

In Barrio Brasil, with spacious gardens and an English-speaking owner who will exchange books, *Hotel Turismo Japón* (☎ 698-4500, *Almirante Barroso 160*) is an excellent value at US$35/45 with breakfast, though it can get a little cool in winter. Some rooms are small at *Hotel Ducado* (☎ 696-9384, *fax 695-1271, Agustinas 1990*), but this good, friendly place charges US$35/45.

In an interesting neighborhood, well-maintained *Hotel Foresta* (☎/fax 639-6262, *fax 632-2996, Subercaseaux 353)* is a first-rate choice for US$33/46 singles/doubles. Opinions differ on *Hotel Cervantes (☎ 696-5318, Morandé 631)*, where some rooms are cramped, with lumpy beds, and others are bright and spacious. Rates are US$26/36 with private bath and breakfast; it also has a decent restaurant.

Friendly, well-located *Hotel Gran Palace (☎ 671-2551, fax 695-1095, Huérfanos 1178)* is also quiet and tidy, starting around US$37/45 with breakfast and cable TV. Other respectable downtown choices include ragged *Hotel Panamericano (☎ 672-3060, Teatinos 320)*, which is also a bit noisy, for US$38/46, and *Hotel El Libertador (☎ 639-4212, fax 633-7128, Alameda 853)* for US$46/55.

On a cul-de-sac off Catedral between Teatinos and Morandé, recommended *Hotel Metrópoli (☎ 672-3987, Sótero del Río 465)* has worn but clean and comfortable rooms with private bath for US$41/49, though readers' opinions are mixed. Try also the professionally run *City Hotel (☎/fax 695-4526, Compañía 1063)* for US$41/50, or the pleasant, better-located *Hotel Riviera (☎ 633-1176, Miraflores 106)*, where smallish rooms cost US$43/50.

One of the best mid-range places is *Hotel Montecarlo (☎ 639-2945, fax 633-5577, Subercaseaux 209)* opposite Cerro Santa Lucía. Rooms are small but cheery, all have private (if tiny) bathrooms and the staff are friendly, but beware of noise from the busy street. Rates are US$43/50. Despite its slightly cheesy remodeling job, cheerful *Hotel Las Vegas (☎ 632-2498, fax 632-5084, Londres 49)* remains one of Santiago's better mid-range bargains for clean, spacious rooms at US$43/51, but breakfast costs US$6 extra.

Accommodations of any kind are scarce in Barrio Bellavista, but *Apart Hotel Monteverde (☎ 777-3607, fax 737-0341, Av Pío Nono 193)* is the exception for US$39/49 with breakfast. Rooms have kitchenettes with microwaves, but the street is noisy Friday and Saturday nights.

Hotel Santa Lucía (☎ 639-8201, fax 633-1844, Huérfanos 779, 4th floor) is also good value for US$50/60; rooms are attractive and have TV, telephone, strongbox, refrigerator and private bath. While the street below can be noisy, double-paned windows make the rooms nearly soundproof. *Hotel Conde Ansurez (☎ 699-6368, fax 696-0807, Av República 25)* offers European atmosphere for US$56/66 (Metro: República).

Top End

Santiago has many expensive, first-rate hotels, including well-known international chains. Most have gourmet restaurants, cafés, bars and money-exchange services for their clients.

Nevertheless, some of the best values are at the low end of the range, such as *Hotel El Conquistador (☎/fax 696-5599, Miguel Cruchaga 920)*, on a passageway off Paseo Estado near the Alameda, starting at US$67 single or double. Enthusiastically recommended *Hotel Principado (☎ 222-8142, fax 222-6065, Av Vicuña Mackenna 30)* charges US$68/79 singles/doubles (Metro: Baquedano). For US$75/86, reader-recommended *Majestic Hotel (☎ 695-8366, fax 697-4051, Santo Domingo 1526)* has fine service but it's close to the freeway and lacks air-conditioning.

Glittering *Hotel Galerías (☎ 361-1911, fax 633-0821, San Antonio 65)* a block from the Alameda, has rooms from US$80/90, breakfast included, and features a swimming pool. In a well-preserved older building, *Hotel Orly (☎ 231-8947, fax 252-0051, Av Pedro de Valdivia 027)* reflects the Providencia of more-dignified, less-commercial times; for US$84/95, rooms are a little small, but the hospitable staff are a big plus (Metro: Pedro de Valdivia).

In Las Condes, *Hotel Montebianco (☎ 233-0427, fax 233-0420, Isidora Goyenechea 2911)* is a sparkling place that has rooms with attractive attached patios. Rates start at US$83/105 for air-conditioned rooms with TV, telephone and continental breakfast. Near Plaza Mulato Gil de Castro, alongside the Instituto Chileno-Francés, the *Hostal del Parque (☎ 639-2694, fax 639-2754, Merced 294)*, which caters to businesspeople, charges US$99/110, including airport transfers, for kitchenette rooms.

Hotel Tupahue (☎ 638-3810, fax 639-2899, San Antonio 477) charges US$110/120, including continental breakfast, but the air-conditioning is suspect and it's a lesser value than Providencia's much newer *Hotel Diego de Velásquez* (☎/fax 234-4400, Diego de Velásquez 2141). Rooms costs US$110/125, including a room-service US-style breakfast, cable television and many other services (Metro: Pedro de Valdivia or Los Leones). Another good choice in Providencia, with an accommodating English-speaking staff, is *Hotel Aloha* (☎ 233-2230, fax 233-2494, Francisco Noguera 146), where rates are US$131/152 singles/doubles (Metro: Pedro de Valdivia).

Rates at downtown's *Holiday Inn Crowne Plaza* (☎ 638-1042, fax 633-6015, Alameda 136) start at US$189/260; the hotel has offices, shops, car rentals and a post office. North of the Mapocho the *Sheraton San Cristóbal* (☎ 233-5000, fax 234-1729, Av Santa María 1742) has rates starting at US$210 double. The *Santiago Park Plaza* (☎ 233-6363, fax 233-6668, Ricardo Lyon 207) in Providencia (Metro: Los Leones), charges US$230/240.

At venerable *Hotel Carrera* (☎ 698-2011, fax 672-1083, Teatinos 180), overlooking Plaza de la Constitución, rates start at US$260 double. It was from here, in 1985, that deadly serious opponents of the dictatorship aimed a time-delayed bazooka at General Pinochet's office at La Moneda – but the recoil was too strong for the photo tripod on which they'd mounted it and the explosion destroyed the hotel room's interior instead.

In Las Condes, the *Hyatt Regency Santiago* (☎ 218-1234, fax 218-2279, Av Kennedy 4601) has rooms starting at US$310 single/double.

PLACES TO EAT

Downtown Santiago has an abundance of eateries from the basic to the elegant, especially around the bus terminals, the Huérfanos and Ahumada pedestrian malls, the Plaza de Armas and the Alameda. The best selection of restaurants, however, is in and around Cerro Santa Lucía, Barrio Bellavista,

and the comunas of Providencia, Las Condes and Ñuñoa.

Among the varied choices are Italian pasta, Indian curry, Middle Eastern stuffed grape leaves, Mexican food (both Tex-Mex and regional cuisine), Peruvian specialties and Chilean *parrillada* (grilled steak and other cuts of beef) and seafood. Sernatur's free publications offer some idea of this formidable range, but the *Centro* volume of CTC's Turistel series also has comprehensive and systematic listings (see Books in the Facts for the Visitor chapter).

Downtown & Vicinity

Avoid greasy McDonald's clones such as *Burger Inn* or *Max Beef* (for that matter, avoid McDonald's). For cheap snacks, pastries and drinks there's a string of stand-up places in the Portal Fernández Concha on the south side of the Plaza de Armas, serving items like hot dogs, sandwiches and fried chicken with fries. In the same arcade, highly regarded *Chez Henry* (☎ 696-6612, Portal Fernández Concha 962) is no longer inexpensive, but neither is it outrageous; for about US$6 their famous *pastel de choclo* (maize casserole filled with vegetables, chicken and beef) is the only meal you'll need all day (other dishes are dearer, but selective diners can still eat well at moderate prices). Portions are huge. But ready-made items from the take-away deli are cheaper and no less appealing.

For lunch, one of Santiago's best choices is the Mercado Central on San Pablo, a few blocks north of the plaza, whose various locales offer a wealth of tremendous seafood dishes: be adventurous. Its lively atmosphere makes the historic building worth visiting in its own right, and the food is often a bargain. The most obviously appealing places are those like *Donde Augusto* (☎ 672-2829, Mercado Central, Local 66 & 166), picturesquely set among the central fruit and vegetable stands, but those restaurants are not dramatically better than the smaller, cheaper places on the periphery.

Carnivores can try *El Novillero* (☎ 699-1544, Moneda 1145). Numerous travelers have enjoyed *Bar Central* (San Pablo 1063), which serves generous portions of excellent seafood and is also popular with Santiaguinos. For Chinese food, try *Kam-Thu* (☎ 639-9511, Santo Domingo 769).

Italian restaurants are good and numerous but surprisingly expensive, including *Da Carla* (☎ 633-3739, MacIver 577), *San Marcos* (☎ 633-6880, Huérfanos 618) and the classic *Le Due Torri* (☎ 633-3799, San Antonio 258). For Italian fast food, try *Pizza Napoli* (☎ 633-0845, Paseo Estado 149).

Serving Chilean specialties such as pastel de choclo, *Bar Nacional 1* (☎ 695-3368, Bandera 317) is a lunchtime favorite with downtown office workers. *Bar Nacional 2* (☎ 696-5986, Huérfanos 1151) is a nearby branch.

A good central place for *onces* (afternoon tea), juices and sandwiches is *100% Natural* (☎ 697-1860, Valentín Letelier 1319), directly west of La Moneda. Try *Au Bon Pain* (Miraflores 235), the North American chain, for sandwiches and croissants.

Cerro Santa Lucía Just south of the Mapocho, several restaurants are clustered in and around Plaza del Mulato Gil de Castro, on Lastarria near Merced; at *Pérgola de la Plaza* (☎ 639-3604, Lastarria 321), the tasty lunch specials (about US$6) are great bargains. Renovated and used as artists' studios, the surrounding buildings house a cluster of galleries and bookstores.

Alongside its namesake cinema, *Café del Biógrafo* (☎ 639-9532, Villavicencio 398) is a neighborhood hangout. Its US$5 lunches are excellent, as are the baguettes and the casual atmosphere, but service can be slow. *Don Victorino* (☎ 639-5263, Lastarria 138) is one of several venues that offer excellent lunches at moderate prices, with an extensive but costlier dinner menu, first-rate service, and a relaxed atmosphere. In the same category are nearby *Gatopardo* (☎ 633-6420, Lastarria 192), which serves Bolivian food, and *Rincón Español* (☎ 633-9466, Rosal 346), for Mediterranean cuisine.

Santiago has a growing number of outstanding Peruvian restaurants, the best of which is probably *Cocoa* (☎ 632-1272, Lastarria 297). It's fairly expensive, but the pisco

sours and desserts are large and exquisite. Closer to downtown, *El Puente de Bórquez* (☎ 633-4021, Miraflores 443) has inexpensive Peruvian lunches and dinners.

French cuisine is the rule at *Les Assassins* (☎ 638-4280, Merced 297-B), where outstanding fixed-price lunches cost only about US$7. It's better to go early or late for lunch, because it has fewer than 20 tables; the downstairs is tobacco-free.

Japanese restaurants tend to be expensive, but there are at least two exceptions. At the plain but very fine *Izakaya Yoko* (☎ 632-1954, Merced 456), it's possible to find excellent, filling meals for around US$5 to US$6 without drinks, which are also reasonably priced. Don't miss the sushi at *Kintaro* (☎ 638-2448, Monjitas 460), a bargain compared with almost anywhere else in the world; taking advantage of Chile's varied finfish and shellfish, a portion large enough for two has recently gone up in price, but still costs only US$9.

Barrio Brasil West of the Via Norte-Sur, Barrio Brasil's dining scene is a combination of older, traditional restaurants and newer, more innovative eateries that, at their best, rival Barrio Bellavista's restaurants – but are substantially cheaper. The nearest Metro stations are Los Héroes and República.

Convenient to Santiago's youth hostel, *Pizzería Gigino* (☎ 698-2200, Agustinas 2015) keeps long hours, with standard pizza and pasta dishes for about US$5, and is also notable for a grossly mismatched collection of paintings that cover virtually every open wall spot, imparting an undisciplined, informal atmosphere.

The new *Las Vacas Gordas* (☎ 697-1066, Cienfuegos 280) serves excellent parrillada and pasta at below-average prices, and drinks are cheap. *Tú y Yo* (☎ 696-4543, Av Brasil 249) is a neighborhood pub-style restaurant with simple but good Chilean dishes.

Ocean Pacific's (☎ 697-2413, Av Ricardo Cumming 221) is a reasonably priced, family-style seafood restaurant with excellent, friendly service and particularly delicious homemade bread, but the menu is misleading; many items listed are often not available. Nearby, slightly more expensive **Ostras Squella** (☎ 699-4883, Ricardo Cumming 94) usually has most of what appears on the menu.

Ostras Azócar (☎ 681-6109, Bulnes 37) is a traditional seafood restaurant, with outstanding quality and service. Nearby are two branches of the popular seafood locale **Tongoy** (☎ 697-1144, Bulnes 91; ☎ 681-4329, Bulnes 72); despite inconsistencies, at their best they're very good, particularly the former.

Moderately priced **Plaza Garibaldi** (☎ 699-4278, Moneda 2319) has outstanding Mexican dishes, beers and margaritas, and an increasingly varied menu as Santiaguinos gradually adapt to spicier food. Santiago's best Peruvian bargain, though the quality is not as high as its counterparts at Cerro Santa Lucía and Bellavista, is **Puente de los Suspiros** (☎ 696-7962, Av Brasil 75). It has changed its name three times in three years without altering its typical lunches, which include an appetizer, main course, wine and dessert for just US$6.

El Chachachá (☎ 699-4360, Av Ricardo Cumming 536) is a new Cuban restaurant that bears watching. **Puro Chile** (☎ 681-9355, Maipú 363) combines wildly imaginative décor with upscale versions of Chilean specialties and outstanding, friendly service. It's popular with the arts crowd.

Barrio Bellavista

North of the Mapocho, a short walk from the Baquedano Metro station, Pablo Neruda's old haunts, especially lively on weekends, offer great dining. Many, though not the best, restaurants line both sides of Av Pío Nono between the bridge and Plaza Caupolicán. There's an array of stylish, new and generally expensive restaurants on the Providencia side of the barrio, while the Recoleta side has more traditional venues (except for its hyperactive nightlife).

El Antojo de Gauguin (☎ 737-0398, Pío Nono 69) is a good Middle Eastern restaurant that's one of few places in the area that offers fixed-price lunches on Saturdays.

Armandita (☎ 737-3409, Pío Nono 108) is an Argentine-style parrilla whose lomo a lo pobre is a good value for US$8, including juice or soft drink, but the service is sluggish. Across the street, **Al Karim** (☎ 737-8129, Pío Nono 127) serves kabobs and other Middle Eastern specialties.

La Venezia (☎ 737-0900, Pío Nono 200) is a moderately priced Chilean picada (informal family restaurant), but standards seem to be falling. Across the street and down the block, **Cristóforo** (☎ 737-7752, Pío Nono 281) serves Greek-Mediterranean food and has comfortable outdoor seating. Its reasonably priced vaina doble (aperitif made with port, cognac, cocoa and egg white) packs a punch.

Café de la Dulcería Las Palmas (☎ 777-4586, Antonia López de Bello 0190) is worth a visit for fresh fruit juices and desserts, but the fixed-price lunches are mediocre. Argentine-run **Pizzas Gloria** (☎ 735-9968, Dardignac 0188) has quality pizza and pasta at bargain prices, primarily at lunchtime.

The outstanding Peruvian restaurant **Cocoa** (☎ 735-0634, Antonia López de Bello 60) has a branch on the Recoleta side. By no means inferior, in spectacular digs across the street, is the equally Peruvian **El Otro Sitio** (☎ 777-3059, Antonia López de Bello 53). Another good Peruvian choice, though probably not quite so good a value, is down-the-block **La Flor de la Canela** (☎ 777-1007, Antonia López de Bello 125), whose service is so rapid and attentive as to almost seem an affront. They have a tobacco-free section.

El Caramaño (☎ 737-7043, Purísima 257), a self-styled 'anti-restaurant' so informal that there's no sign outside (ring the bell to get in) and visitors scribble on the interior walls, has fine Chilean food and friendly service. Across the street, **El Tallarín Gordo** (☎ 737-8567, Purísima 254) serves Italian food but lags behind Bellavista's more innovative locales. **Rodizio** (☎ 777-9240, Bombero Núñez 388) is a great-looking Brazilian parrilla, but even though it's an all-you-can-eat, the US$23 price tag will deter budget watchers as well as dieters.

There are two branches of **Tasca Mediterránea** (☎ 735-3901, Purísima 165;

☎ 737-1542, Dominica 35); the former has excellent fixed-price lunches, good service and Bohemian atmosphere, while the latter is more of a dinner venue. In Recoleta's Patronato district, a bit to the west, *El Rinconcito (Manzano and Dávila Baeza)*, is a very cheap Middle Eastern picada run by a Lebanese immigrant – who arrived by way of Chicago; it is an excellent place for hummus, falafels and the like. More expensive Middle Eastern fare is available at *Omar Khayyam (☎ 777-4129, Av Perú 570)*, the *Club Palestino (Av Perú 659)* and *El Amir Issa (☎ 777-3651, Av Perú 663)*.

Eneldo (☎ 732-0428, Pinto Lagarrigue 195) serves seafood, but the best seafood choice, on the Providencia side, is *Azul Profundo (☎ 738-0288, Constitución 0111)*, which serves fine seafood, at premium prices, amid elaborate maritime decor.

Galindo (☎ 771-0116, Dardignac 098) is a traditional hangout for Bohemians and musicians, with sidewalk seating for lunch. *Di Simoncelli (Dardignac 197)* serves good pizza and modestly priced Italian lunches.

Zen (☎ 737-9520, Dardignac 0175) has appealingly minimalist Japanese decor, but even the midday lunch, around US$10, is a lesser value than its Cerro Santa Lucía counterparts' offers. A better choice is the varied menu at *Muneca Brava (☎ 732-1338, Mallinkrodt 170)*, whose cinematic décor can overshadow very fine food and excellent service; prices are high but not outrageous. Designed by the same architect as Azul Profundo, *Como Agua para Chocolate (☎ 777-8740, Constitución 88)* is a new Mexican place with imaginative décor in primary colors, great use of natural light, an interesting bar and a menu created in consultation with the founder of Barrio Brasil's Plaza Garibaldi.

Providencia

A perennial vegetarian favorite is *Café del Patio (☎ 236-1251, Providencia 1670, Local 8-A)*, near the Manuel Montt Metro station, and even non-vegetarians flock to *El Huerto (☎ 233-2690, Orrego Luco 054)*, internationally renowned for imaginative meatless meals (Metro: Pedro de Valdivia).

It's become more expensive, but the smaller menu at its adjacent café *La Huerta* offers quality food at much lower prices.

Affiliated with Mexico's diplomatic mission, the *Casa de la Cultura de México (☎ 334-3848, Bucarest 162)* features outstanding regional dishes rather than Tex-Mex borderlands food; it also sells superb crafts and runs a bookstore (Metro: Los Leones). In the same area, German food is the fare at *Der Münchner Hof (☎ 233-2452, Diego de Velásquez 2105)*.

You'll find Italian fast food at *Pizza Napoli (☎ 225-6468, Av 11 de Septiembre 1935)*, near Pedro de Valdivia station. Nearby *La Pizza Nostra (☎ 231-9853, Av Providencia 1975)* is only so-so. *Sbarro (Av Suecia 055)* is part of an Italian-style chain that sells food by weight; the selection is ample and the quality's not bad (Metro: Los Leones). *La Vera Pizza (☎ 232-1786, Av Providencia 2630)* offers good variety but is a bit pricey (Metro: Tobalaba).

For sandwiches and onces, one of Santiago's best traditional venues is *Liguria (☎ 235-7914, Av Providencia 1373)*, also a hangout for actors (Metro: Manuel Montt). *Au Bon Pain (☎ 233-6912, Av Providencia 1936)*, the North American chain, serves sandwiches and croissants (Metro: Pedro de Valdivia).

The cheapest fixed-price lunches in town are at *Peters (☎ 204-0124, Marchant Pereira 132)*; weekdays before 1 pm or after 3 pm, four-course meals, including a salad bar, cost only US$2.50 (Metro: Pedro de Valdivia). Homesick Brits will find Santiago's best pub lunches, for about US$7 to $8, at the *Phone Box Pub (☎ 235-9972, Av Providencia 1670)*, whose grapevine arbor patio is a pleasant sanctuary from the busy avenue outside (Metro: Manuel Montt).

For fine ice cream and other desserts, go to *Sebastián (☎ 231-9968, Andrés de Fuenzalida 26)*, midway between the Pedro de Valdivia and Los Leones stations; *Bravíssimo (☎ 235-2511, Av Providencia 1406)* near Manuel Montt station or *La Escarcha (Av Providencia 1763)* near Metro Pedro de Valdivia. The hands-down best ice creamery, though, is the classy Buenos Aires import

Freddo (Av Providencia 2304), near Los Leones station.

Las Condes

Near the Tobalaba Metro station, as are most Las Condes restaurants, the complex of fast-food outlets at the *Food Garden (Av El Bosque Norte and Roger de Flor)* contains a number of decent, inexpensive eateries, including a branch of *Sbarro*, the juice bar *Jugomanía*, and a good frozen yogurt outlet.

There are two branches of *Au Bon Pain* (☎ 366-9145, Av El Bosque Norte 0177; ☎ 331-5048, Av Apoquindo 3575). Though it imports nearly all its ingredients frozen, it's an exception to the rule that foreign franchises are not worth patronizing.

There are better choices, however, such as *Café Melba (☎ 232-4546, Don Carlos 2988)*, which serves North American-style breakfasts all day and is a popular lunch spot. Another possibility is the *New York Bagel Bakery (☎ 246-3060, Roger de Flor 2894)*, which has bagels, cream cheese and muffins.

Although the pun deserves reproach, popular *PubLicity (☎ 246-6414, Av El Bosque Norte 0155)* has excellent meals ranging from simple sandwiches to more elaborate fare. Recently reinvented as a Celtic venue, with Guinness on tap, the informal *Flannery's Irish Geo Pub (☎ 233-6675, Encomenderos 83)* has excellent lunches from US$5 to US$7 and is a popular weekend hangout.

A favorite with professionals on expense accounts, *München (☎ 233-2108, Av El Bosque Norte 0204)* serves German food. Beef eaters dine at the *Hereford Grill (☎ 231-9117, Av El Bosque Norte 0355)*; Italian-food lovers can dine at a branch of downtown's *Le Due Torri (☎ 231-3427, Isidora Goyenechea 2908)*. *Da Dino (☎ 208-1344, Av Apoquindo 4228)* is expensive for pizza, but it's tasty (Metro: Escuela Militar).

The Los Condes Japanese restaurant *Shoogun (☎ 231-1604, Enrique Foster Norte 172)* is more expensive than its Cerro Santa Lucía counterparts, but the quality is not demonstrably superior. *Chang Cheng*

(☎ 212-9718, Av Las Condes 7471) is an excellent, upscale Chinese restaurant, serving both Mandarin and Cantonese cuisine.

Outlying Comunas

Increasingly popular Plaza Ñuñoa offers modest choices like *República de Ñuñoa (Trucco 33)* and *El Amor Nunca Muere (Trucco 43)*, the latter open for dinner only. Across Av Irarrázaval, *La Terraza (☎ 223-3987, Jorge Washington 58)* is more patrician. Decorated in a Cuban motif, *Café de la Isla (☎ 341-5389, Irarrázaval 3465)* prepares good sandwiches and excellent juices to the accompaniment of recorded jazz.

Ñuñoa's upscale restaurant row is along José Domingo Cañas, north of the Estadio Nacional, with venues such as *Solar de Sancho Panza (☎ 225-1413, JD Cañas 982)*, which specializes in the cuisine of Spain. Another fine choice is *Walhalla (☎ 209-8492, Campo de Deportes 329)*, at the corner of JD Cañas, with moderately priced Swiss food and excellent service in attractive surroundings.

So wildly popular that reservations are essential even on weeknights, Vitacura's distractingly noisy, Canadian-run *Santa Fe (☎ 215-1091, Av Las Condes 10690)* features well-prepared Tex-Mex specialties such as fajitas, enchiladas and burritos. The salsas are milder than one would find in the North American borderlands, but given the size of the portions, the US$10 to US$15 entrees are still a good value. Take a taxi colectivo from Escuela Militar Metro or a bus out Av Apoquindo from Las Condes.

ENTERTAINMENT

Santiago's main nightlife districts are Barrio Bellavista (Metro: Baquedano), Providencia's Av Suecia (Metro: Los Leones) and Plaza Ñuñoa (most easily reached by bus or taxi), though other venues are scattered throughout the city. Remember that, in any event, the Metro closes at 10:30 pm – around the time most of these places open.

Bars

The numerous bars clustered around Av Suecia and General Holley (Metro: Los

Leones) in Providencia have adopted the North American custom of holding happy hours (two drinks for the price of one), until midnight in some cases, and serve decent if unexceptional food. Nearly all have live music, usually cover versions of international hits. Among them are *Brannigans* (☎ 232-5172, *Av Suecia 035*), the *Old Boston Pub* (☎ 231-5169, General Holley 2291), *Australian-run* *Boomerang* (☎ 334-5081, General Holley 2285), *Mister Ed* (☎ 231-2624, *Av Suecia 0152*) and *Wall Street* (☎ 232-5548, General Holley 99).

Across Av Providencia, waiters in bolo ties serve reasonably priced beer (including Guinness on tap) and respectable food at the *Electric Cowboy* (☎ 231-7225, *Guardia Vieja 35*), which features live rockabilly music on weekends.

There are two branches of *La Casa en el Aire* (☎ 735-6680, *Antonia López de Bello 0125;* ☎ 222-8789, *0411 Santa Isabel*), which offers theater, poetry and live music. Other Bellavista venues featuring music include *Altazor* (☎ 777-9651, *Antonia López de Bello 0189*) and *Da Lua* (*Antonia López de Bello 0126*).

Near Cerro Santa Lucía, one of Santiago's liveliest, most informal bars is *Bar Berri* (☎ 638-4734, *Rosal 321*); it also has good, inexpensive lunches. *Nichola's Pub* (☎ 246-0277, *Av Apoquindo 3371*), a neighborhood spot in Las Condes, has the cheapest pisco sours in town.

In Ñuñoa, the *Bar Sin Nombre* (*Irarrázaval 3442*), just west of Plaza Ñuñoa, features excellent live, on-the-way-up rock bands. Nearby *La Batuta* (*Jorge Washington 52*) also features quality live rock bands.

For inexpensive espresso and cocoa, go to any of the several stand-up bars, such as *Café Haití* (*Ahumada 140*), *Café Caribe* (*Ahumada 120*) almost next door, or *Café Cousiño* (*Matías Cousiño 107*), all of which have many other branches around town. Some women feel uncomfortable at these coffee bars, colloquially referred to as *cafés con piernas* (cafés with legs), since most of them attract male clientele by requiring their young female staff to dress in tight, revealing minidresses.

Clubs

Dating from 1879, *Confitería Las Torres* (☎ 698-6220, *Alameda 1570*) reinforces its late-19th-century atmosphere, complete with spectacular woodwork, with live tango music on weekends (Metro: Los Héroes). The stage set features enormous blowups of Argentine tango legend Carlos Gardel, and the walls are lined with photographs of Chilean presidents – perhaps the only place in the world where portraits of Allende and Pinochet hang side by side. The food is good but expensive, the service excellent.

Los Adobes de Argomedo (☎ 222-2104, *Argomedo 411*) is a gaudy pseudo-folkloric restaurant-nightclub with music and dance, but the Chilean food is good and varied (Metro: Santa Isabél). Expect to pay around US$25 per person, with wine. Although it's very large, reservations are a good idea, at least on weekends. Dance clubs open late, around 11 pm, and stay open almost all night, at least on weekends.

Bellavista's *Tadeo's* (*Lagarrigue 282*) has a spacious dance floor, with a crowd in the mid-20s range. Also in Bellavista, *Havana Salsa* (*Dominica 142*) cleverly re-creates the ambience of Old Havana, encouraging even neophytes to salsa, and also serves good food.

One of the most fashionable discos in Santiago is the techno-pop *Oz* (☎ 737-7066, *A Manzur 6*), in a converted warehouse on a cul-de-sac just off Antonia López de Bello in Bellavista, but it enforces a hefty cover charge, around US$15 per person. Its Providencia counterpart, a bit cheaper, is *Kasbba* (☎ 231-7419, *Av Suecia 081*).

Bellavista is the focus of Santiago's gay life, thanks to venues such as *Bunker* (☎ 777-3760, *Bombero Núñez 159*). The cover charge is US$12. Also in Bellavista, *Bokhara* (☎ 732-1050, *Pío Nono 430*), primarily a gay venue, is relatively small – although mirrors make it seem larger and even livelier. *Fausto* (☎ 777-1041, *Av Santa María 0832*), farther east in Providencia, is a stylish, multilevel club with techno-pop music (Metro: Salvador).

Music & Theater

Santiago has numerous performing arts venues for music and drama. Most prestigious is the **Teatro Municipal** (☎ 369-0282, Agusti-nas 794), with offerings from opera and symphony orchestras, to musical theater. The box office is open 10 am to 7 pm weekdays, 10 am to 2 pm weekends; members have priority, so seats can be hard to come by.

Teatro Universidad de Chile (☎ 634-5295, Baquedano 043) presents a fall season of ballet, orchestral and chamber music, but it also hosts occasional popular music concerts; acoustics are excellent. A notable Providencia venue is the **Teatro Oriente** (☎ 232-1360, Av Pedro de Valdivia 099), which doubles as a cinema; the theater ticket office is at Av 11 de Septiembre 2214, Oficina 66.

Near Cerro Santa Lucía, the well-established **Teatro La Comedia** (☎ 6391-523, Merced 349) offers contemporary drama Thursday through Sunday. Other downtown venues include the Universidad de Chile's **Sala Agustín Sire** (☎ 696-5142, Morandé 750); the **Teatro Casa Amarilla** (☎ 672-0347, Balmaceda 1301) and the **Teatro Estación Mapocho** (☎ 735-6046, Balmaceda 1301), both in the Centro Cultural Mapocho; and the **Teatro Nacional Chileno** (☎ 671-7850, Morandé 25).

More known for experimental theater, Barrio Bellavista is home to companies such as **Teatro El Conventillo** (☎ 777-4164, Bellavista 173), **Teatro Taller** (☎ 235-1678, Lagarrigue 191), **Teatro Bellavista** (☎ 735-6264, Dardignac 0110) and **Teatro La Feria** (☎ 737-7371, Crucero Exéter 0250).

In summer, there's an inexpensive open-air theater program at Parque General Bustamante (also known as Parque Manuel Rodríguez), south of Plaza Baquedano, in Providencia; check the newspapers for details. One venue, the **Teatro de la Universidad Católica** (☎ 205-5652, Jorge Washington 24) gets much of the credit for Plaza Ñuñoa's renaissance. The **Centro Cultural Las Condes** (☎ 231-3560 Av Apoquindo 3364), also offers live theater.

Cinemas
Commercial Cinemas Santiago's commercial cinema district is along Paseo Huérfanos and nearby side streets, where many former large theaters now have two or three

screens showing different films. There are also venues in suburban comunas like Providencia and Vitacura. Most cinemas have half-price discounts on Wednesdays.

Cine Central
  (☎ 633-3555) Paseo Huérfanos 930
Cine Hoyts
  (☎ 664-1861) Paseo Huérfanos 735
Cine Huelén
  (☎ 633-1603) Paseo Huérfanos 779
Cine Huérfanos
  (☎ 633-6707) Paseo Huérfanos 930
Cine Lido
  (☎ 633-0797) Paseo Huérfanos 680
Cine Lo Castillo
  (☎ 242-1342) Candelaria Goyenechea 3820, Vitacura
Cine Rex
  (☎ 633-1144) Paseo Huérfanos 735
Gran Palace 1-4
  (☎ 696-0082) Paseo Huérfanos 1176
Las Condes
  (☎ 220-8816) Apoquindo & Noruega, Las Condes
Teatro Oriente
  (☎ 231-7151) Pedro de Valdivia 099, Providencia

Art Cinemas For film cycles and unconventional movies, the following cinemas are the best bets. These also usually have half-price discounts on Wednesday.

Centro de Extensión de la Universidad Católica
  (☎ 686-6516) Alameda 390
Cine Alameda
  (☎ 639-2479) Alameda 139
Cine El Biógrafo
  (☎ 633-4435) Lastarria 181
Cine Normandie
  (☎ 697-2979) Tarapacá 1181
Cine Tobalaba
  (☎ 231-6630) Av Providencia 2563, Providencia

SPECTATOR SPORTS
Soccer
Santiago has several first-division soccer teams. Major matches usually take place at the Estadio Nacional, at the corner of Av Grecia and Marathon in Ñuñoa. For tickets, contact the following teams:

Colo Colo
(☎ 695-2251, 695-1094) Cienfuegos 41

Universidad Católica
(☎ 231-2777) Av Costanera Andrés Bello 2782, Providencia

Universidad de Chile
(☎ 239-2793) Campo de Deportes 565, Ñuñoa

Horse Racing

Santiago has two racecourses, which are usually open weekends. The Hipódromo Chile (☎ 736-9276) is at Fermín Vivaceta, north of the Mapocho along Av Independencia in the comuna of Independencia. The Club Hípico de Santiago (☎ 683-5998) is at Almirante Blanco Encalada 2540 (Metro: Unión Latinoamericana).

SHOPPING

Popular artisanal products include lapis lazuli, black pottery and copperware, plus attractively carved wooden moai from Easter Island. There are several well-stocked shops, including Chile Típico (☎ 696-5504) at Moneda 1025, Local 149, and Huimpalay (☎ 672-1395) at Huérfanos 1162.

For the best selection of indigenous crafts from the Mapuche and Aymara people, as well as from Rapa Nui natives, visit the Centro de Exposición de Arte Indígena (☎ 664-1352) at Alameda 499, at the southwestern corner of Cerro Santa Lucía. Across the Alameda is the Centro Artesanal Santa Lucía, bounded by Carmen and Diagonal Paraguay.

Bellavista is a popular area for crafts, both at Pío Nono's weekend street fair and at shops such as Artesanía Nehuen (☎ 777-7367), Dardignac 59, which has a wide selection of materials from throughout the country. A shuttle from the shop will pick up customers at their hotels. Nearby is the Cooperativa Almacén Campesina (☎ 737-2117), Purísima 303.

Several area shops specialize in lapis lazuli jewelry, including Lapiz Lazuli at Av Pío Nono 3, and Lapiz Lazuli House (☎ 732-1419) at Bellavista 014. For antiques, try Arte del Mundo (☎ 735-2507) at Dardignac 67.

Numerous Lonely Planet readers have enjoyed the artisans' village at Los Graneros

del Alba (☎ 246-4360), Av Apoquindo 9085, Las Condes. Another market, open in summer only, is the daily crafts market on the north side of Av Providencia, at the exit from the Pedro de Valdivia Metro station.

In the suburban comuna of Lo Barnechea, the Feria San Enrique features antiques and bric-a-brac, artwork and outstanding crafts with a minimum of kitsch, and presentations on themes like *La Nueva Ola*, the Chilean music of the '60s. For current information, contact the Corporación Cultural de Lo Barnechea (☎ 243-4758). The crafts fair proper starts around 11:30 am Sundays, from October through December only. From San Pablo or Compañía in downtown Santiago, or from Av Providencia, take bus No 203, 205 or 206.

Chileans themselves prefer to flock to disorienting, modern shopping centers, including the Mall Panorámico (☎ 233-2244) at the corner of Av 11 de Septiembre and Ricardo Lyon in Providencia (Metro: Pedro de Valdivia); Parque Arauco (☎ 299-0500) at

Los Dominicos

Popularly known as 'Los Dominicos' after its nearby convent, Los Graneros del Alba boasts Santiago's largest crafts selection, imported from throughout the country, has good food for a variety of budgets, and often features folkloric music and dancing on weekends. Among possible purchases are copperware, huaso horsegear, furniture, sculpture, jewelry and alpaca woolens.

At the east end of Av Apoquindo, Los Dominicos is open 11 am to 7:30 pm daily all year. The quickest way to get there is to take the Metro to the end of Línea 1 at Escuela Militar and then catch a taxi (US$4) out Av Apoquindo, but it's also possible to catch bus No 327 from Av Providencia, No 344 from the Alameda or Av Providencia, No 229 from Catedral or Compañía or No 326 from Alameda and Miraflores.

Av Kennedy 5413, Las Condes (Metro: Escuela Militar); Shopping Center Apumanque (☎ 246-2614), Manquehue Sur 31; and Alto Las Condes (☎ 229-1383), Av Kennedy 9001. Most of these shopping centers have free shuttles from upscale hotels downtown and in the eastern suburbs. Or, catch a bus at Escuela Militar.

GETTING THERE & AWAY
Air

Given Chile's 'crazy geography,' Santiago is an unavoidable reality – nearly every visitor either arrives at the capital or passes through here at one time or another. Many major international airlines have offices or representatives in Santiago. See the Air section in the Getting There & Away chapter for a complete list. For a list of domestic airlines and their Santiago locations, as well as sample one-way domestic coach airfares from Santiago, see the Domestic Air Services section in the Getting Around chapter.

Bus

For information regarding international buses departing Santiago, see the Bus section in Getting There & Away. For a discussion of Santiago's bus terminals, ticket offices, sample fares and bus companies serving various destinations in Chile, see the Bus section in the Getting Around chapter.

Train

For information on trains leaving Santiago, see Train in the Getting Around chapter. (All trains leave from the Estación Central, ☎ 689-5199, Alameda 3322, Metro: Estación Central.)

GETTING AROUND
To/From the Airport

Aeropuerto Internacional Arturo Merino Benítez (☎ 601-9001, 601-9709), which also serves as the airport for most domestic flights, is in Pudahuel, 26km west of downtown Santiago. Note that, although Línea 1 of the Metro ends at Pudahuel, the Metro does *not* reach the airport.

The cheapest transportation to the airport, Centropuerto buses (☎ 601-9883)

charge only US$1.30 from Plazoleta Los Héroes, outside the Los Héroes Metro station, between 5:55 am and 10:30 pm, there are 40 departures daily. Return times from the airport are 6:40 am to 11:30 pm. Slightly more expensive Tour Express (☎ 671-7380), Moneda 1529, charges US$2 one-way, US$3.50 return. The trip takes at least a half hour, depending on traffic.

Buses from the airport leave from the front of the international terminal, and will drop you at the city terminal or just about anywhere along the route.

Minibuses belonging to Delfos (☎ 226-6020) or Transfer (☎ 777-7707) carry passengers door-to-door between the airport and any part of Santiago for US$5 to US$7.50 depending on distance from the airport. Departing passengers should call the day before their flight if possible, but the minibuses will sometimes pick up on short notice.

Taxi fares are negotiable; a cab to or from downtown can cost anywhere from about US$10 (if your Spanish is good) to US$25, and may be shared.

Bus

Santiago's buses go everywhere cheaply, but it takes a while to learn the system; check the destination signs in their windows or ask other passengers waiting at the stop. Many buses now have signed, fixed stops, especially in the downtown area, but that doesn't necessarily mean they won't stop at other points. Fares vary slightly depending on the bus, but all are within a few cents of US$0.40 per trip; hang on to your ticket, since inspectors may ask for it.

For convenience and security reasons, municipal authorities are promoting automatic fare machines, but the expense and difficulty of getting the myriad private companies to adopt the new technology have been daunting.

Metro

Carrying nearly a million passengers daily, Santiago's Metro system has three separate lines that interlink, and farther extensions under construction. For destinations along these lines, it's far quicker than city buses, which must contend with the capital's narrow, congested streets. The Metro operates 6:30 am to 10:30 pm Monday to Saturday, 8 am to 10:30 pm Sundays and holidays. Trains are clean, quiet and frequent, but at most hours it's difficult to get a seat.

Signs on station platforms indicate the direction in which the trains are heading. On east-west Línea 1, 'Dirección Las Condes' heads toward the Escuela Militar station in the wealthy eastern suburbs; 'Dirección Pudahuel' goes to San Pablo (it does *not* reach the international airport). On the north-south Línea 2, 'Dirección Centro' reaches Puente Cal y Canto station a few blocks north of the Plaza de Armas; 'Dirección La Cisterna' heads towards the southern comuna of Lo Ovalle. Los Héroes, beneath the Alameda, is the only transfer station between these two lines.

Línea 5 (planners have apparently decided to skip Líneas 3 and 4) uses Baquedano (on Línea 1) as a transfer station, passing through Ñuñoa and Macul en route to the southeastern comuna of La Florida; a northwestern extension to Línea 2 at Santa Ana, will include new stations at Bellas Artes and Plaza de Armas.

Fares vary slightly depending on the time of day and the line, but they range from about US$0.30 to US$0.50. Tickets can be purchased from agents at each station; a convenient *boleto inteligente* or *boleto valor* (multi-trip ticket) is available at a slight discount. Charges are according to the following schedule; note that weekends and holidays are always middle hours.

hora alta (peak)	media (middle)	baja (low)
7:15 to 9 am	9 am to 6 pm	6 to 7:15 am
6 to 7:30 pm	7:30 to 9 pm	9 to 10:30 pm

Tickets have a magnetic strip on the back. After slipping your ticket into a slot, pass through the turnstile and continue to the platform; your ticket is not returned unless it's a boleto inteligente with remaining value (several individuals may use the same boleto inteligente by simply passing it back across the turnstile). No ticket is necessary to exit the system.

Car

Keep in mind that a car is less useful in Santiago than on excursions beyond the city, since traffic is so congested and parking is difficult and can be expensive. However, Santiago has dozens of car rental agencies, from internationally known franchises to lesser-known local companies that tend to be cheaper. For rate details, see the Getting Around chapter. Many companies have airport offices at Pudahuel in addition to the city offices below:

Alamo
(☎ 233-4343, fax 233-4766) Av 11 de Septiembre 2155, Oficina 1204, Providencia

Atal
(☎ 235-9222, fax 236-0636) Av Costanera Andrés Bello 1051, Providencia

Automóvil Club de Chile (Acchi)
central office: (☎ 212-5702, 274-6261, fax 229-5295) Av Vitacura 8620, Vitacura
tourism & member services: (☎ 225-3790) Fidel Oteíza 1960, Providencia

Avis
(☎ 601-9966, fax 601-9757) Av Santa María 1742, Providencia

Budget
(☎ 220-8292, fax 224-1175) Manquehue Sur 600, Las Condes

Chilean
(☎/fax 737-9650) Bellavista 0185, Providencia/ Barrio Bellavista

Dollar
(☎ 245-6175, fax 228-0995) Málaga 115, Local 101, Las Condes

First
(☎ 225-6328) Rancagua 0514, Providencia

Hertz
(☎ 235-9666, fax 236-0252) Av Costanera Andrés Bello 1469, Providencia

United
(☎ 236-1483) Padre Mariano 420, Providencia

The South Central American Information Club (SCAI Club, ☎ 673-3166, fax 673-3165), in the Hotel Indiana at Rosas 1339, deals largely but not exclusively with Israeli travelers. Daily rates range from US$55 per day for passengers cars to US$89 for 4WD pickups; monthly rates range from US$1300 to US$2200.

Taxi Colectivo

Taxi colectivos are, in effect, five-passenger buses on fixed routes. They are quicker and more comfortable than most buses and not much more expensive – about US$0.75 within Santiago city limits, although some to outlying suburbs like Puente Alto are a bit dearer. Taxi colectivos resemble ordinary taxis but have an illuminated roof sign indicating their destination and a placard in the window stating the fixed fare.

Taxi

Santiago has abundant metered taxis – black with yellow roofs. Fares vary, but it costs about US$0.60 to *bajar la bandera* ('drop the flag,' ie, start the meter) and about US$0.15 per 200m. Most Santiago taxi drivers are honest, courteous and helpful, but a few will take roundabout routes, and a handful have 'funny' meters.

There is also a system of radio taxis, which can be slightly cheaper. Hotels and restaurants are usually happy to make calls for clients.

Bicycle

Except in poorer barrios and upscale neighborhoods, not many people ride bicycles within the city because of the dense auto traffic, narrow streets and the propensity for cars to take the right-of-way. Recreational cyclists often use sidewalks.

Around Santiago

There are many worthwhile sights outside the capital proper but still within the Región Metropolitana, as well as others outside the region but near enough for reasonable day trips.

TEMPLO VOTIVO DE MAIPÚ

In the southwestern suburban comuna of Maipú, this monstrous manifestation of patriotic and ecclesiastical hubris is a 10-story concrete bunker that probably only a structural engineer could appreciate. Its only redeeming feature: stained glass windows. The

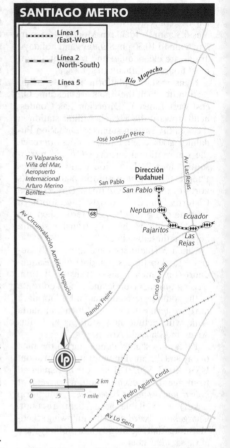

attached **Museo del Carmen** (☎ 247-9669) contains exhibits on religious history and customs, and the Templo's grounds contain late-colonial ruins (fenced off because of earthquake damage).

The Templo is open to the public 8:30 am to 7:30 pm, while the Museo is open 3:30 to 6 pm Saturday, 11 am to 2 pm and 3:30 to 6:30 pm Sundays and holidays.

From the Alameda in Santiago, take any bus that says Templo. Taxi colectivos will also take you there. They leave from the Alameda and Amunátegui.

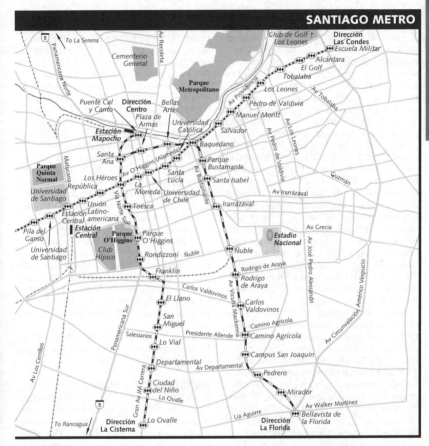

SANTIAGO METRO

POMAIRE

In this small, dusty village near Melipilla, southwest of Santiago, skilled potters spend the days at their wheels producing unique and remarkably inexpensive ceramics. A punchbowl with half a dozen cups, for instance, costs only about US$10. Unfortunately, most items are too large and fragile for travelers to take home, but it's still worth a day trip from the capital for a tour and a small souvenir. For lunch, try *Restaurant San Antonio* (☎ 831-2168, San Antonio and Arturo Prat).

From Santiago, take Buses Melipilla (☎ 776-2060) from Terminal San Borja, Alameda 3250.

WINERIES

While Santiago's growth has displaced many of the wineries that once surrounded the capital, it has spared some, even within the city limits. Besides those mentioned here, see also the entry for Pirque, in the Cajón del Maipo.

The most accessible winery is **Viña Santa Carolina** (☎ 450-3000, ask for Relaciones

Públicas and try to avoid getting passed on to the voice mail system) at Rodrigo de Araya 1341 in the comuna of Macul, near the Estadio Nacional. Although the sprawling capital has displaced the vineyards themselves, the historical *casco* (main house) of the Julio Pereira estate and the *bodegas* (cellars or storehouses) are still here, open to the public with 24 hours' advance notice. Taxi colectivos out Av Vicuña Mackenna pass within easy walking distance.

Also within Santiago city limits, in the comuna of Macul, **Viña Cousiño Macul** (☎ 284-1011, Anexo 45) has opened its bodegas but not its grounds to the public (the grounds are due for a major real estate development as the winery moves its growing activities out of the city). Tours take place at 11 am daily except Sunday, by reservation only, and are free of charge; the sales office is open 9 am to 1 pm and 2 to 6 pm weekdays, 9 am to 1 pm Saturdays. Take bus No 39 or 391 from Santo Domingo out Américo Vespucio Sur to Av Quilín 7100, or No 210 from the Alameda.

In the village of Alto Jahuel, south of the capital and east of Buin, is **Viña Santa Rita** (☎ 821-2707 for reservations), Camino Padre Hurtado 0695. Tours (US$6) take place five times daily Tuesday through Friday, and at 12:30 and 3:30 pm Saturday and Sunday; they include tasting, and there is also an excellent restaurant. By public transport, the simplest way to get here is to take Línea 2 to the end of the line at Lo Ovalle and catch Metrobús No 56, which passes the winery entrance.

Thirty-four kilometers southwest of the capital on the old Melipilla highway between Peñaflor and Talagante, the grounds and buildings of **Viña Undurraga** (☎ 817-2346) are open to the public 10 am to 4 pm weekdays (reservations obligatory). Buses Peñaflor (☎ 776-1025) covers this route from the Terminal San Borja, Alameda 3250; be sure to take the smaller Talagante micro rather than the larger Melipilla bus.

CAJÓN DEL MAIPO

Southeast of the capital, easily accessible by public transportation, the Cajón del Maipo (canyon of the Río Maipo) is one of the main weekend recreation spots for Santiaguinos. The cajón is an excellent place for camping, hiking, climbing, cycling, whitewater rafting and skiing. The area experienced an environmental controversy over the location of a natural gas pipeline from Argentina through the Cascada Las Animas, a private nature reserve. Ultimately, the pipeline was placed to avoid the reserve.

Two main access routes climb the canyon: on the north side of the river, a good paved road passes from the suburban comuna of La Florida to San José de Maipo and beyond, while another narrower, less-traveled paved route follows the south side of the river from Puente Alto. The southern route crosses the river and joins with the other just beyond San José de Maipo.

Among the popular stops in the canyon are El Melocotón, San Alfonso, Cascada de Las Animas, San Gabriel (where the pavement ends and beyond which the main gravel road follows the Río Volcán, a tributary of the Maipo), El Volcán, Lo Valdés, Monumento Natural El Morado and rustic thermal baths at Baños Morales and Termas de Colina.

Buses Cajón del Maipo (☎ 850-5769) leave about every half-hour from the Parque O'Higgins Metro station.

Rafting the Río Maipo

From September to April, several adventure travel companies run descents of the Maipo in seven-passenger rafts, from San Alfonso to Guayacán-Parque Los Héroes. The hourplus descent, passing through mostly Class III rapids with very few calm areas, is rugged enough that it's common for passengers to get tossed in the water. Still, it's perhaps less hazardous than it was when the first kayakers descending in the 1970s found themselves facing automatic weapons as they passed the grounds of General Pinochet's estate at El Melocotón (the narrow bedrock chute here, one of the river's more entertaining rapids, is now known as 'El Pinocho').

Rafting excursions cost anywhere from US$30 to US$75, depending on whether the outing includes lunch, transport to and from Santiago and other amenities; kayak

CAJÓN DEL MAIPO

To Santiago
Río Manzano
Río Colorado
▲ La Tinaja 2509m
Termas del Plomo
El Manzano
Guayacán   Lagunillas
Puente Alto
Río Maipo
Parque los Héroes   San José
de Maipo
Laguna   Embalse
Negra   El Yeso
Viña Concha y Toro
Pirque
To Panamericana
Laguna Lo
Encañado
Río Yeso
Isla de Pirque
El Melocotón
▲ Peladeros 3910m
Río Clarillo
San Alfonso
Monumento Natural El Morado
El Principal
Loma del ▲ Diablo 2324m
Cascada de las Ánimas
Cerro El Morado ▲ 5060m
Reserva Nacional Río Clarillo
San Gabriel
San Pedro ▲ Nolasco 3216m
Río Volcán
Baños Morales
Baños Colina
El Volcán   Lo Valdés   Refugio Alemán

0   5   10 km
0   3   6 miles

descents and lessons are also possible. Operators provide helmets, wet suits and buoyant life jackets, as well as experienced guides and safety kayakers. For operators, see the list in the Facts for the Visitor chapter.

Pirque

One of the gateways to the Cajón, Pirque is an easygoing village just beyond Puente Alto. On weekends a crafts fair features leather workers, goldsmiths and silversmiths. Cyclists will find the paved but narrow route up the south bank of the Maipo much less crowded and more pleasant than the north bank route.

Chile's largest winery, **Viña Concha y Toro** (☎ 821-7000) occupies spacious grounds here. Tours of the vineyards and cellars in English take place at 9:30 and 11:30 am and 3 pm weekdays, and 10 am, noon and 3:30 pm Saturday. Call ahead to be sure of a spot. At the end of the tour you can taste three different wines for about US$1 each.

Spanish-language tours take place at 10:30 am and 2 and 4 pm weekdays, 11 am and 2:30 pm Saturday.

About 3km east of Concha y Toro, on the road up the south side of the Cajón, the **Wailea Coffee Store** has good sandwiches, kuchen and coffee. There is also a string of restaurants, all very popular on weekends, most notably **La Vaquita Echá** (☎ 854-6025, Ramón Subercaseaux 3355), famed for its pastel de choclo.

The quickest way to Pirque is to take Línea 5 of the Metro to the end of the line at La Florida, then catch a bus or taxi colectivo at Paradero 14, just outside the station.

Reserva Nacional Río Clarillo

One of the closest nature reserves to Santiago, 10,000-hectare Río Clarillo is a scenic tributary canyon of the Cajón del Maipo, 23km from Pirque. Its primary attractions are the river and the forest, with sclerophyllous (hard-leafed) tree species unique to the area (though similar to those in other Mediterranean climates, like California's). In addition to abundant bird life, the endangered Chilean iguana also inhabits the reserve, where the admission fee is US$5 per person weekdays, US$7 weekends.

From Pirque, Buses LAC has hourly departures to within 2km of the reserve. Bus No 32 ('El Principal') leaves every three hours or so from Calle Gandarillas, half a block from the Pirque's Plaza de Armas.

Lagunillas

Ranging from 2250m to 2580m above sea level, this small resort, 84km southeast of Santiago via San José de Maipo, is a very modest counterpart to the region's other high-powered ski resorts. Accommodations are available through the Club Andino de Chile (☎ 269-0898), the Refugio Suizo (☎ 205-5423) or in nearby San Alfonso, but it's also an easy day trip from the capital. Ask the Club Andino about transportation.

San Alfonso

San Alfonso is home to **Cascada de las Animas**, a private nature reserve that, a few years back, successfully defied the Chilean government's plans to build a natural gas pipeline over the Andes and through it from Argentina. A former fundo, it also operates a campground and cabañas, and arranges outings ranging from relaxing picnics, day trips and camping to more strenuous activities such as hiking, horseback riding and rafting or kayaking. This is a popular place on weekends and in summer, but much quieter during the week and off-season.

About 20m up the well-marked turnoff to Cascada de las Animas, one of the Cajón's oddest sights is the collection of antique railcars and operating miniature railway belonging to José Sagall, known as 'Pepe Tren' to his neighbors. About 100m farther down the road stands the old station for the military railroad that, until the 1960s, carried Santiaguino weekenders up the Cajón (there is talk of restoration as a tourist train).

From October to April, **Camping Cascada de las Animas** (☎ 861-1303) charges

US$8 per person for shady campsites with good bathroom facilities; the rest of the year, rates are US$4 per person. Comfortable cabañas are also available from US$68 double.

Besides rafting, the Santiago office of Expediciones Las Cascadas (☎ 251-9223, 232-7214), Orrego Luco 040 in Providencia, does a full-day hiking excursion to Cascada de las Animas, including transport to and from Santiago, lunch and pool access at the end of the hike, for US$73 per person. A similar outing on horseback costs US$94.

Refugio Lo Valdés (Alemán)

Overlooking the Cajón from a southside perch above the Río Volcán, across from Baños Morales and surrounded by poplars, the **Refugio Lo Valdés** (☎ 232-0476, terrainc@entelchile.net), popularly known as the Refugio Alemán, is a popular weekend destination throughout the year.

Accommodations with full board cost US$51 per person; children age three to seven pay half, while those two or younger stay free. Accommodations alone cost US$23; rates are US$35 with breakfast, US$45 with half-board, but travelers with their own sleeping bags can crash in the attic for US$11.

The Refugio's restaurant also serves meals separately for nonguests: US$7 for breakfast, US$10 for an elaborate onces of sandwiches, kuchen, ice cream, cookies and coffee, and US$12 for lunch or dinner.

Monumento Natural El Morado

Only 93km from Santiago, this relatively small (3000 hectares) but very scenic park rewards visitors with views of 5060m-tall Cerro El Morado from **Laguna El Morado**, a two-hour hike from the humble hot springs of **Baños Morales**. Although it's a stiff climb at the beginning, the trail soon levels off; motivated hikers can continue to the base of Glaciar El Morado, on the lower slopes of the cerro.

Conaf maintains a small Centro de Información at the park entrance, where rangers collect an admission charge of US$1.25 for adults, US$0.50 for children. Rental horses are available for about US$5 per hour at

Baños Morales, where there's also camping and simple accommodations.

Altué Active Travel (☎ 232-1103), Encomenderos 83, Las Condes, Santiago, arranges day trips (or contracts others to arrange trips), including lunch and transfers, for a minimum of two persons for US$155 per person. Larger parties pay substantially less per person.

T-Arrpue (☎ 211-7165) runs weekend buses from Santiago's Plaza Italia directly to Baños Morales. There are also buses from the Parque O'Higgins Metro at 7 am, returning at 6 pm.

Baños Colina
The road ends at **Baños Colina** (☎ 737-2844), a basic hot springs resort 12km beyond Lo Valdés. For US$5 per person, campers have the right to unlimited use of the thermal baths, but the campsites are bleak and exposed, and tents difficult to pitch in the hard soil. There are also horse rentals; the border is about a six-hour ride away, but only group trips planned far in advance may cross to Argentina here.

From September to April, Expediciones Manzur (☎ 643-5651, 777-4284) provides Saturday and Sunday transport from Plaza Italia for US$14, including access to the baths; in summer, there's an additional Wednesday departure. Miguel Acevedo (☎ 777-3881) does the same trip for US$10 return including access to the baths, from the corner of Alameda and San Ysidro. Try also Buses Cordillera (☎ 777-3881) from Terminal San Borja.

SKI RESORTS
Chile has acquired an international reputation among skiers, and Chile's best downhill skiing is to be found in Middle Chile's high cordillera, primarily up the valley of the Río Mapocho beyond Farellones, and along Ruta 60 to Mendoza, Argentina. Most ski areas are above 3300m; the runs are long, the season is long and the snow is deep and dry. Snowboarders are increasingly welcome at many resorts.

The season generally runs June to early October. Most resorts adjust their rates from

low season (mid-June to early July and mid-September to early October), to mid-season (mid-August to mid-September), to high season, the most expensive (early July to mid-August). For current conditions, check the English-language *Santiago Times* online (www.chip.cl).

El Colorado
One of the closest ski areas, only 45km east of the capital and just beyond Farellones, El Colorado (☎ 211-0426, fax 220-7738) has 19 lifts climbing to 3333m above sea level, with 22 different runs and a vertical drop of 903m. Daily lift tickets cost US$33, with discounts for children and seniors; season passes are also available.

There is lodging at **Refugio Manqui-mávida** (☎ 220-6879, fax 229-5062) for US$64 per person with half-board; meals are available at **El Mirador**.

For information in Santiago, contact Centro de Ski El Colorado (☎ 246-3344, fax 206-4078, ski-colorado@ctcinternet.cl), Av Apoquindo 4900, Local 47/48, Las Condes, which is also the point of departure for direct transport.

La Parva
Only 4km from Farellones, elevations on La Parva's 30 separate runs range from 2662m to 3630m (968m vertical drop). Daily lift tickets range from US$26 in low season to US$33 in high season; multi-day, weekly and seasonal passes are also available. It's also possible to buy an interconnected lift ticket with Valle Nevado (see below).

For accommodations, there's a new hostel, *Albergue Manzanillo*, that charges US$77 to US$110 per person with full board and lift ticket. There's also the *Hotel Condominio Nueva La Parva* for US$1950 to US$2550 per week; for the most current information, contact Centro de Ski La Parva (☎ 264-1466, fax 264-1569), La Concepción 266, Oficina 301, Providencia.

Valle Nevado

Another 14km beyond Farellones, Valle Nevado is a well-planned, high-altitude ski area, ranging from 2805m to 3670m, with 27 runs up to 3km in length. Full-day lift tickets run US$27 on weekdays, US$33 on weekends. Multi-day tickets are also available, but the savings is minimal. Rental equipment is available on site, and there's also a ski school.

At *Hotel Valle Nevado*, rates start at US$1344/2142 singles/doubles per week in low season and reach US$3234/4606 in high season, including half-board and lift tickets. *Hotel Puerta del Sol* is about 30% cheaper, while *Hotel Tres Puntas* is another 15% to 20% cheaper.

Transport to and from the international airport at Pudahuel costs US$60 roundtrip with Andina del Sud (☎ 697-1010); otherwise, more expensive taxi and helicopter service are also available. For bookings, contact Valle Nevado (☎ 206-0027, fax 208-0695, info@vallenevado.com), Gertrudis Echeñique 441, Las Condes. Valle Nevado also has toll-free numbers in the US (☎ 800-669-0554) and Canada (☎ 888-301-3248).

Portillo

Known for its dry powder, Chile's most famous ski resort is the site of several downhill speed records. Altitudes range from 2590m to 3330m on its 11 runs, the longest of which is 1.4km. Just a short distance from the Chilean customs post, on the trans-Andean highway to Mendoza (Argentina), Portillo is 152km from Santiago.

Hotel Portillo is not cheap, starting at US$825 per person for a week's stay in low season, rising as high as US$4615/6550 singles/doubles for a suite; prices include all meals and eight days of lift tickets, but not taxes (foreign visitors, however, are exempt from the 18% IVA). Bunks and shared bath are lower-priced alternatives, but even those run US$640 per person in low season, US$770 in high season.

Depending on demand, ski facilities may or may not be open to nonguests, but lift tickets are in the US$35 daily range. Additional services include a ski school, babysitters, sauna and massage and the like. Meals are available in the hotel restaurant, which has superb views of Laguna del Inca. Moderately priced accommodations are available in the city of Los Andes, below the snow line, 69km to the west.

In summer, the Hotel Portillo charges around US$66/99 to US$77/110 singles/doubles, with breakfast. Contact the Centro de Ski Portillo (☎ 263-0606, fax 263-0595, ptours@skiportillo.com), Renato Sánchez 4270, Las Condes, Santiago (Metro: Escuela Militar), for more information. There's a toll-free US number (☎ 800-829-5325).

Middle Chile

In addition to the Metropolitan Region of Santiago, the country's heartland consists of Regions V (Valparaíso), VI (O'Higgins), VII (Maule) and VIII (Biobío). Its most significant feature is the fertile central valley which, at its widest, extends just 70km between the Andean foothills and the coastal range. Only at the southern edge does the valley floor extend to the Pacific. Endowed with rich alluvial soils, a pleasant Mediterranean climate and Andean meltwater for irrigation, this is Chile's chief farming region, ideal for orchards and vineyards, and for growing cereal.

Since the arrival of Europeans, large estates have dominated Chile's regional economy and society. But landowners' failure to develop their properties efficiently provoked a contentious movement for agrarian reform – spawned by pressure from the landless, and undertaken by the Christian Democrats and subsequent Socialist governments in the 1960s and early 1970s. After the 1973 coup, the Pinochet dictatorship returned many large farms to their former owners and dissolved cooperatives in favor of individual family farms.

Middle Chile contains almost 75% of the country's population and most of its industry. Nearly a third of the region's inhabitants live in the sprawling capital, but Middle Chile also includes the major port of Valparaíso and Chile's most famous resort, the 'garden city' of Viña del Mar. Copper mines dot the sierras of the Metropolitan, Valparaíso and O'Higgins regions, while just north of the Biobío, Concepción (a manufacturing center) and its port, Talcahuano (also home to a naval base), play a key role in the national economy.

Throughout the region, the imposing Andean crest is never far out of sight, and although Argentina is just over the mountain range, the Los Libertadores tunnel northeast of Santiago is the only all-season crossing to Argentina.

Valparaíso & the Central Coast

Northwest of Santiago, Valparaíso and its scenic coastline play a dual role in Chile. Valparaíso is a vital port and one of South America's most distinctive urban areas. Viña del Mar, a resort of international stature, and other coastal towns to its north are favorite summer playgrounds.

VALPARAÍSO
☎ 32

Growing spontaneously along the sea and up the surrounding coast range, Valparaíso – Valpo for short – more closely resembles a medieval European harbor than a 21st-century commercial port. Often called 'La Perla del Pacífico' (Pearl of the Pacific), Chile's second-largest city occupies a narrow, wave-cut terrace, overlooked by precipitous cliffs and hills. The suburbs and shantytowns that cover the hills are linked to the city center by meandering roads, footpaths so steep they resemble staircases.

Built partly on landfill between the waterfront and the hills, the commercial center is no less distinctive, with sinuous cobbled streets, irregular intersections and landmark architecture. In parts of the city where residents pay no garbage tax because their home values are so low, trash tends to pile up; but other areas are improving rapidly. There is a prospect that some neglected older houses will be restored or remodeled as hotels or hostels, and some rehabilitation has begun, particularly on Cerro Concepción.

History

Historians credit Juan de Saavedra, a lieutenant from Diego de Almagro's expedition whose troops met a supply ship from Peru in what is now the Bahía de Valparaíso in 1536, as the founder of the city. Despite Pedro de

MIDDLE CHILE

Valdivia's designation of the bay as the port of Santiago and the building of some churches, more than 2½ centuries passed before the Spanish Crown established a *cabildo* (town council) in 1791. Not until 1802 did Valparaíso legally become a city.

Spanish mercantilism, which favored other cities, such as Lima, Peru, as trade centers, retarded the growth of colonial Valparaíso, but after independence foreigners quickly established their presence. One visitor in 1822 remarked that Englishmen and North Americans so dominated the city that 'but for the mean and dirty appearance of the place, a stranger might almost fancy himself arrived at a British settlement.' Its commerce was disorderly but vigorous:

The whole space between the beach and custom-house was filled with goods and merchandise of various kinds – timber, boxes, iron-bars, barrels, bales, etc – all exposed without any method or arrangement in the open street. Interspersed among them were a number of mules, some standing with loaded, others with unloaded panniers; while the drivers, called peons, dressed in the characteristic garb of the country, made the place ring with their noisy shouts. Here and there porters were busied in carrying away packages; boatmen stood ready to importune you with incessant demands.

Only a few months later, another visitor to Valparaíso had similar impressions, noting that although 'even the governor's house and the custom-house are of poor appearance…all the symptoms of great increase of trade are visible in the many new erections for warehouses.'

Valparaíso's population at independence was barely 5000, but demand for Chilean wheat brought on by the California gold rush prompted such a boom that shortly after the mid-18th century the city's population was about 55,000. Completion of the railroad from Santiago helped to boost the city's population further, and by 1880 it exceeded 100,000. As the first major port of call for ships coming around Cape Horn, the city had become a major commercial center for the entire Pacific Coast and the hub of Chile's nascent banking industry.

A major earthquake in 1906 destroyed many downtown buildings, though some impressive 19th-century architecture remains. The opening of the Panama Canal soon after was an economic blow, as European shipping avoided the longer, more arduous Cape Horn route. Furthermore, Chilean exports of mineral nitrates declined as Europeans found synthetic substitutes, indirectly affecting Valparaíso by further reducing the region's maritime commerce. The Great Depression of the 1930s was a calamity, as demand for Chile's other mineral exports declined. Not until after WWII was there significant recovery, as the country began to industrialize.

Valparaíso remains less dependent on tourism than neighboring Viña del Mar, but many Chilean vacationers make brief excursions to the city from nearby beach resorts. As capital of Region V, the city is an administrative center. Its major industries are food processing and exporting the products of the mining and fruit-growing sectors. Despite port expansion, the city's congested location has diverted cargo south to San Antonio, which handles nearly twice the volume of Valparaíso. The navy's conspicuous presence remains an important factor in the economy.

Orientation

The city of Valparaíso, 120km northwest of Santiago at the south end of the Bahía de Valparaíso, has an extraordinarily complicated layout that probably only a lifetime resident could completely fathom. In the city's congested commercial center, pinched between the port and the almost sheer hills, nearly all major streets parallel the shoreline, which curves north as it approaches Viña del Mar. Av Errázuriz runs the length of the waterfront, alongside the railway, before merging with Av España, the main route to Viña.

Downtown's focal point is remodeled Plaza Sotomayor, facing the port, but several other plazas encourage a vibrant street life. Families frequent Plaza Victoria, for instance, for its lively playground, while Plaza O'Higgins is the site of one of Chile's finest antique markets.

Behind and above the downtown area, Valparaíso's many hills are a rabbit's warren of steep footpaths, zigzag roads and blind alleys where even the best map sometimes fails the visitor. The city map in Turistel's *Centro* volume continues to show improvement, however, and the municipal Departamento de Turismo's cheaper *Valparaíso: Ciudad Puerto* is suitable for short-term visitors.

Information

Tourist Offices Valparaíso's improved, enthusiastic municipal Departamento de Turismo (☎ 221-001), Condell 1490, is open 8:30 am to 2 pm and 3:30 to 5:30 pm weekdays. Its new information office (☎ 236-322) at the Centro de Difusión on Muelle Prat (the pier), near Plaza Sotomayor, employs friendly and well-informed personnel, including English speakers, and distributes free, adequate city maps; the maps for sale are slightly better. It's open 10 am to 7 pm daily.

There is also an office in the *terminal rodoviario* (bus station, ☎ 213-246, Av Pedro Montt 2800), open 10 am to 7 pm in summer and 10 am to 6 pm daily except Monday the rest of the year, and on Plaza Victoria, open the same hours in summer but closed the rest of the year.

Money Valparaíso's exchange houses include Inter Cambio on Plaza Sotomayor and Cambio Exprinter at Prat 895.

Post & Communications Correos de Chile is on Prat at its junction with Plaza Sotomayor. CTC (Telefónica) has long-distance telephone services at Esmeralda 1054, Pedro Montt 2023 and at the bus station. Entel is at Condell 1495 and at the corner of Av Pedro Montt and Cruz. Chilexpress, Av Brasil 1456, has fax, telephone and courier services.

DHL (☎ 881-299) has private courier service at Plaza Sotomayor 55.

Bookstores Librería Crisis (☎ 218-504), Av Pedro Montt 2871, has a good selection of used books on Chilean history and literature.

Cultural Centers The Centro Cultural Valparaíso is at Esmeralda 1083. A branch of the Instituto Chileno-Norteamericano de Cultura (☎ 256-897) is nearby at Esmeralda 1061.

Medical Services Hospital Carlos van Buren (☎ 254-074) is at Av Colón 2454, at the corner of San Ignacio.

Dangers & Annoyances The colorful hill neighborhoods of Valparaíso have an unfortunate reputation for thieves and robbers – local people warn against any ostentatious display of wealth – but with the usual precautions these areas are safe enough, at least during daylight. Visitors to the area west of Plaza Sotomayor and even downtown have reported muggings, so be alert for suspicious characters and ploys to divert your attention. Exercise all reasonable caution, avoid poorly lit areas at night and, if possible, walk with a companion.

Valparaíso has Chile's highest rate of AIDS, associated in part with the sex industry of one of the continent's major ports.

Things to See & Do

Facing the historic **Primera Zona Naval** (ex-Intendencia de Valparaíso), an impressive structure with a mansard roof, **Plaza Sotomayor** is the official heart of Valparaíso, even more so as a new underground parking structure liberates for public use what had, until recently, looked like a used-car dealership. Its dignified statuary crowns a simple, unadorned **Monumento a los Héroes de Iquique**, a subterranean mausoleum paying tribute to Chile's naval martyrs of the War of the Pacific. In addition to the tomb of Arturo Prat, there are tombs of lesser-known figures whose surnames – Reynolds, Wilson and Irving – hint at the role played by northern European immigrants in Chilean history.

Other landmarks surrounding Plaza Sotomayor include the **Aduana Nacional**, or customhouse – one of the port city's most important institutions; **Estación Puerto**, the terminal for Merval commuter trains, which is also noteworthy for its murals; and **Muelle Prat**, the redeveloped port area.

If Plaza Sotomayor is the city's official heart, the **Plaza Matriz** is its historic core, directly uphill from the Mercado Central, where the distinctive hills architecture starts to take shape. The plaza's major landmark is the **Iglesia Matriz**, a national monument dating from 1842. This is the fourth church to occupy this site since construction of the original chapel in 1559.

Southeast of Plaza Sotomayor, where Prat and Cochrane converge to become Esmeralda, the **Edificio Turri** narrows to the width of its namesake clock tower. Topped by a mansard roof at Esmeralda and Ross, the neoclassical **El Mercurio de Valparaíso** (1903) is the home of Chile's oldest continuously published newspaper (since 1827, long antedating the building itself).

At Independencia and Huito, the neoclassical **Palacio Lyon** (1881), once a private mansion, now houses the city's natural history museum and the municipal art gallery. One block east, at the southwest corner of Plaza Victoria, on Independencia between Huito and Molina, the French-style **Club Naval** dates from 1895. Overlooking Plaza Victoria, on Edwards between Av Pedro Montt and Chacabuco, is the **Iglesia Catedral**, the site of ecclesiastical primacy.

At the east end of downtown, toward Viña del Mar, the most imposing landmark is the controversial **Congreso Nacional** (1990), which overlooks **Plaza O'Higgins**. Mandated by Pinochet's 1980 constitution, which moved the legislature away from the Santiago-based executive branch, the last major public works project of the dictatorship had cost US$100 million by its completion in 1990. With an area of 40,000 sq meters, the imposing modern building was built on the site of one of Pinochet's boyhood homes. Since the return to constitutional government, the location of the legislature has been a notable inconvenience – rapid physical communication between the two cities is only possible by helicopter and a number of legislators have been busted for speeding on Ruta 68 between the two cities. Talk of returning the Congreso to Santiago, hitherto opposed by conservative elements, has been gaining steam, but such action

would leave Valparaíso with an unanticipated contemporary historical monument – or white elephant. When the Congreso is in session, the building is open to the public from 3 to 5 pm Friday. It's at the junction of Av Pedro Montt and Av Argentina, opposite Plaza O'Higgins and the bus terminal.

The plaza is also the site of the **Teatro Municipal** (municipal theater; 1931), and of the city's best antiques market on weekends. Two blocks north, the **Universidad Católica** is the city's most prestigious educational institution, but the most imposing edifice, dating from the 1930s, belongs to the **Universidad Técnica Federico Santa María**, which dominates Av España to the northeast.

Valparaíso's redeveloped pier, **Muelle Prat**, at the foot of Plaza Sotomayor, is a lively place on weekends, with a helpful tourist kiosk and a good handicrafts market, the Feria de Artesanías, open 10 am to 4 pm Thursday through Sunday. Do not photograph any of the numerous Chilean naval vessels at anchor.

Hills of Valparaíso

Valparaíso is undoubtedly the single most distinctive city in Chile and one of the most intriguing in all of South America. On a sunny afternoon, it's possible to spend hours riding the 15 *ascensores* (funicular railways), built between 1883 and 1916, and strolling

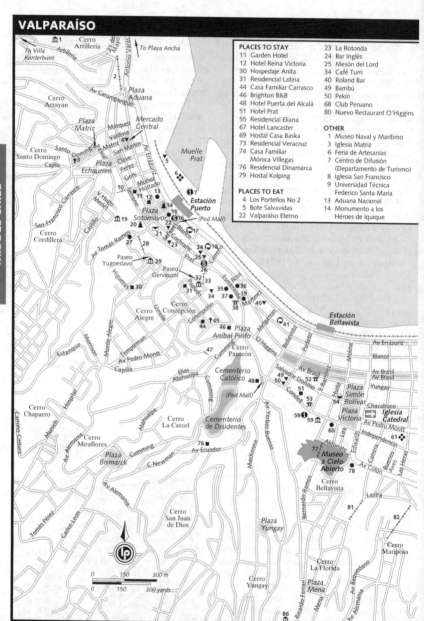

VALPARAÍSO

MIDDLE CHILE

PLACES TO STAY
11 Garden Hotel
12 Hotel Reina Victoria
30 Hospedaje Anita
31 Residencial Latina
44 Casa Familiar Carrasco
46 Brighton B&B
48 Hotel Puerta del Alcalá
51 Hotel Prat
55 Residencial Eliana
67 Hotel Lancaster
69 Hostal Casa Baska
73 Residencial Veracruz
74 Casa Familiar
   Mónica Villegas
76 Residencial Dinamarca
79 Hostal Kolping

PLACES TO EAT
4 Los Porteños No 2
5 Bote Salvavidas
22 Valparaíso Eterno

23 La Rotonda
24 Bar Inglés
25 Mesón del Lord
34 Café Turri
40 Roland Bar
49 Bambú
50 Pekín
68 Club Peruano
80 Nuevo Restaurant O'Higgins

OTHER
1 Museo Naval y Marítimo
3 Iglesia Matriz
6 Feria de Artesanías
7 Centro de Difusión
   (Departamento de Turismo)
8 Iglesia San Francisco
9 Universidad Técnica
   Federico Santa María
13 Aduana Nacional
14 Monumento a los
   Héroes de Iquique

VALPARAÍSO

15 DHL
16 Inter Cambio
17 British Consulate
18 Argentine Consulate
19 Museo del Mar
   Lord Cochrane
20 Primera Zona Naval
21 Post Office
26 Cambio Exprinter, Reloj Turri
27 Tribunales
29 Palacio Baburizza
   (Museo de Bellas Artes)
32 Museo de Lukas
35 El Mercurio de Valparaíso
36 Instituto Chileno-
   Norteamericano de Cultura
37 LanChile
38 CTC (Telefónica)
39 Centro Cultural Valparaíso,
   Centro Cine
41 Peruvian Consulate,
   German Consulate

43 Mirador Diego Portales
45 Iglesia Luterana
52 Chilexpress
53 Entel
54 Buses La Porteña
56 Universidad Católica
58 Municipalidad,
   Departamento de Turismo
59 Palacio Lyon
   (Natural History Museum,
   Municipal Art Gallery)
60 Club Naval
61 Mercado Artesanal
   Permanente
62 CTC (Telefónica)
63 La Puerta del Sol
64 Santiago Wanderers Offices
65 Cine Hoyts
66 Entel
70 Teatro Municipal
71 Bus Station
72 Librería Crisis

78 Sala Herbert Jonckers
83 Hospital Carlos van Buren
84 Comveq Car Rental
86 La Sebastiana,
   Fundación Neruda

ASCENSORES
 2 Ascensor Artillería
10 Ascensor Cordillera
28 Ascensor El Peral
33 Ascensor Concepción (Turri)
42 Ascensor Barón
47 Ascensor Reina Victoria
57 Ascensor Lecheros
75 Ascensor Larraín
77 Ascensor Espíritu Santo
81 Ascensor Florida
82 Ascensor Mariposa
85 Ascensor Polanco
87 Ascensor Monjas
88 Ascensor Cerro La Cruz

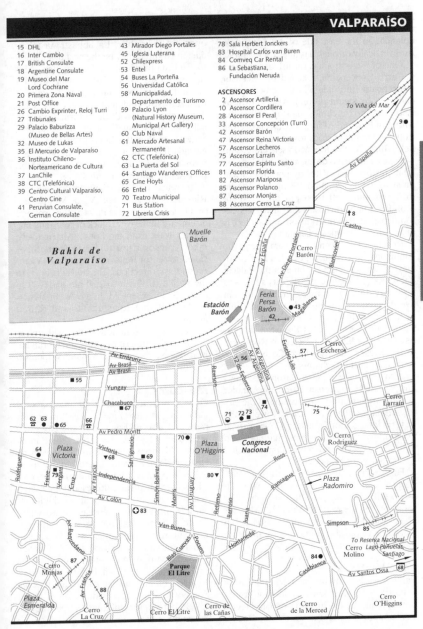

MIDDLE CHILE

back alleys. Some of the ascensores are remarkable feats of engineering – **Ascensor Polanco**, on the east side of Av Argentina, rises vertically through a tunnel, for example.

One of the best areas for urban explorers is Cerro Concepción, reached by **Ascensor Concepción** (the oldest in the city, it originally ran by steam power). Also known as Ascensor Turri, it climbs the slopes from the corner of Prat and Almirante Carreño, across from the landmark clock tower known as the **Reloj Turri**. At the top, at Paseo Gervasoni 448, the new **Museo de Lukas** (☎ 221-344) exhibits historical sketches by porteño caricaturist Renzo Pecchenino. It's open 10:30 am to 2 pm and 3:30 to 6 pm daily except Monday; admission costs US$1. Three blocks southeast, at Paseo Atkinson and Abtao, is the Gothic-style **Iglesia Luterana**.

Reached by **Ascensor El Peral**, near the **Tribunales** (law courts) just off Plaza Sotomayor, Cerro Alegre is home to the **Palacio Baburizza** (1916), housing the city's fine arts museum but presently undergoing an overdue renovation. From here it's possible to loop over to Cerro Concepción, or vice versa. One block north of Plaza Sotomayor, **Ascensor Cordillera** climbs Cerro Cordillera to the **Museo del Mar Lord Cochrane**, described later in this chapter.

Above the Feria Persa Barón (flea market), reached by **Ascensor Barón**, the **Mirador Diego Portales** offers a panorama of the city toward the west; nearby, the bell tower of the historic **Iglesia San Francisco** (1845) served as a landmark for approaching mariners, who gave the city its common nickname 'Pancho' (a diminutive of Francisco).

For a quick, inexpensive tour of Valparaíso's hills, catch the Verde Mar 'O' *micro* (city bus) on Serrano, near Plaza Sotomayor, all the way to Viña del Mar for about US$0.40. This bus also passes Pablo Neruda's Valparaíso home, now a museum (see La Sebastiana).

La Sebastiana

Pablo Neruda probably spent less time at La Sebastiana, his least-known and least-visited house, than at La Chascona or Isla Negra, but he made it a point to watch Valparaíso's annual New Year's fireworks from his lookout on Cerro Bellavista. Restored and open to the public, La Sebastiana (Fundación Neruda) may be the best destination for Neruda pilgrims; it's the only one of his three houses that visitors can wander around at will without having to subject themselves to regimented tours that seem out of character with the informal poet. In addition to the usual assemblage of oddball artifacts within the house, the Fundación Neruda has built a Centro Cultural La Sebastiana alongside it, with rotating exhibitions, a café and a souvenir shop.

To reach La Sebastiana (☎ 256-606), at Ricardo Ferrari 692, take Verde Mar bus 'O' or 'D' on Serrano near Plaza Sotomayor and disembark in the 6900 block of Av Alemania, a short walk from the house. Alternatively, take Acensor Espiritu Santo (sometimes called Ascensor Bellavista) near Plaza Victoria and ask directions. The house is open to the public 10:30 am to 2:30 pm and 3:30 to 6 pm daily except Monday. Admission is US$3, half that for students and retired people.

Neruda's most famous house, with an extensive collection of maritime memorabilia, is at Isla Negra (see the Around Valparaíso section).

Museums

Once a private mansion, the neoclassical Palacio Lyon (1881) merits a visit in its own right, but also houses two of the city's key museums. Most of the large selection of natural history specimens in the **Museo de Historia Natural** are mediocre, but the upper exhibition halls compensate; the story of Chile's pre-Hispanic cultures and their environments is told in outstanding exhibits, including dioramas of subsistence activities. There is superb material on the oceans and their future, a subject of great importance to a maritime country such as Chile. At Condell 1546, the Museo (☎ 257-441) is open 10 am to 1 pm and 2 to 6 pm Tuesday to Friday, 10 am to 6 pm Saturday and 10 am to 2 pm Sunday and holidays. Admission is about US$1, half that for children; it's free Wednesday and Sunday.

In the basement of the building, but with a separate entrance, the **Galería Municipal de Arte** (municipal art gallery) hosts fine arts exhibits throughout the year. At Condell 1550, the Galería (☎ 220-062) is open 10 am to 7 pm daily except Sunday; admission is free.

Designed for an Italian nitrate baron but named for the Yugoslav who purchased it from him, the **Palacio Baburizza (Museo de Bellas Artes),** a landmark Art Nouveau house (1916) is noteworthy for imaginative woodwork, forged-iron details and a steeply pitched central tower. Set among attractive gardens, it was a private residence until 1971, when the city acquired it as a fine arts museum, presently undergoing a much needed renovation with its collections currently in storage, but the building and its grounds alone justify a visit.

On Cerro Alegre's Paseo Yugoeslavo, reached by Ascensor El Peral from near Plaza Sotomayor, the museum (☎ 252-332) is normally open 9:30 am to 6 pm daily except Monday. Admission is free, but donations are accepted.

The **Museo del Mar Lord Cochrane,** overlooking the harbor, was built in 1842 for Lord Thomas Cochrane but never occupied by him. This tile-roofed, colonial-style house above Plaza Sotomayor held Chile's first astronomical observatory – however unlikely a place to observe the heavens Valparaíso might seem, given its constant fogs. Its pleasant gardens offer excellent views, while the museum itself displays an excellent collection of model ships in glass cases, along with acrylic paintings.

To reach the museum (☎ 213-124), take Ascensor Cordillera from the west side of Plaza Sotomayor and walk east to Merlet 195. It's open 10 am to 6 pm daily except Monday; admission costs US$1 for adults, half that for children.

One of the few Chilean museums with sufficient resources for acquisitions and a truly professional presentation, Chile's **Museo Naval y Marítimo** focuses on the War of the Pacific (specifically honoring naval hero and national icon Arturo Prat), but there are also major displays on Lord Cochrane (the navy's

Pablo Neruda

founder), Admiral Manuel Blanco Encalada (an independence-era naval fighter) and other lesser figures. The most interesting displays, though, deal with voyages around the Horn, giving credit to sailors of every European country.

Reached by Ascensor Artillería from the triangular Plaza Aduana (also known as the Plaza Wheelwright), the immaculate museum building served as Chile's Escuela Naval (naval academy) from 1893 to 1967. At the top of the ascensor, Paseo 21 de Mayo offers souvenir stands, a small café with an attractive terrace and outstanding views of the port to the east. Open 10 am to 5:30 pm daily except Monday, the museum (☎ 283-749) charges about US$1 for adults, half that for children.

Between 1969 and 1973, students from the Universidad Católica's Instituto de Arte created the 20 brightly colored abstract murals that cover numerous hillside sites on Cerro Bellavista, reached by Ascensor Espíritu Santo. Concentrated on Calle Aldunate and Paseos Guimera, Pasteur, Rudolph and Ferrari, Valparaíso's **Museo a Cielo Abierto,** or 'open sky museum,' is not great art, but still adds a welcome spot of color to an otherwise rundown area. The tourist kiosk on Muelle Prat distributes a locator map of the area.

MIDDLE CHILE

Special Events

Año Nuevo (New Year's) is one of Valparaíso's biggest events, thanks to the massive fireworks display that brings hundreds of thousands of spectators to the city.

April 17, which marks the arrival of the authorization of the cabildo of Valparaíso in 1791, is the city's official day (imperial Spain's glacial bureaucracy and slow communications across the Atlantic delayed receipt of the authorization for more than three years).

Places to Stay

Nearby Viña del Mar has a broader choice of accommodations in all categories, but Valparaíso has a few alternatives, the most interesting of which are hospedajes in the scenic hills. Phone ahead before visiting any of these places, which can be difficult to find and may have a limited number of beds.

Budget Near the bus terminal, quiet, comfortable and amiable *Casa Familiar Mónica Villegas* (☎ 215-673, *Av Argentina 322*) charges US$9 (with some space for negotiation, especially when it's not crowded) including a simple breakfast. Try also the appealing, comparably priced *Residencial Veracruz* (*Av Pedro Montt 2881*), located opposite the Congreso Nacional, or *Residencial Eliana* (☎ 250-945, *Av Brasil 2164*) for US$12.

On Cerro Concepción, reached by Ascensor Concepción (Turri), family-oriented *Residencial Latina* (☎ 237-733, *Papudo 462*) comes highly recommended at US$10 per person. Also on Cerro Concepción, the friendly *Casa Familiar Carrasco* (☎ 210-737, *Abtao 668*) is a phenomenal value for US$8 to US$10 for a single with shared bath, US$25 for a double with a fireplace and antique furnishings; there are spectacular vistas from the rooftop deck (ideal for New Year's fireworks).

On Cerro Playa Ancha, at the west end of town near Ascensor Artillería, *Villa Kunterbunt* (☎ 288-873, *Av Quebrada Verde 192*) charges US$8 per person without breakfast;

English and German are spoken. On Cerro Panteón, near the Cementerio de Disidentes, *Residencial Dinamarca* (☎ 259-189, *Dinamarca 535*) offers rooms with cable TV and private bath for US$16 per person (there's one single with shared bath for US$12), as well as a bar and cafeteria. On Cerro Alegre, recently renovated *Hospedaje Anita* (☎ 239-327, *Higueras 107*) may be worth a look for US$14 per person.

Conspicuous because of its striking mansard roof but suffering from deferred maintenance and a noisy location, *Hotel Reina Victoria* (☎ 212-203, *Plaza Sotomayor 190*) starts around US$12 per person for 4th-floor singles with shared bath, and increases to US$17/22 for 2nd-floor singles/doubles with private bath and breakfast. Around the corner, the similarly priced *Garden Hotel* (*Serrano 501*) has spacious rooms but is the subject of mixed reports, some of which mention surly staff.

Mid-Range & Top End One of downtown's best values is *Hostal Kolping* (☎ 216-306, *Vergara 622*) on the south side of Plaza Victoria, where singles/doubles are US$18/24 with shared bath, US$25/33 with private bath, breakfast included. Not as good but more expensive are *Hotel Prat* (☎ 253-081, *Condell 1443*) for US$25/29; or the rather better *Hotel Lancaster* (☎ 217-391, *Chacabuco 2362*) for US$25/44. Highly recommended *Hostal Casa Baska* (☎ 234-036, *Victoria 2449*) is a better choice for US$33/38.

On Cerro Concepción, the *Brighton B&B* (☎/fax 223-513, *Pasaje Atkinson 151*) is – despite its classic Valparaíso architecture – a new building, fitted with recycled materials. Also a pub-restaurant, its terrace offers great views of the city over Plaza Aníbal Pinto; rates are US$31/42, but rooms with sea views cost 50% more.

An exception to Valpo's reputation for a shortage of upscale hotels is the new *Hotel Puerta del Alcalá* (☎ 227-478, fax 745-642, *Pirámide 524*). Well-located and architecturally appealing, this business-oriented facility charges US$65 single or double.

Places to Eat

Traditionally, visitors dine in Viña del Mar, but Valparaíso can be an equally good place to eat. For the cheapest eats, try the area around the bus terminal.

Informal *Valparaíso Eterno* (☎ 255-605, *Señoret 150, 2nd floor*) drips with bohemian atmosphere and is also an inexpensive lunch favorite for the city's downtown business crowd. *Los Porteños No 2* (☎ 252-511, *Valdivia 169*) has large portions and excellent service, but the menu is limited. Across the street, the 2nd-floor marisquerías at the *Mercado Central* charge less than US$3 for three-course meals, but the fish is usually fried.

Recommended vegetarian restaurant *Bambú* (☎ 234-216, *Pudeto 450*) sells cheap lunches; nearby *Pekín* (☎ 254-387, *Pudeto 422*) serves Chinese food. Near Parque Italia, in a classic building with high ceilings and chandeliers, the elderly waiters at the *Club Peruano* (☎ 228-068, *Victoria 2324*) serve moderately priced Peruvian specialties. The restaurant has tobacco-free areas. *Nuevo Restaurant O'Higgins* (*Retamo 506*) has a popular Sunday lunch for US$7.

The *Roland Bar* (☎ 235-123, *Av Errázuriz 1152*) serves meat and seafood dishes; its weekday lunch special costs US$5. *Mesón del Lord* (☎ 231-096, *Cochrane 859*) has good lunches (including vegetarian alternatives) in a traditional porteño atmosphere. Another traditional favorite is the *Bar Inglés* (☎ 214-625, *Cochrane 851/Blanco 870*), but prices have risen so that it's no longer a great bargain, even for lunch. At *La Rotonda* (☎ 217-746, *Prat 701*) the lunch menu includes a daily special for about US$10, but consider splitting à la carte dishes from the extensive menu – portions are huge. Both seafood and service are excellent.

Bote Salvavidas (☎ 251-477, *Muelle Prat s/n*) is a traditional but expensive seafood restaurant. *Café Turri* (*Templeman 147*, ☎ 252-091), fronting on Paseo Gervasoni at the upper exit of Ascensor Concepción (Turri), has superb seafood in an agreeable setting, attentive but unobtrusive service and panoramic views of the harbor from the 3rd-floor balcony. It's an exceptional value.

Entertainment

Valparaíso has plenty of sleazy waterfront bars, but most visitors prefer the numerous pubs that line Av Ecuador, climbing the hill toward Cerro Panteón, just east of the Cementerio de Disidentes.

The five-screen *Cine Hoyts* (☎ 594-709, *Pedro Montt 2111*) shows current films. The *Centro Cine* (☎ 216-953, *Esmeralda 1083*) is more of an art house, part of the Centro Cultural Valparaíso.

The *Teatro Municipal* (☎ 214-654, *Av Uruguay 410*) hosts live theater and concerts. The *Sala Herbert Jonckers* (☎ 221-680, *Colón 1712*) also offers live theater.

La Puerta del Sol (*Av Pedro Montt 2037*) has weekend tango shows.

Spectator Sports

Santiago Wanderers (☎ 217-210), Independencia 2061, is Valparaíso's first-division soccer team; they play at the Estadio Municipal at Playa Ancha.

Shopping

For a fine selection of crafts, visit the Mercado Artesanal Permanente at the corner of Av Pedro Montt and Las Heras. Valparaíso may be the best city in Chile for flea markets, such as the Feria Persa Barón, on Av Argentina where it becomes Av España, which is open 9 am to 11 pm daily.

On Saturday, Sunday and holidays, there's a tremendous Feria de Antiguedades y Libros La Merced on Plaza O'Higgins, where the prices aren't cheap but the selection of books and antiques is outstanding. A more general-interest flea market, on Plaza Radomiro Tomic, the median strip between the lanes of Av Argentina, offers some Mapuche crafts among the usual post-industrial dreck. There's also a modest Feria de Artesanías near Plaza Prat.

Getting There & Away

Air LanChile (☎ 251-441, fax 233-374) is in Valparaíso at Esmeralda 1048. There are no flights out of Viña del Mar's Aeropuerto Torquemada at present; Santiago's is the closest operating airport.

Bus – Regional Nearly all bus companies have offices at Valparaíso's bus station (☎ 213-246), Av Pedro Montt 2800, across from the Congreso Nacional. Because services from Valparaíso and Viña del Mar are almost identical, most information (including telephone numbers) appears here.

The company with the most frequent service to Santiago (1¾ hours to two hours) is Tur-Bus (☎ 212-028 in Valpo, 882-621 in Viña). Buses leave every 10 to 15 minutes 6 am to 10 pm. Some Viña buses go direct to Santiago, while others go via Valparaíso, but the fare is identical at about US$4 one way.

Slightly cheaper, Cóndor Bus (☎ 212-927 in Valpo, 882-345 in Viña) leaves every 20 to 30 minutes. Sol del Pacífico (☎ 213-776 in Valpo, ☎ 883-156 in Viña) has hourly departures 6:50 am to 9:30 pm, while Sol del Sur (☎ 252-211 in Valpo, ☎ 687-277) has four daily. Pullman Lit (☎ 237-290) goes every two hours from 8:10 am to 7:10 pm.

Buses La Porteña (☎ 216-568), Molina 366, covers coastal and interior destinations in the northern sector of Region V, including La Ligua (US$2, one hour), Pichidangui (US$3, 1½ hours) and Los Vilos (US$3.50, two hours), four times daily. Sol del Pacífico (☎ 288-577) serves the region's northern beaches from Quintero north as far as Papudo and also goes to La Ligua three times daily. Cóndor Bus (☎ 212-927) goes to La Ligua half-hourly 6:45 am to 9:15 pm.

Buses JM (☎ 256-581) goes half-hourly to Los Andes (US$4, two hours) between 6:45 am and 9:15 pm, while Pullman Bus (☎ 253-125) runs hourly 6:10 am to 10 pm. Buses Dhino's (☎ 221-298) also goes to Los Andes via Limache, Quillota and San Felipe, hourly 5:20 am to 6:50 pm.

Pullman Bus Lago Peñuelas (☎ 224-025) goes to Algarrobo (US$2.50) and nearby Isla Negra (for the Neruda house) every 15 minutes 6:20 am to 10 pm.

Bus – Long-Distance Unless otherwise indicated, the following carriers leave from the main bus terminal. Note that some northbound long-distance buses, especially ones that travel at night, involve connections with buses from Santiago, which can mean waiting on the Panamericana – ask before buying your ticket.

Tur-Bus also runs northbound routes on the Panamericana to Antofagasta (US$29, 15 hours), Iquique (US$35, 20 hours) and Arica (US$40, 24 hours), and southbound to Talca (US$8, six hours), Chillán (US$13, eight hours), Concepción (US$16, 10 hours), Temuco (US$18, 11 hours), Osorno (US$24, 14 hours) and Puerto Montt (US$27, 16 hours).

Buses Zambrano (☎ 258-986 in Valpo, 883-942 in Viña) follows the Panamericana north to Iquique (US$40), Arica (US$50) and intermediate points, at 8 am daily. Similar services are available from Pullman Bus (☎ 256-898 in Valpo, 680-424 in Viña), which has five departures daily.

Flota Barrios (☎ 253-674 in Valpo, 882-725 in Viña), covering the Norte Grande routes, has three departures daily, while Chile Bus (☎ 256-325 in Valpo, 881-187 in Viña) and Fénix Pullman Norte (☎ 257-993 in Valpo) cover the same routes. Transportes Lasval (☎ 214-915 in Valpo, 684-121 in Viña) serves the cities of the Norte Chico, primarily Ovalle (US$12) and La Serena/Coquimbo.

Southbound, Buses Norte (☎ 258-322) goes nightly to Temuco, Valdivia, Osorno and Puerto Montt, and makes connections in Santiago with Turibús for Punta Arenas (US$75). Tas Choapa (☎ 252-921 in Valparaíso, 882-258 in Viña del Mar) goes daily to Santiago and intermediate points on the Panamericana as far south as Puerto Montt. Other companies serving southern destinations include Buses Lit (☎ 237-200 in Valpo, 690-783 in Viña), Intersur (☎ 212-297) and Sol del Sur, with service to Talca, Chillán and Concepción.

Buses JM (☎ 256-581 in Valpo, 883-184 in Viña), has three buses daily to Concepción (US$11 to US$15). Sol del Pacífico also offers southbound services on the Panamericana to Talca (US$10), Chillán (US$13), Concepción (US$14) and Los Angeles (US$14).

Bus – International Unless otherwise indicated, the following carriers leave from the main bus terminal.

Valparaíso and Viña both have direct services to Argentina, bypassing Santiago. All these buses leave between 8 and 9 am; those leaving from Valparaíso also stop in Viña.

Carriers with daily departures to Mendoza (US$25, eight hours) and Buenos Aires (US$50 to US$60) include El Rápido (☎ 257-587 in Valpo, 685-474 in Viña); Buses TAC (☎ 258-922 in Valpo, 685-767 in Viña) and Buses Ahumada (☎ 216-663).

Fénix Pullman Norte has daily runs to Mendoza, while Tur-Bus goes to Mendoza Monday, Wednesday and Friday only. Tas Choapa goes daily to Mendoza, San Juan and Córdoba (US$36). Buses Pluma (☎ 258-322) runs buses Tuesday, Friday and Sunday to Mendoza, Rosario and the Brazilian cities of Florianópolis (US$104), São Paulo (US$108) and Rio de Janeiro (US$112). Buses Géminis (☎ 258-322) goes Monday, Wednesday and Friday to Oruro and La Paz, Bolivia (US$80).

Getting Around

Valparaíso and Viña del Mar are only a few kilometers apart, connected by countless local buses (about US$0.40) and slightly more expensive taxi colectivos.

Metro Regional de Valparaíso (Merval) operates regular commuter trains between the Valparaíso-Viña area and the towns of Quilpué, Villa Alemana and Limache. The area's endemic traffic congestion makes the frequent, inexpensive service between Valparaíso and Viña a superior alternative to either bus or taxi, but fewer trains run around midday and late in the evening; service ceases at around 10 pm. Valparaíso's Estación Puerto (☎ 217-108) is at Plaza Sotomayor 711, corner of Errázuriz, with additional stations at Bellavista (on Errázuriz between Pudeto and Molina) and at Muelle Barón.

Driving in the congested Valparaíso-Viña area makes little sense, but cars can be useful for visiting beach resorts to the north or south. Most car rental agencies have offices in Viña del Mar, but in Valparaíso try Comveq (☎ 212-153) at Av Argentina 850.

AROUND VALPARAÍSO
Reserva Nacional Lago Peñuelas

Not really a lake, Lago Peñuelas is a reservoir built at the end of the 19th century to supply potable water to Valparaíso and Viña del Mar. Nevertheless, this 9260-hectare Conaf reserve along Ruta 68 is a popular site for weekend outings; fishing is possible, and it has a representative sample of coast-range vegetation and lesser fauna and birds.

Lago Peñuelas is 30km southeast of Valparaíso. Any of the frequent buses linking Santiago with Valparaíso and Viña del Mar can drop passengers at the entrance.

MIDDLE CHILE

AROUND VALPARAÍSO & VIÑA DEL MAR

MIDDLE CHILE

Lo Vásquez

Every December 8, Chilean authorities close Ruta 68 as nearly half a million pilgrims converge on this small town's **Santuario de la Inmaculada Concepción**, 32km southeast of Valparaíso and 68km northwest of Santiago. Masses take place hourly from 6 pm the night before until 8 pm on the 8th.

Isla Negra

Even more outlandish than La Chascona in Santiago, Pablo Neruda's favorite house sits on a rocky ocean headland between Valparaíso and Cartagena. Once vandalized by agents of the Pinochet dictatorship, it now houses the Museo Neruda, holding the poet's collections of bowsprits, ships in bottles, nautical instruments, wood carvings and other memorabilia. His tomb is also here.

In summer, Isla Negra (☎ 035-461-284), which is *not*, by the way, an island, is open for visits 10 am to 8 pm Tuesday to Sunday. Reservations are imperative, since there are up to 40 tours daily led by guides whose interest and competence vary greatly. The rest of the year, when Isla Negra is open 10 am to 2 pm and 3 to 6 pm Tuesday through Friday and 10 and to 8 pm weekends, tours are more relaxed. Admission and tour fees are US$2.50 for adults, US$1.25 for children and US$4 for English- or French-language.

Tours last only half an hour, but visitors are permitted to hang around and photograph the grounds as long as they like. Pullman Bus Lago Peñuelas (☎ 224-025 in Valpo) leaves from the main bus terminal in Valpo, and drops pilgrims almost at the door of Isla Negra (US$2.50). You can also catch a bus from Santiago's Terminal Sur.

VIÑA DEL MAR
☎ 32

Viña del Mar (Viña for short) has long been Chile's premier beach resort, but it's also a bustling commercial center. Only a short bus ride north of Valparaíso, it is popularly known as the Ciudad Jardín (Garden City), for reasons obvious to any visitor; beginning with Av España's Reloj de Flores (Clock of Flowers), whose blooms greet visitors at the

entrance to town, Viña's manicured subtropical landscape of palms and bananas contrasts dramatically with the colorful disorder of its blue-collar neighbor. Many moneyed Chileans and other wealthy Latin Americans own houses here, but while Viña is not cheap, neither is it impossibly dear.

Colonial Viña was the hacienda of the prominent Carrera family, who sold it to a Portuguese businessman named Alvarez in the mid-19th century. Alvarez's daughter and sole heir later married into the Vergara family, who have bestowed their name upon many city landmarks. Soon thereafter, Viña's role as the country's Pacific playground began as the railroad linked Valparaíso with Santiago; the porteños of Valparaíso, many of them foreigners, now had easy access to the beaches and broad green spaces to the north, and soon built grand houses and mansions away from the cramped harbor city.

With construction of hotels and subdivision of the sector north of the Estero Marga Marga, Viña became an increasingly attractive and popular weekend destination for Santiaguinos. Viña, though, has recently lost popularity to competing resorts such as La Serena.

Visitors hoping for balmy summer weather are often disappointed; Viña and the entire central coast are subject to cool fogs that don't burn off until early afternoon, and ocean temperatures are downright chilly. Sunseekers and surfers often wish they had brought woolens and wet suits.

Orientation

Viña is about 10km northeast of Valparaíso via the shoreline Av España. It consists of two distinct sectors: an established, prestigious area of traditional mansions south of the Estero Marga Marga, and a newer, more regular residential grid to its north. Several bridges, most notably Puente Libertad, connect the two sectors. North of the heavily polluted Marga Marga, most streets are identified by number and direction, either Norte (north), Oriente (east) or Poniente (west). Av Libertad separates Ponientes from Orientes. These streets are usually written as a numeral, but are sometimes spelled out, so that 1 Norte may also appear as Uno Norte.

The commercial and activity centers of Viña are south of the Marga Marga, on Plaza Vergara and Avs Arlegui and Valparaíso, which parallel the river. South of Alvarez is a zone of turn-of-the-20th-century mansions that belonged to the Santiago and Viña elite, whose centerpiece is the famous Quinta Vergara (see below). Viña's main attractions, of course, are the white-sand beaches that stretch northward from Caleta Abarca to the suburbs of Reñaca and Concón. The city's limited industry is several kilometers inland.

Information

The municipal Central de Turismo e Informaciones (☎ 269-330) is near the junction of Libertad and Arlegui, just north of Plaza Vergara. Most of the year it's open from 9 am to 2 pm and from 3 to 7 pm weekdays, 10 am to 2 pm and 4 to 7 pm Saturday, but in the summer, which is the peak season, it's open from 9 am to 7 pm daily except Sunday. The tourist office distributes an adequate city map and an excellent monthly flyer entitled *Todo Viña del Mar Valparaíso*, including useful information and a calendar of events for both cities.

Sernatur's regional office (☎ 882-285, fax 684-117) is at Valparaíso 507, 3rd floor, but the entrance is a little difficult to find and the staff cater more toward businesses than individuals. It's open 8:30 am to 5:30 pm weekdays. The Automóvil Club de Chile (Acchi; ☎ 689-505) is just north of the Marga Marga at 1 Norte 901.

For US cash or traveler's checks, try Cambios Guiñazú at Arlegui 686 or InterCambio at 1 Norte 655-B.

The post office is at the northwest side of Plaza Vergara, near Puente Libertad. DHL, on Av Libertad between 8 and 9 Norte, has international courier service.

CTC (Telefónica) has long-distance offices at Valparaíso 628, at Valparaíso and Villanelo, and at the corner of Av Libertad and 1 Norte. For cellular communications, contact Entel PCS at Av Libertad 1030,

Startel at Av Libertad 1002 or BellSouth (☎ 975-891) at 9 Norte 870.

The Cyber Blues Café (☎ 690-529, cyber@café.cl), Av Valparaíso 196, offers Internet access.

Among Viña del Mar's private galleries are Galería de Arte Modigliani (☎ 684-991) at 5 Norte 168 and the Arte Gallery at 2 Poniente 671.

There are frequent exhibitions of art and sculpture at the Centro Cultural Viña del Mar (☎ 269-708), Av Libertad 250, which is open 10 am to 1 pm and 3 to 7:30 pm weekdays, 10:30 am to 1:30 pm and 4 to 8 pm weekends. Similar programs take place at the Sala Viña del Mar (☎ 680-633), Arlegui 683, which is open 10 am to 8 pm daily except Sunday, when hours are 10 am to 1 pm.

Viña's international cultural centers include the Instituto Chileno-Norteamericano (☎ 686-191) at 2 Oriente 385 between 3 and 4 Norte, the Instituto Chileno-Británico at (☎ 971-060) at 3 Norte 824, which has up-to-date British newspapers and magazines, and the Alianza Francesa (☎ 685-908) at Alvarez 314.

Conaf (☎ 970-108), 3 Norte 541, has information on protected areas such as Parque Nacional La Campana.

For laundry services, Laverap is at Libertad 902. Lavarápido is at Arlegui 440.

Hospital Gustavo Fricke (☎ 680-041) is east of downtown at Alvarez 1532, at the corner of Cancha.

Summer is the pickpocket season, so keep a close eye on your belongings, especially on the beach.

In-line skaters have become so ubiquitous in Viña that pedestrians must be alert to avoid collisions.

Museums

Specializing in Easter Island archaeology and Chilean natural history, **Museo de Arqueológico e Historia Francisco Fonck** features an original moai from Chile's remote Pacific possession at the approach to its entrance, but the moai may be moved because of repeated vandalism. It has also been the site of the **Biblioteca William Mulloy**, probably the best concentration *(continued on p 178)*

(continued on p 178)

MIDDLE CHILE

VIÑA DEL MAR

PLACES TO STAY
9 Hotel San Martín
12 Hostal Chacras de Coria
19 Residencial 555
20 Crown Royal Hotel
21 Hotel Royal House
25 Hotel Cap Ducal
29 Residencial Helen Misch
37 Hotel Rondó
41 Hotel Balia
42 Hotel Capric
45 Residencial Villarrica
53 Hospedaje Toledo
54 Hospedaje Calderón
56 Residencial Victoria
57 Residencial Blanchait
58 Hotel Rokamar
62 Hotel Marina del Rey
67 Residencial Agua Santa
68 Residencial La Nona
69 Residencial Montaña
73 Residencial La Gaviota
75 Residencial Magallanes
79 Hotel O'Higgins
86 Hotel Español
89 Residencial Ona Berri
101 Hotel Alcázar
103 Residencial France
104 Hotel Quinta Vergara

PLACES TO EAT
5 Ital Burger
8 Ristorante San Marco
10 Santa Fe
15 Delicias del Mar
16 Parrilla El Gaucho
17 Bravíssimo
23 Viña's
27 La Cucina di Vaccarezza
28 Fellini
35 Flavia
36 Don Giovanni
48 Panadería Suiza
49 Don Giacomo
59 Puerto Montt
63 Africa
80 Pau San
81 Anayak
82 Samoiedo
91 Chau San
92 El Sin Nombre
94 Panzoni
95 México Lindo

96 El Mezón con Zeta
97 Cappi Kúa
98 Lennon
99 Timbao

OTHER
1 Reloj del Sol
2 Terminal Shopping Viña
   (Trolley Tour), Cinemark
3 Entel PCS
4 Startel
6 Laverap
11 Estadio Sausalito
11 Arte Gallery
13 DHL
14 BellSouth Celular
18 Galería de Arte Modigliani
22 Instituto Chileno-
   Norteamericano
24 Museo de la Cultura del Mar
   Salvador Reyes
26 Casino Municipal
30 Conaf
31 Centro Cultural Viña del Mar
32 Museo de Arqueológico e
   Historia Francisco Fonck
33 Instituto Chileno-Británico
34 Museo Palacio Rioja
38 Inter-Cambio
39 CTC (Telefónica)
40 Automóvil Club de Chile
43 Avant
44 LanChile, Ladeco
46 Manhattan
47 Aguitur (Galería Fontana)
50 Lavarápido
51 Sernatur
52 Mercado Municipal
55 Reloj de Flores

60 Cyber Blues Café
61 Everton Offices
64 CTC (Telefónica)
65 Scratch
66 Terminal de Buses Viña del Mar
70 Alianza Francesa
71 Palacio Vergara (Museo
   Municipal de Bellas Artes)
72 Anfiteatro
74 Hospital Gustavo Fricke
76 Sala Viña del Mar
77 Post Office
78 Central de Turismo e
   Informaciones
83 Cambios Guiñazú
84 Cine Arte
85 Teatro Municipal
87 Centro Artesanal Viña del Mar
88 Cine Olimpo
90 CTC (Telefónica)
93 El Burro
100 Cine Rex
102 Bert Rent a Car

PACIFIC
OCEAN

Muelle
Vergara

Playa
Acapulco

Av San Martín

9
10
8
15
16
18
Av Perú
17
26
27 28
Av San Martín
6 Poniente
5 Poniente
4 Poniente
3 Poniente
25
24
Av Marina
35
36
37
Puente
Casino
Plaza
México
41
42
Iberia
Callao
Berger
43
44
45
46
47
48 50
49
51
Libertad
Balmaceda
Von Schroeders
Nieto
55
Caleta
Abarca
Av Marina
57
56
59 60
58 61
62
Ecuador
63 64
Traslaviña
Villanelo
Av España
67
68
Estación
Miramar
Agua Santa
Av Portales
70
Viana
Álvarez
Echevers
Quinta
69
Bellavista
To Valparaíso

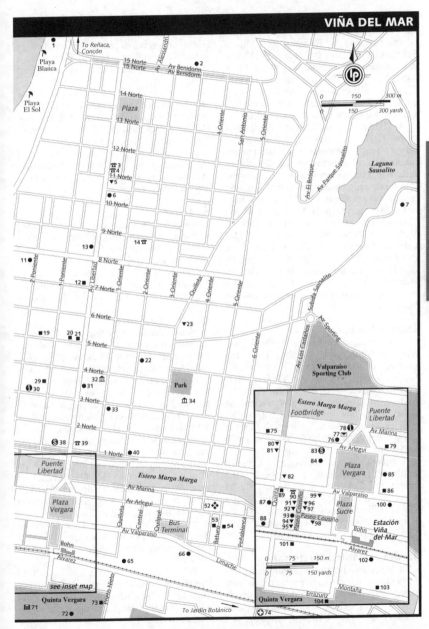

VIÑA DEL MAR

MIDDLE CHILE

of books, maps and documents on the subject of Easter Island, but this facility is due to move to Hanga Roa's Museo Sebastián Englert in the year 2000. Duplicates of most of the material will remain in Viña. At 4 Norte 784, the museum (☎ 686-753) is open 10 am to 6 pm Tuesday to Friday, 10 am to 2 pm weekends; admission costs US$1.50 for adults, US$0.20 for children.

At Quillota 214, the **Museo Palacio Rioja** (☎ 689-665) is a century-old mansion that is now a municipal museum. Also hosting frequent musical and theater presentations, including films, it's open 10 am to 2 pm and 3 to 6 pm daily except Monday; admission is US$0.60 for adults, US$0.20 for children.

On Av Marina near the outlet of the Estero Marga Marga, housed in the Castillo Wulff, the **Museo de la Cultura del Mar Salvador Reyes** (☎ 625-427) is open 10 am to 1 pm and 2:30 to 5:45 pm Tuesday to Friday, 10 am to 2 pm weekends and holidays. Admission costs US$1 for adults, half that for children, and is free on weekends and holidays.

Quinta Vergara

Once the residence of the prosperous Alvarez-Vergara family, now a public park, the grounds of the magnificently landscaped Quinta Vergara contain the Venetian-style **Palacio Vergara**, which dates from 1908. The building houses the **Museo Municipal de Bellas Artes** (fine arts museum; ☎ 680-618), which is open 10 am to 2 pm and 3 to 6 pm daily except Monday. Admission is about US$0.60, US$0.20 for children.

Frequent summer concerts at the Quinta's **anfiteatro** (amphitheater) complement the celebrated Festival Internacional de la Canción (see Special Events later in the chapter). The grounds, whose only entrance is on Errázuriz at the south end of Calle Quinta, are open 7 am to 7 pm daily.

Jardín Botánico Nacional

Chile's national botanical garden comprises 61 hectares of native and exotic plants and, since 1983, has been systematically developed as a research facility with an expanded nursery, a library, educational programs and plaques identifying individual specimens. Conaf has restricted automobile traffic and recreational activities such as soccer and picnicking, making the garden a more interesting and relaxing place to spend an afternoon.

From Calle Viana in downtown Viña, take Bus No 20 east to the end of the line, then cross the bridge and walk about 10 minutes; the Jardín Botánico (☎ 672-566) is on your left. Grounds are open from 9 am to 7 pm daily except Monday in summer; the rest of the year they are open 10 am to 6 pm daily. Admission is about US$0.75 for adults, US$0.20 for children.

Beaches

Many of Viña's beaches are either crowded or contaminated by sewage, but those in the northern suburbs are far better. From 2 Norte, take Pony Bus Nos 1, 10, 10-A (summer only) or 111 north to Reñaca or Concón, for example. For more details, see this chapter's Around Viña del Mar section.

Organized Tours

A pleasant means of getting to know Viña is an hour's ride around town in a horse-drawn carriage, leaving from Plaza Vergara, about US$15 for two people. At 3 and 5 pm daily, Sernatur-sponsored Trolley Tour conducts less expensive, 1½-hour city tours of Viña, leaving from Terminal Shopping Viña on 15 Norte between 2 and 3 Oriente. The cost is US$5 for adults, US$4 for children.

Aguitur, Viña's Asociación de Guias de Turismo (☎ 711-052), has moved out of the municipal tourist office and into the Galería Fontana at Arlegui 364, Oficina 223. It arranges tours of Viña or Valparaíso (US$20, three hours), both Viña and Valparaíso (US$25, four hours), Zapallar (US$35, eight hours), Isla Negra (US$35, eight hours) or Santiago (US$40, 10 hours), as well as a three-hour night tour of Viña and Valparaíso for US$35.

Private guided tours are available from Aguitur for US$40 per half day, US$80 per full day, in English, French, Italian and Greek; Spanish-language rates are about one third less.

Special Events

Viña del Mar's most wildly popular attraction is the annual Festival Internacional de la Canción (International Song Festival), held every February in the amphitheater of the Quinta Vergara. This pompous competition of the kitschiest artistes from the Spanish-speaking world (for balance, there's usually at least one really insipid English-speaking performer) resembles the Eurovision Song Contest; every evening for a week, everything stops as ticketless Chileans gaze transfixed at TV sets in their homes, and in cafés, restaurants and bars. Patient and discriminating listeners may hear some worthwhile folk music. The Latin American TV network Univisión owns the overseas rights and often broadcasts the better-known acts in the USA and elsewhere.

Places to Stay

Accommodations are so plentiful that it would be impossible to list everything, but the entries below form a representative sample. Prices rise in summer, but outside the peak months of January and February supply exceeds demand and prices drop (except on major holidays such as Easter and mid-September's Fiestas Patrias). March is an especially good month, when the weather is often ideal but most Chileans have finished their holidays.

Budget Budget travelers will find several alternatives on or near Agua Santa and Von Schroeders, as well as downtown near the bus terminal. Off-season prices run to about US$10 per person, in season twice that or more, but a weak Argentine economy can also mean negotiable prices even in summer and at mid-range hotels.

Hotel Royal House (☎ 681-965, 5 Norte 683), an outstanding, well-located facility, charges US$12 in the off-season, US$20 in summer. Spruced up *Residencial Montaña* (☎ 622-230, Agua Santa 153) is one of Viña's cheapest, for about US$9 per person, slightly less in the off-season, breakfast included. *Residencial Blanchait* (☎ 974-949, Valparaíso 82-A) charges US$10 per person for room with shared bath.

In an attractive blue Victorian building, *Residencial Agua Santa* (☎ 901-531, Agua Santa 36) charges US$10 in peak season. Almost next door, *Residencial La Nona* (☎ 663-825, Agua Santa 48) charges US$15 per person with breakfast.

Residencial Victoria (☎ 977-370, Valparaíso 40) charges US$12 per person with shared bath, US$16 with private bath. *Hotel Capric* (☎ 978-295, Von Schroeders 39) charges US$13 for singles with shared bath (there's only one such room) and a skimpy breakfast, but the place isn't bad; rooms with private bath cost US$22/33 singles/doubles. *Residencial Ona Berri* (☎ 688-187, Valparaíso 618) has rooms for US$15 per person with shared bath, US$25 with private bath.

Near the bus terminal, across the street from each other, are two friendly, comfortable family lodgings, each charging around US$20 to US$25 double with private bath: *Hospedaje Calderón* (☎ 970-456, Batuco 147) and *Hospedaje Toledo* (☎ 881-496, Batuco 160).

Set back from the street, friendly, family-run *Residencial Magallanes* (☎ 685-101, Arlegui 555) is a rundown place that seems overpriced at US$20 per person with shared bath (US$30/45 with private bath), but the staff are willing to bargain. On the 'wrong side of the tracks' (in Viña, at least), *Residencial France* (☎ 685-976, Montaña 743) is a bit ragged, but friendly for US$16 per person with shared bath. Some rooms are small and boxy, but it has pleasant common areas.

Mid-Range Near the grounds of the Quinta Vergara, family-run *Residencial La Gaviota* (☎ 974-439, Alcalde Prieto Nieto 0332) is a bargain at US$15 per person with shared bath, US$20 per person with private bath, both with breakfast. For US$18/26, *Residencial Villarrica* (☎ 942-807, Arlegui 172) is also a good choice.

In the quieter, more residential area north of the Marga Marga, rates at tranquil, comfortable and well-located *Residencial Helen Misch* (☎ 971-565, 1 Poniente 239) are US$25/30. Award-winning *Residencial*

555 (☎/fax 972-240, 5 Norte 555) is a newish place charging US$25/33 with shared bath, US$32/44 with private bath. **Hotel Royal House** (☎ 681-965, 5 Norte 683) has moderately priced singles with private bath and cable TV for US$27. **Hotel Balia** (☎ 978-310, Von Schroeders 36) charges US$25/37 for singles/doubles, while **Hotel Rokamar** (☎ 690-019, Viana 107) charges US$30/35.

Hostal Chacras de Coria (☎ 901-419, 7 Norte 669) charges US$30/36 with breakfast. English is spoken at reader's choice **Crown Royal Hotel** (☎ 682-450, 5 Norte 655), where doubles with a substantial buffet breakfast cost US$45. Another reader recommendation is **Hotel Español** (☎ 685-145, Plaza Vergara s/n); it's in the same price range at US$37/50.

Service is good at **Hotel Rondó** (☎ 883-144, 1 Norte 157), which charges US$48/61. Enthusiastically endorsed **Hotel Quinta Vergara** (☎ 685-073, fax 691-978, Errázuriz 690) has an English-speaking owner whose room rates are US$50/60 with breakfast. During the annual song festival, though, this can be a noisy location. The new **Hotel Marina del Rey** (☎ 883-505, Ecuador 299), a Best Western affiliate, charges US$65/78.

Top End Top-end accommodations in Viña del Mar start around US$80/109 singles/doubles at **Hotel San Martín** (☎ 689-191, San Martín 667), but readers have criticized the size and quality of rooms, despite its views of Playa Acapulco. **Hotel Alcázar**, (☎ 685-112, Alvarez 646) is a better value for US$82/110. Visitors with a little more green, about US$105/130, can try the oddball **Hotel Cap Ducal** (☎ 626-655, fax 665-478, Av Marina 51), a shipshaped building set on a concrete foundation in the surf ('It's not next to the sea, it's on the sea'), whose restaurant is also worth a try.

At the venerable **Hotel O'Higgins** (☎ 882-016, Plaza Vergara s/n), rates start at US$102/122 singles/doubles, but you can pay up to US$130/146 (including a buffet breakfast) and accumulate a huge room-service bill without even working up a sweat. It's worth mentioning, though, that

this 1934 landmark is past its prime, and the service could stand improvement as well.

Places to Eat

Like many other seaside resorts, Viña is sinking under the weight of hotels and restaurants, and there are good values for diners. **Panadería Suiza** (Arlegui and Villanelo) has good, cheap pastries and kuchen. For good sandwiches, coffee and desserts, try **Anayak** (☎ 680-093, Quinta 134) or **Samoiedo** (☎ 684-610, Valparaíso 637). **Pau San** (☎ 685-257, Quinta 122) serves inexpensive Chinese lunches and dinners.

Several good, moderately priced eateries are clustered on Pasaje Cousiño, a small passageway off Valparaíso near Plaza Vergara. **Panzoni** (☎ 682-134, Cousiño 12-B) features friendly service, excellent atmosphere and fine Italian and Middle Eastern specialties; it's especially popular for lunch. **Chau San** (☎ 884-943, Pasaje Cousiño 10) prepares cheap Cantonese lunches. The modest, inexpensive **México Lindo** (☎ 692-144, Cousiño 136, 2nd floor) serves credible Tex-Mex specialties such as enchiladas and burritos, but the sauces are bland and the drinks expensive. Tobacco-free **El Sin Nombre** (Cousiño s/n) has cheap lunches, as does friendly, inexpensive **Lennon** (Cousiño 16), which doubles as a pub. Other possibilities are **Cappi Kúa** (☎ 977-331, Cousiño 11, Local 4) and **El Mezón con Zeta** (☎ 690-494, Pasaje Cousiño 9), which also provides live music at night.

Misleadingly named **Ital Burger** (Av Libertad 920) has reasonably priced pasta dinners, but most other Italian choices are upscale. **Ristorante San Marco** (☎ 975-304, San Martín 597), **Don Giacomo** (☎ 688-889, Villanelo 135, 2nd floor), **Don Giovanni** (2 Norte and 6 Poniente), **Flavia** (☎ 686-358, 6 Poniente 121) and **La Cucina di Vaccarezza** (☎ 975-790, Av San Martín 180) all serve Italian specialties. **Fellini** (☎ 975-742, 3 Norte 880 is more Franco-Italian, with excellent fish.

Lonely Planet correspondents continue to praise **Puerto Montt** (Valparaíso 158-A), reached by a narrow off-street passageway, for large portions of well-prepared and reasonably priced fish. *Delicias del Mar (☎ 901-837, San Martín 459)* is a good, but expensive, Basque seafood restaurant.

Vina's (☎ 694-655, Quillota and 6 Norte) serves full parrilladas, as does *Parrilla El Gaucho (Av San Martín and 5 Norte)*. Most notable for its outlandish facade and decor, *Africa (☎ 882-856, Valparaíso 324)* serves both meat and seafood. *Santa Fe (☎ 691-719, 8 Norte 303)* is the Viña branch of Santiago's fine and popular but expensive Tex-Mex restaurant.

Timbao (Av Valparaíso 670) and *Bravíssimo (Av San Martín and 4 Norte)* both offer good ice cream.

Entertainment

First-run movies often hit Viña even before Santiago. Try the two-screen *Cine Olimpo (☎ 711-607, Quinta 294)*, *Cine Rex (☎ 685-050, Valparaíso 758)* or the eight-screen *Cinemark (☎ 993-391, 15 Norte 961, Local 224)*. The *Cine Arte (☎ 882-798, Plaza Vergara 142)* is an art house.

Viña may qualify for the title 'Disco Hell' (though the club of that name is in Antofagasta, in the Norte Grande region) thanks to a plethora of nightspots such as *El Burro (Pasaje Cousiño 12-D)*, *Scratch (☎ 978-219, Bohn 970)* and *Manhattan (Arlegui 302, 2nd floor)*.

It's not really a dance club, but *Hotel Alcázar, Alvarez 646)* holds a *noche de tango* every Saturday from 9 pm. There's also dancing Friday and Saturday evenings at top-end *Hotel O'Higgins Plaza Vergara s/n)* and at *Restaurante Don Giacomo (Villanelo 135)*.

Plays, concerts and movies – retrospectives and art films – take place at the *Teatro Municipal (☎ 681-739, Plaza Vergara s/n)*.

The *Casino Municipal de Viña del Mar (☎ 689-200, Av San Martín 199)*, overlooking the beach on the north side of the Marga Marga, offers opportunities to squander your savings on slot machines, bingo and card games – in between dinner and cabaret entertainment. Open daily from 6 pm into the early morning, it collects a US$6 cover charge.

Spectator Sports

Everton, Viña's second-division soccer team, plays at Estadio Sausalito (☎ 978-250). Team offices (☎ 689-504), where tickets are available, are at Viana 161.

Horse racing takes place at the *Valparaíso Sporting Club (☎ 689-393)*, Av Los Castaños 404.

Shopping

The permanent crafts stalls along Pasaje Cousiño are a good place to search for jewelry, copperware and leather goods. The Centro Artesanal Viña del Mar, on Quinta between Viana and Valparaíso, has a large selection of crafts.

Getting There & Away

Air LanChile (☎ 690-365) and Ladeco share offices at Ecuador 80, but all flights leave from Santiago. Avant (☎ 975-532) is at Ecuador 31.

Bus Viña's bus station at Valparaíso and Quilpué, two long blocks east of Plaza Vergara, is currently undergoing a major renovation; at present buses leave from the nearby provisional Terminal de Buses Viña del Mar (☎ 697-680), Limache 1001. Services are virtually identical to those from Valparaíso, and all northbound and international services from the port capital stop in Viña (see the Getting There & Away section for Valparaíso for details).

Getting Around

Running along Arlegui, frequent local buses marked 'Puerto' or 'Aduana' link Viña with Valparaíso.

For easier connections to Valparaíso, the Metro Regional Valparaíso (Merval) has two stations: Estación Miramar at Alvarez and Agua Santa, and Estación Viña del Mar at the southeast corner of Plaza Sucre.

The Viña area is congested and impossible to park in. However for out-of-town excursions, the cheapest car rental rates are at Bert Rent a Car (☎ 685-515) at Alvarez 762. There are several others, including Mach Viña (☎ 259-429) at Las Heras 428, and Euro (☎ 883-559) at Hotel O'Higgins.

MIDDLE CHILE

AROUND VIÑA DEL MAR

North of Viña are several less celebrated but more attractive beach towns, along a coastline with spectacular rock outcrops, crashing surf and blowholes, but Chile's moneyed elite are rapidly appropriating the best sites and cutting off public access in many places.

Reñaca & Concón

Among the nearby beach towns are overbuilt suburbs such as Reñaca, which has its own tourist office (☎ 900-499) at Av Borgoño 14100, plus the area's most extensive beach (also one of the cleanest). Body-boarders frequent Concón's Playa Negra.

The wall-to-wall, multitiered apartment buildings at Reñaca and Concón exemplify urban claustrophobia and mean no budget accommodations, but Reñaca's *Hotel Montecarlo* (☎ 830-397, fax 835-739, Av Vicuña Mackenna 136), has earned readers' recommendations for US$45/70 singles/doubles.

One local treat is the seafood at Concón's *La Picá Horizonte* (☎ 903-665, San Pedro 120,) at Caleta Higuerillas. It's a little hard to find but worth the effort. From the Muelle de Pescadores (Fisherman's Pier), climb the steps (behind Restaurant El Tiburón) and, at the top, walk one short block left along the dirt road to San Pedro. On Sunday afternoons it's hard to get a table, but other nearby restaurants such as *Picá los Delfines* (☎ 814-919, San Pedro 130) are decent alternatives, though the latter's service leaves much to be desired.

The *Cine Plaza* (☎ 837-217, Mall Plaza Reñaca s/n) shows current films. Spots for dancing include Reñaca's *News* (☎ 831-158, Av Borgoño 13101) and *Baby Oh* (Santa Luisa 501) and Concón's *César* at Playa Amarilla.

Quintero

Another 23km beyond Concón, Quintero is a peninsular beach community that was once part of Lord Cochrane's hacienda. **Las Ventanas**, just to the north, is a petroleum port featuring a power plant, an old LPG tanker washed up on the beach, and, incongruously, the **Río Puchuncaví estuary**, a valuable wetland that's essentially an ecopreserve.

From its fabulous architecture, you can tell that *Hotel Monaco* (☎ 032-930-939, 21 de Mayo 1500) must once have been a very fine place; it's now rundown – but cheap – at US$6 with shared bath, US$30 double with private bath. Rates are US$10 per person with shared bath at *Residencial Victoria* (Vicuña Mackenna 1460) which also has a good picada. There are also reasonable accommodations at *Residencial María Alejandra* (☎ 032-930-266, Lord Cochrane 157), where singles with shared bath cost about US$10 and those with private bath are only slightly more expensive. *Residencial Brazilian* (☎ 032-930590, 21 de Mayo 1336), though architecturally drab, has decent rooms and attractive gardens for US$20/36 single/double with breakfast.

You'll find dozens of seafood locales along 21 de Mayo.

Horcón

Across the bay to the north, the quaint working port of Horcón is also something of an artists' colony. Its short, narrow beach is nothing special, but nearby Playa Cau Cau is the place for beach volleyball, bodysurfing and the like. Horcón's clutter of cheap seafood restaurants rank among the area's best. Try *El Ancla*, which also offers accommodations. Sol del Pacífico buses from Viña go directly here.

Maitencillo

Its long, sandy beaches, Playa Larga and Playa Aguas Blancas, attract many visitors, and no one can overlook the five-star *Marbella Resort Hotel* (☎ 032-772-020, fax 772-030, Km 35 Carretera Concón-Zapallar), which has a conference center, three restaurants, two bars, an 18-hole golf course as well as a nine-hole par three, two swimming pools, tennis courts and rental horses. Although it's far from cheap – US$195 single or double with an elaborate buffet breakfast – some more expensive places in Chile offer much less.

Marbella's local mailing address is Casilla 17, Puchuncaví. In Santiago, contact Marbella Resort (fax 228-3198, resorts@chilesat.net), Cruz del Sur 133, Oficina 503, Las Condes.

Zapallar

At Zapallar, the Malibu of Chilean beach resorts, about 80km north of Viña, multi-million-dollar houses cover the densely wooded hillsides from the beach nearly to the ridgetops, but public access is nevertheless excellent.

Residencial La Terraza (☎ *033-741-026, 711-409, Alcalde 142*), two short blocks west of the highway that connects with the Panamericana, and a stiff climb from the beach, has singles/doubles for US$40/50 in season, US$24/30 off-season, and a good restaurant. On the beach, *Restaurant César* (☎ *033-741507, Rambla s/n*), where the view commands premium prices, is popular with upper-income Chileans. However, there are more modest places in Horcón and Zapallar that offer good food for less.

Cachagua

Cachagua, about 3km south of Zapallar, lacks hotels but has plenty of summer houses and a couple restaurants, most notably *Entre Olas*, directly on the beach at the south end of Av Los Eucaliptos. Just opposite the attractive crescent beach is Conaf-administered Isla Cachagua, one of the central coast's major seabird breeding sites – with an odor to match. Humboldt penguins are the most notable species.

On the triangular plaza, scrawny horses and burros are available for rental rides for children.

Papudo

Papudo, 10km north of Zapallar, is less exclusive than Zapallar and has a wider range of accommodations, but high-rise apartment buildings are starting to crowd the waterfront. Sheltered Playa Chica and the more open Playa Grande are the main attractions, linked together by Av Irarrázaval.

Residencial La Plaza (*Chorrillos 119,* ☎ *033-791-391*) is a small, friendly, family-run lodging that maintains prices of US$9 per person all year, with private bath and breakfast; even less with shared bath. *Hotel Restaurant La Abeja* (☎ *033-791-116, Chorrillos 36*), does good business even out of season; room rates are US$30/40.

Several beachfront restaurants line Irarrázaval, most notably the expensive *Banana*; the next-door pub and snack bar *Caleta Papudo* is more economical. At Caleta Zapallar, just beyond the yacht club, there's a shellfish market as well as the *Marisquería Chungunguito* for dining.

Buses up and down the coast connect Papudo with Valparaíso, Viña del Mar and intermediates, and with La Ligua.

LA LIGUA

Inland from Papudo, motorists passing on the Panamericana will notice white-coated vendors hawking the famous *dulces* (sweets) of La Ligua, a modest but tidy agricultural town. Banco de Chile has an ATM at Ortiz de Rosas 485, and there's a good artisans' market on the Plaza de Armas.

The Museo de La Ligua (☎ 033-712-143), Pedro Polanco 698, is a superb archaeological museum. Once the city slaughterhouse, this well-organized and remodeled building recreates a burial site in the Diaguita-Inka style, with materials uncovered in downtown La Ligua. It also displays a selection of materials from the 19th-century mining era and historical photographs of the city's early days. Hours are 9:30 am to 1:30 pm and 3 to 6:30 pm weekdays; admission costs US$0.50.

Accommodations are available for about US$7 with shared bath at *Residencial Regine I* (☎ *033-711-192, Esmeralda 27*) or for about US$11 with private bath at *Residencial Regine II* (☎ *033-711-196, Condell 360*). Modern, well-managed *Hotel Anchimallén* (☎ *033-711-685, Ortiz de Rosas 694*) has rooms with private bath and breakfast for US$33/44. *Restaurant Lihuén* (☎ *033-711-143, Ortiz de Rosas 303*) has good sandwiches and outstanding ice cream.

The bus terminal is on Papudo between Pedro Polanco and Uribe; frequent buses connect La Ligua with Santiago, and with the coastal towns of Papudo and Zapallar.

PARQUE NACIONAL LA CAMPANA

After scaling the 1828m summit of Cerro La Campana, which he called 'Bell Mountain,'

Charles Darwin fondly recalled one of his finest experiences in South America:

The evening was fine, and the atmosphere so clear, that the masts of the vessels at anchor in the bay of Valparaíso, although no less than twenty-six geographical miles distant, could be distinguished clearly as little black streaks. A ship doubling the point under sail, appeared as a bright white speck.

The setting of the sun was glorious; the valleys being black, whilst the snowy peaks of the Andes yet retained a ruby tint. When it was dark, we made a fire beneath a little arbor of bamboo, fried our *charqui* (dried strips of beef), took our *mate*, and were quite comfortable. There is an inexpressible charm in thus living in the open air.

We spent the day on the summit, and I never enjoyed one more thoroughly. Chile, bounded by the Andes and the Pacific, was seen as in a map. The pleasure from the scenery, in itself beautiful, was heightened by the many reflections which arose from the mere view of the Campana range with its lesser parallel ones, and of the broad valley of Quillota directly intersecting them.

Created in 1967 by private donation and managed by Conaf, La Campana occupies 8000 hectares in a nearly roadless segment of the coastal range that once belonged to the Jesuit hacienda of San Isidro. In geological structure and vegetation, its jagged scrubland resembles the mountains of Southern California and protects remaining stands of the roble de Santiago (*Nothofagus obliqua*), the northernmost species of the common South American genus, and the Chilean palm (*Jubaea chilensis*).

The Chilean palm, also known as the Palma de Coquitos for its tasty fruits (one Chilean writer called them miniature coconuts), grows up to 25m in height and measures up to 1.5m in diameter. In more accessible areas, it declined greatly in the 19th century because it was exploited for its sugary sap, obtained by toppling the tree and stripping it of its foliage. According to Darwin, each palm yielded up to 90 gallons of sap, which cutters concentrated into treacle by boiling. In some parts of the park you can see the ruins of ovens that were used for this purpose; there are also old-fashioned charcoal kilns.

Orientation & Information

In the province of Quillota in Region V (Valparaíso), La Campana is about 40km east of Viña del Mar and 110km northwest of Santiago via the Panamericana. There are Conaf stations at each entrance, where rangers collect the small entrance fee (about US$2) and sometimes have maps. The largest of these stations is the Administración at Granizo, on the south side of the park near Olmué, which is open 8 am to 6 pm weekdays.

Geography & Climate

Ranging in altitude from less than 400m above sea level to 2222m on the summit of Cerro Roble, the park has a Mediterranean climate strongly influenced by the ocean. Annual maximum temperatures average 19°C and minimum temperatures 9°C, but these statistics obscure dramatic variation. Summer can be hot and dry; snow brushes higher elevations in winter. Mean annual rainfall, about 800mm, falls almost entirely between May and September. Profuse wildflowers and a reliable water supply make spring the best time for a visit, but the park is open all year.

Cerro La Campana

Thousands of Chileans and increasing numbers of foreign visitors reach the summit of La Campana every year from the Administración at Granizo, most easily accessible from Viña del Mar. It's conceivable to hitchhike to the campground at the abandoned mine site at the end of the old but well-maintained road from the Administración, considerably shortening the hike to the summit, but it's much more interesting and rewarding to hike the trail from the park entrance. Figure at least four hours to the top and three hours back down.

From the Administración, 373m above sea level, the abruptly steep trail to the summit climbs 1455m in only 7km – an average grade of nearly 21%. Fortunately, most of the hike is in shade, and there are three water sources en route: **Primera Aguada**, at an elevation of 580m; **Segunda Aguada** (backcountry camping is possible near a cold, clear spring, about two hours from the Administración); and the drive-in **campground** at the abandoned mine site, where the trail continues to the summit.

At the point where the trail skirts a granite wall, prior to the final vertiginous ascent, is a plaque, placed by Sociedad Científica de Valparaíso and the city's British community, commemorating the 101st anniversary of Darwin's climb (which took place August 17, 1834). At another point slightly beyond this, the Club Montañés de Valparaíso has placed another plaque, honoring climbers who died in 1968 when an earthquake unleashed a landslide.

On a clear day, the view from La Campana, from the ships at anchor in the Pacific harbor to the Andean summit of Aconcagua, is no less spectacular than when Darwin saw it. Unfortunately, many Chileans feel obliged to leave a visible record of their climbing success: you might notice some carrying spray paint in their backpacks.

Sturdy, sensible footwear is essential. Women in high heels have made the summit, but good, treaded hiking boots are the best bet – parts of the trail are slippery even when dry; even sneakers can be awkward.

Palmas de Ocoa

Reached by a sometimes rough gravel road from the village of Hijuelas on the Panamericana, Palmas de Ocoa is the northern entrance to La Campana.

At Casino, 2km beyond the park entrance, a good walking trail connects Palmas de Ocoa (Sector Ocoa) with Granizo, 14km to the north. To reach the high saddle of the Portezuelo de Granizo takes about two hours of steady hiking through the palm-studded canyon of the Estero Rabuco. On clear days, which are becoming rarer, the Portezuelo offers some of the views that so impressed Darwin.

About halfway up the canyon is a good, flat campsite where wild blackberries abound and the fruit from abandoned grapevines ripens in late summer. Water is limited. Farther up the canyon, just below the Portezuelo, is a conspicuous and dependable spring, but elsewhere livestock

have fouled the water, so carry your own. At the Portezuelo, the trail forks: the lower branch plunges into Cajón Grande, while the other follows the contour westward before dropping into Granizo.

The hike from Palmas de Ocoa to Granizo, or vice versa, is an ideal weekend excursion across the coastal range, allowing the hiker to continue to either Santiago or Viña, depending on the starting point. It's probably better to start from Granizo, where public transportation is better; once you've reached Palmas de Ocoa, Conaf rangers will help you get a lift back to the Panamericana, where it's easy to flag a bus back to Santiago.

Also at Sector Ocoa, another foot trail leads 6km to Salto de la Cortadera, an attractive waterfall that is best during the spring runoff. Ask the rangers for directions to the trailhead.

Places to Stay & Eat

Camping is the only alternative in the park proper – Conaf has formal camping areas (US$15 for up to six people) at Granizo, Cajón Grande and Ocoa. Conaf permits backcountry camping, but you need to inform rangers before attempting the routes between Palmas de Ocoa and Granizo or Cajón Grande. This is steep, rugged country, and fire is a serious hazard, especially in summer and autumn.

In the nearby town of Olmué, which is popular on weekends, there are good accommodations at *Hostería Copihue* (☎ 033-441-944, Diego Portales 2203) a luxury complex with pool, tennis courts and other facilities, charging US$94/145 with full board. For dining, there's also *Hostería Aire Puro* (☎ 033-441-381, Av Granizo 7672).

Getting There & Away

La Campana is easily accessible from both Santiago and Viña del Mar. From the Valparaíso and Viña area (US$1, 1¾ hours), Ciferal Express (☎ 953-317) goes to within about 1km of the Granizo entrance, slightly farther from Cajón Grande, every 30 minutes in season; the easiest place to catch the bus is on 1 Norte in Viña. Local transport

MIDDLE CHILE

(Agdabus) leaves every 20 minutes from Limache and Olmué.

Direct access to Sector Ocoa is more problematic. Almost any northbound bus from Santiago will drop you at Hijuelas (there is a sharp and poorly marked turnoff to the park just before the bridge across the Río Aconcagua), but from there you will have to hitch or walk 12km to the park entrance, or else hire a taxi (about US$10).

From October to April, Altué Active Travel (☎ 232-1103, fax 233-6799), Encomenderos 83 in Las Condes, Santiago, runs (or contracts others to run) full-day tours to climb Cerro La Campana for US$155 per person for a minimum of two people. Lunch and transportation are included. Larger parties pay substantially less per person.

LOS ANDES
☎ 34

Founded in 1791 by Ambrosio O'Higgins, Los Andes is a friendly foothill town along the international highway to the legendary ski resort at Portillo, near the Argentine border, and the Argentine city of Mendoza.

Orientation & Information

Los Andes is 77km directly north of Santiago via the congested, two-lane Ruta 57 through Colina, or slightly farther (but more quickly reached) via a combination of the Panamericana, Ruta 71 and Ruta 57. It is 145km northeast of Viña del Mar via Ruta 60, the international highway to Mendoza.

The helpful municipal Quiosco Turístico (☎ 421-121), Av Santa Teresa 333, is open 10 am to 2 pm and 4 to 8 pm weekdays, 10 am to 6 pm weekends. Correos de Chile is at the corner of Santa Rosa and Esmeralda. Entel is at Esmeralda 463, Chilesat at Esmeralda 399. Hospital San Juan de Dios (☎ 421-121, 421-666) is at Av Argentina and Av Hermanos Clark.

Things to See & Do

For a small provincial museum, Los Andes' **Museo Arqueológico**, Av Santa Teresa 398, features surprisingly good presentations on pre-Hispanic local cultures and also exhibits material on forensic anthropology, colonial times and the cultures of the Inka, Mapuche and Easter Islanders. The curator, who once lived in the USA, has translated the exhibit captions into English. The museum (☎ 420-115) is open 10 am to 8 pm daily except Monday; admission costs US$1.

Across the street at Av Santa Teresa 389, dating from the early 19th century but reconstructed during the 1920s, the **Museo Antiguo Monasterio del Espíritu Santo** formerly served as the Convento Carmelitas Descalzas del Espíritu Santo de los Andes, a retreat for Carmelite nuns. It was home to Santa Teresa de los Andes, beatified in 1993; it also includes materials on Laura Vicuña, who legend says willed herself to die at the age of 12, in 1906, in atonement for her widowed mother's taking a married lover.

Facing the nicely landscaped Plaza de Armas, the **Gobernación Provincial** dates from 1850. From 1912 to 1918, Gabriela Mistral taught classes at the former **Colegio de Niñas** (Girls' School, now the restaurant called Círculo Italiano), Esmeralda 246.

Places to Stay & Eat

Residencial Susi (☎ 428-600, Santa Rosa 151) charges only US$5 per person, but it's pretty basic. *Hotel Central* (☎ 421-275, Esmeralda 278) is friendly and passable, and for US$8 per person with shared bath, US$16 with private bath, it's not unreasonable – though some rooms lack windows.

A better but more expensive choice is *Hotel Plaza* (☎ 421-169, fax 426-029, Rodríguez 370), whose entrance faces the north side of the Plaza de Armas at Esmeralda 353 despite its formal street address. Rates are US$39/42 singles/doubles, for comfortable, heated rooms with cable TV, and the café is a good choice for breakfast. There are also *Hotel Los Andes* (☎ 428-484, Av Argentina 1100), charging US$32/36 with breakfast, and *Hotel Don Ambrosio* (☎ 420-441, Freire 472), which charges US$32/45.

Half a block from the museum, the *Centro Español* (O'Higgins 674) has a good daily fixed-price lunch. Another good choice for lunch and dinner is the historic *Círculo*

Italiano, *Esmeralda 246* Try also *El Guatón* (☎ 423-596, *Av Santa Teresa 240*).

Getting There & Away

Los Andes' aging bus station is on Membrillar between Esmeralda and O'Higgins, one block east of the Plaza de Armas, but it's due to move to the old train station at the end of Av Carlos Díaz, the northern extension of Av Santa Teresa. There are many buses to and from Santiago and Valparaíso/Viña del Mar; buses from Santiago to Mendoza, Argentina, stop here, but it's a good idea to buy advance tickets.

Southern Heartland

RANCAGUA
☎ 72

Founded in 1743 on lands 'ceded' by the Picunche cacique Tomás Guaglén, Rancagua played an important role in Chilean independence. In 1814, it was the site of the Desastre de Rancagua (Disaster of Rancagua), at which Spanish Royalist troops vanquished Chilean patriots, many of whom were exiled to the Juan Fernández Archipelago. Although Chilean liberator Bernardo

MIDDLE CHILE

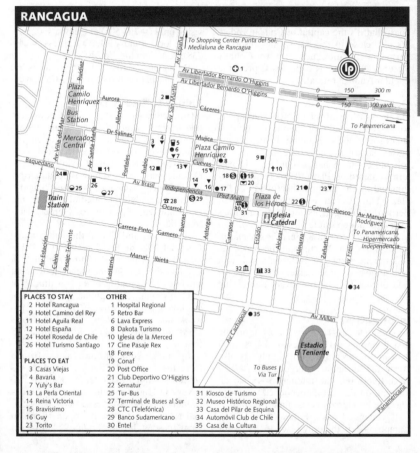

RANCAGUA

PLACES TO STAY	OTHER
2 Hotel Rancagua	1 Hospital Regional
9 Hotel Camino del Rey	5 Retro Bar
11 Hotel Aguila Real	6 Lava Express
12 Hotel España	8 Dakota Turismo
24 Hotel Rosedal de Chile	10 Iglesia de la Merced
26 Hotel Turismo Santiago	17 Cine Pasaje Rex
	18 Forex
PLACES TO EAT	19 Conaf
3 Casas Viejas	20 Post Office
4 Bavaria	21 Club Deportivo O'Higgins
7 Yuly's Bar	22 Sernatur
13 La Perla Oriental	25 Tur-Bus
14 Reina Victoria	27 Terminal de Buses al Sur
15 Bravíssimo	28 CTC (Telefónica)
16 Guy	29 Banco Sudamericano
23 Torito	30 Entel

31 Kiosco de Turismo	
32 Museo Histórico Regional	
33 Casa del Pilar de Esquina	
34 Automóvil Club de Chile	
35 Casa de la Cultura	

O'Higgins went into exile in Mendoza, Argentina, the battle was only a temporary setback for criollo self-determination.

Capital of Region VI, Rancagua is partly an agricultural service center, but the regional economy mostly relies on the huge El Teniente copper mine, in the Andes to the east. The presence of 10,000 mining families and the orientation of many Rancaguans toward Santiago (where they both work and shop because of easy rail connections) has made the city a cultural wasteland – it's the only regional capital without a university. The presence of many single male laborers has in turn fomented social problems such as prostitution.

Despite its shortcomings, Rancagua can boast that it's the capital of Chilean rodeo. It's also close to the hot springs resort of Termas de Cauquenes and to Conaf's Reserva Nacional Río de los Cipreses, a popular Andean retreat.

Orientation

On the north bank of the Río Cachapoal, Rancagua (population about 180,000) is 86km south of Santiago; the Panamericana passes east of the city. Like most cities of colonial origin, it has a standard grid pattern, centered on Plaza de los Héroes. Surrounded by the major public buildings, the plaza features an equestrian statue of Bernardo O'Higgins; its northeast corner has a carved wooden statue of Tomás Guaglén, a Mapuche who fought against the Spaniards. Between Av San Martín and the plaza, the commercial street of Independencia is a pedestrian mall; street names change on each side of San Martín, but street numbering does not.

Information

Sernatur (☎ 230-413, fax 232-297), on the first floor at Germán Riesco 277, is open 8:30 am to 5:15 pm weekdays only. Try also Acchi, the Automóvil Club de Chile (☎ 239-930), Ibieta 09. The municipal Kiosco de Turismo on Paseo Independencia, opposite Plaza de los Héroes, is marginally helpful.

If you need cash, Forex (☎ 235-273), Campos 363, is the only place to cash your traveler's checks, but Banco Sudamericano has an ATM at the corner of Independencia and Bueras.

The post office is on Campos between Cuevas and Independencia. CTC (Telefónica) has a long-distance office at San Martín 440; Entel is at Independencia 468.

At Millán and Cachapoal, four blocks south of Plaza de los Héroes, Rancagua's Casa de la Cultura was the headquarters of royalist Colonel Mariano de Osorio during the battle for the city. Administered by the Municipalidad, it now offers regular exhibitions of paintings and photographs. Hours are 8:30 am to noon and 3 to 8 pm weekdays only.

For information regarding national parks, visit Conaf (☎ 297-505) at Cuevas 480.

The local laundry is Lava Express (☎ 241-738), at Av San Martín 270.

Rancagua's Hospital Regional is on O'Higgins between Astorga and Campos.

Things to See & Do

At the corner of Estado and Cuevas, the **Iglesia de la Merced** is a national monument dating from the mid-18th century, when it served as the Convento y Templo de la Merced de Rancagua. During the battle of Rancagua, the building was headquarters for O'Higgins' patriots. Another religious landmark, the **Iglesia Catedral** at the corner of Estado and Plaza de los Héroes, dates from 1861.

At Estado and Ibieta, the late-colonial **Casa del Pilar de Esquina** (☎ 221-254) belonged to Fernando Errázuriz Aldunate, a key figure in the independence movement and one of the creators of the constitution of 1833. It's open to the public 10 am to 6 pm weekdays except Monday, 9 am to 1 pm weekends and holidays. Admission costs US$1 for adults, US$0.50 for children; it's free on Tuesday.

In another colonial house, across Estado from the Casa del Pilar de Esquina, the **Museo Histórico Regional** (also ☎ 221-254) covers O'Higgins' role in Chilean independence. It also displays a selection of colonial religious artwork. It's open 10 am to 4 pm Tuesday through Friday, 9 am to 1 pm weekends and holidays. Admission is the same as Casa del Pilar de Esquina, and it's also free Tuesday.

Special Events

In early autumn (late March), the Campeonato Nacional de Rodeo (national rodeo championship) takes place at the Medialuna de Rancagua, on Av España, the northward extension of Av San Martín. If planning to stay in Rancagua at this time, make hotel reservations early; otherwise, make it a day trip from Santiago.

Places to Stay & Eat

Easily the cheapest in town is bare-bones *Hotel Rosedal de Chile (Calvo 435)*, near the train station, which charges about US$8 per person. Several travelers have recommended *Hotel España (☎ 230-141, Av San Martín 367)* which has singles/doubles for US$26/40 with private bath. *Hotel Turismo Santiago (☎ 230-855, fax 230-822, Av Brasil 1036)* charges US$39/59 with cable TV and breakfast.

Family-oriented *Hotel Rancagua (☎ 228-158, fax 241-155, Av San Martín 85)* charges US$35 double, but discounts IVA for foreign visitors. The three-star *Hotel Aguila Real (☎ 233-823, Av Brasil 1045)* charges guests US$38/50. Despite its aging facade, *Hotel Camino del Rey (☎ 239-765, fax 232-314, Estado 275)* features a tastefully modernized interior; rates are US$52/77.

Yuly's Bar (Cuevas 745) has simple but inexpensive and well-prepared lunches, as does *Casas Viejas (☎ 230-006, Rubio 216)*. *Bavaria (☎ 241-241, Av San Martín 255)*, the local branch of the countrywide chain, is reliable but uninspiring. *La Perla Oriental (☎ 235-447, Cuevas 714)* is the place to go for Chinese food.

Torito (Zañartu 323) is a parrilla with good atmosphere. *Guy (☎ 226-053, Astorga 319)*, an upscale French-continental restaurant, is probably the classiest in town. *Reina Victoria (Independencia 667)* has good lunches for about US$4 and excellent ice cream. *Bravíssimo (☎ 230-596, Astorga 307)* is a branch of the popular Santiago ice creamery.

Entertainment

The *Cine Pasaje Rex (Independencia and Astorga)*, at the back of a gallery, occasionally shows good movies. For drinks, try the *Retro Bar (☎ 243-556, Av San Martín 226)*.

Spectator Sports

Club Deportivo O'Higgins (☎ 225-630), Cuevas 226, is the perpetual cellar-dweller in Chile's first-division soccer league. Estadio El Teniente is at the corner of Av Freire and Av Millán.

Getting There & Away

Bus Rancagua's bus station is at Dr Salinas 1165, just north of the Mercado Central, but some companies continue to use their own terminals. The focus at the main station is mostly on regional services. Carriers operating out of the station include Via Tur (234-502) to Los Angeles, Puerto Montt and intermediates, and Andimar (☎ 237-818), which goes to some coastal destinations, including Pichilemu.

There are frequent buses to Santiago from the Terminal de Buses al Sur (☎ 230-340), Ocarrol 1039. Tur-Bus (☎ 241-117), at Calvo and Ocarrol, also has frequent service to Santiago and extensive long-distance routes.

Train Rancagua's train station (☎ 225-239) is on Av Viña del Mar between Ocarrol and Carrera Pinto. Metrotrén runs frequent commuter trains to the capital, and EFE's infrequent long-distance passenger services, connecting Santiago with Temuco and Concepción, also stop at Rancagua.

AROUND RANCAGUA
Centro de Esqui Chapa Verde

Some 50km northeast of Rancagua via a mostly paved highway, Chapa Verde (☎ 294-255) is less famous than more prestigious ski centers such as Portillo and Valle Nevado, but has four lifts and eight runs, 2870m above sea level. Created for Codelco (the state-owned mining enterprise) workers but open to the public, its facilities include a ski school, rental equipment, a café and a restaurant.

MIDDLE CHILE

This is a day trip only, and since the road to Chapa Verde is not open to the public, visitors must take Codelco buses from the Hipermercado Independencia, Av Manuel Rodriguez 665, at 9 am on weekdays, or between 8 and 9:30 am weekends.

El Teniente

At Sewell, 55km northeast of Rancagua, El Teniente belonged to the Braden Copper Company and then Kennecott Copper Corporation until its expropriation under the Unidad Popular, and is now part of Codelco. Dating from 1904, the world's largest subsurface copper mine has more than 1500km of tunnels. Sewell itself is now a ghost town, and a monument to 20th-century company-town architecture.

El Teniente and Sewell are open to the public for organized tours only. If you want to visit, contact Turismo Dakota (☎ 072-228-166), Astorga 270, Rancagua. Including a country-club lunch and transport, the full-day trip costs US$125 per person from Santiago, with regular Friday departures with a minimum of four persons.

Termas de Cauquenes

In the Andean foothills east of Rancagua, Cauquenes' thermal baths have received such celebrated visitors as Bernardo O'Higgins and Charles Darwin, who observed that the buildings consisted of 'a square of miserable little hovels, each with a single table and bench.' Improvements since Darwin's day now allow *Hotel Termas de Cauquenes* (☎/fax 072-297-226; ☎ 02-638-1610, fax 632-2365 in Santiago) to charge from US$72/100 for B&B to US$107/200 singles/doubles with full board, in an area that Darwin acknowledged as 'a quiet, solitary spot with a good deal of wild beauty.'

Overlooking the river, the hotel's dining room offers a popular Sunday lunch whose quality doesn't quite merit the US$17 price tag. Nonguests can use the thermal baths, lined in Carrara marble, for US$6.50 per person, slightly more with jacuzzi. The lodgings themselves are comfortable and the surrounding gardens professionally landscaped. For more information or reservations, contact Termas de Caquenes, Casilla 106, Rancagua.

If you can't afford to stay at Cauquenes, only 28km east of Rancagua, you can visit for the afternoon by taking Buses Coya (US$1.50) from Andén 13 of Rancagua's bus station, daily at 9:30 am and 1:30 pm, returning at 11 am and 5:15 pm.

RESERVA NACIONAL RÍO DE LOS CIPRESES

Set among the Andean foothills and cordillera, ranging from 900m to the 4900m summit of Volcán El Palomo in the upper drainage of its namesake river, 37,000-hectare Los Cipreses contains a variety of volcanic landforms, hanging glacial valleys with waterfalls, and fluvial landscapes. Just south of the park boundary, an Uruguayan air force plane carrying the national rugby team crashed in the winter of 1972, resulting in the notorious tale of survival by cannibalism told in Piers Paul Reid's book *Alive!*, which was later turned into an English-language film by director Frank Marshall in 1993.

The reserve is home to extensive forests of cypress, olivillo and other native tree species; its wildlife includes guanaco, fox, vizcacha, condor and many other birds. The reintroduction of pumas a few years back has upset nearby ranchers who graze goats, sheep and cattle in the area, however, and there is also significant poaching of rabbits and other mammals – though not necessarily by locals.

Fox (zorro culpeo)

Orientation & Information

Los Cipreses is 50km southeast of Rancagua. At the park entrance, at the north end of the reserve, Conaf's congenial and dedicated staff has a well-organized **Centro de Visitantes**, with a scale model of the park for orientation and natural history displays, including a full guanaco skeleton (there is also a bone lab here).

There are petroglyphs at several sites; ask Conaf for directions. It's possible to rent horses from local people, and one long trail ascends the valley of the Río de los Cipreses to Uriarte, where Conaf has a simple refugio. *Camping Ranchillos*, 6km south of the park entrance, has grassy campsites for US$8, and also has a swimming pool.

No direct public transport exists, but visitors can take a bus as far as Termas de Cauquenes (see the Termas de Cauquenes section earlier in this chapter) and walk or hitch another 15km to the park entrance. With luck and persuasion, it may be possible to arrange transport with Conaf's Rancagua office.

HACIENDA LOS LINGUES

Probably no other single site can match that of Hacienda Los Lingues, midway between Rancagua and San Fernando, in providing a glimpse into the life of colonial Chilean landowners. Dating from the 17th century, it now offers luxury hotel accommodations and is one of a handful of South American affiliates of the prestigious Relais & Châteaux group, with a reputation for offering outstanding but unobtrusive service in extraordinary surroundings.

The accommodations consist of 10 rooms, all furnished with antiques (but with modern amenities such as private baths), in a 17th-century building with thick adobe walls, modified by 18th- and early-19th-century additions. Also a working farm, Los Lingues grows much of its own produce and breeds thoroughbred horses. Riding, mountain biking, hiking, tennis, swimming and fly-fishing are all possible on its extensive grounds.

For reservations, contact Hacienda Los Lingues (☎ 02-235-5446, 235-2458, fax 235-7604, loslingues@entelchile.net), Av Providencia 1100, Torre C de Tajamar, Oficina 205, Providencia, Santiago. Its rates are US$186 single or double, US$406 per suite. Breakfast costs an additional US$19, lunch US$46, and dinner US$62.

Hacienda Los Lingues is about 32km south of Rancagua, reached by a short gravel lateral just south of the town of Pelequén on the Panamericana. It's possible to get a cab from the turnoff, but Los Lingues provides roundtrip transportation from central Santiago or from the international airport for US$320 for up to 11 persons. Day visits (US$46 per person with lunch including wine, pool access, a tour of the main house and a rodeo) are also permitted, but usually as part of large groups to whom parts of the grounds are closed to protect the privacy of overnight guests.

LAGO RAPEL

In truth a reservoir rather than a lake, Lago Rapel was formed by the Central Hidroeléctrica Rapel, which inundated the basins of the Cachapoal and Tinguiririca rivers in 1968. Since then, it's become a popular site for water sports such as windsurfing, water-skiing and fishing. There are many camping areas east of El Manzano, on the south shore of the reservoir's northern arm, plus reasonable accommodations at the *Hostería y Camping Playas de Llaullauquén* (☎ 072-343-385, Llaullauquén s/n), on the eastern shore of its southern arm, for US$32 for a double room (campsites go for US$20 for up to five people).

Lago Rapel is about 100km west of Rancagua via Pelequén, on the Panamericana. It can also be reached from Santiago (147km) with Buses Navidad from Terminal San Borja, Alameda 3250.

PICHILEMU
☎ 72

Most easily accessible by bus from the city of San Fernando (55km south of Rancagua), Pichilemu has been Region VI's most popular beach resort since the beginning of the 20th century. There's an Oficina de Información Turística (☎ 841-017) in the Municipalidad, Angel Gaete 365.

In summer, the Campeonato Nacional de Surf (national surfing championship) takes place at Punta de Lobos, 6km south of town, with perhaps the best left break in Chile.

Places to Stay & Eat

For camping, try *Pequeño Bosque* (☎ 841-601, Santa Teresa s/n), where shady sites cost US$14 for up to four people (try bargaining for a discount). At Punta de Lobos, *Nalu Surf Club* is cheap (charging per person rather than per site) but lacks shade; most guests here worry more about the waves.

Pichilemu gets crowded in season, but reasonable accommodations are available – try *Residencial Las Salinas* (☎ 841-071, Aníbal Pinto 51), which has singles with shared bath for US$12, or *Residencial San Luis* (☎ 841-040, Angel Gaete 237), which charges US$10 per person with shared bath, US$20 with private bath, including breakfast; the latter also has restaurant facilities. Highly praised *Hotel Chile España* (☎ 841-270, Av Ortúzar 255) caters to surfers; rates are normally US$19 per person with breakfast, US$30 with full board at its restaurant. Prices with shared bath are about 20% less, and there are also substantial off-season discounts.

Getting There & Away

Buses Andimar (☎ 072-841-081), Av Ortúzar 483, connects Pichilemu with San Fernando and Santiago.

Around Pichilemu

About 20km south of Pichilemu is the smaller beach resort and fishing village of **Bucalemu**, where several residenciales have singles for about US$10. Try *Hotel Casablanca* (☎ 072-342-335, Av Celedonio Pastene s/n). From Bucalemu, it's possible to make a two- to four-day beach trek – camping along the way – to the seaside village of **Llico**, a popular windsurfing spot with bus connections to Curicó.

CURICÓ
☎ 75

Founded in 1743 by José Antonio Manso de Velasco, pleasant, attractive Curicó (population about 72,000) is a service center for surrounding orchards and vineyards. While not a major attraction in its own right, it's a good base for excursions to nearby wineries, coastal areas such as Vichuquén and parts of the Andes that are visited by relatively few foreigners, such as the Reserva Nacional Radal Siete Tazas.

Orientation

Beside the Río Guaiquillo, 195km south of Santiago, Curicó lies just west of the Panamericana. Entering town from the Panamericana, broad, tree-lined Av Manso de Velasco skirts the eastern edge of Curicó's central quadrangle. At the north end of Manso de Velasco, Cerro Carlos Condell is a verdant, scenic overlook with a pool to beat the summer heat.

Curicó's palm-studded Plaza de Armas is one of Chile's prettiest, with a delightful, early-20th-century wrought-iron bandstand and cool fountains. On its south side, a local artist has sculpted a tree trunk into an image of a Mapuche warrior.

Curicó's Festival de la Vendimia (wine harvest festival) lasts four days in early March.

Information

Curicó has no formal tourist office, but in summer Sernatur maintains a kiosk at the Edificio Servicios Públicos on Carmen, on the east side of the plaza. Open 9 am to 6:30 pm, it's understaffed and lacks space

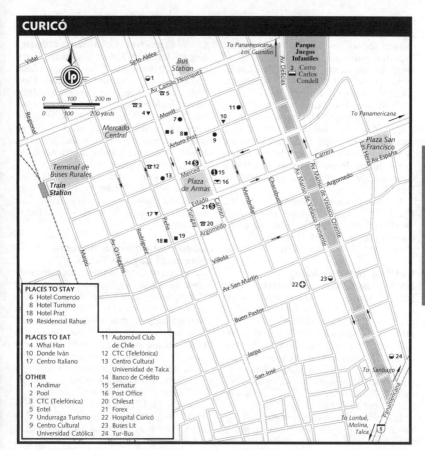

CURICÓ

PLACES TO STAY
6 Hotel Comercio
8 Hotel Turismo
18 Hotel Prat
19 Residencial Rahue

PLACES TO EAT
4 Whai Han
10 Donde Iván
17 Centro Italiano

11 Automóvil Club de Chile
12 CTC (Telefónica)
13 Centro Cultural Universidad de Talca

OTHER
1 Andimar
2 Pool
3 CTC (Telefónica)
5 Entel
7 Undurraga Turismo
9 Centro Cultural Universidad Católica

14 Banco de Crédito
15 Sernatur
16 Post Office
20 Chilesat
21 Forex
22 Hospital Curicó
23 Buses Lit
24 Tur-Bus

MIDDLE CHILE

but does its best. The local branch of Acchi, the Automóvil Club de Chile (☎ 311-156) at Chacabuco 759, is especially helpful.

You'll be able to change US cash and traveler's checks at Forex, Carmen 497. Banco de Crédito has an ATM at Merced 315.

The post office is at Carmen 556, opposite the Plaza de Armas. CTC (Telefónica) provides long-distance services at its offices at Peña 650 and at Camilo Henríquez 412. Entel is at Av Camilo Henríquez 334; Chilesat at Yungay 430.

The local travel agency is Undurraga Turismo (☎ 317-605), at Carmen 737.

The Centro Cultural Universidad de Talca, Merced 437, offers films and concerts on a regular basis and runs a small but good bookstore. The Centro Cultural Universidad Católica, Arturo Prat 220, has similar offerings.

The Hospital de Curicó (☎ 310-252) is on Chacabuco between Av San Martín and Buen Pastor.

Places to Stay & Eat
Friendly *Hotel Prat* (☎ *311-069, Peña 427*) is the budget pick at US$9 per person with shared bath. The rooms vary – some are

large, bright and comfortable, with high ceilings, while others are dark and drab. The showers are hot, there's a shady grape arbor over the patio and it's become a good meeting place. Across the street, *Residencial Rahue (☎ 312-194, Peña 410)* is identically priced and perfectly satisfactory.

At tranquil *Hotel Comercio (☎ 310-014, fax 317-001, Yungay 730)*, rates start at about US$27/40 singles/doubles, but better rooms with private bath cost US$40/58; there are IVA discounts for foreigners. Set on attractive grounds, *Hotel Turismo (☎ 310-823, Carmen 727)* is slightly more expensive at US$48/63.

Try the *Centro Italiano (☎ 310-482, Estado 531)* for US$3 lunches. *Donde Iván (☎ 314-090, Prat 189)* is popular and cheap but only so-so. *Whai Han (☎ 326-526, Yungay 853)* serves Chinese food.

Getting There & Away

Bus Most north-south companies have their offices at Curicó's long-distance bus station on Camilo Henríquez, three blocks north of the plaza. The companies that use their own offices are Buses Lit (☎ 315-648) at Av Manso de Velasco and Buen Pastor, Tur-Bus (☎ 312-115) at Manso de Velasco 0106 and Andimar (☎ 312-000) at Yungay 926, which goes to Santiago, Temuco, and coastal destinations. Buses to Santiago (US$5, 2½ hours) leave about every half hour.

For local and regional services, the Terminal de Buses Rurales is at the west end of Calle Prat, across from the railway station. Companies operating there include Buses Bravo (☎ 312-193), which goes to Lago Vichuquén and the coastal resort of Iloca, and Buses Díaz (☎ 311-905), which goes to Santiago. Buses Hernández (☎ 491-607, 491-179) goes to interior destinations such as Molina and Radal Siete Tazas.

Train Passenger trains between Santiago and Temuco stop at Curicó's train station (☎ 310-028) at Maipú 657, at the west end of Calle Prat, four blocks west of the Plaza de Armas. Fares to Santiago range from US$4 to US$6; to Chillán, US$5 to US$6.50; to Temuco, US$7.50 to US$14.50.

AROUND CURICÓ
Wineries

One of Chile's best-known vineyards, **Bodega Miguel Torres** (☎ 310-455), is on the Panamericana just south of Curicó. Phone ahead and take a taxi colectivo from Camilo Henríquez and Rodríguez in Curicó toward the village of Molina. It'll be easy to catch a colectivo back as well. In summer, the winery is open from 8:30 am to 1 pm and 3 to 6:30 pm daily; the rest of the year and it's open from 8:30 am to 1 pm and 3 to 6 pm weekdays and 8:30 am to 1 pm Saturday.

On the same route, near the village of Lontué, **Viña San Pedro** (☎ 491-517) dates from the early 18th century. Hours are limited – 9 am to 10:30 pm Tuesday to Thursday only.

Lago Vichuquén & Reserva Nacional Laguna Torca

In the coast range only a short distance from the Pacific, 110km from Curicó, **Lago Vichuquén** is a natural lake that is a popular center for water sports. Nearby is **Reserva Nacional Laguna Torca**, a 604-hectare reserve that is home to breeding populations of black-necked swans, coscoroba swans and more than a hundred other species. In especially wet years, the two lakes join to form a single extensive coastal wetland.

Conaf maintains a Centro de Información Ambiental at Laguna Torca, where it collects US$1 admission for adults, US$0.40 for children. There is a US$10 charge for camping in rustic sites with cold showers; no fires or music permitted.

RESERVA NACIONAL RADAL SIETE TAZAS

In the upper basin of the Río Claro southeast of Molina, 5700-hectare Reserva Nacional Radal Siete Tazas is a state-protected area whose territory, which ranges in elevation from 600m to 2156m, marks an ecological transition between the drought-tolerant Mediterranean vegetation to the north and the moist evergreen forests to the south. Its major scenic attraction is a stunning series of waterfalls – the highest of which is about 30m – and pools.

AROUND CURICÓ & TALCA

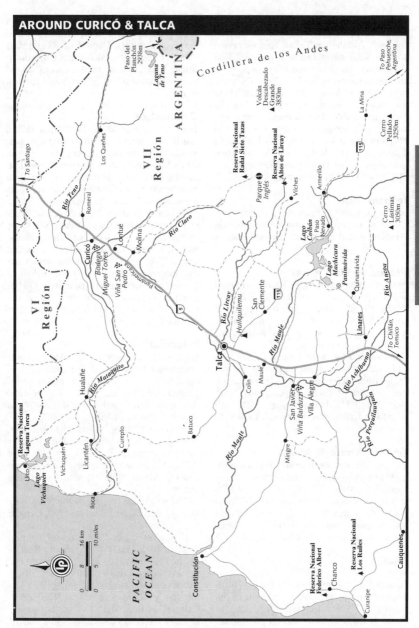

The falls and pools at Siete Tazas (literally, Seven Teacups) are accessible via a short footpath. Another trail leads to a viewpoint for the **Salto de la Leona**, a waterfall that drops more than 50m from a narrow gorge to the main channel of the Río Claro. The same trail continues down to the river itself. There are longer, scenic hiking trails up Cerro El Fraile and at Valle del Indio, and it's also possible to trek across the drainage of the Río Claro to exit at Reserva Nacional Altos del Lircay (see the Reserva Nacional Altos del Lircay section, later in this chapter), taking about two days, but not without a guide.

Information
At Parque Inglés, the entrance to the reserve, Conaf maintains a Centro de Información Ambiental that offers educational talks at 11 am and 7 pm weekends.

Places to Stay & Eat
Free, rustic campgrounds with cold running water are available at **Radal** and **Parque Inglés;** Conaf is attempting to improve the campgrounds and toilets at Parque Inglés. There is also **Camping Los Robles** for US$16 for up to two tents.

Hostería Flor de la Canela (☎ 075-491-613), near Conaf headquarters at Parque Inglés, offers accommodations from December to March for US$38 per person with shared bath, US$43 with private bath, both with full board in its restaurant. A kiosk sells basic supplies.

Getting There & Away
Parque Inglés is 50km from Molina over a good but narrow gravel and dirt road. Buses Hernández (☎ 491-607, 491-179), Maipú 1723 in Molina, goes to Parque Inglés (US$2, two hours) daily at 5:30 pm all year; in January and February, there are up to seven buses daily, some of them direct from Curicó.

TALCA
☎ 71
Founded in 1690 but refounded in 1742 after a major earthquake, Talca was the site of the signing of Chile's declaration of independence in 1818. Since its earliest days, it has

been an important commercial center in a prosperous agricultural region and home to many landowners. Capital of Region VII (Maule), the city is also a notable educational and cultural locus, thanks to its museums, universities, galleries and cultural centers.

Orientation
Talca (population about 140,000) is 257km south of Santiago via the Panamericana, which skirts the city's eastern border; the Río Claro limits its westward expansion. Talca's street plan is no less regular than most Spanish colonial cities, but most streets are numbered rather than named.

Streets north of the Plaza de Armas begin at 1 Norte, those to the south at 1 Sur, those to the east at 1 Oriente and those to the west at 1 Poniente. Frequently '1' is spelled out as 'Uno,' but nearly all other streets use the numeral except for 4 Norte, a divided boulevard known as Av Bernardo O'Higgins. O'Higgins crosses the Río Claro to the Cerro de la Virgen, which offers fine views of the city.

Information
Sernatur (☎ 233-669, fax 226-940, sernatur_talca@entelchile.net), 1 Poniente 1281, is open 8:30 am to 4:30 pm weekdays only. English-speakers are sometimes on duty. Acchi, the Automóvil Club (☎ 232-774), is almost next door at 1 Poniente 1267.

Marcelo Cancino Cortés, 1 Sur 898, Oficina 15, changes US, Argentine and other foreign currencies. Banco Santiago has an ATM at 1 Sur 853, one block east of the Plaza de Armas, while Banco de Crédito has one at 1 Sur 732.

The post office is opposite the plaza, on 1 Oriente. Entel is on 1 Sur between 2 Oriente and 3 Oriente.

If you're in need of a travel agency, Bontour (☎ 234-003) is at 5 Oriente 1080.

The Universidad de Talca's Centro de Extensión Pedro Olmos, 2 Norte 685, offers various cultural events, including films, lectures and exhibitions of artwork. The Centro Cultural de Talca, on 1 Oriente between 1 and 2 Norte, offers theater, concerts and art exhibits. The Centro de Extensión de la Universidad Católica (☎ 226-303), 2 Sur 1525, offers art exhibits throughout the university year, from March through December.

Conaf (☎ 233-148) is at 2 Poniente 1180, but its Patrimonio Silvestre (☎ 228-029), the branch which deals with national parks, is at the corner of 2 Poniente and 3 Sur.

Talca's Hospital Regional (☎ 242-406) is 11 blocks east of the plaza on 1 Norte, just across the railway tracks.

Things to See & Do

The **Museo O'Higginiano y de Bellas Artes,** a late-colonial house dating from 1762 and handsomely furnished in period decor is where Bernardo O'Higgins officially signed Chile's declaration of independence in 1818. Like Rancagua's Casa del Pilar de Esquina, the building has an interesting corner pillar.

The material on O'Higgins is barely worthwhile, but the museum also contains archaeological and numismatic exhibits, as well as collections of Chilean and foreign painting and sculpture, mostly landscapes and portraits. A display on the city from the standpoint of a local 19th-century writer is excellent, and there are occasional special exhibits of regional painters.

At 1 Norte 875, the museum (☎ 227-330) is open 10 am to 5:45 pm Tuesday to Friday, 10 am to 1:45 pm weekends. Admission costs US$1 for adults, US$0.50 for children; on Sundays admission is free.

Travelers with incendiary tendencies can visit the **Museo Bomberil Benito Riquelme** (firemen's museum), in the main fire station at 2 Sur 1172. Its collections of antique firefighting equipment, photographs and miscellanea are open to the public, so long as there's not a serious blaze raging across town. It's free of charge, but has no fixed schedule.

The Municipalidad's **Casa del Arte-Museo Municipal Gabriel Pando,** 1 Norte 931, is a gallery-museum that occasionally hosts films, concerts and other events as well. Hours are 10 am to 1 pm and 3:30 to 7 pm weekdays.

Places to Stay

Budget Talca is relatively short on budget accommodations. The best bargain is

Residencial Ramiro Riquelme (☎ 232-962, 3 Sur 1078), charging US$9 to US$11 single with shared bath. Near the train station, recommended *Hostal Victoria (☎ 239-193, 1 Sur 1737*, is an almost equally good value for US$14 per person.

Mid-Range Remodeled *Hotel Cordillera (☎/fax 221-817, 2 Sur 1360)* has singles with shared bath for US$17; singles/doubles with private bath and TV go for US$25/40. One of Talca's better values is well-kept *Hotel Amalfi (☎/fax 233-389, 2 Sur 1265)*, set among attractive gardens, for US$31/45. Some of its singles are available for as little as US$19.

For US$25/40 plus US$5 for breakfast, try the excellent *Hostal del Puente (☎ 220-930, fax 225-448, 1 Sur 411)*, which has English-speaking management and an attractive riverside site on a cul-de-sac. *Hotel Napoli (☎ 227-373, 2 Sur 1314)* charges US$31/50 with breakfast, private bath and color television. The new *Hotel Inca del Oro (☎ 239-608, 1 Sur 1026)*, is worth a look at US$46/63.

Top End Talca's top-end accommodations are cheaper than in most other Chilean cities. For example, *Hotel Plaza (☎ 22150, 1 Poniente 1141)* starts at US$55/78 with breakfast; *Hotel Marcos Gamero (☎ 223-388, fax 224-400, 1 Oriente 1070)*, charges US$55/70. For US$65/77, the sparkling *Hotel Terrabella (☎/fax 226-555, 1 Sur 641)* is probably Talca's best.

Places to Eat

One of Chile's best bargains is *Picada José Barrera (☎ 224-120, 1 Sur 530)*, jammed with downtown diners in search of tasty, filling three-course lunches that cost around US$2. The *Mercado Central*, bounded by 1 Norte, 5 Oriente, 1 Sur and 4 Oriente, has several economical cocinerías. The *Casino Caja de Empleados Particulares (1 Oriente between 1 and 2 Norte)* has modest lunches that are a good value.

Worthwhile restaurants include the *Centro Español (☎ 224-664, 3 Oriente 1109)* and *Ibiza (1 Sur 1168)*, which also has a take-away

TALCA

PLACES TO STAY
9 Hostal Victoria
10 Hostal del Puente
13 Hotel Terrabella
14 Hotel Plaza
20 Hotel Marcos Gamero
25 Hotel Inca del Oro
29 Hotel Amalfi
34 Hotel Napoli
35 Hotel Cordillera
36 Residencial Ramiro Riquelme

PLACES TO EAT
5 El Alero de Gastón
6 Casino Caja de Empleados Particulares
11 Picada José Barrera
13 Varoli

17 Gobelino
24 Centro Español
26 Lomitón
27 Ibiza

OTHER
1 Centro de Extensión Pedro Olmos (Universidad de Talca)
2 Sernatur
3 Automóvil Club de Chile
4 Centro Cultural de Talca
7 Museo O'Higginiano y de Bellas Artes
8 Casa del Arte, Museo Municipal Gabriel Pando
12 Conaf
15 Banco de Crédito
16 Cine Plaza
18 Post Office

19 Banco Santiago
21 Marcelo Cancino Cortés
22 Entel
28 Bontour
30 Entel
31 Centro de Extensión de la Universidad Católica
32 Tur-Bus
33 Museo Bomberil Benito Riquelme
37 Patrimonio Silvestre (Conaf)

MIDDLE CHILE

rotisserie). ***Lomitón*** *(1 Sur between 4 and 5 Oriente)* is a sandwich spot, while ***Varoli*** *(☎ 224-097, 3 Oriente 1189)* is a beer-and-pizza kind of place, palatable and cheap, but nothing special.

Gobelino *(1 Sur and 1 Oriente)* is one of the best restaurants in town. Relatively expensive ***El Alero de Gastón*** *(☎ 233-785, 2 Norte 858)* also features a broad range of Chilean dishes on its menu. It is also known for its fine service. The restaurant is set in pleasant surroundings including a shady patio, but the food's quality falls a little short of the prices.

Entertainment
The ***Cine Plaza*** *(☎ 232-310, 1 Sur 770)* shows current films.

Getting There & Away
Bus Talca's main Rodoviario Municipal (☎ 243-270) is at 2 Sur 1920, across the tracks but not directly accessible from the nearby train station (1 Sur will get you there). Domestic companies with northbound and southbound services on the Panamericana include Buses Lit (☎ 242-048), Tas Choapa (☎ 243-334), Varmontt (☎ 242-120), Intersur (☎ 245-920), Buses Jac – as far as Temuco –

TALCA

To Curicó,
Santiago

0   150   300 m

0   150   300 yards

2 Norte

1 Norte

16 Oriente

1 Sur

15 Oriente

14 Oriente

13 Oriente

Av San Miguel
To San
Clemente

18 Oriente

Panamericana

Bus
Station

32

To Chillán,
Temuco

and Sol del Pacífico (☎ 244-199) to Valparaíso/Viña del Mar and to Concepción.

Pullman del Sur (☎ 244-039) goes to the coastal resort of Constitución (US$2). Buses Vilches (☎ 243-366) leaves three times daily, at 7 am and at 1 and 4:50 pm, for the village of Vilches Alto and beyond, turning around at the entrance to Reserva Nacional Altos del Lircay.

Tur-Bus (☎ 241-748), utilizing a separate terminal one block south at 3 Sur 1960, travels north and south on the Panamericana. Buses Biotal (☎ 223-727) is the agent for Transporte Pehuenche (☎ 073-212-322 in

MIDDLE CHILE

Linares), a minibus service that crosses the spectacular 2553-m Paso Pehuenche to the Argentine cities of Malargüe (US$40, eight hours) and San Rafael (US$60 10 hours) in the summertime.

Sample fares include Santiago or Chillán (US$6, four hours), Temuco or Valparaíso/Viña del Mar (US$13, six hours) and Puerto Montt (US$18, 11 hours).

Train Note the surrealistic pop-art murals at the train station (☎ 226-254) at 11 Oriente 1000, at the eastern end of 2 Sur. All trains from Santiago's Estación Central to Temuco and points south stop here en route.

In addition to long-distance service, a narrow-gauge passenger train still runs to the coastal resort of Constitución. Well worth a detour for rail aficionados, this threatened service (US$2.25) runs at 7:30 am and 6:10 pm weekdays, 7:30 am only weekends.

AROUND TALCA
Huilquilemu

Once an important *fundo* (hacienda) but now property of the Universidad Católica, this complex of restored 19th-century buildings, 10km east of Talca on the San Clemente highway, houses a variety of galleries and museums (including a fine collection of farm machinery), chapels and regional crafts. There is also a restaurant on site.

The Villa Cultural Huilquilemu Hernán Correa de la Cerda (☎ 242-474) is open 3 to 6:30 pm Tuesday to Friday, 4 to 6:30 pm Saturday and 11 am to 2 pm Sunday; admission costs US$0.70 for adults, US$0.20 for children. All San Clemente micros from Talca's bus station pass the site.

San Javier

About 19km south of Talca, the Panamericana passes the **Puente Maule**, an impressive, 442m-long iron bridge, dating from 1885, spanning the canyon of the Río Maule. Two km farther south, a lateral road leads to San Javier, where **Viñedo Balduzzi** (☎ 073-322-138), Av Balmaceda 1189, is an increasingly popular boutique winery set among spacious gardens and well-kept colonial and modern buildings. It annually produces about 500,000 bottles of chardon-nay, sauvignon blanc and cabernet, most of which is exported to Asia.

Free guided tours and tastings are available 9 am to 6 pm daily except Sunday. Buses to San Javier run frequently from Talca's bus station.

RESERVA NACIONAL ALTOS DEL LIRCAY

Administered by Conaf, this former 'área de protección' occupies 12,163 hectares in the Andean foothills east of Talca, between 600m and 2448m above sea level. Slated for expansion to about 22,000 hectares, Altos del Lircay is also the site of a puma research project with the participation of the Talca office of Codeff, which is a private conservation organization.

Conaf's helpful Centro de Información Ambiental, near the park entrance, has excellent displays on local natural and cultural history (there have been four sequential Indian occupations). The park entrance fee is modest at US$1.60 for adults, US$0.40 for children.

Hiking

Within the park, it's possible to camp in the upper basin of the Río Lircay and to make hiking excursions to the basaltic plateau of **El Enladrillado,** to **Laguna El Alto** and **Laguna Tomate,** and up the canyon of the Valle del Venado. Well-organized trekkers can loop across the drainage of the Río Claro to exit at Conaf's Reserva Nacional Radal Siete Tazas. Since the trail is not always obvious, it's advisable to hire a local guide (see Reserva Nacional Radal Siete Tazas, earlier in this chapter).

Probably the best single hike between Santiago and Temuco, El Enladrillado offers tiring but exhilarating hiking crowned by top-of-the-world views from this unique columnar basalt plateau. About one hour's walk above the entrance station, a signed lateral follows an abandoned logging road for about half an hour to an ill-marked junction (look for an 'E' and an arrow carved in a tree at a small clearing) where the trail

proper begins, just before the logging road begins to drop. Conaf has pledged to improve the trail signage.

From this junction, the trail climbs steeply through dense forest, zigzagging for about an hour before leveling off and winding around various volcanic outcrops and emerging onto El Enladrillado, a site where it seems as if a mad gardener has placed massive hexagonal flagstones for an immense patio and planted prostrate shrubs among them. Like California's Devil's Postpile and Ireland's Giant's Causeway, this striking geological feature resulted from rapid cooling of an igneous intrusion before it reached the earth's surface; erosion of softer surrounding material has slowly exposed the resulting geometric structures to open view.

From the park entrance, figure about five hours up and 3½ hours down for this strenuous but rewarding hike, and allow at least an hour on top. There are two or three potable springs before the trail emerges above treeline, but carry as much water as possible. Close gates to keep livestock from the upper reaches of the trail.

Trekkers can also choose to descend the valley of the Río Lircay, where backcountry camping is possible, and continue north to Radal Siete Tazas, in the Río Claro drainage. This trek, which ends at Parque Inglés, takes about two to three days; see the Radal Siete Tazas section for more detail. Again, hiring a local guide is advisable.

Horseback Riding

Good but inexpensive rental horses, about US$17 to US$21 per day, are available just outside the park entrance. These are a good alternative for visitors with little time to explore the park, but they're not really suitable for the steep trail to El Enladrillado, where the four-legged beasts have caused serious erosion.

Places to Stay & Eat

There is no formal camping within the reserve proper, except for backcountry sites, but near the entrance are several basic private sites, some of which sell supplies, that charge about US$3 per person. Simple meals may also be available here. Choose a site as far away from the dusty highway as possible.

In Vilches Alto, 6km west of the park entrance, *Hostal Alto Vilches* (☎ *071-237-165)* provides comfortable lodging for US$17 per person with full board – and use of the swimming pool.

Getting There & Away

Altos del Lircay is 65km from Talca via paved Chile 115 and a lateral that may be the dustiest road in all of Chile (except in winter, when it's probably the muddiest). From Talca, Buses Vilches goes directly to the park entrance at 7 am and 1 and 4:50 pm, returning at 9 am and 2:30 and 6:30 pm daily. The fare is US$1.50.

CHILLÁN
☎ 42

Birthplace of Chilean liberator Bernardo O'Higgins, the market city of Chillán also marks the approximate northern border of La Frontera, that area over which Spain – and Chile – never really exercised effective control until the state finally subdued the Mapuche in the late 19th century. Founded in 1565 as a military outpost, destroyed and refounded several times after earthquakes and Mapuche sieges, it moved to its present site in 1835. The old city, nearby Chillán Viejo, has never really died.

In addition to its colorful market, perhaps Chile's finest, Chillán has several notable museums and landmark works by the famous Mexican muralist David Alfaro Siqueiros and his colleague Xavier Guerrero. Thanks to this combination of attractions, Chillán is the best stopover of all the cities along the Panamericana between Santiago and Temuco.

Orientation

Chillán (population about 135,000), 400km south of Santiago and 270km north of Temuco, sits on an alluvial plain between the Río Ñuble and its smaller southern tributary, the Río Chillán. The city's heart is an area 12 blocks square, bounded by the divided, tree-lined Avs Ecuador, Brasil, Collín and Argentina. The center proper is the Plaza de Armas, bounded by Libertad, 18 de Septiembre, Constitución and Arauco.

Av O'Higgins leads north to the Panamericana (which passes northwest of the city) and south to the suburb of Chillán Viejo (the city center until the earthquake of 1835), which is now a separate *comuna* (local governmental unit). From Chillán Viejo there is alternative access to the southbound Panamericana.

Information

Sernatur (☎/fax 223-272) is at 18 de Septiembre 455, half a block north of the plaza. It's open 8:30 am to 7:30 pm weekdays all year; from mid-December through February, it's also open weekends, 10 am to 2 pm only. There's also a small information kiosk at the main bus terminal.

Acchi, the Automóvil Club de Chile (☎ 216-410), is at O'Higgins 677.

For cash or traveler's checks, Schüler Cambios, Constitución 608, is open 9 am to 1 pm and 3:30 to 7 pm weekdays, 10 am to 6 pm Saturday and 11 am to 1:30 pm Sunday. Banco Concepción, Constitución 550, also has an ATM.

The post office is at Libertad 505. CTC (Telefónica) long-distance offices are at Arauco 625; Entel is next door at Arauco 623; Chilexpress at 18 de Septiembre 490, Local 201. Phone facilities are also available at the main bus terminal.

Chillán's several travel agencies include Centrotur (☎ 221-306) at 18 de Septiembre 656, Alvatur (☎ 227-392) at 18 de Septiembre 342 and Alto Nivel (☎ 225-267) at Arauco 683, Oficina 5. The Primera Sala Teatro Municipal (☎ 231-048, Anexo 334), 18 de Septiembre 590, is an annex to the municipal theatre. It's open 9 am to 2 pm and 3 to 6 pm weekdays for special exhibitions.

For laundry services, head to Lava Matic at Arturo Prat 357-B.

Chillán's Hospital Herminda Martín (☎ 212-345) is six blocks east of the Plaza de Armas, at the corner of Constitución and Av Argentina.

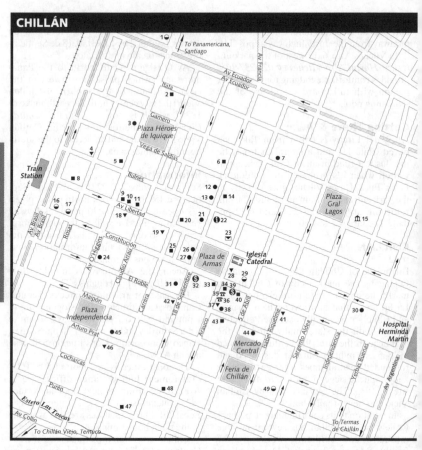

CHILLÁN

To Panamericana, Santiago

Av Ecuador
Av Ecuador
Av Franca

Itata
2 ■

Gamero
3 ● Plaza Héroes
de Iquique

Vega de Saldías

Train
Station
■ 8

Bulnes

4 ▼
5 ■
6 ■
● 7

9 ■
10 ● 11 ■
16 ■
17 ●
Av Libertad
18 ▼

12 ●
13 ● ■ 14

Plaza
Gral
Lagos
血 15

19 ▼
■ 20
21 ●
ℹ 22

Constitución
Av O'Higgins
● 24
Rosas

25 ■
26 ●
27 ●
Plaza de
Armas
23 ▼

Iglesia
Catedral

El Roble
31 ●
32 🛇 33 ■
34 39
35 🛇
36 ☂
37 ▼ 38
40
28 ▼
29

Maipón
Plaza
Independencia

42 ▼
43 ■

44 ●
Mercado
Central

30 ●

Hospital
Herminda
Martín

Arturo Prat
● 45
▼ 46

Cocharcas
Feria de
Chillán
49 ◐

Purén
■ 48
47 ■

Estero Las Toscas
Av Collín
To Chillán Viejo, Temuco

To Termas
de Chillán

Escuela México

After a 1939 earthquake devastated Chillán, the Mexican government of President Lázaro Cárdenas donated a new school to the city. Before its completion, at the urging of Pablo Neruda, Mexican muralist David Alfaro Siqueiros decorated the library with spectacular murals honoring both indigenous and post-Columbian figures from each country's history – the northern wall devoted to Mexico and the southern wall to Chile.

Among the Mexican figures depicted on Siqueiros' murals, which bear the inflammatory title *Muerte al Invasor (Death to the Invader)*, are the Aztec emperor Cuauhtémoc and his Spanish nemesis Hernán Cortés; revolutionary priest Miguel Hidalgo and his contemporary ally José María Morelos; the Zapotec Indian and President Benito Juárez; agrarian rebel Emiliano Zapata; and reformist President Cárdenas and his successor Manuel Avila Camacho. Chilean figures represented on the murals include the Mapuche resistance leaders Caupolicán, Lautaro and Galvarino; independence hero Bernardo O'Higgins; anti-clerical writer Francisco Bilbao; and reformist presidents José Manuel Balmaceda and Pedro Aguirre Cerda.

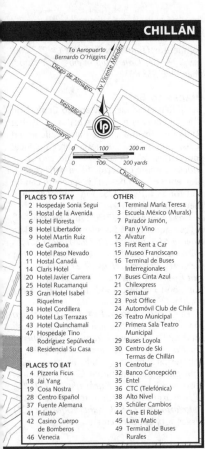

CHILLÁN

To Aeropuerto
Bernardo O'Higgins

Diego de Almagro

Av. Vicente Méndez

República

Sotomayor

Chacabuco

0   100   200 m
0   100   200 yards

PLACES TO STAY
2   Hospedaje Sonia Segui
5   Hostal de la Avenida
6   Hotel Floresta
8   Hotel Libertador
9   Hotel Martín Ruiz
    de Gamboa
10 Hotel Paso Nevado
11 Hostal Canadá
14 Claris Hotel
20 Hotel Javier Carrera
25 Hotel Rucamanqui
33 Gran Hotel Isabel
    Riquelme
34 Hotel Cordillera
40 Hotel Las Terrazas
43 Hotel Quinchamalí
47 Hospedaje Tino
    Rodríguez Sepúlveda
48 Residencial Su Casa

PLACES TO EAT
4   Pizzería Ficus
18 Jai Yang
19 Cosa Nostra
28 Centro Español
37 Fuente Alemana
41 Friatto
42 Casino Cuerpo
    de Bomberos
46 Venecia

OTHER
1   Terminal María Teresa
3   Escuela México (Murals)
7   Parador Jamón,
    Pan y Vino
12 Alvatur
13 First Rent a Car
15 Museo Franciscano
16 Terminal de Buses
    Interregionales
17 Buses Cinta Azul
21 Chilexpress
22 Sernatur
23 Post Office
24 Automóvil Club de Chile
26 Teatro Municipal
27 Primera Sala Teatro
    Municipal
29 Buses Loyola
30 Centro de Ski
    Termas de Chillán
31 Centrotur
32 Banco Concepción
35 Entel
36 CTC (Telefónica)
38 Alto Nivel
39 Schüler Cambios
44 Cine El Roble
45 Lava Matic
49 Terminal de Buses
    Rurales

Siqueiros' countryman Xavier Guerrero also participated in the project. His own simple but powerful murals, *Hermanos Mexicanos (Mexican Brothers)*, flank the library staircase. Unfortunately, the murals' state of preservation is declining.

Although the Escuela México is a functioning school rather than a museum, the staff welcome visitors to the library at O'Higgins 250, between Gamero and Vega de Saldías. It's open 9:30 am to 12:30 pm and 3 to 6 pm daily in summer; the rest of the year, hours are 9 am to 1 pm and 3 to 6 pm weekdays (except for Monday afternoon),

and 9:30 am to 12:30 pm Saturday. Admission is free, but donations are welcome.

Feria de Chillán

Chillán's open-air market, one of Chile's most colorful, is a sprawling affair with a superb selection of local crafts and mountains of fresh produce. Chilean playwright Antonio Acevedo Hernández described the scene as generating

…the sensation of a shattered rainbow fallen on the Feria, or of a fragment of the solar spectrum captured in a glorious instant, or perhaps the delirium of a mad painter projected on a massive pallet. The color is something that shouts, whirls, absorbs light and overwhelms the vision.

Open daily, but especially lively on Saturday, the market occupies the entire Plaza de la Merced, bounded by Maipón, 5 de Abril, Arturo Prat and Isabel Riquelme, but spills over into adjacent streets as well.

Museo Franciscano

Chillán's Franciscan museum displays historical materials of the missionary order that, from 1585, proselytized among the Mapuche in 15 settlements, from Chillán in the north to Río Bueno in the south. Part of its namesake church on Sargento Aldea opposite Plaza General Lagos, the museum (☎ 237-606) is 10 am to 1 pm and 3 to 7 pm open daily except Monday. Admission is free.

Parque Monumental Bernardo O'Higgins

In Chillán Viejo, only a short bus or cab ride from downtown, a tiled mural 60m long and 6m high marks O'Higgins' birthplace and illustrates scenes from his life. The associated **Centro Histórico y Cultural** displays notable objects from O'Higgins' life, but its effort to portray the viceroy's (illegitimate) son as a humble peasant is less than credible. The Centro's collection of paintings by Chilean artists and its photographic natural history display, make up for such shortcomings.

In summer, the Centro (☎ 223-536) is open 8 am to 8 pm daily; the rest of the year, hours are 8 am to 6:30 pm. Admission is free.

Places to Stay

Budget Chillán has a good selection of budget accommodations starting at about US$6.50 per person, the cheapest of which is **Hospedaje Sonia Segui** (☎ 214-879, Itata 288), whose rates include a good, generous breakfast. **Residencial Su Casa** (☎ 223-931, Cocharcas 555) is comparable at US$7. Try also **Hospedaje Tino Rodríguez Sepúlveda** (☎ 216-181, Purén 443), which charges US$8.

Centrally located **Hostal Canadá** (☎ 221-263, Av Libertad 269) is a good value for US$8 with shared bath. Comparably priced places include **Hotel Javier Carrera** (☎ 221-175, Carrera 481), and the so-so **Claris Hotel** (☎ 221-980, 18 de Septiembre 357) for US$9/16 with shared bath, US$16/23 with private bath, but without breakfast.

Mid-Range It's a bit worn, but rooms with shared bath cost only US$13/25 at **Hotel Libertador** (☎ 223-255, Av Libertad 85); rooms with private bath cost US$20/30. Constantly changing names and management (due to a family dispute), the unimpressive **Hotel Martín Ruiz de Gamboa** (☎ 221-013, O'Higgins 497) charges US$14/26 with shared bath, US$21/31 with private bath, again without breakfast.

Rooms are relatively small at **Hotel Floresta** (☎ 222-253, 18 de Septiembre 278), where rates start around US$29/36. The boxy but renovated **Hotel Quinchamalí** (☎ 223-381, fax 227-365, El Roble 634) charges about US$29/47 for singles/doubles. At **Hotel Rucamanqui** (☎ 222-927, Herminda Martín 590), in an alleyway off Constitución, rooms go for US$35/55.

Once a budget hotel, family-run **Hotel Paso Nevado** (☎ 237-788, Av Libertad 219) has undergone major improvements and rates now range from US$37/50 to US$47/56 singles/doubles. At the upper end of the range, **Hotel Cordillera** (☎ 215-211, fax 211-198, Arauco 619) charges US$39/50 but has drawn some flack for untidiness and its noisy location. **Hostal de la Avenida** (☎ 230-256, Av O'Higgins 398) charges US$41/48.

Top End Traditionally, Chillán's most prestigious accommodations are at **Gran Hotel** **Isabel Riquelme** (☎ 213-663, fax 211-541, Arauco 600), starting at US$61/75. Its newer competitor **Hotel Las Terrazas** (☎ 227-000, fax 227-001, Constitución 664, 5th floor) charges US$84/93.

Places to Eat

In Chillán's remodeled **Mercado Central**, on Maipón between 5 de Abril and Isabel Riquelme, several simple but excellent and reasonably priced cocinerías prepare local specialties. Worth a try is the *pastel de choclo*, a maize casserole filled with vegetables, chicken and beef. This specialty can be had for as little as US$3 in summer, when there's fresh corn.

Cosa Nostra (☎ 217-703, Av Libertad 398) serves good breakfasts and desserts. The **Fuente Alemana** (☎ 212-720, Arauco 661) is a fine choice for sandwiches and kuchen. For pizza, try **Pizzería Ficus** (☎ 212-176, Bulnes and Rosas) or **Venecia** (☎ 210-105, Prat 348). For good Chinese food, there's **Jai Yang** (☎ 225-429, Av Libertad 250).

The **Centro Español** (☎ 216-212, Arauco 555) has excellent Spanish-Chilean food and service. The **Casino Cuerpo de Bomberos** (El Roble and 18 de Septiembre) is, like its counterparts in other Chilean cities, a reliable place for traditional Chilean cuisine. Also worth a try is **Kuranepe** (☎ 221-409, O'Higgins 0420), north of the bus terminal.

Friatto (☎ 222-878, Isabel Riquelme 621) serves very good ice cream.

Entertainment

Two-screener **Cine El Roble** (El Roble 770) is in a new downtown shopping mall. During the university year (March to December), the Centro de Extensión de la Universidad del Biobío operates a Cine Arte at the **Teatro Municipal** (18 de Septiembre 580, 3rd floor).

Shopping

Chillán is one of central Chile's major artisan zones. Especially good are ceramics from the nearby villages of Quinchamalí, Paine and Florida. Leatherwork, basketry, horse gear and weavings are also available in the Feria de Chillán.

Getting There & Around

Chillán's modern bus station, Terminal María Teresa (☎ 272-149) is at Av O'Higgins 010, just north of Av Ecuador. A few companies, specifically identified below, still sell tickets and leave from the old Terminal de Buses Interregionales (☎ 221-014) at Constitución 01, at the corner of Av Brasil. Unless otherwise indicated, buses use the new terminal.

Tur-Bus (☎ 212-502), at the Interregionales, runs numerous northbound buses to Talca and Santiago; southbound, it leaves twice daily for Concepción and Los Angeles, and daily for Angol, Temuco, Valdivia, Osorno and Puerto Montt. Línea Azul (☎ 211-192), also at the Interregionales, has many buses that go to Concepción, plus two daily to Santiago. Buses Jota Be (☎ 215-862) makes seven journeys daily to Salto del Laja and Los Angeles, with additional services to Angol. Biotal (☎ 213-223) service includes three to Los Angeles, four to Concepción and seven to Talca. Cinta Azul (☎ 212-505), Constitución 85, goes to Concepción and Santiago.

Tas Choapa (☎ 223-062), at the Interregionales, provides regular service north and south along the Panamericana, direct service to Valparaíso-Viña del Mar and combinations to northern Chile and Mendoza, Argentina (US$33), from Santiago. It also offers direct service to Bariloche, Argentina, daily (US$31).

Sol del Sur and Sol del Pacífico also go to Santiago, Viña and Valparaíso. Buses Lit (☎ 222-960), at the Interregionales, runs similar routes. Other companies covering the Panamericana include Buses Jac, between Temuco and Santiago; Tramaca (☎ 226-922), from Santiago south to Villarrica and Pucón; Via Tur, to Santiago, Temuco and Valdivia; and Inter Sur, to Santiago.

Samples fares and approximate times include Concepción or Los Angeles (US$3, 1½ hours), Angol or Talca (US$4.50, three hours), Temuco (US$6.50, five hours), Valdivia (US$9, six hours), Puerto Montt (US$10 to US$14, nine hours), Santiago (US$8.50, six hours), and Valparaíso/Viña del Mar (US$12, eight hours).

For local and regional services, the Terminal de Buses Rurales (☎ 223-606) is on Sargento Aldea, south of Maipón. Buses Loyola (☎ 217-838), 5 de Abril 594, runs buses to Termas de Chillán in summer only.

Trains between Santiago and Temuco arrive and depart from the train station (☎ 222-424) on Av Brasil, at the west end of Libertad. There are three daily to Santiago, two to Temuco and one to Concepción.

If you prefer to drive, First Rent a Car (☎ 211-218) is at 18 de Septiembre 380.

AROUND CHILLÁN
Ninhue

Arturo Prat, the naval officer who tried to sink a Peruvian ironclad with his sword in Iquique harbor, was born in this village, 40km northwest of Chillán via the Panamericana and another good paved road. Honoring the local hero, its **Santuario Cuna de Prat** is open 10 am to 1 pm and 3 to 6:30 pm Tuesday to Sunday. Admission is free, but the exhibits are mediocre.

Via Itata buses to Ninhue (US$1, one hour) leave from Chillán's Terminal de Buses Rurales on Sargento Aldea.

Termas de Chillán

Long renowned for its **thermal baths**, Termas de Chillán has more recently become celebrated for its skiing, on the southern slopes of 3122m Volcán Chillán. The runs themselves vary from 90m to 700m in vertical drop, and from 400m to 2500m in length; there are two double chairs and five surface lifts. The season ranges from mid-May to mid-October; in summer, the peak is a walkup, with no special equipment necessary. Admission to the heated pools, open all year, costs US$20 per day for adults, US$16 for children.

In peak ski season, weekly accommodations at the resort's *Nuevo Hotel Pirigallo*, including lift tickets and many other amenities, start around US$700 per person, double occupancy, with half-board, rising as high as US$1155 with full board. There are relatively inexpensive bunk accommodations available starting at US$530 to US$955 per week with half-board, including lift tickets.

MIDDLE CHILE

At the more luxurious *Gran Hotel Termas de Chillán*, rates start at US$895 to US$1700 per person. At both, three-day packages are also available.

Reservations can be made at Centro de Ski Termas de Chillán, in Chillán (☎ 223-887, fax 223-576, ventachi@termachillan.cl) at Av Libertad 1042; or in Santiago (☎ 02-233-1313, fax 231-5963, ventanac@termachillan.cl) at Av Providencia 2237, Oficina P-41, Providencia. For more information see the boxed text 'Online Services' in the Facts for the Visitor chapter.

In the summer off-season, the Pirigallo charges US$105/185 for singles/doubles with full board; the Gran Hotel costs US$154/225. At that time, camping is possible at *Camping Termas de Chillán* (☎ 223-404 in Chillán) for US$12 per site. *Parador Jamón, Pan y Vino* (☎ 220-018, fax 225-977), Gamero 607 in Chillán, offers week-long fishing, hiking and camping excursions in the cordillera in and around the springs. Doubles normally cost US$105 with half-board.

Getting There & Away Termas de Chillán is 80km east of the city of Chillán; all but the last 9km of the road is paved. Buses Loyola (☎ 217-838), 5 de Abril 594 in the city provides transportation to the springs in summertime only. Contact ski areas for winter transport; chains are obligatory for all rental cars.

CONCEPCIÓN
☎ 41
Concepción's industry, convenient energy resources, port facilities and universities have combined to make the capital of Region VIII (Biobío) Chile's second most important city after Santiago. Due to earthquakes throughout its history, practically nothing remains of the city's colonial past, but the modern downtown has managed to integrate commerce, industry and education without sacrificing its human scale. Concepción has become a major export point for wood products from southern Chile, but the cost of extracting coal from the mines across the Biobío has made that industry economically unsustainable.

The inhabitants of Concepción are known as *penquistas* after the city's original site at the nearby town of Penco. By the 1992 census, Concepción had a population of about 310,000, and, combined with the port city of Talcahuano, it still comprises a metropolitan area of roughly half a million inhabitants. The creation of a new comuna at San Pedro, on the south bank of the Rió Biobío, has altered the area's political geography, though, and Concepción's population has technically fallen to about 206,000.

History
Founded in 1551 by Pedro de Valdivia, menaced constantly by Indians and devastated by earthquakes in 1730 and 1751, Concepción moved several times before settling at its present site in 1764. After a major Mapuche uprising in 1598, Spain never again seriously contested Mapuche control of the area south of the Biobío, and Concepción remained one of the empire's southernmost fortified outposts. Because they would facilitate seaborne communication with Santiago via Valparaíso, the fine harbors of Talcahuano and San Vicente were major reasons for the city's location.

From accounts of the late colonial period, Concepción much resembled other Chilean cities, where differences in the types of dwellings reflected clear distinctions between social classes. A British visitor in 1804 wrote:

The houses are commonly one storey high, but some are two, built of...*adoves*, large sun-dried bricks, and all of them are tiled. The largest have a courtyard in front, with an entrance through arched porches, and heavy folding doors...The windows have iron gratings, with many parts of them gilt, and inside shutters, but no glass. This article has been too dear, and it is consequently used only in the windows of the principal dwelling apartments of the richer classes. On each side of the court, or *patio*, there are rooms for domestics, the younger branches of the family, and other purposes.

The dwellings of lower classes are on the same plan, except that they have no courts or patios, the fronts being open to the street, but they usually have a garden at the back, where the kitchen is built separately from the house, as a precaution against fire.

This type of construction made the city especially susceptible to earthquake damage, while its low-lying site exposed it to the power of seismic seawaves. After experiencing a major quake near Valdivia in 1835, Darwin entered the Bahía de Concepción to find, as a result of the ensuing tsunami:

...the whole coast being strewed over with timber and furniture as if a thousand ships had been wrecked. Besides chairs, tables, book-shelves etc in great numbers, there were several roofs of cottages, which had been transported almost whole. The store-houses at Talcahuano had been burst open, and great bags of cotton, yerba, and other valuable merchandise were scattered on the shore.

After independence, Concepción's isolation from Santiago, coupled with the presence of lignite (brown coal) near Lota, a coastal town south of Concepción, fomented an autonomous industrial tradition. The export of wheat for the California gold rush market further spurred the area's economic growth, and secondary industries emerged later in the form of glassblowing, timber and woolen and cotton textiles. The railway reached Concepción in 1872 and, after the Mapuche threat receded, the government bridged the Biobío to improve access to the mines and give the city a strategic role in the colonization of La Frontera, the present-day lakes region.

Mining of coal, a scarce resource in South America, took place in westward-sloping seams as much as 3km beneath the sea, but high production costs along with diminishing returns have eliminated the industry. Since WWII, the major industrial project to benefit Concepción has been the Huachipato steel plant, built with US assistance. Inexpensive shipping and local energy supplies – now hydropower – have made the industry competitive despite the fact that the iron ore comes from Coquimbo, 800km north, and limestone comes from the Madre de Diós islands, 1500km south.

Despite Concepción's industrial importance, wages and living standards are relatively low. This, coupled with activism at the Universidad de Concepción, made the city and its industrial hinterland the locus of a highly politicized labor movement that was a bulwark of support for Salvador Allende and the Unidad Popular. As a center of leftist opposition, the area suffered more than other regions under the military dictatorship of 1973–89. The labor movement has remained relatively strong, however. In response to a report questioning Lota's economic viability, the state coal company Enacar's dismissal of nearly 100 workers in mid-1996 occasioned a contentious strike and vigorous protests from miners, who blocked highways in southern Chile.

One indicator of the continuing strength of labor is that the Biobío is the only region in which the left-center Concertación party has been able to win both national senate seats by more than doubling the vote of right-wing parties under Pinochet's custom-drawn constitution. Nevertheless, this was not enough to save the coal industry, and the government bought out the miners with a package of early retirement and training benefits – leaving the undersea seams as a tourist attraction.

Orientation

Concepción sits on the north bank of the Río Biobío, Chile's only significant navigable waterway. Cerro Caracol, a scenic overlook, blocks any eastward expansion so that Concepción and its port of Talcahuano, 15km northwest on the sheltered Bahía de Concepción, are rapidly growing together. Concepción's standard grid centers on Plaza Independencia, a pleasantly landscaped space with an attractive fountain. Few older buildings have survived – the drab Iglesia Catedral and other utilitarian structures on the surrounding streets Aníbal Pinto, Barros Arana, Caupolicán and O'Higgins testify to the city's vulnerability to earthquakes. The bustling plaza is often the site of impromptu performances by actors and street musicians, while Barros Arana and Aníbal Pinto are lively pedestrian malls for two or three blocks to the north and west of the plaza.

Four blocks east of the plaza, Parque Ecuador is a pleasant refuge from the busy downtown. The park's border, Av Lamas, becomes Esmeralda southwest of Prat and

MIDDLE CHILE

MIDDLE CHILE

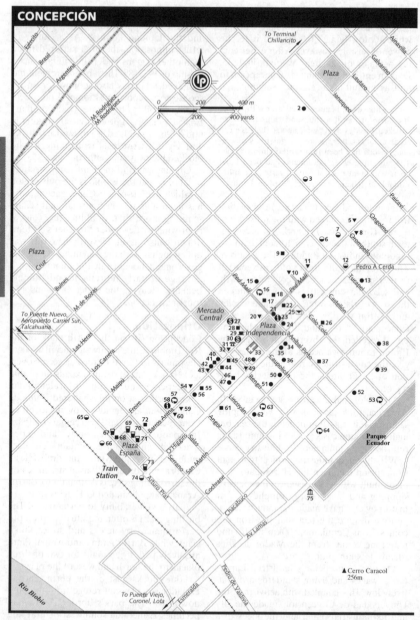

CONCEPCIÓN

To Terminal de Buses
Collao (Puchacay),
Chillán, Santiago

Barrio
Universitario

Plaza
Perú

CAFÉS & PUBS
28 Café Caribe
29 Café Haití
67 El Medio Toro
69 Choripan
70 Mezcal
71 Matador
73 Treinta y Tanto,
   Sandunga, Comanche Pub

OTHER
1 Automóvil Club de Chile
2 Alta Luz
3 Buses Lit
4 Hospital Regional
6 Tur-Bus
7 Buses Tas Choapa
8 Buses Igi Llaima
13 Sala Andes
14 Casa del Arte
15 Feria Artesanal
16 Peruvian Consulate
19 Concepción Soccer
   Club Offices
20 Spanish Consulate
21 EFE Venta de Pasajes
23 Sernatur
24 Librería Caribe
25 Post Office, Chilesat
27 Inter-Santiago
28 La Gruta
30 Afex
31 Entel
33 Iglesia Catedral
34 Librería Manantial
35 Cine Concepción
36 Laverap
38 Budget Rent a Car
39 Instituto Chileno-Alemán,
   Sala Lessing
40 Avant
42 LanChile
47 Cyber Café
48 Ladeco
50 Instituto Chileno-
   Norteamericano
51 Instituto Chileno-Británico
52 Avis Rent a Car
53 French Consulate,
   Instituto Chileno-Francés
56 Cine Regina
57 Italian Consulate
58 Conaf
62 Instituto Chileno-Español
63 Argentine Consulate
64 German Consulate
65 Buses Los Alces
66 Buses Jota Ewert
74 Buses Biobio
75 Galería de Historia

PLACES TO STAY
9 Hotel Cruz del Sur
17 Hotel Ritz
18 Residencial San Sebastián,
   Residencial Antuco
22 Hotel Maquehue
26 Hotel Alonso de Ercilla
28 Hotel El Araucano
37 Hotel della Cruz
41 Hotel Alborada
44 Residencial Metro
45 Hotel San Sebastián
46 Residencial O'Higgins
55 Hotel El Dorado
61 Hotel Terrano
68 Hotel Cecil
72 Hotel Concepción

PLACES TO EAT
5 China Town
8 Casablanca
10 El Novillo Loco
11 Centro Italiano
20 Centro Español
32 Bocatto
43 Chela's
49 Fuente Alemana
54 El Rancho de Julio
59 Chung-Hwa
60 El Naturista

leads to the Puente Viejo (old bridge), which continues south to the *Costa del Carbón* (Coast of Coal), where cities like Coronel and Lota supply the energy for Concepción's industry. A newer and better bridge, the Puente Nuevo, crosses the river to the west.

Information

Sernatur (☎ 227-976, serna08@entelchile.net), Aníbal Pinto 460, is well stocked with maps and brochures and has a helpful, well-informed staff. In summer, when there's usually an English speaker on hand, it's open 8:30 am to 8 pm daily; the rest of the year, hours are 8:30 am to 1 pm and 3 to 5:30 pm weekdays.

Acchi (☎ 311-968), the Automóvil Club de Chile, Freire 1867, is also a good source of information.

Befitting its commercial and industrial importance, Concepción has a number of consulates; see the Facts for the Visitor chapter for addresses and telephone numbers.

For changing traveler's checks, try Inter-Santiago, Caupolicán 521, Local 58, or Afex at Barros Arana 565, Local 57. There are numerous downtown ATMs.

The post office is at O'Higgins 799, corner of Colo Colo; Chilesat is at the same address. Entel is at Barros Arana 541, Local 2.

The Cyber Café (☎ 238-394), O'Higgins 443, offers Internet access.

Alta Luz travel agency (☎ 241-039) is at Paicaví 891. South Expediciones (☎ 09-442-9423), Gesswein 44, leads adventure travel excursions such as river rafting, mountain biking and horseback riding trips.

As a university town, Concepción has a good selection of bookstores. Try Librería Manantial (☎ 223-614) at O'Higgins 680, or Librería Caribe, Aníbal Pinto 450.

Concepción has more than its share of binational cultural centers: the Instituto Chileno-Norteamericano (☎ 225-506) at Caupolicán 315, the Instituto Chileno-Británico (☎ 242-300) at San Martín 531, the Instituto Chileno-Alemán (☎ 229-287) at Chacabuco 840, the Instituto Chileno-Francés (☎ 226-813) at Colo Colo 1 and the Instituto Chileno-Español (☎ 244-573) at San Martín 450, 2nd floor.

MIDDLE CHILE

Ercilla & the Araucanian Wars

In the early colonial times, armed conflict between Spaniards and Chile's Indian peoples was so bloody, protracted and pervasive that Chilean historian Alvaro Jara entitled his history of the period *Guerra y Sociedad en Chile* (War and Society in Chile). Yet, in spite of frequent brutality, the adversaries did not lack respect for each other and some even managed to see the broader picture and tragedy of the era even as they participated in it. The most prominent of these was Spanish soldier-poet Alonso de Ercilla, whose epic poem *La Araucana*, based on personal experience, is one of the classics of colonial Latin American literature.

Born into a noble Basque family in 1533 and educated in the classics, Ercilla entered the service of the Spanish royal family at the age of 15. At 21, on a visit to London, he heard of Pedro de Valdivia's death and resolved to participate in the Spanish campaign against the Araucanians. He spent seven years in the New World, including more than a year and a half exploring Chile and fighting the Indians, before returning to Spain in 1563. Over the course of two decades, starting in 1569, he published his lengthy poem, in three parts. Although the epic form lends itself to romanticizing events, and Ercilla's belief in Spanish superiority is evident, the poem is notable for its fidelity to historical events and its regard for, and analysis of, an opponent feared and denigrated by most Spaniards. While the Araucanians bedeviled Ercilla and his countrymen, he could still admire their courage, tactics and adaptability.

The Araucanians' unconventional tactics were difficult to counter. To offset their opponents' mobility, they retreated into the forest, lured the Spaniards into swampy areas where horses were ineffective and dismounted the riders with ropes and clubs. When possible they fought in the midday heat, quickly exhausting the heavily armored Spaniards, and set traps with sharpened stakes where (in Ercilla's words) surprised soldiers would die 'impaled…in agony.'

Like the North American Plains Indians, the Araucanians themselves became expert horsemen, raiding the Argentine pampas for mounts, taming them and driving them back across the Andes to aid the resistance. Although Spain's commitment to dominate the region south of the Biobío was less than it might have been had the economic incentives been greater

Conaf (☎ 220-094) is at Barros Arana 215, Laverap laundry is at Caupolicán 334, and Concepción's Hospital Regional (☎ 237-445) is at San Martín and Av Roosevelt, eight blocks north of Plaza Independencia.

Galería de Historia

Vivid dioramas of local and regional history are the strong point of this fine museum on the edge of Parque Ecuador near Cerro Caracol. Among the subjects are pre-Columbian Mapuche subsistence, the arrival of the Spaniards and battles between the two peoples (with fine representations of Mapuche battle tactics), construction of fortifications at Penco (the original site of Concepción), treaty signings, military and literary figure Alonso de Ercilla, Chile's declaration of independence, the 1851 battle of Loncomilla, the devastating 1939 earthquake (15,000 houses destroyed) and a finely detailed scale model of a local factory.

At Victor Lamas and Lincoyán, the Galería (☎ 231-830) is open 10 am to 1:30 pm and 3 to 6:30 pm Tuesday to Friday, 10 am to 2 pm and 3 to 7 pm weekends. Admission is free.

Casa del Arte

La Presencia de América Latina, a massive mural by Mexican artist Jorge González Camarena (a protégé of José Clemente Orozco) is the highlight of this university art museum, which also contains two rooms of landscapes and portraits.

In the Barrio Universitario, at Chacabuco and Larenas, the Casa del Arte (☎ 204-290) is open 10 am to 6 pm Tuesday to Friday, 10 am

Ercilla & the Araucanian Wars

(there were no great bonanza mines to grab the Crown's attention), its lack of success against the natives was due to the its hierarchical command system – one that discouraged initiative and improvisation. Conversely, one of the major factors in Araucanian success was the absence of hierarchy and organization; in the more egalitarian Indian society, no single leader was indispensable.

Ercilla openly praised the intelligence and bravery of leaders such as Lautaro, Caupolicán and Colo Colo, some of whom distinguished themselves at a very young age. Captured by the Spaniards at age 15 and forced to serve three years as a scout, Lautaro escaped to play a leading role at the battle of Tucapel (where Colo Colo's forces killed Pedro de Valdivia), and became an important military leader. Caupolicán, named *toqui* by the older Colo Colo, helped defeat the Spaniards at Tucapel and later suffered a gruesome but stoic death – he was only 22 years old – when, in 1557, the Spaniards impaled him on a sharpened wooden pole (although legend says the disdainful cacique threw them off the platform and sat down of his own volition).

Ercilla's literary legacy still permeates Chilean society, from popular culture and tourism to revolutionary politics. The country's most popular soccer team is known simply as Colo Colo. A series of historical markers on the coastal highway south of Concepción marks the Ruta de La Araucana, immortalizing the bravery of caciques such as Galvarino, who quietly suffered the amputation of both his hands but escaped to help lead his people against the Spanish invaders. One of Chile's most troublesome guerrilla movements, which declined to cease its resistance for some time after return of democracy, adopted the name of Lautaro.

The Mapuche, direct heirs of the Araucanian legacy, have regained visibility over the past few years as, in response to incursions on traditional lands by hydroelectric and forestry projects, they have demanded restoration of indigenous rights. While there are disagreements within the Mapuche community as to tactics and even goals, it once again forced the Chilean state to take it seriously.

to 4 pm Saturday and 10 am to 2 pm Sunday. Admission is free.

Barrio Estación
Fronting on Arturo Prat between Maipú and Freire, the area surrounding Concepción's train station is undergoing a renaissance similar to those in Santiago's Barrio Bellavista and Barrio Brasil, with older buildings undergoing rehab as stylish bars and restaurants. Within the next couple of years, the station itself is due to become the Intendencia Regional, or regional government, after construction of a new station farther to the northwest.

Special Events
Organized by the universities, Concepción's Fiesta de la Primavera (Festival of Spring),

commemorating the founding of the city, lasts an entire week in early October.

Places to Stay
Prices for accommodations show little seasonal variability, since Concepción's industrial and commercial importance insulates it from the usual tourist-trade fluctuations. Some of the town's budget accommodations are seriously overpriced and mid-range places are often better values. It's worth asking about IVA discounts for mid-range and top-end hotels.

Budget In summer, when university students vacate the town, there are plenty of inexpensive accommodations, but the rest of the year it can be hard to find something reasonable. ***Residencial Metro*** (☎ 225-305,

Barros Arana 464) has spacious rooms with high ceilings for US$12/20 singles/doubles with breakfast; equally spacious *Residencial O'Higgins (☎ 228-303, O'Higgins 457)* charges US$10 per person with a skimpy breakfast.

Residencial Antuco (☎ 235-485, Barros Arana 741, Departamento 31) charges US$16/26 singles/doubles with shared bath and breakfast. Prices are virtually identical with shared bath at *Residencial San Sebastián (☎ 242-710, fax 243-412, Barros Arana 741, Departamento 35)*, where rooms with private bath cost US$22/33.

Mid-Range In the up-and-coming Barrio Estación, well-worn *Hotel Cecil (☎ 230-677, Barros Arana 9)*, has singles/doubles for US$25/38. *Hotel San Sebastián (☎/fax 243-412, Rengo 463)* is a better value at US$31/41.

On a quiet street but still central, *Hotel della Cruz (☎/fax 240-016, Aníbal Pinto 240)* is a good choice for US$36/52 with a substantial breakfast, but some rooms are small. At *Hotel Ritz (☎ 226-696, fax 243-249, Barros Arana 721)*, rates of US$38/59 seem excessive.

Toward the upper end of the range is *Hotel Alonso de Ercilla (☎ 227-984, fax 230-053, Colo Colo 334)* at US$42/76. *Hotel Concepción (☎ 228-851, fax 230-948, Serrano 512)* charges US$46/67. At amiable *Hotel Maquehue (☎ 238-348, fax 238-350, Barros Arana 786)* rates are US$49/64, but it's worth asking about discounts.

Try also *Hotel Cruz del Sur (☎ 230-944, fax 235-655, Freire 889)*, where rooms go for US$49/67, including breakfast. *Hotel El Dorado (☎ 229-400, fax 231-018, Barros Arana 348)* is the next step up at US$56/71. The newest entry in the hotel scene is *Hotel Terrano (☎ 240-078, O'Higgins 340)*, which starts at US$60/72 and has most modern conveniences, including its own gym.

Top End Concepción has two downtown luxury hotels. *Hotel Alborada (☎/fax 242-144, Barros Arana 457)* charges US$91/99 including a buffet breakfast; there are substantial weekend discounts at this otherwise business-oriented Best Western affiliate. Rates at *Hotel El Araucano (☎ 230-606, fax 230-690, Caupolicán 521)* start at US$78 double, but most of its rooms range US$109 to US$114.

Places to Eat

Concepción's central market, occupying an entire block bounded by Caupolicán, Maipú, Rengo and Freire, has a multitude of cheap and excellent eateries. However beware of waitresses who drag customers – literally – into their venues. There's not much difference among these places in price, quality or decor, but *Don José* offers a superb pastel de choclo, a regional specialty that's a meal in itself.

The *Fuente Alemana (☎ 228-307, O'Higgins 513)* serves good sandwiches and desserts. *El Naturista (☎ 230-928, Barros Arana 244)* offers vegetarian fare at lunchtime only. *Chela's (☎ 243-367, Barros Arana 405)* serves outstanding pastel de choclo, sandwiches, ice cream and cold beer. *Bocatto (☎ 243-334, Barros Arana 533)* serves sandwiches, pizza and ice cream.

Off Barros Arana, *El Novillo Loco (☎ 241-114, Pasaje Portales 539)* and Uruguayan-run *Casablanca (☎ 247-107, Barros Arana 1102)* are good spots for carnivores, along with *El Rancho de Julio (☎ 228-207, Barros Arana 337)*, which also serves pizza. The *Centro Español (☎ 230-685, Barros Arana 675)* and the *Centro Italiano (☎ 230-724, Barros Arana 935)* add a bit of European flavor. For Chinese cuisine, visit *Chung-Hwa (☎ 229-539, Barros Arana 262)* or *China Town (☎ 233-218, Barros Arana 1115)*.

For a cheap stand-up cappuccino, try *Café Haití (☎ 230-755, Caupolicán 511, Local 7)* or *Café Caribe (☎ 241-937, Caupolicán 521, Local 34)*.

Entertainment

Cinema Unlike many Chilean towns where video has meant the demise of the cinema, Concepción still has a couple decent movie theaters: the *Cine Concepción (☎ 227-193, O'Higgins 650)* and the *Cine Regina (☎ 225-904, Barros Arana 340)*. There are also films at the university and at the various cultural institutes mentioned previously in this section.

Theater & Music Concepción has several important music and drama venues, so check the schedule for the *Teatro Concepción (☎ 227-193, O'Higgins 650)*, the *Sala Andes (☎ 227-264, Tucapel 374)*, the Instituto Chileno-Alemán's *Sala Lessing (☎ 229-287, Chacabuco 840)* or the *Casa del Arte (☎ 234-985, Chacabuco and Larenas)* in the Barrio Universitario.

Pubs Southwest of the immediate downtown area, across from the train station, the rejuvenated Barrio Estación is home to several popular pub-restaurants, most notably *Treinta y Tanto (☎ 240-451, Prat 404)*, which has outstanding empanadas and *vino navegado* (mulled wine); it's open for dinner only. Other choices for barhoppers include *Sandunga (Prat 438)*, the *Comanche Pub (Prat 442)*, *Matador (Prat 528)*, *Mezcal (Prat 532)*, *Choripan (Prat 546)* and *El Medio Toro (Prat 592)*.

Spectator Sports
Concepción's first-division soccer team (☎ 242-684) has offices at Colo Colo 486. Matches take place at Estadio Collao, on Av General Bonilla near the main bus terminal.

Shopping
Local and regional crafts are on display in the Mercado Central, the Feria Artesanal at Freire 757 and at La Gruta at Caupolicán 521, Local 64. The best things to look for are woolens, basketry, ceramics, wood carvings and leather goods.

Getting There & Away
Air LanChile (☎ 229-138), Barros Arana 451, averages more than four flights daily to Santiago (US$64 to US$88) and flies to Valdivia weekdays (US$44) and to Punta Arenas Wednesday and Saturday (US$115 to US$158). Ladeco (☎ 248-824), O'Higgins 533, flies four times daily to Santiago except on weekends, when there are two flights daily.

Avant (☎ 246-710), Barros Arana 455, averages almost four flights daily to Santiago (US$69 to US$112). It also flies to Temuco Tuesday, Thursday and weekends (US$26 to US$42), to Temuco and Puerto Montt weekdays (US$79 to US$113), to Valdivia (US$44 to US$79) daily except Saturday and to Puerto Montt and Punta Arenas Saturday (US$146 to US$196).

Bus Concepción has two long-distance bus terminals. Most carriers leave from Terminal de Buses Collao (☎ 316-666), on the outskirts of town at Tegualda 860, a side street off Av General Bonilla (Ruta 148), the highway to Chillán, but a few companies use the separate Terminal Chillancito (☎ 315-036), Camilo Henríquez 2565, the northward extension of Bulnes. Because of the terminals' peripheral locations, many companies maintain a more central office as well. Unless otherwise indicated, companies use Terminal Collao (sometimes called Terminal Puchacay). Buses and taxi colectivos connect downtown with both the Chillancito (from the corner of Maipú and Rengo) and Collao (via Calle San Martín, anywhere in the downtown area) bus terminals.

Tur-Bus (☎ 315-555), Tucapel 530 and at Terminal Chillancito, runs 13 buses daily to Santiago, runs three to Valparaíso-Viña del Mar, and also goes southbound to Temuco, Valdivia and Puerto Montt.

Sol del Pacífico offers 11 buses daily to Santiago, some of them continuing to Valparaíso and Viña del Mar. Buses Lit (☎ 230-722), Orompello 750, runs one each to Santiago and Valparaíso; other companies cover the same route, including Sol del Sur (☎ 313-841, four daily), Estrella del Sur (☎ 321-383, eight daily), Transtur (five daily) and Intersur (nine daily).

Buses Tas Choapa (☎ 312-639), Barros Arana 1081, goes twice daily to Santiago and provides excellent connections to northern Chile and Argentina. Varmontt (☎ 314-010) goes nightly to Puerto Montt, while Buses Igi Llaima (☎ 312-498) at Tucapel 432 leaves five times daily for Temuco and Puerto Montt, as does Cruz del Sur (☎ 314-372). Tur-Bus, Igi Llaima and

Cruz del Sur all provide service to Valdivia as well.

Buses Biobío (☎ 310-764), Arturo Prat 416, has frequent service to Los Angeles, Angol and Temuco, though Jota Be (☎ 312-652) also has numerous services to Los Angeles and to Salto del Laja. Línea Azul (☎ 311-126) is the most frequent to Los Angeles, about every 20 minutes from Chillancito, but Igi Llaima has another 10.

For services down the coast to Coronel, Lota, Arauco, Lebú, Cañete and Contulmo, try Buses Los Alces (☎ 240-855) at Prat 669 or Buses Jota Ewert (☎ 229-212) at Arturo Prat 535.

Ticket prices vary considerably among companies, but typical fares from Concepción are as follows: to Chillán or Los Angeles (US$3, two hours), Angol (US$3, 1½ hours), Talca (US$5 to US$6, four hours), Temuco (US$5 to US$6, four hours), Valdivia (US$7 to US$10, six hours), Puerto Montt (US$10 to US$19, seven hours), Santiago (US$7 to US$14, seven hours) and Valparaíso/Viña del Mar (US$13 to US$18, nine hours).

Train Concepción's train station (☎ 227-777) is on Arturo Prat at the end of Barros Arana, but EFE also has a venta de pasajes (ticket office; ☎ 225-286) at Aníbal Pinto 478, Local 3. Trains leave nightly at 10:30 pm. Fares are US$14 salón, US$24 cama alta, and US$32 cama baja.

Getting Around

To/From the Airport Aeropuerto Carriel Sur is 5km northwest of downtown, on the road to Talcahuano. Several companies run airport minibuses for about US$3, including Airport Express (☎ 236-444), Turismo Ritz (☎ 237-637) and Taxivan (☎ 248-748). All three connect with flights from in front of the appropriate LanChile, Ladeco or Avant offices, but will also pick up passengers at hotels.

Car Concepción has several rental agencies to choose among: the Automóvil Club de Chile (Acchi; ☎ 317-111) at Freire 1867, Budget (☎ 245-550) at Castellón 134 and Avis (☎ 235-837) at Chacabuco 726.

AROUND CONCEPCIÓN
Museo Huáscar

Built in Birkenhead, England, in 1865, captured from the Peruvian navy in 1879 and now on display in Talcahuano, the *Huáscar* was one of the world's earliest ironclad battleships. Despite a nominal display of naval portraits, it's less a museum than an object, owing its remarkable state of preservation to the labor of naval conscripts whose spit-and-polish maintenance work never ends.

From Concepción, take any 'Galaxias' bus that has 'Base Naval' on its placard along Calle San Martín to the Apostadero Naval, beyond Talcahuano's Club de Yates on Av Villaroel. You'll be required to leave your passport at the gate. Photography is permitted, but only with the port of Talcahuano or the open sea as background – do *not* photograph other naval vessels or any part of the base itself. Opening hours are from 9:30 am to 12:30 pm and 1:30 to 5:30 pm daily except Monday. Admission to the museum (☎ 505-016) costs US$1.25 for adults, US$0.80 for children.

La Costa del Carbón

As an advertising slogan, the 'Coast of Coal' may sound improbable, but beach towns south of the Río Biobío draw substantial crowds to and around Coronel (which reeks of fishmeal), Lota, Arauco and Península Lebú. The best day trip is Lota, the site of the 14-hectare **Parque Isidora Cousiño**. The town's mid-century company-town architecture is also worth a look. Open 9 am to 8 pm daily, the park is a remarkable demonstration of the resilient survival of cultivated beauty alongside massive slag heaps. Admission costs US$2.50 for adults, half that for children.

Since the demise of the local coal industry, part of the government's response to worsening economic conditions has been to train former miners as guides to the **Mina Chiflón Carlos**, in the coast range behind Lota. Reservations are essential for visits to the mine, which take place from 9 am to 8 pm daily from November to March, 9 am to 6 pm the rest of the year; contact the Fundación de Chile (☎ 870-682, 871-459). Visits to the mine

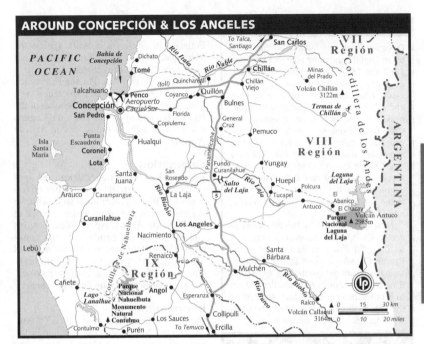

AROUND CONCEPCIÓN & LOS ANGELES

cost US$1.25 for adults, US$0.65 for children; a 45-minute descent into the mine costs US$6 for adults, US$3 for children.

Coronel, just north of Lota, holds a **Muestra Cultural de Folklore** (folklore festival) in early February, during its traditional **Semanas Culturales de Coronel**.

Ruta de La Araucana

Local and regional tourist authorities have established a series of historical markers at famous sites from soldier-poet Alonso de Ercilla y Zuñiga's epic poem *La Araucana*, an account of Mapuche resistance to the Spanish invasions of the 16th century (see the boxed text 'Ercilla & the Araucanian Wars' earlier in this chapter). The first two markers have been placed near Punta Escuadrón, 22km south of Concepción, and near Arauco, about 2km west of the town of Carampangue.

Escuadrón is the site of the **Hito Histórico Galvarino**, commemorating the battle of Lagunillas (1557), where the Mapuche *toqui* (chief) Galvarino submitted stoically as the Spaniards severed both his hands with their swords, after which he placed his own head on the block. The Spaniards refrained from executing him, but he swore revenge. On being recaptured years later, he may have been executed, though some historians believe he killed himself to avoid Spanish retribution.

The **Hito Histórico Prueba y Elección de Caupolicán** marks the site where Mapuche leader Colo Colo chose Caupolicán to lead the indigenous resistance that, ultimately, routed the Spaniards and executed Pedro de Valdivia in 1553.

At Cañete, 135km south of Concepción, the disappointing **Museo Araucano Juan Antonio Ríos** (☎ 611-093) takes its name from a 20th-century Chilean president born nearby, rather than for any of the Mapuche people it presumably esteems. Exhibits detail historical antecedents, economic activities,

Beauty Among the Slag

Designed for the influential Cousiño family by an English landscape architect between 1862 and 1872, Parque Isidora Cousiño is an incongruous plantation; it features exotic trees surrounded by rose gardens and other flower beds, ponds with black-necked swans, and loads of neoclassical statuary (and one representation of Caupolicán). Among its trees are redwoods, cypresses, acacias and the like, but very few Chilean natives. The park seems to prove that beauty can thrive alongside blight, namely, the conspicuous slag heaps to the north. Some plants have even colonized the toxic tailings.

Now administered by the private Fundación Chile, which seems committed to restoring the glories of the Cousiño years, Parque Cousiño is open to the public in spring and summer (September to March) 8 am to 8 pm Monday to Saturday, 10 am to 8 pm Sunday and holidays; the rest of the year it closes at 6 pm. Admission costs US$2 for adults, US$1 for children.

funerary customs and art, particularly silverwork. The museum also includes a small garden of native plants and a model replica of a Spanish fortification. It's open 9:30 am to 12:30 pm and 2 to 6 pm daily. Admission costs US$1, half that for children or retired individuals.

Monumento Natural Contulmo

A worthwhile stop for travelers passing through en route to Angol and Los Angeles, Monumento Natural Contulmo is a small (84-hectare) forest corridor abutting the highway. An 8km trail leads through woods as dense and verdant as a tropical rain forest; plaques identify major tree species, but the giant ferns and climbing vines are just as intriguing. There are picnic facilities, but the nearest camping is at Lago Lanalhue, a few kilometers to the west, where **Camping Municipal** has 40 sites for US$6.

LOS ANGELES
☎ 43

Founded in 1739 as a bulwark against the Mapuche, Santa María de Los Angeles is not Hollywood, and the closest thing to a freeway is the two-lane Panamericana that skirts the town to the east. It does, however, have good access to the upper reaches of the Río Biobío and to Parque Nacional Laguna del Laja, which includes 2985m Volcán Antuco.

Orientation

Los Angeles (population 95,000) is an agricultural and industrial service center 110km south of Chillán. Its commercial downtown is small, mostly contained within a block of the Plaza de Armas. Apart from that, it's almost exclusively residential. The channeled Estero Quilque, two blocks north of the plaza, flows through the city into parklands on its western edge. East of the plaza, Av Alemania leads to the Panamericana.

Information

There's a municipal tourist office (☎ 340-161) on the 2nd floor of the museum at the southeast corner of the Plaza de Armas, but it's inadequately staffed and the information is skimpy. There's also a small private office on Caupolicán, alongside the post office on the south side of the Plaza de Armas, but it's also pretty shaky.

Probably the best source is Cayaquí Turismo (☎ 328-546, fax 322-248), Lautaro 252, a travel agency which also has the best city map at a small charge. Another reliable source of information is the Automóvil Club de Chile (☎ 314-209), Caupolicán 201.

LanChile (☎ 323-324) is at Av Alemania 320 and Ladeco is at Lautaro 188.

Inter Bruna (☎ 313-812), Caupolicán 350, changes money. Banco BHIF has an ATM at Colón 492, but there are several others.

The post office is on Caupolicán, on the south side of the Plaza de Armas. CTC (Telefónica) long-distance offices are at the bus terminal. Entel is at Colo Colo 489, Local 1, Chilesat at Av Alemania 321.

Lavaseco (☎ 321-098), at Lautaro 551, is Los Angeles' laundry.

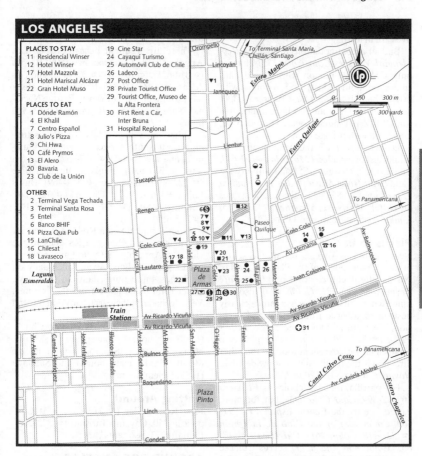

LOS ANGELES

PLACES TO STAY
11 Residencial Winser
12 Hotel Winser
17 Hotel Mazzola
21 Hotel Mariscal Alcázar
22 Gran Hotel Muso

PLACES TO EAT
1 Dónde Ramón
4 El Khalil
7 Centro Español
8 Julio's Pizza
9 Chi Hwa
10 Café Prymos
13 El Alero
20 Bavaria
23 Club de la Unión

OTHER
2 Terminal Vega Techada
3 Terminal Santa Rosa
5 Entel
6 Banco BHIF
14 Pizza Qua Pub
15 LanChile
16 Chilesat
18 Lavaseco

19 Cine Star
24 Cayaquí Turismo
25 Automóvil Club de Chile
26 Ladeco
27 Post Office
28 Private Tourist Office
29 Tourist Office, Museo de
   la Alta Frontera
30 First Rent a Car,
   Inter Bruna
31 Hospital Regional

MIDDLE CHILE

Los Angeles' Hospital Regional (☎ 321-456) is on Av Ricardo Vicuña, just east of Los Carrera.

Museo de la Alta Frontera

Though most of its exhibits are mundane, Los Angeles' municipal museum has an extraordinary collection of Mapuche silverwork that's worth a stopover despite the installation's lack of interpretation or description. The museum is at Caupolicán and Colón, 2nd floor, at the southeast corner of the Plaza de Armas, in the same building as the tourist office.

Organized Tours

Cayaquí Turismo (☎ 322-248), Lautaro 252, offers a city tour for US$18 (minimum two people), as well as day trips to the Alto Biobío (US$58) and to Parque Nacional Laguna del Laja (US$66); both the latter include hotel lunches.

Places to Stay

Los Angeles differs from many other Chilean cities in that many of its accommodations are along the Panamericana rather than in the city itself, because of the Salto del Laja, the area's biggest nearby attraction.

Nevertheless, the most reasonable alternatives are in town.

Budget accommodations are scarce. *Residencial Winser (Colo Colo 335)* charges only US$10 per person with shared bath (these rooms fill up fast), US$34 double with private bath. Its sister *Hotel Winser (☎ 320-348, Rengo 138)* is an excellent alternative for US$12 per person with shared bath, US$30/38 with private bath.

Dating from 1907, the central, architecturally distinctive *Hotel Mazzola (☎ 321-643, Lautaro 579)* charges US$18/23 with private bath. *Gran Hotel Muso (☎ 313-183, Valdivia 222)* charges US$51/67 singles/doubles; rates at *Hotel Mariscal Alcázar (☎ 311-725, Lautaro 385)* start around US$55/70.

Places to Eat

Nearly all of Los Angeles' restaurants are on or near Colón, north of the Plaza de Armas. An excellent choice for breakfast, *Café Prymos (☎ 323-731, Colón 400)* also has sandwiches, outstanding ice cream, a clearly designated tobacco-free section and occasional live music. Down the block, *Julio's Pizza (☎ 314-530, Colón 452)* is part of a small chain with excellent food. In the other direction is the traditional nationwide chain *Bavaria (☎ 315-531, Colón 357)*.

For parrilla, the best choice is *El Alero (☎ 312-899, Colo Colo 235)*, but for more varied fare try the *Centro Español (☎ 311-669, Colón 482)* or the *Club de la Unión (☎ 322-218, Colón 261)*. *Chi Hwa (☎ 313-867, Colón 438, 2nd floor)* serves Chinese food; *El Khalil (☎ 362-536, Colo Colo 555)* is a Middle Eastern venue.

Entertainment

The *Cine Star (Colo Colo between Valdivia and Colón)* shows recent films. For live entertainment in addition to food, there's *Dónde Ramón (Colón between Janequeo and Lincoyán)*, a parrilla that also has peña entertainment, and the *Pizza Qua Pub (Av Alemania near Dario Barrueto)*.

Getting There & Away

Bus Long-distance buses leave from Los Angeles' Terminal Santa María at Av Sor Vicenta 2051 on the northeast outskirts of town, most easily reached via Av Villagrán.

There are frequent buses between Los Angeles and Concepción with Biobío (☎ 314-621), Igi Llaima (☎ 321-666) and Los Alces. Jota Be (☎ 317-180) runs 14 buses daily to Angol, the gateway to Parque Nacional Nahuelbuta, via Renaico (US$2, 1½ hours).

Other Los Angeles bus companies running north-south services along the Panamericana are Biotal (☎ 317-357), Cruz del Sur (☎ 317-630), Fénix Pullman Norte (☎ 322-502), Buses Jac (☎ 317-469), Buses Laja (☎ 316-729), Tas Choapa (☎ 322-266), Unión del Sur (☎ 316-891) and Tur-Bus (☎ 315-610).

From Terminal Santa Rosa, at the corner of Villagrán and Rengo, ERS goes to the village of Antuco, gateway to Parque Nacional Laguna del Laja, seven times daily on weekends, three times daily on weekdays. Other rural buses leave from the Terminal Vega Techada, at the corner of Villagrán and Tucapel.

Sample fares and times include Chillán (US$2, 1½ hours), Concepción (US$3, two hours), Temuco (US$6, four hours), Puerto Montt (US$12, eight hours) and Santiago (US$13, eight hours).

Getting Around

First Rent a Car (☎ 313-812) is at Caupolicán 350. Cayaqui Turismo (☎ 322-248), Lautaro 252, also rents cars.

AROUND LOS ANGELES
Salto del Laja

Just east of the Panamericana, 25km north of Los Angeles en route to Chillán, the Río Laja plunges nearly 50m over a steep escarpment to form a miniature Iguazú Falls before joining the Biobío at La Laja, 40km to the west. Salto del Laja is a popular recreation area, perhaps as much for its accessibility as its scenery. Recent dry years, coupled with erratic releases from the hydroelectric plants on the upper Laja, have left the falls with only a trickle of water.

Year-round camping is possible at *Camping Curanadú (☎ 043-312-686, Km 485)* for about US$10 per site. At the same location, there are also conventional accommodations at *Motel Curanadú* for US$31 double. Nearby alternatives include *Hotel Los Manantiales* (☎/fax 043-314-275, Km 485) for US$40/51 singles/doubles, and *Hostería Salto del Laja* (☎ 043-321-706, fax 313-996, Km 485) from US$69/83 singles/doubles, both with breakfast.

German-run *Hospedaje El Rincón* (☎ 09-441-5019, fax 043-317-168, interbruna@entelchile.net) will pick up passengers at Cruce La Mona, Km 494, or at the Los Angeles bus terminal. Rooms with shared bath and breakfast cost US$17, with full board US$37. English, German and French are spoken, and the proprietors also offer excursions to the Alto Biobío, Laguna del Laja, Parque Nacional Nahuelbuta, Termas de Chillán and the Concepción coastline. Weeklong intensive Spanish courses (five hours daily), with full board, are also available (US$350).

Fundo Curanilahue

This English-owned fundo, just north of Saltos del Laja and 3km east of the Panamericana, offers tourist accommodations on a call-ahead basis – no drop-ins. Relax and ride on a diverse 500-hectare working farm that raises sugar beets, wheat, alfalfa, and beef and dairy cattle, and also dabbles in raising trees, primarily eucalyptus. Set among splendid gardens with expansive lawns and fruit trees, the fundo's five bedrooms all have fireplaces and private baths. Guests share a swimming pool and tennis court outside. The food, prepared with fresh organic ingredients, is excellent; the hospitality gracious.

Rates are US$170 per person with full board, including wine. For details or reservations, contact John or Louisa Jackson at Fundo Curanilahue (☎ 043-372-819, fax 372-829, jacksonmay@entelchile.net), Casilla 1165, Los Angeles.

Rafting the Biobío

By nearly unanimous consent, the Río Biobío southeast of Los Angeles was once South America's premier Class V white water. Even though massive hydroelectric development has disrupted recreational

river running – not to mention the livelihood of the Pehuenche people who live in the region – trips of varying length, difficulty, cost and itinerary are still available, but likely to end before the next edition of this book.

In Concepción, contact South Expediciones (☎ 09-442-9423), Gesswein 44. There are also reliable Santiago operators, including Cascada Expediciones (☎ 02-232-7214, fax 233-9768), Orrego Luco 040, Providencia, Santiago, which charges US$475 for three-day, two-night descents starting from the city of Victoria. Their six-day, five-night trip, including an ascent of Volcán Callaquí, costs US$930 per person. Altué Active Travel (☎ 02-232-1103, fax 233-6799), Encomenderos 83, Las Condes, Santiago, offers similar packages and prices. Both Cascada and Altué have excellent websites (see the boxed text 'Online Services' in the Facts for the Visitor chapter).

For overseas operators running trips on the Biobío and other Chilean rivers, see the Organized Tours entry in the Getting There & Away chapter.

PARQUE NACIONAL LAGUNA DEL LAJA

In *The Voyage of the Beagle*, Darwin remarks that the inhabitants of Talcahuano believed that Concepción's great earthquake of 1835 'was caused by two Indian women, who being offended…stopped the volcano of Antuco.' Whether or not suppressed vulcanism triggered that quake, 2985m Antuco and its lava flows have

Laja River Falls

VICTOR ENGELBERT

MIDDLE CHILE

dammed the Río Laja to form the lake from which this 11,600-hectare national park takes its name. The park protects the mountain cypress *(Austrocedrus chilensis)* and the monkey-puzzle tree *(Araucaria araucana)* at the northern limit of its distribution, as well as other uncommon tree species. Mammals are rare, though puma, foxes and vizcachas do exist in the park. Nearly 50 bird species frequent the area, including the Andean condor.

In some ways, the lake itself belies its violent origins. From an overlook, one 19th-century American visitor described it as nearly sterile:

…green, calm and noiseless beneath. No ripple disturbed the surface – no bird played upon its bosom; and enveloped in morning mist, with mountains rising dark and blue on the farther shore, so gloomy, so deathlike, it seemed a fit companion for desolate Antuco, upon whose vast sides not a blade of grass, nor any other sign of life existed.

Chile's Endangered Rivers

In its drive toward modernization, symbolized by more than a decade of uninterrupted growth until a recent downturn in 1998, Chile has had to deal with limited energy resources. The country provides less than half its petroleum requirements from domestic sources, mainly from onshore and offshore fields in the southern region of Magallanes, which also yield natural gas. Coal has been nearly exhausted in the undersea mines near Concepción, though there remains some exploitable coal north of Punta Arenas. To maintain its growth, Chile requires energy, preferably clean energy to reduce the dense air pollution of Santiago, and perhaps even to encourage industrial development outside the central heartland.

To overcome these shortcomings, successive Chilean governments have made a conscious decision to encourage hydroelectricity. On the face of it, this is a wise decision: in many areas, heavy spring snowmelt in the high Andes feeds raging transverse rivers that pass through narrow canyons; many sites are ideal for dams. Unfortunately, these sites also have major drawbacks – social, cultural, environmental and economic.

The most internationally notorious case is the attempt by the powerful electrical utility Endesa to construct a series of dams on the Río Biobío, revered by rafters and kayakers as one of the world's finest white-water rivers. For years, Pehuenche Indian communities and environmental activists such as the Grupo de Acción por el Biobío (Biobío Action Group) have protested the loss of prime community lands and scenic canyons under stagnant reservoirs like the Pangue dam site, whose rising waters have submerged the Royal Flush rapids.

The Pangue is only one of seven proposed dams on the upper Biobío, expected to provide a substantial percentage of Chile's hydroelectricity. Ironically, none of it is supposed to go to local consumers (96% of Pehuenche households lack electricity). Objections from nine Pehuenche communities, stemming from Endesa's inadequate environmental impact report, have stopped construction on the 570-megawatt Ralco dam, which would inundate 3395 hectares of prime alluvial bottomlands. Endesa has offered a land swap, but the governmental Consejo Nacional de Desarollo Indígena refused to approve it, saying Endesa's proposal substitutes inferior lands; whether Endesa's recent sale to Spanish interests will lead to policy changes is still uncertain. In the meantime, Pehuenche lawsuits have halted construction, so both Chilean and foreign adventure travel companies continue to run the river, attracting tourists and valuable foreign exchange to Chile.

The Biobío is not the only river under threat. Residents in the area of Chile's other world-class white-water site, the Futaleufú near the Argentine border southeast of Chaitén, were shocked to learn that Endesa and two other hydroelectric utilities, Colbún Machicura and Chilgener, had filed claims on water rights to the river's 12,000-cubic-meter-per-second flow – without any fanfare. In response, the locals have formed their own Corporación de

Laguna del Laja presents a less desolate scene now, as pampas grass and other pioneer species have begun to colonize the lava fields and wildlife has returned to many sectors. Still, most visitors find it less appealing than other parks to the south.

Geography & Climate

In the upper drainage of the Río Laja, 95km east of Los Angeles, Laguna del Laja is a natural lake so modified by a variety of hydro-electric projects, including tunnels and dams, that it more closely resembles a reservoir. The park itself, however, is a mountainous area ranging from 1000m to nearly 3000m above sea level. Its most striking feature is Antuco's symmetrical cone, but the higher Sierra Velluda to the southwest, beyond the park boundaries, offers a series of impressive glaciers.

Summer is fairly dry, but more than 2m of precipitation accumulate as rain and snow

---

Chile's Endangered Rivers

Defensa y Desarollo del Río Futaleufú (Codderfu), seeking to create a nationally recognized and protected river corridor. Their supporters include Codeff, Grupo de Acción por el Biobío and the US-based FutaFriends, originally formed by US kayaker Chris Spelius.

Outdoor river-based recreation is making a particularly large contribution to the Futaleufú economy. In addition to the increasing number of white-water rafting companies operating in the area, fishing is a big money earner, as some fly-fishing lodges charge up to US$3000 per guest per week. The opening of the new Futaleufú Adventure Center, modeled on North Carolina's Nantahala Outdoor Center and aided by an improving hotel infrastructure, underscores the area's economic potential.

The Aisén region's other major river, the Río Baker, carries the largest volume of any Chilean river through what is one of the country's least densely populated areas, from the outlet of Lago General Carrera to the Pacific Ocean at Caleta Tortel. There are preliminary plans to construct hydroelectric sites for a new aluminum plant – an industry noted for its high energy consumption.

There are some positive signs. The increasing recognition that erratic rainfall and snowpacks make hydroelectric resources unpredictable is causing some decision-makers to look at alternatives, especially with the recent influx of clean-burning natural gas through pipelines from Argentina and the increasing interconnectedness of the two countries' power grids. The latter is especially improving in providing peak-hours energy supplements, since all of Chile is in the same time zone, while Argentina is usually one hour ahead.

Readers interested in more information can contact the Grupo de Acción por el Biobío (☎ 02-737-1420, fax 777-6414) at Ernesto Pinto Lagarrigue 112, Recoleta, Santiago, or FutaFriends (bgrause@futafriends .org), 25 Needmore Rd, Bryson City, NC 28713, USA.

the rest of the year. The ski season lasts from June to October.

Trekking
Laguna del Laja has trails suitable for day hikes as well as for longer excursions; the best is the circuit around Volcán Antuco, which provides views of both the Sierra Velluda and the lake. For details, consult Lonely Planet's *Trekking in the Patagonian Andes*.

If trekking or camping, buy supplies in Los Angeles, where selection is far better and prices are much lower.

Places to Stay & Eat
In 1999, the park's *Camping y Cabañas Lagunillas* (☎ 043-314-275) was closed, complicating the accommodations possibilities for anyone other than backcountry campers. The closest alternative is Abanico's *Hotel Malalcura* (☎ 043-313-183), 9km west of the park entrance.

In winter, for about US$10 per person, it's possible to stay at the *Refugio Digeder*, operated by Concepción's Dirección General de Deportes y Recreación, at the base of Volcán Antuco. It has beds for 50 skiers, a restaurant and rental ski equipment; it *may* be open in summer. For reservations, contact Digeder (☎ 041-229-054) at O'Higgins 740, Oficina 23, Concepción.

Getting There & Away
From Los Angeles' Terminal Santa Rosa at the corner of Villagrán and Rengo, ERS buses go to the villages of Antuco and Abanico, gateways to Parque Nacional Laguna del Laja, seven times daily on weekends, three times daily on weekdays. The trip takes only about 1½ hours, but it takes another several hours to walk the 11km to Chacay, where Conaf maintains administrative offices and a small visitor center. Hitchhiking is possible, but vehicles are a rare sight except on weekdays.

ANGOL
☎ 45
Founded in 1553 by Pedro de Valdivia as a strategic frontier outpost – and destroyed half a dozen times over three centuries in

the Mapuche wars – Angol de los Confines finally survived the Indian resistance after 1862. Easily reached by southbound travelers from Los Angeles, as well as from Temuco, it provides the best access into mountainous Parque Nacional Nahuelbuta, a forest reserve that protects the largest remaining coastal stands of araucaria pines.

Orientation
Angol (population 39,151), west of the Panamericana, 60km southwest of Los Angeles and 127km north of Temuco, is actually an outlier of Region IX (La Araucanía). It straddles the Río Vergara, an upper tributary of the Biobío formed by the confluence of the Ríos Picoiquén and Rehue. The city's older core, centered on a particularly attractive Plaza de Armas, lies west of the river. Farther west, the coastal Cordillera Nahuelbuta rises to nearly 1600m.

Information
Angol's Oficina Municipal de Turismo (☎ 711-930, 711-255, fax 711-714) is just east of the bridge across the Río Vergara. Open from 9 am to 1 pm and 3 to 7 pm weekdays all year, it has few maps and brochures but boasts a hard-working, well-informed staff. In summer, it's also open from 9 am to 1 pm Saturday.

Angol has no formal cambios, but Boutique Boston (☎ 713-946), Sepúlveda 3-A between Prat and Lautaro, changes US cash from 9 am to 1 pm and 3 to 7 pm weekdays, but try also the travel agencies Turismo Christopher (☎ 715-156), Ilabaca 421 or Nahuel Tour (☎ 715-457), Pedro Aguirre Cerda 307. Banco de Chile, Lautaro 2, has an ATM.

The post office is at Lautaro and Chorrillos, at the northeast corner of the Plaza de Armas. CTC (Telefónica) has long-distance offices at O'Higgins 297, west of the river.

Things to See & Do
Built in 1863, **Convento San Buenaventura,** a Franciscan convent, is the region's oldest church and well worth a visit. It's on Covadonga between Vergara and Dieciocho.

Developed as both a plant nursery and gardens by Anglo-Chilean Manuel Bunster in the 19th century, then acquired by Methodist missionaries in 1920, the **Escuela Agrícola El Vergel (Museo Dillman S Bullock)** is an agricultural college with a national reputation for training gardeners and farmers. Its Museo Bullock, a fine collection of natural history specimens and archaeological artifacts, is the legacy of North American Methodist Dillman S Bullock, who spent nearly 70 years in Chile learning the Mapuche language and publishing articles on the region's biology, natural history and archaeology.

Five km east of Angol but easily reached by taxi colectivo No 2 from the Plaza de Armas, El Vergel's grounds are open 9 am to 7 pm daily; the museum is open 9 am to 1 pm and 3 to 7 pm daily. Museum admission costs US$1 for adults, US$0.30 for children.

Special Events
In the second week of January, the Municipalidad de Angol sponsors Brotes de Chile, a folk song festival with prizes ranging up to US$3000. One of Chile's most important festivals for more than a decade, it features music, dance, food and crafts.

Places to Stay & Eat
Angol has limited but mostly reasonable accommodations, beginning with the basic *Casa del Huésped (Dieciocho 465)* for US$8 per person; *Residencial Olimpia (☎ 711-162, Caupolicán 625)* charges US$14/27 singles/doubles.

Hotel Millaray (☎ 711-570, Prat 420) has rooms with shared bath for US$13/21; but with private bath rates jump to US$23/31. Standards are slipping at *Hostería El Vergel (☎ 712-103, Km 5 Angol-Collipulli)*, on the grounds of the Escuela Agrícola El Vergel, which charges US$33 double with shared bath, US$38 with private bath. Probably the best choice is the *Hotel Club Social (☎ 711-103, Caupolicán 498)*, for US$30/38 with private bath; it has a pool, bar and good restaurant.

For the best selection, try *Las Totoras (Ilabaca and Covadonga)* or the *Club Social*

(Caupolicán 498). As a place to eat, *El Vergel*, on the grounds of the agricultural college, has declined despite an abundance of good, fresh produce. The fast-food outlet *Lomitón (Lautaro and Bunster)* has reliable sandwiches.

Shopping
Angol is renowned for fine ceramics, produced at small factories open to the public. Cerámica Serra is at Bunster 153, while Cerámica Lablé is at Purén 864.

Getting There & Away
For long-distance services, Angol's Terminal Rodoviario is at Caupolicán 200, a block north of the plaza. Buses Biobío (☎ 711-777) has more than a dozen buses daily to Temuco (US$3.50, two hours), plus another five to Concepción (US$2). Tur-Bus (☎ 711-655) has morning and evening departures for Santiago (US$10 to US$18, eight hours). Igi Llaima (☎ 711-920) goes to Los Angeles and Concepción twice daily and to Santiago nightly. Trans Tur has morning and evening buses to the capital (US$8 to US$10).

The Terminal Rural (☎ 712-021), for local and regional services, is at Ilabaca and Lautaro. Buses Thiele (☎ 711-110) has extensive regional services, connecting Angol to the Costa del Carbón via Contulmo, Cañete and Lebú (US$4), and to Concepción via Nacimiento and Santa Juana. Buses Jota Be (☎ 712-262) has 14 buses daily to Los Angeles (US$2) via Renaico.

Buses Angol goes from Angol to Vegas Blancas (US$2), 7km from the entrance to Parque Nacional Nahuelbuta, Tuesday, Thursday and Saturday at 6:45 am and 4 pm, returning at 9 am and 6 pm. For details of park tours, see the following section.

PARQUE NACIONAL NAHUELBUTA
Between Angol and the Pacific, covered with araucaria pines, the coastal range rises to nearly 1600m in Parque Nacional Nahuelbuta. Created in 1939 to protect one of the last non-Andean refuges of the monkey-puzzle tree, whose largest specimens can reach 50m in height and 2m in diameter, this

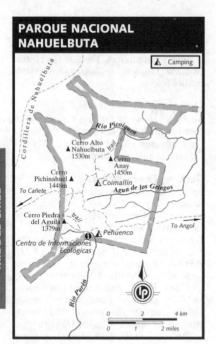

PARQUE NACIONAL NAHUELBUTA

summit of Cerro Alto Nahuelbuta. Unlike the Andes, the coastal range is granitic rather than volcanic.

The park enjoys warm, dry summers, but snow sometimes falls at higher elevations in winter. Mean annual precipitation is about 1000mm, falling almost entirely between May and September. November to April is the best time for a visit.

Things to See & Do

Nahuelbuta has 30km of roads and 15km of footpaths, so car-touring, camping and hiking are all possible. From Pehuenco, a 4km trail winds through pehuen forests, with occasional springs, to the granite outcrop of **Piedra del Aguila**, a 1379m overlook with views from the Andes to the Pacific except to the north-northeast, where the forest crown blocks the view. To the southeast the entire string of Andean volcanoes from Antuco, east of Chillán, to Villarrica and Lanín, east of Pucón, is visible; on a really clear day, even Osorno may appear on the southern horizon.

Piedra del Aguila is only an 800m hike from a shorter approach accessible by car, but it's possible, and more interesting, to loop back to Pehuenco via the valley of the Estero Cabrería to the south via a trail that starts beneath the west side of Piedra del Aguila.

Cerro Anay, 1450m above sea level, has similar views; the trail itself, reached via Coimallín, is relatively short, and has countless wildflowers and huge stands of araucarias. **Cerro Alto Nahuelbuta**, the park's highest peak at 1530m, is off-limits to hikers because of the recent reintroduction of pumas in the area.

Places to Stay

Conaf charges US$10 per site at **Camping Pehuenco** (11 sites, 5km from the park entrance) near park headquarters, and at **Camping Coimallín** (four sites, 5km north of Pehuenco). The Pehuenco site has shady forest clearings with picnic tables and bathrooms with flush toilets and cold showers; the Coimallín is more rustic, lacking running water.

6832-hectare park also features notable stands of *Nothofagus* (southern beech). Occasional sightings of rare mammals such as puma, culpeo (Chiloé fox) and the miniature Chilean deer known as the pudú have been known to happen.

At Pehuenco, on the road from Angol, Conaf maintains a **Centro de Informaciones Ecológicas**, with a small museum, where rangers offer audiovisual presentations on the local environment. Park admission costs US$3.50 for adults, US$1 for children. The park gets heavy weekend use, though the lack of swimming sites keeps some Chileans away.

Geography & Climate

In the province of Malleco in Region IX, Nahuelbuta is about 35km west of Angol. On a mostly flat or undulating plain, some 950m above sea level, permanent streams have cut deep canyons, while jagged peaks rise abruptly, up to 1530m high on the

The Andes tower over Santiago.

Santiago's Mercado Central

Cool kids in Santiago

The capital's speedy Metro

Charming streets and hills of Valparaíso

Steelworker, Talcahuano

Lush Viña del Mar

Valparaíso's holy mackerel

Getting There & Away

Angol's Conaf (☎ 711-870), at Prat and Chorrillos, may be able to offer suggestions for transport to Parque Nacional Nahuelbuta. Buses Angol goes to Vegas Blancas (US$2), 7km from the park entrance, at 6:45 am and 4 pm, returning at 9 am and 6 pm, Tuesday, Thursday and Saturday. In summer, it also offers Sunday tours for US$13 per person, leaving Angol's Terminal Rural at 6:45 am. For motorists with low-clearance vehicles, the steep and dusty road may be difficult in spots. Few mountain bikers will be able to do the ride without dismounting and walking at least part of the time, and water is hard to find.

Norte Grande

The Norte Grande consists of Regions I (Tarapacá) and II (Antofagasta) and the northernmost part of Region III (Atacama). Prior to the arrival of the Spaniards, the oases of this desert region were more closely linked to the Andean highlands of present-day Peru and Bolivia than to coastal areas both north and south. The most prominent geographical features are the Pacific Ocean, the starkly desolate but unique Atacama Desert with its deeply incised canyons and the Andean altiplano (steppe) and its volcanic summits.

The region's conspicuous pre-Hispanic archaeological monuments and colonial remains complement those in Peru and Bolivia. Substantial Indian populations once lived by fishing and by irrigated agriculture in scattered oases and in the valleys that descend from the cordillera to the coast. Many Indians remain despite the influx of immigrants from central Chile to the cities of Arica, Iquique and Antofagasta.

Indian peoples left impressive fortresses, agricultural terraces and huge stylized designs (geoglyphs) made by covering the light sands of the surrounding barren slopes with darker stones. Their representations of llama trains depict the significance of the transverse canyons as pre-Columbian transport routes. Coastal people exchanged products such as fish and guano for maize and *charqui* (sun-dried llama or alpaca meat) with their Andean kin.

The Atacama is the most 'perfect' of deserts; some coastal stations have never recorded measurable rainfall, although infrequent 'El Niño' events can bring brief but phenomenal downpours. Otherwise, the only precipitation comes from the convective fogs known as *camanchaca* or *garúa*, which sometimes condense at higher elevations and support the scattered vegetation of the *lomas* (coastal hills).

Farther inland, rainfall and vegetation increase with elevation and distance from the sea. In the precordillera, or foothills, Aymara farmers still cultivate the terraces, man-made landforms designed for soil conservation and irrigation, that have covered the hillsides for millennia, although alfalfa fodder for livestock has largely replaced *quinoa* (a native Andean grain) and the myriad varieties of potato. Cultivation reaches as high as 4000m; above this level, the Aymara pasture llamas, alpacas and a few sheep on the grasslands of the *puna* (highlands).

Until the late 19th century, the Norte Grande belonged to Peru and Bolivia. Treaty disputes, the presence of thousands of Chilean workers in the Bolivian mines and Bolivian attempts to increase taxation on mineral exports led to the War of the Pacific (1879-1884) against Bolivia and Peru. Within those five years, Chile overpowered its rivals and annexed the copper- and nitrate-rich lands that are now the regions of Tarapacá and Antofagasta.

Most cities in the Atacama, such as Iquique and Antofagasta, owe their existence to minerals, especially nitrates and copper. Nitrate *oficinas* (company towns) such as Humberstone flourished during an early-20th-century boom but withered when new petroleum-based fertilizers superseded mineral nitrates and are now ghost towns. Only a handful continue to operate, as newer methods make processing lower grade ores profitable.

One of the chief beneficiaries of the War of the Pacific was British speculator John Thomas North, the single most important figure in nitrate history. In 1875, prior to the war, Peru expropriated nitrate holdings and issued bonds to their former owners. During the war, the value of these bonds plummeted and North, using Chilean capital, bought as many as he could. When, after the war, Chile decided to restore ownership to bondholders, it was a windfall for North, who moved to gain control of all other industries on which the nitrate industry depended, such as the railroad. Along with a handful of other

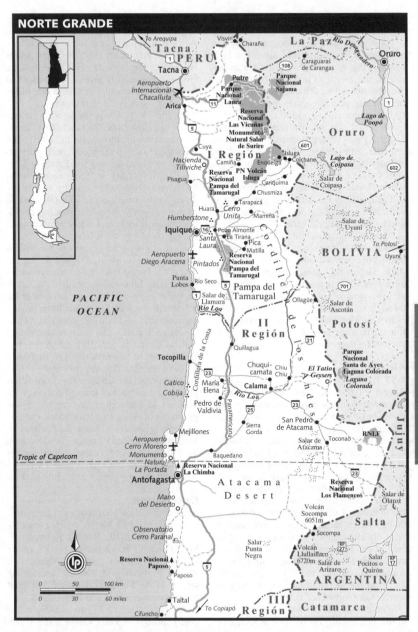

NORTE GRANDE

entrepreneurs, he largely controlled the region's economy.

Chile's economic dependence on nitrates and copper has meant that, since the 19th century, the Atacama has played a major role in the country's political fortunes. The desert's mineral wealth meant a steady flow of revenue into the exchequer, allowing Chilean politicians to postpone dealing with major social and political issues – the mal-distribution of land, in particular – until well into the 20th century; able to depend on mining revenue to finance government services, they failed to devise a broadly based tax system. Militant trade unions first developed in the north, in the late 19th century and early 20th century, introducing a new factor into Chilean politics in general.

After WWI, the nitrate industry declined as synthetic nitrates replaced mineral nitrates, but revenue from copper took up the slack. The world's largest open-pit copper mine is at Chuquicamata, near Calama, and there are many other important new mines throughout the region, such as Cerro Colorado near Mamiña, Collahuasi southeast of Iquique near the Bolivian border, and Zaldívar and La Escondida east of Antofagasta.

ARICA
☎ 58

An early 19th-century English visitor called Arica 'one bleak, comfortless, miserable, sandy waste,' but even before Inka times it had been the terminus of an important trade route, as coastal peoples exchanged their fish, cotton and maize for the potatoes, wool and charqui of their kin in the precordillera and altiplano. With the arrival of the Spanish in the early 16th century, Arica (officially founded in 1565) became the port for the bonanza silver mine at Potosí in Alto Perú (present-day Bolivia). Although Arica became part of independent Peru, its 19th-century development lagged behind the frenzied activity in the nitrate mines farther south, near Pisagua, Iquique and Antofagasta. During the War of the Pacific, Arica became de facto Chilean territory, an arrangement formalized in 1929.

Where Chile and Peru once fought bloody skirmishes, wealthy Bolivians now lounge on the beach, and Quechua and Aymara Indians sell handicrafts, vegetables and trinkets. Arica is a popular year-round resort, with beach weather nearly every day; some adults have never seen rain. Despite its aridity, the city occupies an attractive site at the foot of El Morro, a spectacular headland that offers sweeping ocean and desert views.

In the 1960s, Chile made a conscious effort to industrialize the region by offering tax incentives to automobile and electronics industries to set up shop, powered by diverting the eastward-flowing Río Lauca to a hydroelectric facility in the precordillera. Industrialization failed but, by the 1970s, Arica had become a city of 120,000, a sixfold increase in less than two decades, because of international trade and active promotion of the region as a customs-free zone.

Chile has periodically proposed territorial compensation for Bolivian losses during the War of the Pacific, but offers of a narrow strip between the Lluta valley (north of the Arica-La Paz railway) and the Peruvian border for a Bolivian corridor to the sea have proved unacceptable to Peru, the area's erstwhile sovereign. Traditionally, much of landlocked Bolivia's exports pass through Arica, but Peru's grant of free port rights to Bolivia at Ilo have undercut Arica's economy.

In response, the Chilean government has proposed a number of tax and duty-free incentives to encourage investment in the provinces of Arica and Parinacota, but this has met opposition from authorities in Iquique, whose Zona Franca duty-free area has faltered in recent years. Unemployment in Arica has, in the recent past, exceeded 10%, and the population has fallen slightly.

Orientation

Arica (population 160,000) lies at the northeastern base of El Morro, which rises dramatically out of the Pacific. Between El Morro and the Río San José (which rarely has any surface flow), the city center is a slightly irregular grid. The main shopping street, 21 de Mayo, is a pedestrian mall running between Prat and Baquedano.

At the foot of El Morro are the manicured gardens of Plaza Colón, from which

Av Comandante San Martín (do not confuse with Calle San Martín, east of downtown) snakes west and south towards the city's most popular beaches. In the other direction, Av Máximo Lira swerves sharply at sprawling Parque Brasil to become Av General Velásquez, leading to the Panamericana Norte and the Peruvian border, some 20km to the north. To get to the Panamericana Sur, toward Iquique, take either 18 de Septiembre or 21 de Mayo eastbound.

Information

Tourist Offices Sernatur (☎ 232-101, fax 254-506, sernatur_arica@entelchile.net), Prat 305, 2nd floor, is open from 8:30 am to 5:30 pm weekdays. Its friendly, helpful staff distribute a useful city map, plus a fistful of brochures on Tarapacá and other Chilean regions; if arriving from Peru or Bolivia, this is a good place to orient yourself.

The municipal Dirección de Turismo (☎ 206-243, 206-245, 800-201-489 toll-free) is at Sotomayor 415, but no longer maintains its kiosk on 21 de Mayo.

The Automóvil Club de Chile (☎ 252-678, fax 232-780), Chacabuco 460, offers free information and sells maps. It's open 9 am to 1 pm and 3 to 7 pm weekdays, 9 am to 1 pm Saturday.

Visas To replace a lost tourist card or renew a visa, go to the Departamento de Extranjería (☎ 250-377) at Angamos 990, open 8:30 am to 12:30 pm and 3:30 to 6 pm weekdays. However, given Chilean high visa renewal charges, it would be cheaper to make a day trip to Tacna (Perú) or to go to La Paz (Bolivia) for a couple days.

Money Arica enjoys the best rates and least bureaucracy for changing money north of Santiago, and there are many ATMs, such as the one at Banco de Crédito at Bolognesi 221.

Reliable street changers hang out at the corner of 21 de Mayo and Colón; there are several permanent exchange houses on 21 de Mayo, where you can change US cash and traveler's checks, as well as Peruvian, Bolivian and Argentine currency. Try Marta Daguer at 18 de Septiembre 330 or Turismo Sol y Mar at Colón 610, Oficina 4. On Sunday, when cambios are closed, try the street changers or larger hotels (where rates will be less favorable).

Post & Communications The post office is in the same building as the tourist office at Prat 305. For long-distance phone calls, go to Entel at 21 de Mayo 345, CTC (Telefónica) at Colón 476 or Chilesat at 18 de Septiembre 430. In the alcove outside the tourist office, there is a fiber-optic line with direct connection to overseas operators, but it's accessible only during regular business hours.

Technolabs, Maipú 488, provides cheap Internet access from 10 am to 2 am daily. Cipcomp, 21 de Mayo 694, also has Internet access.

National Parks Conaf's regional office (☎ 250-207, 250-570), Vicuña Mackenna 820, is open 8:30 am to 5:18 pm weekdays.

Laundry Lavandería La Moderna (☎ 232-006) is at 18 de Septiembre 457. Lavandería Radiante is at O'Higgins 554.

Medical Services Hospital Dr Juan Noé (☎ 229-200) is at 18 de Septiembre 1000, a short distance east of downtown.

Things to See & Do

Overlooking the city, with panoramic views of the port and the Pacific, the 110m headland known as **El Morro de Arica** is also a historical monument whose open-air **Museo Histórico y de Armas** (☎ 254-091) commemorates a crucial battle between Chilean and Peruvian forces on June 7, 1880, about a year into the War of the Pacific. It's open 8 am to 9:30 pm daily, accessible by car or by a footpath from the south end of Calle Colón; there's an admission charge of US$0.80.

At the base of El Morro, at the corner of Colón and Yungay, one of downtown's most imposing buildings is the **Casa Bolognesi**, the command center for Peruvian forces in the War of the Pacific and later the Peruvian consulate.

Famous for his Parisian tower, Alexandre Gustave Eiffel designed many prefab landmarks in Latin America, including the **Aduana de Arica** (1874), the former custom-house. Though it once fronted on the harbor, a century of landfill has left it about 200m inland, facing Parque General Baquedano. Restored as the city's Casa de la Cultura (☎ 206-366), it displays historical photographs and occasional art exhibitions on the 2nd floor, reached by a 32-step, wrought-iron spiral staircase.

Arica's other Eiffel monument is the **Iglesia San Marcos** (1875), opposite Plaza Colón. Originally intended for the bathing resort of Ancón, north of Lima, the Gothic-style building replaced a church destroyed by an earthquake in 1868.

The 1924 German locomotive that once pulled trains on the Arica-La Paz line now stands in the **Plazoleta Estación**, part of Parque General Baquedano, at the corner of 21 de Mayo and Pedro Montt. On the north side of the Plazoleta, the **Estación Ferrocarril Arica-La Paz**, the train station, dates from 1913.

Beaches

Arica is one of Chile's best beach resorts, since the Pacific is warm enough for comfortable bathing, but note that all the beaches have strong ocean currents and may be dangerous, some more so than others.

The most frequented beaches are south of town, along Av Comandante San Martín, where there are a number of sheltered coves and seaside restaurants. The closest site is **Playa El Laucho**, just south of the Club de Yates, followed by **Playa La Lisera** 2½ km south of downtown; both have calm surf and are suitable for swimming, but nearby, rougher **Playa Brava** is suitable for sunbathing only. About 10km south of town, **Playa Corazones** is the most southerly accessible beach. Bus No 8, which leaves from General Velásquez and Chacabuco, serves this area.

Beaches along the Panamericana Norte, toward the Peruvian border, are cleaner than those to the south. **Playa Chinchorro**, 2km north of downtown, is suitable for swimming and diving, while **Playa Las Machas**, a few

Eiffel Beyond the Tower

Few are aware that French engineer Alexandre Gustave Eiffel, so renowned for his controversial tower in Paris, also played such a significant role in the New World. New York's Statue of Liberty is his most prominent transatlantic landmark (he designed the steel framework inside it), but his designs also dot the Latin American landscape from Mexico to Chile. Arica's Iglesia San Marcos and restored Aduana (customhouse) are but two of many examples.

In 1868, in partnership with another engineer, Théophile Seyrig, Eiffel had formed G Eiffel et Compagnie, which later became the Compagnie des Etablissements Eiffel. While the bulk of its metal construction work took place in France and French colonies, an aggressive Buenos Aires agent landed many contracts for South American public buildings. In addition to the Arica landmarks, Eiffel's notable creations include the gasworks of La Paz, Bolivia, and the railroad bridges of Oroya, Peru, but his work appears as far north as the Iglesia Santa Bárbara in Santa Rosalía, in the Mexican state of Baja California Sur. Most of these were designed and built in Eiffel's workshops in the Parisian suburb of Levallois-Perret, then shipped abroad for assembly.

What might have been his greatest Latin American monument effectively ended his career. In the late 19th century, he had argued strongly in favor of a transoceanic canal across Nicaragua, and a few years later he obtained a contract to build the locks for Ferdinand de Lesseps' corruption-plagued French canal across Panama. Implicated in irregular contracts, Eiffel was sentenced to two years in prison and was fined a substantial amount; though his conviction was overturned on appeal, he never returned to his career as a builder.

kilometers north, is too rough for swimming but ideal for surfing and fishing. Take bus No 12 from General Velásquez and Chacabuco.

Arica has several surf shops, including Huntington Surf Shop at 21 de Mayo 493, Tropisurf at 21 de Mayo 423-A and Solari Surf Shop at 21 de Mayo 160. For fishing permits, contact the Servicio Nacional de Pesca (Sernap; ☎ 222-684), Serrano 1856, just off 21 de Mayo about 10 blocks east of the hospital. It's open 8:30 am to 1 pm and 3 to 6 pm weekdays.

Poblado Artesanal
On the outskirts of Arica near the Panamericana Sur, this mock altiplano village, complete with church and bell tower, is a good place to shop for ceramics, weavings, musical instruments, carvings and similar crafts, and has an excellent restaurant, El Tambo (see Places to Eat).

At Hualles 2825, the Poblado Artesanal (☎ 222-683) is open 9:30 am to 1:30 pm and 3:30 to 8 pm daily except Monday; there's a *peña* (folk music and cultural club) at 9:30 pm Friday and Saturday evenings. Taxi colectivos Nos 2, 7, 8, 13 and U pass near the entrance, as do buses Nos 2, 3, 5, 7, 9 and 12.

Organized Tours
Numerous travel agencies arrange trips around the city and to the Azapa valley, the precordillera, Parque Nacional Lauca and other altiplano destinations; some run trips themselves, while others contract out. When booking a tour indirectly, confirm the operator's name.

One-day Lauca tours cost about US$20 to US$25 including a late lunch in Putre, but when competition is heavy in summer the price can fall as low as US$15; shop around for the best deal. These tours leave around 7:30 am and return about 8:30 pm. Verify whether the operator carries oxygen for those who suffer from *soroche* (altitude sickness) – this is not a minor issue, as many people become very sick at high altitudes. Avoid overeating, smoking and alcohol consumption.

Tours lasting 1½ days, including a night in Putre, cost around US$60. A 2½-day tour to

Lauca and Surire costs about US$130; a three-day circuit to Lauca, Surire, Isluga and Iquique, returning to Arica late the third night, costs US$180.

Companies running their own trips include well-established, recommended Geotours (☎ 251-675) at Bolognesi 421, which has English-speaking guides and provides oxygen; Ecotours (☎ 250-000) at Bolognesi 460; and Belgian-run Latinorizons (☎/fax 250-007, latinor@entelchile.net), Thompson 236 (French and English spoken).

Other agencies include Turismo Payachatas (☎ 256-981) at Sotomayor 199, Aacción Tour (☎/fax 257-216) at Thompson 251, Parinacota Expediciones (☎/fax 256-227) at Prat 430, Oficina 5 and Turismo Lauca (☎ 252-322) at Prat 430, Local 10.

While there is no longer any regular passenger service to Bolivia, Latinorizons now does a one-day rail tour to Parque Nacional Lauca (US$30 including breakfast and a box lunch), using a 12-passenger ferrobus, a sort of minibus that rides the tracks; it's possible to combine this with an overnight in Putre (US$90) to allow for more time in the park. There are three weekly departures.

Special Events
Arica's unpretentious Carnaval Ginga draws around 15,000 spectators during a three-day weekend in late February; the Municipalidad blocks off Av Comandante San Martín, near El Morro, for a parade that features regional *comparsas* (groups of musicians and dancers) performing traditional precordillera and altiplano dances. The music mostly consists of brass bands, so no one will confuse this with Rio de Janeiro or Bahia, but it's worth a look for visitors who happen to be in town.

The biggest local event is June's Semana Ariqueña (Arica Week), about the same time as the Concurso Nacional de Cueca, a folkloric dance festival in the Azapa valley.

Places to Stay
Arica has abundant accommodations at reasonable prices; though many bottom-end places are cramped and malodorous, and some lack hot water. Others are excellent.

ARICA

PLACES TO STAY
3   Hotel El Paso
6   Residencial Chillán
18 Residencial Tía Anita
19 Residencial Patricia
22 Residencial Madrid
23 Residencial Venecia
24 Residencial Chungará
26 Residencial Las Parinas
29 Hotel Aragón
31 Residencial Blanquita
34 Hotel Lynch
35 Residencial Muñoz
36 Residencial Sur
46 Hostal Chez Charlie
57 Hotel Central
    Best Western
73 Residencial Española
76 Residencial Leiva
77 King Hotel
78 Hotel San Marcos
84 La Casa de Mía Nonna
87 Residencial Caracas
90 Residencial Sotomayor
91 Hotel Diego de Almagro
93 Hotel Tacora
94 Residencial Real
95 Hostal Jardín del Sol
96 Residencial Stagnaro
102 Hotel Savona

PLACES TO EAT
5   El Tacneño
10 Nuevo Mundo
11 Shao Lin
17 Inti-Marka
20 Bavaría
28 Mercado Colón,
    Caballito del Mar,
    El Rey del Marisco
30 Buen Gusto No 2
37 Shanghai
43 Govinda
44 La Scala
46 La Ciboulette
49 Café 21
52 El Arriero
69 Goro
72 La Fontana
74 DiMango
75 Casino La Bomba
80 D'Aurelio
83 Chin Huang Tao
86 Los Aleros de 21
100 Illimani
105 Maracuyá

OTHER
1   Terminal de Buses
2   Terminal Internacional
3   Hertz
4   Estación Ferrocarril
    Arica-Tacna
7   Klasse
8   Tur-Bus
9   Automóvil Club de Chile
12 Italian Consulate
13 Departamento de
    Extranjería
14 Conaf
15 Bus Lluta
16 Buses Martínez

21 Turismo Sol y Mar
25 Lavandería Radiante
27 Radio Taxi Arica
32 Lavandería La Moderna
33 Technolabs
38 Estación Ferrocarril
    Arica-La Paz
39 Parinacota Expediciones,
    Turismo Lauca
40 Cambio Yanulaque
41 Geotours
45 Ecotours
45 Avant
46 Latinorizons
47 Aacción Tour
48 CTC (Telefónica)
50 LanChile
51 Entel

53 Danish, Norwegian
    Consulates
54 Marta Daguer
55 Chilesat
56 Tropisurf
58 Ladeco
59 Huntington Surf Shop
60 Bolivar, Consulate
61 German Consulate
62 American Rent a Car
63 Hospital Dr Juan Noé
64 Parque General
    Baquedano
65 Plazoleta Estación
66 Ex-Aduana,
    Casa de la Cultura
67 Sernatur, Post Office
68 Solari Surf Shop

70 Café 303
71 Turismo Payachatas
79 France Tropicale
81 Dirección de Turismo
82 Radio Taxi
    Aeropuerto Chacalluta
85 Cipcomp
88 Banco de Crédito
89 Taller Artesanal
    San Marcos
92 Lloyd Aéreo Boliviano
97 Museo Histórico
    y de Armas
98 Cine Colón
99 Iglesia San Marcos
101 Casa Bolognesi
103 Peruvian Consulate
104 Club de Yates

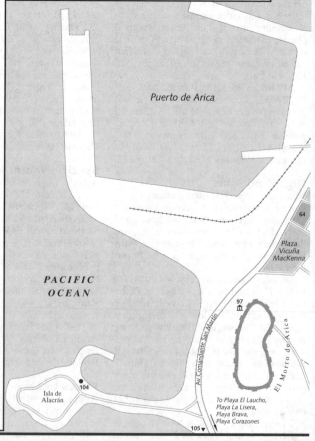

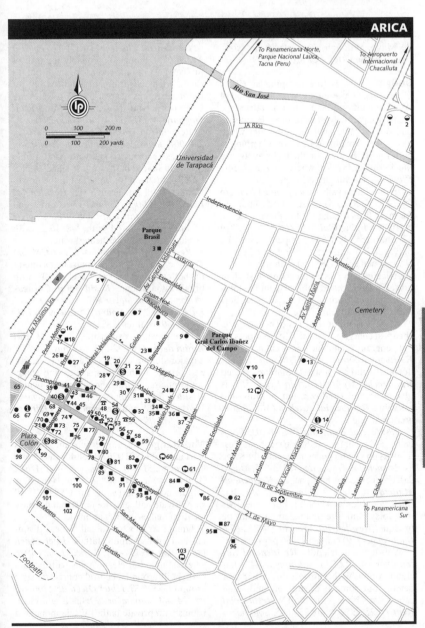

ARICA

Those in search of quiet should look south of the busy thoroughfares of Maipú and 21 de Mayo, although some places on cross-streets in the latter area are fine.

Budget There is free camping at *Playa Corazones*, 8km south of Arica at the end of Av Comandante San Martín, but these highly frequented sites are dirty. Basic supplies are available – but not fresh water, which has to be brought from town. Camping is better north of town, on the highway toward the Peruvian border, where sites including *Playa las Machas* are cleaner.

In the Azapa valley, *Camping El Refugio* (☎ 227-545, Km 1.5) charges US$13 per site for up to five persons. On the Panamericana Norte, *Camping Gallinazo* (☎ 214-144, Km 13) charges only US$4 per person, but the only public transportation is taxi colectivo No 1, which costs US$1.50 each way.

Arica usually has an inexpensive student hostel in January and February, but the location changes from year to year. Ask Sernatur for the current listing.

Arica has numerous residenciales. The cheapest charge as little as US$4 per person, but generally do not include breakfast. Drab *Residencial Sur* (☎ 252-457, Maipú 516) has hot water and clean sheets. Similarly priced *Residencial Muñoz* (Patricio Lynch 565) is ultrabasic and rundown, but friendly and tolerable. *Residencial Patricia* (Maipú 269) is comparable.

Residencial Española (☎ 231-703, Bolognesi 340) charges US$6/10 for singles/doubles on a quiet pedestrian walk, the same as *Residencial Tía Anita* (☎ 252-975, Maipú 25). Frequented by backpackers, *Residencial Madrid* (☎ 231-479, Baquedano 685) has singles/doubles at US$6/11, but sometimes it's noisy and the management can be brusque. *Residencial Venecia* (☎ 252-877, Baquedano 739) charges US$6 per person.

Well-located, friendly *Residencial Sotomayor* (☎ 252-336, Sotomayor 442) has clean rooms with showers for US$8 per person, but some beds are soft and some rooms are a bit close to the TV. *Residencial Real* (☎ 253-359, ☎/fax 250-065, Sotomayor 578) is also a good value for US$8 per person with shared bath.

Residencial Chungará (☎ 231-677, Patricio Lynch 675), though, is probably the pick of this category – some rooms are small, but it's clean, bright, cheerful and quiet (except for the front rooms nearest the TV). Rates are US$8 per person, the same as at *Residencial Stagnaro* (☎ 231-254, Arturo Gallo 294).

Belgian-run *Hostal Chez Charlie* (☎/fax 250-007, latinor@entelchile.net, Thompson 236) has spacious rooms with comfortable beds and shared baths for just US$8/14 plus US$1 per person for breakfast in the downstairs restaurant. French-run *Residencial Leiva* (☎ 232-008, Colón 347) is quiet and well-located; rates are US$9/12 singles/doubles with shared bath, US$16/21 with private bath and solar-heated water.

Residencial Blanquita (☎ 232-064, Maipú 472) is clean; at US$9 per person, it's one of the better budget choices. For US$10/16, with breakfast, intimate *Residencial Caracas* (☎ 253-688, Sotomayor 867) is worth a look. *La Casa di Mia Nonna* (☎ 250-597, 21 de Mayo 660) charges US$11/20.

Quiet, with responsible staff, *Hostal Jardín del Sol* (☎ 232-795, Sotomayor 848) is a major step up at US$12/20 with breakfast and private bath, plus spacious and shady common areas. Others in this range include *Residencial Chillán* (☎ 251-677, Av General Velásquez 747) and *Residencial Las Parinas* (☎ 231-971, Prat 541).

Mid-Range Mid-range accommodations start around US$21/26 at well-located *Hotel Tacora* (☎ 251-240, Sotomayor 540). *Hotel Aragón* (☎/fax 252-088, Maipú 344) offers bright motel-style rooms for US$25/35, all with private bath and breakfast, but the busy location makes it noisy at times.

One of Arica's traditional choices, distinguished for its helpful staff, is *Hotel Lynch* (☎ 251-959, fax 231-581, Patricio Lynch 589), where simple but clean rooms with private bath, built around a central courtyard, start around US$26/37. *Hotel Diego de Almagro* (☎ 224-444, Sotomayor 490) has bright, clean rooms with private bath, TV, telephone and double beds for US$30/36. A good buffet breakfast is also available, at extra cost.

Similar to the Diego de Almagro, the **King Hotel** (☎ 232-094, Colón 376) is slightly dearer at US$33/44. Well-situated **Hotel San Marcos** (☎ 232-970, fax 251-815, Sotomayor 367) charges US$38/45.

Popular with tour groups, fronted by attractive gardens, **Hotel Savona** (☎ 231-000, Yungay 380) charges US$49/61 with breakfast. Somewhat costlier but very convenient is **Hotel Central Best Western** (☎ 252-575, 21 de Mayo 425) for US$54/62.

Top End In the restful Azapa Valley, only a short colectivo ride from downtown, the **Azapa Inn** (☎ 244-537, Guillermo Sánchez 660) has top-end accommodations starting at US$83/100, set among striking gardens with a swimming pool. In town, also set among pleasant gardens, **Hotel El Paso** (☎ 231-041, fax 231-965, elpaso@cepri.cl, General Velásquez 1109) charges US$95/115.

On the beach at the southern end of town, **Hotel Arica** (☎ 254-540, fax 231-133, hotpanam@ctc-mundo.net, Av Comandante San Martín 599) has drawn some flack for its service, especially with rates starting at US$103/122, but has responsive management.

Places to Eat

There are numerous cafés and restaurants along 21 de Mayo, 18 de Septiembre, Maipú, Bolognesi and Colón. Many foreign travelers congregate at **Café 21** (☎ 231-680, 21 de Mayo and Colón), which serves hamburgers, sandwiches, snacks, coffee and excellent lager. For breakfast or onces, try sandwiches and *licuados* (milk shakes) at the modest but excellent **Buen Gusto No 2** (Baquedano 559), which is a nonsmoking place.

Inside the fire station, **Casino La Bomba** (☎ 232-983, Colón 357) is an Arica institution for its excellent midday meals (less than US$5) and attentive service, plus the country's hottest fresh *ají*, a spicy condiment similar to Mexican salsa picante. If you can't find it, listen for its deafening siren at noon.

Bavaria (☎ 251-679, Colón 613) is part of a nationwide chain with standard Chilean dishes. Chile's neighbors are represented at the inexpensive Peruvian **El Tacneño** (Prat and Chacabuco) and the Bolivian **Inti-Marka** (Maipú 1). **Govinda** (☎ 231-028, Bolognesi 430) has cheap vegetarian specials.

Within the Mercado Colón, at Colón and Maipú, **Caballito del Mar** (☎ 241-569) has well-prepared corvina, cojinova and other fish dinners for about US$5 to US$6, though service can be erratic. Upstairs in the same building, **El Rey del Marisco** (☎ 229-232) is a more expensive but worthwhile alternative. For a more elaborate spread in beachfront surroundings there's **Maracuyá** (☎ 227-600, Av Comandante San Martín 0321), south of downtown toward Playa El Laucho.

El Arriero (☎ 232-636, 21 de Mayo 385) is a fine parrilla with pleasant atmosphere and friendly service; it's closed Monday. **Los Aleros de 21** (☎ 252-899, 21 de Mayo 736) is a popular but stodgy parrilla trending toward the upscale; the food is good but the service is almost overpowering. **Illimani** (San Marcos 374) is another good parrilla.

D'Aurelio (☎ 321-471, Baquedano 369) is a very good Italian restaurant with attentive service and exceptionally tasty appetizers such as olives and pickled onions. **La Scala** (☎ 231-680, 21 de Mayo 201) serves pizza. **La Ciboulette** (Thompson 238) offers moderately priced lunches and plans an expanding Italian-oriented menu.

Like other northern Chilean coastal towns, Arica has several chifas of decent quality. Try **Shanghai** (☎ 231-955, Maipú 534), **Chin Huang Tao** (Patricio Lynch 317), **Shao Lin** (☎ 232-338, Chacabuco 735) or **Nuevo Mundo** (Blanco Encalada 810). **Goro** (Bolognesi 347-A) is a Japanese venue.

For traditional Chilean food in agreeable surroundings, at the Poblado Artesanal near the Panamericana Sur, try **El Tambo** (☎ 241-757, Hualles 2825), or the Azapa Valley's **Club de Huasos** (☎ 223-991, Km 3.5). Visitors to the museum at San Miguel de Azapa may enjoy **La Picá del Muertito**, alongside the cemetery.

La Fontana (☎ 254-680, Bolognesi 320) has fine fruit-flavored ice cream. **DiMango** (☎ 224-575, 21 de Mayo 244) also has good ice cream.

Entertainment

The *Cine Colón* (☎ 231-165, 7 de Junio 190) shows reasonably current films.

French-run *France Tropicale* (☎ 257-217, Baquedano 371) has live music, generous drinks and good food in an agreeable setting. *Café 303* (Bolognesi 303) is another popular pub.

Shopping

A narrow passageway off Plaza Colón between Sotomayor and 21 de Mayo, Pasaje Bolognesi has a lively artisans' market in the evenings. There are also many permanent shops along the walkway.

The Gendarmería de Chile (prison service) sells prisoners' crafts at the Taller Artesanal San Marcos, at the corner of Sotomayor and Baquedano (the massive building on the Panamericana Sur, as you approach Arica from Iquique, is a state-of-the-art prison).

See also Poblado Artesanal, earlier in the chapter.

Getting There & Away

Air From Arica, travelers can head north across the Peruvian border to Tacna and Lima, south toward Santiago or east to Bolivia.

The flight between Arica and Santiago is one of South America's most spectacular, with awesome views of the northern coastal desert and the Andes. Sit on the left side southbound and the right side northbound.

LanChile (☎ 252-600), 21 de Mayo 345, has at least two flights daily to Santiago (US$208) via Iquique (US$17); one daily flight also stops in Antofagasta (US$30). Ladeco (☎ 252-021), 21 de Mayo 443, flies three times daily from Arica to Iquique and Santiago; their early morning flight stops in Antofagasta. Fares are almost identical to LanChile's.

LanChile also has international services daily to La Paz, Bolivia (US$92 one-way, US$145 roundtrip). Lloyd Aéreo Boliviano (☎ 251-919), Patricio Lynch 298, flies Tuesday and Saturday to La Paz and Santa Cruz, and Thursday to Santa Cruz and La Paz, all with connections to Cochabamba.

Avant (☎ 232-328), 21 de Mayo 277, flies three times daily to Iquique (US$7 to

US$17), Antofagasta (US$29 to US$56) and Santiago (US$133 to US$233).

Bus Arica now has two main bus terminals. Most major companies have their offices at Arica's Terminal de Buses (☎ 241-390), Diego Portales 948 at Av Santa María, but there's also the newer, misleadingly named Terminal Internacional, which is almost directly alongside it on Portales (many companies with international service use the old terminal). Smaller regional companies usually have separate offices closer to downtown.

Bus – Regional For altiplano destinations including Parinacota (Parque Nacional Lauca), Visviri and Charaña (on the Bolivian border), contact Buses Martínez (☎ 232-265), Pedro Montt 620, or Transportes Humire (☎ 260-164), at the new terminal. Both leave Tuesday and Friday at 10 or 10:30 am. Fares to Parinacota are about US$6, to Visviri US$8.

Buses La Paloma (☎ 222-710), Germán Riesco 2071, accepts phone reservations for travel to the precordillera villages of Socoroma (Tuesday and Saturday, US$3), Belén (Tuesday and Friday, US$4) and to Putre (daily, US$4); all depart Arica at 6:45 am. To reach the terminal, take bus No 7 to Germán Riesco, about 12 blocks east of the hospital, or arrange for their special taxibus (US$0.50) to come to your hotel. La Paloma also goes to the southern precordillera village of Codpa Monday and Friday at 8 am (US$3.50, three hours), returning at 5 pm.

Bus Lluta serves Poconchile from the corner of Chacabuco and Vicuña Mackenna in Arica, six times daily between 5:45 am and 8 pm.

Bus – Long-Distance To Iquique, try Buses Carmelita (☎ 241-591), Pullman Santa Rosa (☎ 241-029) or Cuevas y González (☎ 241-090), which have multiple departures among them. Taxi colectivos to Iquique, faster than buses, charge about US$10 per person. The major companies are Tamarugal (☎ 222-609), Turiscargo (☎ 241-052), Taxis Norte (☎ 224-806) and Turistaxi (☎ 222-671).

Fénix Pullman Norte (☎ 222-457) goes to Antofagasta, La Serena and Santiago, with connections to southern Chile. Buses Zambrano (☎ 241-587) serves Iquique, Valparaíso and Viña del Mar. Tur-Bus (☎ 222-217), which has a downtown ticket office at Chacabuco 314, goes to Calama, Antofagasta, Santiago and intermediate points, as do Carmelita, Cata (☎ 222-218) and Pullman Bus (☎ 223-837).

Fichtur (☎ 241-972), which has more comfortable and expensive semi-cama and salón cama service, and Flota Barrios (☎ 223-587) also go to Santiago. Tramaca (☎ 241-198) goes to Calama, Antofagasta and Santiago, while Géminis (☎ 241-647) also has service to Calama and Antofagasta.

Sample bus fares and travel times include Iquique (US$5, four hours), Calama (US$12 to US$17, nine hours), Antofagasta (US$20, 12 hours), Copiapó (US$30), La Serena (US$32, 19 hours) and Santiago (US$38 to US$56, 26 hours).

Bus – International Adsubliata (☎ 241-972) offers frequent bus service (US$2) to Tacna, Peru. Several companies operate taxi colectivos to Tacna for about US$3 per person; these leave from the new bus terminal whenever they are full, and take about an hour, including a tedious Peruvian customs inspection.

Tas Choapa (☎ 222-817) operates services to Lima, Peru (US$42, 20 hours) Tuesday at 8 pm, but it's cheaper to take local transport to Tacna and then buy a separate ticket to Lima or elsewhere in Peru.

Since completion of the paving of the highway across the altiplano to La Paz, Bolivia (US$21 to US$35, six to eight hours depending on the weather), there has been a proliferation of bus services on the route. Among the carriers are Géminis (☎ 241-647), Cata (☎ 222-218), Chile Bus (☎ 222-817), at Cuevas y González and Ramos Cholele at the main terminal, and Buses Litoral (☎ 254-702), Trans Panamericana and Salvador (☎ 246-064) at the newer terminal. Buses on this route will drop passengers in Parque Nacional Lauca, but expect to pay full fare to La Paz. There are also taxi colectivos to La Paz for around US$55.

Tramaca (☎ 222-586) leaves Monday and Thursday at 11 pm for Salta, Argentina (US$70, 24 hours), via Calama. Géminis (☎ 241-647) may restore service on this route, which is generally heavily booked and operates in summer only.

Train The Ferrocarril Arica-Tacna (☎ 231-115), Máximo Lira 889, still chugs across the Peruvian border around noon and 4 pm Monday, Wednesday and Friday (turn up about half an hour earlier for exit formalities). The 1½-hour journey costs about US$1.50 but is for rail aficionados only – taxi colectivos are faster and more frequent.

Getting Around
To/From the Airport Aeropuerto Internacional Chacalluta (☎ 211-116) is 18km north of Arica, near the Peruvian border. Radio Taxi Aeropuerto Chacalluta (☎ 254-812), Patricio Lynch 371, provides door-to-door service for US$4 (shared taxi) or US$10 (single passenger). Try also Radio Taxi Arica (☎ 250-340), Prat 528.

Bus Local buses and taxi colectivos connect downtown with the main bus terminal. Taxi colectivos, only slightly more expensive than buses, are faster and more frequent. Destinations are clearly marked on an illuminated sign atop the cab.

Car Rental cars are available from Hertz (☎ 231-487), on the grounds of Hotel El Paso at General Velásquez 1109, American (☎ 252-234) at 21 de Mayo 821 and Klasse (☎ 254-498) at General Velásquez 760, Local 25.

Bicycle Latinorizons (☎ 250-007), Thompson 236, rents mountain bikes for US$6 per half day, US$12 per full day. Residencial Caracas (☎ 253-688), Sotomayor 867, also rents mountain bikes.

AROUND ARICA
There are varied sights and recreational opportunities in and near Arica. Most are easy day trips, especially with a car, but some of the more distant ones would be more suitable as overnighters. Closest to Arica is the

AROUND ARICA

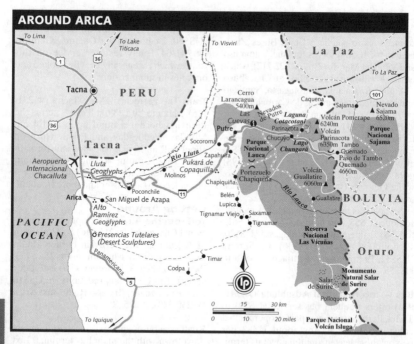

irrigated Azapa Valley, a prodigious producer of olives and tomatoes for export to central Chile, but also an area of major archaeological sites.

Museo Arqueológico San Miguel de Azapa

In the Azapa Valley, the continually improving Museo Arqueológico displays a superb assemblage of exhibits on regional culture sequences from the 7th century BC to the Spanish invasion, in a building expressly designed for the purpose. It is also increasingly interactive, with computers on site, and the museum sells books, journals and artisanal goods.

The staff can point out nearby archaeological sites – ask about early geoglyphs at **Atoca**, Tiwanaku-era (700-1000 AD) fortifications at **Pukará San Lorenzo** and the Incaic **Cerro Sagrado** (1000-1400 AD). Some local tour companies include the museum and other valley sites on their itineraries.

In January and February, the museum (☎ 224-248), 12km east of Arica, is open 9 am to 8 pm daily; the rest of the year hours are 10 am to 6 pm daily. It's closed January 1, May 1 and December 25. Admission costs US$1.50 for adults, US$0.75 for children.

From Parque Chacabuco, at the corner of Chacabuco and Patricio Lynch in Arica, taxi colectivos (US$1) operate between 7 am and 10 pm daily.

Lluta Geoglyphs

About 10km north of Arica, the Panamericana intersects paved Chile 11, which leads east up the valley of the Río Lluta to Poconchile. A short distance inland, a series of restored pre-Columbian geoglyphs cover an otherwise barren slope on the right. These figures, made by grouping dark stones over light-colored soil, include representations of llamas, and recall the importance of pre-Columbian pack trains on the route to

Tiahuanaco, a traffic which only recently disappeared with the construction of good motor roads.

Poconchile

Built in the 17th century, reconstructed in the 19th century, and restored in the 20th century, Poconchile's **Iglesia de San Gerónimo** is one of the oldest churches in the country. Camping is possible along the Río Lluta.

To get to Poconchile, take Bus Lluta from Chacabuco and Vicuña Mackenna in Arica to the end of the line at the carabineros checkpoint.

Copaquilla

As Chile 11 zigzags up the desolate mountainside, there are exceptional views of the upper Lluta valley. Along the route, the very appropriately named *cactus candelabros* ('candle-holder' cactus or *Browningia candelaris*) grows just 5mm to 7mm a year and flowers for only 24 hours. These cacti and other plants absorb moisture from the *camanchaca* (fog) that penetrates inland.

At Copaquilla, overlooking a spectacular canyon, the restored 12th-century fortress **Pukará de Copaquilla** was built to protect Indian farmlands below – notice the abandoned terraces, evidence of a much larger pre-Columbian population. Tours to Parque Nacional Lauca normally make a brief stop here.

Along the highway just west of Copaquilla, the eccentric *Posada Pueblo Maiko* is a surviving remainder of 1994's eclipse mania and a good spot to stop for fresh bread and a drink (including mate de coca from the fresh coca leaf, but *not* Coca-Cola).

Socoroma

On the colonial pack route between Arica and Potosí, Socoroma is an Aymara farming village featuring cobbled streets, the 17th-century **Iglesia de San Francisco** and other colonial remains.

Emilia Humire has a simple hospedaje (three beds) and also offers meals. See the Getting There & Away entry for Arica for transport details.

Belén Precordillera

At Zapahuira, a gravel road leaves the international highway and heads south through a series of villages in an area showcasing numerous archaeological sites, including pre-Columbian fortresses and agricultural terraces, as well as colonial relics comparable to those in many parts of Peru. The highlights are the *pukarás* (pre-Hispanic fortifications) of Belén, Lupica and Saxamar, and there are also colonial churches at Belén and Tignamar Viejo.

This route makes an excellent day trip from Arica for travelers with vehicles, but only Belén has tourist services – María Martínez's simple hospedaje (two beds) , which also serves meals. South of Tignamar, the road deteriorates through a narrow and dusty canyon, but improves beyond the turnoff to Timar and Codpa, where it becomes a wide, smooth dirt road that rejoins the Panamericana 21km south of Arica. At the junction with the Panamericana, the state arts agency Fondart has sponsored a series of desert sculptures known as **Presencias Tutelares** (guardian spirits).

Buses La Paloma (☎ 222-710), Germán Riesco 2071 in Arica, goes to Belén Tuesday and Friday at 6:45 am. La Paloma also goes to Codpa (US$4) and Tignamar Monday and Friday at 4 pm, making a loop on public transportation feasible, though not particularly convenient. This would mean walking or hitchhiking (with very few vehicles on the road) the 13km between Belén and Tignamar. Hitchhiking is never entirely safe in any country in the world, and Lonely Planet does not recommend it. Travelers who decide to hitchhike should understand that they are taking a small but potentially serious risk. People who do choose to hitchhike will be safer if they travel in pairs and let someone know where they are planning to go.

PUTRE
☎ 58

Placed on the international travel map due to the total solar eclipse of 1994, Putre is an appealing Aymara village, 3500m above sea level in the precordillera, where many visitors prefer to spend at least a day acclimatizing before proceeding to Parque Nacional Lauca, on the altiplano. Originally a 16th-century *reducción*, established by the Spaniards to facilitate control of the Indians, Putre retains many houses with late-colonial elements. In the surrounding hills, local farmers raise alfalfa for llamas, sheep and cattle on extensive stone-faced agricultural terraces of even greater antiquity.

Dating from 1670, the adobe **Iglesia de Putre**, on the north side of the Plaza de Armas, was restored two centuries later. To visit its interior, which contains valuable colonial artifacts, ask for the keys and leave a small donation.

Putre's February **Carnaval** is an informal, spontaneous affair in which visitors may be either willing or unwilling participants – fortunately, the locals fill their balloons with flour rather than water, and cover onlookers with *chaya* (multicolored paper dots) rather than fresh fruit. Two noncompetitive groups, the older *banda* and the younger *tarqueada*, provide the music; many participants are returnees from Arica. The event ends with the burning of the *momo*, a figure symbolizing the frivolity of Carnaval.

Information

The post office is at the corner of Carrera and Prat. Entel, on the south side of the Plaza de Armas, is open 9 am to 1 pm and 4 to 8 pm daily.

Organized Tours

Alaskan Barbara Knapton runs Birding Alto Andino (☎ 300-013 for voicemail, fax 222-735), Baquedano 299, which organizes specialized birding tours, as well as more general tours, of Parque Nacional Lauca and other parts of the altiplano as far away as Parque Nacional Volcán Isluga. She also runs a book exchange. Transportation is in a comfortable 4WD vehicle, with oxygen. Discounts on standard rates are available to travelers who have their own camping equipment and prefer to cook their own food, or who have their own vehicles; sometimes accommodations are at Conaf refugios. Trips can start and end in Arica or Putre.

Full-day tours to Las Cuevas, Parinacota, Laguna Cotacotani and Lago Chungará cost US$150 for one or two people, US$175 for three or US$200 for four. The very long full-day trip to the Salar de Surire costs US$288 for one or two people, US$300 for three or US$312 for four.

The overnight trip to Lago Chungará, Parinacota and the Salar de Surire is only slightly dearer than the full-day trip to Surire, at US$325 for one or two persons, US$365 for three or US$400 for four. Prices are identical for the overnight to Parinacota, Caquena and Lago Chungará.

Three-day, two-night excursions include Lago Chungará, Parinacota, Surire and Parque Nacional Isluga, costing US$575 for one or two persons, US$625 for three or US$675 for four; the same trip ending in Pozo Almonte or Iquique costs US$650 for one or two people, US$700 for three or US$750 for four.

Places to Stay & Eat

Restaurant Oasis (Cochrane s/n) serves good, plain meals and offers basic accommodations for US$5 per person, but lacks hot water. *Residencial La Paloma (Baquedano s/n)* has hot showers, clean, spacious rooms and good beds for US$6 per person, but the thin walls mean it's noisy sometimes and it does get cold at night. Meals are also available.

The comparable *Restaurant Rosamel (Cochrane s/n)* also provides modest accommodations and serves lunch to Lauca tour groups. The slightly more expensive regular meals are also a good value. Across from La Paloma, the spotless, friendly *Hostal Cali (Baquedano s/n)* has excellent rooms for US$6 per person with shared bath, US$10 with private bath.

Opposite the army camp, Conaf's comfy *Refugio Putre (O'Higgins s/n)* offers lodging when space permits for about US$10 (slightly cheaper for Chilean nationals). There are six beds, hot showers and cooking facilities.

Casa Barbarita (Baquedano 299), the site of Birding Altoandino (see Organized Tours) also rents out rooms for US$10 per person with kitchen privileges or US$50 for the entire house, which sleeps six. The next-door pub **Kuilin Marka** *(Baquedano s/n)* has good food and atmosphere but stays open late, leading to conflicts with neighbors.

Originally built for mining interests, at the approach to town, **Hostería Las Vicuñas** *(☎ 228-564)* charges from US$46/67 singles/doubles, breakfast and dinner included. It also offers other meals.

Getting There & Away

Putre is 150km east of Arica via paved Chile 11, the international highway to Bolivia. Buses La Paloma (☎ 222-710), Germán Riesco 2071 in Arica, serves Putre daily, departing Arica at 6:45 am, returning in the early afternoon. Buses to Parinacota, in Parque Nacional Lauca (see below), pass the turnoff to Putre, which is 5km from the main highway.

PARQUE NACIONAL LAUCA

One of Chile's most accessible parks, Parque Nacional Lauca is a World Biosphere Reserve harboring vicuña, *vizcacha* (a wild Andean relative of the domestic chinchilla) and more than 150 bird species (including condor and rhea), plus cultural and archaeological landmarks and Aymara herders of llamas and alpacas. Among its spectacular features is Lago Chungará, one of the world's highest lakes, at the foot of the dormant twin Pallachata volcanoes. Slightly to the south, Volcán Guallatire smokes ominously.

Lauca comprises 138,000 hectares of altiplano, between 3000m and 6300m above sea level, 160km northeast of Arica near the Bolivian border. Contiguous to the park, but more difficult to access, are Reserva Nacional Las Vicuñas and Monumento Natural Salar de Surire. Once part of the park, they now constitute technically separate units but are still managed by Conaf and are described below.

The park's altitude, well above 4000m in most parts, requires the visitor to adapt gradually. Do not exert yourself at first and eat and drink moderately; if you suffer anyway, try a cup of tea made from the common Aymara herbal remedy *chachacoma*, readily gathered around the settlements, or *mate de coca*. Keep water at your bedside, as the throat desiccates rapidly in the arid climate, and wear sunblock – tropical rays can be truly brutal at this elevation.

Lauca is currently under siege from mining interests who, with support from some regional officials, have formed a coalition that threatens to amputate the park's western third for a speculative, unquestionably destructive, gold-seeking venture. At the same time, courts have ruled that roughly 80% of the park belongs not to the state, but to Aymara residents, some of whose titles date from the days of Peruvian sovereignty. The next few years are likely to see politically turbulent struggles over control of the land.

Geography & Climate

Beyond Copaquilla, paved Chile 11 climbs steadily but gradually through the precordillera to the park entrance at Las Cuevas, where the altiplano proper begins. Rainfall and vegetation increase with altitude and distance from the coast; it can snow during the summer rainy season, known as *invierno boliviano* (Bolivian winter), when heavy fog often covers the precordillera approaches to the park.

Along the highway and at Las Cuevas, remarkably tame specimens of the vicuña *(Vicugna vicugna)*, a wild relative of the llama, are living advertisements for a major Chilean wildlife conservation success story. Pay special attention to the ground-hugging, bright green *llareta (Laretia compacta)*, a densely growing shrub with a cushionlike appearance that belies the fact that it's nearly as hard as rock – the Aymara need a pick or mattock to break open dead llareta, which they collect for fuel.

The local Aymara pasture their llamas and alpacas on verdant *bofedales* (swampy alluvial grasslands) and the lower slopes of the surrounding mountains, and sell handicrafts woven from their wool in the village of Parinacota and at Lago Chungará.

Information

Conaf's refugio at Parinacota is due to open as a Centro de Información Ambiental.

NORTE GRANDE

The New World Camelids

Unlike the Old World, the Western Hemisphere had few grazing mammals after the Pleistocene, when mammoths, horses and other large herbivores disappeared for reasons that are not entirely clear. Their disappearance is linked to hunting pressure by the earliest inhabitants of the plains and pampas of North and South America. For millennia, however, Andean peoples have relied on the New World camels – the wild guanaco and vicuña, the domesticated llama and alpaca – for food and fiber.

Guanacos and vicuñas are few today, but are the likely ancestors of their domesticated cousins. In fact, they were among very few potential New World domesticates – contrast them with the Old World cattle, horses, sheep, goats, donkeys and pigs which have filled so many vacant niches in the Americas. Of the major domesticated animals from across the Atlantic, only the humped camels have failed to achieve an important role here. While the New World camels

Alpaca

have literally lost ground to sheep and cattle in some areas, they are not likely to disappear.

The range of the guanaco *(Lama guanicoe)* extends from the central Andes to Tierra del Fuego, at elevations from sea level up to 4000m or more. In the central Andes, where the human population is small and widely dispersed but domestic livestock are numerous, its numbers are small, but on the plains of Argentine Patagonia and in reserves such as southern Chile's Parque Nacional Torres del Paine, herds of rust-colored guanaco are still a common sight. Native hunters ate its meat and dressed in its skins.

By contrast the vicuña *(Vicugna vicugna)* occupies a much smaller geographical range, well above 4000m in the puna and altiplano, from south-central Peru to northwestern Argentina. While not so numerous as the guanaco, it played a critical role in the cultural life of pre-Columbian Peru, which assured its survival; its very fine golden wool was the exclusive property of the Inka kings. Spanish chronicler Bernabé Cobo wrote that the ruler's clothing was 'made of the finest wool and the best cloth that was woven in his whole kingdom…most of it was made of vicuña wool, which is almost as fine as silk.'

Strict Inka authority protected the vicuña, but the Spanish invasion destroyed that authority and made the species vulnerable, over the past 500 years, to hunting pressure. By the middle of this century, poaching reduced its numbers from two million to perhaps 10,000 and ensured its placement

Vicuña

The New World Camelids

on Appendix I of the Endangered Species List. But conservation programs such as those in northern Chile's Parque Nacional Lauca have achieved so impressive a recovery that economic exploitation of the species – for cloth that would bring a good price – may soon benefit the communities of the puna. In Lauca and surrounding areas, vicuña numbers grew from barely a thousand in the early 1970s to more than 24,000 nearly three decades later.

The communities of the puna and altiplano – in northern Chile, mostly Aymara Indians – still depend on llamas and alpacas for their livelihood. While the two species appear similar, they differ in several important respects. The taller, rangier and hardier llama *(Lama glama)* is a pack animal whose relatively coarse wool serves for blankets, ropes and other household goods (llama trains are rare in Chile since good roads penetrated the altiplano). It can survive – even flourish – on relatively poor, dry pastures. The smaller, more delicate alpaca *(Lama pacos)* is not a pack animal and requires well-watered, sometimes irrigated grasslands in order to produce a much finer wool with great commercial value. Both llama and alpaca meat are consumed by Andean households and even sold in urban markets – visit Arica's Mercado Benedicto for 'churrasco de alpaca.'

Llama

Meager earnings from wool and meat have not been sufficient to stem the flow of population from the countryside to cities such as Arica and Iquique, but, if international agreement permits it, the commercialization of vicuña wool might help do so. According to one Conaf study, production and sale of vicuña cloth at a price of nearly US$290 per linear meter could earn more than US$300,000 per annum for reinvestment in one of Chile's most remote and poorest areas.

If, as intended, Conaf involves the area's inhabitants and respects their needs and wishes, it could set a precedent that many Latin American governments might emulate in tropical rain forests and other threatened environments. In Santiago, legal purchases of vicuña wool may be possible at Casimiro Castrodonoso at Moneda 950 (☎ 695-4091) and at Bucarest 25, Providencia (☎ 233-4789).

Guanaco

NORTE GRANDE

Otherwise, rangers at the Las Cuevas entrance and at Lago Chungará are available for consultation.

Las Cuevas

At the park's western entrance, Las Cuevas has a permanent ranger station which is a good source of information and an excellent place to view and photograph the vicuña, whose numbers have increased from barely a thousand in the early 1970s to nearly 25,000 today. Over the past decade of protection, they have also become exceptionally tame. Don't miss a soak in the rustic thermal baths nearby, where camping may be possible.

Just beyond Las Cuevas, Conaf has built a new overlook **Mirador Llano de Chucuyo**, featuring a massive, out-of-place sculpture in orange, blue and yellow that partly resembles the Andean *zampoña* (panpipes).

Ciénegas de Parinacota

On the north side of Chile 11, between the tiny settlements of Chucuyo and Parinacota, *guallatas* (Andean geese) and ducks drift on the Río Lauca and nest on the shore, while the curious mountain vizcacha *(Lagidium viscacia)*, a relative of the domestic chinchilla, peeks out from numerous rockeries that rise above the swampy sediments of the park's largest bofedales.

Most of the Aymaras' domestic livestock also graze the *ciénegas* (swamps), which shelter some interesting cultural relics – there's a colonial chapel just below Restaurant Matilde at Chucuyo, and another about half an hour's walk from Parinacota. A small weavers' cooperative sells local woolens in Chucuyo.

Parinacota

Five kilometers off the international highway, Parinacota is a picturesque but nearly depopulated pastoral village whose 17th-century colonial church, reconstructed in 1789, contains surrealistic murals, the work of artists from the Cuzco school. The murals recall Hieronymus Bosch's *Sinners in the Hands of an Angry God*, but note also the depiction of the soldiers bearing Christ to the cross as Spaniards. According to local legend, the small table chained to the wall used to leave the church at night in search of spirits. To visit the church, ask caretaker Cipriano Morales for the key and leave a small donation.

Conaf has a refugio at Parinacota, built originally for a high-altitude genetic research project, (see Places to Stay & Eat, later in this section). Ask rangers for information on surrounding sights such as Laguna Cotacotani and Cerro Guane Guane.

Laguna Cotacotani

Laguna Cotacotani is the source of the Río Lauca, but unfortunate diversions by Endesa, the privatized national electric company, have caused fluctuations in lake levels and undermined its ecological integrity. Still, along its shores, at the foot of sprawling lava flows and cinder cones, you will see diverse bird life and scattered groves of *queñoa (Polylepis tarapacana)*, one of the world's highest-elevation trees, reaching about 5m in height. Though puma are not commonly seen, tracks are not unusual, and foxes are fairly common. Follow the road along the south bank of the Río Lauca from Parinacota.

Cerro Guane Guane

Immediately north of Parinacota, Guane Guane is a 5096m peak with extraordinary panoramic views of the park and beyond. From the village, it's climbable along its eastern shoulder in about four hours, but the last 500m in particular are a difficult slog through porous volcanic sand – one step forward, two steps back. Ask advice from Conaf's rangers, and do not attempt to climb in threatening weather, since there is no shelter from lightning.

Lago Chungará

More than 4500m above sea level, Lago Chungará is a shallow body of water formed when a lava flow dammed the snowmelt stream from 6350m Volcán Parinacota, which dominates the lake to the north. About 28km from Las Cuevas, Chungará is home to abundant, unusual bird life, including the Chilean flamingo *(Phoenicopterus chilensis)*, the *tagua gigante* or giant coot *(Fulica gigantea)* and the Andean gull

(Larus serranus). You can reach the west end of the lake from Parinacota on foot in about two hours, but most of its wildlife is more distant, near the Conaf ranger station on Chile 11 and the Chilean customs post near the border, so you may want to drive to one of these spots and then hike.

Because of Arica's increasing consumption of hydroelectricity and the Azapa Valley's insatiable thirst, Endesa has built an intricate system of pumps and canals that constitute a continuing menace to Lago Chungará's ecological integrity, though they are unused at present. Since the lake is so shallow, any lowering of its level would dramatically reduce its overall surface area and impinge on those parts where wading birds such as the flamingo and giant coot feed and nest.

You'll find woolens and other crafts for sale in the parking lot at the Conaf refugio, many of which come from Bolivia; for locally made goods, try the weavers' cooperative in Chucuyo.

Feria Tambo Quemado

At the east end of Lago Chungará, the border post of Tambo Quemado is also the site of a colorful international market on alternate Fridays.

Places to Stay & Eat

While the park has no formal accommodations, there are several reasonable alternatives. In a pinch, Conaf's *Refugio Las Cuevas*, at the park entrance, may offer a bed.

In Chucuyo, directly on the highway to Bolivia near the junction to Parinacota, *Restaurant Matilde* usually has an extra bed at a very reasonable price. Matilde Morales prepares alpaca steaks and other simple meals, and there are two other inexpensive restaurants. Limited supplies, including food, are available, but it's cheaper and more convenient to bring them from Arica.

Conaf's sparsely furnished *Refugio Parinacota*, 3km from Chucuyo, offers beds for US$8 per night, slightly cheaper for Chilean nationals, but bring your own sleeping bag. The availability of hot showers depends on the sporadic arrival of gas canisters from

Arica. Two small tent campsites are available nearby for US$11.

Conaf charges US$8 per person at its lakeside *Refugio Chungará*, which has eight beds, and US$11 per site for its adjacent *Camping Chungará*, which has picnic tables and 1.2m-high stone walls for shelter from the wind. At 4500m above sea level, it gets frigid at night.

Getting There & Away

Parque Nacional Lauca straddles Chile 11, the Arica-La Paz highway, which is paved all the way to La Paz; the trip from Arica now takes only about three hours. From Arica, there is regular passenger service with Buses Martínez (☎ 232-265), Pedro Montt 620, or Transporte Humire (☎ 253-497). Martínez leaves Tuesday and Friday at 10 am; Humire departs at 10 pm the same days. Fares to Parinacota are about US$6, to Visviri US$7.50.

Several travel agencies in Arica offer tours to the park – for details, see Organized Tours in the Arica section. Although tours provide a good introduction, you spend most of the time in transit, so try to arrange a longer stay at Chucuyo, Parinacota or Chungará – one alternative is renting a car in Arica and driving to the park, providing access to more remote sites like Guallatire, Caquena and the Salar de Surire (the latter only with a high-clearance vehicle, since it involves fording several watercourses). Carry extra fuel in cans – most rental agencies will provide them – but fuel is available from Empresa de Comercio Agrícola (ECA) in Putre and perhaps from Matilde Morales in Chucuyo. Do not forget warm clothing and sleeping gear.

RESERVA NACIONAL LAS VICUÑAS

South of Lauca, Reserva Nacional Las Vicuñas consists of 210,000 sparsely inhabited hectares where the endangered vicuña has proliferated; once part of the park, it was reclassified in the mid-1980s to permit reopening of the gold mine at Choquelimpie, which has since closed.

At the base of smoking Volcán Guallatire, 60km from Parinacota via a roundabout route, the village of Guallatire features a 17th-century church and Conaf's *Refugio Guallatire*, which provides beds for US$9 per person but is not always staffed (ask in Arica, Las Cuevas or Parinacota). South of Guallatire, on the Surire road, are ruins of a colonial silver mill.

Farther south, new bridges cross the Río Viluvio, a tributary of the Lauca, but the road can still be impassable during summer rains, even with 4WD. Carabineros at Guallatire and Chilcaya (farther south) have 4WD vehicles and *may* be able to help vehicles in distress.

MONUMENTO NATURAL SALAR DE SURIRE

En route to Surire, 126km from Putre and 108km from Parinacota, vicuña and flocks of the sprinting *ñandú* (the ostrich-like rhea, *Pterocnemia pennata)* dot the countryside. Formed in 1983 when the Chilean government reduced the size of Parque Nacional Lauca, the monument itself comprises 11,300 hectares around a sprawling salt lake with breeding colonies of three species of flamingos, including the rare James flamingo *(parina chica* or *Phoenicoparrus jamesi)*, which are present from December to April. In 1989, the outgoing military dictatorship gave 4560 hectares to the mining company Quiborax.

Again, there is no public transport, but it may be possible to hitchhike with trucks from the nearby borax mine or with Conaf, whose *Refugio Surire* has beds for US$11. Camping is possible at Polloquere, where there are rustic thermal baths. Please note that hitchhiking is never entirely safe in any country in the world, and Lonely Planet does not recommend it. However this is the only alternative. Travelers who decide to hitchhike should understand that they are taking a small but potentially serious risk.

Although most visitors return to Putre and Arica, it's possible to make a southerly circuit through Parque Nacional Isluga and back to Arica via Camiña or Huara. Do not attempt this without consulting either Conaf or the carabineros. The route is particularly iffy during the summer rainy season.

PISAGUA
☎ 57

Midway between Arica and Iquique, the isolated coastal village of Pisagua has a long, sometimes inglorious history. Several architectural landmarks have survived from one of Chile's largest 19th-century nitrate ports, which became a penal colony after the decline of the nitrate industry. It acquired true notoriety as a prison camp for the military dictatorship of 1973-1989; after the return to democracy, the discovery of unmarked mass graves in the local cemetery caused an international scandal.

With a small population (barely 150), Pisagua occupies a narrow shelf at the foot of the coast range, which rises almost vertically from the shore. There are good campsites and beaches at the north end of town. Visitors not deterred by the town's grim history will find much of interest and, as work proceeds on a road north toward Arica, this stretch of coastline may become as popular as the newly paved Ruta 1 south of Iquique.

Things to See & Do

On a hillock overlooking the town, Pisagua's brightly painted **Torre Reloj** (clock tower) is a national monument dating from the nitrate glory days, when the port had a population of several thousand.

North of the palm-shaded Plaza de Armas, the surf laps at the foundations of the **Teatro Municipal**, a once-lavish theater with a broad stage, opera-style boxes, and ceiling murals of cherubim; the regional government has dedicated substantial resources toward restoring the facade and parts of the interior, and there have even been some presentations on its stage. The building's northern half, which once held dressing rooms, municipal offices and a market, is also worth exploring, but be cautious – one second-story door plunges directly into the ocean. To enter the theater, ask someone for directions to the house of Catarina Saldaña, who keeps the key, on the hill above the carabineros station.

A half-block inland from the plaza, the **Colonia Penal Pisagua** was a conventional

NORTE GRANDE

prison and not the primary site for incarceration of political prisoners after the military coup of 1973. Now the town's only hotel, it seems to be atoning for Pisagua's grisly past by featuring portraits of leftist icons such as poet Pablo Neruda and folksinger Violeta Parra.

Just beyond the police station, the abandoned train station recalls the time when Pisagua was the northern terminus of El Longino, the longitudinal railway that connected the nitrate mines with the ports of the Norte Grande. Just outside town and off the road to the north, the **Monolito Centenario** commemorates a local battle during the War of the Pacific.

About 2km north of town, the faded wooden crosses at Pisagua's **Cementerio** mark tombs from the town's historic past; this was also the notorious site of a mass grave of victims of the Pinochet dictatorship. A memorial plaque proclaims that 'Although the tracks may touch this site for a thousand years, they will not cover the blood of those who fell here.'

Beyond the cemetery, the road continues to **Pisagua Vieja**, with a handful of adobe ruins, scattered, mummified human remains from a pre-Columbian cemetery, and a broad sandy beach. From here, a rough road (appropriate only for 4WD vehicles) continues up the Quebrada de Tana to Hacienda Tiliviche, on the Panamericana. Summer rains, such as those in 1999, can create dangerous washouts.

Places to Stay & Eat

Pisagua's free *Camping Municipal* is basically a large parking lot at Playa Seis, a small but fine sandy beach just beyond the ruins of the former fish processing factory that once incarcerated political prisoners. It has clean toilets and de facto hot showers, since the water piped from the old rail station of Dolores, on the pampas behind Pisagua, runs through surface pipes heated by the desert sun. You can also camp north of town at Playa Blanca, beneath the Monolito Centenario, but there are no facilities.

In the former jail, *Hotel Pisagua* (☎ 731-509) charges US$28 with full board for

Pisagua's famous clock tower

adults, US$15 for children; B&B – lodging and breakfast only – is also available, but there are few other places to eat. All the guest rooms remain labeled for their original institutional occupants – the warden, guards and other prison personnel. Visitors can dine among banana trees and gardenias on the patio; the lunch menu, usually a seafood dish, is very good and costs about US$5. In addition to superb pisco sours, ping-pong and billiard tables provide amusement.

Getting There & Away

Pisagua is 40km west of the Panamericana by a good road from a turnoff 85km south of the carabineros checkpoint at Cuya and 47km north of Huara. All but the last 5km are paved, but wind often covers part of the road with a film of sand that can make the surface more slippery than it looks. There is a taxi (☎ 731-511) that will pick up passengers from the junction with the Panamericana.

IQUIQUE
☎ 57

Prior to the Spanish invasion, Iquique was a minor concentration of coastal Chango Indians who traded fish and guano from offshore islands for maize, potatoes and other products of the precordillera and the altiplano. During the colonial era, guano grew in importance, but the region's real wealth stemmed from the Huantajaya silver mine in the coast range, second only to the bonanza vein at Potosí.

During the 19th century, Tarapacá's minerals and nitrates were shipped by narrow-gauge railways through ports such as Iquique, once little more than a collection of shanties at the base of the barren headlands. In 1835 Darwin observed that Iquique:

...contains about a thousand inhabitants, and stands on a little plain of sand at the foot of a great wall of rock two thousand feet in height, here forming the coast. The whole is utterly desert. A light shower of rain falls only once in very many years; and the ravines consequently are filled with detritus, and the mountain-sides covered by piles of fine white sand, even to a height of a thousand feet...The aspect of the place was most gloomy; the little port, with its few vessels, and small group of wretched houses, seemed overwhelmed and out of all proportion with the rest of the scene.

In a few years, Darwin would barely have recognized Iquique. As the nitrate industry grew, its population exceeded 5000 in the 20 years following his visit, and 40,000 by the turn of the century. Not all the nitrate ports survived, but in those that did, such as Iquique, mining barons built opulent mansions (many of them still standing), while authorities piped in water from the distant cordillera and imported topsoil for public plazas and private gardens. Downtown Iquique reflects this 19th-century boom, its Plaza Prat complete with clock tower and theater with Corinthian columns, as well as many stately wooden Victorian mansions. Nearby ghost towns such as Humberstone and Santa Laura, with their rusting machinery, recall the source of this wealth.

The nitrate era also made Iquique the site of one of the most notorious episodes in Chilean labor history: In 1907, nearly 8500 strikers gathered in and around the Escuela Santa María to protest unemployment and unfair treatment in the salitreras, and to agitate for improved benefits. When they refused to abandon the school, the police and military fired machine guns upon the unarmed strikers, killing hundreds and wounding many more. The Chilean folk group Quilapayún immortalized the incident in their record *Cantata Popular Santa María de Iquique*.

Now a city of more than 140,000, Iquique is still one of the Norte Grande's largest ports, but fishing has supplanted mining as its primary industry – Iquique ships more fishmeal than any other port in the world. Establishment of the Zona Franca (duty-free zone) in 1975 has made it one of Chile's most prosperous cities, and the paving of Ruta 1 to Antofagasta is bringing larger numbers of visitors.

Downtown retains the atmosphere of a 19th-century port, with ramshackle wooden houses, sailors' bars and street life, but the city is spreading south along the coast, where many houses are literally built on sand and, consequently, vulnerable to the area's frequent earthquakes. New high-rise apartment blocks and hotels along the beach remind some visitors of Miami Beach, on a lesser scale. On the desert plain high above Iquique, toward the Panamericana, new housing developments are making the once tiny community of Alto Hospicio an integral part of the city. Alto Hospicio (whose population may be as great as 50,000) is also home to burgeoning shantytowns, as low-skilled, low-wage workers can no longer afford to live in Iquique proper.

Orientation

Iquique sits on a narrow terrace at the foot of the coastal range, which abruptly rises 600m above the city, 1853km north of Santiago by a combination of the Panamericana and Ruta 1, and a roundabout 315km from Arica via the Panamericana and paved Ruta 16, which passes through the spreading hilltop suburb of Alto Hospicio. Blocked by the mountains, Iquique has sprawled north and, especially, south along the coast. Alto Hospicio is growing even more rapidly.

The city's focus is Plaza Prat. Av Baquedano, which runs north-south along the east side of the plaza, is the main thoroughfare, while Calle Tarapacá runs east four blocks to Plaza Condell, a secondary center of downtown activity. Most points of interest are within a roughly rectangular area marked by Sotomayor to the north, Av Costanera to the west, Amunátegui to the east, and Manuel Bulnes to the south. The main beaches are south of downtown, along Av Balmaceda and its extension Av 11 de Septiembre.

Information

Iquique's Sernatur (☎ 427-686, fax 411-523, sernatur_iquiq@entelchile.net) is at Serrano 145, Oficina 303. Open 8:30 am to 5:30 pm weekdays, it's helpful and provides a free city map and brochures, but is less well stocked than its counterparts in other Chilean cities. In December, January and February it has a branch at Aníbal Pinto 486, and another at the Palacio Astoreca, O'Higgins 350. Another good source of information is the Automóvil Club de Chile (☎ 413-206), Serrano 154, across the street from Sernatur.

Afex, on Serrano between Uribe and Patricio Lynch, changes foreign currency and traveler's checks, and there are many ATMs downtown and at the Zona Franca (where there are also cambios).

The post office, Bolívar 458, is open 8:30 am to 12:30 pm and 3 to 7 pm weekdays, 9 am to 1 pm Saturday.

Iquique has several telephone offices, including Telefónica at Ramírez 587 and at the Zona Franca, Módulo 212, 2nd level. Entel is at Gorostiaga 251.

The VIP CyberCafé (☎ 416-011), Latorre 703, provides Internet access.

The Swiss-run Academia de Idiomas del Norte (☎ 411-827, fax 429-343), Ramírez 1345, provides Spanish language instruction.

Lavarápido (☎ 425-338), Obispo Labbé 1446, provides laundry service and charges by weight. Laverap (☎ 420-353) is at San Martín 490. Hospital Regional Doctor Ernesto Torres Galdames (☎ 422-370) is at the corner of Tarapacá and Av Héroes de la Concepción, 10 blocks east of Plaza Condell.

Walking Tour

Because of its 19th-century heritage, rooted in foreign exploitation of nitrates, Iquique's architecture resembles that of few other Latin American cities, and fire is a constant hazard to its distinctive wooden buildings. Many city landmarks are on Plaza Prat, including the **Torre Reloj** (1877) clock tower; the **Teatro Municipal**, a neoclassical structure that has hosted opera, theater and other cultural activities since 1890; and the adjacent **Sociedad Protectora de Empleados de Tarapacá** (1913), one of the country's first labor union buildings. At the northeast corner, facing the plaza, the Moorish-style **Centro Español** (1904) is now a club and restaurant whose interior features murals and oil paintings based on themes from *Don Quijote* and from Spanish history.

South of the plaza, **Av Baquedano** is a preservation zone for Georgian-style buildings dating from 1880 to 1930. Among them are the former **Tribunales de Justicia** (Law Courts; now the Museo Regional) at Baquedano 951; the **Palacio Astoreca**, a nitrate baron's mansion that's also a museum, at Baquedano and O'Higgins; and the **Iquique English College** at Balmaceda and Patricio Lynch.

At Sotomayor and Vivar, four blocks north of Plaza Condell, the erstwhile train station once linked Iquique with the nitrate oficinas of the interior. Built under Peruvian rule, the 19th-century **Edificio de la Aduana**, at the west end of Esmeralda, contains Iquique's Museo Naval (Naval Museum). West of the customhouse, the **Muelle de Pasajeros** (passenger pier) dates from 1901.

About 10 minutes from the pier by launch, in the middle of Iquique harbor, the **Boya Conmemorativa del Combate de Iquique** is a buoy marking the spot where Arturo Prat's corvette *Esmeralda* sank in a confrontation with the Peruvian ironclad *Huáscar* in the War of the Pacific.

It's a bit beyond the central circuit, but the **Iglesia San Antonio de Padua**, at the corner of Latorre and 21 de Mayo, is worth the detour for its twin bell towers.

IQUIQUE

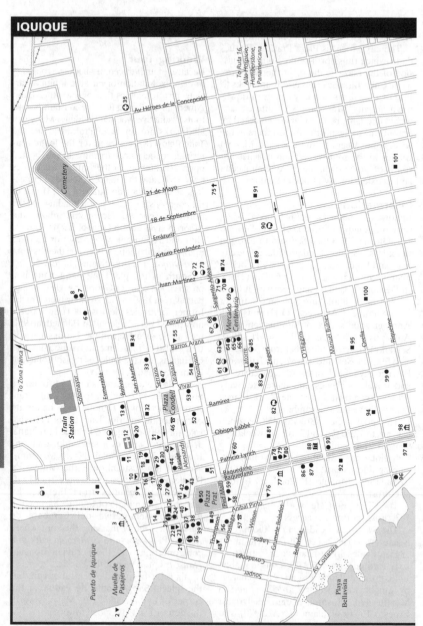

Cemetery

Av Héroes de la Concepción

To Ruta 16, Alto Hospicio, Humberstone, Panamericana

21 de Mayo

18 de Septiembre

Errázuriz

Arturo Fernández

Juan Martínez

Amunátegui

Barros Arana

Tarapacá

Vivar

Ramírez

Obispo Labbé

Patricio Lynch

Baquedano

Aníbal Pinto

Wilson

Sotomayor

Esmeralda

Bolívar

San Martín

Serrano

Thompson

Latorre

Zegers

O'Higgins

Manuel Bulnes

Orella

Riquelme

Sargento Aldea

Mercado Centenario

Plaza Condell

Plaza Prat

Uribe

Thompson

Gorostiaga

Cavancha

Cavancha

Souper

Lagos

Grumete Bolados

Bellavista

Av Costanera

Playa Bellavista

Puerto de Iquique

Muelle de Pasajeros

Train Station

To Zona Franca

Pedro Prat

NORTE GRANDE

To Zona Franca

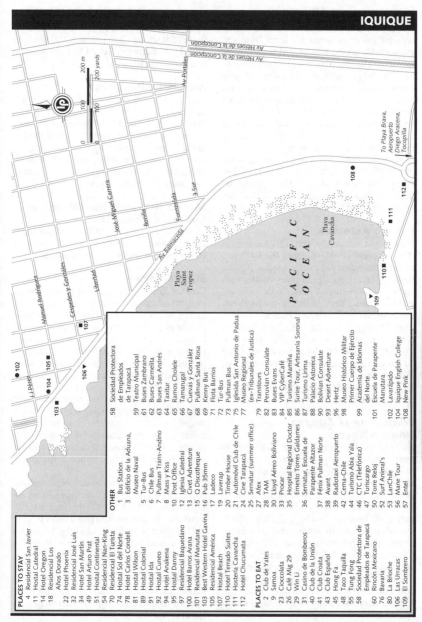

IQUIQUE

NORTE GRANDE

PACIFIC OCEAN

Playa Saint Tropez

Playa Cavancha

To Playa Brava,
Aeropuerto
Diego Aracena,
Tocopilla

Av Heroes de la Concepción
Av Heroes de la Concepción

Av Portales

José Miguel Carrera

Bonilla

Fuenzalida

3 Sur

Av Balmaceda

Libertad

Céspedes y Gonzáles

Manuel Rodríguez

J. J. Pérez

PLACES TO STAY
4 Residencial San Javier
11 Hostal Catedral
14 Hotel Oregon
18 Residencial Los Años Dorado
22 Hotel Phoenix
32 Residencial José Luis
34 Hotel San Martín
49 Hotel Arturo Prat
51 Hostal Continental
54 Residencial Nan-King
70 Residencial El Turista
74 Hostal Sol del Norte
78 Hotel Carlos Condell
81 Hostal Wilson
89 Hostal Colonial
91 Hostal Ida
92 Hostal Cuneo
94 Hotel Anakena
95 Hostal Danny
97 Residencial Baquedano
100 Hotel Barros Arana
101 Residencial Manutara
103 Best Western Hotel Gavina
105 Residencial América
107 Hostal Beach
110 Hotel Terrado Suites
111 Hostería Cavancha
112 Hotel Chucumata

PLACES TO EAT
2 Club de Yates
9 Samoa
23 Cioccolata
26 Café Mig 29
29 Win Li
31 Casino de Bomberos
40 Club de la Unión
41 Club Croata
43 Club Español
45 Hong Fa
48 Taco Taquilla
55 Tung Fong
58 Sociedad Protectora de Empleados de Tarapacá
60 Rincón Mexicano
76 Bavaria
80 La Brioche
106 Las Urracas
109 El Sombrero

OTHER
1 Bus Station
3 Edificio de la Aduana, Museo Naval
5 Tur-Bus
6 Chile Bus
7 Pullman Trans-Andino
8 Mass y Kiss
10 Post Office
12 Iglesia Catedral
13 Civet Adventure
15 Q Discotheque
16 Pub 35mm
17 Ladeco
19 Laverap
20 Timber House
21 Automóvil Club de Chile
24 Cine Tarapacá
25 Sernatur (summer office)
27 Afex
28 TAM
30 Lloyd Aéreo Boliviano
33 Procar
35 Hospital Regional Doctor Ernesto Torres Galdames
36 Sernatur, Escuela de Parapente Altazor
37 Fénix Pullman Norte
38 Avant
39 Radiotaxi Aeropuerto
42 Cema-Chile
44 Turismo Abia Yala
46 CTC (Telefónica)
47 Turiscargo
50 Torre Reloj
52 Surf Animal's
53 LanChile
56 Mane Tour
57 Entel
58 Sociedad Protectora de Empleados de Tarapacá
59 Teatro Municipal
61 Buses Zambrano
62 Buses Carmelita
63 Buses San Andrés
64 Taxitur
65 Ramos Cholele
66 Tamarugal
67 Cuevas y González
68 Pullman Santa Rosa
69 Kenny Bus
71 Flota Barrios
72 Tur-Bus
73 Pullman Bus
75 Iglesia San Antonio de Padua
77 Museo Regional (ex-Tribunales de Justica)
79 Transtours
82 Peruvian Consulate
83 Buses Evans
84 VIP CyberCafé
85 Turismo Mamíña
86 Surire Tour, Artesanía Soronal
87 Turismo Lirima
88 Palacio Astoreca
90 Bolivian Consulate
93 Desert Adventure
96 Hertz
98 Museo Histórico Militar
99 Primer Cuerpo de Ejército, Academia de Idiomas del Norte
101 Escuela de Parapente Manutara
102 Lavarápido
104 Iquique English College
108 New Pink

Museo Regional

Occupying Iquique's former courthouse, the regional museum features a mock altiplano village with adobe houses and mannequins in Aymara dress, plus a large collection of pre-Columbian artifacts, including raft and canoe paddles, fish hooks and sinkers, rope, harpoons, arrows and quivers made from animal hide. There's also an exhibition of Indian ceramics and weaving, photos of Iquique's early days and a fascinating display on the nitrate industry.

At Baquedano 951, the Museo Regional (☎ 411-034) is open 9:30 am to 1 pm and 3 to 6:30 pm weekdays, 10:30 am to 1 pm Saturday. Admission is a modest US$0.60 for adults, US$0.30 for children.

Palacio Astoreca

Built for a nitrate tycoon, this Georgian-style mansion (1904) matches the opulence of the wool barons of Punta Arenas. It has a fantastic interior of enormous rooms with elaborate woodwork and high ceilings, massive chandeliers, stained-glass windows, a gigantic billiard table and balconies.

At O'Higgins 350, the Palacio (☎ 425-600) is now a museum and cultural center which exhibits paintings by local artists. It's open 10 am to 1 pm and 4 to 7:30 pm weekdays, 9:30 am to 1:30 pm Saturday and 11 am to 2 pm Sunday. Admission costs US$0.80 for adults, half that for children.

Edificio de la Aduana (Museo Naval)

Built in 1871 (when Iquique belonged to Peru), the colonial-style customhouse is a two-story structure with meter-thick walls, an octagonal tower and an attractive interior patio. During the War of the Pacific, Peru incarcerated prisoners from the battle of Iquique in the building, which was also the site of armed confrontations during the Chilean civil war of 1891. Unfortunately, the Aduana is deteriorating, and only its naval museum is sufficiently presentable to be open to the public; it contains artifacts salvaged from the sunken *Esmeralda* and biographical material on Prat.

Fronting on Esmeralda between Aníbal Pinto and Baquedano, the Museo Naval is open 9:30 am to 12:30 pm and 2:30 to 6 pm Tuesday to Saturday, 10 am to 1 pm Sunday and holidays. Admission is free.

Muelle de Pasajeros

Just west of the Edificio de la Aduana, Iquique's passenger pier dates from 1901. Harbor tours (US$2.50) leave from here, passing the buoy that marks the site of the *Esmeralda*, and approaching the colony of sea lions that cover the nearby rocks. Depending on the tide, more or fewer of the interestingly constructed steps are exposed to view.

Museo Histórico Militar Primer Cuerpo de Ejército

In the historic district at Baquedano 1396, the Chilean army's military museum is open 10 am to 1 pm and 4 to 7 pm weekdays.

Zona Franca

Created in 1975, this massive monument to uncontrolled consumption is the reason most Chileans visit Iquique and many have moved here. The entire Region of Tarapacá is legally a customs-free zone, but its nucleus is this sprawling shopping center for imported electronics, clothing, automobiles and almost anything else.

The *Zofri*, as it is commonly known, employs more than 10,000 workers in 1500 different companies, helping make Iquique's unemployment rate the lowest in the country. Also benefiting from its proximity to Peru, Bolivia and Argentina, the Zofri turns over around US$3 billion in merchandise per annum.

To see this feeding frenzy of voracious consumers, and maybe replace a lost or stolen camera, take any northbound taxi colectivo from downtown. The Zofri (☎ 214-129) is open 4 to 9 pm Monday, 10 am to 9 pm Tuesday through Friday, and 10 am to 2 pm and 5 to 9 pm Saturday.

Beaches

Playa Cavancha, beginning at the intersection of Balmaceda and Amunátegui, is Iquique's most popular beach, good for swimming and surfing but sometimes crowded. There's also a playground for children.

Farther south, along Av 11 de Septiembre, crashing waves and rip currents at scenic **Playa Brava** make it too rough to go in the water, but it's fine for sunbathing. Toward the hills, look for the massive dunes of Cerro Dragón, which looks like a set for a science fiction film. The easiest way to Playa Brava is by taxi colectivo from downtown.

Much farther south, toward and beyond the airport, the beaches are excellent and less crowded, but the paved highway and improved public transport are a mixed blessing – once-pristine beaches are now so easy to reach that many of them look like rubbish dumps.

Surfing

Surfing is best in winter, when swells come from the north, but is possible at any time of year. Chilean surfers, mostly bodyboarders, sleep late, so there's less competition for early morning waves at Playa Cavancha. Playa Huaiquique, on the southern outskirts of town, is also a good choice, but the sea is warmer farther north near Arica.

Surf Animal's, Ramírez 619, the local surf shop, rents boards.

Paragliding

Iquique's unique geography, with its steep coastal escarpment, rising air currents and the soft, extensive dunes of Cerro Dragón, makes it ideal for *parapente* (paragliding), an activity that involves jumping off a cliff to get airborne. It's theoretically possible to glide all the way to Tocopilla, 240km to the south – but that's not for novices.

The French-run Escuela de Parapente Manutara (☎/fax 418-280, manutarachile@ hotmail.com), 18 de Septiembre 1512, offers short introductory flights for about US$30, with three-day courses available for US$120. Other paragliding enterprises include the Escuela de Parapente Altazor (☎ 431-382), Serrano 145, Oficina 702; and Mane Tour (pager 09-581-1000), Gorostiaga 194, Oficina 2.

Organized Tours

Travelers have voiced dissatisfaction with some Iquique tour operators, but those included here appear to be reliable. Before taking any tour, ask for a detailed explanation to be sure that your expectations coincide with theirs.

Traditional 12-hour excursions take in the nitrate ruins at Humberstone, geoglyph sites at Cerro Unita and Pintados and oases at Pica and Matilla for US$25 to US$30 per person. Three-hour city tours cost around US$13, 10-hour coastal excursions toward the Río Loa are about US$25, the Tarapacá Valley is US$30 and Pisagua (14 hours) costs US$40. Most trips require a four-person minimum; English-speaking guides are available for an extra charge.

Among the established operators are Turismo Abia Yala (☎/fax 472-706), Patricio Lynch 548, Oficina 16; Surire Tour (☎ 445-440, fax 411-795), Baquedano 1035, which will also organize excursions to more out-of-the-way places in the altiplano and the canyons of the precordillera; Transtours (☎/fax 428-984), Baquedano 982; Turismo Lirima (☎ 473-979), Baquedano 1067; Civet Adventure (☎/fax 428-483), Bolívar 684, which organizes bike tours and has English- and German-speaking guides; and Desert Adventure (☎/fax 474-091, desert/advemtire@ entelchile.net), Baquedano 1124.

Places to Stay

Budget *Hostal Sol del Norte* (☎/fax 421-546, Juan Martínez 852) charges US$6 per person, but has few singles and lacks hot water. Close to the bus terminal, friendly *Residencial San Javier* (☎ 427-641, Patricio Lynch 97) is nearly as cheap at US$7 per person, and has undertaken improvements, but the rooms are still tiny. *Hostal Ida* (☎ 425-833, 18 de Septiembre 1064) charges US$7 per person with shared bath, US$10 per person with private bath, while *Residencial Los Años Dorados* (☎ 427-362, San Martín 486) has drawn readers' praise for US$8 per person.

In the heart of the historic district, *Residencial Baquedano* (☎ 422-990, Baquedano 1315) has small but clean singles with firm

NORTE GRANDE

beds for US$8, and now has hot water; breakfast costs US$1 extra. Across the street from the Sol del Norte, simple but spotless **Residencial El Turista** (☎/fax 422-245, Juan Martínez 849-857) has 55 rooms and 16 shared baths, charging US$8/12 singles/doubles; there's a handful of rooms with private bath for US$20.

Clean, friendly **Residencial José Luis** (☎ 422-844, San Martín 601) also gets short-stay trade, so the US$13 downstairs doubles are for couples only; interior singles, for US$8 per person, are quieter. Near Playa Cavancha, **Residencial América** (☎ 427-524, Manuel Rodríguez 550) has hot water and includes breakfast for US$10 per person.

French-run **Residencial Manutara** (☎/fax 418-280, 18 de Septiembre 1512) charges US$10 per person with breakfast and 24-hour hot water; lunch, dinner, kitchen privileges, laundry and Internet service are also available. Several other places also charge around US$10, including **Hostal Danny** (☎ 414-161, Vivar 1266), also easy walking distance to the beach; and **Residencial Nan-King** (☎ 413-311, Thompson 752), which is quiet but often full.

Hostal Cuneo (☎ 428-654, Baquedano 1175) is a very fine place charging US$10 per person with shared bath (breakfast extra), US$18 with private bath, but some interior rooms lack windows; it's decorated with photos of old Iquique. **Hotel San Martín** (☎ 412-260, San Martín 823) has drawn some criticism for small rooms, spongy mattresses and mediocre breakfasts; rates are US$13/21.

A traditional budget favorite is tidy **Hostal Catedral** (☎ 412-184, Obispo Labbé 233), opposite the cathedral, where singles/doubles with shared bath cost US$12.50/23, but rates with private bath are US$25/33 and even then it's often full. Highly recommended, it has two levels of rooms surrounding a spacious courtyard and garden, but it's not the value it once was.

Worth a look is the new **Hostal Beach** (☎ 429-653, Vivar 1707) for US$20/31.

Mid-Range Nondescript **Hostal Continental** (☎ 429-145, Patricio Lynch 679) is passable for US$15 per person with private bath.

Rates start around US$15/25, including breakfast and cable TV, at **Hotel Oregon** (☎ 410-959, San Martín 294). The comparable **Hostal Colonial** (☎ 426-097, Juan Martínez 1020) charges US$21/31.

Iquique's best mid-range value is the central **Hotel Phoenix** (☎ 411-349, Aníbal Pinto 451) with friendly staff and simple but clean and bright rooms for US$23/31 with private bath and breakfast. Its ground floor offers a restaurant, but also a billiard hall, which is noisier than some guests would prefer. Others in this range include **Hostal Wilson** (☎ 423-789, Wilson 422) for US$29/38, and two very appealing historic restorations: **Hotel Anakena** (☎ 426-509, Orella 456) for US$37/46, and **Hotel Carlos Condell** (☎ 424-467, Baquedano 964), known for its helpful staff, for US$39/45.

Prices have risen and it's less central than others in this category, but expanded **Hotel Barros Arana**(☎ 412-840, Barros Arana 1330) continues to draw praise from readers. Though architecturally undistinguished, its clean, fresh-looking rooms with TV and private bath cost from US$36/45 to US$44/54.

Top End There are numerous high-rise hotels along the beaches, such as Playa Cavancha's **Hostería Cavancha** (☎ 431-007, Los Rieles 250), charging US$77/92 single/double, and the newish **Hotel Chucumata** (☎ 435-050, Av Balmaceda 850), charging US$79/94.

Also at Playa Cavancha, the multistory **Best Western Hotel Gavina** (☎ 413-030, Av Balmaceda 1497) offers North American franchise conventionality for US$84/89. Near Playa Brava, the **Holiday Inn Express** (☎ 433-300, Av 11 de Septiembre 1690) is another chain charging US$87/100.

One of Iquique's traditional favorites is **Hotel Arturo Prat** (☎ 411-067, Aníbal Pinto 695), opposite Plaza Prat, but its central location also means some rooms can be noisy. Rates start at US$88/94, but rooms in the new Thompson wing go for US$92/101.

Toward the south end of town, near Playa Brava, the high-rise **Hotel Terrado Club** (☎ 437-878, fax 437-755, Av Aeropuerto 2873) is a Miami Beach-style waterfront hotel for US$91/108. Near Playa Cavancha, its first-rate clone **Hotel Terrado Suites** (☎ 488-000, Los Rieles 126) is slightly more expensive at US$93/111.

Places to Eat

Despite its unprepossessing appearance, one of Iquique's best eating places is the **Mercado Centenario** (Barros Arana between Sargento Aldea and Latorre), where several upstairs cocinerías offer varied seafood at reasonable prices; it has undergone remodeling to make it more attractive and hygienic.

Cioccolata (☎ 413-010, Aníbal Pinto 487) is a good choice for breakfast or onces. **Café Mig 29** (☎ 426-134, Luis Uribe 443) is another good choice for coffee and pastries. **La Brioche** (☎ 415-715, Baquedano 982-A) serves authentic French croissants and pain au chocolat – barely visible through the toxic Gitanes haze.

Samoa (Bolívar 396) has economical fixed-price lunches, as does the historic **Sociedad Protectora de Empleados de Tarapacá** (Thompson 207). The **Casino de Bomberos** (☎ 422-887, Serrano 520) is also a good lunch spot. **Bavaria** (☎ 427-888, Aníbal Pinto 926) is the local outlet of the popular nationwide chain; it also has a delicatessen with good take-out food.

The **Club Croata** (☎ 416-222, Plaza Prat 310) has fine four-course lunches for US$6 and more expensive dinners, but the overworked waiters find it hard to maintain consistent service. Reasonable lunches are also available at **Club de la Unión** (☎ 413-236, Plaza Prat 278, 3rd floor).

Not to be missed are the Moorish interior and artwork at the ornate **Club Español** (☎ 423-284, Plaza Prat 58-A), but it has become expensive. If you can't afford a meal, at least peek through the windows or treat yourself to a drink.

Expensive **El Sombrero** (☎ 423-655, Los Rieles 704) has excellent seafood in agreeable surroundings overlooking Playa Cavancha. Ditto for the **Club de Yates** (☎ 413-385), just west of the Muelle de Pasajeros, where the sea lions lurk for leftovers. **Las Urracas** (☎ 421-493, Balmaceda 431) is also worth a try for seafood.

Iquique has two fine alternatives for Mexican cuisine: the Tex-Mex **Taco Taquilla** (☎ 427-804, Thompson 123) and the more genuinely Mexican **Rincón Mexicano** (☎ 422-301, Patricio Lynch 754), which has excellent service, real corn tortillas and tasty but pricey margaritas. Chinese restaurants are abundant – including **Tung Fong** (☎ 421-548, Tarapacá 835), **Win Li** (☎ 425-942, San Martín 439) and **Hong Fa** (☎ 422-319, Serrano 489).

Entertainment

Cine Tarapacá (☎ 422-329, Serrano 206) shows recent movies from around the world.

There are several downtown pubs, including **Pub 35mm** (☎ 413-851, Bolívar 419), which has live music and a cinema theme. The **Timber House** (☎ 422-518, Bolívar 553) is a pub venue that also serves good food.

Downtown's **Q Discotheque** (Uribe 330) is an exception to the rule that most dance clubs are out by the beach, like **New Pink** (☎ 435-385, Balmaceda 2751). At the south end of town, **Pharo's** (☎ 381-682, Av Costanera 3607) is a monument to kitsch.

Shopping

Most Chilean shoppers swarm to the Zona Franca (see Zona Franca earlier in this chapter), but for regional arts and crafts, Cema-Chile at Plaza Prat 570 is worth a visit, as is Artesanía Soronal (☎ 410-592), Baquedano 1035.

Getting There & Away

Air LanChile (☎ 412-540), Vivar 675, has 27 flights weekly to Santiago (US$126 to US$208), a third of which stop over in Antofagasta (US$30). Flights from Santiago to Iquique usually continue to Arica (US$17), and La Paz (US$103) daily; on Monday, Wednesday, Thursday and Sunday they continue to Asunción, Paraguay.

Lloyd Aéreo Boliviano (☎ 426-750, 427-058), Serrano 442, flies Monday and Friday to La Paz, and Wednesday and Sunday to Santa Cruz, Bolivia (US$167). TAM (☎ 410-155), at Patricio Lynch 467, flies Tuesday, Thursday and Saturday to Asunción, Paraguay (US$212).

NORTE GRANDE

Ladeco (☎ 413-038), at San Martín 428, Local 2, flies four times daily to Santiago, mostly stopping in Antofagasta but once daily in La Serena (US$114). All flights from Santiago continue to Arica. Fares are essentially identical to LanChile's. Avant (☎ 428-800), Aníbal Pinto 555, flies three times daily to Santiago (US$133 to US$150), usually stopping in Antofagasta (US$24), and three times daily to Arica (US$30).

Bus Iquique's shabby bus station (☎ 426-492) is at the north end of Patricio Lynch, but most companies have ticket offices near the Mercado Centenario. Buses leave from the terminal, but passengers may also board at these ticket offices. Services north (to Arica) and south are frequent, but nearly all southbound services now use Ruta 1, the coastal highway to Tocopilla (for connections to Calama) and Antofagasta (for Panamericana connections to Copiapó, La Serena and Santiago).

To Arica, try Pullman Santa Rosa (☎ 428-126) at Sargento Aldea 884, Buses San Andrés (☎ 413-953) at Sargento Aldea 798, Buses Carmelita (☎ 423-766) at Sargento Aldea 790, Cuevas y González (☎ 412-471) at Sargento Aldea 850, Fénix Pullman Norte (☎ 412-423) at Aníbal Pinto 531, or Ramos Cholele (☎ 411-650) at Barros Arana 851. Faster taxi colectivos charge about US$12 per person with Tamarugal (☎ 419-288), Barros Arana 897-B; Taxitur (☎ 414-875), Sargento Aldea 791; and Turiscargo (☎ 412-191) at Serrano 721.

To Calama, Tocopilla, Antofagasta and intermediate points, try Kenny Bus (☎ 414-159) at Latorre 944, Flota Barrios (☎ 426-941) at Sargento Aldea 987, Tramaca (☎ 413-884) at the Rodoviario, and Tur-Bus (☎ 421-702) at its magnificently restored showcase terminal at Esmeralda 594; Tur-Bus has another ticket office (☎ 424-955) at Juan Martínez 788-A.

Numerous bus companies have service to Santiago, including Carmelita, Flota Barrios, Fénix Pullman Norte, Tur-Bus, Buses San Andrés and Buses Evans (☎ 413-462) at Vivar 955-A. Pullman Bus (☎ 428-749), at Juan Martínez and Sargento Aldea, and

Buses Zambrano (☎ 413-215), Sargento Aldea 742, operate between Iquique and Valparaíso/Viña del Mar.

Buses San Andrés and Santa Rosa both go daily to Pica, while Turismo Mamiña (☎ 420-330) at Latorre 779 goes to Pica, Matilla and Mamiña. Taxitur has taxi colectivos to Mamiña and Pica, while Tamarugal goes to Mamiña only. Taxi colectivos to Pozo Almonte (US$2) and Tirana (US$4) leave from the north side of the Mercado Centenario.

Typical destinations and fares include Arica (US$6, four hours), Calama (US$14, six hours), Antofagasta (US$18 to US$20, eight hours), Chañaral (US$26, 12 hours), Caldera/Copiapó (US$28, 15 hours), La Serena (US$32, 18 hours) and Santiago (US$37, 24 hours). Semi-cama services cost around US$32 to Chañaral, US$40 to La Serena and US$46 to Santiago.

Ramos Cholele offers direct service to the Bolivian cities of Oruro (US$32) and La Paz (US$35, 24 hours) daily, as does Chile Bus (☎ 474-363), Esmeralda 978. Mass y Kiss (☎ 417-106), Juan Martínez 182, and Pullman Trans-Andino, Esmeralda 1000, serve the border town of Colchane (US$8), in the altiplano of Iquique; Mass y Kiss continues to Oruro and La Paz. It's also possible to arrange improvised transport with trucks to Colchane from the Shell station at the roundabout on the road to Alto Hospicio.

Tramaca offers Monday and Thursday evening service to Jujuy and Salta, Argentina (US$55), via Calama.

Getting Around

As in Arica, taxi colectivos are the easiest way to get around town. Destinations are clearly marked on an illuminated sign on top of the cab.

To/From the Airport Iquique's Aeropuerto Diego Aracena is 41km south of town on Ruta 1; for about US$5 per person, it's easy to find a taxi colectivo on Plaza Prat to connect with your flight. For door-to-door transportation, contact Radiotaxi Aeropuerto (☎ 415-036), Aníbal Pinto 595.

Volcán Parinacota in Parque Nacional Lauca

WOODS WHEATCROFT

Norte Grande's Valley of the Moon

ANDREW PETERS

Leaping llamas! (Parque Nacional Volcán Isluga)

AARON MCCOY

ERIC WHEATER

Mapuche farmers near Temuco

ROBERT FRIED

Colorful barnacles in Puerto Montt

WAYNE BERNHARDSON

Araucaria bark, Parque Nacional Nahuelbuta

GALEN ROWELL/ODYSSEY/CHICAGO

Smooth sailing near Pucón – until Volcán Villarrica blows its top

Car For rental vehicles, try Procar (☎/fax 413-470), Serrano 796, or Hertz (☎ 426-316), Aníbal Pinto 1303.

AROUND IQUIQUE

Inland from Iquique are numerous geoglyphs, including the enormous human image on Cerro Unita, a hillside in the Quebrada de Tarapacá, east of Huara, and the sprawling murals on the eastern slope of the coastal range at Pintados. Also worth seeing are the nitrate ghost towns of Humberstone and Santa Laura, the regional shrine of La Tirana, the improbable forests of Reserva Nacional Pampa del Tamarugal, the precordillera hot springs villages of Chusmiza, Pica and Mamiña and altiplano settlements such as Colchane, in Parque Nacional Volcán Isluga.

Ruta 1, the paved highway between Iquique and Tocopilla (Region II), has largely superseded the older Panamericana for southbound travelers. There is spectacular coastal desert scenery, but heavy truck traffic has damaged a highway originally intended for recreational traffic, and improved access has also meant that careless campers are rapidly despoiling the beaches with trash.

While most of the beaches south of Iquique are too rocky for surfing, the beach near the customs post at the Río Loa, on the border between Regions I and II, is a good choice. At Río Seco, 96km south of Iquique, there's a private open-air **Museo Parque** with good artifacts from pre-Columbian Chango fishermen and from the nitrate era.

Humberstone & Santa Laura

Once nearly deserted but for scrap metal merchants and a handful of curious travelers, the eerie pampas ghost town of Humberstone is now the center of a legal struggle over its preservation as a historic monument. Around its central Plaza de Armas, nearly all the original buildings, such as the theater, church and market, are still standing. Some are starting to crumble, but others including the church have undergone restoration.

Nitrate oficinas could be hazardous places to work. One now-faded sign reminded miners that 'One accident could destroy all your hopes.' Another warned that workers' contracts prohibited sheltering anyone not associated with the company, which provided housing, health care, food and merchandise (goods were normally purchased only with *fichas*, tokens which took the place of cash and were worthless elsewhere). Union organizers were not welcome.

Despite its paternalistic organization, Humberstone was in some ways a model company town, offering amenities such as tennis and basketball courts. The most impressive recreational feature is the enormous swimming pool, built of cast iron from a shipwreck in Iquique harbor (don't be tempted to plunge off the diving board into the now empty pool). At the west end of town, the electrical power plant still stands, along with the remains of the narrow gauge railway to the older but less well-preserved Oficina Santa Laura, easily visible across the highway.

Originally known as Oficina La Palma when it opened in 1872, Humberstone takes its name from its British manager James Humberstone, who arrived in Pisagua in 1875 under contract to the San Antonio Nitrate & Iodine Company. Perfecting the 'Shanks system' for extracting a larger proportion of nitrates from the raw *caliche* (hardpan) of the pampas, he also became an important administrator and builder of the nitrate railways. Upon his retirement in 1925, La Palma was renamed in Humberstone's honor; he died in Santiago in 1939, but is buried at the curious British Cemetery at Hacienda Tiliviche, on the Panamericana midway between Iquique and Arica.

Most of Humberstone's amenities date from the 1930s, when the De Castro family's Compañía Salitrera de Tarapacá installed the theater, market and sports facilities, but economic realities forced the oficina's closure by 1960, leaving 3000 workers unemployed. Acquired by the Andía family, who paid for the property partly by dismantling it, the remaining buildings became a historical monument – largely a symbolic measure – in 1970. Andía's bankruptcy placed the site in legal limbo, and it has recently become vulnerable to vandalism and unauthorized salvage. It is presently under caretakership by the regional government, but influential rightist politician Francisco Errázuriz, who paid for restoration of the church, is maneuvering to wrest control of the site.

The most accessible of the former mining settlements, Humberstone sits just off the Panamericana, about 45km due east of Iquique. Any eastbound bus from Iquique will drop you off there and it is easy to catch a return bus. Take food, water and a camera, since it is easy to spend many hours exploring the town, but modest supplies are available. Early morning hours are the best time for wandering around, although afternoon breezes often moderate the midday heat.

Given the nebulous legal situation, Humberstone (and nearby Santa Laura) are open to the public without charge, but the Andía family, who have a caretaker on site, request donations for routine maintenance at the entry kiosk, which sells a map and souvenirs. Every year, in early November, nostalgic former residents hold a reunion.

El Gigante de Atacama

The Giant of the Atacama, a geoglyph 14km east of Huara on the southern slope of Cerro Unita, is the largest archaeological representation of a human figure in the world – a massive 86m high.

From the figure's rectangular head, supported by a pencil-thin neck, emanate a dozen rays – four from the top and four from each side. The eyes and mouth are square, the torso long and narrow, the arms bent (one hand appears to be an arrowhead). The size of the feet suggest the figure is wearing boots, and there are odd protrusions from the knees and thighs. Alongside the giant is another odd creature with what appears to be a tail – perhaps a monkey, although a reptile seems likelier in the desert environment.

The two figures are set amidst a complex of lines and circles, and on one side of the hill (facing the Huara-Chusmiza road, visible as you approach the hill) are a number of enormous clearings. The entire Gigante is visible if you stand several hundred meters back from the base of the isolated hill, so avoid climbing it, which damages the site.

The Huara-Colchane road, the main Iquique-Bolivia route, is paved as far as the

village of Chusmiza and should be completely paved to the border in the near future; only the very short stretch (about 1km) from the paved road to the hill itself crosses the desert. Buses leave Iquique infrequently and at inconvenient hours; and returning by bus would be even more awkward, so the best way to visit the site is to rent a car or taxi, or take a tour – limited traffic makes hitching difficult.

Tarapacá

In colonial and early republican times, San Lorenzo de Tarapacá was one of Perú's most important settlements until the nitrate boom spurred the growth of Iquique; the Battle of Tarapacá, during the War of the Pacific, marked the town's eclipse. Today, although its 18th-century **Iglesia San Lorenzo** is being restored, other adobe buildings are crumbling, and the handful of remaining residents are nearly all frail or elderly.

About 5km east of Cerro Unita, a paved lateral drops into the Quebrada de Tarapacá to the still-irrigated but nearly depopulated valley. At the entrance to town, a monument displays a map of the battle, which took place on November 27, 1879, and marks the spot where Chilean military hero Eleuterio Ramírez lost his life. On the battle's anniversary, the Chilean military holds an annual remembrance.

To visit the church, a more interesting monument, ask for the key at the store at the southeast corner of the Plaza de Armas. Tarapacá has neither accommodations nor a restaurant, so bring food.

Chusmiza

At 3200m in the Quebrada de Tarapacá, 106km from Iquique, Chusmiza is a thermal springs resort. It's known both for bottling a popular brand of mineral water and because it is the site of extensive, well-kept pre-Columbian terraces. The only formal accommodations are at the relatively pricey and declining *Hostería Chusmiza* (☎ 422-179 in Iquique). Buses from Iquique pass the turnoff to Chusmiza, which is another 6km from the highway.

Parque Nacional Volcán Isluga

Parque Nacional Volcán Isluga's 175,000 hectares contain natural and cultural features similar to those of Parque Nacional Lauca (see that section, earlier in this chapter), but this more isolated area, home to some of Chile's most traditional peoples, is much less visited than areas farther north.

Parque Nacional Volcán Isluga is 228km from Iquique and 6km west of the village of Isluga, the main gateway to the park. At Colchane, 3750m above sea level on the Bolivian border, it's also possible to cross the border and catch a truck or bus to Oruro.

Conaf's *Refugio Enquelga*, in the village of the same name, charges US$11 per person, while its nearby *Camping Aguas Calientes*, where there are thermal baths, charges US$8 per site. From Isluga, it's possible to travel north to the Salar de Surire and Parque Nacional Lauca and west to Arica, but inquire about the state of roads, especially in the summer rainy season, and do not attempt it without a high-clearance vehicle.

POZO ALMONTE

Only a few kilometers south of the junction of the Panamericana and Ruta 16 to Iquique, the former nitrate service town of Pozo Almonte, which took its name from a freshwater well used by local hacendados during colonial times, is booming again due to its proximity to the paved highways that lead northeast to the copper mine at Cerro Colorado and the hot springs resort of Mamiña, and southeast to the massive new copper mine at Collahuasi.

Pozo Almonte is not exactly a tourist hot spot, but does acknowledge its past through the modest **Museo Histórico Salitrero**, on the south side of the Plaza de Armas, which is open 9 am to 1 pm and 4 to 7:30 pm Tuesday through Saturday. Admission costs US$0.20.

Hotel Anakena (☎ 057-751-201, *Comercio 053*) has the best accommodations, though there are also several cheaper residenciales. There are frequent colectivos to and from Iquique; long-distance buses to Calama from Arica and Iquique also pass through here.

La Tirana

In mid-July, up to 170,000 pilgrims overrun the nearby village of La Tirana (permanent population 250) to pay homage to the Virgin of Carmen by dancing in the streets with spectacular masks and costumes in a Carnival-like atmosphere. One of Chile's most important religious shrines, La Tirana is 72km from Iquique at the north end of the Salar de Pintados, in the Pampa del Tamarugal.

The **Santuario de La Tirana** consists of a broad ceremonial plaza graced by one of the country's most unusual, even eccentric, churches. Although several restaurants surround the plaza, there are no accommodations – pilgrims camp in the open spaces east of town. Have a glance at the **Museo del Salitre** on the north side of the plaza, which has a wild, haphazard assortment of artifacts from the nitrate oficinas. Enter through Almacén El Progreso.

MAMIÑA
☎ 57

Mamiña, a precordillera Aymara village 2700m above sea level, 73km east of Pozo Almonte, has been a popular hot springs resort for residents of the region ever since the nitrate boom, although it is much older than that. Winter is the peak season because of its dry, clear weather, though nights can be very chilly.

Orientation & Information

The village of Mamiña divides, conveniently, into upper and lower sectors, the former clustered around the bedrock outcrop where the church stands, while the latter lies in the valley at the foot of Cerro Ipla, just to the south. A handful of hotels and services are in the upper sector, but most hotels and baths are in the valley below. The best view of the town and its surroundings is from the hilltop cemetery.

There's a public telephone office on the Plaza opposite the church.

Things to See & Do

The **Pukará del Cerro Inca** is a pre-Hispanic fortress on Cerro Ipla, while the **Iglesia de Nuestra Señora del Rosario** is a national

NORTE GRANDE

historical monument dating from 1632. Its twin bell tower is unique in Andean Chile, but the rest of the building has undergone substantial modifications. The **Centro Cultural Kespikala** (☎ 057-425-810 in Iquique) is a gathering place for Aymara artists and artisans.

Places to Stay & Eat

Mamiña has plenty of accommodations in all price ranges; note that most of the telephone contacts below are in Iquique, and that street addresses, while indicated here, don't mean much in village context.

The best bargain is inviting *Residencial Cholele (Ipla s/n)*, with comfortable if utilitarian rooms with a simple breakfast for US$10 per person; other meals are also available. *Hotel Tamarugal* (☎ *414-663, Ipla s/n)* costs about US$25 per person with full board; slightly more expensive, around US$31, is *Hotel Niña de Mis Ojos* (☎ *420-451, Ipla s/n)*. Spanish-run *Hotel La Coruña (cellular 09-543-0370, Santa Rosa 687)* is reasonably priced for US$20/25 singles/doubles with breakfast, and has an attractive bar-restaurant. The modern *Hotel Termas Llama Inn* (☎ *419-893,Ipla s/n)* has spacious shared areas, charging US$40/46 singles/doubles with breakfast, and has good lunches and dinners for about US$8. Try the homemade ice cream.

For US$50 per person with full board, set among beautiful gardens, friendly Lithuanian-run *Hotel Los Cardenales* (☎ *057-438-182, cellular 09-553-0934, 545-1091)* has kitschy décor but each room has a whirlpool tub and there's a large covered pool. Foreigners should ask about IVA discounts. At *Hotel Refugio del Salitre* (☎ *751-203, El Tambo s/n)*, a nitrate-era relic, rates are US$63/117 with full board, but some parts of the building are rundown compared with other nearby places. For nonguests, breakfast costs US$5, lunch or dinner US$10.

Getting There & Away

Buses and taxi colectivos stop in the plaza opposite the church. From Iquique, Turismo Mamiña (☎ 420-330), Latorre 779, provides bus service to Mamiña at 7:30 am and 6 pm daily except Sunday (6 pm only), so it's possible to visit for just a day. Taxitur (☎ 422-044), Sargento Aldea 791 in Iquique, operates taxi colectivos.

RESERVA NACIONAL PAMPA DEL TAMARUGAL

The desolate pampas of the Atacama seem an improbable site for extensive forests, but the dense groves on both sides of the Panamericana, south of Pozo Almonte, are no mirage. Although not a natural forest, the trees are in fact a native species – the tamarugo *(Prosopis tamarugo)* – which covered thousands of square km of the Pampa del Tamarugal until the species nearly disappeared under the pressures of woodcutting for the nitrate mines of the Norte Grande.

Managed by Conaf, the 108,000-hectare Reserva Nacional Pampa del Tamarugal has restored much of this forest, which survives despite excessively saline soils, providing fuelwood for local people and fodder for livestock. Although there is no surface water, seedlings are planted in holes dug through the salt hardpan; after a few months' irrigation, they can reach groundwater which has seeped westward from the Andean foothills. Unfortunately, wells dug to supply the city of Iquique have lowered the regional water table from four to about 15m, desiccating many of the trees within the reserve.

The reserve itself consists of several discrete sectors, the most interesting of which is Pintados. Conaf's **Centro de Información Ambiental** (☎ 751-055) is 24km south of Pozo Almonte, on the east side of the Panamericana, with excellent exhibits on the biology and ecology of the tamarugo and the pampas. It's open 8:30 am to 6 pm daily.

Pintados

At Pintados, one of the world's most elaborate archaeological sites, 355 individual geoglyphs blanket a large hillside in the coast range. From close up it's difficult to discern what most of them represent, but from a distance the outlines of human figures (121), animals (97) including llamas, and various geometric designs (137) become apparent. Most of them date from between 500 and

1450 AD, and served to mark trade routes, indicate the presence of water, identify ethnic groups or express religious meaning.

A derelict nitrate rail yard with a number of ruined buildings and rusting rolling stock, Pintados lies 7km west of the Panamericana via a gravel road 45km south of Pozo Almonte, nearly opposite the eastward turnoff to Pica. It's a long, dry and dusty but not impossible walk from the highway – figure about 1½ to two hours each way, with a possible detour to avoid the caretaker's junkyard dogs. Don't forget food and water. The only other way to visit the site is by car, taxi or tour from Iquique.

Places to Stay

On the west side of the Panamericana, opposite the Centro de Información Ambiental, Conaf maintains a *campground* (shaded sites with tables and benches cost US$8 per night). It also offers a limited number of beds in its guesthouse for US$11 per person. Despite the highway that bisects the reserve, it's a pleasant, restful stopover, with extraordinary views of the southern night sky.

PICA
☎ 57

Spanish conquistador Diego de Almagro skirmished with local Indians near Pica on his expedition to Chile in 1535, but in later colonial times this agreeable oasis became famous for its wines and fruits, which supplied the mines at Huantajaya and beyond. In the 19th century, it supplied wheat, wine, figs, raisins and alfalfa to the nitrate mines of the pampas, then became a sort of 'hill station' for the nitrate barons. Today, supposedly, limes from Pica make the best pisco sours.

Pica was so dependent on outside water that the Spaniards developed an elaborate system of more than 15km of tunnels, like the ganats of the Middle East, to carry groundwater to the village. In the 1920s, American geographer Isaiah Bowman observed:

Unlike most desert towns Pica stands in the midst of the desert without the green valley that elsewhere gives a natural basis for settlement. From its wells and springs and a reservoir in the course of a small stream descending from the piedmont the closely compacted gardens of the village are watered with scrupulous economy.

When Iquique boomed with nitrate exports, the Tarapacá Water Company piped water from Pica, 119km to the southeast, to the coast to accommodate the city's growth. Only 42km from La Tirana by an excellent paved road, Pica (population 1500) has become a more democratic destination, no longer a preserve of the nitrate barons, and is popular on the weekends, with several hotels and restaurants.

Things to See & Do

Most visitors take advantage of the baths at **Cocha Resbaladero**, at the upper end of General Ibáñez, where there's room to swim as well as soak. Admission costs less than US$0.75.

The 19th-century **Iglesia de San Andrés**, opposite the Plaza de Armas, replaced two earlier churches destroyed by earthquakes. The last two days of November, Pica celebrates the **Fiesta de San Andrés**, a religious festival that also includes traditional dances and fireworks.

In the adjacent village of Matilla, 3km west, the **Iglesia de San Antonio** is a national monument dating from 1887, and built on 17th-century foundations. More interesting is the **Lagar de Matilla**, an on-site museum with a colonial winepress.

Places to Stay

Camping Miraflores (☎ 741-338, *Miraflores 4*), the municipal site, charges about US$2.50 per person; it's adequate but crowded, especially on weekends, and lacks shade.

The simple but clean *Hotel Palermo* (☎ 741-129, *Arturo Prat 233*) charges US$7 per person for three-bed rooms with private bath, and also has a restaurant. Near the Resbaladero baths, *Residencial El Tambo* (☎ 741-041, *General Ibáñez 68*) charges US$8.50 per person.

The friendly, ramshackle *Hotel San Andrés* (☎ 741-319, *Balmaceda 197*) is a nonsmoking facility that charges US$10 per person for large rooms with shared bath. In a stylish older building, friendly **Hostal Los Emilios** (☎ *741-126, Lord Cochrane 213*) is a fine place charging US$10 single with breakfast and shared bath. **Cabañas El Resbaladero** (☎ *741-316, General Ibañez 57*) rents six-person cabañas for US$42.

Places to Eat

There are several inexpensive restaurants near the Plaza de Armas, on Balmaceda, but nothing really special. For the best menu, the hands-down winner is **El Edén de Pica** (☎ *741-196, Riquelme 12*), only half a block off the Plaza de Armas, which has pleasant patio dining, but items like seafood, quinoa and juices are not always available. It can also be expensive for nonselective diners.

La Viña (☎ *741-314, General Ibáñez 70*) prepares Chilean specialties, while **Los Naranjos** (☎ *741-318, Esmeralda and Barbosa*) offers inexpensive three-course lunches. **Son Sang** (*Esmeralda 444*) serves Chinese meals.

Getting There & Away

Buses San Andrés and Pullman Santa Rosa run buses and Taxitur and Turismo Mamiña operate taxi colectivos between Pica and Iquique; see the Iquique section for details.

Antofagasta Region

In pre-Columbian times, the sea was the main source of subsistence for the Chango Indians who populated the coast of the present-day Antofagasta region. A Spanish visitor to Cobija in 1581 counted more than 400 Changos, who fished from sealskin canoes and hunted guanaco in those areas where condensation from the winter camanchaca renewed the coastal range pastures. This small population, though, could not support encomiendas, and colonial Spaniards largely ignored the area. Moreover, the population could be hostile, often attacking Spanish naval parties that came ashore in search of fresh water at scattered coastal oases.

The interior of the region was different. Although the landscape was utterly barren for nearly 200km to the east – in all the

Norte Grande, the meandering Río Loa is the only river whose flow consistently reaches the Pacific – irrigated agriculture sustained relatively dense sedentary populations in oases like Calama, on the Loa, and San Pedro de Atacama. At higher elevations shepherds grazed llamas, but the area was generally too dry for the more delicate alpaca. In the very high, arid Puna de Atacama, however, there was too little moisture to support any permanent human habitation – even the 5916m peak of Licancábur has no permanent snow cover.

In the early 18th century, the Spaniards started Cobija, 130km north of modern Antofagasta, as a customhouse; after the wars of independence, this remote outpost became Bolivia's outlet to the sea, despite its poor and scanty fresh water supply. Nearly destroyed by an earthquake and tsunami in 1877, followed by the development of mineral nitrates from the interior, it was superseded by Antofagasta.

Nitrates brought Antofagasta into the modern world. Nineteenth- and 20th-century nitrate ghost towns line both sides of the Panamericana and the highway to Calama, and the oficinas of María Elena and Pedro de Valdivia still function, but copper has supplanted nitrates in the regional and national economy. Chuquicamata, still the world's largest open-pit mine, dominates the mining sector, but fishing and tourism are growing in importance.

There's a wealth of outstanding travel literature on the Atacama. Although much of it is out of print and not widely known, it's worth checking university libraries for titles such as the American geographer Isaiah Bowman's *Desert Trails of Atacama* (1924). Bowman traveled by mule over the length of the Norte Grande and across the high Andean passes between Chile and Argentina and Bolivia, recording his impressions and speculations, and photographing towns and villages off the beaten track.

Decades later William Rudolph, for many years the chief engineer at Chuquicamata, followed Bowman's footsteps in *Vanishing Trails of Atacama* (1963), which chronicled the changing human landscape of the desert.

John Aarons and Claudio Vita-Finzi published an entertaining account of a Cambridge expedition to the Atacama in *The Useless Land* (1960).

ANTOFAGASTA
☎ 55

The port of Antofagasta, the Norte Grande's largest city, handles most of the minerals from the Atacama, especially the copper from Chuquicamata, and is still a major import-export node for Bolivia, which lost the region to Chile during the War of the Pacific. The city's distinctive architecture, resembling Iquique's, dates from the nitrate era.

Founded in 1870, the port of La Chimba (later renamed Antofagasta) replaced Cobija as the region's most important settlement after nitrate mining began in the Salar del Carmen, a short distance inland, and it became apparent that it provided the easiest rail route to the east. By 1877, the railroad reached halfway to Calama, but it was not completed as far as Oruro until after the War of the Pacific, when Chile acquired the territory.

After the war, Antofagasta exported tin and silver from Bolivia, and borax from the Salar de Ascotán, in addition to nitrates from the pampas. The latter commodity underwent a major expansion after the turn of the century, when Antofagasta's port proved inadequate and the nearby harbor of Mejillones took up much of the slack. Later, however, infrastructural improvements restored Antofagasta's pre-eminence and it came to handle the highest tonnage of any South American Pacific port.

Like the rest of the coastal Norte Grande, Antofagasta rarely receives rainfall, but infrequent meteorological events can be catastrophic. In late 1991, for instance, a storm caused a flash flood that obliterated the southern access road between the Panamericana and the city. In general, though, the city has an ideal climate, clear and dry, neither too hot nor too cold at any time of year. In the day, beach weather is the rule and at night, in the words of poet Neftalí Agrella, 'The moon hangs its lantern over Antofagasta.'

Orientation

Like Iquique, Antofagasta (population 225,000) sits on a terrace at the foot of the coastal range, some 1350km north of Santiago and 700km south of Arica. The north-south Panamericana passes inland, about 15km east of the city, but there are paved northern and southern access roads.

Downtown's western boundary is north-south Av Balmaceda, immediately east of the modern port; Balmaceda veers northeast at Uribe and eventually becomes Aníbal Pinto; to the south, it becomes Av Grecia. Streets run southwest to northeast in this central grid, bounded also by Bolívar and JS Ossa. Refurbished Plaza Colón, bounded by Washington, Sucre, San Martín and Arturo Prat, sports rushing fountains amidst its palms, mimosas and bougainvilleas.

Information

Sernatur (☎ 264-016, ☎/fax 264-044), at Maipú 240, is open from 8:30 am to 1 pm and from 3 to 7:30 pm weekdays. It is due to move, however, to the corner of Uribe and San Martín.

In summer, there's a tourist information kiosk (☎ 224-834) on Balmaceda at Prat, in front of Hotel Antofagasta, open 9:30 am to 1:30 pm and 3 to 7 pm daily except Sunday, when it's open 10:30 am to 2 pm. Another good information source is the Automóvil Club de Chile (☎ 225-332), Condell 2330.

Except for the numerous ATMs downtown, changing money in Antofagasta can be surprisingly difficult, but try Cambio San Marcos at Baquedano 524 or Cambio Ancla Inn at Baquedano 508.

The post office is at Washington 2613, opposite Plaza Colón. CTC (Telefónica) long-distance services are at Condell 2527, while Chilesat is at Uribe 645.

Lightnet (☎ 283-173), Baquedano 498, Oficina 24, has inexpensive Internet access.

Australian-run Intitour (☎ 266-185, fax 260-882) is at Baquedano 460.

For information on the region's natural attractions, contact Conaf (☎ 227-804), Av Argentina 2510.

For books, Librería Andrés Bello is at Condell 2421.

ANTOFAGASTA

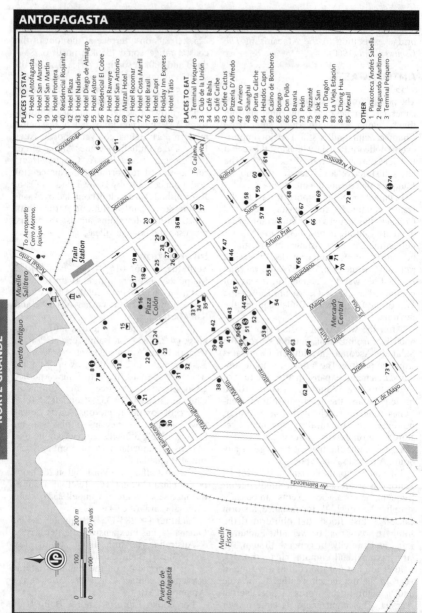

PLACES TO STAY
7   Hotel Antofagasta
10 Hotel San Marcos
19 Hotel San Martín
36 Hotel Frontera
40 Residencial Riojanita
42 Hotel Plaza
43 Hotel Nadine
46 Hotel Diego de Almagro
55 Hotel Astore
56 Residencial El Cobre
57 Hotel Rawaye
62 Hotel San Antonio
69 Marzal Hotel
71 Hotel Rocomar
72 Hotel Costa Marfil
76 Hotel Brasil
81 Hotel Capri
82 Holiday Inn Express
87 Hotel Tatio

PLACES TO EAT
3   Terminal Pesquero
33 Club de la Unión
34 Café Bahía
35 Café Caribe
43 Coffee Cactus
45 Pizzería D'Alfredo
47 El Arriero
48 Shanghai
49 Puerta Caliche
54 Helados Capri
59 Casino de Bomberos
65 Bongo
66 Don Pollo
70 Bavaria
73 Pekín
75 Pizzanté
78 Jok San
79 Un Dragón
83 La Vieja Estación
84 Chong Hua
85 Mexall

OTHER
1   Pinacoteca Andrés Sabella
2   Resguardo Marítimo
3   Terminal Pesquero

ANTOFAGASTA

4 Soquimich
  (Casa de Administración)
5 Museo Regional
6 Géminis, Corsal
8 Tourist Kiosk
9 Ferronor
11 Terminal de Buses Rurales
12 Avis
13 Budget
14 Avant
15 Post Office
16 Torre Reloj
17 Buses Tramaca
18 Fénix Pullman Norte
20 Pullman Bus
21 Hertz
22 Ladeco
23 LanChile
24 Bolivian Consulate
25 Teatro Municipal
26 Bazar Mejillones
27 Bazar Acuario
28 Bazar Mariela
29 Tur-Bus
30 Sernatur
31 Localiza
32 Aerobús
37 Flota Barrios
38 Lloyd Aéreo Boliviano
39 Intitour
41 Lightnet
44 CTC (Telefónica)
50 Cambio Ancla Inn
51 Cambio San Marcos
52 Teatro Pedro de la Barra
53 Librería Andrés Bello
58 Cine Nacional
60 Club Antofagasta Offices
61 Alamo
63 Automóvil Club de Chile
64 Chilesat
67 Sergio Izquierdo
68 Safe Sex
74 Conaf
77 Tramaca
80 Laverap
86 Hospital Regional
88 Wally's Pub
89 Argentine Consulate

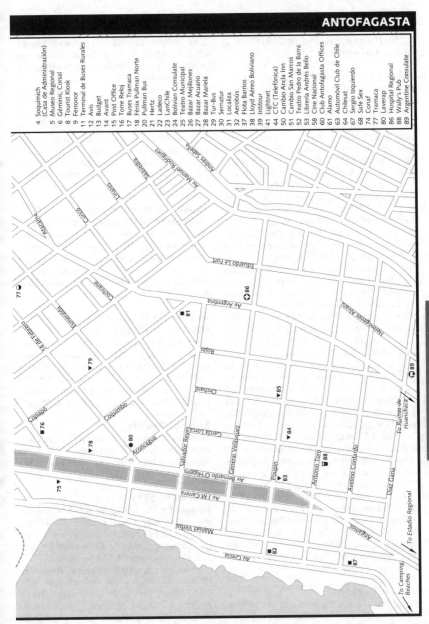

NORTE GRANDE

Laverap laundry (☎ 251-085) is at 14 de Febrero 1802.

The Hospital Regional (☎ 269-009) is at Av Argentina 1962.

Things to See & Do

Like Iquique, Antofagasta is a 19th-century city whose architecture is not stereotypically Latin American. The British community has left a visible imprint in **Plaza Colón** and its **Torre Reloj** replica of Big Ben (where, despite political controversy between the countries, tiled British and Chilean flags still intertwine) and its bandshell. British influence is also palpable in the **Barrio Histórico** between the plaza and the old port, which features many wooden Victorian and Georgian buildings – the **Muelle Salitrero** (Nitrate Pier) at the foot of Bolívar, for instance, was the work of Melbourne Clark, an early partner in the Tarapacá Nitrate Company. At the entrance to the pier is the former **Resguardo Marítimo** (Coast Guard), built in 1910.

Across the patio, at Balmaceda and Bolívar, the former **Gobernación Marítima** (Port Authority) houses the **Pinacoteca Andrés Sabella**, a gallery honoring a local poet. The Pinacoteca is open 10 am to 1 pm and 3:30 to 7 pm Tuesday to Friday, 11 am to 2 pm weekends.

Across the street, originally erected in Mejillones in 1866 by a Chilean mining company then dismantled and transported to its present site in 1888, the former Aduana (Customhouse) now houses the **Museo Regional** (Regional Museum). Across Bolívar, the former **Estación Ferrocarril** (1887) is the restored terminus of the Antofagasta-La Paz railway, though there is no longer passenger service here; the 2nd story was added in 1900. Unfortunately, it's closed to the public.

To the north, across from the colorful **Terminal Pesquero** (fish market), is the Casa de Administración (administrative office) of the Sociedad Química de Chile (Soquimich), once the Lautaro Nitrate Company and then the Anglo Lautaro Nitrate Company until its nationalization in 1968.

Museo Regional

Occupying the historic customhouse, Antofagasta's improved regional museum contains ground-floor exhibits on minerals and fossils, the regional environment and prehistoric immigration and cultural development, ending with the Inka presence. The quality of the artifacts, and particularly the dioramas, is excellent.

At Balmaceda and Bolívar, the museum (☎ 221-836) charges US$1 admission for adults, US$0.50 for kids. From November to March, it's open 10 am to 1 pm and 3:30 to 6:30 pm Monday through Saturday; Sunday hours are 11 am to 2 pm. The rest of the year, hours are 10 am to 1 pm and 3:30 to 6:30 pm Tuesday through Saturday, 11 am to 2 pm only on Sunday.

Museo Arqueológico Universidad Católica del Norte

At Av Angamos 0610, the southern extension of Av Bernardo O'Higgins, the Catholic university's archaeological museum focuses on the Norte Grande. The museum (☎ 255-090, 248-198) is open 9 am to noon and 3 to 6 pm weekdays.

Ruinas de Huanchaca (Minas de Plata)

Hovering over the city, at the south end of Av Argentina, the imposing hillside foundations of a 19th-century British-Bolivian silver-refining plant offer some of the best panoramas of the city. From downtown, take colectivo No 3 and ask for Minas de Plata.

Special Events

February 14, the anniversary of the founding of the city, is a major local holiday. There are fireworks at the Balneario Municipal at the south end of Av Grecia.

Places to Stay

Budget On the coast road south of Antofagasta, *Camping Las Garumas* (☎ 247-764, Anexo 42, Km 9) costs US$10 for up to four people, while *Camping Rucamóvil* (☎ 260-121, Km 11) charges US$4 per person.

Plain but friendly *Residencial Riojanita* (☎ 226-313, Baquedano 464) charges only US$7.50 per person. Recommended *Hotel Brasil* (☎ 267-268, JS Ossa 1978) has spacious rooms with shared bath for US$9/15 with shared bath, US$27 double with private bath; the hot showers are excellent.

Hotel Rawaye (☎ 225-399, *Sucre 762*) is OK and still cheap at US$9/15 singles/doubles with shared bath. At present, long-time budget favorite *Residencial El Cobre* (☎ 225-162, *Prat 749*) is only suitable for an emergency at US$9/15 with shared bath, US$15/24 with private bath.

There's also central *Hotel Frontera* (☎ 281-219, *Bolívar 558*), which has a few budget rooms for US$12/19, but most come with private bath for US$18/26. Renovated *Hotel Capri* (☎ 263-703, *Copiapó 1208*) has become one of Antofagasta's better values for US$10 per person with shared bath, US$14 with private bath. Its main drawback is its inconvenience to the bus stations, but the rooms are immaculate.

Mid-Range Mid-range accommodations start around US$27/38 at *Hotel Costa Marfil* (☎ 269-361, *Prat 950*). Boxy, bleak but tidy *Hotel San Marcos* (☎ 251-763, *Latorre 2946*) has rooms for US$30/43 with private bath. Close to the Terminal de Buses Rurales, it's clean and has its own restaurant.

Hotel San Martín (☎ 263-503, *fax 268-159, San Martín 2781*) charges about US$31/42, while comparable *Hotel Astore* (☎ 267-439, *Matta 2537*) charges US$35/42, *Hotel Rocomar* (☎ 261-139, *Baquedano 810*) has rooms for US$35/45 and appealing *Hotel Nadine* (☎ 227-008, *Baquedano 519*) charges US$38/62.

Hotel San Antonio (☎ 268-857, *Condell 2235*) charges US$41/47. The newish *Marzal Hotel* (☎ 268-063, *Arturo Prat 867*) *charges US$45/54, while rates at well-kept but unimpressive* *Hotel Diego de Almagro* (☎ 268-331, *Condell 2624*) start at US$46/62.

Top End Having started its existence as a cluster of reconditioned tour buses, the once oddball *Hotel Tatio* (☎ 277-602, *Av Grecia 1000*) now charges US$60/72. The more conventional *Hotel Plaza* (☎ 269-046, *Baquedano 461*) has its own restaurant and bar and is fairly quiet; rates are US$69/93.

A recent addition to the hotel scene, the North American chain *Holiday Inn Express* (☎ 228-888, *Av Grecia 1490*) charges US$89 to US$95 single or double, with breakfast. On the beach, widely acknowledged as the city's best, *Hotel Antofagasta* (☎ 268-259, *Balmaceda 2575*) is also the largest in town. Rooms start around US$75/133, with a buffet breakfast.

Places to Eat

At the unpretentious Terminal Pesquero, at the north end of the old port, a collection of inexpensive stands peddle tasty fresh shellfish. It's especially lively on Saturday mornings, but even if you find sea urchins unpalatable, the pelicans that crowd the pier for scraps are always amusing. Similar fare is available at the *Mercado Central*, on Ossa between Maipú and Uribe.

The *Casino de Bomberos* (*Sucre 763*) has good set lunches for about US$4. *Bavaria* (☎ 266-567, *Ossa 2424*) is part of a reliable but uninspired chain. Always crowded, inexpensive *Don Pollo* (☎ 263-361, *Ossa 2594*) specializes in grilled chicken. *Bongo* (☎ 263-697, *Baquedano 743*) is suitable for sandwiches and draft beer, as is *Café Bahía* (☎ 227-551, *Prat 470*).

Carnivores will find *El Arriero* (☎ 268-759, *Condell 2644*) a fine parrilla, with large portions, attentive service, classic decor and, less appealingly, crashing piano duets. Other recommended choices include *La Vieja Estación* (☎ 263-167, *O'Higgins 1456*) and the *Club de la Unión* (☎ 268-371, *Prat 474*).

Definitely worth consideration, at the corner of Orchard and Poupin, is *Mexall* (☎ 223-672), a Mexican pub-restaurant. *Puerto Caliche* (☎ 227-878, *Latorre 2464*) is a seafood possibility.

Pizzería D'Alfredo (☎ 261-643, *Condell 2539*) is a chain that serves pizza at reasonable prices, but Antofagasta's best pizzería is *Pizzanté* (☎ 268-115, *Av JM Carrera 1857*), which also enforces a nonsmoking section. It has large portions, reasonable prices, good service and pleasant ambience, plus a wide selection of appealing sandwiches.

Like other northern Chilean cities, Antofagasta has an array of inexpensive Chinese restaurants, including *Un Dragón* (☎ 221-259, *Copiapó 951*), *Shanghai* (☎ 262-547,

Latorre 2426), **Pekín** (☎ *260-833, Ossa 2135)*, **Jok San** *(Bernardo O'Higgins 1862)* and **Chong Hua** (☎ *251-430, García Lorca 1468)*.

For snacks, coffee, superb ice cream and other desserts, try **Helados Capri** *(Baquedano 632)* and **Coffee Cactus** *(Baquedano 519)* in the Hotel Nadine. For caffeine in a form other than soluble Nescafé, try **Café Caribe** *(Prat 482)*.

Entertainment

The **Cine Nacional** (☎ *269-166, Sucre 735)* shows recent films, as does the **Cine Gran Vía** (☎ *241-380, Angamos 232)*, beyond the stadium. For theater and other performing arts, check **Teatro Pedro de la Barra** (☎ *263-400, Condell 2495)* or the **Teatro Municipal** (☎ *264-919, Sucre 433)*.

Wally's Pub (☎ *223-697, Antonino Toro 982)* is a British-style pub, with a daily happy hour from 6 to 8:30 pm, and also serves meals.

Club Antofagasta (☎ *221-553, Ossa 2755)* is the city's first-division soccer team; it plays at the Estadio Regional, in the south end of town at Av Angamos and Club Hípico.

Shopping

There's a good informal market for historical items like banknotes, coins, fichas from nitrate oficinas and other odds and ends at the foot of the Terminal Pesquero, on the west side of Aníbal Pinto, north of downtown. For Chile's and Antofagasta's most varied (and perhaps only) specialized selection of condoms, Safe Sex is at Sucre 818.

Getting There & Away

Air LanChile (☎ *265-151, 262-526)*, Washington 2552, has four or five nonstops daily to Santiago (US$108 to US$183); about half the northbound flights continue to Iquique (US$24), where one connects Monday, Wednesday, Thursday and Sunday to Santa Cruz, Bolivia, and Arica (US$30), where one connects daily to La Paz, Bolivia. There are also two or three daily flights to Calama (US$22).

Ladeco (☎ *269-170)*, Washington 2589, flies at least three and sometimes four times daily to Santiago, with one midafternoon flight stopping in La Serena (US$93); northbound flights go to Calama daily (twice on Monday) and to Iquique four or five times daily) and Arica (three or four times daily).

Avant (☎ *264-050)*, Arturo Prat 264, flies four or five times daily to Santiago (US$129 to US$144), twice daily to Iquique (US$24) and Arica (US$29), and twice weekdays and once Saturday and Sunday to Calama (US$22).

Lloyd Aéreo Boliviano (☎ *260-618)*, San Martín 2399, no longer flies out of Antofagasta, but can arrange connections to fly out of Iquique or Arica.

Bus Antofagasta has no central long-distance terminal, but most companies operate out of their own terminals near downtown. A few long-distance and most locally based companies use the Terminal de Buses Rurales, Riquelme 513. Nearly all northbound services now use coastal Ruta 1, via Tocopilla, en route to Iquique and Arica.

Tramaca (☎ *200-124)*, Uribe 936 and Sucre 375, has frequent buses to Calama, plus daily service to Arica, Iquique, Santiago and intermediate points. Internationally, Tramaca goes to Jujuy (US$52, 14 hours) and Salta, Argentina (16 hours), Tuesday and Friday mornings, and to the Bolivian destinations of Uyuni (US$17) and Oruro (US$23) Wednesday at 11 pm.

Tramaca's regional destinations include Sierra Gorda, Baquedano, Taltal and the nitrate towns of María Elena and Pedro de Valdivia. Tramaca also handles tickets for the Calama-Oruro railway (see the Calama section later in this chapter), and has direct daily departures to San Pedro de Atacama at 8 am and 6:30 pm. Flota Barrios (☎ *268-559)*, Condell 2782, goes to Calama, María Elena and Pedro de Valdivia, and Tocopilla.

Géminis (☎ *251-796)*, Latorre 3055, goes to Calama and to intermediate stops on the Panamericana between Santiago and Arica. Fénix Pullman Norte (☎ *268-896)*, San Martín 2717, runs nearly identical domestic routes, as does the more expensive Tur-Bus (☎ *266-691)*, Latorre 2751. Pullman Bus (☎ *262-591)*, Latorre 2805, goes to Calama and Chuquicamata three times daily, and runs long-distance routes on the Panamericana between Arica and Santiago.

Many companies operate from the Terminal de Buses Rurales at Riquelme 513. Local carriers include Fepstur (☎ 222-982), Maravilla Bus and El Shadday (☎ 266-724) to Mejillones (US$2) and Buses Tocopilla and Buses Camus (☎ 267-424) to Tocopilla. Corsal, in the Géminis terminal at Latorre 3055, also goes to Mejillones.

Long-distance carriers at the Terminal de Buses Rurales include Carmelita, which covers the southbound Panamericana and continues north to Iquique and Arica; Litoral Bus (☎ 262-175) to Chañaral, Diego de Almagro and El Salvador; Buses Iquique on coastal Ruta 1 north to Iquique; Kenny Bus (☎ 262-216) to Iquique, Santiago and intermediates; Pullman Santa Rosa (☎ 282-763) to Iquique and Arica, Tas Choapa to Iquique, Santiago and intermediates and Ramos Cholele (☎ 251-632) to Tocopilla, Iquique and Santiago.

Bazar Mejillones (☎ 251-332) at Latorre 2715, Bazar Acuario (☎ 224-805) at Latorre 2723 and Bazar Mariela (☎ 227-111) at Latorre 2727 run taxi colectivos to La Portada and Mejillones (US$1.60) all year, and to Juan López (US$2) and Hornitos (US$4) in summer only.

Typical fares and times include Arica (US$20, 10 hours), Iquique (US$18 to US$20, six hours), Tocopilla (US$4, 2½ hours), Calama (US$5.50, three hours), Chañaral (US$19, six hours), Copiapó (US$22, eight hours), La Serena (US$30, 12 hours) and Santiago (US$31 to US$42, 18 hours).

Train There's no train service from Antofagasta proper, but tickets for the Calama-Oruro line are available from Tramaca (☎ 251-770), Uribe 936 or Sucre 375.

Travelers hoping to cross the Andes to Salta, Argentina on the Chilean freight that connects with the famous Tren a las Nubes should contact Ferronor (☎ 224-764, 227-927) at Sucre 220, 4th floor; for more detail, see the Baquedano section later in this chapter.

Getting Around

To/From the Airport Antofagasta's Aeropuerto Cerro Moreno is 25km north of the city, at the south end of Península Mejillones. From the Terminal Pesquero, local bus No 15 goes to the airport for US$0.50, but only every two hours or so from 7:30 am to 10:30 pm.

Shared taxis leave from the stand opposite LanChile's downtown offices for US$3 per person, but Aerobús (☎ 262-727), Baquedano 328, provides door-to-door service for US$6.

Car Rentals are available from Avis (☎/fax 221-073) at Balmaceda 2499, Hertz (☎ 269-043) at Balmaceda 2492, Budget (☎ 251-745) at Prat 206, Local 5, Localiza (☎ 225-370) at Baquedano 300, Alamo (☎ 261-864) at Av Argentina 2779 and Sergio Izquierdo (☎ 263-788) at Prat 801.

AROUND ANTOFAGASTA

North of Antofagasta, paved Ruta 1 leads to Mejillones and Tocopilla, then continues to Iquique as a spectacular desert coastal highway. Between Mejillones and Tocopilla are the fascinating ghost towns of Cobija and Gatico.

Reserva Nacional La Chimba

In the coastal range, 15km northeast of Antofagasta, 2583-hectare La Chimba consists of several tributary canyons, moistened by the camanchaca. This supports a surprisingly varied flora and fauna, the latter including foxes, guanacos, reptiles and many bird species.

Unfortunately, sprawling Antofagasta is encroaching on the reserve, which is presently closed to public access. For the latest information, however, contact the Conaf office in Antofagasta.

Monumento Natural La Portada

Probably the most photographed sight on the Norte Grande coastline, 31-hectare La Portada's centerpiece is an offshore stack of marine sediments, eroded into a natural arch by the stormy Pacific, upon a volcanic base.

About 25km north of Antofagasta, on a short westbound lateral off the highway south of Aeropuerto Cerro Moreno, it's a pleasant spot for a relaxing beach afternoon. Take micro No 15 from Antofagasta's Terminal Pesquero; if driving, leave belongings in the trunk and lock your car; break-ins have occurred at the lot.

Juan López & Bolsico
At the south end of Península Mejillones, just north of La Portada, a paved road leads west to the beach villages of Juan López (take the left fork at Km 11) and Bolsico (take the right fork gravel road). The latter route passes offshore Isla Santa María, a site with several impressive ocean blowholes.

Bazar Mariela (see Antofagasta's Getting There & Away section) runs taxi colectivos to Juan López (US$2).

Mano del Desierto
About 45km south of the junction of the Panamericana and Ruta 28 (the lateral to Antofagasta), 1100m above sea level, Antofagasta sculptor Mario Irarrázaval built this 20m-plus sculpture, an eerie hand rising out of the desert pampa, in 1992. Bus travelers should look to the west side of the highway.

Observatorio Cerro Paranal
Just south of the Mano del Desierto, an ill-marked lateral leaves the Panamericana to follow a steep, dusty mountain road southwest to a wild desert coast comparable to the route between Tocopilla and Iquique. The latter route hits the coast at Caleta El Cobre and eventually ends up at the former nitrate port of Taltal, but an alternative inland route leads past 2664m Cerro Paranal, a major new astronomical facility of the European Space Organization (ESO), about 120km south of Antofagasta.

The observatory, scheduled to have four 8m Very Large Telescopes (VLTs), officially opened in March 1999. A daytime visitor center is in the planning stages but not yet open to the public; for updates, consult ESO's home page.

From Paranal, it's also possible to continue to Taltal, another 120km south, on a good dirt road before descending the Quebrada de Despoblado to the coastal fish camp of Paposo.

MEJILLONES
☎ 55
Once a key Bolivian port, Mejillones (permanent population about 5600) first thrived off guano (transported from the hills above the town by an aerial tramway) and then nitrate, but for decades it's been a weekend beach resort for residents of the regional capital. Construction of a huge thermoelectric plant and a new megaport project seem to be putting the town back on the economic map – perhaps at the cost of its relative tranquillity.

Mejillones' historical landmarks are mostly relics of Bolivian sovereignty and the nitrate era. The oldest is the U-shaped **Aduana** (Customhouse, 1866), Francisco Antonio Pinto 110, which now holds the **Museo de Mejillones** (☎ 621-289), open 10 am to 2 pm and 3 to 9 pm daily; admission costs US$0.50.

At the foot of Manuel Rodríguez, overlooking the Plaza Fuerza Aérea, the **Capitanía del Puerto** (port authority; 1876) is a French-style building with a lighthouse tower. At the corner of Latorre and Almirante Castillo, the **Iglesia Corazón de María** is a striking wooden building that dates from 1906.

About 60km north of Antofagasta via Ruta 1 and a short paved lateral, on the sheltered Bahía de Mejillones, Mejillones' main drag is the beachfront Av San Martín.

Correos de Chile is at Las Heras 205, while CTC (Telefónica) is at Latorre 748.

Three bus companies, Fepstur (☎ 621-644), Latorre 588; El Shadday (☎ 621-561), Latorre 440; and Maravilla Bus, Latorre 549, all connect Mejillones with Antofagasta (US$1.75).

COBIJA & GATICO
Stained white with guano, offshore stacks look like distant snow peaks at the desolate ghost towns of Cobija and Gatico, whose few remaining families eke out a living from

fishing and collecting seaweed. In the early 19th century, though, flourishing Cobija was Bolivia's outlet to the Pacific, serving the mines of the altiplano despite a precarious water supply, whose distribution reflected the early republican hierarchy. According to Isaiah Bowman:

The best well close to the shore was reserved for the government officials and garrison. The rest of the populace was supplied with water from springs in the hills back of town, conducted in pipes and kept under lock and key, the daily quota being delivered to each family. More water might be purchased from a carrier who brought it from the interior. In those days the present of a barrel of sweet water from southern Chile or Peru was highly esteemed.

So was fresh produce. In 1851, when Cobija had a population of 1500, a North American seaman recorded the eagerness with which the settlement's residents greeted a shipment of supplies from the north:

It was a matter of no little interest to witness the avidity of the population on landing the garden-stuff brought from Arica. Probably within 10 minutes after the first boatload of bags had been landed, all over town, Indians, including soldiers, might have been seen stripping the rind from green sugar-cane…housekeepers bearing away piles of maize, sweet potatoes…an hour later the beach – which had served as the impromptu market-place – was again bare.

Today, if you visit Cobija or Gatico, about 130km north of Antofagasta and 60km south of Tocopilla, bring your own supplies. After an earthquake and tsunami nearly obliterated the town in 1877, Cobija's population declined rapidly; by 1907, it had only 35 inhabitants and now there are even fewer.

You may be able to purchase fish, but everything else is at a premium except for free camping among the atmospheric adobe walls overlooking the sea. In a few places, such as the plaza, the church and the cemetery (with its wooden fences and crosses, and a few crumbling adobe crypts), the ruins are obvious. But for the most part visitors must guess the past identity of any given building.

BAQUEDANO

Midway between Antofagasta and Calama, Baquedano was a major rail junction where the *Longino* (Longitudinal Railway) met the Antofagasta-La Paz line. Its **Museo Ferroviario** is an open-air railroad museum with an amazing roundhouse, full of antique locomotives and other ancient railcars. A freight line still hauls borax from the Argentine border at Socompa, where it's possible to make connections with Argentina's famous Tren a las Nubes (Train to the Clouds) to Salta. The Chilean freight is sporadic, agonizingly slow and truly filthy, but may take really persistent passengers on a rarely traveled and scenic route.

For more information on the freight to Socompa, contact Señor Emilio Mavrakis at Ferronor (☎ 055-224-764, 227-927) at Sucre 220, 4th floor, in Antofagasta. Ostensible departures are on Sunday, but delays are common; intending passengers must obtain a notarial certificate absolving Ferronor of legal liability for delays or accidents. The individual in charge in Baquedano is Teodoro Torres (☎ 055-641-910).

MARÍA ELENA

Ten kilometers east of the point where the Panamericana crosses the Tocopilla-Chuquicamata highway is María Elena (population 7700), founded in 1926 and now one of Atacama's last operating nitrate oficinas. Built on a orderly plan that looks better on paper than in practice, its streets form a pattern like the Union Jack.

Now a municipality, María Elena offers such amenities as a theater, supermarket, library, hospital, market and administrative offices; oddly, for a onetime British company town, it also has a baseball field. There is also a **Museo Arqueológico e Histórico** (☎ 055-632-935), on Ignacio Carrera Pinto, open 9 am to 1 pm and 4 to 7 pm Monday to Saturday, 10 am to 1 pm and 5 to 8 pm Sunday. Tours of the nitrate plant are possible with a week's advance notice to Soquimich's public relations office (☎ 055-632-731) in María Elena.

The *Residencial Chacance* (☎ 632-749, *Claudio Vicuña 437*) is the only lodging in town for US$9/13 with shared bath, US$12/21 with private bath, but there is camping at **Balneario María Elena** on the Río Loa on the east side of the Panamericana (swimming is not advisable on this heavily polluted river). Decent food is available in town at the **Club María Elena**.

Tramaca (☎ 055-632-903 in María Elena) buses from Antofagasta continue to Calama, but Flora Barrios, Kenny Bus, Pullman Bus and Camus also provide services to María Elena.

AROUND MARÍA ELENA
Pedro de Valdivia, 40km south of María Elena, is a functioning mine but no longer a town. Founded in 1930, it's open to visits by the public; inquire at the gate. Meals are available at the **Club Pedro de Valdivia**. Tramaca and Flota Barrios buses connect the mine with Antofagasta and María Elena.

There are dozens of nitrate ghost towns in the Antofagasta region, lining both sides of the highway between Baquedano and Calama, and along the Panamericana north of the Tocopilla-Chuquicamata highway. The best-preserved is **Oficina Chacabuco**, a national monument just north of the junction between the two highways, that also served as a concentration camp during the military dictatorship of 1973-89.

TOCOPILLA
☎ 55

The paving of Ruta 1, the coastal highway to Iquique, has made the nitrate port of Tocopilla the beneficiary of a recent tourist boom, as traffic that once followed the inland Panamericana now heads directly north from Antofagasta. For travelers between Iquique and San Pedro de Atacama or Calama, Tocopilla is a far more convenient stopover than Antofagasta.

Despite its apparent isolation, Tocopilla exports the produce of the still operating oficina of María Elena. Since 1929, it has been the site of Codelco's massive thermoelectric plant, which serves the copper-mining complex of Chuquicamata. Fishing is also a significant industry.

Tocopilla (population 25,000) occupies a narrow coastal shelf at the base of the coastal range, 190km north of Antofagasta, 160km west of Calama, and 240km south of Iquique. The main thoroughfare is north-south Arturo Prat, while the main commercial street is 21 de Mayo, one block east. Most services are a few blocks either north or south from Plaza Condell, at the corner of 21 de Mayo and Aníbal Pinto.

In summer, Tocopilla maintains a Caseta de Informaciones at Caleta Boy, at the southern approach to town.

The post office is at the corner of 21 de Mayo and Aníbal Pinto, and Entel is at 21 de Mayo 2066 and Telefónica is at Manuel Rodríguez 1337.

Tocopilla's Hospital (☎ 821-839) is at Santa Rosa and Matta, a few blocks northeast of downtown.

Things to See & Do
Like other northern coastal towns, Tocopilla's smattering of wooden buildings, mostly along Prat and 21 de Mayo, give it a turn-of-the-20th-century atmosphere. At the corner of Prat and Baquedano, the **Torre Reloj** (clock tower) was relocated intact from the nitrate oficina of Coya, near María Elena. **Playa El Salitre**, reached by a staircase from Calle Colón, is the best spot for sunbathing, but the water is too contaminated for swimming.

Tocopilla has a **Museo Arqueológico** (Archaeological Museum) in the Municipalidad, at Aníbal Pinto and 21 de Mayo, 2nd floor.

Places to Stay
Residencial Sonia (☎ 813-086, Washington 1329) is the cheapest in town for about US$6 with shared bath but the staff can be a little brusque; comparably priced **Residencial Royal** (☎ 811-488, 21 de Mayo 1988) also has singles with private bath for US$12/20.

Amiable **Residencial Alvarez** (☎ 811-578, Serrano 1234) charges US$8 per person for spacious, well-kept rooms with high ceilings, set around an attractive patio. Friendly **Hostería Bolívar** (☎ 812-783, Bolívar 1332) is also a good value for US$10 with shared bath. **Hotel Casablanca** (☎ 813-222, 21 de

Mayo 2054) charges US$10 per person; all rooms have private baths.

Hotel Vucina (☎ 812-155, 21 de Mayo 2069) has rooms for US$24/32 including cable TV and breakfast. Newish *Hotel Chungará (☎ 812-737, 21 de Mayo 1440)* charges US$26/32 for rooms that are clean but a little small; they do have private baths, and breakfast is included.

Places to Eat

Tocopilla's top restaurant is the reasonably priced *Club de la Unión (☎ 813-198, Prat 1354)* which has fine four-course Sunday lunches for US$6, including a tasty pisco sour. Service is friendly but can be erratic.

Chinese food is available at *Chifa Ji Kong (21 de Mayo 1848)* and *Chifa Jok San (☎ 811-225, 21 de Mayo 1482)*.

Getting There & Away

Since the paving of coastal Ruta 1, Tocopilla has become a hub for north- and southbound bus services, and for those headed east to Chuquicamata and Calama. Regional bus lines connecting Tocopilla with Iquique and Antofagasta include Buses Camus (☎ 813-102) at 21 de Mayo 1940 and Tocopilla Bus (☎ 811-029) at 21 de Mayo 1250; long-distance companies include Flota Barrios (☎ 811-861) at 21 de Mayo 1720, Tur-Bus (☎ 811-581) at 21 de Mayo 1495, Tramaca (☎ 813-195) at 21 de Mayo 2196 and Pullman Bus at 21 de Mayo 1377.

Taxi colectivos to Chuquicamata and Calama (US$6) leave from the corner of 21 de Mayo and Manuel Rodríguez, just south of Hotel Casa Blanca. Departure times are 7 am and 3 pm.

Sample fares and times include Antofagasta (US$4, 2½ hours), Iquique (US$10, four to five hours, depending on customs delays), Arica (US$18, seven to eight hours), Copiapó (US$25, 11 hours), La Serena (US$30, 15 hours) and Santiago (US$40, 21 hours).

CALAMA
☎ 55

In the interior of Region II, Calama is the commercial center for the world's largest open-pit copper mine at nearby Chuquicamata and claims to be Chile's highest-altitude city. The starting point for visits to 'Chuqui' (the company town that is in fact at a higher elevation than Calama), it's also convenient to historic and archaeological sites such as the Atacameño village of Chiu Chiu and the Pukará de Lasana, the oases of San Pedro de Atacama and Toconao and the El Tatio geysers. Calama is now the western terminus of passenger service on the Calama-Oruro (Bolivia) railway, which formerly ran all the way to Antofagasta.

It's a measure of Calama's own brief history that the city did not acquire its Iglesia Catedral San Juan Bautista until 1906 – until then, it was ecclesiastically subordinate to tiny Chiu Chiu. Major changes are in store, though: By 2002 the entire population of heavily polluted Chuquicamata will relocate to Calama. A new civic center is planned for north of downtown, and other improvements are already underway, as downtown Calle Ramírez becomes an attractive pedestrian mall, Parque El Loa undergoes a refurbishing and the city in general becomes a livelier place. But most visitors will use the city as a brief stopover en route to the sights of the Atacama outback.

Orientation

On the north bank of the Río Loa, 220km northeast of Antofagasta, Calama (population 105,000) sits 2250m above sea level. Though the city has sprawled with the influx of laborers who prefer its slightly milder climate to that of Chuquicamata, the city's central core is still pedestrian-friendly. Named for the date of Calama's occupation by Chile in the War of the Pacific, the modest Plaza 23 de Marzo is the focus of downtown activity.

Information

The Oficina Municipal de Información Turística (☎ 345-345) is at Latorre 1689, near Vicuña Mackenna. It's open 9 am to 1 pm and 3 to 7 pm weekdays (but sometimes stays open later). There's usually an English speaker on duty in summer.

Another good source of information is Acchi, the Automóvil Club de Chile (☎ 342-770), Av Ecuador 1901.

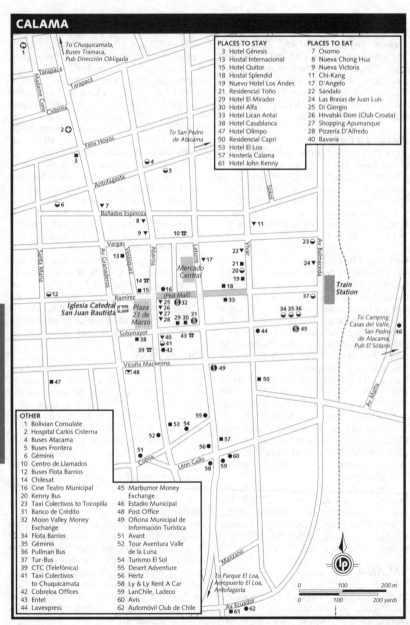

CALAMA

PLACES TO STAY
- 3 Hotel Génesis
- 13 Hostal Internacional
- 15 Hotel Quitor
- 18 Hostal Splendid
- 19 Nuevo Hotel Los Andes
- 21 Residencial Toño
- 29 Hotel El Mirador
- 30 Hotel Alfa
- 33 Hotel Lican Antai
- 38 Hotel Casablanca
- 47 Hotel Olimpo
- 50 Residencial Capri
- 53 Hotel El Loa
- 57 Hostería Calama
- 61 Hotel John Kenny

PLACES TO EAT
- 7 Osorno
- 8 Nueva Chong Hua
- 9 Nueva Victoria
- 11 Chi-Kang
- 17 D'Angelo
- 22 Sándalo
- 24 Las Brasas de Juan Luis
- 25 Di Giorgio
- 26 Hrvatski Dom (Club Croata)
- 27 Shopping Apumanque
- 28 Pizzería D'Alfredo
- 40 Bavaria

OTHER
- 1 Bolivian Consulate
- 2 Hospital Carlos Cisterna
- 4 Buses Atacama
- 5 Buses Frontera
- 6 Géminis
- 10 Centro de Llamados
- 12 Buses Flota Barrios
- 14 Chilesat
- 16 Cine Teatro Municipal
- 20 Kenny Bus
- 23 Taxi Colectivos to Tocopilla
- 31 Banco de Crédito
- 32 Moon Valley Money Exchange
- 34 Flota Barrios
- 35 Géminis
- 36 Pullman Bus
- 37 Tur-Bus
- 39 CTC (Telefónica)
- 41 Taxi Colectivos to Chuquicamata
- 42 Cobreloa Offices
- 43 Entel
- 44 Lavexpress
- 45 Marbumor Money Exchange
- 46 Estadio Municipal
- 48 Post Office
- 49 Oficina Municipal de Información Turística
- 51 Avant
- 52 Tour Aventura Valle de la Luna
- 54 Turismo El Sol
- 55 Desert Adventure
- 56 Hertz
- 58 Ly & Ly Rent A Car
- 59 LanChile, Ladeco
- 60 Avis
- 62 Automóvil Club de Chile

Several downtown banks have ATMs, including Banco de Crédito at Sotomayor 2002. Moon Valley Money Exchange is on Ramírez between Abaroa and Latorre, while Marbumor Money Exchange is at Sotomayor 1837.

The post office is at Vicuña Mackenna 2167. Telefónica has long-distance telephone offices at Abaroa 1756, Entel is at Sotomayor 2027 and Chilesat is at Abaroa 1928.

The Centro de Llamados at Vargas 2014 has Internet access.

Calama has numerous travel agencies that arrange excursions to more remote parts of the desert – though some of these trips can be arranged more cheaply from San Pedro de Atacama. Among them are Tour Aventura Valle de la Luna (☎/fax 310-720, colle-in@ctc-mundo.net) at Abaroa 1620, Desert Adventure (☎ 344-894) at Latorre 1602 and Turismo El Sol (☎ 340-152) on Cobija between Abaroa and Latorre.

Lavexpress (☎ 315-361), Sotomayor 1887, open 9 am to 9 pm daily except Sunday, has excellent laundry service.

Hospital Carlos Cisterna (☎ 342-347) is at Av Granaderos near the corner with Cisterna, five blocks north of Plaza 23 de Marzo.

Parque El Loa

At the south end of Av O'Higgins (the southern extension of Abaroa), Parque El Loa features a riverside swimming pool and a scale model of the famous church at Chiu Chiu, with its twin bell towers. In the park you'll also find Calama's **Museo Arqueológico y Etnológico** (Museum of Archaeology and Ethnology), with exhibits on the peoples of the Atacama, a decent collection of artifacts and good models. However, there's not much interpretive material. Museum admission costs US$0.45 for adults, half that for children; it's open 10 am to 1 pm and 3 to 7 pm, daily except Monday.

Organized Tours

The Corporación Cultural y Turismo de Calama leads city tours (US$5) on Friday and Saturday, walking around the downtown area before boarding a bus to visit the Estación Ferrocarril a Bolivia (railroad station), Parque Loa, the Monolito Topater (a memorial to the War of the Pacific at the junction of Circunvalación and the highway to San Pedro) and Parque Manuel Rodríguez. The Corporación also organizes half-day tours to Lasana and Chiu Chiu (US$15), full-day tours Lasana, Chiu Chiu and Caspana (US$24), full-day tours to Lasana, Chiu Chiu, Caspana, Toconce and the Baños de Turi (US$32),and full-day tours to San Pedro de Atacama, Toconao and Valle de la Luna (US$50). For reservations, visit the municipal tourist office.

Otherwise, similar circuits are available from or through the travel agencies (see Information); the paving of the highways to San Pedro de Atacama and Chiu Chiu has made longer trips more feasible from Calama, though many travelers find San Pedro a better base of operations.

Special Events

Calama's major holiday is March 23, when the city celebrates the arrival of Chilean troops during the War of the Pacific with fireworks and other festivities.

Places to Stay

Budget Tolerable by budget standards but avoided by some travelers, *Residencial Capri* (☎ 342-870, Vivar 1639) charges US$6 per person with shared bath, slightly more with private bath. Tidy *Nuevo Hotel Los Andes* (☎ 341-073, Vivar 1920) charges US$8/14 singles/doubles.

Long popular with foreign visitors, the fairly tranquil *Residencial Toño* (☎ 341-185, Vivar 1970) has clean sheets and provides plenty of blankets for US$9/17, but some of the beds are uncomfortable. *Hostal Splendid* (☎ 341-841, Ramírez 1960) is basic but clean and secure, though some rooms are small and have no exterior windows. Rooms with shared bath cost US$9/15; rooms with private bath cost US$15/25. In the same range is *Hotel Génesis* (☎ 342-841, Av Granaderos 2148) for US$11/15 with shared bath, US$20 double with private bath.

Friendly *Hotel El Loa* (☎ 341-963, Abaroa 1617) offers comfortable, spotless rooms with shared bath (plenty of hot water) for US$11/20. Reader-endorsed *Hostal Internacional* (☎ 342-927, *General Velásquez 1976*) is OK though a bit rundown for US$11/21 with shared bath, US$46 double with private bath.

At the upgraded, improving *Hotel John Kenny* (☎ 341-430, *Ecuador 1991*), rates start at US$13/24 with shared bath; rooms with private bath cost US$27/49.

Mid-Range Mid-range accommodations are relatively scarce in Calama, starting around US$41/52 at the Art Deco-style *Hotel Casablanca* (☎ 341-938, *Sotomayor 2161*), opposite Plaza 23 de Marzo, which is worn but still appealing for its clean, spacious rooms. Boxy, modern *Hotel Olimpo* (☎ 342-367, *Av Santa María 1673*) charges US$57/68.

A major step up is stylish, historic *Hotel El Mirador* (☎/fax 340-329, *Sotomayor 2064*) probably the best value in town for US$62/70. The new *Hotel Quitor* (☎ 341-716, *Ramírez 2116*) charges US$75/90.

Top End Rates are US$93/121 with breakfast at the traditional favorite *Hostería Calama* (☎ 341-115, *Latorre 1521*), and identical at *Hotel Alfa* (☎ 342-496, *Sotomayor 2016*). *Hotel Lican Antai* (☎ 341-621, *Ramírez 1937*) is a newer upscale hotel charging US$119/133.

On the southern outskirts of town, near the airport, is the luxury *Park Hotel de Calama* (☎ 319-900, *Camino Aeropuerto 1392*), which is over the top from US$142 double.

Places to Eat

At the *Mercado Central* (*Latorre between Ramírez and Vargas*); there are several inexpensive cocinerías. *Nueva Victoria* (*Vargas 2102*) is a routine budget eatery, as is *Osorno* (☎ 341-035, *Av Granaderos 2013-B*), which is also a functioning peña.

Facing Plaza 23 de Marzo, the *Hrvatski Dom* (☎ 342-126, *Abaroa 1869*) is the Club Croata or Croatian Club, a slightly upmarket place with good fixed-price lunches. Next-door *Shopping Apumanque* (*Abaroa 1859*) also has good fixed-price meals, but the à la carte menu is much more expensive.

For fine ice cream, other desserts, sandwiches and coffee, head to *Di Giorgio* (☎ 312-353, *Ramírez 2099*). *Bavaria* (☎ 341-496, *Sotomayor 2093*) is part of a reliable but uninspired nationwide chain.

Pizzería D'Alfredo (☎ 319-440, *Abaroa 1835*) is the local branch of a reliable regional chain; the music can be deafening. Caffeine addicts will find capuccinos and espresso here, but try also *D'Angelo* (☎ 312-867, *Latorre 1983*). *Sándalo* (☎ 311-926, *Vivar 1982*) specializes in meat and seafood. *Las Brasas de Juan Luis* (☎ 344-366, *Av Balmaceda 1952*) is an upscale parrilla.

For Chinese food, try *Chi-Kang* (☎ 341-121, *Vivar 2037*), or *Nueva Chong Hua* (☎ 313-387, *Abaroa 2008*), which has fixed-price meals but also a diverse à la carte menu.

Entertainment

The *Cine Teatro Municipal* (☎ 342-864, *Ramírez 2080*) shows current films, along with occasional art exhibits and live theater. Calama has two worthwhile pubs, *Dirección Obligada* (☎ 345-834, *Av Granaderos 2663*) and *El Sótano* (*Av La Paz 436*).

Cobreloa (☎ 341-775, *Abaroa 1757*), the local soccer team, plays at the Estadio Municipal on Av Matta, across the railroad tracks to the east.

Getting There & Away

From Calama travelers can head north to Iquique and Arica, southwest to Antofagasta, west to Tocopilla, northeast by train to Bolivia, or east by bus to San Pedro de Atacama and to Salta, in Argentina.

Air LanChile and Ladeco share offices (☎ 341-394) at Latorre 1499. LanChile flies to Antofagasta (US$22) and Santiago (US$117 to US$179) three times daily except Sunday, when it flies twice. Ladeco flies daily to Antofagasta and Santiago except Monday, when it has two flights.

Avant (☎ 343-066), Cobija 2188, flies to Antofagasta (US$22) and Santiago (US$131 to US$150) twice each weekday and once Saturday and Sunday.

Bus Calama has no central bus terminal, but most bus companies are fairly central, within a few blocks of each other. The exception is Tramaca (☎ 340-404), which has its terminal at Av Granaderos 3048, about 12 blocks north of Plaza 23 de Marzo; it has frequent buses to Antofagasta, plus several daily to Santiago, Arica and Iquique.

Tur-Bus (☎ 316-699), Ramírez 1802, has services north- and southbound on the Panamericana and also goes to San Pedro de Atacama at 11 am daily.

Flota Barrios (☎ 341-497), Ramírez 2298 and on Sotomayor between Vivar and Balmaceda, serves the same destinations along the Panamericana, as does Pullman Bus (☎ 319-665), Sotomayor 1808.

Géminis (☎ 341-993), Antofagasta 2239 and on Sotomayor between Vivar and Av Balmaceda, has daily buses to Santiago, Antofagasta, Arica and Iquique. Kenny Bus (☎ 342-514), Vivar 1954, serves Iquique via María Elena and Pozo Almonte.

Buses Frontera (☎ 318-543), Antofagasta 2041, goes six times daily to San Pedro and daily to Toconao (US$4.50). Buses Atacama (☎ 314-757), Abaroa 2105-B, goes two or three times daily to San Pedro.

Taxi colectivos to Tocopilla leave from the corner of Balmaceda and Vargas, one block north of the Tur-Bus terminal.

Sample fares and approximate times from Calama include Arica (US$17, nine hours), Iquique (US$14, six hours), Antofagasta (US$5.50, three hours), Chañaral (US$23, nine hours), Copiapó (US$25, 11 hours), Vallenar (US$29, 13 hours), La Serena (US$33, 16 hours) and Santiago (US$46). Tur-Bus's semi-cama service to Santiago costs US$55, while their salón cama service costs US$68.

International buses are invariably full, so make reservations as far in advance as possible. Tramaca goes to Jujuy (14 hours) and Salta (US$48, 16 hours), leaving Tuesday and Friday at 10 am.

Train Every Thursday at 3 am there's train service from Calama to Ollagüe, on the Bolivian border, with connections to Uyuni (US$14, 24 hours) and Oruro (US$20, 30 hours). Tickets are available either at Tramaca or at Calama's Estación de Ferrocarril (☎ 342-004), Balmaceda 1777; you may also be able to purchase tickets at Tramaca offices in Antofagasta and in Santiago. Tickets should be purchased by the Saturday prior to departure.

Show your passport when buying tickets and be sure to obtain a Bolivian visa if you need one. There's a Bolivian consulate (☎ 344-413) at Madame Curie 2388, 2nd floor. Temperatures can drop well below freezing on this route, so bring warm clothing and sleeping gear.

Getting Around

Aeropuerto El Loa (☎ 312-348) is only a short cab ride south of Calama.

Frequent taxi colectivos to Chuquicamata leave from Abaroa, a block from Plaza 23 de Marzo, between Vicuña Mackenna and Sotomayor. The fare is about US$0.75.

Calama car rental agencies include Hertz (☎ 340-018) at Latorre 1510, Budget (☎ 341-076) at Av Granaderos 2925, Avis (☎ 319-797) at Pedro León Gallo 1985 and Ly & Ly Rent a Car (☎ 341-873) at the corner of Latorre and León Gallo. To visit the geysers at El Tatio, rent a 4WD or pickup truck – ordinary passenger cars lack sufficient clearance for the area's rugged roads and may get stuck in the mud at river fords.

AROUND CALAMA
Chuquicamata

The seemingly inexhaustible copper reserves at Chuquicamata (or just Chuqui), 16km north of Calama, have made Chile the world's greatest producer of that commodity. Foreign capital originally financed the exploitation of its relatively low-grade ores, with open-pit techniques originally developed in the western USA. Today, it's the world's largest open-pit copper mine and the largest single supplier of copper, producing 650,000 tons per annum, a figure that may double within five years thanks to new technology. Despite Chile's attempts at economic diversification, Chuqui still provides about 43% of the country's total copper output and around 17% of annual export income. In total, copper accounts for nearly 40% of Chilean exports.

Chuqui's perpetual plume of eastward-blowing dust and smoke gives away its location from a great distance in the cloudless desert, but everything here dwarfs the human scale, from the fleet of 115 massive diesel trucks that carry 170- to 330-ton loads on tires more than 3m high (and that cost US$12,000 each), to the towering mountains of *tortas* (tailings, some of which are being reprocessed) that have accumulated over eight decades. The mine complex's single most impressive feature, though, is the massive open pit, 4.3km long, 3km wide and 728m deep, from which the ore comes. Much of the time on two-hour tours is spent simply gazing into the depths of this immense excavation. Unfortunately, the smelter plant is no longer open to the public.

Chuquicamata proper is a clean, well-ordered company town whose landscape is a constant reminder of its history. The **Estadio Anaconda** is a modern football stadium and the **Auditorio Sindical** is a huge theater, whose interior mural commemorates a 1960s strike in which several workers died. A prominent statue near Relaciones Públicas (Public Relations) honors the workers who operated heavy equipment (including the monstrous power shovel that towers nearby), and created the huge excavations and gigantic piles of tailings that surround the town.

Because of persistent environmental problems, though, the entire population will relocate to Calama by the year 2002. Families in the most polluted areas have already begun to move, despite sentimental attachment to the town.

History Prospectors first discovered the Chuquicamata deposits in 1911, but the original North American owner sold it to New York City's Guggenheim brothers, who in turn sold it to the US Anaconda Copper Mining Company, which began excavations in 1915. Out of nothing, the company created a city (current population about 13,000) with housing, schools, cinemas, shops, a hospital and many other amenities, although many Chileans accused the company of taking out more than it put back into the country. At the same time, labor unrest added to the resentment felt toward the huge, powerful corporation.

By the 1960s, Chile's three largest mines (the others were Anaconda's El Salvador, in Region III of Atacama, and Kennecott's El Teniente, in Region VI of Rancagua) accounted for more than 80% of copper production, 60% of total exports and 80% of tax revenues. Anaconda, although it paid a greater percentage of its profits in taxes than other mining companies, became the target of those who advocated nationalization of the industry.

Congressional leftists had introduced nationalization bills since the early 1950s, but support for nationalization grew even among the Christian Democrats and other centrists. During the Christian Democratic government of President Eduardo Frei Montalva in the late 1960s, Chile gained a majority shareholding in the Chilean assets

Copper Processing

Given Chuquicamata's low-grade ore, only large quantities make production practical. The ore is quarried by blasting and power shovels; at the mining stage, material is classified as ore or waste depending on its copper content. Sufficiently rich material is dumped into a crusher, which reduces it to fine particles. The metal is then separated from the rock by a flotation process in which the copper is separated and concentrated through chemically induced differences in surface tension. It is carried to the surface of pools of water – the large pools of blue solution at the processing works are the concentrators where this process takes place. The copper concentrate becomes a thick slurry from which the final product is extracted by smelting.

AROUND CALAMA & SAN PEDRO DE ATACAMA

To Ollagüe, Bolivia

To Panamericana, Chug Chug, Tocopilla

Pukará de Lasana

Chuquicamata

Chiu Chiu

Calama

Río Loa

To Panamericana, Antofagasta

Vegas de Turi

Linzor

Ayquina

Toconce

Caspana

El Tatio Geysers

Cerros de Tocorpuri 5808m

Volcán Putana 5890m

Salar de Chalviri

Cerro Saireçábur 5971m

Termas de Puritama

Cordón Barros Arana

Gautin

Catarpe

Pukará Quitor

Valle de la Luna

San Pedro de Atacama

Solcor

Tulor

Sequitor

Cuyo

RNLF

RNLF

Tambillo

Toconao

RNLF

Salar de Atacama

RNLF

Laguna Chaxa

RNLF

Camar

Socaire

Peine

Talabre

Volcán Lincancábur 5916m

Laguna Verde

Portezuelo del Cajón 4480m

Cerro Toco 5604m

Cerro Redondo 5698m

Cerro Colachi 5631m

Cerro de Pili 6046m

Cerro Lascar 5154m

Laguna Lejía

Cerro Lejía 5793m

Cerro Chiliques 5778m

Laguna Miscanti

Cerro Miscanti 5622m

RNLF

Laguna Miñiques

Laguna Tuyajto

Salar de Tara

Salar de Pujsa

RNLF

Volcán Aguas Calientes 5924m

Paso de Jama

Paso de Guaitiquina 4296m

Salar de Laco

Paso de Lago Sico 4079m

Salar del Rincón

Reserva Nacional Los Flamencos

To Susques, Salta

Parque Nacional Santa de Ayes Laguna Colorada

Laguna Colorada

BOLIVIA

Laguna Caruta

Laguna Grande de Chalviri

Laguna Busch

Potosí

Atacama Desert

Cordillera de Domeyko

Cordillera de la Sal

0   20   40 km
0   10   20 miles

RNLF   Reserva Nacional Los Flamencos

ARGENTINA

NORTE GRANDE

Jujuy

Salta

of Anaconda and Kennecott, partly because the companies feared expropriation under a future leftist regime.

In 1971 Congress approved nationalization of the industry by a large majority that included rightist elements. After 1973, the new military junta agreed to compensate companies for loss of assets, but retained ownership through the Corporación del Cobre de Chile (Codelco), although it has encouraged the return of foreign capital. In early 1996 there was a brief but contentious strike, revealing factionalism in the local labor movement. Some conservative legislators are urging privatization of Codelco, and even left-center, newly elected president Ricardo Lagos has approached the topic, albeit gingerly.

Organized Tours Chuquicamata's Oficina de Relaciones Públicas (public relations office) offers weekday tours, in both English and Spanish, to more than 25,000 people each year. To go on a tour, report to the Oficina Ayuda a la Infancia, at the top of Av JM Carrera, by 9 am, bringing your passport for identification and making a modest donation of about US$2.50. Tours are ostensibly limited to the first 40 arrivals, but if there are at least 15 more visitors they'll add a second bus. Demand is high in January and February, so get there early, but if demand is sufficient there may be afternoon tours as well. Children under age 12 are not permitted.

Tours begin with a 10-minute video shown in Spanish; on completion, those who understand Spanish go directly to the tour bus, while others sit through the English-language version. Visitors should wear sturdy footwear; the mine now permits shorts and casual clothing. Do not arrange the tour through agencies in Calama, which may charge more than Codelco's nominal fee.

Places to Eat Good lunches are available at the *Club de Empleados (JM Carrera s/n)* and the *Arco Iris Center (☎ 326-251, JM Carrera 104)*, both across from the plaza, the *Club de Obreros (Mariscal Alcázar s/n)* two blocks south of the stadium, and *Carloncho (Av Comercial O'Higgins s/n)*.

Getting There & Away From Calama, taxi colectivos leave from Abaroa between Vicuña Mackenna and Sotomayor, just south of Plaza 23 de Marzo. From the taxi rank in Chuqui, it's a short uphill walk to the Oficina Ayuda a la Infancia.

Geoglifos Chug Chug

About 15km west of Chuquicamata, on the paved highway to Tocopilla, a dirt road leads north to Chug Chug, a hillside whose restored geoglyphs are mostly geometric rhomboids; one resembles a pre-Columbian surfer. Some date from Tiwanaku (500 to 1000 AD), while others are regional (dating from about 1100 to 1450 AD), and the remainder Incaic (1450 to 1530 AD).

The Upper Loa & Its Tributaries

Northeast of Calama, a string of typically Andean villages and archaeological monuments dots the landscape of the upper Río Loa and its eastern tributaries – an alternative route to the Tatio geysers. Visitors to this area should be aware that the drinking water of Chiu Chiu and Caspana is contaminated with arsenic. Although this danger may be

alleviated by a new treatment plant, at present it's better to stick to bottled water.

Closest to Calama is **Chiu Chiu**, 33km away via paved Ruta 21. Chiu Chiu boasts the **Iglesia de San Francisco** (a national monument) and the modest *Hotel Tujina (☎ 055-326-386, Esmeralda s/n)*. Graveled Ruta 21 continues north toward the Bolivian border at Ollagüe; a paved parallel road, about 2km west, goes north toward the new El Abra copper mine. After about 8km, a lateral drops into the Loa valley to pass the reconstructed **Pukará de Lasana**, an extensive fortress originally dating from the 12th century AD.

From either Chiu Chiu or Lasana, parallel gravel roads (the more southerly is generally better but sometimes suffers washouts) head east toward **Ayquina**, an agricultural village in the Río Caspana Valley, best known for the **Museo Votivo de Ayquina**, which emphasizes religious artifacts and folkloric dance groups. The museum is open 9 am to 1 pm and 2 to 5:30 pm daily except Monday.

The more northerly of the two eastbound roads passes the **Vegas de Turi**, a thermal spring whose flow, unfortunately, is declining because of water extraction for mining and use by inhabitants of Calama. The road continues toward **Toconce**, known for a church and extensive agricultural terraces. The area's real gem, though, is **Caspana**; nestled in its namesake valley, it's exactly what an Andean village is supposed to look like – verdant terraces, thatched roofs, the colonial **Iglesia de San Lucas** and a **museum**, organized by Maltese anthropologist George Serracino, that would be the pride of many larger communities. Museum admission costs US$0.80.

From Caspana, a road climbs south out of the valley and switchbacks up the Cuesta de Chita, an alternative route to the geysers at El Tatio.

SAN PEDRO DE ATACAMA
☎ 55

Immensely popular with Chilean and foreign visitors, San Pedro de Atacama is a placid oasis of adobe houses at the northern end of the Salar de Atacama, a saline lake that has almost completely evaporated. First visited by Pedro de Valdivia in 1540, in the early 20th century it was a major stop on cattle drives from the Argentine province of Salta to the nitrate oficinas of the desert. Isaiah Bowman, in 1924, observed that:

It takes thirteen to fourteen days for cattle to be driven from Salta to San Pedro de Atacama. They wait at San Pedro one or two days, according to the need for beef at the nitrate establishments, as well as their own condition, which depends largely upon the weather they have experienced in crossing the Puna. The days of waiting are called 'la tablada.' In this time the cattle are fed liberally, and if any of them are ailing or footsore they receive the attention of a veterinary. From San Pedro it takes three days to drive them to the nitrate establishments.

Bowman also chronicled San Pedro's decline as railroad construction across the Andes made stock drives obsolete:

The fame that San Pedro has long enjoyed and the facilities it has for accommodating transient herds and droves attract the stockmen of Catamarca, La Rioja, San Luis, and Córdoba. For years they have sent droves of mules to be sold in the nitrate oficinas of the coastal desert farther north, but…completion of the Antofagasta railroad has greatly disturbed this traffic. In place of mule transport there is now railroad transport.

No longer on the cattle trail, San Pedro has become a popular stop on the 'gringo trail,' though many young Chileans also spend their holidays here. On Saturday nights, while gringo visitors hit the bars and restaurants, locals crowd the evangelical storefront churches that have invaded the town. Novelist Roberto Ampuero's mystery *El Alemán de Atacama* (The German of Atacama, 1996) conveys the ambience of contemporary San Pedro.

Besides tourism, the other main source of local employment is irrigated farming by the indigenous communities *(ayllus)* that surround the village and the Salar. East of the Salar rise immense volcanoes, some active but most extinct. Symmetrical Licancábur, at 5916m, is one of the most conspicuous (believe it or not, one individual has dragged

a mountain bike to the summit). Near San Pedro, the colorful Valle de la Luna (Valley of the Moon), one of the Atacama's most scenic areas, is part of Conaf's Reserva Nacional Los Flamencos.

The same interests who have built the tasteful luxury Hotel Explora in Parque Nacional Torres del Paine have erected an ill-advised equivalent here and simultaneously driven real estate prices through the roof – it's become the proverbial '800-pound gorilla,' doing whatever it wants. Still, despite increasing tourist trade, the town remains an affordable and attractive place, one which still has electricity from sunset until the first cable TV movie is over.

Travelers to and from Argentina and Bolivia clear immigration with the Policía Internacional, as well as customs and agricultural inspections, just outside of town to the east.

Orientation

San Pedro (permanent population about 1000), 2440m above sea level, is some 120km southeast of Calama via paved Chile 23. The village itself is small and compact, with almost everything of interest within easy walking distance of the Plaza de Armas.

While the streets do have names, few villagers use them, and very few buildings have numbers; consequently, it's easiest to refer to the map for directions. The main commercial street, Caracoles, south of the Plaza de Armas, appears as 'O'Higgins' on some maps, but the latter usage is fast disappearing.

Information

San Pedro's helpful, knowledgeable Oficina de Información Turística (☎ 851-019) is on the east side of the Plaza de Armas. It's open 10:30 am to 2:30 pm and 4 to 7:30 pm weekdays, 9 am to 1 pm weekends.

There are two cambios: Money Exchange on Toconao near Solcor, and El Chañar on Caracoles between Tocopilla and Toconao; the former changes traveler's checks, but the rates are poor.

Correos de Chile is on Padre Le Paige, opposite the museum. Entel is at the

SAN PEDRO DE ATACAMA

PLACES TO STAY
6 Residencial Chiloé
8 Camping Cunza
9 Casa Corvatsch
11 Residencial Rayco
12 Residencial Vilacollo
14 Residencial La Florida
20 Hostal Katarpe
25 Residencial El Pukará
26 Hotel Terrantai
31 Residencial Juanita

34 Hostal Supay
36 Camping/Hostal
    Takha Takha
37 Camping/Hostal Puri
39 Hotel Kimal
42 Hotel El Tatio
53 Hostal Tulor
57 Camping Los Perales
58 Residencial
    Licancábur
59 Hostería San Pedro

PLACES TO EAT
1 Quitor
7 La Esquina del Sol
10 Café al Paso Sonchek
35 Fogón del Diablo
38 Paachá
41 La Casona
43 El Adobe
46 La Estaka
47 Todo Natural
51 Tambo Cañaveral
52 Petro Pizza

OTHER
2 Buses Frontera
3 Bus Terminal
4 Buses Atacama
5 Bus Terminal
13 Expediciones
    Corvatsch
15 Iglesia San Pedro
16 Oficina de
    Información Turística
17 Posta Médica
18 Atacama Inca Tour
19 Post Office
21 La Manada
22 Artesanía Sempuray
23 Turismo Colque
24 Pangea
27 Café Etnico
28 Desert Adventure
29 CTC (Telefónica)
30 Entel
32 Casa Incaica
33 Turismo
    Pachamama
40 Labra Turismo
44 Turismo Ollagüe
45 Cosmo Andino
48 H2O
49 El Chañar
50 Turismo Ochoa
54 Money Exchange
55 Rancho Cactus
56 Artesanía La Luna

To Puritama,
El Tatio Geysers

Cemetery

To Pozo 3,
Toconao, Peine,
Customs & Immigration

To Pukará Quitor,
Catarpe

Museo Gustavo
Le Paige

To Calama

Plaza de
Armas

To Yaye,
Sequitor

To Solcor,
Solor

southwest corner of the plaza; CTC (Telefónica), on Caracoles half a block south of the plaza, is open 8:30 am to 8 pm.

Internet service at the Café Etnico, Tocopilla s/n, is relatively expensive.

The Posta Médica (☎ 851-010), on Toconao at the east side of the plaza, is the local clinic.

Local residents, especially the indigenous Atacameño people, can be sensitive to what they perceive to be an overwhelming presence of outsiders. Visitors should make a special effort to behave appropriately and blend in as well as possible.

San Pedro's tap water has a high mineral content, and some visitors react poorly to it. H2O, on Caracoles between Tocopilla and Toconao, sells bottled water.

Things to See & Do

On the east side of the plaza stands the restored adobe **Casa Incaica**, ostensibly built in 1540 for Valdivia, but it might be safer to say that Valdivia slept here. Since it's private property, visits are not possible. On the west side stands the **Iglesia San Pedro**, a colonial church built with indigenous or artisanal materials – adobe, wood from the *cardón* cactus

(Cereus atacamensis) and, in lieu of nails, large leather straps. It dates from the 17th century, though its present walls were built in 1745 and the bell tower was added in 1890.

Museo Gustavo Le Paige

If ordinary deserts are paradise for archaeologists, the Atacama is nirvana because of its nearly rainless environment, which preserves artifacts and other materials for millennia. In 1955, a Belgian priest and archaeologist, Gustavo Le Paige, assisted by the villagers of San Pedro and the Universidad Católica del Norte (Antofagasta), began to organize one of South America's finest museums, offering an overview of this region's cultural evolution through an extraordinary collection of pre-Columbian artifacts. Though primarily an archaeological museum – its explanatory panels on stone tool making are outstanding – it also includes exhibits on the Inka conquest and the Spanish invasion. It's weak on contemporary Atacameño culture, but this issue is due to be redressed.

Among the traditional displays are paleo-Indian mummies, including a child buried in a pottery urn, and skulls that show deliberate malformation. The skulls, in conformity with current anthropological practice respecting indigenous burial practices, are due to be replaced with credible replicas. There are also fragments of ancient weavings, pottery, tools, jewelry and paraphernalia for preparing, ingesting and smoking hallucinogenic plants.

Half a block east of the plaza, on Padre Le Paige, the museum (☎ 851-002) charges an admission fee of US$2, but only US$1 with student ID. Summer hours are 10 am to 1 pm and 3 to 7 pm daily; winter hours are 9 am to noon and 2 to 6 pm daily.

Organized Tours

San Pedro's recent tourist boom has given it the world's highest density of travel agencies for a town of its size, and competition is fierce. Local operators organize tours to Valle de la Luna, the geysers at El Tatio, Laguna Chaxa and the Salar de Atacama, and Toconao, among other sites. Normally,

without a minimum of six persons, there are surcharges. For more detailed information, see the Around San Pedro de Atacama section later in this chapter.

Special Events

In the first days of February, San Pedro celebrates the Fiesta de Nuestra Señora de la Candelaria with religious dances. Carnaval takes place in February or March, depending on the date of Easter. June 29 marks the local Fiesta de San Pedro y San Pablo.

August's Limpia de Canales is the resurrection of an old tradition of the cleaning of San Pedro's irrigation canals prior to the upcoming agricultural season. On August 30, the Fiesta de Santa Rosa de Lima is a traditional religious festival.

Places to Stay

Budget San Pedro has abundant budget accommodations of very good quality but holiday periods, such as Chilean independence days in mid-September, can tax these resources severely.

Camping Los Perales (Tocopilla s/n) is friendly and cheap at US$2.50 per person. *Camping Cunza* (☎ *851-183, Antofagasta s/n)* is also inexpensive, but it's next door to a noisy pub.

Placid *Camping Puri* (☎ *851-049, Caracoles s/n)* and next door *Camping Takha Takha* (☎ *851-038, Caracoles s/n)*, slightly farther west, both charge about US$5 per person for good sites with shade.

About 3km east of San Pedro, beyond the customs post, *Camping Alberto Terrazas* (☎ *851-042)* charges US$4 per person, including access to its swimming pool, and also has a restaurant. Nonguests can also use the popular swimming pool for US$2.

Hostal Puri (☎ *851-049, Caracoles s/n)* charges about US$6 per person, while nextdoor *Hostal Takha Takha* (☎ 851-038) charges US$11 for plain but comfy rooms with shared bath, set among pleasant gardens shared with campers; rooms with private bath are available for US$33/41.

Residencial Vilacollo (☎ *851-182, Tocopilla s/n)* is passable for US$7 with shared bath. For US$8 per person, *Residencial*

NORTE GRANDE

Chiloé (☎ 851-017, *Domingo Atienza s/n*) is only so-so. Comparably priced *Residencial Juanita* (☎ 851-039, *Plaza de Armas s/n*) also has a restaurant.

For US$9/15 singles/doubles, *Residencial El Pukará* (☎ 851-257, *Tocopilla s/n*) is by no means bad. *Residencial Rayco* (☎ 851-008, *Antofagasta s/n*) comes highly recommended for US$9 per person, with hot water 24 hours a day; rooms with private bath cost US$42 double.

Service standards and building conditions continue to erode at *Residencial La Florida* (☎ 851-021, *Tocopilla s/n*), but its restaurant still serves palatable and economical meals. Room rates are about US$9/16. *Casa Corvatsch* (☎ 851-101, *Antofagasta s/n*) has firm beds and shared baths with ample hot water for US$10 per person, and it's also next door to a popular pub that's open late.

Recommended *Residencial Licancábur* (☎ 851-007, *Toconao s/n*) charges US$15/21 with shared bath, US$40 double with private bath. *Hostal Katarpe* (☎ 851-033, *Domingo Atienza s/n*) is a good choice for US$16/30.

Mid-Range Half a block south of the plaza, clean, agreeable *Hostal Supay* (☎ 851-076, *Toconao s/n*)) has rooms with private bath for US$25/38, but there's a rowdy bar almost next door. There are mixed opinions on *Hostería San Pedro* (☎ 851-011, *Solcor s/n*) but it's clearly lost its onetime status as San Pedro's finest. Room rates are US$51/63, including private bath, plus swimming pool, restaurant and solar-heated showers. Its restaurant has drawn praise for both quality and size of portions.

The comfortable, attractively landscaped *Hotel Kimal* (☎ 851-030, *Domingo Atienza s/n*) charges US$55/75 with private bath and breakfast (at what may be San Pedro's best restaurant).

Upgraded *Hotel Tulor* (☎ 851-027, *Domingo Atienza s/n*), offers mid-range accommodations for US$58/71. *Hotel El Tatio* (☎ 851-092, *Caracoles s/n*) charges US$60/71 for relatively small rooms.

Top End Recommended *Hotel Terrantai* (☎ 851-045, *Tocopilla s/n*) is one of the better

recent additions to San Pedro's hotel scene, though it caters mostly to groups. Rates are US$100/112.

Open for package holidays only, the *Hotel Explora San Pedro de Atacama* inexplicably won a 'green architecture' award for its innovative design, passive air-con and sewage treatment plant, but this award glossed over the hotel's insatiable thirst for scarce water, given huge tubs and jacuzzis in every room, *four* swimming pools, and the irrigation needs of its ineptly transplanted mature pepper and algarrobo trees, acquired from local people who had better uses for them. Packages range from four days and three nights for US$1858/2592 singles/doubles to eight days and seven nights for US$3534/4882. All meals and excursions are included; for more information, see Organized Tours in the Getting Around chapter.

Places to Eat

Quitor (☎ 851-190, *Licancábur s/n*) prepares simple but nourishing meals for about US$4. Run by Slovenian immigrants, *Café al Paso Sonchek* (*Calama s/n*) has drawn praise from visitors to San Pedro, particularly for its breakfasts. *Todo Natural* (*Caracoles s/n*) focuses on juices but also has homemade ice cream; *Café Etnico* (*Tocopilla s/n*) is a friendly coffeehouse that now has Internet access.

Traditional favorite *Tambo Cañaveral* (☎ 851-060, *Toconao s/n*) doubles as a popular nightspot, with live Andean music on weekends. *La Estaka* (☎ 851-038, *Caracoles s/n*) has excellent food, including a nightly vegetarian special, and a lively bar with good atmosphere, but prices have risen.

Hotel Kimal's restaurant *Paachá* (☎ 851-030, *Domingo Atienza s/n*) has probably become the best place in town to eat. Although it's not cheap, everything is first-rate and even budget travelers should consider a splurge here.

La Esquina del Sol (☎ 851-183, *Antofagasta s/n*) has good lunches but at night it's better known as a pub. *Petro Pizza* (*Toconao s/n*) has fine Argentine-style pizza and *submarinos* (hot chocolate with steamed milk).

El Adobe (☎ 851-089, Caracoles s/n) gets more points for style than for food, similar to *La Casona* (☎ 851-004, Caracoles s/n). *Fogón del Diablo* (☎ 851-076, Toconao s/n) specializes in parrillada.

Shopping
The Paseo Artesanal, a shaded alley between the plaza and the bus station, is a good place to look for cardón carvings, llama and alpaca woolens and other souvenirs, but much of the stuff is imported from Bolivia. Other artisanal outlets include La Luna, Toconao s/n and Artesanía Sempuray and La Manada, both on Caracoles.

Getting There & Away
San Pedro doesn't have a bus terminal proper; buses load and unload passengers in an open area on Licancábur, across from the Paseo Artesanal. Buses Atacama (☎ 851-057), Licancabur s/n, leaves two or three times daily for Calama. Buses Frontera (☎ 851-117), a couple doors west, runs six buses daily to Calama (US$2.50) except on Sunday, when it runs three. Two leave for Toconao (US$2), at 3 and 8 pm, and one for Socaire at 9 pm daily except Sunday, when it leaves at 10 pm.

Tur-Bus also goes to Calama, at 5:50 pm daily. For reservations, visit Turismo Ochoa, Caracoles s/n; otherwise, buy tickets aboard the bus.

Getting Around
Mountain bikes are a good way to get around San Pedro and vicinity. Be sure to carry water; rentals are available at Pangea (☎ 851-111), Tocopilla s/n.

Rental horses are available at Rancho Cactus, Toconao s/n near Solcor.

AROUND SAN PEDRO DE ATACAMA
Most of San Pedro's attractions are more than walking distance from town and public transportation is limited, but heavy competition among numerous operators keeps tours reasonably priced. The fact that an operator is not listed below does not necessarily mean the agency is unreliable, but it's worth asking detailed questions and seeking the latest information before contracting for a tour. Some operators have drawn criticism for poor service and opportunism, particularly the agencies Ollagüe (criticized by the San Pedro tourist office for poor service, disagreeable and irresponsible guides and even hazardous practices) and Licancábur (criticized for poor service).

Among the most popular tours are destinations Valle de la Luna (US$8), Laguna Chaxa (US$12 plus the Conaf fee of US$3) and the geysers at El Tatio (US$21). Trips to the latter sometimes include an extension to Atacameño villages such as Caspana. Some agencies specialize in currently undervisited areas such as Laguna Lejía (US$42) and Cerro Lascar (US$45), and in leading trekking excursions to destinations such as El Tatio and the mountains and lakes toward the Argentine border for US$60 per person per day.

Among the best-established agencies are Dutch-run Cosmo Andino (☎ 851-069, fax 811-156), Caracoles s/n, which specializes in trekking but also has the best book exchange in Chile; Turismo Pachamama (☎ 851-064), Toconao s/n on the east side of the plaza; Turismo Ochoa (☎ 851-022), Caracoles s/n; Expediciones Corvatsch (☎ 851-021) Tocopilla s/n; Desert Adventure (☎ 851-067), Caracoles s/n; Atacama Inca Tour (☎ 851-034, fax 851-062), Toconao s/n; Labra Turismo (☎ 851-137), Caracoles s/n; and Turismo Ollagüe (☎ 851-106), Caracoles s/n.

Turismo Colque (☎ 851-109), Caracoles s/n, is the only choice for crossing the Bolivian border at Portezuelo del Cajón and continuing to Lago Verde and Uyuni, on the Bolivian side. Chilean operators have run into problems with Bolivian authorities at this legally ambiguous border crossing, which may involve bribes to the Bolivian military. Colque's three-day trip goes to Laguna Colorada, the Salar de Uyuni and intermediate points before ending in the city of Uyuni. The price is a reasonable US$80 to US$90 per person with food; modest lodging is extra at Laguna Colorada and Hotel San Juan, near Chiguana. Travelers clear Chilean immigration at San Pedro and Bolivian immigration on arrival at the city of Uyuni.

Pukará de Quitor & Catarpe

Just 3km northwest of San Pedro, on a promontory overlooking the Río San Pedro, are the ruins of a 12th-century Indian pukará. From the top of the fortifications, part of the last bastion against Pedro de Valdivia and the Spanish, you can see the entire oasis. Archaeologists have reconstructed parts of its ruined walls. Three km farther north, on the east side of the river, are the ruins of Catarpe, a former Inka administrative center.

Termas de Puritama

The Explora company, responsible for the monstrous hotel of the same name in San Pedro, has given these volcanic hot springs, in a box canyon about 30km north of San Pedro en route to El Tatio, a much-needed makeover, including new buildings and wooden walkways. These improvements have come at a price, though – the daily admission charge of US$10 is well beyond the budget of local families who used to frequent the site. Tour operators who once stopped here on the way back from El Tatio rarely do so now because of the price increase.

Since guests at the decidedly elitist Explora have unlimited free access to the baths, one local tour operator has gone so far as to call Explora's policy 'economic apartheid,' and the local community is now involved in a water rights struggle with Explora. Should you decide Puritama is worth the price, it's a 20-minute walk from the junction, where there's an ample parking lot, along an obvious gravel track. The temperature of the springs is about 33°C and there are several falls and pools. Bring food and water.

RESERVA NACIONAL LOS FLAMENCOS

Reserva Nacional Los Flamencos consists of seven geographically distinct sectors, totaling about 74,000 hectares, mostly to the south and east of San Pedro de Atacama. Its varied environments range from the Valle de la Luna and the Salar de Atacama, where Laguna Chaxa is home to breeding colonies of three species of flamingos, and high-altitude salt lakes toward the Argentine border. As the highway to Argentina improves in the coming years, this latter area is likely to become more easily accessible.

Conaf maintains a Centro de Información Ambiental at the *ayllu* (hamlet) of Solcor, about 2km past San Pedro de Atacama's customs and immigration post on the road to Toconao. It's open 10 am to 1 pm and 2:30 to 4:30 pm daily. There's another Conaf office on the southern outskirts of Toconao, and a ranger station at Laguna Chaxa.

Valle de la Luna

Latin Americans prosaically call every place where flood and wind have left an array of oddly shaped polychrome desert landforms the 'Valley of the Moon' – there are others in Bolivia and Argentina – but this area west of San Pedro de Atacama, part of Reserva Nacional Los Flamencos, definitely deserves a visit. At the northern end of the Cordillera de la Sal, it's one of San Pedro's most popular attractions.

If driving, leave the highway to explore the dirt roads and box canyons to the north, but take care not to get stuck in the sand. You can also hitchhike to the desert to hike around, but take plenty of water and food, and smear yourself with heavy sunblock (Lonely Planet does not recommend hitchhiking). Probably a better choice than either driving or walking is mountain biking (see the San Pedro section for bicycle rental details), but keep to the roads and trails. If driving, park only on the shoulder or at other designated areas – do not tear up the fragile desert with tire tracks.

Some visitors enjoy the view and solitude at night under a full moon, in which case you should take warm clothing – at this altitude, nights are cool at any time of year, but drop well below freezing in winter. Moonlight tours from San Pedro cost as little as US$5; note that in this part of Los Flamencos, Conaf no longer permits camping.

Laguna Chaxa

In the midst of the Salar de Atacama, about 25km southwest of the village of Toconao, Laguna Chaxa is the reserve's most easily accessible flamingo breeding site. Besides the operator's tour fees, rangers collect an admission charge of US$3.

Laguna Miniques

From a junction 3km south of Toconao, Ruta 23 heads 46km south toward the village of Socaire (which features an attractive colonial church and a remarkable density of pre-Columbian terraces on relatively gentle slopes), then climbs another 18km to an eastbound turnoff leading to Laguna Miniques, a high-Andean flamingo breeding site. Rejoining Ruta 23 about 15km south of the turnoff, the road heads eastward past several other impressive salt lakes, most notably Laguna Tuyajto, and continues to the Argentine border at 4079m Paso Sico. Many high country tours take this route.

EL TATIO GEYSERS

At 4300m above sea level, the world's highest geyser field is less breathtaking than the intermittent explosions of Yellowstone, but the visual impact of its steaming fumaroles at sunrise in the azure clarity of the altiplano is unforgettable, and the individual structures formed when the boiling water evaporates and leaves behind dissolved minerals are strikingly beautiful. Part of the proposed Parque Nacional Licancábur-Tatio (despite continued pressure for geothermal energy development), the geysers are 95km north of San Pedro de Atacama.

Early morning, about 6 am, is the best time to see the geysers; after about 8:30 am, morning winds disperse the steam, although most tours leave by that hour and you can enjoy the large thermal pool in virtual privacy. Watch your step – in some places, visitors have fallen through the thin crust into underlying pools of scalding water and suffered severe burns.

Places to Stay

Corfo, the state development agency, has a free *refugio* about 2km before the geysers – very rundown, but better than being outside. It's also possible to *camp*, but heavy frosts are nightly events at this elevation. Campers should bring plenty of food, since nothing is available on site.

Getting There & Away

Tours from San Pedro (see Around San Pedro de Atacama earlier in the chapter) include breakfast, often with fresh eggs boiled in geyser pools.

If driving, leave San Pedro no later than 4 am to reach the geysers by sunrise. The route north from San Pedro is signed, but some drivers prefer to follow tour agencies' jeeps and minibuses in the dark (tour drivers do not appreciate this, however). Do not attempt the road, which is very rough in spots and has some difficult stream fords, without a high clearance pickup or jeep, preferably one with 4WD.

If you have rented a vehicle in Calama, it's possible to return via the picturesque villages of Caspana, Toconce, Ayquina and Chiu Chiu (see Calama's Organized Tours section earlier in the chapter) rather than via San Pedro, on much improved roads. Some tours from Calama take this route as well.

TOCONAO

Known for finely hewn volcanic stone, the material for most of its houses, and an intricate irrigation system, the village of Toconao is about 40km south of San Pedro. Its **Iglesia de San Lucas**, with a separate bell tower, dates from the mid-18th century.

Toconao farmers produce almonds, grapes, pomegranates, apples and herbs. Most of their orchards and fields are in the **Quebrada de Jeria**, a delightful place for a walk, rock climbing or even a swim – its water is of such high quality that, in Isaiah Bowman's time, affluent families from San Pedro sent peons with mules to Toconao to fetch casks of drinking water. In the village proper, local women sell fine products woven of llama wool, including ponchos, pullovers, gloves and socks, as well as souvenirs cut from local stone.

Toconao has several inexpensive residenciales and restaurants near the plaza – try *Casa de Pensión Lascar* for good, simple meals and lodging.

Buses Frontera has two buses daily to and from San Pedro.

TALTAL
☎ 55

South of Antofagasta, about 30km beyond the La Negra truck stop, the Panamericana veers inland, roughly paralleling the route of the defunct Longino, before turning coastward again to pass near Taltal (population 11,800), a simple fishing port and modest beach town with a decaying cluster of period architecture from its nitrate export heyday (when its population was 20,000). The population shrank as the oficinas closed between 1940 and 1960, though Oficina Alemania held on until 1977.

Taltal may be in for big changes, though, as Chile's former public works minister and probable president, Ricardo Lagos, plans to extend and eventually pave the coastal route all the way to Antofagasta, opening the area to tourist traffic, while Canadian mining interests have discovered gold reserves of about 1.5 million ounces nearby. The European Space Organization's Very Large Telescope (VLT) at Cerro Paranal is about midway (120km north) between Taltal and Antofagasta.

Orientation & Information
From an intersection on the Panamericana, 300km south of Antofagasta and 115km north of Chañaral, a paved lateral heads northwest to Taltal, where it becomes Av Francisco Bilbao and then Calle O'Higgins. Trending southwest from O'Higgins, the main commercial street of Arturo Prat leads to the central Plaza Arturo Prat, while east of O'Higgins are most of the town's historic monuments.

In summer, Taltal maintains a helpful Oficina de Información Turística, open 10 am to 1 pm and 6 to 10:30 pm daily, on Plaza Arturo Prat.

Correos de Chile is at Prat 515. Telefónica is at Prat 687, Chilesat at San Martín 283.

Things to See & Do
During the nitrate era, this was the headquarters of **The Taltal Railway Company**, whose restored narrow-gauge **Locomotora No 59** (locomotive) sits, along with two restored railcars that serve as a museum, on the east side of O'Higgins, between Esmeralda and Prat. Squatters and tenants inhabit

buildings such as the Company's **Oficinas Generales** (general offices) and **Casa Administrador** (administrator's house). Built by Stothert & Pitt Ltd of Bath, England, the rusting crane on the **Muelle Salitrero** (nitrate pier) dates from 1903. Pick your way carefully out onto the pier, watching your step to avoid falling through the huge gaps into the sea. Taltalinos come here to fish at sunset, though nobody seems to catch anything.

Downtown monuments of the nitrate era include the wooden **Iglesia San Francisco Javier** (1897) and **Teatro Alhambra** (1921), both opposite Plaza Prat. At Prat 642, the **Museo Augusto Capdeville** is the modest municipal museum, with a fine selection of Andean ceramics; the building also serves as Taltal's Casa de la Cultura Sady Zañartu Bustos. On Esmeralda, between Torreblanca and Ramírez, **Plaza Riquelme** overlooks the **Balneario Municipal**, the city beach.

Special Events
The Aniversario de Taltal, July 12, celebrates the city's founding.

Places to Stay
There's free beach camping at **Muelle de Piedra**, about 2km north of town on the road to Paposo.

In summer only, there's an **Albergue Juvenil** (*Av Matta s/n*), opposite the Copec gas station at the eastern approach to the city.

In town, the cheapest lodging is basic **Hotel San Martín** (☎ *611-088, Martínez 279*), which charges US$9/17 singles/doubles with shared bath, but also has doubles with private bath for US$31. **Hotel Verdy** (☎ *611-105, Ramírez 345*) charges US$9 per person with shared bath and breakfast and has doubles with private bath for US$28.

Taltal's best is beachfront **Hostería del Taltal** (☎ *611-173, Esmeralda 671*) which ranges from US$23/29 to US$38/40 with private bath and breakfast. The new **Hostal del Mar** (☎ *611-612, Carrera 250*), charges US$29/38.

Places to Eat
At the Terminal Pesquero (wholesale fish market), **Las Brisas** (*Esmeralda s/n*) has

moderately priced seafood fresh off the boat. All the hotels have restaurants, as does the **_Club Social_** *(☎ 611-258, Torreblanca 162)*. For breakfast and sandwiches, try **_Pastelería La Central_** *(☎ 611-519, Prat 649)* or **_Salón de Té Capri_** *(☎ 611-273, Ramírez 218)*.

Getting There & Away

Tramaca (☎ 611-034), Prat 428, and Tur-Bus (☎ 611-426), Prat 63, provide bus services north- and southbound on the Panamericana. Typical fares include Arica (US$30, 18 hours), Iquique (US$25, 14 hours), Calama or Tocopilla (US$10, six hours), Chañaral (US$8, five hours), Copiapó (US$13, eight hours), La Serena (US$17, 15 hours) and Santiago (US$32).

AROUND TALTAL
Cifuncho

Midway between Taltal and the Panamericana, a gravel lateral heads southwest to Cifuncho, a tiny fishing camp that's also one of the most popular beaches in the area. En route to Cifuncho, a track suitable only for 4WD vehicles heads northwest to isolated Las Tórtolas, an even more attractive area.

Reserva Nacional Paposo

About 30km north of Taltal the coastal range reaches well over 2000m in places, dropping abruptly to the coast, where deep canyons such as **Quebrada El Médano** contain rock-art sites between 500 and 1000 years old, and the camanchaca supports a surprisingly varied flora. Access to this 13,000-hectare reserve, surrounded by a 30,000-hectare private buffer zone, is still difficult, but it may become easier as the highway improves and Conaf provides more information and assistance. There is no longer a Conaf ranger at the village of Paposo, 50km north of Taltal, so ask for details in Antofagasta before making the trip here.

Norte Chico

South of the Atacama proper, the Norte Chico (Little North) is a semiarid transition zone to the central valley's Mediterranean-like climate. Once known as the 'region of 10,000 mines,' this once-great silver mining area is still an important source of copper and iron. Several notable rivers make irrigated agriculture productive, although the region contains only a small percentage of Chile's total arable land.

Geographically, the Norte Chico's northern boundary lies just beyond Copiapó, at about 27°S, while its approximate southern boundary is the Río Aconcagua at about 33°S. Politically, it comprises Region III of Atacama (capital Copiapó) and Region IV of Coquimbo (capital La Serena), which is the area covered in this chapter.

For most travelers, the Norte Chico's major attractions are its balmy coastal climate, pleasant beaches and colonial-style cities, such as La Serena. Off the beaten track of the Panamericana, there are intriguing villages and spectacular mountain scenery in areas where foreign travelers are still a novelty. Not far off the Panamericana are two increasingly popular national parks, Pan de Azúcar and Fray Jorge; only a handful of people visit newer, more remote reserves such as Parque Nacional Llanos de Challe, on the coast north of Huasco, and Parque Nacional Nevado Tres Cruces, northeast of Copiapó, an area that seems likely to gain popularity in the coming years.

One of the Norte Chico's ephemeral attractions is the *desierto florido*, the 'flowering desert' that appears when dormant wildflower seeds sprout in years of sudden, heavy rains. Llanos de Challe is reportedly one of the best places to see this phenomenon, but the region's erratic rainfall patterns make it difficult to predict the best sites in any given year.

HISTORY

In pre-Columbian times the coastal Norte Chico, like the Norte Grande, was home to Chango fisherfolk. Sedentary Diaguita farmers inhabited the fertile river valleys beyond the littoral, and even parts of the less fertile uplands. The Diaguita, who crossed the Andes from present-day Argentina at an undetermined date, cultivated and irrigated maize. At different altitudes, they also raised a variety of complementary crops such as potatoes, beans, squash and quinoa, and they may have herded llamas. While their numbers were smaller and their political organization less complex than those of the major civilizations of Peru and Bolivia, the Diaguita were able to mobilize sufficient labor to build agricultural terraces and military fortifications. Some decades before the European invasion, the Inka Empire began to expand its influence among the Diaguita and other southern Andean peoples, but the area remained peripheral to the Central Andean civilizations.

Europeans first saw the region in 1535, when Diego de Almagro's expedition from Cuzco crossed the Paso San Francisco from Salta. Their first impressions were less than positive. Surviving phenomenal hardship, a member of Almagro's party left a graphic, gruesome account of the group's miserable 800km march over the Puna de Atacama (which took 20 days in the best of times), reporting that men and horses froze to death and that members of later expeditions, finding the undecomposed horses, 'were glad to eat them.'

In the lowlands, at least food and water were available, but Almagro and his men passed quickly through the Copiapó Valley and turned south to the Río Aconcagua before returning to Cuzco through Copiapó and the oases of the Norte Grande. A few years later Pedro de Valdivia's party, following Almagro's return route to establish a permanent Spanish settlement at Santiago, met stiff resistance from Indian warriors at Copiapó; of one party of 30 that Valdivia had ordered back to Cuzco, only the two officers survived.

In the course of his travels, Valdivia founded La Serena in 1541, but Copiapó

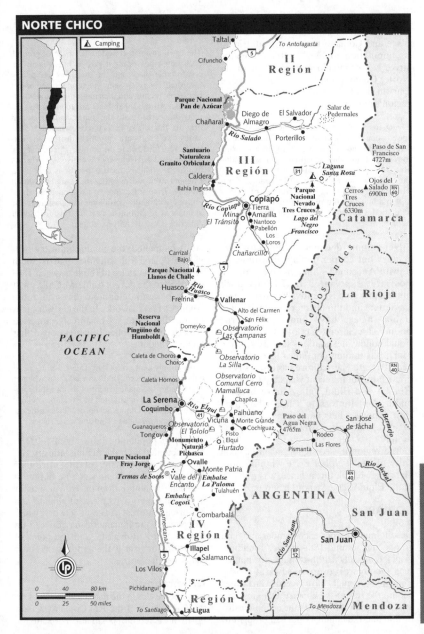

NORTE CHICO

△ Camping

Taltal

To Antofagasta

II Región

Cifuncho

Parque Nacional Pan de Azúcar

Diego de Almagro

El Salvador

Salar de Pedernales

Chañaral

Río Salado

Porterillos

Paso de San Francisco 4727m

Santuario Naturaleza Granito Orbicular

III Región

Laguna Santa Rosa

Ojos del Salado 6900m   RN 60

Caldera

Bahía Inglesa

Copiapó

Tierra Amarilla

Parque Nacional Nevado Tres Cruces

Cerros Tres Cruces 6330m

Catamarca

Río Copiapó

Mina El Tránsito

Nantoco

Pabellón

Los Loros

Lago del Negro Francisco

Chañarcillo

Carrizal Bajo

Parque Nacional Llanos de Challe

Río Huasco

Huasco

Vallenar

Freirina

Alto del Carmen

San Félix

Reserva Nacional Pingüino de Humboldt

Domeyko

Observatorio Las Campanas

La Rioja

Cordillera de los Andes

Caleta de Choros

Choros

Observatorio La Silla

PACIFIC OCEAN

Caleta Hornos

Observatorio Comunal Cerro Mamalluca

Chapilca

La Serena

Coquimbo

Río Elqui

Paihuano

Vicuña

Monte Grande

Cochiguaz

Paso del Agua Negra 4765m

San José de Jáchal

RN 40

Río Bermejo

Guanaqueros

Tongoy

Observatorio El Tololo

Pisco Elqui

Hurtado

Rodeo

Las Flores

Monumento Natural Pichasca

Pismanta

Río Jáchal

Parque Nacional Fray Jorge

Ovalle

Monte Patria

Termas de Socos

Valle del Encanto

Embalse La Paloma

ARGENTINA

Embalse Cogotí

Tulahuén

San Juan

Combarbalá

San Juan

IV Región

Panamericana

Illapel

Salamanca

RP 12

Río San Juan

Los Vilos

Pichidangui

V Región

To Santiago

La Ligua

To Mendoza

Mendoza

0   40   80 km
0   25   50 miles

NORTE CHICO

lagged well behind until its 18th-century gold rush. When gold failed, silver took its place and Copiapó really boomed, tripling its population to 12,000 after a bonanza strike at Chañarcillo in 1832. Even so, the Norte Chico remained a frontier zone. Darwin vividly described the behavior of the region's miners:

Living for weeks together in the most desolate spots, when they descend to the villages on feast-days, there is no excess or extravagance to which they do not run. They sometimes gain a considerable sum, and then, like sailors with prize-money, they try how soon they can contrive to squander it. They drink excessively, buy quantities of clothes, and in a few days return penniless to their miserable abodes, there to work harder than beasts of burden.

Silver mining declined by the late 19th century but copper mining soon replaced it, with Anaconda's huge mine at Potrerillos later supplanted by El Salvador's mining industry. Recently, the area around La Serena and the northern sector around Bahía Inglesa have undergone tourist booms (La Serena has overtaken traditional holiday destinations such as Viña del Mar), but mining continues to be significant. Irrigated agriculture has always been important, but in recent years the Copiapó, Huasco and Elqui Valleys have become major contributors to Chile's booming fruit exports. Their vineyards are notable for producing pisco, Chile's potent grape brandy.

The region is also significant in Chilean cultural life – Nobel Prize-winning poet Gabriela Mistral, for instance, was a native of the Elqui Valley, east of La Serena.

COPIAPÓ
☎ 52

Despite much earlier encomiendas and land grants, and its mid-18th-century founding, Copiapó is really a 19th-century city; but for Juan Godoy's discovery of silver at nearby Chañarcillo, it might have lagged even farther behind the rest of the country. Darwin, visiting Copiapó in 1835, noted the economic distortion that the mining boom had brought to an area whose agriculture sufficed to feed it for only three months a year:

The town covers a considerable space of ground, each house possessing a garden; but it is an uncomfortable place and the dwellings are poorly furnished. Everyone seems bent on the one object of making money, and then migrating as quickly as possible. All the inhabitants are more or less directly concerned with the mines; and mines and ores are the sole subjects of conversation. Necessaries of all sorts are extremely dear; as the distance from the town to the port is eighteen leagues, and the land carriage very expensive. A fowl costs five or six shillings; meat is nearly as dear as in England; firewood, or rather sticks, are brought on donkeys from a distance of two and three days' journey within the cordillera; and pasturage for animals is a shilling a day: all this for South America is wonderfully exorbitant.

As it happened, the mining industry provided Copiapó with a number of firsts: South America's first railroad (built between 1849 and 1852 to the port of Caldera), Chile's first telegraph and telephone lines, and the country's first gasworks. In the early decades of the 20th century, Copiapó so impressed American geographer Isaiah Bowman that he described it as

…beautifully kept, with clean streets, well repaired buildings, and a thoroughly businesslike air, whether we consider the management of its mines, the appearance and administration of its famous college and its still more famous School of Mines, or the excellent administration of land and water rights.

Copiapó's population (now about 100,000) has fluctuated with the mining industry, but the city retains many of the attributes Bowman described, and some he did not – especially pollution from the copper smelter at nearby Paipote. Its pleasant climate and historical interest make it a worthwhile stopover on the Panamericana between La Serena and Antofagasta, and the point of departure for visits to the remote peaks near the Argentine border.

Orientation

Copiapó nestles in the narrow valley floor on the north bank of the Río Copiapó, 330km north of La Serena, 800km north of Santiago and 565km south of Antofagasta. Three blocks north of Av Copayapu (the Panamericana), shaded by massive pepper trees, Plaza Prat marks the city's historical center.

Most areas of interest to the visitor are in or near a roughly rectangular area bounded by Calle Manuel Rodríguez to the north, the Alameda Manuel Antonio Matta to the west, Av Henríquez to the east and the Río Copiapó to the south. Overlooking town from the northwest is the landmark Cerro La Cruz.

Information

Tourist Offices Sernatur (☎ 231-510, fax 217-248, serna03@entelchile.net) occupies a concrete bunker on the northeast side of Plaza Prat, directly in front of the Intendencia Regional at Los Carrera 691. The staff are congenial, helpful, well informed and can provide a list of accommodations, an excellent free map and many brochures. It's open 8:30 am to 5:30 pm weekdays all year, 10 am to 2 pm Saturday in summer only.

Money Copiapó has no currency exchange houses, but there are many downtown banks with ATMs, including Banco de Crédito, Chacabuco 449.

Post & Communications Correos de Chile is in the Intendencia Regional at Los Carrera 691, behind the Sernatur office. CTC (Telefónica) has long-distance telephone offices at the corner of Los Carrera and Chacabuco, on Plaza Prat. Entel is at Colipí 500, at the northeast corner of the plaza. Chilesat is at Atacama 499.

The Biblioteca Regional, on Colipí between Rodríguez and Los Carrera, offers public access to the Internet 10 am to 1 pm Monday through Saturday, 3 to 7:30 pm weekdays. Fees are US$1.50 for 15 minutes, US$3 per half hour, and US$5 per hour.

Travel Agencies Copiapó's main travel agencies are Turismo Atacama (☎ 212-712) at Los Carrera 716, and Cobretur (☎ 211-072) at O'Higgins 640.

Peruvian Tours (☎ 233-017), O'Higgins 12, runs tours of the city, the upper Copiapó valley, Bahía Inglesa, Parque Nacional Pan de Azúcar and more remote destinations such as Parque Nacional Nevado Tres Cruces and Ojos del Salado. Other operators offering backcountry tours include Expediciones Puna Atacama (☎/fax 211-273), Arredondo 154, and Maricunga Expediciones (☎ 210-075, fax 211-191), Maipú 580.

National Parks For information on protected areas in Region III, including Parque Nacional Pan de Azúcar and Parque Nacional Nevado Tres Cruces, contact Conaf (☎ 239-067), Juan Martínez 55, which may be able to offer suggestions for transportation.

Laundry Lavandería Mackenna (☎ 218-775), Mackenna 450, is reliable but fairly expensive.

Medical Services Copiapó's Hospital San José (☎ 212-023, 218-833) is at the intersection of Los Carrera and Vicuña, about eight blocks east of Plaza Prat.

Museums

Founded in 1857 and supported by the Universidad de Atacama (successor to Copiapó's famous School of Mines), the **Museo Mineralógico** literally dazzles, a tribute to the raw materials to which the city owes its existence. Its exhibition hall displays more than

---

A Railroad Remembered

South America's oldest railroad, the Copiapó-Caldera line, opened on Christmas Day, 1851, to carry the produce of the silver mine at Chañarcillo. North American shipping pioneer William Wheelwright attracted a group of investors that formed a who's who of the Chilean mining elite of the time, including Doña Candelaria Goyenechea, Agustín Edwards, Matías Cousiño, Vicente Subercaseaux and others. Although passenger trains no longer carry Copiapinos to the beach, Wheelwright's handiwork is on display at the old railroad station at Juan Martínez 244.

NORTE CHICO

2000 samples, organized according to chemical elements and structure, and a number of mineral curiosities.

At the corner of Colipí and Rodríguez, a block from Plaza Prat, the museum is open 9 am to 1 pm Monday to Saturday, and 3:30 to 7 pm weekdays. Admission costs US$0.60 for adults, US$0.20 for children.

Built in the 1840s, the **Museo Histórico Regional** is a national monument that belonged to the influential Matta family. The museum, at Atacama 98, is open 9:30 am to 12:45 pm and 3 to 7:15 pm Tuesday to Thursday, 9:30 am to 12:45 pm and 3 to 6:15 pm Friday, 10 am to 12:45 pm and 3 to 5:45 pm Saturday, and 10 am to 12:45 pm on Sundays and holidays. Admission costs US$1 for adults, half that for children.

Other Things to See & Do

Shaded by century-old pepper trees, Copiapó's Plaza Prat is the site of a number of historic buildings from its mining heyday, including the **Iglesia Catedral** and the municipal **Casa de la Cultura** (which was a private residence until 1945). On Atacama between Vallejos and Colipí, the **Asociación Minera Copiapó** is a national monument from the early mining days. A little out of the way, on Infante just east of Yerbas Buenas, the **Iglesia de Belén** is a colonial Jesuit building that was rebuilt in the mid-19th century; now functioning as the **Santuario Santa Teresa**, it's open 4:30 to 6:30 pm weekdays.

West of downtown, the **Alameda Manuel A Matta** is an attractive, tree-lined street with a series of monuments dedicated to local figures (including Manuel Antonio Matta, and prospector Juan Godoy, who discovered the Chañarcillo silver deposits) and interesting older buildings in an unfortunate state of decline.

At the corner of Juan Martínez and Batallón Atacama, the **Estación Ferrocarril** was the starting point for the first railroad on the continent. At the southern end of Rómulo Peña, mining magnate Apolinario Soto's **Palacete Viña de Cristo**, built in 1860 from European materials, was once the town's most elegant mansion. Now belong-

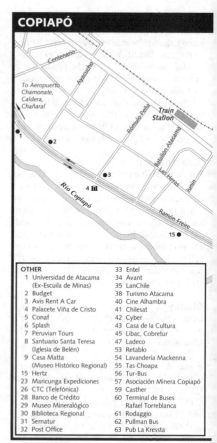

COPIAPÓ

OTHER		
1	Universidad de Atacama	33 Entel
	(Ex-Escuila de Minas)	34 Avant
2	Budget	35 LanChile
3	Avis Rent A Car	38 Turismo Atacama
4	Palacete Viña de Cristo	40 Cine Alhambra
5	Conaf	41 Chilesat
6	Splash	42 Cyber
7	Peruvian Tours	43 Casa de la Cultura
8	Santuario Santa Teresa	45 Libac, Cobretur
	(Iglesia de Belén)	47 Ladeco
9	Casa Matta	53 Retablo
	(Museo Histórico Regional)	54 Lavandería Mackenna
15	Hertz	55 Tas Choapa
23	Maricunga Expediciones	56 Tur-Bus
26	CTC (Telefónica)	57 Asociación Minera Copiapó
28	Banco de Crédito	59 Casther
29	Museo Mineralógico	60 Terminal de Buses
30	Biblioteca Regional		Rafael Torreblanca
31	Sernatur	61 Rodaggio
32	Post Office	62 Pullman Bus
		63 Pub La Kressta

ing to the Universidad de Atacama, it's open 8 am to 7 pm weekdays; admission is free.

A few blocks west, the historic **Escuela de Minas** (School of Mines) is now the Universidad de Atacama; on its grounds is the **Locomotora Copiapó**, the Norris Brothers locomotive that was the first to operate on the Caldera-Copiapó line.

Special Events

Copiapó and the Atacama region celebrate numerous festivals. December 8 marks the founding of the city, while the first Sunday of February is the Festival de Candelaria,

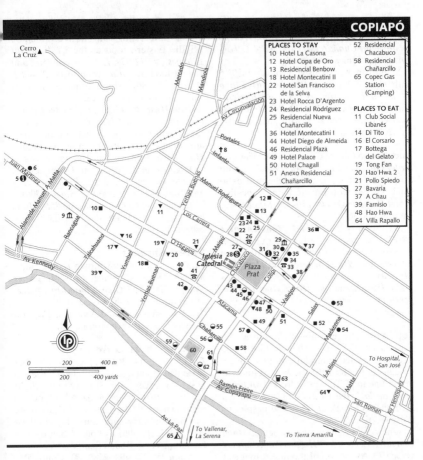

COPIAPÓ

PLACES TO STAY
10 Hotel La Casona
12 Hotel Copa de Oro
13 Residencial Benbow
18 Hotel Montecatini II
22 Hotel San Francisco
   de la Selva
23 Hotel Rocca D'Argento
24 Residencial Rodríguez
25 Residencial Nueva
   Chañarcillo
36 Hotel Montecatini I
44 Hotel Diego de Almeida
46 Residencial Plaza
49 Hotel Palace
50 Hotel Chagall
51 Anexo Residencial
   Chañarcillo
52 Residencial
   Chacabuco
58 Residencial
   Chañarcillo
65 Copec Gas
   Station
   (Camping)

PLACES TO EAT
11 Club Social
   Libanés
14 Di Tito
16 El Corsario
17 Bottega
   del Gelato
19 Tong Fan
20 Hao Hwa 2
21 Pollo Spiedo
27 Bavaria
37 A Chau
39 Farnisio
48 Hao Hwa
64 Villa Rapallo

Cerro La Cruz

celebrated at the Iglesia de la Candelaria at Los Carrera and Figueroa, about 2km east of Plaza Prat. Throughout the region, August 10 is Día del Minero (Miner's Day).

Places to Stay

Budget It's not really a formal campground and can be noisy, but the Copec gas station on the Panamericana just south of Av Copayapu has shade and hot showers. It is especially suitable for self-contained car campers.

Clean, basic *Residencial Rodríguez* (☎ 212-861, Rodríguez 528) is about the cheapest in town at US$6/10 singles/doubles, US$12/20

with private bath. Across the street, *Residencial Benbow* (☎ 217-634, Rodríguez 541) is friendly and almost equally reasonable, at US$7 per person for rooms with shared bath, US$18 with private bath, even though it has noisy moments. Occupying new quarters, *Residencial Chacabuco* (☎ 213-428, O'Higgins 921) is still moderately priced at US$7 per person for rooms with shared bath, US$10 with private bath.

Residencial Chañarcillo (☎ 213-281, Chañarcillo 741) has small but clean rooms with shared bath for US$8 per person, US$14/24 with private bath, but avoid those

NORTE CHICO

too close to the noisy TV lounge. Under the same management, identically priced *Anexo Residencial Chañarcillo* (☎ 212-284, O'Higgins 804) is funky but friendly.

Slightly more expensive, around US$9/15 with shared bath, is *Residencial Plaza* (☎ 212-671, O'Higgins 670). *Residencial Nueva Chañarcillo* (☎ 212-368, Rodríguez 540) charges US$12/19 with shared bath, US$21/28 with private bath.

Mid-Range One of Copiapó's best values is *Hotel Palace* (☎ 212-852, Atacama 741), with attractive rooms around a delightful patio for US$26/38 with private bath. Appealing *Hotel Copa de Oro* (☎ 216-309, Infante 530) charges US$36/42.

At the very fine *Hotel Montecatini I* (☎ 211-363, Infante 766), rates range from US$26/35 to US$35/49. Under the same management, *Hotel Montecatini II* (☎ 211-516, fax 214-773, Atacama 374) charges US$41/55. The newish *Hotel Rocca D'Argento* (☎ 218-744, fax 211-191, Maipú 580) charges US$50/66.

Top End The colonial-style *Hotel La Casona* (☎ 217-278, O'Higgins 150) offers outstanding accommodations in a lovely garden setting for US$48/57; its restaurant serves fine food. The spiffy *Hotel San Francisco de la Selva* (☎ 217-013, Los Carrera 525), merits a look at US$59/70 despite its noisy location.

A new entry is the business-oriented *Hotel Chagall* (☎ 213-775, O'Higgins 760), charging US$65/73. At the top of the line is four-star *Hotel Diego de Almeida* (☎ 212-075, O'Higgins 656), which charges US$70/80.

Places to Eat

For an excellent value, try the grilled chicken at *Pollo Spiedo* (O'Higgins 461). The popular chain *Bavaria* (☎ 217-160, Chacabuco 487) has decent if overpriced sandwiches, but good breakfasts. *Di Tito* (☎ 212-386, Chacabuco 710) is a moderately priced pizzeria. *Farnisio* (☎ 213-880, Chañarcillo 272) has inexpensive fixed-price lunches and seafood.

Occupying an older house with pleasant patio seating, *El Corsario* (☎ 215-374,

Atacama 245) serves varied Chilean food. Other interesting alternatives include Middle Eastern food at the *Club Social Libanés* (☎ 212-939, Los Carrera 350), and Italian food at *Villa Rapallo* (☎ 214-082, Atacama 1080), whose atmosphere outshines the food and service.

Hao Hwa (☎ 213-261, Colipí 340) is one of northern Chile's better Chinese restaurants, with good food, pleasant ambience and attentive service; it has a second branch *Hao Hwa 2*, at Yerbas Buenas between O'Higgins and Atacama. Other chifas include *A Chau* (☎ 212-472, Rodríguez 755) and *Tong Fan* (☎ 212-860, O'Higgins 390).

Bottega del Gelato (Atacama 256) offers homemade ice cream; the fruit flavors are especially good.

Entertainment

Copiapó has two downtown dance clubs: *Splash* (Juan Martínez 46) and *Cyber* (Maipú 279). The *Cine Alhambra* (☎ 212-187, Atacama 455) shows recent films.

At Chañarcillo and Vallejos, *Pub La Kressta* is worth a stop for a drink.

Getting There & Away

Air LanChile (☎ 213-512), Colipí 526, flies twice daily to and from Santiago (US$82 to US$137), except for Sunday (one flight only); one flight from Santiago continues to the town of El Salvador (US$20) daily except Thursday and Saturday. Ladeco (☎ 217-285, 217-406), Colipí 354, flies daily to La Serena (US$33) and Santiago.

Avant (☎ 238-400, 238-962), Colipí 510, flies daily to La Serena (US$33 to US$48) and Santiago (US$97 to US$121).

Bus Regional carriers include Recabarren (☎ 216-991), Muñoz (☎ 213-166) and Casther (☎ 218-889), at Chacabuco and Esperanza, all of which run frequently to Caldera and Bahía Inglesa for about US$2. Casther and Abarcía serve destinations in the upper Copiapó valley, such as Nantoco and Pabellón, Los Loros, Viña del Cerro and Tranque Lautaro. The highest fares are about US$2.

Copiapó's main Terminal de Buses Rafael Torreblanca (☎ 212-577) is at Chacabuco 112, three blocks south of Plaza Prat and just north of the river. Virtually all north-south buses stop here, as well as many to interior destinations. Most bus companies have offices here (some of them shared) but some have downtown offices (whose addresses are listed, when appropriate), and a couple have separate terminals.

In the main terminal, Ramos Cholele (☎ 213-113) links Copiapó with the northern Atacama destinations of Antofagasta, Iquique and Arica; Zambrano, Evans and Carmelita share the same office and serve the same destinations. Carmelita also goes south to La Serena, Coquimbo, Ovalle and Santiago.

Tramaca (☎ 213-979) covers the same Panamericana routes, along with two buses daily to Calama and half a dozen to Taltal. Libac (☎ 212-237), O'Higgins 640, goes to Santiago and intermediate points. Tas Choapa (☎ 213-793), Chañarcillo 631, works the same routes, with connections to spots as far away as Puerto Montt in southern Chile, and to points in Argentina, Uruguay and Paraguay.

Flota Barrios (☎ 213-645) has similar routes, plus buses to Calama, Tocopilla and Viña del Mar. Buses Fénix (☎ 214-929) goes to Arica, Iquique and Santiago. Tur-Bus (☎ 213-050), Chañarcillo 680, covers similar routes on the Panamericana.

Pullman Bus (☎ 211-039), Colipí 109, covers the Panamericana and serves Viña del Mar as well as southerly destinations off the Panamericana, including Illapel and Salamanca. Pullman also goes to northern mining towns such as Diego de Almagro, El Salvador and Potrerillos. In the same terminal, Los Corsarios serves destinations throughout the Norte Chico.

Sample destinations and fares include Arica (US$40, 16 hours), Iquique (US$37, 14 hours), Antofagasta (US$24, eight hours), Calama (US$27, 11 hours), La Serena (US$10, four hours) and Santiago (US$20, 11 hours).

Pullman Bus, Libac, Tramaca and Los Diamantes de Elqui run more expensive but more comfortable *salón cama* (bus with reclining seats) services to Santiago and Viña. Fares are about US$25 to US$30.

Getting Around

To/From the Airport Aeropuerto Chamonate (☎ 214-360) is 15km west of Copiapó, just north of the Panamericana. Transfer (cellular 09-554-0436) offers airport transportation for US$3 per person.

Car Copiapó's several car rental agencies include Hertz (☎ 213-522) at Av Copayapu 173; Avis (☎ 213-966) at Rómulo Peña 102 (west of the train station); Budget (☎ 218-802) at Ramón Freire 466; Rodaggio (☎ 212-153) at Colipí 127; and Retablo (☎ 214-427) at Los Carrera 955.

Rodaggio has the cheapest unlimited mileage rates, at US$33 per day plus 18% IVA for a small car, but pickup trucks, suitable for exploring the backcountry, cost at least US$60 per day, and 4WDs cost at least US$90.

AROUND COPIAPÓ

Up the valley of the Río Copiapó, southeast of the city, many worthwhile sights are accessible by public transport. At nearby Tierra Amarilla, the **Iglesia Nuestra Señora de Loreto** (1898) was the work of Spanish architect José Miguel Retornano. The municipal Casa de Cultura (☎ 320-098; ask for Alejandro Aracena Siares) arranges visits to **Mina El Tránsito**, a former gold mine in the Sierra de Ojancos. Dating from 1743 but reaching its peak in the early 19th century, El Tránsito was once a substantial community as well as a work site, but only the administrator's house, now partly a museum, remains in anything approximating its original condition. Some machinery is still standing, and there are open shafts; plans are under way to restore carts to provide rail rides into the mine and out the other side.

Only 23km from the city, flood-prone **Nantoco** is the site of a colonial church, a 19th-century silver and copper smelter, and the former hacienda of Apolinario Soto, dating from 1870. At Km 34, **Hacienda Jotabeche** belonged to the notable Chilean essayist José Joaquín Vallejo. Better known by his pseudonym, Jotabeche, Vallejo was a pioneer of Chilean literature and a keen observer of his country's customs.

Pabellón, 38km from Copiapó, was the former rail junction to Chañarcillo; it occupies a site in the midst of a vineyard zone that also offers basic camping. **Los Loros**, 64km from Copiapó, is a picturesque village in a rich agricultural zone that yields excellent grapes, watermelons, citrus and other fruits. **Viña del Cerro**, an archaeological monument on a spur off the main valley road, consists of the restored remains of a Diaguita-Inka copper foundry, with associated houses and other constructions, including more than 30 ovens.

Buses Casther (☎ 218-889) runs buses up the valley from Copiapó's bus station.

Chañarcillo

After Juan Godoy found silver at Chañarcillo on May 16, 1832, the town that grew up alongside the mine reached a maximum population of about 7000 before declining, at the end of the 19th century, when water flooded the mines, rendering them unusable. Foxes scurry among its remaining stone and adobe ruins, including public offices, the police station and jail, a theater, hospital and cemetery. Most of these are now difficult to distinguish. One interesting recognizable ruin is the rustic, still-functioning water well; and the cumulative impact of the site itself makes it worth a visit.

To reach Chañarcillo, take the Panamericana south to Km 59, where a dusty but excellent eastbound lateral goes toward Mina Bandurrias, a contemporary mine. The road continues east over scenic desert mountains and through deep canyons before intersecting the paved highway in the upper Río Copiapó, near Nantoco and Pabellón. This very interesting route is inadvisable in a vehicle without high clearance, and 4WD would be desirable. There's an interesting detour that dead-ends at **Mina Tres Marías**, an abandoned ridge-top mine with exceptional panoramas.

PN NEVADO TRES CRUCES

Likely to become a major attraction for adventurous travelers, the recently created Parque Nacional Nevado Tres Cruces protects about 61,000 hectares in two separate sectors of the high Andes east of Copiapó along Ruta 31, the international highway to Argentina via Paso de San Francisco. Flamingos spend the summer season here, but the park is also home to about 200 vicuñas and an equal number of guanacos, plus giant and horned coots, Andean geese and gulls, pumas and other species.

The larger **Sector Laguna Santa Rosa** comprises 49,000 hectares surrounding the lake of the same name, but also includes the Salar de Maricunga to the north. The smaller **Sector Laguna del Negro Francisco** consists of 12,000 hectares surrounding its namesake lake. While flamingos do not nest in the park, the shallow waters (barely a meter deep in most places) are ideal for the 8000 birds that summer here. About 56% are Andean flamingos, 40% are Chilean flamingos, and the remaining 4% are rare James flamingos.

Laguna del Negro Francisco itself consists of two ecologically distinct areas. A peninsula separates the upper Laguna Dulce, whose less saline waters supply plankton to the flamingos' diet, from the lower, saltier Laguna Salada, crustaceans are the main food source. The highest quantity of birds is present from December through February.

Outside the park boundaries proper, 6900m **Ojos del Salado** may be South America's highest peak (its precise height is in dispute and Argentines claim, probably correctly, that 6962m Aconcagua is higher). At the 5100m level, the Universidad de Atacama maintains a rustic refugio that can shelter a dozen climbers; at 5750m, there is another with a capacity of 24.

Because Ojos del Salado straddles the border, climbers must obtain authorization from Chile's Dirección de Fronteras y Límites (Difrol; ☎ 02-698-3502, fax 697-1909, difrol3@minrel.cl), Bandera 52, 5th floor, in Santiago, which oversees border area activities. It's possible to request permission prior to arriving in Chile.

Places to Stay

Conaf's comfortable **Refugio Laguna del Negro Francisco** charges US$10 per person for comfortable beds, cooking facilities, electricity, flush toilets and hot showers.

Ojos del Salado versus Aconcagua

Inglesa's beaches are more sheltered and attractive, but Caldera is livelier and cheaper.

Bahía Inglesa takes its name from the British privateers who took refuge here in colonial times. Now popular with visitors from central and northern Chile, it gets crowded during the January-February peak, but the weather is just as good or better in the off-season, when it's cheaper and more pleasant. In addition to tourism, the area's economy depends on fishing and mining. Locally cultivated scallops, oysters and seaweed are also exported, although some are consumed locally.

Conaf plans to build a campground at Laguna Santa Rosa, which at present has a tiny, free refugio, with space to sleep and eat out of the wind and cold.

Getting There & Away

Sector Laguna Santa Rosa is 146km east of Copiapó via Ruta 31 and another road that climbs up the scenic Quebrada de Paipote. Sector Laguna del Negro Francisco is another 85km south via a roundabout road that passes Mina Marte, a defunct gold mine, and drops into the valley of the Río Astaburuaga to arrive at the lake. Note that the road that passes directly west from the Conaf refugio to Mina Aldabarán to Quebrada San Miguel is not passable.

There is no regularly scheduled public transport to the park, but visitors planning a trip to the park should ask Conaf's Copiapó office about current alternatives. For planned tours of the area, see the Travel Agencies entry in Copiapó's Information section.

CALDERA & BAHÍA INGLESA
☎ 52

A minor colonial port, Caldera grew dramatically after the silver strikes east of Copiapó. Arrival of the railroad in the mid-19th century provided residents of Copiapó easy access to the beach and, along with nearby Bahía Inglesa, Caldera is still Region III's most popular beach resort. Bahía

Orientation & Information

Caldera, which is on the south shore of the Bahía de Caldera, is 75km west of Copiapó and just west of the Panamericana, which continues north to Chañaral. Av Diego de Almeyda, which links Caldera with the Panamericana, continues south as Av Carvallo to nearby Bahía Inglesa, on the north shore of the eponymous bay.

For tourist information, try the summer tourist office in the bus terminal at Vallejos and Gallo (note that it's not always staffed).

For postal service, go to Correos de Chile, at Edwards 325. CTC's (Telefónica) long-distance telephone office is at Edwards 360, Entel at Tocornal 383, and Chilesat at Ossa Cerda 370.

The travel agency Turismo Tour Mar (☎ 316-612), Diego de Almeyda 904, does coastal tours.

Things to See & Do

At the eastern approach to town, along Av Diego de Almeyda, the **Cementerio Laico** was Chile's first non-Catholic cemetery. Note the forged ironwork. Most of the tombs belong to English, Welsh, Scots and German immigrants, but there are also some Chinese sepulchers.

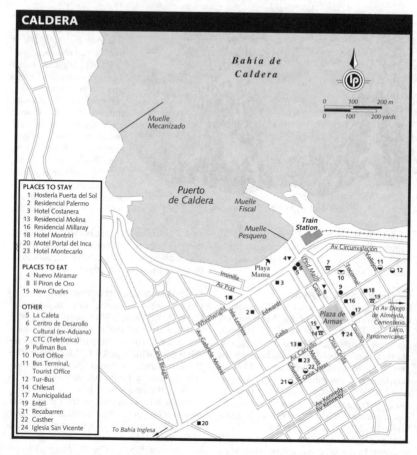

CALDERA

PLACES TO STAY
1 Hostería Puerta del Sol
2 Residencial Palermo
3 Hotel Costanera
13 Residencial Molina
16 Residencial Millaray
18 Hotel Montriri
20 Motel Portal del Inca
23 Hotel Montecarlo

PLACES TO EAT
4 Nuevo Miramar
8 Il Piron de Oro
15 New Charles

OTHER
5 La Caleta
6 Centro de Desarollo
   Cultural (ex-Aduana)
7 CTC (Telefónica)
9 Pullman Bus
10 Post Office
11 Bus Terminal,
   Tourist Office
12 Tur-Bus
14 Chilesat
17 Municipalidad
19 Entel
21 Recabarren
22 Casther
24 Iglesia San Vicente

Around the plaza and toward the colorful **Muelle Pesquero** (fishing jetty), the many distinctive 19th-century buildings include the **Iglesia San Vicente** (1862) with its gothic tower; the **Estación de Ferrocarril** (the 1850 train station, currently undergoing restoration befitting its historical monument status); and several private houses. The **Municipalidad**, the former **Aduana** (customhouse) at Gana and Wheelwright, is now the Centro de Desarollo Cultural, which contains the local museum, open 6 pm to 1 am daily (admission US$0.40).

In addition to swimming and sunbathing, windsurfing is a popular pastime at Bahía Inglesa; rental equipment is not available.

Visit *La Caleta (Wheelwright and Ossa Cerda)*, to hear live music.

There's a small handicrafts market on the Gana pedestrian mall, between Wheelwright and Edwards.

Places to Stay

Outside the peak summer season, prices drop considerably.

Camping Bahía Inglesa (☎ 315-424), on Playa Las Machas just south of Bahía Inglesa, has good facilities, but costs nearly US$30 per site in high season. It also has cabañas, ranging from US$40 to US$70 for up to five persons, with private bath.

The cheapest options are the simple *Residencial Millaray* (☎ 315-528, Cousiño 331) and run-down *Residencial Molina* (☎ 315-941, Montt 346), both charging about US$9 per person.

Hotel Montriri (☎ 319-055, Tocornal 371) charges US$20/28 with private bath and breakfast, while *Hotel Montecarlo* (☎ 315-388, Av Carvallo 627) charges US$21/35 with private bath and kitchenette. At *Residencial Palermo* (☎ 315-847, Cifuentes 150), rooms cost US$24 double with private bath, while rates at *Hotel Costanera* (☎ 316-007, Wheelwright 543) are about US$22/30 with private bath.

Toward the upper end of the scale is *Hostería Puerta del Sol* (☎ 315-205, Wheelwright 750), where rates start at US$35/55. On the road to Bahía Inglesa, *Motel Portal del Inca* (☎ 315-252, Av Carvallo 945) charges US$56/70.

Midway between Caldera and Bahía Inglesa, *Motel Umbral de Bahía Inglesa* (☎ 315-000) charges US$100 to US$120 for up to six persons. In Bahía Inglesa proper, with a restaurant and swimming pool, is the four-star *Apart Hotel Rocas de Bahía* (☎ 316-005, El Morro s/n); rooms cost US$64/88, but it also has US$140 cabañas for up to seven persons.

Places to Eat

Seafood is the only reasonable choice when dining out. *Il Piron di Oro* (☎ 315-109, Cousiño 218) gets so-so reviews, so try *Nuevo Miramar* (☎ 315-381, Gana 90), overlooking the fishing pier. Despite its anglophone name, the popular restaurant *New Charles* (☎ 315-348, Ossa Cerda 350) specializes in Chilean cuisine, especially seafood.

In Bahía Inglesa, the upscale *El Coral* (☎ 315-331, El Morro 564) offers superb seafood, including local scallops. It's expensive, but if you choose your meal wisely you may be able to eat here without shattering your budget.

Getting There & Around

Everything in Caldera is easily accessible on foot. Buses and taxi colectivos shuttle visitors from Caldera to Bahía Inglesa in about 10 minutes.

For long-distance buses, see Pullman Bus (☎ 315-227), with offices at Cousiño 297 but leaving from the terminal at Gallo and Vallejos, and Tur-Bus, with its own terminal on Gallo northeast of Vallejos. Fares and times resemble those from Copiapó; add an hour southbound, and subtract an hour northbound.

Recabarren (☎ 315-034), Ossa Varas 710, goes frequently to Copiapó, as does Casther (☎ 316-300), Ossa Varas 660.

AROUND CALDERA

On the scenic coastline about 12km north of Caldera, **Santuario Naturaleza Granito Orbicular** is a geological oddity that consists of a number of irregularly shaped mineral conglomerates. It is not part of Conaf's wildlands system, but instead is under the administration of the education ministry. About a mile or two away there's an offshore sea lion colony.

CHAÑARAL
☎ 52

On the boundary between Regions II and III, Chañaral is a dilapidated but intriguing mining and fishing port set among the rugged headlands of the Sierra de las Animas. It dates from 1833, almost a decade after Diego de Almeyda discovered the nearby Las Animas copper mine; the area's economic powerhouse is the huge copper mine at El Salvador, in the mountains to the east.

For the people of Chañaral, El Salvador has been a mixed blessing – providing their economic livelihood but also polluting the town they call home. Their 1988 court action, which forced the mine's powerful owner, Codelco, to prevent toxic runoff into the Río Salado and onto Chañaral's broad sandy beach, was the first of its kind in Chile.

Just north of Chañaral, the coastal Parque Nacional Pan de Azúcar (see separate entry below) straddles the regional border. This increasingly popular, scenic destination, which offers excellent camping, is the best reason for a stopover in the area.

Orientation & Information

About 165km northwest of Copiapó and 400km south of Antofagasta, Chañaral (population 12,000) has two distinct sections: the industrial port sprawling along the shoreline and the Panamericana, and a residential zone scaling the hills south of the highway. Steep sidewalks and staircases link Chañaral's streets, which respect the natural contours of the highly irregular terrain more than in most other Chilean cities.

Chañaral's new tourist office is at Merino Jarpa and Conchuelas, half a block northeast of the bus terminal; the office schedule is erratic.

The post office is on Comercio, at the west end of town. The CTC (Telefónica) long-distance telephone offices are at Los Carrera 618; Entel is at Merino Jarpa 1197.

Barquito

Barquito, 2km west of Chañaral via the Panamericana, contains the mechanized port facilities through which El Salvador's copper passes. It's an interesting, ramshackle kind of landscape, with a large rail yard and many antique railcars among the steep headlands.

Places to Stay & Eat

Accommodations are limited. The marginal *Hotel Jiménez* (☎ *480-328, Merino Jarpa 551*) is the cheapest at US$8 per person without breakfast (there's one single with private bath for US$17); across the street, the slightly more expensive *Hotel Marina* (*Merino Jarpa 562*) is a better value. *Hotel Nuria* (☎ *480-903, Av Costanera 302*) charges US$12 with breakfast, a good value. The best in town is the appealing *Hostería Chañaral* (☎ *480-055, Miller 268*), where rooms start at US$42/48.

For a town of its size, Chañaral has several surprisingly good, if modest, restaurants. Facing the Plaza de Armas, *Nuria* (*Yungay 434*) offers well-prepared, reasonably priced seafood, salads and snacks, with friendly and attentive service. *El Rincón Porteño* (*Merino Jarpa 567*) is also worth a

visit. *Alicanto* (☎ *481-168, Panamericana Sur 49*), at the southwestern approach to town, has good dining with coastal views.

Getting There & Around

Chañaral's main bus terminal is at Merino Jarpa 854, with Tur-Bus next door at Merino Jarpa 858. Other companies with offices in town are Flota Barrios (☎ 480-071) at Merino Jarpa 567 and Pullman Bus (☎ 480-153), which also serves Diego de Almagro and El Salvador, at Merino Jarpa and Los Baños.

Turismo Chango (☎ 480-484, 480-668), Comercio 265, leaves for Parque Nacional Pan de Azúcar at 8:30 am and 3 pm daily in summer, less frequently the rest of the year; the early bus returns immediately, the latter leaves at 8 pm. It departs from opposite the Municipalidad, at Merino Jarpa and Los Baños.

For car rental, contact Rodrigo Zepeda (☎ 480-015), San Martín 407. He may also arrange excursions to Parque Nacional Pan de Azúcar for about US$100 per day with driver.

PN PAN DE AZÚCAR

Only 30km north of Chañaral, Parque Nacional Pan de Azúcar comprises 43,754 hectares of coastal desert and cordillera, with sheltered coves, white sandy beaches, stony headlands, abundant wildlife and unique flora. There's excellent camping in some coastal areas, but the park is becoming an increasingly popular and crowded summer destination.

Information

Conaf's Centro de Información Ambiental at Caleta Pan de Azúcar, open 8:30 am to 12:30 pm and 2 to 6 pm daily, offers slide presentations about the park's environment and also has a cactarium. At the southern entrance, rangers collect an admission charge of US$7 for foreigners, US$3 for children up to 18 years of age.

Geography & Climate

Park altitudes range from sea level to 900m. The park has a humid coastal desert climate with abundant fog and cloud cover (which usually burns off in the afternoon). The mean annual temperature is about 16°C.

In the coastal zone, the cool Humboldt Current supports a variety of marine life, such as otters and sea lions, and many birds, including pelicans, cormorants and the Humboldt penguin. At higher elevations, moisture from the *camanchaca* (fog) nurtures a unique collection of more than 20 species of cacti and succulents. Farther inland, guanacos and foxes are common sights.

Isla Pan de Azúcar

About 2000 Humboldt penguins, plus other seabirds, nest on the island of Pan de Azúcar, which seems to float on the ocean as the camanchaca advances inland at twilight. With a good pair of binoculars, the birds are visible from the shore, but local fishermen also approach the 100-hectare island by boat for better views (the island proper is a restricted area).

Launches charge about US$5 to US$7 per person for up to 10 people from Caleta Pan de Azúcar. Rodrigo Carvajal Robles' Pingüi Tour (☎ 052-480-563, 09-429-2132, carvajalrodrigo@hotmail.com) has regularly scheduled departures.

Places to Stay

As of this writing, Conaf had not yet chosen a permanent replacement for an unsatisfactory concessionaire who operated campgrounds at Playa Piqueros (25 sites) and Caleta Pan de Azúcar (29 sites). Current charges are US$12 per site; facilities include toilets, water, picnic tables and shade, but there are no showers. There are also two private cabañas, with kitchens, that sleep up to six people for US$83 per night, and two Conaf cabañas for US$73 per night (make reservations at Conaf's Copiapó office, especially in January and February and on weekends). A small market at Caleta Pan de Azúcar has limited supplies, and fresh fish is also available from local residents, but supplies are cheaper and more abundant at Chañaral.

Getting There & Away

Pan de Azúcar is 30km north of Chañaral by a smooth but unpaved road. For public

PARQUE NACIONAL PAN DE AZÚCAR

transport to and from the park, see the Getting There & Around entry for Chañaral, above. It's also possible to hire a taxi from Chañaral

If you're driving and approaching from the direction of Antofagasta, there's also an ill-marked park entrance at Las Bombas, 45km north of Chañaral on the Panamericana, where a good road descends Quebrada Pan de Azúcar to the coast.

EL SALVADOR

In the mountains, 62km east of Chañaral, 2300m above sea level, the Codelco company town of El Salvador is a legacy of the Andes Mining Company, a subsidiary of US-owned Anaconda, which had a strong presence in Chile for much of the 20th century. Its city plan, resembling a giant amphitheater with the Plaza de Armas as the stage, reflects the influence of Brasilia and its famed architect Oscar Niemeyer.

As a service center, El Salvador supports both the mine of that name and the older Mina Potrerillos, 32km southwest by a winding paved road. An unpaved road continues southeast past the Salar de Maricunga and Parque Nacional Nevado Tres Cruces before heading east toward the Argentine border at Paso San Francisco (4726m). All travelers in both directions must stop at the customs post at the Salar de Maricunga, but only those crossing the border must go through immigration and customs formalities.

Places to Stay & Eat
El Salvador has several hotels but nothing really economical. The most reasonably priced is *Hostería El Salvador* (☎ *052-475-749, Av Potrerillos 003)*, which charges US$8/15 singles/doubles with shared bath, US$21/35 with private bath, and *Hotel Pucará (☎ 052-475-558, Av 18 de Septiembre 2308)*, which charges US$15/24 with shared bath, US$26/40 with private bath. Neither includes breakfast.

The luxury *Hotel Camino del Inca* (☎ *475-252, Av El Tofo 330)*, charges US$100/120 singles/doubles with breakfast.

Cosquín (Av 18 de Septiembre 2312) has plain but good, moderately priced lunches.

Getting There & Away
LanChile (☎ 475-590), Wheelwright 619-A, flies daily except Thursday and Saturday to Copiapó (US$20), La Serena (US$42) and Santiago (US$115 to US$145) from Aeropuerto El Salvador, 18km west of town.

There are regular bus connections to and from Chañaral, leaving from the Pullman bus terminal at the corner of Av 4 de Julio and Av Glover.

VALLENAR
☎ 51
In the valley of the Río Huasco, roughly midway between Copiapó and La Serena, Vallenar dates from the late 18th century, when colonial governor Ambrosio O'Higgins applied the name of his native Ballenagh, Ireland, to the area – 'Ballenagh' became 'Vallenar.' Darwin later visited the area on horseback during his travels aboard the *Beagle*.

Like the rest of the Norte Chico, Vallenar's development was based on mining, but irrigated agriculture has also been critically important; olives are the local specialty. After serious earthquake damage occurred in 1922, Vallenar was rebuilt with wood instead of adobe, but the city's buildings still rest on unconsolidated sediments.

Orientation
Motorists often bypass Vallenar (population 42,000), 145km south of Copiapó and 190km north of La Serena, because Puente Huasco (Huasco Bridge), which spans the valley, does not drop down into the town, readily visible below. At the south end of the bridge, the Vallenar-Huasco highway leads east into town, crossing the river via Puente Brasil. Everything in town is within easy walking distance of the central Plaza O'Higgins, at the intersection of Prat and Vallejos.

Municipal authorities have turned part of the northern riverbank, from Vallejos eastward across Av Brasil, into an attractive park. Prat has become a semi-peatonal, a wide sidewalk with a single automobile lane, east of Plaza O'Higgins.

Information
Vallenar's tourist office is a kiosk at the junction of the Panamericana and the Vallenar-Huasco highway, at the south end of Puente Huasco, but regional budget crises have closed it down for the time being.

For cash, try the ATM at Banco de Crédito, Prat 1070.

Correos de Chile is at the northeast corner of Plaza O'Higgins. The CTC (Telefónica) long-distance telephone office is at Prat 1035; Entel is on Prat between Brasil and Colchagua. Chilesat is at the corner of Prat and Colchagua.

The Cyber Café, Prat 862, offers Internet access.

Vallenar's hospital (☎ 611-202) is at the corner of Merced and Talca.

Things to See & Do
Vallenar's **Iglesia Parroquial**, on the east side of Plaza O'Higgins, is notable for the copper dome on its wooden tower.

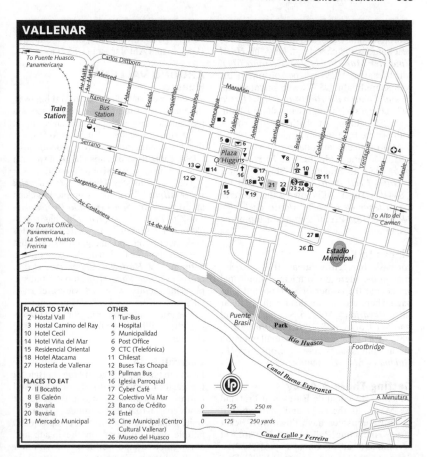

VALLENAR

To Puente Huasco, Panamericana

Carlos Dittborn

Merced

Marañón

Train Station

Ramirez Bus Station

Prat

Serrano

Faez

Sargento Aldea

Av Costanera

To Tourist Office,
Panamericana,
La Serena, Huasco
Freirina

14 de Julio

Plaza O'Higgins

Estadio Municipal

To Alto del Carmen

A Manutara

Ochandia

Puente Brasil

Park

Río Huasco

Footbridge

Canal Buena Esperanza

Canal Gallo y Ferreira

0   125   250 m
0   125   250 yards

PLACES TO STAY	OTHER
2 Hostal Vall	1 Tur-Bus
3 Hostal Camino del Ray	4 Hospital
10 Hotel Cecil	5 Municipalidad
14 Hotel Viña del Mar	6 Post Office
15 Residencial Oriental	9 CTC (Telefónica)
18 Hotel Atacama	11 Chilesat
27 Hostería de Vallenar	12 Buses Tas Choapa
	13 Pullman Bus
PLACES TO EAT	16 Iglesia Parroquial
7 Il Bocatto	17 Cyber Café
8 El Galeón	22 Colectivo Vía Mar
19 Bavaria	23 Banco de Crédito
20 Bavaria	24 Entel
21 Mercado Municipal	25 Cine Municipal (Centro Cultural Vallenar)
	26 Museo del Huasco

The historical **Museo del Huasco**, Sargento Aldea 742, has a modest collection of local artifacts and materials, including an excellent photo collection. It's open 10 am to 12:30 pm and 4 to 7 pm Tuesday to Friday, 10 am to 12:30 pm weekends, but the curator sometimes admits visitors even when the museum is officially closed. Admission costs US$0.50 for adults, US$0.25 for children.

The ***Cine Municipal*** (☎ *611-501, Prat 1094*) is part of the city's Centro Cultural Vallenar.

Try a regional specialty, the sweet wine known as *pajarete*, available in local wine shops.

Special Events

January 5 is a local holiday celebrating the founding of the city; the local song festival, Festival Vallenar Canta, takes place later in the month. In the village of San Félix, 58km up the valley of the Río Huasco, the annual grape harvest in February is the occasion for the Festival de la Vendimia.

Places to Stay

The cheapest accommodations are ***Residencial Oriental*** (☎ *613-889, Serrano 720*), where singles with shared bath, set around an attractive patio, cost US$7. Nearby ***Hotel***

Atacama (☎ *615-395, Serrano 873*) is a little dearer, around US$8, and noisier. Vallenar's best value is the cheerful, family-run *Hotel Viña del Mar* (☎ *611-478, Serrano 611*), which charges US$8 per person for rooms with shared bath, US$12 with private bath. *Hostal Camino del Rey* (☎ *613-184, Merced 943*) charges US$16/22 with shared bath, US$22/32 with private bath, but the rooms with private baths fill up fast.

Mid-range accommodations start around US$35/40 singles/doubles at *Hostal Vall* (☎ *613-380, Aconcagua 455*). Slightly dearer is *Hotel Cecil* (☎ *614-071, Prat 1059*) for US$44/54. The finest in town is the *Hostería de Vallenar* (☎ *614-379, Alonso de Ercilla 848*), for US$64/76; it also has a top-notch restaurant.

Places to Eat

For basic, inexpensive meals, try the cocinerías in the Mercado Municipal (municipal market) at the corner of Serrano and Santiago. There are two locales for the popular chain *Bavaria* (☎ *614-255, Santiago 678* and ☎ *613-504, Serrano 802*). *Il Bocatto* (☎ *614-609, Plaza O'Higgins s/n*) has small but good pizzas and snacks. For seafood, try *El Galeón* (☎ *614-641, Ramírez 934*).

Getting There & Away

Vallenar's Terminal de Buses is at Prat and Av Matta, at the west end of town, but several companies have downtown ticket offices, including Pullman (☎ 612-461) at Serrano 551 and Tas Choapa (☎ 613-822) at Serrano 580. Flota Barrios (☎ 614-295), Diamantes de Elqui (☎ 612-574) and Carmelita (☎ 613-037) are at the terminal only. Tur-Bus (☎ 611-738), with its own terminal on Prat opposite the main terminal, has extensive north- and southbound routes.

North-south transport routes closely resemble those going to and from Copiapó, but buses and taxi colectivos also connect Vallenar with the port of Huasco and the village of Freirina, and travel up the valley. For these regional services, contact Buses Tal (☎ 612-574) at the terminal. Colectivo Via Mar, Serrano 959, runs shared taxis to Huasco.

Sample fares include Copiapó (US$4), La Serena (US$5), Caldera (US$6), Santiago (US$12) and Antofagasta (US$21).

AROUND VALLENAR
Huasco

An hour west of Vallenar by paved highway, the picturesque fishing port of Huasco is a pleasant surprise, with good beaches, decent hotels and fine seafood. En route to Huasco, the village of Freirina is worth a stop to see its Iglesia Santa Rosa de Lima (1869), a wooden church with an impressive bell tower.

For places to stay, Huasco's *Residencial La Ovallina* (*Craig 340*) is simple but clean and tidy. *Hostal San Fernando* (☎ */fax 051-531-726, Pedro de Valdivia 176*) has a spacious older section with shared baths for US$9 per person, and an equally spacious but newer section for US$20 double with private bath and TV. *Hostería Huasco* (☎ *531-026, Ignacio Carrera Pinto 110*), an older but still pleasant facility with sea views, charges US$24/36 off-season, US$37/47 in summer.

For information on transport to Huasco, see the Vallenar section earlier in the chapter.

Carrizal Bajo

From the farming village of Huasco Bajo, at the eastern approach to Huasco, a paved northbound road soon turns into a good but sandy coastal road that continues to Carrizal Bajo, a quasi ghost town where up to 3000 people come to camp on the beach and among abandoned buildings on summer weekends. Speculators are trying to snap up land in the area because of rumored construction of an improved coastal highway. Concrete buttresses support the crumbling adobe walls of its landmark church, a national monument.

Carrizal Bajo gained a certain fame (or notoriety) in 1986, when the leftist Frente Patriótico Manuel Rodríguez (FPMR) chose the deserted port to smuggle in a large cache of weapons to aid its armed struggle against the Pinochet dictatorship – the same year the FPMR made an attempt on General Pinochet's life in the Cajón del Maipo.

PN Llanos de Challe

Designated a national park in 1994 for its unique flora, most notably the endemic *Garra de León (Leontochir ovallei*, an endangered species that is possibly Chile's rarest and most beautiful flower), Llanos de Challe comprises 45,000 hectares of coastal desert, 50km north of Huasco. During wet years, it's one of the best places to see the wildflower display of the *desierto florido*, but there is also a selection of cacti to be seen, as well as guanacos and foxes (despite continued poaching in the northern part of the park).

Accessible only by private vehicle, Llanos de Challe consists of a coastal sector south of Carrizal Bajo around Punta Los Pozos, where Conaf plans to install a campground, and an inland sector along the Quebrada Carrizal, 15km southeast of Carrizal Bajo. In addition to the road north from Huasco Bajo, a slightly shorter route to Llanos de Challe leaves the Panamericana 15km north of Vallenar.

RN PINGÜINO DE HUMBOLDT

Consisting of several offshore islands on the border between Regions III and IV, the 860-hectare Reserva Nacional Pingüino de Humboldt is one of the best possible excursions in the Norte Chico and is most easily reached from La Serena. It takes its name from the nesting Humboldt penguin, but there are also many cormorants, gulls and boobies in remarkable numbers, as well as marine mammals such as sea lions, dolphins and otters.

Orientation & Information

From a turnoff on the Panamericana, about 78km north of La Serena near Trapiche, a rough gravel road passes through **Choros**, an oasis of olive trees that was one of Spain's earliest settlements in the area (1605), and continues to Caleta de Choros, site of Conaf's small but outstanding Centro de Información Ambiental, where visitors pay a park admission charge of US$3.

At Caleta de Choros, it's possible to hire a launch to Isla Damas and around Isla Choros (where landing is not permitted).

Isla Chañaral, the largest and most northerly of the three islands comprising the reserve, is less easily accessible, but its wildlife is similar to that around Isla Choros.

Things to See & Do

Hired launches from Caleta de Choros, charging around US$70 total for up to seven people, carry passengers along the east coast of 320-hectare **Isla Choros**, which has it all – pods of bottle-nosed dolphins that dive and surface alongside the boat, a large sea lion colony, groups of otters and Humboldt penguins, and massive rookeries of cormorants, gulls and boobies.

Isla Damas, a 60-hectare metamorphic outcrop capped by a low granitic summit, is usually visited on the return from Isla Choros. It has two main beaches: **Playa La Poza** at the landing point, and the attractive white-sand **Playa Tijeras**, roughly a 1km walk.

Chile Sub (☎ 032-834-626 in Viña del Mar, chilesub@entelchile.net) operates a summer diving camp on Isla Damas. Limited climbing is possible on the granite heights of Damas, but none of the faces is big enough to be really challenging.

Places to Stay & Eat

Conaf's *campground* at Playa La Poza, charging US$16 per site for up to six people, has clean toilets but no potable water, so bring your own water and food (it's also possible to buy fresh fish from the nearby fishermen's camp). Isla Damas is crowded in summer and on weekends (although most visitors are daytrippers); on weekdays and in the off-season it's pretty deserted. Campers must bring bags to pack out trash.

Getting There & Away

While there is no regular public transport to Caleta de Choros, several travel agencies in La Serena offer visits to Isla Choros and Damas as day trips. It's possible to leave one day and return another after camping on Isla Damas, but this is more difficult outside the peak season, when demand for tours is lower.

NORTE CHICO

LA SERENA

☎ 51

Fast supplanting Viña del Mar as Chile's premier beach resort, La Serena is also one of Chile's oldest cities and is the capital of Region IV (Coquimbo). Thanks to President Gabriel González Videla's 'Plan Serena' of the late 1940s, La Serena maintains a colonial facade, but there are only a handful of genuine colonial buildings and recent upscale developments are rapidly overshadowing the city's historical legacy. Water shortage remains a serious concern in this semidesert area.

Besides its beaches, La Serena has numerous attractions in the surrounding countryside, including quaint villages such as Vicuña (home to Nobel Prize-winning poet Gabriela Mistral), with its nearby vineyards, and several international astronomical observatories, which take advantage of the region's exceptional atmospheric conditions.

History

Encomendero Juan Bohón, Pedro de Valdivia's lieutenant, founded La Serena in 1544, but after Bohón died in an Indian uprising, his successor Francisco de Aguirre refounded the city in 1549. Following Chilean independence, silver and copper became the backbone of its economy, supported and supplemented by irrigated agriculture in the Elqui Valley. Silver discoveries were so significant that the Chilean government created an independent mint in the city.

Orientation

La Serena (population approaching 130,000) lies on the south bank of the Río Elqui, about 2km above its outlet to the Pacific, 470km north of Santiago. The Panamericana, known as Av Juan Bohón, skirts the western edge of town.

Centered on the Plaza de Armas, the city plan is a regular grid, complicated by a few diagonals toward the east, but orientation is easy. Most areas of interest fall within a rectangular area marked by Av Bohón and Parque Pedro de Valdivia to the west, the Río Elqui to the north, Calle Benavente to the east and Av Francisco de Aguirre to the south.

LA SERENA

PLACES TO STAY
1 Hostal de Colón
2 Hotel El Escorial
3 Hostal de Turismo Croata
4 Residencial Suiza
8 Hotel Pucará
13 Hotel de Turismo Brasilia
14 Residencial El Loa
16 Residencial Lorena
17 Hotel Francisco de Aguirre
36 Hotel Casablanca
37 Residencial La Casona de Cantournet
39 Hotel Pacífico
42 Residencial Lido
43 Residencial Chile
48 Hotel Berlín
54 Residencial Petit
56 Hotel Mediterráneo
59 Hotel Costa Real
66 Hotel Alameda
74 Residencial Limmat (HI)
83 Hotel Los Balcones de Alcalá
84 Residencial Jofré
88 Hotel Soberanía
89 Albergue Santo Tomás
92 Residencial El Silo

PLACES TO EAT
5 Donde El Guatón
6 Gelatería Mammamia
9 Boccaccio
12 El Cedro
15 Taiwan
23 Café Plaza Real
26 Café do Brasil
35 Mai Lan Fan
51 Diavoletto
52 Rincón Oriental
53 Grill Bar Serena
55 Quick Biss Dos
81 Restaurant y Bar Croata

OTHER
7 Café del Patio, Talinay Adventure Expeditions
10 Cámara de Turismo
11 Iglesia La Merced
18 Post Office
19 Sernatur
20 Museo Histórico Gabriel González Videla
21 Iglesia Catedral
22 Municipalidad, Tribunales
24 Turismo San Bartolomé
25 Viajes Torremolinos
27 CTC (Telefónica)
28 Librerías Universitarias
29 Ladeco
30 Chilesat
31 Entel
32 Compucenter
33 Gira Tour
34 Iglesia San Agustín
38 Iglesia Santo Domingo
40 Conaf
41 Net Café
44 Tur-Bus
45 Diaguitas Tour, Librería Andrés Bello
46 Banco Santander
47 Cine Centenario
49 Buses Tal, Los Diamantes de Elqui
50 Tas Choapa
57 Museo Arqueológico
58 Covalle Bus
60 Ingservtur
61 Intijalsu
62 Avant
63 Intercam
64 LanChile
65 Automóvil Club de Chile
67 Buses Libac
68 Iglesia San Francisco, Museo Colonial de Arte Religioso
69 Línea Ruta 41, Tacso Taxi Colectivos
70 Electric Net
71 Pullman Bus, Los Corsarios
72 Callergari (Car Rental)
73 Lasval/Inca Bus
75 Flota Verschae (Car Rental)
76 Hertz
77 Avis
78 Buses Serenamar
79 Laverap
80 Salón Stylo
82 Centro Latinoamericano de Arte y Cultura, Afro Son
85 Hospital Emergency Entrance
86 Museo Mineralógico Ignacio Domeyko
87 Bus Terminal
90 Gala
91 Ciclomanía

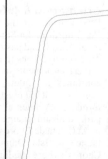

To Beaches, Bahía de Coquimbo, Lighthouse

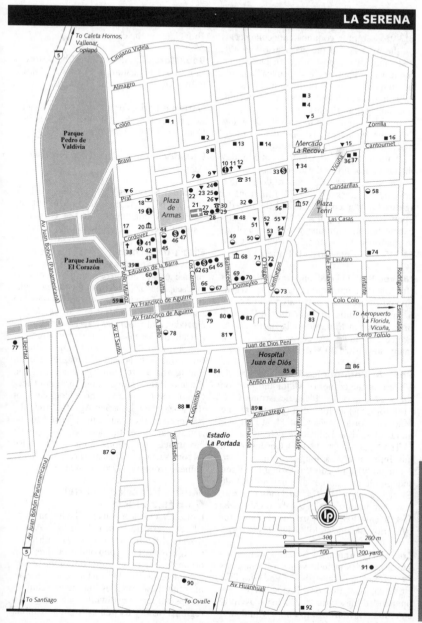

LA SERENA

To Caleta Hornos,
Vallenar,
Copiapó

5

Cirujano Videla

Almagro

Colón

Brasil

Parque
Pedro de
Valdivia

Prat

Av Juan Bohón (Panamericana)

Parque Jardín
El Corazón

5

To Santiago

Plaza
de
Armas

Cordovez

Eduardo de la Barra

Av Francisco de Aguirre
Av Francisco de Aguirre

Estadio
La Portada

To Ovalle

Hospital
Juan de Diós

Juan de Dios Peni

Anfión Muñoz

Amunátegui

Av Huanhuali

Mercado
La Recova

Plaza
Tenri

Zorrilla

Cantournet

Gandarillas

Las Casas

Colo Colo

To Aeropuerto
La Florida,
Vicuña,
Cerro Tololo

NORTE CHICO

0   100   200 m
0   100   200 yards

Information

Tourist Offices Sernatur (☎ 225-199, fax 213-956, sernatur_coquim@entelchile.net) is on the west side of the plaza, at Matta 461, just south of the post office. In December, January and February, it's open 8:45 am to 7 or 8 pm daily; the rest of the year, it closes at 5:30 pm weekdays, and at noon on weekends. It usually has an English-speaker on duty.

In conjunction with the private Diaguitas Tour, the Municipalidad operates an information office at the bus terminal, open 9:30 am to 1 pm and 3:30 to 9 pm Monday through Saturday, and 9 am to 2 pm Sunday.

La Serena's private Cámara de Turismo operates a kiosk (☎ 227-771) in front of Iglesia La Merced, at Prat and Balmaceda, open 10 am to 2 pm and 5 to 9 pm daily except Sunday. Another good source of information is the Automóvil Club de Chile (☎ 225-279), Eduardo de la Barra 435.

Money Both US cash and traveler's checks (for a small commission), as well as Argentine pesos, are easily negotiated at any of La Serena's cambios. Try Gira Tour at Prat 689 or Intercam at Eduardo de la Barra 435-A. Banco Santander, Cordovez 351, is one of many downtown ATMs.

Post & Communications Correos de Chile is at the corner of Matta and Prat, on the west side of the Plaza de Armas. CTC (Telefónica) has long-distance telephone offices at Cordovez 446; Entel is at Prat 571; and Chilesat is at Balmaceda 469.

The Net Café (☎ 212-187), Cordovez 285, has Internet access, long hours (10 am to 2 am daily) and good, reasonably priced snacks. Other Internet alternatives include Electric Net (☎ 212-224), at Domeyko 550, and Compucenter (☎ 211-594), at Cordovez 588, Oficina 403. Rates are low at Ingservtur (see Travel Agencies, following this entry).

Travel Agencies La Serena's numerous travel agencies include Viajes Torremolinos (☎ 223-946), at Balmaceda 437, and Gira Tour (☎ 223-535), at Prat 689. Readers have recommended Ingservtur (☎ 220-165, ingsvtur@ ctcreuna.cl), Matta 611, where you'll find friendly, English-speaking staff, and cheap, fast Internet access (see also Organized Tours later in the chapter).

Bookstores La Serena's best bookstore is Librerías Universitarias, Cordovez 470. Librería Andrés Bello is at Matta 510.

National Parks For information on Region IV's national parks and other reserves, visit Conaf (☎ 225-685) at Cordovez 281.

Laundry Laverap is located at Francisco de Aguirre 447.

Medical Services Hospital Juan de Diós (☎ 225-569) is at Balmaceda 916, but the emergency entrance is at the corner of Larraín Alcalde and Anfión Muñoz.

Plaza de Armas

Many of La Serena's key features, several of them churches, are on or near the beautifully landscaped Plaza de Armas. On the east side, the **Iglesia Catedral** dates from 1844. Just to its north, at Prat and Carrera, are the **Municipalidad** and **Tribunales** (law courts), built as a result of González Videla's Plan Serena.

Southwest of the plaza, facing a smaller but attractively landscaped plaza, the colonial **Iglesia Santo Domingo** is a relic from the mid-18th-century. At the corner of Cienfuegos and Cantournet, three blocks east of the plaza, the **Iglesia San Agustín** originally belonged to the Jesuits, then passed to the Agustinians after the Jesuits' expulsion. It has undergone serious modifications since its construction in 1755, most recently due to damage from the 1975 earthquake.

Museo Histórico Gabriel González Videla

González Videla, a native of La Serena, was Chile's president from 1946 to 1952. A controversial figure, he took power with communist support but soon outlawed the party, driving poet Pablo Neruda out of the senate and into exile. Exhibits on González Videla's life omit these episodes, but the museum includes other worthwhile materials on regional history, as well as rotating exhibits of works by Chilean artists. The adjacent **Plaza González Videla**, between the museum and the post office, is the site of the annual book fair (see below).

The museum (☎ 215-082) is at Matta 495, at the southwest corner of the Plaza de Armas. In summer, it's open 9 am to 1 pm and 4 to 7 pm Tuesday to Saturday, and 10 am to 1 pm Sunday. Admission costs US$1, but is free Sunday.

Museo Arqueológico

La Serena's archaeological museum repeats many of the same themes of the González Videla museum, but also has a valuable collection of Diaguita Indian artifacts from before the Inka conquest, which truncated the autonomous cultural development of the Chilean coast. There is a good map of the distribution of Chile's aboriginal population.

At the intersection of Cordovez and Cienfuegos, the museum (☎ 224-492) keeps identical hours to the González Videla. The museums share a common admission policy – admission to one is valid for the other.

Museo Colonial de Arte Religioso

Occupying an annex of the colonial **Iglesia San Francisco** at Balmaceda 640, this museum features polychrome sculptures from the Cuzco School and paintings from 17th-century Quito, Ecuador. The church itself, completed in 1627 but reconstructed several times, contains 18th-century carvings on the sacristy beams. Closed for some time, it is uncertain when it will reopen.

Museo Mineralógico Ignacio Domeyko

La Serena's mineral museum, housing more than 2000 samples, is one of the best in a country whose economy depends on mining (the mineral museum in Copiapó is perhaps even better). At Anfión Muñoz 870, between Benavente and Infante, the museum (☎ 204-096) is open 9:30 am to 12:30 pm, weekdays only. Admission costs US$0.60.

Parque Jardín El Corazón

Along Av Juan Bohón, La Serena's relatively new Japanese garden has come a long way in

a short time, but the landscaping still needs time to mature. Between the Panamericana and the downtown area, at the foot of Cordovez, the gardens (☎ 217-013) are open 10 am to 6 pm daily. Admission costs US$1 for adults, US$0.40 for children.

Activities

From the west end of Av Aguirre, south to Coquimbo, are a multitude of beaches suitable for various activities. On a two-week vacation in La Serena, you can visit a different beach every day, but strong rip currents make some of them unsuitable for swimming. Safe beaches include Playa Canto del Agua, Playa Las Gaviotas, Playa El Pescador, Playa La Marina, Playa La Barca, Playa Mansa, Playa Los Fuertes, Playa Blanca, Playa El Faro (Sur) and Playa Peñuelas (Coquimbo). Suitable only for sunbathing and paddleball are Playa Cuatro Esquinas, Playa El Faro (Norte), Playa Changa (Coquimbo), Playa Punta de Teatinos, Playa Los Choros, Playa Caleta Hornos, Playa San Pedro and Playa Chungungo. All of these have regular bus and taxi colectivo service from downtown La Serena.

Besides swimming and sunbathing, other popular activities include sailing (if you make friends with a member of the yacht club), surfing (Playa El Faro is a favorite with bodyboarders) and windsurfing. Windsurfers who do not respect the rights of swimmers within 200m of the beach may run afoul of the naval Gobernación Marítima.

Organized Tours

The last few years have seen a proliferation of agencies offering a variety of excursions, ranging from conventional city tours and visits to nearby national parks, nighttime astronomical trips and even New Age pyramid schemes at Cochiguaz.

Several companies run half-day city tours (around US$15) and full-day trips (in the US$30 to US$40 range) in the Limarí and Elqui valleys to sites including Valle del Encanto, Parque Nacional Fray Jorge, Termas de Socos, Vicuña, the Pichasca petrified forest and Region IV beaches. Among them are

Diaguitas Tour (☎ 214-129, fax 217-265), Matta 510, Oficina 6; Turismo San Bartolomé (☎ 211-670, fax 221-992), Balmaceda 417, Departamento 28; and Ingservtur (☎ 220-165, ingsvtur@ctcreuna.cl), Matta 611, which also does astronomy tours.

There are several English-speaking guides at Talinay Adventure Expeditions (☎/fax 218-658, juan-pe@starmedia.com), Prat 470, which does full-day trips to the Elqui Valley and Cochiguaz (US$40), Reserva Nacional Pingüino de Humboldt (US$70) and the La Silla or La Campana observatories (US$70). Talinay also conducts spring horseback excursions to Alcohuaz (US$65 for a day trip) and Cochiguaz (US$190, two days and one night). It also offers two- and three-day trips across the Andes to the Argentine hot springs resort of Pismanta via the Agua Negra pass, a scenic route over which there is no regular public transportation.

Cycling specialist Ciclomanía (☎/fax 210-172), Huanhualí 900, does a variety of half-day bike tours, with support vehicles, in the immediate La Serena area (US$11 to US$14), full-day tours to the Elqui Valley, Cochiguaz and Paihuano (US$30), and overnight trips in the Elqui valley (US$56). Chile Adventours (☎/fax 239-280, goose@entelchile.net), Av El Santo 3375, Departamento 102, specializes in 'surfin' safaris.' Intijalsu (☎ 217-945, intijalsu@entelchile.net), Matta 621, consists of professional astronomers offering archaeoastronomy and ethno-astronomy tours, integrating serious science with traditional Andean culture; see also boxed text 'Online Resources' in Facts for the Visitor.

Special Events

In the second week of January, the city hosts the Jornadas Musicales de La Serena, a series of musical events with nearly a decade and a half of history.

In the first fortnight of February, the Feria del Libro, the annual book fair, displays the latest works from national and foreign publishing houses. Many prominent Chilean authors visit the city and give public readings during this time.

Places to Stay

Many families who house students from the university rent to tourists only in summer, but some may also have a spare bed at other times. Seasonal price differentials in La Serena are substantial; the prices below are high-season (January and February) prices; off-season prices may be only a fraction of these.

Budget La Serena's Hostelling International affiliate is highly praised *Residencial Limmat* (☎ 211-373, Lautaro 914), charging US$10 per person for spotless rooms (some of them small) with firm beds; it also has attractive common spaces.

Open in summer only, *Albergue Santo Tomás (Amunátegui 570)* has hostel accommodations with kitchen privileges and hot showers for US$3.50.

Residencial El Loa (☎ 210-304, O'Higgins 362) charges US$8.50 per person with shared bath; some rooms are dark, but others are fine. Pick of the cheapies is friendly, well-kept *Residencial Lorena* (☎ 223-380, Cantournet 950), where spacious rooms with shared bath cost only US$9; during the school year (March to December), though, university students occupy most of the generally quieter rooms at the back. Others in the same range include *Residencial Petit* (☎ 212-536, Eduardo de la Barra 586) and, some distance from downtown, *Residencial El Silo* (☎ 213-944, Larraín Alcalde 1550).

Close to the bus terminal, reader-endorsed *Residencial Jofré* (☎ 222-335, Regimiento Coquimbo 964) charges US$10 per person for rooms with private bath and breakfast, plus kitchen privileges. Half a block from the plaza, recommended *Residencial Chile* (☎ 211-694, Matta 561) has pleasant garden singles/doubles with shared bath for US$10 per person but also has a 1 am curfew (an unusual policy for a resort town). Breakfast costs an additional US$1.60. Nearby, friendly *Residencial Lido* (☎ 213-073, Matta 547), which has rooms for US$11, seems to be slipping.

Residencial La Casona de Cantournet (☎ 226-439, Cantournet 815) has spacious singles with comfy beds and excellent hot showers for about US$12 per person, but the quality of individual rooms varies dramatically. The entrance is through Hotel Casablanca, Vicuña 414.

Still recommended *Hotel Pacífico* (☎ 225-674, *Eduardo de la Barra 252*) has rooms for US$10/15 with shared bath, US$14/22 with private bath. Highly regarded central *Hostal de Turismo Croata* (☎ 224-997, *Cienfuegos 248*) charges US$16/24 with private bath.

Mid-Range Mid-range accommodations start around US$20/31 with private bath at *Hotel Alameda* (☎ 213-052, *Av Aguirre 452*). Though not really Swiss-run, the remodeled *Residencial Suiza* (☎ 216-092, *Cienfuegos 250*), friendly and tidy, charges US$21/38.

Hotel de Turismo Brasilia (☎ 225-248, *fax 211-883, Brasil 555*) charges US$24/43 with breakfast, but rooms vary considerably; check for lower off-season prices. For non-hostel accommodations, *Residencial Limmat* (☎ 211-373, *Lautaro 914*) charges US$25/33. Some rooms are a little cramped at *Hotel Soberanía* (☎ 227-672, *Regimiento Coquimbo 1049*), a colonial-style family hotel charging US$25/39.

Hotel El Escorial (☎ 224-793, *fax 221-433, Brasil 476*) is an older building with some newer rooms that are less charming but more functional. Rates are US$30/40 (US$40/50 in summer), breakfast included. The family-style *Hostal de Colón* (☎ 223-979, *Colón 371*) charges US$29/35 in the off-season, US$38/42 in summer for rooms with private bath and TV, and also offers free transport to and from the airport or bus terminal.

Modern, boxy *Hotel Pucará* (☎ 211-966, *Balmaceda 319*) is a full-service hotel that charges US$36/44 with breakfast, but there are slightly cheaper rooms on the 3rd floor. Rates at *Hotel Casablanca* (☎ 223-506, *Vicuña 414*) are US$42/51 with breakfast, but some otherwise-comfortable rooms are dark and small.

Top End Recently upgraded, *Hotel Berlín* (☎ 222-927, *fax 223-975, Cordovez 535*) now costs US$57/76. The tasteful new *Hotel Costa Real* (☎ 221-010, *Av Francisco de Aguirre 170*) is one of La Serena's more appealing places, with rooms for US$60/90. The very central *Hotel Mediterráneo* (☎ 225-837, *fax 225-838, Cienfuegos 509*) has rooms with private bath for US$65/83, while reader-recommended *Hotel Los Balcones de Alcalá* (☎ 225-999, *Av Aguirre 781*) charges US$69/80.

The beachfront *Hotel La Serena Plaza* (☎ 225-745, *Av Francisco de Aguirre 0660*), near the lighthouse, has spacious rooms with cable TV and pool for US$80/87. For US$106/125 with breakfast, the handsome *Hotel Francisco de Aguirre* (☎ 222-991, *Cordovez 210*) comes highly recommended, but guests who are not early risers may be disturbed by the bells at the nearby Iglesia Santo Domingo.

Places to Eat

For superb, moderately priced seafood, almost any of the numerous restaurants in the Mercado La Recova complex at Cienfuegos and Cantournet may be a good choice. Competition among them is so intense that diners can often get a free pisco sour with lunch, but some hawkers are getting unpleasantly aggressive. One personal favorite is *Caleta Hornos* (☎ 221-152, *Local 220*). Next door, *Serena* (*Local 219*) is also good, as is *Lidia* (☎ 214-076, *Local 218*).

The best fast-food choice, with a wide selection of surprisingly good cafeteria fare at low prices, is *Quick Biss Dos* (☎ 226-300, *Cienfuegos 545, 2nd floor*). It also has a separate tobacco-free area. Popular *Grill Bar Serena* (*Eduardo de la Barra 614*) serves cheap seafood.

Café Plaza Real (☎ 217-166, *Prat 465*) has good breakfasts and fixed-price lunches. The *Restaurant y Bar Croata* (☎ 224-663, *Balmaceda 871*) has decent fixed-price lunches for about US$5, but the food is Chilean, rather than Balkan.

El Cedro (☎ 221-427, *Prat 568*) is a recommended, though pricey, Chilean-Middle Eastern restaurant in pleasant surroundings. *Donde El Guatón* (☎ 211-519, *Brasil 750*) has good beef and good service.

Rincón Oriental (*O'Higgins 570*) is one of La Serena's better Chinese restaurants, but *Taiwan (☎ 214-407, Cantournet 844)* and *Mai Lan Fan (☎ 214-828, Cordovez 740)* are also worth consideration.

Coffee, ice cream and desserts are outstanding at *Boccaccio (☎ 222-296, Prat 490)*, but *Gelatería Mammamia (☎ 216-032, Prat 220)* and *Diavoletto (O'Higgins 535)* are also good choices. For coffee, snacks and sandwiches, try *Café do Brasil (Balmaceda 461)*.

There are also many places to eat along the beach, heading south from the lighthouse toward Peñuelas, including the seafood restaurant *Tololo Beach (☎ 242-656, Av del Mar s/n)* and *El Atojo (Av del Mar s/n)* for credible Mexican specialties and live music.

Entertainment
The *Cine Centenario (Cordovez 399)* shows recent films, but there's also a multiscreen cinema at the Plaza La Serena shopping mall, south of the bus terminal.

Café del Patio (Prat 470) is a small café that turns into a lively jazz and blues venue and offers good bar food on Friday and Saturday nights, but it keeps long hours every day of the week. In summer, some of Santiago's best play the club, but the local bands that play the rest of the year are still worth hearing. Owner Rodrigo Sugg Pierry speaks good English.

In a 130-year-old house, part of the Centro Latinoamericano de Arte y Cultura, *Afro Son (Balmaceda 824)* has live Chilean folk music. Across the street, *Salón Stylo (Balmaceda 841)* offers live tango music and dancing.

Shopping
Check Mercado La Recova, at Cienfuegos and Cantournet, for musical instruments, woolens and dried fruits from the Elqui Valley. Other crafts are available for purchase at the Cema-Chile artisans' gallery, at Los Carrera 562.

Getting There & Away
Air LanChile (☎ 221-531), Eduardo de la Barra 435-B, flies twice daily to and from Santiago (US$67 to US$97) except Sunday (once); all flights from Santiago continue to

Copiapó (US$33), five of them to the town of El Salvador (US$42). Ladeco (☎ 225-753), Cordovez 484, flies twice daily to Santiago, daily to Copiapó, and daily to Antofagasta (US$93) and Iquique (US$114).

Avant (☎ 219-275, 219-276), Eduardo de la Barra 417, flies twice each weekday and once Saturday and Sunday to Santiago (US$71 to US$115), and daily except Sunday to Copiapó (US$33 to US$48).

Bus – Regional La Serena's Terminal de Buses (☎ 224-573) is southwest of downtown, at Amunátegui and Av El Santo. Many companies have offices downtown as well; where no address appears below, you may assume the office is at the terminal. Buses to Vicuña and the Elqui Valley also stop at the Plaza de Abasto, at the corner of Colo Colo and Esmeralda.

For regional transportation, Buses Serenamar (☎ 248-725), Andrés Bello 862, runs eight buses daily to Guanaqueros (US$1.25) and Tongoy (US$1.50), between 6:45 am and 7:30 pm.

Fares to other regional destinations range from US$3 to US$5. Via Elqui (☎ 225-240) has five buses daily to Vicuña. Frontera Elqui (☎ 221-664) serves the upper Elqui Valley destinations of Vicuña, Paihuano, Monte Grande and Pisco Elqui daily.

Los Diamantes de Elqui (☎ 225-555), Balmaceda 594, goes to Vicuña and Ovalle, as does Expreso Norte (☎ 224-857, 225-503). Other carriers serving Ovalle include Tas Choapa (☎ 225-959, 224-915) at O'Higgins 599; Lasval/Inca Bus (☎ 225-627) at Cienfuegos 698; Buses Tal (☎ 226-148, 225-555) at Balmaceda 594; and Buses Palacios (☎ 224-448). Los Corsarios and Pullman Bus (☎ 225-284), O'Higgins 663, go daily to the upper Choapa Valley destinations of Illapel and Salamanca, northeast of Los Vilos.

Bus – Long-Distance Many carriers ply the long-distance Panamericana routes, from Santiago north to Arica. Those serving Santiago include Buses Tal (☎ 225-555, usually the cheapest), Géminis (☎ 224-018), Lasval/Inca Bus (☎ 224-795), Tramaca (☎ 225-575), Flota Barrios (☎ 213-394, 226-

361), Los Diamantes del Elqui, Tas Choapa, Buses Palacios, Expreso Norte, Buses Libac (☎ 226-101, 225-172) at Francisco de Aguirre 452 and Pullman Bus. Los Corsarios (☎ 225-157), O'Higgins 663, Lasval/Inca Bus and Pullman Bus all serve Valparaíso and Viña del Mar.

For Copiapó and other northern destinations as far as Iquique and Arica, try Inca Bus, Flota Barrios, Pullman, Tramaca, Tur-Bus (☎ 331-104) at Cordovez 309, or Fénix Pullman Norte (☎ 225-555, 226-148).

Destinations and typical fares include Santiago (US$15, seven hours), Valparaíso/Viña del Mar (US$15, seven hours), Los Vilos (US$8, three hours), Vallenar (US$6, 2½ hours), Copiapó (US$10, four hours), Chañaral (US$12.50, six hours), Antofagasta (US$27, 13 hours), Calama (US$32, 15 hours), Iquique (US$38, 17 hours) and Arica (US$42, 21 hours). Add about 30% for semi-cama services, 50% for salón cama.

Bus service also links La Serena with other South American countries. In the summer months, departing Wednesdays and Sundays at 11 pm, Covalle Bus (☎ 213-127), Infante 538, connects La Serena with the Argentine cities of Mendoza (US$35, 12 hours) and San Juan (US$45, 14 hours). Cata (☎ 218-744) provides service to Mendoza (US$36) Wednesday, Friday and Sunday.

Tas Choapa takes passengers to Tacna and Lima, Peru, leaving Monday at 10 pm.

Taxi Colectivo Many regional destinations are more frequently and rapidly served by taxi colectivo. Tacso (☎ 224-517), Domeyko 524, goes to Andacollo, Ovalle, and the Elqui Valley. Línea Ruta 41 (☎ 224-517), also at Domeyko 524, goes to upper Elqui Valley destinations such as Vicuña (US$4) and Pisco Elqui (US$6).

Getting Around
Cabs to La Serena's Aeropuerto La Florida, a short distance east of downtown on Chile 41, the route to Vicuña and the Elqui Valley, cost only US$3 to US$4.

For rental cars, try the Automóvil Club de Chile (☎ 225-279) at Eduardo de la Barra 435, Avis (☎ 227-049) at Av Aguirre 063,

Hertz (☎ 225-471) at Aguirre 0225 or Budget (☎ 296-890) at Balmaceda 3850. Lesser-known local agencies include Gala (☎ 221-400) at Huanhualí 435, Callegari (☎ 211-688) at O'Higgins 672, and Flota Verschae (☎ 227-645) at Av Francisco de Aguirre 0240.

AROUND LA SERENA
Caleta Hornos
About 25km north of La Serena, directly on the Panamericana, this small fishing settlement is known for its good, inexpensive seafood picadas, most notably **Brisas Marinas**, that serve the catch fresh off the boat.

Observatorio Cerro Tololo
Operated by the Tucson-based Association of Universities for Research in Astronomy (Aura, a group of about 25 institutions including the Universidad de Chile), Observatorio Interamericano Cerro Tololo sits 2200m above sea level, 88km southeast of La Serena. Its 4m telescope, once the Southern Hemisphere's largest, has since been superseded by 8m giants at Cerro Paranal, south of Antofagasta, but it is still a popular excursion for visitors to the Norte Chico, thanks to guided tours led by knowledgeable staff, all of whom speak English (although most visitors are Chilean).

Tours to Cerro Tololo, a futuristic-looking multi-domed campus on a hill, take place Saturdays only and are free of charge. They feature visits to two of the main telescopes, including the 4m giant, and an audiovisual program with images of some of the observatory's 'stellar' discoveries of the past decade or so. Despite the fact that it's a daytime visit – and, in any event, the observatory has no telescopes that any astronomer actually peers through, since all the data are fed into computers and re-sorted into monitor images that the human eye can handle – Tololo is a worthwhile excursion. To see the nighttime skies, try a visit to Mamalluca near Vicuña (see the Around Vicuña section later in this chapter).

To visit Cerro Tololo, make reservations by contacting Aura, at Colina El Pino s/n, La Serena (☎ 225-415, fax 205-212; see also the

The Starry Southern Skies

Inland from the perpetually fogbound coast, in the western foothills of the Andes, the Norte Chico hosts the most important cluster of astronomical observatories in the Southern Hemisphere, and one of the most important in the world. Within 150km of La Serena are three major facilities: above the Elqui Valley is the Cerro Tololo Interamerican Observatory (CTIO); at La Silla, the European Southern Observatory (ESO); and the Carnegie Institution's Observatorio Las Campanas, are both east of the Panamericana on the border between Regions III and IV.

The importance of these and other observatories is likely to increase in the coming years with the construction of several major telescopes. The biggest project to date is ESO's Cerro Paranal observatory, 120 km south of Antofagasta in Region II, where four 8.2m trapezoidal Very Large Telescopes (VLTs) superseded CTIO's 4m instrument as the Southern Hemisphere's largest. The Carnegie Institution is also adding two 6.5m units at Las Campanas.

Even more massive is the planned Atacama Large Millimeter Array (ALMA), consisting of 64 12m radio telescopes or antennas spread over a 10km area. Set to be built on the Llano de Chajnantor, 5000m above sea level and 40km east of San Pedro de Atacama, it's part of the US National Science Foundation's (NSF) Project Gemini. With multinational participation, it will complement a similar facility on Hawaii's Mt Mauna Kea. In what sounds like a case of celestial hubris, the area may be the site for a projected Overwhelmingly Large Telescope (OWT), budgeted at US$1 billion (perhaps the next step is the ILT- Impossibly Large Telescope).

Chile is doing its best to encourage research (as Congress has granted customs benefits to astronomers), but the country also hopes to foment more local participation through supervision by its Comisión Nacional de Ciencia y Tecnología (National Commission on Science and Technology). Chile's small community of 30 or so astronomers will be guaranteed a certain amount of research time on facilities.

One problem that concerns astronomers, though, is the urbanization of Chile's northern deserts. Once-remote areas such as Cerro Tololo are now vulnerable to light pollution from growing towns and cities such as Vicuña and La Serena. To ensure Chile's astronomical future, the Comisión Nacional del Medio Ambiente (Conama, the national environment commission) will help implement a new law requiring downward-pointing screens over all outdoor lights in the Norte Chico and Norte Grande.

boxed text 'Online Services' in the Facts for the Visitor chapter.) There is no public transport to the observatory, so renting a car or hiring a taxi are pretty much the only options. The well-marked, gated turnoff to Tololo is 52km east of La Serena via Ruta 41, where vehicles that have contracted tours ascend the smooth but winding gravel road in a caravan.

COQUIMBO

In the rocky hills of Península Coquimbo, between the Bahía de Coquimbo and the smaller Bahía Herradura de Guayacán, the bustling port of Coquimbo (population 106,000) takes its name from a Diaguita word meaning 'place of calm waters' – even Darwin observed that it was 'remarkable for nothing but its extreme quietness.' Though now livelier, especially on a Saturday night, it's a less attractive place to stay than La Serena.

The staff at Coquimbo's municipal tourist office, at Melgarejo and Las Heras, try to be helpful but they don't have much expertise or material. They do have a modest **Museo de Sitio** of a pre-Columbian graveyard discovered serendipitously when clearing a lot for expanding the Plaza de Armas. It dates from the Las Animas cultural complex, 900 to 1100 AD, which predated the Diaguita.

Half-hour boat tours of the harbor depart from the Av Costanera daily between 10 am and 8 pm, charging US$1 for adults and US$0.50 for children. There are very popular beaches along the Bahía Herradura de Guayacán, easily reached from either Coquimbo or La Serena.

Places to Stay & Eat
Excellent budget accommodations are available at *Hotel Iberia* (☎ 312-141, *Lastra 400*) for about US$15/26 singles/doubles with private bath and TV. For a change of gastronomic pace, try the Middle Eastern fare at *Restaurant Arabe* (*Alcalde 527*), the good Chinese food at *Mai Lan Fan* (☎ 315-615, *Av Ossandón 1*) or Italian at *Tavola Calda* (*Bilbao 451*). For seafood, visit *La Picada* (☎ 311-214, *Av Costanera s/n*) or *Sal y Pimienta* (*Aldunate 769*), or, for *parrillada* (grilled meat), *El Brasero* (*Av Alessandri 113*).

Getting There & Away
Coquimbo's Terminalde Buses is on Varela between Borgoño and Barriga. Long-distance services are similar to those to and from La Serena; many local buses and taxi colectivos also link the two cities.

GUANAQUEROS
At the south end of Bahía Guanaqueros, 30km south of Coquimbo and 5km west of the Panamericana, Guanaqueros' long, white, sandy beach makes it one of the area's most popular resorts. It's suitable for a day trip, but *Hotel La Bahía* (☎ 391-380, *Av Costanera 274*) is open all year for accommodations. *El Pequeño Restaurant* (☎ 391-341, *Av Costanera 306*) has traditionally been a favorite for Chilean food.

Buses and taxi colectivos run frequently from Coquimbo and La Serena and continue to Tongoy; see the La Serena and Tongoy sections in this chapter for more information.

TONGOY
On a rocky peninsula 58km south of La Serena, the lively beach resort of Tongoy is like Blackpool or the Jersey shore with a Latin feel, thanks to its artisans' market, family-oriented beachfront restaurants and souvenir shops. The moderately priced *marisquerías* (seafood restaurants) along the south side of Playa Grande are enjoyable places to spend the afternoon and watch the action, but Playa Socos, on the north side of the peninsula, is more sheltered and popular for bathing.

Places to Stay & Eat
Friendly *Residencial D'Pardo* (*Fundición Norte 668*) charges US$10 per person for plain rooms, set among pleasant gardens, with shared bath. The upscale *Hotel Yachting Club* (☎ 391-259, *Av Costanera 200*) charges US$62 for a double, but it has seen better days. *Hostería Tongoy* (☎ 391-203, *Costanera 10*) is a better choice, at US$66 double.

Getting There & Away
From Coquimbo's bus terminal, Alfa Mar taxi colectivos reach Tongoy in about 45 minutes (US$2); slightly cheaper Serenamar buses (☎ 248-725) from Andrés Bello 862, La Serena, take about an hour.

VICUÑA
☎ 51
In the upper Elqui Valley, logos bearing the names of Capel, Control and Tres Erres piscos are as conspicuous as international soft-drink billboards in the rest of the country. Vicuña (population 7700), 62km east of La Serena, is a quiet village of adobe houses in an area that grows avocados, papayas and other fruits, but most notably provides the raw grapes that local distilleries transform into Chile's powerful brandy. Vicuña holds its annual grape harvest festival, Festival de la Vendimia, in February; it ends February 22, the anniversary of the city's founding. Suitable either for a day trip or a few days' stay, Vicuña and its surrounding communities have also acquired a reputation of attracting oddballs since the arrival of several groups convinced that UFOs frequent the area, most notably in nearby Cochiguaz.

From Vicuña, eastbound Ruta 41 leads over the Andes to Argentina. A rugged,

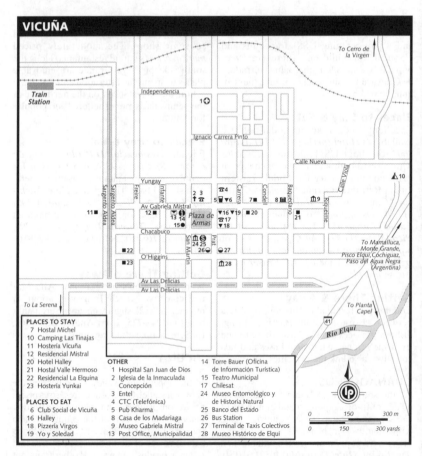

VICUÑA

Train Station

To Cerro de la Virgen

Independencia

Ignacio Carrera Pinto

Calle Nueva

Yungay

Av Gabriela Mistral

Plaza de Armas

Chacabuco

O'Higgins

Av Las Delicias

Av Las Delicias

To La Serena

To Mamalluca, Monte Grande, Pisco Elqui, Cóchiguaz, Paso del Agua Negra (Argentina)

To Planta Capel

Río Elqui

0   150   300 m
0   150   300 yards

PLACES TO STAY
7   Hostal Michel
10 Camping Las Tinajas
11 Hostería Vicuña
12 Residencial Mistral
20 Hotel Halley
21 Hostal Valle Hermoso
22 Residencial La Elquina
23 Hostería Yunkai

PLACES TO EAT
6   Club Social de Vicuña
16 Halley
18 Pizzería Virgos
19 Yo y Soledad

OTHER
1   Hospital San Juan de Dios
2   Iglesia de la Inmaculada
    Concepción
3   Entel
4   CTC (Telefónica)
5   Pub Kharma
8   Casa de los Madariaga
9   Museo Gabriela Mistral
13 Post Office, Municipalidad

14 Torre Bauer (Oficina
    de Información Turística)
15 Teatro Municipal
17 Chilesat
24 Museo Entomológico y
    de Historia Natural
25 Banco del Estado
26 Bus Station
27 Terminal de Taxis Colectivos
28 Museo Histórico de Elqui

dusty secondary road leads south to the town of Hurtado, the modest petrified forest of Monumento Natural Pichasca and the city of Ovalle.

Orientation
On the north bank of the Río Elqui, across a narrow bridge from Ruta 41, Vicuña has a geometric town plan centered on the wooded Plaza de Armas. Av Gabriela Mistral, running east-west off the plaza, is the main commercial street. Every important service or feature is within easy walking distance.

Information
The Municipalidad's Oficina de Información Turística (☎ 209-125) in the Torre Bauer at the northwest corner of the Plaza de Armas, is open 8:30 am to 1 pm and 2 to 5:30 pm weekdays except in January and February, when it's open weekends as well and does not close for lunch.

Banco del Estado, on the south side of the Plaza de Armas, offers poor exchange rates for cash only (no traveler's checks), and its ATM recognizes only its own cards; it's better to change money in La Serena.

Correos de Chile is in the Municipalidad, near the corner of Mistral and San Martín. The CTC (Telefónica) long-distance office is at Prat 378, half a block north of the plaza. Entel is on the north side of the plaza at Gabriela Mistral 351; Chilesat is on the east side, on Prat.

Hospital San Juan de Dios (☎ 411-263) is at the corner of Independencia and Prat, a few blocks north of the plaza.

Things to See & Do

Built by a former German mayor, the **Torre Bauer** (1905), an unusual clock tower on the west side of the Plaza de Armas, resembles a castle with wooden battlements. Just to its south, the **Teatro Municipal** (1950) has Art Deco touches.

At Chacabuco 334, on the south side of the plaza, the **Museo Entomológico y de Historia Natural** (☎ 411-283) specializes in insects. It's open 11:30 am to 1:30 pm and 3:30 to 6:30 pm daily except weekends, when it does not close for lunch. Admission costs US$0.50.

Dating from 1875, the **Casa de los Madariaga** (☎ 411-220), Gabriela Mistral 683, contains furnishings and artifacts from an influential family. It's open 10 am to 1 pm and 3 to 6 pm daily; admission costs US$0.60. The **Museo Histórico de Elqui** (☎ 412-104), Prat 90, has Diaguita artifacts; it's open 10 am to 6 pm weekdays (admission US$0.50).

The hike up **Cerro de la Virgen**, just north of town, offers vast panoramas of the entire Elqui Valley, but it's hot and exposed – bring plenty of water and snacks. There's a road most of the way to the summit, but it's less than an hour's walk from the Plaza de Armas.

Museo Gabriela Mistral Vicuña's landmark museum is a tangible eulogy to one of Chile's most famous literary figures, born Lucila Godoy Alcayaga in 1889, in the nearby village of Monte Grande. Exhibits include a handsomely presented photographic history of her life (including a picture of a sculpted bust that makes her seem a particularly strict and severe school-

marm), modest personal artifacts such as her desk and a bookcase, and a replica of her adobe birthplace. Her family tree indicates Spanish, Indian and even African ancestry. Like Pablo Neruda, she served in the Chilean diplomatic corps.

The museum (☎ 411-223) is on Av Gabriela Mistral between Riquelme and Baquedano. Admission costs US$1. It's open 10 am to 1 pm daily, 2:30 to 7 pm weekdays, and 3 to 6 pm Saturday.

Planta Capel Capel, a cooperative with member growers throughout the Norte Chico from Copiapó to Illapel, distills some of its product at this facility, where grapes arrive in vehicles ranging from tractors and pickups to 18-wheelers. The cooperative also has its only bottling plant here. The process of distilling takes eight to 12 months, depending on the desired strength of the pisco.

Across the bridge from Vicuña, tours take place every half-hour from 9:30 am to 6 pm daily in summer; the rest of the year, 9:30 am to 12:30 pm daily and 2:30 to 6 pm weekdays. The plant is closed January 1, May 1,

Gabriela Mistral

September 20, November 8 and December 25. Mornings are best, since many Chileans are late risers and there is no minimum attendance required – guides literally provide individual attention if only one person shows up, and free samples are served on conclusion. In addition to pisco, the sales room also offers *pajarete*, the region's delicious dessert wine.

Places to Stay

Camping is available at shady *Las Tinajas* (☎ 411-731, Chacabuco s/n) for US$6 per person, including access to the large municipal swimming pool.

Clean, friendly *Residencial Mistral* (☎ 411-278, Gabriela Mistral 180) charges US$6 per person for rooms with shared bath, breakfast US$1.50, lunch US$4. Plain but spacious *Hostal Michel* (☎ 411-060, Gabriela Mistral 573) is moderately priced, at US$8 with private bath but without breakfast.

Warmly recommended *Residencial La Elquina* (☎ 411-317, O'Higgins 65) charges US$10/18 singles/doubles with shared bath, US$18/30 with private bath, in an attractive house with lush gardens and fruit trees (although some rooms are cramped). Friendly *Hostal Valle Hermoso* (☎ 411-206, Gabriela Mistral 706) charges US$15 per person, with breakfast, for comfortable rooms with private bath in a century-old, Spanish-style adobe. *Hotel Halley* (☎ /fax 412-070, Gabriela Mistral 542) occupies a beautifully restored colonial-style building with antique furnishings, modern bathrooms and a swimming pool; rates are US$30/36.

Toward the upper end of the scale, rooms at the *Hostería Yunkai* (☎ 411-593, O'Higgins 72) cost US$35/43 off-season, US$50/64 in summer, breakfast included. Vicuña's ritziest accommodation's are at *Hostería Vicuña* (☎ 411301, fax 411-144, Sargento Aldea 101), where singles/doubles cost US$57/78 off-season, US$66/89 in summer, but there are occasional bargains as low as US$40/50. It also has the town's finest restaurant, a pool, tennis courts, TV and video.

Places to Eat

There are several modest restaurants, including *Yo y Soledad* (☎ 411-368, Mistral 448) and the nearby *Halley* (☎ 411-225, Mistral 404), recommended for its pastel de choclo. *Pizzería Virgos* (☎ 411-090, Prat 234) is so-so.

The *Club Social de Vicuña* (411-853, Mistral 445) is expensive but has a good menu in an attractive setting. Consider also the hotel restaurants, especially the one at Hostería Vicuña.

Pub Kharma (Av Gabriela Mistral 417) is the only notable nightspot.

Getting There & Away

Vicuña's Terminal de Buses is at Prat and O'Higgins, one block south of the plaza. Elqui Mar, Frontera Elqui and Vía Elqui all go to La Serena, Coquimbo and Pisco Elqui (US$2).

Pullman Bus (☎ 411-466) goes to Santiago and Valparaíso/Viña del Mar, while Los Diamantes de Elqui, Buses Tal (☎ 411-404) and Expreso Norte (☎ 411-348) also go to Santiago. There's a wider choice of destinations, especially northbound, in La Serena; fares are only a couple of dollars higher than those from La Serena.

Across Prat from the bus terminal is the separate Terminal de Taxis Colectivos, the departure point for shared taxis to La Serena and up the Elqui Valley. Fares to Paihuano are US$1, to Monte Grande US$1.20 to US$1.50 and to La Serena US$2.

AROUND VICUÑA
Observatorio Comunal
Cerro Mamalluca

Filling a need that the region's research observatories are unable to satisfy, Vicuña's new and charming municipal facility allows visitors to view the southern night skies through a 12-inch telescope, magnifying selected stars such as Alpha Centauri up to 140 times – not nearly what Cerro Tololo and others can do, but at those observatories you can't look through the telescopes.

Led by astronomy students and enthusiastic amateurs, all well prepared, guided tours take place nightly at 8 and 10 pm and midnight, starting with a slide show on the history of astronomy. Depending on its size, the group then moves inside the observatory proper to peer through the computer-controlled telescope, or splits up, with half moving outside to observe the stars with the naked eye; later, the two groups switch places. The weather is usually almost cloudless, but moonless nights are best for observing distant stars.

Contact the Municipalidad (☎ 411-352, fax 411-255, obser_mamalluca@yahoo.com), Av Gabriela Mistral 260 in Vicuña, for tour reservations. There is also a website; see boxed text 'Online Resources' in Facts for the Visitor for details. Adults pay US$6, while children age five to 12 pay US$2; there are discounts for groups larger than 15 persons.

There is no public transport, but some La Serena tour agencies arrange trips; it's also possible to hire a cab in Vicuña. Vehicles go by convoy to the site, which is difficult to find without knowing the route in advance, as it climbs a dark, winding mountain road.

Monte Grande

Reached by local bus or taxi colectivo from Vicuña, Monte Grande is Gabriela Mistral's birthplace. Her burial site, on a nearby hillside, is the destination of many Chilean and literary pilgrims. She received her primary schooling at the **Casa Escuela y Correo**, a modest museum open 9:30 am to 1 pm and 3 to 7 pm daily except Monday in summer; the rest of the year, hours are 10 am to 1 pm and 3 to 6 pm.

Monte Grande has no accommodations itself, but there are hotels in Pisco Elqui, just up the valley, and several cabañas in the nearby village of Cochiguaz (see below). Monte Grande's restaurant **Mesón del Fraile** is worth stopping at for a meal.

Cochiguaz

Considered a significant location by New Age adherents, Cochiguaz is, according to one brochure, a 'place among the mountains that concentrates cosmic energy,' but you needn't be a believer to enjoy the secluded valley, which is also the starting point for hikes and horseback rides in the backcountry.

There is camping for US$16 per site, for up to four persons, at **Camping Cochiguaz** (☎ 327-046). Accommodations cost US$30/40 singles/doubles without meals at **Apart Hotel Naturista Las Pirámides de Cochiguaz** (☎ 411-871, fax 411-246) where, 'Under one of the clearest starry skies on the planet, with a great possibility of seeing luminous extraterrestrial objects, you can rest under a parabolic pyramid, relax and meditate on existence, awakening the psychotronic power slumbering in the mind.'

Paso del Agua Negra

East of Vicuña, Ruta 41 climbs the valley of the Río Turbio to the Chilean customs and immigration post at Juntas del Toro. It then continues south along the Río de La Laguna before switchbacking steeply northeast to 4765m Paso del Agua Negra, one of the highest Andean passes between Chile and Argentina. Once mined by the Argentine military during tensions over the Beagle Channel in 1978, the route is usually open to vehicular traffic from mid-November to mid-March or April, and a fair number of cyclists enjoy this steep, difficult route for its spectacular mountain scenery.

Leading to the hot springs resort of Termas de Pismanta in Argentina, and to the provincial capital of San Juan, Agua Negra is one of the best areas to see the frozen snow formations known as *penitentes*, so called because they resemble a line of monks

UFOs and pisco

garbed in tunics. There are also accessible glaciers on both the Chilean and Argentine sides. The road is passable for any passenger vehicle in good condition, and La Serena tour operators may soon offer short trips across to Pismanta.

PISCO ELQUI

Renamed to publicize the area's most famous product, the former village of La Unión is a placid community in the upper drainage area of the Río Claro, a tributary of the Elqui. Its main attraction, the **Solar de Pisco Elqui**, produces the premium Tres Erres brand; while they're a bit disorganized as far as tours go, it's a nice place to taste free samples and inspect the antique machinery of the old distillery and bodegas.

According to local legend, Chilean President Gabriel González Videla personally changed La Unión's original name to undermine Peruvian claims of having originated the beverage (the provincial city of Pisco, in the valley of the same name south of Lima, also produces the drink). Despite producers' complaints of competition from foreign imports such as whiskey, acreage planted to grapes seems to have skyrocketed in the past few years – an apparent pisco boom – and several new labels have appeared on the market.

Places to Stay & Eat

Camping El Olivo (☎ 451-790 in Vicuña) charges US$7 per adult, US$3 per child, including pool access and showers, and also has a simple restaurant. Congenial *Hostal Don Juan* (☎ 451-087, Arturo Prat s/n) charges US$7.50 per person in a dilapidated, mysterious building that, in the words of travel writer Sara Wheeler, is 'straight out of a Gothic horror novel.'

Hotel Elqui (☎ 451-083, O'Higgins s/n) charges US$17 per person, including breakfast and use of the pool, but off-season prices drop to US$10; non-guests may use the pool for US$6. Lunches are reasonably priced, at about US$6. *Hotel Gabriela Mistral* (☎ 451-086, Prat 59) has good food but is less appealing than the Elqui; rates are US$37 double, but at off-

season rates of US$10 per person it's an outstanding value.

German-run *El Tesoro de Elqui* (☎ 451-958, elqui@bigfoot.com, Prat s/n) has attractive cabañas for US$18/28 with shared bath and breakfast, US$30/40 with private bath and breakfast, and a good restaurant. Opposite the Plaza de Armas, shady *Jugos Naturales* serves huge fresh juices from oranges, papayas, pineapples and apricots.

Getting There & Away

Frequent taxi colectivos link Pisco Elqui with Vicuña.

OVALLE

☎ 53

Founded as a satellite of older La Serena in early republican times, Ovalle is the spotlessly clean capital of the prosperous agricultural province of Limarí. Although the city is half an hour east of the Panamericana, many north-south buses pass through here.

Orientation

Ovalle (population 51,000-plus) sits on the north bank of the Río Limarí, 90km south of La Serena and 30km east of the Panamericana. Everything of interest is within easy walking distance of the Plaza de Armas, which is beautifully landscaped and has both sunny and shady areas.

Information

Ovalle's tourist office is an erratically staffed kiosk at the southeast corner of the Plaza de Armas, theoretically open 10 am to 9 pm daily from November to March, 10 am to 2 pm and 4 to 7:30 pm the rest of the year. Should you find the kiosk closed, try the Automóvil Club de Chile (☎ 620-001) at Coquimbo 187, where the staff are friendly, helpful and competent.

It's better to change money in a larger town, but try Agencia Tres Valles (☎ 629-650), at Carmen and Libertad, for exchanging US cash only. There are several ATMs, including Banco de Crédito and Banco Santander, on opposite corners at Vicuña Mackenna and Victoria.

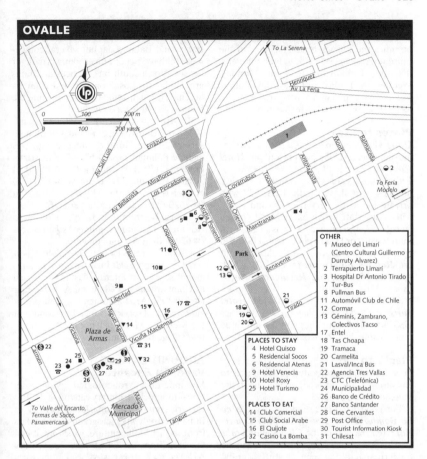

OVALLE

To La Serena

Henríquez
Av La Feria

0   100   200 m
0   100   200 yards

Errázuriz

Av San Luis

Av Bellavista

Miraflores

Los Pescadores

Covarrubias

Ariztía Oriente

Ariztía Poniente

Maestranza

Coquimbo

Arauco

Socos

Libertad

Miguel Aguirre

Victoria

Vicuña Mackenna

Carmen

Independencia

Maipú

Tangue

Benavente

Tirado

Park

Plaza de
Armas

Mercado
Municipal

To Valle del Encanto,
Termas de Socos,
Panamericana

To Feria
Modelo

Antofagasta

Tocopilla

Balmaceda

Maipú

OTHER
1 Museo del Limarí
   (Centro Cultural Guillermo
   Durruty Alvarez)
2 Terrapuerto Limarí
3 Hospital Dr Antonio Tirado
7 Tur-Bus
8 Pullman Bus
11 Automóvil Club de Chile
12 Cormar
13 Géminis, Zambrano,
   Colectivos Tacso
17 Entel
18 Tas Choapa
19 Tramaca
20 Carmelita
21 Lasval/Inca Bus
22 Agencia Tres Vallas
23 CTC (Telefónica)
24 Municipalidad
26 Banco de Crédito
27 Banco Santander
28 Cine Cervantes
29 Post Office
30 Tourist Information Kiosk
31 Chilesat

PLACES TO STAY
4 Hotel Quisco
5 Residencial Socos
6 Residencial Atenas
9 Hotel Venecia
10 Hotel Roxy
25 Hotel Turismo

PLACES TO EAT
14 Club Comercial
15 Club Social Arabe
16 El Quijote
32 Casino La Bomba

Correos de Chile is opposite the plaza, on Vicuña Mackenna between Victoria and Miguel Aguirre. The CTC (Telefónica) long-distance telephone office is at Vicuña Mackenna 499, a block west of the plaza; Entel is at Vicuña Mackenna 115 and Chilesat is at Vicuña Mackenna 232.

Hospital Dr Antonio Tirado (☎ 620-042) is at the north end of Ariztía Poniente, between Socos and Los Pescadores.

Museo del Limarí

Ovalle's archaeological museum, part of the new Centro Cultural Guillermo Durruty Alvarez, is a modest endeavor stressing the trans-Andean links between the Diaguita peoples of coastal Chile and northwest Argentina. There are also pieces from the earlier Huentelauquén and Molle cultures. Some of the larger ceramics are in excellent condition.

In new quarters at the former train station, at the corner of Covarrubias and Antofagasta, the museum is open 10 am to 8 pm daily except Monday in summer; the rest of the year, hours are 10 am to 1 pm and 4 to 7:30 pm. Admission costs US$1 for adults, US$0.50 for children.

Feria Modelo de Ovalle

Ovalle's lively fruit and vegetable market occupies the former repair facilities of the railroad. Also a good place to look for crafts, it's open from 8 am to 4 pm Monday, Wednesday, Friday and Saturday. Follow Vicuña Mackenna east across Ariztía, where its name changes to Av Benavente.

Places to Stay

Hotel Venecia (☎ 620-968, Libertad 261), is inexpensive, at US$8 per person, but *Hotel Roxy* (☎ 620-080, Libertad 155) is one of Chile's best values for US$9/16 singles/doubles with shared bath, US$13/23 with private bath. It's very friendly and clean, with a huge, attractive patio. *Hotel Quisco* (☎ 620-351, Maestranza 161) has singles with shared bath for US$10 per person, US$20/30 with private bath. Also worth checking out are *Residencial Atenas* (Socos 12), which has a restaurant, and *Residencial Socos* (Socos 22).

Ovalle's finest, the remodeled *Hotel Turismo* (☎ 623-258, Victoria 295) charges US$35/50 singles/doubles, but it's not three times better than the Roxy.

Places to Eat

There are many moderately priced places to eat along Calle Independencia, near the Mercado Municipal.

For good fixed-price lunches, try *Casino La Bomba* (Aguirre 364), the *Club Comercial* (Aguirre 244) or the *Club Social Arabe* (☎ 620-015, Arauco 255), which offers Middle Eastern specialties such as stuffed grape leaves. A personal favorite, though, is the unrepentantly political *El Quijote* (☎ 620-501, Arauco 298), where the walls are covered with images of leftist icons including Salvador Allende and Federico García Lorca, poems by Pablo Neruda, and the Universal Declaration of Human Rights, but the staff still manages to serve excellent meals with friendly but unobsequious service.

Entertainment

Cine Cervantes (Vicuña Mackenna s/n), on the south side of the Plaza de Armas, shows recent films.

Getting There & Away

There is a new Terrapuerto Limarí at Maestranza and Balmaceda, but several companies still have ticket offices along Ariztía or nearby. North-south bus services and fares are similar to those going to and from La Serena, although some companies using the Panamericana bypass Ovalle.

Tur-Bus (☎ 623-659), Ariztía Poniente 143, has extensive north- and southbound services. Other long-distance companies include Pullman Bus (☎ 621-476) at Ariztía Poniente 159, Tas Choapa (☎ 620-500) at Ariztía Poniente 371, Tramaca (☎ 620-656) at Ariztía Poniente 379 and Carmelita (☎ 620-656) at Ariztía Poniente 391. Géminis, Zambrano and Colectivos Tacso (for La Serena and Coquimbo) share offices (☎ 620-430) at Ariztía Poniente 245.

Lasval/Inca Bus (☎ 621-574, 620-886) is at Ariztía Oriente 398; Inca Bus provides regional service to interior destinations such as Combarbalá and Chañaral Alto. Cormar (☎ 620-195), Ariztía Poniente 219, also provides regional services. Línea Las Condes, at the Mercado Municipal, goes to the mountain village of Punitaqui.

AROUND OVALLE
Valle del Encanto

Monumento Arqueológico Valle del Encanto, a rocky tributary canyon of the Río Limarí, contains a remarkable density of Indian petroglyphs, pictographs and mortars from the El Molle culture, which inhabited the area from the 2nd to the 7th century AD. The rock art is best viewed in the early afternoon, when shadows are fewer, but it can be very hot at that time of day.

Both picnicking and camping (with permission) are possible at Valle del Encanto, 19km west of Ovalle. To get there, take any westbound bus out of Ovalle toward Termas de Socos and disembark at the highway marker; Valle del Encanto is an easy 5km walk along a clearly marked gravel road, but with luck, someone will offer to give you a lift. Bring water for the hike, although there is potable water in the canyon itself.

Operated under the protection of the Municipalidad of Ovalle, the Monumento

Arqueológico charges US$1 admission for adults, US$0.50 for children. On weekends, a concessionaire sells sandwiches and snacks. Hours are 8 am to 7:30 pm daily.

Termas de Socos

Termas de Socos, a short distance off the Panamericana at Km 370, 100km south of La Serena and 33km west of Ovalle, has great thermal baths and swimming pools. Private tubs cost US$6 per person for a half-hour's hot soak; access to the public pool also costs US$6 for non-guests.

Camping Termas de Socos (☎ 053-681-021; 02-779-6475 in Santiago) charges US$8 per person, including pool access. Accommodations at *Hotel Termas de Socos* (☎ 621-373; 02-681-6692 in Santiago) start at US$38 per person, including breakfast, and rise to US$66 per person, including full board.

Monumento Natural Pichasca

In the foothills 45km northeast of Ovalle, Pichasca guards 128 hectares of petrified araucaria forest along the Río Hurtado, but it's only fair to say that so many fossil trees were carted away before the area acquired Conaf protection that it's barely worth a detour for anyone expecting to see a large petrified forest. Also within the monument, a natural overhang known as **Casa de Piedra** has a smattering of pre-Columbian Molle rock art, but smoke from decades of campfires lit by stock drivers who camped here has damaged the paintings.

Pichasca is open 9 am to 6 pm daily. Admission costs US$2.50 for adults, US$1 for children. Local M&R buses from Ovalle's Feria Modelo go as far as Hurtado, passing the lateral to Pichasca, a 2km uphill walk in the summer heat. Motorists can take the dusty, winding gravel road north or south, to or from Vicuña.

PN FRAY JORGE

Moistened by the Pacific Ocean camanchaca, Parque Nacional Fray Jorge is an ecological island of Valdivian cloud forest (rain forest found around Valdivia, several humdred kilometers south) in an otherwise semiarid region, 110km south of La Serena

and 82km west of Ovalle. Illapel, for instance, gets only about 150mm of rainfall per annum, but Fray Jorge receives up to 10 times that, supporting vegetation that is more like the verdant forests of southern Chile than the Mediterranean scrub that covers most of the Norte Chico. Elevations range from sea level to 600m.

Of Fray Jorge's 10,000 hectares, there remain only 400 hectares of this truly unique vegetation – enough, though, to make it a Unesco World Biosphere Reserve. Some scientists believe this relict vegetation is evidence of dramatic climate change, but others argue that humans are responsible for the destruction of these forests, using them for fuel, farming and timber.

The first recorded European visitor was a Franciscan priest named Fray Jorge in 1672. Darwin, surprisingly and unfortunately, overlooked the area when he turned inland from the coastal road and passed through Illapel instead. What he missed, at elevations above 450m where the effect of the ocean fog is most pronounced, were stands of *olivillo (Aetoxicon punctatum), arrayán* (myrtle, *Myrceugenia correaeifolia*) and *canelo (Drimys winteri)*, plus countless other shrubs and epiphytes. The few mammals include two species of fox *(Dusicyon culpaeus* and *Dusicyon griseus)*, skunks and sea otters. There are some 80 bird species, including the occasional Andean condor.

Information

Fray Jorge is open to the general public in summer (January 1 to March 15) from 8:30 am to 6 pm Thursday to Sunday, plus holidays; the rest of the year, it's open weekends only. Note that, because of staff limitations, the gated road may be locked outside these hours so that theoretically no one can enter or leave, but in practice, they're a bit more flexible.

Park admission is US$4 for Chilean citizens, US$5 for foreigners; children pay half. The Centro de Información remains under development, with interesting photographic displays, but progress has been slow over the past several years.

Activities

In late afternoon, the rising camanchaca moistens the dense vegetation at **Sendero El Bosque**, a so-called interpretive trail that runs for 1km along the ridge above the ocean (the interpretation consists of labeling common Spanish names for a few of the most conspicuous tree species). The best time to appreciate the forest's ecological characteristics is early morning, when condensation from the fog leaves the plants dripping with moisture.

A short distance inland from the main forest, contrasting with the parched semidesert of the surrounding hills, discontinuous patches of green suggest that the forest at one time must have been far more extensive. The trail is at the end of the road from the Panamericana, 7km from the campground at El Arrayancito. Hikers will find the last segment of the road to the trailhead very steep and dusty.

With permission from Conaf, it's possible to walk down the fire trail from the ridge to the coast. Three kilometers from the Centro de Información is the park Administración, a historic building that was once the *casco* (big house) for a local hacienda. From there it's possible to walk 15km to a beach campsite, but Conaf discourages hikers from taking this route because part of it goes through private property.

Places to Stay

The only option for staying overnight within the park is to camp at sheltered El Arrayancito, 3km from the visitor center and 7km west of El Bosque. For US$10, each of its 13 sites has a firepit (firewood is available), a picnic table, potable water, clean toilets and cold showers, and plenty of annoying bugs. It's possible that, before the next edition of this book, Conaf will authorize construction of cabañas within the park.

Bring all supplies, since nothing is available in the park itself (except for free figs and pears – in late summer).

Getting There & Away

Fray Jorge is reached by a westward lateral off the Panamericana, about 15km north of its junction with the paved highway to Ovalle and about 2km north of a carabineros checkpoint. There is no regular public transport, but several agencies offer tours out of La Serena (see the La Serena section earlier in this chapter).

North-south buses can drop you at the clearly marked junction, which is 22km from the park itself – walking it is no picnic; Ask tour companies if you can leave the tour and perhaps even return another day.

LOS VILOS
☎ 53

Up to 20,000 visitors jam the working-class beach resort of Los Vilos (permanent population 8000) in the peak summer season. Midway between Santiago and La Serena, it has plenty of inexpensive accommodations and fine seafood, and is especially lively Sunday mornings when the Caleta San Pedro market offers live fresh crab, dozens of kinds of fish, a roving hurdy-gurdy man and thousands of colorful balloons.

According to local legend, the name Los Vilos is a corruption of *Lord Willow*, a British privateer that shipwrecked nearby. An alternative explanation is that it comes from the Araucanian *vilú*, a term that means serpent or snake and is common elsewhere in the region.

Held the second week of February, **Semana Vileña** (Vilos Week) is the town's biggest celebration.

Orientation

Los Vilos consists of two distinct areas, an older part with a regular grid west of the railroad tracks, and a newer, less regular section between the tracks and the Panamericana. Av Costanera, leading to the beach, is more of a focus of activity than is the Plaza de Armas. Most hotels and restaurants are along Av Caupolicán, which links the town with the Panamericana.

Information

In January and February, Sernatur sponsors a tourist representative at the municipal Corporación Cultural at Caupolicán 278, open 10 am to 2:30 pm and 4 to 8 pm daily. The staff are competent and helpful.

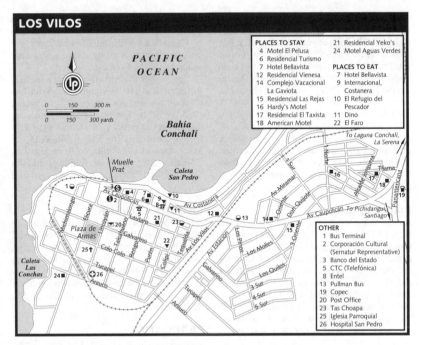

LOS VILOS

PLACES TO STAY
4 Motel El Pelusa
6 Residencial Turismo
7 Hotel Bellavista
12 Residencial Vienesa
14 Complejo Vacacional La Gaviota
15 Residencial Las Rejas
16 Hardy's Motel
17 Residencial El Taxista
18 American Motel
21 Residencial Yeko's
24 Motel Aguas Verdes

PLACES TO EAT
7 Hotel Bellavista
9 Internacional, Costanera
10 El Refugio del Pescador
11 Dino
22 El Faro

OTHER
1 Bus Terminal
2 Corporación Cultural (Sernatur Representative)
3 Banco del Estado
5 CTC (Telefónica)
8 Entel
13 Pullman Bus
19 Copec
20 Post Office
23 Tas Choapa
25 Iglesia Parroquial
26 Hospital San Pedro

PACIFIC OCEAN

Bahía Conchalí

Muelle Prat

Caleta San Pedro

Caleta Las Conchas

Plaza de Armas

To Laguna Conchalí, La Serena

To Pichidangui, Santiago

Banco del Estado is on Caupolicán near Muelle Prat, but foreign visitors are few and rates are poor, so it's better to exchange money in Santiago or La Serena.

Correos de Chile is opposite the plaza, at the corner of Lincoyán and Galvarino. The CTC (Telefónica) long-distance telephone offices are on Caupolicán between Rengo and Talcahuano; Entel is at Caupolicán 597.

Los Vilos' Hospital San Pedro (☎ 541-061) is at Lincoyán and Arauco, two blocks south of the plaza.

Things to See & Do

In addition to the usual beach activities, local launches approach seabird colonies at Isla de Huevos (US$2 per person) and the 1400-strong sea lion colony of Isla de Lobos (US$10 per person), from 9 am to 7 pm daily. These leave from Caleta San Pedro, which also has a lively fish market with several cheap restaurants.

Places to Stay

For US$7 per person, friendly ***Residencial Yeko's*** *(Purén 168)* has a restaurant and spacious rooms with shared bath in an attractive garden setting, but it lacks hot water as yet. Nearer the highway than the beach, ***Residencial El Taxista*** *(Tilama 247)* has comfortable singles with TV and shared bath for the same price. Although the entrance is through a bar, it's friendly and quiet, and not at all bad.

Complejo Vacacional La Gaviota *(☎ 541-326, Caupolicán 1259)* has singles/doubles for US$7/11. Beware of overcharging at ***Residencial Las Rejas*** *(☎ 541-026, Caupolicán 1310)*, which should cost about US$9.50.

Popular, central ***Hotel Bellavista*** *(☎ 541-073, Rengo 020)* charges US$8 per person for rooms with shared bath and breakfast, US$12.50 with private bath; it also has a fine restaurant that serves huge portions. There are good reports on ***Residencial Turismo*** *(☎ 541-176, Caupolicán 437)*, which charges

NORTE CHICO

US$12 per person. Friendly, appealing *Residencial Vienesa* (☎ 541-143, Av Los Vilos 11) charges US$12.50 per person but is often full.

Los Vilos has several US-style motels (and not the by-the-hour type that the term implies elsewhere in Chile). *Motel Aguas Verdes* (Elicura 701) charges US$42 double, while rooms at *Hardy's Motel* (☎ 541-098, Av 1 Norte 248) cost US$38/50. Rates at the more central *Motel El Pelusa* (☎ 541-041, Caupolicán 411) are US$43/49. In shady grounds at the junction of Caupolicán and the highway, the excellent *American Motel* (☎ 541-020, fax 541-163, Panamericana Km 224) charges US$50/69.

Places to Eat
In addition to the Hotel Bellavista restaurant, *El Faro* (☎ 541-190, Colipí 224) has attentive service, large portions and good fish dishes. Beachfront cafés along the costanera are cheap and good, especially *El Refugio del Pescador* (Av Costanera s/n) at Caleta San Pedro, and *Costanera* (☎ 541-010, Purén 80) and *Internacional* (also Purén 80), both facing the beach. *Dino* (Purén between Av Costanera and Av Caupolicán) also serves seafood.

Getting There & Away
Los Vilos proper has remade the former railroad station, at the west end of Caupolicán, into its Terminal de Buses, but some companies also maintain separate offices on

Caupolicán. It's also possible to flag a bus going either north or south from the junction of Caupolicán with the Panamericana – if you get hungry waiting, there's a decent snack bar at the Copec gas station.

Companies that do stop in town include Pullman Bus (to Santiago and Arica) at Caupolicán and Av Estación, Tas Choapa (☎ 541-032; to Santiago, Illapel and Salamanca) at Caupolicán 784, Dhino's (to Santiago), Inter-Bus (to Valparaíso/Viña del Mar), Incaval (to Santiago), Inca Bus-Los Corsarios (☎ 541-578, to Santiago and La Serena) and Tur-Bus (to Santiago and Arica).

LAGUNA CONCHALÍ
Near the new Muelle Mecanizado de Minera Los Pelambres, a mechanized mining port just north of Los Vilos, Laguna Conchalí is a coastal wetland harboring coots, storks, egrets, herons and other birds as well as coypu and several endangered plants. The fenced area is open during the day for picnics only.

PICHIDANGUI
Thirty kilometers south of Los Vilos, Pichidangui is a small, pleasant but more exclusive beach resort with several hotels and campgrounds. *Residencial Lucero* (☎ 533-106, Albacora s/n), in addition to its accommodations for US$15 per person, has an excellent seafood restaurant with reasonable prices.

La Araucanía & Los Lagos

Few landscapes surpass the beauty of those beyond the Río Biobío, where Fuji-like volcanic cones, blanketed by glaciers, tower above deep blue lakes, ancient forests and verdant farmland. Outside the cities, the loudest sound is the roar of waterfalls spilling over cliffs into limpid pools. But it was not always so tranquil. In the early 17th century, Mapuche resistance reduced Spanish settlements south of the Biobío to ashes and ruin.

The region's most important cities are Temuco, Valdivia, Osorno and Puerto Montt, but half the region's population lives in the countryside. Tourism plays a major role in the economy, but logging (chain saws can drown out some waterfalls), cereal production, dairy farming and livestock raising are also important. Local industries, such as sawmills and leather works, depend on these primary products.

Temuco, in Region IX of La Araucanía, is the starting point for exploring the area. From Temuco, travelers can visit Parque Nacional Conguillío and the upper reaches of the Biobío, head south to Lago Villarrica and Pucón, work their way to Lican Ray beside Lago Calafquén, on to Lago Panguipulli, and then to Futrono on Lago Ranco.

Farther south, east of Osorno, the Lago Puyehue route offers an easy land crossing to Argentina via Parque Nacional Puyehue, while Puerto Varas and Ensenada, on Lago Llanquihue, are stops on the route to Lago Todos los Santos in Parque Nacional Vicente Pérez Rosales, with a ferry from Petrohué to Peulla. From Peulla, it's possible to cross to Bariloche, Argentina, by a combination of boats and buses.

Puerto Montt, on the Seno de Reloncaví, is the capital of Region X (Los Lagos) and gateway to the Chiloé Archipelago and the remote, enthralling regions of Aisén and Magallanes. Despite construction and improvements on Ruta 7, the Camino Austral, the southern mainland of Region X remains accessible by road only through the Argentine province of Chubut. While the segment

of this highway from Caleta Gonzalo and Chaitén south to the Río Palena is part of Region X, it is covered in the Aisén chapter.

Travelers intending to visit the many national parks in these areas should acquire Lonely Planet's *Trekking in the Patagonian Andes*, which covers extended hikes in Conguillío, Huerquehue, Villarrica, Puyehue, Vicente Pérez Rosales and Alerce Andino national parks. It also includes several hikes across the border in Argentina.

HISTORY

South of Concepción, Spanish conquistadors found small quantities of precious metals, good farmland and a large potential Indian workforce; some lands were so tempting that conquistadors surrendered their central valley encomiendas for grants south of the Biobío. Despite their optimism, this area was a dangerous frontier and its settlements were constantly under threat from Mapuche attack or natural hazards, such as volcanoes, earthquakes and floods. Spanish soldier-poet Alonso de Ercilla immortalized the Mapuche resistance in his epic *La Araucana,* a classic of its genre and of Spanish literature; see the boxed text 'Ercilla & the Araucanian Wars' in the Middle Chile chapter.

The Mapuche constantly besieged settlements such as Osorno and Valdivia, especially in the general rebellion of 1598. By the mid-17th century, the Spaniards had abandoned most of the area except for a resettled and heavily fortified Valdivia; another century passed before they reclaimed settlements south of the Biobío. In the early 19th century, foreign travelers commonly referred to 'Arauco' as a separate country, and it was not until the 1880s that treaties made the area safe for European settlement.

The present towns and cities of Curacautín, Cunco, Victoria, Lonquimay, Temuco, Villarrica and Pucón owe their origins to military outposts along the Malleco, Cautín and Toltén rivers. Today, several hundred thousand Mapuche remain in the provinces

LA ARAUCANÍA

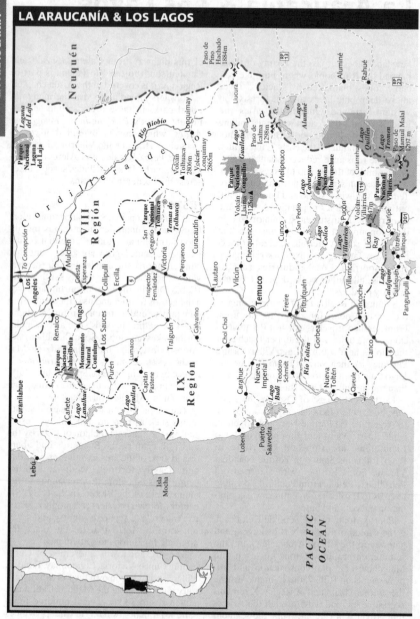

LA ARAUCANÍA & LOS LAGOS

Neuquén

Laguna del Laja

Parque Nacional Laguna del Laja

Río Biobío

Lonquimay

Paso de Pino Hachado 1884m

BP 13

Aluminé

Rahué

BP 23

C o r d i l l e r a   d e   l o s   A n d e s

VIII Región

To Concepción

Mulchén

Cuesta Esperanza

Los Angeles

Collipulli

Ercilla

5

Angol

Renaico

Los Sauces

Parque Nacional Nahuelbuta

Monumento Natural Contulmo

Curanilahue

Cañete

Lago Lanalhue

Lago Lleulleu

Purén

Lumaco

Capitán Pastene

Lebú

Isla Mocha

San Gregorio

Parque Nacional Tolhuaca

Termes de Tolhuaca

Inspector Fernández

Victoria

Perquenco

Curacautín

Volcán Tolhuaca 2806m

Volcán Lonquimay 2865m

Lago Gualletue

Paso de Icalma 1298m

Melipeuco

Volcán Llaima 3125m

Parque Nacional Conguillio

Lago Caburgua

Parque Nacional Huerquehue

Curarrehue

Lago Aluminé

Lago Quillén

Lago Tromen

Paso de Mamuil Malal 1207 m

Lautaro

Vilcún

Cherquenco

Cunco

San Pedro

Lago Colico

Lago Villarrica

Villarrica

Pucón

Volcán Villarrica 2847m

Parque Nacional Villarrica

119

Curarrehue

Coñaripe

201

Lican Ray

Lago Calafquén

Calafquén

Coñaripe

Eltrán

Pullinque

IX Región

Chol Chol

Galvarino

Traiguén

Temuco

Freire

Pitrufquén

Gorbea

Río Toltén

Nueva Toltén

Villarrica

Loncoche

Lanco

5

Panguipulli

Carahue

Nueva Imperial

Teodoro Schmidt

Lago Budi

Lobería

Puerto Saavedra

Queule

PACIFIC OCEAN

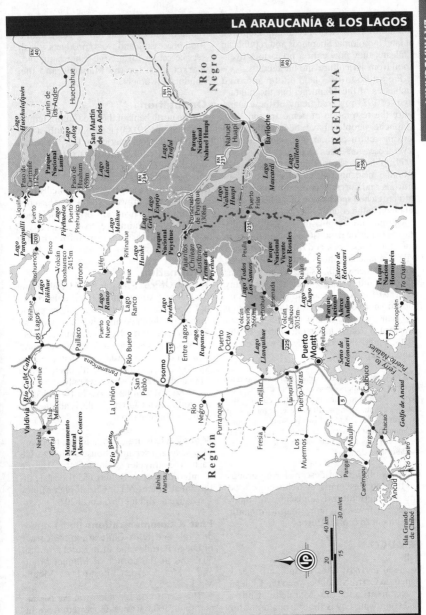

LA ARAUCANÍA & LOS LAGOS

between the Biobío and the Río Toltén, still commonly known as 'La Frontera.' Deprived of land by colonial Spaniards and republican Chileans, they now earn a precarious livelihood from agriculture and handicrafts.

From 1965 to 1973, land reform improved the status of the Mapuche, but the military coup of 1973 reversed many of these gains. Since the restoration of democracy in 1989, Mapuche peoples have been militant in seeking return of their lands and have, on several occasions, been successful. In 1998 and 1999, political resistance flared up again, with sporadic incidents that alarmist government officials and forestry companies magnified into farfetched speculation of a Chiapas-style rebellion in the countryside.

German immigrants in the 19th century started many local industries, including breweries, tanneries, brick and furniture factories, bakeries, machine shops and mills. Although their influence is still visible in cities such as Valdivia and Osorno, which have many central-European-style buildings, visitors should not overestimate the lingering German influence in the region. American geographer Mark Jefferson, writing in the 1920s, found the claims of German dominance exaggerated:

Puerto Montt was said to speak German and read German newspapers. I was even told I should find people there who were born in the country but could speak no Spanish. All this is exaggeration of the grossest sort...I found two persons who spoke no Spanish, but both were German-born. No street in the city has a German name, nor is German used on signs.

Chileans of German descent have perhaps left their greatest marks in architecture, food and the agricultural landscape of dairy farms, but few have more than a romantic attachment to central Europe.

TEMUCO
☎ 45

Founded in 1881, after a landmark treaty signed on Cerro Ñielol between the Chilean government and the Mapuche, Chile's fastest-growing city is the starting point for excursions to nearby indigenous settlements and Andean national parks. Supporting a range of industries, including steel, textiles, food processing and wood products, it is the service center for a large hinterland, and a market town for the Mapuche and their handmade woolens.

Orientation
On the north bank of the Río Cautín, Temuco (population 210,000) is 675km south of Santiago via the Panamericana. Despite its late founding, it still conforms to the conventional grid of the Spanish colonial city, but the Panamericana (known as Av Caupolicán through town) slices the city diagonally from northeast to southwest. To the north, across Av Balmaceda, historic Cerro Ñielol overlooks the city and the river. The city is growing, but travelers can still reach most sites of interest on foot.

Information
Tourist Offices Sernatur (☎ 211-969), facing the Plaza de Armas Aníbal Pinto at the corner of Claro Solar and Bulnes, has city maps and many free leaflets, and there's usually an English speaker on duty. In January and February, it's open 8:30 am to 7:30 pm weekdays, 8:30 am to 5 pm Saturday, and 10 am to 2 pm Sunday. The rest of the year, it's open 9 am to 1 pm and 3 to 5 pm weekdays only.

At San Martín 0278, Acchi (☎ 215-132), the Automóvil Club de Chile, is also a good source of information.

Money ATMs are abundant, but there are also several exchange houses. Change US cash and traveler's checks at Casa de Cambio Global at Bulnes 655, Local 1, Intercam at Bulnes 743 or Christopher Money Exchange at Bulnes 667, Local 202.

Post & Communications Both Correos de Chile and Telex-Chile are at the corner of Diego Portales and Prat. Entel is at Prat 505, and at the corner of Manuel Montt and J M Carrera. Chilesat is at Vicuña Mackenna 557.

The Centro de Llamados on Av Alemania, about 100m west of Hochstetter, has Internet access.

Common Mapuche Words & Phrases

Mapudungun, Chile's mostly widely spoken indigenous language, has great practical significance to its native speakers, who use it daily, and symbolic importance to Chileans that goes deeper than the use of Mapuche for many place names. Though the great majority of Mapuche also speak Spanish, the following sample of Mapudungan vocabulary may prove useful to visitors. Pronunciation is less consistently phonetic than Spanish, but still fairly straightforward. A few words have obviously been adapted from Spanish.

thank you	caltumay	9	pura
hill	pichi huincul	10	mari
volcano	pillán	11	mari quiñe
boy	pichi huentro	12	mari epu
girl	pichi hilcha	13	mari quila
mother	ñuque	14	mari meli
woman	somo	15	mari quechu
brother	peñi	16	mari callu
sister	sella	17	mari regle
house	ruca	18	mari ailla
dog	tre gua	19	mari pura
cow	wuaca	20	epu mari
sheep	ofisa	30	quila mari
condor	ñancú	40	meli mari
flower	rayen	50	quechu mari
water	co	60	callu mari
beans	quilli	70	regle mari
wine	pulco	80	ailla mari
white wine	blan pulco	90	pura mari
1	quiñe	100	quiñe pataca
2	epu	110	quiñe pataca quiñe mari
3	quila	200	epu pataca
4	meli	210	epu pataca quiñe mari
5	quechu	220	epu pataca epu mari
6	callu	230	epu pataca quila mari
7	regle	240	epu pataca meli mari
8	ailla	250	epu pataca quechu mari

Travel Agencies Multitour (☎ 237-913, fax 233-536), Bulnes 307, Oficina 203, operates reasonably priced excursions including city tours, visits to Mapuche villages and explorations of the national parks of the cordillera, and has English-speaking guides. Similar services are available from Turismo Ñielol (☎ 239-497) at Claro Solar 618, Oficina 1, and Turismo Sur de América (☎/fax 212-535), Antonio Varas 424, Departamento 28. For sample prices, see the Organized Tours entry later in this chapter.

Bookstores For materials on the Mapuche and regional history, visit Librería Universitaria, Portales 861.

Cultural Centers Temuco's Centro Cultural Municipal, at the junction of Av Balmaceda, Caupolicán and Prat, contains the city library, the Teatro Municipal (continued on p 336)

TEMUCO

PLACES TO STAY
1 Hotel Terraverde
9 Hotel Estacionamiento
15 Hospedaje Aroca
16 Hotel Bayern
19 Hospedaje Espejo
22 Hostal Francia 199
23 Hospedaje Muñoz
28 Residencial Temuco
38 Hotel Oriente
46 Hospedaje Montt
47 Hotel Nicolás
49 Nuevo Hotel Chapelco
51 Hostal Austria
56 Hospedaje Millaray
65 Hostal Casablanca
66 Hotel Espelette
69 Hotel Turismo
81 Hotel Continental
82 Nuevo Hotel
   de la Frontera
85 Hotel de la Frontera
87 Hotel Aitué
88 Hospedaje Tolosa
91 Hostal Aldunate

PLACES TO EAT
20 Pepperoni's
26 Tien Xiang
27 Bavaria
33 Dino's
36 Nuevo Pehuén
44 Il Gelato
45 Centro Español
48 Centro Arabe
50 Jairo's
52 Pizzería Madonna
76 Quincho de la Empanada
78 Club Alemán

OTHER
2 Conaf
3 Terminal de Buses Rurales
4 Flota Erbuc
5 Centro Cultural Municipal
6 Buses Panguisur
7 Buses Varmontt
8 Buses Ruta Sur
10 Buses Unión del Sud
11 Buses Inter Sur, Tur-Bus
12 Buses San Martín
13 Buses Igi Llaima, Nar-Bus
14 Rodoviario Curacautín
17 Buses Biobio
18 Buses Power
21 Jalisco
24 Club de Esquí Llaima
25 Casa de la Mujer Mapuche
29 Centro de Llamados
30 Centro de Extension de la
   Universidad Católica
31 Hospital Regional
32 Post Office, Telex-Chile
34 Librería Universitaria
35 Multitour
37 Centro de Ski
   Las Araucarias
39 Lavandería Autoservicio
   Marva
40 Club Temuco Soccer
   Team Offices

41 Avis Rent a Car
42 El Boliche de la Toñi
43 Transportes Aéreos Neuquén
53 Taller Artesanal
   Universidad Católica
54 Museo Regional
   de la Araucanía
55 Entel
57 Tur-Bus
58 Buses Fénix
59 Buses Bonanza
60 Chilesat
61 Entel
62 Ladeco, Avant
63 Ferrocarriles del Estadio
64 Sernatur
67 Cóndor Bus
68 Turismo Ñielol
70 Buses Tas Choapa

71 Buses Cruz del Sur,
   Pullman Sur
72 Casa de Cambio Global
73 Christopher Money
   Exchange
74 LanChile
75 Gerónimo
77 Del Turista
79 Turismo Sur de America
80 Buses Jac
83 Mosquito's Pub
84 Intercam
86 First Rent a Car
89 Tour Gira
90 Pub-Restaurant Emperador
92 Full Fama's Rent a Car
93 Automóvil Club de Chile
94 Hertz Rent a Car
95 Buses Lit

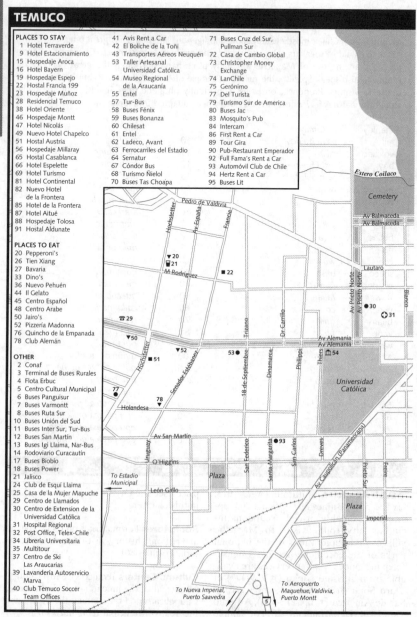

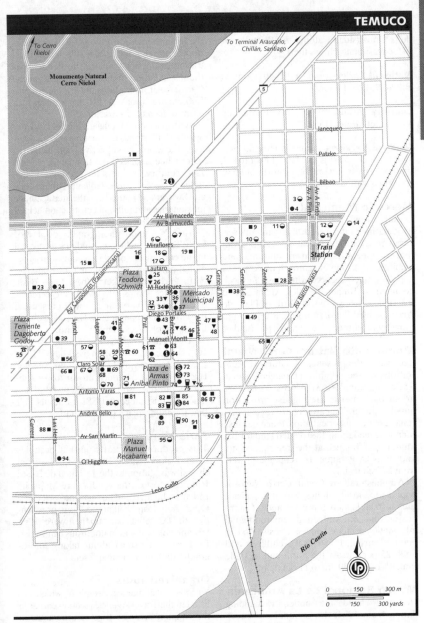

TEMUCO

Pablo Neruda (for shows and concerts), and an exhibition hall. The Centro de Extensión de la Universidad Católica, Av Prieto Norte 371, occasionally shows films.

National Parks Conaf (☎ 210-407) is at Av Bilbao 931, 2nd floor.

Laundry Lavandería Autoservicio Marva is at Manuel Montt 415.

Medical Services Temuco's Hospital Regional (☎ 212-525) is at Manuel Montt 115, six blocks west and one block north of Plaza de Armas Aníbal Pinto.

Mercado Municipal

Dating from 1929, the municipal market building integrates practical community services (fresh food and functional clothing) with tourist appeal (seafood restaurants and quality crafts). One of central Temuco's most popular attractions, occupying most of a block bounded by Bulnes, Portales, Aldunate and Rodríguez, it's two blocks north of Plaza de Armas Aníbal Pinto. Hours are 8 am to 7 pm Monday to Saturday, 8:30 am to 2 pm Sunday.

Monumento Natural Cerro Ñielol

Because of the presence of natural concentrations of the copihue *(Lapageria rosea,* Chile's national flower), this 85-hectare urban park merits the highest protection possible under Chilean forestry regulations. It has greater historical importance because Mapuche leaders, in 1881, ceded land for the founding of Temuco at the tree-shaded site known as **La Patagua**. The copihue flowers from March to July.

Administered by Conaf, Cerro Ñielol is popular for local outings, with many picnic sites, a small lagoon, footpaths and a Centro de Información Ambiental (environmental information center). Admission costs US$1.25 per pedestrian, US$0.30 for children and US$1.25 per car. At the north end of Calle Prat, it's open 8:30 am to 11 pm daily.

Museo Regional de La Araucanía

Housed in a handsome frontier-style building dating from 1924, the regional museum's permanent exhibits recount the history of the Araucanian peoples before, during and since the Spanish invasion. One particularly memorable presentation is a textile mural illustrating distinctions among the Pehuenches (hunter-gatherers of the cordillera), Mapuche (farmers of the plains and valleys) and Lafkenches (coastal fisher-gatherers) in terms of means of subsistence.

A display on Mapuche resistance to the Spaniards illustrates native weapons, but overlooks the Mapuche's effective guerrilla tactics. After Chile stabilized the frontier in the late 19th century, immigrants from Germany, Belgium, Spain, France, Holland, Britain, Italy and Switzerland poured into the area. Catholic missionaries and railroad construction helped consolidate Chilean authority.

There's a good photographic display of early Temuco, including buildings destroyed in the earthquake of 1960; a collection of regional paintings; and a sample of Mapuche crafts, including basketry from Lago Budi; and textiles, looms, silverwork and ceremonial objects. Everything is well-presented, but labeled in Spanish only. The 5000-volume library emphasizes Mapuche culture.

At Av Alemania 084, the museum (☎ 211-108) is open 9 am to 5 pm weekdays, 11 am to 5 pm Saturday, and 11 am to 2 pm Sunday. Bus No 9 runs from downtown to Av Alemania, but it's also reasonable walking distance. Admission costs US$1 for adults, half that for children; it's free on Sunday.

Feria Libre

This produce and crafts market occupies several blocks along Barros Arana – from the railway station to the Terminal de Buses Rurales. Most of the vendors are Mapuche Indians who arrive in horse or bullock carts. Open daily from 9:30 am to 4 pm, or whenever the last sellers pack up their wares, it's a vibrant, colorful and malodorous can't-miss. Be *very* circumspect about taking photographs, though, as people resent it.

Organized Tours

Various travel agencies, some of which are listed in the Travel Agencies section earlier in the chapter, organize trips to attractions in and around the city. However, it may be more convenient to arrange some of these trips in Villarrica or Pucón. A city tour of Temuco costs about US$20 per person. Sample fares for full-day excursions, with lunch, include Lican Ray (US$32), Termas de Huife (US$34), Termas del Palguín (US$34), Parque Nacional Conguillío (US$34), Valdivia and Niebla (US$56) and Lago Budi and Puerto Saavedra (US$37). Discounts are often available for groups as small as two or three.

Places to Stay

Prices for accommodations have stabilized in recent years, but it can still pay to call ahead or look around. Some of the places closest to the train station and the Feria Libre are less than reputable, but some otherwise mid-range places have rooms with shared bath at budget rates.

Budget The friendly HI affiliate *Residencial Temuco* (☎ 233-721, Rodríguez 1341, 2nd floor) charges US$8.50 per person with breakfast, but it's small and often full in summer.

Clean, friendly *Hospedaje Espejo* (☎ 238-408, Aldunate 124) has singles for US$7; breakfast costs US$1 more. For about US$7.50, *Hospedaje Tolosa* (☎ 323-290, Las Heras 832) is a friendly but simple family-run place on a quiet street, though it may have to move because of lease complications. In the US$8.50 range are *Hospedaje Montt* (☎ 211-856, Manuel Montt 965, Departamento 301) and amiable *Hospedaje Aroca* (☎ 234-205, Lautaro 591).

Hospedaje Muñoz (☎ 230-268, Rodríguez 361) charges US$9.50 but may be negotiable. *Hostal Aldunate* (☎/fax 231-128, Aldunate 864) *charges US$10 per person with shared bath*. Well-located *Hospedaje Millaray* (☎ 211-384, Claro Solar 471) charges US$10 with shared bath, US$12 with private bath.

Hostal Casablanca (☎/fax 212-740, Manuel Montt 1306) has singles for US$10 with shared bath and breakfast, US$16 with private bath, breakfast and cable TV. *Hotel Espelette* (☎ 234-805, Claro Solar 492) compares favorably for US$11 per person with shared bath, but rooms with private bath cost US$26/35. Rates at *Hotel Oriente* (☎ 233-232, Manuel Rodríguez 1146) are US$11/19 with shared bath, US$18/33 with private bath.

Mid-Range In residential west Temuco, *Hostal Austria* (☎/fax 247-169, Hochstetter 599) is an outstanding choice for US$15 per person with IVA discounted. Also in west Temuco, *Hostal Francia 199* (☎ 235-594, Francia 199) charges US$18 per person with shared bath and breakfast, but only US$20 with private bath.

Family-run *Hotel Turismo* (☎ 210-583, fax 212-932, Claro Solar 636) has spacious rooms with comfy beds from US$15/28 singles/doubles with breakfast and shared bath, but rooms with private bath cost US$31/41. The oddly named *Hotel Estacionamiento* (☎ 215-503, Balmaceda 1246) charges US$25/30 for carpeted rooms with private bath, cable TV and hot tub. *Nuevo Hotel Chapelco* (☎ 213-473, General Cruz 401) is comparable for US$27/33.

For over a century, rambling *Hotel Continental* (☎ 238-973, fax 233-830, Varas 709) has hosted guests such as poets Gabriela Mistral and Pablo Neruda, and presidents Pedro Aguirre Cerda and Salvador Allende. Rates begin at US$19/31 for singles/doubles with general bath (down the hall), while rooms with shared baths (one for every two rooms) cost US$33/38, and rooms with private bath cost US$40/44. Even if you don't stay at this singular hotel, you can enjoy a reasonably priced lunch in its classic dining room, or a drink at its equally classic bar. Though past its prime, it's still professionally run.

Top End The *Hotel Nicolás* (☎ 210-020, fax 213-468, General Mackenna 420), with smallish but bright and cheery rooms with private bath and TV for US$41/52, is a good choice, and the restaurant's meals are a good value. *Hotel de la Frontera* (☎/fax 200-400), Bulnes 733) charges US$52 single or double, including access to the indoor pool and other facilities of its across-the-street sister *Nuevo Hotel de la Frontera* (☎ 200-401, Bulnes 726), which charges twice as much.

Try also *Hotel Bayern* (☎ 213-915, fax 212-291, Prat 146), whose rates of US$57/73, with buffet breakfast, may be negotiable. Despite its unimpressive exterior, *Hotel Aitué* (☎ 211-917, fax 212-608, Varas 1048) is a good value at US$59/75.

On the northern outskirts of town, the *Holiday Inn Express* (☎ 233-300, fax 224-100, Av Rudecindo Ortega 1800) is a North American chain charging US$100 single or double. Rates at *Hotel Terraverde* (☎ 239-999, fax 239-455, hotpanam@ctc-mundo.net, Prat 0220), a new luxury high-rise near Cerro Ñielol, are US$122/141.

Places to Eat

Temuco's cheapest food is available around the train station and the Terminal de Buses Rurales, but the best value is the seafood at various *puestos* (stands) in the Mercado Municipal at Portales and Aldunate – don't leave Temuco without trying it. *El Caribe*, Puesto 45 in the market, is an outstanding value, but the slightly more formal and upscale *La Caleta* (☎ 213-002) is worth a splurge. *Don Jeyo* (☎ 214-335) at Puesto 55, *El Turista* (☎ 238-056) at Puesto 32 and *El Criollito* (☎ 212-583) at Puestos 38 and 39 are other good choices. Market restaurants close early, around 7 pm.

For fast food, try *Dino's* (☎ 213-660, Bulnes 360), *Bavaria* (☎ 213-401, Manuel Rodríguez 1073), or the relocated *Pizzería Madonna* (☎ 249-191, Av Alemania 0660). Traditional Chilean cuisine is the rule at *Quincho de la Empanada* (☎ 216-307, Aldunate 698) and *Nuevo Pehuén* (☎ 214-468, Bulnes 317). *Tien Xiang* (☎ 214-485, Prat 295) is the choice for Chinese cuisine.

For Mediterranean food, check out the *Centro Español* (☎ 238-664, Bulnes 483), but for heartier middle-European fare try the *Club Alemán* (☎ 240-034, Senador Estébanez 772). The *Centro Arabe* (☎ 215-080, General Mackenna 462) serves Middle Eastern food, while *Pepperoni's* (☎ 261-271, Hochstetter 425) specializes in pizza and pasta. *Jairo's* (☎ 248-849, Av Alemania 0830) is for seafood. *Il Gelato* (Bulnes 420) has fine ice cream.

Entertainment

The Universidad Católica (☎ 210-773), Montt 56, shows quality films.

Club Temuco (☎ 211-004), Lagos 459, is the city's first-division soccer team. It plays in the Estadio Municipal, at the west end of León Gallo.

Temuco now has a number of pub-restaurants that are best described as gathering places, but the food is usually palatable. Among them are *Mosquito's Pub* (☎ 213-920, Bulnes 778); *Gerónimo* (☎ 230-041, Varas 983); the sandwich-oriented *Pub-Restaurant Emperador* (Bulnes 853); and the Tex-Mex *Jalisco* (☎ 243-254, Hochstetter 435).

Shopping

Despite a lot of junk and kitsch, the Mercado Municipal remains a good place to find Mapuche woolen ponchos, blankets and pullovers, jewelry, pottery, polished stone mortars and musical instruments such as *zampoñas* (pan pipes) and drums. Many women also hawk these goods on the streets.

Run by a cooperative of 135 women, the Casa de la Mujer Mapuche (☎ 233-886), Prat 283, sells a wide selection of traditional indigenous crafts, most notably textiles and ceramics. Profits benefit members of the cooperative in the form of literacy classes, crafts training and cash. The artisans are often available to discuss their work.

Other good places to look for crafts are the Galería de Arte beneath the bandstand in the Plaza de Armas, El Boliche de la Toñi at Montt 743 Interior and the Taller Artesanal Universidad Católica at Av Alemania 0422.

Del Turista, on Hochstetter near the corner of Holandesa, is the local branch of an Argentine chain of specialist chocolates.

Getting There & Away

Air LanChile (☎ 211-339), Bulnes 687, has 17 flights weekly to Santiago (US$78 to US$120); there are two flights daily Monday and Tuesday, and one every Wednesday, Thursday and Saturday to Osorno (US$30), and weekend flights to Valdivia (US$20). Ladeco (☎ 213-180), at Prat 565, Local 2, has 11 flights weekly to Santiago, daily flights to

Valdivia, and Wednesday, Friday and weekend flights to Osorno.

Avant (☎ 270-670), Prat 565, Local 101, flies 18 times weekly to Santiago (US$73 to US$105), occasionally via Concepción (US$28), twice each weekday and once Saturday and Sunday to Puerto Montt (US$32), the Saturday flight continuing to Punta Arenas (US$75 to US$135), and Saturday to Valdivia (US$15).

Transportes Aéreos Neuquén or TAN (☎ 210-500), Portales 840, connects Temuco with Neuquén, Argentina, on Monday, Wednesday, Friday and Sunday. Fares range from US$70 to US$88.

Bus Temuco is a major transport hub; its new and long overdue Terminal Araucario (☎ 255-005) is on Av Rudecindo Ortega, at the northern approach to town, but most long-distance companies have ticket offices in or near downtown. Times and frequencies vary throughout the year, with fewer buses in winter.

Besides destinations on or near the Panamericana between Puerto Montt and Santiago, there are frequent connections to nearby national parks such as Conguillío, to Curarrehue and to lakeside resorts such as Villarrica and Lican Ray. There are also international services to the Argentine cities of San Martín de los Andes, Zapala and Neuquén, to Bariloche via Osorno, and to Mendoza and Buenos Aires via Santiago.

The Terminal de Buses Rurales (☎ 210-494) is at Av Balmaceda and Av Pinto; for local and regional destinations not mentioned below, check the schedules of the many companies at the terminal. The Rodoviario Curacautín, Barros Arana 191, is the departure point for buses to Curacautín, Lonquimay and the upper Biobío.

Many companies operate between Santiago and Puerto Montt, most of them also serving Concepción and Valdivia. Among them are Cruz del Sur (☎ 210-701), Vicuña Mackenna 671, which also serves the island of Chiloé; Pullman Sur, at the same office; Tas Choapa (☎ 212-422), Varas 609, which has a nightly direct service (11:15 pm) to Valparaíso

and Viña del Mar without transfer in Santiago; Fénix (☎ 212-582), Claro Solar 609; Tur-Bus (☎ 234-349), Lagos 538. There's also Buses Lit (☎ 211-483), San Martín 894; Igi Llaima (☎ 210-364), Miraflores 1535; Varmontt (☎ 211-114), Bulnes 45; the inexpensive Buses Power (☎ 236-513), Bulnes 178; Inter Sur (☎ 234-278) at Balmaceda 1372, where Tur-Bus has another ticket office; and Bonanza (☎ 213-094), Vicuña Mackenna 586.

Cóndor Bus (☎ 230-979), Claro Solar 598, the inexpensive Tur-Bus subsidiary, goes to Santiago, Pucón and intermediates. Buses Jac (☎ 210-313), Vicuña Mackenna 798, offers about 29 buses daily to Villarrica and Pucón, plus four daily to Coñaripe, and a daily service to Curarrehue. Panguisur (☎ 211-560), Miraflores 871, has 11 buses daily to Panguipulli, plus three nightly to Santiago.

Buses Biobío (☎ 210-599), Lautaro 853, runs frequent services to Angol, Los Angeles and Concepción. Nar-Bus (☎ 233-958), Miraflores 1535, and Flota Erbuc (☎ 212-939), at Av Balmaceda 1415, have regular buses to Lonquimay, on the upper Biobío near the Argentine border.

Sample fares and times include Curacautín (US$3, 1½ hours) Panguipulli (US$3), Angol (US$3.50, two hours), Coñaripe or Curarrehue (US$4, 2½ hours), Ancud (US$12, seven hours), Osorno (US$6, three hours), Puerto Montt (US$8, five hours), Castro (US$14, eight hours), Quellón (US$17, 11 hours), Valdivia or Los Angeles (US$4, three hours), Chillán (US$6.50, four hours), Concepción (US$7.50, 4½ hours), Talca (US$10, seven hours), Santiago (US$15 to US$17, eight hours) and Valparaíso-Viña del Mar (US$18 to US$20, 10 hours). Salón cama buses to Santiago cost around US$30.

Services across the Andes to Argentina are becoming more frequent, but usually leave very early, between 3 and 6 am. Competition has been driving prices down. Igi Llaima, Nar-Bus, Buses San Martín (☎ 234-017), Balmaceda 1598, and Buses Ruta Sur (☎ 233-043), Miraflores 1151, connect Temuco with Junín de los Andes, San Martín de los Andes (US$19, six hours), Zapala and Neuquén

(US$30, 10 hours). These services usually go via Paso Mamuil Malal east of Pucón, but occasionally over Paso Pino Hachado, directly east of Temuco via Curacautín and Lonquimay, along the upper Biobío.

Tas Choapa, Cruz del Sur and Unión del Sud (☎ 232-257), Miraflores 1285, have daily services to Bariloche (US$30), via Paso Cardenal Samoré east of Osorno.

Train The train from Temuco goes north to Santiago (about 11½ hours) at 8 pm nightly, stopping at various stations en route. Fares are US$12 for económica, US$14 for turista, US$20 for salón, US$33 cama alta, and US$44 cama baja.

Buy tickets either at the Estación de Ferrocarril (☎ 233-416), on Av Barros Arana eight blocks east of Plaza de Armas Aníbal Pinto, or at the downtown office of Ferrocarriles del Estado (EFE; ☎ 233-522), Bulnes 582. Fares to Santiago are about US$15 económica, US$26 salón, US$36 cama alta, and US$56 cama baja.

Getting Around

While Temuco has begun to sprawl, with the railway station and main bus terminal some distance from downtown, any taxi colectivo will quickly take you there. Bus No 1 runs from downtown to the train station.

Temuco's Aeropuerto Maquehue is 6km south of town, just off the Panamericana. Taxis leaving from the west side of the Plaza de Armas take passengers for US$5. Tour Gira (☎ 272-041), Andrés Bello 870, Local 5, will also take you to the airport, with notice.

From downtown Temuco, Micro No 7 goes directly to the new Terminal Araucario (☎ 255-005), on Av Rudecindo Ortega near Lemunao.

Car rental is worth considering for access to the surrounding national parks and Mapuche settlements. Vehicles are available from the Automóvil Club (☎ 215-132) at San Martín 0278, Hertz (☎ 235-385) at Las Heras 999, Avis (☎ 238-013) at Vicuña Mackenna 448 and at the airport, and First (☎ 233-890) at Varas 1036. Full Fama's (☎/fax 215-420), Andrés Bello 1096, has probably the cheapest rates.

CHOL CHOL

Mapuche oxcarts ply the dusty streets of Chol Chol, a village of wooden, tin-roofed bungalows with traditional Mapuche *rucas* (wood and thatch houses) on its outskirts. Chol Chol retains the atmosphere of a frontier town where time has stood still, or at least run slowly.

From Temuco's Terminal de Buses Rurales, Buses Epaza and Huinca Bus (☎ 210-494) travel about 1½ hours to Chol Chol, the former via Nueva Imperial and the latter direct, for US$1. The bus is likely to be jammed with Mapuches returning from the market with fruits and vegetables.

PARQUE NACIONAL TOLHUACA

Nestled in the precordillera northeast of Temuco, on the north bank of the Río Malleco, 6400-hectare Tolhuaca is one of the Chilean park system's best-kept secrets, a tranquil forested getaway with excellent camping, fishing and hiking. In January and February it sometimes gets crowded, especially on weekends, but poor roads and the absence of public transport generally help keep the peace.

Laguna Malleco, the park's most conspicuously accessible feature, is a glacial relic slowly becoming a meadow as *junquillos* (reeds) colonize the shoreline sediments from the surrounding volcanic mountains. Elevations range from 850m around Laguna Malleco to 1830m on the summit of Cerro Colomahuida; 2806m Volcán Tolhuaca is beyond the park boundaries. Rainfall reaches 3000mm per year, but summer is relatively dry.

Activities

Where it passes through the campground at Inalaufquén, the westward-flowing Río Malleco has several pools suitable for swimming. Shallow **Laguna Malleco** is a good spot for watching waterfowl or fishing (ask the Conaf ranger for oars to the rowboat).

Along the north shore of Laguna Malleco, a signed nature trail leads through dense forest of raulí, coigüe, quila (both species of southern beech) and araucaria to its outlet, where the **Salto Malleco** (Malleco

Falls) tumbles 50m over resistant columnar basalt into a deep pool, surrounded by massive nalcas and water-loving ferns and mosses. The trail continues down to the river, through even denser vegetation.

From the north shore of Laguna Malleco, another trail climbs steeply to the **Prados de Mesacura**, and continues east to **Lagunillas** through an araucaria forest with outstanding panoramas. Water is scarce on this trail, which is a full-day excursion; carry sufficient food as well.

The park's best overnight backpacking trip goes to **Laguna Verde**, reached via a trailhead about 5km east of Laguna Malleco, on the road to Termas de Tolhuaca. The trail crosses the Río Malleco and passes several waterfalls before reaching campsites on the north side of 1605m Cerro Laguna Verde.

Places to Stay
On the southeastern shore of Laguna Malleco, Conaf's *Camping Inalaufquén* has secluded woodsy sites for US$13, including running water, firepits, picnic tables and immaculate toilets with cold showers. Backpackers may negotiate a smaller per person charge.

Getting There & Away
From Victoria's Terminal de Buses Rurales, on the Panamericana, Buses San Gregorio goes weekdays at 4 pm to the village of San Gregorio; from there it's about a 20km walk to the campground at Laguna Malleco. Beyond San Gregorio, the road narrows rapidly and deadfalls may be a problem after storms, but any carefully driven passenger car can pass in good weather. This would be an ideal mountain bike route, as it climbs gradually into the precordillera.

From the town of Curacautín, north of Parque Nacional Conguillío, taxi colectivos ply a rugged but passable gravel road to the hot springs resort of Termas de Tolhuaca (see the section of that name later in this chapter), but the 10km-long logging road between the Termas and Laguna Malleco is impossible for ordinary passenger cars and difficult even with high clearance, making 4WD desirable.

PARQUE NACIONAL CONGUILLÍO
Created primarily to preserve the distinctive araucaria, or monkey-puzzle tree, Conguillío shelters 60,835 hectares of alpine lakes, deep canyons and native forests surrounding 3125m Volcán Llaima. Since 1640, Llaima has experienced 34 violent eruptions, most recently in 1957. Some 2000 years ago, a lava flow off Llaima's northern flank dammed the Río Truful-Truful to form Laguna Conguillío, Laguna Arco Iris and Laguna Verde.

Geography & Climate
In the Region IX province of Cautín, Conguillío is about 80km directly east of Temuco via Vilcún and Cherquenco, but about 120km via the northern access point of Curacautín or the southern access point of Melipeuco. Its most conspicuous feature is Llaima's smoldering, snow-covered cone, but rugged lava fields cover much of the rest of the park. The glaciated peaks of the Sierra Nevada, north of Laguna Conguillío, consistently exceed 2500m, but park elevations descend as low as 700m.

Conguillío experiences warm summers, but up to 3m of snow can accumulate in winter. Mean annual precipitation is about

PARQUE NACIONAL CONGUILLÍO

1 Los Ñirres, Los Carpinteros
2 Cabañas Conguillío
3 Laguna Captrén
4 Playa Curacautín, Centro de Información Ambiental
5 El Estero
6 La Caseta
7 Playa Linda
8 Refugio Escuela Ski
9 Centro de Ski Las Arucarias

2000mm, falling almost entirely between May and September. November to April is the best time for a visit.

Flora & Fauna

Conguillío's woodlands are more open than the denser Valdivian rain forest to the south. At lower elevations, around 1000m to 1150m, they consist of *coigue (Nothofagus dombeyi)* and *roble (Nothofagus obliqua)*, but roble gives way to *raulí (Nothofagus alpina)* between 1200m and 1400m. Above 1400m, mixed forests of araucaria, coigue and *ñirre (Nothofagus antarctica)* predominate, while the highest elevations consist of araucaria and *lenga (Nothofagus pumilio)*.

Known to Spanish-speakers as *paragua* (the umbrella) because of its unusual shape, the araucaria is *pehuén* to the Mapuche, who have traditionally gathered nuts from its cones as food. Often colloquially bunched with pines, the araucaria family is limited to the Southern Hemisphere, but once enjoyed a much wider distribution into North America; its presence has made Conguillío a Unesco Biosphere Reserve.

Information

Conaf's **Centro de Información Ambiental** at Laguna Conguillío is usually open 10 am to 1 pm and 3 to 7:30 pm daily. It offers a variety of programs in January and February, including slide shows and ecology talks, hikes to the Sierra Nevada, outings for children and boat excursions on the lake. Excursions usually take place in the morning, nature talks in the afternoon or early evening.

Rowboats rent for about US$2 per hour on Laguna Conguillío.

Sierra Nevada

One of Chile's finest short hikes, the trail to the base of the Sierra Nevada leaves from the small parking lot at Playa Linda, at the east end of Laguna Conguillío. Climbing steadily northeast through dense coigue forests, the trail passes a pair of lake overlooks, the second and more scenic of which is sited where solid stands of araucarias begin to supplant coigues on the ridgetop.

On the more exposed second half of the hike, continuing along the ridgetop, biting tábanos are a problem unless there's a breeze. Natural history lovers will take more pleasure from the abundant *lagartija (Liolaemus tenuis*, a tiny lizard) and the rosette succulent *añañisca (Rhodophiala andina)*, growing where humus formed from fallen ñire leaves has begun to mix with volcanic ash to form an incipient soil.

Conaf discourages all but the most experienced, well-prepared hikers from continuing north over the Sierra Nevada to Termas Río Blanco, an excursion detailed in *Trekking in the Patagonian Andes*, because route finding is so difficult and at least one person has died on the trip. Nevertheless, anyone can undertake the two-hour hike to the ridgetop, which provides superb views of Laguna Conguillío, expansive araucaria forests and numerous waterfalls.

Sector Los Paraguas

Experienced climbers can tackle Volcán Llaima from Sector Los Paraguas on the west side of the park, where there is a refugio on the road from Cherquenco, or from Captrén on the north side. Before climbing, ask permission from Conaf in Temuco.

In winter, when snow may close the road to Laguna Conguillío, there is downhill skiing at Los Paraguas, whose Centro de Ski Las Araucarias (☎ 045-562-313) has provided long-overdue new installations; its Temuco office (☎ 045-274-141) is at Bulnes 351, Oficina 47. Contact also the Club de Esquí Llaima (☎ 237-923), Las Heras 299 in Temuco, which offers classes and rental equipment.

Other Things to See & Do

Near the visitor center, the **Sendero Araucarias** is a half-hour walk through a verdant rain forest. At present, backcountry camping is not permitted within the park, but Conaf still hopes to open the so-called **Ruta de los Pehuenches**, a series of Indian trails from the precordillera into the mountains. Likewise, within a few years, the park may be open for winter use and accessible for cross-country skiing.

Formed when lava flows from **El Escorial** dammed the river, **Laguna Arco Iris** is worth a stop for travelers in the southern part of the park; the nearby **Casa del Colono**, an early pioneer's cabin, is a historical monument of minor significance. At **Laguna Verde**, a short trail goes to La Ensenada, a peaceful beach area; in 10 million years or so, as the weaker volcanic rock erodes, the granitic outcrops across the lake could become another Torres del Paine.

Travelers interested in vulcanism should visit the canyon of the **Río Truful-Truful**, whose colorful strata, exposed by the rushing waters, are a vivid record of Llaima's numerous eruptions. Near the trail an attractive waterfall plunges into a small but lush rain forest basin, while there are also some impressive hexagonal basalt columns. The shorter **Los Vertientes** trail leads to an open spot among rushing springs.

Places to Stay & Eat
At present, backcountry camping is not permitted. A private concessionaire has taken control over campgrounds at *Los Ñirres* (44 sites), *El Estero* (10 sites), *Los Carpinteros* (12 sites) and *La Caseta* (20 sites), all on or near the south shore of Laguna Conguillío. In January, February and during Semana Santa (Holy Week) these are expensive at US$25 for two tents with up to five persons; the rest of the year, they are half-price. Conaf reserves a limited number of backpacker sites for US$5 per person at El Estero, specifically for those arriving on foot or bicycle. At *Laguna Captrén*, at the northwest entrance to the park, sites are available for US$25 from mid-January to the end of February; they go for only US$10 the rest of the year.

At the southwest end of Laguna Conguillío, *Cabañas Conguillío (☎ 214-363, 211-493 in Temuco)*, a Conaf-authorized concessionaire, operates accommodations, a restaurant and a small store from mid-December to early March. Built around the trunks of araucaria trees, their cabañas cost US$63 per night for four people, US$104 for six. Though the price includes stove, fuel and cooking utensils, the cabañas are overpriced for what is basic, if picturesque, accommodations.

These are due to be demolished and replaced in the near future.

At Sector Los Paraguas, the *Refugio Escuela Ski (☎ 045-237-923 in Temuco)* has 70 beds and a restaurant, but has become rundown. The new Centro de Ski Las Araucarias (☎ 045-562-313) rents six-bed apartments for US$84, but there are also dormitory accommodations for US$12 per person; lift tickets cost US$14 weekdays, US$18 weekends. Weeklong packages with dormitory accommodations, including full board and lift tickets, cost only US$220 – but you need your own sleeping bag. For more details, including transport suggestions, contact the Temuco office (☎ 045-274-141), Bulnes 351, Oficina 49.

Getting There & Away
There are several ways to approach the park. To reach Sector Los Paraguas from Temuco's Terminal de Buses Rurales, take one of Flota Erbuc buses (☎ 212-939), which run a dozen times daily to the village of Cherquenco (US$1). From Cherquenco it's necessary to walk or hitchhike 17km to the ski lodge at Los Paraguas.

It's possible to approach Sector Conguillío from either the north or south. The northern route takes the Panamericana to Victoria, then the paved highway east to Curacautín, which is 42km from the park headquarters (an alternative to Curacautín goes via a gravel road from Lautaro). Erbuc has six buses daily via Victoria (US$2) and four via Lautaro (US$2.50). Two buses weekly, Monday and Friday at 6 am, go as far as the park entrance at Guardería Laguna Captrén in summer; the rest of the year they go only to the junction of the rugged road (4WDs only) to Sector Los Paraguas. Otherwise, from Curacautín it may be necessary to hitchhike the 15km to Laguna Conguillío. In heavy rain, ordinary passenger vehicles may not be able to pass the road from Laguna Conguillío to Laguna Captrén.

The southern route to Sector Conguillío passes through the villages of Cunco and Melipeuco. Nar-Bus (☎ 045-211-611) in Temuco runs seven buses daily to Melipeuco (US$2.50) where Hostería Huentelén can arrange a cab to park headquarters. Travelers who can afford to rent a car can combine these two routes in a loop trip from Temuco.

CURACAUTÍN
☎ 45

Curacautín (population 12,700), the northern gateway to Parque Nacional Conguillío, is also a convenient staging point for excursions into the upper Biobío drainage. The scenic road from Victoria, on the Panamericana, continues eastward to Lago Galletué, the starting point for rafting trips down the endangered river.

Curacautín's Oficina de Informaciones Turísticas is at the bus terminal, on the north side of the Plaza de Armas. Money can be changed at Turismo Christopher, Yungay 206. Entel is at Serrano 175.

Places to Stay & Eat

Curacautín's best value is *Hostal Rayén* (*Manuel Rodríguez 104*), a family-run place with comfortable rooms and excellent showers in a spacious shared bathroom for about US$10 per person. *Residencial Rojas* (*Tarapacá 249*) is also inexpensive.

The *Hotel Turismo* (☎ *811-116, Tarapacá 140*) charges US$11/20 singles/doubles, while *Hotel Plaza* (☎ *881-256, Yungay 175*) is ordinary but passable for US$17 per person.

Facing the Plaza de Armas, *La Cabaña* (*Yungay 157*) has good sandwiches.

Getting There & Away

Curacautín's Terminal Rodoviario is at Arica and Manuel Rodríguez, directly on the highway to Lonquimay. Erbuc goes to Conguillío (US$1.20) Monday and Friday at 6 am, four times daily to Lonquimay, and also connects to Temuco (US$3) six times daily via Victoria, and four times via Lautaro. Some buses to Argentina, via Paso de Pino Hachado, pass through Curacautín, but these usually fill up in Temuco.

TERMAS DE TOLHUACA

Some 35km north of Curacautín via a rough but passable gravel road, Termas de Tolhuaca is a modest hot springs resort that has undergone substantial remodeling. A long,

hot soak at the fairly rustic baths costs only about US$6 for adults, half that for children. Camping costs US$10 for up to six persons, while rooms at *Hotel Termas de Tolhuaca* cost US$52 per person with full board. For more information, contact Transporte, Turismo y Agrícola Tolhuaca (☎ 045-881-211), Calama 240, Curacautín.

From Termas de Tolhuaca, a rugged, dusty logging road, best suited to 4WDs and hazardous without high clearance, leads to Parque Nacional Tolhuaca, described earlier in the chapter.

LONQUIMAY & UPPER BIOBÍO

The paved highway east of Curacautín leads climbs to the hot springs resort of **Manzanar**, where *Hotel Abarzúa* (☎ *045-870-011*) has decent lodging for US$10 to US$12 per person and a reasonable orchard campground (US$5 per site) with hot showers, but barking dogs and mooing cows can disturb the peace; its restaurant is expensive but mediocre. *Hotel Termas de Manzanar* (☎ *045-881-200*), at Km 18, is a traditional spa resort with rates as low as US$19 per person for shared-bath accommodations (US$45 with full board) up to US$49 per person with private hot tubs (US$93 with full board).

The road then passes Conaf's 31,305-hectare **Reserva Nacional Malalcahuello**, which has some hiking trails; at Km 28, Swiss-run *El Encuentro* (☎ *09-884-9541, fax 045-881-892*) offers camping for US$4 per person, dormitory accommodations for US$7 per person with breakfast, and cabañas for US$9 per person with breakfast. Túnel Las Raíces, a converted railway tunnel, is open for alternating one-way traffic that emerges into the drainage of the upper Biobío. The road, by now a gravel surface, forks north to the town of Lonquimay, which has an unusual oval street plan, a tourist office, and various tourist services including hotels (these may all be closed out of season). A shorter but steeper and dustier route to Lonquimay, over the Cuesta la Raíces, passes the modest **Centro de Esquí Lonquimay** (☎ 045-881-106) at the foot of 2865m Volcán Lonquimay, part of Reserva Nacional Malalcahuello.

The main road's southern fork passes Conaf's **Reserva Nacional Galletué,** where there's the basic, Pehuenche-run *Camping del Nacimiento del Río Biobío* for US$6 per site at Lago Galletué, source of the Biobío. The river then brushes the Argentine border at the post of Icalma (several Pehuenche-run campgrounds), before heading west toward Melipeuco, the southern approach to Parque Nacional Conguillío. East of Lonquimay, a gravel road reaches 1884m Paso Pino Hachado, a border crossing that leads to the Argentine cities of Zapala and Neuquén.

MELIPEUCO

Melipeuco, the southern gateway to Conguillío, is 90km east of Temuco via Cunco. It has a summer-only tourist office on Pedro Aguirre Cerda, alongside the YPF gas station, where it's possible to exchange dollars or Argentine pesos, but at poor rates.

Reasonable accommodations and so-so food are available at *Hostería Huetelén (☎ 581-005, Pedro Aguirre Cerda 1)* starting at US$21 single or double with private bath. Accommodations are nearly as good, and cheaper at US$10 per person, at *Hospedaje Muñoz (Aurelio Letelier 80)*, which also offers orchard camping and river access. Try also simple *Hospedaje Icalma (Pedro Aguirre Cerda 729)* for US$6.50 per person.

From Temuco's Terminal de Buses Rurales, Nar-Bus has seven buses daily to Melipeuco. Although there's no scheduled transport from Melipeuco to Conguillío, it's possible to hire a cab or car to the visitor center for about US$15.

VILLARRICA
☎ 45

Sharing its name with the smoldering, snow-capped volcano that dominates its skyline and the lake on which it lies, Villarrica is a traditional resort town that, while it remains popular, has lost ground to nearby Pucón. Some visitors, though, prefer Villarrica's tranquil stability to Pucón's chaotic transience.

Founded in 1552 by Gerónimo de Alderete, Santa María Magdalena de Villarrica failed to withstand repeated Mapuche attacks during colonial times. According to

one commentator of the era, the Indians were well beyond Spanish authority:

The ruins of this city are yet visible, particularly those of the walls of orchards and of a church. The town stood on the side of a lake…about 25 miles in circumference, and abounding with fish. The soil is very fertile, and the Indians raise maize, potatoes, quinoa, peas, beans, barley and wheat. Apple, pear, peach and cherry-trees are seen growing where they were planted by the Spaniards before the destruction of the city. The Indians neither admit missionaries nor comisario. They have all kinds of cattle and poultry, which they exchange with other tribes for ponchos, flannels, being very averse to trade with the Spaniards.

Not until 1883 did the Mapuche toqui Epuléf allow the Chilean state, in the person of Colonel Gregorio Urrutia, to maintain a permanent presence in the territory. German colonists have left a visible legacy.

Orientation

On the southwest shore of Lago Villarrica, where the Río Toltén drains the lake toward the Pacific, Villarrica is 86km southwest of Temuco. The city itself (permanent population about 20,000) displays a fairly regular grid pattern, bounded by the irregular lakeshore on the north, Av JM Carrera to the west, the diagonal Presidente JA Ríos on the south and Aviador Acevedo to the east. The important commercial streets are Av Pedro de Valdivia (the major thoroughfare) and Camilo Henríquez (which becomes Alderete south of Pedro de Valdivia).

Information

The municipal Oficina de Turismo (☎ 411-162, villamun@entelchile.net) is at Pedro de Valdivia 1070, near Aviador Acevedo. From January 1 to March 31, it's open 8:30 am to 11 pm daily; the rest of the year, hours are 8:30 am to 1 pm and 2:30 to 6:30 pm, except for December, when it's open 8:30 am to 8:30 pm. The staff are helpful, providing many leaflets, including the useful *Datos Utiles Villarrica*, and a current list of accommodations and prices. Banco de Crédito has an ATM at the corner of Pedro de Valdivia and Gerónimo

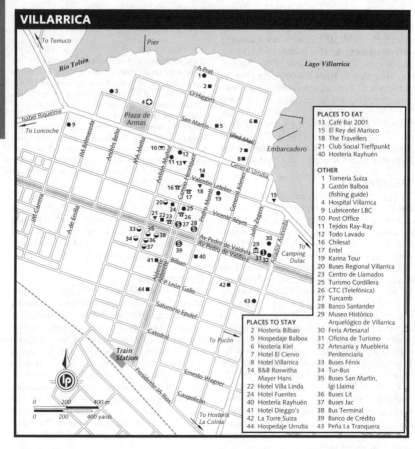

VILLARRICA

PLACES TO EAT
13 Café Bar 2001
15 El Rey del Marisco
18 The Travellers
21 Club Social Treffpunkt
40 Hostería Rayhuén

OTHER
1 Tornería Suiza
3 Gastón Balboa
   (fishing guide)
4 Hospital Villarrica
9 Lubricenter LBC
10 Post Office
11 Tejidos Ray-Ray
12 Todo Lavado
16 Chilesat
17 Entel
19 Karina Tour
20 Buses Regional Villarrica
23 Centro de Llamados
25 Turismo Cordillera
26 CTC (Telefónica)
27 Turcamb
28 Banco Santander
29 Museo Histórico
   Arqueológico de Villarrica
30 Feria Artesanal
31 Oficina de Turismo
32 Artesanía y Mueblería
   Penitenciaria
33 Buses Fénix
34 Tur-Bus
35 Buses San Martín,
   Igi Llaima
36 Buses Lit
37 Buses Jac
38 Bus Terminal
39 Banco de Crédito
43 Peña La Tranquera

PLACES TO STAY
2 Hostería Bilbao
5 Hospedaje Balboa
6 Hostería Kiel
7 Hotel El Ciervo
8 Hotel Villarrica
14 B&B Roswitha
   Mayer Hans
22 Hotel Villa Linda
24 Hotel Fuentes
40 Hostería Rayhuén
41 Hotel Dieggo's
42 La Torre Suiza
44 Hospedaje Urrutia

de Alderete, while Banco Santander has one at Pedro de Valdivia 778.

Turcamb, Camilo Henríquez 570, changes US cash and traveler's checks.

Correos de Chile is at Anfión Muñoz 315. CTC (Telefónica) long-distance offices are at Henríquez 544, Entel is at Camilo Henríquez 446 and Chilesat at Henríquez 473.

La Torre Suiza (see Villarrica's Places to Stay section later in this chapter) has Internet access at Bilbao 969, as does the Centro de Llamados at Camilo Henríquez 565.

Turismo Cordillera (☎ 413-027), Vicente Reyes 737, arranges day trips to national parks and surrounding areas for US$19. Karina Tour (☎ 412-048) is at Valentín Letelier 825.

Todo Lavado (☎ 414-452) offers laundry servies at General Urrutia 699, Local 7.

Hospital Villarrica (☎ 411-169) is at San Martín 460.

Museo Histórico y Arqueológico de Villarrica

Mapuche artifacts, including jewelry, musical instruments and roughly hewn wooden masks – powerful carvings despite their simplicity – are the focus of the municipal museum. Gracing the grounds in front of the museum is a Mapuche ruca, oblong with thatched walls and roof, traditionally built by four men in four days under a reciprocal labor system known as *minga*. Reeds from the lake provide the thatch, so skillfully intertwined that water cannot penetrate even in this very damp climate.

At Pedro de Valdivia 1050, alongside the tourist office, the museum (☎ 413-445) is open 9 am to 1 pm and 3 to 7:30 pm weekdays. Admission costs US$0.50.

Other Things to See & Do

Directly behind the tourist office, Villarrica's **Feria Artesanal** (artisans' market) has a fine selection of local crafts and offers the chance to sample traditional Mapuche food.

For launch excursions on the lake, visit the Embarcadero at the foot of San Martín and General Körner, opposite Hostería Kiel.

Local fishing is good, especially on the Río Toltén, but first obtain a license from the Cámara de Turismo in Pucón. Travelers have recommended Gastón Balboa, San Martín 348, as a well-equipped, knowledgeable fishing guide.

Special Events

At the annual Muestra Cultural Mapuche, in January and February, local artisans display their wares to the public; there is also indigenous music and ritual dance. Late January's Jornadas Musicales de Villarrica is a music festival with nearly two decades of history.

Places to Stay

Budget Villarrica has substantial seasonal price differentials, with a summer peak in January and February. Prices may also rise during the ski season.

There are more than half a dozen campgrounds on the road between Villarrica and Pucón, but the most convenient is *Camping Dulac* (☎ 412-097), 2km east of town. It can be crowded, but the shady sites provide reasonable privacy for US$19 per night. It has excellent hot showers and a restaurant, and sells supplies.

Many places offer seasonal accommodations only for around US$6.50/11 singles/doubles with shared bath, US$7.50/12 with private bath; the tourist office provides the most current information. Among the possibilities are *Hospedaje Balboa* (☎ 411-098, San Martín 734) and *Hospedaje Urrutia* (☎ 411-415, Alderete 821).

Popular with some travelers but unappealing to others, one of the cheapest permanent places is *Hotel Fuentes* (☎ 411-595, Vicente Reyes 665) for about US$8 per person with shared bath, US$14 with private bath. Rooms are basic, but the downstairs bar and restaurant provide a cozy winter hearth. Ask for a room with a window, however, and watch your head on the staircase.

In a stylishly renovated and spacious older house, the increasingly popular *La Torre Suiza* (☎/fax 411-213, info@torresuiza.com, Bilbao 969) charges US$5 per person for garden camping (with use of indoor facilities), US$8 for dorm accommodations, and US$10 per person for double rooms, including an outstanding breakfast. Cyclists get discounts, there's Internet access, the showers are five-star, and there's a no-smoking inside policy.

English, German and French are spoken at remodeled, Austrian-run *B&B Roswitha Mayer Hans* (☎ 09-883-4711, Valentín Letelier 748), which has large rooms for US$12.50/21 singles/doubles. *Hotel Villa Linda* (☎ 411-392,

Pedro de Valdivia 678) offers singles with shared bath for US$14, while doubles with private bath cost US$30.

Mid-Range Managed by extroverted, English-speaking Gualberto López, *Hostería Rayhuén* (☎ 411-571, Pedro Montt 668) is a charming place featuring hot showers, well-heated rooms and a fine restaurant with outdoor dining space. Rates, including an abundant breakfast, are US$24/36.

In part because of street noise, and perhaps because it's changed hands several times, travelers have mixed opinions of *Hotel Dieggo's* (☎ 411-370, Alderete 709), where rates are US$25/40 with breakfast. The friendly, quieter *Hostería Bilbao* (☎ 411-186, Henríquez 43) charges US$30/40.

Top End *Hotel Villarrica* (☎/fax 411-641, Körner 255) has motel-style cabins from US$33/48. Set among attractive grounds on a hillside site well above its street address, Oregonian-owned *Hostería de la Colina* (☎/fax 411-503, Presidente Ríos 1177, aldrich@entelchile.net) has singles/doubles for US$80/97, but also slightly cheaper rooms without views of Llaima and Villarrica volcanoes. There is also a well-stocked library.

Hostería Kiel (☎/fax 411-631, Körner 153) has rooms from US$50/70 off-season to US$65/85 in high season, and a good restaurant. *Hotel El Ciervo* (☎ 411-215, fax 411-426, Körner 241) is one of several good hotels along the same street; rooms with breakfast start at US$70/80 in summer, but can go for half price the rest of the year.

Places to Eat

Most of Villarrica's restaurants are along Pedro de Valdivia and Alderete/Henríquez. *Café Bar 2001* (☎ 411-470, Henríquez 379) seems typical of the region's tourist cafés, with its selection of sandwiches and kuchen.

Don't overlook the hearty fixed-price lunches at *Hostería Rayhuén* (☎ 411-571, Pedro Montt 668) with its friendly but erratic service. The popular *Club Social Treffpunkt* (☎ 411081, Valdivia 640) serves German cuisine and Chilean seafood.

English and German are spoken at the Sino-Chilean *The Travellers* (☎ 412-830, Valentín Letelier 753), which features a varied menu of Chilean, Chinese, Thai and Mexican dishes, in congenial surroundings.

El Rey del Marisco (☎ 412-093), Valentín Letelier 1030) is nothing fancy, but serves excellent fish and other seafood, with entrees from about US$6. Special mention goes to their *pescado a la vasca*, spiced with garlic and garnished with red peppers, white asparagus, tasty baguettes and *ají* (hot sauce). Service can be less congenially erratic than that at Hostería Rayhuén, however.

Peña La Tranquera, Acevedo 761, is a bar and folk club with live music as well as typical Chilean food.

Shopping

Besides the Feria Artesanal, there are several other places to look for Mapuche silverwork, baskets, woolens and carvings. Visit Tejidos Ray-Ray (☎ 412-006) at Anfión Muñoz 386, or the Tornería Suiza (☎ 411-610) at Prat 675.

Prisoners' crafts are for sale at the Artesanía y Mueblería Penitenciaria (☎ 411-308) at the corner of Acevedo and Pedro de Valdivia.

Getting There & Around

Villarrica's main bus terminal is at Pedro de Valdivia 621, though a few companies have separate offices nearby. Services to Santiago and many regional destination are frequent, but most southbound services on the Panamericana leave from Temuco (so you have to backtrack to Temuco to catch many southbound buses). Long-distance fares are similar to those from Temuco, only an hour away.

It's possible to shorten southbound trips by transferring at Freire, the northern junction with the Panamericana, or (more conveniently) by taking a Valdivia-bound bus as far as Loncoche, the southern junction with the Panamericana.

Regular international services are available to the Argentine towns of Zapala, Neuquén and San Martín de los Andes, but for services to Bariloche it's necessary to return to Temuco.

Lubricenter LBC (☎ 411-333), at JM Carrera 366, is the only car-rental agency.

Bus – Regional Buses Jac (☎ 411-447), Bilbao 610, goes to Pucón (US$0.60) and Temuco (US$3) half-hourly, to Valdivia (US$3.50) five times daily, half-hourly to Lican Ray (US$0.60), and to Coñaripe (US$1.25) eight times daily. It also goes thrice daily to Caburgua (US$2) via Pucón. Buses Regional Villarrica (☎ 411-871), Vicente Reyes 619, has frequent buses to Pucón, but less frequent services to Curarrehue and Puesco.

Bus – Long Distance Many companies have nightly service to Santiago, including Buses Jac, Tur-Bus (☎ 411-534) at Anfión Muñoz 657, Igi Llaima (☎ 412-733) at Anfión Muñoz 604, Buses Power (☎ 411-121), Inter Sur (☎ 411-534), Buses Fénix (☎ 410-378) at Anfión Muñoz 615 and Buses Lit (☎ 411-555) at Anfión Muñoz 640.

Fares to Santiago can be as low as US$10 but as high as US$20, depending on seasonal demand. Prices for more comfortable salón cama sleepers can be as high as US$38.

Other bus destinations include Valdivia (US$3.50, served by Tur-Bus and Jac), Los Angeles (US$6, Tur-Bus and Igi Llaima), Concepción (US$7.50, Tur-Bus and Igi Llaima) and Puerto Montt (US$7, Tur-Bus).

Bus – International Igi Llaima leaves at 6:15 am Monday, Wednesday, Friday and Sunday for San Martín de los Andes (US$23), Zapala and Neuquén (US$35, 16 hours) via Paso Mamuil Malal. Buses San Martín (☎ 411-584), Anfión Muñoz 604, operates similar international services Tuesday, Thursday and Saturday.

PUCÓN
☎ 45

With its burgeoning travel agencies offering hiking, climbing, mountain biking, windsurfing, whitewater rafting and kayaking excursions, Pucón resembles Wyoming's Jackson Hole in its youthful vitality – as well as its

faux rusticity. At least until the next major eruption of Volcán Villarrica obliterates it, this lakeside resort will remain the focus of Chile's adventure tourism industry and a locus of environmental activism. It also has a wide range of accommodations in all categories, and superb food.

In the days leading up to New Year's, Pucón is a beehive of around-the-clock activity, as bars and restaurants make last minute preparations for the summer in a boom-or-bust atmosphere of total improvisation. Villarrica may be cheaper (and safer – don't buy a Pucón condo unless it's guaranteed lava-proof), but Pucón is livelier. The season is gradually lengthening at both ends of the January-February rush, but many businesses are still closed outside this time.

Orientation
Pucón (population about 8000) is 25km from Villarrica at the east end of Lago Villarrica, between the estuary of the Río Pucón to the north and Volcán Villarrica to the south. Structured along a conventional grid system, this very compact town is bounded by the lake to the north, the Costanera Roberto Geis to the west, the flanks of the volcano to the south, and Av Colo Colo to the east. To the northwest, a wooded peninsula juts into the lake, forming the sheltered inlet La Poza at the west end of Av Libertador Bernardo O'Higgins, (often called just Av O'Higgins) the main commercial street and thoroughfare.

Information
Tourist Offices The private Cámara de Turismo (☎ 441-671) has new quarters at Brasil 115, open 8 am to midnight in January and February, 10 am to 1 pm and 4 to 9 pm the rest of the year. Annual fishing licenses are also available here for US$2.

Money Changing money is not difficult, but rates are better in Santiago and Temuco. Cambios include Turismo Christopher at O'Higgins 335 and Conexion at O'Higgins 472. Supermercado Eltit, O'Higgins 336, will change US and Argentine cash and now has an ATM.

PUCÓN

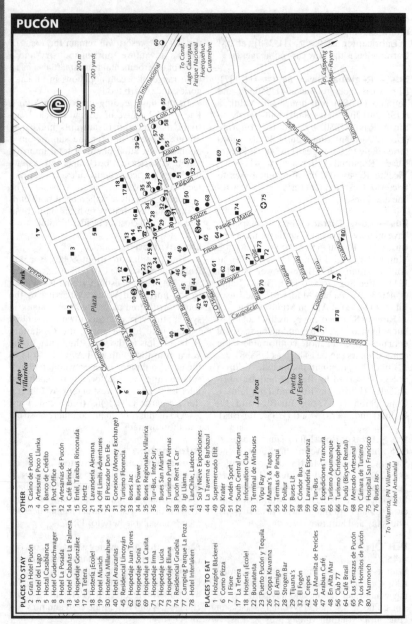

PLACES TO STAY
2 Gran Hotel Pucón
3 Hotel del Lago
5 Hostal Casablanca
8 Hotel Gudenschwager
9 Hotel La Posada
13 Hotel Cabañas La Palmera
16 Hospedaje González
17 La Tetera
18 Hostería ¡Ecole!
19 Hotel Munich
30 Hostería Millarahue
40 Hotel Araucarias
45 Residencial Lincoyán
62 Hospedaje Juan Torres
63 Hospedaje Sonia
65 Hospedaje La Casita
71 Hospedaje Irma
72 Hospedaje Lucía
73 Hospedaje Eliana
74 Residencial Graciela
77 Camping Parque La Poza
78 Hotel Interlaken

PLACES TO EAT
1 Holzapfel Bäckerei
6 Como Pizza
7 Il Fiore
17 La Tetera
18 Hostería ¡Ecole!
22 Buonatesta
23 Puerto Pucón y Tequila
26 Coppa Kavanna
27 El Amigo
28 Strogen Bar
29 Tijuana's
32 El Fogón
42 Crepes
46 La Marmita de Pericles
47 Arabian Café
48 En Alta Mar
56 Club 77
64 Café Brasil
65 Las Terrazas de Pucón
79 Los Hornitos de Pucón
80 Marmonch

OTHER
3 Casino de Pucón
4 Artesanía Poco Llanka
10 Banco de Crédito
11 Post Office
12 Artesanías de Pucón
14 Café Brinck
15 Entel, Taxibus Rinconada
20 Hertz
21 Lavandería Alemana
24 Off Limits Adventures
25 El Pescador Don Ele
31 Conexión (Money Exchange)
32 Turismo Florencia
33 Buses Jac
34 Buses Power
35 Buses Regionales Villarrica
36 Tur-Bus, Inter Sur,
   Buses San Martín
37 Turismo Punta Arenas
38 Pucón Rent a Car
39 Igi Llaima
41 LanChile, Ladeco
43 Sol y Nieve Expediciones
44 La Taverna de Barbazul
49 Supermercado Elit
50 Krater
51 Anden Sport
52 South Central American
   Information Club
53 Terminal de Minibuses
54 Vipu Ray
55 Mama's & Tapas
55 Termas de Panqui
56 Politur
57 Buses Lit
58 Condor Bus
59 Lavandería Esperanza
60 Tur-Bus
61 Expediciones Trancura
65 Turismo Apumanque
66 Turismo Christopher
67 Pudú (Bicycle Rental)
68 Mercado Artesanal
70 Cámara de Turismo
75 Hospital San Francisco
76 Buses Jac

To Villarrica, PN Villarrica,
Hotel Antumalal

Banco de Crédito has an ATM at Alderete and Fresia.

Post & Communications Correos de Chile is at Fresia 183. Entel is at Ansorena 299.

For Internet services, visit Café Brinck, Ansorena 243, or the South Central American Information Club (☎ 443-449), Palguín 465, for US$2 per half hour.

Travel Agencies On Pucón's Av Bernardo O'Higgins, Chile's adventure travel mecca, numerous companies arrange climbing, river rafting, mountain biking (including rentals), horseback riding and fishing trips. You can watch the video replays of the day's excursions on the sidewalk in front of the business. For details and prices, see the Organized Tours section later in this chapter.

Among the agencies are reader-recommended, Colombian-American Sol y Nieve Expediciones (☎/fax 441-070, solnieve@entelchile.net) at O'Higgins 192, Expediciones Trancura (☎/fax 441-189, turismo@trancura.com) at O'Higgins 211-C, Turismo Apumanque (☎ 441-085, fax 441-361) at O'Higgins 323, Andén Sport (☎ 441-048, fax 441-236) at O'Higgins 545, Politur (☎ 441-373) at O'Higgins 635, Turismo Punta Arenas (☎ 449-510) at O'Higgins and Palguín, Turismo Florencia (☎ 441-472) at O'Higgins 480 and Off Limits Adventures (☎ 441-210, fax 441-604) at Fresia 273, which specializes in fishing. Some of these operate in summer only.

National Parks Conaf (☎ 441-261) is east of town, at Camino Internacional 1355.

Language Courses Hostería ¡Ecole!, the HI affiliate, at General Urrutia 592, offers intensive Spanish language instruction in an activities-oriented context, both during the summer (hiking, rafting and the like) and winter (skiing). Rates are US$50 for two hours for individuals or small groups, while six-day programs with half-board cost US$745 for one-person, US$415 for each additional person. A full schedule of activities costs US$285 for one person, US$190 for each additional person.

Laundry Lavandería Alemana (☎ 441-106) is at Fresia 224; Lavandería Esperanza (☎ 441-379) is at Colo Colo 475.

Medical Services Pucón's Hospital San Francisco (☎ 441-177) is at Uruguay 325.

Casino de Pucón
Despite its pseudo-European design, Pucón's massive casino is totally out of proportion to its surroundings, occupying a full block bounded by Ansorena, Holzapfel, Palguín and Pedro de Valdivia. At Ansorena 23, the Casino (☎ 441-873) contains a hotel and functions as a performing arts venue.

Organized Tours
Competition is heavy among tour companies, but prices vary less than the quality of services among them; for names and addresses, see the Travel Agencies section earlier in the Pucón section of this chapter. Climbing Volcán Villarrica, a day and one night's camping – if the weather holds – costs about US$45 to US$60 per person. A 2½-hour rafting trip (including transfers) down the lower Río Trancura costs as little as US$10 to US$15, but a three-hour excursion on the more rugged upper Trancura costs US$25 to US$35. A series of dry years has left the latter smoother than usual in some parts, but several Class IV falls still make for exciting moments.

For climbing Volcán Villarrica, it's best to use your own boots, so long as they can be fitted with crampons; bring extra high-energy snacks. Colombian-American Sol y Nieve is more expensive than most of Pucón's adventure travel agencies, but provides better equipment for climbing and rafting, and additional services (such as a sumptuous end-of-the-day barbecue). Apumanque and Politur are also well established. El Pescador Don Ele, Urrutia 384, organizes fishing trips and sells gear.

Besides traditional excursions, Hostería ¡Ecole! (☎ 441-675, fax 441-660) organizes hiking trips to the Fundación Lahuen's Santuario Cañi, a private nature reserve, and to other, more remote destinations such as the Fiordo de Cahuelmó (part of the proposed

Parque Natural Pumalín, another private reserve), in Region X. In conjunction with the Proyecto Indígena Alto Biobío, ¡Ecole! also arranges summer hiking and winter cross-country skiing on El Sendero Pehuenche, the traditional Pehuenche trail of the endangered upper Biobío drainage, and offers suggestions for visitors who prefer to undertake independent excursions. For information in the USA, contact Ancient Forests International (☎ 800-447-1483; ☎/fax 707-923-3001), Box 2453, Redway, CA 95560.

Special Events

Mid-January's Jornadas Musicales de Pucón is an annual musical festival that's been going for more than a decade. A more recent event, in keeping with the growth in outdoor recreation, is February's Triatlón Internacional de Pucón (Pucón International Triathlon).

Places to Stay

Pucón has abundant accommodations, including budget alternatives, but the seasonal differential is substantial, and good mid-range values are hard to find. Prices below are from the January/February high season

unless otherwise indicated; figure about 20% less the rest of the year.

Budget *Camping Parque La Poza* (☎ 441-435), on shady grounds at Av Costanera Roberto Geis 769, charges US$5 per person.

The HI affiliate, *Hostería ¡Ecole!*, (☎ 441-675, fax 441-660, trek@ecole.mic.cl, Urrutia 592), is in a category of its own (most fun). It charges US$10 with hostel card, US$12 per person without, though it looks more expensive. It also has a superb vegetarian restaurant and a book exchange, holds parties and dances, and organizes informal tours to nearby attractions.

Budget accommodations start around US$10, usually with breakfast or kitchen privileges, at places such as *Hospedaje Eliana* (Pasaje Chile 225), tidy and friendly *Hospedaje Juan Torres* (☎ 441-248, Lincoyán 445), *Hospedaje Lucía* (☎ 441-271, Lincoyán 565), *Hospedaje La Casita* (☎ 441-712, Palguín 555), *Hospedaje Irma* (Lincoyán 545) and *Residencial Lincoyán* (☎ 441-144, Lincoyán 323).

Congenial *Hospedaje Sonia* (☎ 441-269, Lincoyán 485), a good place to meet people, charges US$10 per person with breakfast and kitchen privileges. *Residencial Graciela* (☎ 441-494, Pasaje Roland Matus 521) normally charges US$10 per person but has rooms that sleep four for US$31. It also has a restaurant.

Known as one of Pucón's better breakfast or dessert choices, next-door *La Tetera* (☎ 441-462, Urrutia 580) has added equally good accommodations for about US$15 per person. Lackluster but acceptable *Hospedaje González* (☎ 441-491, General Urrutia 484) charges the same.

Mid-Range Mid-range accommodations are relatively scarce, but for US$33 double, *Hostería Millarahue* (☎ 441-610, O'Higgins 460) also has a fine restaurant with seafood specialties. *Hostal Casablanca* (☎ 441-450, Palguín 136) provides reasonable accommodations for US$31/52 with breakfast. *Hotel Cabañas La Palmera* (☎/fax 441-083, Ansorena 221) charges US$58/68.

Top End Top-end accommodations start around US$70/99 at *Hotel Interlaken* (☎ 441-276, fax 441-242, Caupolicán s/n) near Costanera Geis. Recovering some of its former luster, *Hotel Araucarias* (☎ 441-286, araucari@cepri.cl, Caupolicán 243) charges US$73/94.

Germanic influence is palpable in chalet-style architecture like that of the *Hotel Gudenschwager* (☎ 441-156, Pedro de Valdivia 12), but its venerable style conceals thin walls and creaking floors. Doubles with views across the lake cost US$78. Once a mid-range place, the *Hotel La Posada* (☎ 441-088, Pedro de Valdivia 191) is no longer a bargain for US$83/102. *Hotel Munich* (☎ 442-292, Alderete 275) is a better value at US$83/91, with helpful English- and German-speaking staff.

Part of the new casino, *Hotel del Lago* (☎ 291-000, Ansorena 23) charges US$186/200. Built by Ferrocarriles del Estado (the state railroad corporation) in the depths of the Great Depression, the imposing *Gran Hotel Pucón* (☎ 441-001, Holzapfel 190) offers lakefront luxury for US$189/252.

Overlooking the lake at Km 2 on the road to Villarrica, each of the 20 rooms at *Hotel Antumalal* (☎ 441-011/2, fax 441-013, antumalal@entelchile.net) comes with a picture window view, a fresh fruit basket, and a fireplace, plus lake access and a heated pool. Its most impressive asset is the spectacular, rambling hillside garden, brightly punctuated by flower beds set among winding paths, pools and waterfalls, magnificent arrayanes and other native tree species. Its only drawback is the noise from jet skis on the lake in summer. Rates are US$180/250 with half-board in high season (mid-December to March). The off-season rates of US$120/140 are a bargain.

Places to Eat

Most hotels have their own restaurants, but there are scores of other appealing places to eat, some of them open only in summer. For fast food, there are fine empanadas at *Los Hornitos de Pucón* (Caupolicán 710). For cheap but decent eats, try the sandwiches and lunches at *Coppa Kavanna* (☎ 449-033)

or *El Amigo*, alongside each other at Urrutia 407, or the *Strogen Bar* (Urrutia 417).

The inexpensive vegetarian specialties at nonsmoking *Hostería ¡Ecole!* (☎ 441-675, Urrutia 592) are one of Pucón's special attractions. For breakfast or onces, you can't do much better than Swiss-run *La Tetera* (☎ 441-462, General Urrutia 580), which also has a book exchange with a good selection in English and Spanish, less so in German and French.

Specializing in regional cuisine, *Marmonch* (☎ 441-972, Ecuador 175) has a different, inexpensive fixed-price lunch daily. *Club 77* (O'Higgins 635) offers traditional Chilean and regional specialties like pastel de choclo, baked empanadas and smoked trout. *Café Brasil* (☎ 441-593, Fresia 477) is recommended for trout and sandwiches. *En Alta Mar* (Urrutia and Fresia) has drawn praise for its seafood.

Highly regarded for pizza, pancakes, meat and seafood, *Las Terrazas de Pucón* (☎ 441-085, O'Higgins 323) has outdoor patio dining. *Il Fiore* (☎ 441-565, Holzapfel 83) specializes in upscale pasta, meat and seafood. Next-door *Como Pizza* (☎ 441-109, Holzapfel 71) serves the obvious. *Buonatesta* (☎ 441-434, Fresia 243) has an excellent Argentine-style pizza menu.

Puerto Pucón y Tequila (☎ 441-592, Fresia 245) is a decent if slightly overpriced Spanish-Mexican restaurant worth consideration. *Tijuana's* (Ansorena 303) also serves Mexican cuisine.

La Marmita de Pericles (Fresia 300) serves crepes and fondue. Pricey *Crepes* (☎ 441-347, Lincoyán 372) is worth a look. *El Fogón* (☎ 444-904, O'Higgins 480) is a parrilla. The *Arabian Café* (☎ 443-469, Fresia 354) is an upscale Middle Eastern venue.

For exquisite sweets in a pleasant garden seating, try the *Holzapfel Bäckerei* (☎ 441-334, Holzapfel 524), which specializes in raspberry kuchen and other Germanic goodies, as well as ice cream.

Entertainment

La Taverna de Barbazul (Lincoyán 361) is a popular summer hangout for Pucón's youthful adventure-oriented crowd. *Krater* (☎ 441-339, O'Higgins 447) is a pub and karaoke bar. Another possibility is *Mama's & Tapas* (☎ 449-002, O'Higgins 587).

Shopping

Pucón's a better place to do things than to buy things, but there's a Mercado Artesanal on Ansorena between O'Higgins and Brasil. Artesanías de Pucón is on Alderete between Fresia and Ansorena, while Artesanía Poco Llanka is at Lincoyán 12.

Getting There & Away

Air LanChile (☎ 443-514), Urrutia 102, has occasional summer flights to and from Santiago, but it and Ladeco (at the same location) normally fly out of Temuco.

Bus Long-distance services closely resemble those from Villarrica, and consequently are not mentioned in detail here. The locations of the companies and their terminals, however, are scattered around town and currently undergoing changes. The two major carriers have new terminals: Buses Jac at Uruguay and Palguín, and Tur-Bus on Camino Internacional just east of town, but both maintain ticket offices elsewhere as well. The Terminal de Minibuses Vipu Ray, on Brasil between Palguín and Arauco, is the spot for services to Villarrica, Lican Ray and Coñaripe.

Long-distance carriers include Tur-Bus (☎ 441-965), Buses San Martín (☎ 441-965) and Inter Sur, all at Palguín 383; Buses Power (☎ 441-706), the cheapest – but also least comfortable – at Palguín 360; Buses Lit (☎ 441-055) at the corner of O'Higgins and Colo Colo; Igi Llaima (☎ 442-061) at O'Higgins and Colo Colo; and Cóndor Bus, on Colo Colo just south of O'Higgins.

Buses Jac (☎ 442-069), also at O'Higgins 492, has countless departures from Pucón to Villarrica (½ hour, US$0.65), serves Valdivia six times daily and adds local service to Caburgua (US$1.25) and Paillaco five times daily, between 7 am and 5 pm, and to Curarrehue four times daily. Buses Regionales Villarrica (☎ 441-706), on Palguín alongside Tur-Bus, has four buses daily to Curarrehue

and Puesco, the last stop before the border crossing to Junín de los Andes in Argentina.

Taxibuses Rinconada, Ansorena 299, goes to Termas de Huife (US$1.60) and Los Pozones at 12:30 and 5 pm, and to other hot springs at Palguín and Menetué.

Getting Around

The South Central American Information Club (SCAI Club, ☎ 443-449, fax 443-436), Palguín 465, deals largely but not exclusively with Israeli travelers. Daily rates range from US$55 for passenger cars to US$89 for 4WD pickups; monthly rates range from US$1300 to US$2200. Pucón Rent a Car (☎ 441-922), Camino Internacional 1395-1510, is comparably priced; it also has an office on O'Higgins between Palguín and Arauco. Hertz (☎ 441-664) has a local representative at Alderete and Fresia.

Most of the adventure travel agencies mentioned earlier in the Pucón section rent bicycles; try also Pudú (☎ 442-312), at Ansorena 435.

AROUND PUCÓN
Casa Fuerte Santa Sylvia

In colonial times, the Villarrica region was one of the continent's southernmost encomiendas, but the widespread Mapuche uprising of 1599 caused the Spaniards to abandon the area and ended the forced labor system. Revealing evidence of that rebellion, excavations have found broken roofing tiles that apparently belonged to the encomendero's residence. There were also a chapel, houses for Mapuche servants and several graves. Small gold deposits attracted the Spaniards here, but determined Mapuche resistance soon drove them away.

Santa Sylvia is 18km east of Pucón on the road to Termas de Huife; at the Huerquehue junction, take the road to the right. It's open 9 am to noon and 3 to 6 pm daily.

Hot Springs Resorts

La Araucanía's volcanic terrain means a multitude of hot springs, many of them in the Pucón area. **Termas de Huife**, only 30km northeast of Pucón on the Río Liucura, is an upscale location whose *Hotel Termas de*

AROUND PUCÓN

Huife (☎/*fax 045-441-222*) is a chalet with singles/doubles for US$102/152 with half-board. Day visitors, however, can use the baths all day for US$11 in summer, US$9 the rest of the year, and meals are available in the cafeteria. More economical is the rustic **Termas Los Pozones**, a few kilometers beyond Huife, where admission costs US$4. For transportation details, see Pucón's Getting There & Away section.

Termas de Palguín, 30km southeast of Pucón on the Río Palguín, used to feature the elegant German-built chalet *Hotel Termas de Palguín* (☎/*fax 045-441-968*), built

in the mid-1940s. However, it burned to the ground a few years ago. Reconstruction of a smaller hotel in the same style has begun, but for the moment there are cabañas and newer hotel accommodations that lack the character of the old place. A rugged southbound road crosses Parque Nacional Villarrica to Coñaripe from here; for details, see the Coñaripe section later in this chapter.

Accommodations start around US$48 per person with shared bath and full board, while rooms with private bath cost around US$98/133 for singles/doubles with full board. Day visitors can use the baths for

US$6.50 and eat in the hotel restaurant; camping is possible nearby. At **Rancho de Caballos** (☎ 045-441-575), in nearby Palguín Alto, cabaña accommodations are available for US$10 per person with hot showers and a good breakfast; three-hour to three-day horseback tours are available. For transport details, see Pucón's Getting There & Away section.

The unorthodox **Termas de Panqui**, 58km east of Pucón via an improved road whose last few kilometers can still be difficult for low clearance vehicles, is a North American deep ecology enclave (with Chilean participation at the business end) that offers accommodations in Sioux (Lakota) tipis and Mapuche rucas, vegetarian meals, hot pools, mud baths, yoga, tai chi, meditation and the like. There are also hiking trails in the vicinity. Admission costs US$10, tipi accommodations another US$10 and full board around US$20, plus IVA. Make reservations and arrange transportation through Termas de Panqui (☎ 045-442-039, fax 442-040), O'Higgins 615, in Pucón.

Santuario Cañi

Purchased and administered by the Fundación Lahuen to rescue it from a logging threat, Chile's first private nature reserve protects about 400 hectares of ancient araucaria forest, 21km east of Pucón. As part of an educational project to train local guides in natural history, the Fundación organizes overnight treks in the Cañi through its offices at Hostería ¡Ecole! (☎ 045-441-675, fax 441-660), Urrutia 592 in Pucón.

PARQUE NACIONAL HUERQUEHUE

Mountainous Huerquehue is a compact 12,500-hectare reserve of rivers and waterfalls, alpine lakes and araucaria and nothofagus forests, with superb views across the Río Pucón Valley to Volcán Villarrica. There are occasional sightings of the Andean condor, but woodpeckers and thrushes are far more common.

Conaf maintains a Centro de Educación e Intepretación Ambiental at the park entrance at Lago Tinquilco, where rangers collect a US$4 admission fee. The Centro is open 10 am to 8 pm daily during the summer.

Geography & Climate

On the eastern shore of Lago Caburgua, 35km northeast of Pucón, Huerquehue offers pleasant hiking and good camping. Rushing snowmelt streams have cut deep canyons whose flanks rise up to 2000m on Cerro Araucano.

The park enjoys warm summers, but snow accumulates at higher elevations in winter. The mean annual precipitation of 2000mm of rain falls almost entirely between May and September, so November to April is the best time for a visit.

Lago Verde Trail

Leaving from park headquarters at Lago Tinquilco, this very fine day excursion switchbacks from 700m to 1300m through dense lenga forests and past several waterfalls. Frequent forest clearings reveal striking views of Volcán Villarrica to the south. At upper elevations are solid stands of araucaria trees.

At the outlet of Lago Chico, the first of three clustered lakes, there are fine pools for swimming on warm days. Well-marked trails continue to Lago Toro and to Lago Verde, a 7km walk that takes about two or three hours each way from Lago Tinquilco. Backcountry camping is not allowed at present, but Conaf's **Refugio Renahue** offers accommodations for US$17 per night. It's possible to continue through the park to Termas de Río Blanco, a hot springs resort accessible by a gravel road from Cunco, Lago Colico and the north end of Lago Caburgua.

Places to Stay

At Conaf's 18-site **campground** on Lago Tinquilco, rates are about US$17 per site. It's technically outside the park boundaries, but the new Canadian-Chilean **Refugio Tinquilco** (☎ 02-777-7673, fax 735-1187, in Santiago, tinquilco@lake.mic.cl), at the Lago Verde trailhead, offers hostel-style bunks (US$12 without sheets, US$14 with), as well as doubles with shared bath (US$42) and private bath (US$52). Breakfast costs

US$1.50, lunch or dinner US$5, or full board US$10.

Getting There & Away

From Pucón, Buses Jac provides regular transport to Paillaco, at the south end of Lago Caburgua; for details, see Pucón's Bus section earlier in this chapter. It's another 8km on a dusty, winding road to the park entrance at Lago Tinquilco; hitchhiking may be feasible, but it's probably wiser to start walking and hope for a lift. Some motorists find this road difficult without 4WD, especially after a rain.

Most Pucón adventure travel agencies have excursions to Huerquehue among their offerings.

PARQUE NACIONAL VILLARRICA

In his 16th-century epic *La Araucana*, a classic of colonial literature, Spanish poet Alonso de Ercilla paid homage to the perpetually smoldering cone of 2847m Volcán Villarrica, now the centerpiece of one of Chile's most accessible national parks:

> Great neighbor volcano,
> That they call Vulcan's forge
> That belches ceaseless fire...

Established in 1940 to protect its remarkable volcanic scenery, Villarrica's 60,000 hectares also embrace inactive volcanoes such as 2360m Quetrupillán and, along the Argentine border, a section of 3746m Lanín, which has given its name to an equally impressive park across the frontier (Lanín must be climbed from the Argentine side).

Geography & Climate

Only 12km from Pucón, this is an area of active vulcanism – a major 1971 eruption opened a 4km-wide fracture in Volcán Villarrica that emitted 30 million cubic meters of lava and displaced several rivers. One flow, down the Río Challupén, was 14km long, 200m wide, and 5m high.

Where lava flows have not penetrated, at elevations up to 1500m, dense forests of southern beech and araucaria cover the mountain's flanks – Volcán Quetrupillán is

the southern limit of the araucaria's natural range. The climate resembles that of nearby Parque Nacional Huerquehue, though Villarrica tends to be rainier.

Administratively, the park consists of three sectors. Sector Rucapillán, closest to Pucón, is most popular for its access to Volcán Villarrica; Sector Quetrupillán and Sector Puesco are more remote but still accessible. At present, Conaf does not collect an admission charge.

Activities

Villarrica's accessibility makes it a mecca for hikers and climbers. The popular climb to the summit of Villarrica, which is physically but not technically demanding, requires equipment and either experience or a guide who knows the route; nonguided climbers require a special permit from Conaf. Do not hesitate to turn back in bad weather. For most visitors, the best bet is to arrange a full-day excursion with one of Pucón's many adventure travel companies for about US$45 to US$60 per person. However, Conaf also grants up to four climbing permits per day to well-equipped individuals who wish climb without a guide.

The most convenient trek circles Villarrica's southern flank and leaves the park at Termas de Palguín. From Termas de Palguín there's another route to Puesco, near the Argentine border, where there is public transport back to Pucón. For trekking details, see Lonely Planet's *Trekking in the Patagonian Andes*.

On the lower slopes of the volcano, *Refugio Villarrica* accommodates skiers in wintertime; for details, contact the Centro de Ski Volcán Villarrica (☎ 441-176, 441-901), in the Gran Hotel Pucón, Holzapfel 190. Lift tickets run about US$23 to US$27 per day.

Getting There & Away

Although Sector Rucapillán is only a few kilometers from Pucón, there is no scheduled public transport. However a shared taxi should cost no more than US$8 to US$10 total. To Sector Puesco, there is regular transport from Pucón with Buses Regional Villarrica.

LICAN RAY
☎ 45

On the north shore of island-studded Lago Calafquén, surrounded by mountains and jammed with high-season refugees from Santiago, fashionable Lican Ray draws its name from a Mapuche phrase meaning 'flower among the stones.' It boasts one of the region's best beaches in the Playa Grande, a long strip of dark volcanic sand. After sunset on summer nights, most visitors promenade on its only paved street, Av General Urrutia, filling the restaurants and cafés.

Orientation
Lican Ray (population about 4000), a compact grid between the estuaries of the Río Muilpún and the Río Melilahuén, is 30km south of Villarrica. General Urrutia, the main commercial street, is the southern extension of the paved Villarrica highway. Av Punulef, running along Playa Grande, is the western boundary; Av Manquel, along the Playa Chica, is the southern limit. A rough gravel road goes west to Panguipulli and a newly paved road follows the north shore of the lake east to Coñaripe.

Information
Lican Ray's municipal Oficina de Turismo (☎ 431-201), directly on the Plaza de Armas at General Urrutia 310, distributes maps, brochures and a list of hotels. In summer it's open 9 am to 11 pm daily; the rest of the year, hours are 9 am to 12:30 pm and 2:30 to 6 pm weekdays only.

Lican Ray has no exchange houses, but Supermercado Jumbito, on Urrutia between Millañanco and Huenumán, may change small amounts of US cash. The nearest permanent cambio is at Villarrica.

The post office is on Curiñanco between Huenumán and Marichanquín. CTC (Telefónica) has a long-distance office on Huenumán near the corner of Urrutia, while Entel is on Huenumán between Urrutia and Curiñanco.

Turismo Trancura, which arranges adventure tourism activities in Pucón, has a summer office at the corner of General Urrutia and Marichanquín.

There's a *posta médica* (first-aid station) on Esmeralda, behind the Plaza de Armas.

Places to Stay & Eat
Passable **Residencial Temuco** (☎ 431-130, Gabriela Mistral 515) is fairly basic for US$8, with sagging beds, breakfast and a downstairs restaurant. Doubles with private bath cost US$31. Woodsy, friendly **Residencial Catriñi** (☎ 431-093, Catriñi 140) costs about US$10 per person with breakfast, but the eight beds in two-plus upstairs rooms take up almost all the floor space and also sag a bit; there's one single room.

Other comparably priced lodgings include **Hospedaje López** (☎ 431-012, Urrutia 145) and **Hospedaje San Cristóbal** (Millañanco 145), which also rents mountain bikes. **Hospedaje Los Nietos** (☎ 431-078, Manquel 125) is slightly dearer at US$15 per person.

Fronting on Playa Grande, **Hotel Refugio Inaltulafquén** (☎ 412-543, Punulef 510) chargesUS$25 per person with shared bath. The more upscale **Hotel Becker** (☎ 431-156, Manquel 105) charges US$63 double with private bath and breakfast.

There are several cafés, restaurants and bars along General Urrutia and the Playa Grande. **The Ñaños** (☎ 431-021, Urrutia 105) is one of the town's most popular establishments for its Chilean specialties. **Guido's** (☎ 431-046, Urrutia 405) specializes in meat, seafood and trout. Open in summer only, **Madonna** (Urrutia 201) has a wider selection of toppings than most Chilean pizzerías.

Shopping
In summer, Lican Ray hosts two nightly crafts fairs. The first, on Esmeralda behind the tourist office, consists of works by local artisans. The second, the Centro Artesanal Nehuen, Urrutia 315, displays goods from other places in the region and around the country.

Getting There & Away
Buses Jac (☎ 431-185), which has its own terminal at General Urrutia and Marichanquín, has frequent services to and from Villarrica (45 minutes), direct service to Santiago (10 hours), and also goes to Coñaripe (US$0.60, ½ hour), with connections around the lake to

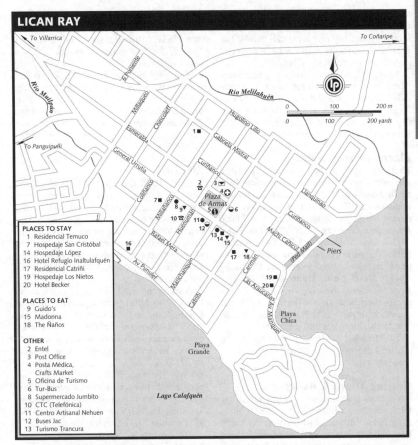

LICAN RAY

To Villarrica
To Coñaripe
Río Maichín
Río Melilahuén
To Panguipulli

PLACES TO STAY
1 Residencial Temuco
7 Hospedaje San Cristóbal
14 Hospedaje López
16 Hotel Refugio Inaltulafquén
17 Residencial Catriñi
19 Hospedaje Los Nietos
20 Hotel Becker

PLACES TO EAT
9 Guido's
15 Madonna
18 The Ñaños

OTHER
2 Entel
3 Post Office
4 Posta Médica,
   Crafts Market
5 Oficina de Turismo
6 Tur-Bus
8 Supermercado Jumbito
10 CTC (Telefónica)
11 Centro Artisanal Nehuen
12 Buses Jac
13 Turismo Trancura

Plaza de Armas
Piers
(Ped Mall)
Playa Chica
Playa Grande
Lago Calafquén

Panguipulli. Buses Guarda goes to Panguipulli (US$2, ½ hour) via Calafquén daily at
7:30 am; Vipu Ray goes to Panguipulli at
8:30 am and 4 pm. Tur-Bus (☎ 431-260),
Marichanquín 190, also offers long-distance
services, and Villarrica has many other carriers offering various destinations and departure times. Buses Guarda and Vipu Ray
leave from the Buses Jac terminal.

COÑARIPE
☎ 063

Across the regional border, 22km east of
Lican Ray, Coñaripe is a modest resort

whose black-sand beaches sprout multicolored tents during the summer holidays.
Completion of the paved highway along the
north shore of Lago Calafquén promises to
convert it into another Lican Ray. At the
east end of town the main drag, Av Guido
Beck Ramberga, intersects Ruta 201, the international highway to Junín de los Andes,
Argentina; at the bifurcation, the westbound
fork leads to Panguipulli and the southeast
to Termas de Coñaripe, Liquiñe and the
border crossing at Paso Carririñe.

A ruggedly exciting 4WD road also heads
north, traversing Parque Nacional Villarrica,

to Termas de Palguín and Pucón. Many Santiaguinos test their 4WDs here, but others seem to think any rental car can handle this narrow, hazardous route, which is better suited to motorcycles and bicycles.

From December through February, Coñaripe's municipal Oficina de Información Turística (☎ 317-403), on the Plaza de Armas, is open 9 am to 9 pm daily. Entel, at the corner of Beck Ramberga and Los Robles, provides long-distance services.

Places to Stay & Eat

There are several good, moderately priced accommodations, including **Hospedaje Iván de la Jara**(☎ 317-227), on Beck Ramberga opposite the Plaza de Armas, for US$10 per person with breakfast. Behind the Plaza, **Hospedaje Chumay** (☎ 317-289, Las Tepas 201) is slightly dearer at US$13 per person, but its restaurant is one of the better places to eat in town. Also opposite the Plaza, the newish **Hotel Entre Montañas**(☎ 317-298, Beck Ramberga 496), has singles for US$14 per person with shared bath, US$26 per person with private bath, both with breakfast. It also has a bar and restaurant.

El Mirador, on Beck Ramberga at the east end of town, is an attractive place for a leisurely meal.

Getting There & Away

All the bus companies have terminals along Beck Ramberga. Buses Jac has several buses daily from Villarrica to Coñaripe via Lican Ray (US$2). Buses San Pedro runs three buses daily from Coñaripe to Panguipulli (US$1.50); Buses Carrasco has one bus daily, Buses Panguipulli six daily. Buses Pirihueico goes to Panguipulli and Valdivia daily at 5 pm. There's also minibus service to Liquiñe, a nearby hot springs resort, daily at 1 pm.

CENTRO TURÍSTICO TERMAL COÑARIPE

About 15km east of Coñaripe, on the road to Liquiñe, the **Centro Turístico Termal Coñaripe** (☎ 063-317-330, 02-242-2578, fax 558-9738 in Santiago) is a diverse hot springs resort, featuring the the usual spa and swimming pools, but also tennis courts, hiking and

horseback trails and even its own trout farm for fresh fish dinners at the restaurant. Rates are US$195 double with full board, or US$297 for four-person cabañas, with seasonal variations.

The pool facilities are also open to day-trippers, who pay US$10 per person (US$5 for children ages two to 10), plus US$10 extra for access to the indoor pool and spa. Roundtrip transportation is available from Temuco airport (US$26) or from Villarrica (US$8.50).

LIQUIÑE

Liquiñe, 31km southeast of Coñaripe along Ruta 201, is an affordable hot springs resort with appealing hospedajes and hotels, along its namesake river. Horseback riding and fly-fishing excursions are particularly popular here. Note that there is a single public telephone (☎/fax 063-311-060), where messages can be left for accommodations that do not have extensions.

Among the available lodgings, all in the US$8.50 to US$12 range, are **Residencial Lagos**, **Residencial La Frontera**, and especially **Residencial La Casona**. The most elaborate accommodations are the rustically deluxe cabañas at **Termas Río Liquiñe** (☎ 311-060, Anexo 2), where full board and private thermal baths cost US$56 per person; with in-room hot tub, rates are US$6 more. For reservations, contact the Sociedad Turística Termal Río Liquiñe (☎ 063-317-377), Casilla 202, Villarrica.

Only a few kilometers north of town, **Termas Manquecura** has a swimming pool, thermal tubs and mud baths for US$4 per person per day. Cabañas rent for US$38 for up to six people; meals cost extra.

There are two buses daily to and from Villarrica from the Igi Llaima office in Villarrica, and one to Panguipulli, at 6:45 am, with Pirihueico.

PANGUIPULLI
☎ 63

At the northwest end of Lago Panguipulli, the town of Panguipulli (population 8300) is quieter, slower-paced and less touristy than many other lake resorts. About 115km northeast of Valdivia by a paved highway, via Lanco on the Panamericana, it has sensational views across Lago Panguipulli to Volcán Choshuenco. The street plan is irregular, but Panguipulli is small enough that orientation is no problem.

Information

The Oficina Municipal de Turismo (☎ 311-311, Anexo 731) fronts directly on Plaza Arturo Prat. It's open 9 am to 9 pm daily from December to mid-March, but keeps shorter hours the rest of the year.

Banco de Crédito is at Martínez de Rozas and Portales, on Plaza Arturo Prat, but has no ATM. Christopher Money Exchange, Martínez de Rozas 705, changes US cash and traveler's checks.

Correos de Chile is on Plaza O'Higgins, a block north of Plaza Prat. Telefónica del Sur is on Portales between JM Carrera and Martínez de Rozas.

To obtain a fishing license, visit the Municipalidad's Departamento de Rentas y Patentes, O'Higgins 793, or Librería Colón, O'Higgins 528.

Outdoor Activities

Expediciones Panguipulli (☎ 311-757), Martínez de Rozas 556, offers white-water rafting on the Río San Pedro, horseback riding and trekking excursions, and also rents mountain bikes.

Special Events

In early February, Panguipulli celebrates the town's founding during the Semana de las Rosas, with parades, folkloric music and similar events.

Places to Stay

Camping El Bosque (☎ 311-489), only 200m north of Plaza Prat, has 15 tent sites (no drive-in sites) and hot showers for US$4.50 per person.

Several unassuming hospedajes are in the US$8 to US$10 range, including the excellent *Hospedaje Berrocal* (☎ 311-812, Portales 72), which is also a neighborhood picada with good, moderately priced dinners. *Hospedaje Halabi* (☎ 311-483, Los Ulmos 62) and *Hospedaje Monserrat* (☎ 311-443, O'Higgins 1112) are comparable.

Cabañas Tío Carlos (☎ 311-215, Etchegaray 367) charges US$10.50 per person for a triple with private bath and a shared kitchen. Friendly *Hotel Central* (☎ 311-331, Pedro de Valdivia 115) has airy rooms and clean bathrooms with hot water (and even bathtubs) for US$12.50 per person; upstairs rooms are quieter and larger.

At *Hostal España* (☎ 311-166, O'Higgins 790), rooms with private bath cost US$20/33 singles/doubles with breakfast in homey surroundings. Prices are slightly higher, US$25/45 with breakfast, at the *Hostería Quetropillán* (☎ 311-348, Etchegaray 381), at a quiet location near the corner of Freire, but it's less congenial.

Places to Eat

Try *El Chapulín* (☎ 311-560, Martínez de Rozas 639) for meat and seafood (though the menu is sometimes limited), or reader-recommended *Girasol* (Martínez de Rozas near Matta). *El Criollo* (Matta between JM Carrera and Martínez de Rozas) also serves meat and seafood.

The modernized *Café Central* (☎ 311-495, Martínez de Rozas 880) serves snacks and onces in an attractive covered patio with hanging plants and natural light. *Gardylafquen* (☎ 311-887, Martínez de Rozas 722), is a new café-restaurant worth a visit, particularly for salmon.

Getting There & Away

Panguipulli's main Terminal de Buses (☎ 311-055) is at Gabriela Mistral 100, corner of Diego Portales, but Tur-Bus (☎ 311-377) has its own terminal at JM Carrera 784, corner of Pedro de Valdivia.

Tur-Bus has two morning buses to Temuco and Santiago, a route also served by Intersur (☎ 311-309) and Igi Llaima (☎ 311-347) at the main terminal. Panguisur (☎ 311-502) has many buses daily to Temuco, and two daily to Santiago, at 6:30 and 8:15 pm. Buses Pirehueico (☎ 311-497) has daily buses to Valdivia (2½ hours) and Puerto Montt, and one to Liquiñe.

Buses San Pedro (☎ 311-502) has daily service to Coñaripe (US$1.75), with connections to Liquiñe, Lican Ray and Villarrica. Buses Guarda goes to Calafquén at noon and 4 pm. Buses Hua Hum (☎ 311-199) has several crowded buses daily to Choshuenco, Neltume and Puerto Fuy. Buses Ríos also goes to Neltume.

CHOSHUENCO
☎ 063

Choshuenco, little more than two streets at the east end of Lago Panguipulli, survives from agriculture, a local sawmill and visitors who enjoy its enticing black-sand beach. There are many fine walks in the nearby countryside, at the foot of 2415m Volcán Choshuenco.

Places to Stay & Eat

Beachfront camping costs US$5 per tent, plus US$0.80 per hot shower and US$0.20 every time you use the toilet.

Beachfront *Hotel Rucapillán* (☎ 224-402, Anexo 220, San Martín 85) is tidy and well heated, with a good restaurant, hot showers and friendly staff. Rooms cost about US$21 double with shared bath, US$25 with private bath. *Hotel Choshuenco* (☎ 224-402, Anexo 214, Padre Bernabé s/n) charges US$17 per person and also has a restaurant.

Just outside of town on the road to Enco at the east end of Lago Riñihue, *Hostería Pulmahue* (☎ 224-402, Anexo 224) sits among gardens overlooking the lake. Pleasant rooms with private bath cost US$32 double with breakfast, but rooms with shared bath cost only US$25.

Getting There & Away

Buses from Panguipulli to Puerto Fuy pass through Choshuenco, taking about two hours and returning to Panguipulli early the next morning. In January and February, from Puerto Fuy, the ferry *Mariela* (☎ 063-311-334 in Panguipulli) carries passengers and vehicles to Puerto Pirehueico (two hours) at 7 am and 1 and 6 pm daily, returning at 10 am and 3:30 and 8 pm. In March-April and November-December, the ferry operates at 7 am and 2 pm daily except

Sunday, returning at 10 am and 5 pm; the rest of the year, it sails at 7 am and 12:30 pm, returning at 10 am and 3 pm.

Automobiles pay US$21; pickup trucks, jeeps and vans pay US$31. Pedestrians pay only US$1, motorcyclists US$4. The *Mariela* has a capacity of just 21 vehicles, so make reservations.

VALDIVIA
☎ 63

After languishing throughout the colonial era, Valdivia owes much of its present character to mid-19th-century German immigration. This influence has declined, but remains palpable in the city's architecture, German surnames (among the population and of street and place names) and, in particular, the delicious regional cuisine. Though the major earthquake of 1960 destroyed many older landmarks, there are still several European-style buildings and mansions along General Lagos, near the riverfront.

On orders from Pedro de Valdivia, Juan Pastene took formal possession of this area in 1544. Valdivia himself decreed the foundation of the city of Santa María La Blanca de Valdivia in early 1552, on the site of a Mapuche settlement known as Guadalauquén. After Mapuche resistance obliterated Valdivia in 1599 and the Dutch had attempted to occupy the area, the Spaniards eventually rebuilt the city as a military encampment. There remain colonial fortifications at nearby Corral and Niebla, at the mouth of the Río Valdivia.

Orientation

Valdivia (population 124,000), 160km southwest of Temuco and 45km west of the Panamericana, sits on the south bank of the Río Calle Calle where it becomes the Río Valdivia, near its confluence with the Río Cau Cau and the Río Cruces. Shaped in part by the meandering river, the core of the *Ciudad de los Ríos* (City of the Rivers) is a compact, triangular area between Calle Arauco and the riverfront.

Within this core, the Av Costanera Arturo Prat (more conveniently known as Prat) is a major focus of activity, but most important public buildings are on the central Plaza de la República. From the Panamericana, Av Ramón Picarte is the main eastern approach. To the west, the Puente Pedro de Valdivia crosses the river to Isla Teja, a leafy suburb which is the site of the Universidad Austral.

Information

Tourist Offices Sernatur (☎/fax 213-596, serna13a@entelchile.net), on the riverfront at Prat 555, is open 8:30 am to 1 pm and 2:30 to 6:48 pm weekdays, 10 am to 4 pm Saturday, and 10 am to 2 pm Sunday, but does not close at midday in summer. There is also an Oficina de Informaciones (☎ 212-212) at the bus terminal, Anfión Muñoz 360, open 8:30 am to 10 pm daily.

The Automóvil Club de Chile (☎ 250-376, 250-377), García Reyes 440, is also a good source of information.

Money For both cash and traveler's checks, Cambio Arauco is at Arauco 331, Local 24, Cambio La Reconquista at Carampangue 329. Downtown ATMs are abundant.

Post & Communications Correos de Chile is at O'Higgins 575, opposite Plaza de la República. Telefónica del Sur has a Centro de Llamados at San Carlos 107. Entel is at Pérez Rosales 601, Local 1, Chilesat at Pérez Rosales 712.

Public Access Internet (☎ 294-300) is upstairs at Letelier 236, on the north side of Plaza de la República.

Travel Agencies At Arauco 436, Turismo Cochrane (☎ 212-213) arranges air and bus tickets and rents cars. Similar agencies include Turismo Cono Sur (☎ 212-757) at Maipú 129, and Turismo Paraty (☎ 215-585) at Independencia 640.

Bookstores Libros Chiloé, Caupolicán 410, has a good selection of books by Chilean and foreign authors.

Cultural Centers The Centro Cultural El Austral (☎ 213-658), Yungay 733, hosts public arts and music events. The Corporación Cultural de Valdivia (☎ 219-690), Prat 549, also promotes local cultural activities and is the location of Sala Ainlebu, a theater venue.

Laundry Lavamatic, Walter Schmidt 305, is open 9:30 am to 8:30 pm daily except Sunday. Lavandería Manantial is at Camilo Henríquez 809.

Medical Services Valdivia's Hospital Regional (☎ 214-066) is south of downtown at Bueras 1003, near Aníbal Pinto.

Museo de Arte Contemporáneo

Valdivia's new modern art museum, almost alongside the older archaeological museum on Isla Teja, sits atop the foundations of the former Cervecería Anwandter, the onetime brewery that tumbled during the cataclysmic 1960 earthquake. With fine views across the river to the city, the museum (☎ 221-968) is open 10 am to 1 pm and 3 to 7 pm daily except Monday. Admission costs US$1 for adults, US$0.50 for children.

Museo Histórico y Arqueológico Mauricio van de Maele

Housed in a fine riverfront mansion on Isla Teja, one of Chile's most beautiful museums features a large, well-labeled collection from pre-Columbian times to the present, with particularly fine displays of Mapuche Indian artifacts and household items from early German settlements. Well-organized tours, in Spanish only, are a bit rushed but the guides are happy to answer questions at the end.

To get to the museum (☎ 212-872), which sits across the Río Valdivia from the Puerto Fluvial, take the bridge across the Río Valdivia, turn left at the first intersection and walk about 200 meters; the entrance is on the left (east) side, at Los Laureles 47. December to March, it's open 9 am to 1 pm and 2:30 to 6 pm; the rest of the year, hours are 10 am to 1 pm and 2 to 6 pm. Admission is about US$1.25 for adults, US$0.50 for children.

Parque Saval On Isla Teja, Parque Saval is a shady botanical garden (admission US$0.30) with a riverside beach. A pleasant trail follows the shoreline of Laguna de los

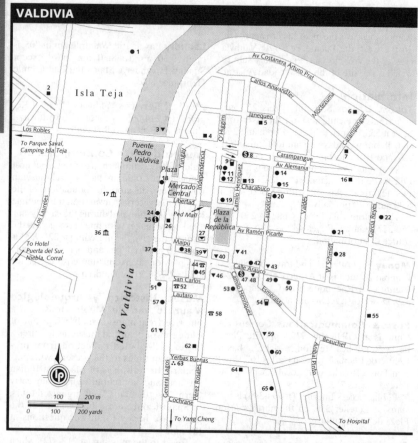

VALDIVIA

Isla Teja

• 1

■ 2

Av Costanera Arturo Prat

Carlos Anwandter

Janequeo
▼ 5

Moctezuma

Carampangue

6 ■

Los Robles

To Parque Saval,
Camping Isla Teja

3 ▼

■ 4

Puente
Pedro
de Valdivia

O'Higgins

$ 8

Carampangue

7 ■

Av Alemania

Plaza
•18

Yungay

Independencia

9 ▼
10 ●
▼ 11
▼ 12

Camilo Henríquez

● 14

14

● 15

16 ■

Mercado
Central
Libertad

Chacabuco

■ 13

Caupolicán

● 20

Valdés

17 🏛

● 19

Plaza
de la
República

García Reyes

● 22

24 ●
25 🛈
● 26

Ped Mall

36 🏛

27 ▼

Av Ramón Picarte

● 21

To Hotel
Puerta del Sur,
Niebla, Corral

Los Laureles

Maipú

37 ●
●38
39 ▼   ▼ 40

▼ 41

● 28

W Schmidt

Río Valdivia

44 ▼
☎
●45

Calle Arauco

▼ 42

▼ 43

$
47 48 ●
●

49 ●

50

▼ 46

San Carlos

51 ●   ☎ 52

Lautaro

53 ●

Camilo Henríquez

Esmeralda

54 🍷

■ 55

57 ●

☎ 58

61 ▼

62 ■

▼ 59

Beauchef

Anibal Pinto

● 60

General Lagos

Yerbas Buenas
∴ 63

Pérez Rosales

64 ■

65 ●

Cochrane

To Yang Cheng

To Hospital

0   100   200 m
0   100   200 yards

Lotos, covered with lily pads. It's a good place to see birds. Opposite the park entrance, at the north end of Los Laureles, the Universidad Austral operates a first-rate dairy outlet which sells very fine ice cream, yogurt and cheese at bargain prices.

Other Things to See & Do

Valdivia's **Feria Fluvial**, a riverside market north of the Sernatur office, is a great place to buy a bag of cherries and just watch the river flow. On Sundays, Valdivianos flock to the area to buy fish and fruit for the week,

float downstream to Niebla and Corral, or just plain sit in the sunshine.

East of the bus terminal, the **Torreón del Barro** is the turret of a Spanish fort built in 1774. A 17th-century turret, the **Torreón de los Canelos**, stands at the corner of Yerbas Buenas and General Lagos, facing the Río Valdivia.

At Km 5 on the road to Niebla, there are guided visits to the **Cervecería Kunstmann** (☎ 292-969), Valdivia's largest brewery, which also includes the **Museo de la Cerveza** (beer museum) and a pub-restaurant. Any Niebla bus will drop visitors at the door.

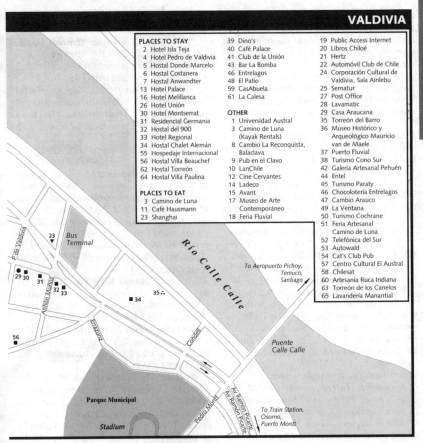

VALDIVIA

PLACES TO STAY
2 Hotel Isla Teja
4 Hotel Pedro de Valdivia
5 Hostal Donde Marcelo
6 Hostal Costanera
7 Hostal Anwandter
13 Hotel Palace
16 Hotel Melillanca
26 Hotel Unión
30 Hotel Montserrat
31 Residencial Germania
32 Hostal del 900
33 Hotel Regional
34 Hostal Chalet Alemán
55 Hospedaje Internacional
56 Hostal Villa Beauchef
62 Hostal Torreón
64 Hostal Villa Paulina

PLACES TO EAT
3 Camino de Luna
11 Café Hausmann
23 Shanghai

39 Dino's
40 Café Palace
41 Club de la Unión
43 Bar La Bomba
46 Entrelagos
48 El Patio
59 CasAbuela
61 La Calesa

OTHER
1 Universidad Austral
3 Camino de Luna
   (Kayak Rentals)
8 Cambio La Reconquista,
   Balaclava
9 Pub en el Clavo
10 LanChile
12 Cine Cervantes
14 Ladeco
15 Avant
17 Museo de Arte
   Contemporáneo
18 Feria Fluvial

19 Public Access Internet
20 Libros Chiloé
21 Hertz
22 Automóvil Club de Chile
24 Corporación Cultural de
   Valdivia, Sala Ainlebu
25 Sernatur
27 Post Office
28 Lavamatic
29 Casa Araucana
35 Torreón del Barro
36 Museo Histórico y
   Arqueológico Mauricio
   van de Maele
37 Puerto Fluvial
38 Turismo Cono Sur
42 Galería Artesanal Pehuén
44 Entel
45 Turismo Paraty
46 Chocolotería Entrelagos
47 Cambio Arauco
49 La Ventana
50 Turismo Cochrane
51 Feria Artesanal
   Camino de Luna
52 Telefónica del Sur
53 Autowald
54 Cat's Club Pub
57 Centro Cultural El Austral
58 Chilesat
60 Artesanía Ruca Indiana
63 Torreón de los Canelos
65 Lavandería Manantial

LA ARAUCANÍA

Just north of Puente Pedro de Valdivia, on the Costanera, there are kayak rentals near the floating restaurant Camino de Luna.

Special Events

Valdivia's numerous summer events are all subsets of Verano en Valdivia, a two-month-long celebration that includes many minor happenings and more significant ones such as late January's Festival Musical de Valdivia; February's Aniversario de la Ciudad (on the ninth), a commemoration of the city's founding; and Noche de Valdivia, the third Saturday in February, which features decorated riverboats and fireworks.

Places to Stay

Valdivia's accommodations scene is a bit unusual, with plenty of budget choices, at least in the summer, relatively few lower-mid-range places, and a number of good upper-middle to top-end choices. For most of the year, students from the Universidad Austral monopolize the cheapest lodging, but many of these same places vigorously court travelers in summer. Some hospedajes take their name from the street where they're located, so don't be surprised to find three or more with identical names – if someone recommends a place, be sure to get the exact street number.

Hospedajes are heavily concentrated on Av Ramón Picarte and Carlos Anwandter. Sernatur keeps a roster of seasonal accommodations, which change from year to year.

Budget *Camping Isla Teja* (☎ 213-584) is about half an hour's walk across Puente Pedro de Valdivia, at the end of Calle Los Robles and Los Cipreses. It's a pleasant orchard setting – free apples in late summer – with good sanitary facilities and a riverside beach. Rates are US$13 for two persons, with a small charge for each additional person.

The HI affiliate, *Residencial Germania* (☎ 212-405, *Av Ramón Picarte 873*), charges US$8.50 per person for clean rooms with hot showers, breakfast and friendly German-speaking owners.

Friendly *Hotel Regional* (☎ 216-027, *Picarte 1005*) is plain but clean, with hot water and a small restaurant for US$6 per person with shared bath; doubles with private bath cost US$20. *Hotel Unión* (☎ 213-819, *Prat 514*) is clean, central and economical at US$10/16 per head, but suffers from brusque management.

Hospedaje Internacional (☎ 212-015, *García Reyes 658 Interior*) has a hospitable German-speaking owner who charges US$10/19 singles/doubles. Near the bus terminal, clean and attractive *Hostal del 900* (☎ 213-055, *Picarte 953*) charges US$12 per person with shared bath, but without breakfast. *Hostal Villa Beauchef* (☎ 216-044, *Beauchef 844*) has rooms for US$13/21 with shared bath, US$21/35 with private bath.

Residencial Germania (☎ 212-405, *Picarte 873*) is a very decent place for US$15 per person with breakfast, hot showers, heated rooms, a restaurant and friendly, German-speaking owners. Another popular choice is *Hotel Montserrat* (☎ 215-401, *Picarte 849*), with small but clean and bright rooms for US$15/25 with breakfast. *Hostal Costanera* (☎ 250-042, *Av Prat 579*) has spacious rooms for US$16 per person with

breakfast, but the plumbing fixtures could use an upgrade.

Well-located, inviting *Hostal Donde Marcelo* (☎/fax 205-295, *Janequeo 355*) charges US$17 per person with breakfast and cable TV, but the ownership has drawn some criticism for rigidity. Popular *Hostal Anwandter* (☎ 218-587, *Anwandter 601*) has rooms with shared bath and breakfast from around US$17/23, as well as rooms with private bath for US$25/33, but the hot water is sometimes balky.

Mid-Range & Top End Mid-range accommodations start around US$29/50 with breakfast at homey, consistently improving *Hostal Torreón* (☎ 212-622, *Pérez Rosales 783*). *Hostal Chalet Alemán* (☎/fax 218-810, *Picarte 1134*) charges US$37/57. The very central *Hotel Palace* (☎ 213-319, *fax 219133, Chacabuco 308*) has small but pleasant rooms from US$42/48.

Charming *Hostal Villa Paulina* (☎ 212-445, *fax 216-372, Yerbas Buenas 389*) charges US$42/56 with private bath. Across Puente Pedro de Valdivia, one of Valdivia's best values is *Hotel Isla Teja* (☎ 215-014, *fax 214-911, Las Encinas 220*), which offers rooms that start at US$49/59 in a tranquil but still convenient setting.

At *Hotel Melillanca* (☎ 212-509, *fax 222-740, Av Alemania 675*), rates start at US$49/69 and range to US$72/95, but it's a questionable value for the money. The city's classic hotel is *Hotel Pedro de Valdivia* (☎/fax 212-931, *Carampangue 190*), a traditional pink palace with elaborate gardens for US$99/128 with breakfast. On woodsy Isla Teja, *Hotel Puerta del Sur* (☎ 224-500, *Av Los Lingues 950*) is a resort facility charging US$110/122.

Places to Eat

Valdivia has a variety of good-to-excellent restaurants in all price categories. For inexpensive seafood, visit any of the several restaurants at the renovated *Mercado Central*, bounded by Chacabuco, Yungay, Libertad and the Costanera.

For some reason, *Café Palace* (☎ 213-539, *Pérez Rosales 580*) remains popular with young people, especially on Saturday mornings, but some of the sandwiches are almost inedible. For pastries and desserts, try instead the venerable *Café Hausmann* (☎ 213-878, *O'Higgins 394*), which also has fine lunches.

Dino's (☎ 213-061, *Maipú 191*) is a branch of the popular southern Chilean chain. *El Patio* (☎ 215-238, *Arauco 343, 2nd floor*) is a worthwhile choice for beef and seafood. *CasAbuela* (☎ 218-807, *Camilo Henríquez 746*) offers home-style Chilean cooking, with lunches from US$5.

Opposite the plaza, the *Club de la Unión* (☎ 213-377, *Camilo Henríquez 540*) offers filling, well-prepared three-course meals, with tea or coffee, for about US$6. Try also *Bar La Bomba* (☎ 213-317, *Caupolicán 594*), which has good meals, reasonable prices and, occasionally, live music.

Valdivia has two Chinese restaurants, *Yang Cheng* (☎ 224-088, *General Lagos 1118*), relocated after a fire burned its previous locale to the ground, and *Shanghai* (☎ 212-577, *Anwandter 898*).

La Calesa (☎ 213-712, *Yungay 735*) serves Peruvian dinners and seafood. *Camino de Luna* (☎ 213-788. *Prat s/n*), is a floating seafood restaurant on the Costanera.

There are good desserts and ice cream at *Entrelagos* (☎ 218-333, *Pérez Rosales 630*).

Entertainment

Cine Cervantes (*Chacabuco 210*) is the only place to see first-run movies.

Downtown pubs and discos include *La Ventana* (☎ 218-806, *Arauco 425*); *Pub en el Clavo* (☎ 211-229, *Av Alemania 299*); *Balaclava* (*northeast corner of Av Alemania and Camilo Henríquez*); and the *Cat's Club Pub* (☎ 207-546, *Esmeralda 657*), a restored older building with great atmosphere.

Shopping

Chocolates are a regional specialty, with several different outlets including Chocolatería Entrelagos at Pérez Rosales 622.

For artisanal goods, visit the new Feria Artesanal Camino de Luna, at the corner of Yungay and San Carlos. Other outlets include the Galería Artesanal Pehuén (☎ 251-412) at

Arauco 340 and, for Mapuche crafts, Artesanía Ruca Indiana at Camilo Henríquez 758 or Casa Araucana at Picarte 841.

Getting There & Away

Air LanChile (☎ 218-841), O'Higgins 386, flies weekdays to Concepción (US$44) and Santiago (US$120), and Saturdays and Sundays to Temuco (US$15) and Santiago. Ladeco (☎ 213-392), Caupolicán 364, Locales 7 & 8, flies nightly to Temuco and Santiago.

Avant (☎ 251-431), Chacabuco 408, Local 27, flies daily except Saturday to Concepción (US$44) and Santiago (US$98 to US$106), and Saturday to Temuco (US$15) and Santiago.

Bus Valdivia's Terminal de Buses (☎ 212-212) is at Anfión Muñoz 360. Tur-Bus (☎ 226-010), Tas Choapa (☎ 213-124), Buses Norte (☎ 212-800), Igi Llaima (☎ 213-542), Buses Lit (☎ 212-835) and Cruz del Sur (☎ 213-840) have frequent buses to destinations on or near the Panamericana between Puerto Montt and Santiago. Typical fares are Temuco US$3.50, Puerto Montt US$6.50, Concepción US$10, Talca US$14 and Santiago US$17.

Regional carriers include Línea Verde and Pirehueico (☎ 218-609) to Panguipulli (US$3), Bus Futrono (☎ 202-225) to Futrono, Buses Jac (☎ 212-925) to Villarrica and Temuco (US$3) and Buses Cordillera Sur (☎ 229-533) to other interior lake district destinations.

Tas Choapa, Cruz del Sur, Andesmar (☎ 224-665) and Buses Norte provide international service to Bariloche (US$18).

Getting Around

From the bus terminal, any bus marked 'Plaza' will take you to Plaza de la República. Buses from the plaza to the terminal go down Arauco before turning onto Picarte. There are also taxi colectivos.

To/From the Airport Valdivia's Aeropuerto Pichoy is 29km north of the city via the Puente Calle Calle. Transfer Valdivia (☎ 225-533) provides on-demand minibus service to the airport (US$3.50).

Car Rental cars are available from Hertz (☎ 218-317) at Picarte 640, and Autowald (☎ 212-786) at Henríquez 610.

CORRAL, NIEBLA & ISLA MANCERA

Southwest of Valdivia, where the Río Valdivia and the Río Tornagaleones join the Pacific, there are 17th-century Spanish fortifications at Corral, Niebla and Isla Mancera. Largest and most intact is the **Castillo de Corral**, consisting of the Castillo San Sebastián de la Cruz (1645), the gun emplacements of the Batería de la Argolla (1764) and the Batería de la Cortina (1767). Nearby **Fuerte Castillo de Amargos**, a half-hour's walk north of Corral, lurks on a crag above a small fishing village.

Allowing Spanish forces to catch potential invaders in a crossfire from its location on the north side of the river, **Fuerte Niebla** also dates from 1645, but the remaining ramparts of Castillo de la Pura y Limpia Concepción de Monfort de Lemus (1671) are the oldest remaining ruins; the former commandant's house, now restored, is the

---

Museo Fuerte Niebla, open 9 am to 8 pm daily November through March, 10 am to 5:30 pm daily except Monday the rest of the year. Isla Mancera's **Castillo San Pedro de Alcántara** (1645) guarded the confluence of the Valdivia and the Tornagaleones, but then became the residence of the military governor.

In January and February, at 4 and 6 pm daily, there is a historical reenactment of Spanish military maneuvers at Corral. As a popular bathing resort for Valdivianos, Niebla has a tourist office, open 9 am to 1 pm and 2:30 to 7 pm daily in summer. The Niebla restaurant *Canto del Agua* serves fish fresh off the boat, while in quieter Corral, several waterfront restaurants serve huge plates of curanto.

Getting There & Away

The best alternative is a leisurely float on the regular launches from Valdivia's Puerto Fluvial, near the Sernatur office, returning by bus in the afternoon. Departures vary according to the day and season; the trip takes about 2½ hours from Valdivia to Corral via Isla Mancera, Amargos and Niebla. Prices vary depending on the level of service, but range from about US$3 to US$10.

Among the choices are the *Neptuno* (☎ 218-952), the *Orion III* (☎ 210-533), the *Reina Sofía* (☎ 207-120), the *Río Calle Calle* (☎ 202-223) and the *Isla del Río* (☎ 225-244). All services are less frequent outside the summer high season.

From 8:30 am to 9 pm, buses to Niebla leave from the corner of Yungay and Chacabuco in Valdivia. There are 24 launches daily across the river between Niebla and Corral for US$0.60 per person; there is also a car ferry charging US$7.50 per vehicle.

HE Tours (☎ 210-533), Libertad 23 in Valdivia, offers half-day (six-hour) tours down the Río Valdivia to Corral that include a stopover for lunch at Isla Huapi, a small private nature reserve on the Tornagaleones. The US$32 price includes admission to the historical reenactment at Corral.

Chile's Scottish Savior

In 1820, a single Chilean warship under Scotsman Lord Thomas Cochrane launched an audacious but successful assault on Spanish forces at what one of his subordinates later, with some hyperbole, called the 'Gibraltar of South America.' Boldly seizing a Spanish vessel in the harbor, Cochrane landed 300 musketeers who took Corral by surprise – no mean feat, since it was defended by more than 700 soldiers and 100 cannons.

Lord Cochrane himself had a diverse and colorful career. Convicted of fraud and jailed in Great Britain, he became one of the world's highest-ranking mercenaries, serving Brazil and Greece as well as Chile. Britain restored his rank in 1842 and even promoted him to Admiral in 1854.

FUTRONO
☎ 63

On the north shore of Lago Ranco, Futrono is a small, quiet and dusty town (permanent population 3000), 102km from Valdivia via Paillaco, on the Panamericana. While the lakeshore is attractive, public access is limited and awkward. The main street, Av Balmaceda, continues east to Llifén and Lago Maihue; although the road around the east side of Lago Ranco is very poor beyond Llifén, travelers to the town of Lago Ranco can make connections there.

Futrono's municipal Oficina de Turismo (☎ 481-389) is at O'Higgins and Balmaceda, at the western approach to town.

Places to Stay & Eat
Modest but friendly *Hospedaje Futronhué* (☎ *481-265, Balmaceda 90*), is clean and tidy and has hot showers for US$11/20 singles/doubles. *Hostería Rincón Arabe* (☎ *481-406, Manuel Montt s/n*) overlooks the lake, with a swimming pool and a fine restaurant serving Middle Eastern and Chilean meals. Rooms cost about US$14 per person with private bath, without breakfast.

Getting There & Away
From offices on Av Balmaceda. Buses Futrono, Buses Pirehueico and Buses Cordillera Sur each operate several buses daily to Valdivia (US$3) via Paillaco. Cordillera Sur continues to Llifén and Riñinahue, for connections to the town of Lago Ranco.

LLIFÉN
☎ 63

Llifén, at the east end of Lago Ranco via a rather poor road, is a more attractive but significantly more expensive resort than Futrono. Lodging is available at *Hostería Lican* (☎ *215-757, fax 213-155*) for US$30 double without breakfast (but there is a restaurant), or at *Hostería Huequecura* (☎ *09-653-5450, 218-125*) starting at US$25/42. *Hostería Chollinco* (☎ *481-205 in Valdivia)*, a short distance up the road to Lago Maihue, charges US$30 for campsites, not to mention US$40 per person for accommodations with breakfast.

LAGO RANCO
☎ 63

On the south shore of its namesake lake, the village of Lago Ranco is a modest working-class resort (permanent population about 2000) in pleasant but unspectacular country, 124km from Valdivia via Río Bueno. The Mapuche reserve of Isla Huapi, in the middle of the lake, lends a strong indigenous presence.

Information
Staffed by enthusiastic and well-informed locals, Lago Ranco's municipal tourist office (☎ 491-212) has free maps and leaflets on the Lake District. On the north side of Av Concepción, the main road from Río Bueno, it's open 8:30 am to 12:30 pm and 2:30 to 6:30 pm daily in summer only. The Municipalidad also maintains an office at the junction with Ruta 5, the Panamericana, open December through March only.

Turihott (☎ 491-201), Valparaíso 111, runs auto trips around Lago Ranco and has a launch for excursions to Isla Huapi. Specializing in Mapuche ceramics, the **Museo Arqueológico de Lago Ranco**, Santiago s/n, is open 8:30 am to 1 pm and 2:30 to 7 pm daily between mid-December and mid-March. Admission is free.

Special Events
Visitors are welcome to the Mapuche festival Lepun, which takes place on Isla Huapi in late January, but photography is strictly forbidden.

Places to Stay & Eat
Camping Lago Ranco, on a crowded lakefront site with limited shade, charges US$13 per site. Hot showers are available on a limited schedule. Otherwise the most economical alternative is *Hospedaje Alto Pino* (☎ *491-356, Concepción 197* at about US$10 per person. Lakefront *Hostería Casona Italiana* (☎ *491-225, Viña del Mar 145)* is a cheerful place with moderate prices, about US$21/38 singles/doubles with breakfast, and also offers other meals. Almost next door, *Hostería Phoenix* (☎ *491-226, Viña del Mar 141)* charges US$30/32 with full board.

Getting There & Away

Weekdays at 9 am, Buses Obando goes to Río Bueno, with connections both north and south on the Panamericana. Buses San Martín also goes to Río Bueno, while Buses Ruta 5 goes to Osorno via Río Bueno.

Buses Lagos del Sur also goes to Osorno and to Riñinahue, at the east end of Lago Ranco. Obando also has buses to Riñinahue, with connections to Futrono: this entails crossing the Río Calcurrupe on a current-driven barge.

RÍO BUENO
☎ 64

Just east of the Panamericana, 40km north of Osorno, Río Bueno (population 13,000-plus) is a crossroads for Lago Ranco. Dating from 1778, its colonial **Fuerte San José de Alcudia** commands a bluff overlooking the river, while the **Museo Arturo Moller Sandrock**, Pedro Lagos 640, is open 9 am to noon and 2:30 to 6 pm Tuesday through Friday, 10 am to 12:30 pm weekends. The museum contains Mapuche ceramics, antique firearms, and documentation on German colonization in the region.

Reasonable accommodations are available for about US$10 per person at *Hospedaje Río Bueno* (☎ 341-860, *Patricio Lynch 1491*) or at *Hotel Richmond* (☎ 341-363, *Comercio 755*). There are several buses daily to Lago Ranco with Obando, Buses del Sur, San Martín and Buses Ruta 5.

OSORNO
☎ 64

Founded in 1558 by García Hurtado de Mendoza, by the end of the 16th century San Mateo de Osorno had a population of more than 1000 Spaniards and mestizos, supported directly or indirectly by encomiendas of 80,000 Indians. After the Mapuche rebellion of 1599 forced the city's inhabitants to flee to Chiloé, Spaniards failed to re-establish the settlement until 1796. Even after Chilean independence from Spain, growth was slow, as Mapuche control of the countryside made overland communications difficult and dangerous.

Since the mid-19th century, German immigrants have left their mark on the city and the region, particularly in manufacturing and dairy farming. By the turn of the 20th century, the population reached 5000, the city had its first newspapers and the railroad had arrived from Santiago. The local economy still relies on agriculture and its subsidiary industries, but tourism is increasing significantly, thanks to nearby lake resorts and the excellent communications both north and south, as well as across the Andes to Argentina. Commerce still outweighs tourism as a contributor to the local economy, however.

Orientation

At the confluence of the Río Rahue and the Río Damas, Osorno (population 105,000) is 910km south of Santiago and 110km north of Puerto Montt via the Panamericana. The city is a key road-transport hub, especially to Lago Puyehue, Lago Rupanco, Parque Nacional Puyehue and Pajaritos (the major border crossing to Argentina).

Most places of interest to the visitor are within a few blocks of the Plaza de Armas, in an area bounded by the Río Rahue to the west, the Río Damas to the north, Av Bilbao to the south and Calle Angulo to the east.

Information

Tourist Offices Sernatur (☎ 237-575) is on the ground floor of the Edificio Gobernación Provincial, on the west side of the Plaza de Armas. Well-stocked with maps, pamphlets and information on Osorno and the entire region, it's open weekdays 8:30 am to 1 pm and 2:30 to 7 pm. In summer, there's usually an English speaker on duty.

From mid-December through March, the municipal Departamento de Turismo operates an information kiosk at the northwest corner of the Plaza de Armas. Its hours are 10 am to 1:30 pm and 2:30 to 8 pm Monday through Saturday, 10 am to 2 pm Sunday.

There is a private information office (☎ 234-149), coordinated with Sernatur, at the main Terminal de Buses, Errázuriz 1400. Another good source of information is the

Automóvil Club de Chile (☎ 232-269), Manuel Bulnes 463.

El Diario Austral, Osorno's daily newspaper, publishes a useful monthly *Guía de Servicios* in summer.

Money Turismo Frontera (☎ 236-394), at Ramírez 959, Local 11, and Cambiotur (☎ 234-846), Juan Mackenna 1004, change US and Argentine cash and US traveler's checks. Banco de Osorno has an ATM at the corner of Ramírez and Matta.

Post & Communications The post office vis at O'Higgins 645, opposite the Plaza de Armas. Entel is at Ramírez 1107, Chilesat is at O'Higgins 645 and the private Centro de Llamados is at Ramírez 816.

Olivetti, Los Carrera 821, offers Internet access.

Travel Agencies In addition to Turismo Frontera (see Money), Lagos Austral (☎ 234-137), Ramírez 949, Local 11, runs tours to Parque Nacional Puyehue.

British-run Anytime Adventures (☎/fax 317-520, anytime@pearshaped.com), Errázuriz 1520, offers tours throughout the region and the country in a customized bus.

Cultural Centers Osorno's Centro Cultural (☎ 238-898), Av Matta 556, offers rotating exhibitions of painting, photography and other events. It's open 9 am to 1 pm and 3 to 7:30 pm daily.

The Alianza Francesa is at Los Carrera 753 and the Instituto Chileno-Norteamericano is at Los Carrera 770.

National Parks Conaf (☎ 234-393) is at Martínez de Rozas 430.

Laundry Lavandería Limpec is at Prat 678.

Medical Services Osorno's Hospital Base (☎ 235-572) is on Av Bühler, the southward extension of Arturo Prat.

Museo Histórico Municipal

Osorno's well-arranged historical museum includes exhibits on Mapuche culture, the city's shaky colonial origins, German colonization and 19th-century development, local naval hero Eleuterio Ramírez and natural history.

Housed in an impressive neocolonial building dating from 1929, the musem holds several uncommon and noteworthy objects. A very unusual collection of antique firearms includes a pistol that seems to be attached to an early Swiss army knife. One historical photograph of Termas de Puyehue, east of Osorno, depicts the modest origins of what is now an elegant, expensive resort.

At Matta 809, the museum (☎ 238-615) is open 10 am to 12:30 pm and 2:30 to 5 pm weekdays; additional summer hours are 11 am to 1 pm and 4 to 7 pm Saturday. Admission is free.

Other Things to See & Do

Between the Plaza de Armas and the **Estación de Ferrocarril** (train station; 1912), new construction is threatening many of the deteriorating but intriguing buildings in Osorno's **Distrito Histórico** (historic district), which includes obsolete factories and weathered Victorian houses. Some, however, have been well restored, such as the silos of the **Sociedad Molinera de Osorno**, an early grain mill.

West of the railway station, the bulwarks of Osorno's **Fuerte Reina Luisa**, built in 1793 on the orders of Governor Ambrosio O'Higgins (father of Bernardo O'Higgins), once guarded riverine access to Osorno. While the well-restored ruins are unspectacular, they're a pleasant site for a lunchtime breather.

At Mackenna 949, the **Casa Mohr Pérez** (1876) is Osorno's oldest surviving Germanic construction, but the 1000 block of Mackenna, between Cochrane and Freire, preserves a solid row of early Germanic houses. The **Cementerio Católico** (Catholic cemetery), at Manuel Rodríguez and Eduvijes, has immense, ornate family crypts with numerous German surnames, reflecting the town's history from the 19th century to the present. There is also a large **Cementerio Alemán** on Los Carrera, between Arturo Prat and Angulo.

LA ARAUCANÍA

OSORNO

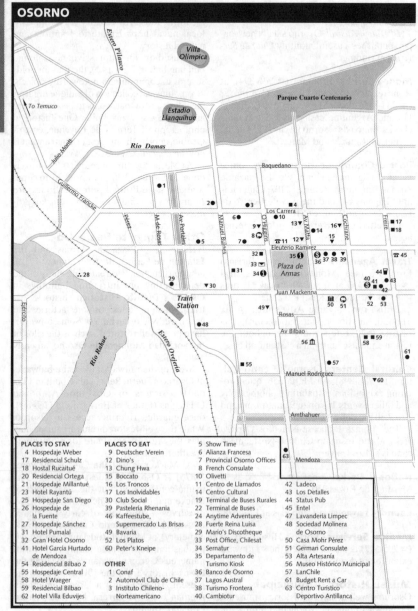

Villa Olímpica

Estero Pilauco

To Temuco

Estadio Llanquihue

Parque Cuarto Centenario

Río Damas

Baquedano

Julio Montt

Guillermo Francke

Peter

M. de Rosas

Av. Portales

Manuel Bulnes

O'Higgins

Los Carrera

Av. Matta

Cochrane

Freire

Eleuterio Ramírez

Plaza de Armas

Juan Mackenna

Ejército

Río Rahue

Train Station

Estero Ovejería

Rosas

Av. Bilbao

Manuel Rodríguez

Amthahuer

Mendoza

PLACES TO STAY
4 Hospedaje Weber
17 Residencial Schulz
18 Hostal Rucaitué
20 Residencial Ortega
21 Hospedaje Millantué
23 Hotel Rayantú
25 Hospedaje San Diego
26 Hospedaje de
   la Fuente
27 Hospedaje Sánchez
31 Hotel Pumalal
32 Gran Hotel Osorno
41 Hotel García Hurtado
   de Mendoza
54 Residencial Bilbao 2
55 Hospedaje Central
58 Hotel Waeger
59 Residencial Bilbao
62 Hotel Villa Eduvijes

PLACES TO EAT
9 Deutscher Verein
12 Dino's
13 Chung Hwa
15 Boccato
16 Los Troncos
17 Los Inolvidables
30 Club Social
39 Pastelería Rhenania
46 Kaffeestube,
   Supermercado Las Brisas
49 Bavaria
52 Los Platos
60 Peter's Kneipe

OTHER
1 Conaf
2 Automóvil Club de Chile
3 Instituto Chileno-
   Norteamericano
5 Show Time
6 Alianza Francesa
7 Provincial Osorno Offices
8 French Consulate
10 Olivetti
11 Centro de Llamados
14 Centro Cultural
19 Terminal de Buses Rurales
22 Terminal de Buses
24 Anytime Adventures
28 Fuerte Reina Luisa
29 Mario's Discotheque
33 Post Office, Chilesat
34 Sernatur
35 Departamento de
   Turismo Kiosk
36 Banco de Osorno
37 Lagos Austral
38 Turismo Frontera
40 Cambiotur

42 Ladeco
43 Los Detalles
44 Status Pub
45 Entel
47 Lavandería Limpec
48 Sociedad Molinera
   de Osorno
50 Casa Mohr Pérez
51 German Consulate
53 Alta Artesanía
56 Museo Histórico Municipal
57 LanChile
61 Budget Rent a Car
63 Centro Turístico
   Deportivo Antillanca

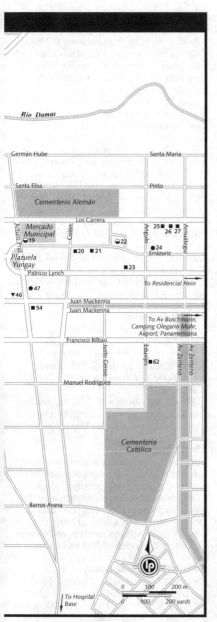

Special Events

Osorno's Festival Regional del Folklore Campesino, for two days in mid-January, presents and promotes typical music, dance, crafts and food. Toward the end of the month, the town hosts the Semana Osornina, a weeklong celebration of the city's colonial origins and Germanic heritage.

Places to Stay

Budget *Camping Olegario Mohr* (☎ 204-860), on the south bank of the Río Damas just off the Panamericana, is a shady municipal site, with picnic tables and firepits, but it lacks hot water and has only two toilets each for men and women. It now costs US$8.50 per site, and the attendants lock the front gate between midnight and 8 am, so it's impossible to leave or enter during those hours. Any taxi colectivo out Av Buschmann will drop you at the Panamericana, within a few minutes' walk of the site.

Close to the bus terminal, *Hospedaje Sánchez* (☎ 232-560, Los Carrera 1595) charges US$8.50 per person with breakfast and kitchen privileges. *Hospedaje Central* (☎ 231-031, Bulnes 876) is also cheap at US$9 plus US$1 for breakfast.

Spotlessly clean but with some sagging beds, *Hospedaje de la Fuente* (☎ 239-516, Los Carrera 1587) charges about US$8 per person, with breakfast, after amicable haggling. Improved *Hospedaje San Diego (Los Carrera 1551)* is also worth a look.

Clean and comfortable, with English-speaking management, *Hospedaje Weber* (☎ 248-413, Los Carrera 872) charges US$9 per person, including breakfast. Renovated *Residencial Ortega* (☎ 232-592, Colón 602) is an excellent value for US$9 with breakfast and shared bath; it's simple but very clean and airy, with pleasant common spaces.

Recently relocated, congenial, well-kept *Residencial Hein* (☎ 236-542, Errázuriz 1757) charges US$14/24 singles/doubles with shared bath, US$18/30 with private bath.

Mid-Range Osorno's mid-range accommodations are a good value, starting at appealing *Hospedaje Millantué* (☎ 242-480, Errázuriz 1339), across from the bus terminal, for US$22/38. **Residencial Schulz** (☎ 237-211, Freire 530) charges US$29 to US$38 double.

Highly recommended, clean and friendly **Hotel Villa Eduvijes** (☎/fax 235-023, Eduvijes 856) a few blocks south of the bus terminal, is an exceptional value at US$30/52 with breakfast. Service is outstanding at well-regarded **Hostal Rucaitué** (☎ 239-922, Freire 546), for US$31/48 with breakfast, TV and private bath.

The superlative **Residencial Bilbao** (☎ 242-244, fax 231-111, Francisco Bilbao 1019) charges about US$32/43. Rates and telephone numbers are identical at its sister hotel, **Residencial Bilbao 2** (Juan Mackenna 1205).

Facing the Plaza de Armas since 1930, the Art Deco **Gran Hotel Osorno** (☎ 232-171, fax 239111, O'Higgins 615) has slipped from the top-end category, mostly because other places have superseded it (in terms of cost and luxury). Rates start at about US$38/55; though not really grand, the rooms are simple and clean, and have phones and private baths.

Top End The modern but stylish **Hotel Pumalal** (☎/fax 242-477, Bulnes 630) charges US$40/65. Other modern top-end places include **Hotel García Hurtado de Mendoza** (☎ 237-111, fax 237-113) at Mackenna 1040 for US$57/91, and the very fine **Hotel Rayantú** (☎ 238-114, fax 238-116, Patricio Lynch 1462) charges US$58/81.

The more traditional, German-run **Hotel Waeger** (☎ 233-721, fax 237-080, Cochrane 816) gives special attention to German speakers. Perhaps Osorno's most elegant lodgings, it has rooms with private bath and breakfast for US$64/90, and a very good restaurant.

Places to Eat

The Mercado Municipal's **La Naranja** (Prat and Errázuriz, Local 13) has very good and inexpensive food, but there are many comparable places; don't overlook the basement comedores (inexpensive restaurants). In the Supermercado Las Brisas, the **Kaffeestube** (☎ 230-262, Mackenna 1150) serves good cafeteria food.

Facing the Plaza, **Dino's** (☎ 233-880, Ramírez 898) is a good place for drinks, snacks and sandwiches. **Bocatto** (☎ 238-000, Ramírez 938) serves pizza, sandwiches and very good ice cream. For fine pastries and light meals, try **Pastelería Rhenania** (☎ 235-457, Ramírez 977).

Los Platos (☎ 233-693, Mackenna 1027) has cheap lunchtime dishes for about US$4. **Los Troncos** (☎ 231-998, Cochrane 527) serves pizza. **Chung Hwa** (☎ 233-445, Matta 517) is the local Chinese restaurant, good and reasonably priced. **Los Inolvidables** (Freire 530) serves Middle Eastern food.

The **Deutscher Verein** (☎ 232-784, O'Higgins 563) is more typically Chilean than its German moniker would suggest, but offers good food with fine service at reasonable prices. **Bavaria** (☎ 231-302, O'Higgins 743) is part of a chain specializing in beef and seafood. The singular **Club Social** (Juan Mackenna 634) has a good Chilean menu. For a splurge, try the German food at **Peter's Kneipe** (☎ 232-083, Manuel Rodríguez 1039).

Entertainment

Osorno's only movie theater is the two-screen **Show Time** (☎ 233-890, Ramírez 650).

There are a number of central pubs and discos, including the **Status Pub** (Freire 677) and **Mario's Discotheque** (☎ 234-978, Mackenna 555).

Provincial Osorno (☎ 233-211, Ramírez 766-B) has fallen into the second division of Chile's professional soccer league.

Shopping

Local and regional crafts, including wood carvings, ceramics and basketry, are available at the Mercado Municipal, Errázuriz 1200, Locales 2 & 3; Alta Artesanía (☎ 232-446), Mackenna 1069; and Los Detalles (☎ 238-462), Mackenna 1100. There's another small artisans' market at Plazuela Yungay, at the corner of Prat and Ramírez.

Getting There & Away

Air LanChile (☎ 236-688), Matta 862, Block C, flies once or twice daily to Santiago (US$86 to US$120), usually via Temuco (US$23) but sometimes nonstop. Ladeco (☎ 234-355),

Mackenna 1098, flies Wednesday, Friday and weekends to Temuco and Santiago.

Bus – Regional Buses to local and regional destinations leave from the Terminal de Buses Rurales (☎ 232-073) in the Mercado Municipal, two blocks west at the corner of Errázuriz and Prat. Many smaller destinations in the region are most conveniently reached from Osorno.

Buses Puyehue (☎ 236-541), at the Mercado Municipal, has several buses daily to Termas de Puyehue, en route to Aguas Calientes (US$2), and to Chilean customs and immigration at Pajaritos (US$3), within Parque Nacional Puyehue. Expreso Lago Puyehue (☎ 243-919) goes to Entre Lagos (US$1.25) many times daily, Sundays to Aguas Calientes (US$2.50). Geosur also goes to Aguas Calientes. Taxi colectivos go to Entre Lagos all year, and to Aguas Calientes in summer only.

Buses Ruta 5 (☎ 237-020), at the main Terminal de Buses (☎ 234-149), Av Errázuriz 1400, near Angulo, serves Río Bueno, with connections to Lago Ranco and Lago Rupanco. Buses Pirihueico (☎ 233-050) goes to Panguipulli via Valdivia four times daily except Sunday.

Transur (☎ 234-371), which shares the Igi Llaima offices at the Terminal de Buses, goes to Las Cascadas (US$2.50), on the eastern shore of Lago Llanquihue at the foot of Volcán Osorno. Buses Via Octay (☎ 237-043), also in the same terminal, serves Puerto Octay (US$1) and Frutillar on Lago Llanquihue. Mini Buses Puerto Octay, at the same office, also goes to Puerto Octay. Buses to Octay leave every 20 to 30 minutes.

Across the Río Rahue, Buses Mar (☎ 236-166), Tarapacá 799, and Maicolpué (☎ 234-003), Valdivia 501, connect Osorno with Bahía Mansa (two hours, US$2), the only easily accessible ocean bathing resort between Valdivia and Chiloé.

Bus – Long Distance Long-distance buses also use the main terminal, (☎ 234-149) at Av Errázuriz 1400, near Angulo.

Many companies offer services to Puerto Montt and other Panamericana destinations,

including Tas Choapa (☎ 233-933), Varmontt (☎ 232-732), and Tur-Bus (☎ 234-170). There's also Buses Lit (☎ 234-317), Intersur (☎ 231-325), Igi Llaima (☎ 234-371), Buses Norte (☎ 236-076), Turibús (☎ 233-633) and Cruz del Sur (☎ 232-777).

Typical fares include Puerto Montt (US$3, 1½ hours), Temuco (US$5.50, three hours), Ancud (US$6, 3½ hours), Concepción (US$13, nine hours), Santiago (US$19, 14 hours), and Valparaíso/Viña del Mar (US$21, 16 hours). Many but not all of these services originate in Puerto Montt; for more details, see the Getting There & Away section for Puerto Montt, later in this chapter.

Bus – International From its main bus terminal, Osorno has international services to Bariloche and other Argentine destinations via the Cardenal Samoré pass over the Andes. Tas Choapa has connections for Mendoza and Buenos Aires via the Libertadores tunnel northeast of Santiago. Buses to destinations in Chilean Patagonia, such as Coihaique, Punta Arenas and Puerto Natales also go via Cardenal Samoré. Other principal companies are Buses Norte, Igi Llaima, Cruz del Sur and Río de La Plata (☎ 233-633). Most of these services originate in Puerto Montt; see that section's Getting There & Away entry for more details.

Fares to Bariloche are about US$19, to Mendoza US$40 and to Buenos Aires US$95.

Getting Around
To/From the Airport Osorno's Aeropuerto Carlos Hott Siebert (sometimes known as Cañal Bajo) is 7km east of downtown, across the Panamericana via Av Buschmann. An airport cab costs about US$3.50.

Car For rental cars, try the Automóvil Club de Chile (☎ 232-269), at Bulnes 463, or Budget (☎ 235-303), at Freire 848.

AROUND OSORNO
Along with Puerto Montt, Osorno is one of the best centers for exploring the Chilean lakes. From Osorno, you can go east to Lago Puyehue with its thermal baths, and continue

to Parque Nacional Puyehue, or south to Lago Llanquihue and the resorts of Puerto Octay and Frutillar.

Entre Lagos

Entre Lagos is an unpretentious resort 50km east of Osorno, on the southwest shore of Lago Puyehue. Eight kilometers east of town, quiet, sheltered **Camping No Me Olvides** (☎ 064-371-633) is an outstanding facility with private sites large enough for two tents, abundant firewood and excellent showers and toilets, but for US$25 it's no bargain.

For hotel accommodations, try **Hostería Entre Lagos** (☎ 064-371-225, Ramírez 65), which has singles/doubles for US$36/50; US$25/35 in the low-season. **Pub del Campo** (☎ 064- 371-220), about 100m west of town on the road to Osorno, comes highly recommended for meals.

Termas de Puyehue

One of Chile's most famous hot springs resorts, Termas de Puyehue is 76km east of Osorno, where paved Chile 215 forks; the north fork goes to Anticura and the Argentine border, while the southern lateral leads to Aguas Calientes and ends in Antillanca, in Parque Nacional Puyehue.

Set in elegant grounds at the junction of the two roads, the baronial **Hotel Termas de Puyehue**(☎ 064-232-157, fax 02-283-1010 in Santiago, puyehue@ctcreuna.cl) truly recalls an old-world alpine resort. Singles/doubles start at US$63/98 with breakfast; half-board and full-board are also available.

PARQUE NACIONAL PUYEHUE

Created in 1941 to protect 65,000 hectares of humid evergreen forest and starkly majestic volcanic scenery, Puyehue has since expanded to 107,000 hectares. It is Chile's most popular national park in terms of numbers of visitors, but this is a bit misleading – most Chileans head for the developed hot springs at Aguas Calientes and take only short walks on nearby nature trails, missing the truly high and wild backcountry. There is also skiing at Antillanca.

Flora & Fauna

In Puyehue's lower Valdivian forest, the dominant tree species is the multi-trunked ulmo (*Eucryphia cordifolia*), accompanied by olivillo (*Aextoxicon punctatum*), tineo (*Weinmannia trichosperma*) and southern beech (*Nothofagus* spp). The dense undergrowth includes the delicate, rust-barked arrayán (*Myrceugenella apiculata*, a member of the myrtle family), quila (*Chusquea* spp), a genus of solid, rather than hollow bamboo which make some areas utterly impenetrable), and wild fuchsia. At higher elevations, the southern beeches lenga and coigue predominate.

In such dense forest, wildlife is scarce or hard to see. In more open areas there are occasional sightings of puma or pudú, but birds are the most common animals. On the peaks, hikers may glimpse the Andean condor; along the rivers, look for the Chilean torrent duck (*Merganetta armata, pato cortacorriente* in Spanish), which flourishes in Class V rapids.

Puma

Pudú

Geography & Climate

Mountainous Puyehue is about 75km east of Osorno via Chile 215, the international highway to Argentina, which is now paved as far as the Chilean immigration post at Pajaritos. Altitudes range from 250m on the delta of the Río Golgol where it enters Lago Puyehue, to 2236m on the summit of Volcán Puyehue.

The park has a humid, temperate climate, with an annual rainfall of about 4200mm at Aguas Calientes. The annual mean temperature is about 9°C, with a summer average of about 14°C, which falls to 5°C in winter. January and February, the driest months, are best for visiting the high country, but the park is open all year and there's good skiing in winter.

Despite Puyehue's moist climate, many areas north of the highway are no less barren than the Atacama, as plants recolonized only slowly after a major eruption of Volcán Puyehue in 1960. On the volcano's western slopes are many extinct fumaroles and very lively hot springs.

Aguas Calientes

One of the highlights at Aguas Calientes is the **Sendero El Pionero**, a steep 1800m nature trail that offers, at the end of the trail, splendid views of Lago Puyehue, the valley of the Río Golgol and Volcán Puyehue. En route you will see the nalca *(Gunnera chilensis)*, resembling an enormous rhubarb, with edible stalks and leaves almost large enough to serve as umbrellas. There are

exceptionally fine specimens of the multi-trunked ulmo, which grows as tall as 45m and is covered with white flowers in summer. Chileans greatly prize *miel de ulmo,* the honey from the pollen bees extract from these flowers.

An easier nature trail is the **Sendero Rápidos del Chanleufú**, which follows the river for 1200m. For a longer excursion, take the 11km trail to **Lago Bertín**, where there is a basic refugio (some of these backcountry refugios have recently been closed because of hantavirus concerns). After hiking along the nature trails, or completing a longer trek, you can soak or swim in a heated pool filled with the therapeutic mineral waters that gave Aguas Calientes its name. This place is a more economical alternative than Termas de Puyehue.

Conaf's **Centro de Información Ambiental**, open 9 am to 1 pm and 2:30 to 8:30 pm daily, has a simple but informative display on Puyehue's natural history and geomorphology, with slide presentations at 5 pm. Usually, Conaf provides basic maps and brochures, despite occasional shortages.

Conaf rangers no longer lead overnight backpack trips to Lago Paraíso, Volcán Puyehue, Lago Constancia and Pampa Frutilla, but it is possible to make these trips independently. At Pampa Frutilla, near the border, it's essential to have official authorization from Conaf rangers at Anticura.

Antillanca

For some of the finest views of Puyehue and the surrounding area, visit Antillanca, a popular ski resort at the foot of Volcán Casablanca. The ski season runs from early June to late October; the ski area itself has three surface lifts, 460m of vertical drop and a friendly, clublike atmosphere.

At the end of the 18km road beyond Aguas Calientes, the resort is also open in summer, when there is good backcountry hiking and camping. The nearest formal campground is at Aguas Calientes. For details on ski packages, contact the Centro Turístico Deportivo Antillanca (☎ 064-232-297, fax 238-877), Casilla 765, O'Higgins 1073, Osorno.

Anticura

Anticura, 17km northwest of the Aguas Calientes turnoff, is the best base for exploring the park's wilder sectors. The international highway follows the course of the Río Golgol, but the finest scenery is the magnificently desolate plateau at the base of Volcán Puyehue, reached only by an overnight hike from El Caulle, 2km west of Anticura.

On the western slope of Puyehue, a steep morning-plus walk from El Caulle, Conaf has a well-maintained refugio that is a good place to lodge or camp (ask Conaf rangers at Anticura about access to the refugio, which

has recently been closed because of the hantavirus scare). From the refugio, it's another four hours or so through a moonscape of massive lava flows and extinct fumaroles to a spring with rustic thermal baths, which is a fine and private place to camp. Trekkers can continue north to Riñinahue, at the south end of Lago Ranco, or return to Anticura.

Some of Puyehue's best backcountry lies in the remote area between Chilean customs and immigration at Pajaritos station and the actual border, which was heavily fortified when Argentina threatened war over the Beagle Channel in 1979. Signs of these

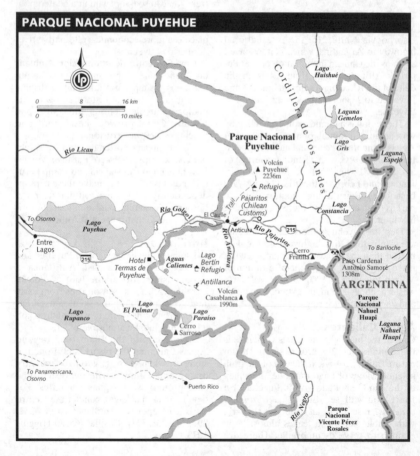

PARQUE NACIONAL PUYEHUE

preparations have disappeared, but to visit Pampa Frutilla, the upper drainage of the Río Golgol and Lago Constancia, visitors need permission from Conaf rangers here.

Another worthwhile sight, easily reached from the highway, is the **Salto del Indio**, an attractive waterfall on the Golgol where, according to legend, a lone Mapuche hid to escape encomienda service in a nearby Spanish gold mine.

Conaf has another **Centro de Información** at Anticura, but it's less elaborate than the one at Aguas Calientes.

Places to Stay & Eat

Now under private concession from Conaf, the rustic but attractive *Camping Catrué (☎ 064-234-393)*, near Anticura, has fresh water, picnic tables, firepits and basic toilets for US$8.50 per site. At Aguas Calientes, private concessionaires also operate *Camping Chanleufú (☎ 064-236-988 in Osorno)*, which costs US$15 per site for up to four persons, and *Camping Los Derrumbes*, which costs US$13 for up to four persons. Neither has hot showers, but fees entitle you to use the nearby thermal baths. In January and February, Catrué is a better alternative to these crowded, noisy sites.

Hostería y Cabañas Aguas Calientes (☎ 064-236-988) rents doubles for US$50 and four-bed cabins for US$95. Its restaurant offers reasonably priced meals, groceries and other supplies (much cheaper, with greater variety, in Osorno).

Hotel Antillanca (☎ 064-235-114) has accommodations for US$98/136 singles/doubles, breakfast included, but lunch and dinner cost extra; there are half-price bargains in summer. Its gymnasium, sauna, disco, boutique and shops seem horribly out of place in a national park.

Getting There & Away

Buses and taxi colectivos from Osorno's Mercado Municipal, at Errázuriz and Colón, pass Termas de Puyehue en route to Aguas Calientes and to Chilean customs and immigration at Pajaritos; for details, see the Osorno Getting There & Away section. In winter, there are direct services to the ski lodge at Antillanca; contact the Centro Turístico Deportivo Antillanca (☎ 064-232-297), O'Higgins 1073, Osorno.

Auto traffic is heavy enough that hitchhiking from Osorno's eastern outskirts should not be difficult if the bus schedule proves inconvenient. Because it is never entirely safe, Lonely Planet does not recommend hitchhiking.

PUERTO OCTAY

☎ 64

In the early days of German settlement, when poor roads made water transport critically important, the Lago Llanquihue harbor of Puerto Octay was a key transport link between Puerto Montt and Osorno. While modern roads long ago supplanted the lake as a freight route, the 2500 permanent residents of this bucolic village, 50km from Osorno at the north end of the lake, still provide a certain level of Eastern European *Gemütlichkeit* for visitors to the region. There are a handful of architectural landmarks and an excellent museum.

Puerto Octay's Oficina Municipal de Turismo (☎ 391-491) is on Calle Esperanza, on the east side of the Plaza de Armas. It's open 9 am to 9 pm daily in December, January and February.

Museo El Colono

Puerto Octay's surprisingly professional museum includes a superb cartographic display on German colonization, relevant and well-labeled historical photographs and a rundown on local architecture. At Independencia 591, it's open 10 am to 1 pm and 3 to 7 pm daily except Monday. Admission costs US$1.

Some of the museum's larger exhibits, mostly farm machinery, are displayed in a barn on Andrés Schmoelz (the road to Península Centinela) at the southern edge of town.

Special Events

Over the course of the summer, Puerto Octay hosts several festivals, which vary from year to year. Among them is the Encuentro Regional de Bandas del Sur, a big-band music event.

Places to Stay & Eat

About 2km north of town on the Osorno road, **Puerto Octay Backpacker** (*☎/fax 391-575*) is a custom-built, Swiss-run hostel-style facility whose only drawbacks are its relative isolation (also a strength) and its embryonic landscaping (an eventual strength). At US$6.50 per person without breakfast but with kitchen privileges, it's a bargain, and rental bicycles are also available.

Several travelers have complimented clean, comfortable and friendly **Hospedaje La Cabaña** (*☎ 391-260, German Wulf 712*), with rooms for US$7.50 without breakfast, US$8.50 with breakfast. Across the street, the same folks run **Restaurant Cabañas** (*Pedro Montt 713*). Other possibilities in the US$8 to US$9 price range include **Hospedaje Costanera** (*☎ 391-329, Pedro Montt 306*) and **Hospedaje Barrientos** (*☎ 391-381*), at Independencia 488.

A few kilometers south of town, on Península Centinela, the plain but agreeable **Hostería La Baja** (*☎ 391-269*) charges US$9 per person with breakfast and shared bath, or US$10 with private bath. Shady **Camping La Baja** (*☎ 391-251*) is Puerto Octay's municipal site, charging US$10 per site, but it gives backpackers and cyclists a break by charging only US$4.50 per person.

Farther on is **Hotel Centinela** (*☎/fax 391-326, Andrés Schmoelz s/n*), a massive chalet at the end of the road that runs along the peninsula. Its simple but spacious rooms, commanding fine views across the lake, cost US$21 per person with private bath. It also has a large restaurant.

For empanadas, try **La Naranja** (*☎ 391-219, Independencia 560*). **Baviera** (*☎ 391-460, Germán Wulf 582*) has a varied menu. For parrillada, there's **El Fogón de Anita** (*☎ 391455, Esperanza and Balmaceda*). **Tante Valy** (*☎ 391-461*), at Km 3 on the Frutillar highway, specializes in desserts and onces.

Getting There & Away

Puerto Octay's bus stop is on German Wulf just south of Amunátegui. Via Octay (*☎ 230-118 in Osorno*), connects Puerto Octay with Osorno's main bus terminal several times daily, while Thaebus goes to Puerto Montt.

At 5 pm weekdays, Arriagada goes south to Las Cascadas.

LAS CASCADAS

Named for nearby waterfalls, Las Cascadas is a tiny settlement fronting on a black-sand beach, on the eastern shore of Lago Llanquihue. The bus ride from Puerto Octay offers grand views of Volcán Osorno as it passes through dairy country with many small farms and tiny, shingled churches with corrugated metal roofs. The road south to Ensenada is a popular bicycle route, but it's very exposed and cyclists are vulnerable to the irritating, biting flies known as tábanos.

Places to Stay & Eat

Recommended **Hostería Irma**, 1km south of town on the Ensenada road, has a bar that also serves meals. Rates remain about US$15 per person with breakfast. Diagonally opposite the hostería, alongside the lake, is a peaceful, quiet and free campsite with few facilities.

Camping Las Cañitas (*☎ 064-238-336*), 3km down the Ensenada road, charges US$19 per site with hot and cold showers. It also rents five-person cabañas for US$55.

Getting There & Away

From Puerto Octay, one late-afternoon bus each weekday goes to Las Cascadas, but there's no bus service farther south toward Ensenada, the entry point to Parque Nacional Vicente Pérez Rosales. Consequently, southbound visitors must either walk or hitch south, or return to the Panamericana and take the bus from Puerto Varas.

The bus from Puerto Octay arrives at Las Cascadas early in the evening, so unless you can continue the 22km to Ensenada (a four- to five-hour walk) you'll have to spend the night in Las Cascadas.

FRUTILLAR
☎ 65

Seemingly floating on the horizon, snow-capped Volcán Osorno dominates the landscape across Lago Llanquihue from Frutillar, one of Chile's most captivating and popular lake resorts. Founded in 1856 and noted for its meticulously preserved Germanic architecture, Frutillar consists of two distinct parts: the resort area by the lake is Frutillar Bajo (Lower Frutillar), while the bustling commercial section near the Panamericana is Frutillar Alto (Upper Frutillar), about 2km west. Between them, the two have a permanent population of about 5000.

While its scenery and the quality of travelers' services is high, Frutillar may be just a little too perfect and orderly for some – municipal regulations are so strict as to prohibit picnics on the beach, for example. The landmark Hotel Casona del Lago, which burned to the ground a few years back, is under reconstruction as an event center.

Orientation

Frutillar Bajo is about 70km south of Osorno and 40km north of Puerto Montt via the Panamericana. The main street, Av Philippi, runs north-south along the lakeshore; most hotels and other points of interest are along its west side, with fine sandy beaches on the east. Av Carlos Richter connects Frutillar Bajo with Frutillar Alto.

Information

Frutillar's municipal Oficina de Información Turística (☎ 421-198) is a kiosk just south of the Municipalidad, on Av Philippi between San Martín and O'Higgins. The seasonal staff are a bit perfunctory toward visitor inquiries. The summer hours (December to March) are 10 am to 9 pm, while the rest of the year it's open 10 am to 6 pm.

Exchange, Av Philippi 883, changes cash and traveler's checks. Banco Santander, Av Philippi 555, has an ATM.

Correos de Chile is at Pérez Rosales and San Martín. There's a Centro de Llamados near the corner of Av Philippi and Manuel Rodríguez. CTC (Telefónica) and Entel are in Frutillar Alto.

Lavandería Frutillar (☎ 421-555) is at Carlos Richter 335, in Frutillar Alto.

Visitors can shower for US$0.50 at the municipal Baños Públicos (public baths) on O'Higgins, between Philippi and Pérez Rosales.

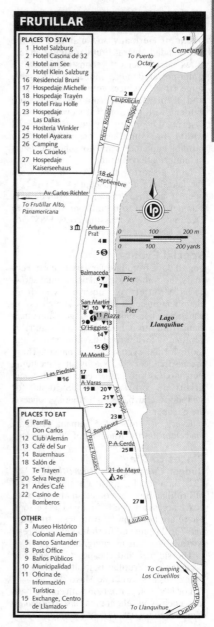

FRUTILLAR

PLACES TO STAY
1 Hotel Salzburg
2 Hotel Casona de 32
4 Hotel am See
7 Hotel Klein Salzburg
16 Residencial Bruni
17 Hospedaje Michelle
18 Hospedaje Trayén
19 Hotel Frau Holle
23 Hospedaje Las Dalias
24 Hostería Winkler
25 Hotel Ayacara
26 Camping Los Ciruelos
27 Hospedaje Kaiserseehaus

PLACES TO EAT
6 Parrilla Don Carlos
12 Club Alemán
13 Café del Sur
14 Bauernhaus
18 Salón de Te Trayen
20 Selva Negra
21 Andes Café
22 Casino de Bomberos

OTHER
3 Museo Histórico Colonial Alemán
5 Banco Santander
8 Post Office
9 Baños Públicos
10 Municipalidad
11 Oficina de Información Turística
15 Exchange, Centro de Llamados

Museo Histórico Colonial Alemán

Built with assistance from the Federal Republic of Germany and managed by the Universidad Austral, Frutillar's museum features nearly perfect reconstructions of a water-powered mill, a smithery with a usable forge (that produces souvenir horseshoes) and a mansion set among manicured gardens with phenomenal views of Volcán Osorno. Displayed on the grounds and within the buildings are 19th-century farming implements and household artifacts in immaculate condition.

Only a short walk up Arturo Prat from the lakeshore, the museum (☎ 421-142) is open 10 am to 2 pm and 3 to 6 pm daily in summer, 10 am to 6 pm from March 15 to December 15. Admission costs US$2 for adults, US$1 for children.

Special Events

For 10 days, from late January to early February, the Semana Musical de Frutillar showcases a variety of musical styles from chamber music to jazz. This annual event, which began in 1968, hosts singers and musicians from throughout the country and Argentina, with informal daytime shows and more formal evening performances. There are also concerts in nearby sites including Futrono, Osorno and Puerto Montt. Some tickets are costly at about US$10-plus for symphony and ballet, but midday concerts are cheaper.

Every November, the Semana Frutillarina celebrates the founding of the town.

Places to Stay

Budget *Camping Los Ciruelillos* (☎ 339-123), on a small peninsula at the south end of Frutillar Bajo, has quiet, shady sites with beach access for US$17 for up to six persons. There are hot showers from 8 am to 11 am and 7 to 11 pm, and fresh homemade bread is available in the morning.

The simpler and cheaper *Camping Los Ciruelos* is in Frutillar Bajo, at the corner of Pérez Rosales and 21 de Mayo.

For US$7.50 per person with shared bath and a hearty, excellent breakfast, *Hospedaje Kaiserseehaus* (☎ 421-387, Philippi 1333)

has earned enthusiastic recommendations. Rooms with private bath are only slightly dearer, about US$10.

For US$10 per hostal members only, there are official HI accommodations at *Hostería Winkler* (☎ 421-388, Philippi 1155); regular rooms are in the mid-range category.

Away from the lakeshore, but open only in summer, *Residencial Bruni* (☎ 421-309, Las Piedras 60) charges a very reasonable US$12 per person. Plain but friendly *Hospedaje Michelle* (☎ 421-463, Antonio Varas 75) is also open in summer only, charging US$15 with breakfast. *Hospedaje Trayén* (☎ 421-346, Philippi 963) is open all year, with rooms with private bath for US$17 and a highly regarded restaurant.

Mid-Range Mid-range accommodations are more abundant than budget choices. For US$31 per person, *Hostería Winkler* (☎ 421-388, Philippi 1155) is one of Frutillar's better values. *Hotel Casona del 32* (☎/fax 421-369, Caupolicán 28) charges US$38/54, while *Hospedaje Las Dalias* (☎ 421-393, Philippi 1095) has singles/doubles for US$38/63 with private bath and breakfast.

Directly opposite the beach, *Hotel am See* (☎ 421-539, Philippi 539) charges US$48/86. *Hotel Frau Holle* (☎ 421-345, Antonio Varas 54) charges US$58/63.

Top End Occupying a remodeled 1910 house, *Hotel Ayacara* (☎/fax 421-550, Philippi 1215) is open September to April; rates start at US$72 double. *Hotel Klein Salzburg* (☎ 421-201, fax 421-750, Philippi 663) charges US$84/112, while its sibling *Hotel Salzburg* (☎ 421-569, fax 421-599), at the north end of town on the road to Puerto Octay, has luxury lodging for US$111/157.

Places to Eat

Frutillar's best value is the *Casino de Bomberos* (☎ 421-588, Philippi 1065), which serves four-course lunches for about US$5 plus drinks. Part of its namesake hostería, *Salón de Te Trayen* (Philippi 963) specializes in onces and breakfasts. *Café del Sur* (☎ 421-467, Philippi 775) and the *Andes Café* (Philippi 1057) are good choices for light meals. The **Bauernhaus**, just across O'Higgins from Café del Sur, has superb kuchen.

The **Club Alemán** (*☎ 421-249, San Martín 22*) has fixed-price lunches for about US$10. The **Selva Negra** (*☎ 421-164, Antonio Varas 24*) serves delicious desserts and kuchen. **Parrilla Don Carlos** (*☎ 09-643-5909, Balmaceda near Philippi*) serves mixed Argentine grills.

Shopping
Local specialties include fresh raspberries – delicious and cheap in season – plus raspberry jam and kuchen. The Museo Colonial sells miniature wood carvings of museum buildings.

Getting There & Around
Cruz del Sur (*☎ 421-552*), Alessandri 360 in Frutillar Alto, has the most frequent services from Osorno or Puerto Montt. Tur-Bus (*☎ 421-390*), Diego Portales 150 in Frutillar Alto, also provides long-distance services. Thaebus, at the Alessandri terminal, has five buses daily to Puerto Octay.

Inexpensive taxi colectivos cover the short distance between Frutillar Alto and Frutillar Bajo.

PUERTO VARAS
☎ 65
An important lake port during the 19th-century German colonization, Puerto Varas is the gateway to Parque Nacional Vicente Pérez Rosales and the popular boat-bus crossing, via Lago Todos los Santos, to the Argentine lake resort of Bariloche. A popular travel destination in its own right for its access to Lago Llanquihue and the national park, Puerto Varas also contains perhaps the best-preserved concentration of Middle European architecture in the entire country.

Orientation
On the southern shore of Lago Llanquihue, Puerto Varas (population roughly 30,000) is only 20km north of Puerto Montt. Unlike most Chilean cities, its hilly topography and the curving shoreline have resulted in an irregular street plan, but most services are within a small grid bounded by Portales, San Bernardo, Del Salvador and the lakeshore. Outside this area, street numbers can be chaotic; on one street, three consecutive houses bear the numbers 62, 140 and 48.

The escarpment of Cerro Calvario, a steep hill southwest of downtown, has diverted Puerto Varas' growth east and west along the lakeshore. Av Costanera, an eastward extension of Del Salvador, becomes paved Chile 225 to Ensenada, Petrohué, and Lago Todos los Santos.

Information
Tourist Offices Puerto Varas' municipal Oficina de Información Turística (*☎ 232-437, puertovaras@munitel.cl*), San Francisco 431, has a friendly, well-informed staff, and provides free maps and brochures about the entire area, but there may not be English-speakers on duty at all times. In summer, it's open 9 am to 9 pm daily; the rest of the year, hours are 10 am to 2 pm and 4 to 6 pm.

Money There are numerous downtown ATMs, including Banco de Crédito at the corner of Del Salvador and San Pedro, but change cash and traveler's checks at Turismo Los Lagos, Local 11 in the Galería Real at Del Salvador 257, or at TravelSur (*☎ 236-000*), San José 261, Local 4.

Post & Communications The post office is at the corner of San Pedro and San José. Entel is at San José 413; Chilesat is on San José between San Pedro and Santa Rosa.

Internet Puerto Varas (*☎ 311-901*) is on the 2nd floor at Av Gramado 560. Turismo Nieve (*☎ 232-299*), San Bernardo 406, also has Internet access.

Travel Agencies For more conventional travel services and standard tours, including the bus-boat excursion across the Andes to Argentina, try Andina del Sud (*☎/fax 232-511*), Del Salvador 72, or Turismo Nieve (*☎ 233-000*), San Bernardo 406. TravelSur (*☎/fax 236-000, travelsu@travelsur.com*), San José 261, Oficina 4, has English-speaking personnel, changes money, and arranges rental cars.

PUERTO VARAS

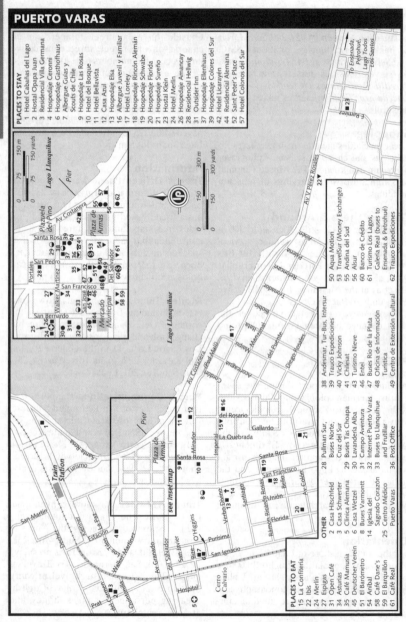

PLACES TO STAY
1   Hotel Cabañas del Lago
2   Hostal Opapa Juan
3   Residencial Villa Germana
4   Hospedaje Ceronni
6   Hospedaje Gasthofhaus
7   Albergue Guías y
    Scouts de Chile
9   Hospedaje Las Rosas
10 Hotel del Bosque
11 Hotel Bellavista
12 Casa Azul
13 Hospedaje Elsa
16 Albergue Juvenil y Familiar
17 Hotel Loreley
18 Hospedaje Rincón Alemán
19 Hospedaje Schwabe
20 Hospedaje Florida
21 Hospedaje Sureño
23 Hostal Klein
24 Hotel Merlin
26 Hospedaje Amancay
28 Residencial Hellwig
31 Outsider Inn
37 Hospedaje Ellenhaus
39 Hospedaje Colores del Sur
42 Hotel Licarayén
44 Residencial Alemana
52 Saint Peter's Place
57 Hotel Colonos del Sur

PLACES TO EAT
15 La Confitería
22 Ibis
24 Merlin
27 Espigas
31 Open Café
34 Asturias
35 Café Mamusia
45 Deutscher Verein
51 El Barómetro
54 Anibal
58 Café Dane's
59 El Barquillón
61 Café Real

OTHER
2   Casa Hitschfeld
3   Casa Schwerter
5   Clínica Alemana
6   Casa Wetzel
8   Buses Varmontt
14 Iglesia del
    Sagrado Corazón
25 Centro Médico
    Puerto Varas
28 Pullman Sur,
    Buses Norte,
    Cruz del Sur
29 Buses Tas Choapa
30 Lavandería Alba
31 Campo Aventura
32 Internet Puerto Varas
33 Buses to Llanquihue
    and Frutillar
36 Post Office
38 Andesmar, Tur-Bus, Intersur
39 Trauco Expediciones
40 Vicky Johnson
41 Chilesat
43 Turismo Nieve
46 Entel
47 Buses Rio de la Plata
48 Oficina de Información
    Turística
49 Centro de Extensión Cultural
50 Aqua Motion
53 TravelSur (Money Exchange)
55 Andina del Sud
56 Alsur
60 Banco de Crédito
61 Turismo Los Lagos,
    Galería Real (buses to
    Ensenada & Petrohué)
62 Trauco Expediciones

Puerto Varas is also one of the major regional centers for adventure tourism activities such as trekking, climbing, white-water rafting and kayaking, mountain biking and birding. Among the local operators are Aqua Motion (☎/fax 232-747, aquamotn@telsur.cl) at San Pedro 422; Alsur (☎/fax 232-300, alsur@telsur.cl), Del Salvador 100; and Trauco Expediciones (☎ 338-588), Santa Rosa 318, which also has an office at Del Salvador and San Juan.

English and German are spoken at Campo Aventura (☎/fax 232-910, outsider@telsur.cl), San Bernardo 318, which offers tours of the spectacular Cochamó valley, southeast of Puerto Varas. For details, see the entry for Cochamó, below.

Cultural Centers The Centro de Extensión Cultural, Del Salvador 322, occupies part of the former Hotel Antonio Varas.

Laundry Lavandería Alba (☎ 232-908) is at Walker Martínez 511.

Medical Services Puerto Varas' Clínica Alemana (☎ 232-336) is at Hospital 810, on Cerro Calvario near Del Salvador's southwest exit from town. There's also the Centro Médico Puerto Varas (☎ 232-792), Walker Martínez 576.

Things to See & Do

Puerto Varas' architecture gives it a distinctive middle European ambience, thanks in part to imposing landmarks such as the **Iglesia del Sagrado Corazón** (1915), overlooking downtown from a promontory at the corner of San Francisco and Verbo Divino. Most other notable constructions are private houses from the early decades of this century. The useful brochure *Paseo Patrimonial,* which suggests a walking tour of 28 different houses, was due to be reprinted and should be available at the tourist office. Several of these houses serve as hospedajes, including the **Casa Schwerter** (1941–42) at Nuestra Señora del Carmen 873, the **Casa Hitschfeld** (1930) at Arturo Prat 107 and the **Casa Wetzel** (1930) at O'Higgins 608.

Lago Llanquihue and the surrounding area provide opportunities for recreational activities such as swimming, windsurfing and cycling. For sailing on the lake, contact Tours Náutico (☎ 243-260 or 09-436-0338), which leaves from the main dock at the foot of San José.

Check adventure travel companies (mentioned in Puerto Varas' Travel Agencies section) for rental bicycles and equipment for other sports.

Organized Tours

Andina del Sud and others (see Travel Agencies earlier in this chapter) arrange conventional excursions such as city tours of Puerto Montt (US$13) and Frutillar (US$15), and bus trips to Saltos del Petrohué (US$10). See also Puerto Montt's Organized Tours section.

Several agencies offer treks in Parque Nacional Vicente Pérez Rosales and Parque Nacional Alerce Andino, climbing expedicions on Volcán Osorno, mountain bike rides throughout the area, birding excursions on the Río Maullín and rafting trips on the Río Petrohué. For more information, see Puerto Varas' Travel Agencies section, as well as individual national park entries.

Special Events

The prolonged Aniversario de Puerto Varas, comprising the last week of January and the first week of February, celebrates the city's founding in 1854. In the second week of February, the annual Concurso de Pintura El Color del Sur attracts painters from throughout the country for a contest and exhibition.

Places to Stay

For the most current information on budget accommodations, check the Oficina de Información Turística at San Francisco 431.

Budget In the Liceo Pedro Aguirre Cerda (a secondary school), the ***Albergue Juvenil y Familiar*** *(corner of Rosario and Imperial)* offers beds for US$5 in January and February only. During the same months, the ***Albergue Guías y Scouts de Chile*** *(☎ 232-774, San Ignacio 879)* also charges US$5 per person; hot showers, meals and kitchen privileges are all available.

Puerto Varas' most reasonable accommodations are its many hospedajes, mostly in the US$10 range per person. Some of these are seasonal, so it's better to phone ahead unless you happen to be in the immediate vicinity.

Among the cheapest alternatives, all in the US$8.50 range, are *Hospedaje Sureño* (☎ 232-648, *Colón 179*), the spacious but rather gloomy *Residencial Hellwig* (☎ 232-472, *San Pedro 210*) and friendly *Hospedaje Florida* (☎ 233-387, *Florida 1361*).

Central, well-regarded *Hospedaje Ellenhaus* (☎ 233-577, *Walker Martínez 239*), charges US$9 per person. In a quiet location alongside the Iglesia del Sagrado Corazón, *Hospedaje Elsa* (☎ 232-803, *María Brun 427*) is an excellent choice for US$10 per person with breakfast. Recommended *Hospedaje Ceronni* (☎ 232-016, *Estación 262*) charges US$10 per person, but US$15 with an elaborate breakfast.

In the US$12 range fall *Hospedaje Schwabe* (☎ 233-165, *Ramón Ricardo Rosas 361*); popular, Norwegian-run *Hospedaje Colores del Sur* (☎ 338-588, *Santa Rosa 318*); and well-located, German-run *Casa Azul* (☎ 232-904, *casaazul@telsur.cl, Mirador 18*), a remodeled traveler's hangout offering spacious, comfortable bedrooms and kitchen privileges (you can also buy breakfast). Slightly dearer *Saint Peter's Place* (☎ 236-208, *San Pedro 416*), an attractively refurbished downtown B&B, is a fine value.

Mid-Range Mid-range accommodations start around US$17 per person with breakfast at *Hospedaje Amancay* (☎ 232-201, *Walker Martínez 564*) and highly recommended *Hospedaje Las Rosas* (☎ 232-770, *Santa Rosa 560*), which has excellent views and serves an ample breakfast of kuchen, fruit and cheese. In the same range are convenient *Residencial Alemana* (☎ 232-419, *San Bernardo 416*) and attractive *Hospedaje Rincón Alemán* (☎ 232-087, *San Francisco 1004*). The stylish, immaculate, German-run *Outsider Inn* (*San Bernardo 318*, ☎ 232-910*), charging US$27/38 singles/doubles, is

one of Chile's best deals; breakfast in the downstairs café costs an additional US$3.

Three of Varas's landmark houses offer distinctive lodgings just outside the commercial downtown. In the Casa Wetzel, *Hospedaje Gasthofhaus* (☎ 233-378, *O'Higgins 608*) charges US$13 per person with private bath, plus US$5 for an elaborate breakfast. Rates at *Residencial Villa Germana* (☎ 233-162, *Nuestra Señora del Carmen 873*), in the Casa Schwerter, are US$13.50 with shared bath, US$15.50 with private bath, plus US$2 for breakfast. In the Casa Hitschfeld, German is spoken at *Hostal Opapa Juan* (☎ 232-234, *Arturo Prat 109*), which charges US$21 per person with private bath with breakfast.

Hotel Loreley (☎ 232-226, *Maipú 911*) has doubles for US$42, while *Hostal Klein* (☎/fax 233-109, *Ramírez 1255*) charges US$22 per person with breakfast. Offering sweeping views of Puerto Varas and Lago Llanquihue, with attentive service and comfortable beds, *Hotel del Bosque* (☎ 232-897, *fax 233-085, travelsu@chilesat.net, Santa Rosa 710*) charges US$34/50 with private bath. *Hotel Merlín* (☎/fax 233-105, *Walker Martínez 584*) is an appealing place that also features one of Chile's finest restaurants; rates are US$35/50.

Top End Past its prime, the lakefront, chalet-style *Hotel Licarayén* (☎ 232-305, *fax 232-955, San José 114*) may be better to look at than to stay in, with rates ranging from US$55/70 to US$70/90. Also on the lakefront, notable for its views, is *Hotel Bellavista* (☎ 232-011, *Vicente Pérez Rosales 60*), from US$84/103 in the summer. The modern *Hotel Colonos del Sur* (☎ 233-369, *Del Salvador 24*) charges US$90/110. *Hotel Cabañas del Lago* (☎ 232-291, *fax 232-707, Klenner 195*) starts at US$100/109.

Places to Eat

Café Real (*Del Salvador 257, 2nd floor*) has cheap fixed-price lunches. *Asturias* (☎ 232-283, *San Francisco 302*) features sandwiches and desserts. The *Open Café* (*San Bernardo 318*) serves excellent breakfasts and more elaborate, though not extravagant, lunches and dinners, all at reasonable prices.

Café Dane's (☎ 232-371, *Del Salvador 441*) is particularly good for *onces*, but don't overlook the tasty *humitas* and *pastel de choclo* (the latter made with chicken breast rather than leg meat). *Espigas* (☎ 310-529, *Walker Martínez 417, Local 3*) serves vegetarian specialties. *Aníbal* (☎ 235-222, *Del Salvador and Santa Rosa*) serves varied Argentine-style pizza.

In the Mercado Municipal at Del Salvador 582 are two upscale seafood restaurants: *El Mercado* and the erratic *El Gordito* (☎ 233-425). The *Deutscher Verein* (☎ 232-246, *San José 415*) offers midday Middle European meals at moderate prices. *Café Mamusia* (☎ 233-343, *San José 316*) serves excellent Chilean specialties in attractive surroundings, accompanied by powerful pisco sours.

Several readers have testified that *Ibis* (☎ 232-017, *Pérez Rosales 1117*) is worth a splurge, and travelers go out of their way to sample the imaginative cuisine at *Merlín* (☎ 233-105, *Walker Martínez 584*), part of its namesake hotel. While not cheap, it's not extravagantly costly to dine at one of Chile's finest restaurants.

El Barómetro (*San Pedro 418*) is worth a stop for coffee or dessert, as is *La Confitería* (☎ 338-188, *Imperial and Del Rosario*) for its kuchen. *El Barquillón* (*Del Salvador 401*) serves Varas's best ice cream.

Shopping

The local Feria Artesanal, on Plazuela del Vino near the lakefront, has a fine selection of local handicrafts. Vicky Johnson (☎ 232-240), Santa Rosa 318, sells Puerto Varas' finest coffee and chocolates.

Getting There & Around

Puerto Varas has no central terminal, but most bus companies have convenient downtown offices within a few blocks of each other. Fares and times closely resemble those from nearby Puerto Montt, and northbound buses from Puerto Montt often pick up passengers here.

Buses Varmontt (☎ 232-592), San Francisco 666, has daily buses to Santiago and intermediates, and more than two dozen daily to Puerto Montt. Other Santiago carriers include Pullman Sur, Buses Norte and Cruz del Sur (☎ 233-008), all at San Pedro 210, in the same location as Residencial Hellwig; the latter has extensive services to Chiloé.

Several other carriers are nearby at Walker Martínez 227-B: Andesmar (which crosses the Andes to Bariloche, Argentina), Tur-Bus and Intersur. Buses Tas Choapa (☎ 233-831) is across the street at Walker Martínez 230. Buses Río de la Plata, San Francisco 447, also goes daily to Bariloche (US$19).

From September to March, Andina del Sud (☎ 232-511), Del Salvador 72, goes daily to Ensenada and Petrohué, connecting with the bus-boat crossing to Bariloche. These buses leave Puerto Montt at 8:30 am, returning at 5 pm; from April to mid-September, they run Wednesday to Sunday, leaving Puerto Montt at 10 am and returning at 5 pm.

Buses to Frutillar and Llanquihue frequently leave from corner of San José and San Bernardo. Services to Ensenada and Petrohué, with a company popularly known as Mitsubishi for their minivans, leave from the Galería Real, Del Salvador 257, up to eight times daily.

Turismo Nieve (☎ 232-299), San Bernardo 406, arranges transport to Puerto Montt's Aeropuerto Tepual for US$14 for one to three passengers, US$18 for four to 10 passengers.

ENSENADA

At the southeast corner of Lago Llanquihue, at the base of snow-capped, 2660m Volcán Osorno, Ensenada is a tranquil stopover on Chile 225 to Petrohué and Lago Todos los Santos. To the south is the jagged crater of Volcán Calbuco, which blew its top during the Pleistocene.

Places to Stay & Eat

There is good camping at *Camping Playa Trauco* (☎ 212-033), at Km 43, for US$4 to US$7.50 per person, depending on proximity to the beach. Since the outstanding

Hostería Ruedas Viejas burned to the ground recently, the best remaining budget choice is *Hospedaje La Arena* (☎ 212-037), at Km 43 on Chile 255, which charges US$13 per person with breakfast. At Km 42, *Hostería Canta Rana* (☎ 212-010) has drawn praise for its accommodations (US$17 per person) and, in particular, for its restaurant.

Top of the range is the *Hotel Ensenada* (☎ 212-017), the first large building on the road to Las Cascadas and Puerto Octay, beyond the Petrohué turnoff. Resembling Puerto Octay's Hotel Centinela, it has a large restaurant festooned with odd bits of ironwork and machinery, and a raging fireplace. Room rates start at US$80 double with breakfast.

Getting There & Away

From Puerto Montt, Expreso JM runs half a dozen buses daily to Ensenada. Informal Mitsubishi minibuses make another seven trips. Andina del Sud (☎ 232-511), Del Salvador 72 in Puerto Varas, also has buses to Ensenada and Petrohué, connecting with the bus-boat crossing to Bariloche. Buses Fierro (☎ 253-022) travels three times daily to and from Puerto Montt (US$1.75).

Crossing the Lakes

One of the most popular traditional excursions in the entire lakes region is the bus-boat crossing from Puerto Montt and Puerto Varas to the Argentine city of San Carlos de Bariloche.

Andina del Sud, with offices in both Puerto Varas and Puerto Montt, is the Chilean representative for the trip, though tickets may also be purchased at Petrohué's dock. Fares for each stretch are Puerto Montt to Petrohué (US$7), Petrohué to Peulla (US$25), Peulla to Puerto Frías, Argentina (US$54). Other fares are Puerto Frías to Puerto Blest (US$5), Puerto Blest to Puerto Pañuelo (US$14) and Puerto Pañuelo to Bariloche (US$5). The total fare from Puerto Montt or Puerto Varas to Bariloche is US$110.

There is no public transport between Ensenada and Las Cascadas, a distance of 22km on the road to Puerto Octay, but hitch-hiking may be feasible. For pedestrians and cyclists, this is a hot, exposed route infested with tábanos. Lonely Planet does not recommend hitchhiking.

PN VICENTE PÉREZ ROSALES

Beneath the flawless cone of Volcán Osorno, Lago Todos los Santos is the centerpiece of Parque Nacional Vicente Pérez Rosales and the jewel of Chile's southern mainland lakes. A glacial basin scoured between densely forested ridges, the lake offers dramatic views of the volcano, at least when the clouds clear. The needle point of Volcán Puntiagudo lurks to the north; to the east, craggy Monte Tronador marks the Argentine border.

Established in 1926 to protect this extraordinary scenery, 251,000-hectare Pérez Rosales was Chile's first national park, ironically honoring a man who, according to US geographer Mark Jefferson, 'arranging the first important settlement of Germans near Lake Llanquihue…hired the Indians to clear away the woods by fire.' Ecologically, the park's Valdivian rain forest and other plant communities resemble those of Parque Nacional Puyehue, which borders it to the north.

Pérez Rosales has a much longer history, however. In pre-Columbian times, the Camino de Vuriloche was a major trans-Andean crossing for the Mapuche. Later, Jesuit missionaries traveled from Chiloé, continuing up the Estuario de Reloncaví and crossing the pass south of Tronador to Lago Nahuel Huapi, avoiding the riskiest crossings of the region's lakes and rivers. For more than a century after the Mapuche uprising of 1599, the Indians successfully concealed this route from the Spaniards.

Geography & Climate

Parque Nacional Vicente Pérez Rosales is about 50km east of Puerto Varas via paved Chile 225. Altitudes range from only 50m above sea level near the shores of Lago Llanquihue to 3491m on the summit of Tronador.

PARQUE NACIONAL VICENTE PÉREZ ROSALES

Other high points include 2490m Puntiagudo and 2660m Osorno, a popular – and challenging – climb. Because lava flows from Osorno have blocked the former westward drainage into Lago Llanquihue, the Río Petrohué (the outlet from Todos los Santos) now flows south into the Golfo de Reloncaví.

The park has a humid temperate climate, with an annual precipitation of about 2500mm near Ensenada, rising to about 4000mm at higher altitudes where much of it falls as winter snow. The annual mean temperature is about 11°C, with a summer average of about 16°C, falling to 6.5°C in winter. There are more than 200 days of rain annually, but January and February are the driest months.

Volcán Osorno

Adventure travel companies in Puerto Varas offer guided climbs of Volcán Osorno, which requires snow and ice-climbing gear, but experienced and well-equipped climbers should be able to handle it alone. Because of at least one accident and increasingly dangerous conditions on the mountain, Conaf now requires one guide for every three people. This makes the full-day excursion, which leaves at 5:30 am, pricey at US$200 per person. Independent climbers may still scale the mountain, but must obtain Conaf permission, providing detailed personal qualifications as well as lists of equipment and intended routes.

The **Refugio Teski Ski Club** (☎ 065-212-012), just below snow line, has outstanding views of Lago Llanquihue. Take the Ensenada-Puerto Octay road to a signpost about 3km from town and continue 9km up the lateral. The refugio is open all year, but getting there entails a long, uphill trek; it's difficult, particularly with a heavy pack. Beds are available for US$10 per night; breakfast costs US$5, lunch or dinner US$9. Climbing equipment – ice axes, ropes and crampons – rent for US$20 per person.

Petrohué

In the shadow of Volcán Osorno, Petrohué is the point of departure for the ferry excursion to Peulla, over the deep blue waters of Todos los Santos. Ferries leave for Peulla early in the morning and return after lunch. At 3 pm daily in summer, Andina del Sud runs boat trips to **Isla Margarita,** a wooded island with a small interior lagoon. The roundtrip lasts about two hours and costs US$6.50 for adults, US$6 for children.

Conaf's **Centro de Visitantes,** opposite Hotel Petrohué, displays material on the park's fauna and flora, geography, geology and history. From the hotel, a dirt track leads to **Playa Larga,** a long black-sand beach much better than the one near the hotel. After passing through a former military campground, look for the sign pointing to the beach, which is half an hour's walk away. The **Sendero Rincón del Osorno** is a 5km-long trail on the western shore of Lago Todos los Santos. Six km southwest of Petrohué, the **Sendero Saltos del Petrohué** is one of a number of short recreational trails along the rapids of the river; Conaf collects a US$2 admission charge here.

From Cayutué, on the southern arm of Lago Todos los Santos, it's possible to trek to Ralún, at the north end of the Estuario de Reloncaví. For this, you must hire a fisherman's launch for the 45-minute trip to Cayutué, which is about four hours' walk from Lago Cayutué (excellent camping) and another five hours to Ralún, where three or four buses travel back to Puerto Varas each day. The track is easy to follow.

Aqua Motion, the Puerto Varas adventure travel operator, maintains an office at Petrohué, where it's possible to arrange climbs of Volcán Osorno (US$200 per person), rafting on the Río Petrohué (US$40) and full-day 'canyoning' excursions that involve climbing (with and without ropes), hiking and swimming to explore the gorge of the Río León (US$80).

Places to Stay & Eat Other than camping, there are only two lodging alternatives at Petrohué. The cheaper of the two is basic, even rugged **Hospedaje Küscher**, across the river, for which you'll have to hire a rowboat. Rooms cost US$10 per person, but camping is possible for US$5. Rates at the distinctive **Hotel Petrohué** (☎fax 065-258-042), the other option, start at US$58/85 single/double with breakfast, US$74/105 with half-board; the restaurant is open to the general public. Things are quieter after March 1, the best time for a visit, but facilities are open all year.

Campers should buy food and supplies in Puerto Montt or Puerto Varas rather than in Petrohué, whose only shop charges premium prices.

Getting There & Away Bus services from Puerto Montt and Puerto Varas are more frequent than they used to be. From Puerto Montt, Expreso JM has five buses daily to Petrohué from December through March, but only two daily the rest of the year. Intersur also has service from Puerto Montt.

From September to March, Andina del Sud (☎/fax 257-797), Varas 437 in Puerto Montt, has daily buses to Ensenada and Petrohué via Puerto Varas, with connections for its own bus-boat crossing to Bariloche. These leave Puerto Montt at 8:30 am and return at 5 pm; from April to mid-September, they run Wednesday to Sunday, leaving Puerto Montt at 10 am and returning at 5 pm.

Andina del Sud's ferry departs Petrohué early in the morning for Peulla, a three-hour trip that is the first leg of the journey to Bariloche. Purchase tickets at the kiosk near the jetty for US$27 roundtrip for adults, US$19 for children; with lunch, the fare is US$48 for adults, US$31 for children. Tickets are also available at Andina del Sud offices in Puerto Varas and Puerto Montt.

Peulla

Approaching Peulla, Todos los Santos' deep blue waters turn to an emerald green. This tiny settlement, which has a hotel, a school and a post office, bustles in summer as tourists pass through customs and immigration en route to Bariloche.

There is an easy walk to **Cascada de Los Novios**, a waterfall just a few minutes from Hotel Peulla. For a longer excursion, try the 8km **Sendero Laguna Margarita**, a rugged but rewarding climb.

Places to Stay & Eat One km from the dock, *Hotel Peulla* (☎ 065-258-041) charges US$111/152 for singles/doubles with half-board but is slowly declining. Several readers have complained about prices and quality at the restaurant *Tejuela*, and recommend bringing your own food in lieu of the expensive buffet.

There's a campsite opposite the Conaf office, and it may also be possible to get a room with a local family – several readers have recommended the home of Elmo and Ana Hernández, on the right side as you leave the jetty, for US$10.

From either Puerto Montt or Puerto Varas, the Andina del Sud travel agency leads overnight excursions to Peulla, with lodging at Hotel Peulla, for US$93 per person with half-board.

COCHAMÓ

At the end of the paved highway, 79km southeast of Puerto Varas, the Río Petrohué discharges into the Seno de Reloncaví at **Ralún**, where people fish from the bridge and there are several campgrounds. Beyond Ralún, a decent gravel road leads another 16km south to the village of Cochamó, home to the landmark Chilote-style **Iglesia Parroquial María Inmaculada** and gateway to the

awesomely scenic valley of the upper Río Cochamó, whose Yosemite-like granite domes rise above the verdant rain forest. The area is eminently worthy of national park status, but nearly all the land is privately owned.

Independent hikers, prepared for rain and mud, can hike up the valley to La Junta and beyond, but Cochamó is also the base for Campo Aventura (see Travel Agencies in the Puerto Varas section earlier in this chapter), which organizes two- to 10-day horseback trips to its backcountry camp at La Junta and on into Argentina. About 70% of its clients are first-time riders.

Part of the route follows a 19th-century road made out of logs, built for oxcarts, which carried seafood from Reloncaví to the Argentine side. La Junta, 17km from Cochamó and about 600m above sea level, is a good base for climbers attracted to the impressive granite walls. Unlike Yosemite, though, the falls are numerous narrow ribbons rather than broad, thunderous cascades.

For nonclimbers, there's a nature trail to **Cascada Stede**, a ribbonlike waterfall where there's a simple shelter and a place to prepare tea. However, the wind and spray off the waterfall can make it uncomfortable to spend more than a few minutes there. If fording the river from Campo Aventura's La Junta camp to get back to the main trail up the valley, carry a walking stick for balance and do not cross if the water is too high or fast.

Places to Stay & Eat

The village of Cochamó has two basic accommodations for around US$8 per person: *Hospedaje Moreno (Av Prat and Sargento Aldea)* and *Hotel Cochamó* (☎ 065-216-212). Open October 1 to April 15, Campo Aventura has three splendid cabañas (each with an upstairs sleeping loft), a kitchen and indoor and outdoor dining areas at Cochamó, while the La Junta backcountry camp (run by Campo Aventura) has comfortable dormitory accommodations and wood-fired hot showers. While the Cochamó facility is primarily for horseback-tour clients, the cabañas are open to the general public on a space available basis. Three-day, two-night trips cost around US$250 per person with full board.

Campo Aventura's 80-hectare La Junta site has two resident employees who handle meals and accommodations. The house itself, decorated with distinctive wood carvings of huasos and horsegear, has three bedrooms, one with five bunks and the other two with double beds (all with Thermarest pads), a kitchen and a dining room with a central woodstove to keep it cozy. The major concession to rusticity is the outhouse 30m up the hill. Outside there are covered porches with room to dry clothes.

Campo Aventura has a campground under construction at La Junta, where sites will be available for US$4 per person. Otherwise, accommodations in bunks cost US$15, breakfast US$5, lunch or dinner US$8, wine US$8, and fresh bread US$2.

Getting There & Away

Buses Fierro has two buses daily from Puerto Montt (US$3), at noon and 5 pm, that pass through Puerto Varas; they return from Río Puelo, 31km south of Cochamó, at 7 am and 4 pm. For Campo Aventura, disembark at the bridge over the Río Cochamó, about 5km south of Cochamó village. The cabañas are about 500m east of the bridge, on the south side of the river.

PUERTO MONTT

☎ 65

Settled by German colonists in the mid-19th century, Puerto Montt still presents a middle-European façade of what Jan Morris described, in 1967, as a townscape of 'houses…faced with unpainted shingles, very Nordic and sensible, and here and there stand structures in the Alpine manner, all high-pitched roofs and quaint balconies.' One of southern Chile's most important cities, it enjoys a spectacular setting that may remind visitors from Seattle or Vancouver of Puget Sound or the Strait of Georgia. Built entirely of alerce in 1856, the Iglesia Catedral on the Plaza de Armas is the oldest building. A commercial construction boom is transforming the downtown area.

As a gateway to the southern lakes, Chiloé and Chilean Patagonia, Puerto Montt has air, bus and train links in virtually all directions except to the west. Its maritime orientation is conspicuous to the most casual observer. Even more conspicuous are the mountains of wood chips, at the port of Angelmó, that have become a symbol of uncontrolled exploitation in southern Chile's temperate forests. But these may disappear as the chips begin to fly, equally controversially, in the Cascada Chile wood chip project at the smaller mainland port of Ilque.

Orientation

Capital of Region X of Los Lagos, Puerto Montt (population 87,000) is 1020km south of Santiago via the Panamericana, which skirts the northern edge of the city as it continues to Chiloé.

The city center occupies a narrow terrace, partly on landfill, behind which hills rise steeply. The waterfront Av Diego Portales turns into Av Angelmó as it heads west to the small fishing and ferry port of Angelmó. To the east, Av Soler Manfredini continues on to the bathing resort of Pelluco, connecting with the rugged Camino Austral, a combination of ferries and gravel roads that ends far south, at Villa O'Higgins in Region XI (Aisén).

Information

Tourist Offices Abundantly supplied with maps and brochures, Puerto Montt's Oficina Municipal de Turismo (☎ 261-700, Anexo 823) is a kiosk at Varas and O'Higgins, facing the south side of the Plaza de Armas. It's open 9 am to 1 pm and 3 to 6 pm weekdays and 9 am to 1 pm Saturday except in January and February, when it's open 9 am to 9 pm daily.

Sernatur, on the west side of the Plaza de Armas, is open 8:30 am to 1 pm and 2 to 6 pm weekdays except in January and February, when it's open 9 am to 7 pm. Sernatur's administrative office (☎ 252-720), which also provides information, overlooks the city from the 2nd floor of the annex of the Edificio Intendencia Regional, O'Higgins 480 – a stiff climb from the waterfront.

It's open 8:30 am to 1 pm and 1:30 to 5:45 pm weekdays.

Acchi (☎ 252-968), the Automóvil Club, is at Esmeralda 70, east of downtown off Av Egaña.

Money There are several cambios, including Turismo Los Lagos at Varas 595, Local 3, Eureka Turismo at Antonio Varas 449 and La Moneda de Oro at the bus terminal. There are many downtown ATMs, including Banco de Crédito at Antonio Varas and Pedro Montt.

Post & Communications Correos de Chile is at Rancagua 126. Entel is at Varas 567, Local 2, with a smaller office just outside the ferry port at Angelmó. Chilesat is at Talca 70.

Mundo Internet, Varas 629, provides Internet access, as does Latin Star Communication Center, Av Angelmó 1684, which keeps long hours.

Travel Agencies English-run Travellers (☎/fax 258-555, gochile@entelchile.net), Av Angelmó 2456, makes special efforts to cater to overseas travelers. Besides arranging guides and equipment for Volcán Osorno and other adventure trips, director Adrian Turner sells IGM topographic maps and travel books (including Lonely Planet guides) and will reserve flights, rental cars and ferry trips. They also operate a used paperback-book exchange, and have an upstairs café with a message board, Internet access and other conveniences.

Alsur (☎ 287-628, alsur@telsur.cl), Antonio Varas 445, leads adventure travel trips in and around Puerto Varas and at the private Parque Natural Pumalín. Lahuén-Tur, at the Pueblito de Melipulli artisans market opposite the bus terminal, arranges tours with Pucón's Hostería ¡Ecole! Cruceros Skorpios (☎ 252-996), which offers luxury cruises to Laguna San Rafael and the Chilean fjords, is at Av Angelmó 1660.

Bookstores Sotavento Libros (☎ 256-650), Portales 580, has a good selection of books on local history and literature.

National Parks Conaf (☎ 290-711) is at Amunátegui 500.

Medical Services Puerto Montt's Hospital Base (☎ 253-991) is on Seminario, the street that runs behind the Intendencia Regional (the building that houses Sernatur's regional office).

Casa del Arte Diego Rivera

The upstairs Sala Hardy Wistuba at the Casa del Arte Diego Rivera, a joint Mexican-Chilean project finished in 1964, displays work by local and foreign artists and photographers. The downstairs Sala de Espectáculos offers theater, dance and a selection of quality films that changes frequently.

At Quillota 116, the gallery (☎ 261-817) is open 10 am to 1 pm daily except Sunday, and 3 to 9 pm weekdays. Admission to exhibitions is free.

Museo Juan Pablo II

Puerto Montt's improving waterfront museum has begun to stress more locally oriented materials than it did a few years back, when the transitory euphoria of the 1984 papal visit led to the renaming of the former Museo Vicente Pérez Rosales. There are now displays on natural history, archaeology, the island of Chiloé, maritime history and weapons, religious iconography, German colonization and local urbanism. There are also rotating exhibits.

At Av Diego Portales 991, immediately east of the bus terminal, the museum (☎ 261-822) is open 9 am to 7 pm daily in summer, 9 am to noon and 2 to 6 pm the rest of the year. Admission costs US$0.50.

Angelmó

Puerto Montt's picturesque fishing port has an outstanding crafts market, with a range of goods including handmade boots, curios, copperwork, ponchos, woolen sweaters, hats and gloves. Waterfront cafés serve tasty seafood, especially curanto, but overfishing of native species and the glut of commercially cultivated salmon has meant that tastier local specialties such as *sierra* (sawfish) are less common on the menu than they once were.

PUERTO MONTT

PLACES TO STAY
3 Hotel Le Mirage
7 Residencial Benavente
9 Residencial Urmeneta
10 Hostal Panorama
12 Hotel Viento Sur
13 Hostal Yelcho
14 Residencial El Talquino
15 Residencial La Nave
20 Residencial Millantú
22 Hotel El Candil
24 Hotel Millahue
25 Hospedaje Emita
28 Escuela No 1
31 Residencial Los Helechos
32 Hostal Marazul
33 Hospedaje Suizo
34 Residencial Independencia
37 Residencial Torres del Paine
38 Residencial Costanera
39 Hotel O'Grimm
42 Hotel Gamboa
43 Hospedaje Puerto Montt
59 Hotel Montt
61 Gran Hotel Don Luis
67 Hotel Colina
73 Hotel Burg
78 Hotel Vicente Pérez Rosales

PLACES TO EAT
11 Islas de Chiloé
16 Embassy
17 El Bodegón
18 Apetito's
19 Deutscher Verein
41 Centro Español
44 Heladería La Reina
50 Dino's
51 Di Napoli
52 Café Real
53 Pastelería Alemana
58 Mykonos
60 Balzac
64 Pastelería Nueva Lisel
65 Kaffeeschatz
69 Rincón Sureño
74 Amsel

OTHER
1 Budget
2 Pub Sitges
4 Sernatur (Edificio
  Intendencia Regional)
5 Hospital Base
6 Avis
8 Timón Austral
21 Aerosur
23 Hertz
26 Autowald
27 Pueblito de Melipulli,
  Lahuén-Tur
29 Bus Terminal
30 Museo Juan Pablo II
35 Latin Star
  Communication Center
36 Cruceros Skorpios
40 Aerovip
45 LanChile, Ladeco, TAN
46 Petrel Tours
47 Línea Aérea Aquelarre
48 OK Corral

49 Banco de Crédito
54 Spanish Consulate
55 Post Office
56 Sernatur
57 Avant
62 Casa del Arte Diego Rivera
63 Argentine Consulate
66 Mundo Internet
67 Colina
68 Turismo Los Lagos
70 Chilesat
71 Sotavento Libros
72 Entel
75 German Consulate
76 Full Fama's
77 Eureka Turismo
79 Alsur
80 Andina del Sud
81 Oficina Municipal de Turismo

To Panamericana

El Vergel

Crucero

Allende

Frederic Segundo Godoey

Pérez Rosales

Díaz

Calbuco

Ecuador

Benavente

Lota

Rodríguez

Urmeneta
● 6

Araud

Ebenberger

Los Manuís

Los Guindos

Manzanal

Figueroa

Trigal

Philippi

A Goecke

Chorrillos

Miraflores

Juan Mira

■ 14

15 ■

13 ■

Chiloé

Constitución

■ 25

28 ■

27 ●

◗ 29

26 ●

Linares

Buenos Aires

Ecuador

Ñuble

31 ■

Pudeto

32
■

26 ●

35 ● 36

37 ■ 38 ■

33 ■

34 ■

Independencia

Av Angelmó

To Camping
Los Paredes,
Angelmó,
Isla Tenglo

Port

Canal Tenglo

Isla
Tenglo

PUERTO MONTT

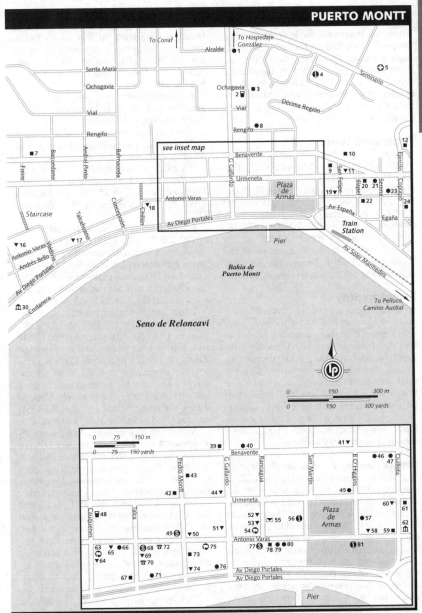

Easily reached by frequent local buses and taxi colectivos, Angelmó is about 3km west of downtown Puerto Montt. It is the terminus for ferries to Chaitén, Puerto Chacabuco, Laguna San Rafael and Puerto Natales. Off-shore **Isla Tenglo**, reached by inexpensive launches from the docks at Angelmó, is much quieter than bustling Puerto Montt, but recent fires have destroyed much of the island's former forest cover.

Organized Tours

Several agencies offer city tours of Puerto Montt (US$8), Puerto Varas (US$12), Frutillar (US$20), Ancud and Castro (US$30), Parque Nacional Puyehue (US$45), Petrohué and Lago Todos los Santos (US$30) and Peulla (US$34, transportation only). Well-established Andina del Sud (☎ 257-797), Varas 437, is group-oriented, with fixed itineraries, but reader-recommended Petrel Tours (☎ 251-780), Benavente 327, has drawn praise for their individual attention.

Places to Stay

At the northern approach to Puerto Montt, mobs of hawkers line Av Salvador Allende with signs offering accommodations, just as they do at the bus terminal. Indeed, Puerto Montt has such abundant budget accommodations that seasonal price differentials are relatively small. However many of these hospedajes are 'pirate' accommodations that do not pay taxes and some have dubious standards. Generally, if a hospedaje has no formal sign or does not require you to sign a register, it is probably unlicensed.

Budget *Camping Los Paredes* (☎ 258-394), 6km west of town on the road to Chinquihue, charges US$14 for pleasant sites with hot showers, but backpackers might get away as cheaply as US$3.50 per person. There's plenty of hot water in the showers which, however, are a little hard to regulate. Local buses from the bus terminal will drop you at the entrance.

Farther out the road toward Panitao, on the shores of the Bahía de Huequillahue, *Camping Anderson* is somewhat remote and inconvenient, but that very remoteness adds to its appeal. Sites cost US$3 per

person, including hot showers. Fresh provisions such as eggs, vegetables, cheese and bread are available on site. Buses Bohle makes the 20km trip from Puerto Montt six times daily except Sunday, at 7 and 11:30 am, and at 12:30, 4, 5 and 8 pm; catch the Panitao bus from the main terminal.

Summer hostel accommodations are available for US$3.50 at *Escuela No 1* (*Lillo and Lota*), opposite the bus terminal. Cold showers, an 11:30 pm curfew and the lack of bedding (bring your own sleeping bag) may deter some travelers.

Try either of two locations of the HI affiliate *Residencial Independencia* (☎ 277-949, *Independencia 167;* ☎ 257-938, *Av Angelmó 2196*). The former charges US$10, the latter US$11.

Friendly but a bit noisy, *Hostal Yelcho* (☎ 262-253, *Ecuador 1316*) charges US$7 per person with breakfast, with three beds to a room. *Residencial Los Helechos* (☎ 259-525, *Chorrillos 1500*) charges the same, or slightly more with private bath, but some rooms lack windows. Breakfast costs US$2 more.

Convenient to the ferry port at Angelmó, *Hostal Marazul* (☎ 256-567, *Ecuador 1558*) charges US$7.50 with shared bath, US$10 with private bath and breakfast. *Hospedaje Emita* (☎ 250-725, *Miraflores 1281*) is a reasonable alternative at US$7.50/10 singles/doubles with firm beds, shared bath and hot showers. Also near the port, *Residencial Torres del Paine* (☎ 258-193, *Portales 1568*) charges US$8 with shared bath and breakfast.

Nearer the bus terminal, *Residencial El Talquino*(☎ 253-331, *Pérez Rosales 114*) is a bargain at only US$8 per person without breakfast; kitchen privileges cost an extra US$1. At friendly, north-of-town *Hospedaje González* (*Gallardo 552*), spacious, sunny rooms cost US$9 with breakfast, hot water and kitchen privileges. *Hospedaje Rocco* (☎ 272-897, *hospedajerocco@entelchile.net, Pudeto 233*) roughly midway between the bus terminal and the Angelmó Navimag offices, charges US$9 with breakfast in attractive surroundings, plus kitchen facilities. It also has cable TV and Internet access.

Run by gregarious Rossy Oelckers, a Swiss-Chilean artist, *Hospedaje Suizo*

(☎ 252-640, 257-565, *Independencia 231*) is one of Puerto Montt's better values for US$13 with shared bath, plus another US$1.50 for a generous breakfast. It's straight up the hill from the mountain of wood chips at the entrance to the port at Angelmó.

Residencial Costanera (☎ 255-244, *Angelmó 1528*), charges US$10 per person with breakfast. *Residencial Benavente* (☎ 253-084, *Benavente 948*) is comparably priced for US$10 with shared bath; rooms with private bath cost US$21/32. Charging US$10/17 with private bath, aptly named *Hostal Panorama* (☎ 277-940, *San Felipe 192*) has a misleading street address, as it actually fronts on Benavente via a steep footpath.

Mid-Range Some rooms lack exterior windows at friendly but slightly gloomy *Residencial Urmeneta* (☎ 253-262, *Urmeneta 290, 2nd floor*) where rates are US$16/25 with shared bath, US$25/38 with private bath. Readers' choice *Residencial La Nave* (☎ 253-740, *Ancud 103*) charges US$25 double with private bath and TV, and has a good restaurant downstairs.

Helpful *Hotel Gamboa* (☎ 252-741, *Pedro Montt 157*) charges a very reasonable US$29 for spacious doubles with shared bath and breakfast, though some rooms are dark; those with private bath are only slightly dearer. At downtown *Hospedaje Puerto Montt* (☎ 252-276, *Pedro Montt 180*) doubles with private bath cost US$30 per person. Rates at *Hotel El Candil* (☎ 253-080, *Varas 177*) are US$21/32.

Showing its age, *Residencial Millantú* (☎ 252-758, *fax 263-550, Illapel 146*) still charges US$25/38 with private bath and breakfast. From US$35/42, *Hotel Colina* (☎ 253-501, *fax 259-331, Talca 81*) has excellent accommodations with waterfront views and private bath, and friendly and competent staff, but the walls are surprisingly thin and there's a noisy music store nearby. *Hotel Millahue* (☎ 253-829, *Copiapó 64*) charges US$35/44.

Rates may be negotiable at friendly *Hotel Le Mirage* (☎ 255-125, *fax 256-302, Rancagua 350*), which normally charges US$52/63 including breakfast and TV.

Reader feedback is ambivalent about *Hotel Montt* (☎ 253-651, *fax 253-652, Varas 301*), but off-season prices, nearly 50% cheaper, make it worth consideration.

Top End Top-end accommodations start around US$66/75 at waterfront *Hotel Burg* (☎ 253-941, *Pedro Montt 86*). *Hotel O'Grimm* (☎ 252-845, *Gallardo 211*) charges US$80/90.

Overlooking downtown from its east end perch, *Hotel Viento Sur* (☎ 258-701, *Ejército 200*) has drawn praise for comfort, helpful and efficient staff and an outstanding restaurant; rates start at US$81/93. Starting at US$82/94, the newish *Gran Hotel Don Luis* (☎ 259-001, *fax 259-005, Quillota 146*) has made good impressions. *Hotel Vicente Pérez Rosales* (☎ 252-571, *fax 255-473, Varas 447*) has long been the city's top hotel, charging from US$85/99, but it's seen better days.

Places to Eat

El Bodegón (*Varas 931*) is popular with locals and sometimes has live music at night, but some travelers have criticized its hygiene. *Dino's* (☎ 252-785, *Varas 550*) is the local representative of an ordinary but reliable chain. The waterfront *Amsel* (☎ 253-941, *Pedro Montt 56*) has so-so food and service, as does inexpensive *Rincón Sureño* (☎ 254-597, *Talca 84*). *Mykonos* (☎ 262-627, *Antonio Varas 326*) has good, moderately priced lunches.

Puerto Montt's best pizzería, Italian-run *Di Napoli* (☎ 254-174, *Gallardo 119*) is a tiny venue that gets crowded and stuffy – the ventilation is better downstairs. The rejuvenated *Deutscher Verein* (☎ 252-551, *Varas 264*) offers Eastern European fare.

Don't leave Puerto Montt without sampling curanto or other regional seafood specialties at Angelmó's waterfront cafés – among the recommended choices are the aggressively tourist-oriented *Marfino* (☎ 259-044, *Av Angelmó 1856*) and the less pretentious *Asturias* (☎ 258-496, *Av Angelmó 2448-C*). Downtown seafood choices include *Embassy* (☎ 252-232, *Ancud 106*); the *Centro Español* (☎ 255-570, *O'Higgins 233*), renowned for its paella; highly regarded *Balzac* (☎ 259-495, *Urmeneta 305*; and *Islas de Chiloé* (☎ 256-981, *Benavente 21*).

For drinks, snacks and kuchen, there's *Pastelería Alemana* (☎ 254-721, Rancagua 117), nearby *Café Real* (☎ 253-750, Rancagua 137), *Kaffeeschatz* (☎ 254-275, Varas 629) or *Apetito's* (☎ 252-470, Chillán 96). *Pastelería Nueva Lisel* (Cauquenes 82) is a fine bakery. *Heladería La Reina* (☎ 253-979, Urmeneta 508) has the best ice cream in town.

The bathing resort suburb of Pelluco, east of downtown via Av Juan Soler but easily reached by taxi colectivo, is a good hunting ground for restaurants – try the parrillada at *Fogón Las Tejuelas* (☎ 252-876, Los Pinos s/n) or any of several other beachfront restaurants.

Entertainment

If you've come to Chile for country music and line dancing, the *OK Corral* (☎ 266-287, Cauquenes 128) is the place to go. *Pub Sitges* (☎ 257-926, Rancagua 355) is another local favorite.

Shopping

Timón Austral, Rengifo 430-A, sells antiques and used books. For crafts, visit the lively waterfront market Pueblito de Melipulli, opposite the bus terminal.

Getting There & Away

Air LanChile and Ladeco, both at O'Higgins 167, Local 1-B (☎ 253-315), fly several times daily to Punta Arenas (US$83 to US$159), Balmaceda/Coihaique (US$43 to US$77) and Santiago (US$88 to $US159), usually nonstop but sometimes via Temuco or Concepción.

Avant (☎ 258-277), on O'Higgins between Urmeneta and Varas, averages four flights daily to Santiago (US$88 to US$159), often via Temuco; and flies daily to Balmaceda (US$43 to US$73), and eight times weekly to Punta Arenas (US$81 to US$117).

Transportes Aéreos Neuquén (TAN; ☎ 284-299), also at O'Higgins 167, flies Tuesday and Friday mornings to the Argentine cities of Bariloche (US$73) and Neuquén (US$114), the only international flights from Aeropuerto El Tepual.

Several small airlines serve communities along the Camino Austral. Aerosur (☎ 252-523), Urmeneta 149, flies daily except Sunday

to Chaitén (US$36). Línea Aérea Aquelarre (☎ 268-499), Benavente 305, flies twice daily except Saturday to Chaitén. Aerovip (☎ 256-969), Benavente 476, is a new service to Chaitén that has recently suspended its flights, but seems likely to resume them.

Bus – Regional Puerto Montt's bus terminal (☎ 294-533) is on the waterfront, at Av Portales and Lota. There are services to all regional destinations, Chiloé, Santiago, Coihaique, Punta Arenas and Argentina. Services down the Camino Austral are still limited but improving.

To nearby Puerto Varas (US$0.65), try Expreso Puerto Varas (the most frequent) or Varmontt (☎ 254-110). Full Express and Thaebus both go to Frutillar (US$1.25); Thaebus also goes to Puerto Octay. Buses Fierro (☎ 253-022) goes to Lenca, the turnoff for the southern approach to Parque Nacional Alerce Andino, and Chaica (US$1.50) five times daily. Fierro also goes to Lago Chapo (US$1.75), the northern approach to Alerce Andino, four times daily, and to Ralún (US$4), Cochamó (US$4.50) and Río Puelo via Puerto Varas.

Other rural destinations include the coastal town of Maullín (US$1.25), served by Buses Bohle (☎ 254-494) and ETM (☎ 256-253), and the fishing village of Calbuco (US$1.50), served by Bohle and Buses Calbuco (☎ 252-926). Buses Pirehueico (☎ 252-926) goes to Panguipulli.

Buses Fierro has three buses daily, at 8 am and 1:30 and 3 pm, to Hornopirén on the Camino Austral (US$6, three hours), where there are summer ferry connections to Caleta Gonzalo. There is, however, no regular public transport for the 56km between Caleta Gonzalo and the mainland port of Chaitén, which is more easily reached by ferry both from Puerto Montt or from Quellón, on Chiloé. Since conditions and traffic on the Camino Austral are erratic, transport information changes rapidly; check details on arrival in Puerto Montt.

Bus – Long Distance Cruz del Sur (☎ 254-731) and Transchiloé (☎ 254-934) have frequent services to Ancud, Castro and other destinations on Chiloé. Varmontt (☎ 254-410), Igi Llaima (☎ 254-519) and Buses Lit (☎ 254-011) all go to Concepción and to various stops along the Panamericana as far as Santiago. Other companies serving Santiago include Bus Norte (☎ 252-783), Tas Choapa (☎ 254-828), Tur-Bus (☎ 253-329), and Vía Tur (☎ 253-133). Buses Lit and Tur-Bus have daily service to Valparaíso/Viña del Mar.

For the long trip (30 to 36 hours) to Punta Arenas (US$50), via Argentina's Atlantic coast, contact Turibús (☎ 253-345), Ghisoni (☎ 256-622) or Bus Sur (☎ 252-926). Turibús also goes to Coihaique (US$33) daily via Argentina.

Sample fares and times include Ancud (US$4, two hours), Castro (US$6, three hours), Quellón (US$9, five hours), Osorno (US$2, 1½ hours), Valdivia (US$5, 3½ hours), Temuco (US$8, five hours), Concepción (US$15, nine hours), Santiago (US$11 to US$20, 16 hours) and Valparaíso/Viña del Mar (US$25, 18 hours).

Bus – International Bus Norte, Cruz del Sur and Río de La Plata (☎ 253-841) travel daily to Bariloche, Argentina (US$19, eight hours), via the Cardenal Samoré pass east of Osorno. Andesmar goes to Bariloche and Neuquén (US$46) Sunday, Wednesday and Friday.

Buses Andina del Sud (☎ 257-797) offers daily bus-boat combinations to Bariloche, Argentina (about US$110) via Puerto Varas, Ensenada, Petrohué and Peulla. These depart Puerto Montt in the morning, arriving in Bariloche early in the evening.

Boat The most appealing route to Chile's far south is by sea from Puerto Montt. Ferry or bus-ferry combinations connect Puerto Montt with Chiloé and Chaitén in Region X; ferries to Chiloé leave from the port of Pargua, on the Canal de Chacao. Some ferries from Puerto Montt continue to Puerto Chacabuco (the port of Coihaique) in Region XI (Aisén) or go to Puerto Natales in Region XII (Magallanes) via Puerto Edén.

Ferries also visit truly remote spots such as Laguna San Rafael; information about these trips appears in the Aisén chapter. Travelers prone to motion sickness should consider taking medication prior to crossing the Golfo de Penas, which is exposed to gut-wrenching Pacific swells.

At Angelmó's Terminal de Transbordadores, Av Angelmó 2187, Navimag (☎ 253-318, fax 258-540) sails roll-on, roll-off ferries (ones that vehicles can drive on and off) through Chile's southern seas. The *Evangelistas* goes to Puerto Chacabuco (twice weekly) and Laguna San Rafael, while the *Puerto Edén* sails to Puerto Natales (weekly), a spectacular three-day cruise through the Chilean fjords that's comparable to Alaska's Inside Passage or New Zealand's Milford Sound (see boxed text 'Sailing the Fjords'). The *Alejandrina* goes to Chaitén and Quellón three times weekly, Tuesday, Thursday and Saturday.

Fares from Puerto Montt to Puerto Chacabuco range from US$38 for a reclining seat, to US$167/292 singles/doubles for suites, all meals included. Slightly cheaper cabins with bunks (US$104 to US$125) are also available. These sailings continue to Laguna San Rafael; see the Aisén chapter for more details.

Passenger fares to Chaitén range from US$21 to US$31. Bicyclists pay US$10, motorcyclists US$31 and drivers of automobiles or light trucks US$94.

For fares from Puerto Montt to Puerto Natales, see the Puerto Natales entry in the Magallanes chapter. If possible, try to book passages between Puerto Montt and Puerto Natales at Navimag's Santiago offices (see the Getting Around chapter). In Puerto Montt, Travellers has a good record for getting its clients a berth, but last-minute arrivals at the port sometimes manage to get on.

Transmarchilay (☎ 270-416, fax 270-415), also at the Terminal de Transbordadores, sails the ferries *La Pincoya* to Chaitén (10 hours) Friday and *El Colono* to Puerto Chacabuco (23 hours) Tuesday and Friday. Fares to Chaitén range from US$25 for a fixed seat to US$33 for a recliner. Comparable accommodations to Chacabuco cost US$36 to US$50, but there are also sleeper cabins for US$73.

Sailing the Fjords

Almost everyone who travels to southern Chile entertains the idea of sailing the nearly unin-habited Chilean fjords, a scenic area comparable to Alaska's Inside Passage, New Zealand's Milford Sound or Norway's North Atlantic coastline, where glaciers reach the sea or sprawl within easy view during good weather.

In the not-so-distant past, before Chilean shippers grasped the tourist potential of this route, travelers begged passages in cramped bunks on rusty state-run freighters that carried cargo between Puerto Montt and Puerto Natales, or negotiated with truckers for a berth on ferries such as the *Evangelistas* (truckers were entitled to bunks but usually slept in their own, more comfortable cabs). Now Navimag's *Puerto Edén* makes weekly four-day, three-night sailings in each direction (for fares, see page 400).

Increasing numbers of visitors are taking advantage of the improved service. Once on board in the port of Puerto Montt, the crew segregates passengers by class – those with cabin accommodations to the left, those in multibunk clase económica to the right. The trip begins with an orientation talk and slide show by a bilingual guide who covers indigenous people and the region's history and conducts guided visits to the bridge and engine room.

Leaving Angelmó, the sight of Osorno's perfect cone and shattered Volcán Calbuco presage even more impressive scenery to the south, as the ferry sails between Chiloé and the mainland. The route stays in relatively sheltered waters such as the Canal Moraleda, passing the lonely lighthouse at Melinka in the Guaitecas Archipelago, before entering Aisén's maze of narrow channels.

Approaching the south end of the Canal Moraleda, Puerto Chacabuco's fishing fleet floats nearby, accompanied by tremendous numbers of albatross, petrels, cormorants, penguins and skuas, while orcas do tailstands and sea lions sun themselves on the rocks. At the south end of Canal Errázuriz, the ferry heads west through the constricted Canal Chacabuco to enter the dreaded Golfo de Penas, where Pacific swells can make all but the most experienced sailors queasy.

For most passengers, it's a relief to escape the Golfo de Penas and enter the Canal Messier where, after navigating the Angostura Inglesa (a passage so confined that the ship seems to graze the shoreline on both sides), the Puerto Edén drops anchor at its namesake settlement, a small fishing port and the last outpost of the region's Qawashqar Indians. If schedules and conditions permit, passengers may sometimes go ashore; in any event, lighters pick up cen-tolla (king crab) for the Punta Arenas market and a handful of Qawashqar come aboard to offer king baskets and model canoe souvenirs.

To the south, the route becomes increasingly scenic as the channels become narrower, the snow peaks get closer, and hundreds of waterfalls tumble from U-shaped glacial valleys. Even the second week of January, during mid-summer, the snow line on the nearest hills is proba-bly below 400m, just below the cloud banks that often cover the highest points. As Darwin remarked after navigating the fjords of Tierra del Fuego and Laguna San Rafael:

> I was astonished when I first saw a range, only from 3000 to 4000 feet in height, in the latitude of Cumberland, with every valley filled with streams of ice descending to the sea coast.

The natural grandeur of Aisén and Magallanes is the reason most people make the trip, but the social experience has become a highlight in itself. An increasing number of Chileans are

doing the trip, and the interaction is gratifying for foreigners. It begins in the waiting room on shore and improves as, on the first evening, the crew provides complimentary pisco sours. While there are separate galleys for cabin passengers and those in clase económica, the two groups mix readily outside mealtimes, enjoying the scenery and the conversation. After crossing the Golfo de Penas, the passengers delight each other with tales of how they survived the pitching and rolling (some feel fine after 'feeding the fish').

The last evening is the most sociable of the trip, as people who were strangers a few days earlier share the wine they've purchased in Puerto Montt or Puerto Natales, and everyone dances beneath a mirror ball to incongruous medleys of salsa, technopop and oldies. Only a handful make the next morning's breakfast, but before disembarking, the crew says goodbye and sometimes distributes 'diplomas' to everyone who finished the voyage of 900 nautical miles – probably the longest in the world for a vessel of its kind. Many who met on board continue to encounter other 'boat people' in Puerto Natales and Torres del Paine.

Practical Pointers Most four-passenger cabins on the *Puerto Edén* have a toilet, sink, shower and closet, plus additional storage beneath the bunks, but some have toilet and shower outside the cabin. Unless you're really claustrophobic, the porthole views in the ship's 'A' cabins do not justify the extra expense – most people prefer the views from the decks or common areas. The bunks themselves are comfortable.

Some passengers have called clase económica the 'dungeon', but the bunks are comfortable and have curtains for privacy, though some have low ceilings. In fact, clase económica has the atmosphere of a floating youth hostel, though it can get hot and noisy (especially if you're near the engine room). The main shortcoming is the lack of space to store gear. And don't leave things on the floor, as they can get wet.

Meals on board are generally well prepared but simple; portions are ample but not huge. The main courses are usually seafood, chicken, hamburgers and sausages, but vegetarian meals are available if requested in advance. Beer, wine and pisco sours are available at the bar, but it's cheaper to bring your own.

Neither galley has enough seats for everyone, so that clase económica dines in shifts, while cabin passengers are staggered. You spend a lot of time standing in line. Breakfast is less crowded due to the absence of late risers. Smoking is prohibited in cabins and common areas. Videos games are available. At certain times, passengers may visit the bridge.

Weather can be changeable, but this means there's usually good visibility at some time during the trip; dress for cold and wind. December and January have the longest days.

Passengers prone to seasickness might want to refrain from eating prior to crossing the Golfo de Penas, which can be extremely rough. If the crossing is at night, you may be able to sleep through it in your bunk, but you may also feel like a human gyroscope as the boat pitches in the heavy seas, even if there is no storm – what counts is what's happening in the open ocean. The bunks have low sides, but the stewards make the beds so tight that it's hard to fall out.

Increasing numbers of travelers are bringing along Global Positioning Systems (GPSs) in conjunction with marine charts to trace the route as they go, though it's also possible to do this on the bridge, which is often open to passengers. At the scale of 1:750,000, the British *Admiralty's Hydrographer of the Navy Chart No 561, Cabo Pilar to Golfo Coronado*, is the best single source to accompany the GPS.

Sailing the Fjords

Fares per person, which vary according to view and private or shared bath, are approximately as follows:

cabina armador	high season	low season
single	US$1513	US$1405
double	US$792	US$738
triple	US$551	US$515

literas (bunks)	high season	low season
AA	US$398	US$354
A	US$345	US$302
B	US$318	US$275
económica	US$297	US$256

Passenger vehicles and pickup trucks cost US$250 northbound, US$170 southbound. Motorcycles cost US$58 either direction; bicycles US$30.

El Colono's Friday sailing picks up additional passengers at Puerto Chacabuco before continuing to Laguna San Rafael; for details, see the Parque Nacional Laguna San Rafael section in the Aisén chapter. Passenger fares from Puerto Montt to Laguna San Rafael and back run from US$277 to US$378 with full board; bunks cost US$550 per person.

Transmarchilay's automobile fares to Chaitén are US$93 for vehicles less than 4m long, US$103 for vehicles longer than 4m. Bicycles cost US$10, motorcycles US$25. To Puerto Chacabuco, automobile fares are US$133 for vehicles less than 4m long, US$154 for vehicles longer than 4m. Bicycles cost US$10, motorcycles US$28.

Transmarchilay and Cruz del Sur also operate auto-passenger ferries from Pargua, 60km southwest of Puerto Montt, to Chacao, on the northern tip of the Isla Grande de Chiloé (see the Chiloé chapter). Fares are about US$1 for passengers or US$12 per car, no matter how many passengers. There is no extra ferry charge for passengers on buses to Chiloé.

Getting Around

To/From the Airport Local ETM buses connect downtown Puerto Montt with Aeropuerto El Tepual (☎ 252-019), 16km west of town, for all incoming and outgoing flights.

Car Regional destinations such as Lago Llanquihue, Petrohué and Lago Todos los Santos are most conveniently explored by car. Rental cars are available from the Automóvil Club (☎ 254-776) at Esmeralda 70, Budget (☎ 254-888) at Gallardo 450, Autowald (☎ 256-355) at Portales 1330, Hertz (☎ 259-585) at Varas 126, Avis (☎ 253-307) at Urmeneta 1037, Full Fama's (☎ 258-060, fax 259-840) at Portales 506 and Colina (☎ 258-328) at Talca 79.

Autowald and Full Fama's are small, local agencies that will help get notarial permission for taking rental vehicles into Argentina. Daily rates range from about US$45 plus IVA and insurance for a small vehicle, to US$100-plus for a pickup truck or Jeep. Weekly rates range from about US$250 to US$500-plus.

AROUND PUERTO MONTT
Calbuco

Founded in 1604 by Spanish survivors of the destruction of Osorno, and connected to the mainland by a causeway, this island fishing village is 51km south of Puerto Montt on a spur off the Panamericana. It has a wealth of restaurants and reasonable accommodations. The rates are US$15 per person with shared bath, US$35 double with private bath at ***Residencial Aguas Azules*** (☎ 461-427, Av Oelckers 159). For seafood, try ***Costa Azul*** (☎ 461-516, Vicuña Mackenna 202).

Calbuco's municipal Oficina de Informaciones (☎ 461-807) is at Av Los Héroes s/n. Buses Bohle and Buses Calbuco (☎ 252-926) and Aguas Azules provide transport from Puerto Montt.

Aqua Motion, the Puerto Varas tour operator, does a yacht tour daily except Monday from Puerto Montt's Muelle Oxean, which is 2.5km west of Calbuco on the road to Chinquihue. This full-day trip, from 10 am to 7 pm, costs US$40 for adults, including a substantial *curanto* (seafood stew) enjoyed on Isla Quenu, with discounts for children (US$32) and for students and retired people (US$35).

Maullín

Southwest of Puerto Montt, Maullín is a small, sedate port on the estuary of the Río Maullín, which in many ways is as much a highway as the paved route to Puerto Montt. People cross from shore to shore constantly, and sail up and down the river. Opposite the Copec petrol station, *Residencial Toledo* (☎ 065-451-246, *Gaspar del Río 147*) has accommodations for US$7.50 per person. There's a good restaurant in the bus terminal on the Costanera.

Five kilometers west of Maullín, at the seaside resort of **Pangal**, the *Cabañas Pangal* (☎ 065-451-244) has four-bed cabañas for US$63, camping for US$12.50 per site and a well-regarded restaurant. *Camping Punta Pangal* (☎ 065-451-242) is slightly cheaper, but charges extra for hot showers.

At the end of a gravel road, 17km south of Maullín, **Carelmapu** is a scenic fishing village with a couple of good restaurants, *Mi Rincón* and *La Ruca*, and modest lodging at an anonymous residencial on O'Higgins (ask a local where it is). Camping is possible at *Mar Brava*, on a cliff overlooking the Pacific. On February 2, the village celebrates the **Fiesta de la Virgen de Candelaria**.

Among them, ETM, ETC and Carelmapu have about 30 buses daily from Puerto Montt (US$2) to and from Carelmapu via Maullín, between 7:30 am and 8 pm.

PARQUE NACIONAL ALERCE ANDINO

Created in 1982, 40,000-hectare Parque Nacional Alerce Andino protects some of the last remaining forests of alerce *(Fitzroya cupressoides)*, a conifer resembling California's giant sequoia in appearance and longevity. Its attractive and durable timber has made the species vulnerable to commercial exploitation, but alerce forest still dominates more than half the park's surface, a remarkable fact considering its proximity to populated areas.

AROUND PUERTO MONTT

Geography & Climate

Rising from sea level to 1558m on the summit of Cerro Cuadrado, mountainous Alerce Andino is only 40km from Puerto Montt via the partly paved segment of Ruta 7, the Camino Austral, that runs to La Arena, on the Estero de Reloncaví. The park consists of three main sectors: Sector Correntoso on the Río Chamiza at the northwestern end, Sector Lago Chapo only a few kilometers to the east and Sector Chaicas at the southwestern approach.

Exposed to Pacific frontal systems, Alerce Andino receives annual precipitation of 3300mm to 4500mm, often in the form of snow above 800m. The average temperature is 15°C in January and 7°C in July. The largest of several glacial lakes is Lago Chapo, on the park's northern border, which is now unfortunately exploited for hydroelectricity and fish farming, but there are several other attractive lakes in more remote areas, generally at higher altitudes.

Flora & Fauna

Though not so tall as the sequoia, reaching only 40m, a 3000-year-old alerce can reach 4m in diameter. It is found primarily between 400m and 700m above sea level, coexisting with species such as coigue, tineo, mañío and canelo. Evergreen forest, ranging from sea level to 900m, consists of species such as coigue and ulmo, as well as ferns, climbing vines and dense thickets of quila, a solid bamboo. Coigue and lenga dominate the park's highest elevations.

The park's fauna is much less conspicuous, but there are occasional sightings of mammals such as pumas, pudús, foxes and skunks, as well as birds, including condors, kingfishers and several species of waterfowl.

Organized Tours

In conjunction with the Travellers agency of Angelmó, Alerce Mountain Lodge (see the Places to Stay section later in this chapter) offers a full-day excursion with lunch and transfers from Puerto Montt for US$75.

Hiking & Trekking

Backcountry hiking is the best reason for visiting Alerce Andino. Between the Correntoso and Río Chaica sectors, there is a good trail with several refugios along the route, but recent severe winters have covered the trail with many deadfalls that Conaf has been slow to remove. Several Puerto Montt agencies, including Travellers in Angelmó, organize trips to the park, but it is also possible to hike and trek independently.

From the campground at Río Chaica, the river has washed out part of the 4WD road, which has become a de facto trail. From Guardería Chaica, Lago Triángulo is only 9½km; the last part of the trail, beyond Laguna Chaiquenes, has been cleared of deadfalls. The earlier, more open part of the trail is full of tábanos in early summer.

Places to Stay

Camping is the only option in the park proper. Conaf has a five-site campground (US$6.50 per site) at Correntoso on the Río Chamiza, at the northern end of the park, and another six-site campground near the head of the Río Chaica Valley. For trekkers, backcountry camping is another possibility, but Conaf also maintains rustic trailside refugios at Río Pangal, Laguna Sargazo and Laguna Fría.

In the vicinity of the park, at Km 36 on the Camino Austral, the new *Alerce Mountain Lodge* (☎ 286-969, *smontt@telsur.cl*), is a four- to five-star facility set among well-preserved alerce forests, with trekking and horseback riding options in the area. Three-day, two-night packages with full board cost US$530/920; four-day, three-night packages US$785/1360; and five-day, four-night packages US$1015/1760.

Getting There & Away

From Puerto Montt, Buses Fierro has four buses daily to the village of Correntoso, only 3km from the Río Chamiza entrance on the northern boundary of the park, continuing to Lago Chapo (US$1.75). Fierro also runs five buses daily to the crossroads at Lenca (US$1.50), on the Camino Austral, where a narrow lateral road climbs 7km up the valley of the Río Chaica. This journey offers slightly better access to a number of lakes and peaks, and is probably a better choice for the non-trekker.

At the park entrances, Conaf collects a fee of US$2 per visitor. The gate on the Río Chaica side is open 9 am to 5 pm only, so visitors out for a long day's hike should park outside the gate (which is only half an hour's walk from the end of the road) unless they're planning an overnight stay at Río Chaica campground.

HORNOPIRÉN

Southbound travelers on the Camino Austral often stop in this scenic village, formerly known as Río Negro, on the north shore of the sheltered Canal Hornopirén, directly opposite Isla Pelada and only a few kilometers west of Parque Nacional Hornopirén. The village is the southern terminus of bus service on the segment of Ruta 7 from Puerto Montt, and the northern terminus of the summer ferry to Caleta Gonzalo, on Fiordo Reñihue, the point where the highway continues south.

Places to Stay & Eat

Tent camping is free at Hornopirén's shoreline park, but there are no sanitary facilities. Rambling **Hotel Hornopirén** (*☎ 263-062, Anexo 256, Carrera Pinto 388*) is a family-run establishment with loads of personality, good rooms for US$10 per person with shared bath, and an excellent restaurant. **Restaurant Central Plaza** has good, moderately priced sandwiches, but is nothing special.

Getting There & Away

Although Hornopirén is directly on the Camino Austral, it's necessary to cross the Estuario de Reloncaví from Caleta La Arena to Puelche on the Transmarchilay ferry *Tehuelche*. From mid-December to the end of March, there are 10 sailings daily between 8 am and 9:30 pm; in the other direction, times are 7:15 am to 8:45 pm. The 30-minute trip costs US$10 for people with cars, US$13 for those driving pickup trucks, US$1 for pedestrians. Bus passengers pay no extra charge.

Buses Fierro, on the Plaza de Armas, has three buses daily to and from Puerto Montt (US$6, three hours), at 5:30 and 6:30 am and 1:45 pm.

In summer, Transmarchilay's ferry *Mailén* makes the six-hour trip to Caleta Gonzalo daily at 3 pm. Most car and pickup-truck drivers pay US$90. Passengers pay US$14. Cyclists pay an additional US$9, while motorcyclists pay US$16 more.

Archipiélago de Chiloé

About 180km long but only 50km wide, the Isla Grande de Chiloé is a well-watered, densely forested island of undulating hills, linked to the Chilean mainland by frequent ferries across the Canal de Chacao. Between the Isla Grande and the mainland, the Golfo de Ancud and the Golfo Corcovado are dotted with many smaller islands of archipelagic Chiloé. Politically, the province of Chiloé belongs to Region X of Los Lagos.

Prior to the arrival of the Spaniards in the 16th century, Huilliche Indians cultivated potatoes and other crops in Chiloé's fertile volcanic soil. Spain took possession of Chiloé in 1567 and founded the city of Castro the following year. Jesuit missionaries were among the first settlers, but early-17th-century refugees from the Mapuche Indian uprising on the mainland also established settlements. During the wars of independence, Chiloé was a Spanish stronghold; the Spanish resisted criollo attacks in 1820 and 1824 from heavily fortified Ancud, until the final Spanish defeat in 1826.

Distinctive shingled houses with corrugated metal roofs line the streets of Chiloé's towns and punctuate the verdant countryside. For much of the year, rain and mist obscure the sun, which, when it finally breaks through the clouds, reveals majestic panoramas across the Golfo de Ancud to the mainland's snowcapped volcanoes.

Ancud and Castro are the only sizable towns. Some towns, most notably Castro, have picturesque neighborhoods of *palafitos,* rows of houses built on stilts over the water, where boats on a rising tide can anchor at the back door. Other palafitos can be found at Quemchi, Chonchi and smaller ports.

Do not miss the smaller villages, with more than 150 distinctive wooden churches up to two centuries old, nine of them national monuments. Achao, Chonchi, Quilquico, Isla Quinchao and Villupulli have 18th-century churches, and churches in Dalcahue, Nercón and Rilán date from the 19th century. Castro's gaudy Iglesia San Francisco is an early-20th-century construction.

Nearly all Chiloé's 140,000 inhabitants live within sight of the sea. More than half make their living from subsistence agriculture, but many others depend on fishing for food and money. The nearly roadless western shores and interior still preserve extensive forests, and the densely settled eastern coastal region contributes wheat, oats, vegetables and livestock to a precarious economy. Despite great natural beauty, Chiloé has contemporary parallels with the 19th century, when the island was one of Chile's poorest areas and Darwin commented that

the climate is not favourable to any production which requires much sunshine to ripen it. There is very little pasture...and in consequence, the staple articles of food are pigs, potatoes and fish...The arts, however, are in the rudest state – as may be seen in their strange fashion of ploughing, their method of spinning, grinding corn, and in the construction of their boats...Although with plenty to eat, the people are very poor: there is no demand for labour, and consequently the lower orders cannot scrape together money sufficient to purchase even the smallest luxuries. There is also a great deficiency of circulating medium. I have seen

Chilote Church

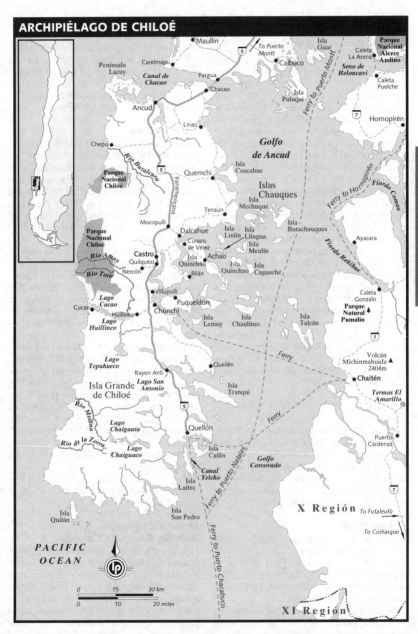

a man bringing on his back a bag of charcoal, with which to buy some trifle, and another carrying a plank to exchange for a bottle of wine.

Because of perpetual economic hardship, many Chilotes (natives of the archipelago) have reluctantly left for employment elsewhere, from the copper mines of the Norte Grande to the sheep estancias of Argentine and Chilean Patagonia. To metropolitan sophisticates, 'Chilote' is synonymous with 'bumpkin,' but the island has a rich tradition of folklore and legend that has made great contributions to Chilean literature.

In part, at least, Chiloé's reputation derives from its insularity – the waters of the Canal de Chacao are so rough that, in days of sail, settlers only reluctantly crossed to and from the mainland. This isolation has encouraged self-reliance but also an unexpected courtesy and hospitality toward visitors that has changed little since Darwin remarked, more than a century and a half ago, 'I never saw anything more obliging and humble than the manners of these people.'

Now, of course, ferries sail frequently from Pargua to Chacao, and there are imminent prospects of a 2.5km bridge that would span the channel. In 2001, the government will accept bids for an estimated US$300 million crossing that will reduce the travel time from a half hour to 2½ minutes.

ANCUD
☎ 65

Founded in 1767 to defend Spain's Chilean coastline from foreign intrusion, the onetime fortress of Ancud is now Chiloé's largest town (population 23,000), an attractive fishing port on a promontory overlooking the Bahía de Ancud. The town's regional museum is a fine introduction to life on the island.

Orientation

At the north end of the Isla Grande, Ancud sits on a small peninsula facing the Canal de Chacao, with the Golfo de Quetalmahue to the west. The Península Lacuy, farther west, shelters the harbor from the swells and storms of the open Pacific.

Ancud's irregular topography has caused an atypical street plan, but the town is small and compact enough that directions are easy to follow. Most points of interest are within a few blocks of the north-south Av Doctor Salvador Allende (the recently renamed costanera) and the asymmetrical Plaza de Armas, on the hill above it. Calle Aníbal Pinto leads to the Panamericana, which continues to Quellón on the island's southern tip.

Information

Sernatur (☎ 622-800) is at Libertad 665, opposite the Plaza de Armas. In summer, it's open 8:30 am to 8 pm weekdays, 10 am to 1:30 pm and 3 to 7:30 pm weekends; the rest of the year, hours are 8:30 am to 1 pm and 2:30 to 6 pm weekdays. It has plenty of brochures, town maps and lists of accommodations. It's better to change currency in Puerto Montt, where there are more ATMs and better exchange rates, but Banco de Crédito has an ATM at Ramírez 257.

Correos de Chile is at the corner of Pudeto and Blanco Encalada. Entel is at Pudeto 219, but there's another Centro de Llamados on Ramírez between Chacabuco and Maipú.

The Centro Internet (☎ 622-607) is at Av Salvador Allende 740.

Turismo Ancud (☎ 623-019) is at Pudeto 219, within the Hotel Lacuy. MB Turismo (☎ 624-349, 09-443-6546), on the Plaza de Armas, offers 2½-hour city tours for US$5, goes to the market at Dalcahue (US$5) and also offers US$25 excursions to Achao, Parque Nacional Chiloé and Quellón. Turismo Huaihuén (☎ 623-800), Pudeto 135, 2nd floor, also offers tours.

The Clean Center laundry (☎ 623-838) is at Pudeto 45.

The Hospital de Ancud (☎ 622-356) is at Almirante Latorre 405, at the corner of Pedro Montt.

Museo Regional Aurelio Bórquez Canobra

Colloquially known as the Museo Chilote, this building houses ethnographic and historical materials (including an outstanding selection of photographs) and a superb natural history display. Surrounded by towers and battlements like a small fortress, its sunny patio displays sculptured figures from Chilote

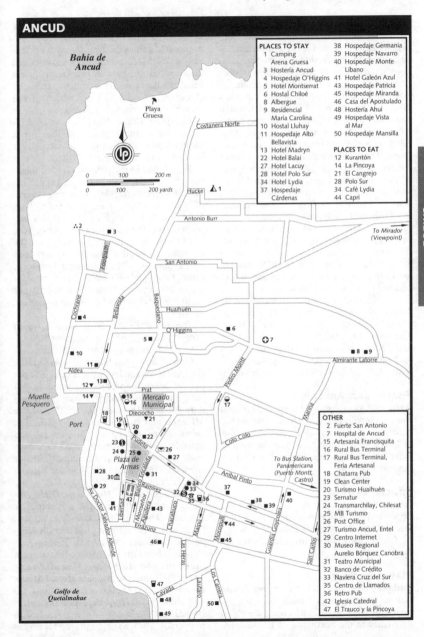

ANCUD

PLACES TO STAY
1 Camping
  Arena Gruesa
3 Hostería Ancud
4 Hospedaje O'Higgins
5 Hotel Montserrat
6 Hostal Chiloé
8 Albergue
9 Residencial
  María Carolina
10 Hostal Lluhay
11 Hospedaje Alto
  Bellavista
13 Hotel Madryn
22 Hotel Balai
27 Hotel Lacuy
28 Hotel Polo Sur
34 Hotel Lydia
37 Hospedaje
  Cárdenas
38 Hospedaje Germania
39 Hospedaje Navarro
40 Hospedaje Monte
  Libano
41 Hotel Galeón Azul
43 Hospedaje Patricia
45 Hospedaje Miranda
46 Casa del Apostulado
48 Hostería Ahui
49 Hospedaje Vista
  al Mar
50 Hospedaje Mansilla

PLACES TO EAT
12 Kurantón
14 La Pincoya
21 El Cangrejo
28 Polo Sur
34 Café Lydia
44 Capri

OTHER
2 Fuerte San Antonio
7 Hospital de Ancud
15 Artesanía Francisquita
16 Rural Bus Terminal
17 Rural Bus Terminal,
  Feria Artesanal
18 Chatarra Pub
19 Clean Center
20 Turismo Huaihuén
23 Sernatur
24 Transmarchilay, Chilesat
25 MB Turismo
26 Post Office
27 Turismo Ancud, Entel
29 Centro Internet
30 Museo Regional
  Aurelio Bórquez Canobra
31 Teatro Municipal
32 Banco de Crédito
33 Naviera Cruz del Sur
35 Centro de Llamados
36 Retro Pub
42 Iglesia Catedral
47 El Trauco y la Pincoya

CHILOÉ

folklore, such as the mermaid La Pincoya (symbol of the ocean's fertility) and the troll-like Trauco. In recent years the museum has become more professional in its presentations and more interactive, with the introduction of videos and matching game panels.

Among the fine exhibits are scale models of several of the island's shingled wooden churches – note the variety of designs among the shingles. A very fine three-dimensional relief map of Chiloé indicates major settlements. There's also a replica of the schooner *Ancud,* which sailed the treacherous fjords of the Strait of Magellan to claim Chile's southernmost territories in the mid-19th century, and Chile's first fire engine, sent from Europe to Valparaíso in 1852.

One of Ancud's most intriguing restaurants is the thatched-roof Chilote house on the museum's patio, whose traditional kitchen, dug into the earth through an opening in the floor, serves a savory *curanto* (a seafood stew) on weekends.

On Libertad just south of the Plaza de Armas, the museum (☎ 622-413) is open 10 am to 7 pm daily in January and February. The rest of the year, hours are 9 am to 1 pm and 2:30 to 7 pm Tuesday to Saturday, 10 am to 1 pm and 3 to 6 pm Sunday. Admission costs US$1 for adults, US$0.25 for children.

Fuerte San Antonio

At the northwest corner of town, late-colonial cannon emplacements still look down on the harbor from the early-19th-century remains of Fuerte San Antonio. During the wars of independence, this was Spain's last Chilean outpost.

Special Events

For a week in January Ancud observes the Semana Ancuditana (Ancud Week), which includes the annual Encuentro de Folklore de Chiloé, promoting the island's music, dance and cuisine.

Places to Stay

Budget The grassy sites at *Camping Arena Gruesa* (☎ 623-428, *Costanera Norte s/n, entrance on Hucke),* six blocks from the Plaza de Armas at the north end of Baquedano,

overlook the sea and have small cooking shelters, but they lack shade and the neighborhood has many barking dogs. Sites ostensibly cost US$13, including hot showers and firewood, but the friendly proprietors give a break to backpackers or small parties by charging around US$3 per person if the campground is not too crowded.

Camping Playa Gaviotas (☎ 09-653-8096), 5km northeast of town on Ruta 5, has similar facilities and good beach access, but little shade or shelter, for US$18.

Better than its dilapidated exterior might suggest, but up for sale at last pass, the informal *Albergue* (☎ 622-065, *Almirante Latorre 478)* provides floor space for sleeping bags for US$1.50 per night, but travelers can pitch tents in the patio for US$1 per person.

In December, January and February, the church-sponsored *Casa del Apostulado* (☎ 623-256), on Chacabuco near Errázuriz, offers floor space for US$2, mattresses for US$3 and proper beds for US$4.50 per night. Visitors can use the kitchen from 8 am to 10 pm.

The HI affiliate is *Hospedaje Vista al Mar* (☎ /fax 622-617, *Av Salvador Allende 918),* which charges US$10 per person.

Other than hostels, hospedajes provide the cheapest accommodations, at about US$7 per person. Many hospedajes are seasonal, but some that are open all year include *Hospedaje Navarro (Pudeto 361)* and *Hospedaje Miranda* at Errázuriz and Mocopulli. For clean rooms and baths, hot showers and amiable hosts, the Miranda is an especially good choice. *Hospedaje Patricia (Monseñor Aguilera 756)* charges US$7.50 for a room with shared bath and cable TV.

Spacious, friendly *Hospedaje O'Higgins* (☎ 622-266, *O'Higgins 6)* is a spectacular mansion charging US$8.50 with breakfast. Open in summer only, tiny but friendly *Hospedaje Cárdenas* (☎ 622-535, *Pudeto 331)* charges US$9. Other hospedajes in the same range include *Hospedaje Mansilla (Los Carrera 971)* and the pleasant *Hostal Monte Líbano* (☎ 622-172, *Aníbal Pinto 419).*

Well-regarded *Hospedaje Alto Bellavista* (☎ 622-384, *Bellavista 449)* charges US$10 per person. For US$12 per person for rooms with breakfast and shared bath, **Residencial María Carolina** (☎ 622-458, Almirante Latorre 558) has many things going for it, including its quiet location, attractive common spaces and spacious gardens.

Mid-Range Mid-range accommodations start around US$14 per person, with shared bath, at **Hospedaje Germania** (☎ 622-214, Pudeto 357); rates are US$35 for doubles with private bath. Highly recommended by many readers, **Hotel Madryn** (☎ 622-128, Bellavista 491) charges around US$15 for singles with breakfast. **Hostal Chiloé** (☎ 622-869, O'Higgins 274) charges US$16 per person for friendly family accommodations, with private bath and a substantial breakfast. Comparable accommodations at waterfront **Hotel Polo Sur** (☎ 622-200, Av Salvador Allende 630) cost US$17 per person, but without breakfast.

Despite an unimpressive exterior, **Hotel Lydia** (☎ 622-990, fax 622-879, Pudeto 256) has agreeable rooms starting at US$15/28 with shared bath; rooms with private bath cost US$27/39. The hotel also has a highly regarded restaurant. For US$23, **Hostal Lluhay** (☎ 622-656, Cochrane 458, lluhay@entelchile.net) has singles with private bath and breakfast. The hotel has sea views and good common spaces. **Hotel Lacuy** (☎ 623-019, Pudeto 219) comes recommended at US$29/38 for rooms with breakfast and private bath, but has thin walls and can be noisy because of its central location.

Directly opposite the Plaza de Armas, **Hotel Balai** (☎ 622-541, Pudeto 169) charges US$27/38. Homey, well-located **Hotel Montserrat** (☎ 622-957, Baquedano 417) charges US$33/50. At the southern end of downtown, **Hostería Ahuí** (☎ 622-415, Av Salvador Allende 906) charges US$34/50.

Top End The hillside **Hotel Galeón Azul** (☎ 622-567, Libertad 751) charges US$69/83. Overlooking the sea and Fuerte San Antonio, with superb views from the bar, is Ancud's top hotel, **Hostería Ancud** (☎ 622-340, San Antonio 30, 02-696-5599 in Santiago). Rooms cost US$79/100, with breakfast and private bath.

Places to Eat
Visiting Chiloé without sampling seafood is like going to Argentina without tasting beef. Excellent, reasonably priced local specialties are available at **El Sacho**, in the Mercado Municipal on Dieciocho between Libertad and Blanco Encalada, which has featured such creatively mistranslated dishes as 'poultry baked, brailed or bailed' and 'sauce made of seafood, butter cornstarch wine and spice spice.'

Other seafood choices include **Polo Sur** (Av Salvador Allende 630), in its namesake hotel; the waterfront **La Pincoya** (☎ 622-613, Prat 61), most notable for its views; and **Capri** (Mocopulli 710). **El Cangrejo** (Dieciocho 155), another good place to eat, gets more notice for its decor. Business cards and other scrawls on the walls make it seem that just about every visitor to Ancud has eaten there at least once.

For good dinners, desserts and coffee, try **Café Lydia** (☎ 622-990, Pudeto 256). **Kurantón** (☎ 622-216, Prat 94) has a varied menu, including the dish for which it's named, curanto (seafood stew), plus beef, fish and shellfish and pizza.

Entertainment
Ancud has several popular pubs, including the **Chatarra Pub** (☎ 622-178, Av Salvador Allende 580), the appropriately named **Retro Pub** on Maipú between Ramírez and Pudeto, which features a '60s ambience and music, and **El Trauco y la Pincoya** at Av Salvador Allende and Los Cavada, which has live music at night.

The **Teatro Municipal**, on Blanco Encalada opposite the Plaza de Armas, hosts concerts and other cultural events.

Shopping
Ancud has a plethora of outlets for artisanal goods such as woolens, carvings and pottery. Besides the Museo Chilote and the Mercado Municipal, try Artesanía Francisquita at Libertad 530. In summer, there's a small but good Feria de Artesanos on the north side of the Plaza de Armas. There's also a new Feria Artesanal at the corner of Prat and Pedro Montt.

CHILOE

Getting There & Away

Nearly all traffic reaches and leaves the Isla Grande de Chiloé by the ferry between Pargua, on the mainland 56km southwest of Puerto Montt, and Chacao, at the northeast corner of the island. Bus fares to and from the mainland include the half-hour ferry crossing; if you're hitching and walk on board, you will have to pay US$2 for the privilege; cars cost about US$12. The pier at Pargua is a good place to ask for a lift, but it's crowded in summer.

Bus All of Ancud's bus companies have finally moved from downtown to the new Terminal de Buses, at Aníbal Pinto and Marcos Vera, east of downtown.

Cruz del Sur (☎ 622-265) has a dozen buses daily to Puerto Montt; some of these continue to Osorno, Valdivia, Concepción, Temuco and Santiago. It has a dozen buses daily to Castro and several more to Chonchi and Quellón. Cruz del Sur also goes to Bariloche, Argentina, at 8:30 am Thursday and Sunday, but Bus Norte is cheaper and departs at 8:30 am daily.

Turibús (☎ 622-289) goes to Concepción and Santiago, and to Punta Arenas and Puerto Natales Tuesday, Thursday and Saturday. Queilén Bus goes to Punta Arenas at 8:25 am Monday and Friday.

Varmontt (☎ 623-049) goes to Puerto Montt, Temuco and Santiago and south to Quellón. Transchiloé (☎ 622-876) has several buses daily to Castro, Chonchi, Quellón and Puerto Montt.

Some sample bus fares and approximate travel times include Castro (US$2, one hour), Puerto Montt (US$5, two hours), Quellón (US$5, three hours), Temuco (US$14, seven hours), Concepción (US$19, 11 hours), Santiago (US$27, 18 hours), Bariloche (US$19 to US$25) and Punta Arenas (US$85, 48 hours).

For buses to other destinations on Chiloé, go to one of the two rural bus terminals: on Pedro Montt opposite Prat, and at the corner of Prat and Libertad. Buses Mar Brava has three buses weekly to Chepu, at the northern end of Parque Nacional Chiloé (US$1.25). Buses Chepu also goes there.

Boat Although ferries don't leave from Ancud, Transmarchilay (☎ 622-317, fax 623-067) has an office at Libertad 669 alongside Sernatur, and sails from Quellón to Chaitén, and to Puerto Chacabuco in the Aisén Region (see the Quellón entry later in this chapter). It also runs ferries between Pargua and Chacao, as does Naviera Cruz del Sur (☎ 622-506), Chacabuco 672. For automobiles, the fare between Pargua and Chacao is about US$12, including as many passengers as can fit.

DALCAHUE

Sunday's crafts market, traditionally the most important on the Isla Grande, is the primary attraction of the small fishing port of Dalcahue, which takes its name from the *dalca,* a type of canoe in which indigenous Chilotes went to sea. The tsunami of 1960 washed away Dalcahue's palafitos, though the town still features a 19th-century church. The shipwrights at work in the harbor are worth a visit. Dalcahue (population 2300) is also the Isla Grande gateway to Quinchao, one of archipelagic Chile's most interesting and accessible islands.

Orientation & Information

On the east coast of Chiloé, Dalcahue is 20km northeast of Castro and opposite the island of Quinchao, to which there are ferry-bus connections.

The tourist office, a small storefront on the costanera alongside the Centro de Llamados via Entel, keeps erratic hours.

Aitué Excursiones (☎ 641-251), O'Higgins 013, provides excursions to outlying islands.

Things to See

Artisans from offshore islands travel great distances for Sunday morning's nonchalant **feria artesanal**, which has a variety of woolens, wooden crafts, basketry and good cheap seafood restaurants. Sellers often drop their prices without even hearing a counteroffer. Unfortunately, imported manufactured goods have diluted the feria's overall quality.

The nearby **Centro Cultural Dalcahue** has replaced the former Museo Regional; its fossils, stuffed birds and antique household implements are better displayed than in the past. On the Plaza de Armas, the neoclassical **Iglesia Dalcahue**, with Doric columns, dates from 1854. It is not in especially good repair, but has a truly grisly statue of the crucified Christ, with movable arms attached with leather straps.

Special Events
The annual fiesta is the Semana Dalcahuina, in the second week of February.

Places to Stay & Eat
Dalcahue has remarkably good budget accommodations from about US$6 per person. Try friendly **Residencial Playa** (☎ 641-397, *Rodríguez 009)*, which also has a fine restaurant. If it's full, the comparably priced but less amiable **Residencial La Feria** *(Rodríguez 011)*, where the rooms are small but beds are comfortable and the hot showers are excellent, is nearby. Opposite the plaza, **Residencial San Martín** (☎ 651-207, *San Martín 001)* has singles for US$6.50 and moderately priced three-course meals.

Hospedaje Mary *(Teniente Merino 010)*, east of the church, permits camping and offers moderately priced lodging. **Pensión Pulemún** (☎ 651-330, *Freire 305)* is an excellent value at US$8 single. The best place to stay in town, though, is the new **Hotel La Isla** (☎ 641-241, *Av Mocopulli 113)*, a new three-star establishment that blends traditional architecture with modern conveniences. Rates are US$42/48 singles/doubles.

For good cheap food and waterfront atmosphere, try **Brisas Marinas**, on palafitos above the feria artesanal. **La Dalca** *(Freire 502)* is especially notable for fresh clams and other seafood, with cordial service and large portions.

Getting There & Away
The main bus terminal is on Freire opposite O'Higgins, but buses also load and unload at the Feria Artesanal. Expreso Dalcahue, on Freire near Eugenio, has weekday buses to and from Castro every half-hour, but fewer on weekends. However, frequent taxi colectivos from Castro charge just over US$1 for the half-hour trip.

The motor launch *Ultima Esperanza* connecting Dalcahue with the outlying Islas Chauques leaves at 2 pm Tuesday and Friday. There are also ferries and buses across the estuary to Isla Quinchao, with connections to the village of Achao and its landmark 18th-century church. Pedestrians go free on these ferries; the roundtrip automobile fare of US$5 is slightly cheaper than two one-way fares.

CASTRO
☎ 65

Emblematically Chilote, thanks in large part to the vernacular architectural distinction of its waterfront palafitos and their crafted *tejuelas* (shingles), Castro is the capital of Chiloé province. Founded in 1567 by Martín Ruiz de Gamboa, the town languished through colonial and early republican times. When Darwin visited in 1834, he found it 'a most forlorn and deserted place' where

the usual quadrangular arrangement of Spanish towns could be traced, but the streets and plaza were coated with fine green turf, on which sheep were browsing...The poverty of the place may be conceived from the fact, that although containing some hundred of inhabitants, one of our party was unable anywhere to purchase either a pound of sugar or an ordinary knife. No individual possessed either a watch or a clock; and an old man, who was supposed to have a good idea of time, was employed to strike the church bell by guess.

Charles Darwin

CHILOÉ

CASTRO

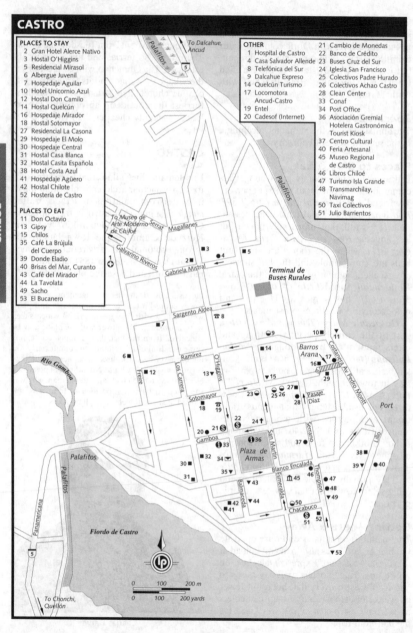

PLACES TO STAY
2 Gran Hotel Alerce Nativo
3 Hostal O'Higgins
5 Residencial Mirasol
6 Albergue Juvenil
7 Hospedaje Aguilar
10 Hotel Unicornio Azul
12 Hostal Don Camilo
14 Hostal Quelcún
16 Hospedaje Mirador
18 Hostal Sotomayor
27 Residencial La Casona
29 Hospedaje El Molo
30 Hospedaje Central
31 Hostal Casa Blanca
32 Hostal Casita Española
38 Hotel Costa Azul
41 Hospedaje Agüero
42 Hostal Chilote
52 Hostería de Castro

PLACES TO EAT
11 Don Octavio
13 Gipsy
15 Chilos
35 Café La Brújula
    del Cuerpo
39 Donde Eladio
40 Brisas del Mar, Curanto
43 Café del Mirador
44 La Tavolata
49 Sacho
53 El Bucanero

OTHER
1 Hospital de Castro
4 Casa Salvador Allende
8 Telefónica del Sur
9 Dalcahue Expreso
14 Quelcún Turismo
17 Locomotora
    Ancud-Castro
19 Entel
20 Cadesof (Internet)
21 Cambio de Monedas
22 Banco de Crédito
23 Buses Cruz del Sur
24 Iglesia San Francisco
25 Colectivos Padre Hurado
26 Colectivos Achao Castro
28 Clean Center
33 Conaf
34 Post Office
36 Asociación Gremial
    Hotelera Gastronómica
    Tourist Kiosk
37 Centro Cultural
40 Feria Artesanal
45 Museo Regional
    de Castro
46 Libros Chiloé
47 Turismo Isla Grande
48 Transmarchilay,
    Navimag
50 Taxi Colectivos
51 Julio Barrientos

Castro overcame the economic depression of the 19th century, though its most conspicuous attraction – the bright and incongruously painted Iglesia San Francisco opposite the Plaza de Armas – dates from 1906. Like Ancud, the city is a popular summer destination, attracting many Chilean and Argentine tourists.

Orientation

On a sheltered estuary on the eastern shore of the Isla Grande de Chiloé, 90km south of Ancud, most of the city of Castro (population 18,000) sits on a bluff above the water. Only the Costanera Av Pedro Montt has direct access to the shore. Nearly every point of interest is within a couple of blocks of the Plaza de Armas, bounded by Gamboa, O'Higgins, Blanco Encalada and San Martín. The Panamericana enters town from the direction of Ancud and exits south toward Quellón, the end of the line for this branch of the longitudinal highway.

Information

The private Asociación Gremial Hotelera Gastronómica funds the small tourist kiosk on the north side of the Plaza de Armas, which has town maps, a hotel price list (including only those that belong to the association) and some information on the surrounding countryside. It's open 9 am to 9 pm daily in summer, but the rest of the year hours are 9 am to 1 pm and 3 to 7 pm weekdays, 9 am to 1 pm Saturday.

For the best exchange rates, try Julio Barrientos (☎ 625-079) at Chacabuco 286 or Cambio de Monedas, at Gamboa 411. Banco de Crédito has an ATM at the corner of O'Higgins and Gamboa.

Correos de Chile is at O'Higgins 388, on the west side of the Plaza de Armas. For long-distance telephone services, go to Entel at O'Higgins 480 or Telefónica del Sur at O'Higgins 667.

Cadesof (☎ 632-629), Gamboa 447, 2nd floor, offers reasonably priced Internet access 9 am to 1 pm daily except Sunday and from 3 to 7 pm weekdays.

Castro has a more vigorous tourist industry and better infrastructure than Ancud. Helpful Turismo Isla Grande (☎ 632-384), Thompson 241, is a full-service travel agency.

Turismo Queilén Bus (☎ 632-173) at the main bus terminal, San Martín 689, offers tours to sights such as Parque Nacional Chiloé, the islands of Quinchao, Lemuy and Mechuque and the market at Dalcahue.

Libros Chiloé, Blanco Encalada 202, has a good selection of books on both regional and general Chilean subjects, along with a good selection of Chilean music.

The Clean Center laundry is at Serrano 490.

The Hospital de Castro (☎ 632-445) is at Freire 852, at the foot of Cerro Millantuy.

Iglesia San Francisco de Castro

Built in 1906 at the north end of the Plaza de Armas, the Iglesia San Francisco assaults the vision with its gaudy exterior paint job – salmon with violet trim. The varnished-wood interior is more soothing, despite some gruesome portrayals of the crucifixion and other religious statuary. Termites and dry rot have begun to cause problems for this landmark wooden structure.

Locomotora Ancud-Castro

On Av Pedro Montt, near Hotel Unicornio Azul, stands the original, German-made locomotive from the narrow-gauge railway that connected Castro with Ancud via Pupelde, Coquiao, Puntra, Butalcura, Mocopulli

¡Más rápido!

and Pid Pid. According to legend, the only difference between 1st and 3rd class was that the conductor would order 3rd-class passengers off the train to help push the locomotive over the crest of even gentle slopes. Service on this line ended with the massive earthquake and tsunami of 1960.

Palafitos
All around Castro, shingled houses on stilts stretch out into estuaries and lagoons; at high tide, resident fishermen tie their boats to the stilts, but from the street these houses resemble any other in town. This truly singular architecture, now the subject of determined preservation efforts, can be seen along Costanera Pedro Montt at the north end of town, at the feria artesanal on the south end (where some are restaurants) and at both ends of the bridge across the Río Gamboa, where the Panamericana heads south to Quellón.

Museo Regional de Castro
In attractive quarters on Esmeralda, half a block south of the Plaza de Armas, the regional museum houses an idiosyncratic but well-organized collection of Huilliche relics, traditional farm implements and exhibits on the evolution of Chilote urbanism. In the past few years, it has made great leaps forward in ethnography, cartography and photography – its black-and-white photographs of the 1960 earthquake are remarkable.

In summer (January and February), the museum is open 9:30 am to 8 pm daily except Sunday, when it's open from 10:30 am to 1 pm. The rest of the year, it's open 9 am to 1 pm and 3 to 7 pm daily, 10:30 am to 1 pm Sunday. Admission is free.

Museo de Arte Moderno de Chiloé
Castro's spacious modern art museum, in an imaginatively recycled warehouse divided into five separate exhibition halls, features over 300 works by contemporary Chilean artists, many of them Chilotes producing innovative work. Most of these works are paintings, but there's also some imaginative multimedia work.

Located in the Parque Municipal, at the west end of Galvarino Riveros, the underfunded museum (☎ 635-454) is open 10 am to 7 pm daily, in summer only.

Feria Artesanal
Castro's waterfront market has a fine selection of woolen ponchos and sweaters, caps, gloves and basketry. Note the bundles of dried seaweed and the rhubarblike *nalca*, both part of the local diet, and the blocks of peat Chilotes use for fuel. The market has several excellent, inexpensive seafood restaurants, and has become more diverse and interesting than its more highly publicized counterpart at Dalcahue.

Special Events
In late January, the Festival de Huaso Chilote pays homage to local cowboys. In mid-February, Castro celebrates the Festival Costumbrista, a weeklong party with folk music and dance and traditional foods.

Places to Stay
Budget *Camping Llicaldad* (☎ 635-080), 5km south of town on the Fiordo de Castro, charges US$13 per four-person site. *Camping Pudú* (☎ 632-476), 10km north of Castro on the Dalcahue road, charges US$9 per site for reasonable facilities, but is a bit far out of town.

For barebones summer hostel accommodations, go to the *Albergue Juvenil* (☎ 632-766, Freire 610), in the Gimnasia Fiscal, which charges about US$2.50 per person.

Castro has an abundance of inexpensive hospedajes, mostly along San Martín and O'Higgins, and their immediate side streets. At *Hospedaje Central*, at Los Carrera between Blanco Encalada and Gamboa, spotless but small and spartan rooms with firm beds cost US$7 (including a *very* late breakfast). The shared baths have excellent hot showers. In the same range is *Residencial Mirasol* (San Martín 815).

Despite its attractive setting, *Hotel Costa Azul* (☎ 632-440, Lillo 67) is reported to be 'damp and cold and a little bleak.' Rooms cost US$8.50 per person with shared bath, but don't hesitate to haggle. Rooms with private bath cost twice as much. Rates are comparable at **Hostal O'Higgins** (☎ 632-016, O'Higgins 831 Interior), small but tidy and friendly **Hostal Sotomayor** (☎ 632-464, Sotomayor 452), and spacious **Hospedaje Aguilar** (☎ 634-214, Sargento Aldea 516).

At an excellent location on a pedestrian staircase, exceptionally friendly **Hospedaje El Molo** (☎ 635-026, Barros Arana 140) charges only US$8 per person, with breakfast, cable TV and kitchen privileges. If it's full, try **Hospedaje Mirador** (☎ 633-795, Barros Arana 127), across the street, which has family atmosphere, good hot showers and sea views. **Residencial La Casona** (☎ 632-246, Serrano 496) charges US$9.

For US$10 per person, with breakfast, **Hospedaje Agüero** (☎ 635-735, Chacabuco 449) is recommended and enjoys a quiet location with views of the sea and Castro's southern palafitos. Nearby **Hostal Chilote** (☎ 635-021, Aldunate 456) is spotless and spacious for US$10 with shared bath.

Mid-Range Mid-range accommodations are relatively scarce, but **Hostal Casa Blanca** (☎ 632-726, Los Carrera 308) has rooms with shared bath for US$12 per person, with breakfast; doubles with private bath and color TV cost US$42. Friendly **Hostal Quelcún** (☎ 632-396, San Martín 581) charges US$29/38 singles/doubles with private bath, but also has some bargain rooms for just US$10 per person with shared bath.

Rates are US$42/52 at **Hostal Casita Española** (☎ 635-186, Los Carrera 359). The comparable **Hostal Don Camilo** (☎ 632-180, fax 635-533, Ramírez 566) charges US$50 double.

Top End Top-end accommodations start around US$50/64 at **Gran Hotel Alerce Nativo** (☎ 632-267, fax 632-309, O'Higgins 808), a good value with private bath, telephone and TV. Taking its name from a popular song by Cuban singer Silvio Rodríguez, the waterfront **Hotel Unicornio Azul** (☎ 622-359, Pedro Montt 228) has Castro's most architecturally oddball accommodations. Simple but attractive rooms cost US$69/83 with breakfast (in what was once a budget hotel).

Conspicuous for its exaggerated chalet design, the **Hostería de Castro** (☎ 632-301, fax 635-688, Chacabuco 202) has good harbor views. Rates are US$70/80 with private bath and breakfast.

Places to Eat

The palafito restaurants at the waterfront Feria Artesanal on the south end of town have the best food for the fewest pesos. **Brisas del Mar** and **Curanto** both have fixed-price lunches for about US$5, as well as more expensive specialties.

Don Octavio (☎ 632-855, Pedro Montt 261), across from Hotel Unicornio Azul, is no longer a budget choice but it's still a good value for seafood. Try **Chilos** (☎ 635-782), at Sotomayor and San Martín, for meat and seafood, and **Sacho** (☎ 632-079, Thompson 213) for curanto. Other seafood choices include **Donde Eladio** (☎ 635-285, Lillo 97) and the newish palafito restaurant **El Bucanero**, at Lillo and Thompson, which is good and moderately priced.

Café La Brújula del Cuerpo (O'Higgins 308) is an excellent choice for sandwiches, coffee and desserts, as is **Café del Mirador** (☎ 633-958, Blanco Encalada 388). **La Tavolata** (☎ 633-882, Balmaceda 245) is a good, moderately priced pizzería. For Chinese food, try **Gipsy** (O'Higgins 552).

Entertainment

Casa Salvador Allende (Gabriela Mistral 357) holds a Saturday night peña (folk music performance). Castro's **Centro Cultural** (Serrano 320) is open 11 am to 1 pm and 4 to 9 pm daily.

Getting There & Around

There are many buses on Chiloé; ferry transport plays a major role as well. If you prefer to pedal, Quelcún Turismo (☎ 632-396), San Martín 581, rents mountain bikes for reasonable rates in peak season.

Bus From its central location, Castro is the major hub for bus traffic on Chiloé, both local and long distance. The misleadingly named Terminal de Buses Rurales, on San Martín near Sargento Aldea, also hosts several long-distance carriers; most others have offices nearby.

Buses Arroyo (☎ 635-604) has two to three buses a day to Huillinco and Cucao, the entrance to Parque Nacional Chiloé on the west coast, and Ocean Bus (☎ 635-492) has two daily buses on the same route. Since most of these buses leave early in the morning and return in the early evening, it's possible to visit the park on a day trip. The fare is about US$2.50 one way.

Dalcahue Expreso (☎ 635-164), at Ramírez 233, goes every half-hour to Dalcahue on weekdays, but less often on weekends. Arriagada, in the Cruz del Sur terminal at San Martín 486, goes to Dalcahue and to Achao, on Isla Quinchao. Buses Cárdenas covers the Dalcahue route less frequently, but also goes to smaller towns like Quetalco, San Juan and Calén.

Buses Lemuy serves Chonchi (US$1.40) and destinations on Isla Lemuy, including Puqueldón, as does Buses Gallardo. Buses Queilén (☎ 632-173), which also operates tours around Chiloé, has regular service to Queilén and intermediate points.

Taxi colectivos to Chonchi leave from Chacabuco near Esmeralda. Colectivos Padre Hurtado (☎ 632-501), Sotomayor 268, goes to Quellón, and Colectivos Achao Castro is at Sotomayor 262.

For long-distance bus service, Cruz del Sur (☎ 632-389), in its own terminal at San Martín 486, has a dozen buses daily to Ancud and Puerto Montt, several of which continue to Santiago and intermediate stops. It also has several buses daily to Chonchi and Quellón, as does Regional Sur (☎ 632-071), at the bus terminal. Transchiloé (☎ 635-152), at the Cruz del Sur terminal, has several buses daily north to Ancud and Puerto Montt, and south to Chonchi and Quellón.

Castro enjoys direct bus service, via Argentina, to Punta Arenas (US$70) and Puerto Natales, twice weekly with Buses Ghisoni (☎ 632-358) and two to four times weekly with Bus Sur at the terminal. Turibús (☎ 635-088) goes to Puerto Montt, Concepción and Punta Arenas (36 hours, about US$85 in

summer, a bit cheaper the rest of the year). Buses Queilén also goes to Punta Arenas.

Sample fares and times include Ancud (US$3, one hour), Quellón (US$4, two hours), Puerto Montt (US$7, three hours), Puerto Varas (US$8, 3½ hours), Valdivia (US$13), Temuco (US$15, eight hours), Concepción (US$22, 12 hours) and Santiago (US$27, 19 hours).

Boat Transmarchilay (☎/fax 635-691) has no ferries from Castro, but makes reservations at its offices at Thompson 273. So does Navimag, at the same location.

ACHAO
On the elongated offshore island of Quinchao, the village of Achao is a charming destination with a landmark church and outstanding vernacular architecture, fine food and accommodations and friendly people. Its annual folk festival, in early February, deserves a detour from mainland Chile.

Orientation & Information
Achao is 25km southeast of Dalcahue via a short ferry crossing and a good gravel road that traces Isla Quinchao's hilly topography. While Achao is more than 250 years old, it does not follow the standard grid pattern of most Chilean towns, and its rectangular Plaza de Armas almost seems peripheral compared to the waterfront Calle Prat and the commercial district of Calle Serrano, which terminates in the fishing jetty.

Achao's helpful Oficina de Información Turística is a small kiosk at the corner of Serrano and Ricardo Jara, which keeps long summer hours and also arranges excursions to offshore Isla Llingua (see Around Achao).

Correos de Chile is on Serrano between Ricardo Jara and Progreso, and there's a telephone office on Pasaje Freire, south of Pedro Montt. The hospital is at the corner of Progreso and Riquelme.

Iglesia Santa María de Achao
Crowned by a 25m tower, sided with alerce shingles and held together by wooden pegs rather than nails, Achao's 18th-century Jesuit church, on the south side of the Plaza de

Armas, is now a national monument. At this writing, the church is still undergoing restoration for termite damage and dry rot.

Special Events
Early February's Encuentro Folklórico de las Islas del Archipiélago, nearing its 20th year, attracts musical groups from throughout the archipelago. The quality of the groups is almost uniformly excellent, and the festival organization is very professional. A simultaneous event is the Muestra Gastronómica y Artesanal, where visitors can taste traditional Chilote specialties, see and purchase local crafts and view demonstrations of antique machinery like apple presses and grain mills.

Places to Stay & Eat
In the busy summer season, there's informal camping – for free or negligible cost – on Delicias between Sargento Aldea and Serrano. The cheapest regular accommodation is *Hospedaje São Paulo* (☎ 661-245, Serrano 052), which charges US$8.50 per person and also has a restaurant with an extensive menu. Nearby, *Hospedaje Achao* (☎ 661-373, Serrano 061) charges US$10 for a room with shared bath.

Achao's best choice may be friendly *Hospedaje Sol y Lluvia* (☎ 661-383, Ricardo Jara 09), where comfortable, spotless rooms with shared bath and a superb breakfast cost US$12 per person; rates with private bath are US$16. *Hospedaje Chilhue* (Zañartu 025) also deserves a look.

At *Hostal Plaza* (☎ 661-283, Amunátegui 20), doubles with private bath and breakfast cost US$18. *Hostería La Nave* (☎ 661-219, Prat s/n), facing the beach, charges US$18 for a double with shared bath, US$26 with private bath, but the latter are in short supply.

Mar y Velas (☎ 661-375, Serrano 02), at the foot of the pier, has outstanding seafood, including particularly tasty oysters. Try also *Restaurant de los Amigos* at Delicias and Sargento Aldea.

Getting There & Away
Transportes Arriagada, at the Terminal de Buses at the east end of town, runs nine buses daily to Castro via Dalcahue, between 7:15 am and 5:30 pm daily. There are also taxi colectivos to Castro.

AROUND ACHAO
Isla Llingua
Half an hour from Achao by launch, Isla Llingua is a small island whose century-old church is a local landmark (legend says that Chono Indians burned the first two churches on the site to get the nails). Well-trained local guides take visitors past Chono shell middens, into the church and its bell tower, up the local mirador for a panorama of the tiny settlement, and into the island's small but excellent artisans' market, which specializes in basketry.

For information on tours, which cost US$5 and last about two hours, contact Achao's Oficina de Información Turística at the corner of Serrano and Ricardo Jara.

Curaco de Vélez
Midway between Dalcahue and Achao, the village of Curaco de Vélez dates from 1660, when a Jesuit mission was built there. It features a modern church (built in 1971 after the historic church burned to the ground) and a small but organized museum in its Centro Cultural on the Plaza de Armas. The rest of the village, though, is a treasure of vernacular Chilote architecture, including eight traditional water mills recently restored with government and municipal help.

CHONCHI
Known as the Ciudad de los Tres Pisos (City of Three Floors) for its abrupt topography, Chonchi's more colorful indigenous name literally means 'slippery earth.' The town dates from 1767, though its landmark **Iglesia San Carlos de Chonchi**, with its three-story tower and multiple arches, dates from the mid-19th century. Other noteworthy vernacular architecture is along Calle Centenario.

Orientation & Information
Chonchi (population about 4000) occupies a site above Canal Lemuy, 23km south of Castro and 3km west of the Panamericana. It is connected by launch to the port of

Ichuac and by ferry to Chulchuy, both on Isla Lemuy.

Chonchi's Oficina de Información Turística, at the intersection of Sargento Candelaria and Centenario, is open 9 am to 7 pm daily from January to March. Correos de Chile is almost next door.

The Semana Verano Chonchi, in early February, is a weeklong municipal festival with folk music, art exhibits, dances and rodeos and other sports events.

Places to Stay & Eat
Camping los Manzanos (☎ 671-263, *Pedro Aguirre Cerda 409*) has sites with covered cooking areas and hot showers for US$10.

Several hospedajes fall into the US$6 to US$7.50 range, including *Hospedaje Andrea* (☎ 671-655, *Andrade 236*), *Hospedaje Emarley* (☎ 671-202, *Irarrázaval 191*), *Hospedaje Gómez* (☎ 671-224, *Andrade 298*), *Residencial Turismo* (☎ 671-257, *Andrade 299*) and *Hospedaje El Mirador* (☎ 671-351, *Ciriaco Alvarez 198*).

English and German are spoken at beachfront *Hospedaje La Esmeralda* (☎ 671-328, *Irarrázabal s/n, gredycel@entelchile.net*), which charges US$5.50 for bunks, US$7.50 to US$10 for rather better accommodations with shared and private bath. English owner Carl Brady also serves popular salmon dinners, rents mountain bikes and fishing gear and has a small loaner rowboat.

Hotel Huildín (☎ 671-388, *fax 635-030, Centenario 102*) has singles with breakfast and shared bath for US$8.50 per person. *Hospedaje Chonchi* (☎ 671-288, *O'Higgins 379*) has comparably priced rooms with shared bath; rooms with private bath cost US$10 per person.

Dating from 1935 and built of native timber, *Posada El Antiguo Chalet* (☎ 671-221, *Gabriela Mistral s/n*) is in a quiet location and is the best place to stay in town, for US$38/63 singles/doubles.

For Chilote seafood specialties, try *El Trébol* (☎ 671-203, *Irarrázaval s/n*), on the 2nd floor of the mercado municipal or *La Quila* (☎ 671-389, *Andrade 183*). *Los Tres Pisos* (☎ 671-433, *O'Higgins 359*) serves *kuchen, empanadas* and the like.

Shopping
For Chilote woolens, try Ismenia Vidal (☎ 671-317), Sargento Candelaria 051.

Getting There & Away
Bus & Colectivo Opposite the Plaza de Armas, Cruz del Sur (☎ 671-218) and Transchiloé have several buses daily between Castro and Chonchi. Taxi colectivos (US$1) are also numerous; in Castro, these leave from Chacabuco near Esmeralda.

A new summer bus service to Parque Nacional Chiloé, leaving Chonchi at 8:30 am and 12:30 pm, was due to start as of publication. For current information, check with Carl Brady of Hospedaje La Esmeralda (see Places to Stay & Eat earlier in the chapter).

Boat There are launches to the port of Ichuac on Isla Lemuy. The ferry *El Caleuche* leaves every half-hour between 8 am and 8 pm daily from Puerto Huichas, 5km to the south, except Sunday, when it is hourly. The ferry lands at Chulchuy, with connections to Puqueldón.

From September to May, the new *Esmeralda de Chonchi* (☎ 671-326) sails to Chaitén at 8 am Tuesday and Thursday, arriving at 4 pm. Low-season fares (September to November, March to May) are US$10 per person, but high-season fares (December, January, February) are US$16. The ship can carry bicycles but not motorcycles. You can purchase tickets at the corner of Centenario and the waterfront, or at Hospedaje La Esmeralda.

PARQUE NACIONAL CHILOÉ
Nowhere in South America can travelers follow Darwin's footsteps more closely than in Parque Nacional Chiloé. The great naturalist left so vivid a record of his passage to the village of Cucao, now the gateway to the park, that it merits lengthy citation:

At Chonchi we struck across the island, following intricate winding paths, sometimes passing through magnificent forests, and sometimes through pretty cleared spots, abounding with corn and potato crops. This undulating woody country, partially cultivated, reminded me of the wilder parts of England, and therefore had to my eye a most fascinating aspect. At Vilinco (Huillinco), which is situated on the borders of the lake of Cucao, only a few fields were cleared...

The country on each side of the lake was one unbroken forest. In the same periagua (canoe) with us, a cow was embarked. To get so large an animal into a small boat appears at first a difficulty, but the Indians managed it in a minute. They brought the cow alongside the boat, which was heeled towards her; then placing two oars under her belly, with their ends resting on the gunwale, by the aid of these levers they fairly tumbled the poor beast, heels overhead into the bottom of the boat, and then lashed her down with ropes.

The village of Cucao has grown rapidly with the park's increasing popularity, and now sports several residenciales and hospedajes, several good restaurants and even a regular bus terminal. The late Bruce Chatwin, the gifted travel writer and novelist, left a brief but illuminating essay on Cucao and the people of rural Chiloé in his collection *What Am I Doing Here?*

Indigenous Huilliche communities in and around the park are ambivalent, at best, about Conaf's management plan, which they feel has restricted their access to traditional subsistence resources. Again, there are conspicuous parallels with Darwin's time, when the great scientist wrote:

The district of Cucao is the only inhabited part on the whole west coast of Chiloé. It contains about 30 or 40 Indian families, who are scattered along four or five miles of the shore. They are very much secluded from the rest of Chiloé, and have scarcely any sort of commerce, except sometimes in a little oil, which they get from seal-blubber. They are tolerably dressed in clothes of their own manufacture, and they have plenty to eat. They seemed, however, discontented, yet humble to a degree which it was quite painful to witness. These feelings are, I think, chiefly to be attributed to the harsh and authoritative manner in which they are treated by their rulers.

Established in 1982, 43,000-hectare Parque Nacional Chiloé is about 30km west of Chonchi and 54km west of Castro, on the island's Pacific coast. It is reached via the paved Panamericana and a normally passable gravel lateral to Huillinco and Cucao.

Altitudes range from sea level to 850m on the heights of the Cordillera de Piuchén. The annual average temperature in the temperate maritime climate is about 10°C, with a mean annual rainfall at Cucao of 2200mm, evenly distributed throughout the year. The park is open all year, but fair weather is more likely in summer, the best time for a visit.

Parque Nacional Chiloé protects extensive stands of native coniferous and evergreen forest, plus a long and almost pristine coastline, in a nearly roadless portion of the island. The majestic alerce reaches its southern limit within the park, in pure stands at altitudes above 600m, and a few endemic animal subspecies can be found, most notably the Chiloé fox *(Dusicyon fulvipes.)* The reclusive pudú inhabits the shadowy forests of the contorted *tepú (Tepualia stimulais)*, but sightings of this miniature Chilean deer are rare in the wild. The 110 species of bird include the occasional penguin.

The park's northern sector, including Chepu and Isla Metalqui (which has a sea lion colony) are less easily accessible without a car or, in the case of Metalqui, highly restricted because of ecological concerns. See the Ancud entry for suggestions about tours.

Rental horses are available at Cucao for US$4 per hour or US$18 for the entire day. Be selective in choice of horses, since their quality varies considerably.

Sector Chanquín

Chanquín, across the suspension bridge from Cucao, is the starting point for almost all excursions into the park. Park admission costs US$2.

About 1km from the bridge, Conaf's Centro de Visitantes, open 9 am to 7:30 pm daily, has good displays on local flora and fauna, the indigenous Huilliche peoples, the early mining industry and island folklore. Outside are wooden carts and sleighs, used to haul heavy loads over wet ground in damp weather, a gold extractor and a *chicha* (apple cider) press.

Near the Chanquín campground is the **Sendero Interpretivo El Tepual**, a short nature trail built on tree trunks, which loops through dense, gloomy forest where you might expect

CHILOÉ

to meet the Trauco, a troll-like figure from Chilote folklore. There are several other trails, including the **Sendero Dunas de Cucao**, which goes from the visitor center through a remnant of coastal forest to a series of dunes behind a long, white sandy beach. After the earthquake of 1960, a tsunami obliterated much of the coastal plant cover and the dunes advanced for some years, but they have since stabilized. The beach is attractive, but the cold water and dangerous currents make swimming inadvisable.

Day hikers or trekkers can follow the coast north on a 3km trail to **Lago Huelde**, where there is a Huilliche community. At Río Cole Cole, about 12km north of Chanquín, and at Río Anay, another 8km north, there are rustic *refugios* in reasonable shape, but a tent is not a bad idea in this changeable climate. Wear water-resistant footwear and woolen socks since, in Darwin's words, 'everywhere in the shade the ground soon becomes a perfect quagmire.' Biting flies make insect repellent a good idea.

Places to Stay & Eat
Local families run numerous camping sites in and around Cucao and across the bridge between Cucao and the park entrance; rates are about US$2 per person. Within the park proper, about 200m beyond Conaf's visitor center, **Camping Chanquín** has secluded sites with running water, firewood, hot showers and toilets for US$10 per person. At refugios or along trails, camping is free of charge.

Travelers not wishing to camp will find several hospedajes within easy walking distance of the park entrance, all reachable by leaving a message through Cucao's single public telephone (☎ 633-040). *Hospedaje El Paraíso*, *Hospedaje Pacífico*, *Hospedaje y Albergue La Pincoya* and *Albergue y Hospedaje Los Pinos* all charge around US$6.50 per person with breakfast; *Posada Cucao* charges around US$8.50. All offer reasonably priced meals. At Chanquín, Conaf concessionaire Luis Olivares and Alvaro Crow (☎ 065-631359, vidasur@ netscape.net) rent cabañas for US$36 off-season, US$80 in summer.

German-run *Parador Darwin*, across the *pasarela* (footbridge) from Cucao, has an innovative menu based on local specialties. The food at *Doña Rosa* in the Arroyo bus station is more strictly local. Limited supplies are available in Cucao, but everything except fresh fish and a few vegetables is cheaper in Castro.

Getting There & Away
Cucao is 54km from Castro and 34km west of Chonchi via a bumpy gravel road, passable in all but the most inclement weather. There is regular bus transport between Castro and Cucao with Ocean Bus (☎ 635-492 in Castro) and Buses Arroyo (☎ 635-604 in Castro). Schedules vary, but there are usually four to five buses daily, with a fare of US$2.50. A new service to Chonchi leaves at 10 am and 3 pm daily in summer.

Buses Mar Brava has three buses weekly from Ancud to Chepu, at the northern end of the park (US$1.50).

QUELLÓN
Chiloé's southernmost port, the departure point for ferries to Chaitén, offers superb views of surrounding islands, including Cailín, a former Jesuit estancia which, in Darwin's day, was the 'last outpost of Christianity.'

Orientation & Information
On the sheltered Canal Yelcho, at the southeast corner of the Isla Grande, Quellón (terminus of Ruta 5, the Panamericana) is 98km south of Castro. Like Chonchi, the town has an irregular terrain that does not lend itself easily to the standard Hispanic grid, but it's small enough that it's simple to find your way around.

Most visitor services are concentrated in an area bounded by the Costanera Pedro Montt, Pedro Aguirre Cerda, Ladrilleros and Freire. From December to March, Quellón maintains an obliging Caseta de Información Turística at the corner of Gómez García and Santos Vargas. It's open 9 am to 9 pm daily.

Change your money before coming to Quellón, since Banco del Estado at Ladrilleros and Freire is the only possibility for cash or traveler's checks, and charges

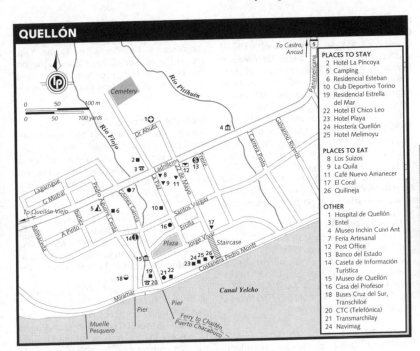

QUELLÓN

To Castro, Ancud

Panamericana

PLACES TO STAY
2 Hotel La Pincoya
5 Camping
6 Residencial Esteban
10 Club Deportivo Torino
19 Residencial Estrella del Mar
22 Hotel El Chico Leo
23 Hotel Playa
24 Hostería Quellón
25 Hotel Melimoyu

PLACES TO EAT
8 Los Suizos
9 La Quila
11 Café Nuevo Amanecer
17 El Coral
26 Quilineja

OTHER
1 Hospital de Quellón
3 Entel
4 Museo Inchin Cuivi Ant
7 Feria Artesanal
12 Post Office
13 Banco del Estado
14 Caseta de Información Turística
15 Museo de Quellón
16 Casa del Profesor
18 Buses Cruz del Sur, Transchiloé
20 CTC (Telefónica)
21 Transmarchilay
24 Navimag

CHILOÉ

unreasonable commissions. Correos de Chile is on 22 de Mayo between Ladrilleros and Santos Vargas. Telefónica is on the Costanera Pedro Montt between Aguirre Cerda and Gómez García, and Entel's long-distance office is at Ladrilleros 405. The Hospital de Quellón (☎ 681-443) is at Dr Ahués 305.

Things to See & Do
Admiration for Chilote technological ingenuity, in the form of uniquely local artifacts fashioned with basic materials, is the rationale behind the **Museo Inchin Cuivi Ant (Nuestro Pasado)**, a new and surprisingly good museum. The outstanding explanatory panels are a bonus alongside displays of items like *cercos tejidos* (living fences; fences woven of living shrubs and trees), *bongos* (local watercraft resembling dalcas), flour mills, apple presses and sledges for moving heavy loads across soggy terrain. The nascent botanical garden of native trees and shrubs will improve with time.

The museum, at Ladrilleros 225, charges US$1 admission. Hours are 9:30 am to 1:30 pm and 2:30 to 8 pm daily. The municipal **Museo de Quellón** is at the corner of Gómez García and Ercilla, down the block from the tourist office. The **Casa del Profesor**, on La Paz between Santos Vargas and Ercilla, is a cultural center that offers art exhibits.

Special Events
The Semana Quellonina, the second week of February, consists of theater and folklore presentations, art and artisanal exhibits, a rodeo and other activities.

Places to Stay
Camping There's informal garden *camping* for US$1 per person at a house at the corner of Aníbal Pinto and Aguirre Cerda.

Hostels The *Club Deportivo Torino* (*La Paz 316*) operates a summer hostel where mattress spots cost US$2 per night.

Hotels & Residenciales The *Hotel El Chico Leo* (☎ 681-567, *Pedro Montt 325*) has rooms for US$8 per person, excellent food and attentive service. Placid *Residencial Esteban* (☎ 681-438, *Aguirre Cerda 353*) offers small, simple but comfortable and tidy rooms for US$8.50 per person with shared bath; it also has a popular restaurant.

On the waterfront, a few doors from the Transmarchilay office, *Hotel Playa* (☎ 681-278, *Pedro Montt 427*) is a decent place, with hot water and a good cheap restaurant, charging US$9 per person. Despite its shabby exterior, the comparably priced *Residencial Estrella del Mar* (*Gómez García 18*) is OK inside – spartan, but with hot water and palatable food.

Hotel La Pincoya (☎ 681-285, *La Paz 64*) is a comfortable place with a friendly staff and hot water, charging US$15/23 singles/doubles with shared bath and breakfast; doubles with private bath cost US$35. In the same range are *Hostería Quellón* (☎ 681-250, *Pedro Montt 383*) and *Hotel Melimoyu* (☎ 681-310, *Pedro Montt 360*).

Places to Eat
Besides the hotel restaurants mentioned above, Quellón has fine seafood in the restaurants near the jetty and at *La Quila* (☎ 681-206, *La Paz 385*), *El Coral* (☎ 681-472, *22 de Mayo 215*) and *Quilineja* (☎ 681-441, *Pedro Montt 363*).

Los Suizos, at Ladrilleros and La Paz, is a new venue worth consideration. *Café Nuevo Amanecer* (☎ 682-026, *22 de Mayo 344*) is a popular Quellón café that transforms itself into a nightspot.

Shopping
For Chilote crafts, visit the feria artesanal at the corner of Ladrilleros and Gómez García. At Rayen Anti, 22km north of Quellón, the Huilliche Indian community of Huequetrumao sells woolens, wood carvings and basketry.

Getting There & Away
Bus Services to Castro (US$4, two hours) are frequent with Cruz del Sur (☎ 681-284) and Transchiloé, which share offices at Aguirre Cerda 52. There are also services to Puerto Montt (US$8, three hours). There are taxi colectivos to Castro.

Boat Transmarchilay (☎ 681-331) is at Pedro Montt 457, and Navimag has a seasonal office, most recently at Pedro Montt 383. Ferry schedules change seasonally, so verify the information given here at Transmarchilay or Navimag offices.

Transmarchilay's car ferry *La Pincoya* sails to Chaitén (five hours) at 3 pm Wednesday, and to Puerto Chacabuco (18 hours) at 7 pm Saturday via several small island and mainland ports. Passenger fares on the Quellón-Chaitén trip range from US$16 to US$24, depending on the quality of seat. Vehicle size determines the cost of transporting a car: rates range from US$82 (less than 4m) to US$94 (longer than 4m). Bicycles pay US$8, and motorcycles US$20. Fares to Chacabuco resemble those from Puerto Montt.

Navimag's *Alejandrina* sails to Chaitén Monday, at 4 pm Friday and Sunday, at midnight Wednesday. For fares, see the Chaitén entry in the Aisén chapter.

Aisén & the Camino Austral

Beyond Puerto Montt and the Isla Grande de Chiloé, the islands, fjords and glaciers of the Region XI of Aisén (formally known as Región Aisén del General Carlos Ibáñez del Campo) mirror the landscapes of Alaska's Inside Passage, New Zealand's South Island and Norway's subarctic coastline. The still rudimentary Camino Austral Longitudinal (Southern Longitudinal Highway) awkwardly links Puerto Montt with widely separated towns and hamlets from Chaitén to Puerto Yungay, and should soon reach Villa O'Higgins. But the most convenient connections are by air or ferry from Puerto Montt, by ferry from Chiloé or overland through the Argentine province of Chubut.

For thousands of years, Chonos and Alacaluf Indians fished, gathered and hunted among western Aisén's intricate canals and islands, while their Tehuelche counterparts hunted guanaco and other game on the mainland steppes. The rugged geography of Aisén deterred European settlement for centuries – even after Francisco de Ulloa first set foot on the Península de Taitao in 1553. Fortune seekers believed the legendary 'City of the Caesars' to be in Trapananda, as Aisén was first known, but Jesuit missionaries from Chiloé were the first Europeans to explore the region intensively. In the late 17th century, Bartolomé Díaz Gallardo and Antonio de Vea came upon Laguna San Rafael and the Campo de Hielo Norte, the northern continental ice sheet.

Recounting his many experiences in the Archipiélago Guayaneco, the shipwrecked British seafarer John Byron, grandfather of the famous poet Lord Byron, made it apparent why Europeans did not flock to the inclement region. From the shore, the sailor known as 'Foulweather Jack' wrote:

A scene of horror presented itself: on one side the wreck...together with a boisterous sea, presented us with the most dreary prospect; on the other, the land did not wear a much more favourable appearance: desolate and barren, without sign of culture, we could hope to receive little other benefit from it than the preservation it afforded from the sea...Exerting ourselves, however, though faint, benumbed and almost helpless, to find some wretched cover against the extreme inclemency of the weather, we discovered an Indian hut...within a wood, in which as many as possible, without distinction, crowded themselves, the night coming on exceedingly tempestuous and rainy.

A great many expeditions (including Captain Robert Fitzroy's British expedition for which Darwin served as a naturalist) visited the area in the late 18th and early 19th centuries, some in search of a protected passage to the Atlantic. Argentine expeditions reached the area from the east, becoming the first non-native people to see Lago General Carrera (Lago Buenos Aires to Argentines). In the early 1870s, Chilean naval officer Enrique Simpson made the most thorough survey up to that time, mapping areas as far south as the Península de Taitao.

Not until the early 20th century did Chile actively promote colonization of the region, granting the Valparaíso-based Sociedad Industrial Aisén a long-term lease for exploitation of livestock and lumber. This measure fomented a wave of spontaneous immigration from mainland Chile and the Argentine province of Chubut that threatened the monopoly of the Sociedad. Small-scale colonists successfully resisted ejection from the Río Simpson valley, but the company still controlled much of the land – nearly a million hectares in and around Coihaique – and dominated the regional economy. Part of its legacy is the destruction of much of Aisén's native southern beech forest in a series of fires that raged for nearly a decade in the 1940s. Encouraged by a Chilean law that rewarded clearance with land titles, the company and colonists burned nearly three million hectares of lenga forest. While this burning was intentional, some fires raged out of control and the bleached trunks of downed trees now litter hillsides from Villa Mañihuales to Puerto Ibáñez.

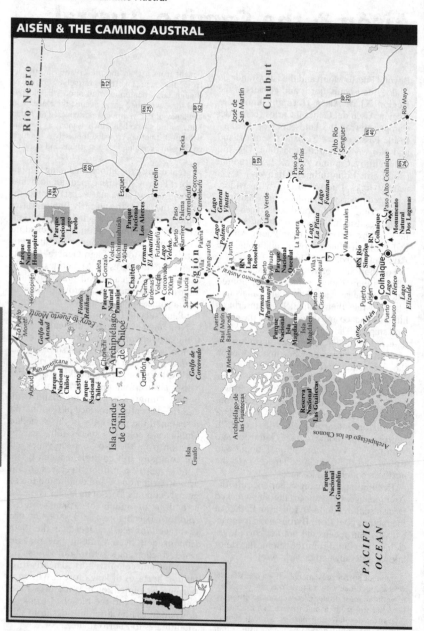

AISÉN & THE CAMINO AUSTRAL

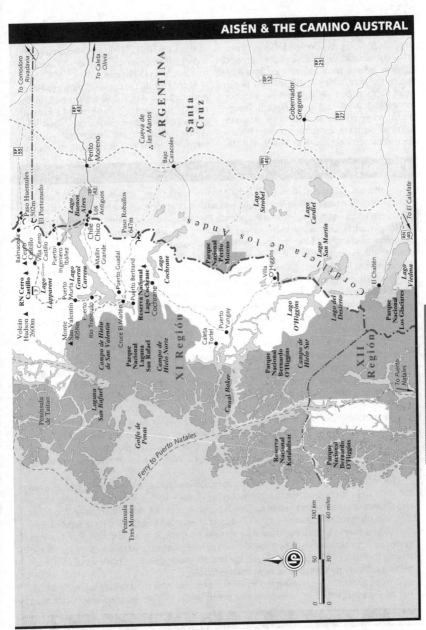

AISÉN & THE CAMINO AUSTRAL

AISÉN

Since the agrarian reform of the 1960s, the influence of the Sociedad and other large landowners has declined. Better maritime communications and the improved highway system have encouraged immigration to the area, which is still sparsely populated. Salmon farming is becoming a major economic activity, causing ecological disruption in some coastal areas, and the region's rivers are under threat from proposed hydroelectric projects on the Río Baker and the Río Futaleufú. Argentina and Chile recently settled their last remaining border dispute at the Campo de Hielo Sur, the continental icefield that overlaps Regions XI and XII south of Villa O'Higgins.

Recognizing that despite improved communications, Aisén has lagged behind the rest of the country, the Eduardo Frei administration developed a so-called *Plan Aysén* for the region's economic advancement. This includes continuing infrastructural

Pinochet's Folly

Near the old railroad station on Puerto Montt's waterfront, where Av Diego Portales becomes Av Juan Soler Mefredini, a fading, vandalized sign declares the beginning of Ruta 7, the Carretera Longitudinal Austral Presidente Pinochet, more popularly referred to as the Camino Austral. Only a few kilometers east, beyond the beach suburb of Pelluco, a smooth concrete roadway becomes the spine-rattling washboard that is one of the most ambitious and, to this point, least productive public works projects ever undertaken in Chile.

Starting at Puerto Montt, Chilean maps depict Ruta 7 as a continuous road, paralleling the Argentine border for more than 1100km to the pioneer outpost of Puerto Yungay. The real road, however, is discontinuous, requiring several ferry crossings unlikely to ever be bridged or circumvented because of the phenomenal expense this would entail. Ruta 7 was scheduled to reach Villa O'Higgins, 220km south of Cochrane at the foot of the Campo de Hielo Sur, by the end of 1999; some politicians have fantasized extending it another 950km through the fjords and islands of extreme southern Chile to Puerto Natales.

Maintenance is a nightmare. In Parque Nacional Queulat, a conspicuous road sign warns motorists not to stop for any reason in one 400m stretch where an ominous debris flow threatens to slither across the highway at any moment. Smaller slides are common and, in the far south, the road sits barely 1m above the flood-prone Río Baker, which carries the greatest flow of any Chilean river.

The population of the entire region, from Puerto Montt to Villa O'Higgins, is barely 80,000, and nearly half of those people live in the city of Coihaique, the only sizable population center between Puerto Montt and Punta Arenas. Why then did Chile invest an initial US$300 million (and 11 lives) to serve so few people? While the public rationale is development, the initial motive was geopolitics.

Like many other Southern Cone military men, General Augusto Pinochet Ugarte believed the state to be an organic entity that must grow or die – that is, it must effectively occupy and develop all the territory within its formal boundaries or risk losing that territory to other states. In his textbook *Geopolítica* (1977), Pinochet asserted that the state is 'a superperson, the highest form of social evolution.' As an organic entity, it must maintain an integrated system of communications, which are 'the nerves which unite the different zones within and among themselves.' By Pinochet's logic, the longitudinal highway is Chile's spinal cord, connecting the country's extremities to its brain in Santiago.

Chilean geopoliticians, among whom Pinochet has been the most influential public figure, still perceive Argentina as an expansionist threat in the thinly populated south – much as

improvements; increasing contacts with the Argentine provinces of Chubut and Santa Cruz; promoting private investment in the agriculture, forestry, fishing and energy sectors; and allowing greater administrative autonomy.

Some of the region's advocates continue to have unrealistic expectations, however – one local senator has even insisted that the area could support five million people, and he has favored large-scale immigration from Russia, South Africa and the former Yugoslavia. More promising are benefits from increased integration along the so-called *Corredor Bioceánico* (Bioceanic Corridor) linking Argentina's Atlantic port of Comodoro Rivadavia, 600km to the east, with Aisén's Pacific port of Puerto Chacabuco. It is unclear, however, whether there are any practical advantages to improved links between two thinly populated areas with parallel economies.

Pinochet's Folly

Argentine geopoliticians view Chile. For Chileans, this interpretation is not unreasonable, since the two countries barely avoided armed conflict over the Beagle Channel in 1979, and Argentina, acting on its own geopolitical impulses, invaded and occupied the British-held Falkland Islands for two and a half months in 1982. Since restoration of civilian rule, relations between the two countries have been more cordial, but the military obsession with territorial security lurks in the background. Pinochet has even suggested that the highway bear the name Ejército de Chile (Army of Chile).

In the meantime, the near completion of the Camino Austral by the Cuerpo Militar de Trabajo (Army Corps of Engineers), which will soon hand it over to the civilian Dirección de Vialidad (Highway Department), has had unanticipated consequences. To some degree, it has encouraged economic development in forestry, fisheries and mining, but these are extractive industries that take out more than they leave. In many areas, abundant cow patties symbolize the economic marginality of a road that carries almost no traffic.

Without continued major improvements and expenditure, the odds that the Camino Austral will achieve Pinochet's goal of establishing an effective communications network to link the region with the Chilean heartland are poor. The several short ferry links on the highway between Puerto Montt and Chaitén have proved inadequate for commercial traffic, which prefers the longer ferries from Puerto Montt and Chiloé to Chaitén and Puerto Chacabuco. Most tourists also find these routes more practical.

The Camino Austral is primarily a penetration road, and travel is generally difficult in any direction other than north-south. The few existing laterals, ironically, have made communication with Argentina better than ever – so much better that buses between Coihaique and Puerto Montt pass through the Argentine provinces of Chubut and Río Negro rather than use the much slower Chilean route. Argentine tourists flock across the border to Aisén and, should they ever need to, so could the Argentine military. This is probably not what General Pinochet had in mind, but on the other hand, the road linking the two countries was probably inevitable.

In any case, the opening of the Camino Austral has created opportunities for adventurous travelers to explore areas that were previously the province of hard-core long-distance trekkers. Remote destinations such as Chaitén and Coihaique, and national parks such as Queulat are now readily accessible by road, even though public transport still tends to be limited and seasonal. It's difficult to see the road's benefits to the country as a whole, but visitors who want to see a rugged, remote territory can now do so in relative comfort. Some sectors, from Coihaique north to Villa Mañihuales and south to Villa Cerro Castillo, are even being paved.

AISÉN

While this chapter focuses on Region XI, it also includes parts of Region X – on and around the Camino Austral from Caleta Gonzalo south – that are only accessible by air or sea from Puerto Montt, Chiloé or Hornopirén, or overland through Argentina.

COIHAIQUE
☎ 67

Founded in 1929 at the foot of the basalt massif of Cerro Macay, the regional capital of Coihaique was Aisén's first major town. Initially a service center for the properties of the Sociedad Industrial, it has outgrown its pioneer origins to become a modest but tidy city with a population of about 38,000. Coihaique's most unusual feature is the pentagonal Plaza de Armas, the work of carabineros general Marchant González, who based his confusing city plan on the shape of the national police force's emblem. It recently acquired its first traffic signals.

Most visitors arrive by air from Puerto Montt or by ferry at Puerto Chacabuco, continuing overland to Coihaique, but increasing numbers are traveling the length of the Camino Austral.

Orientation

At the confluence of the Río Simpson and the Río Coihaique, Coihaique is linked by a paved highway to Puerto Chacabuco to the west, and by partly paved roads to Puerto Ibáñez to the south and Chaitén to the north. It's also accessible from Argentine Patagonia to the east.

For travelers accustomed to the standard Latin American grid, Coihaique's street plan can be disorienting. Its focus is the pentagonal Plaza de Armas, from which 10 streets radiate like spokes from a wheel, but within a block or two in every direction, this irregularity gives way to a more conventional pattern. One way to orient yourself is to walk once around the plaza, noting landmarks such as the cathedral, and then wander once around the outer pentangle bounded by Arturo Prat, General Parra, 21 de Mayo, Eusebio Lillo and Francisco Bilbao. This isn't foolproof, but it helps.

Av General Baquedano, which skirts the northeast side of town, eventually connects with the paved highway to Puerto Chacabuco and a gravel road east to the Argentine border at Coihaique Alto. Av Ogana heads south to Balmaceda, Puerto Ibáñez and other southerly points on the Camino Austral.

Information

Tourist Offices Sernatur (☎ 233-949, sernatur_coyhaiq@entelchile.net) at Bulnes 35, half a block from the Plaza de Armas, is one of the best-organized, most helpful offices in the country. Normal hours are 9 am to 1 pm and 3 to 7 pm weekdays, but in summer it's open 8:30 am to 9 pm weekdays, 11 am to 8 pm weekends.

Coihaique's Dirección Municipal de Turismo (☎/fax 232-100, 234-051) is at Baquedano 310. Another source of information is the Automóvil Club de Chile (☎ 231-649), Bolívar 194.

Conaf (☎ 212-125) is at Bilbao 234.

Money Exchange cash and traveler's checks at Turismo Prado, 21 de Mayo 417, or Cambios Emperador, Bilbao 222. Banco Santander has an ATM at the corner of Condell and 21 de Mayo.

Post & Communications Correos de Chile is at Cochrane 202 near the Plaza de Armas. Entel is at Arturo Prat 340, and Chilesat is at 21 de Mayo 472.

For Internet access at US$3 per half hour, try the Centro de Capacitación, Bilbao 144, but be aware of very strict timekeeping – if you're even a minute over, you pay for an extra half hour.

Travel Agencies Most of Coihaique's travel agencies arrange fishing holidays or visits to Laguna San Rafael, but they can be surprisingly indifferent to more unconventional alternatives. Among them are Turismo Prado (☎/fax 231-271) at 21 de Mayo 417, which has English-speaking staff, and Turismo Queulat (☎/fax 231-441) at 21 de Mayo 1231.

More adventure-oriented are Expediciones Coihaique (☎/fax 232-300) at Portales 195, which specializes in pricey fishing

COIHAIQUE

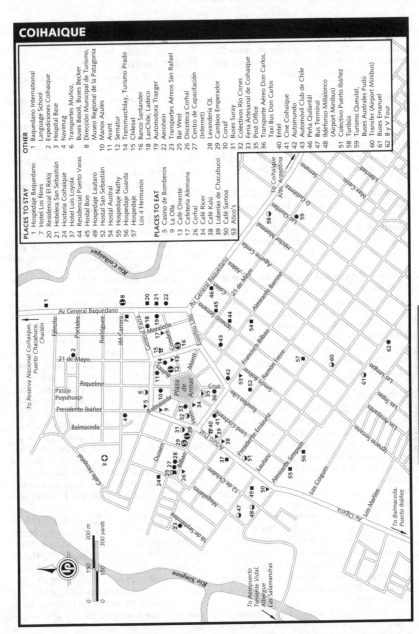

PLACES TO STAY
1 Hospedaje Baquedano
7 Hotel Los Ñires
20 Residencial El Reloj
21 Hotelera San Sebastián
24 Hostería Coihaique
37 Hotel Luis Loyola
44 Residencial Puerto Varas
45 Hostal Bon
49 Hospedaje Lautaro
52 Hostal San Sebastián
54 Hostal Austral
55 Hospedaje Nathy
56 Hospedaje Guarda
57 Hospedaje
   Los 4 Hermanos

PLACES TO EAT
5 Casino de Bomberos
9 La Olla
13 Café Oriente
17 Cafetería Alemana
26 Corhal
34 Café Ricer
38 Café Kalú
39 Loberías de Chacabuco
50 Café Samoa
53 Atico's

OTHER
1 Baquedano International
   Language School
2 Expediciones Coihaique
3 Hospital Base
4 Navimag
6 Transportes Muñoz,
   Buses Basoli, Buses Becker
8 Dirección Municipal de Turismo,
   Museo Regional de la Patagonia
10 Manos Azules
11 Avant
12 Sernatur
14 Transmarchilay, Turismo Prado
15 Chilesat
16 Banco Santander
18 LanChile, Ladeco
19 Automotora Traeger
22 Aerohein
23 Transportes Aéreos San Rafael
25 Bar West
26 Discoteca Corhal
27 Centro de Capacitación
   (Internet)
28 Lavandería QL
29 Cambios Emperador
30 Conaf
31 Buses Suray
32 Colectivos Río Cisnes
33 Feria Artesanal de Coihaique
35 Post Office
36 Transporte Aéreo Don Carlos,
   Taxi Bus Don Carlos
40 Entel
41 Cine Coihaique
42 Automundo
43 Automóvil Club de Chile
46 Peña Quilantal
47 Bus Terminal
48 Ildefonso Millalonco
   (Airport Minibus)
51 Colectivo Puerto Ibáñez
58 Turibús
59 Turismo Queulat,
   Buses Australes Pudú
60 Transfer (Airport Minibus)
61 Buses Emanuel
62 B y V Tour

AISÉN

holidays from Coihaique to Cochrane, and Expediciones Lucas Bridges (☎/fax 233-302, cellular 09-892-5477, lbridges@aisen.cl), which is located on the outskirts of town and is easiest to contact by phone.

Language Schools The Baquedano International Language School (☎ 232-520, fax 231-511, pguzmanm@entelchile.net), Baquedano 20, offers intensive Spanish-language instruction at various levels (four hours per day for two weeks, six days a week). The US$300 weekly price includes room and board.

Laundry Try Lavandería QL (☎ 232-266), Bilbao 160, for prompt and efficient service.

Medical Services Coihaique's Hospital Base (☎ 231-286) is on Calle Hospital, at the west end of JM Carrera.

Museo Regional de la Patagonia

Coihaique's regional museum, at Baquedano 310, has a fine collection of labeled photographs on regional history, plus some miscellaneous pioneer artifacts. It's open 8:30 am to 1 pm and 2:30 to 8 pm in summer, but winter hours are more limited. Admission costs US$0.75 for adults, children are admitted free.

Activities

Fishing in summer and skiing in winter are the most popular pastimes in and around Coihaique. On most lakes and rivers, the fishing season runs from November to May, but in a few popular areas it is restricted to a shorter period. Brown and rainbow trout are the most common species. Some of the travel agencies mentioned earlier in this section arrange fishing trips.

From June to September, skiers can test the facilities at the Centro de Ski El Fraile (☎ 231-690), only 29km south of Coihaique. It has two lifts and five different runs, up to 2km in length and ranging in difficulty from beginner to expert. Rental equipment is available, and there is also a café. Hours are 9 am to 5 pm daily.

Near Puerto Ibáñez, 81km south of Coihaique, the Centro de Ski Los Maillines

has steeper slopes but no formal infrastructure and is suitable only for experienced skiers.

Places to Stay

Spanish-run *Albergue Las Salamandras* (☎ 211-865), in a woodsy area about 2km south of town on the road to the old airport, charges US$10 per person, which includes kitchen privileges and extensive common spaces. Inexpensive camping is also possible.

Family-run *Hospedaje Los 4 Hermanos* (☎ 232-647, Colón 495) charges US$7.50 per person, making it one of Coihaique's better values. Friendly, comparably priced *Hospedaje Nathy* (☎ 231-047, Almirante Simpson 417), which permits garden camping, is also worth checking out.

In a spacious, conveniently located house with cable TV, *Hospedaje Lautaro* (☎ 238-116, Lautaro 269) charges US$8.50 per person, including kitchen privileges. Basic *Hostal San Sebastián* (☎ /fax 231-762, Freire 554) has US$9 singles that will do in a pinch.

For US$10 per person *Hospedaje Baquedano* (☎ 232-520, Baquedano 20) has both house and simple cabaña accommodations in a quiet location, as well as garden camping with spectacular views.

Some travelers enjoy *Residencial Puerto Varas* (☎ 233-689, Serrano 168), but others have found the rooms cramped and occasionally noisy, and the management can be indifferent or even brusque. Rates are US$10 per person, which includes breakfast and hot showers. The restaurant is passable. *Hospedaje Guarda* (☎ 232-158, Simpson 471) has commodious rooms in a garden setting for US$12 per person and serves a decent breakfast, but some of the mattresses are too soft and the scalding hot water can be difficult to regulate.

A former budget choice, upgraded *Hostal Bon* (☎ 231-189, Serrano 91) now has bright and comfortable singles for US$30/46. Well-established *Residencial El Reloj* (☎ 231-108, Baquedano 444) charges US$31/42. Under new ownership, *Hotel Los Ñires* (☎ 232-261, Baquedano 315) has singles/doubles for US$37/50 with breakfast and private bath. *Hotelera San Sebastián* (☎ 233-427, Baquedano 496) charges US$38/50.

Hotel Luis Loyola (☎ /fax 234-200, Prat 455) has most amenities, including central heating and cable television, for US$45/59. Rooms at *Hostal Austral* (☎ 232-522, Colón 203) cost US$52/67. In a class by itself is highly regarded *Hostería Coihaique* (☎ 231-137, Magallanes 131) with singles/doubles for US$89/114.

Places to Eat

Café Samoa (☎ 232-864, Prat 653) is a cozy little bar and restaurant with cheap meals and snacks. *Café Kalú* (☎ 233-333, Prat 402) is a modest café with decent sandwiches and inexpensive lunches.

There are good desserts and light meals at *Café Oriente* (☎ 231-622, Condell 201). Under the same ownership, the upgraded *Cafetería Alemana* (☎ 231-731, Condell 199) is a popular local hangout with similar fare.

Just off the Plaza de Armas, *Café Ricer* (☎ 232-920, Horn 48) has good fixed-price lunches with large portions and fine service; its upstairs restaurant has a more elaborate menu. The *Casino de Bomberos* (☎ 231-437, General Parra 365) has fine meals at moderate prices.

For seafood, there are two excellent choices: *Loberías de Chacabuco* (☎ 239-786, Prat 386) and *Corhal* (☎ 233-125, Bilbao 123). *Atico's* (☎ 234-000, Bilbao 563) specializes in beef and seafood, with a worthwhile lunch menu, but the tacky mirrors and wide-screen television detract from the atmosphere and make it hard to enjoy the food. *La Olla* (☎ 234-700, Prat 176) is an upscale venue, but the midday lunch specials are within reach of most budgets.

Entertainment

The *Cine Coihaique* (Cochrane 321) is open erratically.

Bar West (☎ 231-617, Bilbao 110) is self-consciously Western (in the US sense).

In new quarters, *Peña Quilantál* (☎ 234-394, Baquedano 791) features live folk music; shows may start considerably later than advertised.

Discoteca Corhal (☎ 232-869, Bilbao 123) shares a building with its namesake seafood restaurant, but stays open much later.

Shopping

Several crafts outlets sell woolens, leather goods, wood carvings and seashells. The Feria Artesanal de Coihaique, on the Plaza de Armas, and Manos Azules (☎ 230-719), Riquelme 435, are both worth a look.

Getting There & Away

Air LanChile (☎ 231-188), Moraleda 402, has morning flights to Puerto Montt (US$43 to US$77) and Santiago (US$115 to US194); Ladeco (☎ 231-300), at the same address, flies in the afternoon. Avant (☎ 237-570), General Parra 202, also flies daily to Puerto Montt (US$42 to US$73) and Santiago (US$134 to US$165).

Transporte Aéreo Don Carlos (☎/fax 231-981), Subteniente Cruz 63, flies small craft to Cochrane (US$60) Monday and Wednesday, to Villa O'Higgins (US$110) Wednesday, and to Chile Chico (US$34) daily except Sunday.

Don Carlos and the air-taxi charters Aerohein (☎/fax 232-772), Baquedano 500, and Transportes Aéreos San Rafael (☎ 232-048, fax 233-408), 18 de Septiembre 469, fly to Laguna San Rafael on demand; for details, see the Parque Nacional Laguna San Rafael entry later in this chapter.

Bus Coihaique's dingy bus station is at the corner of Lautaro and Magallanes, but most companies operate out of offices elsewhere in town, as indicated below (unless indicated, you can assume a carrier uses the main station). Regional and interregional bus services along the Camino Austral are improving in frequency and quality.

For frequent buses to Puerto Aisén and Puerto Chacabuco (US$2, one hour), try Taxi Bus Don Carlos (☎ 231-981) at Cruz 63, Buses Suray (☎ 238-387) at Arturo Prat 265, and Buses Cordillera at the main terminal.

Transportes Mañihuales at the terminal runs daily northbound buses on the Camino Austral to Villa Ortega and Villa Mañihuales (US$3) at 1 pm. Transportes Fidel Pinilla (☎ 232-452) goes to Villa Mañihuales daily at the same hour.

Transportes Muñoz (☎ 232-167), General Parra 337, goes to Villa Mañihuales and

Puerto Cisnes (US$10), on a lateral off the Camino Austral, Wednesday and Saturday at noon; Buses Basoli, at the same office, goes to Cisnes Monday and Thursday at 2 pm. Colectivos Río Cisnes (☎ 231-859), Horn 51, has buses to Cisnes (US$12) at 2:30 pm daily.

Buses Becker (☎ 232-167), also at General Parra 337, goes to Chaitén (US$23, 12 hours) Monday and Thursday, while Buses Emanuel (☎ 231-555), in the Hostal San Cayetano at Simpson 829, goes there Tuesday, Friday and Sunday. B y V Tour (☎ 231-793), Simpson 1037, goes to Chaitén Tuesday, Thursday and Sunday at 9 am.

Colectivo Puerto Ibáñez (☎ 251-073) heads southbound on the Camino Austral from the corner of Arturo Prat and Errázuriz to Puerto Ibáñez (US$6), connecting with the ferry to Chile Chico. Other carriers to Puerto Ibáñez include Transportes Ali (☎ 250-346) and Transportes Molina (☎ 237-672).

Buses Australes Pudú (☎ 231-008), 21 de Mayo 1231, goes Wednesday and Saturday morning to Villa Cerro Castillo (US$9), Bahía Murta (US$12), Puerto Tranquilo (US$13), Puerto Guadal (US$16), Puerto Bertrand (US$17) and Cochrane (US$20). Taxi Bus Don Carlos and Acuario 13 (☎ 232-067) and Los Ñadis (☎ 211-585), both at the main terminal, have similar services; Don Carlos runs Monday and Saturday morning, while Acuario 13 goes Friday morning. Los Ñadis has service Sunday morning.

Turibús (☎ 231-333), Baquedano 1171, leaves Tuesday and Saturday at 5 pm for Osorno and Puerto Montt (US$32) via Argentina. Bus Sur, at the main terminal, goes Tuesday at 4 pm to Punta Arenas (US$51), also via Argentina.

Buses Giobbi (☎ 232-067), at the terminal, has buses to Comodoro Rivadavia, Argentina (US$28), Tuesday and Saturday at 8:30 am. Turibús goes to Comodoro Monday and Friday at 11 am.

Boat Ferries to Chiloé, Chaitén and Puerto Montt leave from Puerto Chacabuco, two hours west of Coihaique by bus, but ferry companies have their offices in Coihaique. Schedules are subject to change. For transport to Puerto Chacabuco, see the Bus section above.

Transmarchilay (☎ 231-971), upstairs at 21 de Mayo 417, runs the ferry *El Colono* from Puerto Chacabuco to Puerto Montt (24 hours) Monday at 4 pm and Wednesday at midnight. Navimag (☎ 223-306, fax 233-386), at Presidente Ibáñez 347, Oficina 1, also sails from Puerto Chacabuco to Puerto Montt, Sunday and Friday in summer, three or four times monthly the rest of the year. For fares, see the Getting There & Away section for Puerto Montt in the Araucanía & Los Lagos chapter.

Getting Around

To/From the Airport From downtown, shared cabs to Aeropuerto Teniente Vidal, about 5km south of town, cost about US$4, but only small craft use this airport.

Commercial flights use the airport at Balmaceda, 50km southeast of Coihaique. The completely paved road to Balmaceda still means nearly an hour's bus or minibus ride, but services (about US$2) are frequent with Buses Ali (☎ 232-788), at the main terminal. There are also minibus services (US$4) with Transfer (☎ 233-030) at Lautaro 828 or Ildefonso Millalonco (☎ 236-718) at 12 de Octubre 135.

Car Because public transport in Region XI is infrequent, sometimes inconvenient and focused on major destinations along the Camino Austral, many travelers rent cars to see the countryside. The local supply is limited, so advance reservations are advisable.

Shop around because prices vary considerably, but try Automotora Traeger (☎ 231-648, fax 231-264) at Baquedano 457, Automundo (☎ 231-621, fax 231-794) at Bilbao 510, or Turismo Prado (☎/fax 231-271) at 21 de Mayo 417. The Automóvil Club (☎ 231-649), Bolívar 194, is exceptionally friendly and helpful; staff meets clients at the airport and picks up the cars there as well.

RESERVA NACIONAL COIHAIQUE

Given its proximity to the city, barely an hour's walk away, the 2150-hectare Reserva Nacional Coihaique is startlingly wild country, with exhilarating panoramas of Coihaique and the enormous basalt columns of Cerro Macay behind it, and other nearby and distant peaks. Native southern beech forests of coigue and lenga, along with introduced species such as pine and larch, cover the hillsides.

There are short nature trails at Laguna Verde and Laguna Venus, but the reserve's real attractions are the extraordinary views. It's a convenient, popular retreat for the residents of Coihaique, but spacious enough so that it never feels oppressively crowded.

Geography & Climate
On the southern slopes of Cerro Cinchao, Reserve Nacional Coihaique is only 5km north of town via the paved road toward Puerto Chacabuco and a steep dirt lateral to the entrance. Altitudes range from 400m to 1000m above sea level. Summers are warm and relatively dry, with a mean temperature of about 12°C. Most of the 1100mm of annual precipitation, both rain and snow, falls in winter.

Places to Stay
It's easy enough to make this a day trip from Coihaique, but with a tent, you can stay at rustic Conaf campgrounds (☎ 212-125 in Coihaique) at *Laguna Verde* (three sites) and *Casa Bruja* (10 sites) for US$7.50 for up to six persons. The basic facilities consist of picnic tables, fresh water and firepits. Be sure to bring as much food as you'll need for the duration.

Getting There & Away
Local drivers can and do take ordinary vehicles up the very steep dirt road, but it's not really a good idea without 4WD. From Coihaique, it's a snail's-pace uphill hike of about 1½ hours to the park entrance, where Conaf collects an admission fee of US$1.25 and US$0.45 for children, and then another hour to Laguna Verde.

MONUMENTO NATURAL DOS LAGUNAS
On the road to Coihaique Alto and the Argentine border, this 181-hectare wetland reserve has abundant bird life, including black-necked swans, coots and grebes, in an area that is ecologically transitional from southern beech forest to semiarid steppe. Around Laguna El Toro and Laguna Escondida, the two lakes that give the monument its name, Conaf maintains a self-guided nature trail, a campground (US$7.50 for up to six persons) and a picnic area. While the park lacks regular public transport, Conaf may be able to offer suggestions for getting there. Admission costs US$1.20 per person.

RESERVA NACIONAL RÍO SIMPSON
Straddling the paved highway between Coihaique and Puerto Chacabuco, this 41,000-hectare reserve is an accessible, scenic area where streams from tributary canyons cascade over near-vertical cliffs to join the broad valley of the Río Simpson. The native flora consists of evergreen forest, mostly southern beech species. Despite being downgraded from national park status, it's well worth a visit for travelers to the region.

Geography & Climate
Altitudes in Reserva Nacional Río Simpson range from 100m to 1900m above sea level. The climate is damp, with up to 2500mm rainfall in some sectors, but summers are mild and pleasant, with mean maximum temperatures of 15° to 17°C.

Things to See & Do
At Km 37 from Coihaique on the Puerto Chacabuco-Coihaique highway, the Conaf Centro de Visitantes, consisting of a small **natural history museum** (admission US$0.60) and **botanical garden**, is a good introduction to

Black-necked swan

regional ecology and wildlife. There is a beach for swimming, and many people take advantage of the river's proximity for fishing. Note that the visitor center is due to move to a new location at Las Chimeneas (Km 30).

A short distance from the current visitor center, **Cascada La Virgen** is a shimmering waterfall on the north side of the highway. Near the confluence of the Río Simpson and the Río Correntoso, 22km from Coihaique, there's a good hike up the canyon to Laguna Catedral that requires an overnight stay. Although the access is through Conaf property, hikers should be aware that this is private land.

Places to Stay
Five kilometers east of the visitor's center, Conaf's rustic **Camping San Sebastián** charges US$7.50 for up to six persons. **Camping Río Correntoso** (☎ 232-005) at Km 24 west of Coihaique has 50 spacious riverside sites, plus hot showers, for US$15.

Getting There & Away
Visitors can take any of the frequent buses between Coihaique and Puerto Aisén with Don Carlos; see Coihaique's Bus section for details.

PUERTO CHACABUCO
At the east end of a narrow fjord, Puerto Chacabuco displaced nearby Puerto Aisén as the port of Coihaique when the latter's harbor silted up. Reached by ferry from Puerto Montt or from the port of Quellón on Chiloé, and connected to Coihaique by an excellent paved highway, it's one of the most frequent ports of entry to Aisén.

Places to Stay & Eat
Just outside the harbor compound, convenient for late arrivals on the ferries, **Hotel Moraleda** (☎ 351-155, O'Higgins 82) charges US$8 per person but is distinctly mediocre. **Hotel Loberías de Aisén** (☎ 351-115, JM Carrera 50) is far better but also far more expensive for US$58/75. It also has a superb, but reasonably priced seafood restaurant with outstanding service.

Getting There & Away
Bus Buses from Coihaique, 82km from Puerto Chacabuco by paved highway, meet arriving and departing ferries (see the Coihaique Bus section for details).

Boat At the port, Navimag (☎ 351-111, fax 351-192) and Transmarchilay (☎/fax 351-144) connect Puerto Chacabuco to Quellón at the southern tip of the Isla Grande de Chiloé and to Puerto Montt; for details, see Coihaique's Boat section.

PN LAGUNA SAN RAFAEL
Dense with floating icebergs calved from the Campo de Hielo Norte, the massive northern Patagonian ice sheet, Laguna San Rafael is a memorable sight even beneath the somber clouds that so often hang like gloomy curtains over surrounding peaks. Established in 1959, the 1.7-million-hectare Parque Nacional Laguna San Rafael where glaciers brush the sea is the region's single most impressive and popular attraction despite the difficulty and expense of getting there. Visitors will see considerable wildlife, mostly birds, including flightless steamer ducks, black-browed and sooty albatross and Magellanic penguins. Otters, sea lions and elephant seals also frequent the icy waters, while pudú, pumas and foxes inhabit the surrounding forests and uplands.

Geography & Climate
Laguna San Rafael proper is a nearly enclosed inlet of the sea, 225km southwest of Puerto Chacabuco via a series of longitudinal channels between the Chonos Archipelago and the Península de Taitao on the west and the Patagonian mainland on the east. Only the low-lying Istmo de Ofqui, linking Taitao with the mainland, impedes access to the Golfo de Penas. In 1940 the Chilean government began a canal to connect the two, abandoning the project after proceeding only 300m, but proposals to build a road across the isthmus, for transshipment of cargo between vessels, surfaced as late as the 1980s.

Altitudes range from sea level to 4058m on the summit of Monte San Valentín, the southern Andes' highest peak. The park is damp and humid, with 3500mm of precipitation in coastal areas. At higher elevations, more than 5000mm of rain and snow nourish the 19 major glaciers that coalesce to form the Campo de Hielo Norte, which covers about 300,000 hectares. Because of the maritime influence of the Pacific Ocean, the mean annual temperature is a relatively mild 8°C. Possibly as a result of global warming, the glacier has receded dramatically over the past several decades.

Activities

Sight-seeing around the San Rafael glacier is clearly the major attraction. Most visitors arrive by sea, shifting to smaller craft and rubber rafts to approach the glacier and weave among the multitudinous icebergs that have calved off its 60m face. Unfortunately, visitors arriving by sea spend only a few hours at the glacier and are unable to set foot on land.

Nevertheless, climbing and hiking are also possible for well-equipped travelers in top physical condition, who usually arrive by air, though the usual stopover for day-trippers is only an hour. Visitors intending to hike should heed Darwin's caution:

The coast is so very rugged that to attempt to walk in that direction requires continued scrambling up and down over the sharp rocks of mica-slate; and as for the woods, our faces, hands and shin-bones all bore witness to the maltreatment we received, in attempting to penetrate their forbidding recesses.

Visitors who arrive by plane or otherwise manage to set foot in the park pay a US$5 admission fee. Arrivals by sea do not pay, since technically they do not enter the park.

Places to Stay & Eat

Since most visitors stay on board ship, Laguna San Rafael has no permanent accommodations except *Camping Laguna Caquenes* near the former hotel that serves as park headquarters; in case of emergency, Conaf allows people to stay in a shed nearby. No food is available at the park, so bring everything from Coihaique or Puerto Chacabuco.

Getting There & Away

The only access to and from Laguna San Rafael is by air or sea, so travel tends to be either expensive or time-consuming (or both). A new road proceeding westward from Puerto Río Tranquilo (on the Camino Austral) to Bahía Exploradores on the Estuario San Francisco may improve access in the near future, but this is still about 65km north of the glacier.

Air Charter flights from Coihaique land at Laguna San Rafael's 775m gravel airstrip and usually spend only an hour at the glacier before returning. Contact Aerohein (☎ 231-028, fax 232-772) at Baquedano 500, Transportes Aéreos San Rafael (☎ 232-048, fax 233-408) at 18 de Septiembre 469 or Transporte Aéreo Don Carlos (☎/fax 231-981) at Cruz 63. Small planes carry five passengers for about US$600 to US$700 roundtrip for the 1½-hour flight.

Boat There are several alternatives for sea access to Laguna San Rafael, roughly (in more than one sense) a 16-hour voyage from Puerto Chacabuco.

Transmarchilay (☎ 231-971), 21 de Mayo 417 in Coihaique, runs the 230-passenger *El Colono*, which leaves Puerto Montt at 4 pm Friday, picking up additional passengers at Puerto Chacabuco. Fares from Chacabuco to Laguna San Rafael and back range from US$202 for a reclining seat to US$404 per person for a bunk. A four-person suite costs US$604 per person. After spending most of Sunday at Laguna San Rafael, the ship sails back to Chacabuco at 6 pm.

Another relatively inexpensive alternative is the ferry *Evangelistas*, operated by Navimag (☎ 233-306, fax 233-386), Presidente Ibáñez 347 in Coihaique, which sails every four or five days in summer but only three or four times monthly the rest of the year. From Puerto Montt, the cruise takes five days and four nights. See the boxed text '*Evangelistas* Ferry Rates' later in this chapter, for fare information.

Turismo Rucaray (☎ 332-862, fax 332-725), Teniente Merino 848 in Puerto Aisén, charters

Evangelistas Ferry Rates

Approximate fares from Puerto Montt and back:

	cabina armador	cabina a	litera	butaca a	butaca b	butaca
single	US$1000	US$950	US$375	US$350	US$325	US$213
double	US$600	US$550				
triple		US$500				

Fares from Puerto Montt to Laguna San Rafael and back to Puerto Chacabuco:

	cabina armador	cabina a	litera	butaca
single	US$875	US$825	US$350	US$225
double	US$563	US$500		
triple		US$438		

Approximate fares from Puerto Chacabuco to Laguna San Rafael and back to Puerto Montt:

	cabina armador	cabina a	litera a	litera b	butaca
single	US$750	US$700	US$300	US$275	US$188
double	US$475	US$425			
triple		US$350			

the 10-passenger luxury launch *Patagonia I* for US$6000. The Hostería Coyhaique (☎ 231-137), Magallanes 131 in Coihaique, operates the 70-passenger *Iceberg Expedition* for US$235 per person. This includes meals and an open bar.

Patagonia Connection (☎ 67-325-103 in Puyuhuapi) sails the 70-passenger catamaran *Patagonia Express* to Laguna San Rafael (four hours) every Friday for US$250 per person, including all meals and an open bar. Its Santiago office (☎ 02-225-6489, fax 274-8111) is at Fidel Oteíza 1951, Oficina 1006, Providencia. Passengers should arrive early to claim the best window seats in the event of iffy weather – a high probability. Because of the catamaran's speed, the outside decks can be a bit uncomfortable except at the stern, which is out of the wind. Visitors spend about two hours at the glacier.

Northern Aisén

North of Coihaique, the Camino Austral passes through a number of pioneer villages and past Parque Nacional Queulat to Chaitén (the port for ferries from Quellón on the Isla Grande de Chiloé and from Puerto Montt) and Caleta Gonzalo (the summer port for ferries from Hornopirén). The town of Futaleufú, east of the main highway on its namesake river near the Argentine border, is a magnet for rafters and kayakers from around the world and is reached by public transport only via Chaitén.

VILLA MAÑIHUALES

Founded in 1962, 73km north of Coihaique via a soon-to-be-paved segment of the Camino Austral, Villa Mañihuales is acquiring an air of permanency that it previously lacked. It now has a couple hospedajes, including *Residencial Maniguales* (US$8 per person), and some simple cafés. The highway southwest toward Puerto Aisén and Puerto Chacabuco is now completely paved.

VILLA AMENGUAL

At the southern approach to Parque Nacional Queulat, Villa Amengual is a pioneer village with a Chilote-style shingled chapel. At the foot of 2760m Cerro Alto Nevado, it has modest but good accommodations and food at *Residencial El Paso* (rooms for

US$10 including breakfast). A comparable, recent addition is *Hospedaje El Michay*.

A few kilometers to the north, a lateral road climbs the valley of the Río Cisnes to the Argentine border, but the road is in questionable shape beyond Estancia La Tapera. The closest Argentine settlement is Alto Río Senguer, about 170km from Villa Amengual, but Argentine authorities may close this rarely used border crossing.

PUERTO CISNES
Dolphins seeking salmon dinners from floating fish farms cavort in the Canal Puyuhuapi near the growing village of Puerto Cisnes, at the mouth of its namesake river. This town is 35km west of the Camino Austral via a good gravel lateral. The surrounding scenery is dazzling when the weather clears, but the town itself may be most notable for having two gasoline stations in an area where it's possible to drive hundreds of kilometers on the main highway without encountering any place to fill the tank. The population is about 2000.

Recommended *Hospedaje Bellavista* (☎ 346-408, Séptimo de Línea 112) is Cisnes' most economical lodging at US$8 per person. *Hostería El Gaucho* (☎ 346-514, Holmberg 140) charges around US$15 per person, while the upgraded *Hostal Michay* (☎ 346-462, Gabriela Mistral 112) has rooms for US$25. For a meal, try reader-recommended *Guairao* (☎ 346-473, Piloto Pardo 58).

Getting There & Away
Buses Basoli (☎ 346-693), Aguirre Cerda 048, has buses to Coihaique (US$10) Tuesday at 11 am, and Thursday, Friday and Sunday at noon. Colectivos Río Cisnes (☎ 346-757), Gabriela Mistral 540, leaves daily at 6:30 am (US$12). No company runs services northbound on the Camino Austral from town, though you can flag down a northbound bus at the highway junction.

PARQUE NACIONAL QUEULAT
Straddling the Camino Austral midway between Chaitén and Coihaique, 154,000-hectare Parque Nacional Queulat is a wild domain of steep-sided fjords, rushing rivers, evergreen forests, creeping glaciers and high volcanic peaks. Created in 1983, it has rapidly gained popularity since completion of the highway, but it still qualifies as an off-the-beaten-track destination.

Geography & Climate
Queulat, 200km south of Chaitén and 220km north of Coihaique, rises from sea-level Canal Puyuhuapi to 2225m. Moisture-laden Pacific frontal systems drop up to 4000mm of rain per year on the park, nurturing southern beech forests at lower altitudes and adding snow to sizable glaciers at higher elevations. Mean annual temperatures range from 4° to 7°C, depending on elevation. Large streams such as the Río Cisnes and the glacial fingers of Lago Rosselot, Lago Verde and Lago Risopatrón offer excellent fishing.

Information
Conaf is building a new Centro de Información Ambiental at the parking lot for the lookout toward the Ventisquero Colgante, the highly visible hanging glacier that is the park's most popular feature. For ideas on excursions, consult rangers here, at the Administración in La Junta or at guard stations at Pudú (the southern approach to the park), Puerto Puyuhuapi or El Pangue. Rangers collect an admission charge of US$3 at Sector Ventisquero.

Activities
Queulat has become a popular destination for adventure travel companies, but it also offers superb hiking, camping and fishing opportunities for independent visitors, although heavy brush inhibits off-trail exploration.

From Conaf's Centro de Información, 22km south of Puerto Puyuhuapi, a bridge crosses the Río Guillermo, where a short 600m trail leads to the misnamed **Laguna Témpanos** (there are no icebergs in the lake). A longer 3.2km trail follows the crest of a moraine on the river's north bank to excellent views of the **Ventisquero Colgante**, where ice-falls crash periodically onto the rocks below.

Just north of Guardería Pudú, the southern entrance to the park, a damp trail climbs the valley of the **Río de las Cascadas** through a dense forest of delicate ferns, copihue vines, tree-size fuchsias, podocarpus and lenga. The heavy rainfall never directly hits the ground but seems to percolate through the multistoried canopy. After about half an hour, the trail emerges at an impressive granite bowl where half a dozen waterfalls drop from hanging glaciers.

At Km 175, just north of the Portezuelo de Queulat, the view of the Queulat Valley rivals anything in California's Yosemite. From the highway here, a 200m staircase drops to an overlook of the **Salto Río Padre García**, an especially impressive waterfall.

Places to Stay
Camping Ventisquero, near the Ventisquero Colgante, has attractive sites with covered barbecues and picnic tables for US$15, but the glacial meltwater that comes out of the showers in the spotless bathrooms will test anyone's resolve to get clean. The sites themselves are a bit rocky for pitching tents easily.

On Lago Risopatrón, 15km north of Puerto Puyuhuapi, Conaf's **Camping Angostura** charges US$15 per site in a sopping rainforest, but the facilities are good (cold showers only).

Getting There & Away
Renting a car in Coihaique provides flexibility but can be expensive without several people to share the cost. Buses connecting Chaitén and Coihaique via the Camino Austral will drop passengers at Puerto Puyuhuapi or other points along the western boundary of the park. It's also possible to take the bus from Coihaique to Puerto Cisnes. See the Chaitén and Coihaique sections for details.

PUERTO PUYUHUAPI
At the northern end of the Seno Ventisquero, a scenic fjord that's part of the larger Canal Puyuhuapi, Puerto Puyuhuapi was one of the earliest settlements along what is now the Camino Austral. Settled by German immigrants in the 1940s, this modest service center is also the northern gateway to Parque Nacional Queulat and convenient to Termas de Puyuhuapi, one of Chile's most prestigious hot springs resorts.

Puerto Puyuhuapi's single biggest attraction is its **Fábrica de Alfombras**, which has produced handmade woolen carpets since 1945. Half-hour tours (US$2 for adults and US$1 for children) take place weekdays at 10:30, 11 and 11:30 am and at 4, 4:30 and 5 pm; weekends and holidays at 11:30 am.

Places to Stay & Eat
In Puyuhuapi proper, alongside the gas station, **Camping Puyuhuapi** is a free site (though it's customary to make a donation to the caretaker). The best bargain in town is friendly **Hostería Marily** (☎ 325-102, Uebel s/n) with rooms for US$8 per person with shared bath and breakfast, US$11 with private bath; it has firm beds and spacious common areas. **Hostería Elizabeth** (☎ 325106, Circunvalación s/n) has B&B accommodations for US$8.50 per person and good meals in a comfortable environment.

Mid-range lodging is available at **La Casona de Puyuhuapi** (☎ 325-131, Camino Austral s/n), at the southern approach to town, for US$37/48 singles/doubles, or at **Hostería Alemana** (☎ 325-118, Uebel 450) for US$42/48. For meals and kuchen, there's the so-so **Café Rossbach** (Aisén s/n).

At Km 205, about 10km south of town, **Hospedaje Las Toninas** is a simple but attractive Chilote-style shingled house, set among spectacular flower gardens, offering lodging for US$7, beachfront camping for US$10 per site, and out-of-this-world fresh crab salads. It's a real treat for cyclists and backpackers, and worth a stop even for upscale travelers.

Getting There & Away
Buses that run between Coihaique and Chaitén will drop passengers in Puerto Puyuhuapi.

TERMAS DE PUYUHUAPI
In an extraordinarily lush forest setting on the western shore of the Seno Ventisquero,

the luxurious but tasteful and unpretentious *Hotel Termas de Puyuhuapi* (☎ 067-325-103, 02-225-6489, fax 274-8111, Fidel Oteíza 1921, Oficina 1006, Santiago) is a prestigious hot-springs resort just 11km south of Puerto Puyuhuapi at Bahía Dorita. For the most part, its elaborate new spa facilities attract an older crowd, but there's usually a handful of middle-aged professionals and younger people. There are frequent Argentine, European and North American visitors in the mix.

Hotel rates range from US$130/240 for singles/doubles from Christmas to mid-March, to only US$118/220 the rest of the year and include an ample buffet breakfast. Fixed-price lunches and dinners cost US$17, while a more elaborate buffet dinner costs US$26. For information on four-day, three-night packages, see the Organized Tours section in the Getting Around chapter. The hotel also arranges hiking, fly-fishing and other excursions around the resort and along the Camino Austral.

Nonguests can use the thermal pools for US$10 in low season, US$15 in high season (half price for children); massages and seaweed therapies are also available in the new spa building (gym and pool), which is not open to the public at large. Lunch or dinner costs US$20; children pay half price. The cafeteria at the thermal pools, open only in the daytime, is cheaper than the hotel restaurant but has a more limited menu. After the day-trippers return to the mainland, the evening is extraordinarily peaceful.

Termas de Puyuhuapi is accessible only by water; transport from the mainland dock, near the Puerto Puyuhuapi airstrip just off the Camino Austral, costs US$5 each way. Launches leave the dock at 9:30 am, noon and 7 pm, returning at 10 am and 12:30 and 7:30 pm, but there are often unscheduled crossings as well.

LA JUNTA
At the confluence of the Río Palena and the Río Figueroa, just south of the boundary between Regions X and XI, the crossroads settlement of La Junta, near the turnoff to Reserva Nacional Lago Rosselot and Lago

Verde, is a former estancia that is becoming a village. Unlike most towns in this mountainous region, it enjoys a broad, open valley site.

Hostería Copihue (☎ 314-108, Varas 611) and nearby *Residencial Valderas* (☎ 314-105) both charge about US$9 to US$10 per person. Some northbound buses stop for the night at *Residencial Patagonia* (☎ 314-115, Patricio Lynch 331), which charges only US$6 per person.

LAGO YELCHO
Surrounded by forested peaks and fed by the raging Río Futaleufú, long and narrow Lago Yelcho covers 11,000 hectares. Until the completion of the Camino Austral, the only settlements were a number of small ports such as **Puerto Cárdenas**, where the Río Yelcho drains the lake toward the west. There is now a gravel highway along the south shore, east to Futaleufú and Palena, continuing to the Argentine border, but if plans to build a huge hydroelectric facility on the river succeed, this road will disappear. Puerto Cárdenas has three modest choices for accommodations, all open in summer only: *Hospedaje Lulu*, *Residencial Yelcho* and *Residencial Los Pinos*.

Only 15km south of Puerto Cárdenas, the Puente Ventisquero (Glacier Bridge) is the starting point for a muddy two-hour hike to the **Ventisquero Cavi**, a large hanging glacier. The nearby resort *Yelcho en la Patagonia* (☎ 65-731-337, ☎ 02-334-1309 in Santiago, yelcho@chilecom.com) has campsites for US$44 (yes, you read right) for up to four people; double cabañas with shared bath range from US$75 to US$168. Note that sometimes Yelcho's phone service is cut off during the winter.

At Villa Santa Lucía, 78km south of Chaitén, the south shore lateral leads eastward to **Puerto Ramírez** at the southeast corner of the lake before bifurcating toward Futaleufú (to the northeast) and Palena (farther southeast). At the junction, *Hospedaje El Cruce* and *Hostería Verónica* offer shelter for about US$12 per person with breakfast, US$25 with full board; the Verónica also has camping.

FUTALEUFÚ

At the confluence of the Río Espolón and the Río Futaleufú in a forested basin close to the Argentine towns of Trevelin and Esquel, and to Argentina's Parque Nacional Los Alerces, Futaleufú is a world-class destination for fishing, kayaking and white-water rafting. Only 8km from the border, the town is 155km southeast of Chaitén via an indirect route around Lago Yelcho. It's distinguished by an attractive Plaza de Armas studded with topiary shrubs.

Note that the Futaleufú border post, open 8 am to 8 pm daily, is far quicker and more efficient than the crossing at Palena (see the Palena section later in this chapter), opposite the Argentine border town of Carrenleufú.

Information

In summer, there's a Sernatur office at the border and a helpful municipal Oficina de Información Turística at O'Higgins 536 on the south side of the Plaza de Armas. The post office is directly east at the corner of Manuel Rodríguez. Banco del Estado at O'Higgins and Manuel Rodríguez is the only choice for changing money.

Telephone Telefónica del Sur is at Balmaceda 419. As of this writing, isolated Futaleufú lacked direct dial services and calls were being routed through ☎ 065-258-633 or 258-644, both Puerto Montt numbers, and the appropriate *anexo* (extension) as indicated on each of the telephone numbers below. However, in the future, the town is likely to get direct dial service with the same area code (065) but with the prefix 731 added to each anexo.

White-Water Rafting & Kayaking

Several US rafting and kayaking outfitters operate in the area in summer; for details, see the Organized Tours section in the Getting There & Away chapter. For Santiago-based operators, see the Getting Around chapter.

There are also local agencies that do the Río Espolón and segments of the more difficult Futaleufú, including Expediciones Futaleufú at the Hostería Río Grande, O'Higgins 397, Local 3; Juan Pablo Cerón's Rockside Expediciones at the municipal tourist office, O'Higgins 536; and the Club de Rafting y Kayak (☎ 298) at Pedro Aguirre Cerda 545.

An easy floating descent of the Espolón costs about US$12, a Class III rafting trip US$20; a short Class IV run on the Futa costs about US$30, while a half-day Class IV-V descent costs about US$50.

Places to Stay & Eat

Camping is available at several nearby sites, including *Camping Puerto Espolón*, just south of town on the road to Puerto Ramírez.

Otherwise, reasonable accommodations are available from about US$5 per person at *Residencial Carahue (☎ 260, O'Higgins 332)*. For US$8 per person, *Hospedaje Adolfo (O'Higgins 302)* provides comfy beds and a diverse breakfast in a quiet, pleasant family atmosphere. Several others fall in the same range, including *Hospedaje El Campesino (☎ 275, Prat 107)*, *Hospedaje Los Pioneros (☎ 212, Hermanos Carrera 400)* and *Hospedaje Ely (☎ 205, Balmaceda 409)*.

Hospedaje Cañete (☎ 214, Gabriela Mistral 374) charges US$8 for rooms with shared bath, US$12 with private bath. *Hotel Continental (☎ 222, Balmaceda 595)* charges about the same with breakfast, but it's only US$17 with full board.

The new, spiffy *Hostería Río Grande (☎ 320, O'Higgins 397)* has doubles for US$52 (US$62 with breakfast) and also has a good restaurant. *Posada Campesina La Gringa (☎ 260, Sargento Aldea 456, ☎ 02-235-9187 in Santiago)* has spacious gardens and a quiet location for US$62/83 singles/doubles with breakfast.

Escorpio (☎ 228, Gabriela Mistral 255) specializes in *curanto* but also serves a variety of chicken and meat dishes, as well as sandwiches. Other choices with varied menus include *Futaleufú (☎ 295, Pedro Aguirre Cerda 407)*, *Hanga Roa (☎ 281, Pedro Aguirre Cerda 697)* and *Encuentro (☎ 247, O'Higgins 633)*. Also try the restaurant at *Hostería Río Grande*.

Shopping
Local leather and woolens are available at the artisanal outlet at Pedro Aguirre Cerda and Manuel Rodríguez on the northeast side of Plaza de Armas.

Getting There & Away
Buses Codao carries passengers to the Argentine border, where it's possible to make connections to the nearby towns of Trevelin and Esquel.

Buses Futaleufú, on Sargento Aldea between Balmaceda and Pedro Aguirre Cerda, goes to Chaitén at 7 am daily and also has Tuesday and Thursday buses to Osorno (US$33) and Puerto Montt via Argentina.

Buses Cordillera (☎ 248), Balmaceda 539, also goes to Chaitén at 7 am daily (US$8, four to five hours).

PALENA
Palena, 43km southeast of Puerto Ramírez, is only 8km west of the Argentine border, but the crossing on the Chilean side is water-torture slow, and the Argentine officials are only marginally better. Since there's no regular public transport across the Paso Palena Carrenleufú to the Argentine town of Corcovado, south of Trevelin, it's better to cross at Futaleufú.

Still, some visitors come here to enjoy otherwise inaccessible segments of the Río Futaleufú, and early February's **Rodeo de Palena** may be worth a stop. At last visit, a new tourist information kiosk was under construction on the Plaza de Armas. Like Futaleufú, Palena lacks direct dial service and relies on the same Puerto Montt operator (☎ 065-258-633 or 258-644) for telephone connections.

For inexpensive accommodations (about US$7 per person) try *Residencial La Chilenita (☎ 212, Pudeto 681)* or the more expensive *Residencial Pasos (☎ 226, Pudeto 661)* (about US$12).

Buses Palena on the Plaza de Armas goes to Chaitén Monday, Wednesday and Friday at 7:30 am.

CALETA GONZALO (PARQUE NATURAL PUMALÍN)
Caleta Gonzalo, the summer ferry port to Hornopirén, is the de facto center for US entrepreneur and conservationist Douglas Tompkins' Parque Natural Pumalín, a remarkable forest conservation effort that has, to date, protected 270,000 hectares of southern Chilean rain forest stretching from near Hornopirén in the north almost to Chaitén in the south. Pumalín has, however, drawn severe opposition from nationalist Chilean politicians, not all of them right-wingers, and to date the park has no formal legal standing despite improved relations with the government.

If hiking here or in other southern Chilean rain forests, watch for tiny *sanguijuelas*

Parque Natural Pumalín

Although Chile has one of Latin America's best national park systems, some observers believe the country could, and should, do more to preserve its representative ecosystems. To many conservationists, both Chileans and foreigners, the mountains of wood chips awaiting shipment from Puerto Montt to Japan are a palpable symbol of the overexploitation of Chile's woodlands. Boise Cascade's ambitious forestry project at nearby Ilque and an equally controversial multinational scheme to exploit southern Tierra del Fuego's lenga forests have aroused opposition but, ironically, no single undertaking has caused more conflict than US conservationist Douglas Tompkins' attempt to create the private Parque Natural Pumalín to protect thousands of square kilometers of temperate rain forest, including alerce and other native species, in Region X (Los Lagos).

Tompkins, an entrepreneur who made his fortune as the founder of the Esprit clothing company, became acquainted with Chile on recreational visits during the 1960s. In the early 1990s, after cashing out his interest in Esprit, he quietly began to acquire various fundos, consisting of three large blocks of native forest totaling about 270,000 hectares (including some small agricultural parcels) in the area south of Hornopirén and north of Chaitén, between the ocean and the Argentine border. The effort to finalize the project has run into political obstacles, though the situation has recently improved.

First offering to donate the projected park to the state, Tompkins found that Conaf lacked funds to administer such a large new acquisition. Alternatively, he created the Puerto Montt-based Proyecto Pumalín, due to become a nonprofit foundation, to hold and administer it. The foundation needs final government approval to ensure the park's legal status and to transfer the property, even though there are no formal legal obstacles.

One problem is geopolitical, as conservative politicians have questioned foreign ownership of so much land so close to an international border – even though some of the earlier fundos were foreign-owned, the project's entire board (except for Tompkins and his wife, Kristine) is Chilean and the park's administration would be financed by an independent endowment. One of Tompkins' most vociferous critics is former Interior Subsecretary Belisario Velasco, who had the ear of President Eduardo Frei Ruiz-Tagle and personally obstructed Tompkins' purchase of 30,000 hectares owned by Valparaíso's Universidad Católica at Huinay, which would have united two geographically separated sectors of Pumalín. The eventual purchaser was the Spanish-controlled utility company Endesa.

Anti-Tompkins rhetoric, mostly but not exclusively right-wing, can be intemperate or worse. According to Christian Democrat Senator Sergio Páez, Tompkins is part of a group of foreign investors trying to take extraterritorial control of thinly populated areas along the Argentine border: 'This is a very real threat to our national sovereignty; it is a geopolitical

(leeches), which are bothersome but not dangerous.

Information

Pumalín's new Centro de Visitantes, at Caleta Gonzalo, has brochures, photographs and environmental information on the park, and also sells artisanal goods from the region. If it's locked, ask someone at the café to open it for you.

Things to See & Do

Near the café at Caleta Gonzalo, the **Sendero Cascadas** is an undulating footpath, through dense forest, that ends at a large waterfall. The round-trip takes about three hours.

Parque Natural Pumalín

catastrophe. If these investors achieve their aims they will become owners of a vast tract of our southern frontiers.' Páez failed to name any of these investors, however.

Other opponents include the right-wing UDI party and the fringe Movimiento Nacionalista Chileno (Chilean Nationalist Movement), which has gone so far as to threaten (at least rhetorically) the impresario's life, replacing the slogan 'Tompkins fuera de Chile' (Tompkins out of Chile) with 'Muera Tompkins' (Death to Tompkins). Some opponents have concocted wild accusations of money laundering, speculated on the presence of massive gold deposits on the property (a favorite fantasy about the area ever since the 16th century), and even hallucinated the creation of a new Jewish state.

Another source of opposition is a sector of the Catholic Church, which distrusts Tompkins' association with the California-based Foundation for Deep Ecology, suspecting it of a pro-choice stance on abortion rights. The church also worries that deep ecologists do not consider humans superior to nature. (The Catholic Church has a strong influence. One measure of this is the fact that Chile is the only Western democracy with no divorce law.)

On the face of it, the most substantive criticism could be the impact of the park's creation on local land rights, since numerous small-scale *colonos* (agricultural colonists) occupy scattered landholdings throughout the area. Consequently, Tompkins and the Proyecto have pledged to respect existing land rights, most of those rights have been regularized, and the project has dedicated 5% of its area to experimental agroecological plots, livestock raising and beekeeping.

Still, it's not hard to imagine that disputes could develop. In the area north of Chaitén, for example, boatwrights have secretly stripped alerce bark for caulking, a practice that, if uncontrolled, eventually kills the trees. Even if this could be regulated to limit stripping to a sustainable level, it would be unacceptable under a Chilean law that protects the alerce as a national monument.

In the interim, the Proyecto has prepared a management plan that foresees increased tourist visitation and has also begun to provide facilities, such as a free hostel with hot showers at the Caleta Gonzalo ferry port, for the use of local residents only, along with market-rate cabañas and a fine restaurant. Actively courting local support, Tompkins has invited local officials to his home at Fundo Reñihue, east of Caleta Gonzalo, and sponsored an annual January folk festival there. How quickly this advances the goals of Parque Pumalín may not be clear for some time, though newly elected president Ricardo Lagos has support from many Chilean environmental groups.

For more information on Parque Pumalín, contact the Proyecto Pumalín (☎ 251-910, 251-911, fax 255-145), Buin 350 in Puerto Montt, or the Foundation for Deep Ecology (☎ 415-771-1102, fax 771-1121), 1555 Pacific Avenue, San Francisco, California 94109.

About 12km south of Caleta Gonzalo, the marked route to **Laguna Tronador** is not so much a trail as it is – often literally – a staircase. Beginning as a boardwalk, it crosses a rushing stream on a *pasarela* (hanging bridge) before ascending a series of wooden stepladders where the soil is too steep and friable for anything else. After about an hour's climb, at the saddle, there's a *mirador* (platform) with fine views of Michinmáhuida above the forest to the south. The trail then drops toward the lake, where there's a two-site campground with sturdy picnic tables (one set on a deck) and a latrine.

One kilometer farther south, only a few minutes off the highway to Chaitén, **Sendero los Alerces** crosses the river to a substantial grove of alerce trees where, in a few places,

AISÉN

locals have stripped bark fiber off the trees to caulk their boats – consequently killing the trees, even though cheap artificial materials are available for the purpose. At **Cascadas Escondidas**, 14km south of Caleta Gonzalo, another short trail leads from the campground to a waterfall.

Organized Tours

Alsur (alsur@telsur.cl), at Antonio Varas 445 in Puerto Montt (☎ 65-287-628) and Del Salvador 100 in Puerto Varas, organizes extended outings in Pumalín (☎/fax 65-232-300), specializing in sea kayaking, sailing and trips to the Cahuelmó hot springs, an area accessible only by sea.

Places to Stay & Eat

On the shores of Fiordo Reñihué, at Caleta Gonzalo, Tompkins's *Camping Río Gonzalo* is a state-of-the-art walk-in campground, with firepits and a stylish shelter for cooking, charging US$2 per person, but there are cold showers only. Fourteen kilometers south of Caleta Gonzalo, for US$10 per site, *Auto-Camping Cascadas Escondidas* is a drive-in campground, with cold showers, clean toilets, and covered sites for eating.

At Caleta Gonzalo, there are cabañas (☎ 065-250-079 for reservations) for rent for US$50/70 singles/doubles, plus US$10 for each additional person. The cabañas lack kitchen facilities, but *Café Caleta Gonzalo*, looking as if it had been airlifted intact from Aspen, prepares superb four-course meals, including fresh homemade bread, for about US$7 to US$10. It's the only place to eat and an ideal place to wait for the ferry.

Getting There & Away

Transmarchilay's ferry *Mailén* sails to Hornopirén daily at 9 am in summer only – from the first week of January to the end of February. For fares, see the Hornopirén section in the Araucanía & Los Lagos chapter. For transportation to and from Chaitén, see the Getting There & Away section for Chaitén, earlier in this chapter.

CHAITÉN
☎ 65

On clear days, the view from Chaitén, a pioneer port of 3600 people, toward the northern end of the Camino Austral, includes 2404m Volcán Michinmáhuida to the northeast and 2300m Corcovado to the southwest. Like nearly every other Chilean town, Chaitén shudders to a midday blast from the fire station; on Sunday it seems this blast is the town's alarm clock.

While Chaitén proper offers little to see, it's the main staging point for trips down the highway and to numerous outdoor destinations, including Parque Natural Pumalín, a spacious private forest reserve that's increasingly accessible to visitors. Transmarchilay and Navimag ferries link the town to Quellón at the south end of Chiloé and to Hornopirén and Puerto Montt.

Orientation

Chaitén, 56km south of Caleta Gonzalo and 45km north of Puerto Cárdenas, consists of a few wide, puddled streets in a regular grid pattern between the Bahía de Chaitén and the Río Blanco. The Plaza de Armas, bounded by O'Higgins, Almirante Riveros, Pedro Aguirre Cerda and Libertad, is two blocks east of the bay, where the Costanera Av Corcovado connects the town with the ferry port, about a 10-minute walk to the northwest. Most other hotels, restaurants and shops are between the Costanera and the plaza.

Information

The municipal Oficina de Información Turística, at the foot of Todesco, has a handful of leaflets and a list of hospedajes. In January and February it's open 9 am to 1 pm Monday through Saturday and 3 to 7 pm weekdays.

Change money before coming to Chaitén. Banco del Estado, at Libertad and O'Higgins, may change US cash but gives poor rates, and does not exchange traveler's checks. There are no ATMs.

The post office is opposite the plaza at Riveros and O'Higgins. There are several long-distance offices, including Teléfonica del Sur on the Costanera just north of

O'Higgins, and Chilesat at O'Higgins 53, alongside the bus terminal.

The new Entel office at Pedro Aguirre Cerda 300, on the east side of the Plaza de Armas, has Internet access.

Lavandería Masol (☎ 731-566) offers laundry services at Todesco 272, Local B.

The Hospital de Chaitén (☎ 731-244) is on Av Ignacio Carrera Pinto between Riveros and Portales.

Organized Tours

American-run Chaitur (☎ 731-429, fax 731-266, nchaitur@hotmail.com), at the bus terminal or at Diego Portales 350, arranges trips with bilingual guides to the Pumalín, the Yelcho glacier, Termas de Amarillo and beaches including Playa Santa Bárbara.

Places to Stay

The nearest campground is *Los Arrayanes* (☎ 218-202), 4km north of town, where beachfront sites cost US$2.50 per person, plus US$0.60 per vehicle and per tent. There are hot showers.

Rooms at *Hospedaje Casa de Rita* at the corner of Almirante Riveros and Prat, Chaitén's Israeli hangout, cost US$5 per person. Family-run, friendly and quiet *Hospedaje Don Carlos* (☎ 731-287, Almirante Riveros 53) charges US$6 with shared bath, US$7 with breakfast.

Other good choices in a similar price range include *Hotel Triángulo* (☎ 737-312, Todesco 2), *Hospedaje Sebastián* (☎ /fax 731-225, Todesco 188), and *Hospedaje Santana* (Pedro de Valdivia 129).

Waterfront *Hostería Llanos* (☎ 731-332, Corcovado 378) is a work-in-progress with spacious rooms that will eventually have private baths, but at present some rooms are cramped with too many beds. Rates are US$10 with breakfast; it also has a restaurant, and corner rooms enjoy views of

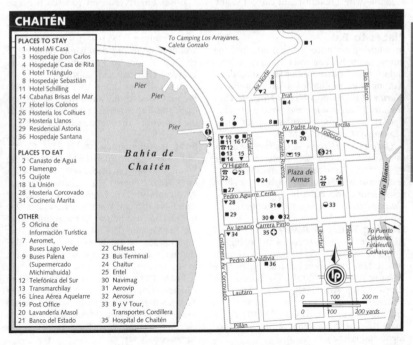

CHAITÉN

PLACES TO STAY
1 Hotel Mi Casa
3 Hospedaje Don Carlos
4 Hospedaje Casa de Rita
6 Hotel Triángulo
8 Hospedaje Sebastián
11 Hotel Schilling
14 Cabañas Brisas del Mar
17 Hotel los Colonos
26 Hostería los Coihues
27 Hostería Llanos
29 Residencial Astoria
36 Hospedaje Santana

PLACES TO EAT
2 Canasto de Agua
10 Flamengo
15 Quijote
18 La Unión
28 Hostería Corcovado
34 Cocinería Marita

OTHER
5 Oficina de Información Turística
7 Aeromet, Buses Lago Verde
9 Buses Palena (Supermercado Michimahuida)
12 Telefónica del Sur
13 Transmarchilay
16 Línea Aérea Aquelarre
19 Post Office
20 Lavandería Masol
21 Banco del Estado
22 Chilesat
23 Bus Terminal
24 Chaitur
25 Entel
30 Navimag
31 Aerovip
32 Aerosur
33 B y V Tour, Transportes Cordillera
35 Hospital de Chaitén

To Camping Los Arrayanes, Caleta Gonzalo

Pier
Pier
Pier

Bahía de Chaitén

Av Norte
Río Blanco
Prat
Av Padre Juan Todesco
Ercilla
Almirante Riveros
O'Higgins
Plaza de Armas
Pedro Aguirre Cerda
Av Ignacio Carrera Pinto
Costanera Av Corcovado
Pedro de Valdivia
Lautaro
Pillán
Libertad
Piloto Pardo
Río Blanco

To Puerto Cárdenas, Futaleufú, Coihaique

0   100   200 m
0   100   200 yards

AISÉN

Corcovado. **Residencial Astoria** (☎ 731-263, Corcovado 442) also charges about US$10, but the new petrol station across the street blocks the ocean view. **Hotel los Colonos** (☎ 266-650, fax 251-548, Todesco 77) charges US$12 per person including breakfast.

The newish **Hostería los Coihues** (☎ 731-461, Pedro Aguirre Cerda 398) charges US$19 per person with breakfast off-season, US$24 per person in peak season. Cheerful **Hotel Schilling** (☎ 731-295, Corcovado 230) has singles/doubles for US$21 per person with shared bath, and doubles with private bath for US$50.

Hotel Mi Casa (☎ 731-285, Av Norte 206) is a large hilltop place with its own restaurant. The rooms are simple but clean and spacious, and rent for US$48/67 singles/doubles including breakfast. New, attractive **Cabañas Brisas del Mar** (☎ 731-266, fax 731-284, Av Corcovado 278) charges US$63 for a double with breakfast and cable TV, and also has a restaurant.

Places to Eat
In addition to hotel restaurants, try the simple but appealing restaurants on Corcovado for seafood and other local specialties. Among the possibilities are **Cocinería Marita** (Corcovado 478) and **Hostería Corcovado** (Corcovado and Pedro Aguirre Cerda), or the more expensive, elaborate **Flamengo** (Corcovado 218).

Quijote (O'Higgins 42), serves seafood, sandwiches and espresso. **Canasto de Agua** (☎ 731-550, Prat 65) is a new, stylish pub and restaurant with fine fish dishes, excellent pisco sours, and equally fine service. **La Unión** (Riveros 242) is another option.

Getting There & Away
Air Several air-taxi services fly to Puerto Montt (US$35 to US$43), including Aerosur (☎ 731-228), at Carrera Pinto and Almirante Riveros; Aeromet (☎ 731-275), Todesco 42; Línea Aérea Aquelarre (☎ 731-800), on Todesco between Corcovado and Portales; and the start-up Aerovip (☎ 731-401), Almirante Riveros 453, which recently suspended flights but is likely to resume.

Bus Transport details for the Camino Austral change rapidly as the road undergoes improvements. Unless otherwise indicated, departures are from the main bus station (☎ 731-429), O'Higgins 67.

Tuesday and Friday at 9 am, Buses Becker takes the Camino Austral south to Coihaique (US$23, 12 hours). Monday, Wednesday and Saturday at the same hour, Transportes Emanuel goes to Coihaique. In winter, Becker and Emanuel sometimes go to La Junta, Puerto Cisnes, Lago Verde and Palena.

B y V Tour (☎ 731-390), Libertad 432, goes Thursday and Saturday at 8 am to Coihaique. It also goes to Caleta Gonzalo (US$5) daily at 7 am in summer, and occasionally at other times.

Transportes Cordillera, also at Libertad 432, goes daily at 3:15 pm to Futaleufú. Transportes Futaleufú goes to Futaleufú (US$8) at 3:30 pm daily except Sunday, when it goes at 5 pm.

Buses Lago Verde, on Todesco between Corcovado and Portales, goes to Puerto Cárdenas, Villa Santa Lucía, Villa Vanguardia and La Junta (US$10) at 4 pm Monday, Wednesday and Friday, while Campos de Hielo Sur goes to La Junta at 3:30 pm, Tuesday, Thursday and Saturday.

Buses Palena goes to Palena (US$8) Monday, Wednesday and Friday at 3:30 pm from the Supermercado Michimahuida at the corner of Corcovado and Todesco.

Boat Transmarchilay (☎ 731-272), Corcovado 266, sails to Puerto Montt (10 hours) Wednesday at 9 pm on the ferry *Pincoya*; for fares, see the Puerto Montt section in the La Araucanía & Los Lagos chapter. Transmarchilay also sails Wednesday and Saturday to Quellón (five hours), at the south end of the Isla Grande de Chiloé, on the *Pincoya*; for fares, see the Quellón entry in the Chiloé chapter. Schedules change, so confirm them at any Transmarchilay office.

From Caleta Gonzalo, 56km north of Chaitén, Transmarchilay sails daily except Monday to Hornopirén, where there are bus connections to Puerto Montt; see the Caleta Gonzalo section below for details. This is a summer-only service.

Navimag (☎ 731-570, fax 730-571), Ignacio Carrera Pinto 188, sails the spacious auto-passenger ferry *Alejandrina* to Quellón Monday, Wednesday, Friday and Sunday, and to Puerto Montt Tuesday, Thursday and Saturday; the food is less than appealing, so bring something along. Fares to Quellón are US$17 to US$24 for passengers, US$10 for bicycles, US$23 for motorcycles, and US$83 for cars or light trucks. For fares to Puerto Montt, see the Getting There & Away section in the Araucanía & Los Lagos chapter.

From September to May, the new *Esmeralda de Chonchi* sails to Chonchi, on the Isla Grande de Chiloé, Wednesday and Friday at 8 am; for fares, see the Chonchi entry in the Chiloé chapter. Purchase tickets through Chaitur (☎ 731-429) at O'Higgins 67.

TERMAS EL AMARILLO

About 25km southeast of Chaitén, on a spur north off the Camino Austral, Termas El Amarillo is a simple hot springs, with 20 walk-in campsites and a restaurant that has been the subject of a tug-of-war between would-be concessionaires. Until the Municipalidad sorts out the details of improvements on this run-down site, it's a better day trip than overnight excursion.

Admission to the pools costs US$4, while campsites cost US$6.50. Nearby *Residencial Marcela* (☎ 65-264-442), at the crossroads, charges US$10/19 for singles/doubles with breakfast and shared bath.

Southern Aisén

South of Coihaique, settlements are fewer and farther apart. Part of the area was devastated by the 1991 eruption of Volcán Hudson, a relatively inconspicuous 1369m peak that dumped tons of ash over thousands of square kilometers in both Chile and Argentina, ruining cropland and killing livestock by burying pasture grasses. The only substantial towns are Chile Chico, on the south shore of Lago General Carrera near the Argentine border, and Cochrane on the Camino Austral. The highway presently ends at Puerto Yungay, south of the Río Baker, but is slowly proceeding toward Villa O'Higgins.

PUERTO INGENIERO IBÁÑEZ

Buried in ash by the eruption of Volcán Hudson, Puerto Ingeniero Ibáñez, on the north shore of emerald green Lago General Carrera, has recovered more quickly than other affected towns in the area. Surrounded by steep mountains and barren hills, the town has regular ferries to Chile Chico, where there are bus connections to the Argentine border at Los Antiguos. Across the border, Lago General Carrera is known as Lago Buenos Aires.

Cattle and sheep are the backbone of the economy. Local *huasos*, the Chilean equivalent of the Argentine gaucho, drive their herds along the roads. Orchard crops also do well in the low-altitude microclimate along the lake. Long lines of poplars, planted as windbreaks, separate the fields; black-necked swans and pink flamingos crowd the river and its shores.

The town itself is of little interest, but the surrounding countryside is very worthwhile if you can afford to rent a car. From Puerto Levicán, on the lake, there are panoramic views of the Río Ibáñez Valley when dust from Volcán Hudson doesn't obscure the horizon.

Places to Stay & Eat

Opposite the ferry dock, *Residencial Ibáñez* (☎ 423-227, Dickson 31) has unheated singles with plenty of extra blankets for US$6.50 including breakfast; other meals are available. Nearby *Residencial Vientos del Sur* (☎ 423-208, Dickson 282) is comparably priced.

Getting There & Away

For ground transport from Coihaique to Puerto Ibáñez, see the Coihaique section, earlier in this chapter. Naviera Sotramin (☎ 234-240), Portales 99 in Coihaique, crosses to Chile Chico (2½ hours), on the south shore of Lago General Carrera, in the ferry *El Pilchero* daily except Sunday. Departures are at 9 am except for Saturday (10 am).

The passenger fare from Puerto Ibáñez to Chile Chico is US$3.50 per person, but students and children pay half fare. Bringing

AISÉN

bicycles or motorcycles costs US$3, while the fee for passenger vehicles is US$42.

RN CERRO CASTILLO
Reaching nearly 2700m and flanked by three major glaciers on its southern slopes, the basalt spires of Reserva Nacional Cerro Castillo tower above southern beech forests in this sprawling 180,000-hectare reserve, 75km south of Coihaique. This is fine, but rarely visited, trekking country (not to be confused with the settlement of Cerro Castillo near Parque Nacional Torres del Paine.

Sight-seeing, fishing and trekking are popular recreational options. There is an excellent four-day trek from Km 75, at the north end of the reserve, to Villa Cerro Castillo at the south end, which is described in Lonely Planet's *Trekking in the Patagonian Andes*.

Places to Stay
On the Camino Austral, 67km south of Coihaique, Conaf operates a modest but sheltered and shady *campground* at Laguna Chaguay for US$5 per site, but tent camping is free in the spectacular backcountry. Be sure to check in with the ranger, since trekking is potentially hazardous, even though bridges now cross rushing meltwater streams that once required fording.

VILLA CERRO CASTILLO
At the south end of the reserve, on a short gravel lateral from the Camino Austral about 10km west of the Puerto Ibáñez junction, Villa Cerro Castillo is a typical pioneer settlement of cement block houses with corrugated metal roofs, plus a few scattered samples of Chilote shingle houses. There is now a tourist office, open 10 am to 8 pm daily in January and February only.

Pensión El Viajero has a few rooms for US$6 per person, as well as a bar and a cheap restaurant. There's an increasing and improving number of places to stay, though the food is nothing to speak of.

PUERTO RÍO TRANQUILO
One of the larger settlements on the Camino Austral between Coihaique and Cochrane, Puerto Río Tranquilo was one of several

ports linked by ferry to Puerto Ibáñez, Chile Chico and smaller lakeside outposts. Now a convenient stopover for those passing through the area, it is the junction for a new road under construction northwest to Bahía Exploradores, which will improve access to Laguna San Rafael.

Places to Stay & Eat
Directly on the highway, *Residencial Carretera Austral* (☎ 419-500, 1 Sur 223) charges US$15 per person but also has a selection of inexpensive cabañas that cost about US$9 per person. *Residencial Los Pinos* (☎ 411-637, 2 Oriente 41), just west of the highway, charges US$25/38 singles/doubles and has a restaurant with fixed-price meals for US$6 (salmon is a good choice).

Getting There & Away
Regular buses between Coihaique and Cochrane will drop off and pick up passengers here. Transportes Ales goes to Chile Chico (US$16, six hours) Wednesday mornings.

PUERTO GUADAL
At the west end of Lago General Carrera, 13km east of the junction with the Camino Austral on the highway to Chile Chico, Puerto Guadal's shingled houses are palpable evidence of Chilote immigration over the past two decades.

The only formal accommodations in town are at homey *Hostería Huemules* (☎ 411-202, Las Magnolias 382), charging a very reasonable US$10 per person with a good restaurant to boot, but there are also acceptable free campsites along the lake. *Café de la Frontera* (Los Lirios 399) has a diverse menu; it's not cheap, but still reasonable.

Buses Australes Pudú, on the Plaza de Armas, has Sunday and Thursday buses to Coihaique; there is also service Wednesday and Saturday to Chile Chico (US$9); Ales' Tuesday service from Chile Chico continues to Río Tranquilo, while the Friday service goes to Cochrane. Sergio Haro goes Thursday and Sunday to Chile Chico (US$9).

There are several rural resort accommodations in the vicinity of Puerto Guadal. At Cruce El Maitén, the junction of the Camino

Austral (Km 274) and the highway to Chile Chico, *Hacienda Tres Lagos* (☎ 411-323) has attractive lakeside cabañas and a restaurant. Rates are US$83/123 for singles/doubles; there is also a lakeside sauna, horse rentals and launches for fishing.

Other nearby alternatives include *Bahía Catarina* (☎ 232-920) at Km 268, which has both camping and cabañas (US$63 for three people) and *Pasarela Lodge* (☎ 411-425) at Km 265, which has self-catering fishing cabañas (US$169) for up to five people.

CHILE CHICO
☎ 67

Founded in 1928 by immigrant fortune seekers of several nationalities – Argentine, Brazilian, Chilean, French, German and Italian – Chile Chico derived its early prosperity from copper, the blue-tinged ore still visible in the rocky hills. The broad, recently paved Av O'Higgins is a tangible reminder of the optimism of the first settlers but, after miners exhausted the copper, the economy declined rapidly. It revived with the opening of US-based Coeur d'Alene Exploration's Fachinal gold and silver mine in 1995. However, initial optimism has evaporated as production has fallen (allegations of fraud led to a lawsuit in Colorado).

Before recent developments, cultivation of high-quality fruit in Chile Chico's balmy microclimate kept the town alive if not truly prosperous; the warm, sunny weather encouraged production of apples, pears, plums and cherries equal to those from the Chilean heartland. Even many street trees are fruit-bearing apricots and peaches, rather than strictly ornamentals, but fruit is economically marginal because markets other than Coihaique are distant and transport is difficult and expensive.

Ash from the 1991 eruption of Volcán Hudson smothered local orchards, jeopardizing the town's future, and when there are high winds the skies still darken. Despite the arrival of foreign capital and improved streets, Chile Chico still has a more forlorn aspect than nearby Los Antiguos, across the border in Argentina. Many residents have left to work in Argentina or elsewhere, and the permanent population of 2300 is only about half of what it was in the 1960s. Remittances from expatriate workers, or those in other parts of Chile, are a main source of income, but some residents make a living catering to the Argentine tourist trade.

The mountainous road west from Chile Chico to the junction with the Camino Austral is one of the region's highlights, a scary experience that several mountain bikers have enjoyed despite its steepness. If driving, proceed very slowly; there are many blind curves, and in some places the roadway is barely wide enough for a single vehicle.

Orientation

On the southern shore of Lago General Carrera, Chile Chico is a compact village only a few kilometers from the Argentine border at Los Antiguos. One block south of the lakeshore, westbound Av O'Higgins becomes the hair-raising highway to Puerto Guadal and Cruce El Maitén, on the Camino Austral just north of Cochrane.

Information

At the corner of O'Higgins and Lautaro, Chile Chico's Oficina de Información Turística is part of the Casa de la Cultura (see the section by that name, immediately following). It's open Tuesday through Saturday 10 am to 1:30 pm and 2:30 to 7:30 pm, Sunday 10 am to 1 pm. Conaf is at Blest Gana 121.

From 10 am to 1 pm weekdays, the bureaucratically lethargic Banco del Estado, González 112, changes US cash only at reasonable rates, but collects a US$12 commission on traveler's checks, regardless of the amount cashed.

The post office is at Manuel Rodríguez 121. Entel is on O'Higgins between Pedro Montt and Lautaro; Fonosol is almost next door. Chilexpress is at O'Higgins 409 and there's also a CTC (Telefónica) phone at Café Elizabeth y Loly, Pedro González 25.

The operators of Hostería Austral (see the Places to Stay section, later in the chapter) arrange fishing excursions, horseback riding and other trips to natural attractions including Lago Jeinimeni and the Río Baker. They also rent Suzuki jeeps for backroads travel.

Traveling through Argentine Patagonia

Without flying or sailing, the only way from Aisén to the far southern Chilean region of Magallanes is through Argentine Patagonia. For an outline of the formalities of visiting Argentina, see the Getting There & Away chapter. A brief summary of practical information on traveling in Argentina and the main routes to Magallanes follows. For full details, see Lonely Planet's *Argentina, Uruguay & Paraguay*.

Visas

There is no Argentine consulate between Puerto Montt and Punta Arenas, so if you need a visa, get one at the Argentine consulate in Santiago.

Getting Around

In Argentine Patagonia, distances are immense, roads can be very bad, and some travelers find the desert monotonous, so the occasional flight is sometimes a welcome relief. Argentina's three major airlines, Aerolíneas Argentinas, Austral and Líneas Aéreas del Estado (LADE), have extensive networks in southern Patagonia and Tierra del Fuego. LADE fares are very cheap, in some cases less than the bus fare for the same route, but demand is high, especially in summer. Try the airport if LADE staff insist that flights are completely booked. Other regional airlines are making inroads on the established carriers.

Argentine buses, resembling those in Chile, are modern, comfortable and fast. Most large towns have a central bus terminal, though some companies operate from their own private offices. In some more remote and less populated areas, buses are few or even non-existent, so be patient.

Traffic in Patagonia and Tierra del Fuego is sparse and there may be long waits between lifts, since the few private vehicles are usually full with families. Paved Ruta Nacional 3, on the Atlantic coast, is the fastest route south. Much improved Ruta Nacional 40 is a dirt and gravel highway that still carries little traffic south of Esquel. If hitchhiking, be sure to have warm, windproof clothes and carry snack food and a water bottle (Lonely Planet does not recommend hitchhiking).

Coihaique to Comodoro Rivadavia

One of the main routes to Argentine Patagonia is from Coihaique to Comodoro Rivadavia, an oil town on the Atlantic coast. Buses run about four times weekly (see Coihaique's Bus section, earlier in this chapter).

Antonio Rodríguez (☎ 411-209), Pedro González 253, rents horses (US$8 half day, US$12 full day) and arranges excursions to Laguna Jeinimeni, Cueva de las Manos (Argentina) and other nearby sites.

Casa de la Cultura

Chile Chico's museum and cultural center, at O'Higgins and Lautaro, features a ground floor collection of works by regional artists and a second floor assemblage of local arti-

facts, including minerals and fossils; unfortunately, the interpretive material is scanty. Outside is the restored *Los Andes*, a boat that once carried passengers and freight around the lake.

Places to Stay

Chile Chico's selection of accommodations has recently improved. Friendly *Hospedaje No Me Olvides*, about a kilometer east of downtown on the highway to Argentina, is a

Traveling through Argentine Patagonia

Comodoro (population about 100,000) is southern Argentine Patagonia's largest city, but most foreign visitors spend only a few hours here. The surrounding oil fields supply about a third of Argentina's crude, and travelers should not miss the **Museo del Petróleo**, one of Argentina's most impressive and professional museums. Since Comodoro is a transport hub, air and road connections are good to all parts of the country, especially southbound to Río Gallegos.

Chile Chico to Caleta Olivia

From Chile Chico, there are up to three buses daily to the Argentine village of Los Antiguos, which has buses to the town of Perito Moreno (not to be confused with the rarely visited national park or the famous glacier of the same name) or to Caleta Olivia, on the coast. From Caleta Olivia, there are daily buses to Río Gallegos and frequent buses on the short hop to Comodoro Rivadavia. A new service, almost daily in summer but less frequent the rest of the year, connects Los Antiguos and Perito Moreno with El Chaltén, at the Fitzroy sector of Argentina's Parque Nacional Los Glaciares.

Like Chile Chico, Los Antiguos was blanketed with ash deposits from the eruption of Volcán Hudson, but its site on Lago Buenos Aires is incomparably beautiful and its mild climate is a pleasure. From Perito Moreno, Tuesday LADE flights go to El Calafate (US$43), Río Gallegos (US$58) and Ushuaia (US$94); Thursday flights go to El Calafate, Río Turbio (US$55) and Río Gallegos.

Caleta Olivia is a miniature version of Comodoro Rivadavia, a plain but friendly oil town with frequent bus connections.

To/From Río Gallegos

Río Gallegos, 800km south of Comodoro Rivadavia, is a sizable sheep-farming town that's the starting point for many trips to El Calafate, near Argentina's Parque Nacional Los Glaciares, and to Ushuaia, on the island of Tierra del Fuego. From Río Gallegos there are daily buses to Puerto Natales and Punta Arenas in Chile. Several Argentine airlines have air connections north and south, and Aerolíneas Argentinas' transpolar flights to and from Australia stop here.

There are daily buses to El Calafate from Río Gallegos. In summer, there are regular buses from Calafate to Puerto Natales, Chile, but this trip is difficult in winter, when snow sometimes blocks the road from El Calafate to Chile.

Another crossing from Argentina to Chile is by bus from Río Gallegos to Puerto Natales, via the coal town of Río Turbio. Take one of the daily buses from Río Gallegos to Río Turbio, then catch one of the frequent workers' buses from Río Turbio to Puerto Natales. LADE flies Thursday to Río Gallegos (US$20) and Friday to El Calafate (US$20.)

popular budget choice for US$7.50 per person, and also offers camping and serves reasonable meals. *Hospedaje Alicia* (☎ 411-265, Freire 24) is worth a look for US$8.50 per person, as is *Hospedaje Monique* (O'Higgins 420).

The best value in town is *Hospedaje Don Luis* (☎ 411-384, Balmaceda 175), a spotless and friendly place that charges US$10 per person without breakfast, but *Hospedaje Brisas del Lago* (☎ 411-204, Manuel Rodrí-

guez 443) offers good lake views in the same price range. The staff at *Residencial Aguas Azules* (☎ 411-320, Manuel Rodríguez 252) has an attitude problem and, for US$25 single, it's no bargain. Its cheaper annex, at the corner of Balmaceda and Manuel Rodríguez, is overpriced at half the cost – the walls are paper-thin and the beds sag like hammocks.

The sparkling *Hostería Austral* (☎/fax 411-461, O'Higgins 501) offers Chile Chico's most impressive accommodations; room rates are US$31/46 singles/doubles. There are, however, two new hotels that may soon supersede it: *Hotel Fachinal* (☎ 411-460, O'Higgins s/n) and *Hotel Los Dos* (☎ 411-710, Carrera 290).

Places to Eat
For snacks and drinks, try the congenial *Café Elizabeth y Loly* (☎ 411-288, Pedro González 25), opposite the plaza, or *Rapanui* (☎ 411-475, Blest Gana 22-A). *Café Holiday* (☎ 411-382, González 115) has fine simple meals. The restaurant at *Hostería Austral* is erratic and fairly expensive, but salmon dinners and fresh local raspberries, when available, are good reasons to dine here. It also serves espresso.

El Minero (☎ 411-521, Carrera 205) is a pub and restaurant that has a US$5 fixed-price lunch. Try also *Pub Tagonia* (☎ 411-401, Manuel Rodríguez 70), which has occasional live entertainment.

Getting There & Away
Air Transporte Aéreo Don Carlos (☎ 411-490), in the Panadería La Espiga at O'Higgins 264, flies daily except Sunday to Coihaique (US$38). The airfield is just outside town, on the road to the Argentine border.

Bus Transportes Padilla (☎ 411-224), O'Higgins 424, crosses the border to Los Antiguos (US$2.30), just 9km east, four times daily except on weekends, when it goes only once. Acotrans (☎ 411-582), which leaves from in front of the Fonosol office on O'Higgins, crosses five times daily. From Los Antiguos, travelers can make connections to Perito Moreno, Caleta Olivia, El Chaltén and southern Argentine Patagonia.

Transportes Ales (☎ 411-739), Rosa Amelia 800, goes Tuesday at 10 am to Guadal and Río Tranquilo (US$16, six hours), and Friday at 10 am to Guadal and Cochrane (US$16, six hours). Sergio Haro (☎ 411-251), Manuel Rodríguez 30, goes Wednesday and Saturday at 10 am to Guadal (US$9, three hours) and El Cruce (US$11), on the Panamericana.

Boat Naviera Sotramin's auto-passenger ferry *El Pilchero* sails weekdays at 5:30 pm and Sunday at 3 pm to Puerto Ibáñez, on the north side of the lake. For fares, see the entry for Puerto Ibáñez, above.

PUERTO BERTRAND
On the southeast shore of Lago Bertrand, 11km south of Cruce El Maitén, Puerto Bertrand is a small but scenic village with a cluster of places to stay and eat, none of them particularly cheap. This scenic spot is becoming a center of outdoors activity.

About 40km south of Puerto Bertrand and 17km north of Cochrane, at the scenic confluence of the Río Baker and Río Nef, a decent gravel road climbs eastward up the valley of the Río Chacabuco to the Argentine border at Paso Roballos.

Organized Tours
US-run Patagonia Adventure Expeditions (☎/fax 67-411-330, riobaker@entelchile.net) is a small but ambitious start-up offering rafting on the powerful Río Baker and climbing and riding in the nearby mountains. Their postal address is Casilla 519, Coihaique, but excursions can also be arranged through Albergue Las Salamandras in Coihaique and in the USA (☎ 303-670-8918, fax 303-674-1024), where their mailing address is 5259 Elk Ridge Rd, Evergreen, CO 80439.

Half-day trips on the Río Baker cost US$30, while a 150km, six-day descent of the river from its source to the sea costs US$600 per person. Kayak instruction costs US$100 per day. Horseback trips cost US$70 for one day, US$135 per day for overnights, while flyfishing trips on the Río Baker cost US$110 per half day and US$185 per full day (US$150 per person for two people). Climbing trips are also possible.

Places to Stay & Eat
Puerto Bertrand's small but charming *Camping Municipal*, on the riverside, costs US$2 to US$3 per person. Otherwise, the most reasonable options are *Hospedaje Vargas*, charging US$10 per person with breakfast, and *Hostería Puerto Bertrand* for

US$17 per person with breakfast. The latter also serves good, abundant lunches and dinners.

With an attractive sitting room and a deck looming above the water, the **Hostería Río Baker** (☎ 67-411-447) charges US$80/120 singles/doubles for a beautiful riverside location; it also has Argentine contact numbers in Buenos Aires (☎ 54-11-4863-9373) and Mendoza (☎ 54-261-420-2196).

At the highway junction is the luxury **Lodge Río Baker** (☎ 67-411-499), which charges US$240 for four-person cabañas that are a bit too close together; the service falls short of the price.

COCHRANE
☎ 67

Cochrane, 345km south of Coihaique, is almost the end of the road. Although the Camino Austral continues south to Puerto Yungay and will eventually go to Villa O'Higgins, public transport turns around and heads back north. Directly west are the southern outliers of the Campo de Hielo Norte, while a few kilometers to the east is Lago Cochrane, a popular recreational area that is known as Lago Pueyrredón across the Argentine border. There is no public transport across the border, and traffic is generally scarce.

Now paving most of its streets, the small but growing town has an attractively landscaped Plaza de Armas and the last notable tourist services on the Camino Austral. From October to March, its tourist information kiosk, on the plaza, is open 10 am to 1 pm and 2:30 to 8 pm daily except Sunday. The rest of the year, try the nearby Municipalidad for information.

For information on Reserva Nacional Lago Cochrane, north of town, visit Conaf (☎ 522-164) at Río Nef 417. Correos de Chile is at Esmeralda 199, and there's a telephone office at the corner of San Valentín and Las Golondrinas. The hospital (☎ 522-131) is at O'Higgins 755.

Places to Stay & Eat
Free but windy and exposed campsites with no services are available at the **Central Náutico** on Lago Cochrane, about 3km east of town. A few kilometers farther on, Conaf's **Camping Las Correntadas** charges US$12 per site; admission to Reserva Nacional Tamango costs US$3 more.

Otherwise, Cochrane has several basic hotels for about US$10 per person including **Residencial El Fogón** (☎ 522-240, San Valentín 651), which has a good restaurant with outdoor seating, and, with friendly but distracted staff, **Residencial Sur Austral** (☎ 522-150, Prat 281), which also serves meals. Reader-recommended **Hospedaje Cochrane** (☎ 522-377, Dr Steffens 451) charges about US$11 per person, with garden camping also possible.

A bit run-down despite its attractive gardens, **Hotel Wellmann** (☎ 522-171, Las Golondrinas 36) is still one of the best in town for US$25/38 singles/doubles with breakfast, but **Hotel Ultimo Paraíso** (☎ 522-361, Brown 450) is muscling in on its territory. Rates there are US$47/58.

Rogeri (☎ 522-264, Teniente Merino 502) is a good, reasonably priced restaurant.

Getting There & Away
Air Transporte Aéreo Don Carlos (☎ 522-150), Prat 281 alongside Residencial Sur Austral, flies Monday to Coihaique (US$60). The southbound flight from Coihaique continues to Villa O'Higgins (US$50).

Bus Buses Don Carlos (☎ 522-150), Prat 281, goes to Coihaique (US$15) at 8:30 am Wednesday and Sunday, and slightly more expensive Buses Pudú, at Teniente Merino and Río Maitén, goes Thursday and Sunday at 8:15 am. Transportes Ales goes to Puerto Guadal and Chile Chico Saturday morning.

CALETA TORTEL
About 20km north of Puerto Yungay, a rustic A-frame shelter (no insulation, but a woodstove) marks Río los Vagabundos, the departure point for Caleta Tortel, a picturesque fishing village at the mouth of the Río Baker. The villagers of Caleta Tortel have petitioned for a highway extension to link them to the Camino Austral. However, for the moment, the only way to get there is to be fortunate

enough to arrive at Río Los Vagabundos when there's a boat, or else have the carabineros from Cochrane radio ahead from the Municipalidad to have someone meet you in a launch. This is expensive, however – US$115 for up to five passengers – unless you catch the municipally subsidized service at 9 am Tuesday and Sunday.

PUERTO YUNGAY

Puerto Yungay, 1125km from Puerto Montt and 113km from Cochrane, was, until recently, the southern end of the Camino Austral. But a government ferry now hauls passengers to the east end of the Fiordo Mitchell, where the Cuerpo Militar de Trabajo (CMT; Army Corp of Engineers) has recently turned over the last likely segment of the southern highway, the stretch to Villa O'Higgins, to the Ministerio de Obras Públicas (Public Works Ministry). Yungay has no tourist services, though it's likely some will appear in the coming years.

The stretch of highway from Río los Vagabundos to Puerto Yungay is rugged, difficult for vehicles without high clearance and subject to slides; beyond Fiordo Mitchell it's likely to remain rough for some years. Before continuing south toward Puerto Yungay and Villa O'Higgins, it's a good idea to consult carabineros in Cochrane about road conditions.

VILLA O'HIGGINS

At the north end of a narrow arm of Lago O'Higgins (known as Lago San Martín on the Argentine side), isolated Villa O'Higgins is a pioneer village of about 300 souls, but completion of the Camino Austral is likely to bring big changes. The only accommodations are at *Hospedaje Patagonia* (☎ 234-813, *Río Pascua 1956*) for US$10 per person including breakfast.

There are weekly flights from Coihaique and Cochrane with Transporte Aéreo Don Carlos, but no public transport yet on the rugged highway from Puerto Yungay. There's an improved stretch of road south to the main basin of Lago O'Higgins, but it's not easy to cross the border here.

Magallanes & Tierra del Fuego

Chile's Region XII, the Región de Maga-llanes y de la Antártica Chilena, takes in all the country's territory beyond about 49° S, including the western half of the Isla Grande de Tierra del Fuego (whose eastern half is Argentine), the largely uninhabited islands of the Tierra del Fuego Archipelago, and the slice of Antarctica claimed by Chile. This chapter also includes information on Argentine Tierra del Fuego and the southeast corner of Argentina's Santa Cruz province, which includes the popular destinations of El Calafate as well as Parque Nacional Los Glaciares.

Magallanes

Battered by westerly winds and storms that drop huge amounts of rain and snow on the seaward slopes of the Andes, Magallanes is a rugged, mountainous area, geographically remote from the rest of the country. From Aisén or the Chilean mainland, Magallanes and its capital Punta Arenas are accessible by road only through Argentine Patagonia, or else by air or sea.

Alacaluf and Tehuelche Indians, subsisting through fishing, hunting and gathering, were the region's original inhabitants. While the Alacalufes and Tehuelches survive in reduced numbers, there remain very few individuals of identifiable Ona, Haush or Yahgan.

Magellan, who in 1520 became the first European to visit the region, left it his name, but early Spanish colonization attempts failed. Tiny Puerto Hambre (Port Famine), at the southern end of the Strait of Magellan, is a reminder of these efforts. Nearby, the restored wooden bulwarks of Fuerte Bulnes recall Chile's first colonization in 1843, when President Manuel Bulnes ordered the army south to the area, which at the time was sparsely populated by indigenous peoples.

Increased maritime traffic spurred by the California gold rush gave birth to Punta Arenas, whose initial prosperity came from the ships that passed through the straits between Europe and California and Australia. With the opening of the Panama Canal and the reduction of traffic around Cape Horn (Cabo de Hornos), the port's international importance diminished. Later wealth was earned from the wool and mutton industries, which transformed both Argentine and Chilean Patagonia in the late 19th century.

Besides wool, Magallanes' modern economy depends on commerce, petroleum development and fisheries, which have made it prosperous, with some of the country's highest levels of employment and school attendance, and some of its best quality housing and public services, but recent global events, most notably the Asian crisis and declining oil reserves, have undercut the economy. Some farmers have taken to selling lambs out of their own trucks to avoid middlemen.

Its impressive natural assets, particularly Parque Nacional Torres del Paine, have made Magallanes an increasingly popular tourist destination, but the region also manifests symptoms of the global environmental crisis. The continuing deterioration of the ozone layer over Antarctica has impacted southern South America more than any other permanently inhabited area on earth, directly affecting both the human population and the local livestock economy. Native forest conservation has become a major issue in the remotest corners of both Chilean and Argentine Tierra del Fuego.

PUNTA ARENAS
☎ 61

At the foot of the Andes on the western side of the Strait of Magellan, Patagonia's most interesting city features many mansions and other impressive buildings dating from the wool boom of the late 19th and early 20th centuries. As the best and largest port for thousands of kilometers, Punta Arenas (population 113,000) still attracts ships from the South Atlantic fishery but has lost out to the Argentine city of Ushuaia as a port for Antarctic research and tourist vessels.

Free port facilities have promoted local commerce and encouraged immigration from central Chile; luxury items such as automobiles are cheaper here, but the basic cost of living is higher. The economy has been affected by recent difficulties as a result of declining fisheries and petroleum production.

Punta Arenas has experienced a large influx of foreign visitors, compared to their relative paucity in Argentina, but the town can be utterly dead on Sunday, which is a good day to explore some of the surrounding area or start a trip to Torres del Paine.

History

Founded in 1848, Punta Arenas was originally a military garrison and penal settlement that proved to be conveniently situated as a stopover for ships headed to California during the gold rush. Compared to the initial Chilean settlement at Fuerte Bulnes, 60km south, the town had a better, more protected harbor, and superior access to wood and water. For many years, English maritime charts had called the site 'Sandy Point,' which became its rough Spanish equivalent.

In Punta Arenas' early years, its economy depended on wild animal products, including sealskins, guanaco hides and feathers; mineral products, including coal, gold and guano; and firewood and timber. None of these was a truly major industry, and the economy did not take off until the last quarter of the 19th century, after the territorial governor authorized the purchase of 300 purebred sheep from the Falkland Islands. This successful experiment encouraged others to invest in sheep and, by the turn of the century, nearly 2 million animals grazed the territory.

In 1875, Magallanes' population was barely 1000, but European immigration accelerated as the wool market boomed. Among the most notable immigrants were Portuguese businessman José Nogueira; Irish doctor Thomas Fenton, who founded one of the island's largest sheep stations; and José Menéndez, an Asturian entrepreneur who would become one of the wealthiest and

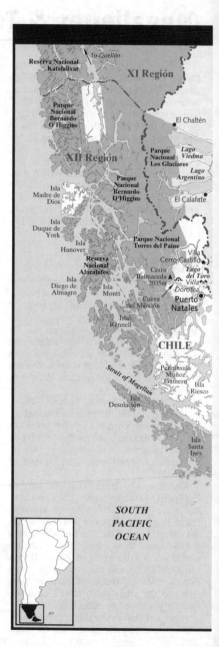

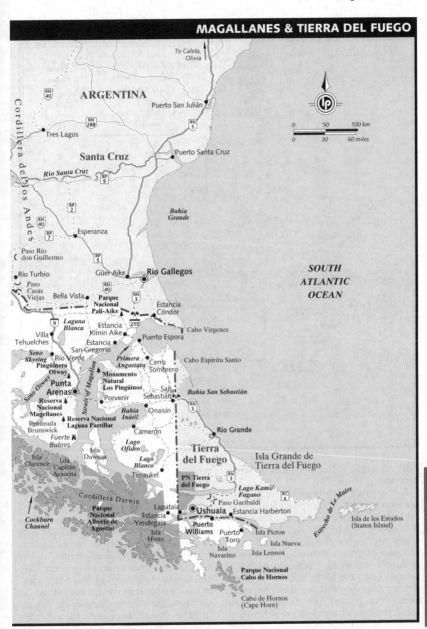

MAGALLANES & TIERRA DEL FUEGO

To Caleta, Olivia

ARGENTINA

Puerto San Julián

RN 40

RN 288

RN 3

Tres Lagos

Cordillera de los Andes

Santa Cruz

Puerto Santa Cruz

Río Santa Cruz

RP 9

Bahía Grande

0   50   100 km
0   30   60 miles

RP 2

RN 40

RP 7

Esperanza

RP 5

Paso Río don Guillermo

Río Turbio

Güer Aike

Río Gallegos

SOUTH ATLANTIC OCEAN

Paso Casas Viejas

Bella Vista

RN 40

RN 3

Parque Nacional Pali-Aike

Estancia Cóndor

Laguna Blanca

Estancia Kimiri Aike

255

Cabo Vírgenes

Villa Tehuelches

Estancia San Gregorio

Puerto Espora

9

Seno Skyring

Río Verde

Primera Angostura

Cabo Espíritu Santo

Pingüinera Otway

Cerro Sombrero

Seno Otway

Strait of Magellan

Monumento Natural Los Pingüinos

Punta Arenas

San Sebastián

Bahía San Sebastián

Reserva Nacional Magallanes

Porvenir

RN 3

Bahía Inútil

Onaisín

Península Brunswick

Reserva Nacional Laguna Parrillar

Cameron

Río Grande

Fuerte Bulnes

Isla Dawson

Lago Ofidro

Tierra del Fuego

Isla Grande de Tierra del Fuego

Isla Clarence

Isla Capitán Aracena

Lago Blanco

Timaukel

PN Tierra del Fuego

RN 3

Lago Kami Fagano

RC 8

Cordillera Darwin

Lapataia

Paso Garibaldi

Estrecho de le Maire

Cockburn Channel

Parque Nacional Alberto de Agostini

Estancia Yendegaia

Ushuaia

Estancia Harberton

Isla de los Estados (Staten Island)

Puerto Williams

Puerto Toro

Isla Picton

Isla Hoste

Isla Navarino

Isla Nueva

Isla Lennox

Parque Nacional Cabo de Hornos

Cabo de Hornos (Cape Horn)

MAGALLANES

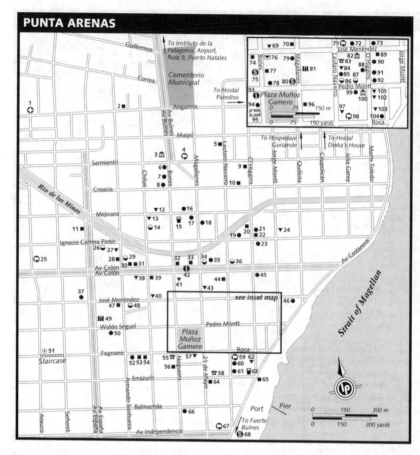

PUNTA ARENAS

most influential individuals in all of South America.

First engaged solely in commerce, Menéndez soon began to acquire pastoral property. He founded the famous Sociedad Explotadora de Tierra del Fuego, which controlled nearly a million hectares in Magallanes alone and other properties across the border – one of Argentina's greatest estancias, near Río Grande, bears the name of his wife, María Behety. Together with another important family, the Brauns, the descendants of Menéndez figured among the wealthiest and most powerful regional elites in Latin America. Although few remain in Punta Arenas (having relocated to Santiago and Buenos Aires), their mansions remain as symbols of Punta Arenas' golden age.

Menéndez and his colleagues could not have built their commercial and pastoral empires without the labor of immigrants from many lands: England, Ireland, Scotland, Croatia, France, Germany, Spain, Italy and others. On all sides of José Menéndez' opulent mausoleum, modest tombstones in the municipal cemetery suggest the origins of those whose efforts made his and other wool fortunes possible. Ever since the ex-

PUNTA ARENAS

PLACES TO STAY
2 Hostal Sonia (HI)
5 Hostal Carpa Manzano
9 ¡Ecole! Patagonia
10 Hostal de la Patagonia
11 Hostal Rubio
20 Hospedaje Manuel
22 Albergue Backpacker's Paradise
28 Residencial Coirón
30 Hostal de la Avenida
31 Hotel Cóndor de Plata
32 Hotel Tierra del Fuego
33 Hotel Finis Terrae
39 Hotel Montecarlo
44 Hostal Calafate
47 Hostal Oasis
53 Residencial Oasis
54 Hotel Mercurio
56 Hotel Plaza
64 Hotel Isla Rey Jorge
65 Hostal O'Higgins
70 Residencial Roca
74 Hotel Los Navegantes
77 Hotel José Nogueira
89 Hostal Calafate II
96 Hotel Cabo de Hornos

PLACES TO EAT
12 222
13 El Mercado
24 El Mesón del Calvo
27 Rotisería La Mamá
38 Golden Dragon
40 La Carioca
41 Café Calipso
43 El Infante
57 Centro Español
62 Sotito's Bar
69 Lomit's

84 Asturias
97 Quijote
101 La Casa de Juan
102 La Taberna de Silver
103 El Beagle

OTHER
1 Hospital Regional
3 Museo Regional Salesiano Mayorino Borgatello
4 Netherlands Consulate
6 Southern Patagonia Souvenirs & Books
7 Tres Arroyos
8 Austro Internet
10 Ecotour Patagonia
14 Transportes Polo Sur
15 Nómade
16 Solovidrios
17 Sala Estrella
18 Turismo Aonikenk
19 Arka Patagonia
21 Canadian Institue
23 Chile Típico
25 Brazilian Consulate
26 Buses Punta Arenas
29 Buses Fernández, Buses Pingüino, Turibús
34 Bus Sur
35 Operatur Patagónica
36 Buses Pacheco
37 Turismo Cordillera Darwin
42 Kiosko de Informaciones
45 Gabriela Mistral Mural
46 Conaf
48 Bus Sur
49 Milward's Stone Castle
50 Internacional Rent a Car
51 Mirador La Cruz
52 Turismo Viento Sur

55 CTC (Telefónica)
57 Teatro Cervantes
58 Chilexpress
59 Belgian Consulate
60 Turismo Pali Aike
61 Ladeco
63 Olijoe Pub
66 Chile Tours
67 Turismo Comapa, Navimag, Norwegian Consulate
68 Pingüi Tour (Casa de Cambio)
71 Spanish Consulate
72 Turismo Pehoé
73 Aerovías DAP
75 RedBanc (ATM)
76 Post Office
78 Club de la Unión
79 Lubag Rent a Car
80 Citibank (ex-Sociedad Menéndez Behety)
81 Casa Braun-Menéndez
82 Museo Militar de la Quinta División del Ejército
83 Entel
85 LanChile
86 Buses Ghisoni, Tecni-Austral
87 Transfer Austral
88 Budget Rent a Car
90 Automóvil Club de Chile
91 Lavasol
92 Hertz
93 Sernatur
94 Intendencia Regional
95 Cathedral
98 British Consulate
99 Disco Splash
100 Museo Naval y Marítimo
104 Emsa, Avis

propriation of the great estancias, including those of the Sociedad Explotadora, in the 1960s, land tenure has been more equitable. Energy production and fishing have eclipsed wool in the regional economy.

Orientation

Punta Arenas sits on a narrow shelf between the Andes to the west and the Strait of Magellan to the east. Consequently, the city has spread north and south from its original center between the port and the Plaza de Armas, properly known as Plaza Muñoz Gamero. Street names change on either side of the plaza, but street addresses fronting on the plaza bear the name Muñoz Gamero. Most landmarks and accommodations are within a few blocks of here. Mirador La Cruz, at Fagnano and Señoret, four blocks west of the plaza, provides a good view of town and the strait.

Most city streets are one-way, although grassy medians divide Av Bulnes and a few other major thoroughfares. There are two main routes out of town: Av Costanera leads south to Fuerte Bulnes, and Av Bulnes heads north past the airport eventually becoming Ruta 9 to Puerto Natales, which branches off to Ruta 255 to Río Gallegos, Argentina. Travelers coming from Argentina will find Chilean traffic much less hazardous than the Argentine variety.

Information

Sernatur (☎ 225-385, serna12a@entelchile .net), the Chilean state tourist agency, is at Waldo Seguel 689, just off Plaza Muñoz Gamero. It's open 8:30 am to 5:45 pm weekdays, but it has extended January and February hours: 8:30 am to 8 pm weekdays, 11 am to 7 pm Saturday and 11 am to 3 pm Sunday. It has a friendly, helpful and well-informed staff that includes English speakers, publishes an annually updated list of accommodations and transport and provides a message board for foreign visitors.

The municipal Kiosko de Informaciones (☎ 223-798), in the 700 block of Av Colón, between Bories and Magallanes, is open 9 am to 7 pm weekdays all year, and 9 am to 7 pm Saturday in summer.

The Automóvil Club de Chile (Acchi; ☎ 243-675), O'Higgins 931, provides information for motorists, rents cars and honors auto club memberships from other countries.

Money changing is easiest at the cambios and travel agencies along Lautaro Navarro, which are open weekdays and Saturday morning, but not on Sunday. Traveler's checks are more widely accepted than in Argentina, but many hotels and restaurants also accept US dollars at a fair rate of exchange. Bus Sur, at Magallanes and Colón, cashes traveler's checks for Saturday afternoon arrivals.

Redbanc has an ATM at Bories 970, half a block north of the plaza, and there are several others ATMs in the vicinity.

Correos de Chile is at Bories 911, one block north of Plaza Muñoz Gamero.

Long-distance telephone calls can be made at CTC, Nogueira 1116, on Plaza Muñoz Gamero; Chilexpress, Errázuriz 856; and Entel, Lautaro Navarro 931.

For Internet access, try Austro Internet (☎ 229-297), Croacia 690; the Canadian Institute (☎ 227-943), O'Higgins 694; or the Albergue Backpacker's Paradise, Ignacio Carrera Pinto 1022.

For information on national parks, Conaf (☎ 223-841) is at José Menéndez 1147.

In addition to the agencies listed under Organized Tours, try also Turismo Pehoé (☎ 241-373), José Menéndez 918, or Turismo Cordillera Darwin (☎/fax 224-637, c_darwin@ patagonian.com), José Menéndez 386, which arranges trips to remote parts of Tierra del Fuego.

A good, reliable place for film developing, including slides, is Todocolor, Chiloé 1422, between Av Independencia and Boliviana.

Southern Patagonia Souvenirs and Books, Bories 404, has a good selection of printed material and maps, including some in English.

Lavasol (☎ 243-607), O'Higgins 969, isn't cheap, but it's fast with your laundry.

The Hospital Regional (☎ 244-040) is at Arauco and Angamos.

Walking Tour

Punta Arenas' compact downtown rewards walkers. The logical starting place is the lovingly maintained **Plaza Muñoz Gamero**, landscaped with a variety of exotic conifers and a Victorian kiosk (1910) that sometimes contains handicraft displays. In the plaza's center is a monument to the 400th anniversary of Magellan's voyage, donated by wool baron José Menéndez in 1920; Magellan stands on a pedestal, and on a lower level stand a Selknam Indian, symbolizing Tierra del Fuego, and a Tehuelche, symbolizing Patagonia. Behind the Portuguese navigator are a globe and a copy of his log; beneath him is a mermaid with Chilean and regional coats of arms.

Around the plaza are the **Club de la Unión** (once the Sara Braun mansion, built by a French architect and now a hotel and restaurant), the **Catedral**, the restored **Intendencia Regional** and other monuments to the city's early-19th-century splendor. At the northeast corner of the plaza, the present Citibank was the headquarters of the powerful Sociedad Menéndez Behety.

Half a block north, at Magallanes 949, is the spectacular **Casa Braun-Menéndez**, the famous family's mansion which is now a cultural center and regional history museum.

Three blocks west of the plaza, the outlandish **stone castle** at Av España 959 belonged to Charly Milward, whose equally eccentric exploits inspired his distant relation Bruce Chatwin to write the extraordinary travelogue *In Patagonia*.

Four blocks south of the plaza, at the foot of Av Independencia, is the entrance to the **puerto** (port), which is open to the public. At the end of the pier, you may see ships and sailors from the Chilean navy, as well as from Spain, Poland, Japan, France, the USA, and many other countries, not to mention local fishing boats and countless seabirds. At the corner of Colón and O'Higgins, four blocks northeast of the plaza, is a very fine **mural** of Nobel Prize-winning poet Gabriela Mistral.

Six blocks north of the plaza, at Bories and Sarmiento, is the **Museo Salesiano** (Salesian Museum). Another four blocks north is the entrance to the **Cementerio Municipal** (Municipal Cemetery), an open-air historical museum in its own right.

Casa Braun-Menéndez

Also known as the Palacio Mauricio Braun, this opulent mansion testifies to the wealth and power of pioneer sheep farmers in the late 19th century. After the last remaining daughter of Mauricio Braun (brother of Sara Braun) and Josefina Menéndez Behety (daughter of José Menéndez and María Behety) died some years ago in Buenos Aires, the family donated the house to the state. Much of it, including original furnishings, remains as it did when still occupied by the family. At present, only the main floor is open to the public, but restoration may permit access to the upper floors.

The Casa Braun-Menéndez (☎ 244-216) also has excellent historical photographs and artifacts of early European settlement. The admission fee is modest (US$1.60, US$0.80 for children, free on holidays), but there's an extra charge for photographing the interior. Hours are 11 am to 5 pm Tuesday to Friday, 11 am to 2 pm weekends and holidays. Access to the grounds is easiest from Magallanes, but the museum entrance is at the back of the house.

Museo Regional Salesiano Mayorino Borgatello

Especially influential in European settlement of the region, the Salesian order collected outstanding ethnographic artifacts, but its museum takes a self-serving view of the Christian intervention, simplistically portraying missionaries as peacemakers between Indians and settlers. The moldy natural history specimens are nothing to speak of, however. The best materials are on the mountaineer priest Alberto de Agostini and the various indigenous groups. A real surprise is the cross salvaged from the grave of Pringle Stokes, an officer who died on the *Beagle* in 1828; the rotting cross was replaced by another on site.

Hours at the Museo (☎ 241-096), Av Bulnes 374, are 9 am to noon and 3 to 6 pm daily except Monday. Admission is US$2 for adults, US$1 for children.

Museo Naval y Marítimo

In addition to its formal military music and romantic viewpoint on Chile's presence in the southern oceans, Punta Arenas' naval and maritime museum has various exhibits on model ships, naval history (including the obligatory homage to patriotic icon Arturo Prat) and the unprecedented visit of 27 US warships to Punta Arenas in 1908.

Also on view are materials on southern Patagonia's Canoe Indians, and a fine account of the Chilean mission that rescued famous British explorer Sir Ernest Shackleton's crew from Antarctica. The most imaginative display is a ship's replica, complete with bridge, maps, charts and radio room, which really gives the sense of being on board a naval vessel.

At Pedro Montt 981, the Museo (☎ 205-558) is open 9:30 am to 12:30 pm and 3 to 6 pm Tuesday through Saturday. Admission is US$0.60 for adults, US$0.40 for children.

Museo Militar de la Quinta División del Ejército

The army museum (☎ 240-230), José Menéndez 961, is open 9 am to 5 pm daily except Monday. Admission is free.

MAGALLANES

Cementerio Municipal

In death as in life, Punta Arenas' first families flaunted their wealth – wool baron José Menéndez's extravagant tomb is, according to Bruce Chatwin, a scale replica of Rome's Vittorio Emanuele monument. Sara Braun's remains rest on a plot larger than many of the city's gardens, but the headstones among the topiary cypresses in the walled municipal cemetery, at Av Bulnes 949, also tell the stories of the Anglo, German, Scandinavian and Yugoslav immigrants who supported the wealthy families with their labor.

There's also a monument to the Onas, now nearly extinct, and another to German casualties of the 1914 Battle of the Falklands, during which Admiral Graf Spee was the highest-ranking of those who died on any of the ships the *Gneisenau*, *Nürnberg* and *Scharnhorst*.

Open daily, the cemetery is about a 15-minute walk from Plaza Muñoz Gamero, but you can also take any taxi colectivo from the entrance of the Casa Braun-Menéndez on Magallanes. At the entrance, the city has posted a map of the most significant gravesites.

Instituto de la Patagonia

Part of the Universidad de Magallanes, the Patagonian Institute's **Museo del Recuerdo** features a collection of antique farm and industrial machinery imported from Europe, a typical pioneer house and shearing shed (both reconstructed) and a wooden-wheeled trailer that served as shelter for shepherds. Visitors can wander among the outdoor exhibits at will, but you should ask the caretaker at the library for admission to the buildings.

The library also has a display of historical maps and a series of historical and scientific publications for sale to the public. A rather overgrown botanical garden, a small zoo and experimental garden plots and greenhouses are also open to the public.

Admission to the museum (☎ 207-196), Av Bulnes 01890, is US$1 for adults, free for children. Hours are 8:30 am to 12:30 pm and 2:30 to 6 pm weekdays, 8:30 am to 12:30 pm on Saturday. Any taxi colectivo to the *Zona Franca* (duty-free zone) will drop you across the street.

Organized Tours

Several agencies run trips to the important tourist sites near Punta Arenas, as well as to more distant destinations such as Torres del Paine.

Turismo Pali Aike (☎/fax 223-301), Lautaro Navarro 1129, goes to Cerro Mirador in the Reserva Nacional de Magallanes (US$5 roundtrip), west of town, at 10:30 am and 2:30 pm Tuesday to Sunday; to the Seno Otway (Otway Sound) penguin colony (US$10 to US$12) daily at 4 pm; to Fuerte Bulnes (US$12) daily at 10 am; and, less frequently, to Río Verde (US$15). All tours include sandwiches and soft drinks.

Other agencies running similar trips include Arka Patagonia (☎ 248-167), Ignacio Carrera Pinto 946; Turismo Aonikenk (☎ 228-332), Magallanes 619; Turismo Viento Sur (☎ 225-167), Fagnano 565; Chile Tours (☎ 244-505), Balmaceda 707; and Transportes Polo Sur (☎ 243-173), Chiloé 873. There's also Ecotour Patagonia (☎ 223-670, ecopatagonia@entelchile.net), Croacia 970; and Operatur Patagónica (☎ 240-513), Av Colón 822. Since the outings are short enough, most of these companies do both the Seno Otway and Fuerte Bulnes trips in the same day.

For penguin enthusiasts, a better though more expensive alternative is trip to the Isla Magdalena penguin colony run by Turismo Comapa (☎ 241322, tcomapa@entelchile .net), Av Independencia 830, 2nd floor. The ferry *Melinka*, which regularly connects Punta Arenas with Porvenir, also carries passengers to Isla Magdalena (US$30) Tuesday, Thursday and Saturday from December to February. Total time on the island is only about one and a half hours, and the crossing takes two hours each way, but the density of birds is higher and the scenery better.

Boat Cruises From September through April, Turismo Comapa (☎ 241-437, fax 224-526), Av Independencia 830, the local representative of Cruceros Australis, arranges weeklong luxury cruises on the 100-passenger

Terra Australis from Punta Arenas through the Cordillera de Darwin, the Beagle Channel and Puerto Williams, Ushuaia (Argentina), and back. It is possible to do the leg between Punta Arenas and Ushuaia, or vice versa, separately. For details, see boxed text 'Border Crossings with Argentina' in the Getting There and Away chapter.

From the beginning of November through February, Comapa also arranges Antarctic cruises with Russian ships, though most such trips now leave from Ushuaia, on Argentine Tierra del Fuego. It is also the Punta Arenas representative for Navimag's *Puerto Edén*, which plies the fjords from Puerto Natales to Puerto Montt.

Special Events

At the end of March, the **Carnaval de Invierno** welcomes the winter with two days of parades and floats, also celebrating the city's anniversary.

Places to Stay

Prices for accommodations have risen recently, but there are still good values to be found. Sernatur maintains a very complete list of accommodations and prices. Note that, at some hotels, guests paying in US dollars may be exempt from IVA.

Budget Open November through March, the hostel *Albergue Backpacker's Paradise* (☎ 222-554, bparadise@ctcreuna.cl, Ignacio Carrera Pinto 1022) charges US$6 for dark, cramped dormitory accommodations, but it has pleasant common rooms, a kitchen, Internet access and cable TV.

Six blocks south of Plaza Muñoz Gamero, *Colegio Pierre Fauré* (☎ 226-256, Bellavista 697) is a private school that operates as a hostel in January and February. Singles cost US$7 with breakfast, US$6 without, but campers can also pitch a tent in the side garden for US$4 per person. All bathrooms are shared, but there's plenty of hot water, and it's a good place to hook up with other travelers.

Hostelling International-affiliated *Hostal Sonia* (☎ 248-543, Pasaje Darwin 175), north of downtown, charges US$10 with hostel membership card.

Sernatur has reclassified most of the city's hospedajes and residenciales as hostales, but this is pretty much a semantic issue. Popular *Hostal Dinka's House* (☎ 226-056, fax 244-292, Caupolicán 169), on a quiet street, costs only US$7.50 with breakfast and shared bath, US$10 with private bath, but it's often full. Avoid their nearby annexes, which are unpleasant.

Homey *Hospedaje Guisande* (☎ 243-295, JM Carrera 1270), near the cemetery, has earned exuberant recommendations from readers for its accommodations, which cost US$9 with breakfast. *Hospedaje Manuel* (☎ 220-567, O'Higgins 648) has similar accommodations for US$9/15 and also organizes tours. In the port zone, south of downtown, are *Hospedaje Carlina* (☎ 247-687, Paraguaya 150) and *Hospedaje Nena* (☎ 242-411, Boliviana 366). Both charge about US$9 per person with breakfast; Nena's breakfast gets raves.

At recommended *Hostal O'Higgins* (☎ 227-999, O'Higgins 1205), near the port, rates are US$12 per person. Popular *Residencial Roca* (☎ 243-903, Magallanes 888, 2nd floor), which has moved to new quarters, has singles/doubles for US$12/22 with breakfast and shared bath.

Other modest and modestly priced alternatives include *Residencial Oasis* (☎ 223-240, Fagnano 583) with singles for about US$13, and friendly *Residencial Coirón* (☎ 226-449, Sanhueza 730), across from the Fernández bus terminal, which has spacious, sunny singles for US$13 with breakfast.

The lively Pucón cooperative ¡Ecole! has recently opened *¡Ecole! Patagonia* (☎ 221-764, O'Higgins 424), where singles cost US$14 with breakfast. It also plans to be a clearinghouse for environmental information in southern Chile and Argentina. *Hostal Rubio* (☎ 226-458, Av España 640) is a good value, at US$15/21 singles/doubles with shared bath, and US$25/40 with private bath, both with breakfast.

Recommended *Hostal Calafate II* (☎ 241-281, José Menéndez 1035) charges US$16/30 for singles/doubles with shared bath, while *Hostal Oasis* (☎ 226-849, José Menéndez 485) is slightly dearer at US$17/30.

MAGALLANES

Hostal Paradiso (☎/fax 224-212, Angamos 1073) is an excellent value, at US$18/20 for singles/doubles with shared bath, US$25/30 with private bath. In addition to hostel accommodations, *Hostal Sonia* (☎ 248-543, Pasaje Darwin 175) has regular rooms for US$22/40.

Rehabbed *Hotel Montecarlo* (☎ 223-438, Av Colón 605) charges US$21/35 for singles/doubles with shared bath, US$38/52 with private bath. Recommended *Hostal Calafate* (☎ 248-415, Lautaro Navarro 850) charges US$25/38 for singles/doubles and serves a substantial breakfast.

Mid-Range Mid-range accommodations are relatively scarce compared with the number of budget and top-end places. *Hostal de la Patagonia* (☎/fax 249-970, Croacia 970) costs US$30/44 with private bath, but has some doubles with shared bath for US$30. *Hostal Carpa Manzano* (☎ 242-296, fax 248-864, Lautaro Navarro 336) is also worth a try, at US$36/44, as is *Hostal de la Avenida* (☎/fax 247-532, Colón 534), at US$44/50.

Comfortable, modern *Hotel Cóndor de Plata* (☎ 247-987, fax 241-149, Av Colón 556) charges US$48/60, a good value. *Hotel Mercurio* (☎ 223-430, Fagnano 595) is also modern, clean and comfortable, charging US$49/63 with breakfast. Convenient *Hotel Plaza* (☎ 241-300, fax 248-613, Nogueira 1116) charges US$57/68.

Top End There are good initial reports on the new *Hotel Tierra del Fuego* (☎/fax 226-200, Av Colón 716). It charges US$98/109 singles/doubles. Once the best in town, the declining but still passable *Hotel Los Navegantes* (☎ 244-677, fax 247-545, José Menéndez 647) has rooms for US$100/126. Another relatively new top-end choice is *Hotel Isla Rey Jorge* (☎/fax 222-681, 21 de Mayo 1243), for US$105/130.

On the east side of Plaza Muñoz Gamero, refurbished *Hotel Cabo de Hornos* (☎/fax 442-134), charges US$131/155. It has a good but expensive bar, and its solarium displays a number of stuffed birds, including rockhopper and macaroni penguins, which visitors to local penguin colonies are unlikely to see.

Hotel Finis Terrae (☎ 228-200, fax 248-124, Av Colón 766) costs US$127/144.

Part of the Sara Braun mansion has become *Hotel José Nogueira* (☎ 248-840, fax 248-832, Bories 959), half a block from Plaza Muñoz Gamero. Rooms cost US$151/180 singles/doubles, but selective backpackers can still enjoy a drink or a meal in its conservatory-restaurant, beneath what may be the world's most southerly grapevine arbor.

Places to Eat

At *222* (☎ 224-704, Mejicana 654), you'll find good pizza and tasty sandwiches. *Quijote* (Lautaro Navarro 1087) also has reasonably priced lunches. *La Carioca* (☎ 224-809, José Menéndez 600) has good sandwiches and lager beer, although its pizzas are, like most Chilean pizzas, small and relatively expensive. *Rotisería La Mamá* (☎ 225-812, Sanhueza 720), across from the Fernández bus terminal, is a small, family-run place with excellent, moderately priced lunches.

A good choice for breakfast, *onces* (afternoon tea) and people-watching is *Café Calipso* (☎ 241-782, Bories 817), whose 'selva negra' chocolate cake is served in portions large enough for two, as are their sandwiches. *Lomit's* (☎ 243-399, José Menéndez 722) also serves excellent sandwiches.

A local institution, *El Mercado* (☎ 247-415, Mejicana 617, 2nd floor), an upstairs restaurant with an inconspicuous ground-level entrance, prepares a spicy *ostiones al pil pil* and a delicate but filling *chupe de locos*; prices are generally moderate. It's open 24 hours a day but adds a 10% surcharge between 1 and 8 am.

The *Centro Español* (☎ 242-807), above the Teatro Cervantes on the south side of Plaza Muñoz Gamero, serves delicious *cóngrio* and ostiones, among other specialties. *Golden Dragón* (☎ 241-119, Colón 529), a Chinese restaurant, is also very good.

Highly regarded *Sotito's Bar* (☎ 245-365, O'Higgins 1138) serves outstanding but pricey dishes such as *centolla* (king crab), but it also has reasonably priced items. The same is true of nearby *El Beagle* (☎ 243-057, O'Higgins 1077). Prices are moderate at *La*

Taberna de Silver (☎ 225-533, O'Higgins 1037), although its fish is often deep-fried. Another recommended restaurant, specializing in lamb, is *El Mesón del Calvo* (☎ 225-015, Jorge Montt 687), but sometimes the food isn't as good as the atmosphere.

Asturias (☎ 243-763, Lautaro Navarro 967), at the upper end of the scale, is worth a try, as is *El Infante* (☎ 241-331, Magallanes 875). *La Casa de Juan* (☎ 223-463, O'Higgins 1021) is a seafood venue.

Entertainment

Chilean nightlife is more exuberant than it was under the late military dictatorship, but no one will mistake Punta Arenas for Buenos Aires. *Café Calipso* (see Places to Eat) has a lively crowd late into the evening and sometimes has live entertainment. *Nómade* (☎ 240-893, Mejicana 733) is a pub with fajitas and the like, and occasional live music. Try *Disco Splash* (☎ 223-667, Pedro Montt 951) and the *Olijoe Pub* (Errázuriz and O'Higgins) for dancing.

Two cinemas often show North American and European films: *Teatro Cervantes* (☎ 223-225), on the south side of Plaza Muñoz Gamero, and the *Sala Estrella* (☎ 241-262, Mejicana 777).

On the outskirts of downtown, on Av Bulnes, are the *Club Hípico* (municipal racetrack) and the *Estadio Fiscal* (stadium), where the local entry in the Chilean soccer league plays.

Shopping

Punta Arenas' *Zona Franca* (duty-free zone) is a good place to go to replace a lost or stolen camera and to buy film and other luxury items. Fujichrome slide film, 36 exposures, costs about US$5 per roll without developing, but it is increasingly difficult to find; print film is correspondingly cheap. Taxi colectivos run frequently from downtown to the Zona Franca, which is open daily except Sunday.

Chile Típico (☎ 225-827), Ignacio Carrera Pinto 1015, offers artisanal items in copper, bronze, lapis lazuli and other materials. Tres Arroyos (☎ 241-522), Bories 448, sells a variety of chocolates.

To replace a shattered windshield on a private car – not an unusual occurrence on Patagonian roads – go to Solovidrios (☎ 224-835), Mejicana 762. Prices here are a fraction of what they are in Argentina.

Getting There & Away

Sernatur distributes a useful brochure containing information on all forms of transportation, including modes of travel to and through Argentina and route schedules to and from Punta Arenas, Puerto Natales and Tierra del Fuego. Note that discount airfares are available from the major airlines between Punta Arenas and mainland Chile but usually involve some restrictions.

Air From Punta Arenas, there are flights to domestic destinations, including Chilean Antarctic bases, and to Argentine Patagonia and the Falkland Islands. There are, however, no direct flights to Ushuaia, in Argentine Tierra del Fuego; travelers must fly to Río Grande and catch a connecting flight on an Argentine airline.

LanChile (☎ 241-232), Lautaro Navarro 999, flies daily to Santiago (US$141 to US$284) via Puerto Montt (US$83 to US$155), and Wednesday and Saturday via Concepción (US$113 to US$158). It also flies Saturday to the Falkland Islands (US$200 one-way); one Falklands flight per month stops in the Argentine city of Río Gallegos. Ladeco (☎ 244-544), Lautaro Navarro 1155, flies twice daily to Santiago via Puerto Montt.

Avant (☎ 227-221, fax 228-322), Roca 924, flies daily to Santiago (US$133 to US$206) via Puerto Montt (US$77 to US$127) except Sunday (two flights); one Sunday flight stops in Temuco, while the other stops in Concepción (US$108 to US$156).

Aerovías DAP (☎ 223-340, fax 221-693), O'Higgins 891, flies to Porvenir (US$22) and back at least twice daily except Sunday. It flies to and from Puerto Williams on Isla Navarino on Tuesday, Thursday and Saturday (US$66 one-way). In summer, it also flies daily except Sunday to Río Grande (US$79). DAP also flies monthly to Chile's Teniente Marsh air base in Antarctica (US$1000); the schedule permits a stay of one or two nights in Antarctica before returning to Punta Arenas.

Bus Punta Arenas has no central bus terminal; each company has its own office from which its buses depart, although most of these are within a block or two of Av Colón. There are direct buses to Puerto Natales, to the Argentine cities of Río Gallegos, Río Grande and Ushuaia, and to mainland Chilean destinations via Argentina. It makes sense to purchase tickets at least a couple of hours in advance.

Buses Fernández (☎ 242-313), Armando Sanhueza 745, has seven buses daily except Sunday to Puerto Natales (US$7, three hours) and a reputation for excellent service. Transfer Austral (☎ 229-613), Pedro Montt 966, goes to Natales at 5 and 6:30 pm daily.

Bus Sur (☎ 244-464), at Magallanes and Colón and at José Menéndez 565 (☎ 247-139), has five buses daily to Natales; it also goes Monday to Coihaique (US$52) and Tuesday to Osorno and Puerto Montt (US$97).

Buses Punta Arenas (☎ 249-868), Ignacio Carrera Pinto 457, makes the journey to Puerto Montt (US$71) Wednesday and Saturday at 8:30 am. Turibús (☎ 227-970), Armando Sanhueza 745, leaves Monday, Thursday and Saturday for Puerto Montt (US$75), Castro (US$85), Concepción (US$95) and Santiago (US$100). The trips take up to two days, but these comfortable buses make regular meal stops.

There are numerous services to Río Gallegos, Argentina (US$13 to US$18 one-way, five hours; the fare in the opposite direction exceeds US$20). The most frequent is Buses Pingüino (☎ 221-812, 242-313), Armando Sanhueza 745, daily at 12:45 pm. Buses Ghisoni (☎ 222-078), Lautaro Navarro 971, leaves Monday, Wednesday, Thursday and Saturday at 11 am. Buses Pacheco (☎ 242-174), Av Colón 900, leaves Tuesday, Friday and Sunday at noon for Río Gallegos and Monday, Wednesday and Friday at 8:30 am for Río Grande (US$27), with connections to Ushuaia. Tecni-Austral (☎ 223-205), Lautaro Navarro 975,

goes direct to Río Grande (US$30) and Ushuaia (US$51) Tuesday, Thursday and Saturday at 7 am.

Boat Transbordador Austral Broom (☎ 218-100, fax 212-126), Av Bulnes 05075, ferries passengers (US$7), motorcycles (US$15) and automobiles (US$38) between Punta Arenas and Porvenir in 2½ hours; the *Melinka* sails Tuesday, Wednesday and Friday at 9 am; Thursday and Saturday at 8 am; and Sunday at 9:30 am from the terminal at Tres Puentes, readily accessible by taxi colectivo from the Casa Braun-Menéndez. The return from Porvenir normally leaves at 2 pm; on Sundays and holidays, when the ferry departs at 5 pm, it's possible to do this as a day trip.

Broom is also the agent for the ferry *Crux Australis*, which sails weekly to Puerto Williams on Isla Navarino. Reclining Pullman seats on the 38-hour trip cost US$120, including meals; bunks cost US$150.

Turismo Comapa (☎ 224-256, fax 225-804) Av Independencia 830, is the local representative for Navimag, which offers a weekly car and passenger ferry service from Puerto Natales to Puerto Montt on the *MV Puerto Edén*, via the spectacular Chilean fjords. The ferry operates year-round, although dates and times vary according to weather and tides. The four-day, three-night voyage is heavily booked in summer, so advance reservations are recommended. It's generally easier to get a berth going northbound.

Getting Around

To/From the Airport Aeropuerto Presidente Carlos Ibáñez del Campo is 20km north of town. Transfer Austral (☎ 220-766), Pedro Montt 966, operates scheduled service (US$2) two hours before each flight from the respective airline office. It also provides door-to-door transfers (US$4) by reservation, as does Transportes Polo Sur (☎ 243-173), Chiloé 873.

Some long-distance bus companies on the Puerto Natales-Punta Arenas route, most notably Bus Sur and Fernández, will drop their passengers at the airport to meet their outgoing flights, eliminating the need to backtrack from downtown Punta Arenas. Travelers should verify this service in advance, however.

Bus & Taxi Colectivo Although most points of interest are within easy walking distance of downtown, public transportation is excellent to outlying sights, such as the Instituto de la Patagonia and the Zona Franca. Taxi colectivos, with numbered routes, are only slightly more expensive than buses (about US$0.40, and a bit more late at night and on Sunday), much more comfortable and much quicker.

Car Punta Arenas' numerous rental agencies include Hertz (☎ 248-742, fax 244-729), O'Higgins 987; Emsa-Avis (☎/fax 241-182), Roca 1022; Budget (☎/fax 241-696), O'Higgins 964; the Automóvil Club de Chile (☎ 243-675, fax 243-097), O'Higgins 931; Internacional (☎ 228-323, fax 226-334), Waldo Seguel 443; and Lubag (☎/fax 242-023), at Magallanes 970.

AROUND PUNTA ARENAS
Pingüineras (Penguin Colonies)
Also known as the jackass penguin for its characteristic braying sound, the Magellanic penguin *Spheniscus magellanicus* comes ashore in spring to breed and lay its eggs in sandy burrows or under shrubs a short distance inland. There are two substantial colonies near Punta Arenas; the easier one to reach is the mainland pingüinera at **Seno Otway**, about an hour northwest of the city, while the larger (50,000 breeding pairs) and more interesting **Monumento Natural Los Pingüinos** is accessible only by the ferry *Melinka* to Isla Magdalena in the Strait of Magellan. Several cormorant and gull species are also commonly found there, along with rheas and southern sea lions.

Magellanic penguins are naturally curious and tame, although if approached too quickly they will scamper into burrows or toboggan awkwardly across the sand back into the water. If you get too close, they will bite, and their bills can open a cut large enough to require stitches – never stick your hand or face into a burrow. The least disruptive way

to observe or photograph them is to seat yourself among the burrows and wait for their curiosity to get the better of them.

Penguins are usually present from October to April, but the peak season is December through February. Visitors who have seen the larger colonies in Argentina or the Falkland Islands may be less impressed than those who have not seen penguins elsewhere. If you have a choice, Isla Magdalena more than justifies the extra expense; even though, strictly speaking, it's transport rather than a tour, Conaf rangers are on hand to answer questions.

At Otway, the grounds are fenced to prevent visitors from having too close an encounter; a morning tour is generally better for photography because the birds are mostly backlit in the afternoon. En route to Isla Magdalena, birders will spot South American terns, black-browed albatrosses, and kelp gulls as well as Magellanic penguins. The landscape – both beaches and headlands – is more appealing than that at Otway.

From the shore at Isla Magdalena, there's a trail to Conaf's **Centro de Visitantes**, a restored 1902 lighthouse that contains brief accounts of the island's history and natural history in English (alongside lengthier ones in Spanish). It's possible to climb the steep and narrow spiral staircase for a panoramic view – and virtually every open spot on this grassy island hosts a penguin burrow. The downside is that you get only about an hour on shore.

Since there is no scheduled public transport to either penguin colony, it's necessary to rent a car or take a tour to visit them. For details, see Organized Tours in Punta Arenas. Admission to the Otway site costs US$4 per person, while the cost of admission is included in the price of the Isla Magdalena ferry trip. There's a small snack bar at the Otway site, while the *Melinka* sells sandwiches and soft drinks.

Puerto Hambre & Fuerte Bulnes
Founded in 1584 by an overly confident Pedro Sarmiento de Gamboa, 'Ciudad del Rey Don Felipe' was one of Spain's most

inauspicious (and short-lived) American outposts. Not until the mid-19th century was there a permanent European presence at suitably named Puerto Hambre ('Port Famine'); a plaque in Puerto Hambre commemorates the 125th anniversary of the arrival of the Pacific Steam Navigation Company's ships *Chile* and *Peru* in 1965.

Named for the Chilean president who ordered occupation of the territory in 1843, the once-remote outpost of Fuerte Bulnes is 55km south of Punta Arenas. Only a few years after its founding, it was abandoned because of its exposed site, scant potable water, rocky soil and inferior pastures.

A good gravel road runs from Punta Arenas to the decaying wooden fort, itself a restoration, where a fence of sharpened stakes surrounds the blockhouse, barracks and chapel, but there is no explanatory material whatsoever. Nor is there any scheduled public transport, but several travel agencies make half-day excursions to Fuerte Bulnes and Puerto Hambre, now a quiet fishing village where visitors can see the ruins of an early church; for details, see the Organized Tours entry for Punta Arenas. There are good picnic sites and pleasant trails along the coast.

Río Verde
About 50km north of Punta Arenas, a graveled lateral leads northwest toward Seno Skyring (Skyring Sound), passing the former Estancia La Mirna before rejoining Ruta 9 at Villa Tehuelches. Visitors with a car should consider making this interesting detour to one of the best-maintained assemblages of Magellanic architecture in the region, including the impressive **Escuela Básica**, a boarding school for the surrounding area and the estancia's shearing shed. The school's **Museo de Fauna** charges US$0.50 admission. Note the town's topiary cypresses.

Six kilometers south of Río Verde proper, 90km from Punta Arenas, *Hostería Río Verde* (☎ *311-122*) is well known for its large portions of lamb, pork or seafood served at its Sunday lunches, for about US$10. Despite the rustic exterior, it also offers snug, comfortable accommodations for US$30 with private bath.

Río Rubens
Roughly midway between Villa Tehuelches and Puerto Natales on Ruta 9, Río Rubens is a fine trout-fishing area and an ideal spot to break up the journey from Punta Arenas, at least for travelers with their own transport. The cozy, comfy *Hotel Río Rubens* is the closest thing to a country-style inn in the region, and at US$14 per person with breakfast and private bath, it's a bargain. The restaurant serves outstanding meals, including lamb and seafood.

Estancia San Gregorio
Some 125km northeast of Punta Arenas, straddling Ruta 255 to Río Gallegos (Argentina), this once-enormous estancia (originally 90,000 hectares) is now a cooperative. Since the abandonment of most of the main buildings (employee residences, warehouses, chapel and *pulpería*, or general store), it has the aspect of a gigantic ghost town. The *casco* still belongs to Alfonso Campos, a lawyer and a descendant of the influential Menéndez family, but the cooperative uses the large shearing shed. Also worth a look are the rusting hulks of the *Ambassador* and the steamer *Amadeo*, the latter intentionally beached here in the 1940s after half a century's service to the Menéndez-Behety regime.

The nearest accommodations are at *Hostería Tehuelche* (☎ *221-270*), 29km northeast, where buses to and from Río Gallegos stop for lunch or dinner; this is also the junction for the road to the ferry that crosses the Strait of Magellan from Punta Delgada to Chilean Tierra del Fuego. Until 1968, the hostería was the casco for Estancia Kimiri Aike, pioneered by the Woods, a British immigrant family. Open November to May only, it has clean, comfortable rooms for US$30/38 singles/doubles and a good restaurant and bar. Hotel staff will change US dollars at fair rates, but Argentine currency is better changed before leaving Río Gallegos.

Parque Nacional Pali Aike
Along the Argentine border, west of the Monte Aymond border crossing to Río

Gallegos, this 5030-hectare park is an area of volcanic steppe where, in the 1930s, Junius Bird's excavations at **Cueva Pali Aike** (Pali Aike Cave) yielded the first Paleo-Indian artifacts associated with extinct New World fauna such as the milodon and the native horse *Onohippidium*. Bird, a self-taught archaeologist affiliated with the American Museum of Natural History, spent two and a half years here and excavated **Fell's Cave**, just outside the park boundaries. Research conducted here has suggested that environmental change rather than hunting pressure led to the extinction of these animals.

The park has several hiking trails, including a 1700m path through the rugged lava beds of the **Escorial del Diablo** to the impressive **Crater Morada del Diablo**; wear sturdy shoes or your feet could get shredded. There is ample wildlife to be seen along the road, including guanaco, fox, bandurria (avocet) and rhea, but the real treat is the volcanic landscape. There's also a 9km trail from Cueva Pali Aike to **Laguna Ana**, where there's another shorter trail to a site on the main road, 5km from the park entrance.

Cueva Pali Aike itself measures 5m high and 7m wide at the entrance, and 17m deep. Bird's excavations in 1936 and '37 unearthed three cremated human skeletons, plus milodon and native horse bones, that were 9000 years old.

Parque Nacional Pali Aike is 196km northeast of Punta Arenas via Ch 9, Ch 255, and a graveled secondary road from Cooperativa Villa O'Higgins, 11km north of Estancia Kimiri Aike. There's also an access road from the Chilean border post at Monte Aymond, but this is more difficult to follow. There is no public transport, but Punta Arenas travel agencies can arrange tours.

There's a ranger at the main park entrance, but no regular accommodations or food and water; camping is permitted but fires are not.

PUERTO NATALES
☎ 61

Black-necked swans and sea kayakers paddle serenely around the gulls and cormorants that perch on the rotting jetties of scenic Puerto Natales, on the eastern shore of Seno Última Esperanza (Last Hope Sound). Dependent on its wool, mutton and fishing industries, this port of 18,000 people is the southern terminus for the scenic ferry from Puerto Montt and an essential stopover for hikers and other visitors en route to Parque Nacional Torres del Paine. It also offers the best access to Glaciar Serrano in Parque Nacional Bernardo O'Higgins and the famous Cueva del Milodón, and many travelers continue on to Argentina's Parque Nacional Los Glaciares via the coal-mining town of Río Turbio.

The visitor season starts in October and runs until April, although the peak is January and February. During the rest of the year, access to attractions such as Torres del Paine and the Balmaceda Glacier may be reduced, but the season continues to lengthen.

History
The first Europeans to visit Última Esperanza were the 16th-century Spaniards Juan Ladrillero and Pedro Sarmiento de Gamboa, in search of a route to the Pacific, but their expeditions left no permanent legacy. In part because of Indian resistance, no Europeans settled here until the late 19th century, when German explorer Hermann Eberhard established a sheep estancia near Puerto Prat, the area's initial settlement (later superseded by Puerto Natales).

The dominant economic enterprise was the slaughterhouse and meat packing plant at Bories, operated by the Sociedad Explotadora de Tierra del Fuego, which processed livestock from southwest Argentina as well. This factory still operates, though its importance has declined.

Orientation
About 250km northwest of Punta Arenas via Ruta 9, which should be completely paved by press time, Puerto Natales is compact enough that walking suffices for nearly all purposes. Its grid is more irregular than those of many Chilean cities, but most destinations are easily visible from the waterfront, where the Costanera Pedro Montt runs roughly east-west. Municipal authorities have undertaken

PUERTO NATALES

PLACES TO STAY
2 Casa Cecilia
12 Residencial Lago Pingo
13 Hotel Juan Ladrilleros
14 Hotel Eberhard
15 Residencial Almirante Nieto
17 Hotel Martín Gusinde
20 Residencial Patagonia
　Aventura
23 Hotel Natalino
27 Hostal La Cumbre
38 Residencial Temuco
40 Hotel Ludovieks
41 Hostal Indigo
42 Hospedaje Tequendama
45 Hostal Los Antiguos
46 Hotel Glaciares
47 Residencial Sutherland
49 Hostal Puerto Natales
53 Residencial La Casona
54 Hotel Milodón
55 Residencial Carahue
56 Hotel Bulnes

60 Hostal Lady Florence Dixie
61 Hotel Laguna Azul
64 Hotel Costa Australis
66 Hotel Palace
67 Hotel Lago Sarmiento
71 Hotel Blanquita
72 Hospedaje Teresa Ruiz
73 Residencial Asturias
75 Residencial Bernardita
78 Hospedaje Tierra del Fuego

PLACES TO EAT
19 Restaurant Midas
21 Última Esperanza
22 Pub Café Acris
34 La Repizza
39 La Frontera
41 Café Indigo
44 Los Pioneros
50 Gelatería Bruna
51 Los Glaciares
58 Gelatería Bruna
59 La Tranquera

65 El Marítimo
68 La Burbuja
70 La Herradura
79 Café Andrés

OTHER
1 Sernatur
3 LanChile, Ladeco
4 Tío Cacho
5 Turismo Cutter 21
　de Mayo
6 Ñandú Artesanía
7 Turismo Luis Díaz
8 Buses Lagoper
9 Turis Sur
10 Cootra
11 Entel
16 Catch
18 Chile Express
24 Post Office
25 Gobernación Provincial
26 Municipalidad
28 Turismo Zaahj

29 Buses JB
30 Buses Fernández
31 Andescape, Onas Patagonia
32 Banco Santiago
33 Cambio Mily
35 CTC (Telefónica)
36 Emsa, Avis
37 Southern Patagonia
　Souvenirs & Books
41 Concepto Indigo
43 Turismo Cutter 21 de Mayo
48 Tanspatagónica Express
52 Cambios Sur
57 Servilaundry
61 Stop Cambios
62 Transfer Austral
63 Navimag
69 Museo Histórico Municipal
74 Conaf
76 Bus Sur
77 Navimag Sala de Espera
80 Hospital Puerto Natales

To Puerto Bories, Cueva del
Milodón, Punta Arenas,
Torres del Paine

Seno Última Esperanza

Estero Natales

Stadium

Plaza
de
Armas

Cemetery

Plaza

Pier

Pier

To Residencial
María José

To Residencial La Bahía,
Museo Salesiano

MAGALLANES

an improvement program on the Costanera, creating a small amphitheater and several viewpoints, and shifting the city's sewage discharge away from the downtown area. Further improvements are likely to take place in the next few years.

The other main commercial streets are Av Manuel Bulnes, running north-south, and Av Baquedano, running east-west. Bories and the Cueva del Milodón are north of town on the graveled highway to Torres del Paine.

Information

Sernatur (☎/fax 412-125), which has maps along with hotel, restaurant and transport information, occupies an A-frame at the Costanera Pedro Montt 19, near the Philippi diagonal. Hours are 8:30 am to 1 pm and 2:30 to 6:30 pm weekdays all year, and 9 am to 1 pm weekends in summer (December to March) only.

Several cambios change US dollars and traveler's checks: try Stop Cambios, Baquedano 380; Cambio Mily, Blanco Encalada 266; and Cambios Sur, Eberhard 285. Banco Santiago, Bulnes 598, has an ATM.

Correos de Chile is directly on the Plaza de Armas at Eberhard 429. CTC (Telefónica), Blanco Encalada and Bulnes, operates long-distance telephone service 8 am to 10 pm daily, as does Chile Express, at Tomás Rogers 143. Entel is on Baquedano between Valdivia and Bulnes.

For access to the Internet, try La Repizza (☎ 410-361), Blanco Encalada 294, although it has better computer access than it does pizza. Casa Cecilia (see Puerto Natales' Places to Stay section) also has Internet access.

Information on national parks can be found at Conaf (☎ 411-438), O'Higgins 584.

Southern Patagonia Souvenirs and Books, Bulnes 688, has a selection of books and maps on the area, including some in English.

For laundry service, go to Servilaundry (☎ 412-869), Bulnes 513, or Catch, Bories 218.

Hospital Puerto Natales (☎ 411-533) is at O'Higgins and Ignacio Carrera Pinto.

Things to See

Recently expanded, Puerto Natales' **Museo Histórico Municipal** has natural history items (mostly stuffed animals), archaeological artifacts, such as stone and whalebone arrowheads and spearpoints, ethnographic materials such as a Yahgan canoe and Tehuelche bolas, details on agricultural colonization, and historical photographs of Captain Eberhard and of Puerto Natales' urban development. At Bulnes 285, the museum (☎ 411-263) is open 8:30 am to 12:30 pm and 2:30 to 6 pm weekdays, and 2:30 to 6 pm weekends. Admission is free.

As in Punta Arenas, the Salesian missionaries have a **Museo Colegio Salesiano** (☎ 411-258), at Padre Rosas 1456, focusing on natural history. It's open daily 10 am to 1 pm and 3 to 6 pm; admission is free.

Organized Tours

Puerto Natales' many travel agencies offer visits to the main local attractions, including Bories, the Cueva del Milodón and Torres del Paine. Among them are Turismo Luis Díaz (☎ 411-654, fax 411-050), Blanco Encalada 189, which also offers trips to Argentina's Parque Nacional Los Glaciares; Servitur (☎ 411-858), Prat 353; and Onas Patagonia (☎ 412-707), Eberhard 599, which leads sea kayaking and trekking trips. Most of these and other companies rent camping equipment as well.

Places to Stay

Particularly popular with budget travelers, Puerto Natales has over 70 different accommodations in all categories, so competition keeps prices reasonable. Off-season prices can drop dramatically, especially in mid-range to top-end lodgings, but many places close at summer's end.

Budget When your bus arrives, you may be besieged by people handing out business cards or slips of paper offering budget accommodations, almost all including breakfast. Quality is usually decent and may even be excellent.

Residencial María José (☎ *412-218, Magallanes 646*) is about the cheapest in town, at US$5 per person. Prices are as low as US$6 at *Residencial Lago Pingo* (☎ *413-848, Bulnes 808*). *Hospedaje Tierra del Fuego*

(☎ 412-138, Bulnes 23), convenient to the ferry, charges US$6 with breakfast and shared bath, as do **Residencial Asturias** (☎ 412-105, Prat 426), and enthusiastically recommended **Hospedaje Teresa Ruiz** (☎ 410-472, Esmeralda 463).

Residencial Patagonia Aventura (☎ 411-028, Tomás Rogers 179), which costs US$7, has drawn readers' praise for congeniality. In the same range are recommended **Residencial Almirante Nieto** (☎ 411-218, Bories 206) and attractive **Residencial La Casona** (☎ 412-562, Bulnes 280).

Hospedaje Tequendama (☎ 412-951, Ladrilleros 141) serves a good breakfast, but rooms are basic, and some are very dark, at US$7.50. Friendly, Scots-Chilean-run **Residencial Sutherland** (☎ 410-359, Barros Arana 155) charges US$7.50. **Hotel Bulnes** (☎ 411-307, Bulnes 407) charges US$8 per person with shared bath, and US$18/27 with private bath.

In the US$9 to US$10 range are **Residencial Bernardita** (☎ 411-162, O'Higgins 765), **Residencial Temuco** (☎/fax 411-120, Ramírez 310) and **Residencial Carahue** (☎ 411-339, Bulnes 370). Comparably priced **Residencial La Bahía** (☎ 411-297, Serrano 434), three blocks south of Yungay, also has a superb restaurant.

Nearly legendary for its delicious breakfasts with fresh bread and sweets, the impressively remodeled Swiss-Chilean-run **Casa Cecilia** (☎ 413-875, fax 411-797, Tomás Rogers 60, redcecilia@entelchile.net) has managed to keep prices reasonable, at US$10 to US$16 per person, depending on whether the facilities have private bath. The bright new atrium is a brilliant touch, encouraging guests to socialize, and there's a kitchen especially for guests.

More businesslike than friendly, well-kept **Hostal Los Antiguos** (☎ 411-885, Ladrilleros 195) charges US$11 single. **Hostal Puerto Natales** (☎ 411-098, Eberhard 250) charges US$12 per person for a room with private bath.

Puerto Natales' **Hostal Indigo** (☎ 410-678, info@conceptoindigo.com, Ladrilleros 105) is becoming a travelers' hangout, partly due to the downstairs pub-café (which closes early enough, however, for guests to get a good night's sleep) and the rock-climbing wall outside. Rates are US$15 in multibed rooms or US$35 double, but if it's not crowded they'll give you a single at the lower price. **Hostal La Cumbre** (☎ 412-422, Eberhard 533) charges US$17 per person.

Mid-Range Hotel **Blanquita** (☎ 411-674, Ignacio Carrera Pinto 409) charges US$21/25 for a room with private bath, plus an abundant breakfast. At recommended **Hotel Natalino** (☎ 411-968, Eberhard 371) rooms with private bath are US$25/31.

Hotel Laguna Azul (☎/fax 411-207, Baquedano 380) charges US$40/55, but there are also several other good values: **Hotel Lago Sarmiento** (☎ 411-542, Bulnes 90) has rooms for US$80/100; **Hotel Milodón** (☎ 411-727, fax 411-286, Bulnes 356) for US$35/52; and **Hotel Ludovieks** (☎ 412-580, Ramírez 324) for US$46/63. At the upper end of the range, set back off the street, the attractive **Hostal Lady Florence Dixie** (☎ 411-158, Bulnes 659) charges US$50/65.

Top End Clearly showing its age, the worn **Hotel Palace** (☎/fax 411-134, Ladrilleros 209) charges US$64/73. Rates at the stylishly new **Hotel Glaciares** (☎/fax 412-189, Eberhard 104) are US$83/96, but service is only so-so. Somewhere between the two in quality, but more expensive than both, is **Hotel Juan Ladrilleros** (☎ 411-652, fax 412-109, Pedro Montt 161) where rooms go for US$85/95. The new **Hotel Martín Gusinde** (☎ 412-770, fax 412-401, Bories 278) is an outstanding value at US$110/133.

With rooms for US$90/99, the waterfront **Hotel Eberhard** (☎ 411-208, fax 411-209, Costanera Pedro Montt 25) is overpriced despite an excellent dining room with panoramic harbor views. Also on the waterfront, at the corner of the Costanera Pedro Montt and Manuel Bulnes, the **Hotel Costa Australis** (☎ 412-000, 411-881, Pedro Montt 262) has rooms that start at US$130/147 with a town view, rising to US$164/181 with a harbor view.

Places to Eat

For a small, provincial town, Puerto Natales offers excellent dining, specializing in good, reasonably priced seafood. Open for lunch only, recommended *La Frontera (Bulnes 819)* has superb home-cooked meals for only US$4, but the service can be inconsistent. Popular *El Marítimo (Costanera Pedro Montt 214)*, a moderately priced seafood choice, is still doing excellent business, but has become self-consciously touristy, and its troubadours can be overbearing. Down the block, *Los Pioneros (☎ 410-783, Pedro Montt 166)* has a decent if unexceptional *salmón al ajo* (garlic salmon), large portions and friendly service.

Its walls covered with museum-quality bric-a-brac, *La Tranquera (☎ 411-039, Bulnes 579)* has good food, friendly service and reasonable prices. Another good and lively place is *Restaurant Midas (☎ 411-045, Tomás Rogers 169)*, on the Plaza de Armas. Only a handful of foreigners patronize the excellent *Última Esperanza (☎ 411-391, Eberhard 354)*, which has huge portions (salmon is a specialty) and fine service and is less expensive than it looks.

Another seafood choice is *Café Andrés (☎ 412-380, Ladrilleros 381)*, whose hardworking cook-owner keeps long hours. Other spots include *La Burbuja (☎ 411-159, Bulnes 291)*, *Los Glaciares (☎ 412-007, Eberhard 261)*, and *La Herradura (☎ 412-538, Bulnes 371)*, which has seafood and parrillada.

The dining room at unpretentious *La Bahía (☎ 411-297, Serrano 434)* can accommodate large groups for a superb *curanto* (seafood stew), with sufficient notice. It's less central than most other restaurants in town but still within reasonable walking distance.

Pub Café Acris (☎ 412-710, Eberhard 351), serves excellent pizza, but the tobacco-smoke-laden atmosphere may be a serious negative for nonsmokers. At *La Repizza (☎ 411-036, Blanco Encalada 294)*, the pizza is mediocre and the service is slow, but the other dishes are OK.

Rhubarb-flavored ice cream is a local specialty at *Gelatería Bruna (☎ 411-656, Bulnes 585, Eberhard 217)*.

Entertainment

In addition to good food, *Pub Café Acris (☎ 412-710, Eberhard 351)* offers live music on weekends. Another pub worth visiting is *Tío Cacho (☎ 411-021)*, Philippi 553, but it's only rarely open. Downstairs, the nightly slide shows at *Café Indigo (Ladrilleros 105)* are complemented by food and drinks and offer a good introduction to the Natales area.

Shopping

Ñandú Artesanía, Eberhard 586, has a small but good selection of crafts, and it also sells local maps and books.

Getting There & Away

Air Since the collapse of the short-hop airline Alta, Puerto Natales' small airfield, a few kilometers north of town on the road to Torres del Paine, has no regularly scheduled flights. Rumors of future commercial service persist, but there is political resistance from Punta Arenas, whose merchants fear (probably correctly) that many Paine-bound travelers would bypass their city.

The local LanChile and Ladeco offices (☎ 411-236) are in the same spot, at Tomás Rogers 78. Buses from Puerto Natales will drop passengers at Punta Arenas' Aeropuerto Presidente Carlos Ibáñez del Campo.

LADE, the Argentine air force passenger service, has flights to and from Río Turbio, just across the border.

Bus Puerto Natales has no central bus terminal, but several companies stop at the junction of Valdivia and Baquedano.

Bus service to Punta Arenas (US$7, three hours) is provided by Buses Fernández (☎ 411-111), at Eberhard 555, and Bus Sur (☎ 411-859), at Baquedano 534, with eight buses (between the two) Monday to Saturday, and four on Sunday. Transfer Austral (☎ 412-616), Baquedano 414, leaves Monday to Saturday at 7:30 am and 1 pm daily except for Sunday, when the bus leaves at 8 am.

In summer, Bus Sur goes daily to Parque Nacional Torres del Paine (US$9 one-way, US$16 roundtrip), twice each weekday and once Sunday to Río Turbio (US$4 one-way),

MAGALLANES

five times weekly to El Calafate, as well as Tuesday and Thursday at 6:30 am to Río Gallegos (US$19 one-way). El Pingüino, at the Fernández terminal, goes Wednesday and Sunday at 11 am to Río Gallegos (US$18 one-way).

Andescape (☎ 412-877), Eberhard 599, goes twice daily to Paine, at 7 am and 1 pm, returning at noon and 5:30 pm. Other carriers going to Paine include Buses JB (☎ 412-824), Prat 258; Transpatagónica Express (☎ 410-565), Eberhard 244; and Buses Gómez, which has no fixed office but sells tickets through hospedajes.

Services to El Calafate, Argentina (5½ hours, US$23) are increasing since the improvement of RN40 on the Argentine side. In season, Turismo Zaahj (☎ 412-260), Prat 236, serves El Calafate daily except Wednesday and Sunday; Zaahj also does a one-day tour to the Moreno Glacier (US$70), a very long day trip. Bus Sur also leaves for Coihaique Monday at 8:30 am and for Osorno and Puerto Montt Tuesday at 7 am.

Buses Lagoper (☎ 411-831), Angamos 640, and Cootra (☎ 412-785), Baquedano 244, have frequent buses to Río Turbio (US$4), where it's possible to make connections to both Río Gallegos and Calafate. Turis Sur (☎ 413-353), Valdivia 652, also leaves for Río Turbio and Villa Cerro Castillo, the 'gateway' to Torres del Paine, and near the Paso Río Don Guillermo border crossing, Monday at 7 am and 5 pm, Wednesday and Friday at 5 pm, and Saturday at 8:30 am.

Car Emsa (the local Avis affiliate) (☎ 410-775), Bulnes 632, rents cars for around US$80 per day. Todoauto (☎ 412-837), in the Hotel Costa Australis at Bulnes 20, also rents vehicles.

Boat Navimag (☎ 411-421, fax 411-642), Costanera Pedro Montt 380, operates the car and passenger ferry *MV Puerto Edén* to Puerto Montt weekly all year, but dates and times vary according to weather and tides. The four-day, three-night voyage is heavily booked in summer, so try to reserve as early as possible. It's generally easier to get a

berth northbound. Thursday is the scheduled departure day from Puerto Natales, but this means that passengers spend Thursday night on board for an early Friday departure. Navimag has stuck together a couple of shipping containers as a Sala de Espera (waiting room) across O'Higgins from its ticket office.

AROUND PUERTO NATALES
Puerto Bories
Built in 1913 with British capital, the Sociedad Explotadora's Puerto Bories **frigorífico** (meat freezer), once processed enormous quantities of beef and mutton, and it also shipped tallow, hides and wool from estancias in Chile and Argentina for export to Europe. Its operations, 4km north of Puerto Natales, have now ceased, but there remain several unique metal-clad buildings and houses, classic representatives of hybrid Victorian-Magellanic architecture.

Puerto Bories has accommodations at the modern *Hotel Cisne Cuello Negro*, whose Punta Arenas contact is Turismo Pehoé (☎ 061-244-506, fax 248-052), José Menéndez 918. There are 39 single/double rooms with private baths, and two suites; rates are US$95/120 with breakfast. The restaurant serves other meals as well.

Puerto Prat
About 12km west of Bories, Puerto Prat is where natalinos go to swim – on those rare occasions when the weather warms the sheltered cove's waters sufficiently. Camping is possible, and there are fine views up Seno Última Esperanza toward the Balmaceda glacier.

Travelers with their own vehicles can continue north and then east to rejoin the main Torres del Paine highway near the Cueva del Milodón.

Monumento Natural Cueva del Milodón
In the 1890s, Hermann Eberhard discovered the well-preserved remains of an enormous ground sloth, or milodon, in a cave at this national monument, 24km northwest of Puerto Natales. Twice the height of a human,

the milodon was a herbivorous mammal that pulled down small trees and branches in order to eat their succulent leaves; like the mammoth and many other American megafauna, it became extinct near the end of the Pleistocene.

Bruce Chatwin's classic literary travelogue *In Patagonia* recounts many fanciful stories about the milodon, including legends saying that Indians kept it penned as a domestic animal and that some specimens remained alive into the last century. Paleo-Indians existed simultaneously with the milodon, occupying the cave as a shelter, and they may have contributed to the animal's extinction, through hunting. The best summary information on the milodon can be found in US archaeologist Junius Bird's *Travel and Archaeology in South Chile* (1988), edited by John Hyslop of the American Museum of Natural History.

A new **Museo de Sitio** at the cave is open 8 am to 8 pm daily. A kitschy, full-size replica of the animal stands in the cave, which is 30m high, 80m wide and 200m deep. The cave itself was formed at the base of a Cretaceous conglomeratic submarine channel fill of the Lago Sofía formation, overlying more easily eroded mudstones and sandstones of the Cerro Toro Formation, which was later uplifted from depths between 1000m and 2000m.

Although the closest hotel accommodations are at Puerto Natales, *camping* and picnicking are possible near the site. Conaf charges US$4 admission, less for Chilean nationals and for children. Buses to Torres del Paine will drop you at the entrance, which is a walk of several kilometers from the cave proper. Alternatively, take a taxi or hitchhike from Puerto Natales. (Because it is never entirely safe, Lonely Planet does not recommend hichhiking).

Parque Nacional Bernardo O'Higgins

This otherwise inaccessible park is the final destination of a dramatic four-hour boat ride from Puerto Natales through Seno Última Esperanza, passing Glaciar Balmaceda (Balmaceda Glacier), to the jetty at Puerto Toro, where a footpath leads to the base of Glaciar Serrano (on a clear day, the Torres del Paine are visible in the distance to the north). En route, passengers glimpse the meat freezer at Bories, several small estancias, numerous glaciers and waterfalls, a large cormorant rookery, a smaller sea lion rookery and occasional Andean condors. The return trip takes the same route.

Daily in summer, weather permitting, Turismo Cutter 21 de Mayo, at Eberhard 554 (☎ 411-978, 21demayo@chileaustral.com) and Ladrilleros 171 (☎ 411-176) in Puerto Natales, runs its cutter *Ladrilleros* or the motor yacht *Alberto de Agostini* to the park, and additional trips may be added if demand is sufficient. The trip costs US$56 per person, including a snack on board, as well as hot and cold drinks, but it's better to bring along some extra refreshments.

Rather than returning to Puerto Natales, a better option is to continue up the Río Serrano to Torres del Paine via Zodiac rafts, a unique way to approach the park, with Onas Patagonia (☎/fax 412-707, onas@chileaustral .com), Eberhard 599 in Puerto Natales. The open rafts permit passengers to appreciate the landscape; Onas has a full supply of foul-weather gear, including rain jackets and pants, ski masks and life jackets. A brief portage is necessary because the Zodiac cannot climb or descend the Serrano rapids, but most passengers find this to be a relatively easy route, which includes a lunch stop alongside the river. The cost is US$80 for the seven-hour trip (from Puerto Natales), which ends near the Río Serrano campground; it's also possible in the opposite direction.

VILLA CERRO CASTILLO

Capital of the comuna of Torres del Paine, once part of the Sociedad Explotadora properties, this tiny village has 250 permanent inhabitants, a well-hidden gas station and a pretty sad museum that also serves as local tourist office (you'll get much better information in the park). The border crossing at Río Don Guillermo, known as Cancha Carrera on the Argentine side, is the shortest route from Torres del Paine to El Calafate and Parque Nacional Los Glaciares.

There are inexpensive lodgings at *Residencial Loreto*. Open September to April, *Hostería El Pionero* (☎ 691-932, Anexo 722; ☎ 413-953, fax 412-911 in Puerto Natales) was once the Sociedad Explotadora's administrator's house but now offers comfortable accommodations for US$57/65 singles/doubles, serves good restaurant meals and rents horses.

PARQUE NACIONAL TORRES DEL PAINE

Soaring almost vertically more than 2000m above the Patagonian steppe, the Torres del Paine (Towers of Paine) are spectacular granite pillars that dominate the landscape of what may be South America's finest national park, a miniature Alaska filled with shimmering turquoise lakes, roaring creeks, rivers and waterfalls, sprawling glaciers, dense forests and abundant wildlife. The issue is not whether to come here, but how much time to spend.

Before its creation in 1959, the park was part of a large sheep estancia, and it's still recovering from nearly a century of overexploitation of its pastures, forests and wildlife. Part of the United Nations' Biosphere Reserve system since 1978, it shelters large and growing herds of guanacos, flocks of the flightless ostrichlike rhea (known locally as the *ñandú*), elusive *huemul* (Andean deer), Andean condors and flamingos and many other species.

The park's outstanding conservation success has been the guanaco (*Lama guanicoe*), which grazes the open steppes where its main natural enemy, the puma, cannot approach undetected. After more than a decade of effective protection from hunters and poachers, the guanaco barely flinches when humans or vehicles approach.

For hikers and backpackers, this 240,000-hectare reserve is an unequaled destination, with a well-developed trail network as well as opportunities for cross-country travel. The weather is changeable – clouds move across the sky as fast as images on a TV weather map – but long summer days make outdoor activities possible late into the evening. Good foul-weather gear is essential, and a warm sleeping bag and good tent are imperative for those undertaking the extremely popular Paine Circuit.

Guided day trips from Puerto Natales are possible, but they permit only a glimpse of what the park has to offer. It's better to explore the several options for staying at the park, including camping at backcountry or improved sites, or staying at guest houses and hotels near park headquarters and at Lago Pehoé. Roads into the park are much improved, largely for the benefit of guests of the new luxury hotels.

Orientation & Information

Parque Nacional Torres del Paine is 112km north of Puerto Natales via a decent but sometimes bumpy gravel road that passes Villa Cerro Castillo, where there is a seasonal border crossing into Argentina at Cancha Carrera. The road continues for 38km north, where there's a junction with a 27km lateral along the south shore of Lago Sarmiento de Gamboa, which goes to the little-visited Lago Verde sector of the park.

Three kilometers north of this junction the highway forks west along the north shore of Lago Sarmiento to the Portería Sarmiento, the park's main entrance; it's another 37km to the Administración (Park Headquarters). About 12km east of Portería Sarmiento, another lateral forks north, and, 3km farther, forks again; the northern branch goes to Guardería Laguna Azul, and the western branch goes to Guardería Laguna Amarga, the starting point for the Paine Circuit, and continues to the Administración.

At the Administración, Conaf's **Centro de Informaciones Ecológicas** features a good exhibit on the park's carnivores, including the puma, two species of fox, and Geoffroy's cat, all of which depend largely on the introduced European hare (although half the puma's diet consists of *chulengos*, or juvenile guanacos).

Entry There is an entry charge of US$14 per person (less for Chilean nationals), but it's only US$7 from May 1 to September 30. The fee is collected at Portería Sarmiento, where maps and informational brochures are available, or at Guardería Laguna Amarga (where most buses stop inbound), Guardería Lago Verde or Guardería Laguna Azul.

Visitors should be aware that, because of pressure on park resources, Conaf is likely to institute restrictions during periods of heavy usage, especially in January and February, when reservations may be necessary in some parts of the park.

Climbing Permits Climbers headed for the Torres should know that Conaf charges a climbing fee of US$100 (a considerable reduction of the former US$825 fee for a maximum of seven climbers). Before being granted permission, climbers must present a current résumé, emergency contact numbers and authorization from their consulate.

Climbers must also get permission from the Dirección de Fronteras y Límites (Difrol) in Santiago, which takes 48 hours, but if you ask for enough time it keeps you in the park for months and eliminates the need for a separate fee each time you enter. Still, a climber pretty much has to cool his or her heels for 48 hours in Puerto Natales before being allowed to climb. A good way to avoid delays is to arrange permissions with a Chilean consulate prior to arrival in the country. For more information, contact the Gobernación Provincial (☎ 411-423, fax 411-992), on the south side of the Plaza de Armas in Puerto Natales.

Books, Maps & Trekking Information
The Sociedad Turística Kaonikén in Puerto Natales and Almacén El Puma in Punta Arenas publish good topographic maps of the park at a scale of 1:100,000 with 100m contour intervals, which include detailed routes of the Paine Circuit and other park trails. Both are widely available in Punta Arenas, Puerto Natales and the park itself; the Puma map is more current and detailed, but either is suitable for exploring the park.

Conaf's inexpensive *Torres del Paine*, at a scale of 1:160,000, is less detailed and less frequently updated. JLM Mapa's *Torres del Paine Trekking Map*, at a scale of 1:100,000 with 100m contours, is probably the most frequently updated source on the park.

For more information on trekking and camping, including detailed contour maps, consult Clem Lindenmayer's Lonely Planet guidebook *Trekking in the Patagonian Andes*. Bradt Publications' *Backpacking in Chile and Argentina* and William Leitch's *South America's National Parks* both have useful chapters on Torres del Paine but are less thorough on practicalities. A well-intentioned but awkwardly translated brochure entitled *Guide, Pathway of Excursions National Park Torres del Paine* is also available.

On wildlife, Lonely Planet readers have recommended *The Fauna of Torres del Paine*, by Gladys Garay N and Oscar Guineo N, available in the Museo Salesiano in Punta Arenas.

Paine Circuit

Fast approaching gridlock, this inordinately popular trek usually begins at Guardería Laguna Amarga, where most hikers disembark from the bus and do the route counterclockwise. It's also possible to start at Portería Sarmiento, adding two hours to the hike, or at the Administración, which means a much

Ñandú

Huemul

longer approach. Hikers must register with the rangers at the guarderías or at the Administración and give their passport number.

In some ways, the Paine Circuit is less challenging than in past years, since simple but sturdy bridges have replaced log crossings and once-hazardous stream fords, and park concessionaires have built comfortable refugios offering hot showers and meals at regular intervals along the trail. In theory, this makes it possible to walk from hut to hut without carrying a tent, but a few stretches are long and the changeable weather makes bringing a tent desirable because of the possibility of being caught in between huts. Camping is possible at designated sites; there is a small charge for camping near the new refugios.

While the trek is tamer than it once was, it is not without difficulty and hikers have suffered serious injuries; some have even died. For this reason, Conaf no longer permits solo treks, but it's not difficult to link up with others. Allot at least five days, preferably more for bad weather; consider at least one layover day for resting, since the route is strenuous, especially the rough segments on the east side of Lago Grey and over the 1241m-high pass to or from the Río de los Perros. The opening of a trail along the north shore of Lago Nordenskjöld, between Hostería Las Torres and the Campamento Italiano at the foot of the Río de los France-

ses, means it's no longer necessary to start from park headquarters and it's possible to exit, as well as enter, at Laguna Amarga.

Be sure to bring food, since prices at the small grocery at Hostería Río Serrano near park headquarters are at least 50% higher than in Punta Arenas or Puerto Natales, and the selection is minimal. In late summer, the abandoned garden at Refugio Dickson still produces an abundance of gooseberries.

Puerto Natales' Andescape (☎ 412-877, fax 412-592, andescape@chileaustral.com), at Eberhard 599 in Puerto Natales, has opened *refugios* at Lago Pehóe (crowded and cramped; reservations recommended), Lago Grey and Lago Dickson, as well as a *campground* at Río de los Perros. For trekkers from Guardería Laguna Amarga, this would mean a roughly 11-hour hike to the first refugio at Dickson, although there is a rustic shelter at Campamento Coirón, about three hours earlier.

Andescape's refugios have 32 bunks for US$18 per night, including kitchen privileges and hot showers, but sheets and sleeping bags are not provided. Breakfast is available for US$4.50, lunch for US$7.50 and dinner for US$10, or full board for US$20.50. A bunk plus full board costs US$34.50. Campers pay US$4 per person; with showers, an additional US$2. Rental camping equipment is also available at reasonable prices, but sometimes there are shortages, so it's best to reserve or bring a sleeping bag from Natales.

A division of Hostería Las Torres, Fantástico Sur (☎ 226-054, fax 222-641, lastorres@chileaustral.com), Magallanes 960 in Punta Arenas, operates *Refugio Las Torres*, *Refugio Chileno* and *Refugio Los Cuernos*, all on the route but formally outside the park boundaries. The spacious Refugio Los Cuernos is a beautifully designed but uninsulated building whose angled windows take full advantage of the view of the Cuernos just to the northwest.

Rates for beds at these very comfortable facilities, which also serve excellent meals (although vegetarians will have a hard time) and have entertaining staff, are US$14 at Refugio Chileno and US$18 at Refugio Las Torres and Refugio Los Cuernos; with full

Chapel, Villa Amengual, Aisén

River crossing, Parque Nacional Queulat

AARON MCCOY

Chiloé fishing fleet

WAYNE BERNHARDSON

WAYNE BERNHARDSON

Tranquil waters of Ancud, Isla Grande de Chiloé's largest town

DANIEL RIVADAMAR/ODYSSEY/CHICAGO

Parque Nacional Torres del Paine's Cuernos del Paine (Horns of Paine)

Incredible icebergs, Torres del Paine

Punta Arenas, lively city on the Strait of Magellan

PARQUE NACIONAL TORRES DEL PAINE

9 Campamento Torres
10 Refugio & Campamento Chileno
11 Hostería & Camping Las Torres
12 Guardería & Camping
   Laguna Amarga
13 Refugio & Camping Grey
14 Campamento Italiano
15 Refugio & Campamento Cuernos
16 Refugio & Camping Lago Pehoé
17 Refugio Pudeto,
   Guardería Lago Pehoé
18 Portería Sarmiento,
   Camping Lago Sarmiento
   & Guardería
19 Refugio Zapata
20 Refugio Pingo
21 Hostería & Guardería Lago Grey
22 Hostería Pehoé
23 Camping Lago Pehoé
24 Hotel Salto Chico
25 Hostería Mirador del Payne
26 Guardería Lago Verde
27 Hostería Río Serrano,
   Refugio Lago Toro
28 Park Administration (Conaf)
29 Camping Río Serrano
30 Hostería Lago Tyndall

1 Guardería & Refugio Lago Paine
2 Refugio & Camping Dickson
3 Campamento Coirón
4 Campamento Serón
5 Camping Laguna Azul
6 Guardería Laguna Azul
7 Refugio & Camping
   Río de los Perros
8 Campamento Británico

board, rates are US$44 per person. Campgrounds at all three sites charge US$4.50 per person with hot showers. Rental camping equipment is also available.

Other Paine Trails

Visitors lacking time to hike the circuit, or those who prefer a bit more solitude, have alternatives within the park. The next best choice for seeing the high country is the shorter but almost equally popular trail up the **Río Ascencio** to a treeless tarn beneath the eastern face of the Torres del Paine proper. From Guardería Laguna Amarga,

there's a narrow but passable road to Hostería Las Torres, which provides inexpensive minibus transport (US$4) that saves a couple of hours' walk.

Just west of Hostería Las Torres, a footbridge avoids a sometimes hazardous river ford, before the trail continues up the canyon to *Refugio & Campamento Chileno* and *Campamento Torres*, the only legal campsites (US$5 per site). From Campamento Torres, a steep and sometimes poorly marked trail climbs through patchy southern beech forests to the barren tarn above, which provides dramatic views of the nearly vertical Torres. This is a feasible day hike from Laguna Amarga, and a fairly easy one from Hostería Las Torres, but it's also an exceptional area for camping despite its popularity (arrive early to get the best sites).

The main trail along the north shore of Lago Nordenskjöld, part of the Paine Circuit, continues west to the *Refugio & Camping Los Cuernos* and to the popular, free and sheltered site at *Campamento Italiano*. From Campamento Italiano, the trail up the **Valle Francés** passes between 3050m-high Paine Grande to the west and the lower but still spectacular Cuernos del Paine (Horns of Paine) to the east. It's also a seven-hour (one-way) hike from the Administración. Trekkers can pitch tents at the *Campamento Británico*, at the head of the Valle Francés, or at the estancia's *Camping y Refugio Los Cuernos*, about a two hours' walk east of the Campamento Italiano.

Floods in the early 1980s destroyed several bridges, requiring Conaf to relocate the part of the Paine Circuit that formerly crossed the Río Paine at the outlet of **Lago Paine**, whose northern shore is now accessible only from Laguna Azul. This four-hour (one-way) hike, offering far greater solitude than the Paine Circuit, leads to the rustic *Refugio Lago Paine*, a former outside house on the former estancia.

From the outlet of Lago Grey, 18km northwest of the Administración by a passable road, a good trail leads to **Lago Pingo**, on the eastern edge of the Campo de Hielo Sur (Southern Continental Ice Field). Much less frequented than other park trails, this route has two very rustic refugios en route.

For a shorter day hike, walk from Guardería Lago Pehoé, on the main park highway, to **Salto Grande**. This powerful waterfall, between Lago Nordenskjöld and Lago Pehoé, destroyed an iron bridge that once was a key part of the Paine Circuit. From Salto Grande, an easy hour's walk leads to **Mirador Nordenskjöld**, an overlook with superb views of the lake and cordillera.

Horseback Riding

At Río Serrano, contact Baqueano Zamora (☎ 412-911). Rates are about US$15 for two hours or US$55 per full day, the latter with lunch included.

Places to Stay & Eat

Other places to stay along the route are listed in the Paine Circuit section, earlier in this chapter.

Camping The most central organized campsites are *Camping Lago Pehoé* (☎ 41-068), which charges US$21 for up to six people, and *Camping Río Serrano*, which costs US$15. Fees include firewood and hot showers, the latter available in the morning (evenings by request only).

At Guardería Laguna Amarga, Conaf has a free *camping area* with a very rustic refugio and pit toilets. Only river water is available at this site, which is usually frequented by recent arrivals to the park or people waiting for the bus to or from Puerto Natales.

On the grounds of Estancia Cerro Paine, *Camping Las Torres* charges US$5 per person and is popular with hikers taking the short trek up the Río Ascencio before doing the Paine Circuit. Although covered with cow patties, the sites themselves are pleasant and scenic, but the inadequate water supply has put pressure on the modern but overburdened toilet and shower facilities.

At the more remote *Camping Laguna Azul*, rates are US$21 per night.

Hotels & Hosterías Despite a construction boom within park boundaries, accommodations are crowded in summer and reservations are a good idea. Low-cost and even free accommodations exist, however – a short walk from the Administración, *Refugio Lago Toro* has bunks for US$6, plus US$2 for hot showers. A sleeping bag is essential. Other refugios are free but very rustic; the refugio at Pudeto on Lago Pehoé may start to charge a fee in the near future.

Hostería Río Serrano (☎ 410-684, fax 412-349), a remodeled estancia house near the Administración, has rooms with shared bath for US$40/70; those with private bath go for US$50 per person. It has a reasonably priced restaurant and bar, with occasional informal, live entertainment, but several readers consider it a poor value and report management attitude problems. *Hostería Mirador del Payne* (formerly Hostería Estancia Lazo), with eight cabins and a spacious farmhouse at the park's Laguna Verde sector, charges US$105/120 and has drawn some very favorable commentary. Its Punta Arenas representative is Turismo Viento Sur (☎/fax 228-712, Fagnano 565, Oficina E).

Well worth considering is *Hostería Lago Grey* (☎ 410-220), at the outlet of the lake of the same name, which costs US$156/180. Breakfast is included, but other meals cost US$24. The Punta Arenas contact is Complejo Turístico Lago Grey (☎ 229-512, fax 225-986, hgrey@ctcreuna.cl), Lautaro Navarro 1061-65. It also arranges excursions.

Hostería Pehoé (☎ 244-506), on a small island in the eponymous lake and linked to the mainland by a footbridge, charges US$120/135 plus IVA for panoramic views of the Cuernos del Paine and Paine Grande. Even though the service is good, many of the small, simple rooms need a full-scale rehab and wouldn't cost more than US$30 in Puerto Natales. Service is shoddy at the bar-restaurant, the exchange rate is poor, and the management sometimes does not take credit cards.

Hostería Las Torres (☎ 226-054, fax 222-641), 7km west of Guardería Laguna Amarga, charges US$79/89 to US$98/107 in low season (mid-April to end of September) and US$131/149 to US$163/179 the rest of the year. It also has a restaurant-bar.

The most extravagant lodgings are at *Hotel Salto Chico* (☎ 02-206-6060, fax 228-4655 in Santiago, 61-411-247 in Puerto Natales, explora@entelchile.net), near the Salto Chico waterfall at the outlet of Lago Pehoé, which specializes in packages ranging from four days and three nights for US$1347/2080 singles/doubles in the least expensive room, to eight days and seven nights for US$5388/6738 in the most expensive suite, including transportation from Punta Arenas. The building's exterior is unappealing but also unobtrusive; the interior, however, in the words of one visiting writer, 'redefines *room with a view*' with its outlook on the expansive panorama of the Paine massif.

Just outside the park, near the Río Serrano campground but reached by a launch across the river, *Hostería Lago Tyndall* (☎ 211-504 in Punta Arenas, or contact Onas Patagonia or Andescape in Puerto Natales) is nowhere close to the glacier and lake for which it is named, but it has 24 cozy rooms with private baths. There is electricity from 7 pm to 1 am only, and the hostería also has an adequate but fairly expensive restaurant. The staff are friendly and helpful, but cows and cheap cabañas mar the view from the otherwise attractive dining room. Rates are US$90/120 singles/doubles with breakfast; there's an additional charge for other meals.

Getting There & Away

For details of transportation to the park, see the Puerto Natales section, earlier in the chapter. Bus service drops you at the Administración at Río Serrano, although you can disembark at Portería Lago Sarmiento or Guardería Laguna Amarga to begin the Paine Circuit, or elsewhere upon request. Hitchhiking from Puerto Natales is possible, but competition is heavy (since it is never entirely safe, Lonely Planet does not recommend hitchhiking). Roundtrip tickets are slightly cheaper, but they limit you to one bus company.

Summer bus services are sometimes available between Torres del Paine and El Calafate, Argentina, the closest settlement to Parque Nacional Los Glaciares. Inquire at the Administración.

Getting Around

Hikers to Lago Grey or Valle Francés can save time and effort by taking the 30-passenger catamaran *Lady of Snow* (US$15) from Refugio Pudeto, at the east end of Lago Pehoé, to Refugio Pehoé, at the west end of the lake.

Service on the 38-passenger *Tetramarán Grey I*, which makes a three-hour excursion between Hostería Grey and Glaciar Grey (US$45), was suspended in early 1999, but it is expected to resume.

MAGALLANES

Hostería Las Torres (see Places to Stay & Eat) offers vehicle, hiking and horseback tours to Las Torres, Los Cuernos, Valle Encantado, Lago Nordenskjöld, Lago Grey, Salto Grande and Lago Pehoé, Laguna Azul, Laguna Amarga and Laguna Sarmiento and Sendero Cerro Paine. It also provides regular transport from Laguna Amarga to the Hostería, a major starting point for hiking trips into the Paine.

EL CALAFATE (ARGENTINA)
☎ 02902
Gradually overcoming its reputation as a tourist trap, El Calafate remains an almost inescapable – but now more agreeable – stopover en route to some of Argentina's most impressive sights. Formally founded in 1927, this one-time stage stop takes its name from the wild barberry *(Berberis buxifolia)*, which grows abundantly in the area. The improved highway from Puerto Natales has meant a significant increase in transport options, and many visitors to Chile make at least a brief detour here.

Once an oversized encampment of rapacious merchants bent on making a year's income in a few short months by selling goods at high prices to visitors, El Calafate (population 4000) still swarms with Buenos Aires tourists, who parade up and down the sidewalks of Av del Libertador San Martín, to the accompaniment of roaring motorcycles, before and after spending a few hours at the Moreno Glacier. In recent years, though, greater competition has slowed rising prices and reduced gouging; some merchants are even showing courtesy to customers.

January and February are the most popular months; if possible, plan your visit just before or just after peak season. From May to September, visitors are fewer and prices may drop, but days are shorter and the main attractions less accessible.

Orientation
El Calafate is 320km northwest of Río Gallegos via paved RP 5 and RP 11, and 32km west of RP 5's junction with northbound RN 40, which heads toward the El Chaltén section of Parque Nacional Los Glaciares.

Westbound RP 11 goes to the southern sectors of Parque Nacional Los Glaciares and the Moreno Glacier. RN 40 south to Río Turbio has been greatly improved, permitting any vehicle to cut 100km off the trip to Torres del Paine by avoiding the lengthy La Esperanza route.

El Calafate's main thoroughfare is Av del Libertador General José de San Martín, more manageably known as 'Av Libertador' or 'San Martín.' Because the town is small, most everything is within easy walking distance of Av Libertador.

Information
El Calafate's Ente Municipal Calafate Turismo (Emcatur; ☎ 491-090, 492-884), at the bus terminal, is open 8 am to 10 pm daily November to March, 8 am to 8 pm the rest of the year. It keeps a list of hotels and prices and has maps, brochures and a message board; there's usually an English-speaker on hand.

The Automóvil Club Argentino (ACA, ☎ 491-004), the counterpart to Chile's Acchi, is at Primero de Mayo and Av Roca.

Although (or because) El Calafate is a tourist destination, changing money has traditionally been problematic, but the federal government's rigid convertibility policy has curtailed foreign exchange profiteering by local merchants. For the most part, US dollars are welcome as Argentine currency.

Banco de la Provincia de Santa Cruz, Av Libertador 1285, changes traveler's checks (for a substantial commission), but it's open 10 am to 3 pm weekdays only; its ATM is often out of service. El Pingüino, Av Libertador 1025, also changes money, but it imposes a substantial commission on traveler's checks.

Correo Argentino is at Av Libertador 1133; the postal code is 9405. El Calafate's Cooperativa Telefónica is at Espora 194; collect calls are not possible, and discounts are available only after 10 pm.

El Calafate now has Internet access at Lago Digital (☎ 492-328) on Av Libertador, opposite Casa Blanca.

The Parques Nacionales office (☎ 491-755, 491-005), Av Libertador 1302, is open 7 am to 2 pm weekdays and has brochures including a decent (though not adequate for trekking) map of Parque Nacional Los Glaciares.

All of El Calafate's travel agencies can arrange excursions to the Moreno Glacier and other attractions. Among them are Interlagos Turismo (☎ 491-018) at Av Libertador 1175; Solo Patagonia (☎ 491-298, fax 491-790) at Av Libertador 963; Los Glaciares (☎ 491-159) at Av Libertador 924; and Cal Tur (☎ 491-117) at Av Libertador 1080.

El Lavadero, on San Martín between 25 de Mayo and 9 de Julio, charges US$8 per laundry load and is open every day, including Sunday afternoons.

El Calafate's Hospital Municipal Dr José Formenti (☎ 491-001) is at Av Roca 1487.

Things to See & Do

West and north of El Calafate, **Parque Nacional Los Glaciares** offers several of the most spectacular natural attractions in South America: the **Moreno Glacier**, the **Upsala Glacier** and the **Fitzroy Range** of the southern Andes. For details, see the separate entry for the park later in this chapter.

The **Museo Regional El Calafate**, Av Libertador 557, has been closed for remodeling – a seemingly permanent state of affairs.

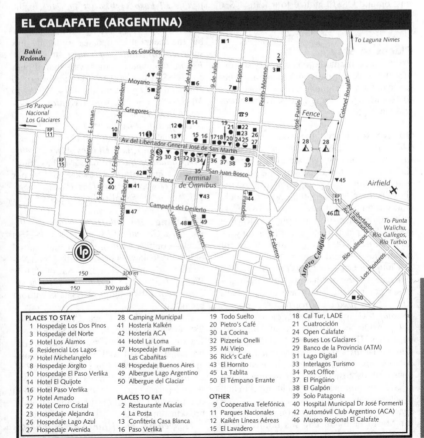

EL CALAFATE (ARGENTINA)

PLACES TO STAY	28 Camping Municipal	19 Todo Suelto	18 Cal Tur, LADE
1 Hospedaje Los Dos Pinos	41 Hostería Kalkén	20 Pietro's Café	21 Cuatrocéción
3 Hospedaje del Norte	42 Hostería ACA	30 La Cocina	24 Open Calafate
5 Hotel Los Álamos	44 Hotel La Loma	32 Pizzería Onelli	25 Buses Los Glaciares
6 Residencial Los Lagos	47 Hospedaje Familiar	35 Mi Viejo	29 Banco de la Provincia (ATM)
7 Hotel Michelangelo	Las Cabañitas	36 Rick's Café	31 Lago Digital
8 Hospedaje Jorgito	48 Hospedaje Buenos Aires	43 El Hornito	33 Interlagos Turismo
10 Hospedaje El Paso Verlika	49 Albergue Lago Argentino	45 La Tablita	34 Post Office
14 Hotel El Quijote	50 Albergue del Glaciar	50 El Témpano Errante	37 El Pingüino
16 Hotel Paso Verlika			38 El Galpón
17 Hotel Amado	PLACES TO EAT	OTHER	39 Solo Patagonia
22 Hotel Cerro Cristal	2 Restaurante Macías	9 Cooperativa Telefónica	40 Hospital Municipal Dr José Formenti
23 Hospedaje Alejandra	4 La Posta	11 Parques Nacionales	42 Automóvil Club Argentino (ACA)
26 Hospedaje Lago Azul	13 Confitería Casa Blanca	12 Kaikén Líneas Aéreas	46 Museo Regional El Calafate
27 Hospedaje Avenida	16 Paso Verlika	15 El Lavadero	

Alongside the lakeshore, north of town, the former sewage pond known as **Laguna Nimes** has become, since its reclamation, a prime bird habitat.

There is authentic aboriginal rock art at **Punta Walichu** (☎ 491-059), 7km east of town near the shores of Lago Argentino, but this grossly commercialized site is a reminder of old Calafate – its hokey reproductions of similar sites, such as northern Santa Cruz's Cueva de las Manos, epitomize the Argentine slang term *trucho* (bogus). Whatever integrity it might have had before its privatization, its exorbitant fees – US$7 admission and US$10 guided tour (plus US$6 for transfers) – make it one of the country's most flagrant tourist rip-offs.

Places to Stay

Prices for accommodations can vary seasonally; the peak is usually in January and February, but it can extend from early November to late March at some places. Many places close in winter.

Budget Now fenced, the woodsy *Camping Municipal* (☎ 491-829, José Pantín s/n), straddling the *arroyo* (watercourse) just north of the bridge into town, has separate areas for auto and tent campers, good toilets, hot showers, firepits and potable water; the entrance is on the east side of the arroyo. Easy walking distance from any place in town, it costs US$4 per person; in summer only, an additional US$4 per tent and US$3 for parking are charged.

Camping Los Dos Pinos (☎ 491-271, 9 de Julio 218), at the north end of town, charges US$4 per person. There are also orchard sites at *Hospedaje Jorgito* (☎ 491-323, Moyano 943) for US$5 per person.

Open October to the end of March, El Calafate's HI-affiliated hostel is *Albergue del Glaciar* (☎/fax 491-243, alberguedelglaciar@cotecal.com.ar, Los Pioneros s/n), east of the arroyo. Beds cost US$10 for members and US$12 for nonmembers, including kitchen privileges, laundry facilities and access to a spacious, comfortable common room. Director Mario Feldman and his family speak English, provide visitor information and

email service (small extra charge) and organize minibus excursions to local attractions. Travelers who are financially challenged can crash for US$5 per person in the loft above the restaurant, while those with bigger bucks will find comfortable private rooms.

There are also several unofficial hostels. *Albergue Lago Argentino* (☎ 491-423, Campaña del Desierto 1050), opposite the bus terminal, charges US$5 for those with their own sleeping bag, US$9 for those who rent sheets. *Hospedaje Los Dos Pinos* (☎ 491-271, 9 de Julio 358) has hostel accommodations for US$8 per person, as does *Hospedaje El Paso Verlika* (☎ 492-216), at the corner of Av Libertador and 7 de Diciembre.

Prices vary considerably with the season, but the cheapest hospedajes are family inns such as *Hospedaje Alejandra* (☎ 491-328, Espora 60), where rooms with shared bath cost US$10 per person; identically priced *Hospedaje Lago Azul* (☎ 491-419, Perito Moreno 83); and *Hospedaje Avenida* (☎ 491-159, Av Libertador 902).

Hospedaje Jorgito (☎ 491-323, Moyano 943) is slightly dearer at US$12. Near the bus terminal, *Hospedaje Buenos Aires* (☎ 491-147, Ciudad de Buenos Aires 296) has drawn mixed commentary; rates are US$15 per person. *Hospedaje Los Dos Pinos* (☎ 491-271, 9 de Julio 358) also charges US$15.

Mid-Range *Hospedaje del Norte* (☎ 491-117, Los Gauchos 813) charges US$25/30 singles/doubles with breakfast and shared bath, US$36/45 with private bath. Open November through Semana Santa (Holy Week), *Hotel Paso Verlika* (☎ 491-009, Av Libertador 1108) charges US$30/45 without breakfast.

Attractive *Hotel Cerro Cristal* (☎ 491-088, Gregores 989) charges US$20/30 off-season, US$30/50 in peak season, but breakfast is US$4 to US$5 extra. Recommended *Residencial Los Lagos* (☎ 491-170, 25 de Mayo 220) charges US$25/40 off-season (breakfast US$5 extra), and US$30 per person December through February, breakfast included.

Hospedaje Familiar Las Cabañitas (☎ 491-118, Valentín Feilberg 218) charges

US$32/46 in peak season, US$25/36 off-season; breakfast is an additional US$6. Several readers have praised **Cabañas del Sol** (☎ 491-439, Av Libertador 1956), west of downtown, which charges US$35/40 in low season, US$45/52 in peak season.

Hotel La Loma (☎ 491-016, Av Roca 849) costs US$35/50 to US$45/70 singles/doubles in the November-to-March high season, with breakfast, but is cheaper the rest of the year. **Hotel Amado** (☎ 491-134, Av Libertador 1072) charges US$38/56. Members pay US$52/69 at the **Hostería ACA** (☎ 491-004, Primero de Mayo 50), while nonmembers are welcome for US$65/86.

Top End Several hotels charge upward of US$50 per person, including pleasant **Hostería Kalkén** (☎ 491-073, Valentín Feilberg 119), which serves an excellent breakfast. Rates are US$87/100 November to March, but only US$74/84 in April and May.

Hotel Michelangelo (☎ 491-045, Moyano 1020) charges US$87/110 with breakfast, but is about 20% cheaper in April and May. **Hotel El Quijote** (☎ 491-017, fax 491-103, Gregores 1191) charges US$110/136, but US$70/87 off-season. In a class by itself is four-star **Hotel Los Álamos** (☎ 491-144, Moyano 1355), set among spectacular gardens, where rates are US$174/180 in peak season, US$129/135 off-season, plus US$5 for breakfast.

Places to Eat

There are several good values in El Calafate's improving restaurant scene. **Confitería Casa Blanca** (☎ 491-402, Av Libertador 1202) has good pizza and reasonably priced beer, but beware of the US$3.50 *submarino* (steamed hot chocolate); **Pizzería Onelli** (☎ 491-184, Libertador 1197), across the street, is also popular. **Paso Verlika** (☎ 491-009, Av Libertador 1108), in the hotel of the same name, is popular, and the fare is reasonably priced, especially the pizza. **Pietro's Café** (Av Libertador 1640) also serves pizza, as does **El Hornito** (☎ 491-443, Buenos Aires 155), half a block south of the bus terminal.

The kitchen at **Hotel Michelangelo** (☎ 491-045, Moyano 1020) offers decent food but microscopic portions, and it's not cheap. More reasonable are **La Tablita** (☎ 491-065, Coronel Rosales 24), near the bridge, and **Restaurante Macías** (Los Gauchos s/n), opposite Hospedaje del Norte.

La Cocina (☎ 491-758, Av Libertador 1245) has an innovative Italian menu. **Mi Viejo** (☎ 491-691, Av Libertador 1111) is a good and popular but pricey *parrilla*.

El Témpano Errante (☎ 491-243), the new restaurant at the Albergue del Glacier on Los Pioneros, is one of El Calafate's best values, well worth a try even for visitors from upscale hotels. Much dearer, but perhaps not much better except for its upscale ambience, is **La Posta** (☎ 491-144), at Bustillo and Moyano (it's part of Hotel Los Álamos, across the street).

Rick's Café (Av Libertador 1105) is a new confitería that's worth a look. **Todo Suelto** (☎ 491-114, Av Libertador 1044) prepares a dozen types of tasty Argentine empanadas, including ones made with trout.

Shopping

Open Calafate, Av Libertador 996, has books and souvenirs. In the past few years there's been a proliferation of shops on Av Libertador offering good but expensive homemade chocolates.

Getting There & Away

Air As facilities improve at El Calafate's airfield, due to open for jet aircraft in November 2000, it's likely that some of the major airlines will fly directly here. For the moment only two smaller airlines serve the town.

LADE (☎ 491-262), Av Libertador 1080, has flights Tuesday to Río Gallegos (US$25), Río Grande (US$49) and Ushuaia (US$56); Thursday to Río Turbio (US$20) and Río Gallegos; and Thursday and Friday to Gobernador Gregores (US$23), Perito Moreno (US$43) and Comodoro Rivadavia (US$62).

Kaikén Líneas Aéreas (☎ 491-266), 25 de Mayo 23, flies daily except Sunday to Río Gallegos (US$55) and Ushuaia (US$93).

Bus El Calafate's hilltop Terminal de Ómnibus is on Av Roca, easily reached by a pedestrian staircase from the corner of Av Libertador and 9 de Julio.

El Pingüino (☎ 491-273), Interlagos (☎ 491-018) and Quebek Tours (☎ 491-843) all cover the 320km of RP 5 and RP 11, which is now completely paved between El Calafate and Río Gallegos (US$20, six hours).

Turismo Zaahj (☎ 491-631), along with Bus Sur, connects El Calafate with Puerto Natales, Chile (US$25), daily except Monday and Thursday. Cootra (☎ 491-444) goes daily except Saturday to Río Turbio (US$18) and Puerto Natales (US$23, US$45 roundtrip). In winter, these services may only leave once per week.

At 7:30 am daily in summer, Buses Los Glaciares (☎ 491-158) leaves El Calafate for El Chaltén (US$25 one-way, US$50 with open return) and the Fitzroy Range. The return service leaves El Chaltén at 5 pm; winter schedules may differ. Cal Tur (☎ 491-842) goes to Chaltén half an hour earlier, but returns at 5 pm, while Chaltén Travel (☎ 491-833) leaves at 8 am and return service leaves at 6 pm.

Almafuerte Travel's new Rotativo Patagónico minibus service runs from El Calafate to the town of Perito Moreno (US$50, 9½ hours) daily in January and February, less frequently the rest of the year. From Perito Moreno, it's possible to cross to the town of Chile Chico, Aisén, via the Argentine town of Los Antiguos.

Getting Around

Cuatrociclón (☎ 492-180), on Espora near the corner of San Martín, rents mountain bikes for US$6 per hour, US$9 for two hours, US$16 for a half day and US$25 for a full day.

ESTANCIA EL GALPÓN

About 20km west of El Calafate, Estancia El Galpón is a working ranch that, like many others, has opened itself to the tourist trade. Afternoon excursions, which include tea served upon arrival, observation of herding and sheep shearing, a birding walk and a lamb asado for dinner, cost US$55 including transportation. They also offer horseback riding to nearby Cerro Frías (US$50) and even to the Moreno Glacier.

For more details contact El Galpón (☎/fax 491-793, elgalpon@cotecal.com.ar), Av Libertador 1015 in El Calafate, or, in Buenos Aires (☎ 011-4312-4473, fax 011-4313-0679) at Av Leandro Alem 822, 3rd floor.

PARQUE NACIONAL LOS GLACIARES (ARGENTINA)

Nourished by awesome glaciers that descend from the Andean divide, Lago Argentino and Lago Viedma in turn feed southern Patagonia's largest river, the Río Santa Cruz. Along with the Iguazú Falls, this amalgam of ice, rock and water is one of the greatest sights in Argentina and all of South America.

Its centerpiece is the breathtaking **Moreno Glacier** which, due to unusual local conditions, is one of the planet's few advancing glaciers, although topography prevents it from making a net advance. A low gap in the Andes allows moisture-laden Pacific storms to drop their loads east of the divide, where they accumulate as snow. Over millennia, under tremendous weight, this snow has recrystallized into ice and flowed slowly eastward. The 1600-sq-km trough of Lago Argentino, the country's largest single body of water, is unmistakable evidence that glaciers were once far more extensive than today.

Fifteen times between 1917 and 1988, as the 60m-high glacier has advanced, it has dammed the **Brazo Rico** (Rico Arm) of Lago Argentino, causing the water to rise. Several times, the melting ice below has been unable to support the weight of the water behind it and the dam has collapsed in an explosion of ice and water. To be present when this spectacular cataclysm occurs would be an unforgettable experience, but the dam hasn't formed since 1988 and it's impossible to predict when or even if it might happen again.

Even in ordinary years, though, the Moreno Glacier merits a visit. It is both an auditory and visual experience, as huge icebergs on the glacier's face calve and collapse into the **Canal de los Témpanos** (Iceberg

PARQUE NACIONAL LOS GLACIARES (ARGENTINA)

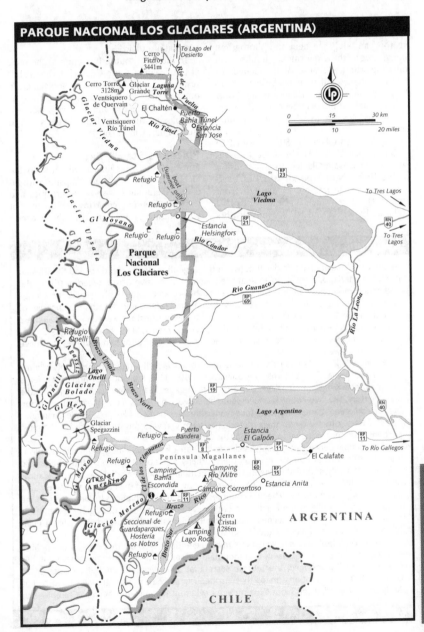

Cerro Fitzroy 3441m

To Lago del Desierto

Río de la Vuelta

Cerro Torre 3128m

Glaciar Grande

Laguna Torre

Ventsiquero de Quervain

El Chaltén

Puerto Bahía Túnel

Ventsiquero Río Túnel

Río Túnel

Estancia San Jose

Glaciar Viedma

Refugio

boat (summer only)

Lago Viedma

RP 23

To Tres Lagos

Refugio

Gl Moyano

RP 21

RN 40

To Tres Lagos

Refugio

Refugio

Estancia Helsingfors

Río Cóndor

Glaciar Upsala

Parque Nacional Los Glaciares

Río Guanaco

RP 69

Refugio Onelli

Gl Onelli

Gl Agassiz

Brazo Upsala

Lago Onelli

Glaciar Bolado

Brazo Norte

RP 19

Lago Argentino

RN 40

Gl Heim

Glaciar Spegazzini

Refugio

Puerto Bandera

Estancia El Galpón

RP 11

Gl Mayo

Refugio

RP 8

Refugio

Península Magallanes

RP 60

RP 15

El Calafate

To Río Gallegos

Glaciar Ameghino

Cl de los Témpanos

Camping Bahía Escondida

Camping Río Mitre

Camping Correntoso

Estancia Anita

Glaciar Moreno

Refugio

Brazo Rico

RP 11

Cerro Cristal 1286m

ARGENTINA

Seccional de Guardaparques, Hostería Los Notros

Camping Lago Roca

Brazo Sur

Refugio

CHILE

0   15   30 km
0   10   20 miles

MAGALLANES

Channel). From a series of catwalks and vantage points on the Península Magallanes visitors can safely see, hear and photograph the glacier as these enormous chunks crash into the water. Because of the danger of falling icebergs and their backwash, it's no longer permissible to descend to the shores of the canal. Another danger of falling icebergs is flying ice chips, which come at bullet speed.

The Moreno Glacier is 80km west of El Calafate via RP 11. The massive but less spectacular **Upsala Glacier**, on an extension of the Brazo Norte (North Arm) of Lago Argentino, is accessible by launch from Puerto Bandera, which is 45km west of El Calafate by RP 11 and RP 8. Many visitors recommend the trip for the hike to iceberg-choked **Lago Onelli**, where it is possible to camp at a refugio.

In the most southerly section of the park at La Jerónima, **Cerro Cristal** is a rugged but rewarding hike beginning at the concrete bunker near the campground entrance. Hikers reaching the summit earn a view encompassing Torres del Paine in the south to Cerro Fitzroy in the north.

Places to Stay & Eat

On Península Magallanes, en route to the glacier, are two organized campsites with facilities including hot showers, fire pits, and the like: *Camping Río Mitre* is 53km west of El Calafate and 27km from the Moreno

Bordering on the Absurd

Above the Uspallata pass, midway between the Argentine city of Mendoza and the Chilean capital of Santiago, a bronze plaque at the base of the massive *Cristo Redentor* (Christ the Redeemer) monument commemorates the British-mediated settlement, in 1902, of a long-standing border dispute: 'Sooner shall these mountains crumble into dust than the peoples of Argentina and Chile break the peace sworn at the feet of Christ the Redeemer.' For all these lofty sentiments – perhaps attributable to the lack of oxygen 4200m above sea level – Southern Cone travelers will find countless contradictions, especially for two countries that have never been to war.

Argentina's 2.8 million sq km make it the world's eighth-largest country, only slightly smaller than India. Chilean territory is only about 800,000 sq km – but still larger than Texas or the United Kingdom. Still, ever since uniting to expel Spain from South America in the 19th century, the two countries have squabbled over tiny tracts along their long common border, sometimes almost tragically (nearly warring over Tierra del Fuego's Beagle Channel in 1978). Just as often though, their rhetoric has been inadvertently comic and, for the most part, inversely proportional to the size of the area involved.

After independence, both countries claimed the area known as Patagonia, Chile establishing the settlement of Punta Arenas on the southerly Strait of Magellan by the 1840s. Still, neither effectively occupied Patagonia until Argentina brutally invaded the former Araucanian Indian territory in the 1880s. Chile, distracted by the War of the Pacific against Peru and Bolivia, could barely protest. The two countries arrived at an ambiguous border based on the vague principle 'Chile in the Pacific, Argentina in the Atlantic' without agreeing what this meant – Argentina preferred a line traced along the highest Andean peaks while Chile argued for its possession of all westward watersheds.

In practice, border issues have led to strained, emotional – sometimes even zany – politics in a region where the same lakes and mountain passes commonly change names on either side. In 1997, for instance, the tourism secretariat of Argentina's Chubut province spent US$240,000 on promotional maps that erroneously placed the fruit-growing town of Los Antiguos not in adjacent Santa Cruz province where it belongs, nor even in Chubut – but

Glacier, while ***Camping Bahía Escondida*** is 72km from El Calafate and only 7km from the glacier; the latter costs US$4 per person. Three km east of Bahía Escondida, ***Camping Correntoso*** is free but dirty; backpackers can also camp a maximum of two nights near the Seccional de Guardaparques, the ranger station at the glacier. Also at the glacier, the Unidad Turística Ventisquero Moreno has a *snack bar* (sandwiches in the US$3 to US$5 range, plus coffee and desserts), and a *restaurant* with full meals in the US$14 to US$18 range.

Hostería Los Notros (☎ 02-902-491-437, *fax 491-816 in El Calafate, notros@lastland .com*), not far from the Seccional de Guardaparques at the glacier, has 20 rooms with glacier views starting at US$235/244 singles/doubles off-season (September and May) and rising to US$270/280 in peak season (October through April) with breakfast; lunches and dinners cost US$35. Prompt in responding to fax or email reservation requests, the Hostería is geared toward two- to four-night packages with full board.

At ***Camping Lago Roca*** (☎ 02-902-49500) at La Jerónima on Brazo Sur, fishing (rental equipment is available) and horseback riding (US$10 per hour) are also possible. Camping prices are US$6 per adult, US$4 per child; there's a ***confitería*** with meals for US$12, and hot showers are available from 7 to 11 pm.

Bordering on the Absurd

across the line in Chile. Dropping all other matters, the irate Santa Cruz legislature demanded that the pamphlet 'be urgently removed from circulation.' An apologetic Chubut official lamented that 'The issue is not the money we spent, but the shame we bear.'

Meanwhile, in Santa Cruz's Parque Nacional Los Glaciares, the Argentine government has built a bumpy *camino de penetración* from the tiny settlement of El Chaltén to the disputed Laguna del Desierto, 30km north, where Argentine tourists appear to be reinforcing their country's claim with pretentious plaques, toilet paper and cigarette butts. Jorge Figueroa, president of Chile's self-proclaimed Corporación de Defensa de la Soberanía (Corporation for the Defense of Sovereignty), who mourns that the loss of Laguna del Desierto was 'like having lost a son,' would probably interpret the Argentine use of 'penetration' in a Freudian sense.

Figueroa, whose organization claims 150,000 members, has even denounced General Augusto Pinochet's military dictatorship of having succumbed to Argentine pressure – though most international observers thought papal mediation in the Beagle Channel favored Chile. According to Figueroa, global warming could melt Chile's southern glaciers and provide Argentina with Pacific access – even though, given the size of the area, this is likelier to be a problem in geologic rather than historic time. Just in case, though, the Chilean air force has built a base directly on the ice.

Even Lonely Planet hasn't avoided the cartographic hysteria. When a customs inspector saw the 2nd edition of LP's *Argentina, Uruguay & Paraguay*, he refused to release the shipment to the Buenos Aires distributor until the latter had placed a disclaimer in each copy indicating that the locator map – on a scale so small that only a paranoid could find any geopolitical significance in it – did not compromise Argentina's borders.

Argentines say Cristo Redentor faces east because He favors Argentina, turning his back on Chile. Chileans say He doesn't dare turn His back on the untrustworthy Argentines. Maybe there's a kernel of truth in both sayings, but fortunately most citizens of both countries seem to share the attitude of former Chilean president Patricio Aylwin, who once told his countrymen not to worry about 'a little piece more or less of territory.'

Getting There & Away

The Moreno Glacier is about 80km from El Calafate via RP 11, a rugged gravel road. Bus tours are frequent and numerous in summer, but off-season transportation can still be arranged. El Calafate's tour operators offer trips to all major tourist sites but concentrate on the Moreno and Upsala Glaciers; for specific operators see the entry for El Calafate or just stroll down Av Libertador. Some, such as Interlagos, have English-speaking guides. The roundtrip fare to Moreno Glacier runs US$20 to US$30 for the 1¼ hour (each way) trip, depending on the departure time. Park admission costs an additional US$5.

El Calafate's Albergue del Glaciar runs its own minivan excursions, leaving about 8:30 am and returning about 5 pm. Many visitors feel that day trips allow insufficient time to appreciate the glacier, especially if inclement weather limits visibility. The changeable weather is almost sure to allow a view of the glacier at some time during your trip, but it's also worth exploring options for camping nearby.

Several travel agencies offer brief hikes across the glacier itself. After crossing Brazo Rico in a rubber raft, you hike with guides through the southern beech forest and onto the glacier. This all-day 'minitrekking' excursion from El Calafate costs US$65. Full-day bus/motor launch excursions to the Upsala Glacier cost about $55. Meals are extra and usually expensive; bring your own food. For more information, see El Calafate's Travel Agencies section, earlier in this chapter).

FITZROY RANGE (ARGENTINA)

Leisure-oriented tourists can enjoy the Moreno Glacier, but the Fitzroy Range is the mecca for hikers, climbers and campers. The staging point for these activities is the tiny settlement of **El Chaltén** (area code ☎ 02962), a monument to Argentina's prodigious capacity for bureaucracy. At one time in this town, where Chile and Argentina have settled all but one of their almost interminable border disputes, virtually every resident was a government employee.

Once a desolate collection of pseudo-chalets pummeled by the almost incessant wind, El Chaltén is becoming a village rather than just a bureaucratic outpost seemingly airlifted onto the exposed floodplain of the Río de las Vueltas. While it still has drawbacks, its magnificent surroundings and improving services – hotels, hostels, campgrounds, restaurants, phone service and even a pharmacy – make El Chaltén more agreeable every day. The name itself, signifying 'azure' in the Tehuelche language, was the name applied to Cerro Fitzroy.

Orientation & Information

While El Chaltén is a bit spread out and street addresses are almost unknown, everything is easy to find. The Parques Nacionales office (☎ 493-004), at the entrance to town just before the bridge over the Río Fitzroy, provides information and issues climbing permits from 8 am to 8 pm daily. The several hostels in town are also good sources of information. There's no place to change money, but there is phone service and, after many years, YPF, an Argentine oil company, has placed a gas station here.

Things to See & Do

One of many fine hikes in the area goes to **Laguna Torre**, and continues to the base camp for climbers of the famous spire of **Cerro Torre**. There's a signed trailhead between the chalets and the rustic Madsen campground along the road to the north. After an initial gentle climb, it's a fairly level walk through tranquil beech forests and along the Río Fitzroy until a final, steeper climb up the lateral moraine left by the receding Glaciar del Torre. From Laguna Torre, there are stunning views of the principal southern peaks of the Fitzroy Range. Allow at least three hours each way.

Clouds usually enshroud the summit of 3128m-high Cerro Torre, but try for a glimpse of the 'mushroom' of snow and ice that caps the peak. This precarious formation is the final obstacle for serious climbers, who sometimes spend weeks or months waiting for weather good enough for an ascent. Protected *campsites* are available in the beech forest above Laguna Torre.

Another exceptional, but more strenuous, hike climbs steeply from the pack station at the Madsen campground; after about an hour, there's a signed lateral to excellent backcountry *campsites* at **Laguna Capri**. The main trail continues gently to **Río Blanco**, a base camp for climbers of Cerro Fitzroy, and then climbs very steeply to **Laguna de los Tres**, a high alpine tarn named in honor of the three Frenchmen who first scaled Fitzroy. Condors glide overhead and nest in an area where, in clear weather, the views are truly extraordinary. Allow about four hours each way, and leave time for contemplation and physical recovery after the last segment, where high winds can be a real hazard.

If the weather doesn't permit climbing to the Laguna – or even if it does – consider a one-hour detour down the Río Blanco to **Glaciar Piedras Blancas**, the last part of which is a scramble over massive granite boulders to a turquoise lake with dozens of floating icebergs and constant avalanches on the glacier's face.

Ambitious hikers can make a circuit through the Fitzroy Range that is shorter than the one in Torres del Paine but still worthwhile; another possibility is Laguna del Desierto, north of El Chaltén. The owner of *Los Troncos*, a good private campground along the circuit, restricts access through his land, making it an obligatory overnight, and there may be other restrictions; ask for details at the ranger station in El Chaltén.

At **Lago del Desierto**, 30km north of El Chaltén, visitors from Argentina appear to be enforcing their country's territorial claim against Chile with pretentious plaques and by leaving behind toilet paper and cigarette butts. There is, however, a 500m trail to an overlook with magnificent views of the lake and surrounding mountains and glaciers, although the weather often intervenes to prevent photography. Powered by twin outboards, the enclosed *Mariana II* (☎ 02902-491-103 in El Calafate), cruises the length of the lake (80 minutes) thrice daily for US$30 roundtrip. Chaltén Travel minibus service

to Lago del Desierto, leaving at 11 am and returning at 4:30 pm daily, costs US$15 return.

Adventurous hikers may opt to take three- to 15-day guided hikes over the **Hielo Patagónico Continental** (Continental Ice Field); for details, contact Parques Nacionales or the local representative of the Asociación Argentina de Guías de Montaña (☎ 493-017). Rates range from US$75 to US$150 per day.

From the north shore of Lago Viedma, at Puerto Bahía Túnel, it's possible to visit the Finnish pioneer **Estancia Helsingfors**, on the south shore, by taking the *Embarcación Huemul*, which also passes the Viedma Glacier. The eight-hour excursion costs US$55; it's possible to continue to El Calafate for another US$15. Buses to Puerto Bahía Túnel leave from Confitería La Senyera. It's also possible to get to Helsingfors and El Chaltén directly from El Calafate (US$65); make reservations at Nova Terra (☎ 02902-491-726), 25 de Mayo 23.

The highly regarded *Hostería Helsingfors* (☎/fax 011-4824-6623 in Buenos Aires, landsur@wam.com.ar) has accommodations with full board for US$125/210 singles/doubles from November to mid-December and in March, while prices during Semana Santa are US$140/260. Children under 12 pay half. There are also three-day, two-night packages that include transport from El Calafate and continue to El Chaltén, for US$365/650 singles/doubles with full board and excursions; two-day, one night packages cost US$225/410. For the latest details, see the Helsingfors home page (www.wam.com.ar/tourism/estancs/helsingfors/).

Places to Stay

Budget There's free camping at Parques Nacionales' *Camping Madsen* in El Chaltén, with running water and abundant firewood, but no toilets – you must dig a latrine. There's another free, but less sheltered, site across the road from Parques Nacionales' information office. If you don't mind walking for 10 minutes or so, you can shower at Confitería La Senyera for about US$2.

Most commercial campgrounds, such as **Posada Lago del Desierto** and **El Relincho**, charge about US$5 per person, sometimes charging extra for hot showers. **Ruca Mahuida** (☎ 493-018) charges US$6 per person, has meals and hot showers and arranges local excursions.

El Chaltén has three HI-affiliated hostels. **Albergue Los Ñires** (☎ 493-009) is a small eight-bed hostel that charges US$10 per member, US$12 per nonmember, and US$5 per person for camping. The larger but homier Dutch-Argentine-run **Albergue Patagonia** (☎ 493-019, patagoni@hostels.org.ar) charges US$12 plus US$2 for kitchen privileges; reasonable meals are also available, and it stays open all year.

The spacious 44-bed **Albergue Rancho Grande** (☎/fax 493-005, bigranch@hostels.org.ar, rancho@cotecal.com.ar) costs US$10 for HI members, US$12 for nonmembers. You might want to opt for a US$75 package that includes return transportation from Calafate, one night's lodging, dinner and breakfast; two-night packages cost US$100. To make reservations from El Calafate, contact Chaltén Travel (☎ 02902-491-833), Av Libertador 1177, Santiago.

Top-End *Hotel Lago del Desierto* (☎ 493-010) has comfortable four-bed apartments, with kitchen facilities, private bath and hot water, for US$80; its hotel has doubles for US$70. Meals are expensive. *Cabañas Cerro Torre* (☎ 493-061) has four-bed cabins with private bath for US$20 per person (US$25 with breakfast). At the *Fitzroy Inn* (☎ 493-062), rates are US$75/80 singles/doubles with breakfast, US$95/120 with half board.

Places to Eat
La Senyera del Torre (☎ 493-063) serves enormous portions of tasty chocolate cake, plus other high-quality snacks and light meals. *The Wall* (☎ 493-092) is a popular pub-restaurant.

Confitería Carrilay Aike (☎ 493-060) has good homemade bread, teas and the like for breakfast. *Josh Aike* (☎ 493-008) has drawn praise for its pizzas, desserts and breakfasts, but the best place to eat is *Ruca Mahuida*

(☎ 493-018), part of the eponymous campground, which has tasty and creative cuisine in a smoke-free environment. *La Casita* (☎ 493-042) comes recommended by locals, but the food can't match Ruca Mahuida and poor ventilation makes the smoke-laden atmosphere almost lethal.

Groceries (including fresh bread) are available at *Kiosko Charito* and *El Chaltén*.

Getting There & Away
El Chaltén is 220km from El Calafate via paved RP 11, rugged RN 40 and improved but still rugged RP 23. See El Calafate's Bus section, earlier in the chapter for details on daily buses to El Chaltén; buses normally return from El Chaltén at 5 or 6 pm. There is also direct service from Río Gallegos with Transportes Burmeister, which drops off and picks up passengers at The Wall, and with Chaltén Patagonia, which stops at Albergue Rancho Grande.

Northbound on RP 40, the nearest gas station is at Tres Lagos, 123km east of El Chaltén. Beyond the RP 23 junction, RN 40 is very bad and carries little traffic. Daniel Bagnera (☎ 011-4302-9533 in Buenos Aires) operates the minibus service Itinerarios y Travesías to the lakeside town of Los Antiguos, near the Chilean border town of Chile Chico in the Aisén region, twice weekly in October and April, four times weekly in November and March, six times weekly from December through February, and weekly from May to September. Including a 2½-hour stop at the impressive cave painting site of Cueva de las Manos, the trip takes 18 hours and costs US$92. While the price may seem high, it's the only fixed transport on this route, which is rough on vehicles, and compared with backtracking to Río Gallegos or flying from Punta Arenas to Coihaique it's pretty cheap. For the latest information in El Chaltén, ask at Albergue Patagonia or, in El Calafate, at Cal-Tur (☎ 02902-491-368), Av Libertador 1080, or at Albergue Lago Argentino (☎ 02902-491-139).

Between Tres Lagos and Bajo Caracoles, the highway has been greatly improved, permitting speeds between 65 and 80kph en route to Perito Moreno and Los Antiguos, but loose gravel can make this route hazardous in places, especially for less stable, high-clearance vehicles.

Tierra del Fuego

Ever since the 16th-century voyages of Magellan and the 19th-century explorations of Fitzroy and Darwin on the *Beagle*, this 'uttermost part of the earth' has held an ambivalent fascination for travelers of many nationalities. For more than three centuries, its climate and terrain discouraged European settlement, yet indigenous people considered it a 'land of plenty.' Its scenery, with glaciers descending nearly to the sea in many places, is truly enthralling.

The Yahgan Indians, now nearly extinct, built the continuous, warming fires that inspired Europeans to give this region its name, now famous throughout the world. It consists of one large island, Isla Grande de Tierra del Fuego, and many smaller ones, only a few of which are inhabited. The Strait of Magellan separates the archipelago from the South American mainland.

History

While Magellan passed through the strait that bears his name in 1520, neither he nor anyone else had any immediate interest in the land or its people. In search of a passage to the spice islands of Asia, early navigators feared and detested the stiff westerlies, hazardous currents and violent seas that impeded their progress. Consequently the Ona, Haush, Yahgan and Alacaluf peoples who populated the area faced no immediate competition for their lands and resources.

All these groups were mobile hunters and gatherers. The Ona, also known as Selknam, and Haush subsisted primarily on terrestrial resources, hunting the guanaco for its meat and its skins, while the Yahgans, also known as the Yamana, and Alacalufes, known collectively as 'Canoe Indians,' lived primarily on fish, shellfish and marine mammals. The Yahgans, consumed the 'Indian bread' fungus *(Cytarria darwinii)* that parasitizes the *ñire*, a species of southern beech. Despite frequently inclement weather, they wore little or no clothing, but constant fires (even in their bark canoes) kept them warm.

The *Beagle* sails the Strait of Magellan.

The decline of Spain's colonization of the Americas slowly opened the area to European settlement and began the rapid demise of the indigenous Fuegians, whom Europeans struggled to understand. Darwin, visiting the area in 1834, wrote that the difference between the Fuegians, 'among the most abject and miserable creatures I ever saw,' and Europeans was greater than that between wild and domestic animals. On an earlier voyage, Captain Robert Fitzroy of the *Beagle* had abducted several Yahgans, whom he returned to their home after several years of missionary education in England.

From the 1850s, there were attempts to Christianize the Fuegians, the earliest of which ended with the death by starvation of British missionary Allen Gardiner. Gardiner's successors, working from a base at Keppel Island in the Falklands, were more successful despite the massacre of one party by Fuegians at Isla Navarino. Thomas Bridges, a young man at Keppel, learned to speak the Yahgan language and became one of the first settlers at Ushuaia, in what is now Argentine Tierra del Fuego. His son Lucas Bridges, born at Ushuaia in 1874, left a fascinating memoir of his experiences among the Yahgans and Onas entitled *The Uttermost Part of the Earth*.

Although the Bridges family and many of those who followed had only the best motives, the increasing European presence exposed the Fuegians to diseases such as typhoid and measles, to which they had had no exposure and had little resistance. One measles epidemic wiped out half of the native population in the district, and recurrent contagion nearly extinguished them over the next half-century. Some early sheep ranchers made things worse with their violent persecution of the Indians, who had resorted to preying on domestic flocks as guanaco populations declined.

Since no European power had any interest in settling the region until Britain occupied the Falklands in the 1770s, Spain too paid little attention to Tierra del Fuego, but the successor states of Argentina and Chile felt differently. The Chilean presence on the Strait of Magellan, from 1843, and increasing British mission activity spurred Argentina to formalize its authority at Ushuaia in 1884, with the installation of a territorial governor the following year. International border issues in the area were only finally resolved in 1984, when an Argentine plebiscite ratified a diplomatic settlement of a dispute over three small islands in the Beagle Channel, which had lingered for decades and nearly brought the two countries to open warfare in 1979.

Despite minor gold and lumber booms, Ushuaia was for many years primarily a penal settlement for both political prisoners and common criminals. Sheep farming brought great wealth to some individuals and families and is still the island's economic backbone, although the northern area near San Sebastián has substantial petroleum and natural gas reserves. Since the 1960s, the tourist industry has become so important that flights and hotels are often heavily booked in summer. The spectacular mountain and coastal scenery in the immediate countryside of Ushuaia, including Parque Nacional Tierra del Fuego, attracts both Argentines and foreigners.

Geography & Climate

Surrounded by the South Atlantic Ocean, the Strait of Magellan and the easternmost part of the Pacific Ocean, the archipelago of Tierra del Fuego has a land area of roughly 76,000 sq km, about the size of Ireland or South Carolina. The Chilean-Argentine border runs directly south from Cape Espíritu Santo, at the eastern entrance of the Strait of Magellan, to the *Canal Beagle* (Beagle Channel), where it trends eastward to the channel's mouth at Isla Nueva. Most of Isla Grande belongs to Chile, but the Argentine side is more densely populated, with the substantial towns of Ushuaia and Río Grande. Porvenir is the only significant town on the Chilean side.

The plains of northern Isla Grande are a landscape of almost unrelenting wind, enormous flocks of Corriedales and oil derricks, while the island's mountainous southern part offers scenic glaciers, lakes, rivers and seacoasts. The mostly maritime climate is surprisingly mild, even in winter, but its changeability makes warm, dry clothing important, especially when hiking or at higher elevations. The mountains of the Cordillera Darwin and the Sierra de Beauvoir, reaching as high as 2500m in the west, intercept Antarctic storms, leaving the plains around Río Grande much drier than areas nearer the Beagle Channel.

The higher southern rainfall supports dense forests of southern beech *(Nothofagus)*, both deciduous and evergreen, while the drier north features extensive native grasses and low-growing shrubs. Storms batter the bogs and truncated beeches of the remote southern and western zones of the archipelago. Guanaco, rhea and condor can still be seen in the north, but marine mammals and shorebirds are the most common wildlife around tourist destinations along the Beagle Channel.

Books

Even though its practical information is badly out of date, the third edition of Rae Natalie Prosser Goodall's detailed, bilingual guidebook *Tierra del Fuego* is the most informed single source on the island's history and natural history. A new edition seems unlikely very soon, but the old one is still for sale in local bookshops in Ushuaia.

Dangers & Annoyances

Note that collecting shellfish is not permitted because of toxic red-tide conditions. Hunting is also illegal throughout the Argentine part of Tierra del Fuego.

Getting There & Around

Overland, the simplest route to Argentine Tierra del Fuego is via Porvenir, across the Strait of Magellan from Punta Arenas; for details, see Punta Arenas' boat section, earlier in the chapter. Transbordadora Austral Broom (☎ 218-100, Anexo 21 in Punta Arenas) operates the roll-on, roll-off auto ferry *Bahía Azul* across the narrows at Primera Angostura, from Punta Delgada to Chilean Tierra del Fuego, but no public transportation connects with it. The ferry operates from 8 am to 11 pm daily; the half-hour crossing costs US$2 for passengers and

US$13 for automobiles or pickup trucks. There are occasional breaks in service because of weather and tidal conditions.

The principal border crossing is at San Sebastián, a truly desolate place about midway between Porvenir and Río Grande. Roads have improved considerably in recent years. Although they are unpaved on the Chilean side, Argentine RN 3 is smoothly paved from San Sebastián past Río Grande as far as Tolhuín on Lago Kami, and about half the stretch of the Ushuaia-Tolhuín portion had been finished by 1999, leaving the stretch over Paso Garibaldi to be completed. Winter weather and a provincial financial crisis have slowed work recently.

PORVENIR
☎ 61

Founded barely a century ago to service the new sheep estancias across the Strait of Magellan from Punta Arenas, Porvenir is the largest settlement on Chilean Tierra del Fuego. Many of its 5083 inhabitants claim Yugoslav (mostly Croatian) descent, dating from the brief 1880s gold rush that is commemorated by several monuments and a pleasant waterfront park.

Porvenir becomes visible only as the ferry from Punta Arenas approaches its sheltered, nearly hidden harbor. The waterfront road, or *costanera*, leads from the ferry terminal to a cluster of rusting, metal-clad Victorians that belie the town's optimistic name ('the future'). The beautifully manicured Plaza de Armas has a worthwhile museum, but for most travelers Porvenir is a brief stopover en route to or from Ushuaia, on the Argentine side of Tierra del Fuego.

Motorists will find the gravel road east, along Bahía Inútil to the Argentine border at San Sebastián, in excellent condition but a bit narrow in spots. Northbound motorists from San Sebastián should take the equally good route from Onaisín to Cerro Sombrero and the crossing of the Strait of Magellan at Punta Delgada-Puerto Espora, rather than the heavily traveled and rutted truck route directly north from San Sebastián.

Changes might be in store for Porvenir. The multinational Trillium Corporation's

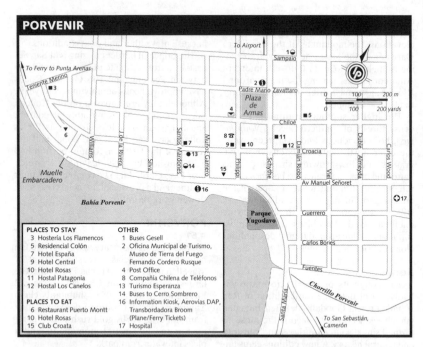

PORVENIR

To Airport

To Ferry to Punta Arenas

Teniente Merino

Padre Mario Zavattaro

Plaza de Armas

Sampaio

Chiloé

Croacia

Muelle Embarcadero

Bahía Porvenir

Av Manuel Señoret

Parque Yugoslavo

Guerrero

Carlos Bories

Fuentes

Chorrillo Porvenir

Santa María

To San Sebastián, Camerón

0   100   200 m
0   100   200 yards

José la Rivera · Santos · Muñoz Gamero · Silva · Schythe · Philippi · Damián Riobó · Viel · Almeyda · Carlos Wood · Duble

Williams

PLACES TO STAY
3 Hostería Los Flamencos
5 Residencial Colón
7 Hotel España
9 Hotel Central
10 Hotel Rosas
11 Hostal Patagonia
12 Hostal Los Canelos

PLACES TO EAT
6 Restaurant Puerto Montt
10 Hotel Rosas
15 Club Croata

OTHER
1 Buses Gesell
2 Oficina Municipal de Turismo, Museo de Tierra del Fuego Fernando Cordero Rusque
4 Post Office
8 Compañía Chilena de Teléfonos
13 Turismo Esperanza
14 Buses to Cerro Sombrero
16 Information Kiosk, Aerovías DAP, Transbordadora Broom (Plane/Ferry Tickets)
17 Hospital

controversial forestry initiative in southern Tierra del Fuego, presently on hold due to its alleged environmental shortcomings, may result in construction of new port facilities in Porvenir costing as much as US$35 million.

Information

Tourist information may be found at the much-improved Oficina Municipal de Turismo (☎ 580-636), upstairs at Padre Mario Zavattaro 402, open from 9 am to 5 pm weekdays only. But information is also available at the kiosk on the costanera between Mardones and Muñoz Gamero.

Correos de Chile is at Philippi 176, on the Plaza de Armas. Telephone service is provided by the Compañía Chilena de Teléfonos, at Philippi 277.

If you need medical attention, Porvenir's hospital (☎ 580-034) is on Carlos Wood between Señoret and Guerrero.

Museo de Tierra del Fuego Fernando Cordero Rusque

This small but intriguing museum has some unexpected materials, including Selknam mummies and skulls, musical instruments used by mission Indians on Isla Dawson, stuffed animals from the region, a display on the evolution of Chilean police uniforms, and another on the enigmatic Julio Popper, the onetime 'dictator' of Tierra del Fuego. Perhaps the most improbable exhibit is one on early Chilean cinematography. On the Plaza de Armas, housed in the same building as the tourist office, museum hours are 9 am to 5 pm weekdays; in January and February, it's also open 11 am to 5 pm weekends.

Organized Tours

Turismo Esperanza (☎ 580-432, cellular 09-640-0162), Croacia 675, offers a 'Ruta de Oro' horseback tour of Porvenir's nearby Córdon Baquedano, a small mountain range that saw somewhat of a turn-of-the-19th-century gold rush and still has some small-scale gold miners.

Places to Stay & Eat
For its size, Porvenir has good accommodations and food, but prices have recently risen. The cheapest rooms are at **Residencial Colón** (☎ 580-108, Damián Riobó 198), where singles with shared bath and breakfast cost US$7. **Hotel España** (☎ 580-160, Croacia 698) has singles with shared bath for US$12 per person, singles/doubles for US$14/26 with private bath. **Hotel Central** (☎ 580-077), at Philippi and Croacia, is a good value for US$19/33 per person for rooms with shared bath, US$24/35 with private bath.

Across the street, **Hotel Rosas** (☎ 580-088, Philippi 296) charges US$24/37 with private bath and has a good seafood restaurant. Two newer choices are **Hostal Patagonia** (☎ 580-372, Schythe 230), which charges US$24/30 but has some doubles with shared bath for US$18, and **Hostal Los Canelos** (☎ 580-247, Croacia 356), which charges US$24/33. For upscale comfort, try **Hostería Los Flamencos** (☎ 580-049, Teniente Merino s/n), overlooking the harbor; however, over the past few years prices have nearly doubled to US$105/126.

The **Club Croata** (☎ 580-053, Manuel Señoret 542) is worth a try for lunch or dinner, as is the simple **Restaurant Puerto Montt** (☎ 580-207, Croacia 1199), near Hostería Los Flamencos.

Getting There & Away
Air Aerovías DAP (☎ 580-089), on Manuel Señoret near Muñoz Gamero, flies across the Strait to Punta Arenas (US$22) at least twice daily except Sunday.

Bus Buses Gesell (☎ 580-162), Sampaio 300, departs Tuesday and Saturday at 2 pm for Río Grande (US$17, seven hours), where there are connections to Ushuaia.

There are also buses to Camerón and Timaukel (US$6, 2½ hours), in the southwestern part of the island, Wednesday at 3 pm; these leave from the DAP offices on Señoret. Monday, Wednesday and Thursday

at 5 pm, there's a bus to Cerro Sombrero (US$6, 1½ hours), departing from Santos Mardones 330.

Boat Transbordadora Broom (☎ 580-089) operates the car-passenger ferry *Melinka* to Punta Arenas (2½ hours, US$7 per person, US$45 per vehicle) Tuesday through Saturday at 2 pm, Sunday and holidays at 5 pm.

Getting Around
The bus to the ferry terminal, departing from the waterfront kiosk about an hour before the ferry's departure, provides a farewell tour of Porvenir for US$1. Taxis cost at least four times as much.

CERRO SOMBRERO
This orderly but half-abandoned town at the north end of Tierra del Fuego, 43km south of the ferry crossing at Primera Angostura, is a company town belonging to Chile's Empresa Nacional de Petróleo (ENAP, National Petroleum Company). It has oddball '60s architecture, a bank, a modern cinema, cheap lodgings, a restaurant open until 3 am and, of all things, an astronomical observatory. The only scheduled public transport comes from Porvenir; return buses to Porvenir leave Monday, Wednesday and Thursday at 8 am.

On the highway outside of town **Restaurant El Conti** serves a chicken soup that's the perfect choice for a cold, windy day (buses between Río Grande and Punta Arenas stop here).

LAGO BLANCO
Excellent fishing can be had at Lago Blanco, in the southern part of Chilean Tierra del Fuego, accessible only by private car. The nearest formal lodgings are in the village of Timaukel, just south of the large estancia at Camerón (which, despite the Spanish accent, takes its name from a Scottish pioneer sheep-farming family). The native forests in this area are presently under pressure from a controversial forestry project that would allow the US-based Trillium Corporation to log substantial areas in return for replanting and preserving others.

ESTANCIA YENDEGAIA

In the Cordillera Darwin, nestled between Argentina's Parque Nacional Tierra del Fuego and Chile's Parque Nacional Alberto de Agostini, Estancia Yendegaia consists of 44,000 hectares of native Fuegian forest, due to become a private national park similar to Doug Tompkins' Parque Natural Pumalín (See the boxed text 'Parque Natural Pumalín' in the Aisén & the Camino Austral chapter). In the works are a series of hiking trails. There will also be postings of park rangers and informational material on environment and archaeological sites. The founders would like to create an alternative to forest megaprojects such as Trillium in what could be a new Torres del Paine, but this is a long-term goal.

Unfortunately, access is difficult and expensive at present. Infrequent naval boats from Punta Arenas to Puerto Williams will drop passengers at the southern approach. There's also an airstrip at Caleta María, at the northern end of the property, that can handle small planes, but the easiest approach would be to hike from Lago Roca on the Argentine side. However, there's no legal border crossing here.

For information on visiting the park, which is accessible only by air or boat, contact Turismo Cordillera Darwin (☎/fax 061-224-637, c_darwin@patagonian.com), José Menéndez 386, Punta Arenas.

PUERTO WILLIAMS

Captain Robert Fitzroy encountered the Yahgan Indians who accompanied the *Beagle* back to England near this Chilean naval settlement on Isla Navarino, directly across the Beagle Channel from Argentine Tierra del Fuego. Missionaries in the mid-19th century and fortune-seekers during the local gold rush of the 1890s established a permanent European presence.

A few people of Yahgan descent still reside near Puerto Williams (population 1800), which is named for the founder of Fuerte Bulnes. A dispute over the three small islands of Lennox, Nueva and Picton, east of Navarino, nearly brought Argentina and Chile to war in 1978, however papal intervention defused the situation and the islands remain in Chile's possession.

Puerto Williams is an official port of entry for yachts, and also a jumping-off point for excursions to Cape Horn, the Cordillera Darwin and Antarctica. The original bow of the *Yelcho*, which saved Ernest Shackleton's Antarctic expedition from Elephant Island in 1916, is also on display here.

Information

There is a cluster of public services, including a telephone, post office, supermarket and tourist office, at President Ibáñez 3. Money exchange is possible at Banco de Chile, Turismo Isla Navarino (☎ 621-140) in the Centro Comercial, and at Sim Turismo, Ricardo Maragano 168, but there is no ATM and traveler's checks are unwelcome.

Things to See & Do

The **Museo Martín Gusinde** (☎ 621-043), honoring the German priest and ethnographer who worked among the Yahgans from 1918 to 1923, has exhibits on natural history and ethnography. It's open 10 am to 1 pm weekdays, and 3 to 6 pm daily. Admission costs US$2.

East of town, at **Ukika**, live the few remaining Yahgan people. There is good hiking in the surrounding countryside, but the changeable weather demands warm, water-resistant clothing.

Organized Tours

German-run Turismo Sim (☎ 621-150, 621-225, fax 621-227, sim@entelchile.net), Ricardo Maragano 168, arranges yacht tours to Antarctica and around the Beagle Channel, as well as trekking, climbing and riding expeditions on Isla Navarino.

Places to Stay & Eat

The new ***Backpacker's Coirón*** (☎ 621-150, sim@entelchile.net, Ricardo Maragano 168) has accommodations for US$13 per person, with kitchen privileges and shared bath. ***Hostería Camblor*** (☎ 621-033) is basic but clean and comfortable for US$13 with breakfast, US$31 with full board, both with private bath. ***Residencial Onashaga*** (☎ 621-081) and

Pensión Temuco (☎ 621-113) charge slightly more, with shared bath; the latter has good meals.

Camping is possible near the upscale, highly recommended *Hostería Wala* (☎ 621-114), which has singles/doubles at US$40/50 (winter prices may be negotiable). Both hotels serve meals. The *Club de Yates Micalvi* has a popular bar and also serves food.

Getting There & Away
Aerovías DAP flies to and from Punta Arenas Tuesday, Thursday and Saturday (US$67 one-way). Seats are limited and advance reservations essential. DAP flights to Antarctica make a brief stopover here.

Regular connections between Puerto Williams and Ushuaia, on Argentine Tierra del Fuego, are due to resume soon; the probable schedule for the Ushuaia-based *Mariana I* is Tuesday, Thursday and Saturday at 4 pm. For the most current information, contact the Gobernación Marítima (☎ 621-090), the Club de Yates (yacht club; ☎ 621-041, Anexo 4250, at night only) or Turismo Sim.

USHUAIA (ARGENTINA)
☎ 02901

Over the past two decades, fast-growing Ushuaia has mutated from a sleepy seaside village into a homely city of 43,000, sprawling and spreading from its original site. The

---

The Frozen South

One of the unanticipated, ironic dividends of the end of the Cold War has been the increasing accessibility of Antarctica at relatively reasonable prices. About 80% of Antarctica's tourists leave from Ushuaia, where it's possible to arrange visits to the frozen continent on Russian research vessels that once benefited from Soviet subsidies but must now pay their own way. To do so, they have begun to take paying passengers on 10- to 17-day Antarctic cruises on well-equipped, remodeled vessels.

Many Antarctic tours are expensive, as much as US$20,000 for a month-long cruise, but trips to the Antarctic peninsula, the region closest to South America, are more reasonably priced. If space is available it's sometimes possible to travel aboard these vessels for as little as US$2000 for a week's voyage, everything included. Several Ushuaia travel agencies arrange Antarctic excursions, but it's also worth going to the port and asking around. Private yachts sometimes carry paying passengers, but they're more expensive.

Adventurous travelers may be able to secure passage on a Chilean navy vessel, resupplying Antarctic stations, from the port of Punta Arenas. You need to be persistent, however, and ask many people in the port, since officially such vessels do not carry passengers. You may also have to be patient, and wait several weeks in Punta Arenas, because it may be that long before a ship returns from a resupplying voyage. The fare is approximately US$80 per day, payable in US cash only, upon return to port. These voyages do not provide the educational lectures and guides offered on commercial trips, and a knowledge of Spanish is desirable.

Overseas operators arranging Antarctic tours include Abercrombie and Kent International (☎ 708-954-2944), 1520 Kensington Rd, Oak Brook, IL 60521; Marine Expeditions (☎ 416-964-9069, 800-263-9147, fax 416-964-2366), 13 Hazelton Ave, Toronto, Ontario M5R 2E1 Canada; Quark Expeditions (☎ 203-656-0499), 980 Post Rd, Darien, CT 06820; Society Expeditions (☎ 800-548-8669), 2001 Western Ave, Suite 300, Seattle, WA 98121; and Zegrahm Expeditions (☎ 800-628-8747), 1414 Dexter Ave N, No 327, Seattle, WA 98109.

Available guidebooks to Antarctica include Lonely Planet's *Antarctica* (2000), by Jeff Rubin, Ron Naveen's *Oceanites Site Guide to the Antarctic Peninsula* (1997) and Tony Soper's *Antarctica: A Guide to the Wildlife* (1994).

setting is still dramatic, however, with jagged glacial peaks rising from sea level to nearly 1500m. The city's drawbacks include its tacky commercialism and shabby new construction, but the countryside offers activities such as trekking, fishing and skiing, as well as the opportunity to venture to the most southerly point accessible by road – RN 3 ends at Bahía Lapataia in Parque Nacional Tierra del Fuego, 3242km from Buenos Aires.

In 1870, the British-based South American Missionary Society made Ushuaia its first permanent outpost in the Fuegian region. Now only artifacts, shell mounds, memories and Thomas Bridges' famous dictionary remain of the Yahgan Indians who once flourished here. Nearby Estancia Harberton, now open to visitors, still belongs to descendants of the Bridges family.

Between 1884 and 1947, Argentina incarcerated many of its most notorious criminals and political prisoners here and on remote Isla de los Estados (Staten Island). Since 1950, Ushuaia has been an important naval base that Argentina has used to support its Antarctic claims, and in recent years it's become an important tourist destination.

Wages are higher than in mainland Argentina, thanks to industrial successes in electronics assembly, fishing and food processing, but so are living expenses. The boom is subsiding, and the city is set to lose the preferential tax treatment it now enjoys, with the imposition of IVA in 2003.

Orientation

Running along the north shore of the Beagle Channel, the beautified Av Maipú becomes Av Malvinas Argentinas west of the cemetery and, as RN 3, continues west to Parque Nacional Tierra del Fuego. The waterfront – its harbor protected by the nearby peninsula (site of the expanded airport) – is a good place to observe shorebirds.

Ushuaia has no central plaza. Most hotels and visitor services are on or within a few blocks of Av San Martín, the principal commercial street, one block north of Av Maipú. North of Av San Martín, streets rise very steeply, offering good views of the Beagle Channel.

Information

Tourist Offices The municipal Dirección de Turismo (☎ 424-550, 0800-333-1476 on the Argentine side of the island of Tierra del Fuego), Av San Martín 660, also has an airport branch for visitors arriving on planes and another at the port for those arriving on ships. They maintain a complete list of accommodations with current prices and will assist in finding a room with private families; after closing time they post a list of available lodgings. They also have a message board, and the friendly, patient and helpful staff usually includes an English speaker and, less frequently, a German, French, or Italian speaker. Hours are 8 am to 9 pm weekdays, 9 am to 8 pm weekends and holidays.

The provincial Instituto Fueguino de Turismo (Infuetur; ☎ 423-340) is on the ground floor of Hotel Albatros at Maipú and Lasserre. The Automóvil Club Argentino (ACA, ☎ 421-121) is at Malvinas Argentinas and Onachaga.

Consulates Chile has a consulate (☎ 422-177) at Jainén 50, open 9:30 am to 1 pm weekdays. Germany maintains a consulate (☎ 430-763) at Alem 966.

Immigration The Dirección Nacional de Migraciones (☎ 422-334) is at Beauvoir 1536.

Money Several banks on Maipú and San Martín have ATMs. The best bet for cashing traveler's checks (2% commission) is Banco de la Provincia, San Martín 396. CrediSol, on San Martín between Rosas and 9 de Julio, takes 5% commission for cashing traveler's checks.

Post & Communications Correo Argentino is at Av San Martín and Godoy. The postal code is 9410. Locutorio del Fin del Mundo is at Av San Martín 957, and Locutorio Cabo de Hornos is at 25 de Mayo 112.

The Dirección de Turismo has a convenient telephone line for collect and credit-card calls to Brazil, Chile, France, Italy, Japan, Spain, Uruguay and the United States (AT&T, MCI, Sprint). The Oficina Antarctica Infuetur (☎ 424-431), on the

USHUAIA (ARGENTINA)

PLACES TO STAY			
2	Hostal del Bosque	19	Volver
4	Hostal América	20	Club Náutico
5	Hospedaje Torres al Sur	21	La Salchicha Austral
8	Hostería Mustapic	35	Barcleit 1912
9	El Refugio del Mochilero	37	Helados Bobby
24	Hotel Maitén	38	Café de la Esquina
26	Residencial Fernández	42	Barcito Ideal
29	Hospedaje Malvinas	44	La Estancia
30	Hospedaje Hilda Sánchez	45	La Don Juan
32	Hotel Cabo de Hornos	46	Tante Sara
36	Hotel César	64	Moustacchio
57	Hotel Canal Beagle	67	La Casa de los Mariscos
59	Hotel Albatros		

PLACES TO EAT		OTHER	
3	Kaupé	1	Tres Marías Excursions
6	Mi Viejo	7	Sheik
13	Tante Sara	10	Museo Marítimo
15	Pizzería El Turco		(ex-Presidio de Ushuaia)
16	Opíparo	11	Administración de
			Parques Nacionales

12	Avis/Tagle Rent A Car
14	Locutorio del Fin del Mundo
17	Banco de Tierra del Fuego
18	Iglesia de la Merced
22	Oficina Antarctica Infuetur
23	Hospital Regional
25	Casa de la Cultura
27	Automóvil Club Argentino
28	Chilean Consulate
31	Los Tres Angeles
33	CrediSol
34	Ansa International (AI)
39	Locutorio Cabo de Hornos
40	Banco de la Provincia
	de Santa Cruz
41	Aerolíneas Argentinas
43	Post Office
47	Kaikén Línea Aéreas
48	Optica Eduardo's, Genesys
49	Seven Deportes
50	BanSud

51	Club Andino Ushuaia
52	All Patagonia (American Express)
53	Crafts Market,
	Biblioteca Sarmiento
54	Dirección de Turismo
55	Lapa
56	Tecni-Austral
58	LADE
59	Instituto Fueguino de Turismo
	(Infuetur), Localiza Rent a Car
60	Poder Legislativo
61	Banco de la Provincia
62	Rumbo Sur/Línea B
65	Banca Nazionale del
	Lavoro (ATM)
66	Antartur
68	Banco de la Nación
69	Museo Territorial Fin del Mundo
70	Asociación Caza y Pesca
71	Transportes Pasarela
72	Buses Eben-Ezer, Kaupén

waterfront Muelle Comercial, has email services (antartida@tierradelfuego.ml.org) for a small charge. Genesys, on San Martín near 9 de Julio, also offers email access.

National Parks The Administración de Parques Nacionales (☎ 421-315), San Martín 1395, is open 9 am to noon weekdays.

Travel Agencies Ushuaia has nearly twenty travel agencies. Among them are: Rumbo Sur (☎ 422-441, rumbosur@satlink.com), at Av San Martín 342 and at the Muelle Turístico; Antartur (☎ 423-240), at Maipú 237; and All Patagonia (☎ 430-725), Juana Fadul 26, which is the American Express representative.

Laundry Los Tres Angeles (☎ 422-687) is at Juana M de Rosas 139.

Medical Services Ushuaia's Hospital Regional (☎ 422-950, 107 for emergencies) is at Maipú and 12 de Octubre.

Museo Territorial Fin del Mundo

The city has restored the original facade of this unusual block construction, dating from 1903. Atypical of Magellanic architecture, the building once belonged to the family of territorial governor Manuel Fernández Valdés. An informed, enthusiastic staff oversees exhibits on Fuegian natural history, aboriginal life, the early penal colonies (complete with a photographic rogues' gallery) and replicas of an early general store and bank. The prize exhibit, though, is a copy of Thomas Bridges' Yamana-English dictionary. There is also a bookstore and a specialized library.

On the waterfront at Av Maipú and Rivadavia, the museum (☎ 421-863) charges US$5 admission, but ask about student discounts. It's open 10 am to 1 pm and 3 to 7 pm Monday to Saturday in summer, 4 to 8 pm the rest of the year.

Museo Marítimo

As early as 1884, Argentina's federal government established a military prison on Isla de los Estados (Staten Island), at the east end of Tierra del Fuego, partly to support its territorial claims in a region inhabited only by hunters and gatherers with no state allegiance. In 1902, the prison was shifted to Ushuaia and, in 1911, it merged with the Carcel de Reincidentes, which had incarcerated civilian recidivists since 1896.

One of Ushuaia's most famous inmates was Russian anarchist Simón Radowitzky, who assassinated Buenos Aires police chief Ramón Falcón with a bomb after a police massacre of laborers on May Day in 1909. Too young for the death penalty, Radowitzky received a life sentence at Ushuaia, but briefly escaped to Chile with the aid of Argentine anarchists before being caught and brought back to Ushuaia. In 1930 radical president Hipólito Yrigoyen ordered him released, but then the military dictatorship that overthrew Yrigoyen confined several radical political figures to the Ushuaia prison, including writer Ricardo Rojas, diplomat and former presidential candidate Honorio Pueyrredón and Pueyrredón's vice-presidential candidate Mario Guido. Héctor Cámpora, who served as president before Juan Perón's last term, also did time here.

Closed as a penal institution since 1947, the present building, when operational, held up to 800 inmates in 380 cells designed for one prisoner each. Officially, it is now the Museo Marítimo, with scale models of famous ships such as the *Beagle* and polar explorer Roald Amundsen's *Fram*, and a 1:1 replica of Isla de los Estados' (Staten Island) Faro San Juan de Salvamento, featured in Jules Verne's story 'The Lighthouse at the End of the World.' There are also numerous Antarctic materials.

Incorporated into the naval base at the east end of Av San Martín, the museum (☎ 424-058) is open 10 am to 1 pm and 4 to 8 pm daily and also has a café. Admission is US$7, with discounts for children, students and seniors; use the entrance at Yaganes and Gobernador Paz rather than the base entrance at Yaganes and San Martín.

Other Things to See

Ushuaia is capital of the province, and the **Poder Legislativo** (Provincial Legislature; built in 1894) occupies a very traditional Magellanic building at Maipú 465. At Av San Martín 674, a crafts market operates outside the former **Biblioteca Sarmiento** (1926), Ushuaia's first public library. Built with convict labor, the century-old **Iglesia de la Merced**, at Av Maipú and Don Bosco, is currently undergoing restoration.

Activities

All of Ushuaia's travel agencies arrange activities such as trekking, horseback riding, canoeing, mountain biking and fishing in and around Parque Nacional Tierra del Fuego and elsewhere on the island. See the Dirección de Turismo for a listing that rates these activities from *sin dificultad* (easy) to *pesado* (very difficult).

Fishing Fishing is a popular pastime for both Argentines and foreign visitors; there are two kinds of permits, one for the national park and one for the island at large. For the former, which costs US$10 daily, US$30 weekly, US$60 monthly and US$100 for the season, visit the Administración de Parques Nacionales (see Ushuaia's Information section, earlier in the chapter). For the latter, visit the Asociación Caza y Pesca (☎ 423-168), at Maipú 822, or Optica Eduardo's

(☎ 433-252), at San Martín 830. These licenses cost US$10 daily, US$20 weekly, US$30 for 15 days and US$40 monthly.

Spinning and fly casting are the most common means of hooking brown trout, rainbow trout, Atlantic salmon and other species. The nearest site is Río Pipo, 5km west of town on RN 3. It is possible to visit the Estación de Piscicultura (trout hatchery) at Río Olivia, 2km east of town.

Mountain Biking From October to April, local operators arrange mountain-bike excursions ranging from a full day in Parque Nacional Tierra del Fuego to weeklong tours over Paso Garibaldi to Lago Kami, Lago Yehuin and Río Grande. Distances range from 50km to 95km per day; fortunately, the wind is usually at your back. For rentals, try Seven Deportes (☎ 437-604), San Martín 802.

Skiing From June to mid-September, the nearby mountains provide opportunities for both downhill and cross-country skiing, although only the period around Argentine winter holidays in early July is really busy. The main downhill area is **Centro de Deportes Invernales Luis Martial** (☎ 421-423, 423-340), 7km northwest of town, which has one 1300m run on a 23° slope, with a double-seat chairlift (maximum capacity 244 skiers per hour). The Club Andino Ushuaia (☎ 422-335), Fadul 50, has a smaller area only 3km from downtown on the same road.

East of Ushuaia, along RN 3 toward Paso Garibaldi, are cross-country ski areas at the Club Andino's Pista Francisco Jermán, 5km from town; at Valle de los Huskies (☎ 431-902), 17km from town; at Tierra Mayor (☎ 437-454), 21km from town; at Las Cotorras (☎ 499-300), 26km from town; and at Haruwen (☎/fax 424-058), 37km from town. Rental equipment is available at each site for around US$30 per day. Each center provides its own transportation from downtown Ushuaia.

Ushuaia's biggest ski event is the annual **Marcha Blanca**, a symbolic re-creation of José de San Martín's historic crossing of the Andes, taking place on August 17, the date of the great man's death. Attracting up to 450 skiers, it starts from Las Cotorras and climbs to Paso Garibaldi.

Organized Tours

Overland Trips Local operators (see Travel Agencies earlier in this chapter) offer tours to the principal attractions in and around Ushuaia, including a half-day city tour (US$15 including the museum). Tours of Parque Nacional Tierra del Fuego (US$15 to US$20) and historic Estancia Harberton (US$55 to US$70), east of Ushuaia, and excursions over Paso Garibaldi to Lago Kami/Fagnano (US$30 full-day) and Río Grande.

Boat Trips Popular boat trips, with destinations such as the sea lion colony at Isla de los Lobos, leave from the Muelle Turístico (tourist jetty) on Maipú between Lasserre and Roca. The most commonly seen species is the southern sea lion *Otaria flavescens*, whose thick mane will make you wonder why Spanish-speakers call it *lobo marino* (sea wolf). Fur seals, nearly extinct because of commercial overexploitation during the past century, survive in much smaller numbers; they usually arrive in early January. Isla de Pájaros, also in the Beagle Channel, has many species of birds, including extensive cormorant colonies.

See travel agencies for trips on the luxury catamarans *Ana B*, *Ezequiel B* and *Luciano Beta*, which cost about US$30 for a 2½-hour excursion to Isla Lobos; with an extension to Bahía Lapataia or the penguin colony near Estancia Harberton, they cost US$50. Trips to Estancia Harberton cost US$70.

Héctor Monsalve's Tres Marías Excursiones (☎/fax 421-897), Romero 514 and at the Muelle Turístico, charges US$45 for a four-hour morning or afternoon excursion on the Beagle Channel, including the king cormorant colony on Isla Alicia, the fur seal and sea lion colony on Isla de Lobos, and a short but interesting hike on Isla Bridges, which has a rock cormorant colony, shell mounds, and the occasional king penguin.

For weeklong sailboat excursions around Cape Horn or the Cordillera Darwin (about US$1200 per person), contact travel agencies such as All Patagonia or Rumbo Sur.

Places to Stay

In the summer high season, especially January and February, demand is very high and no one should arrive without reservations; at least, try to arrive early in the day, before everything fills up. If nothing is available, the 24-hour *confitería* at the Hotel del Glaciar (at Km 3.5 on the road to Glaciar Martial) is a good place to stay up drinking coffee. The tourist office posts an outside list of available accommodations after closing time.

Budget For camping, Ushuaia's *Camping Municipal*, 8km west of town on RN 3 to Parque Nacional Tierra del Fuego, has minimal facilities but an attractive setting for US$1 per tent plus US$5 for use of their parrillas. The *Camping del Rugby Club Ushuaia*, 5km west of town, charges US$5 per person up to a maximum of US$15 per tent. Far more central but still a steep uphill walk, *La Pista del Andino* (☎ 02901-1556-8626, *Alem 2873*), at the Club Andino's ski area, charges US$5 per person and offers the first transfer free. It has a bar-restaurant with good atmosphere (you can also crash in the refugio upstairs), but it could use more showers and toilets.

Other *campsites*, both free and for a fee, are at Parque Nacional Tierra del Fuego and out RN 3 toward Río Grande and Valle de los Huskies. *Camping Río Tristen*, at the Haruwen winter sports center, has a dozen sites, with bathrooms and showers, for US$5 per tent (one or two people).

The local affiliate of Hostelling International, highly regarded *Hospedaje Torres al Sur* (☎ 430-745, *torresur@hostels.org.ar, Gobernador Paz 1437*) charges US$10 in low season, US$12 in summer. For non-HI members, it charges US$15 for a single.

Deservedly popular hostel *El Refugio del Mochilero* (☎ 436-129, *25 de Mayo 241*) is not an official HI affiliate, but it has excellent facilities and great ambience for US$13.

At the Martial Glacier, the Club Andino's *Refugio de Alta Montaña* offers hostel accommodations for US$7.

The Dirección de Turismo discourages visitors from *Hospedaje Hilda Sánchez*

(☎ 423-622, *Deloquí 391*), but many travelers have found her place congenial, if crowded and a bit noisy at times. Rates are US$15 per person, and it's open all year.

Run by a Croat national, *Hostería Mustapic* (☎ 421-718, *Piedrabuena 230*) costs US$25/35 with shared bath, US$30/45 with private bath.

The tourist office can help arrange for rooms in *casas de familia*, or private homes, which tend to be cheaper than hotels, but these are usually available only seasonally and change from year to year. Prices are typically in the US$20 per person range, and, occasionally, slightly cheaper.

Mid-Range Mid-range accommodations start around US$35/50 at *Hotel Maitén* (☎ 422-745, *12 de Octubre 140*). Nearby, popular *Residencial Fernández* (☎ 421-192, *Onachaga 72*) also has rooms at US$35/50, while *Hostal América* (☎ 423-358, *Gobernador Paz 1665*) charges US$40/50.

On the waterfront, ACA's *Hotel Canal Beagle* (☎ 421-117, *Av Maipú 599*) is a good value for members and affiliates at US$40/60 but nonmembers pay US$54/80. Other possibilities in this range include *Hotel César* (☎ 421-460, *Av San Martín 753*) for US$45/55 and *Hospedaje Malvinas* (☎ 422-626, *Deloquí 609*) for US$50/60. Boxy *Hotel Cabo de Hornos* (☎ 422-187), Av San Martín at Rosas, charges the same.

Top End On the hillside, *Hostal del Bosque* (☎ 421-723, *Magallanes 709*) has rooms for US$64/80. At *Hotel Ushuaia* (☎ 430-671, *Lasserre 933*) rates are US$60/80, while rooms at quiet *Hotel Tolkeyén* (☎ 434-883), 5km west of town on RN 3, go for US$85/100.

Somewhat overpriced *Hotel Albatros* (☎ 433-446, *Av Maipú 505*) charges US$120 single or double with breakfast, but the restaurant has great harbor views. For US$150, *Hotel del Glaciar* (☎ 430-640, fax 430-636), at Km 3.5 on the road to Glaciar Martial, is probably a better choice, but it's still hard to call it a good value. Five-star *Las Hayas Resort Hotel* (☎ 430-710), at Km 3 on the Glaciar Martial road, charges

US$165/175, but sometimes lacks sufficient staff to provide all the services of a hotel in its category.

Places to Eat

On the waterfront near the Muelle Turístico, informal *La Salchicha Austral* (☎ 424-596) is among the most reasonable places in town. *Pizzería El Turco* (☎ 424-711, San Martín 1440) is also good and relatively inexpensive. *Opíparo* (☎ 434-022, Maipú 1255) specializes in varied, moderately priced pizza and pasta. *Barcleit 1912* (☎ 433-422, Fadul 148) serves pizza plus *minutas* (short orders) with live music Friday and Saturday.

The US$10 *tenedor libre* (buffet) at lively *Barcito Ideal* (☎ 430-614, Av San Martín 393) can be a bargain for travelers making it their only meal of the day. *Mi Viejo* (☎ 423-565, Gobernador Campos 758) also has a tenedor libre special, as does the traditional (but more expensive) favorite *Moustacchio* (☎ 423-308, Av San Martín 298).

At pricier restaurants, reservations are essential for groups of any size. *La Don Juan* (☎ 422-519, San Martín 193) is Ushuaia's main parrilla, but *La Estancia*, on San Martín between Godoy and Rivadavia, offers some competition.

La Casa de los Mariscos (☎ 421-928, San Martín 232) specializes in fish and shellfish, most notably crab. *Tía Elvira* (☎ 424-725, Maipú 349) also has a good reputation for seafood, along with *Volver* (☎ 423-977, Maipú 37). *Kaupé* (☎ 422-704, Roca 470), is the town's most elegant restaurant, especially memorable for crab, but the waterfront *Club Náutico* (☎ 424-028, Maipú and Belgrano) is also a good choice.

Café de la Esquina (☎ 421-446, San Martín 601) is Ushuaia's most popular confitería. *Tante Sara* (San Martín 175), and at the corner of San Martín and Don Bosco, has outstanding ice cream and other desserts. *Helados Bobby* (San Martín 621) features deliciously unusual ice-cream flavors, such as rhubarb and *calafate*, or wild barberry.

Entertainment

Since the *Cine Pakawaia* burned to the ground in May 1998, the only current cinema is at the *Casa de la Cultura*, at Maipú and 12 de Octubre.

Sheik, at Gobernador Paz and Roca, is a good place for drinks and music.

Shopping

Ushuaia is ostensibly a duty-free zone, but overseas visitors will find few bargains compared to Punta Arenas. Locally made chocolates deserve a taste.

Getting There & Away

Air A new 3800m runway at Aeropuerto Internacional Malvinas Argentinas now permits planes larger than 737s to land safely, and Aerolíneas Argentinas' loss of a landing monopoly has allowed some competition from other long-distance carriers. Note that the airport taxes here are the most expensive in the country: US$4 to Río Grande, US$13 elsewhere in Argentina, and US$20 international.

Aerolíneas Argentinas (☎ 421-091), Roca 116, flies twice daily, with an additional flight on Monday, Thursday and Sunday, to Buenos Aires' Aeroparque (US$147 to US$252); the Monday flight stops in Trelew (US$79 to US$157).

Lapa (☎ 422-150), 25 de Mayo 64, flies daily except Saturday to Trelew (US$90 to US$156) and Aeroparque (US$149 to US$245); the flights on Tuesday, Thursday and Sunday first stop at Río Gallegos (US$35 to US$61).

LADE (☎ 421-123), in the Galería Albatros at Av San Martín 564, flies Wednesday and Thursday to Río Grande (US$20), Río Gallegos (US$35 to US$61), and El Calafate (US$56), continuing Thursday only to Gobernador Gregores (US$68), Perito Moreno (US$94) and Comodoro Rivadavia (US$100).

Kaikén Líneas Aéreas (☎ 432-963), San Martín 880, flies daily to Río Grande (US$28 to US$36, unfortunately the only way to make a connection to Punta Arenas), Río Gallegos (US$39 to US$49), Comodoro Rivadavia (US$119 to US$142), Trelew (US$129 to US$157) and Bahía Blanca (US$180 to US$221). It also flies daily except Sunday to Bariloche (US$209 to

US$380), Neuquén (US$238 to US$355) and Mendoza (US$265 to US$350).

Bus Tecni-Austral (☎/fax 423-396), in the Galería del Jardín at 25 de Mayo 50, goes to Río Grande (US$21, four hours) at 7:30 am and 6 pm daily. The Monday, Wednesday and Friday morning services continue to Punta Arenas (US$51, 14 hours).

For transportation to Parque Nacional Tierra del Fuego, see the Getting There & Away section for the park, later in this chapter.

Sea The *MV Terra Australis* runs luxury sightseeing cruises, with accommodations and all meals included, to Punta Arenas; for details, see the Punta Arenas entry and local travel agents.

Regular connections between Ushuaia and Puerto Williams, on Chile's Isla Navarino, are due to resume soon; the probable schedule for the Ushuaia-based *Mariana I* is Tuesday, Thursday and Saturday at 9 am. The trip three-hour trip costs US$40.

The *Piratur* (☎ 423-875), a 12-passenger boat, has suspended its service between Puerto Almanza, east of Ushuaia, and Puerto Williams, but this may again become a possibility. Check with the tourist office for an update.

Getting Around
To/From the Airport Aeropuerto Internacional Isla Malvinas is on the peninsula across from the waterfront. Cabs are moderately priced, and there's also bus service along Av Maipú.

Car Although rural public transport is better than at Río Grande, it's still limited. Rental rates for a Fiat Spazio start around US$30 per day, plus US$0.30 per km and at least US$15 for insurance daily. Rental companies include Avis-Tagle (☎ 422-744), at San Martín and Belgrano; AI (☎ 436-388), San Martín 847; and Localiza (☎ 430-663), at Hotel Albatros. Rates go up to US$170 per day plus mileage and insurance for a 4WD pickup.

AROUND USHUAIA
Glaciar Martial
Just within the borders of Parque Nacional Tierra del Fuego lies Glaciar Martial, which hikers can reach via a magnificent walk that begins from the west end of Av San Martín, passes the Parques Nacionales office, and climbs the zigzag road (there are many hiker shortcuts) to the ski run 7km northwest of town. Transportes Pasarela (☎ 433-712, 434-706), leaving from the YPF station at Av Maipú and Fadul, runs five buses daily (US$5 return) to the Aerosilla del Glaciar, a chairlift that is open 10 am to 4:30 pm daily except Monday. Buses Eben-Ezer (☎ 431-133) leaves Maipú and 25 de Mayo 10:30 am and 1, 2:30 and 4 pm, returning at 11 am and 1:30, 4 and 4:45 pm. Kaupén (☎ 434-015) goes at 10:30 am and 12:30 and 3:30 pm.

From the base of the Aerosilla (which costs US$5 and saves an hour's walk), the glacier is about a two-hour walk, offering awesome views of Ushuaia and the Beagle Channel. The weather is changeable, so take warm, dry clothing and sturdy footwear.

Ferrocarril Austral Fueguino
Originally constructed to assist the logging industry during presidio days, Ushuaia's short-line, narrow-gauge railroad has reopened as a tourist train under a 30-year concession and now has permission to enter Parque Nacional Tierra del Fuego as far as Cañadón del Toro. It stops at Cascada La Macarena, whose tourist-trap reconstruction of a Selknam-Ona camp would fit better in Disneyland.

From Ushuaia's Plaza Cívica on the waterfront at the Muelle Turístico, Tranex (☎ 431-600, fax 437-696) sells tickets for the 3½-hour train excursion, which would be a poor value at even a small fraction of the US$26 cost. A bus leaves for the starting point at the municipal campground, 8km west of town, 45 minutes before the 10 am and 3 and 5:30 pm departures.

Estancia Harberton
Fuegian pioneer Thomas Bridges, a missionary from the Falkland Islands, founded this

historic estancia on the north shore of the Beagle Channel, 80km east of Ushuaia via RN 3 and RC-i, but his son Lucas made it famous with his memoir of life among the Yahgan Indians, *The Uttermost Part of the Earth*. Still owned by the Goodalls, direct descendants of the Bridges, the estancia now provides well-organized tours (English is usually spoken) around the Bridges family cemetery, a small native botanical garden with credible replicas of Yahgan dwellings, and the estancia's wool shed, carpenter shop, boathouse, and gardens. Since the severe winter of 1995, the estancia itself has only about 1500 sheep on 20,000 hectares.

Rae Natalie Prosser de Goodall, a North American biologist who married into the family, has also created a bone museum focusing on the region's marine mammals. It's also possible to visit nearby penguin rookeries via the *Piratur*, the small vessel that sometimes crosses to Puerto Williams, Chile.

Estancia Harberton (☎ 422-742, fax 422-743) is open to visitors (US$6 per person for tours) in the summer months. Its *Casa de Té Mánacatush*, serving afternoon tea for US$9, can't match Chubut's Welsh teahouses in northern Argentine Patagonia, but it's not bad and the setting is incomparable. The Goodalls permit *camping* at several sites on their property, but asking permission is obligatory. Several Ushuaia travel agencies offer boat tours (around US$70) of the Beagle Channel that make a short stop at Harberton, but overland visits are more leisurely.

PARQUE NACIONAL TIERRA DEL FUEGO (ARGENTINA)

Bays, lakes, rivers, peaks and glaciers attract many visitors and hikers to Argentina's first coastal national park, a 63,000-hectare unit extending from the Beagle Channel in the south along the Chilean border to beyond Lago Kami/Fagnano in the north. Just 18km west of Ushuaia via RN 3, the park lacks the integrated network of hiking trails of Chile's Torres del Paine. There are several short trails, but the one major trek is now off-limits because of policies that have declared

large but lightly impacted portions of the park *reserva estricta*, closed to all access except for scientific research, while permitting the more accessible *zona de recreación* to get trashed almost beyond belief.

Information
Parques Nacionales maintains a Centro de Información at the park entrance on RN 3, where visitors must also pay the US$5 admission charge.

Flora & Fauna
Three species of the southern beech *(Nothofagus)*, known by their common names coihue, lenga and ñire, dominate the dense native forests. The evergreen coihue and deciduous lenga thrive on heavy coastal rainfall at lower elevations, and the deciduous ñire tints the Fuegian hillsides red during the fall months. Other tree species are less significant and not so conspicuous.

Sphagnum peat bogs in low-lying areas support ferns, colorful wildflowers and the insectivorous plant *Drosera uniflora*; these may be seen on the self-guided nature trail **Sendero Laguna Negra**. To avoid damage to the bog and danger to yourself, stay on the trail, part of which consists of a catwalk for easier passage across the swampy terrain.

Land mammals are scarce, although guanacos and foxes exist; marine mammals are most common on offshore islands. Visitors are most likely to see two unfortunate introductions, the European rabbit and the North American beaver, both of which have caused ecological havoc and proved impossible to eradicate from the park. The former animal numbers up to 70 per hectare in some areas, while the latter's handiwork is visible in the ponds and by the dead beeches along the **Sendero de los Castores** (Trail of the Beavers) to Bahía Lapataia. Originally introduced at Lago Kami-Fagnano in the 1940s, beavers quickly spread throughout the island.

Bird life is much more abundant, especially along the coastal zone, including Lapataia and Bahía Ensenada. The Andean condor and the maritime black-browed albatross overlap ranges here, although neither is common. Shorebirds such as cormorants, gulls, terns, oystercatchers, grebes, steamer ducks and kelp geese are common. The large, striking upland goose *(cauquén)* is widely distributed farther inland.

Books

William Leitch's *South America's National Parks* has a useful chapter on Parque Nacional Tierra del Fuego, emphasizing natural history. Several authors have contributed to Bradt Publications' *Backpacking in Chile & Argentina*, which describes treks in the area around Ushuaia but is skimpy on maps. The second edition of Clem Lindenmayer's Lonely Planet guidebook, *Trekking in the Patagonian Andes* is more detailed.

Two useful guides for birders are Claudio Venegas Canelo's *Aves de Patagonia y Tierra del Fuego Chileno-Argentina* and Ricardo Clark's *Aves de Tierra del Fuego y Cabo de Hornos*. Claudio Villegas' *Aves de Magallanes* is also a worthwhile purchase.

Things to See & Do

Most park trails are very short, and the only remaining trek permitted is a mere 6km through lakeside lenga forest along the level northern shore of Lago Roca to the unimposing border marker at **Hito XXIV**.

Cauquén

Because of Argentina's perpetual fiscal crisis and the military's proprietary attitude toward border zones, there are no official, detailed, easily available maps, but the route is fairly straightforward. Probably the best detailed walking map is the one contained in Lonely Planet's *Trekking in the Patagonian Andes*.

From Bahía Ensenada, Isla Verde-Yishka Turismo runs boat circuits to and from Bahía Lapataia via Isla Redonda, a small island in the Beagle Channel, from 10 am to 6 pm daily.

Places to Stay

Since Hostería Alakush at Lago Roca burned to the ground several years ago, camping is the only alternative for visitors wishing to stay in the park, but it's best not to follow the Argentine example of cutting live wood for your *asado* (campfire).

The only site with hot showers is *Camping Lago Roca*, which charges US$5 per person and also has a confitería and a small grocery, although supplies are cheaper in Ushuaia. *Camping Las Bandurrias, Camping Laguna Verde* (☎ 421-433) and *Camping Los Cauquenes* are improved and improving sites charging US$1 to US$2 per person, while *Camping Ensenada* and *Camping Río Pipo* are free sites that, unfortunately, can be disgracefully filthy. Since they lack even pit toilets and few people bother to dig latrines, toilet paper (and worse) is scattered everywhere.

Getting There & Away

In summer, Transporte Pasarela (☎ 433-712) goes to the park from Ushuaia's YPF station at Av Maipú and Fadul six times daily between 8 am and 10:15 pm, returning between 9 am and 11 pm. The roundtrip fare is US$10, and you need not return the same day.

Buses Eben-Ezer (☎ 431-133) leaves from Maipú and 25 de Mayo five times daily between 9 am and 6 pm, returning between 9:45 am and 7 pm. Kaupén (☎ 434-015) leaves from the same location seven times daily between 9:30 am and 9 pm, returning between 10:15 am and 8 pm.

RÍO GRANDE (ARGENTINA)
☎ 02964

Founded in 1894 on the estuary of the river for which it is named, this bleak, windswept wool and petroleum service center is making a genuine effort to beautify and improve itself, but it still has far to go. A recent economic boom, sparked by a change to duty-free status, has subsided and the local economy has stagnated. Most visitors pass through quickly en route to Ushuaia, but it has a good new museum and the surrounding countryside is not devoid of interest.

Orientation
Río Grande (population 59,813) faces the open South Atlantic on RN 3, which leads 190km southwest to Ushuaia and 79km north to the Chilean border at San Sebastián. The main street is Av San Martín, which runs northwest-southeast and crosses Av Islas Malvinas-Santa Fe, as RN 3 is known through town. Most visitor services are along Av San Martín and along Av Manuel Belgrano between San Martín and the waterfront. Do not confuse the similarly named parallel streets 9 de Julio and 11 de Julio, which are two blocks (as well as two days) apart.

Information
The local tourist office, the Instituto Fueguino de Turismo (Infuetur, ☎ 422-887, infuerg@satlink.com), is located in the lobby of Hotel Los Yaganes, at Belgrano 319; hours are 10 am to 5 pm weekdays.

There are several banks with ATMs on and near Av San Martín.

Postal services are offered at Correo Argentino, on Rivadavia between Moyano and Alberdi; the postal code is 9420.

Locutorio Cabo Domingo, offering telephone services, is at Av San Martín 458.

El Lavadero, offering laundry services, is at Perito Moreno 221.

Río Grande's Hospital Regional (☎ 422-088) is at Av Belgrano 350.

Museo de Ciencias Naturales e Historia
Río Grande's new natural sciences and history museum, at Elcano 159, challenges visitors' preconceptions about the region's aboriginal inhabitants ('Could you maintain your family with these tools?'). It also has good displays on Fuegian natural history, cartography, communications (postal, aerial and electronic) and even astronomy. It's open 9 am to 5 pm daily.

Places to Stay
Patience and perseverance are necessary in order to find quality budget accommodations, which often fill up fast.

Budget *Hospedaje Noal (☎ 422-857, Rafael Obligado 557)* charges US$15 per person for rooms with shared bath, US$18/35 singles/doubles with private bath, but without breakfast. At *Hostería Antares (☎ 421-853, Echeverría 49)*, rates are US$15 per person.

Hotel Rawson (☎ 425-503, fax 430-352, JM Estrada 750) is probably the best budget choice, at US$22/33 for small but spotless and well-heated rooms with private bath and cable TV. Another of Río Grande's better choices, *Hotel Villa (☎ 422-312, San Martín 277)* charges US$25/35 singles/doubles.

Mid-Range & Top End The *Hotel Los Yaganes (☎ 430-822, Belgrano 319)* costs US$38/46 for members and affiliates of the Automóvil Club Argentina (ACA), but US$50/61 for nonmembers. *Hotel Isla del Mar (☎ 422-883)*, on Güemes just north of the bus terminal, has rooms with ocean views for US$48/60.

Hotel Federico Ibarra (☎ 430-071, Rosales 357) charges US$63/75, while rates at *Hotel Atlántida (☎ 422-592, Av Belgrano 582)* are US$65/80. Enthusiastically recommended *Posada de los Sauces (☎ 432-895, Elcano 839)* charges US$78/90.

Places to Eat
Hotel Villa, *Hotel Federico Ibarra* and *Hotel Los Yaganes* all have restaurants. For short orders and sandwiches, there are several *confiterías* (confectioner's shop) in and around downtown, including one at *Hotel Rawson*, and *Café La Esquina*, at the corner of Perito Moreno and Espora. At Av Belgrano 464, *La Nueva Piamontesa*

RÍO GRANDE (ARGENTINA)

PLACES TO STAY
2 Hotel Rawson
5 Hotel Atlántida
9 Hotel Los Yaganes
12 Hotel Isla del Mar
13 Hospedaje Noal
18 Posada de los Sauces
19 Hostería Antares
21 Hotel Federico Ibarra
24 Hotel Villa

PLACES TO EAT
2 Hotel Rawson
3 Café Sonora
6 La Nueva Piamontesa
8 El Portal
9 Hotel Los Yaganes
20 La Colonial
21 Hotel Federico Ibarra
22 Estancia Chica
24 Hotel Villa

25 Café La Esquina

OTHER
1 Kaikén Líneas Aéreas
4 Aerolíneas Argentinas
7 Hospital Regional
9 Instituto Fueguino de Turismo (Infuetur)
10 Ansa International (AI)
11 Bus Station
14 Tecni-Austral
15 Post Office
16 Locutorio Cabo Domingo
17 LADE
23 Bansud (ATM)
26 Banco de la Nación
27 El Lavadero
28 El Cine 1 & 2
29 Lapa
30 Banco de Tierra del Fuego (ATM)
31 Aerovías DAP

(☎ 421-977) is an outstanding *rotisería* (grill-room) with reasonably priced take-out meals.

Café Sonora (Perito Moreno 705) has fine pizza at reasonable prices. Popular *La Colonial*, on J Fagnano between Av San Martín and Rosales, is primarily a pizzería but also has other Italian dishes. *El Portal (Belgrano 383)* and *Estancia Chica*, on Espora between Av San Martín and Rosales, are both parrillas.

Entertainment
El Cine 1 & 2 (☎ 433-260, Perito Moreno 211) shows recent films.

Getting There & Away
Air Aeropuerto Internacional Río Grande is only a short cab ride from downtown.

Aerolíneas Argentinas (☎ 422-748), San Martín 607, flies daily to Río Gallegos and Aeroparque in Buenos Aires. Lapa (☎ 432-

620), 9 de Julio 747, flies daily to Río Gallegos, Bahía Blanca and Aeroparque.

LADE (☎ 421-651), located at Lasserre 447, flies Tuesday and Wednesday to Ushuaia; Wednesday and Thursday to Río Gallegos and El Calafate; and Thursday to Gobernador Gregores, Perito Moreno and Comodoro Rivadavia.

Kaikén Líneas Aéreas (☎ 430-665), Perito Moreno 937, flies five times daily except Sunday (three times) to Ushuaia and four times daily to Río Gallegos; it also serves El Calafate, Comodoro Rivadavia, Trelew, Bariloche, Neuquén, Mendoza and Bahía Blanca.

Aerovías DAP (☎ 430-249), 9 de Julio 597, flies Monday, Wednesday and Friday at 11 am to Punta Arenas, Chile (US$79).

Bus Río Grande's bus station (☎ 421-339) is at the foot of Av Belgrano on the waterfront, but most companies have offices elsewhere in town as well.

A chorus of moai, Easter Island

Present-day castaways, Isla Robinson Crusoe

Whale bones, Isla Alejandro Selkirk

Hanga Roa's Ahu Tahai, Easter Island

King cormorants colonize the Falklands.

Penguins rule at Falkland's Volunteer Point.

Port Howard farm, West Falkland

Tecni-Austral (☎ 430-610), Moyano 516, goes to Ushuaia (US$21, four to five hours) at 7:30 am and 6 pm daily, stopping en route at Tolhuin (US$10), and also goes to Punta Arenas at 11:30 am Monday, Wednesday and Friday. It also sells tickets for Transporte Gesell (☎ 421-339), which leaves at 8 am Wednesday and Saturday for Porvenir (US$25, seven hours) in Chilean Tierra del Fuego, meeting the ferry to Punta Arenas.

Buses Pacheco (☎ 423-382) has buses that leave for Punta Arenas (US$30) Tuesday, Thursday, and Saturday at 7:30 am. Prevensur (☎ 420-465), at the terminal, goes to Tolhuin at 9 am and 3 pm daily.

Getting Around

Given the region's limited public transportation options, fishing and other excursions outside town are much simpler when done in a rental car, available from Ansa International (AI; ☎ 422-657), at Ameghino 612.

AROUND RÍO GRANDE

The most interesting historic site is the **Museo Salesiano**, 10km north of town on RN 3, established by the missionary order that converted the Indians in this part of the island. Its several distinctive buildings contain a wealth of geologic, ethnographic and natural history artifacts, but unfortunately the order does little with them. It's open 10 am to 12:30 pm weekdays and 3 to 7 pm every day; admission is US$2 for adults, US$1 for children.

Historic **Estancia María Behety**, 17km west of town via RC-c, features the world's largest shearing shed. **Estancia José Menéndez**, 25km southwest of town via RN 3 and RC-b, is another historic ranch.

The entire coastline of northeastern Tierra del Fuego, from south of Río Grande north to Bahía San Sebastián, is a migratory bird sanctuary known as **Reserva Provincial Costa Atlántica de Tierra del Fuego**; part of this area, near the San Sebastián border crossing, is the particularly dense marshland habitat **Refugio de Vida Silvestre Dicky**.

Lago Fagnano, also known as Lago Kami, fills the huge glacial trough on RN 3 between Río Grande and Ushuaia; about 100km from Ushuaia on the south shore, beautifully sited *Hostería Kaikén* (☎ 02964-492-208) offers lodging for US$25/35 single/double, but it's often full. Its restaurant has good but rather costly meals, with indifferent service (at best). Pasarela buses (US$25) go to Ushuaia at 2 pm daily, Antartur buses (US$20) at 4 pm, but the Tecni-Austral buses at 9:45 am and 8:15 pm cost only US$10.

Fishing

Fishing is a popular activity here. For information on guided trips on the Fuego, Menéndez, Candelaria, Ewan and MacLennan Rivers, contact the Club de Pesca John Goodall (☎ 424-324), Ricardo Rojas 606 in Río Grande. One recommended place is *Hostería San Pablo* (☎ 02964-424-638), 120km southeast of Río Grande via RN 3 and RC-a, where there is good fly-fishing for trout and salmon on the Río Irigoyen. Rooms cost US$30/35 singles/doubles with breakfast; lunch or dinner costs an additional US$13.

Archipiélago Juan Fernández

Scottish maroon Alexander Selkirk left a peculiar legacy to the Juan Fernández Archipelago. In 1966 the Chilean government, motivated explicitly by tourist concerns, renamed Isla Masatierra, the only inhabited island of the group, 'Isla Robinson Crusoe' in honor of literature's most renowned castaway. Selkirk, who spent more than four years in utter isolation on Masatierra, was the real-life model for Daniel Defoe's fictional character, Robinson Crusoe. Though set in the Caribbean, Defoe's fictionalized account of Selkirk's experiences became the enduring classic for which Isla Robinson Crusoe is now named.

The history of Isla Robinson Crusoe, though, is much more than that of Alexander Selkirk's sojourn, and the island is much more than a hermit's hideaway. Singularly serene, it is also a matchless national park and a Unesco World Biosphere Reserve, with much to offer the motivated traveler. Despite the government's intentions, it, along with Isla Alejandro Selkirk and Isla Santa Clara, the other islands that comprise the Juan Fernández Archipelago, is not a major holiday destination and is not likely to become one because of the near impossibility and clear undesirability of significantly expanding its tourist infrastructure. Between December and March, about 40 to 50 foreigners per month visit the island; the rest of the year, visitation drops off dramatically.

HISTORY

Uninhabited when Spanish mariner Juan Fernández discovered them in November 1574, the islands as a group still bear his name. The modest Fernández named them the 'Islas Santa Cecilia,' and two decades passed before Spain attempted even a temporary occupation. For more than two centuries, the islands were largely a refuge for pirates and sealers who sought the pelts of the endemic Juan Fernández fur seal *(Arctocephalus phillippi)*.

According to one account, North American sealers took nearly three million sealskins off the even more remote Masafuera between 1788 and 1809. Single cargoes of 100,000 pelts were not unusual, bringing the species nearly to extinction by the early 19th century. When North American sealer Benjamin Morrell visited in 1824, he speculated oddly that the absence of these seals had to do with the establishment of a Chilean penal colony:

Fur and hair-seals formerly frequented this island; but of late they have found some other place of resort, though no cause for the change has been assigned. Perhaps the moral atmosphere may have been so much affected by the introduction of three hundred felons as to become unpleasant to these sagacious animals.

Whether or not Morrell gave the fur seal too much credit for virtue and wisdom, the Juan Fernández Archipelago was most renowned for the adventures of Scotsman Alexander Selkirk, who spent more than four years marooned on Masatierra after being put ashore (due to a dispute with the captain), at his own request, from the privateer *Cinque Ports* in 1704. This was tantamount to a death sentence for most castaways, who soon starved or shot themselves, but Selkirk survived, adapting to his new home and enduring his desperate isolation.

Ironically the Spaniards, who vigorously opposed the presence of privateers in their domains, had made his survival possible. Unlike many small islands, Masatierra had abundant water, but the absence of food could have been a problem if the Spanish had not introduced goats. Disdaining fish, Selkirk tracked these feral animals, attacked them with his knife, devoured their meat and dressed himself in their skins. Sea lions, feral cats and rats – the latter two European introductions – were among his other companions.

Every day, Selkirk climbed to a lookout above Cumberland Bay (Bahía Cumberland) in hope of spotting a vessel on the horizon, but not until 1708 did his savior, Commander Woodes Rogers of the British privateers *Duke* and *Duchess,* arrive with famed privateer William Dampier as his pilot. Rogers recalled first meeting with Selkirk when the ship's men returned from shore:

Immediately our Pinnace return'd from the shore, and brought abundance of Craw-fish, with a man Cloth'd in Goat-Skins, who look'd wilder than the first Owners of them.

After signing on with Rogers and returning to Scotland, Selkirk became a celebrity.

After Selkirk's departure, privateers (persona non grata on the South American mainland) frequented the islands even more for rest and relaxation, of a sort, and to hunt seals. In response, Spain reestablished a presence at Bahía Cumberland in 1750, founding the village of San Juan Bautista. Occupation was discontinuous, though, until Chile established a permanent settlement in 1877.

After the turn of the 19th century, Masatierra played a notorious role in Chile's independence struggle, as Spanish authorities exiled 42 criollo patriots to the island after the disastrous Battle of Rancagua in 1814. The exiles, including prominent figures such as Juan Egaña and Manuel de Salas, neither accepted nor forgot their relegation to damp caves above San Juan; for many years, the island remained a nearly escapeproof political prison for the newly independent country. During WWI, it once again played a memorable historic role, as the British naval vessels *Glasgow* and *Orama* confronted the German cruiser *Dresden,* scuttled by its crew at Bahía Cumberland before it could be sunk.

Since then, the islands have played a less conspicuous but perhaps more significant role in global history. In 1935, in order to protect the islands' unique flora and fauna,

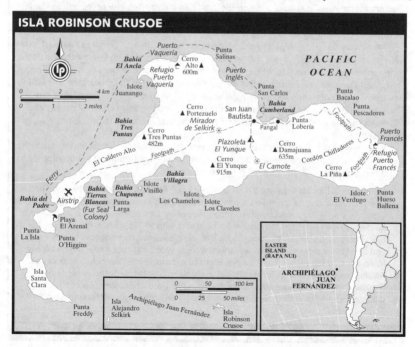

ISLA ROBINSON CRUSOE

the Chilean government declared them a national park, and, later, undertook a program to remove the feral goats (on whose predecessors Selkirk depended so much for his subsistence.

Isla Robinson Crusoe made the news again in 1998 when US communications engineer Bernard Keiser claimed to have detected, by remote sensing, a buried treasure near the site of Selkirk's house at Puerto Inglés. However, substantial excavations in the vicinity found nothing. The possibility of buried treasure has not completely disappeared, however, and Keiser hopes to resume his activities.

GEOGRAPHY & CLIMATE

Separated from Valparaíso by 670km of the open Pacific, the Juan Fernández Archipelago consists of Isla Robinson Crusoe (formerly Masatierra), Isla Alejandro Selkirk (formerly Masafuera) and Isla Santa Clara. The original Spanish names are prosaic: Masatierra simply means 'closer to land,' ie, to the South American continent, while Masafuera means 'farther out' – it is another 170km away from the continent. Tiny Isla Santa Clara, known to early privateers as Goat Island, is only 3km off the southern tip of Isla Robinson Crusoe.

Who Was Friday?

Europeans receive credit for many achievements that others accomplished first. Five hundred years after Columbus stumbled onto the Bahamas, thinking he had reached Japan, he is still known for 'discovering' a continent that Asian immigrants reached at least 12,000 years earlier. Sophisticated Polynesian navigators crossed the Pacific to South America long before Spaniards ever imagined the splendor of the Inkas. And a Miskito Indian from Nicaragua spent several years in solitary exile on the Juan Fernández Islands decades before Captain Stradling of the *Cinque Ports* put Alexander Selkirk ashore or Daniel Defoe made Robinson Crusoe an enduring figure in world literature.

Admittedly the young Miskito, Will, would never have seen Juan Fernández without 'help' from Europeans. Accompanying the famous English privateer William Dampier to the Pacific after meeting him in the Caribbean, Will was inadvertently left ashore when Spanish forces surprised Dampier's expedition at Cumberland Bay in 1681. For three years, he successfully evaded Spanish detection for, as Dampier wrote, 'The Moskitos are in general very civil and kind to the English...but they do not love the French, and the Spaniards they hate mortally.' Even today, the Miskito of Nicaragua and Honduras prefer English to Spanish as a second language.

Will's life in the Caribbean prepared him well for his isolation in the Juan Fernández islands. Knowing the ingenuity and adaptability of the Miskito, Dampier was not surprised to find that Will had made the most of limited resources:

He had with him his Gun and a Knife, with a small Horn of Powder and a few Shot; which being spent, he contrived a way by notching his Knife, to saw the Barrel of his Gun into small Pieces, wherewith he made Harpoons, Lances, Hooks and a long Knife, heating the pieces first in the Fire, which he struck with his Gunflint, and a piece of the Barrel of his Gun, which hardened...The hot pieces of Iron he would hammer out and bend as he pleased with Stones, and saw them with his jagged Knife; or grind them to an edge by long labour, and harden them to a good Temper as there was occasion. All this may seem strange to those that are not acquainted with the Sagacity of the Indians; but it is no more than these Moskito Men are accustomed to in their own Country, where they make their own Fishing and Striking Instruments, without either Forge or Anvil...

The islands' land areas are very small, but their topography is extraordinarily rugged as, geologically, the entire archipelago is a group of emergent peaks of the submarine mountain range known as the Juan Fernández Ridge, which trends east-west for more than 400km at the southern end of the Chile Basin. Isla Robinson Crusoe comprises only 93 sq km, with a maximum length of 22km and a maximum width of 7.3km, but reaches an altitude of 915m on the peak of Cerro El Yunque (The Anvil), which hovers above the island's only settlement, the village of San Juan Bautista. Isla Alejandro Selkirk is even more mountainous, rising to 1650m on Cerro Los Inocentes, where snow has fallen.

The archipelago is far enough from the continent for subtropical water masses to moderate the chilly subantarctic waters of the Humboldt Current, which flows northward along the Chilean coast. The climate is distinctly Mediterranean, with clearly defined warm, dry summers and cooler, wet winters. At San Juan Bautista the maximum mean monthly temperature is 21.8°C, while the minimum mean is 10.1°C, in August. Mean annual precipitation is 1000mm, of

Who Was Friday?

In Central America, the Miskito lived by hunting, fishing, gardening and gathering in the forests and on the shores of the western Caribbean. On Masatierra, without a canoe or dory (a word adapted from Miskito into English), Will could not hunt the green turtle that formed the core of Miskito subsistence, but he could fish the inshore waters of the island. There were no wild deer in Masatierra's dense forests, but he could track and kill the feral goats on which Selkirk later lived. In fact, wrote Dampier, Will was so comfortable that he could afford to be selective in his diet:

He told us that at first he was forced to eat Seal, which is very ordinary Meat, before he had made Hooks: but afterwards he never killed any Seals but to make Lines, cutting their Skins into Thongs. He had a little House or Hut half a Mile from the Sea, which was lin'd with Goats Skins; his Couch or Barbecu of Sticks lying along about two foot distant from the Ground, was spread the same, and was all his Bedding…He saw our Ship the Day before we came to an Anchor, and did believe we were English, and therefore kill'd three Goats in the Morning…and drest them with Cabbage, to treat us when we came ashore.

Dampier's return also reunited Will with a countryman named Robin ('These were names given them by the English, for they had no Names among themselves'), who 'first leap'd ashore, and running to his Brother Moskito Man, threw himself flat on his face at his feet, who helping him up, and embracing him, fell flat with his face on the Ground at Robin's feet…'

This was extraordinary, but the Miskito were no strangers to remote places. It was no coincidence that Defoe placed Robinson Crusoe's fictional island in the Caribbean, where European interlopers had long depended on the Miskito for fishing, hunting and sailing skills by which 'one or two of them in a Ship, will maintain 100 Men…'

In reality, not just one but hundreds of Fridays helped thousands of Crusoes survive the unfamiliar and unwelcoming surroundings in the New World. While the fictional Crusoe may have overshadowed the genuine Selkirk, Friday's real-life Miskito predecessor was more than just a product of Daniel Defoe's imagination. Few knew the names of Will and his countrymen except the English privateers and others 'of whom they receive a great deal of Respect.'

which 70% falls between April and October; less than 10% falls in summer (December to February). Winds often exceed 25 knots.

Because of the islands' irregular topography, rainfall varies greatly over short distances. In particular, the Cordón Chifladores (of which Cerro El Yunque is the highest point) intercepts most of the rainfall, creating a pronounced rain shadow on the southeast portion of Isla Robinson Crusoe – a difference as great as that between Amazonia and the Atacama. By contrast, the area north of the range is dense rain forest, with a high concentration of the endemic species for which the islands were designated a national park and biosphere reserve.

The Pacific Ocean surrounds the islands, but the adjacent seafloor drops abruptly to more than 4000m below sea level on all sides. This leaves relatively little continental shelf to support marine fauna and flora – according to one estimate, the total area exploited for fishing is only about 325 sq km. Those maritime resources that are present, particularly the Juan Fernández lobster *(Jasus frontalis,* really a crayfish), are in great demand on the mainland and provide a substantial income for some of Isla Robinson Crusoe's residents.

FLORA

Like many oceanic islands, the Juan Fernández Archipelago is a storehouse of rare plants and, to a lesser degree, animals, that evolved in isolation and adapted to very specific environmental niches. The indigenous biota have suffered from the introduction of ecologically exotic species, particularly the goats that sustained Selkirk but devoured much of the original vegetation. More opportunistic plant species, resistant to grazing and to fires set by humans, colonized areas goats had degraded.

Still, a great deal of the native flora remains in sectors where even an invader as agile as the goat could neither penetrate nor completely dominate. In places, the terrain is so steep that one can only proceed by grasping branches of the nearly impenetrable foliage. Once, pursuing a feral goat, Selkirk plunged over a sheer cliff and survived only because the animal's body cushioned his fall.

The vegetation of the islands presents an extraordinary mixture of geographic affinities, from the Andes and subantarctic Magallanes to Hawaii and New Zealand. In their oceanic isolation, though, the plant life has evolved into something very distinct from its continental and insular origins. Of 87 genera of plants on the islands, 16 are endemic, found nowhere else on earth; of 140 native plant species, 101 are endemic. These plants survive in three major communities: the evergreen rain forest, evergreen heath and herbaceous steppe.

The evergreen rain forest is the richest of these environments, with a wide variety of tree species such as the endemic *luma (Nothomyrcia fernandeziana)* and the *chonta (Juania australis),* one of only two palm species native to Chile. Perhaps the most striking vegetation, however, is the dense understory of climbing vines and the towering endemic tree ferns *Dicksonia berteroana* and *Thyrsopteris elegans.* The forest was also a source of edible wild plants collected by the crews of visiting ships, as Rogers indicated:

The Cabbage Trees abound about three miles in the Woods, and the Cabbage very good; most of 'em are on the tops of the nearest and lowest mountains.

Evergreen heath replaces rain forest on the thinner soils of the highest peaks and exceptionally steep slopes. Characteristic species are the tree fern *Blechnum cyadifolium* and various tree species of the endemic genus *Robinsonia.* The steppe, which is largely confined to the arid eastern sector of Isla Robinson Crusoe and to Isla Santa Clara, consists of perennial bunch grasses such as *Stipa fernandeziana.*

Exotic mainland species have provided unfortunate competition for native flora. At lower elevations, the wild blackberry *(Rubus ulmifolius)* and the shrub *maqui (Aristotelia chilensis)* have proven to be aggressive colonizers, despite efforts to control them (incidentally, lobstermen use branches from the maqui for their traps). Visiting ships, seeking fresh provisions, once collected edible wild species such as cabbage and even planted gardens that they, and others, later harvested.

FAUNA

The only native mammal, the Juan Fernández fur seal, was nearly extinct a century ago, but has recovered to the point that nearly 9000 individuals now inhabit the seas and shores of Robinson Crusoe and Santa Clara. The southern elephant seal *Mirounga leonina,* hunted for its blubber, no longer survives here. Of 11 endemic bird species, the most eye-catching is the Juan Fernández hummingbird *(Sephanoides fernandensis).* The male is conspicuous because of its bright red color; the female is a more subdued green, with a white tail. Only about 250 hummingbirds survive, feeding off the striking Juan Fernández cabbage that grows in many parts of San Juan Bautista, but the birds do best in native forest.

Introduced rodents and feral cats have endangered nesting marine birds, such as Cook's petrel *(Pterodroma cookii defilippiana),* by preying on their eggs or young. Another mammal that has proliferated since its introduction in the 1930s is the South American coatimundi *(coatí* in Spanish).

BOOKS

Available in many editions, Defoe's classic *Robinson Crusoe* is an obvious choice, but there are many accounts of voyages that stopped at least briefly in the islands. One of the most accessible is Captain Rogers' *A Cruising Voyage Round the World,* available in a Dover Publications facsimile edition (1970). The most thorough history in English is Ralph Lee Woodward's *Robinson Crusoe's Island* (1969).

If you read Spanish and have a general interest in remote oceanic islands, look for Juan Carlos Castilla's edited collection *Islas Oceánicas Chilenas* (1988), which includes articles on various aspects of the natural history of Juan Fernández, Easter Island, San Félix and San Ambrosio (1000km west of Chañaral, and inhabited only by the Chilean navy) and the uninhabited Salas y Gómez, 400km east of Rapa Nui. There are summaries of all the articles in English.

GETTING THERE & AWAY
Air

From Santiago, three companies operate air taxis to Juan Fernández almost daily in summer but less frequently the rest of the year. Flights may be postponed when bad weather makes landing impossible on Isla Robinson Crusoe's improved airstrip. Travel arrangements should be flexible enough to allow for an extra two or three days' stay on the island if necessary. Airlines offer charter flights for up to five passengers, but on a per person basis these are no cheaper than regularly scheduled flights.

Lassa (☎ 02-273-5209, 273-1458 fax 273-4309, lassa@entelchile.net) flies out of Aeródromo Tobalaba, at Av Larraín 7941 in the eastern Santiago comuna of La Reina, where its offices are; the San Juan Bautista office is behind the gymnasium but most easily reached from the pier.

Transportes Aéreos Isla Robinson Crusoe (☎ 02-534-4650, fax 531-3772, tairc@cmet.net), which has offices at Av Pajaritos 3030, Oficina 604 in the southwestern comuna of Maipú, flies out of Santiago's Aeropuerto Los Cerrillos. The island representative is at La Pólvora 226 (☎ 751-099).

Servicios Aéreos Ejecutivos (SAE, ☎ 211-2443, ☎/fax 229-3419, servicio.aereo002@chilnet.cl), Av Apoquindo 7850, Torres 3, Local 4, Las Condes, Santiago, also flies out of Los Cerrillos; their island representative is María del Mar (☎ 751-098).

Roundtrip fares to Isla Robinson Crusoe are around US$390 to US$405, but Lassa has occasional discount packages, including airfare, accommodations and full board at Hostería El Pangal, for US$595 per person, double occupancy. Transportes Aéreos Isla Robinson Crusoe charges US$470.

San Juan Bautista is about 1½ hours from the airstrip by a combination of 4WD (down a frighteningly steep dirt road) to the jetty at Bahía del Padre and motor launch (the best part of the trip, sailing halfway around the island's awesome volcanic coastal escarpments). Both the flight and the rest of the voyage, however, can be rough, so travelers prone to motion sickness may want to consider preventative medication. The cost of the launch, normally about US$15 return, should be included in your air ticket, but check to be certain.

Sea

It's becoming easier to sail to Juan Fernández (and Easter Island) from Valparaíso. Quarterly naval supply ships are the cheapest option, carrying passengers for about US$32 per day, though their infrequency is an obvious drawback – but try contacting the Comando de Transporte (☎ 032-506-354) at the Primera Zona Naval, Plaza Sotomayor 592, Valparaíso.

Naviera del Sur (☎ 032-594-304), Blanco 1041, Oficina 18, Valparaíso, sails to San Juan Bautista in the first fortnight of every month on the small freighter *Navarino*. Since the ship has only four bunks for passengers, reservations are essential. The fare is US$240 return; the trip takes 60 hours out but only 48 back (with favorable currents).

A contract for government-subsidized freight-passenger service from Valparaíso to Juan Fernández and Easter Island is still up in the air.

GETTING AROUND

Getting around Isla Robinson Crusoe presents no major problems but is not necessarily cheap, since it requires hiring a fishing boat or, perhaps more economically, accompanying the lobster catchers to their grounds. To arrange a launch, contact the Municipalidad or ask at the jetty. A launch to Puerto Inglés, for example, costs US$15 for up to eight passengers. Conaf rangers visiting outlying sites in their launch may be willing to take along passengers.

Getting to and from Isla Alejandro Selkirk, rarely visited by foreigners, presents serious problems, but fishing boats will sometimes carry passengers. During lobster season, a Conaf ranger stays on the island. If you manage to get there, you may have to stay for months.

SAN JUAN BAUTISTA

☎ 32

San Juan Bautista, Isla Robinson Crusoe's only settlement, has a permanent popula-

tion of about 500, of whom perhaps 100 are transplanted mainlanders. With only a handful of motor vehicles (not counting launches) and few roads, San Juan Bautista is one of Chile's most tranquil places. Immigrants from the mainland soon adjust to the relaxed pace of island life. Most visitors to Juan Fernández stay here or at nearby Pangal, although it's possible to camp in parts of the national park.

The island economy depends on fishing, mostly for lobster that are afterwards flown to Santiago by air taxi. Most of the 120 fishermen work in open boats, but a handful of them have cabins on their launches. Leaving early in the morning to check their 30 to 40 traps each, they return in the evening to sell their catch to individuals, hotels and the several mainland companies that purchase the lobsters for about US$20 each.

Competition from Peru and Australia, where production costs are lower and transport is cheaper, has undercut the local economy, but a successful lobsterman can usually average half a dozen per day, earning a very substantial income in a place where living costs are low – except for the price of a few imported luxuries. Some do so well in the lobster season, which runs from October through May, that they can afford to take the rest of the year off. Others spend the winter in search of *bacalao* (cod), which they salt and send to the mainland.

Links to the Chilean mainland are significant, since there is no indigenous population, but many islanders rarely or never visit the 'continent.' Children attend school locally up until the eighth grade, after which the most academically talented can obtain grants to finish their secondary education elsewhere in Chile.

In the past few years the town has grown and evidence of affluence has become more palpable – there are sturdier houses, numerous telephones, satellite TV, and more stores, accommodations, restaurants and motor vehicles – despite the fact that there are probably less than 3km of driveable roads in town.

Orientation

Surrounded by forests of exotic conifers and eucalyptus (planted to stem erosion on the nearby hills), San Juan Bautista occupies a protected east-facing site on Bahía Cumberland where, in the evening, schools of flying fish skim across the water. Away from the village, the island's vegetation is more strictly indigenous.

Launches from Bahía del Padre land at the jetty, a short walk from the main street, Larraín Alcalde, which intersects the pleasant Costanera El Palillo a few hundred meters to the south. Other streets – La Pólvora, Subida El Castillo, El Yunque and Vicente González – climb steeply from the shore. There is a bridge across Estero Lord Anson, a stream that flows into the bay. A short distance south of the jetty, there is a landing site for the Chilean navy's roll-on-roll-off cargo vessels. This serves as San Juan Bautista's beach, but there is better swimming and diving off the rocks at El Palillo, at the southern end of the Costanera.

Information

Conaf, in a small kiosk on Larraín Alcalde near the plaza, distributes Sernatur leaflets with decent maps and information about San Juan Bautista and Isla Robinson Crusoe, plus more detailed information on the national park.

There is no bank or other money-changing facilities on the island, so bring all the money you need from the mainland, preferably in small bills. Hostería El Pangal and other hotels normally accept US dollars in payment for lodging, but credit cards are not usually accepted.

Correos de Chile is on the south side of the plaza, and magnetic phonecards are available there.

Conaf's main offices (☎ 751-004, 751-022) are at the top of Vicente González, about 500m above the Costanera. For information on visiting any part of the park outside the immediate environs of San Juan Bautista, it's advisable to contact Conaf in

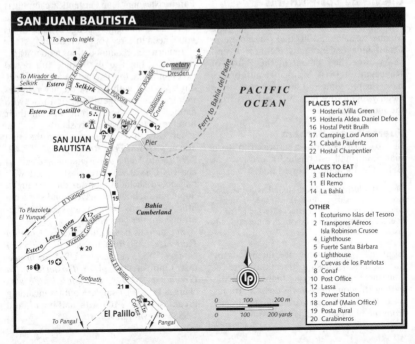

SAN JUAN BAUTISTA

To Puerto Inglés

To Mirador de Selkirk

Estero Selkirk

Estero El Castillo

SAN JUAN BAUTISTA

Cemetery
Dresden

Estero Lord Anson

To Plazoleta El Yunque

To Pangal

El Palillo

To Pangal

Bahía Cumberland

PACIFIC OCEAN

Ferry to Bahía del Padre

Pier

Footpath

| 0 | 100 | 200 m |
| 0 | 100 | 200 yards |

PLACES TO STAY
9 Hostería Villa Green
15 Hostería Aldea Daniel Defoe
16 Hostal Petit Bruilh
17 Camping Lord Anson
21 Cabaña Paulentz
22 Hostal Charpentier

PLACES TO EAT
3 El Nocturno
11 El Remo
14 La Bahía

OTHER
1 Ecoturismo Islas del Tesoro
2 Transpores Aéreos
   Isla Robinson Crusoe
4 Lighthouse
5 Fuerte Santa Bárbara
6 Lighthouse
7 Cuevas de los Patriotas
8 Conaf
10 Post Office
12 Lassa
13 Power Station
18 Conaf (Main Office)
19 Posta Rural
20 Carabineros

advance. Ask for a tour of its plant nursery, where both native and exotic tree species are cultivated, the latter for planting near the town.

The Posta Rural (☎ 751-067), a government clinic, is also on Vicente González, just below the entrance to Conaf's grounds.

Cemetery
San Juan's cemetery, at the north end of Bahía Cumberland near the lighthouse, provides a unique perspective on the island's history, with its polyglot assortment of Spanish, French and German surnames – the latter survivors of the sinking of the *Dresden*.

Just beyond the cemetery, fur seals frolic offshore beneath a spot where, after missing the German cruiser *Dresden*, shells from British ships lodged in the volcanic cliffs. The *Dresden*, however, took enough disabling hits that its captain chose to scuttle it rather than let it fall into British hands.

Cuevas de Los Patriotas
Reached by a short footpath from Larraín Alcalde, these caverns sheltered Juan Egaña, Manuel de Salas and 40 other participants in Chile's independence movement for several years after their defeat in the Battle of Rancagua in 1814. Municipal authorities have cleared some of the eucalyptus in the vicinity to improve the caves' visibility from the shore.

Fuerte Santa Bárbara
In 1767 a British visitor, surprised to learn that Spain had established a presence at Bahía Cumberland, reported that:

This fort, which is faced with stone, has eighteen or twenty embrasures, and within it a long house, which I supposed to be barracks for the garrison: five and twenty or thirty houses of different kinds are scattered round it.

Built in 1749 to discourage incursions by pirates, these Spanish fortifications were reconstructed in 1974. To get there, follow the path north along the Cuevas de los Patriotas past the lighthouse, or else climb directly from the plaza via Subida El Castillo.

Organized Tours
Ecoturismo Islas del Tesoro (☎ 751-058, ☎ 02-335-4325 in Santiago, cellular 09-438-8319), La Pólvora 532, organizes tours on and around the archipelago, including diving, hiking, horseback riding and sightseeing on Isla Alejandro Selkirk. It is possible to pay with credit cards (Visa, MasterCard, American Express) here.

Special Events
June 29 is the Fiesta de San Pedro, in honor of the patron saint of fishermen. On November 22, the anniversary of the original Spanish discovery, islanders celebrate Día de la Isla.

Places to Stay
San Juan's woodsy municipal *Camping Lord Anson*, on Vicente González just above the Costanera, has inexpensive sites with bathrooms and cold showers. There is another, less convenient site at *Plazoleta El Yunque* (see the Parque Nacional Juan Fernández section, later in the chapter). Elsewhere in Parque Nacional Juan Fernández, camping is permitted just about anywhere except in the park's *zona intangible*, though in some areas you'll need to carry your own water.

Otherwise, accommodations tend towards the costly, but usually include full board (keep in mind, this may mean lobster every day). Visitors with special dietary requirements, such as vegetarians or those who cannot eat seafood, should inform their hotel prior to arrival in the islands.

Opposite the carabineros station, the good and new *Hostal Petit Bruilh* (☎ 751-107, 02-741-0186 in Santiago, Vicente González s/n) charges US$20 with breakfast, US$31 with half-board, including lobster the first night. Some guests, however, have found service a little too attentive (the owner's curiosity befitting a former policeman).

Set among beautiful gardens, *Cabaña Paulentz* (☎ 751-108, Costanera El Palillo s/n) charges US$25 single, plus US$5 for breakfast. Opposite the plaza, *Hostería Villa Green* (☎ 751-044, Larraín Alcalde s/n) charges US$41/67 singles/doubles including breakfast, US$72/100 with half-board, and US$85/130 with full board.

Hostería Aldea Daniel Defoe (☎ 751-075, Costanera El Palillo s/n) has seemingly ramshackle shoreline cabins that are surprisingly comfortable, for US$60/80 singles/doubles with breakfast. Half-board and full board are available, and the hotel also serves meals to non-guests, although the food is dearer and no better than that at other restaurants. The staff will, however, prepare lobster for one person.

Hostal Charpentier (☎ 751-070, fax 751-020, Costanera El Palillo s/n) charges US$65/100 with half-board, US$80/120 with full board.

Lassa runs *Hostería El Pangal (☎ 02-273-4354, fax 273-4309 in Santiago)*, which can be reached by launch from the San Juan Bautista jetty, or by a 45-minute walk south along an interesting trail with excellent views of the village and Cerro El Yunque en route. Part of the area around Pangal is badly eroded, and it's less convenient to other areas around the park, but it's also comfortable and peaceful, with great sunset views from the deck. It can be expensive at US$125 single or US$200 double with full board, but does have relatively economical but still comfortable bunks from US$21 single without meals, US$69 with full board.

Places to Eat

If you're not staying or eating at one of the hotels, it's better to give restaurants several hours' or even a day's notice if you want lunch or dinner – at least if you want lobster. If there's no lobster, try the *vidriola,* a particularly tasty fish that's much cheaper.

On the east side of the plaza, *El Remo (☎ 751-030)* serves only sandwiches and drinks, but keeps long hours. *El Nocturno (☎ 751-113, Alcalde Larraín s/n)* has large portions of fresh fish and good french fries. Try the ceviche at *La Bahía (Larraín Alcalde s/n)* which, despite its modest appearance, is one of Chile's best value places, though health problems have caused cook and owner Jorge Angulo to reduce his activities.

Nonguests wishing to dine at *Hostería El Pangal*, which has no telephone, should make reservations by radio-telephone at the police station.

PN JUAN FERNÁNDEZ

Parque Nacional Juan Fernández includes every square inch of the archipelago, a total of 9300 hectares, though the township of San Juan Bautista is a de facto exclusion. Perhaps the best way to see the park in its entirety is to circumnavigate the island's precipitous shoreline in a hired launch from San Juan Bautista, seeing all the major landmarks and pausing at fur seal colonies at Bahía Tierras Blancas (about 1750 seals, the only place they're easily accessible from land), Punta O'Higgins (about 900), Playa El Arenal (about 250) and Bahía Tres Puntas (about 1000). At US$150 for the four- to five-hour trip this isn't cheap, but it's often possible to arrange a group to share the cost. The seals, for their part, frolic in the water, follow the launch and generally make a joyful noise.

Mirador de Selkirk

To see what Selkirk saw, hike to his *mirador* (lookout) above San Juan Bautista. The 3km walk, gaining 565m in elevation, takes about 1½ hours of steady walking but rewards the climber with views of both sides of the island, despite frequent cloud cover. Start as early in the morning as possible and take at least a light cotton shirt since the overlook, exposed to wind and weather, can be much cooler than at sea level. If it's been raining, the trail can be muddy and slippery; a walking stick is a good idea.

On the saddle, there are two metal plaques commemorating Selkirk's exile on the island. The first, minted by John Child & Son of Valparaíso and placed here by officials of the Royal Navy, reads:

In memory of Alexander Selkirk, Mariner, a native of Largo, in the county of Fife, Scotland, who lived on this island in complete solitude for four years and four months.

He was landed from the *Cinque Ports* galley, 96 tons, 16 guns, A D 1704 and was taken off in the *Duke*, privateer, 12th Feb, 1709.

He died lieutenant of *HMS Weymouth*, AD 1723, aged 47 years.

This tablet is erected near Selkirk's lookout, by Commodore Powell and the officers of *HMS Topaze*, AD 1868.

More than a century later, a Scottish relative added his own tribute:

Tablet placed here by Allan Jardine of Largo, Fife, Scotland, direct descendant of Alexander Selkirk's brother David. Remembrance 'Till a' the seas gang dry and the rocks melt in the sun.' January 1983.

The trail to the Mirador begins at the south end of the plaza of San Juan Bautista, climbs the Subida El Castillo, and follows the north side of Estero El Castillo before zigzagging up Cerro Portezuelo to Selkirk's lookout – fill your canteen before continuing up the hillside through dense thickets of maqui and blackberry, which gradually give way to native ferns and trees. Beyond Selkirk's overlook, the trail continues to the airstrip. If you're camping west of the pass, it's possible to walk there to catch your flight back to the mainland, but make arrangements before leaving San Juan Bautista or you could lose your reservation – or have to camp an extra night at the airstrip if the weather delays flights.

Travelers bound to or from the airfield will find the simple *Refugio Villagra* about

TONY WHEELER

Lobster traps, Isla Alejandro Selkirk

an hour's walk from the Mirador, on the south side of the island. Conaf's inexpensive brochure (Spanish only) entitled *Sendero Interpretativo Mirador Alejandro Selkirk* is a detailed guide to the trail's environment.

Plazoleta El Yunque & El Camote
Plazoleta El Yunque, half an hour's walk from San Juan Bautista via a road that becomes a footpath, just beyond the power station at the south end of Larraín Alcalde, is a tranquil forest clearing with picnic and camping areas. A German survivor of the *Dresden* once homesteaded here; the foundations of his house are still visible.

Beyond the plazoleta is a very difficult, poorly marked trail to a saddle at El Camote, which has a splendid view of the south coast of Isla Robinson Crusoe and the offshore Islote (Islet) El Verdugo, a vertical stack that rises 157m out of the sea. This short but exhausting hike is very rewarding but, as part of the *zona intangible*, entry is restricted without special permission. Conaf rangers may accompany motivated hikers who, in any event, will not be able to locate the trail without them. Some of the park's best-preserved flora can be found in this area.

Puerto Inglés
Only a 15-minute boat ride from San Juan Bautista, Puerto Inglés offers a reconstruction of the shelter in which Selkirk passed his years on Masatierra. There are also ruins of a cowherd's shelter and adequate water for camping, but no firewood. If you don't care to pay up to US$15 for a very short boat ride, there is a steep, tiring trail from the top of Calle La Pólvora that will take you over the ridge in about two hours.

Puerto Inglés is the site of US researcher Bernard Keiser's search for millions of dollars worth of buried gold, though so far his quest would have to be qualified as quixotic.

Puerto Vaquería
On the north shore of the island, reachable by launch but with a difficult landing, Puerto Vaquería has a Conaf refugio and a colony of about 100 seals. It's about 30 minutes from San Juan Bautista.

Puerto Francés

On the east shore of the island, Puerto Francés was a haven for French privateers, whose presence motivated Spain to erect a series of fortifications in 1779, the ruins of which still sit atop the hill. It's about 30 minutes by launch from San Juan, but there's also a footpath from Pangal. Another footpath climbs from Puerto Francés, where there's a Conaf refugio, to **Cerro La Piña**, a well-preserved area of native forest.

Bahía Tierras Blancas

Isla Robinson Crusoe's main breeding colony of Juan Fernández fur seals is at Bahía Tierras Blancas, a short distance east of the landing strip above Bahía del Padre. The trail, which connects the airstrip with San Juan Bautista via Mirador de Selkirk, passes close to the colony. There is no drinking water, so bring your own if you plan to camp.

If you can't visit Tierras Blancas or other seal colonies, you can still see pods of fur seals at Bahía del Padre on your arrival, or at the north end of Bahía Cumberland, just beyond the cemetery in San Juan Bautista. Although the seals will not come up on the rocks, you can get within about 10m of them.

ISLA ALEJANDRO SELKIRK

It's difficult and expensive but not impossible to get to Isla Alejandro Selkirk. In San Juan Bautista, contact Julia González (☎ 751-062) or Juanita Díaz at Ecoturismo Islas del Tesoro (see Organized Tours, earlier in the chapter).

Easter Island (Rapa Nui)

How Pacific Islanders arrived at Easter Island (Rapa Nui), one of the world's most remote inhabited islands, is no less an enigma than how their descendants could design and sculpt hundreds of colossal *moai* from hard volcanic tuff, transport these tall and heavy statues great distances from quarry to coast and erect them on great stone *ahu* (platforms).

Residents and visitors have applied various names to this small, isolated volcanic landmass. Polynesian settlers named it Rapa Nui, but the view of the seemingly infinite sea from the summit of Terevaka, the island's highest point, reveals why they also called it Te Pito o Te Henua – the Navel (Center) of the World. From Easter Island, a vessel can sail more than 1900km in any direction without sighting inhabited land.

Dutch mariner Jacob Roggeveen, the first European to sight the island, named it Easter Island, after the date of his discovery; the Spaniards first called it San Carlos (after King Carlos III). Other mariners dubbed it Davis's Land after confusing it with territory identified by the 17th-century English pirate Edward Davis. Roggeveen's legacy survived among Europeans: English speakers call it Easter Island; Spanish speakers refer to Isla de Pascua; Germans to Osterinsel.

A further word on terminology: What exactly to call the island, its inhabitants and their language has been a topic of hairsplitting contention. Some people argue that the two-word term 'Rapa Nui' is an imperial imposition, that the single word 'Rapanui' more closely approximates usage in other Polynesian languages. For purposes of convenience, this chapter uses 'Rapa Nui' to refer to the island as a geographical entity and 'Rapanui' to refer to the people and their language.

HISTORY

In archaeology and the study of antiquity, Rapa Nui raises issues totally disproportionate to its size (only 117 sq km) and population (about 3000 according to recent estimates, with another thousand scattered worldwide).

The nearest populated landmass, 1900km west, is even tinier Pitcairn Island of HMS *Bounty* fame, and the next nearest inhabited 'neighbors' are the Mangarevas (Gambier) Islands, 2500km west, and the Marquesas, 3200km northwest. The South American coast is 3700km to the east. Yet Rapa Nui is central to some very big questions.

The most obvious questions are where the original islanders came from, how they arrived at such an unlikely destination, what inspired them to build the imposing statues for which Rapa Nui is so famous and how the islanders transported those statues from quarry to site. Even larger questions deal with the existence and frequency of transpacific contacts and cultural exchanges between peoples for whom the world's greatest ocean ought to have been an insurmountable barrier.

Five centuries ago, encounters between Europe and the Americas marked the beginning of a global transformation that no one could have anticipated when Columbus, thinking he had reached Japan, set foot in the Bahamas. Everyone knows, of course, that Europeans crossed the Atlantic long before Columbus, but their transient presence made little impact upon North America. Could transpacific crossings have been more significant?

There is a broad consensus that the first Americans were Asiatic peoples who crossed the Bering Strait into Alaska via a land bridge, which disappeared as the sea level rose with the melting of the continental ice sheets at the end of the Pleistocene, about 12,000 years ago. Exact dates are in dispute (some argue that crossings took place during even earlier glacial epochs), but no one doubts that such migrations ceased with the rising oceans. These immigrants reached the southernmost extremes of South America and created the great civilizations of Mexico and Peru. For millennia they were isolated from their Asiatic origins.

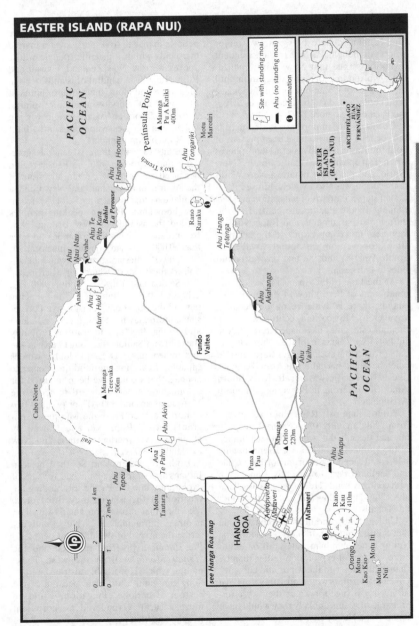

EASTER ISLAND (RAPA NUI)

But how isolated, and for how long? Among scholars of prehistory, there is a long-running debate between two major schools of thought: Partisans of 'independent invention' argue that New World civilizations evolved in geographical isolation until the voyages of Columbus, and 'diffusionists' posit contacts and cultural exchanges across the Pacific long before 1492.

Economically important plants, such as the coconut, appear to have been present in both the Eastern and Western Hemispheres when Europeans first came to the New World, and the sweet potato, a New World domesticate, was also a widely diffused Polynesian staple. Patterns of navigation and settlement in the Pacific are central to the diffusionists' arguments, and Rapa Nui is a key piece in a complex puzzle, the last possible stopover on eastbound voyages to South America and the first on westbound ones to Polynesia.

At the time of the Spanish invasion, the inhabitants of Peru knew of distant Pacific islands; there is evidence of long coastal voyages to Mexico and, centuries before, their ancestors may have sailed to Rapa Nui. In 1947 Norwegian explorer Thor Heyerdahl proved that such voyages were feasible when he sailed his balsa raft *Kon-Tiki*, built like early Pacific watercraft, from South America to Raroia, in Polynesia's Tuamotu Archipelago.

After sailing past Rapa Nui on a voyage from Chile, an early-19th-century European mariner described a strong southern branch of the Humboldt (or Peru) Current that, he said, could speed vessels from northern Chile and southern Peru toward this island, even with contrary winds. He strongly advised that all sailing ships follow this route to the South Sea Islands.

Under these conditions it's conceivable that South American Indians reached Rapa Nui by pre-Columbian watercraft on deliberate voyages of exploration rather than by chance drifting with the winds and currents. Given that drifters would probably not have survived a voyage for which they were unprepared, it seems unlikely they would have found Rapa Nui by chance.

It is more probable that Polynesians settled the island from the west. These peoples managed to disperse over a myriad of islands within a gigantic triangle whose apexes were at New Zealand, Hawaii and Rapa Nui, plus a handful of islands deep in Melanesia and along the southern limits of Micronesia. Orthodox academic opinion currently favors an Asiatic origin for the Polynesian peoples who, apparently, built the Rapa Nui monuments.

Details vary, but there is general agreement that migration into the Pacific region began 50,000 years ago, when ancestors of the Australian aboriginals and New Guinea highlanders first crossed the sea in search of new homelands. Papuan-speaking peoples settled the islands of New Britain, New Ireland and perhaps the Solomons no later than 10,000 years ago – possibly much earlier.

Malay-Polynesian speakers, who had colonized the western islands of Micronesia, Fiji, Samoa and Tonga by about 1000 BC, achieved the settlement of the Pacific beyond the Solomons. A distinctive Polynesian culture may have developed on Samoa and Tonga; the final migrations probably started from Samoa and Tonga early in the first millennium AD. Large double canoes capable of carrying the food and domestic animals that would have been required for colonization sailed eastward to settle the Marquesas around 300 AD, or perhaps two centuries earlier. From the Marquesas, migrants settled Rapa Nui and Hawaii by about 800 AD (perhaps earlier) and New Zealand by 900 AD.

Both Polynesians and South American Indians appear to have launched voyages of exploration into the Pacific, establishing the position of the islands they discovered, recording that information, and passing it on to others. Intriguingly, Rapa Nui legends describe the arrival of two different peoples – the *Hanau Eepe* from the east and the *Hanau Momoko* from the west. These names, which Heyerdahl mistranslated as 'long ears' and 'short ears' because of the custom of earlobe elongation, would be more accurately rendered as 'corpulent people' and 'thin people.'

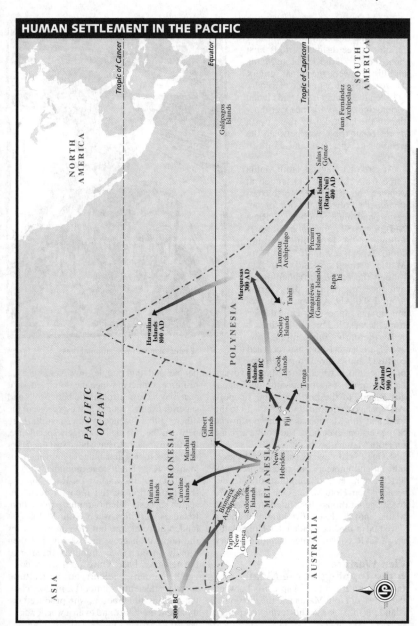

HUMAN SETTLEMENT IN THE PACIFIC

EASTER ISLAND

Legend of Hotu Matua

By oral tradition, Rapa Nui's history falls into three distinct periods. First came the arrival of King Hotu Matua and his followers, the initial settlers. There followed a period of rivalry between the Hanau Eepe and Hanau Momoko, ending with the extermination of the latter. Lastly, there was a more recent tribal war between the peoples of the Tuu and Hotu-iti regions.

According to legend, Hotu Matua came from the east and landed at Anakena on the island's north coast (*matua* is a Polynesian word for 'ancestor' and means 'father' on Rapa Nui). Some 57 generations of kings followed him. From this account, some experts estimate that Hotu Matua arrived around 450 AD, though the earliest archaeological evidence of people dates from around 800 AD. A second group of immigrants supposedly arrived later, from the west, led by Tuu-ko-ihu.

By the early 20th century, however, European visitors had recorded confused and contradictory versions of this legend, in which Hotu Matua's voyage had a number of starting points: the Galápagos Islands to the northeast, the Tuamotu Archipelago to the northwest, Rapa Iti to the west and the Marquesas to the northwest. Some versions even have Tuu-ko-ihu arriving on Hotu Matua's boats.

Trying to date events using genealogies is difficult and imprecise; researchers have collected a number of different lists of kings descended from Hotu Matua. One, estimating 20 to 30 generations descended from Hotu Matua until the last native king died after a slave raid in 1862, concluded that Hotu Matua arrived at Rapa Nui as late as the 16th century.

Clan Warfare & the Toppling of the Moai

In local oral tradition, a gap exists between the arrival of Hotu Matua and the division of islanders into clans. The terms 'corpulent

Easter Islander in ceremonial dress

people' and 'thin people,' however, suggest a resource conflict in which the dominant Miru clan may have controlled the better soils and superior fishing grounds at the expense of the other. At this distance in time, the difference between the two clans is largely speculative, but there appears to have been sustained clan warfare, resulting in damage or destruction of many of Rapa Nui's stone monuments.

What explains warfare on Rapa Nui and the destruction of the moai? Recent research suggests a demographic explanation: islanders were few when Hotu Matua first landed at Anakena, but over the centuries the population grew, first slowly and then rapidly, so that sheer numbers threatened the resource base. Once intensively cultivated gardens yielded an agricultural surplus sufficient to support a priestly class, the artisans and laborers who produced the moai and their ahu, and even a warrior class.

There were limits to this intensification, however. Irrigation, for instance, was difficult or impossible in an environment that lacked surface streams. Forest resources, probably used for timber to move the moai to their ahu, declined greatly, a situation exacerbated by the use of fire for military purposes. Marine food resources were too few and dispersed to provide more than a supplement to agriculture.

Conflict over land and resources erupted in warfare by the late 17th century, only shortly before the European arrival; accounts by later European visitors provide snapshots of the results of what must have been a protracted struggle in which population declined even before slave raids in the mid-19th century. Alfred Metraux estimated a population of up to 4000 for the early 19th century; Katherine Routledge speculated on a maximum population of about 7000, but other informed guesses range up to 20,000.

Dissension between different families or clans led to bloody wars and cannibalism, and many moai were toppled from their ahu. According to one account, tribes or clans were highly territorial and proud of their moai. Enemy groups would topple the moai to insult and anger the statues' owners. Natural disasters – earthquakes and tsunamis – may have contributed to the damage. The only moai standing today have been restored this century.

Arrival of the Dutch

Spanish vessels entered the Pacific from South America in the early 16th century, but in April 1722 a Dutch expedition under Admiral Jacob Roggeveen became the first Europeans to set foot on Rapa Nui. Roggeveen recorded his observations in the ship's log, and another crew member, Carl Behrens, published an account of the voyage. Since they landed on Easter Sunday, by common European custom Rapa Nui acquired the name Easter Island.

The Dutch found the islanders, who subsisted primarily on produce from intensively cultivated gardens and secondarily on the limited wealth of the sea, very friendly. The

A Shaky Explanation

Most of the moai have fallen by human agency, but earthquakes may have contributed to the destruction. Close inspections have shown that some statue bases are broken but still in place; seismic shocks could have caused statues to bounce up and down, cracking their bases and, in some cases, toppling. If this happened at a time when wood was scarce, the moai would not have been put back up. One legend tells of an angry sorcerer who kicked a house post at night, causing statues to fall.

great moai, though, baffled the Dutch, despite obvious religious significance. According to Roggeveen:

What the form of worship of these people comprises we were not able to gather any full knowledge of, owing to the shortness of our stay among them; we noticed only that they kindle fire in front of certain remarkably tall stone figures they set up; and, thereafter squatting on their heels with heads bowed down, they bring the palms of their hands together and alternately raise and lower them.

Behrens recorded that the islanders

relied in case of need on their gods or idols which stand erected all along the sea shore in great numbers, before which they fall down and invoke them. These idols were all hewn out of stone, and in the form of a man, with long ears, adorned on the head with a crown.

Behrens mentioned that some islanders wore wooden blocks or discs in their elongated earlobes – some of which were so long that, after removing the plugs, islanders hitched the lobe over the top of the ear to keep it from flapping. Behrens concluded that islanders with blocks or discs who also shaved their heads were probably priests. Those islanders who did not cut their hair wore it long, either hanging down the back or else plaited and coiled on the top of the head.

EASTER ISLAND

The Spanish Expedition

Not until 1770 did Europeans again visit Rapa Nui, when a Spanish party from Peru under Don Felipe González de Haedo claimed the island for Spain and renamed it San Carlos. The Spaniards recorded that male islanders generally went unclothed, wearing only plumes on their heads, although a few wore a sort of colored poncho or cloak. Women wore hats made of rushes, a short cloak around the breasts and another wrap from the waist down.

Most islanders inhabited caves, but others lived in elliptical boat-shaped houses, probably the type seen earlier by the Dutch. The islanders' only weapons were sharp obsidian knives. The absence of goods and metal implements suggested no commerce with the outside world, but gardens with sugarcane, sweet potatoes, taro and yams provided a healthy subsistence. An expedition officer recorded that the islanders' appearance

[did] not resemble that of the Indians of the Continent of Chile, Peru or New Spain in anything, these islanders being in colour between white, swarthy and reddish, not thick-lipped nor flat nosed, the hair chestnut coloured and limp, some have it black, and others tending to red or a cinnamon tint. They are tall, well built and proportioned in all their limbs; and there are no halt, maimed, bent, crooked, luxated, deformed or bow legged among them, their appearance being thoroughly pleasing, and tallying with Europeans more than with Indians.

Captain Cook

In 1774, the celebrated Englishman Captain James Cook led the next European expedition to land on Rapa Nui. Cook, familiar with the Society Islands, Tonga and New Zealand, concluded that the inhabitants of Rapa Nui belonged to the same general lineage. Later accounts concurred on their Polynesian origins; in 1864 Eugene Eyraud, the first European missionary on the island, commented on the islanders' appearance:

These savages are tall, strong, and well built. Their features resemble far more the European type than those of the other islanders of Oceania. Among all the Polynesians the Marquesans are those to which they display the greatest resemblance. Their complexion, although a little copper-coloured, does neither differ much from the hue of the European, and a great number are even completely white.

Cook conjectured that islanders no longer regarded the moai as idols and thought them monuments to former kings; the ahu appeared to be burial sites. His account is the first to mention that, though some moai still stood and carried their topknots, others had fallen and their ahu were damaged. Cook found the islanders poor and distressed, describing them as lean, timid and miserable.

It seems probable, then, that conflict had raged since the Spanish visit in 1770, reducing the population to misery and destroying some of the moai. Another theory is that the islanders, wary of foreigners, hid in caves from Cook's crew, but this contradicts Roggeveen's account of friendly islanders. It's possible that a number of moai had been toppled even before the Spanish and Dutch visits but that those sailors did not visit the same sites as Cook.

Only one other 18th-century European, the Frenchman La Perouse, visited Rapa Nui. After his two ships crossed from Chile in 1786, he found the population calm and prosperous, suggesting a quick recovery from any catastrophe. In 1804, a Russian visitor reported more than 20 moai still standing, including some at the southern coastal site of Vinapu. Existing accounts from ensuing years suggest another period of destruction, so that perhaps only a handful of moai stood a decade later.

European Colonialism

Whether or not the people of Rapa Nui experienced a period of self-inflicted havoc, their discovery by the outside world nearly resulted in their annihilation. After the European voyages of the late 18th century, European and North American entrepreneurs saw the Pacific as an unexploited 'resource frontier.' First came the whalers – many of them North American – who ranged the Pacific from Chile to Australia. Then came planters who set out to satisfy an increasing European demand for tropical commodities like rubber, sugar, copra and coffee. This often resulted in indigenous peoples becoming slaves or wage laborers on their own lands, or in the importation of foreign labor where local labor proved insufficient, inefficient or difficult to control.

Then came slavers who either kidnapped Polynesians or – to give the trade a veneer of legitimacy – compelled or induced them to sign contracts to work in mines and plantations in lands as remote as Australia and Peru. Many islanders died from the rigors of hard labor, poor diet, disease and maltreatment. Christian missionaries, undermining and degrading local customs, also entered the region. Events on Rapa Nui in the 19th century closely followed this pattern.

Violent encounters had occurred between Europeans and islanders ever since Roggeveen's landing, but in 1862, catastrophe occurred when Peruvian slavers made a vicious and ruthless raid on Rapa Nui. The slavers abducted about a thousand islanders (including the king and nearly all the *maori* or 'learned men') and took them to work the guano deposits on Peru's Chincha Islands. After Bishop Jaussen of Tahiti protested to the French representative at Lima, Peruvian authorities ordered the return of the islanders to their homeland, but disease and hard labor had already killed about 90% of them. On the return voyage, smallpox killed most of the rest, and the handful who survived brought an epidemic that decimated the remaining inhabitants of the island, leaving perhaps only a few hundred.

The first attempts at Christianizing the island occurred after this disaster. Eugene Eyraud, of the Chilean branch of the French Catholic *Société de Picpus,* initially met resistance and left in 1864, but he returned in 1866. With the assistance of other missionaries, he converted the remaining islanders within a few years.

Commercial exploitation of the island began in 1870, when the Frenchman Jean-Baptiste Dutroux-Bornier settled at Mataveri, at the foot of Rano Kau. Importing sheep, he intended to transform the entire island into a ranch and expel the islanders to the plantations of Tahiti. The missionaries, who planned to ship the islanders to mission lands in southern Chile or the Mangarevas,

opposed his claims to ultimate sovereignty over the island and its people.

Dutroux-Bornier armed local followers and raided the missionary settlements, burning houses and destroying crops, leaving many people dead or injured and forcing the missionaries to evacuate in 1870 and 1871. Most islanders reluctantly accepted transportation to Tahiti and the Mangarevas, leaving only about a hundred people on the island. Dutroux-Bornier ruled until the remaining islanders killed him in 1877.

Annexation by Chile

Spain never pursued its interest in Rapa Nui and, in any event, lost all its South American territories early in the 19th century. On the advice of naval officer Policarpo Toro, who had visited as early as 1870, Chile officially annexed the island in 1888 during a period of expansion that included the acquisition of territory from Peru and Bolivia after the War of the Pacific (1879-84).

With its vigorous navy, Chile was capable of expanding into the Pacific. It valued the island partly for its agricultural potential, real or imagined, but mostly for geopolitical purposes as a naval station, to prevent its use by a hostile power, for its location on a potentially important trading route between South America and East Asia, and for the prestige of having overseas possessions – any possessions – in an age of imperialism.

However, because the Chilean government had no clear policy, attempts at colonization came to nothing. By 1897, Rapa Nui fell under control of a single wool company run by Enrique Merlet, a Valparaíso businessman who had bought or leased nearly all the land. Control soon passed into other hands, however.

Williamson, Balfour & Company

In 1851, three Scottish businessmen in Liverpool founded S Williamson & Company to ship British goods to the west coast of South America. Its Chilean branch, Williamson, Balfour & Company, officially came into being in 1863, when the company controlled a substantial fleet and had expanded its interests to include a wide range of products and countries. In the early 20th century, the company acquired Merlet's Rapa Nui holdings, managing the island under lease from the Chilean government through its Compañía Explotadora de la Isla de Pascua (Cedip). The company became the island's de facto government, continuing the wool trade until the middle of the century.

How islanders fared under this system is the subject of differing accounts, but there were several uprisings against the company. One result of foreign control was the genetic transformation of the islanders, as they intermarried with immigrants of many countries. By the 1930s, perhaps three-quarters of the population were of mixed descent, including North American, British, Chilean, Chinese, French, German, Italian, Tahitian and Tuamotuan stock.

In 1953, when Chile was seeking to consolidate its control over its far-flung, unwieldy territories, the government revoked Cedip's lease. The navy took charge of the island, continuing the imperial rule to which islanders had been subject for nearly a century.

Chilean Colonialism

Rapa Nui continued under military rule until the mid-1960s, followed by a brief period of civilian government, until the military coup of 1973 once again brought direct military control. In the 1960s, the island was a Chilean colony pure and simple. The islanders' grievances included unpaid labor, travel restrictions, confinement to the Hanga Roa area, suppression of the Rapanui language, ineligibility to vote (Chilean universal suffrage did not extend to Rapa Nui) and arbitrary naval administration. However, increased contact with the outside world soon developed after establishment of a regular commercial air link between Santiago and Tahiti in 1967, with Rapa Nui as a refueling stop, and things began to change.

For a variety of reasons, including islanders' dissatisfaction, increased immigration from the continent, international attention and tourist potential, and the assumption of power by former president Frei Montalva, the Chilean presence soon became more benevolent, with advances in medical care, education, potable water and electrification.

In August 1985, General Pinochet approved a plan allowing the USA to expand Aeropuerto Internacional Mataveri as an emergency landing site for the space shuttle, arousing opposition both locally and on the continent. But the Rapanui people had no say in the decision. In 1990, though, islanders protested fare increases by LanChile (the only air carrier) and successfully occupied Mataveri airport – even preventing the landing of a jet full of carabineros by blocking the runway with cars and rubble. The global impulse toward self-determination has reached even this remote place, as some islanders argue vocally for the return of native lands and speak hopefully of independence – or at least autonomy. Their aspirations are tempered by realism though; when asked if he would like to expel the Chileans, one islander responded, 'We can't – but we'd like them to leave.'

Since the declaration of Rapa Nui as a national park in 1935, land rights have become an issue; the park comprises more than a third of the island's surface, and nearly all of the remainder belongs to the state. Another contentious matter has been Unesco's proclamation of the park as a world heritage site without consulting the local population. In the words of Mayor Pedro Edmunds Paoa, 'I cannot accept that a group of people claiming to be experts – I don't know who they are – take decisions behind our backs.'

The Frei administration began to deal with some of these matters. In late 1996, it agreed to return about 1500 hectares of land to islanders from the state development company, Corfo; local elected leaders were to determine the distribution of the land among 200 applicants. The government has also expanded the airport and paved the road to Anakena.

A native-rights organization that called itself the Consejo de Ancianos (Council of Elders) demanded the park be returned to its aboriginal inhabitants, who control almost no land outside Hanga Roa proper, and because of lack of faith in the Chilean judiciary have even taken their cause to the

United Nations. At present, though, there are two competing Consejos de Ancianos, prosaically known as No 1 and No 2, split over the issue of formal recognition as an indigenous people within Chile, one group arguing that such recognition condemns islanders to second-class citizenship.

GEOGRAPHY & GEOLOGY

Rapa Nui, just south of the tropic of Capricorn, is a tiny volcanic island formed where lava from three separate cones of different ages coalesced in a single triangular landmass. Its total area is just 117 sq km, and its maximum length 24km. At its widest point, the island is only 12km.

All three major volcanoes are now extinct. Terevaka, the largest, rises 652m above sea level in the northern part of the island, and Pu A Katiki (about 400m) forms the eastern headland of the Poike peninsula; Rano Kau (about 410m) dominates the southwest corner. Smaller craters include Rano Raraku, from whose volcanic tuff islanders carved their giant moai, and Puna Pau, northeast of Hanga Roa, which provided the reddish scoria that forms the statues' topknots. At Orito, islanders quarried black obsidian for spear points and cutting tools. Rano Kau and Rano Raraku both contain freshwater lakes.

For the most part, Rapa Nui's volcanic slopes are gentle and grassy, except where wave erosion has produced nearly vertical cliffs. In contrast, rugged lava fields cover much of the island's interior. Despite this, several areas have soil adequate for cultivation – Hanga Roa and Mataveri on the west coast, Vaihu on the south coast, the plain southwest of Rano Raraku, and inland at Vaitea.

Vulcanism has left numerous caves, many in seaside cliffs. Some caves, consisting of larger and smaller chambers connected by tunnels through which a person can barely squeeze, extend for considerable distances into the lava. These were often used as permanent shelters, refuges in wartime or storage or burial sites.

Rapa Nui rests on a submarine platform some 50m or 60m below the ocean's surface,

but 15 to 30km off the coast, the platform ends and the ocean floor drops to between 1800m and 3600m. There are three islets just off Rano Kau: Motu Nui, Motu Iti and Motu Kao Kao. Motu Nui, the largest, was once a nesting ground for thousands of sooty terns, but overexploitation of the eggs has nearly eliminated the birds.

Although some coral occurs in shallow waters, Rapa Nui does not have coral reefs. In the absence of reefs, the ocean has battered the huge cliffs, some of which rise 300m. Those cliffs composed of lava are usually lower but extremely rugged. There are a few shallow bays, but no natural sheltered harbor, and Anakena on the north coast has the only broad sandy beach.

Rapa Nui's rainfall supports a permanent cover of coarse grasses, but its volcanic soil is so porous that water quickly drains underground. Without permanent streams, water for both humans and livestock comes either from the volcanic lakes or from wells.

CLIMATE

Winds and ocean currents strongly influence Rapa Nui's subtropical climate. The hottest months are January and February, and the coolest are July and August. The average maximum summer temperature is 28°C and the average minimum 15°C, but these figures understate what can be a fierce sun and formidable heat. The average winter maximum is 22°C and the minimum 14°C, but it can seem much cooler when Antarctic winds lash the island with rain. Light showers, however, are the most frequent form of precipitation. May is the wettest month, but tropical downpours can occur during all seasons.

FLORA & FAUNA

Vegetation was once more luxuriant on Rapa Nui – including forests with palms, conifers and other species now extinct – but islanders cut the forests long ago. Most of today's trees, like the eucalyptus, were planted only within the past century. Like other remote islands, Rapa Nui lacks entire families of plants and is particularly poor in native fauna; even seabirds are relatively few.

Some plants are endemic, most notably the tree species toromiro (*Sophora toromiro*) and several genera of ferns. Although the last native toromiro died in 1962, Conaf reintroduced 162 European-cultivated saplings into Rano Kau crater in 1995. About 30 of these have survived, but there is concern that the genetic pool is not large enough to conserve the species; in any event, the competition from more than 60 other introduced trees and shrubs, coupled with a legacy of soil erosion from livestock, have made long-term viability unlikely.

Rapa Nui's original Polynesian immigrants brought small domestic animals such as chickens and rats, and the Norway (brown) rat escaped from European vessels; Europeans also brought horses and sheep in the 19th century.

Conaf's informational booklet *Vegetación de Rapa Nui: Historia y Uso Tradicional*, by Marcos Rauch, Patricia Ibáñez and José Miguel Ramírez, is a useful summary of the island's flora, including native and cultivated plants, medicinal properties, and horticulture. The booklet also contains a selection of illustrations; it sells for US$5 at Conaf offices.

RAPA NUI ANTIQUITIES

Although the giant moai are the most pervasive image of Rapa Nui, islanders created several other types of stonework, most notably the large *ahu* on which the moai were erected, burial cairns (large piles of rock where bodies were entombed) and the foundations of the unusual *hare paenga* (boat-shaped thatched houses). One of the most striking things about the island is the remarkable density of ruins, indicating a much larger population in the past than at present.

Although many structures were partially demolished or rebuilt by the original inhabitants and the moai fell during intertribal wars, Cedip's regime was also responsible for major damage. Many ahu, burial cairns, house foundations and other structures were dismantled and used to build various structures, such as piers at Caleta Hanga Roa and Caleta Hanga Piko and stone walls around grazing areas. Windmills were constructed over native stone-lined wells to provide water for sheep, cattle and horses.

Collectors have pillaged other sites. Only a few moai were removed, but museums and private collections in Chile and elsewhere now feature wooden Rongo-Rongo tablets, painted wall tablets from houses at Orongo, small wood and stone moai, weapons, clothing, skulls and other artifacts. Islanders themselves were responsible for removing building materials from sites like Orongo.

On the other hand, archaeologists have restored a number of sites over the last 30 years. These include Ahu Tahai, Ahu Akivi, the Orongo ceremonial village, Ahu Nau Nau and Ahu Tongariki. Others, such as Ahu Vinapu and Ahu Vaihu, lie in ruins but are nonetheless impressive.

Conaf's *Archaeological Field Guide, Rapa Nui National Park*, written by Claudio Cristino, Patricia Vargas and Roberto Izaurieta, contains useful material in a credible English translation. It's available at Conaf offices for US$3.

Ahu

About 350 ahu form an almost unbroken line along the coast, except for headlands around Península Poike and Rano Kau. They tend to be sited at sheltered coves and areas favorable for human habitation, but only a few were built inland.

Of several varieties of ahu, built at different times for different reasons, the most impressive are the *ahu moai* that support the massive statues. Each is a mass of loose stones held together by retaining walls and paved on the upper surface with more or less flat stones, with a vertical wall on the seaward side and at each end. The moai on these platforms range from 2m to almost 10m in height. Even larger moai were under construction in the quarry at Rano Raraku as work gradually ceased, probably for lack of timber to move and raise the moai.

Usually a gently sloping ramp, paved with rounded boulders or tightly placed slabs of irregular stones, comprises the landward side of the platform. Next to the ramp is a large, perhaps artificially leveled, plaza; in a few cases, these are outlined by earthworks, which form rectangular or irregular enclosures. Sometimes there are small rectangular platforms, which may be altars, or large circles paved with stones, which are either burial sites (as at Ahu Tahai) or *paina* (as at Vaihu), places where feasts paid tribute to deceased ancestors. Early islanders used one- and two-person reed boats, and much larger reed boats were probably launched from *apapa* (stone ramps) leading into the sea alongside the ahu.

Researchers have learned little about the ceremonies connected with these ahu complexes. One theory is that the moai represented clan ancestors and that the ceremonies were part of an ancestor cult. Ahu were also burial sites: Originally bodies were interred in stone-lined tombs in the ahu ramps and platforms but, after the moai had been toppled, bodies were placed around them and on other parts of ramps then covered with stones. Other bodies were cremated at ahu sites, but whether these were bodies of deceased clan members or remains of sacrifices is unknown; oral tradition tells of sacrifice by fire.

Hare Paenga

On or near the restored plaza at Ahu Tahai are several interesting features, among them the foundations of hare paenga. Long and narrow, these houses resembled an upturned canoe, with a single narrow doorway at the middle of one side; the floor shape is outlined by rectangular blocks or curbstones with small hollows on their upper surfaces. To support the walls and roof, islanders inserted poles into these hollows, then arched them across the center of the structure and, where they crossed, lashed them to a ridgepole.

As the space to be covered narrowed near the ends, the roofing poles decreased in length, lowering the roof level. A crescent-shaped stone pavement often covered the entry. These dwellings varied enormously in size; some could house more than 100 people, but others held but half a dozen.

Moai

Although all moai are similar, few are identical. The standard moai at Rano Raraku has its base at about where the statue's hip would be. In general, the statues' arms hang stiffly, and the hands, with long slender fingers, extend across a protruding abdomen. The heads are elongated and rectangular, with heavy brows and prominent noses, small mouths with thin lips, prominent chins and elongated earlobes, which are often carved for inserted ear ornaments. Hands, breasts, navels, and facial features are clear, and elaborately carved backs possibly represent tattoos. Moai vary greatly in size; some are as short as 2m, and the longest is just under 21m. This colossus is unique; the face alone is just over 9m long, it measures just over 4m across the shoulders, and the body is about 1.5m thick. Carvers completed the front and both sides, but never liberated it from the rock below. However, very few are shorter than 3m, and the usual length is from 5.5m to 7m.

It is interesting to speculate on the models for the moai, since their physical features – long straight noses, tight-lipped mouths, sunken eyes, and low foreheads – do not seem Polynesian. Large stone statues have also been found on the Marquesas, Raivavae, and other islands of eastern Polynesia, but also in western South America.

Since the moai at the quarry at Rano Raraku show all stages of carving, it's easy to visualize the creation process. Most moai were carved face up, in a horizontal or slightly reclining position. Workers excavated a channel large enough for the carvers around and under each moai, leaving the statue attached to the rock only along its back. Nearly all the carving, including the fine detail, occurred at this stage. The moai was then detached and somehow transported down the slope (sometimes a vertical wall), avoiding others below. At the base of the cliff at Rano Raraku, workers raised the moai into a standing position in trenches, where sculptors carved finer details on the back and decorated the waist with a belt surrounded by rings and symbols. Basalt *toki,* thousands of which once littered the quarry site, were the carving tools. In *Aku-Aku: The Secret of Easter Island,* Heyerdahl recalls hiring a number of islanders to carve new moai at Rano Raraku; they quit after three days, but their efforts suggested that two teams working constantly in shifts would need perhaps 12 to 15 months to carve a medium-size moai. When carving was finished, moai were moved to their coastal ahu (see the boxed text 'Moving the Moai,' later in this chapter).

Imagine that, having carved a moai from volcanic tuff, you must remove it from its cavity and lower it down the cliff face – which must have been both difficult and dangerous. Broken moai suggest that ropes snapped or workers slipped. After standing the moai up at the base of the slope (probably by sliding it into a trench cut for the occasion) and carving the back, you transport it several kilometers to the coast and stand it upright on a raised platform.

Many of the moai have distinctive features. One displays a three-masted sailing ship on its chest; from the bow, a line extends downward to a circular figure of what might be a head and four short legs. The figure is so crude that it almost certainly has no connection with the carving of the moai itself. This may represent a European ship or a large *totora* reed vessel, and the figure below may be an anchor of some sort, or it could be a turtle or tortoise held by a fishing line. Moai mostly depicted males, but several specimens have carvings that clearly represent breasts and vulva.

A unique discovery at Rano Raraku is the kneeling Moai Tukuturi, which was almost totally buried when found. Slightly less than 4m high, it now sits on the southeastern slope of the mountain. Placing it upright required a jeep, tackle, poles, ropes, chains, and 20 workers. It has a fairly natural rounded head, a goatee, short ears, and a full body squatting on its heels, with forearms and hands resting on its thighs. It has a low brow with curved eyebrows, hollow and slightly oval eyes, and pupils marked by small, round cavities. Both the nose and lips are considerably damaged, but the cheeks are round and natural.

Islanders placed 300 moai on ahu or left them along the old roads in various parts of the island. There are several explanations for this feat, but any valid one must account

for the transport and erection of the biggest moai ever placed on an ahu – the 10m giant at Ahu Te Pito Kura.

Topknots

In the past, archaeologists thought the reddish cylindrical topknots on many moai were hats, baskets or crowns, but there is now a consensus that these *pukao* reflect a male hairstyle common on Rapa Nui when Europeans first visited the island. Quarried from the small crater at Puna Pau, the volcanic scoria from which pukao are made is relatively soft and easily worked. The pukao at Anakena had a clearly marked knot on the top and a partly hollow underside that allowed them to be slotted onto the moai's heads.

Since only about 60 moai had topknots, another 25 of which remain in or near the quarry, they appear to have been a late development. Carved like the moai, the topknots may have been simple embellishments, which were rolled to their final destination and then, despite weighing about as much as two elephants, somehow placed on top of moai up to 10m tall. Early Europeans recorded that moai were still standing on their ahu with the topknots mounted.

Some archaeologists believe that islanders carved the knot on top of the stone and its hollow underside only after transporting the pukao to its ahu – to prevent breaking it in transport and to allow measurement of the head in order to carve a proper-sized hollow – but there are also hollow topknots within the crater itself. Oral tradition says that islanders built a ramp of stones to roll the topknot to the moai's head, but North American archaeologist William Mulloy thought the most likely method of attachment was to tie the topknot to the moai and raise the two simultaneously.

Moai Kavakava

Of all the carved figures that islanders produce, the most common, and at the same time the most exotic, are the *moai kavakava,* or the 'statues of ribs.' Each is a human figure carved in wood, with a large, thin and aquiline nose, protruding cheekbones that accentuate hollow cheeks, extended earlobes, and a goatee that curls back on the chin. Protruding ribs in a sunken abdomen imply starvation.

According to oral tradition, at Puna Pau, King Tuu-ko-ihu chanced upon two *aku aku* (sleeping ghosts) with beards, long hooked noses and pendulant earlobes reaching down to their necks. They were so thin that their ribs stood out. Tuu-ko-ihu returned home and carved their portrait in wood before he forgot their appearance, and since then islanders have always carved these statues.

BOOKS & FILM

For general background on geography and environment, the most thorough source is Juan Carlos Castilla's edited collection, *Islas Oceánicas Chilenas,* which also deals with Chile's other insular possessions, including the Juan Fernández Archipelago.

Though dated, one of the most thorough works on Rapa Nui proper is *Reports of the Norwegian Archaeological Expedition to Easter Island & the East Pacific. Volume 1: Archaeology of Easter Island.* Summarizing the findings of the initial Heyerdahl expedition, it's fully illustrated, with detailed descriptions of all important sites (though none had been restored at the time). More readily accessible are Heyerdahl's popular account of his voyage in *Kon-Tiki* and his *Aku-Aku: The Secret of Easter Island.*

Englishwoman Katherine Routledge was head of the first archaeological expedition, a private venture in 1914. The expedition's scientific notes disappeared, but she published *The Mystery of Easter Island: The Story of an Expedition.* Other pre-Heyerdahl accounts include J MacMillan Brown's *The Riddle of the Pacific* and anthropologist Alfred Metraux's *Ethnology of Easter Island,* based on field research conducted during a French-Belgian expedition in the 1930s.

Bavarian priest Sebastián Englert spent 35 years on Rapa Nui, until his death in 1970; his *Island at the Center of the World* retells the island's history through oral tradition. If you read Spanish, his *La Tierra de Hotu Matua* is a worthwhile acquisition. Englert also analyzed indigenous speech in *Idioma Rapanui – Gramática y Diccionario del Antiguo Idioma de la Isla de Pascua.*

Moai Kavakava (statue of ribs)

Another German, Thomas Barthel, offered a unique perspective on local history via obscure indigenous manuscripts in *The Eighth Land: The Polynesian Discovery and Settlement of Easter Island.*

As the 'Navel of the World,' Rapa Nui is also a focus of the anthropological debate

EASTER ISLAND

over diffusion, independent invention and transpacific contacts. Heyerdahl's *American Indians in the Pacific: The Theory Behind the Kon-Tiki Expedition* compares South American Indian and Pacific cultures, legends, religion, stonework, watercraft, physical characteristics and cultivated plants.

Though the elderly Heyerdahl holds to his conclusions on South American immigration, there is now a consensus that the initial settlers were in fact Polynesians who arrived by way of the Marquesas. For a review of transpacific migration, see Peter Bellwood's 'The Peopling of the Pacific' in *Scientific American* (Vol 243, No 5, November 1980) or his *Man's Conquest of the Pacific*, which also includes a lengthy section on Rapa Nui and the Polynesian-American argument.

A very valuable but diverse collection, dealing partly with pre-Columbian contacts across the Pacific, is *Man Across the Sea*, edited by Carroll L Riley, J Charles Kelley, Campbell W Pennington and Robert L Rands. Based on meticulous research, it deals with a wide variety of related topics, particularly the diffusion of cultivated plants and domestic animals as indicators of human movement.

Some scientists have devised computer simulations of both drift and navigated voyages to try to resolve the matter of Polynesian peoples in the Pacific. One of these is *The Settlement of Polynesia: A Computer Simulation*, by Michael Levison, R Gerard Ward and John Webb.

The Peruvian slave raid on Rapa Nui was no isolated incident; in the early 1860s, many Polynesian islands suffered such attacks, detailed in Henry Maude's *Slavers in Paradise: The Peruvian Labor Trade in Polynesia, 1862-1864*. For an account of the island from the mid-1800s almost to the present, see *The Modernization of Easter Island* by J Douglas Porteous. In a coffee-table format, try Michel Rougie's *Isla de Pascua*, whose superb photos record all the major sites, with text in Spanish, French and English. German speakers will enjoy a collection of articles entitled *1500 Jahre Kultur der Osterinsel*, but anyone can appreciate its lavish illustrations,

not just of moai and archaeological sites, but of other indigenous artwork as well.

Anthropologist Steven Fischer has begun to unravel the enigmas of the famed Rongo-Rongo tablets in his books *Glyphbreaker*, which is inexpensive and oriented toward popular audiences, and the more strictly academic and far more expensive *Rongo-rongo: The Easter Island Script, History, Tradition, Texts*. Georgia Lee analyzes petroglyphs and the like in *The Rock Art of Easter Island*.

The best source for current information on Rapa Nui research and travel is the quarterly *Rapa Nui Journal*, available from the Easter Island Foundation (fax 805-534-9301, rapanui@compuserve.com), PO Box 6774, Los Osos, CA 93412-6774. Rates are US$30 for one year, US$55 for two years. Besides the journal, the foundation has published a number of books, among them Ana Betty Paoa Rapahango and William Liller's phrasebook titled *Speak Rapanui! ¡Hable Rapanui!*, Liller's *The Ancient Observatories of Rapa Nui: The Archaeoastronomy of Easter Island* and the edited collection *Easter Island in Pacific Context*, by Christopher M Stevenson, Lee and William Morin.

Rapa Nui has infinite potential for cinema, but Kevin Costner's Hollywood megaproduction *Rapa Nui* was a colossal waste of money that marginalized local participants and damaged archaeological sites at Rano Raraku. Film critic Roger Ebert characterized director Kevin Reynolds' results as 'sublimely silly.'

MAPS

Most maps of Rapa Nui are poor, but *Isla de Pascua-Rapa Nui: Mapa Arqueológico-Turístico* (Santiago: Ediciones del Pacífico Sur), at a scale of 1.30,000, is outstanding. Unfortunately, it's now out of print and hard to find. Good alternatives include JLM Mapas' *Isla de Pascua*, published in Santiago, and ITM's *Easter Island*, which is more readily available overseas.

GETTING THERE & AWAY

For most visitors, the only practical way to reach Easter Island is by air. LanChile has

Rongo-Rongo Tablets

One Rapa Nui artifact that, until recently, resisted explanation was the *Rongo-Rongo* script. Eugene Eyraud, the first European to record its existence, noted that every house on the island contained wooden tablets covered in some form of writing or hieroglyphics. He could find no islander who could or would explain the meaning of these symbols. The complete name of the tablets was *ko hau motu mo rongorongo*, literally meaning 'lines of script for recitation.' According to oral tradition, Hotu Matua brought these tablets, along with learned men who knew the art of writing and reciting the inscriptions. Most of the tablets are irregular, flat wooden boards with rounded edges, each about 30cm to 50cm long and covered in tidy rows of tiny symbols including birds, animals, possibly plants and celestial objects and geometric forms. The hundreds of different signs are too numerous to suggest a form of alphabet. Only a few such tablets, carved of toromiro wood, survive.

Oral tradition describes three classes of tablets: One class recorded hymns in honor of the native deity Makemake or other divinities; another recorded crimes or other deeds of individuals; and the third commemorated those fallen in war or other conflicts. Tablets recording genealogies may also have existed. Bishop Jaussen attempted to translate the script in 1866, with assistance from an islander said to be able to read the symbols, but this and other attempts failed; informants appeared to be either reciting memorized texts or merely describing the figures, rather than actually reading them. The last truly literate islanders had died, either as a result of 1862's slave raid or the subsequent smallpox epidemic.

Researchers have proposed various theories, most of them fanciful, of the nature of the script. One researcher suggested that Rongo-Rongo was not readable text at all, but rather a series of cues for reciting memorized verse, and another claimed that the characters were ideographs like Chinese script. Another researcher even suggested a connection between Rongo-Rongo script and a similar script from antiquity in the Indus River valley, in modern Pakistan.

In his exhaustive *Rongorongo, the Easter Island Script: History, Text, Traditions*, Polynesian linguistics expert Steven Fischer argues that surviving Rongo-Rongo tablets are religious chants, in the form of 120 different pictograms, elaborating a series of copulatory creation myths. This volume is scholarly, technical and phenomenally expensive (US$175); Fischer's *Glyphbreaker* is a more accessible – both in language and economically – account of his decipherment of Rongo-Rongo and an earlier Minoan script.

two flights weekly (three in the summer) between Santiago and Tahiti, stopping at Easter Island. The standard fare from Santiago is about US$800 to US$898 roundtrip, depending on the season. There are significant off-season discounts from April to October, but some of these are for Chilean citizens only.

Travelers from North America or Europe can get Rapa Nui as a relatively inexpensive add-on if their international travel is with LanChile. Travelers from Australia or New Zealand can take a Melbourne/Sydney-Tahiti flight with Qantas or an Auckland-Tahiti flight with Air New Zealand and then transfer to LanChile for the onward flight to Rapa Nui and Santiago. For fare details, see the Getting There & Away chapter.

Flights to and from Rapa Nui can be crowded, especially in the peak summer season, so be certain to reconfirm at both ends or you may arrive at the airport to find your reservation canceled. The flight from Santiago takes 5½ tiring hours, but LanChile's service is excellent and attentive. The return flight is at least an hour faster because of the prevailing westerlies and the jet stream.

Travelers bound for or leaving from Santiago pay the US$7 domestic airport tax, but westbound international passengers pay US$18. Note that flights from Rapa Nui land at Santiago's international terminal, but that passengers who are returning to mainland Chile, rather than continuing from Tahiti, can avoid baggage inspection by flashing their boarding passes to Chilean customs officers.

GETTING AROUND

The only formal public transport on Rapa Nui is a Sunday bus to Playa Anakena. It leaves from outside the church in Hanga Roa, but it has no set schedule.

Other than the bus, rented horses, mountain bikes, motorcycles and cars are the main options. It's possible to walk around the island in a few days, but the summer heat, lack of shade and scattered water supply are good reasons not to do so. While distances appear small on the map, visiting numerous archaeological sites can be tiring and time-consuming. With good transport, it's possible to see all the major archaeological sites, at least superficially, in about three days, but many people take longer.

If you walk or ride a horse, mountain bike or motorcycle around the island, carry a day pack, a lightweight long-sleeved shirt, sunglasses, a large hat to shade the face and neck and a powerful sunblock for the subtropical rays. Also carry extra food and water, since neither is easily available outside Hanga Roa.

Car & Motorcycle

Established hotels and agencies rent Suzuki jeeps for US$60 to US$80 per eight-hour day, slightly more per 24 hours, but locals charge around US$40 or US$50 per 24-hour day – ask at residenciales or at Sernatur. Hotels and agencies generally accept credit cards, but private individuals expect US cash. Outside high season, prices may be negotiable.

Oceanic Rent a Car rents motorcycles, but many private individuals rent their own for about US$25 to US$40 per eight-hour day. Given occasional downpours, a jeep is more convenient and can be more economical, especially for two or more people.

Gasoline, subsidized by the Chilean government, costs about a third less than it does on the continent, so it's not a major expense for the island's relatively short distances. Outside Hanga Roa, only the two-lane road to Anakena is paved. The rest are unsurfaced, but most are in decent enough condition if you proceed with reasonable caution.

Bicycle

Mountain bikes, readily available in Hanga Roa for about US$15 per day, are more reliable than some horses.

Horse

Horses are good for visiting sites near Hanga Roa, like Ahu Tepeu, Vinapu, Ahu Akivi and Orongo, but for more distant places, like Rano Raraku and Anakena, motorized transport is superior. Horses can be hired for about US$20 to US$30 per day, but see the beast before renting it. Pastures are poor for the large number of animals, and you won't want to risk being impaled by protruding ribs as your mount collapses under you. Most horse gear is basic and potentially hazardous for inexperienced riders, but Hotel Hanga Roa may organize riding excursions and locate a horse with proper saddle, stirrups and reins.

Around the Archaeological Sites

It's possible to take in all the major sites on three loops out of Hanga Roa – the Southwest Route, the Northern Loop and the Island Circuit. These three routes involve minimal backtracking.

Southwest Route From Hanga Roa take the road to the top of the Rano Kau crater and the Orongo ceremonial village. Backtrack to Hanga Roa; then follow the road, called Av Hotu Matua in town, along the northern edge of the airport to Orito, site of the old obsidian quarries. From here head southward to Ahu Vinapu with its impressive, finely cut stonework.

Northern Loop Take the route from Hanga Roa to the Puna Pau crater, source of the reddish volcanic scoria for the topknots of the moai. From here, continue inland to the seven moai of restored Ahu Akivi. From Ahu Akivi follow the track to Ahu Tepeu on the west coast, said to be the burial site of Tuu-ko-ihu. Then head south to Hanga Roa, stopping at Ahu Akapu, Ahu Tahai and Ahu Tautira, all of which have been restored and their moai re-erected. Because the trail-road is poorly marked between the coast and Ahu Akivi, it's easier to go from Hanga Roa to Ahu Akivi and then cut cross-country to Ahu Tepeu rather than the other way round.

Island Circuit From Hanga Roa, follow the southern coast, stopping at Vaihu and Aka-hanga, with their massive ahu and giant toppled moai. Continue east from Akahanga and detour inland to Rano Raraku, source of the volcanic tuff for most of the island's moai, where statues in all stages of production still lie in place. Leaving Rano Raraku, follow the road east to recently restored Ahu Tongariki, whose moai and masonry were hurled some distance inland by a massive tsunami after the Chilean earthquake of 1960.

From Tongariki, follow the road to the north coast to Ahu Te Pito Kura, which boasts the largest moai ever erected on an ahu. Continue west to the beach at Ovahe and then to Anakena, the island's main beach and the site of two more restored ahu. The paved road returns to Hanga Roa from here.

Organized Tours

Several agencies, some of which have offices in Santiago as well as on the island, organize local tours; the addresses below include both local and Santiago information, the latter when appropriate. If you're only in transit en route to Tahiti or Santiago, Anakena Viajes y Turismo (☎ 100-292 in Hanga Roa, 02-334-4549, fax 02-334-4791), Av Providencia 1945, Oficina 601, Providencia, Santiago, offers a whirlwind excursion from Mataveri to Ahu Tahai and then back for your flight. This excursion can also be arranged on the spot.

Visitors contracting tours should verify whether their guides belong to the Asociación de Guías de Turismo de Isla de Pascua,

Site Distances

The following are approximate road distances to key archaeological sites from Hanga Roa:

site	distance from Hanga Roa
Ahu Tahai	1.5km
Orito	2km
Vinapu	5km
Orongo	6km
Vaihu	9.5km
Ahu Akivi	10km
Akahanga	12.5km
Puna Pau	15km
Rano Raraku	18km
Ahu Tongariki	20km
Ahu Te Pito Kura	26km
Ovahe	29km
Anakena	30km

recently organized to establish standards of qualifications. Before contracting a tour, clarify your expectations with the operator and determine what is included, hour of departure and return, whether there is a meal, and the like. Just because someone speaks English, French or German does not necessarily mean he or she is qualified to discuss complex questions on which even many experts do not agree.

One of the best-equipped agencies is Kia Koe Tour, which has drawn some criticism but also considerable praise. Guides Ramón Edmunds Pacomio and Josefina Nahoe Mulloy (☎ 100-274, haumaka@entelchile.net), at Aloha Nui Guest House, are fluent English speakers; Josefina is the granddaughter of archaeologist William Mulloy. Here are some other agencies:

Aku Aku Tour (☎/fax 100-297, 100-591), Hotel Manutara Estado 115, Oficina 703, Santiago Centro (☎/fax (02-632-8173, fax 633-2491, aku.aku@chilenet.cl; Metro: Universidad de Chile)

Hotu Matu'a (☎/fax 100-242) Hotel Hotu Matu'a, Av Pont s/n

EASTER ISLAND

EASTER ISLAND

Kia Koe Tour (☎/fax 100-282, kiakoe@entelchile
.net) Atamu Tekena s/n Napoleón 3565, Oficina
201, Las Condes (☎ 02-203-7209, fax 203-7211;
Metro: El Golf)

Mahinatur Services (☎/fax 100-220) Residencial O
Tama Te Ra'a, Hotu Matua s/n

Manu Iti (☎/fax 100-313) Residencial Sofia
Gomero, Av Tu'u Koihu s/n

Martín Travel Rapa Nui (☎/fax 100-228) Rapa Nui
Inn, Atamu Tekena s/n

Ota'i Tour (☎ 100-250, fax 100-482) Hotel Ota'i, Te
Pito o Te Henua s/n

Pacific Images (☎/fax 100-600, 100-690,
pacific_images@entelchile.net) Atamu Tekena s/n

Rapa Nui Travel (☎ 100-548, fax 100-105, rntravel@
entelchile.net) Tu'u Koihu s/n

Tiki Tour (☎ 100-327, fax 100-115) Residencial
Villa Tiki, Av Pont s/n

HANGA ROA
☎ 32

According to the latest estimates, about 3000
people live on Rapa Nui, nearly all of them in
Hanga Roa. About 70% are predominantly
Polynesian, considering themselves more
Rapanui than Chilean, and most of the remainder are immigrants from the Chilean
mainland. Nearly everyone depends directly
or indirectly on the tourist trade, but there is
some fishing, livestock (mostly cattle) ranching
and kitchen gardens that grow fruit and vegetables within and beyond the village. Government agencies and small general stores are
the only other source of employment.

Orientation
Hanga Roa, on the western shore of Rapa
Nui, is a sprawling, decentralized tropical
village with an irregular street plan. Although many of the streets bear formal
names, in practice those names are rarely
used, there are almost no street numbers
and few street signs, and most locals identify
places with reference to landmarks such as
the harbor at Caleta Hanga Roa, the Gobernación, the market or the church.

Although this section gives street directions whenever possible, it's easier to rely on
the map than on street names. Visitors should
be aware, however, that local authorities
recently switched the names of the parallel

PLACES TO STAY	OTHER
2 Residencial Mahina Taka Taka Georgia	1 Museo Antropológico Sebastián Englert
3 Chez Goretti	5 Rent a Car Puna Pau
4 Residencial Chez Cecilia	7 Toroko
5 Cabañas Vai Moana	12 O Ta'i Tour
6 Pensión Tahai	15 Mercado Artesanal
11 Hotel Ota'i	16 Soccer Field
13 Hostal Manavai	17 Sernatur
14 Hotel Poike	18 Banco del Estado
25 Residencial Tekena Inn	19 Gobernación
26 Residencial El Tauke	20 Feria Municipal
28 Residencial Vai Kapua	21 Post Office
30 Residencial Tahiri	22 Plaza Policarpo Toro
39 Hotel Orongo Easter Island	25 Tekena Inn Rent a Car, Anakena Viajes y Turismo
41 Hotel Chez Joseph	29 Iglesia Hanga Roa
42 Residencial Sofia Gomero	33 Entel
43 Hostal Martín y Anita	35 Oceanic Rent a Car
45 Hotel Hangaroa	36 Tiaki Travel Agency
46 Residencial Ana Rapu	37 Mahina Tea Rent a Car, Lavendería Moane
47 Cabañas Taha Tai	38 Pacific Images (Galería Tumu Kai)
48 Hotel Topara'a	40 Bazar Island Rent a Car
49 Residencial Tiare Anani	42 Manu Iti
50 Residencial Atariki	44 Hospital Hanga Roa
56 Residencial Kona Tau	51 Banana Café
57 Residencial Villa Tiki	52 Rent a Car Mamá Sabina
58 Residencial Vai A Repa	53 Kia Koe Tour
59 Hotel Victoria	54 T&T Rent a Car
60 Residencial O Tama Te Ra'a	55 LanChile
61 Aloha Nui Guest House	57 Tiki Tour
63 Residencial Rapa Nui Inn	58 Rapa Nui Travel
65 Hotel Hotu Matua	62 Tea Tea (Hertz)
66 Residencial Vinapu	63 Martín Travel Rapa Nui
67 Hotel Manutara	67 Aku Aku Tour
71 Hotel Iorana	68 Piriti
	69 Gas Station
PLACES TO EAT	70 Mahinatur Services
8 La Taverne du Pecheur	
9 Avarei Pua	
10 La Caleta	
12 La Tinita	
23 Azul Tahai	
24 Fuente de Soda Tavake	
27 Kopa Kavana	
31 Playa Pea	
32 Ki Tai	
34 Kona Koa	
64 Pérgola Aringa Ora	

0   250   500 m

0   250   500 yards

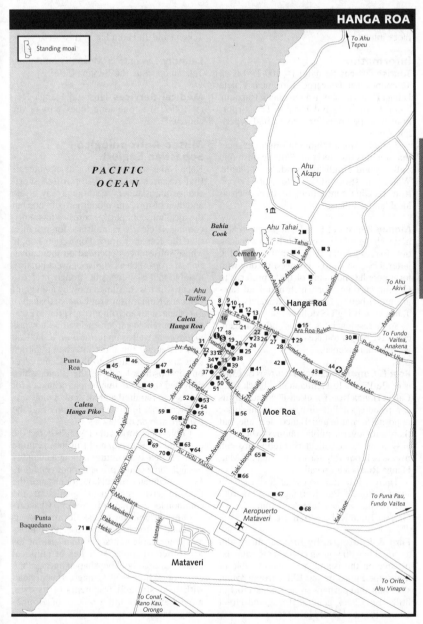

streets Atamu Tekena, which formerly ran along the harbor, with Policarpo Toro, one block inland.

Information

Tourist Offices Sernatur (☎ 100-255) is on Tuumaheke at Policarpo Toro, near Caleta Hanga Roa. The staff usually speak Rapanui, Spanish, English and French. The airport branch is open only for arriving and departing planes.

Te Rapa Nui, a tabloid information sheet that appears quarterly in good Spanish and not-so-good English, is widely available. While tourist-oriented, it does not refrain from tackling contentious matters, such as local land conflicts.

Money Banco del Estado, adjacent to Sernatur, changes US cash and traveler's checks, but charges a hefty 10% commission on the latter. US cash can be changed readily with local people, and many of them prefer it to Chilean currency, for which mainland rates are much better. Eastbound travelers from Tahiti *must* bring US dollars.

Some residenciales, hotels and tour agencies have begun to take credit cards, but this is far from universal.

Post & Communications Correos de Chile is on Te Pito o Te Henua, half a block from Caleta Hanga Roa. Entel, easily located by its conspicuous satellite dish, is on a cul-de-sac opposite Sernatur and Banco de Chile, but there are several public phones, where it's easy to make a collect or credit-card call overseas. From Valparaíso and Viña del Mar, Hanga Roa is a local call.

There's Internet access at Swiss citizen Josef Schmid's Pacific Images (☎/fax 100-600, pacific-images@entelchile.net), in the Galería Tumu Kai on Atamu Tekena.

Film & Photography Bring as much film as possible with you, since it's scarce and expensive on the island. You may be able to find some Fujicolor and Ektachrome 35mm slide film, and perhaps some Kodak 110, but little else. Check general stores, and Hotel Hanga Roa or Hotel Hotu Matua.

Travel Agencies The Tiaki Travel Agency (☎ 100-579) is at the corner of Atamu Tekena and Tu Haka He Vari.

Laundry Lavandería Moana is on Atamu Tekena opposite the Banana Café.

Medical Services Hospital Hanga Roa (☎ 100-215) is one long block east of the church.

Museo Antropológico Sebastián Englert

Rapa Nui is so renowned for its monuments that researchers and visitors often short-change the islanders' traditional way of life and their historic and modern experience, but the local museum partly redresses this short-coming. It clearly establishes, for instance, that the Rapanui are a Polynesian people whose subsistence depended on the cultivation of crops such as *kumara* (sweet potato), a staple that islanders still strongly prefer to wheat, which is consumed most by immigrant Chileans. Kumara, taro root, *maika* (banana), *toa* (sugarcane) and other crops grew in excavated household garden enclosures known as *manavai,* as well as on terraces on Rano Kau crater. Among the most interesting garden sites are the entrances to the volcanic caves on the northwest side of the island, which provided sheltered, humid microclimates for plants that required a great deal of moisture. Garden tools, including the *okauve* and the *oka,* are also on display.

Copies of historical photographs depict the encounter of Rapanui and European culture since the mid-19th century, although humidity has left some of the prints in poor condition. Legal documents reveal how, for instance, the Chilean civil register Hispanicized the common local surname Te Ave into Chávez.

Other exhibits include skulls from bodies originally entombed in ahu, basalt fishhooks and other implements, obsidian spearheads and other weapons, sketches of elliptical houses, circular beehive-shaped huts and the ceremonial houses at Orongo, a moai head with reconstructed fragments of its eyes, moai kavakava and replicas of Rongo-Rongo tablets.

Just outside the museum building stands the unusual reddish moai Mata Mea, about 2.5m high, found near the modern Hanga Roa cemetery and placed here by the Norwegians. With a triangular head and large sunken eyes, it appears crudely made, but may have been damaged or eroded. Within the museum are several oblong stone heads, known as 'potato heads,' with eye sockets and rudimentary features, including one with round ears. Thought to be the oldest carvings on the island, these may have preceded the Rano Raraku figures.

Named for the German priest who spent many years on the island and devoted much of his career to Rapa Nui's people and their history, Hanga Roa's museum is midway between Ahu Tahai and Ahu Akapu. Admission costs about US$2. Opening hours are 9:30 am to 12:30 pm and 2 to 5:30 pm Tuesday to Friday, 9:30 am to 12:30 pm weekends.

Things to See & Do

The **Iglesia Hanga Roa**, the island's Catholic church, is well worth a visit for its spectacular wood carvings, which integrate Christian doctrine with Rapanui tradition.

Overlooking the sea near Ahu Tahai, Hanga Roa's colorful **cemetery** is full of tombstones with Polynesian names and is also the site of ritual visits at Eastertime. Rapa Nui's shortage of broad, sandy beaches places it outside many traditional tropical island pursuits, but fishing, diving and surfing are all possible at sites around the island, though rental equipment is hard to come by. There is a lighted soccer field alongside the post office on Policarpo Toro.

Special Events

Every February islanders observe the Tapati Rapa Nui, a fortnight-long celebration with music, dance and other cultural events. Much of the impetus comes from Resguardo Cultural, an islanders' organization committed to preserving local traditions.

March 19, Día de San José, is a Catholic religious festival. Given the island's links to Christianity through the date of its European discovery, Easter has a special resonance, and the Sunday morning mass is a particular attraction. After the mass, islanders and visitors gather for a *curanto* (seafood stew) near the church.

June 21's Ceremonia Culto al Sol is a more indigenous event commemorating the winter solstice. Late November's Día de la Lengua Rapanui is a cultural festival celebrating the local language.

Places to Stay

Rapa Nui is not inexpensive, but visitors can control costs by staying at one of the many residenciales or with a family. Hosts often meet incoming flights at the airport with discount offers – say US$10 per person with breakfast – but most residenciales charge from about US$20/35 to US$45/70 singles/doubles with breakfast or from US$45/75 to US$70/130 with full board. Full board is not convenient if you spend the day at distant archaeological sites and cannot return to Hanga Roa for lunch, but residenciales also offer half-board options

Except in the summer high season – and especially during the Tapati festival – reservations are not essential. Instead, listen to offers from locals and hotel proprietors who flock to meet the incoming flights and wait outside the arrival area. Make sure you are talking to people from the hotels themselves and not an agent who will book you into any of several places and take a commission. You will also get transport into town, which is helpful, since Hanga Roa is so spread out that walking to some places would take an hour or more in the heat and humidity. There are also taxis.

If the place is unsatisfactory, you can always move the next day; scout the competition, talk to other travelers or ask Sernatur for help. Neither streets nor residenciales are consistently signposted, and buildings and houses lack numbers, so it's easier to locate places by referring to the Hanga Roa map. Phone ahead before walking across town in the midday heat.

Budget Some residenciales offer garden camping. Outside Hanga Roa, camping is officially permitted only at Conaf's free Playa

Anakena site, which now has toilets and drinking water (trucked in from Hanga Roa), but there are no showers.

The comfortable HI-affiliate **Residencial Kona Tau** (☎ 100-321, Avareipua s/n, konatau@entelchile.net) is a friendly family house, serving an ample breakfast with fresh mangos from the garden, for US$20 per person with private bath.

Residenciales start around US$18 per person with breakfast, but there remain very few at the low end. Try **Residencial Ana Rapu** (☎ 100-540, Apina Iti s/n), where garden camping is possible for US$5 per person and good meals are available for about US$7.

On the northern outskirts of town on the road to Ahu Tahai, María Hey's **Pensión Tahai** (☎ 100-395, fax 100-105) is a bungalow set amidst a spacious, relaxing garden. The prices for rooms have fallen – it now charges US$25/40 with breakfast – but there are persistent complaints from readers.

Near the airport, the musty **Residencial Rapa Nui Inn** (☎ 100-228, fax 100-105, Atamu Tekena s/n) needs remodeling, and they do have plans for it. Rates are US$25/40 with breakfast and private bath (though the baths are separated by curtains rather than proper walls). Prices are identical at **Residencial Tahiri** (☎ 100-570, fax 100-105, Ara Roa Rakei s/n) and at **Residencial O Tama Te Ra'a** (☎ 100-635, fax 100-220, Atamu Tekena s/n). **Hotel Topara'a** (☎ 100-225, fax 100-353, Hetereki s/n) charges US$30/40.

The intimate **Residencial Mahina Taka Taka Georgia** (☎ 100-452, fax 100-105, Atamu Tekena s/n) is a real find. Its gregarious owner takes the trouble to introduce her guests to each other and encourages garden barbecues and the like. Rates are US$25 per person. Friendly **Residencial Vai Kapua** (☎ 100-377, fax 100-105, Te Pito o Te Henua s/n) and popular **Residencial El Tauke** (☎ 100-253, fax 100105, Te Pito o Te Henua s/ n) also charge US$25 per person.

Though it's drawn some reader criticism in the past, **Residencial Chez Cecilia** (☎/fax 100-499, Atamu Tekena s/n) was immaculate at last pass; rates are US$30/50. Other residenciales in the same range include **Residencial Vai A Repa** (☎ 100-331, fax 100-105, Tu'u Koihu s/n), **Residencial Tekena Inn** (☎ 100-289, fax 100-105, Atamu Tekena s/n), recommended **Chez Goretti** (☎/fax 100-459, Atamu Tekena s/n) and **Residencial Tiare Anani** (☎/fax 100-249, Atamu Tekena s/n).

Mid-Range Most mid-range places call themselves hotels, but a few better residenciales rank among them. Rates start around US$35/50 at spacious **Cabañas Taha Tai** (☎ 100-623, fax 100-105, Apina s/n) and rise to US$35/60 at attractive and equally spacious **Cabañas Vai Moana** (☎/fax 100-626, Atamu Tekena s/n) and **Residencial Sofía Gomero** (☎/fax 100-313, Tu'u Koihu s/n).

Newly remodeled, cabaña-style **Residencial Atariki** (☎ 100-329, fax 100-105, Atamu Tekena s/n) charges US$35 per person, as does recommended **Residencial Vinapu** (☎ 100-393, fax 100-105, Av Pont s/n).

Another recommended place is secluded **Hotel Victoria** (☎/fax 100-272, Av Pont s/n), which has panoramic views from a hillock on the southeast edge of town, midway between the airport and the settlement. Rates are US$40/60 with breakfast. Rates start around US$40/70 at friendly, intimate (five-room) **Hotel Orongo Easter Island** (☎/fax 100-294, Atamu Tekena s/n) and US$45/70 at **Residencial Villa Tiki** (☎/fax 100-327, Av Pont s/n).

Several Lonely Planet readers have complimented **Hostal Martín y Anita** (☎ 100-593, Simón Paoa s/n, hmanita@entelchile .net), across from the hospital, where plain but private rooms in a lush garden setting cost US$45/70. The hotel staff speaks English. **Hotel Chez Joseph** (☎/fax 100-281, Avareipua s/n) is slightly more expensive, for US$45/85. In the US$50/80 range are **Hotel Poike** (☎/fax 100-283, Petero Atamu s/n) and **Hostal Manavai** (☎ 100-670, fax 100-658, Te Pito o Te Henua s/n).

Top End **Aloha Nui Guest House** (☎/fax 100-274, haumaka@entelchile.net, Atamu Tekena s/n) has excellent spacious rooms with private bath, set among attractive gardens, for US$60/100 with breakfast, US$80/140 with half board, US$100/170 with full board. English and German are spoken.

The traditional favorite, **Hotel Ota'i** (☎ 100-250, fax 100-560, Te Pito o Te Henua s/n), charges from US$65/94 including breakfast. It now has a swimming pool. Service is outstanding at **Hotel Manutara** (☎/fax 100-297, Hotu Matua s/n), which charges US$78/121 and also has a pool.

At **Hotel Iorana** (☎/fax 100-312, Policarpo Toro s/n) rates are US$89/121 for rooms in a quiet area (except during the infrequent landings at the nearby airport) with outstanding coastal views, but the restaurant has drawn criticism for small portions and the hotel service is suspect. There is a swimming pool.

For US$90/140, **Hotel Hotu Matua** (☎ 100-242, fax 100-444, Av Pont s/n) is closer to the airport than to town, but it has a pool. Near Caleta Hanga Piko, **Hotel Hangaroa** (☎/fax 100-299, Av Pont s/n) is a walk from the middle of town, but also has a pool, bar and restaurant and souvenir shops. Rooms cost US$100/120, considerably more with full board.

Places to Eat

Residenciales and hotels will rent a room with breakfast, half board or full board. The least expensive rooms will be about US$15 per person with breakfast. Other meals may cost upwards of US$10 each, but Hanga Roa has several good, reasonably priced restaurants. You can also feed yourself with local produce – available mornings, along with fish, at the feria municipal, the open-air market on Policarpo Toro, alongside the Gobernación.

There are provisions such as canned food, bottled drinks (soft drinks, wine, beer), fresh vegetables, fruit and eggs at supermarkets and bakeries on or near the main avenue, Policarpo Toro. When you arrive from Papeete or Santiago, your bags may be checked for fresh produce, which may not be imported from overseas.

Food at Hanga Roa's restaurants, which are increasing in number, is pleasantly surprising, especially the seafood. Prices are mostly reasonable (except for lobster, which is very dear). **La Caleta** (☎ 100-617, Te Pito o Te Henua s/n), serving fish, hamburgers,

and other items, is the local fast-food outlet, though that's less pejorative than it may sound.

Other modest possibilities include **Fuente de Soda Tavake** (☎ 100-300, Atamu Tekena s/n), near Plaza Policarpo Toro, for sandwiches; **Kopa Kavana** (☎ 100-447, Ava Rei Pua s/n); **Ki Tai** (☎ 100-641, Policarpo Toro s/n), near the south end of Caleta Hanga Roa; and the relocated **Pérgola Aringa Ora** (☎ 100-394, Hotu Matua s/n), opposite the airport.

The ocean laps at the verandah of **Playa Pea** (☎ 100-382, Policarpo Toro s/n), at Caleta Hanga Roa, which has fine seafood and good service. **La Tinita** (☎ 100-813, Te Pito o Te Henua s/n) also has good fish and soups. Brusque service and rising prices tarnish the appeal of French-run **La Taverne du Pecheur** (☎ 100-619, Caleta Hanga Roa s/n). **Avarei Pua** (☎ 100-431, Policarpo Toro s/n), across the street, is simpler but a better value.

Run by a santiaguino who's incorporated the tasty Argentine submarino (hot chocolate) into the breakfast menu, **Azul Tahai** (Atamu Tekena s/n) has superb fish and Polynesian sweet-and-sour chicken, plus delectable mango ice cream. Next to Entel, upscale **Kona Koa** (☎ 100-415, Oho Vehi s/n) has drawn favorable commentary, and also offers folk entertainment.

Entertainment

The **Banana Café** (Atamu Tekena s/n) is a bar with live music on the style of the Hendrix version of 'The Star-Spangled Banner.' There are two discotheques: **Toroko** (Policarpo Toro s/n) gets the younger, rowdier crowd, and **Piriti** (Av Hotu Matua s/n) draws an older, more sedate clientele. Both keep very late hours.

There are folk floor shows for around US$20 at **Hotel Hanga Roa** and the restaurant **Kona Kau**.

Shopping

Hanga Roa has numerous souvenir shops, mostly on Atamu Tekena (where they tend to be dearer than elsewhere) and on Te Pito o Te Henua, leading up to the church. The best selection and prices (open to haggling) are at the reconstructed mercado artesanal

EASTER ISLAND

(crafts market) across from the church and at the feria municipal at Atamu Tekena and Tu'u Maheke. For transit passengers or desperate last-minute shoppers, airport stalls have a selection of crafts and souvenirs, but prices are noticeably higher.

Look for small stone or carved wooden replicas of standard moai and moai kava-kava, replicas of Rongo-Rongo tablets and cloth rubbings of them and fragments of obsidian from Orito (sometimes made into earrings).

It's possible to get custom-made carved stone moai of just about any reasonable size, though large ones take some time and air freight may be prohibitively expensive. Ask at Sernatur for references.

Getting There & Away
Air Aeropuerto Mataveri is at the south end of Hanga Roa, on Av Hotu Matua, about a 20-minute walk from downtown Mataveri. LanChile (☎ 100-279), the only airline that flies to Rapa Nui, has its office on Atamu Tekena near Av Pont.

Sea At present, a subsidized contract for private passenger-freight service from Valparaíso remains up in the air. Quarterly naval supply ships do carry passengers to Hanga Roa for about US$32 per day, including a berth and meals; they take about a week and anchor for six days or so before returning to the mainland. For dates, and to request a reservation, contact the Comando de Transporte (☎ 032-506-354) at the Primera Zona Naval, Plaza Sotomayor 592, Valparaíso. The contact number in Hanga Roa is ☎ 100-222.

Getting Around
There is now on-demand taxi service with Radiotaxi Avareipua (☎ 100-990), but most visitors also do a fair amount of walking around this very spread-out village. To explore the rest of the island, you really need independent transport. See the general Getting Around section, earlier in this chapter.

Among the car rental agencies are the local Hertz affiliate Tea Tea (☎ 100-654, Atamu Tekena s/n), Kia Koe Tour (☎ 100-282,

Atamu Tekena s/n), T&T Rent a Car (☎ 100-337, Atamu Tekena s/n), Oceanic Rent a Car (☎ 100-385, Atamu Tekena s/n), Rent a Car Puna Pau (☎ 100-626, Atamu Tekena s/n), Mahina Tea Rent a Car (Atamu Tekena s/n) alongside Lavandería Moana, Rent a Car Mamá Sabina (☎ 100-566, Atamu Tekena s/n), Bazar Rent a Car (☎ 100-350, Atamu Tekena s/n), and Tekena Inn Rent a Car (☎ 100-289, Atamu Tekena s/n) or any of several other places that have signs in their windows.

PARQUE NACIONAL RAPA NUI
Since 1935, all of Rapa Nui's archaeological monuments have been part of the national park of the same name, administered by Conaf as an 'open-air museum.' Although the government, in cooperation with foreign and Chilean archaeologists and local people, has done a remarkable job in restoring monuments and attracting visitors, it is worth mentioning that some islanders view the park as just another land grab on the part of invaders who, to the islanders, differ little from Dutroux-Bornier or Williamson, Balfour & Company. Many islanders, however, work for Conaf and other government agencies. Conaf's main office (☎ 100-236), on the road to Rano Kau, is open 8:30 am to 6 pm weekdays; there are ranger information stations at Orongo, Anakena and Rano Raraku. In case of emergency, rangers have two-way radios.

West Coast
Lined up along the island's west coast are four major ahu complexes. Ahu Tautira is next to Hanga Roa's small pier; from here a road-track leads north to the Ahu Tahai complex, which is connected to Ahu Akapu and Ahu Tepeu by another coastal track. Ahu Tautira overlooks Caleta Hanga Roa, the fishing port at the foot of Te Pito o Te Henua. The torsos of two broken moai have been re-erected on the ahu.

A short walk north of Hanga Roa, is a site that contains three restored ahu. North American archaeologist William Mulloy directed the restoration work in 1968. Ahu Tahai is the ahu in the middle, supporting a large, solitary moai with no topknot. To one side of Ahu Tahai is Ahu Ko Te Riku, with a large, solitary moai with its topknot in place. Despite its size, it is relatively lightweight, only about a quarter the weight of the giant moai at Ahu Te Pito Te Kura on the north coast. On the other side is Ahu Vai Uri, which supports five moai of varying sizes.

Ahu Akapu, with its solitary moai, stands on the coast north of Ahu Tahai. North of here, the road is rough but always passable if you drive slowly.

Large Ahu Tepeu is on the northwest coast, between Ahu Akapu and Cabo Norte. To the northeast rises Maunga Terevaka, the island's highest point, and to the south is a large grassy plain over a jagged lava flow. To the west, the Pacific Ocean breaks against rugged cliffs up to 50m high. The seaward side of the ahu is its most interesting feature, with a wall about 3m high near the center composed of large, vertically placed stone slabs. A number of moai once stood on the ahu, but all have fallen. Immediately east is an extensive village site with foundations of several large boat-shaped houses and the walls of several round houses, consisting of loosely piled stones.

Puna Pau
The small volcanic crater at Puna Pau has a relatively soft, easily worked reddish scoria from which the pukao were made. Some 60 of these were transported to sites round the island, and another 25 remain in or near the quarry.

Ahu Akivi
This inland ahu, restored in 1960 by a group headed by Mulloy and Chilean archaeologist Gonzalo Figueroa, sports seven moai. Unlike most others, these look out to sea, but Georgia Lee comments that 'Their function was to look out over the ceremonial area...the ocean just happens to be out there in the distance.' The site has proved to have astronomical significance, however: at the equinoxes, the seven statues look directly at the setting sun.

In raising the moai, Mulloy and Figueroa used methods similar to those used at Ahu

Ature Huki and steadily improved their speed and technique. Mulloy later wrote:

Clearly the prehistoric islanders with their hundreds of years of repetition of the same task must have known many more tricks than modern imitators were able to learn.

Mulloy believed that the large number of stones in front of Ahu Akahanga on the south coast were leftovers of stones used to raise the moai, and that one moai appeared to have fallen sideways in the process. He also pointed to the tremendous numbers of stones near many ahu, including Ahu Te Pito Te Kura, as evidence that the moai may have been erected using stones for support.

Mulloy calculated that 30 men working eight hours a day for a year could have carved the moai and topknot at Ahu Te Pito Te Kura, and 90 men could have transported it from the quarry over a previously prepared road in two months and raised it in about three months. Even if Mulloy was correct, there are complications with raising the topknots to the heads of the moai.

Ana Te Pahu
After visiting Ahu Akivi, you can follow the faint, rough but passable track to Ahu Tepeu on the west coast. On the way, stop at Ana Te Pahu, a site of former cave dwellings whose entrance is via a garden planted with sweet potatoes, taro, bananas and other plants from the Polynesian horticultural complex.

Orongo Ceremonial Village
Nearly covered in a bog of floating totora reeds, the crater lake of Rano Kau appears to be a giant witch's cauldron. Perched 400m above, on the edge of the crater wall, the ceremonial village of Orongo occupies one of the island's most dramatic landscapes. Despite its ceremonial significance, it's a much later construction than the great moai and ahu. It is also demonstrably fragile, and visitors should keep to beaten paths and step carefully.

From the winding dirt road that climbs from Hanga Roa to Orongo, there are spectacular views of the entire island. Orongo,

The Birdman Cult

Makemake, the birdman cult's supreme deity, is said to have created the earth, sun, moon, stars and people, rewarding the good and punishing the evil, and expressing his anger in thunder. In times of trouble, he required the sacrifice of a child. Makemake is also credited with bringing the birds and presumably the bird cult to Rapa Nui, although Haua, another deity, aided him in this venture.

No complete record of the cult's ceremonies exists, and there are conflicting accounts with respect to schedules and duration. At a given time, worshipers would move up to Orongo, where they lived in stone houses, recited prayers, made offerings, held rites to appease the gods and participated in fertility dances.

The climax of the ceremonies was a competition to obtain the first egg of the sooty tern (*Sterna fuscata*), which bred on the tiny islets of Motu Nui, Motu Iti and Motu Kao Kao, just off Cabo Te Manga. Each contestant or his *hopu* (stand-in) would descend the cliff face from Orongo and, with the aid of a small reed *pora* (raft), swim out to the islands. He who found the first egg became 'birdman' for the ensuing year. If a hopu found the egg, he called out his master's name to a man in a cave in the cliffs below Orongo. The fortunate master's head, eyebrows and eyelashes were then shaved. His face was painted red and black, and he became birdman and was sequestered in a special house. The reasons for the birdman's celebrity are vague, but whoever found the first egg certainly won the favor of Makemake and great status in the community. The last ceremonies took place at Orongo in 1866 or 1867, a few years after the Peruvian slave raid that decimated the native community in 1862.

overlooking several small *motu* (offshore islands), was the focus of an islandwide bird cult linked to the gods Makemake and Haua in the 18th and 19th centuries.

Partly restored, the Orongo ceremonial village occupies a magnificent site overlooking the ocean. Built into the side of the slope, the houses have walls of horizontally overlapping stone slabs, with an earth-covered arched roof of similar materials, giving the appearance of being partly subterranean. Since walls were thick and had to support the roof's weight, the doorway is a low narrow tunnel, barely high enough to crawl through. At the edge of the crater is a cluster of boulders carved with numerous birdman petroglyphs with a long beak and a hand clutching an egg.

A short distance before the ceremonial village, a footpath descends into the crater, where the dense vegetation includes abandoned orange trees and grapevines whose fruit local people collect in autumn. It is possible to hike around the crater, but it is slow going – give yourself a full day and take plenty to drink, since the water in the crater lakes is muddy and brackish.

Admission charges to the Orongo ceremonial village, collected by rangers at the site, are about US$10 for non-Chileans. These fees are valid for the length of your stay.

Ahu Vinapu

For Ahu Vinapu, follow the road from Mataveri Airport to the end of the runway. Then follow the road south between the airstrip and some large oil tanks to an opening in a stone wall. A sign points to nearby Ahu Vinapu, where there are two major ahu.

Both once supported moai that are now overturned, most broken and lying facedown. Accounts by 18th- and early-19th-century visitors suggest that the moai were not overturned simultaneously, but were all tipped over by the mid-19th century. Some had their foundations undermined, and others may have been pulled down with ropes.

One interesting find is a long brick-red stone, shaped rather like a four-sided column, standing in front of one of the ahu. Closer inspection reveals a headless moai with short legs, unlike the mostly legless moai elsewhere, and resembling pre-Inkan column statues in the Andes. Originally, this was a forked, two-headed moai between whose heads ran a wooden platform on which islanders placed corpses that, when desiccated, were finally interred.

Vinapu's fine stonework, especially Ahu No 1, superficially resembles that of Inkan Cuzco and pre-Inkan Tiahuanaco, enough so that some researchers have concluded South American origins. South American archaeologist Vince Lee, however, notes that Vinapu and similar sites differ from Inka constructions in that the former were merely facades for rubble fills, but the latter consisted of solid, tightly fitted blocks.

Orito

The early Rapanui made weapons from hard black obsidian quarried at Orito. The *mataa*, a common artifact, was a crudely shaped blade of obsidian used as a spearhead; embedded in the edges of flat wooden clubs, such blades made deadly weapons. Nonlethal artifacts included obsidian files and drill bits that would have been attached to a wooden shaft and used to drill bone, wood or stone.

From the slopes of Rano Kau, the quarry resembles an enormous gray rectangle on Orito's southern slope, but quarrying actually took place around its whole circumference. Orito is not the only obsidian quarry – there are others on Motu Iti off Cabo Te Manga, and another on the northeast edge of the Rano Kau crater.

South Coast

On the south coast, east of Ahu Vinapu, enormous ruined ahu and their fallen moai testify to the impact of warfare. Ahu Vaihu has eight large moai that have been toppled and now lie facedown, their topknots scattered nearby. Akahanga is a large ahu with large fallen moai, and across the bay is a second ahu with several more. On the hill slopes opposite are the remains of a village, including foundations of several boat-shaped houses and ruins of several round houses.

Also on the coast, the almost completely ruined Ahu Hanga Tetenga has two large moai, both toppled and broken into fragments. Just beyond Hanga Tetenga, a faint track off the main road branches inland towards the crater quarry of Rano Raraku, which is readily visible.

Fundo Vaitea

Midway between Anakena and Hanga Roa, Vaitea was the center of food and livestock production under Dutroux-Bornier and Williamson, Balfour & Company, who used the island as a gigantic sheep farm. The large building on the east side of the road is the former shearing shed. The property on the west side belongs to Corfo, which raises fruit and vegetables, but may be returned to the islanders.

Anakena

This sheltered, white-sand beach is Rapa Nui's largest, very popular for swimming and sunbathing. Anakena is a pleasant place to spend the afternoon or to overnight at Conaf's pleasant campground; bring food from Hanga Roa, though Conaf now provides drinking water. Anakena Beach is the storied landing place of Hotu Matua. One of several caves is said to have been Hotu Matua's dwelling as he waited for completion of his boat-shaped house, but Thor Heyerdahl and his Norwegian archaeological team found no evidence of very early habitation, despite nearby remains of an unusually large elliptical house, about 25m long. Of greater interest are Ahu Ature Huki and Ahu Nau Nau.

On the hillside above Playa Anakena stands Ahu Ature Huki and its lone moai, re-erected by the Norwegians and islanders. In *Aku-Aku: the Secret of Easter Island*, Heyerdahl described raising the moai onto its ahu with wooden poles:

the men got the tips of their poles in underneath it, and while three or four men hung and heaved at the farthest end of each pole, the mayor lay flat on his stomach and pushed small stones under the huge face...When evening came the giant's head had been lifted a good three feet from the ground, while the space beneath was packed tight with stones.

The process continued for nine days, the giant on an angle supported by stones and the logs being levered with ropes when the men could no longer reach them. After another nine days and the efforts of a dozen people, the moai finally stood upright and unsupported.

During the excavation and restoration of Anakena's Ahu Nau Nau in 1979, researchers learned that the moai were not 'blind' but actually had inlaid coral and rock eyes, some of which were reconstructed from fragments at the site. Of the seven moai at Ahu Nau Nau, four have topknots, while only the torsos remain of two others. Fragments of torsos and heads lie in front of the ahu.

Ovahe

At Ovahe, between La Perouse and Anakena, is a small, attractive and less-frequented beach with interesting caves.

Ahu Te Pito Kura

On the north coast, overlooking a fishing cove at Bahía La Perouse (look for the sign by the road), is the largest moai ever moved from Rano Raraku and erected on an ahu. The ahu's name comes from a particular stone called *te pito kura,* presumably meaning 'navel of light,' but the legend that Hotu Matua himself brought this stone, symbolizing the navel of the world, to Rapa Nui, is likely apocryphal.

According to oral history, a certain widow erected the moai to represent her dead husband; it was perhaps the last moai to fall, although Heyerdahl's expedition has made that claim for the moai re-erected at Anakena. In height, proportion and general appearance it resembles the tall moai still buried up to their necks at Rano Raraku. If

Moving the Moai

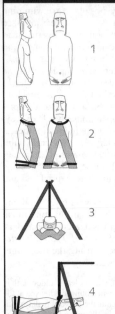

Just moving the moai (figure 1) to the site must have been an even greater problem than removing them from the rock and lowering them down the cliff. Legend says that priests moved the moai by the power of *mana*, an ability to make the moai walk a short distance every day until it eventually reached its destination. After suggestions that islanders could have moved the moai with a Y-shaped sledge made from a forked tree trunk, pulled with ropes made from tree bark, Heyerdahl organized 180 islanders to pull a 4m moai across the field at Anakena and speculated that they could have moved a much larger one with wooden runners and more labor. Another explanation is that islanders inserted round stones under the moai, which were pushed, pulled and rolled to their destinations like a block on marbles, but this fails to explain how they were moved without harming the fine details carved at the quarry.

North American archaeologist William Mulloy proposed a different method of moving the moai that, though difficult, would have been physically possible with enough labor and is consistent with the shape and configuration of the moai. First, islanders would have fitted a wooden sledge to the moai (figure 2); the distribution of the statue's weight would have kept the relatively light and fragile head above ground when tipped over. The islanders would then have set up a bipod astride the statue's neck, at an angle to the vertical (figures 3 & 4) and tied a cable attached to the moai's neck to the bipod's apex and pulled it forward. The head of the moai would then rise slightly and the moai would be dragged

those standing at the quarry site are the last to have been made, the Te Pito Te Kura moai was probably the last erected on an ahu.

Nearly 10m long, the moai lies facedown on the inland slope of the platform. Its ears alone are more than 2m long. A topknot – oval rather than round as at Vinapu – lies nearby. The sheer density of remains at sites like nearby Hanga Hoonu is even more impressive.

Rano Raraku

Known as 'the nursery,' the volcano of Rano Raraku is the quarry for the hard tuff from which the moai were cut. Moai in all stages of progress cover its southern slopes and the crater, which contains a small lake. Most moai on the south slope are upright but buried up to their shoulders or necks in the

earth, so that only their heads gaze across the grassy slopes. Park near the entrance gate (located in a stone wall). A trail leads up a slope from the gate to a 21m giant – the largest moai ever carved. Follow a trail to the right to several other large moai still attached to the rock, or turn left along the trail that leads over the rim and into the crater.

Within the crater are about 20 standing moai, a number of fallen ones and others only partly finished – about 80 in all. On the outer slope stand another 50. Note also the great holes at the crater rim that were used to maneuver the statues down the crater rim.

At the foot of the mountain and on the seaward plain lie another 30 moai, all fallen and, with few exceptions, facedown. In the quarries above are about 160 unfinished moai so that, when work stopped, some

Moving the Moai

forward. When the bipod passed vertical, the statue's own weight would carry it forward along its belly. By moving the legs of the bipod forward, the entire process could be repeated.

This repetitive series of upward and forward movements recalls the islanders' legend that the moai 'walked' to their ahu. It could also explain broken moai along the old transport routes; the rope or bipod may have slipped or broken when the moai was raised, and the statue fallen to the ground.

More recently, Charles Love and Joanne van Tilburg have experimented with moving statues on a sledgelike apparatus pushed along on rollers, and there is a broad consensus for this approach. Though it's unlikely the details will ever be known – feasibility doesn't prove the Mulloy and Love-van Tilburg methods were the actual means of moving the moai – both methods are theoretically possible.

Vince Lee, an Andeanist, has offered an alternative explanation that involves a system of levers, rather like rowing a boat, that required less labor and facilitated rotating the moai in tight quarters, as when raising the statue onto an ahu. He admits, however, to limited experience on Easter Island and that his method is feasible but unproven. All these methods, however, provide a partial explanation for deforestation of the island.

Once at its ahu, the moai had to be raised onto an elevated platform. Restoration of seven moai in the 1960s by Mulloy and Gonzalo Figueroa (see the Ahu Akivi section, earlier in this chapter) suggests that leverage and support with rocks may indeed have raised the moai. Lee, again, hypothesizes the use of wooden levers.

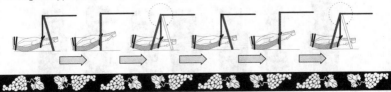

320 moai had been completed but not yet erected on ahu, or were being worked on. The total number of moai from the Rano Raraku quarries is nearly a thousand, but there may be evidence of even more in the mounds at the quarry.

Ahu Tongariki

Between 1992 and 1995, the Japanese company Tadano re-erected 15 moai at this site, the largest ahu ever built, east of Rano Raraku. A 1960 tsunami, produced by an earthquake between Rapa Nui and the South American mainland, had flattened the statues and scattered several topknots far inland. Only one topknot has been returned to its place atop a moai.

Several petroglyphs, near the bend of the road some distance from the moai, include figures of a turtle with a human face, a tuna fish, a birdman motif and Rongo-Rongo figures.

Península Poike

The eastern end of the island is a high plateau called Península Poike, crowned by the extinct volcano Maunga Pu A Katiki. Its western boundary is a narrow depression called Ko te Ava o Iko (Iko's Trench), which runs across the peninsula from north to south.

According to legend, this was a manmade trench that served a defensive function during clan warfare. Filled with branches and tree trunks, it was ready to be set on fire in event of an invasion from the west, but espionage allowed the invaders to penetrate the line and drive the defenders into their own firepit.

There is now consensus, though, that the legend was just that, a legend. While excavations revealed thick layers of ash and charcoal, evidence of a fire that produced very intense heat or else burned for some time, archaeologists have found no evidence of weapons, tools or bones that would have indicated a battlefield site. Once covered with a giant palm forest, Poike could have been the site of a natural conflagration that left extensive charcoal remains.

Falkland Islands (Islas Malvinas)

In the South Atlantic Ocean, 300 miles (500km) east of Argentine Patagonia, the controversial Falklands consist of two large islands and many smaller ones.

FACTS ABOUT THE ISLANDS
History
Despite a possible early Indian presence, the islands were unpeopled when 17th-century European sailors began to frequent the area. Their Spanish name, Malvinas, derives from French navigators of St Malo.

In 1764, French colonists settled at Port Louis, East Falkland, but soon withdrew under Spanish pressure. Spain expelled a British outpost from Port Egmont, West Falkland, in 1767, but restored it under threat of war; the British later abandoned Port Egmont in ambiguous circumstances. Spain placed a penal colony at Port Louis, and then abandoned it to whalers and sealers.

In the early 1820s, after the United Provinces of the River Plate claimed successor rights to Spain, Buenos Aires entrepreneur Louis Vernet attempted a livestock and sealing project. Vernet's seizure of American sealers, however, triggered reprisals that damaged Port Louis beyond recovery. Buenos Aires then maintained a token force, which was expelled by the British Royal Navy in 1833.

The Falklands languished until wool became an important commodity in the mid-19th century. The Falkland Islands Company (FIC) became the islands' largest landholder, and the population, mostly stranded mariners and holdover gauchos, grew with the arrival of English and Scottish immigrants. A few of these immigrants consolidated the remaining pasturelands not claimed by the FIC into large holdings. Half the population resided in the port capital of Stanley, founded in 1844, while the rest worked on sheep stations. Most of the original landowners lived and worked locally, but their descendants often returned to Britain, running their businesses as absentees.

From the late 1970s, local government encouraged subdivision of large landholdings to benefit family farmers. Change became even more rapid with the 1982 Falklands War, subsequent expansion of deep-sea fishing and, most recently, preliminary offshore petroleum exploration.

Although Argentina had persistently claimed the Falklands since 1833, successive British governments were slow to publicly acknowledge the claim's seriousness. By 1971, however, the Foreign & Commonwealth Office (FCO) reached a communications agreement giving Argentina roles in air transport, fuel supplies, shipping and even immigration. Concerned about Argentina's chronic instability, islanders and their UK supporters thought the agreement ominous, and suspected the FCO of secretly arranging transfer of the islands. This process dragged on for a decade, during which Argentina's brutal 'Dirty War' gave islanders more reason for concern.

Facing pressure from Argentines fed up with corruption, economic chaos and totalitarian ruthlessness, General Leopoldo Galtieri's disintegrating military government invaded the islands on April 2, 1982. Seizure of the Malvinas briefly united Argentina, but Prime Minister Margaret Thatcher of Britain, herself in shaky political circumstances, sent a naval task force to retake the islands. Experienced British ground troops routed ill-trained, poorly supplied Argentine conscripts; Argentina's surrender averted Stanley's destruction.

Geography & Climate
The land area of 4700 sq miles (12,176 sq km) is equivalent to Northern Ireland or the US state of Connecticut. Falkland Sound separates East and West Falkland; only a few smaller islands have settlements. Despite a dismal reputation, the oceanic climate is temperate (if windy). Summer temperatures rarely reach 75°F (24°C), and sustained subfreezing temperatures are

FALKLAND ISLANDS (ISLAS MALVINAS)

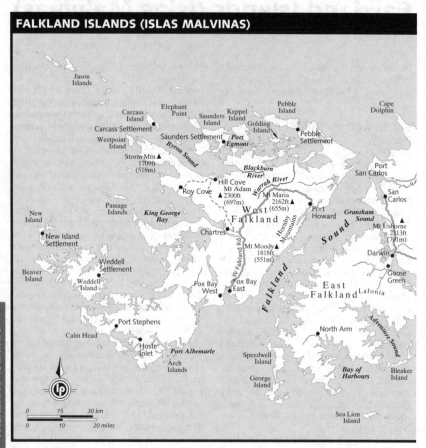

unusual. Annual rainfall is only about 24 inches (600mm).

Except for East Falkland's low-lying Lafonia peninsula, terrain is hilly to mountainous, rarely exceeding 2300 ft (705m). The most interesting geological features are 'stone runs' of quartzite boulders descending from many ridges and peaks. Bays, inlets, estuaries and beaches form an attractive coastline that is home to abundant wildlife.

Every part of the Falklands outside Stanley is known colloquially as 'camp,' including those parts of East Falkland accessible by road from Stanley, all of West Falkland, and the numerous smaller islands.

Flora & Fauna

Grasses and prostrate shrubs dominate the flora. Native tussock grass once lined the coast but proved vulnerable to overgrazing and fire. Most pasture is rank white grass (*Cortaderia pilosa*), supporting only one sheep per four or five acres.

Beaches, headlands and estuaries support large concentrations of subantarctic wildlife.

SOUTH
ATLANTIC
OCEAN

have been observed offshore. Killer whales are common, but not the larger South Atlantic whales.

Over the past decade or so, local government has encouraged nature-oriented tourism by constructing small lodges at outstanding sites, but there are also less-structured opportunities.

Government & Politics

A London-appointed governor administers the Falklands, but the locally elected legislative council (Legco) exercises significant power. Five of its eight members come from Stanley; the remainder represent camp. Selected Legco members advise the governor as part of the executive council (Exco).

Economy

Traditionally, the economy depended almost entirely on wool, but fishing has eclipsed agriculture as a revenue-producer. Licensed Asian and European fleets have funded improvements in public services such as schools, roads, telephones and medical care. Local government issued the first offshore oil exploration licenses in 1996, a matter about which islanders feel ambivalent because of the potential environmental impact. Results from the earliest test wells are inconclusive.

Most Stanley residents work for Falkland Island Government (FIG) or FIC. While FIC has sold all its pastoral property, it continues to provide shipping and other commercial services. In camp, nearly everyone is involved in wool production on relatively small, widely dispersed, family-owned units. Farmers are struggling economically because of low wool prices. Tourism is economically limited, but facilities are always adequate and often excellent.

Population & People

According to the 1996 census, the population was 2564, two-thirds living in Stanley, the rest in camp. Over 60% of permanent residents are native-born, some tracing their ancestry back seven generations. Most others are immigrants or temporary residents from

Five penguin species breed regularly: the Magellanic (jackass), rockhopper, macaroni, gentoo and king.

One of the most beautiful breeding birds is the black-browed albatross, but there are also striated and crested caracaras, cormorants, gulls, peregrine falcons, hawks, oystercatchers, snowy sheathbills, sheldgeese, steamer ducks and swans, among others. Most are present in large, impressive colonies, that are easily photographed.

Elephant seals, sea lions and fur seals breed on shore, while six species of dolphin

FALKLAND ISLANDS

the UK. Islanders' surnames indicate varied European backgrounds, but all residents speak English.

Because of their isolation and small numbers, Falklanders are versatile and adaptable. They are also hospitable, often welcoming strangers for 'smoko,' the traditional midmorning tea or coffee break, or for a drink. This is especially true in camp, where visitors can be infrequent. It is customary to bring a small gift – rum is a special favorite.

About 2000 British military personnel (squaddies) reside at Mt Pleasant Airport, about 35 miles (56km) southwest of Stanley, and at a few other scattered sites.

FACTS FOR THE VISITOR

In many ways the Falklands are a small country, with their own immigration and customs regulations, currency and other unique features. Wildlife, particularly penguins, attracts most visitors, but there are also historical sites.

Planning

From October to March, migratory birds and mammals return to beaches and headlands. Very long daylight hours permit outdoor activities even if poor weather spoils part of the day.

Visitors should bring good waterproof clothing; a pair of rubber boots is useful. Summer never gets truly hot and high winds can lower the ambient temperature, but the climate does not justify Antarctic preparations. Trekkers should bring a sturdy tent with a rain fly and a warm sleeping bag.

Excellent DOS topographic maps are available from the Secretariat in Stanley for about £2 each. The two-sheet, 1:250,000 map of the islands is suitable for most uses, but 1:50,000 sheets have more detail. ITM publishes a 1:300,000 single-sheet version, field checked by the author of this book.

Tourist Offices

Besides their Stanley office and Falkland House (see the Visas & Documents section), the Islands have tourist representation in Europe and the Americas.

Chile
  British Consul John Rees, Avant Airlines
  (☎ 61-228312) Roca 924, Punta Arenas
Germany
  HS Travel & Consulting
  (☎/fax 61-05-1304) PO Box 1447, 64529 Moerfelden
  This is no longer officially affiliated with the Tourist Board, but it still provides up-to-date information.
USA
  Tread Lightly Travel
  (☎ 860-868-1710, fax 860-868-1718; patread@ aol.com) One Titus Road, Washington Depot, CT 06794

Visas & Documents

All nationalities, including British citizens, must carry valid passports. For non-Britons, visa requirements are generally the same as those for foreigners visiting the UK; since August 1999, Argentine passport holders may travel to the islands. Because of the shortage of accommodations, all visitors must book in advance.

For further details, consult Falkland House (☎ 020-7222-2542, fax 020-7222-2375; rep@figo.u-net.com), 14 Broadway, Westminster, London SW1H 0BH, or the Falkland Islands Tourist Board (☎ 22215, fax 22619, manager@tourism.org.fk).

Customs

Customs regulations are few except for limits on alcohol and tobacco, which are heavily taxed.

Money

The Falkland Islands pound (£), divided into 100 pence (p), is at par with the British pound. There are banknotes for £5, £10, £20 and £50, and coins for 1p, 2p, 5p, 10p, 20p, 50p and £1. Sterling circulates alongside local currency, which is not valid in the UK.

Credit cards are becoming more widely used and traveler's checks are also readily accepted. Britons with guarantee cards can cash personal checks up to £50 at Standard Chartered Bank.

Costs Recent development has encouraged short-stay accommodations at prices around

£50 per day (meals included), but B&Bs in Stanley start around £15. Cheaper, self-catering cabins are available in camp, as are opportunities for trekking and camping; some isolated families still welcome visitors without charge.

Air travel within the Falklands costs approximately £1 per minute. See the Getting Around section for sample fares.

Food prices are roughly equivalent to the UK, but fresh meat (chiefly mutton) is cheap. Stanley restaurants are expensive, except for short orders and snacks.

Post & Communications

Postal services are good. There are one or two airmails weekly to the UK, but parcels heavier than 1 pound (0.45 kg) go by sea four or five times yearly. The Falkland Islands Government Air Service (FIGAS) delivers to outer settlements and islands. Correspondents should address letters to Post Office, Stanley, Falkland Islands, via London, England.

Cable and Wireless PLC operates both local and long-distance telephones; local numbers have five digits. The international country code is ☎ 500, valid for numbers in Stanley and in camp.

Local calls cost 5p per minute, calls to the UK are 15p for six seconds, and calls to the rest of the world are 18p per six seconds. Operator-assisted calls cost the same but have a three-minute minimum. Reverse-charge (collect) calls are possible only locally and to the UK.

Internet Resources

Internet connections are recently installed but rapidly improving. The Tourist Board has an informative website (www.tourism.org.fk).

Books

The most readily available general account is Ian Strange's *The Falkland Islands*, 3rd edition (1983). For a summary of the Falklands controversy, see Robert Fox's *Antarctica and the South Atlantic: Discovery, Development and Dispute* (1985). On the war, try Max Hastings and Simon Jenkins' *Battle for the Falklands* (1983).

Robin Woods' *Guide to Birds of the Falkland Islands* (1988) is a detailed account of the islands' birdlife. Strange's *Field Guide to the Wildlife of the Falkland Islands and South Georgia* (1992) is also worth a look. Trekkers should acquire Julian Fisher's *Walks and Climbs in the Falkland Islands* (1992).

Radio & TV

The Falkland Islands Broadcasting Service (FIBS) produces local programs and carries BBC news programs from the British Forces Broadcasting Service (BFBS). The nightly public announcements, to which people listen religiously, are worth hearing.

Television is available through BFBS and via cable. The only print media are the *Teaberry Express* and the weekly *Penguin News*.

Time

The Falklands are four hours behind GMT/UTC. In summer, Stanley observes daylight saving time, but camp remains on standard time.

Electricity

Electric current operates on 220/240V, 50Hz. Plugs are identical to those in the UK.

Weights & Measures

The metric system is official, but most people use imperial measures colloquially. There's a conversion table at the back of this book.

Health

No special precautions are necessary, but carry adequate insurance. Flights from Britain may be diverted to yellow fever zones in Africa, so authorities recommend vaccination.

Wind and sun can combine to burn unsuspecting visitors severely. Wind also contributes to the danger of hypothermia in inclement weather.

Stanley's King Edward VII Memorial Hospital, on St Mary's Walk, has excellent medical and dental facilities.

Useful Organizations

Based in both the UK and Stanley, Falklands Conservation is a nonprofit organization promoting wildlife conservation research as well as the preservation of shipwrecks and historic sites. Membership is available from Falklands Conservation (☎ 020-8346-5011), 1 Princes Rd, Finchley, London N3 2DA, England. In Stanley, the representative (☎ 22247, fax 22288) is on Ross Rd, opposite Malvina House Hotel.

The Falkland Islands Association (☎ 020-7222-0028), 2 Greycoat Place, Westminster, London SW1P 1SD, is a political lobbying group that publishes a quarterly newsletter.

Dangers & Annoyances

Near Stanley and in a few camp locations on both East and West Falkland, there remain unexploded plastic land mines, but minefields are clearly marked and no civilian has ever been injured. Never enter a minefield: mines bear the weight of a penguin or even a sheep, but not of a human. Report suspicious objects to the Explosive Ordnance Disposal office (☎ 22229), near Town Hall, which has free minefield maps.

Despite its firm appearance, 'soft camp,' covered by white grass, is very boggy, though not dangerous.

Business Hours

Government offices are open weekdays 8 am to noon and 1:15 to 4:30 pm. Most larger businesses in Stanley stay open until 7 or 8 pm, but smaller shops may open only a few hours daily. Weekend business hours are reduced. Camp stores keep limited schedules but often open on request.

Public Holidays & Special Events

In the past, when most Falklanders lived in physical and social isolation, the annual sports meetings provided a regular opportunity to share news, meet new people and participate in friendly competitions such as horse racing, bull riding and sheepdog trials.

In late February, the rotating camp sports meeting on West Falkland maintains this tradition, hosting 'two-nighters.' Islanders party till they drop, sleep a few hours, and get up and start all over again. Independent visitors are welcome, but arrange accommodations (usually floor space for your sleeping bag) in advance.

The following holidays are observed:

New Year's Day
    January 1
Camp Sports
    Late February (dates vary)
Good Friday
    March/April (date varies)
Queen's Birthday
    April 21
Liberation Day
    June 14
Falklands Day
    August 14
Battle of the Falklands (1914)
    December 8
Christmas Day
    December 25
Boxing Day-Stanley Sports
    December 26–27

Activities

Wildlife is the major attraction. Penguins, other birds and marine mammals are easily approached, even at developed sites such as Sea Lion Island, but there are other equally interesting, undeveloped areas. Keep a respectful distance.

Fishing can be excellent; early March to late April is the best season for hooking sea trout, which requires a license (£10) from the Stanley post office. Trekking and camping are feasible, though the tourist board and some landowners discourage camping because of fire danger and potential disturbance to stock and wildlife. It's also possible to visit the 1982 battlefields.

Accommodations

Stanley has several B&Bs and hotels, and some farms have converted surplus buildings into comfortable lodges. Others have self-catering cottages, trailers or Portakabin shelters. (These are modular units resembling cargo containers with added doors and windows. Many were left on the islands by the British military.)

In areas not frequented by tourists, islanders often welcome houseguests; many farms have 'outside houses' or shanties that visitors may use with permission. Camping is possible only with permission.

Food & Drinks

Mutton, the dietary staple, is very cheap. Islanders usually consume their own produce, but a hydroponic market garden now produces aubergines (eggplant), tomatoes, lettuce and other salad greens.

Stanley snack bars offer fish and chips, muttonburgers, pizza, sausage rolls and pasties. Hotels have decent restaurants. At pubs, beer and hard liquor, particularly whisky and rum, are the favorites.

GETTING THERE & AWAY
Air

From RAF Brize Norton, in Oxfordshire, England, there are regular flights to Mt Pleasant International Airport (16 hours, plus an hour's layover on Ascension Island). Southbound flights leave Brize Norton Monday and Thursday; northbound flights leave Mt Pleasant Wednesday and Saturday.

The return fare is £2302, but reduced Apex fares cost £1414 with 30-day advance purchase. Groups of six or more pay £1192 each. Travelers continuing to Argentina or Chile can purchase one-way tickets for half the return fare.

For reservations in London, contact Gail Spooner at Falkland House (☎ 020-7222-2542), 14 Broadway, Westminster SW1H 0BH. In Stanley, contact the Falkland Islands Company (☎ 27633), on Crozier Place.

From Santiago, LanChile flies to Mt Pleasant every Saturday via Punta Arenas. Santiago fares are US$410 one way, US$680 return (US$370 one way, US$630 return with seven-day advance purchase). Punta Arenas fares are US$320 one way, US$490 return (US$280 one way, US$420 return with seven-day advance purchase). Though the Chilean government briefly suspended LanChile flights in mid-1999 in retaliation for the detention of General Pinochet in London, flights resumed in mid-August of the same year; one flight per month in each direction now stops in the Argentine city of Río Gallegos.

Sea

Byron Marine Ltd (☎ 22245, fax 22246), at Waverly House in Stanley, will carry passengers to and from Punta Arenas, Chile, on the roughly monthly sailings of its freighter *MV Tamar*. At about £180 per person, the fare is about the same as the lowest one-way airfare and includes three meals per day, but the 60-hour crossing is not for anyone subject to seasickness.

GETTING AROUND

Outside the Stanley-Mt Pleasant area the only regular flights are provided, on demand, by FIGAS. Sample return fares from Stanley include Salvador (£50), Darwin (£76), San Carlos (£78), Port Howard (£94), Sea Lion Island (£95), Pebble Island (£106), Fox Bay East or West (£121) and Carcass Island (£145). Some grass airstrips only accept a limited payload, and baggage is limited to 30 pounds (14kg) per person.

Rental vehicles are available in Stanley, and visitors may use their own state or national driving licenses in the Falklands for up to 12 months. Some lodges provide 4WDs with drivers or guides for their guests.

Byron Marine Ltd (see the Sea section in Getting There & Away, earlier in this chapter) carries a small number of passengers on its freighter *MV Tamar* while picking up wool and delivering other goods to outlying settlements. Berths are limited; day trips cost £20, while overnights cost £25.

STANLEY
☎ 500

Stanley's metal-clad houses, brightly painted corrugated metal roofs and large kitchen gardens make a striking contrast to the surrounding moorland. Founded in 1845, the new capital was a supply and repair port, but Cape Horn shipping began to avoid it when boats were scuttled under questionable circumstances. In the late 19th century, Stanley grew more rapidly as the transshipment point for wool sent from camp to the UK.

As the wool trade grew, so did the influence of the Falkland Islands Company, Stanley's largest employer. Although its political and economic dominance was uncontested, its relatively high wages and good housing offered a paternalistic security. 'Tied houses,' however, were available only while the employee remained with FIC.

Stanley remains the service center for the wool industry, but has also become a significant port for Asian and European fishing fleets.

Orientation
On a steep north-facing hillside, Stanley has sprawled east and west along Stanley Harbour. Ross Rd, the main street, runs the length of the harbor, but most government offices, businesses and houses are within a few blocks of each other.

Information
Tourist Offices The Falkland Islands Tourist Board (☎ 22215 or 22281, fax 22619; manager@tourism.org.fk), at the public jetty, distributes an excellent guide to Stanley, as well as other useful brochures. It's open from 8 am to noon and 1:15 to 4:30 pm weekdays.

The Mount Pleasant Travel Office (☎ 76691) is at 12 Facility Main Reception, at Mt Pleasant International Airport.

Money Standard Chartered Bank, on Ross Rd between Barrack and Villiers Sts, changes foreign currency and traveler's checks, and cashes personal checks drawn on UK banks. Hours are 8:30 am to noon and 1:15 to 3 pm weekdays.

Post & Communications The post office is in Town Hall, on Ross Rd at Barrack St. Cable & Wireless PLC, on Ross Rd West near Government House, operates phone, telegram, telex and fax services. Magnetic cards are cheaper than operator-assisted overseas calls. Counter hours are 8:30 am to 5 pm, but public booths are open 24 hours.

Medical Services King Edward VII Memorial Hospital (☎ 27328 for appointments, ☎ 27410 for emergencies), at the west end of St Mary's Walk, may be the best facility in the world for a community of Stanley's size.

Things to See & Do
Distinguished **Christ Church Cathedral** (1892), is a massive brick-and-stone construction with attractive stained-glass windows. On the small nearby plaza, the restored **Whalebone Arch** commemorates the 1933 centennial of British rule.

Since the mid-19th century, London-appointed governors have inhabited rambling **Government House** on Ross Rd. Just beyond it, the **Battle of the Falklands Memorial** commemorates a WWI naval engagement, while the **Falkland Islands Museum** is a recent project, with professional exhibits on history and natural history.

Just opposite the Secretariat, on Ross Rd, is the **1982 War Memorial**, designed by a Falklander living overseas, paid for by public subscription and built with volunteer labor. At the east end of Ross Road, the islands' dead rest at **Stanley Cemetery**, where surnames such as Felton and Biggs are as common as Smith and Jones are in the UK.

Activities
Stanley's swimming pool, on Reservoir Rd, has become very popular. There are also sites for squash, badminton, basketball and the like.

Fishing for sea trout, mullet and smelt is popular on the Murrell River, which is walking distance from Stanley, but there are many other suitable places. Some are easily accessible from the Mt Pleasant highway.

Special Events
The Stanley Sports, held after Christmas, features horse racing (with betting), bull riding and other events. In March, the competitive Horticultural Show displays the produce of kitchen gardens in Stanley and camp, plus a variety of baked goods, and includes a spirited auction. The July Crafts Fair presents the work of local weavers, leatherworkers, photographers and artists. There are many talented illustrators and painters; watercolorist James Peck has exhibited his paintings in Buenos Aires.

Places to Stay
Accommodations in Stanley are good, but limited and not cheap; reservations are

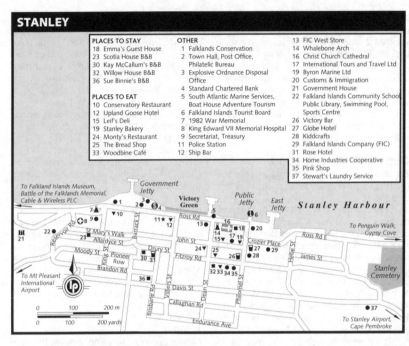

STANLEY

PLACES TO STAY	OTHER	13 FIC West Store
18 Emma's Guest House	1 Falklands Conservation	14 Whalebone Arch
23 Scotia House B&B	2 Town Hall, Post Office,	16 Christ Church Cathedral
30 Kay McCallum's B&B	Philatelic Bureau	17 International Tours and Travel Ltd
32 Willow House B&B	3 Explosive Ordnance Disposal	19 Byron Marine Ltd
36 Sue Binnie's B&B	Office	20 Customs & Immigration
	4 Standard Chartered Bank	21 Government House
PLACES TO EAT	5 South Atlantic Marine Services,	22 Falkland Islands Community School,
10 Conservatory Restaurant	Boat House Adventure Tourism	Public Library, Swimming Pool,
12 Upland Goose Hotel	6 Falkland Islands Tourist Board	Sports Centre
15 Leif's Deli	7 1982 War Memorial	26 Victory Bar
19 Stanley Bakery	8 King Edward VII Memorial Hospital	27 Globe Hotel
24 Monty's Restaurant	9 Secretariat, Treasury	28 Kiddcrafts
25 The Bread Shop	11 Police Station	29 Falkland Islands Company (FIC)
33 Woodbine Café	12 Ship Bar	31 Rose Hotel
		34 Home Industries Cooperative
		35 Pink Shop
		37 Stewart's Laundry Service

advisable. Breakfast is always included; inquire about full board. The most economical is homey *Kay McCallum's B&B* (☎ *21071, 14 Drury St*) charging £16 per person. Nick and Sheila Hadden's *Willow House B&B* (☎/fax *21014, 27 Fitzroy Rd*) also charges £16, while Bob and Celia Stewart's *Scotia House B&B* (☎ *21191, 12 St Mary's Walk*) charges £18.50.

Places to Eat

Two bakeries serve bread, snacks and light meals: *The Bread Shop (Dean St)*, open daily 7:30 am to 1:30 pm, and *Stanley Bakery (Philomel St)*, at Waverley House, open weekdays 8:30 am to 3:30 pm, Saturday 9 am to 12:30 pm. The *Woodbine Café (29 Fitzroy Rd)* serves fish and chips, pizza, sausage rolls and similar items. *Leif's Deli (23 John St)* has specialty foods and snacks.

The upscale *Malvina House Hotel (3 Ross Rd)* has beautiful grounds and runs an excellent conservatory restaurant. The venerable *Upland Goose Hotel (20/22 Ross Rd)*,

in a mid-19th-century building, also serves good meals.

Entertainment

Of Stanley's several pubs, the most popular is the *Globe Hotel* on Crozier Place, but try also the *Rose Hotel* on Brisbane Rd and the *Victory Bar* on Philomel St. The Upland Goose Hotel houses the *Ship Bar*, and Monty's Restaurant, on John St, also has a bar, *Deano's*.

In winter, the pubs sponsor a darts league, with tournaments in Town Hall, where there are also dances with live music throughout the year. There are no cinemas, but hotels and guesthouses have video lounges.

Shopping

For locally spun and knitted woolens, visit the Home Industries Cooperative on Fitzroy Road. Kiddcrafts, 2-A Philomel St, makes stuffed penguins and other soft toys with great appeal for children. The Pink Shop,

33 Fitzroy Rd, sells gifts and souvenirs, Falklands and general-interest books (including selected Lonely Planet guides) and excellent wildlife prints by owner Tony Chater.

Postage stamps, available from the post office and from the Philatelic Bureau, are popular with collectors. The Bureau also sells stamps from South Georgia and British Antarctic Territory. The Treasury, in the Secretariat behind the Liberation Monument, sells commemorative coins.

Getting There & Around

For international flight information, see the Getting There & Away section earlier in this chapter.

From Stanley, FIGAS (☎ 27219) serves outlying destinations in nine-passenger aircraft, arranging itineraries by demand; contact FIGAS when you know where and when you wish to go, and listen to FIBS at 6:30 pm the night before to learn your departure time. Occasionally, usually around holidays, flights are heavily booked and seats may not be available. Passage may also be arranged through the Tourist Board on the public jetty.

Mt Pleasant International Airport is 35 miles southwest of Stanley by road, while Stanley Airport is about 3 miles east of town.

Falkland Islands Tours and Travel (☎/fax 21775) takes passengers to Mt Pleasant for £13 each; call for reservations the day before. They will also take groups to Stanley Airport or meet them there. For cabs, contact Ben's Taxi Service (☎ 21191) or Lowe's Taxis (☎ 21381).

AROUND STANLEY
Stanley Harbour Maritime History Trail

See the Tourist Board for a brochure on wrecks and condemned ships. There are informational panels near vessels such as the *Jhelum*, a sinking East Indiaman deserted by its crew in 1871, whose hulk is still visible above the water; the *Charles Cooper*, an American packet still used for storage; and the *Lady Elizabeth*, a three-masted freighter that struck a rock in 1913.

Penguin Walk & Gypsy Cove

The Falklands' most convenient penguin colonies are about 1½ hours' walk from Stanley. By foot, from the east end of Ross Rd, continue beyond the cemetery and cross the bridge over the inlet known as the Canache, keep going past the *Lady Elizabeth* and Stanley Airport to Yorke Bay.

Penguins crowd the sandy beach where, unfortunately, the Argentines buried plastic mines; get your views of the birds by walking along the minefield fence. Further on, at Gypsy Cove, are nesting Magellanic penguins (avoid stepping on burrows) and other shorebirds.

Kidney Island

Covered with tussock grass, Kidney Island is a small reserve that supports a wide variety of wildlife, including rockhopper penguins and sea lions. Dave Eynon's South Atlantic Marine Services (☎ 21145, fax 22674, sams@horizon.co.fk), on Ross Rd, offers tours in a rigid inflatable boat for £30 per person.

CAMP
☎ 500

Nearly everyone in 'camp' (a term for all of the Falklands outside Stanley) is engaged in sheep ranching. Camp settlements began as company towns, hamlets near sheltered harbors where coastal shipping could collect the wool. Lone shepherds lived at 'outside houses' that still dot the countryside.

Many wildlife sites are on smaller offshore islands such as Sea Lion Island and Pebble Island, where there are comfortable but fairly costly tourist lodges. These are described in detail below, but there are some alternatives for budget travelers.

East Falkland

East Falkland's road network consists primarily of a good highway to Mt Pleasant International Airport and Goose Green, with a spur to San Carlos. From Pony's Pass on the Mt Pleasant Hwy there is a good road north to the Estancia (a farm west of Stanley) and Port Louis, and an excellent road west from Estancia toward Douglas

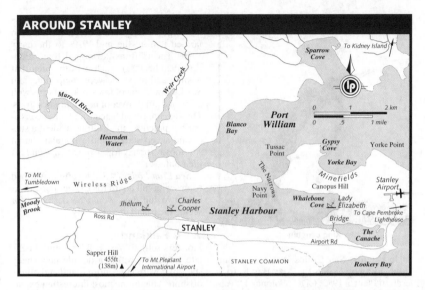

AROUND STANLEY

To Kidney Island
Sparrow Cove
Port William
Blanco Bay
Weir Creek
Murrell River
Hearnden Water
Tussac Point
Gypsy Cove
Yorke Point
Yorke Bay
Minefields
The Narrows
To Mt Tumbledown
Wireless Ridge
Canopus Hill
Stanley Airport
Moody Brook
Jhelum
Charles Cooper
Navy Point
Whalebone Cove
Lady Elizabeth
Stanley Harbour
Bridge
To Cape Pembroke Lighthouse
Ross Rd
STANLEY
The Canache
Airport Rd
Sapper Hill 455ft (138m)
To Mt Pleasant International Airport
STANLEY COMMON
Rookery Bay

0   1   2 km
0   .5   1 mile

and Port San Carlos. Most other tracks are for 4WDs only.

Several Stanley operators run day trips to East Falkland settlements, including Tony Smith's Discovery Tours (☎ 21027, fax 22304), Sharon Halford's Ten Acre Tours (☎ 21155, fax 21950), Montana Short's Photographic Tours (☎/fax 21076) and Dave Eynon's South Atlantic Marine Services (☎ 21145, fax 22674; sams@horizon.co.fk). South Atlantic Marine Services is the only one you can visit in person.

Port Louis Dating from the French foundation of the colony in 1764, Port Louis is the Falklands' oldest settlement. One of the colony's oldest existing buildings is an ivy-covered 19th-century farmhouse, still occupied by farm employees, but there are also ruins of the French governor's house and fortress and Louis Vernet's settlement scattered nearby. Visit the grave of Matthew Brisbane, Vernet's lieutenant, murdered by gauchos after the British left him in charge of the settlement in 1833.

It is possible to trek from Port Louis along the northern coast of East Falkland to

Volunteer Beach, a scenic itinerary with an extraordinary abundance of wildlife. To visit the settlement or seek permission for the trek, contact manager Michael Morrison (☎ 31004).

Volunteer Beach Volunteer Beach, part of Johnson's Harbour Farm, is east of Port Louis. It has the Falklands' largest concentration of king penguins, a growing colony of about 150 breeding pairs. At Volunteer Point, several hours' walk east, is an offshore breeding colony of southern fur seals (bring binoculars). Return along Volunteer Lagoon to see more birds and elephant seals. If attempting the trip on your own, contact owner George Smith of Johnson's Harbour (☎ 31399) for permission.

San Carlos In 1982, British forces came ashore at San Carlos, on Falkland Sound; in 1983, the sheep station there was subdivided and sold to half a dozen local families. There is fishing on the San Carlos River, north of the settlement. Comfortable *Blue Beach Lodge* (☎ 32205) charges £55 with full board and offers boat excursions.

King penguin

Just across San Carlos Water, but four hours away by foot, is the Ajax Bay Refrigeration Plant, a 1950s CDC (Colonial Development Corporation) boondoggle. Gentoo penguins wander through its ruins, which served as a field hospital in 1982. Take a flashlight if you plan to explore.

Darwin & Goose Green At the narrow isthmus that separates Lafonia from northern East Falkland, Darwin was the site of an early *saladero*, where gauchos slaughtered feral cattle and tanned their hides. It later became the center of FIC's camp operations and, with nearby Goose Green, the largest settlement outside Stanley. The heaviest ground fighting of the Falklands War took place at Goose Green, site of the Argentine Cemetery.

Sea Lion Island Off East Falkland's south coast, tiny Sea Lion Island is less than a mile across, but teems with wildlife, including five penguin species, enormous cormorant colonies, giant petrels, and the charmingly bold predator known as the Johnny rook (striated caracara). Hundreds of elephant seals crowd the island's sandy coastline, while sea lions dot the narrow gravel beaches below its southern bluffs or lurk in the towering tussock.

Much of the credit for Sea Lion's wildlife has to go to Terry and Doreen Clifton, who farmed it from the mid-1970s to the early 1990s. The Cliftons developed their 2300-acre (920-hectare) ranch with the idea that wildlife and livestock were compatible, and Sea Lion was one of few working farms with any substantial cover of native tussock grass. Through improved fencing and other conscientious practices, the Cliftons made it a successful sheep station and a popular tourist site, mostly for day trips from Stanley and Mt Pleasant.

Sea Lion Lodge (☎ *32004*) offers twin-bed rooms with full board for £55 per person. At least two full days would be desirable for seeing the island in its entirety.

West Falkland

Pioneers settled West Falkland only in the late 1860s, but within a decade new sheep stations covered the entire island and others offshore. One of the most interesting experiments was the Keppel Island Mission for Indians from Tierra del Fuego.

West Falkland (nearly as large as East Falkland) and the adjacent islands have fine wildlife sites. The only proper roads run from Port Howard on Falkland Sound to Chartres on King George Bay and south to Fox Bay, with a northwestward extension toward Hill Cove. The Fox Bay road is being extended southwest to Port Stephens, but a system of rough tracks is suitable for Land Rovers and motorcycles, and there is good trekking in the mountainous interior. Only a few places have formal tourist facilities.

Port Howard Scenic Port Howard, at the foot of 2158ft (658m) Mt Maria, remains intact after local managers purchased it in 1987. About 50 people live on the station, which has its own dairy, grocery, slaughterhouse, social club and other amenities. It will be the West Falkland port for the anticipated ferry across Falkland Sound.

The immediate surroundings offer hiking, riding and fishing; wildlife sites are more remote. Visitors can view sheep-shearing and other camp activities, and there is a small war museum. Accommodations at the *Port*

FALKLAND ISLANDS

Howard Lodge (☎/*fax 42187*), the former manager's house, cost £55 per person with full board.

It's possible to hike up the valley of the Warrah River, a good trout stream, and past Turkey Rocks to the Blackburn River and Hill Cove, another pioneer farm. Ask permission to cross property boundaries, and remember to close gates; where the track is faint, look for old telephone lines. There are longer hikes south toward Chartres, Fox Bay and Port Stephens. Mt Maria makes a good day hike.

Pebble Island Off the north coast of West Falkland, elongated Pebble Island has varied topography, extensive wetlands and a good sample of wildlife. *Pebble Island Hotel* (☎/*fax 41093*) charges £47.50 per person with full board, but ask for self-catering cottages at the settlement. *Marble Mountain Shanty*, at the west end of the island, charges £15 per night.

Keppel Island In 1853, the South American Missionary Society established itself on Keppel to catechize Yahgan Indians from Tierra del Fuego and teach them to grow potatoes. Because the government suspected that the Yahgans had been brought against their will, the settlement was controversial, but remained until 1898.

Interesting ruins include the chapel, the bailiff's house and the stone walls of Indian dwellings. Keppel is also a good wildlife site, but visits are difficult to arrange because it has no permanent residents. If interested in visiting, contact Mr LR Fell (☎ 41001).

Saunders Island In 1767, Spanish forces temporarily dislodged the British from Port Egmont, site of the first British garrison (1765), and nearly precipitated a war. After the British left in 1774, Spain razed the settlement, but extensive ruins still remain.

Saunders has plenty of wildlife and good trekking to 'The Neck,' whose sandspit beach links it to Elephant Point peninsula, about four hours from the settlement. Near The Neck is a huge colony of black-browed albatrosses and rockhopper penguins, along with a few king penguins and a solitary chinstrap penguin; farther on are thousands of Magellanic penguins, kelp gulls, skuas and a colony of elephant seals.

David and Suzan Pole-Evans (☎ 41298) rent a comfortable self-catering cottage at Saunders settlement for £10 per person per night, as well as a six-bunk Portakabin (bedding supplied), with a gas stove and outside chemical toilet, at The Neck. Fresh milk and eggs are usually available, but otherwise visitors should bring their own food. Depending on the farm workload, transportation to The Neck is available for £10 per person. Inexpensive mountain bikes are for rent.

Port Stephens Port Stephens' rugged headlands, near the settlement's sheltered harbor, host thousands of rockhoppers and other seabirds. Calm Head, about two hours' walk, has excellent views of the jagged shoreline and powerful South Atlantic. One longer trek goes to the abandoned sealing station at Albemarle and past huge colonies of gentoo penguins. The Arch Islands, inaccessible except by boat, take their name from the huge gap that the ocean has eroded in the largest of the group.

If interested in visiting Port Stephens and trekking in the vicinity, contact Peter or Anne Robertson (☎ 42307) at the settlement or Leon and Pam Berntsen (☎ 42309) at Albemarle Station.

Weddell Island Scottish pioneer John Hamilton acquired this western offshore island, the third largest in the archipelago, to experiment with tussock grass restoration and forest plantations and to import Highland cattle, Shetland ponies, and exotic wildlife such as guanacos, Patagonian foxes and otters. The abundant local wildlife includes gentoo and Magellanic penguins, great skuas, night herons, giant petrels and striated caracaras.

Farm owners John and Steph Ferguson (☎ 42398) welcome guests at *Seaview Cottage*, *Hamilton Cottage* or the *Mountain View House* for £15 per person (self-catering) or £30 per person with full board.

FALKLAND ISLANDS

New Island The Falklands' most westerly inhabited island was a refuge for British and North American whalers from the late 18th century well into the 19th century. There remain ruins of a shore-based Norwegian whaling factory that failed simply because there were not enough whales.

On the precipitous west coast are large colonies of rockhopper penguins and black-browed albatrosses and even a rookery of southern fur seals. Potential visitors to the island should contact Tony or Annie Chater (☎ 21399), or Ian or María Strange (☎ 21185) in Stanley.

Language

Every visitor to Chile should attempt to learn some Spanish, whose basic elements are easily acquired. If possible, take a short course before you go. Even if you can't do so, Chileans are gracious hosts and will encourage your Spanish, so there is no need to feel self-conscious about vocabulary or pronunciation. There are many common cognates, so if you're stuck try Hispanicizing an English word – it is unlikely you'll make a truly embarrassing error. Do not, however, admit to being *embarazada* (sounds like 'embarrassed') unless you are in fact pregnant!

Note that in American Spanish, the plural of the familiar 'tu' is *ustedes* rather than *vosotros*, as in Spain. Chileans and other Latin Americans readily understand Castilian Spanish, but may find it either quaint or pretentious.

Chilean Spanish

Chilean speakers relax terminal and even some internal consonants almost to the point of disappearance, so that it can be difficult to distinguish plural from singular. For example, *las islas* (the islands) may sound more like 'la ila' to an English speaker. Chileans speak rather more rapidly than other South Americans, and rather less clearly – the conventional *¿quieres?* (do you want?) sounds more like 'querí' on the tongue of a Chilean.

Other Chilean peculiarities include pronunciation of the second person familiar of 'ar' verbs as 'ai' rather than 'as,' so that, for instance, *¿Adónde vas?* (Where are you going?) will sound more like '¿Adónde vai?' Likewise, the common interjection *pues* (well...) at the end of a phrase becomes 'pueh' or 'po,' as in 'sí, po.'

Vocabulary There are many differences in vocabulary between Castilian and American Spanish, and among Spanish-speaking countries in the Americas. There are also considerable regional differences within these countries not attributable to accent alone –

Chilean speech, for instance, contains many words adopted from Mapuche, while the residents of Santiago sometimes use *coa*, a working-class slang. Check the glossary for some of these terms.

Chileans and other South Americans normally refer to the Spanish language as *castellano* rather than *español*.

Phrasebooks & Dictionaries

Lonely Planet's *Latin American Spanish phrasebook*, by Anna Cody, is a worthwhile addition to your backpack. Another exceptionally useful resource is the *University of Chicago Spanish-English, English-Spanish Dictionary*, whose small size, lightweight and thorough entries make it ideal for travel.

Visitors confident of their Spanish (and judgment) can tackle John Brennan's and Alvaro Taboada's *How to Survive in the Chilean Jungle* (1996), jointly published by Dolmen Ediciones and the Instituto Chileno Norteamericano, an enormously popular book that has gone through nine editions explaining Chilean slang to the naïve.

Pronunciation

Spanish pronunciation is, in general, consistently phonetic. Once you are aware of the basic rules, they should cause little difficulty. Speak slowly to avoid getting tongue-tied until you become confident of your ability.

Pronunciation of the letters f, k, l, n, p, q, s and t is virtually identical with English, and y is identical when used as a consonant; ll is a separate letter, pronounced as 'y' and coming after l in the alphabet. Ch and ñ are also separate letters; in the alphabet they come after c and n respectively.

Vowels Spanish vowels are very consistent and have easy English equivalents:

a is like 'a' in 'father'
e is like the 'e' in 'met'; at the end of a word it's like the 'ey' in 'hey'

i is like 'ee' in 'feet'

o is like 'o' in 'for'

u is like 'oo' in 'boot'; after consonants other than 'q,' it is more like English 'w'

y is a consonant except when it stands alone or appears at the end of a word, in which case its pronunciation is identical to Spanish 'i'

Consonants Spanish consonants generally resemble their English equivalents, but there are some major exceptions:

b resembles its English equivalent, but is undistinguished from 'v'; for clarification, refer to the former as 'b larga,' the latter as 'b corta' (the word for the letter itself is pronounced like English 'bay')

c is like the 's' in 'see' before 'e' and 'i', otherwise like English 'k'

d closely resembles 'th' in 'feather'

g before 'e' and 'i' like a guttural English 'h'; otherwise like 'g' in 'go'

h is invariably silent; if your name begins with this letter, listen carefully when immigration officials summon you to pick up your passport

j most closely resembles English 'h,' but is slightly more guttural

ñ is like 'ni' in 'onion'

r is nearly identical to English except at the beginning of a word, when it is often rolled

rr is very strongly rolled

v resembles English, but see 'b,' above

x is like 'x' in 'taxi' except for very few words for which it follows Spanish or Mexican usage as 'j'

z is like 's' in 'sun'

Diphthongs Diphthongs are combinations of two vowels which form a single syllable. In Spanish, the formation of a diphthong depends on combinations of 'weak' vowels (i and u) or strong ones (a, e and o). Two weak vowels or a strong and a weak vowel make a diphthong, but two strong ones are separate syllables.

A good example of two weak vowels forming a diphthong is the word *diurno* (during the day). The final syllable of *obligatorio* (obligatory) is a combination of weak and strong vowels.

Stress Stress, often indicated by visible accents, is very important, since it can change the meaning of words. In general, words ending in vowels or the letters n or s have stress on the next-to-last syllable, while those with other endings have stress on the last syllable. Thus *vaca* (cow) and *caballos* (horses) both have stress on their next-to-last syllables.

Visible accents, which can occur anywhere in a word, dictate stress over these general rules. Thus *sótano* (basement), *América* and *porción* (portion) all have the stress on the syllable with the accented vowel. When words are written all in capitals, the accent is often not shown, but it still affects the pronunciation.

Basic Grammar

Nouns in Spanish are masculine or feminine. The definite article ('the' in English) agrees with the noun in gender and number; for example, the Spanish word for 'train' is masculine, so 'the train' is *el tren*, and the plural is *los trenes*. The word for 'house' is feminine, so 'the house' is *la casa*, and the plural is *las casas*. The indefinite articles (a, an, some) work in the same way: *un libro* (a book) is masculine singular, while *una carta* (a letter) is feminine singular. Most nouns ending in 'o' are masculine and those ending in 'a' are generally feminine. Normally, nouns ending in a vowel add 's' to form the plural – *unos libros* (some books), *las cartas* (the letters) – while those ending in a consonant add 'es': *los reyes* (the kings) is the plural of *el rey* . Gender also affects demonstrative pronouns: *este* is the masculine form of 'this,' while *esta* is the feminine form and *esto* the neuter; 'these,' 'that' and 'those' are formed by adding 's.'

Adjectives also agree with the noun in gender and number, and usually come after the noun. Possessive adjectives like *mi* (my), *tu* (your) *su* (his/her/their) agree with the thing possessed, not with the possessor. For example 'his suitcase' is *su maleta*, while 'his suitcases' is *sus maletas*. A simple way to indicate possession is to use the preposition *de* (of). 'Juan's room,' for instance, would be *la habitación de Juan*, literally, 'the room of Juan.'

Personal pronouns are usually not used with verbs, except for clarification or emphasis. There are three main categories of verbs: those which end in 'ar' such as *hablar* (to speak), those which end in 'er' such as *comer* (to eat), and those which end in 'ir' such as *reir* (to laugh); there are many irregular verbs, such as *ir* (to go) and *venir* (to come).

To form a comparative, add *más* (more) or *menos* (less) before the adjective. For example, *alto* is 'high,' *más alto* 'higher' and *lo más alto* 'the highest.'

Greetings & Civilities

In their public behavior, Chileans are exceptionally polite and expect others to reciprocate. Never, for example, approach a stranger for information without extending a greeting like *buenos días* or *buenas tardes*. Most young people use the informal 'tú' and its associated verb forms among themselves, but if in doubt you should use the more formal 'usted' and its forms.

Hello	*hola*
good morning	*buenos días*
good afternoon	*buenas tardes*
good evening, night	*buenas noches*
goodbye	*adiós, chau*
please	*por favor*
thank you	*gracias*
you're welcome	*de nada*

Useful Words & Phrases

yes	*sí*
no	*no*
and	*y*
to/at	*a*
for	*por, para*
of/from	*de, desde*
in	*en*
with	*con*
without	*sin*
before	*antes*
after	*después*
soon	*pronto*
alread	*ya*
now	*ahora*
right away	*en seguida, al tiro*
here	*aquí*

there	*allí*
Where?	*¿Dónde?*
Where is…?	*¿Dónde está…?*
Where are…?	*¿Dónde están…?*
When?	*¿Cuando?*
How?	*¿Cómo?*
I would like…	*Me gustaría…*
coffee	*café*
tea	*té*
beer	*cerveza*
How much?	*¿Cuanto?*
How many?	*¿Cuantos?*

I understand	*entiendo*
I don't understand	*no entiendo*

I don't speak much Spanish.
   No hablo mucho castellano.
Is there…? Are there…?
   ¿Hay…?

Getting Around

plane	*avión*
train	*tren*
bus	*ómnibus,* or just *bus*
small bus	*colectivo, micro, liebre*
ship	*barco, buque*
car	*auto*
taxi	*taxi*
truck	*camión*
pickup	*camioneta*
bicycle	*bicicleta*
motorcycle	*motocicleta*
hitchhike	*hacer dedo*
airport	*aeropuerto*
train station	*estación de ferrocarril*
bus terminal	*terminal de buses*
first/second class	*primera/segunda clase*
one way/roundtrip	*ida/ida y vuelta*
left luggage	*guardería, equipaje*
tourist office	*oficina de turismo*

I would like a ticket to…
   Quiero un boleto/pasaje a…
What's the fare to…?
   ¿Cuanto cuesta el pasaje a…?
When does the next plane/train/bus leave for…?
   ¿Cuando sale el próximo avión/tren/ ómnibus para…?
student/university discount
   descuento estudiantil/universitario

first/last/next
   primero/último/próximo

Accommodations

hotel	*hotel, pensión, residencial*
single room	*habitación single*
double room	*habitación doble*
per night	*por noche*
full board	*pensión completa*
shared bath	*baño compartido*
private bath	*baño privado*
too expensive	*demasiado caro*
cheaper	*mas económico*
May I see it?	*¿Puedo verlo?*
I don't like it	*No me gusta.*
the bill	*la cuenta*

What does it cost?
   ¿Cuanto cuesta?
Can you give me a deal?
   ¿Me puede hacer precio?

Toilets

The most common word for 'toilet' is *baño*, but *servicios sanitarios*, or just *servicios* (services) is a frequent alternative. Men's toilets will usually bear a descriptive term such as *hombres, caballeros* or *varones*. Women's toilets will say *señoras* or *damas*.

Post & Communications

post office	*correo*
letter	*carta*
parcel	*paquete*
postcard	*postal*
airmail	*correo aéreo*
registered mail	*certificado*
stamps	*estampillas*
person to person	*persona a persona*
collect call	*cobro revertido*

Geographical Expressions

The expressions below are among the most common you will encounter in this book and in Spanish language maps and guides.

bay	*bahía*
bridge	*puente*
farm	*fundo, hacienda*
glacier	*glaciar, ventisquero*
highway	*carretera, camino, ruta*
hill	*cerro*
lake	*lago*
marsh, estuary	*estero*
mount	*cerro*
mountain range	*cordillera*
national park	*parque nacional*
pass	*paso*
ranch	*estancia*
sound	*seno*
river	*río*
waterfall	*cascada, salto*

Countries

The list below includes only countries whose spelling differs in English and Spanish.

Canada	*Canadá*
Denmark	*Dinamarca*
England	*Inglaterra*
France	*Francia*
Germany	*Alemania*
Great Britain	*Gran Bretaña*
Ireland	*Irlanda*
Italy	*Italia*
Japan	*Japón*
Netherlands	*Holanda*
New Zealand	*Nueva Zelandia*
Peru	*Perú*
Scotland	*Escocia*
Spain	*España*
Sweden	*Suecia*
Switzerland	*Suiza*
United States	*Estados Unidos*
Wales	*Gales*

I am from
   Soy de…
Where are you from?
   ¿De dónde viene?
Where do you live?
   ¿Dónde vive?

Numbers

1	*uno*
2	*dos*
3	*tres*
4	*cuatro*
5	*cinco*
6	*seis*
7	*siete*

8	*ocho*
9	*nueve*
10	*diez*
11	*once*
12	*doce*
13	*trece*
14	*catorce*
15	*quince*
16	*dieciseis*
17	*diecisiete*
18	*dieciocho*
19	*diecinueve*
20	*veinte*
21	*veintiuno*
22	*veintidós*
23	*veintitrés*
24	*veinticuatro*
30	*treinta*
31	*treinta y uno*
32	*treinta y dos*
33	*treinta y tres*
40	*cuarenta*
41	*cuarenta y uno*
42	*cuarenta y dos*
50	*cincuenta*
60	*sesenta*
70	*setenta*
80	*ochenta*
90	*noventa*
100	*cien*
101	*ciento uno*
102	*ciento dos*
110	*ciento diez*
120	*ciento veinte*
130	*ciento treinta*
200	*doscientos*
300	*trescientos*
400	*cuatrocientos*
500	*quinientos*
600	*seiscientos*
700	*setecientos*
800	*ochocientos*
900	*novecientos*
1000	*mil*
1100	*mil cien*
1200	*mil doscientos*

2000	*dos mil*
5000	*cinco mil*
10,000	*diez mil*
50,000	*cincuenta mil*
100,000	*cien mil*
1,000,000	*un millón*

Ordinal Numbers

1st	*primero/a*
2nd	*segundo/a*
3rd	*tercero/a*
4th	*cuarto/a*
5th	*quinto/a*
6th	*sexto/a*
7th	*séptimo/a*
8th	*octavo/a*
9th	*noveno/a*
10th	*décimo/a*
11th	*undécimo/a*
12th	*duodécimo/a*

Days of the Week

Monday	*lunes*
Tuesday	*martes*
Wednesday	*miércoles*
Thursday	*jueves*
Friday	*viernes*
Saturday	*sábado*
Sunday	*domingo*

Time

Eight o'clock is *las ocho*, while 8:30 is *las ocho y treinta* (literally, 'eight and thirty') or *las ocho y media* (eight and a half). However, 7:45 is *las ocho menos quince* (literally, 'eight minus fifteen') or *las ocho menos cuarto* (eight minus one quarter).

Times are modified by morning *(de la mañana)* or afternoon *(de la tarde)* instead of am or pm. It is also common to use the 24-hour clock, especially with transportation schedules.

What time is it?	*¿Qué hora es?*
It is…	*Es la una…*
	or *Son las…*

Glossary

This list includes common geographical and biological terms as well as slang terms from everyday speech. RN indicates that a term is a Rapa Nui (Easter Island) usage, while FI means a Falklands Islands (Islas Malvinas) usage.

aerosilla – chairlift

afuerino – casual farm laborer

aguas – herbal teas

ahu (RN) – large stone platforms on which moai (statues) were erected

alameda – avenue or boulevard lined with trees, particularly poplars

albergue juvenil – youth hostel

alerce – *Fitzroya cupressoides*, large coniferous tree, resembling California redwood, for which Parque Nacional Alerce Andino is named

almuerzo – lunch

alpaca – *Lama pacos*, a wool-bearing domestic camelid of the central Andes, related to but with finer and more valuable wool than the llama

altiplano – high plains of northern Chile, Bolivia, southern Peru and northwestern Argentina, that are generally higher than 4000m

anexo – telephone extension

apapa (RN) – stone ramp used to launch boats

apunamiento – altitude sickness

Araucanians – major grouping of indigenous peoples, including the Mapuche, Picunche and Pehuenche Indians

arrayán – reddish-barked tree of the myrtle family, common in southern Chile's Valdivian forests

arroyo – watercourse

ascensores – picturesque funiculars that connect the center of Valparaíso with its hillside neighborhoods

ayllu – indigenous community of the Norte Grande; ayllus are more kinship-based rather than geographical, although they usually possess community lands

Aymara – indigenous inhabitants of the Andean altiplano of Peru, Bolivia and northern Chile

bahía – bay

balneario – bathing resort or beach

barrio – neighborhood or borough

bencina – petrol or gasoline

bencina blanca – white gas used for camping stoves; usually available in hardware stores or chemical supply shops

bidón – spare fuel container

bodega – cellar or storage area for wine

bofedal – swampy alluvial pasture in the altiplano, used by the Aymara to graze alpacas

boleadoras – weapon of round stones joined by a leather strap, used by Patagonian Indians for hunting guanaco and rhea; also called 'bolas'

boleto inteligente – multitrip ticket for Santiago Metro; also known as 'boleto valor'

cabildo – colonial town council

cacique – Indian chieftain

calefón – hot water heater; in most inexpensive accommodations, travelers must ask to have the calefón turned on before taking a shower

caleta – small cove

caliche – hardpan of the pampas of the Norte Grande; a dry, hard layer of clay beneath the soil surface from which mineral nitrates are extracted

callampas – shantytowns on the outskirts of Santiago, literally 'mushrooms' since they seemed to spring up overnight around the capital. Some have now become well-established neighborhoods.

cama – bed; also a sleeper-class seat on a bus or train

camanchaca – dense convective fog on the hills of the coastal Atacama desert. The camanchaca usually dissipates in late morning and returns with the sea breeze in late afternoon.

camarote – sleeper class on a ship or ferry

caracoles – winding roads, usually in a mountainous area; literally 'snails' or 'spirals'

carretera – highway

casa de cambio – money exchange house that usually buys foreign cash and travelers' checks

casa de familia – modest family accommodations, usually in tourist centers

casco – 'big house' on a fundo or estancia

casino de bomberos – in many Chilean cities and towns, a fire station restaurant, often run by a concessionaire, offering excellent meals at reasonable prices

cena – dinner

cerro – hill

certificado – registered, as in mail

chachacoma – *Senecio graveolens*, a native Andean plant; Aymara Indians brew a tea from the leaves that helps to relieve altitude sickness

charqui – dried llama or alpaca meat

chifa – Chinese restaurant; term most commonly used in the Norte Grande

Chilote – inhabitant of the archipelago of Chiloé; in certain contexts, the term has the connotation of 'bumpkin' despite the islands' rich cultural traditions

ciervo – deer

cine arte – art cinema (in contrast to mass commercial cinema), generally available only in Santiago and at universities

ciudad – city

cobro revertido – reverse charge (collect) phone call

Codelco – Corporación del Cobre, the state-owned enterprise that oversees Chile's copper mining industry

colación – lunch

colectivo or **taxi colectivo** – shared taxi

comedor – inexpensive market restaurant; also, dining room of a hotel

comida corrida – a cheap set meal

comparsa – group of musicians or dancers

comuna – local governmental unit, largely administrative in the very centralized Chilean state

confitería – confectioner's shop

con gas – 'with gas'; carbonated, as in soft drinks

congregación – in colonial Latin America, the concentration of dispersed native populations in settlements, usually for political control or religious instruction; see also *reducción*

congrio – conger eel, a popular and delicious seafood

cordillera – chain of mountains, mountain range

costanera – coastal road; any road along a sea coast, riverside or lakeshore

criollo – in colonial times, a person of Spanish parentage born in the New World

curanto – Chilean seafood stew

desayuno – breakfast

desierto florido – in the Norte Chico, the flowering of dormant wildflower seeds in the desert during a rare year of heavy rainfall

elaboración artesanal – small-scale production, often by a family

encomendero – individual Spaniard or Spanish institution (such as the Catholic Church) exploiting Indian labor under the encomienda system

encomienda – colonial labor system under which Indian communities were required to provide workers for *encomenderos,* in exchange for which the encomendero was to provide religious and language instruction. In practice, the system benefited the encomendero far more than native peoples.

esquí en marcha – cross-country skiing

estancia – extensive cattle- or sheep-grazing establishment with a dominant owner or manager and dependent resident labor force

estero – estuary

FCO (FI) – British Foreign and Commonwealth Office, which appoints the governor of the Falkland Islands

feria – artisans' market

FIBS (FI) – Falkland Islands Broadcasting Service

FIC (FI) – Falkland Islands Company

ficha – token used in lieu of cash in the nitrate *oficinas* of the Norte Grande or the *fundos* of the Chilean heartland

FIGAS (FI) – Falkland Islands Government Air Service

fuerte – fort

fundo – Chilean term for *hacienda*, usually applied to a smaller irrigated unit in the country's central heartland

garúa – coastal desert fog; see also the entry for *camanchaca*

geoglyph – in the Norte Grande, pre-Colombian figures or abstract designs made by grouping dark stones over light-colored soil on hillside sites

golfo – gulf

golpe de estado – coup d'etat, a sudden, illegal seizure of government

guanaco – a type of police water cannon, named after the spitting wild camelid (*Lama guanicoe*).

hacendado – owner of a hacienda, who was usually resident in the city and left day-to-day management of his estate to underlings

hacienda – throughout Latin America, a large but often underproductive rural landholding, with dependent resident labor force, under a dominant owner. In Chile, the term *fundo* is more common, though it generally applies to a smaller irrigated unit.

hare paenga (RN) – elliptical (boat-shaped) house

hospedaje – budget accommodations, usually a large family home with one or two extra bedrooms for guests and a shared bathroom

hostería – inn or guesthouse that serves meals, usually outside the main cities

hotel parejero – urban short-stay accommodation, normally patronized by young couples in search of privacy

huaso – horseman, a rough Chilean equivalent of the Argentine gaucho

ichu – bunch grass found on the altiplano

IGM – Instituto Geográfico Militar; mapping organization whose products are available and useful to travelers

inquilino – tenant farmer on a *fundo*

intendencia – Spanish colonial administrative unit

invierno boliviano – 'Bolivian winter'; summer rainy season in the Chilean altiplano, so-called because of the direction from which the storms come

isla – island

islote – small island, islet

istmo – isthmus

IVA – *impuesto de valor agregado*, value-added tax (VAT) often added to restaurant or hotel bills

kuchen – sweet, German-style pastries

kumara (RN) – Polynesian word for sweet potato

La Frontera – region of pioneer settlement, between the Río Biobío and the Río Toltén, dominated by Araucanian Indians until the late 19th century

lago – lake

laguna – lagoon

latifundio – large landholding, such as a *fundo*, *hacienda* or *estancia*

lenga – a deciduous species of southern beech

lista de correos – poste restante

llano – plain, flat ground

llareta – *Laretia compacta*, a dense compact shrub in the Chilean altiplano, with a deceptive, cushionlike appearance, used by Aymara herders for fuel

local – a numbered addition to a street address indicating that a business occupies one of several offices at that address; for example, Maturana 227, Local 5

lomas – in the Atacama desert, coastal hills on which condensation from the *camanchaca* (convective fog) supports relatively dense vegetation

machista – male chauvinist (normally used as an adjective)

manavai (RN) – excavated garden enclosures

maori (RN) – learned men, reportedly able to read *Rongo-Rongo* tablets

Mapuche – indigenous inhabitants of the area south of the Río Biobío

marae (RN) – platforms found on Polynesian islands that resemble the ahu of Rapa Nui

marisquería – seafood restaurant, usually reasonably priced with excellent quality, in family-oriented beach resorts

mataa (RN) – obsidian spearhead

matua (RN) – ancestor, father; associated with Hotu Matua, leader of the first Polynesian immigrants

media pensión – half-board, in a hotel

mestizo – a person of mixed Indian and Spanish descent

micro – small bus, often traveling along the back roads

minga – reciprocal Mapuche Indian labor system

minifundio – small landholding, such as a peasant farm

mirador – lookout point, usually on a hill but sometimes in a building

moai (RN) – large anthropomorphic statues, carved from volcanic tuff

moai kavakava (RN) – carved wooden 'statues of ribs'

momios – 'mummies,' upper-class Chileans resistant to social and political change

motu (RN) – small offshore islet

municipalidad – city hall

museo – museum

música funcional – muzak

nalca – *Gunnera chilensis*, a plant resembling an enormous rhubarb, with large leaves and edible stalks; gathered for food on Chiloé and elsewhere in southern Chile

ñandú – large, flightless bird known in English as a rhea; similar to the ostrich

nevado – snowcapped mountain peak

Norte Chico – 'Little North,' the semi-arid region between the province of Chañaral and the Río Aconcagua

Norte Grande – 'Big North,' the very arid portion of the country north of Chañaral

Nueva Canción Chilena – the 'New Chilean Song' movement, which arose in the 1960s and combined traditional folk themes with contemporary political activism

oferta – promotional fare, often seasonal, for plane or bus travel

oficina – in the Norte Grande, a 19th- and early 20th-century nitrate mining enterprise, in some cases almost a small city, with a large dependent labor force

onces – 'elevenses,' Chilean afternoon tea

palafitos – on the islands of Chiloé, rows of houses built on stilts over the water, where boats can anchor at their back doors on a rising tide

pampa – in the Norte Grande, a vast desert expanse where mineral nitrates were often mined

parada – bus stop

parque nacional – national park

parrilla – restaurant specializing in grilled meats

parrillada – grilled steak and other beef

pastel de choclo – maize casserole filled with vegetables, chicken and beef

peatonal – pedestrian mall, usually in the center of larger cities

pehuén – *Araucaria auracana*, the monkey-puzzle tree of southern Chile; its nuts are a staple of the Pehuenche Indians' diet

peña – folk music and cultural club; many originated in Santiago in the 1960s as venues for the New Chilean Song movement

penquista – inhabitant of Concepción, deriving from the city's original site at nearby Penco

pensión – family home offering short-term budget accommodation; may also take permanent lodgers

pensión completa – full board, in a hotel

picada – informal family restaurant

pingüinera – penguin colony

playa – beach

pora (RN) – small reed raft used for paddling to offshore islets (*motu*)

Porteño – a native or resident of the port city of Valparaíso

portezuelo – mountain pass

posta – clinic or first-aid station, often found in smaller towns that lack proper hospitals

postre – dessert

precordillera – the foothills of the Andes mountains

propina – a tip, at a restaurant or elsewhere

puente – bridge

puerto – port

pukao (RN) – the topknot on the head of a moai; once a common hairstyle for Rapa Nui males

pukará – a pre-Columbian hilltop fortress in the Andes

pulpería – company store on a *fundo*, *estancia* or *nitrate* oficina

puna – Andean highlands, usually above 3000m

punta – point

quebrada – ravine

quila – a solid bamboo found in southern Chilean rain forest, often forming impenetrable thickets; also known as 'chusquea'

quinoa – native Andean grain, a dietary staple in the pre-Columbian era, still grown by Aymara farmers in the precordillera of the Norte Grande

Rapa Nui – the Polynesian name for Easter Island

Rapanui – the Polynesian name for the people of Easter Island and their language

reducción – the concentration of Indians in towns modeled on the Spanish grid pattern, for purposes of political control or religious instruction; the term also refers to the settlement itself

refugio – a shelter, usually rustic, in a national park or other remote area

reserva nacional – national reserve, a category of land use

residencial – budget accommodations, sometimes seasonal; in general, residenciales occupy buildings designed expressly for short-stay lodging

rhea – large, flightless bird, called *ñandú* in Spanish, similar to the ostrich

río – river

rodeo – annual roundup of cattle on an *estancia* or *hacienda*

Rongo-Rongo (RN) – an indecipherable script on wooden tablets that some have thought to be an alphabet or other form of native writing

roto – 'ragged one,' a dependent laborer on a Chilean *fundo*

ruca – traditional thatched Mapuche house

ruta – route; highway

SAG – Servicio Agrícola Ganadero, the Agriculture and Livestock Service; its officials inspect baggage and vehicles for prohibited fruit and meat imports at Chilean border crossings

saladero – an establishment for salting meat and hides

salar – salt lake, salt marsh or salt pan, usually in high Andes or Patagonia

salón cama – bus with reclining seats

salón de té – literally 'teahouse,' but more like an upscale cafetería

Santiaguino – native or resident of the city of Santiago

seno – sound, fjord

servicentro – large gasoline station with spacious parking lot, restaurants and toilet facilities, including inexpensive hot showers

sierra – mountain range

siesta – afternoon nap during the extended midday break of traditional Chilean business hours

sin gas – 'without gas,' non-carbonated mineral water

smoko (FI) – midmorning tea or coffee break, usually served with cakes and other homemade sweets

s/n – 'sin número,' indicating a street address without a number

soroche – altitude sickness

Southern Cone – in political geography, the area comprising Argentina, Chile, Uruguay and parts of Brazil and Paraguay; so called after the area's shape on the map

squaddies (FI) – British enlisted men on four-month tours of duty in the Falkland Islands

tábano – horsefly

tajamares – dikes built to control flooding of the Río Mapocho in late-colonial Santiago

tejuelas – in archipelagic Chile, especially Chiloé, shingles of varying design that typify the region's vernacular architecture

teleférico – gondola cable car

tenedor libre – all-you-can-eat fare

todo terreno – mountain bike

toki (RN) – basalt carving tool

toqui – Mapuche Indian chief

tortas – mine tailings, literally 'cakes'

totora (RN) – type of reed used for making rafts

turismo aventura – nontraditional forms of tourism, such as trekking and river rafting

two-nighter (FI) – a traditional party for visitors from distant sheep stations, who would invariably stay the weekend

Unidad Popular – 'Popular Unity,' a coalition of leftist political groups that supported Salvador Allende in the 1970 presidential election

vaina doble – common Chilean aperitif consisting of port, cognac, cocoa and egg white

Valle Central – Central Valley, the Chilean heartland that extends south from the Río Aconcagua to near the city of Concepción; this area contains most of Chile's population and its industrial and agricultural wealth

ventisquero – glacier

vicuña – *Vicugna vicugna*, wild relative of domestic llama and alpaca, found only at high altitudes in the Norte Grande

villa – village, small town

vizcacha – *Lagidium vizcacha*, a wild Andean relative of the domestic chinchilla

volcán – volcano

Yahgans – indigenous inhabitants of the Tierra del Fuego Archipelago

zampoñas – pan pipes

zona franca – at Iquique and Punta Arenas, duty-free zone where imported goods are available at very low prices

Climate Charts

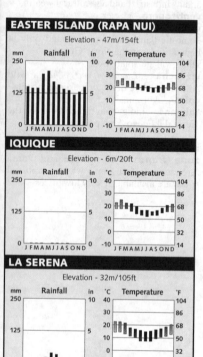

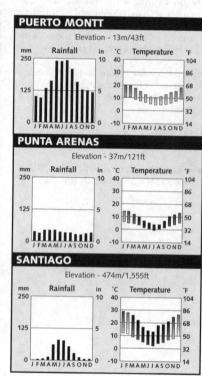

CLIMATE CHARTS

Acknowledgments

THANKS

Many thanks to the travelers who used the last edition of *Chile & Easter Island* and wrote to us with helpful hints, useful advice and interesting anecdotes.

Maria Abel, Noel Aflague, Barbara S. Ainslie, Ester van den Akker, Ximena Alfaro, Lucy W de Alió, Tim Allman & Rebecca Lush, Loreto Alvarez, Jeff Ames, W G Amesz, Frederico Amorim, Daniel Anderbring, Cherie Anderson & Dairne Fitzpatrick, Lillemor Andersson, David Anderson, Ina Anderson, Matt Anderson, Corthout Andre, Bill Angus, Sue Applegate & San Vriens, Joeri Apontoweil & Bianca Dijkstra, Cathy Archbould & Joyce Majiski, Molly Arévalo, Robert Arévalo, Dominique Argenson, Bob Aronoff, James Aronson, Marc Arts, Paul Arundale, Godfrey & Patricia Ash, Soco Astorga, Svein Otto Aure, Jerry Azevedo, Juan Carlos Azócar, Christine Badre, Stan Bach, Harris Baldascini, James R Ball, Barbara Banks, Nancy Bannister, Alison Barber & John Murphy, Paul Bardwell, Pamela Barefoot, CBH Barford, Steven Barger, Valérie Barnich, Craig Barrack, Sue Barreau, Michael C Barris, Irmgard Bauer, Alistair Baxendale, John & Pamela Beard, Irmengard Beckett, Michael Beckmann, John Becken, Joanne Below, Kristel Beltman, Jean-Paul Benglia, Marisa Beretta, Kate M. Berg, Marloes Bergmans & Stefan Rooyackers, Lian van Berkel, Steve Bertrand, Anne Bianchi, Jiri Biciste, Warren Bilkey, Jens Birk, Gillian Birkby, Elaine Birn, Erwin Bittnet, Bruce Blanch, María-José Blass and Reto Westermann, Charlotte Blixt & Dirk Schwensen, Steve Blume, Daniel Boag, Robert Boardman, Benajmin Boccas, Andre Boessenkool, Astrid Bombosd, Robert Bond, Inge Bollen, Alistair Bool, Charlotte & Paul Boorge, Hildegard & Christa Bornemann, Paul Bouwman, Gareth Brahams, Virginia Brand, Kerstin Brandes, Nigel & Sally Branston, Kathleen Brient & Ben Schiemer, Katja Breitenbücher, Elizabeth Briggs, Colin Broadley, Barbara Brons, Thomas Brostean, Berne Broudy, Fraukje Brouwer & Wim van Westrenen, Suzanne Brown, Vanessa T Brown, Richard Brownsword, Maud Bruemmer, Marlis Bruse & Jürgen Boje, Sharon Buccino & Jay Fowler, Alexander Bucka, Sergio Bueno, Jean Bullard, Tim Burford, Juergen Burkhart, Stuart Buxton, Gary Byrne, Richard Caelius, Mojka Cajnko, Fernanda Caiuby, Frank Campbell, Leticia Cárcamo S, PJ Carey, Juan Carlos, Britta-Stina Carlsson, Chris Carlson, Rafael Caro V, Roxana Carolin, Colin S. Carr, TE John Carrington-Birch, PJ Cary, Mike Cavendish, Dennis Chambers, Roberto Chatfield, Philip P. Chen, Anne Chevallier, L Clerke, Stephan Cludts, Linda & Larry Cohen, Pat Coleman & Sara Tizard, Patrick Collins, Richard Collyer-Hamlin, Colleen Cook, Kit Cooper, Sergio Cortez, Bryce Coulter, Peter Coutts, Andrew Cowan, James Cowie, Bob Crabb, Keith Crandall, Paula Crotty, Paul Crovella & Julie Pike, Meryl Cumber, Ryan Cummings, Leah Cutter, Phillip A Dale, Craig Daly, F Damsteeg-Knapen, Emma Dean, Jodie Deignon, Jean-Charles Dekeyser, Matthew Denniger, Rene & Patricia de Heek, Daan de Vries, Marian Dey, Verónica Díaz Rocco, Jörg Digmayer, JP Dilapuin, Katy van Dis, Buck Dodson, Raija Doertbudak, Jorg Dofmayer, Eva Dolne & Denis Duysens, Luis Eduardo Donoso, Andreas Dörr, Luciana & Luis Eduardo Dosso, Dim Douwes, JP Drapkin, Sabine Dressmann, Wolfgang Drexel, Zbynek Dubsky, Kathy Dunham, Julian Dunster, Denis Duysens, John Eastlund, David Edelstein, Andre Efira, Ilona Ehrlich, Vincent WJ Eijt, Amy Eisenberg, Daniel Eisenberg, Don Ellis III, PJ Ellis, Carlijn Engelhart, Donald C. Erbe, Martin Erdmann, Lene & John Eriksen, Sam Esmiol, James Etheridge, Robin Ette & Susan Turner, Minden Ten Eyck, Igor Fabjan, Peter Fahrney, Diego Falcone, Douglas Fears, Lucia Fell, Ninfa Fergadiotti, José Alberto Fernández, Sofia Fernández Catalán, Alfonso Fernández Manso, John

Ferreira, Sarah & Marcelo Ferrer, Caterina Ferrone, Maru & Shiman Fink, Dieter & Renate Finsker, Alan Firth, Molly E Fitz-Gerald, Dairne Fitzpatrick & Cherie Anderson, John C Foitzik, Alan D Foster, Simone Fredriksz, Jonathan Freeman, Lesley Freeness, Dirk Frewing, Brigitte Friedrich, Marjolein Friele, John Foitzik, Alan D Foster, Lesley Furness, Jose Alberto Fernandez Gaete, Paola Galasso, Andres Garcia-Huidobro, Hillary J Gardner, Steve Garnsey, Reg & Diane Gates, Katrin Geissler, Michael Giacometti, Alice Gilbey, Shaun AB Giles, Declan Gilmurray, Thomas & Alcke Girtz, Lisa Glass & Kristin Nali, Otilia Góngora Bravo, Andries Goossens, Leila Gorosito, Christophe Grandjean, Glenn Grant, Robert Grant, Karen H Gray, Laura Grego, DN Griffiths, Jorrit Groen Nienke Groen, Tony & Irena Grogan, Ian & Lynn Grout, J Camilo Guzmán S, Rodrigo Guzman P, Patrick Hagans, Marit Hagel, Callem Hamilton, Claire & Duncan Hamilton, Colleen Hamilton, JT Hamilton, Ross Hamilton, Andy Hammann, Anne Hammersbad & Adam Roberts, Doug Hanauer & Ann Rodzai, Rhonda Hankins, Andrew Hanscom, Nicky Harman, Lynda Harpley, S Harrel, Bill Hart, Julian & Jacquie Hart, Sue Harvey Michael Hasan, James & Jennifer Hatchell, Lorena Haug, Glenn Havelock, Francis Hawkings, Rhonda Hawkins, Franci Hawtangs, Jeremiah Hayes, Charles Hayne, Richard Haywood, Garry J Hazzard, Susan Heap, David Heatwole, René & Patricia de Heek, Eileen & Henk Heetveld, Onno Heijdens, Cyndi Heller, Jim Hendrickson, Clive Henman Siobhan Hennessy, Rodrigo Molina Henriquez, John Henzell, Elmar Herhuth, Sandra van Heyste & Gerd van Lancker, Nicky Heyward, Alan Hickey, Michal ben Hillel, Susanne Hillmer, Scott Hills, Julia Hinde, Lorena Hirschberg, Alexandra & Bohumil Hladky, Gigi Hoeller, Sabina Hoff, Eva Hoffman, Brett Hogan, John Holborow, Vanessa Smith Holburn, R Dieter Hollstein, Andreas Holsten, William Hood, Elva Hoover, Jennifer Hoover, Sanna Hopea, Dawn & Kevin Hopkins, Grenville & Georgina Hopkins, Elizabeth Hoskins, Jean Houlder, Chris Houser, Melissa Hunnibell, Patricia P Hunt, Sandy Hunter, Vickie Hutter, Eric P Havolbøll, Judith R Iave, Javier Ibar Muñoz, Ernestein Idenburg, Juan Iglesias Sesnic, Holger Illi, Ricardo Imai, Niels Iversen, Michael Jacob, Jannette & Marcel, Christopher Jessee, Ken Jewkes, Ana Jofré, Carolyn Johnson & Craig Barrack, Ripton Johnson, Erika Jones, Ali Judd, Horst Jung, Kristine Jürs, JC Noriyuki Kaitsuka, Henny Kanen, C Karp, Tessa Katesmark, James C. Kautz, Luke Kay, Christian Keil, Christopher D. Keivit, Bill Kemball, Alan Kendall, Steven Kennedy, Ton Kersbergen, Nancy Kershaw, Nathan Kesteven & Jessica Lowe, Fred Ketting, Edwin Kirk, Carlo Klauth, Charles Kloch, Karyn Knight, Brigitte Knoetig, Gabi Koch, Eric Koehler, Ray Kohlscheen, Jeffrey Kok, Martin Korff, Peter Korning, Carl Koskey, Michael Kosnett, Kai Kottwitz, Lutz Kral, Gen Kramer, Dale & Adrienne de Kretser, John Krieg, Eric Kuhn & Susan Webb, Avril Kuhrt & Steven Abramovitch, Anne Kuiper & Ruth Bitterlin, Joe Kutza, Rene LaBerge, Peter Lambert, Selena Lamlough, Nicholas La Penna, Francisco Larraín, Judith R Lave, Barbara Leighton, Raoul van Lennep, Albrecht Lenz, Brian & Lorna Lewis, Fernando Libedinsky, Heather Linson Lindberg, Sarah Llewellyn, Rafael Pintos Lopez, Karl Loring, Agnes & Antoine Lornier, Jaqueline & Mila Low, Jessica Lowe & Nathan Kesteven, Eduardo Lucero, Philipp Luginbühl, Diederik Lugtigheid, Joanna Luplin, Rebecca Lush & Tim Allman, Nyi Nyi Lwin, David Lyttle, Eric Maar, Isabel MacDougall, Iain MacKay, Ian Mackley, Bob Magnus, Kate Mahoney, Joyce Majiski & Cathie Archbould, Richard Manasseh, Amy-Jocelyn Mandel, Alfonso Fernandez Manso, Michael Mansour, Mario Marchese, Robert Marincin, Delsignore Marisa, Will Markle, L Martin, Maximiliano Martínez Espinoza, Anna Maspero, Kyle Mathis, Gabriela Matus Quintanilla, Gerhard Maucher, Jim McAdam, Joanne McAdam, Jason McCormack, Brian McDonald, Denise & Malcolm McDonaugh, Teresa McDonough, Sara McFall, Nigel McGrath, Dave McJannet, Tony McKevitt, Dean McNally, Margaret McOnie, Amanda Mead, Ulla Melchiorsen, Les Melrose, Ed Menning, Philippe Merien, John & Tessa Messenger, J Mickleson, Jay & Pete Mickleson, Sylvie

Micolon, Christopher Milenkevich, Cathy & Dimitri Minaretzis, Doug Mitchell & Sharlene Matten, Earle & Olga Moen, John Moffat, Stefan Molenaar, Carlos Ovalle Molina, Rodrigo Molina Henríquez, RS Moneta, Jamie Monk, Michael J Monsour, Fernando Miguel Moreno Olmedo, RS Moreta, Karen & Karim Moukaddem, Carmen Moya, Arun Mucherjee, Lisa & Greg Mueller, Patricio Muñoz, Paudie Murphy, Linda Murray, Kristin Nalli, Alex Nash, Katrina Natale, Bruce & Marcia Nesbitt, Pui Ng, D M Nicholls, Don Nicholls, Iris & Stefan Niederberger, Julie Nield, Gerardo Niklitschek, Mark Nilsson, Anna Noakes, Irene Patricia Nohara, Timo Noko, Justin Norman & Helen Hagan, Lennart Norstrand, Geoff Nuzun, Patty A O'Connell, Donna O'Daniel, Paul Oldaker, Fernando Miguel Moreno Olmedo, Moreno Olmedo, Sara Ominsky, David Onyango, Jose Antonio Opazo, Mitzie V Ortiz, Shannon Orton, Dieter Ottlewski, Luz Ovalle, David Owen, Rick Owen, Cory Owens, Perry de Paauw, Nick Pace, Mercedes Pacin, Astrid Padberg, Joan Paluzzi, Graham Parker, Aristea Parissi & George Kechagioglou, David Parsons, Evert te Pas, Don Paskovich, Caron Patterson, Robert Patterson, John Payson, Douglas Peacocke, Theon Pearce, Richard Pearcy, Elizabeth Pegg, Grace Peng, Carsten Perkuhn, Caterina Perrone, Wilhelmina Hentiette Persoon, James Grant Peterkin, Ginger & Jim Peterson, Bill & Huguette Petruk, Richard & Alison Pett, Laura Pezzano, Anja Pferdmenges, Tim Phipps, Kathie Piccagli, Lise Picert, Adrienne Pitts, Mario Poblete, April Pojman, Michael Pößl, Mario Poblete, Emma Pollard, Lucy Porter, Felix Portmann, Stephen Portnoy, Robert Postle, María Carmen Prado Laguna, Robbie Prater, Natalie Price, Bill Pringle, Bill & Alison Proctor, Rodrigo Proust, Donna Pyle, Jessica Quantes & Joshua Thomases, Alberto Quesada, Trish Quilaran & Daniel Moylan, Sabine Raab, Diane & Michael Rabinowitz, Aldo Raicich, Sweet Rain, Peggy & Chris Raphael, Diederik Ravesloot, Nick Read, Terence & Frances Reardon, JF Regis de Morais, Frances Reid & Lili Pâquet, Malcolm Reid, Michael Rhodes, Elise Richards, JP Richards, Mary Richards, David Roberts, WN

Roberts, Ann Rodzai & Doug Hanauer, Maureen Roe, Caroline Roels, Clive Rogers, Roy & Becey Rogers, Tom J van Rooij, Rachael Rook & Ishbel MacDougall, Stefan Rooyackers, Richard Rothenberger, RF Rudderham, JD Ruehl, Bruce Rumoge, Robert Runyard, Philipp Rusch, Sandra Rüttger, Ofer Sadan, Enrique L Salgado, Mike Salusky, Maria Sanchez de Campaña, Ron Sanchez, Tomás Sánchez, Paul Sanders, Marc Sanford, Hedda Sasburg, Uwe Sauerteig, Emily Sayce, Heidi Schanz, Andrea Schuechner, Henrik Schinzel, Astrid Schloz, Olivier Schmeltzer, Katrina Schneider, Michael Schneider, Gutta E Schoefl, Astrid Scholz, Nicole Schöenholzer, Mark Schottlander, Toralf Schrinner, Laurent Schyns & Elizabeth Walhin, Paul Scotchmer, Martin Scott & Jacky Upson, Stephen Scott, Gour Sen, Jerome Sgard, Annik Shahani, Florence & Peter Shaw, Sarah Shay, Tan Meng Shern, Karen S Shouse, Christopher Siddon, Mark Sigman, Sergio B Silva, Aruna Sinngh, Stephan Sludts, Brian Smith, Curtis & Marion Smith, Duncan Smith, Jonathan Smith, Rachel Smith, Charlotte Snowden, Keith Sohl, Erland Sommerskog, Robert Sonntag, Luca Sorbello, Chris Spelius, Sandra Spies, William Spurgeon, Robert Stanich, Alex Starr, Roland Steffen, Robert Steiner, Edward Steinman, JEM Stephens, Britta Stina-Carlsson, Lea Stogdale, Alexander Stoll, Ralph E. Stone, Ann & Bill Stoughton, Melanie Surry, Pieter Swart, A Sweet, Cate Swinburn, Katherine Tabailloux, Francisca Tapia, Minden Ten Eyck, Paul Tetrault, Julie Tilghman, Barbara Tily, Giles Thomas, Sara Tizard & Pat Coleman, Elvira Toledo de Oporto, Nick Toll, Barbara Tomas, Maria Torlaschi, Debbie Triff, Phill & Charlotte Trzcinski, Alois Tuna, Melissa Turley, Jackie Turner, Lena Tvede, BL Underwood, Cheyenne Valenzuela, Jeremy Valeriote, Llan van Berkel, Esther van den Akker, Frederik Vandenbrouche, Emese Melinda van der Hilt, Koosje van der Horst, Michael van der Valk, Katy van Dis, Sandra van Heyste & Gert van Lancker, Gert van Lancker & Sandra van Henste, Raoyl vanLennep, Bart Van Overmeire, Tom J van Rooij, Wim van Westrenen & Fraukje Brouwer, Jozef Varnagy, Jeroen Verberk, Sven Vestdens, Agustin Vezzani,

Natalie Vial, Christophe Vidal, RW Visser, Jennifer Vogel, Harold Volz, Pam Wadsworth, Kaspar Waelti, Ursula Wagner, Debbie Waldman, Michael Walensky, Clive Walker, Katharina Walldow, Stephne Waller, Susanne Wallnöfer, Tamonn Walsh, Ricardo Wang, Joachim Warnecke, JP Watney, Adrian Watson, Claire Watson, Matthew Watson, Susan Webb & Eric Kuhn, Thomas A Weber, Shane Anna Weiss, Armin Weissen, Stefan Westergard, Reto Westermann & Maria-José Blass, Greg Weston, Andy Whittaker, RD Wicks, Mieke Wieland, Gwyn Williams, Jennifer Williams, Robert Williamson, Anne Wilshin, Greer Wilson, Andrew Woolley, Heather Wright, Sebastian Wright, Ernesto Scabini Yadrievic, Karen Yanez, Sonia Kuscevic Yankovic, Jack Yates, Richard Yeomare, Rosemarie Yevich, Bill Young, Simon Young, Johanna Zevenboom, Rok Zizek

LONELY PLANET

Phrasebooks

Lonely Planet phrasebooks are packed with essential words and phrases to help travellers communicate with the locals. With color tabs for quick reference, an extensive vocabulary and use of script, these handy pocket-sized language guides cover day-to-day travel situations.

- handy pocket-sized books
- easy to understand Pronunciation chapter
- clear & comprehensive Grammar chapter
- romanization alongside script to allow ease of pronunciation
- script throughout so users can point to phrases for every situation
- full of cultural information and tips for the traveller

'...vital for a real DIY spirit and attitude in language learning'
– *Backpacker*

'the phrasebooks have good cultural backgrounders and offer solid advice for challenging situations in remote locations'
– *San Francisco Examiner*

Arabic (Egyptian) • Arabic (Moroccan) • Australian *(Australian English, Aboriginal and Torres Strait languages)* • Baltic States *(Estonian, Latvian, Lithuanian)* • Bengali • Brazilian • Burmese • Cantonese • Central Asia • Central Europe *(Czech, French, German, Hungarian, Italian, Slovak)* • Eastern Europe *(Bulgarian, Czech, Hungarian, Polish, Romanian, Slovak)* • Ethiopian (Amharic) • Fijian • French • German • Greek • Hebrew • Hill Tribes • Hindi/Urdu • Indonesian • Italian • Japanese • Korean • Lao • Latin American Spanish • Malay • Mandarin • Mediterranean Europe *(Albanian, Croatian, Greek, Italian, Macedonian, Maltese, Serbian, Slovene)* • Mongolian • Nepali • Papua New Guinea • Pilipino (Tagalog) • Quechua • Russian • Scandinavian Europe *(Danish, Finnish, Icelandic, Norwegian, Swedish)* • South Pacific Languages • South-East Asia *(Burmese, Indonesian, Khmer, Lao, Malay, Tagalog Pilipino, Thai, Vietnamese)* • Spanish (Castilian) *(also includes Catalan, Galician and Basque)* • Sri Lanka • Swahili • Thai • Tibetan • Turkish • Ukrainian • USA *(US English, Vernacular, Native American languages, Hawaiian)* • Vietnamese • Western Europe *(Basque, Catalan, Dutch, French, German, Greek, Irish)*

FREE Lonely Planet Newsletters

We love hearing from you and think you'd like to hear from us.

Planet Talk

Our FREE quarterly printed newsletter is full of tips from travellers and anecdotes from Lonely Planet guidebook authors. Every issue is packed with up-to-date travel news and advice, and includes:

- a postcard from Lonely Planet co-founder Tony Wheeler
- a swag of mail from travellers
- a look at life on the road through the eyes of a Lonely Planet author
- topical health advice
- prizes for the best travel yarn
- news about forthcoming Lonely Planet events
- a complete list of Lonely Planet books and other titles

To join our mailing list, residents of the UK, Europe and Africa can email us at go@lonelyplanet.co.uk; residents of North and South America can email us at info@lonelyplanet.com; the rest of the world can email us at talk2us@lonelyplanet.com.au, or contact any Lonely Planet office.

Comet

Our FREE monthly email newsletter brings you all the latest travel news, features, interviews, competitions, destination ideas, travellers' tips & tales, Q&As, raging debates and related links. Find out what's new on the Lonely Planet Web site and which books are about to hit the shelves.

Subscribe from your desktop: www.lonelyplanet.com/comet

LONELY PLANET

Mail Order

Lonely Planet products are distributed worldwide. They are also available by mail order from Lonely Planet, so if you have difficulty finding a title please write to us. North and South American residents should write to 150 Linden St, Oakland, CA 94607, USA; European and African residents should write to 10a Spring Place, London NW5 3BH, UK; and residents of other countries to Locked Bag 1, Footscray, Victoria 3011, Australia.

INDIAN SUBCONTINENT Bangladesh • Bengali phrasebook • Bhutan • Delhi • Goa • Healthy Travel Asia & India • Hindi & Urdu phrasebook • India • Indian Himalaya • Karakoram Highway • Kerala • Mumbai (Bombay) • Nepal • Nepali phrasebook • Pakistan • Rajasthan • Read This First: Asia & India • South India • Sri Lanka • Sri Lanka phrasebook • Tibet • Tibetan phrasebook • Trekking in the Indian Himalaya • Trekking in the Karakoram & Hindukush • Trekking in the Nepal Himalaya
Travel Literature: The Age of Kali: Indian Travels and Encounters • Hello Goodnight: A Life of Goa • In Rajasthan • A Season in Heaven: True Tales from the Road to Kathmandu • Shopping for Buddhas • A Short Walk in the Hindu Kush • Slowly Down the Ganges

ISLANDS OF THE INDIAN OCEAN Madagascar & Comoros • Maldives • Mauritius, Réunion & Seychelles

MIDDLE EAST & CENTRAL ASIA Bahrain, Kuwait & Qatar • Central Asia • Central Asia phrasebook • Dubai • Hebrew phrasebook • Iran • Israel & the Palestinian Territories • Istanbul • Istanbul City Map • Istanbul to Cairo on a shoestring • Jerusalem • Jerusalem City Map • Jordan • Lebanon • Middle East • Oman & the United Arab Emirates • Syria • Turkey • Turkish phrasebook • World Food Turkey • Yemen
Travel Literature: Black on Black: Iran Revisited • The Gates of Damascus • Kingdom of the Film Stars: Journey into Jordan

NORTH AMERICA Alaska • Boston • Boston City Map • California & Nevada • California Condensed • Canada • Chicago • Chicago City Map • Deep South • Florida • Great Lakes • Hawaii • Hiking in Alaska • Hiking in the USA • Honolulu • Las Vegas • Los Angeles • Los Angeles City Map • Louisiana & The Deep South • Miami • Miami City Map • New England • New Orleans • New York City • New York City City Map • New York City Condensed • New York, New Jersey & Pennsylvania • Oahu • Out to Eat – San Francisco • Pacific Northwest • Puerto Rico • Rocky Mountains • San Francisco • San Francisco City Map • Seattle • Southwest • Texas • USA • USA phrasebook • Vancouver • Virginia & the Capital Region • Washington DC • Washington, DC City Map • World Food Deep South, USA • World Food New Orleans
Travel Literature: Caught Inside: A Surfer's Year on the California Coast • Drive Thru America

NORTH-EAST ASIA Beijing • Beijing City Map • Cantonese phrasebook • China • Hiking in Japan • Hong Kong • Hong Kong City Map • Hong Kong Condensed • Hong Kong, Macau & Guangzhou • Japan • Japanese phrasebook • Korea • Korean phrasebook • Kyoto • Mandarin phrasebook • Mongolia • Mongolian phrasebook • Seoul • Shanghai • South-West China • Taiwan • Tokyo
Travel Literature: In Xanadu: A Quest • Lost Japan

SOUTH AMERICA Argentina, Uruguay & Paraguay • Bolivia • Brazil • Brazilian phrasebook • Buenos Aires • Chile & Easter Island • Colombia • Ecuador & the Galapagos Islands • Healthy Travel Central & South America • Latin American Spanish phrasebook • Peru • Quechua phrasebook • Read This First: Central & South America • Rio de Janeiro • Rio de Janeiro City Map • Santiago • South America on a shoestring • Santiago • Trekking in the Patagonian Andes • Venezuela
Travel Literature: Full Circle: A South American Journey

SOUTH-EAST ASIA Bali & Lombok • Bangkok • Bangkok City Map • Burmese phrasebook • Cambodia • Hanoi • Healthy Travel Asia & India • Hill Tribes phrasebook • Ho Chi Minh City • Indonesia • Indonesian phrasebook • Indonesia's Eastern Islands • Jakarta • Java • Lao phrasebook • Laos • Malay phrasebook • Malaysia, Singapore & Brunei • Myanmar (Burma) • Philippines • Pilipino (Tagalog) phrasebook • Read This First: Asia & India • Singapore • Singapore City Map • South-East Asia on a shoestring • South-East Asia phrasebook • Thailand • Thailand's Islands & Beaches • Thailand, Vietnam, Laos & Cambodia Road Atlas • Thai phrasebook • Vietnam • Vietnamese phrasebook • World Food Thailand • World Food Vietnam

ALSO AVAILABLE: Antarctica • The Arctic • The Blue Man: Tales of Travel, Love and Coffee • Brief Encounters: Stories of Love, Sex & Travel • Chasing Rickshaws • The Last Grain Race • Lonely Planet Unpacked • Not the Only Planet: Science Fiction Travel Stories • Lonely Planet On the Edge • Sacred India • Travel with Children • Travel Photography: A Guide to Taking Better Pictures

Index

A

accommodations 79–81. *See also* places to stay *for individual locations*
  camping & refugios 79–80
  casas de familia 80
  hospedajes, pensiones & residenciales 81
  hostels 55, 80–1
  hotels & motels 81
  long-term rentals 80
  reservations 79
Achao 418–9
activities 77–8. *See also individual activities*
acute mountain sickness (AMS) 70–1
addresses 60
administrative regions 29, 40, **30–1**
Aguas Calientes 377
ahu 532, 537–8, 551, 552–3, 554–5, 556
AIDS. *See* HIV/AIDS
air pollution 33
air travel
  domestic 106–7
    glossary 90–1
  international 88–99
  airlines 88–9
airports 88, 115–6
Aisén 32, 425–56, **426–7**
Alacaluf. *See* Qawashqar
alcoholic drinks 84–5
alerce 403, 404, 445
Alerce Andino, PN 403–4
Alessandri, Jorge 23–4, 25–6
Alessandri Palma, Arturo 22, 23, 40
Allende, Isabel 25, 46
Allende, Salvador 15, 23–4, 25–7, 43, 49, 66, 133, 135
Almagro, Diego de 17, 161, 261, 290
alpacas 242–3
altitude sickness 70–1

Altos del Lircay, RN 200–1
Ampuero, Roberto 47, 281
Anakena 553–4
Ancud 408–12, **409**
Andes 32–3
Angelmó 393
Angol 222–3
Antarctica 41–2, 457, 501
Anticura 378–9
Antillanca 377
antiques 87, 171
Antofagasta (city) 263–70, **264–5**
Antofagasta (region) 262–89
Antuco 219–20
Arancibia Clavel, Enrique 43
Araucanians 210–1, 215. *See also* Mapuche
araucaria (monkey-puzzle tree) 223, 343
archaeological sites 238–9
  Catarpe 286
  Chug Chug geoglyphs 280
  Cueva Pali Aike 470–1
  El Gigante de Atacama 258
  Lluta geoglyphs 238–9
  Pintados 260–1
  Pukará de Copaquilla 239
  Pukará de Quitor 286
  Rapa Nui 536–9, 542–3, 550–6
  Valle del Encanto 324–5
  Viña del Cerro 298
Archipiélago de Chiloé. *See* Chiloé
Archipiélago Juan Fernández 514–25
  flora & fauna 518–9
  geography & climate 516–8
  history 514–6
  transportation 519–20
Argentina
  border crossings 100–2, 452–3, **101**

  geopolitical disputes with 42, 428–9, 490–1
  Patagonia 452–3
  visiting 98
Arica 228–39, **232–3**, **238**
  places to stay 231, 234–5
  day trips 237–9
  entertainment 236
  history 228
  organized tours 231
  places to eat 235
  shopping 236
  special events 231
  transportation 236–7
astronomy 270, 312, 315–6, 320–1
Atacama Desert 226, 228, 262–3
Atacameño 17, 45, 283
ATMs 59
Aylwin, Patricio 28, 40, 44, 131
Aymara 16, 17, 29, 45, 151, 226, 228, 241, 244
Ayquina 280

B

backpacking. *See* hiking & backpacking
Bahía Inglesa 299–301
Bahía Tierras Blancas 525
Balmaceda, José Manuel 22, 135
Baños Colina 159
Baños Morales 158
Baquedano 271
bargaining 59
Bariloche (Arg) 388
Barquito 302
Barrio Bellavista 133–5, **134**
Barrio Brasil 135, 137
Barrio Ecológico 140
bars 86, 148–9
Basques 19, 45
beaches
  Easter Island 553–4
  La Araucanía 359

Middle Chile 178, 182–3, 214
Norte Chico 299, 306, 307, 311, 317, 328
Norte Grande 230–1, 252–3, 270, 289
Beagle Channel 490, 496
Belén Precordillera 239
Bernardo O'Higgins, PN 477
Berríos, Eugenio 43
bicycling. *See* cycling
birds 34–5, 36, 220, 244–5, 303, 509–10. *See also* *individual species*
Bolívar, Simón 20
Bolivia, border crossings to/from 99–100
Bolsico 270
books 62–3, 66–7. *See also* literature
border crossings 99–103
  Argentina 100–3, 452–3, **102**
  Bolivia 99–100
  Peru 99
Bridges, Thomas 502, 504, 509
Büchi, Hernán 28, 40
buses
  domestic 107–10
  international 99–103
  local 116
business hours 76

C

Cachagua 183
Cajón del Maipo 156, **157**
Calama 273–80, **274**, **279**
Calbuco 402–3
Caldera 299–301, **300**
Caleta Gonzalo 443–6
Caleta Hornos 315
Caleta Olivia (Arg) 453
Caleta Tortel 455–6
California, similarities to 24–5
Camino Austral 425, 428–9, **426–7**

Camp (FI) 566–70
camping. *See* accommodations
carabineros 76
Carrizal Bajo 306
cars 111–3
  accidents 76
  costs 112
  driver's licenses 54–5
  insurance 113
  purchasing 113
  regulations 112
  renting 112–3
  road assistance 112
  shipping 113
Casa Braun-Menéndez 463
Casa del Arte 210–1
Casa del Arte Diego Rivera 393
Casa Fuerte Santa Sylvia 354
casas de familia. *See* accommodations
Cascada de las Animas 158
Casino de Pucón 351
Caspana 280
Castro 413–8, **414**
Catarpe 286
Caupolicán 18, 211, 215
cauquén 510
cell phones 62
cemeteries 135, 464, 522
Central Coast 161–87
Centro de Esquí Chapa Verde 189–90
Centro Turístico Termal Coñaripe 360
Cerro Castillo, RN 450
Cerro El Morado 158
Cerro Guane Guane 244
Cerro La Campana 184–5
Cerro Ñielol, MN 336
Cerro Paranal 270
Cerro San Cristóbal 134–5
Cerro Santa Lucía 133
Cerro Sombrero 499
Cerro Tololo 315–6
Chaitén 446–9, **447**
Chañaral 301–2
Chañarcillo 298
Chango 17, 248, 262, 290
children, traveling with 74, 94

Chile Chico 451–4
Chillán 201–6, **202–3**
Chiloé 32, 406–24, **407**
Chiloé, PN 420–2
Chiu Chiu 280
Chol Chol 340
Chonchi 419–20
Chono 17, 419, 425
Choros 307
Choshuenco 362
Christian Democrats 23–7
Chug Chug 280
Chuquicamata 277–80
Chusmiza 258
Ciénegas de Parinacota 244
Cifuncho 289
cinemas 85–6, 150. *See also* film
Circle Pacific tickets 93
climate 28–33, 582
climbing 78, 298, 342, 351, 357, 389–90, 479, 492–3
clubs 86, 149
coal mining 214–5
Cobija 270–1
Cochamó 391–2
Cochiguaz 321
Cochrane 455
Cochrane, Thomas 20, 169, 368
Coihaique (city) 430–4, **431**
Coihaique, PN 434–5
Colo Colo 211, 215
Comodoro Rivadavia (Arg) 452–3
Coñaripe 359–60
Concepción 206–16, **208–9**, **215**
  places to stay 211–2
  day trips 214–6
  entertainment 212–3
  history 206–7
  restaurants 212
  shopping 212–3
  special events 211
  transportation 213–4
Concón 182
Conguillío, PN 341–4, **341**
consulates 56–7
Contreras, Manuel 43, 139

Contulmo, MN 216, 219
Convento y Museo de San Francisco 132
Cook, James 532
Copaquilla 239
Copiapó 292–8, **294–5**
copihue 336
copper mines 23, 26, 29, 43, 190, 262, 273, 277-80, 292
Coquimbo 316–7
Corral 368
costs 59
courier flights 95
crafts 87
credit cards 59
crime 59, 75
Cristo Redentor 490, 491
cruises 117, 464–5
Crusoe, Robinson 37, 514, 516–7
Cueva del Milodón, MN 476–7
Cueva Pali Aike 470–1
Cuevas de Los Patriotas 522
Cunco 17
Curacautín 344
Curaco de Vélez 419
Curicó 192–4, **193**, **195**
currency 58
customs 55
cycling 77, 104, 114, 312, 505

D

Dalcahue 412–3
Dampier, William 515, 516–7
dams 220–1
Darwin, Charles 63, 184, 185, 190, 207, 219, 248, 292, 304, 316, 406–7, 413, 420–1, 425, 437, 495–6
Darwin (FI) 568
Defoe, Daniel 16, 37, 514, 516, 517
deforestation 33, 45, 444
Diaguita 17, 290
diarrhea 71–2
DINA 27, 43, 139
disabled travelers 73–4, 94
diving 78
documents 54–5
Donoso, José 46
Dorfman, Ariel 48–9, 63

Dos Lagunas, MN 435
drinks 84–5
driving. See cars
dysentery 71–2

E

earthquakes 75
East Falkland (FI) 566–8
Easter Island (Rapa Nui) 526–56, **527**
  antiquities 536–9, 541
  books & film 539–40
  climate 535, 582
  flora & fauna 535–6
  geography & geology 535
  history 526, 528–35, **529**
  maps 540
  transportation 540–4
ecology 33, 66
economy 43–5
ecotourism 103
Edificio de la Aduana (Museo Naval) 252
education 46
Eiffel, Alexandre Gustave 229–30
El Calafate (Arg) 484–8, **485**
El Camote 524
El Chaltén (Arg) 492
El Colorado 159
El Gigante de Atacama 258
El Molle 324
El Morado, MN 158–9
El Salvador 303–4
El Tatio geysers 287
El Teniente 190
electricity 69
email 62
embassies 56–7
employment 79
encomiendas 18–9
endangered species 34–5
Ensenada 387–8
Entre Lagos 376
environmental issues 33
  dams 220–1
  deforestation 33, 45, 444
  organizations 74
  pollution 33
Ercilla, Alonso de 210–1, 215, 329

Escuela México 202–3
Estancia El Galpón 488
Estancia Harberton (Arg) 508–9
Estancia San Gregorio 470–1
Estancia Yendegaia 500
etiquette 50
exchange rates 58

F

Falkland Islands 557–70, **558–9**
  accommodations 562–3
  books 561
  business hours 562
  climate 557–8
  customs 560
  dangers 562
  economy 559
  flora & fauna 558–9
  food & drinks 563
  geography 557–8
  government & politics 559
  history 557
  holidays & special events 562
  Internet resources 561
  money 560–1
  planning 560
  population 559–60
  post & communications 561
  radio & TV 561
  tourist offices 560
  transportation 563
  visas & documents 560
fauna 34–5, 36, 376, 519. See also individual species
fax services 62
Fernández, Juan 514
ferries 115, 399–402, 437–8
Ferrocarril Austral Fueguino (Arg) 508
film 47. See also cinemas
fishing 104, 432, 442, 499, 504–5, 513, 562, 564
Fitzroy, Robert 495, 496, 500
Fitzroy Range (Arg) 492–5
fjords 400–2
flora 33–5, 376, 518–9. See also individual species
food 70, 81–4

Fray Jorge, PN 325–6
Frei Montalva, Eduardo 23–5, 28, 140, 278, 534
Frei Ruiz-Tagle, Eduardo 28, 40, 41, 44, 131, 444
Friday 516–7
Frutillar 380–3, **381**
Fuerte Bulnes 469–70
Fuerte San Antonio 410
Fuerte Santa Bárbara 522
Fundo Curanilahue 219
Fundo Vaitea 553
Futaleufú 442–3
Futrono 369

G

Galería de Historia 210
Galería Municipal de Arte 169
Galletué, RN 345
Galvarino 211, 215
gardens
    Jardín Botánico Nacional 178
    Parque Jardin El Corazón 311
Gatico 270–1
gay & lesbian travelers 73
geoglyphs 238–9, 257, 258, 260–1, 280
geography 28–33
geopolitics 41–2, 67, 429
geysers 287
glaciers 436–7, 488, 490, 508
González, Manuel 50
González Videla, Gabriel 23, 49, 308, 310, 322
Goose Green (FI) 568
government 39–43
Graef-Marino, Gustavo 47
guanacos 242, 243, 478
Guanaqueros 317
Guane Guane 244
guidebooks 63
Guzmán, Jaime 39, 40
Gypsy Cove (FI) 566

H

Hacienda Los Lingues 191
Hanga Roa 544–50, **544–5**

hare paenga 537
Haush 457, 495
health issues 69–73
    altitude sickness 70-71
    climate-related conditions 70–1
    diseases 71–2
    guides 69–70
    medical kit 70
    vaccinations 70
    women's 72–3
heat exhaustion 71
hiking & backpacking 77–8
    Aisén 439–40, 444–6
    books 63
    Chiloé 421–2
    Fitzroy Range (Arg) 492–3
    La Araucanía 340–1, 342, 356
    Los Lagos 377–8, 404
    Magallanes 478–82
    Middle Chile 184–5, 200, 222, 225
    Norte Chico 326
    tours 104
history 17–28, 66–7, 22
hitchhiking 114–5
HIV/AIDS 72
holidays 76–7
Horcón 182
Hornopirén 404–5
horse racing 151, 181
horseback riding 200, 482, 488, 542
hospedajes. See accommodations
hostels. See accommodations
hot springs. See thermal springs
hotels. See accommodations
Hotu Matua 530, 541
Huasco 306
huemul 480
Huerquehue, PN 356–7
Huilliche 17, 406, 421, 422, 424
Huilquilemu 199
human rights 41, 42–3
Humberstone 257–8
hypothermia 71

I

Ibáñez del Campo, Carlos 22, 23, 131
Iglesia Santa María de Achao 418
independence movements 19–20
indigenous peoples 51, 132, 133, 210–1, 226. See also individual cultures
Inkas 16, 17, 18, 242, 286
Instituto de la Patagonia 464
insurance
    car 113
    travel 54
international health card 55
international transfers 59
Internet
    access 62
    resources 64–5
Iquique 248–59, **250–1**
    places to stay 253–5
    climate 582
    day trips 257–9
    entertainment 255
    history 248
    organized tours 253
    places to eat 255
    transportation 255–7
Irarrázaval, Mario 50
Isla Alejandro Selkirk 525
Isla Llingua 419
Isla Mancera 368
Isla Negra 174
Isla Pan de Azúcar 303
Isla Robinson Crusoe 514, **515**
Islas Malvinas. See Falkland Islands
Isluga 37, 259
itineraries, suggested 52
Izurieta, Ricardo 41

J

Jara, Victor 47, 66
Jardín Botánico Nacional 178
Jodorowsky, Alejandro 47
José Romero, María 50
Juan Fernández Archipelago. See Archipiélago Juan Fernández
Juan López 270

K

kayaking 78, 104, 116, 442
Keppel Island (FI) 569
Kidney Island (FI) 566

L

La Araucanía 28, 32,
    329–405, **330–1**
La Campana, PN 183–6
La Chascona (Museo Neruda)
    135
La Chimba, RN 269
La Costa del Carbón 214–5
La Junta 441
La Ligua 183
La Parva 159–60
La Portada, MN 269–70
La Sebastiana 168
La Serena 308–16, 582,
    308–9
La Tirana 259
Lago Blanco 499
Lago Chungará 244–5
Lago Peñuelas, RN 173
Lago Ranco 369–70
Lago Rapel 191
Lago Vichuquén 194
Lago Yelcho 441
Lagos, Ricardo 40, 279, 445
Laguna Chaxa 286–7
Laguna Conchalí 328
Laguna Cotacotani 244
Laguna del Laja, PN 219–22
Laguna Miniques 287
Laguna San Rafael, PN 436–8
Laguna Torca, RN 194
Lagunillas 158
land reform 23, 24
language
    courses 78–9, 140, 351,
        432
    indigenous 51, 333
    Spanish 51, 571–5
Las Cascadas 380
Las Condes **139**
Las Cuevas 244
Las Vicuñas, RN 245–6
latifundios 19, 67
Lauca, PN 241, 244–5
laundry 69
Lautaro 18, 211

Lavín, Joaquín 40, 42
legal issues 76
lesbians. See gay & lesbian
    travelers
Letelier, Orlando 28, 43, 66,
    135
Lican Ray 358–9, **359**
Liquiñe 360
literature 46–7. See also books
Littín, Miguel 47, 67
Llaima 38, 342
llamas 243
Llanos de Challe, PN 307
Llifén 369
Lluta geoglyphs 238–9
Lo Vásquez 174
Lonquimay 344–5
Los Andes 186–7
Los Angeles 216–9, **215**, **217**
Los Antiguos (Arg) 453
Los Dominicos 151
Los Flamencos, RN 286–7
Los Glaciares, PN (Arg)
    488–92, **489**
Los Lagos 29, 32, 329–405,
    330–1
Los Loros 298
Los Pingüinos, MN 469
Los Vilos 326–8, **327**

M

Magallanes 32, 457–95,
    458–9
magazines 67–8
Magellan, Ferdinand 457, 495
mail 59–60
Maitencillo 182
Makemake 552
Malalcahuello, RN 344
Mamiña 259–60
Mano del Desierto 270
Manzanar 344
maps 52–3
Mapuche 16, 17, 18, 20, 21,
    25, 29, 45, 118–20, 151,
    203, 206, 210, 211, 215,
    222, 329, 332, 333, 345,
    354, 362, 369, 370
María Elena 271–2
Matta, Roberto 50
Maullín 403

measurements 69
medical kit 70
Mejillones 270
Melipeuco 345
Menéndez, José 458, 460, 464
Middle Chile 29, 161–225,
    162
military 26, 27–8, 40–1, 66–7,
    76
milodon 477
MIR (Movimiento de Izquierda
    Revolucionario) 24, 26
Mistral, Gabriela 46, 48–9,
    133, 186, 292, 319, 321
MN. See monumentos natu-
    rales
moai 530–1, 532, 537–9, 551,
    554–5
money 55, 58–9
monkey-puzzle tree. See
    araucaria
Monte Grande 321
Montt, Jorge 22
monumentos naturales (MN)
    30–1
    Cerro Ñielol 336
    Contulmo 216
    Cueva del Milodón 476–7
    Dos Lagunas 435
    El Morado 158
    La Portada 269–70
    Los Pingüinos 469
    Pichasca 325
    Salar de Surire 246
Moreno Glacier (Arg) 488
motels. See accommodations
motorcycles 111–3, 117
mountain biking. See cycling
mountaineering. See climbing
murals 202–3, 244
Murieta, Joaquín 25
museums
    Casa del Arte 210–1
    Convento y Museo de San
        Francisco 132
    Edificio de la Aduana
        (Museo Naval) 252
    Galería de Historia 210
    Galería Municipal de Arte
        169
    Huilquilemu 199

La Chascona (Museo Neruda) 135
Museo a Cielo Abierto 169
Museo Antiguo Monasterio del Espíritu Santo 186
Museo Antropológico Sebastián Englert 546
Museo Araucano Juan Antonio Ríos 215–6
Museo Arqueológico (La Serena) 311
Museo Arqueológico (Los Andes) 186
Museo Arqueológico de Santiago 133
Museo Arqueológico San Miguel de Azapa 238
Museo Arqueológico Universidad Católica del Norte 266
Museo Arqueológico y Etnológico 275
Museo Artequín 138
Museo Chileno de Arte Precolombino 132
Museo Colegio Salesiano 473
Museo Colonial de Arte Religioso 311
Museo de Arqueológico e Historia Francisco Fonck 175, 178
Museo de Arte Contemporáneo 363
Museo de Arte Moderno de Chiloé 416
Museo de Ciencia y Tecnología 137
Museo de Ciencias Naturales e Historia (Arg) 511
Museo de Historia Natural 168
Museo de la Alta Frontera 217
Museo de la Cultura del Mar Salvador Reyes 178
Museo de La Ligua 183

Museo de la Solidaridad Salvador Allende 133
Museo de Lukas 168
Museo de Santiago 132
Museo de Tierra del Fuego Fernando Cordero Rusque 498
Museo del Carmen 154
Museo del Huasco 305
Museo del Huaso 138
Museo del Limari 323
Museo del Mar Lord Cochrane 169
Museo del Recuerdo 464
Museo del Salitre 259
Museo Dillman S Bullock 223
Museo El Colono 379
Museo Ferroviario 271
Museo Franciscano 203
Museo Gabriela Mistral 319
Museo Gustavo Le Paige 283
Museo Histórico Colonial Alemán 382
Museo Histórico Gabriel González Videla 310–1
Museo Histórico Militar Primer Cuerpo de Ejército 252
Museo Histórico Municipal (Osorno) 371
Museo Histórico Municipal (Puerto Natales) 473
Museo Histórico Regional (Copiapó) 294
Museo Histórico Regional (Rancagua) 188–9
Museo Histórico Salitrero 259
Museo Histórico y Arqueológico de Villarrica 346–7
Museo Histórico y Arqueológico Mauricio van de Maele 363
Museo Histórico y de Armas 229
Museo Huáscar 214
Museo Inchin Cuivi Ant 423
Museo Infantil 137

Museo Juan Pablo II 393
Museo Marítimo (Arg) 504
Museo Mineralógico 293–4
Museo Mineralógico Ignacio Domeyko 311
Museo Municipal de Bellas Artes 178
Museo Nacional de Historia Natural 137
Museo Naval y Marítimo (Punta Arenas) 463
Museo Naval y Marítimo (Valparaíso) 169
Museo Palacio Rioja 178
Museo Regional (Antofagasta) 266
Museo Regional (Iquique) 252
Museo Regional Aurelio Bórquez Canobra 409, 411
Museo Regional de Castro 416
Museo Regional de La Araucanía 336
Museo Regional de la Patagonia 432
Museo Regional Salesiano Mayorino Borgatello 463
Museo Salesiano (Arg) 513
Museo Territorial Fin del Mundo (Arg) 503–4
Museo Votivo de Ayquina 280
Palacio Astoreca 252
Palacio Baburizza (Museo de Bellas Artes) 168, 169
Palacio Cousiño 132–3
Palacio de Bellas Artes 50, 132
Parque Museo Ferroviario 138
music 47, 86, 149–50

N

Nahuelbuta, PN 223–5, **224**
ñandú 479
Nantoco 297
national parks. See parques nacionales

Bold indicates maps.

national reserves. *See* reservas nacionales
natural monuments. *See* monumentos naturales
Neruda, Pablo 25, 46, 47, 48–9, 135, 168, 169, 174, 202, 310
Nevado Tres Cruces, PN 298–9
New Island (FI) 570
newspapers 67–8
Niebla 368
Ninhue 205
nitrate ghost towns 257–8, 262, 270–1, 272
nitrate industry 21, 67, 226, 228, 248, 288
Norte Chico 29, 290–328, **291**
Norte Grande 29, 226–89, **227**
North, John Thomas 226, 228
Northern Aisén 438–49

O

Observatorio Cerro Paranal 270
Observatorio Cerro Tololo 315–6
Observatorio Comunal Cerro Mamalluca 320–1
Oficina Chacabuco 272
O'Higgins, Bernardo 20, 21, 187–8, 190, 201, 203
Ojos del Salado 37, 298
Ona (Selknam) 17, 457, 495
online services 64–5
organizations 74–5
Orito 553
Orongo 551–2
Osorno 370–6, 389–90, **372–3**
Ovalle 322–5, **323**

P

Pabellón 298
packing 53
painting 50
Palacio Astoreca 252
Palacio Baburizza (Museo de Bellas Artes) 168, 169
Palacio Cousiño 132–3
Palacio de Bellas Artes 50, 132

Palacio de la Moneda 131
palafitos 416
Palena 443
Pali Aike, PN 470–1
palm, Chilean 184
Palmas de Ocoa 185
Pampa del Tamarugal, RN 260–1
Pan de Azúcar, PN 302–3, **303**
Pangue dam 220
Panguipulli 360–2
Paposo, RN 289
Papudo 183
paragliding 78, 253
Parinacota 244
Parque Isidora Cousiño 214, 216
Parque Jardin El Corazón 311
Parque Monumental Bernardo O'Higgins 203
Parque Museo Ferroviario 138
Parque Natural Pumalín 443–6
Parque O'Higgins 138
Parque por la Paz 139
Parque Quinta Normal 137–8
parques nacionales (PN) 36, 37–8, **30–1**
    Alerce Andino 403–4
    Bernardo O'Higgins 477
    Chiloé 420–2
    Coihaique 434–5
    Conguillío 341–4, **341**
    Fray Jorge 325–6
    Huerquehue 356–7
    Juan Fernández 523–5
    La Campana 183–6
    Laguna del Laja 219–22
    Laguna San Rafael 436–8
    Lauca 241, 244–5
    Llanos de Challe 307
    Los Glaciares (Arg) 488–92, **489**
    Nahuelbuta 223–5, **224**
    Nevado Tres Cruces 298–9
    Pali Aike 470–1
    Pan de Azúcar 302–3, **303**
    Puyehue 376–9, **378**
    Queulat 439–40
    Rapa Nui 550–6
    Tierra del Fuego (Arg) 509–10

Tolhuaca 340–1
Torres del Paine 478–84, **481**
Vicente Peréz Rosales 388–91, **389**
Villarrica 357
Volcán Isluga 259
Parra, Marco Antonio de la 46–7, 49
Parra, Violeta 47
Paso del Agua Negra 321–2
passports 54
Pebble Island (FI) 569
Pedro de Valdivia 272
Pehuenche 17, 220
penguins 465, 469, 566, 568
Península, Poike 556
pensiones. *See* accommodations
Pérez Rosales, Vicente 25, 38
Peru, border crossings to/from 99
Petrohué 390–1
Peulla 391
phones 60–2
photography 68
Pica 261–2
Pichasca, MN 325
Pichidangui 328
Pichilemu 191–2
Picunche 17
Pincheira, Máximo 50
Pingüino de Humboldt, RN 307
Pinochet Ugarte, Augusto 15, 27–8, 40–3, 49, 66–7, 131, 156, 306, 428–9, 534
Pintados 260–1
Pirque 157
Pisagua 246–7
Pisco Elqui 322
Pizarro, Francisco 17
planning 52
Planta Capel 319–20
plants. *See* flora
Plaza Ñuñoa 138
Plazoleta El Yunque 524
PN. *See* parques nacionales
Poblado Artesanal 231
Poconchile 239
poetry 46

police 76
politics 39–43, 66–7
pollution 33
Pomaire 155
population 45
Port Howard (FI) 568–9
Port Louis (FI) 567
Port Stephens (FI) 569
Portales, Diego 21
Portillo 160
Porvenir 497–9, **498**
postal services 59–60
pottery 155, 223
Pozo Almonte 259
Prat, Arturo 169, 205, 463
Prats, Carlos 27, 43
pregnancy 73
Providencia 135, **136–7**
Pucón 349–56, **350**, **355**
pudú 376
Puelche 17
Puerto Bertrand 454–5
Puerto Bories 476
Puerto Cárdenas 441
Puerto Chacabuco 436
Puerto Cisnes 439
Puerto Francés 525
Puerto Guadal 450–1
Puerto Hambre 469–70
Puerto Ingeniero Ibáñez 449–50
Puerto Inglés 524
Puerto Montt 392–9, 402–3, 582, **394–5**, **403**
Puerto Natales 471–7, **472**
Puerto Octay 379–80
Puerto Prat 476
Puerto Puyuhuapi 440
Puerto Ramírez 441
Puerto Río Tranquilo 450
Puerto Vaquería 524
Puerto Varas 383–7, **384**
Puerto Williams 500–1
Puerto Yungay 456
Pukará de Copaquilla 239
Pukará de Quitor 286
Pumalín, Parque Natural 443–6

pumas 376
Punta Arenas 457–8, 460–71, 582, **460–1**
Putre 239–41
Puyehue, PN 38, 376–9, **378**

Q

Qawashqar (Alacaluf) 17, 400, 425, 457, 495
Quechua 228
Quellón 422–4, **423**
Queulat, PN 439–40
Quinta Vergara 178
Quintero 182

R

Radal Siete Tazas, RN 194, 196
radio 68
Ralún 391
Rancagua 187–90, **187**
Rano Raraku 535, 537–8, 555–6
Rapa Nui. See Easter Island
Rapanui (people) 526, 528, 530, 534, 546, 553
Refugio Lo Valdés (Alemán) 158
refugios. See accommodations
religion 50–1
Reñaca 182
reservas nacionales (RN) 36, 38–9, **30–1**
   Altos del Lircay 200–1
   Cerro Castillo 450
   Galletué 345
   La Chimba 269
   Lago Peñuelas 173
   Laguna Torca 194
   Las Vicuñas 245–6
   Los Flamencos 286–7
   Malalcahuello 344
   Pampa del Tamarugal 260–1
   Paposo 289
   Pingüino de Humboldt 307
   Radal Siete Tazas 194, 196
   Río Clarillo 157–8
   Río de los Cipreses 190–1
   Río Simpson 435–6
residenciales. See accommodations

restaurants 81–4. See also places to eat for individual locations
revolutionary wars 20
Río Baker 221, 428
Río Biobío 219, 220, 344–5, **221**
Río Bueno 370
Río Clarillo 157–8
Río de los Cipreses, RN 190–1
Río Futaleufú 220–1, 428
Río Gallegos (Arg) 453
Río Grande (Arg) 511–3, **512**
Río Loa 280
Río Maipo 156–7
Río Rubens 470
Río Simpson 435–6
Río Verde 470
river running. See white-water rafting
RN. See reservas nacionales
road assistance 112
Roggeveen, Jacob 526, 531
Rongo-Rongo tablets 541
Round-the-World (RTW) tickets 89, 93
Ruiz, Raúl 47
Ruta de la Araucana 215–6

S

safety issues
   crime 59, 75
   natural hazards 75–6
   for women 73
Salar de Surire, MN 246
Salto del Laja 218–9
San Alfonso 158
San Carlos (FI) 567–8
San Javier 199–200
San Juan Bautista 520–3, **521**
San Martín, José de 20
San Pedro de Atacama 280–6, **279**, **282**
73, 176–7cier 436–7
Santa Laura 257–8
Santiago 118–60, **119**, **121**, **124–5**, **154–5**
   places to stay 141–4
   Barrio Bellavista 133–5, 146–7, **134**
   Barrio Brasil 135, 137, 145–6

Barrio Ecológico 140
Centro 127–33, **128–9**
climate 582
day trips 154–60
entertainment 148–50
history 118–20
language courses 140
Las Condes 148, **139**
organized tours 140–1
Parque O'Higgins 138
Parque por la Paz 139
Parque Quinta Normal
    137–8
Plaza Ñuñoa 138, 148
Providencia 135, 147–8,
    136–7
places to eat 144–8
shopping 151–2
special events 141
sports 150–1
transportation 152–4
walking tour 131
Santuario Cañi 356
Santuario de la Inmaculada
    Concepción 174
Santuario de La Tirana 259
Santuario Naturaleza Granito
    Orbicular 301
Saunders Island (FI) 569
scuba diving. See diving
sculpture 50, 270
Sea Lion Island (FI) 568
sea lions 505
seafood 83
seals 514, 519, 525
Selkirk, Alexander 16, 37,
    514–7, 518, 523–4
Selknam. See Ona
senior travelers 74
Seno Otway 469
Sepúlveda, Luis 46, 63
sexually transmitted diseases
    72
shipwrecks 566
shopping 87, 151–2
Sierra Nevada 342
Skármeta, Antonio 46, 47
skiing 77, 105, 159–60,
    189–90, 205–6, 377, 432,
    505
snorkeling 78

soccer 77, 86, 150–1
society 50
Socoroma 239
Southern Aisén 449–56
Southern Heartland 187–225
Spanish invasion 17–8, 210–1
Spanish language 51, 571–5
special events 76–7
sports 77, 86–7, 150–1
Stanley (FI) 563–6, **565**, **567**
Strait of Magellan 495, 496
student cards 55
sunburn 71
surfing 78, 253, 311
swan, black-necked 435
swimming 75. See also
    beaches

T

Talca 196–200, **195**, **198–9**
Taltal 288–9
Tarapacá 258
taxes 59
taxis 116
Tehuelche 17, 457
telegraph 62
telephones 60–2
Templo Votivo de Maipú 154
Temuco 332–40, **334–5**
termas. See thermal springs
theater 48–9, 86, 149–50
thermal springs
    Aguas Calientes 377
    Baños Colina 159
    Baños Morales 158
    Centro Turístico Termal
        Coñaripe 360
    Chusmiza 258
    Liquiñe 360
    Manzanar 344
    Termas de Cauquenes 190
    Termas de Chillán 205–6
    Termas de Huife 354–5
    Termas de Palguín 355–6
    Termas de Panqui 356
    Termas de Puritama 286
    Termas de Puyehue 376
    Termas de Puyuhuapi
        440–1
    Termas de Socos 325
    Termas de Tolhuaca 344

Termas El Amarillo 449
Termas Los Pozones 355
Termas Manquecura 360
Vegas de Turi 280
Tierra del Fuego 32, 495–513,
    458–9
Tierra del Fuego, PN (Arg)
    509–10
time zones 69
tipping 59
Toconao 287
Toconce 280
Tocopilla 272–3
toilets 69
Tolhuaca, PN 340–1
Tompkins, Douglas 443,
    444–5
Tongoy 317
Torres del Paine, PN 478–84,
    481
tourist cards 54
tourist offices 53
tours, organized 103–5, 116–7
trade unions 40
trains 110–1, 116, 271, 293,
    508
transportation
    domestic 106–17
    international 88–105
travel insurance 54
travel literature 63, 66
traveler's checks 58
trekking. See hiking & back-
    packing
TV 68

U

UP (Unidad Popular) 25, 27,
    66, 133
Upsala Glacier (Arg) 490
Ushuaia (Arg) 501–9, **503**

V

vaccinations 70
Valdivia 362–8, **364–5**
Valdivia, Pedro de 17–8, 118,
    133, 161, 163, 206, 210,
    215, 222, 281, 282, 290,
    362
Valle de la Luna 286
Valle del Encanto 324–5

Valle Nevado 160
Vallenar 304–7, **305**
Valparaíso 161–74, **166–7,
    173**
    places to stay 170
    day trips 173–4
    entertainment 171
    history 161, 163
    places to eat 171
    shopping 171
    special events 170
    transportation 171–3
Vegas de Turi 280
Vicente Peréz Rosales, PN
    388–91, **389**
Vicuña 317–22, **318**
vicuñas 242–3
video 68
Villa Amengual 438–9
Villa Cerro Castillo 450, 477–8
Villa Mañihuales 438
Villa O'Higgins 456
Villarrica (town) 345–9, **346**
Villarrica (volcano) 38, 345,
    351, 357
Viña del Cerro 298
Viña del Mar 174–83, **173,
    176–7**

places to stay 179–80
day trips 182–3
entertainment 181
history 174
organized tours 178
places to eat 180–1
shopping 181
special events 179
transportation 181
visas 54
volcanoes 33, 75
    Antuco 219–20
    Hudson 449, 451, 453
    Isluga 37, 259
    Llaima 38, 342
    Lonquimay 344–5
    Osorno 389–90
    Puyehue 38
    Rano Raraku 535, 537–8,
        555–6
    Villarrica 38, 345, 351, 357
Volunteer Beach (FI) 567

water pollution 33
Web sites 64–5
Weddell Island (FI) 569
weights 69
West Falkland (FI) 568–70
white-water rafting 78, 104,
    116, 156–7, 219, 442, 454
wildlife. See fauna
windsurfing 192, 311
wine 84–5, 155–6, 157, 194,
    199–200
women travelers
    attitudes toward 73
    health of 72–3
    safety precautions for 73
work 79

War of the Pacific 21, 226,
    228, 229, 252, 258, 263,
    533
water, drinking 70

yacht charters 116
Yahgan. See Yamaná
Yamaná (Yahgan) 17, 457,
    495, 500, 502, 509
youth cards 55, 75

Zapallar 183
Zona Franca 252

Boxed Text

Air Travel Glossary 90–1
Beauty Among the Slag 216
The Birdman Cult 552
Bordering on the Absurd 490–1
Carrier Codes 61
The Chile-California Connection 24–5
Chile's Endangered Rivers 220–1
Chile's Scottish Savior 368
Common Mapuche Words & Phrases 333
Copper Processing 278
Crossing the Lakes 388
Eiffel Beyond the Tower 230
Embassies & Consulates 56–7
Endangered Species 34–5
Ercilla & the Araucanian Wars 210–1
Evangelistas Ferry Rates 438
The Frozen South 501
Los Dominicos 151

Moving the Moai 554–5
The New World Camelids 242–3
Online Services 64–5
Parque Natural Pumalín 444–5
The Paths of Mistral & Neruda 48–9
Pinochet's Folly 428–9
A Railroad Remembered 293
Rongo-Rongo Tablets 541
Sailing the Fjords 400–2
Sample Bus Fares from Santiago 110
Sample Train Fares from Santiago 111
A Shaky Explanation 531
Site Distances 543
The Starry Southern Skies 316
Ticket Options 92
Traveling through Argentine Patagonia 452–3
Visiting Argentina 98
Who Was Friday? 516–7

MAP LEGEND

BOUNDARIES

·—··—··—··	International
···—···—···	Región, Province

HYDROGRAPHY

	Water
	Coastline
	Beach
	River, Waterfall
	Swamp, Spring

ROUTES & TRANSPORT

	Freeway
	Toll Freeway
	Primary Road
	Secondary Road
	Tertiary Road
===== -----	Unpaved Road
	Pedestrian Mall
– – – –	Trail
················	Walking Tour
– – – –	Ferry Route
+++++++++	Railway, Train Station
—•••—	Mass Transit Line & Station

ROUTE SHIELDS

⑤	Chile Ruta Nacional	RN③	Argentina Ruta Nacional
⑨	Paraguay Highway	RP㉑	Argentina Ruta Provincial
①	Peru Carretera Sistema Nacional	601	Bolivia Red Complementaria
⑧	Uruguay Ruta Nacional	①	Bolivia Red Fundamental

AREA FEATURES

	Park
	Cemetery
	Building
	Plaza
	Golf Course

MAP SYMBOLS

✪	NATIONAL CAPITAL	✈	Airfield	⚓	Monument
◉	State, Provincial Capital	✈	Airport	▲	Mountain
●	LARGE CITY	∴	Archaeological Site, Ruins	🏛	Museum
●	Medium City	⑤	Bank	⌂	Observatory
●	Small City	⇑	Beach	←	One-Way Street
•	Town, Village	✦	Border Crossing	♠	Park
○	Point of Interest	⊖	Bus Depot, Bus Stop	Ⓟ	Parking
		⊞	Cathedral	) (	Pass
		⌢	Cave	⊐	Picnic Area
■	Place to Stay	✝	Church	★	Police Station
▲	Campground	◩	Dive Site	⚏	Pool
⬛	RV Park	☎	Embassy	✉	Post Office
⌂	Shelter, Refugio	✎	Fish Hatchery	⚓	Shipwreck
		⊱	Footbridge	❖	Shopping Mall
▼	Place to Eat	⟊	Fort	⚐	Skiing (Alpine)
⬗	Bar (Place to Drink)	✿	Garden	⚑	Skiing (Nordic)
☕	Café	⛽	Gas Station	⋔	Stately Home
		⊕	Hospital, Clinic	☎	Telephone
		❶	Information	⚶	Trailhead
		光	Lighthouse	♓	Winery
		※	Lookout	🐘	Zoo

Note: Not all symbols displayed above appear in this book.

LONELY PLANET OFFICES

Australia
PO Box 617, Hawthorn 3122, Victoria
☎ 03 9819 1877 fax 03 9819 6459
email talk2us@lonelyplanet.com.au

USA
150 Linden Street, Oakland, California 94607
☎ 510 893 8555, TOLL FREE 800 275 8555
fax 510 893 8572
email info@lonelyplanet.com

UK
10A Spring Place, London NW5 3BH
☎ 020 7428 4800 fax 020 7428 4828
email go@lonelyplanet.co.uk

France
1 rue du Dahomey, 75011 Paris
☎ 01 55 25 33 00 fax 01 55 25 33 01
www.lonelyplanet.fr

World Wide Web: www.lonelyplanet.com *or* AOL keyword: lp
Lonely Planet Images: lpi@lonelyplanet.com.au